THE LIFE OF BENJAMIN DISRAELI
EARL OF BEACONSFIELD

The Earl of Beaconsfield
1881
from the portrait by Sir John Millais
in the possession of Viscount Hambleden

THE LIFE OF
BENJAMIN DISRAELI
EARL OF BEACONSFIELD

By WILLIAM FLAVELLE MONYPENNY
AND
GEORGE EARLE BUCKLE

NEW AND REVISED EDITION
IN TWO VOLUMES

VOL. II. 1860—1881

WITH PORTRAITS AND ILLUSTRATIONS

*Read no history, nothing but biography, for that
is life without theory.*—CONTARINI FLEMING.

LONDON
JOHN MURRAY, ALBEMARLE STREET, W.
1929

DATES OF FIRST PUBLICATION

VOL.	I.	By W. F. MONYPENNY.	*October*, 1910
VOL.	II.	,, ,,	*November*, 1912
VOL.	III.	By G. E. BUCKLE.	*November*, 1914
VOL.	IV.	,, ,,	*May*, 1916
VOL.	V.	,, ,,	*June*, 1920
VOL.	VI.	,, ,,	*June*, 1920

NEW EDITION IN TWO VOLUMES
REVISED BY G. E. BUCKLE
1929

CONTENTS

IV (*Continued*)

V

CONTENTS

VI

ILLUSTRATIONS

IV

CHAPTERS VIII.–XVI.　1860–1868

BY GEORGE EARLE BUCKLE

CHAPTER VIII.

DISRAELI AND GLADSTONIAN FINANCE.

1860–1863.

John Bright and the majority of the Reformers had preferred to trust Russell's promises in 1859 rather than Disraeli's, and had accordingly taken an active part in upsetting the Conservative Government. A bitter disillusionment was in store for them. The Palmerston Administration only introduced one Reform Bill during the whole duration of a six years' Parliament, and did not prosecute even that solitary effort into the Committee stage. Palmerston's indifference on the subject proved to be a reflection of the public mind; and Russell had to console himself by immersion in foreign affairs—a change of front facilitated by his removal in 1861 from the Commons to the Lords.

But at the beginning of 1860 it looked as if Reform was seriously meant, and as if the Government hoped to pass a Bill by agreement with the Opposition. On January 4 Disraeli wrote to Derby: 'A Cabinet Minister '—it was Charles Villiers, a personal friend of Disraeli's—' has sounded me, and said communications would be confined, and strictly confined, to P[almerston] and J. R[ussell]. I replied I was ready to listen, of course telling you everything, though engaging that, at present, it should not go further.' Derby was surprised at Villiers's revelations. 'I confess that the signature of your correspondent rather startled me; for a correspondence with a member of the Cabinet on such a subject has rather a surprising appearance; but if the correspondence be sanctioned by the Head

3

of the Government and his chief supporter (and rival), I do not see that it is our duty to remonstrate on the part of the rest of the Cabinet; and we are certainly under no obligation to abstain from such communications.' Eventually Ministers abandoned the idea of coming to an arrangement with the Opposition to pass an agreed Bill; perhaps because neither party was really in earnest about passing any Bill at all.

To Lord Derby.

GROSVENOR GATE, *Jan.* 8, 1860.—. . . As at present advised, it is on the cards—nay, probable—that the following proposition will be submitted to you :

1. £10 county franchise—if the Lords carry £20, to be accepted.

2. £7 value—boroughs.

3. Disfranchisement in a separate Bill, and to take its chance.

I should like to have had your view of this proposition without troubling you with my own; but as we are separated, and time is hurrying on, I will venture to observe, though with great diffidence, that these seem terms which we may substantially obtain without entering into any engagement, and that they are prompted as much by the feelings of their own party as by a desire to conciliate ours. I doubt whether the difference between a £6 and a £7 value is one of Conservative importance: while at the same time it keeps up the mischievous imposture that there is a Conservative party in the Cabinet, on which the Peelites intrigue, as they are doing already, and trying to break up our ranks. A majority of the Committee was in favor of an £8 value, but ultimately yielded to the sense of the ridiculous in turning us out for identity and then proposing £10 and £8. An £8 would have estranged the Radicals: they will grumble about the £7, but take it, I think.

I was asked what we considered a 'temperate measure,' assuming that after what had occurred in Parliament identity was out of the question. I declined to give our opinion on the subject, but said I thought that public opinion would recognise, as a temperate measure equal to the occasion, £20 for county; £8 for boroughs; and the scale of disfranchisement in Lord Derby's Bill. It was said, if that course were taken, the Radicals would take the first opportunity of turning them out. I replied we were sincerely desirous of not disturbing the Government at present, and that, if we agreed on a Reform Bill, we should, as a matter of course, wish to give them a general support till it had passed, which alone would carry them through the session.

I was pressed as to our conduct in case of a motion on foreign politics. I declined to hold out any expectation of our binding ourselves on that subject. We must always be free to assert our own principles and policy on such a subject, but I did not hesitate to say that we certainly should not encourage any motions on foreign policy brought forward by the Radicals to disturb them; that we should deplore returning to power by their aid. . . .

Confidential. GROSVENOR GATE, *Jan.* 18, 1860.—There was a Cabinet on Monday. . . . Nothing settled. The Committee of the Cabinet, being quite unable to come to any agreement, and it being impossible any longer to delay some general discussion, the question, quite crude, was thrown, like a piece of raw meat, into the assemblage of nineteen last Monday. My correspondent told Palmerston and Lord John that, having commenced the negotiation with me, and after what had passed, it was impossible, he felt, to continue silent, and they agreed that, whatever might occur, they were bound to deal frankly with us. . . .

I gathered that the moderate party is much stronger in tone at this moment, and that Lord John is checked. I suspect he has enough on his hands of another character. . . .

With the beginning of the session on January 24, it became evident that Reform would not occupy the fore-front of the Parliamentary stage. Disraeli wrote to Derby on the following day : ' I have frequently observed that, until the Houses meet, it is impossible to hit upon what will be the question of the session, often very different from that anticipated. From all I hear and observe it will be the Commercial Treaty.' This was the treaty with France which Cobden had just negotiated at Paris, and on which was built Gladstone's great Budget of 1860. Popular and Parliamentary interest in the sphere of domestic legislation became concentrated on the financial proposals of the Government, which were revealed in February; and it was to an indifferent and not overfull House that Russell on March 1 expounded his new Reform Bill. It established a £10 occupation franchise in the counties, and reduced the borough franchise to £6. The redistribution proposed was hardly on a more extensive scale than in the Conservative Bill of the preceding year; twenty-five boroughs were deprived of one member each, fifteen of these seats being allotted to populous counties, nine to populous boroughs, and one to London University. Russell recommended the plan as a simple one, containing as little novelty as possible. Similar Reform Bills were also introduced for Ireland and Scotland.

The proposals were not substantially different from those which Disraeli had expressed his readiness to accept, with a view to a settlement, in his negotiations with Roebuck, Lindsay, and their Radical friends, in the preceding June. But the Parliamentary atmosphere had changed; the apathy steadily manifested by the country about Reform had invaded Parliament; while the bulk, not only of the Conservatives, but of the Whigs and Moderate Liberals, profoundly disliked both the lowering of the borough franchise to £6 and the prospect, if the Bill were passed, of a third dissolution within three years. Disraeli was quick to perceive that, while there was no opportunity for a settlement of the Reform question, there was plenty of opportunity for successful opposition; that dilatory tactics and contemptuous treatment must eventually secure the withdrawal of the Bill and the discredit of the Government. The reception which the Whigs had accorded to his own Bill debarred them from any claim to consideration. On the second reading,[1] Disraeli said it was a bad Bill, which would not even admit so many new electors as his own; it put numbers before fitness; it would only enfranchise a single homogeneous class; it tended to diminish the just and salutary influence of the land. He would not oppose the second reading; but he recommended Russell to withdraw an ' unnecessary, uncalled-for, and mischievous Bill.' The debate was prolonged, in a desultory manner, over six weeks; it was not till May 3 that the Bill, which secured Bright's approval as an instalment, but was openly opposed by many

[1] March 19.

Liberals, was read a second time. Disraeli wrote to Mrs. Willyams on March 24: 'The new Reform Bill is like the *Great Eastern*, and sticks on its stays. It will not be launched, and, if ever it do float, I think it will founder; then all will be right.' The more it was looked at, the less it was liked. Disraeli had some difficulty in keeping his colleagues on the front bench to the purely passive and waiting tactics which the situation demanded.

To Lord Derby.

HUGHENDEN MANOR, *May* 27, 1860.—. . . The front bench has long been restless—desiring many things, either dangerous or impracticable. Pakington wants a Royal Commission to inquire into the whole subject of Reform, which is madness: John Manners wants to meet the motion by ' previous question,' which cannot be moved on going into Committee: Estcourt wants ' something to be done,' but has no conception of what it should be. The fact is our tactics are to watch circumstances, and not to attempt to create them. The cards will play into our hands if we are quiet. . . .

The Opposition did keep quiet, save to intimate to Palmerston that he could rely on their support in case of a difference with Russell on Reform. The end came a fortnight later. On June 4, on the motion to go into Committee, Russell abandoned the Scottish and Irish Bills, and even in regard to the English Bill announced his readiness to accept in Committee a raising of the figure for the borough franchise. In fact, commented Disraeli, Russell would accept anything, if the House would but agree to something that might shuffle this great impediment to progress out of the course. Thus the high policy which had destroyed a Ministry and dissolved a Parliament had melted away ! Palmerston gave the Bill perfunctory support in a speech which hardly disguised his willingness to acquiesce in its failure; and a proposal to adjourn the debate was only defeated by 21 votes.

To Lord Derby.

Private. Sunday [*June* 10, 1860], 7 *o'clock.*—I have seen the Bear [Ellice]. He says he thinks the Government will give up the Bill to-morrow: he hopes so. . . . The division was exactly the right thing; the Government expected between 40 and 50 majority, which would have encouraged the violent party; but a small majority indicates the only honorable course—withdrawal. He has seen Johnny, who, he says, is low, but he thinks resigned. By his own account he appears to have said to him everything most disagreeable, having explained to him that he does not understand the question, and that, if Reform is ever treated again, it must be treated on quite different principles. . . .

Disraeli's information was correct. The Government withdrew the Bill on June 11, thus taking, as he said, ' a wise and not an undignified course.' They never introduced another Reform Bill, but contented themselves with passing in the next session a short Act allotting the four vacant seats, two to the West Riding of Yorkshire, one to South Lancashire, and one to Birkenhead—almost exactly the arrangement which the Liberals resisted when proposed by the first Derby-Disraeli Government eight years before.[1] When attention was drawn in 1861, in the debate on the Address, to the absence of Reform from the Government programme, Disraeli expressed his approval of the omission, and Russell sadly confessed that there was not sufficient public support to carry a satisfactory Bill.[2] Bright complained bitterly, and with perfect justice, that the failure to proceed with Reform was a breach of the most explicit pledges, public and private, given by the Government in order to obtain office; but he received scant sympathy, as neither warning nor experience had deterred him from trusting the promises of the Whigs and placing them in power. Even Locke King's motion for identity of suffrage, which had been regularly carried for years, was defeated by ' the previous question ' in 1861. Palmerston said that the present was a time for waiting and not for action; and Disraeli's argument, that Parlia-

[1] See Vol. I., pp. 1183, 1184.
[2] Stanley wrote to Disraeli from Knowsley on October 13, 1860: ' I have seen from time to time a good many manufacturers, merchants, and men of the towns; all agree in their politics; all were frightened by Lord John's Bill, all praise your tactics, and will discourage a renewal of agitation. The towns are full of money—and of Conservative opinion, disguised as Moderate Liberalism.'

ment ought only to deal with a comprehensive measure, had a success which had hitherto been denied it. Russell accepted an earldom at the close of the 1861 session; Reform disappeared finally from all the Queen's Speeches for which Palmerston was responsible, and was hardly advocated seriously even by private members till the Parliament was nearing its term. Disraeli had indeed ' pricked the imposture ' of Whig professions to be earnest Reformers.

Reform, therefore, was speedily shelved in the Parliament of 1859-1865; and the principal contentions between parties turned on finance, foreign policy, and the Church. Gladstone was back at the Exchequer, and his dæmonic energy forced finance to the front. 1860 was the year in which his famous Budget of 1853 was to have its full fruition. Terminable annuities to the amount of two millions were due to fall in; and, with that sum in hand, the income tax, which was to have gradually diminished through a period of seven years, was in this year absolutely to cease. Such was the attractive forecast drawn in 1853; the actual fact in 1860 was very different. The Crimean War entirely dislocated the arrangements for the years 1854 to 1856; nevertheless, after it, in 1857 and 1858, not only Gladstone, but Disraeli, anxious to promote both public economy and continuity of policy, impressed upon Parliament the extreme desirability of so ordering finance as to bring about the promised abolition of income tax in 1860. But once again military preparations, due this time to apprehensions of France and to war with China, swelled expenditure; and in his belated Budget of 1859 Gladstone found himself driven to increase income tax instead of diminishing it. This was a bad omen for 1860; and, when that year came, he effected a complete transformation, and built his Budget, not on abolition of income tax, but on a commercial treaty with France, involving a serious loss of Customs dues on wine and brandy and silk, which had to be made good. Entirely regardless of the hopes held out in 1853, and renewed in 1857 and 1858, he once more employed a reimposed and, indeed, largely augmented income tax, as Peel had done in 1842 and 1845, and he himself in 1853, as the engine by which duties could be abolished on a large scale and the tariff simplified. Though he found a deficit, he did not hesitate to make it larger, trusting that the expansion of trade which might be expected to follow a general relief from tariff shackles would produce an abundant and buoyant revenue. It was a bold policy, and, as regards the public purse, proved in the long run to be a successful one. But it was a repudiation of his own previous arrangements, and a direct challenge to an Opposition which had after some misgiving accepted those arrangements, and had in 1857 and 1858 based its own financial policy upon them.

That challenge Disraeli took up. He did not object to improving our commercial relations with France; on the contrary, he had laboured when in office for the same end. But why had the Government negotiated a treaty on the principle of reciprocity, a principle which had been absolutely rejected in our own commercial system ? Why had they engaged us by treaty for what must have been done without any treaty whatever ? Apart from this question of principle, he maintained that the actual treaty was not a good one; and confirmation of this view from a very competent source is found in a letter written in 1877, when the wine duties again came under review by a Government of which Beaconsfield was the head:

Sir Louis Mallet to Montagu Corry.

May 10, 1877.—. . . Our present wine duties were, as you know, fixed by Mr. Gladstone with a view to the treaty of 1860.

Mrs. Cobden's recent death has placed in my hands all Mr. Cobden's correspondence with Mr. Gladstone on the subject, and I have for the first time read it. The melancholy result of this perusal is to me that the great objects which I presume both Governments had in view on that occasion have been frustrated by the exorbitant amount of our wine duties, which no one at that time knew.

But, whatever may be the case with France, it is incontestable that both Spain, Portugal, Italy, and our own Colonies, have ever since protested against the scale. . . .

In spite of his disapproval of many of its terms, Disraeli
did not directly attack the treaty, though he protested
unsuccessfully against the procedure which, in disregard
of Pitt's precedent in 1787, asked the House for a sanction
of the Budget founded on the treaty before submitting
the treaty itself for consideration.   Where he joined issue [1]
was on the policy of augmenting an existing deficit by
surrendering Customs dues, and then obtaining the necessary revenue by disappointing the legitimate expectations of the country in regard to income tax.   This he
considered improvident and profligate finance.[2]   He recalled the failure of the Budget of 1853, owing to ' external circumstances that were not foreseen by one who
ought to have been prescient.'   That should teach Ministers not to be too sanguine now, in view of the troubled
state of Italy.   But Disraeli disclaimed any idea of wishing to displace the Government.

Neither I nor my colleagues . . . are at all anxious to
attempt to reoccupy the places we then[3] filled.   I may, at
least, say for myself that, having for more than two years led
this House in a minority, I shrink from the unparalleled anxiety
and responsibility of such a post; and I would recommend
no gentleman ever to adopt that position who has any regard
for his nervous system.   The important office which the
Chancellor of the Exchequer fills gives ample opportunity to
his eager mind and his impetuous rhetoric.   Perhaps in
moments of solitary aspiration he has wished to occupy the
proud post of leader of the House of Commons, which no one
could fill more efficiently.   But from what I have observed
of the right hon. gentleman's temperament, I think I may

[1] Feb. 21.
[2] The disappearance, without appreciable relief to the taxpayer, of the
£2,000,000 derived from the falling in of the terminable annuities, was
described by Disraeli with great humour on the hustings in 1865.   The
House, he said, was very full on Budget night, as it was known that Gladstone was going to perform a considerable feat.   Gladstone had two millions
of taxation which was dying a natural death.   It was a fund to which
Englishmen had been looking for relief for half a century.   What did
he do with it ?   By a feat of legerdemain exceeding that of a professional conjurer ' he took one million and turned it into ducks; then
he took another million and turned it into drakes; and for half an hour
these ducks and drakes flew cackling about the House of Commons, until
at last we got ashamed of one another, and we ordered strangers to withdraw, and determined to keep it a profound secret till Parliament was
dissolved.'   [3] In the spring of 1859.

tell him that it is well for him, however eminent his position, that he reposes at least for a time beneath the *mitis sapientia* of the noble lord the Foreign Secretary and the calm patience of the noble Premier.

Disraeli's attack, which was very indifferently supported by his party, was easily repulsed by a majority of 116. The debates of this month of February, Disraeli told Mrs. Willyams, were ' noisy Parliamentary fights,' but really ' sham battles.' Greville oddly writes of them that Disraeli ' betrays in the House of Commons a sort of consciousness of his inferiority to Gladstone, and of fear of encountering him in debate.' This judgment may be set against the corresponding picture drawn by Lord Houghton, in 1867, of Gladstone ' quite awed by the diabolical cleverness of Dizzy.' Lord Morley declines to accept ' awe ' as the right word.[1] In the same way, no one who studies Disraeli's life will accept ' fear ' as the right word. Disraeli never hesitated, throughout his career, to encounter any of his eminent adversaries in debate. But he was always generous in his appreciation of an opponent's powers; and Gladstone, both in opening his financial scheme and in his numerous speeches in this month in defence of the Budget and of the treaty, surpassed himself, and earned Disraeli's tribute.

As the session proceeded, and the details of the Budget came to be examined, the glamour of Gladstone's eloquence wore off. ' Not more than three months ago,' wrote Greville on May 12, ' Gladstone was triumphant and jubilant. . . . There never was a greater reaction in a shorter time. Everybody's voice is now against him, and his famous treaty and his Budget are pronounced enormous and dangerous blunders.' Two days later Disraeli told Mrs. Willyams that Gladstone's reputation had ' collapsed more suddenly and completely than anything since Jonah's gourd.' The demands on the Exchequer for the China War and for national defence increased, and it was felt that the yield from the duties to be repealed was

---

[1] *Gladstone*, Bk. V., ch. 14.

wanted.   The principal of these was the paper duty, the
last of the hindrances to a cheap Press.   Its repeal was
to cost the revenue a million; accordingly, as the financial
pressure increased, the majority for repeal fell from 53
to 9.   Disraeli disliked ' taxes on knowledge,' as he had
frequently shown; but most of the newspaper duties had
already been swept away, and he entered heartily into the
Conservative campaign to retain this particular one at
this moment.   Even the Prime Minister agreed with the
Opposition in resisting his colleague's plan, and wrote to
the Queen that if the Lords threw out the repealing Bill
' they would perform a good public service.'   The Lords
did throw out the Bill, thereby provoking a constitutional
dispute with the Commons as to their rights in regard to
taxation.   Gladstone and the Radicals advocated violent
measures against the Lords; the Conservatives rallied
to the Prime Minister.   Derby sent Malmesbury to Lady
Palmerston to ' assure her of the support of our whole
party against the Radicals, and to give a positive promise
that we will not coalesce with them in or out of office.
Disraeli,' adds Malmesbury, ' is equally determined on this
point.'[1]   Palmerston therefore was able to restrain the
Commons from taking any action beyond the mild protest of comparatively innocuous resolutions; and Disraeli
in the debate had the satisfaction, in Derby's words, of
' knocking J. Russell's and Gladstone's heads together.'
Gladstone had to put up with temporary defeat over the
Excise duty on paper, but he had some consolation at the
close of the session by carrying resolutions for the reduction of the corresponding Customs duty.[2]   Disraeli had
hoped for a further success, though he subsequently protested that he had never really contemplated it; but
Palmerston's representations, that the approval of the
treaty which Parliament had already expressed bound
members to fulfil their engagements under it, prevailed
over the reluctance of many Liberals to continue their
support of Gladstone's proposals.   The numbers were

---

[1] *Memoirs*, June 1, 1860.   [2] Aug. 6.

266 to 233. 'I hear you have left town not a little disgusted,' wrote Derby to Disraeli. 'It is, however, satisfactory that, if we were defeated on Monday, it was from no defection of our own people, nor even any miscalculation on the part of our Whips; but a gross violation of pledges on the part of the so-called Liberals.'

The long session of 1860 lasted till the end of August. Besides his action on the Reform Bill and the Budget, Disraeli intervened with effect both in the discussion of French and Italian affairs [1] and in defence of Church rates.[2]

To Mrs. Brydges Willyams.

CARLTON CLUB, *June* 20.—It is a long time since I wrote, but the course of affairs has been very critical, and, indeed, is so intense at the present moment that I have not been able to free myself from the absorption of public duties sufficiently to realise private correspondence.

The withdrawal of the Reform Bill was the culminating point of three months of masterly manœuvres on the part of the Opposition, and has shaken the Government to the centre. They are dispirited and discredited; and have to cope with numerous difficulties, to meet and manage which requires both reputation and courage. I myself wish to maintain them for a season, but I begin to doubt the possibility of doing so.

Yesterday the King of the Belgians sent for me at Buckingham Palace, and I had a most interesting conference with him on foreign affairs. He is the wisest Prince in Europe: natural abilities and great experience; his judgment of men and things very mature. He proposed that we should in future maintain together a confidential correspondence.

To-morrow we dine with the Queen. It is unusual to ask the Leader of Opposition to dine more than once during the season at the Palace, and I suspect this second invitation will excite comments. There was a leading article in some of the Radical journals a few weeks ago, on the enormity of Lord Derby having dined three times at Court since December.

Friday will be a very hard day for me: for at twelve o'clock the Committee of the House of Commons meets, which is to draw up the report on the famous question of the right of the Lords to throw out the Bill for the repeal of the paper duty; at six o'clock precisely I am to take the chair for the Prince

[1] See Ch. 9.   [2] See Ch. 10.

Consort, at the anniversary dinner of the ' Society of Arts, Manufactures and Commerce '; and as soon as I can get away from St. James's Hall, where the dinner of four hundred of the ablest men in London takes place, I am going, with Mrs. Disraeli, to a ball at the Palace. I would, for her sake, gladly escape the latter, as on the following day, Saturday, she gives a great morning fête, in honor of the Queen's review of the Volunteers in Hyde Park, and has invited upwards of seven hundred members of the *beau monde*. I fear the terrible weather will spoil the fête, and that we shall all be drowned. . . .

To Mrs. Disraeli.

July 16, 1860.—No income tax. I could not myself have brought forward a more Conservative Budget ;[1] though I would sooner have cut off my right hand than have done so under the same circumstances. Gladstone looked like a beaten hound, and ate no ordinary quantity of dirt.

Bright has not only to pay a paper tax, but it is to be applied to a China War! What a combination of injuries and insults !

To Mrs. Brydges Willyams.

GROSVENOR GATE, *July* 23.—An interesting and exhausting session is drawing to a close. Until the last ten days, the existence of the Government, in its integrity, has been in daily danger—so it beat fox-hunting. The hours very late, some- times four o'clock in the morning. I have borne it well, as I have contrived to sleep my hours all the same, and with a due quantum of sleep, health and vigor seem to me a mere matter of course. But rising thus at noon, and being obliged to be in your place in the House at four o'clock, your day is neces- sarily very brief, and all correspondence and general business fall into terrible arrear. . . .

It has been a very gay and brilliant social season; at least Mrs. Disraeli tells me so, for I never go anywhere except Wednesdays off and Saturdays—with rare exceptions. I went, however, to two fêtes on Thursday and Friday last, which amused me. The first was at the Russian Ambassador's, at Chesham House, and was really like a festival in a play, or a masquerade. There were a dozen servants in scarlet liveries, who never left the entrance hall, only bowing to those who arrived, and ushering you to one of the finest and most fantastical staircases in London, reaching to the roof of the

---

[1] This was Gladstone's supplementary financial statement, rendered necessary by the increased expenditure for the China War and by the failure of the repeal of the paper duty.

house, and full of painted and gilded galleries. All the other attendants, who swarmed, were in Court dresses and wore swords.

The other entertainment, which amused me, was a ball, given by the Duchess of Wellington, at Apsley House. I had never been there since the death of the famous old Duke. This magnificent mansion has been entirely redecorated, and with consummate taste and splendor. The gallery, where he used to give his Waterloo banquets, now hung with ruby silk and covered with rare pictures, the spoils of Spain and Portugal, is one of the most effective rooms in this city. The banqueting room, hung with full-length portraits of the sovereigns and notabilities at the Congress of Vienna, most interesting at this moment, when the pact has really become history, and the famous settlement of 1815 is disturbed, and perhaps about to be superseded.

I closed my season last night by making my bow to the wife of my rival, Lady Palmerston, whose crowded saloons at Cambridge House were fuller even than usual, for she had invited all the deputies of the Statistical Congress, a body of men who, for their hideousness, the ladies declare were never equalled: I confess myself to a strange gathering of men with bald heads, and all wearing spectacles. You associate these traits often with learning and profundity, but when one sees 100 bald heads and 100 pairs of spectacles the illusion, or the effect, is impaired.

I hope you are quite well. Summer has set in, as Horace Walpole says, with its usual severity. Lady Ebury said to me the other night that she lived only for climate and the affections. . . .

In his first letter to the King of the Belgians, Disraeli gave his own summary of the results of the session.

To the King of the Belgians.

Aug. 23, 1860.—As the session of Parliament is about to close, it may be convenient to place before your Majesty its results, so far as it has influenced the position of the two great parties.

In the audience which your Majesty was graciously pleased to grant to me in the month of June, I indicated to your Majesty the three causes which had mainly contributed to the consolidation of the Conservative party during this year:

1. The withdrawal by the Government of their Reform Bill.

2. The successful assertion of the authority of the House of Lords.

3. The appearance of a Church party in the House of Commons for the first time since 1840, and the fact of the clergy throughout the country again generally acting with the Conservatives.

Later in the session the discontent with the French treaty, and probably a jealousy of Mr. Gladstone, which a section of the Whig party wished publicly to express, rendered it expedient that a decided opposition should be given to the repeal of the duty on foreign paper. This struggle elicited another important feature in the relative state of parties: viz., the complete alienation of the Roman Catholic party from the present Government, avowedly caused by their Italian policy. On that occasion, while many independent Roman Catholic Irish members voted with the Conservatives, as has been their custom of late, the Whig Roman Catholic members for the first time evinced their disapproval of the Ministry, rose, and in a body left the House, including among many others the leading names of Lord Ed. Howard, Mr. More O'Ferrall, Mr. Monsell, and Sir John Acton.[1]

Had not the very Whig section which had originated the resistance against the repeal of the foreign duty on paper wheeled round in this emergency and supported the Government, Lord Palmerston would have been in a minority, which I was far from desiring and had never contemplated.

Your Majesty will therefore perceive that the course of Italian politics may have a most important influence upon affairs in this country.

What that course may be I will not presume to speculate on, when addressing so wise and well informed a Prince as your Majesty. I should rather be grateful were I to receive on this head an intimation of your Majesty's views.

But assuming I was right in my observations expressed more than two years ago in Parliament, that Lord John Russell was counting without his host in supposing that Italian Liberals would be content merely to take the mild form of English Whiggery, and that he must be prepared to encounter the long-matured machinations of the secret societies in whose existence Lord John then would never believe, events may occur which may render war, and even a general war, a necessity for Louis Napoleon.

The English will enter into a war with France with reluctance, but, once embarked in it, they will never cease until their entire object is attained. If there is to be that war, it is of importance that Lord Palmerston should begin it.

[1] Lord E. Howard, W. Monsell, and Sir J. Acton, the historian, were afterwards raised to the peerage, on Gladstone's recommendation, as Lords Howard of Glossop, Emly, and Acton.

The consolidation of the Conservative party, of which Disraeli boasted to the King, was certainly greater at the close than at the beginning of the session, owing largely to his own adroit handling of a delicate situation; but it was still very imperfect. Indeed, throughout the Palmerston Administration the difficulties of Disraeli's leadership were considerable. Following Derby's advice, the bulk of the party were content to keep Palmerston in office, so long as they could exercise a general control over him. They suspected Disraeli, not without cause, of fretting, now and again, under these tactics, though he professed a general acquiescence in them, and even, at times, actively promoted them; and many Conservatives were ready to break away from his leadership on any sign of a serious attack on Ministers, especially if there were a likelihood that the attack would be supported by the Radicals. Derby warned him early in January, 1860: ' I think I ought to tell you that I hear of a cabal getting up among our people, some of whom will have it that you have come to an understanding with the Radicals and mean to throw them over on Reform. . . . I hear that Big Ben[1] (of course) is among the leaders of this *fronde.*' Further details were sent him in the following month by a friendly follower.

From Sir James Fergusson.[2]

Private. 27, CHESHAM STREET, *Feb.* 20, 1860.—. . . I know, from authority I believe to be certain, that lately there was an imminent risk of a defection among those who act with you, so serious that the strong party you had in the House of Commons would not have been at your command: that a considerable number of ' Conservatives ' were prepared to impugn supposed acts of yours, and this so recently as on the eve of the meeting of Parliament. . . . This bad feeling, temporarily allayed, I believe, by Lord Derby, was in a great degree dispelled by your speech upon the Bill for the Abolition of Church Rates, as it is said, among other occasions, to have been excited by one upon the Reform Bill last session.

[1] See Vol. I., p. 1444.   [2] Afterwards Governor of Bombay.

It is represented to me that the loyalty of the party towards you now depends upon your course with regard to the question of the treaty and the Budget: that the general desire of the party is identical with the views which I told Earle had been expressed in conversation with me by Mr. Horsman, viz., that it would be in the last degree distasteful, not only to the great body of the Conservative party, but to most of your late colleagues, were you to attempt to turn out the present Government, with a view to Lord Derby's Administration again taking office; but that you would consolidate and strengthen the party by checking the present dangerous policy of the Government, defeating their measures, while you threw back upon them the language held two years since by Lord Palmerston, and commanded them to keep their places in the face of such defeat. . . .

Though Disraeli's policy during the session was to a large extent such as Fergusson recommended, and though it was remarkably successful, the discontent was only very partially appeased. Greville's diary for 1860 is full of references to the ' disorganisation ' of the party and to what he calls ' their undisguised dislike of their leader.' On February 22, in regard to ' Gladstone's triumph ' in one of the early Budget debates, he writes that it ' did not seem to be matter of much grief to many of the Conservative party; for I hear that, however they may still act together on a great field-day, the hatred and distrust of Disraeli is greater than ever in the Conservative ranks, and Derby himself, when he heard how his colleague had been demolished, did not seem to care much about it.' On March 18 he repeats a story that ' an eminent Conservative, who had begged not to be quoted, had said that he knew Derby was violently discontented with Disraeli, and prepared to dissolve their political connection.' There is no other evidence of Derby's discontent than the gossip retailed to Greville; and, if it existed, it was only a passing mood. But the disorganisation of the party was undoubted; and in April the most authoritative organ of Conservatism, the *Quarterly Review*, which had ignored Disraeli, both as a novelist and as a politician, till about 1850, and had since then mentioned him only occasionally,

and with obvious dislike, made an attack of calculated
bitterness on his leadership. If the invective lacked
finish, it certainly did not lack gall. Disraeli was described as a 'favourite of misfortune,' who 'went forth
blundering and to blunder,' who had 'unrivalled powers
of conducting his party into the ditch.' The policy of
the late Derby Ministry in adopting Reform was singled
out for special condemnation. There was no difficulty,
the writer held, in divining 'the real parentage' of the
Bill of 1859.

It was of a piece with a policy which had long misguided
and discredited the Conservative party in the House of
Commons. To crush the Whigs by combining with the
Radicals was the first and last maxim of Mr. Disraeli's Parliamentary tactics. He had never led the Conservatives to
victory as Sir Robert Peel had led them to victory. He
had never procured the triumphant assertion of any Conservative principle, or shielded from imminent ruin any
ancient institution. But he had been a successful leader to
this extent, that he had made any Government, while he was
in Opposition, next to an impossibility. His tactics were so
various, so flexible, so shameless—the net by which his combinations were gathered in was so wide—he had so admirable
a knack of enticing into the same lobby a happy family of
proud old Tories and foaming Radicals, martial squires jealous
for their country's honour, and manufacturers who had
written it off their books as an unmarketable commodity—
that so long as his party backed him no Government was
strong enough to hold out against his attacks. They might
succeed in repelling this sally or that; but sooner or later their
watchful and untiring enemy, perfectly reckless from what
quarter or in what uniform he assaulted, was sure to find out
the weak point at which the fortress could be scaled.

'Opponents,' the writer added, 'were wont to speak of
the laudable discipline of the Tory party. They little
knew the deep and bitter humiliation that was masked
by the outward loyalty of its votes.' Disraeli's speeches
and tactics might well induce the nation to believe that
'Conservatives registered and organised, and lavishly
spent their money and their labour, merely that the ambition of a few, or of one, might be contented.' The party

could only regain the nation's trust ' if, with their leaders
or without their leaders, they resolutely refuse the fellowship of those who abhor their creed.'   But if ' fidelity to
a leader who has been tried and has been found wanting
is to be preferred to all other considerations,' then ' woe
to the blind that lead, woe to the blind that follow !'

It was a wholesale denunciation, hardly qualified by a
recognition, in one sentence, of ' some improvement of
tone ' in Disraeli's conduct in the session of 1860.   The
effect, indeed, was rather spoilt by the admiration expressed, in contrast to Disraeli's shiftiness, for the consistent Conservatism of Peel—Peel, who took over Roman
Catholic Emancipation from the Whigs, and Free Trade
from the Radicals !   The writer really went behind Peel,
and his article was a plea for a return to the Eldonian
policy of exclusion and restriction.   The great work of
Conservatism was apparently to be purely negative—
to arrest the march of democracy; the party was envisaged
as a territorial and not as a national party.   Tories were
advised, by one who spoke for many besides himself, to
reduce themselves to the state of hopeless inefficiency and
narrowness from which Disraeli's genius had rescued them.

Attention was called to this bitter article in the
House of Commons by Russell, who naturally inquired
who was now the leader of the Tories.   *The Times* took
the matter up.[1]   The leading journal was at that time
a strong supporter of Palmerston; but it was able to do
justice to some extent to Disraeli, though it assumed
rather a patronising air, and insinuated, quite unjustifi-
ably, that he had never been sincere in his advocacy of
Protection.   The following passages give, in substance, a
true picture of his work:

The Tory party, when Mr. Disraeli first took the lead of
them, were in a position of the most marked and violent
hostility to the material interests of the whole country, and
embarked on a career which seemed to tend to something
little short of political annihilation.   With untiring patience

[1] June 6.

Mr. Disraeli set himself to bring order out of this chaos. . . .
It would be unjust, ungrateful, and ungenerous, in the party
which he has redeemed from absolute disorganisation, and
made once more a real and effective power in the State, to
forget for a single moment its signal obligations to him. . . .
He has taught them to profess, at any rate, and probably to
feel, a sympathy for the great body of their countrymen, and
to recognise the necessity of looking to opinion for support.
When he found the Tory party they were armed in impenetrable prejudice; under him they have become no longer an
impediment, but competitors with the Liberals in the career
of progress. Twice has he led them to office. . . . Having
uniformly to fight an uphill battle and to sustain a losing
cause, he has acquitted himself in a manner to gain the
sympathy of those most keenly opposed to his policy, and
to prove that he possesses talents which, under happier
circumstances, might have made his Administration eminently
creditable to himself and useful to his country.

Russell described the author of the *Quarterly* article
as an obscure writer. But there was little secret about
the authorship; and the writer was not obscure, but
was a rising Conservative politician, Lord Robert Cecil,
member for Stamford; who, as political society found it
piquant to reflect, in denouncing the actions of the Ministry of 1858-59 and the conduct of Disraeli, was attacking
his own father, the late President of the Council, and that
father's personal friend and colleague. Family disagreement, which had made it necessary for him to earn money
by his pen, may have sharpened his natural dislike of a
policy repugnant to his high Toryism, and of a personality
which appeared to him, as it had originally to Derby, on
the surface uncongenial. As a *Saturday Reviewer*, Robert
Cecil had been for some time associated with Disraeli's
severest critics; and from this period onwards, in opposition or in office, till foreign politics brought the two men
together in the late seventies, he was a leader of the anti-
Disraeli section of the Tory party—rather perhaps in the
Press than by overt action in Parliament. 'He has written
anonymous articles* against me before and since I was
his colleague; I do not know whether he wrote them when
he was my colleague,' said Disraeli in 1868. Happily, the

misunderstandings were finally cleared up, and the reviewer came to appreciate the high qualities of the man
whom he had spent his earlier political life in condemning
and counterworking.

With this flagrant proof of indiscipline and ill-feeling
laid before the world by the oracle of Toryism, it is rather
pathetic to find Mrs. Disraeli assuring Mrs. Willyams on
May 6 that 'D. was never on better terms with his party,'
and on June 6 that ' he never was so popular with his party
—all right. The person who wrote against him in the magazine is angry because Dizzy did not give him office—Lord
Robert Cecil.' It is true that, except Cecil, no person of
real authority in the party lent himself to the attacks.
Even Gathorne Hardy, though for some years he distrusted Disraeli, and once in a moment of irritation
described him as ' a hateful leader,' was wont to say to
complainants: 'I found him your leader; what has he
done to deserve deposition ?'[1] But Disraeli himself had
no illusions. To such an extent did he resent the ingratitude with which his services to the party had been met,
that once again he threatened, and apparently seriously
contemplated, resignation in preference to further experience of such unworthy treatment.

To Sir William Miles.

HOUSE OF COMMONS, *June* 11, 1860.—You were speaking
to me, the other night, of the state of the party, your regret
at its discontented condition, and your hope that, before you
left us, those sitting behind me might yet become my supporters. I could not, at the moment, pursue the conversation, because our position was then so critical that it required
unceasing vigilance, and I could not venture to be frank.

Out of those dangerous waters we have now steered, and
the course which I pursued some months ago in great difficulties has succeeded, and, I hope, saved us. I may now,
therefore, communicate to you without reserve.

I think it is fourteen years ago since yourself, then the
leader of the country gentlemen, and another county
member—alas ! no more—called upon me at my private
residence, and appealed to me to assist you at a moment of

---

[1] Gathorne Hardy's *Cranbrook*, Vol. I., p. 124.

apparently overwhelming disaster. I ultimately agreed to do so, but with great unwillingness, and only because ultimately I found Lord George Bentinck, with whom I had no acquaintance, had undertaken to fulfil the duties of leadership, if I, with others, would support him; and because, from my earliest years, my sympathies had been with the landed interest of England.

I need say nothing of the years 1846-7-8. They were not inglorious to the country party.

When the catastrophe occurred at the end of 1848, and we lost Lord George, Lord Derby, with whom I had very slight relations, wrote to me, and asked me to undertake, under certain conditions, the management of our party. I declined to do so, though honoring duly the offer. I saw personal difficulties ahead, and the engagement on my part would have involved the sacrifice of several thousands a year, which I would willingly, having no children, have relinquished, if I possessed the confidence of the gentlemen of England, but which, without that great reward, I was not willing to give up.

After long and earnest representations, principally urged by Lord Derby, the present Duke of Rutland, yourself, and Lord Henry Bentinck, I undertook the office of leading the somewhat shattered remnants of the country party. They had divided on Lord G. Bentinck's great party motion on Irish Railways *120*. This was the condition in which affairs were put in my hands. Before three years had passed, by a series of motions on agricultural burdens made by myself, they had become a moiety of the House of Commons, while I left no stone unturned to reconstruct the Tory party by bringing back the Peelite section to our colors.

This was my unvarying effort, and for this I have always been prepared to make the greatest personal sacrifices. The leadership was offered twice to Lord Palmerston, and once, even so late as 1858, after the Ellenboro' disaster, to Sir James Graham: frequent offers, if not of a precise, of a flattering, nature have been made to Mr. Gladstone—and all at my instance, and, generally, personally.

Nevertheless they failed, and although Lord Derby and myself were unwilling to accept office ever without this reconstruction, we were obliged, in order to save the party from political annihilation, on two occasions to accept the responsibility—always in a great minority; on the last occasion the minority was 120. It was clear that such a state of affairs must always conclude in a dissolution; it was as clear that a dissolution could only restore Tory strength, not establish Tory power.

Of course our measures could not be carried after such dissolutions, great as might be our gain. But the strength of the party was restored. I have, however, to bear the brunt of disaster, and the measures of the Cabinet are called my measures, and I am held as alone to blame for their production.

This from my opponents I could bear, as I have had to bear much; but it is unreasonable that I should endure it from those who ought to be my friends.

The Tory party, as an Opposition, has never stood in a more solid—I would say prouder and more powerful—position than at this moment. The finance of Mr. Gladstone has blown up. The House of Lords exercises a real authority in the State. For the first time since 1841 (say 1839), there has been a real Church party in the House of Commons: the question of Parliamentary Reform has ceased to be a party question, and the Tories are cleared of the taint of opposition to popular franchise: they command half the House, and stand high in the country.

So long as they were in distress, I have borne without a murmur the neglect, the desertion, the personal insults, that I have experienced; so long even as these were confined to our own ranks, and not the scandal of the world, I would, for party sake, have been silent. But the Tories are no longer in distress—they have abundance of friends; and, with respect to the privacy of their feelings towards me, they chalk the walls in the market-place with my opprobrium.

I must therefore now take a step, which I wished to have done at the meeting of Parliament, and which nothing but the extreme difficulties and dangers of the party prevented my fulfilling. I must resign a leadership which I unwillingly accepted, and to which it is my opinion that fourteen years of unqualified devotion have not reconciled the party.

I will not communicate this resolve in the first instance to my colleagues, because I do not think that is a fair course to them, or to the party generally.

Your position is independent; you were originally deputed to solicit my undertaking the office; and you are in every respect best qualified to take the steps necessary in the present conjuncture. They should be taken with tact, and without unnecessarily exciting attention until all arrangements are completed. . . .

P.S.—I read with pain, but I felt the truth of the statement, in a Liberal journal, a day or two ago, that my leadership of the party was one of 'chronic revolt and unceasing conspiracy.'

It was a dignified, if not in every detail historically accurate,[1] letter, setting out a record of great and unimpeachable services. Miles received it with consternation, and immediately consulted with a few of the leading members of the party, such as Walpole, Henley, Trollope, Lord Hotham, and Seymer. They all spoke so highly of Disraeli's conduct of business that he was finally persuaded to take the letter back and treat it as not having been written. Miles reminded him that, ' when the pinch comes, notwithstanding their murmuring and cavil, [the party] come to the scratch like men.' He added: ' I do not think you are sensitive to attacks from our enemies; do not be too susceptible of the follies of our friends. . . Depend upon it that by advocating well-considered and moderate progress, and the necessity, for the cause of reliligion, of an Established Church, your lukewarm friends may be converted into ardent supporters, and so thorough a bond of union may be established between yourself and party as may render you irresistible.'

Disraeli's success during the session was so marked that even Cecil was fain, in the *Quarterly* for July, to write of ' Conservative Reaction,' and to temper, in a grudging way, some of his strictures of April, even pretending, in spite of the unambiguous phrases we have quoted, that there had never been any question of change of leadership. At the same time he justified the April article as ' plainly speaking out what everyone was saying of [Disraeli] in private, and no one would say in public.' Now the sinner was treated as repentant. In the session just drawing to a close, ' he has shown no inclination to flinch from the assertion of Conservative principles; he has made no attempts to boil them down to suit the palates of Radical allies. . . . We have a right to assume that the change is permanent, and that Mr. Disraeli has abandoned for ever the '' unholy alliances '' and the trimming tactics of which events have proved the hollowness and the shame.' It was not a very generous acknowledgment; but it

[1] See Vol. I., III., chs. 4 and 5.

is true that, in the Parliament of 1859-1865, Disraeli, sensitive as ever to the political atmosphere, appeared rather in the character of the defender of the institutions of his country, than in that of their reformer in the social and political spheres; and that, at any rate in the first part of the period, he avoided rather than welcomed Radical co-operation.

The summer and autumn of 1860 were occupied with momentous developments in foreign affairs. Garibaldi landed in Sicily, and produced a revolution both there and subsequently in Naples, with the result of the incorporation in the kingdom of Victor Emmanuel of all Italy except Venetia and a remnant of the Papal States; and in America the first decisive step towards Civil War was taken in the declaration by South Carolina of her secession from the Union. The success of the Italian revolution, which was warmly welcomed in England, strengthened the Government; and Disraeli, recognising that the time was not ripe for adopting the offensive, suggested in the winter that the tender of support which Malmesbury had been authorised to make to Palmerston in the previous session should be renewed in a more formal way for the coming year. ' I should fancy,' he wrote to Derby on December 8, ' that the Ministry have no longer a majority; certainly not, if we show indifference. But however this may be, it is expedient that they should be kept in.'

How Malmesbury carried out his leaders' wishes appears in detail from the Prime Minister's report to the Queen:

Lord Palmerston to Queen Victoria.

PICCADILLY, *Jan.* 27, 1861.—. . . Viscount Palmerston saw Lord Malmesbury on Friday before the Cabinet. . . . [Lord Malmesbury] said that he was charged by Lord Derby and Mr. Disraeli with a message similar to that which he had conveyed last year, namely, that if Mr. Gladstone were to propose a democratic Budget making a great transfer of burthens from indirect to direct taxation, and if, the Cabinet refusing its concurrence, Mr. Gladstone were to retire, the Conservative party would give the Government substantial

support except in the case of the Government wishing to take
an active part in war against Austria. That this did not, of
course, mean an abstinence from usual attacks and criticisms
in debate, but that no step would in such case be taken to
produce a change of Government. In fact, said Lord Malmesbury, neither the Conservative leaders nor the party wish at
present to come into office, and have no intention of taking
any step to turn the present Government out. Mr. Bright
had, indeed, proposed to Mr. Disraeli to join together with the
Radical party the Conservatives, for the purpose of turning
out the present Government, and especially to get rid of
Viscount Palmerston and Lord John Russell. Mr. Bright
said he would in that case give the Conservative Government
a two years' existence, and by the end of that time the country,
it might be hoped, would be prepared for a good and real
Reform Bill, and then a proper Government might be formed.
This proposal, which it must be owned was not very tempting, Lord Malmesbury said had been declined. He also
said that Count Persigny, on returning from one of his trips
to Paris, had brought a similar proposal from Mr. Cobden
for a co-operation of Radicals and Conservatives to overthrow
the present Government; but that also had been declined.
Viscount Palmerston requested Lord Malmesbury to convey his
thanks to Lord Derby and Mr. Disraeli for the handsome
communication which they had thus made to him, and to
assure them that he fully appreciated the honourable and
patriotic motives by which it had been prompted. . . .[1]

The offer of the Opposition to Palmerston was the more
handsome and valuable as the by-elections in the country
were turning in their favour. ' The Whig candidate won't
fight in Aberdeenshire,' wrote Disraeli to Mrs. Willyams
on January 19; ' the Whig candidate is beaten in Pem-
brokeshire; the Whig candidates will be beaten in Wiltshire and Leicester.' The Court, which desired both to
keep the Palmerston Administration in office and to
strengthen its conservative side, and which always used
its influence to mitigate, if not to deprecate, party warfare, was greatly pleased with the arrangement; and the
Disraelis received an invitation to stay at Windsor—an
attention to the Opposition which gave the quidnuncs
occasion for gossip.

[1] *Queen Victoria's Letters.*

To Lord Derby.

GROSVENOR GATE, *Jan.* 28, 1861.—. . . They[1] were very gracious and very communicative. They appeared to me greatly distressed and disgusted with public affairs. I had occasion to mention the state of our own party—its numbers, compactness, general good understanding, its increase of strength; and I ventured to say that we should probably win every impending election. ' But you have no newspapers,' he exclaimed pettishly, ' the country is governed by newspapers ! and all the Liberal journals are in the pay of foreign Powers. So much for the liberty of the Press. However, when Parliament is sitting their influence is less.'

We get from the *Life of the Prince Consort* the Prince's account of Disraeli's conversation. Disraeli said that the Conservative Opposition formed a compact body of 300 members; but they had no wish for the return of their leaders to office, and, indeed, were anxious to strengthen the hands of the Government in a bold national policy. A movement for the reduction of the expenses of our armaments, which had been initiated by Cobden and his friends, and which had taken the shape of a letter to Palmerston, signed by about sixty members of Parliament, had shown the existence of a considerable division in the ranks of the Ministerial supporters. But the Conservative party were in no way inclined to take advantage of this state of things. On the contrary, they were prepared to support the Government, and even to help them out of scrapes, if they got into any; all they required from them in return being that they should not enter into a line of ' democratic finance.'[2]

To Mrs. Brydges Willyams.

GROSVENOR GATE, *Feb.* 9, 1861.—. . . I think I have got everything now in good order, and have brought the troops into the field in ample numbers and in fine condition.

The difficulty is to keep them in: but forbearance and patience are clearly our game, and though I could, the first night, have destroyed the Government, I was wise enough to refrain. In the meantime, we win every election, and time is big with great events, which will demand a strong, patriotic, and Conservative Government. . . .

[1] The Queen and the Prince.   [2] Martin's *Prince Consort*, Vol. V., p. 286.

Gladstone's Budget for 1861 did not propose any great transference of burdens from indirect to direct taxation, and so did not bring into active working the arrangement of the Conservative leaders with Palmerston. But, while taking a penny off the income tax, it selected the paper duty for relief instead of the war taxes on tea and sugar, thus, in the opinion of the Opposition, prosecuting the constitutional quarrel with the Lords at the expense of the real interests of the country. One of the main features of Gladstone's speech was a strong protest against the increasing national expenditure, which amounted this year to nearly 70 millions. Income tax could be dispensed with, he said, if the country was contented to be governed at a cost of 60 millions; but if 70 millions were wanted income tax was necessary. Disraeli was justifiably severe on this ineffectual outburst.

There is no innovation so gigantic as a Chancellor of the Exchequer denouncing the expenditure as profligate for which he is supplying at the same time the ways and means. If he believes the expenditure to be impolitic, to use the mildest term, on what principle can he vindicate his sitting on that bench ? . . . The right hon. gentleman insinuates that the Government as well as himself are recommending and pursuing an expenditure that is contrary to their conviction of public necessity. It is someone or other, some unknown but irresistible force, that urges them on. Sometimes it appears to be the country, sometimes the House, but never the Ministry.

Under Disraeli's guidance, the Opposition took the line of endeavouring to substitute a reduction of the duty on tea for the repeal of the duty on paper. Such a policy would be at least equally beneficial to the country, would leave the existing sources of revenue undiminished, and would avoid humiliating the Lords. Northcote, who first established his Parliamentary reputation by his speeches in the numerous debates on this Budget, thought the game a good one, but was afraid his leader might spoil it by over-cleverness. ' Disraeli,' he wrote to Lady Northcote on April 19, ' is in the highest spirits because the battle is to be fought by tactics and not by brute force, and he thinks he is going to display great powers of generalship. I am always a little afraid of his manœuvring, especially when he has a good game, because he always spoils it by overdoing something or other.'[1]   Whether Disraeli was to blame or not, Gladstone's vigour overcame both the luke-warmness of his own chief and the attacks of the Opposition.   A motion to reduce the tea duty was defeated by 18 votes—it was not a majority, said Disraeli, as it was only in its teens; and the repeal of the paper duty was carried by 15: 296 to 281.[2]   This was not a handsome victory for the Government, but it sufficed; and the House of Lords made no effort to continue the fight.

In truth, it is always difficult and thankless to organise opposition with a view to dictating to the Executive which of two taxes it shall remit.   Moreover, in this case the constitutional question rendered the Conservative position peculiarly embarrassing.   Gladstone determined to include all the financial proposals in one Bill, so as to make it impossible for the House of Lords (who had the right to reject, but not to amend, a tax Bill) to pick and choose among the taxes.   While this procedure was strongly resented by the Tories, it was felt by many of them to be impossible to declare it to be unconstitutional; and, as Graham pointed out in debate, ' Up with the Lords and down with the Commons ' would not be a good hustings cry for the Opposition at elections.   On the constitutional point Walpole and Heathcote declared their support of the Government, and Stanley showed a disposition to take the same view.

From Lord Derby.

St. James's Square, *May* 2, 1861.—Stanley came home with me last night, and I did not like his tone; he was very reserved, but I much fear he is going wrong.   He has been talking with Malins[3] (this I heard from M.) and Walpole. Surely there is no fear of the latter ?   If anybody can keep Stanley right, you can. . . .

[1] Lang's *Northcote*, p. 104.   [2] May 30.
[3] Afterwards Vice-Chancellor Sir Richard Malins.

Disraeli was able to prevail on Stanley to keep silence in debate; but, with a party thus divided, he naturally discouraged opposition to the second reading of the Finance Bill, and concentrated his efforts on resisting in Committee the clause relating to the paper duty. Even here he had the greatest difficulty to bring Walpole and Heathcote into line.

To Sir William Heathcote.

[*May* 27, 1861.]—I attribute such importance to the unity of the Conservative party that I should, as a general rule, always be ready to waive any course, which I might think it desirable for us to pursue, rather than endanger our complete concord.

Under these circumstances, it is with the utmost pain that I learn the step you and Walpole contemplate taking with reference to the question of the paper duty. The policy of resisting its repeal was adopted after great deliberation, at which Walpole assisted; and although after that decision I felt it my duty to take every step that I thought likely to effect the desired result, I have been so scrupulous not to move again without materially advancing our object that I have continually refrained from acting, though ever with a distinct reservation of my right to do so, and even an assertion of my future purpose.

It was my opinion that nothing would justify our again trying the issue unless we were assured of the assistance of some of the most eminent members of the Whig party, and even of the course being originated by one of that body. There was a very general and very urgent disposition in our party to support the division of the Budget Bill; but in deference to your opinions and those of Walpole on that subject I would not sanction the attempt. I inferred, however, from your declaration in your speech that your objection to the financial policy was unchanged.

In the midst of the Whitsun week I received a communication that some of the most influential Whig gentlemen were prepared to speak and vote against the paper clause in Committee, if our party were still prepared to support them. And on this I resolved upon our course.

It was impossible to consult anyone, for everyone was absent; but with great deference and with no assumption of arrogance, which I hope is foreign from my nature, I would observe that, although the individual entrusted with the conduct of a Parliamentary party would act very unwarrantably in deciding upon a policy without consulting his principal friends, it is a very different case with respect to the tactics which are to carry that policy into effect. These must necessarily depend upon constantly changing circumstances, and often are the decision of a moment.

If the leader of a Parliamentary party cannot be trusted with deciding on tactics, he really can be entrusted with nothing, and it would be very much like the old Aulic Councils, which, full of prudence and science, always conducted the Austrian armies to discomfiture. . . .

Believing that I was carrying the wishes of the united party entirely into effect by my present course, I view with dismay and the deepest sense of personal vexation your contemplated course.

Upon my representations, some hundreds of gentlemen at great trouble, and even at great expense, have hurried up to the House of Commons. What must be their irritation and their disappointment to find voting against them men like yourself—the principal personages of the party ! I entreat you to think of the effect of their mortified feelings on the mustering of our party on subjects of less exciting, but of far more important interest, than a tax or a duty. The labours of two sessions will be destroyed.

Since we have acted together, I have done everything in my power to meet your views, and would without hesitation have prevented the present movement, had I supposed it would have separated us. I write to you with deep emotion, for I know how much is at stake. I entreat you to consider well the course you are taking. I feel persuaded that, if you will view the circumstances in which we are placed deeply and dispassionately, you will not only support me at this moment, but use all your great and just influence with those who are guided by your example. . . .

Besides pleading thus specially with Heathcote and Walpole, who responded to his appeal, Disraeli sent out an urgent letter to others among his followers, warning them that Derby was very anxious that the impending division should prove the unity of the Conservative party. But in spite of all his efforts more than twenty Conservatives absented themselves from the division,[1] a number sufficient to have turned the Government majority of 15 into a minority. Disraeli in consequence, records Henry Cecil Raikes on June 15, ' withdrew himself from the House

---

[1] May 30.

altogether for three or four days, and declined to return until he had received a satisfactory apology from the malcontents.'[1]   But he was anxious not to emphasise the existence of this undercurrent of discontent, and declined a flattering proposal of a demonstration in his favour from his loyal friends.

To Sir Matthew White Ridley.[2]

GROSVENOR GATE, *June* 7, 1861.—I am honored, and deeply gratified, by the invitation which yourself, and others of my friends, have, this morning, brought me from those members of the Carlton Club who are also members of the House of Commons, to meet them at dinner ' as a testimony of the undiminished value they set upon my services to the Conservative party, and of their earnest and friendly feeling towards myself.'

My services are at all times amply rewarded by the indulgent belief of my friends, that they contribute, however slightly, to the progress and welfare of the party whose interests with me, I trust, will always be paramount to any personal consideration.

If, therefore, I presume to decline a proposition so flattering as this invitation, it is only because I feel its acceptance at this moment might lead to misconception, and foster a notion as unfounded as it might be mischievous, that there is any material want of concord in the Conservative ranks.

Colleagues as well as followers added to Disraeli's worries at this critical time. When he returned to his seat in the House after his calculated absence, he was met by a long letter of complaint from one who had sat with him in both of Derby's Governments, the essence of the grievance being insufficiency of consultation. Disraeli justified himself in similar terms to those contained in his letter to Heathcote, adding:

After all, politics is like war—roughish work. We should not be over-sensitive. We have enough to do and to bear without imaginary grievances. Somebody must lead—but

---

[1] H. C. Raikes's *Life*, p. 32.   Sir Henry Edwards, M.P., wrote to Disraeli in June of the following year: ' Am I at liberty to state in the Carlton and elsewhere that last year—after our defeat—you resigned the leadership of the party, and were pressed into its service again by Trollope, who represented a very influential section of the landed interest in the House of Commons ?'

[2] The 4th baronet, M.P. for N. Northumberland 1859-1868.

I wish to live with my colleagues on terms of perfect equality; and after reading your long letter of complaints over again, you will permit me to say that I do not think they are very substantial.

Disraeli had spoken frequently throughout this prolonged fight against a financial policy which created, he said, an artificial surplus in order to perpetuate a financial caprice. The details of dead-and-gone financial debates are wearisome, but a passage may be rescued in which he vindicated the House of Lords. Its power, he said, had no doubt greatly diminished, as that of the Commons had increased.

But the House of Lords still possess a great and growing influence in the conviction of the national mind that an intermediate body between the popular branch of the legislature and absolute legislation is a great security for public liberty and for temperate government. The people of England feel that the existence of a body of that kind is a great blessing; and all the public experience of Europe has assured them that it is a body which cannot be artificially created. They therefore consider it a very fortunate circumstance for this country that such an intermediate body should have risen, supported by property, by tradition, and by experience, ready to act with the critical faculty which is necessary when precipitate legislation is threatened, and at least to obtain time, so that upon all questions of paramount importance the ultimate decision should be founded on the mature opinion of an enlightened nation.

To Mrs. Brydges Willyams.

GROSVENOR GATE, *March* 16, 1861.—It was most kind of you to write after my health. *Between ourselves*, I took advantage of a very slight indisposition to absent myself from some debates, where, had I been present, more serious consequences might have occurred than I care, at this moment, to accomplish.

It is difficult, almost impossible, to keep the present Government in, though the sudden death of the Duchess of Kent,[1] which took place last night, will assist that result. . . .

There was a pitched battle in the Commons last Wednesday, on the county franchise, and the Conservatives gained a great victory in a full House. This has been our second

---

[1] Queen Victoria's Mother.

great effort before Easter, the first being on the Church rate, when we were only in a minority of 15; and after Easter I think, we shall win on this also. . . .[1]

CARLTON CLUB, *April* 24, 1861.—. . . I have endeavoured to keep the Ministry in, but they tempt their fate, and a critical position has occurred.

On Monday I executed a reconnaissance in force, which will be continued for some days. I hope in the interval to discover the weak part of the enemy's position, and I count in about ten days to give him battle.

This is the real state of affairs. I am quite exhausted in listening to aide-de-camps, instructing generals of division, and writing endless despatches. . . .

HOUSE OF COMMONS, *May* 17, 1861.—. . . I had a very difficult task on Wednesday, in having to propose the health of the Duc d'Aumale, as Chairman of the Literary Fund. I could not allude to the most celebrated of his literary compositions—viz., the pamphlet which he has just published on the present state of affairs in France, and which you have no doubt heard of, perhaps read. It is a masterpiece of composition—of trenchant sarcasm and incisive logic; not unworthy of Junius, or even Pascal. However, I got through my task without blundering, and, I may venture to say to you, with great applause. It was the most brilliant meeting of the kind I ever attended.

The young Princes of France were at different parts of the table, mingling among three hundred distinguished guests. The youths are distinguished in their appearance, with winning manners, and highly educated, bearing wondrous names of historic renown—the Count of Paris, the Duc de Chartres, Gaston of Orleans, Count of Eu, the Prince de Condé, the Duc d'Alençon !

They are exiles, but they are young, and full of hope and dignity—and favored by Nature. . . .

HOUSE OF COMMONS, *June* 3, 1861.—The great battle which commenced this day week, and which, if concluded on that night, would have ended in the defeat of Ministers, terminated on Friday morning at two o'clock, and later, by their escape—by a slight majority. In the very hour of victory, when the signal for the last charge was given, I had the mortification, great for a general indeed, to see a division of my own troops march from the field of contest. One bears this, however, as one bears many things, when the heat of youth is over, and one has experienced, in one's time, what is the surest, perhaps the only, support under discomfiture—the memory of former success.

[1] See below, Ch. 10.

A Government saved by the too prudential forbearance of a section of their foes is not in a proud or a strong position, and I must say I look to the future without dismay. . . .

CARLTON CLUB, *Tuesday, July* 30, 1861.—. . . The end of the session, generally so exhausted and insipid, has been this year of a peculiarly exciting character: reconstructions of Governments, unexpected elevations to the peerage, unexpected death of young Ministers on whose future much depended—and now a great contested election in the City of London, where there has not been such a thing for twenty years—and a Tory in, or nearly in. I don't think the Lord Mayor will quite succeed; for at this hour, three o'clock, he is 100 behind—not much when they had polled 10,000. Such a state of affairs marks a great change in opinion, which has long been occurring. . . .[1]

They say there were never so many marriages as this year, almost all my unappropriated friends are destined in a few days, more or less—the Marquis of Bath, Lord John Manners,[2] Lord Mexborough, etc., etc. Thus the world wags! Strange events every day; the most extraordinary, the retirement of Lord John Russell from the House of Commons!

The retirement and death of Sidney Herbert, recently created Lord Herbert of Lea, coincided with the close of the session; the death of Graham followed in October; Aberdeen and Dalhousie had passed away in the previous year. Of the eminent Peelites with whom Disraeli had so often contended, none were left in the House of Commons at the end of the autumn save the most eminent of all—Gladstone. Even so the tale of deaths was not complete. The Prince Consort passed away in December.

To Lord Derby.

HUGHENDEN MANOR, *Nov.* 15, 1861.—We are engaged to be at Alnwick on the day you so kindly invite us to Knowsley, and having fixed the time ourselves, after much hesitation, I cannot venture to propose a new arrangement. This I much regret, as it would have given me great pleasure to have seen, and conversed with, you.

As for public affairs, no difficulty is solved, or even approaching solution. The recess, hitherto, has advanced

---

[1] The final numbers were—Wood (L.), 5747, Cubitt (C.), 5241. The vacancy was caused by Russell's elevation to the peerage.

[2] This was Lord John's second marriage, to Janetta Hughan. His first wife had died in 1854.

nothing, while the general decomposition proceeds. To be, at the same time, head of the Revolution and head of the Latin race is an inconsistent position, and this is the cause of the perplexities of the Emperor of France; but the Latin race will carry the day, and the compromise with revolution, sooner or later, must be an European war.   Our part in it is another question.

Since the days of the House of Atreus, there has never been a tragedy like the Peelites. Incredible that, since the fatal Act of 1846, Peel, Goulburn, Dalhousie, Aberdeen, Graham, Herbert, have all disappeared, and Lincoln getting as blind as Œdipus, while Palmerston, the senior of all, is rollicking ! The Mayor of Oxford told me yesterday that Cardwell had been in imminent danger, from dysentery : but this would only have been an affair of the lesser Ajax. Strange that, after all their loves and hates, Graham and Tom Duncombe should die in the same month, and of the same complaint

To Mrs. Brydges Willyams.

ALNWICK CASTLE, *Nov.* 24, 1861.—Three hundred men, for the last seven years, have been at work daily at this wondrous place, and they are to work for three years more. The result, that the ancient Castle of Hotspur is externally restored in perfect style; while the interior has all the refinement, fancy, and magnificence, of an Italian palace, in the palmiest days of Italian art. . . .   The Duke [of Northumberland] has formed a school of carvers in wood, where there are about thirty men, chiefly youths, working like Gibbons or Cellini. . . .

SEAHAM HALL, *Dec.* 8, 1861.—. . . This is a remarkable place, and our hostess[1] is a remarkable woman. Twenty miles hence she has a palace (Wynyard) in a vast park, with forest rides and antlered deer, and all the splendid accessories of feudal life. But she prefers living in a hall on the shores of the German Ocean, surrounded by her collieries, and her blast-furnaces, and her railroads, and unceasing telegraphs, with a port hewn out of the solid rock, screw steamers and four thousand pitmen under her control. One day she dined the whole 4,000 in one of the factories. In the town of Seaham Harbour, a mile off, she has a regular office, a fine stone building with her name and arms in front, and her flag flying above; and here she transacts, with innumerable agents, immense business—and I remember her five-and-twenty years ago, a mere fine lady; nay, the finest in London ! But one must find excitement, if one has brains. . . .

[1] Frances Anne Lady Londonderry.   She died Jan. 20, 1865.

The fascination of Gladstone's oratory and the force of his resolution had procured, though not without serious setbacks, a general success for his financial policy in 1860 and 1861. But in 1862, partly owing to the American War, but partly to Ministerial miscalculations, the national balance-sheet was a gloomy one, and, but for supplemental grants, the revenue would have shown a serious deficit. The policy of parting lightly with sources of revenue received a distinct check, and the Budget only proposed a few minor changes of taxation. It was, as Disraeli said, ' the sober hour that follows the financial flourishes,' and he thought the time had come for a critical examination of Gladstonian finance. He maintained[1] that the policy of the past two years had resulted in an accumulated deficiency of £4,000,000, and that during those years Gladstone had anticipated the resources of the country to the amount of £3,500,000; so that he had exceeded the ordinary revenue by the enormous sum of £7,500,000, at a time when that ordinary revenue was sustained by war taxation—a war income tax, and war duties on tea and sugar. ' But is that all ? It seems impossible that there can be any aggravation of such aggravated circumstances. And yet I can show the House that hitherto they have not measured the amount of the prodigality of the right hon. gentleman; for not only has he exceeded during two years the ordinary revenue of the country by £7,500,000, that revenue being sustained by war taxation, but he has done this at a period when the charges for the National Debt had diminished to the extent of £2,000,000 by the lapse of terminable annuities.'

The peroration of Disraeli's speech was a fine specimen of Parliamentary invective. He maintained that Gladstone should have spoken frankly about the income tax; that he had no right to ' fritter away the resources of the country and leave that tax pressing upon us.'

There is something in the speeches of the right hon. gentleman on this subject, and, indeed, on the whole of our financial

[1] April 7, 1862.

system, that fills me with perplexity; which, I think, conveys to the country a sentiment, not merely of perplexity, but of distrust; and it is this, that, while the right hon. gentleman is without parallel or exception the most profuse Finance Minister that ever directed the affairs of this country in time of peace, he is perpetually insinuating—to use the mildest term—both to this House and to the country, that he disapproves of our expenditure, and that he is burning to denounce it. Now, I say that is not a legitimate position for the right hon. gentleman to occupy. If he disapproves of this profuse expenditure, why does he sit on that bench, and lend to its enactment and enforcement all the authority of his character and all the lustre of his reputation ? . . . The right hon. gentleman has gained the confidence and support of a party, not very numerous, but still distinguished by talent, perseverance, and, I will add, integrity—I mean the party that calls for a reduction of our expenditure. How is it that that party, which preaches retrenchment and reduction, which believes that all our estimates, and especially the naval and military estimates, are much too extravagant; who are opposed to fortifications, and who do not much like iron ships, always support the Minister who brings forward these excessive estimates, and who provides for this enormous expenditure ? This is a great question. This, at least, we know, that while this spendthrift is weeping over pence, while this penurious prodigal is proposing his enormous expenditure, he always contrives to repeal some tax to gratify the interests or feelings of the party of retrenchment. No wonder, then, we no longer hear the same character given of the income tax; no wonder we are no longer reminded of that compact entered into by the House and accepted by the country for its gradual abolition. . . .

I remember some years ago, when the right hon. gentleman was at the head of a small and select party of politicians who were not then absorbed in the gulf of Liberalism, they were accustomed to prattle much about ' political morality.' What then most distinguished the right hon. gentleman and his friends was their monopoly of that admirable quality. They were perpetually thanking God they were not as other men and always pointing their finger at the unfortunate wights who sat opposite to them. Now we see what is the end of political morality. We see the position to which political morality has brought the finances of a great nation. I denounce this system as one which is detrimental to the character of public men, and most injurious to the fortunes of the realm.

Gladstone disputed the accuracy of Disraeli's figures, but he did not deny that the finances of the country demanded grave attention; and Disraeli was justified in the complacency with which he narrated the story of the debate to Mrs. Willyams.

To Mrs. Brydges Williams.

Private. GROSVENOR GATE, *April* 14, 1862.—The first portion of our Parliamentary campaign has closed, and it ended with a great financial duel. I believe there is no doubt who was the conqueror. In fact the circumstances were so grave and strong that they had only to be put powerfully and clearly before the country to carry conviction.

Nevertheless, it has taken both the House of Commons and the kingdom by surprise. They had heard so much, and so long, of financial skill and prosperity, that, when the balance-sheet was fairly put before them, all were as surprised and startled as if Baring or Rothschild had failed. It was a *coup d'état*—and nobody talks of anything else. It will influence events, though, myself, I trust the tottering government will still totter on. . . .

In truth, Gladstone's position in Palmerston's Cabinet of 1859-1865 was a somewhat false one. On perhaps the most important domestic question throughout its continuance, whether there should be a considerable expenditure on national defence, or a severe policy of national economy, the Chancellor of the Exchequer was in direct and constant conflict with the Prime Minister. In the early years Gladstone was usually worsted in Cabinet on this question, and the fortifications and the iron ships which Palmerston and the services thought necessary were provided. Nevertheless, if Gladstone often tendered his resignation, he as often recalled it; and the country was treated to the undignified spectacle which Disraeli described again and again in biting language. ' We need not maunder in antechambers,' he said, ' to discover differences in the Cabinet, when we have a patriotic Prime Minister appealing to the spirit of the country; and when at the same time we find his Chancellor of the Exchequer, whose duty it is to supply the ways and

means by which those exertions are to be supported,
proposing votes with innuendo, and recommending expenditure in a whispered invective.' In 1862, when the
necessary defences had been provided, and the financial
outlook was grave, that policy of economy, which all Gladstone's exertions in the Cabinet and his hints in public
had failed to enforce, was warmly supported and driven
home by Disraeli and the Opposition, who resented, in
accord with public opinion, the continuance of war taxation in time of peace. Lord Morley has drawn attention to the contrast between the rise of naval and military
expenditure during the first half of the Administration,
and its decline in the second half to a figure below that
at which it stood at the beginning; but he has omitted
to refer to this movement of Disraeli's, which was one of
the most conspicuous features of the session of 1862, and
nearly brought about the downfall of Palmerston's Government. Derby, who always, and rightly, put defence
above economy, was a little doubtful about some of the
features of the campaign; Disraeli's most active supporter and confidant throughout it was Northcote.

To Lord Derby.

Confidential. GROSVENOR GATE, *May* 21, 1862.—. . .
There is a Committee on Public Accounts now sitting, of
which N[orthcote] is a member. This has greatly assisted
him. The revelations before it are frightful, and prove that
' the outlay on stores, during the last two or three years, has
been perfectly reckless.' This Committee will of course
report. Cobden is on it. ' Money voted for iron ships has
been applied to all kinds of purposes.' The general conclusion
is that the ' enormous expenditure has outgrown all control.'
The report of this Committee will in all probability greatly
affect public opinion, and will prove the wisdom, I think,
especially when connected with a falling revenue, of the
position which we have assumed, and which Gladstone had
his eye on. . . .

From Lord Derby.

ST. JAMES'S SQUARE, *May* 21, 1862.—. . . My only fear
has been, and would be, that of holding out expectations

(and especially if they were to lead to an assumption of office) which we could not practically realise without endangering the defences of the country; and especially those connected with the Navy, which we gained so much credit for strengthening, and with which I am sure you would be as unwilling to interfere as I should. I cannot forget that we entered on our examination of the state of the Navy and its expenditure with the hope, and intention, of effecting considerable reductions, and that hope founded also on what seemed very good authority; and that the result was an enormous increase, and the beginning of the 'reconstruction.' . . .

Disraeli used, in a debate on May 8 on expenditure and policy, a phrase which stuck. Instead of acting in cordial alliance with France, he said that we had been trying to govern by a new system of what was called moral power, which meant 'bloated armaments' in time of peace, and produced misconceptions, broils, and distrust, while taxation had found its limit and was sapping the strength of England. The phrase itself at once produced misconception. Disraeli referred to a system which had become general in Europe, and was not confined to, though it was accepted by, this country; and Derby loyally came to his defence in the Lords. Disraeli explained his position in the debate on June 3, in which the movement for retrenchment culminated. Cobden and the Radicals were naturally pressing, side by side with the regular Opposition, for retrenchment; and Stansfeld, then one of their most advanced men, proposed a resolution to the effect that the national expenditure was capable of reduction without compromising the safety, the independence, or the legitimate influence, of the country. This was exactly Disraeli's view, and the Conservative leaders met and determined, while avoiding an alliance with the Radicals, to push their policy in debate and in the division lobby. Palmerston had given notice of an amendment expressing satisfaction at the economy already effected and expectation of more, but insisting rather on the obligation of home defence and of protection of interests abroad. To this it was arranged that Walpole should move a further amendment, pointing more

decidedly to economy, especially to 'diminishing the
burden of those taxes which are confessedly of a temporary and exceptional character.'

The contention of the Opposition, which represented
indeed the general feeling both of the House and of the
country, was so reasonable that Palmerston felt that
strong measures must be taken; and before the debate
opened he announced that the Government would treat
Walpole's amendment as a question of confidence.   Walpole, forgetful of the agreement at Derby's house, to which
he was a party, and remembering only the Conservative
desire to keep Palmerston in office, quailed; and Disraeli
had to carry on the debate under the shadow of certain
defeat owing to the disaffection of friends.   This did not
affect the spirit with which he attacked the Government.
Further military outlay, he maintained, was not needed,
as, owing to the great efforts made by successive Administrations in the last ten years—the creation of the Militia
and the Volunteers, and the strengthening of the fleet and
the forts—the country was now adequately defended.   He
declined to believe in the treachery of the French, who
were still, as in the time of the Crimean War, our allies.
The people of England, though not the most excitable,
were the most enthusiastic in the world, especially on the
question of national defence.   'In this country, protected
by 400,000 men and a commanding fleet in the Channel,
to say that freemen are in danger of a midnight invasion
from cordial allies is a mystification too monstrous for
belief.'

What was the real cause, Disraeli continued, of the
permanent influence that this country exercised upon the
Continent ?   It was this:

England is the only country which, when it enters into a
quarrel that it believes to be just, never ceases its efforts
until it has accomplished its aim; whereas . . . it was always
felt in old times and generations that are past—and honourable gentlemen can ascertain whether the present state of
Europe makes any difference in this matter—that, with
scarcely an exception, there was not a State in Europe, not

even the proudest and most powerful, that could ever enter into a third campaign. Well, what gave us this power of continuing war into which we had entered, and in which we were ready to persevere because we believed it to be just? It was the financial reserve of England. It was the conviction that the reserves of England, when we once chose to engage in a quarrel, were such that it was not a question of one, two, or three campaigns, but that, as we have proved in old days, our determination, supported by our resources, would allow us to prepare for an indefinite struggle when we had an adequate and worthy object in view. If, however, you allow your finances to be sapped and weakened, you are at the same time weakening this prime source of your authority.[1]

It was, therefore, essential to make such reductions as would equalize the charge and the revenue of the country. Palmerston, he added, had proposed an 'awkward and shambling vote of confidence in his own Government,' and had thereby 'appalled' his right honourable friend, Walpole. But the Opposition had not really intended an assault on the Treasury bench, but had merely desired to assert a temperate and practicable policy which they felt sure the House must ultimately adopt and public opinion sanction. 'To-morrow (Derby Day) I believe we shall all be engaged elsewhere. I dare say that many hon. gentlemen who take more interest than I do in that noble pastime will have their favourites. I hope they will not be so unlucky as to find their favourites bolting. If they are placed in that dilemma, they will be better able to understand and sympathise with my feelings on this occasion.' Walpole having withdrawn, Palmerston's resolution was accepted by a great majority.

To Mrs. Brydges Willyams.

Confidential. HOUSE OF COMMONS, *May* 27, 1862.—The newspapers have made you aware of the change that has taken place in public affairs. I have been, as it were, bringing large bodies of troops into the field during the month, and

---

[1] In a subsequent speech on the question of fortifications, Disraeli said that Palmerston seemed to think that ' posterity is a packhorse, always ready to be loaded.'

the Government have suddenly found themselves, almost
without notice, surrounded, surprised and endangered.   The
state of the finances gave this opening, and I availed myself
of it.   It will ultimately produce their fall, but I wish,
myself, rather to discredit than to defeat them.   It should
go on for eight or ten months more, if possible, when the
state of the country, the decline of the revenue, the want of
employment in Lancashire, and their profuse and extravagant foreign policy, will combine for their permanent discomfiture. . . .

  Confidential.   GROSVENOR GATE, *June* 13, 1862.—When I
wrote to you last, I hinted at the financial crisis, that was
slowly gathering.   The House of Lords followed up the
movement of the Commons, and a resolution, then unwisely
announced by a Radical member, precipitated affairs.   The
papers will have told you the result.   My second in command
lost his head and heart the moment the trumpets sounded
for battle.   Such an incident never before happened in the
House of Commons, and I hope may never happen again.
They say you should see everything once.   I did what I
could to cover the retreat, and mitigate the humiliation of
my troops.   Between ourselves, as you well know, I had no
wish whatever to disturb Lord Palmerston, but you cannot
keep a large army in order without letting them, sometimes,
smell gunpowder. . . .

The fiasco of the debate left both sections of the Conservatives sore.   Disraeli resented the desertion of his
colleague, Walpole and his friends the sarcasms of Disraeli.
Derby wrote to his lieutenant: ' I will do my best to
smooth matters; but I fear it will require time to reunite
the party.   My own opinion is that you were the person who
had the most reason to complain.'   Disraeli's admirable
temper enabled him after awhile to bring his colleagues
together again; so that Earle could report to him on
September 13 that Walpole had recently said: ' Several
members of the party have been to me to ask me to lead
them, but I am under so much obligation to Lord D.
and to Disraeli that I could never think of doing anything
that could possibly weaken their hands.'

Though Disraeli's immediate Parliamentary success
was spoilt by Walpole, the effect of the movement on
the Government remained.   In the following year, 1863,

there was a distinct return to the principles of the
'frugal' Government of the Duke of Wellington, which
Disraeli praised in the debate on the Address. Retrenchment was effected in military expenditure. The duty on
tea was reduced, and twopence was taken off the income
tax; and Disraeli claimed this as a victory for the House of
Commons, and inferentially for the Opposition. The
Budget in its main features was, he said, the Budget of
the House. The arguments used last year had had their
effect. It was no longer held to show subserviency to
France to obtain by the most legitimate means a reduction of the burdens of the people. It was the House of
Commons that had reduced the tea duty and the income
tax.

After 1862 the financial debates ceased to be the most
crucial issues for the Palmerston Government. Economy
was enforced, and the large surpluses which the buoyant
trade of the country and the Chancellor of the Exchequer's
skilful management provided were mainly utilised, as
Disraeli had recommended, in reducing the income tax
and the tea and sugar duties. This chapter may, however, be fitly concluded by chronicling two instances in
1863 in which Disraeli took a prominent part in financial
discussions. One concerned Gladstone's attempt to
subject charities to income tax, on the ground that to
exempt them was in effect to make them a contribution
from the public funds. Though the Chancellor put forth
all his rhetorical powers in the cause, Parliamentary and
public feeling was too strong for him, and he had to
withdraw. Disraeli pointed out that income tax was a
tax on persons, not on property, and that Gladstone's
proposals amounted to a confiscation of endowments.
Gladstone had bolstered up his argument by denouncing
the abuses which had arisen from endowments; but
Disraeli had little difficulty in showing that for such evils
the application of the income tax was a very inappropriate
and inadequate remedy.

The other question was that of a proposed commercial

treaty with Italy.   Disraeli was all for commercial treaties,
such as the great Tory Ministers, Bolingbroke and the
younger Pitt, had negotiated with France; but they must
be based on the old Conservative principle of reciprocity.
That had been given up: in existing circumstances a
commercial treaty was an anachronism.

The age of commercial treaties is past, because you have
no means and no materials for negotiation.   All you can do
is to exercise that moral influence, of which we hear so much,
with foreign countries with which you are placed in communication, to lead them by your own example and your own
prosperity. . . .   From the contemplation of that prosperity,
the conviction will grow in those countries that with immense
resources they are producing small revenues; that they are
not raising revenues that bear a due relation to their resources,
and you may trust to that to lead to reciprocal exchanges
and mutual benefits in commercial transactions.   But you
will gain that as completely, and perhaps sooner, without the
embarrassment of commercial treaties than you would with
these conventions.   I regret that, through the conduct of
the Government, and through the extraordinary behaviour
of the Free Trade party in patronising artificial agreements
of exchange, there has arisen in this country the impression
that the best and most politic mode of stimulating commerce
is to have recourse to that method.   That was a good theory
twenty years ago, and not only a good theory, but a good
theory which could be put in beneficial practice. . . .   You
have adopted unrestricted competition as the principle of
your commercial code.   By accident certain articles were
excepted, and two years ago you used them as a means of
negotiating a treaty of commerce with a great country, with
a large population, and with very rich and valuable resources.
You have played all your cards; and to attempt at the present
moment—to pretend that you can assist and support the
commerce of this country by commercial treaties is a mere
delusion.[1]

[1] Feb. 13, 1863.

CHAPTER IX.

RUSSELL'S FOREIGN POLICY.

1860–1864.

While Disraeli demanded public economy at home, he consistently deprecated a policy of adventure abroad. In the debate on the Address in 1860 he laid down what he conceived to be the proper principles of British foreign policy. They are substantially those which he was advocating in the late forties against the intermeddling diplomacy which Palmerston pursued as Russell's Foreign Minister.[1] Russell now, under Palmerston, was carrying on Palmerston's system, but with less dexterity and a rasher enthusiasm. But the House of Commons, Disraeli maintained, was opposed to adventures, and was in favour of what was popularly but incorrectly called a policy of non-interference—non-interference, be it observed, in the domestic affairs of foreign nations.

I do not know any member of this House—either among my colleagues or among those who sit on the other side of the House—who has ever maintained the monstrous proposition that England ought never, under any circumstances, to interfere in the affairs of foreign States. There are conditions under which it may be our imperative duty to interfere. We may clearly interfere in the affairs of foreign countries when the interests or the honour of England are at stake, or when in our opinion the independence of Europe is menaced. But a great responsibility devolves upon that Minister who has to decide when those conditions have arisen. . . . The general principle that we ought not to interfere in the affairs of foreign nations unless there is a clear necessity, and that,

1 See Vol. I., III., ch. 7, especially pp. 1002, 1003.

generally speaking, it ought to be held a political dogma that the people of other countries should settle their own affairs without the intervention of foreign influence or foreign power, is one which, I think, the House does not only accept, but, I trust, will cordially agree to.

Special point was given to this passage by the recent efforts of Palmerston and Russell to engage this country during the recess in a policy of active intervention on behalf of the unity of Italy—efforts only checkmated by the determined opposition of the Court. Palmerston professed in the debate that the policy of the Government was that the people of Italy should settle their own affairs; but it is now admitted that the suspicions of Disraeli and the Opposition were well founded.

To Lord Derby.

GROSVENOR GATE, *Jan.* 8, 1860.—. . . I hear from Paris that the Emperor has proposed to our Government to enter into a *treaty* for the settlement of Italian affairs, and that Palmerston is highly favorable to the proposition, which was, no doubt, concocted between them without the knowledge of Lord P.'s colleagues. Such a treaty will, I think, be looked upon by the country with very great suspicion, to use the mildest term; and I should think the Cabinet will hesitate before they enter into it. But the Emperor is positive and peremptory. It is the only way by which he can extricate himself, with dash and lustre, from his difficulties, and he offers everything—Suez Canal to be opposed; peace between Spain and Morocco, etc., etc., and government by us to be always impossible. It will be rather ludicrous, after the volunteers and the 10 million loan, should the new session be inaugurated with not only *une entente cordiale*, but an absolute alliance. . . .

Secret. GROSVENOR GATE, *Jan.* 14, 1860.—. . . Lord Cowley came over from the Emperor with a distinct proposal for an alliance, ' *offensive and defensive,*' and, strange to say, enforced it, as his own opinion, in the strongest manner. The Emperor had completely got over him. The Court, finding this out, was much disgusted—and countermined. Lord Palmerston and Lord John had held out to the Emperor every hope of success. Gladstone, furiously Italian, was gained to absolute interference, by the mirage of a Commercial Treaty; but when the Cabinet met, the business being opened by Lord John, the strong opinion of Lord Cowley duly dwelt on, and Lord Palmerston very decisive, they were thoroughly beaten by the Court party !

This is the real state of affairs. You may depend upon its accuracy, and form your own conclusions as to the probable result.

Four foreign questions of great importance successively —and indeed, in some cases, simultaneously—occupied public attention during Palmerston's last Government; and in all of them Disraeli urged, with success, the policy of non-intervention. In regard to three of them, the Italian Risorgimento, with the corollary of the transference of Savoy and Nice from Sardinia to France, the American Civil War, and the Polish insurrection, there were certainly no sufficient British interests involved to warrant armed interference, and Disraeli's action was thoroughly beneficial. There is more doubt about the Schleswig-Holstein dispute between Germany and Denmark; and indeed, in Disraeli's opinion, decided action at an early stage might have averted the catastrophe. But by the time the matter came up for discussion in Parliament, the blunders of Russell's diplomacy had placed serious difficulties in the way of any course of action, and acquiescence in a wrong which England had failed to prevent seemed to be the least unsatisfactory outcome. In regard to all these questions, Russell had at some stage, usually with the active support of the Prime Minister, written strong despatches or taken other steps calculated to lead to armed conflict, only to draw back afterwards, not always without humiliation, under pressure from the Court, or the Cabinet, or the Opposition, or the country. His one great success, accomplished, owing to the prudence of the Court, without fighting, was materially to have advanced by his diplomacy the unity of Italy. But his mismanagement of our relations with America left the country a legacy of bitterness and the *Alabama* claims; and in regard to Poland and Denmark, his well-meant interference, followed as it was by undignified retreat, did nothing but harm to those whom he hoped to befriend. Disraeli may fairly claim to have helped to diminish the evil consequences of the blunders of Ministers in foreign policy, and to have done much to secure the emergence of the country from her troubles without serious material loss, if with some damage to her reputation in the world. His action was the more praiseworthy as he was generally in opposition to the public feeling of the moment, counselling moderation when passions were excited; and on the two most important questions, the American Civil War and the Schleswig-Holstein dispute, the prejudices of the great majority of his own party were strongly arrayed against him.

To Mrs. Brydges Willyams.

GROSVENOR GATE, *Jan.* 16, 1860.—. . . The Emperor of the French has introduced a new system of governing mankind—by anonymous pamphlets, and by letters from himself addressed to Mr. Reuter of the Electro-Telegraph! Wonderful man ! He delights England with his Protestantism and Free Trade; and when public opinion is conciliated and regained, he intends to propose that Savoy shall be surrendered to France, in order to guard her fertile plains from Sardinia, who will then be too powerful for him. And the people of England, who last month believed he was going to conquer them, will also believe that. The fact is, the Emperor is in a scrape, but he is so clever that his scrapes are preferable to other persons' success.

G. G., *Jan.* 28, 1860.—. . . Politics most absorbing, and more mysterious than ever. The Imperial Free Trader is now going to seize Savoy and Nice. The ' natural boundaries ' of the Empire are fast developing, and in 1861 he will be on the Rhine. It is said that all nations that speak French belong to France ! Our uncle at Belgium does not like affairs.

The English people were entirely disinterested in their strong sympathy with the Italian movement for unity, but they had no intention of going to war to promote it; and they were very indignant when they discovered that the French Emperor and people, who had actually fought for the cause, did not propose to imitate their disinterestedness, but to obtain an accession of territory as a reward. Few annexations have been better justified

than those of Savoy and Nice to France; and the violent
anger which they aroused in England, and to a less degree
on the Continent, would be difficult to understand, if
we did not bear in mind the widespread apprehensions
in 1860 of a revival by Napoleon III. of the ambitious
policy of Napoleon I. Savoy and Nice were on the
French side of the Alpine range which forms the natural
boundary of Italy; they were transferred as the result,
not of conquest, but of a friendly arrangement between
allied States; the transference was subject to a popular
vote which proved in each case to be overwhelmingly
in its favour; and the two provinces rapidly became
thoroughly contented portions of the nation to which
they were united. Bright's exclamation in the House
of Commons, ' Perish Savoy !' rather than have a war
on the question between England and France, though
severely reprobated at the time, contained excellent sense.
Disraeli kept his head much better than the Foreign
Secretary and other leading politicians on both sides. He
realised that our alliance with France could not be unilateral; and that we were bound to place a favourable
construction on her policies, as we expected her to do on
ours. Accordingly, he preferred rather to criticise
Ministers who failed to realise the obvious policy of
France, than to attack France, who had only acted as
might have been expected. If the doctrine of ' natural
boundaries ' led to sanguinary wars in Europe, the blame
must be laid on the shortsightedness of Ministers. To
Vitzthum, however, who was busily fanning mistrust of
Napoleon in England, he talked sympathetically on
January 17.

Our course is to keep a sharp watch over Palmerston and
Russell, and force them to pursue our foreign policy. For
the present we are more useful and powerful in Opposition
than on the Ministerial bench. If we oppose every territorial
aggrandisement on the part of France, we shall in the end
paralyse Palmerston and show Napoleon that his alliance
with the noble Viscount does not bring him all the tangible
advantages he had expected. . . . The most important thing

for us is to know exactly how far we can depend upon Austria.
In spite of all her defeats, we regard her as the centre and
nucleus of all Conservative efforts in the field of European
politics. If Austria is nowhere, what can we do ?[1]

Though he had begun to mistrust Napoleon's policy,
Disraeli did not change his mind as to the importance
of preserving the French alliance. He was, moreover,
constantly fascinated by the personality of the French
Emperor, and was flattered by the parallelism between
their characters and careers on which the newspapers of
the day were insisting. In sending Mrs. Willyams on
May 6 a couple of articles of this kind, Mrs. Disraeli wrote :
' I like both, for who would not be delighted to be thought
like so great a man as the Emperor? Mr. Gladstone,
and many papers, all have made lately the same comparison, " the great similitude." ' Earle was encouraged
by Disraeli to go to Paris this spring, though not as
Disraeli's ' emissary,' to see the Emperor again and
sound him on his projects. He found him naturally
disgusted with his treatment by England.

From Ralph A. Earle.

Secret and confidential. [PARIS, *April*, 1860]. . . . The
Emperor said that nothing could be more ridiculous than
the clamour which had been raised about the Swiss annexation, and, taking me to the window, where an elaborate plan
of the Swiss cantons and bordering provinces of France was
exposed, he showed me in detail that the new frontier would
involve Switzerland in no new peril. He then continued :
' The policy which I have always wished to adopt with
respect to England is this: I wish to help her where her
interests are principally concerned, but in return I claim for
France a corresponding consideration from her ally. If you
disapprove of these annexations, which are insignificant in
themselves, which are made with the consent of the Sovereign
who loses them, and with that of the people whose nationality
is changed—is not the inference inevitable that you will
object to any expansion of France, however unexceptionable
its character ? These views were accepted by Lord Palmerston and Mr. Disraeli when in opposition, but since they
have been Ministers their ideas are changed. . . .'
The Emperor then entered into some general considerations

[1] Vitzthum, Vol. II., pp. 21-23. See Vol. I., p. 1448.

about the English alliance. . . . The English had lost a great opportunity of consolidating for ever their relations with France. If they had said, ' These annexations do not concern us. We wish well to France, and shall be glad to see her objects attained,' the whole of France would not only have accepted, but would have demanded a close alliance with England. . . .

The Italian Revolution ran a rapid course through the spring, summer, and autumn of 1860, till by winter practically the whole of Italy, with the exception of Rome and Venetia, was united under the House of Savoy.

To Mrs. Brydges Willyams.

May 14, 1860.—. . . Affairs abroad very critical, and great events may be expected every day. Garibaldi's pirate expedition[1] is a spark that will lead to a general conflagration. Who was its promoter ? . . .

HUGHENDEN, *Sept.* 16, 1860.— . . . What an immense event is the Italian Revolution ! Since 1792 we have not had such affairs. This is real history—and what an imbroglio ! A race between the red flag of Mazzini wafted on by the passions of centuries, and the cold diplomatic standard of mere Sardinian ambition. The sovereigns and statesmen of Europe have raised a spirit they will find it difficult to quell. Look out for great events.

Oct. 18, 1860.—. . . Strange news came from Naples last night; more confounding than anything that has happened. Garibaldi is like an eel. Is he playing a cross with Cavour ? Is he a Masaniello ? Is he a Washington ? A great many other questions will be asked before it is all finished.

Dec. 13, 1860.—. . . What is preparing ? A greater revolution, perhaps, in Austria, than ever occurred in France. Then it was ' the rights of *man* '; now it is ' the rights of *nations*.'

Once I said, in *Coningsby*, there is nothing like Race: it comprises all truths. The world will now comprehend that awful truth.

Dec. 18, 1860.—. . . It is our privilege to live in a wonderful age of rapid and stirring events; and if time, as the poets say, is not to be counted by calendars, but by incidents and sensation, all our existences will be patriarchal. Lord Mendip, a friend of my father's, used to say that by the parish register and the Peerage he was only 60; but, having lived through the French Revolution, he considered he was a hundred at least !

[1] The famous expedition to Sicily.

We have got Italian and Austrian Revolutions, and a great many others coming; and Eastern wars, whether in India, China, or Japan, which beat all the marvels of the Arabian Nights. . . .

The great increase of power which the rise of Italy promised to give to her friend and ally, France, perturbed the King of the Belgians, whose position could only be secure if there were a balance of power on the Continent.

From the King of the Belgians.

Private.   LAEKEN, *Dec.* 19, 1860.

MY DEAR SIR,—You will think me very ungrateful not to have acknowledged sooner your kind communication,[1] but I can plead not guilty to that. The state of Europe is very strange. There is after all a certain sameness in human affairs, but the present time is distinguished by a sort of *leger-de-main*, which is unlike to what history generally shows, and one is constantly tempted to ask: *qui trompe-t-on ici ?* Much is owing to the Oriental war; it has brought about, what at all times was justly feared, an understanding between France and Russia, and has given to France a complete supremacy on the Continent.

Happily England has felt the necessity, for its own independence, of being well armed. If that had been neglected, England would have had a sort of existence on sufferance, and would have been exposed to great danger. I trust that the Conservative party will remain faithful to its policy, as it was the first that awakened to the danger. But it is not only in this case that the Conservative party is of the most vital importance; no constitutional Government can be carried on without it, and it is a great misfortune that in the present Parliament there is such a tendency to split into fragments instead of uniting for the public good.

The affairs of Italy are very strangely appreciated in England. Whatever may be the future consequences, the immediate practical result is to give to France allies against Germany, and I don't think that by so doing the real interests of England are wisely consulted. Whatever weakens still more the power of Germany exposes us also here to new dangers, and we can only see this with just apprehension.

I hope that these lines will find you well, and remain, with sentiments of the highest regard and esteem, ever, my dear sir, most faithfully yours, LEOPOLD.

[1] See above, pp. 16, 17.

To the King of the Belgians.

Dec. 23, 1860.

SIR,—Your Majesty's letter reached me only to-day, but, as I am informed that a courier leaves this for Brussels to-morrow, I will not hesitate to have the honor of addressing to you, Sir, a few lines, feeling your Majesty will pardon them for being written *currente calamo.*

The *leger-de-main* which now distinguishes public affairs, and to which your Majesty so graphically refers, appears to me attributable to this circumstance, which the English Government either does not recognise or never sufficiently appreciates.

The French Emperor, to use a homely image, always runs two hares. His first hare was the old traditionary policy of the French Cabinet: a divided Italy and French supremacy. Lord John Russell thought that in bringing about Italian unity he had checkmated Buonaparte; but he only threw the Emperor on his second hare, a much more dangerous animal—*i.e.*, natural headship of the Latin race; Venetia secured by France to Sardinia; and an offensive and defensive alliance between France and Italy, in order that France, in possession of their united resources, may obtain some great object.

Had the Treaty of Villafranca been sedulously supported, instead of systematically decried, by the English Government, there might have been a resting-point, perhaps for some years; and during the interval all our energies might have been applied to what should be the great object of English statesmen, viz., to terminate or at least to counteract the understanding between France and Russia.

At present, if all is dark and perplexing to your Majesty, what must it be to me ?

There are no doubt ample materials in Italy, if France chooses to recur to her first policy, to disturb, perhaps destroy, Italian unity in the spring. The coast (Liguria) is republican; the country reactionary; and as for the great towns, each of them not only desires, but *expects*, to be the capital. But these elements to be effective require French manipulation; and it is to be feared that the blind exertions of England will force France to the larger and more dangerous scheme.

Mundy, our Admiral, says the King spoke much against the French, praised the English (though complaining of the brigade), and said that Lord J.'s despatch was ' plus qu'amical, c'était magnifique.'   When Mundy left the presence, the King shook his hand so violently that he broke his nail.   He does not think favorably of the King's prospects; he says he never witnessed so frigid a reception as that of Victor Emmanuel at the Opera.

One thing is quite clear: Napoleon meditates next year some accession of territory. Otherwise he would not court the English people. One of his principles is always to distinguish between them and their Government, in the hope that, when he makes the great *coup*, public opinion in England may restrain the English Government from resisting him.

Mr. Cobden enforces these views very much on the Emperor, and we must remember that, to the Emperor, Mr. Cobden is the Minister of the Queen of Great Britain. This is another of the injurious consequences of that ' untoward affair.'

With respect to the state of the Conservative party in the House of Commons, I can report very favorably of it. It has become very consolidated during the recess, and even increased its numbers by some elections. Our characteristic ignorance respecting foreign politics renders it, however, extremely difficult to direct this immense power to an effective and beneficial end; but the difficulty is only one of time, and opportunities must be taken gradually and skilfully to guide their sentiments.

On the 5th February, on the Address, such an occasion would naturally offer, when I am expected to speak generally on affairs without contemplating any trial of strength. I trust I do not count entirely without reason on the condescension of your Majesty in assisting me in the interval by your counsel.

The Roman Catholic party, as I anticipated in my last, has made an overture to me for the overthrow of the Government. I discouraged the proposition, though with courtesy.

In his speech on the Address in 1861, Disraeli followed the line of thought suggested in this correspondence, and conjured up a picture of the Emperor of the French coming forward as the head of the Latin race, the emancipator of Italy, with a million bayonets behind him, and in a position to dominate Europe—all through the recklessness of Russell's diplomacy : the 'candid' policy which substituted a speech in the House of Commons for what in old times, in the days of secret diplomacy, would have been the whisper of Downing Street. On the other hand, he called special attention to the French support of the Papal States against the Sardinian Government. 'The contemplated capital of Italy is not in the possession of the Italians. In this age of jubilant nationality Rome is still garrisoned by the Gauls.'

Regarding the Pope, as he did, as ' an old man on a Semitic throne,' baffling ' the modern Attilas,' Disraeli did not share the general wish of Englishmen for the overthrow of the Temporal Power; and this attitude helped to secure for him not a few Roman Catholic votes which would otherwise have gone to the Liberals. The Pope told Odo Russell in July, 1859: ' Mr. Disraeli was my friend; I regret him.' Earle visited Rome in February, 1861, and reported to Disraeli: ' The Cardinal Minister of the Holy Father sends you a great many messages of compliment, and his Sovereign blessed me on hearing me mentioned as your secretary.' Two months later Earle went to see Cardinal Wiseman, and obtained his good offices towards a working alliance between the Conservative leaders and the Roman Catholic vote in Parliament.

From Ralph A. Earle.

St. Leonards, *April* 26, 1861.—. . . The Cardinal, I am sorry to say, is looking very ill, being here for his health and attending to no business of any kind. He promises to do all in his power, ' as he knows well that, by helping us, he would please those whom it is his highest duty and pleasure to serve.'

In Ireland, he says, there is a very good feeling towards us, and some of those who declined his invitation to help us in 1859 held out hopes of eventual assistance, which is now likely to be realised.

Monsell, Bowyer, and Hennessy, he thinks a very good combination, as they influence three different coteries. The first has great influence with the Irish Bishops and clergy.

The Cardinal . . . concluded by observing that we were quite right in looking to the R.C.'s for our majority, for they could give it us. If there were any prospect of a Government being formed that would carry out a respectable foreign policy, the Catholic constituents and their members would all support it.

Of great exertion he is not capable, and he cannot put himself forward in politics, but quietly he will do whatever may occur to him as likely to serve us. . . .

Instead of putting himself at the head of a militant Franco-Italian alliance, the Emperor of the French, under the influence of the French clergy and of the Empress, resolutely supported the Pope, and Earle reported from Florence towards the close of the year that ' the failure of the Whigs to dislodge the French from Rome is complete.' The cause of Italian unity had another set-back this year in the death of Cavour.

To Mrs. Brydges Willyams.

GROSVENOR GATE, *March* 16, 1861.—. . . An immense suspense in foreign affairs; but what questions! The temporal existence of the Pope: the union of the American States: the dissolution of the Ottoman Empire: the unity of Italy: each of them sufficient for a generation! It is a privilege to live in such an age; to say nothing of ' Essays and Reviews,' which convulses Christendom, and seems to have shaken down the spire of Chichester Cathedral.

HOUSE OF COMMONS, *April* 11, 1861.—. . . When I was Chancellor of the Exchequer, ten years ago, Cavour was travelling in this country, in order to study the art of taxation, and had letters of introduction to me; and I knew him well.

CARLTON CLUB, *June* 11, 1861.—The death of Cavour is an immense event! It is impossible to see the end of the effects it will produce. . . . He was a thorough Italian statesman of the middle ages; most fertile in device, and utterly unscrupulous; an almost unrivalled union of subtilty and vigor. . . .

HOUSE OF COMMONS, *Wednesday, June* 19, 1861.—. . . Yesterday, according to royal appointment, I paid my visit to the King of the Belgians at Buckingham Palace, and had a very interesting audience of an hour. The King, who is a statesman, talked to me very freely on the present state of affairs, which remain most critical, and probably will for several years. This is an age of great and rapid events: their quick succession as remarkable as their importance; and, to a certain extent, mutually mitigating their exciting consequences. The restless and revolutionary spirits, distracted by the choice of materials, pause in the selection; not from satiety, but from sheer perplexity to decide where most mischief can be accomplished. Garibaldi does not know where to begin— Venice or Hungary—and talks of going to America ! . . .

Disraeli's view of the subsequent treatment of the
Italian question by Palmerston and Russell is shown in
an amusing passage from a speech which he delivered in
1863:

Since the death of Cavour, the programme of the national
party in Italy has been ' movement, development, unity,
Rome '—immense words, *verba sesquipedalia*, used by men
of very little minds and very slight resources. What have
they leant upon ? They have leant upon the support of
England. In the English Parliament some gentlemen, if
not with the absolute co-operation of, at least with social encouragement from, the noble lord, constantly brought forward
the subject of the state of Italy. It was let out like a bag-
fox, and followed with a full halloo. Every year we had
the noble lord presented to us as the regenerator of Italy,
the saviour of the country; and the performance ended with
invectives directed against the Pope, and a promise . . .
that Rome should be the capital of a United Italy before the
end of the session. . . . And now, where has all this ended ?
Cavour withdrawn from the scene—no commanding mind in
Italy; France naturally jealous of our uncertain and irritating
policy; Rome alarmed; Rome and France leagued against
the unity of Italy; the noble lord conducting a policy of
words, speeches, and despatches; and the Italian Government,
without a leader, still hanging on the accents of English
Ministers, perpetually adopting a line which nothing could
justify except commanding genius and commanding legions,
and holding out to the people the immediate expectation of
Rome being made their capital by the overpowering interference of their English ally.

It may be added that Disraeli, true to his disapproval
of the 'piratical' means by which Italy had been unified,
and anxious to preserve the threatened authority of
the Pope in Rome, absolutely refused to meet Garibaldi
when London went wild over that wonderful Italian's visit
in April, 1864. Derby and other Tory leaders paid their
respects to the visitor at Stafford House or elsewhere;
but when Mrs. Gladstone asked the Disraelis to come to
a party at Carlton House Terrace to meet him, the reply
was a polite but firm ' no '; and the same curt answer
was sent to all similar invitations. Gladstone overlooked
Garibaldi's hostility to religion in view of his services to

liberty; Disraeli regarded him as essentially the foe of
constituted authority in both Church and State, and declined to countenance the orgy of enthusiasm with which
he was welcomed in England both by the populace and
by Society.

As the Italian question became less acute, the American
difficulty increased. Disraeli wrote to Northcote on
September 12, 1861: 'Our friend Jonathan seems in a
pretty state; it's like the failure of some immense house;
one can hardly realise the enormous results. . . . It is a
privilege to live in such a pantomimic age of glittering
illusions and startling surprises.' Disraeli's view that
the United States were breaking down was the general
opinion among the governing and educated classes in
this country; but he had the wisdom, denied to other
leading statesmen, to keep his view to himself and his
private friends. His 'thoughtfulness and statesmanship'
were shown throughout, as John Bright confessed in Parliament, by not saying a word from the front Opposition
bench likely to create difficulty with America. The
irritation provoked by the sympathy widely expressed in
England for the South bade fair to lead to war this
autumn, when relations were strained over the seizure
by the Federals of Confederate envoys on the British
steamship *Trent*. Happily, the despatch containing the
British demand for their release was so modified in its
language by the dying Prince Consort as to facilitate
the withdrawal of the United States Government from an
untenable position.

In the debate on the Address in 1862, Disraeli, who
had before laid stress on the duty of diplomacy to say
rough things, if they were necessary, kindly, and not
kind things roughly, praised the firm but temperate
course of the Government; and he added some happy
words of recognition of the honourable manner in which
America had offered reparation. 'When I consider the
great difficulties which the statesmen of North America
have to encounter, when I consider what I may call the

awful emergency which they have been summoned suddenly to meet, and which, without giving any opinion upon the causes of these transactions, I would venture to say they have met manfully and courageously, I think it becomes England, in dealing with the Government of the United States, to extend to all which they say at least a generous interpretation, and to their acts a liberal construction.' He was determined that Great Britain should preserve neutrality, and should avoid occasions of provocation and irritation; and in this spirit had protested in the previous session against the precaution which the Government had taken of sending 3,000 men to Canada. This, he held, was not an act of sound policy, as the United States would infer from it that the British Government looked forward with suspicion to the contingency of hostilities. He had another ground for objection, as he explained in a further debate in 1862, that to send troops damped the ardour of the Canadians by indicating a desire to monopolise their defence. The result had been that Canada had refused to pass a Militia Bill. Adderley, the Colonial Reformer, wished to have Canada told that, unless she took measures for self-defence, the British troops would be withdrawn; but Disraeli, who said he trusted to the sense and spirit of the Canadians, would not go that length.

To Charles E. Adderley.

GROSVENOR GATE, *Jan.* 26, 1862.—. . . You have placed your views before the country in a clear and complet light, but what is taking place convinces me that the theme is beyond the domain of mere reasoning, however just and wise. The passions of the people are very high at the present moment, and if the Ministry chose to send 50,000 men to Canada they would be supported.

When our Colonial System was reconstructed, either the Colonies should have had direct representation, or the military prerogatives of the Crown should have been so secured that the faculty of self-defence in the Colonies should always have been considerable. . . .

Foreign politics and foreign personalities naturally bulked largely in Disraeli's correspondence at this time.

To Mrs. Brydges Williams.

Private. GROSVENOR GATE, *July* 8, 1862.—If it had not
been for the Court being in deep mourning, and the unceasing
summer rain, London, this season, would have been a Carnival.
There are so many great sights, and such gatherings of innumerable thousands ! Of all these, however, I think the
most remarkable was the Show of the Royal Agricultural
Society. It gave me an idea of one of those great Tartar
hordes of which we read—of Genghis Khan and Attila. It
was so vast, so busy, and so bovine !

The Pacha of Egypt,[1] who speaks very good French, is
the royalty who most exhibits himself. The newspapers have
told you of the banquet which the Lord Mayor gave him; and
we also met His Highness at a state dinner given to him by
the Speaker of the House of Commons and Lady Charlotte
Denison, though that was a very small and very select party.

That happened to me which, a year ago, many would have
betted 100 to 1 would not have happened to any Englishman
in the year of grace 1862. I was asked to dine on the same
day by the two rival French Princes—the Duke d'Aumale
and the Prince Napoleon ! I fulfilled my previous engagement with His *Royal* Highness, but, two days after, I had a
long and interesting audience with His *Imperial* Highness,
who conversed very frankly and very confidentially on great
affairs. The Prince is a true Buonaparte in mind and visage;
a very striking likeness of the great Emperor, and all his
charlatanry of manner and expression—for he is picturesque
and eloquent. On the other hand, the Bourbon Prince is
thought to resemble, both in character and physically, his
great ancestor, Henri IV.

Private. GROSVENOR GATE, *July* 26, 1862.—The whirl—
political and social—begins a little to slacken its fascinating
velocity, and the sudden burst of sunshine and blue skies
begins to make people remember that there is another and a
better world ' out of town.' We have never been home for
eight months. . . .

Notwithstanding the Court being in seclusion, London has
been full of royal blood this season. The Prince of Carignan,
the Prince of Orange, the Princes of Saxony, *cum multis aliis*
—all Royal Highnesses ; and one *crowned* head, the Grand
Duke of Saxe-Weimar. Strange to say, this, though the
greatest, was my guest—a great honor. I knew him in early
years, when he was Crown Prince only; very literary and
accomplished, and proud of the German Athens over which
his father ruled, and where Wieland and Herder, Goethe

---

[1] The Khedive Ismail.

and Schiller, blazed at the same time.   He deigns to be an admirer of my writings, and has often asked me to Weimar, which, unfortunately, I have never visited.   So, instead of my being H.R.H.'s guest, he deigned to honor my roof, and met a very choice party—among them Lord and Lady Derby, the Duke of Hamilton, the Russian Ambassador, etc.   I shall enclose you the bill of fare, if I can find it.   It may amuse a moment. . . .

HUGHENDEN MANOR, *Dec.* 9, 1862.—. . . They say that the Greeks, resolved to have an English King, in consequence of the refusal of Prince Alfred to be their monarch, intend to elect Lord Stanley.   If he accepts the charge, I shall lose a powerful friend and colleague.   It is a dazzling adventure for the House of Stanley, but they are not an imaginative race, and, I fancy they will prefer Knowsley to the Parthenon, and Lancashire to the Attic plain.

It is a privilege to live in this age of rapid and brilliant events.   What an error to consider it an utilitarian age !   It is one of infinite romance.   Thrones tumble down and crowns are offered, like a fairy tale, and the most powerful people in the world, male and female, a few years back, were adventurers, exiles, and demireps.

Vive la bagatelle !

GROSVENOR GATE, *Wednesday, Jan.* 21, 1863.—We are now going to Hatfield, where we shall make a rather longer visit than usual, as I have a great deal to do; and Lord and Lady Salisbury, who are real friends, let me do what I like, and not come down to breakfast, and all that sort of thing, so that I can work, and prepare for the coming campaign.   A week of quiet mornings is what I now require, in order to digest all I have heard and planned during the last fortnight.   I could not well go to Hughenden, as it is full of workmen, and I have this advantage at Hatfield, that it is a palace, full of company, changing every day, and all the most distinguished persons in the country, especially of my own party, in turn appearing.   I meet and converse with all these, after the solitude of the morning, every day at dinner, and in the evening, which is very advantageous and suggestive.   It allows me to feel the pulse of the ablest on all the questions of the day.   God bless you !

Feb. 7, 1863.—. . . My party was distinguished and brilliant, and I am going to give a series of dinners to my Parliamentary friends of both Houses.   The members of the House of Commons like very much to meet members of the House of Lords who have themselves, in their time, sat in the House of Commons.   It is like old schoolfellows meeting; the memories of the past are interesting, and from old

II.   3*

experience they understand all the fun of the present. The
Duke of Buckingham, the Earl of Shrewsbury, and the
Marquis of Normanby, who were all of them a long time in
the House of Commons, dine with me on Wednesday, and
meet a number of the Lower House.

Lord Derby seems very well, and in good spirits. His
conduct during the Lancashire distress appears to have gained
him golden opinions from all parties. His subscription of
many thousands was munificent, but his administrative
talent in managing the vast sums entrusted to the Central
Committee by the nation not less admirable. . . .

The Greeks really want to make my friend Lord Stanley
their King. This beats any novel. I think he ought to
take the crown, but he will not. Had I his youth, I would
not hesitate, even with the earldom of Derby in the distance.

The indiscretions of leading statesmen about the
American War culminated in a remarkable utterance by
Gladstone in the course of a triumphal progress—the
first of many such progresses—which he made upon the
Tyne in October, 1862. He said: 'There is no doubt that
Jefferson Davis and other leaders of the South have
made an army; they are making, it appears, a navy;
and they have made what is more than either, they have
made a nation.' The world naturally jumped to the
conclusion that the British Government were about to
recognise the independence of the Confederate States; and
Cornewall Lewis, speaking a week later at Hereford, had
specifically to contradict the inference. Disraeli, in his
speech on the Address in 1863, after animadverting on
Gladstone's apparent departure from the policy of
neutrality, said that, for his part, while he had the
greatest respect for the Southern States, he felt that
there was due from England to the existing authorities in
America a large measure of deference in the difficulties
which they had to encounter. He had accordingly exerted
whatever influence he might possess in endeavouring to
dissuade his friends from embarrassing Her Majesty's
Government in their position of 'politic and dignified
reserve.' He made some unconventional reflections on
the general situation.

I have always looked upon the struggle in America in the light of a great revolution. Great revolutions, whatever may be their alleged causes, are not likely to be commenced or to be concluded with precipitation. Before the civil war commenced the United States were colonies; because we should not forget that such communities do not cease to be colonies because they are independent. They were not only colonies, but they were colonising, and they existed under all the conditions of colonial life except that of mere political dependence. But even before the civil war I think that all impartial observers must have been convinced that in that community there were smouldering elements which indicated the possibility of a change, and perhaps of a violent change. The immense increase of population; the still greater increase of wealth; the introduction of foreign races in large numbers as citizens, not brought up under the laws and customs which were adapted to a more limited, and practically a more homogeneous race; the character of the political constitution, consequent perhaps on these circumstances; the absence of any theatre for the ambitious and refined intellects of the country, which deteriorated public spirit and lowered public morality; and, above all, the increasing influence of the United States upon the political fortunes of Europe—these were all circumstances which indicated the more than possibility that the mere colonial character of these communities might suddenly be violently subverted, and those imperial characteristics appear which seem to be the destiny of man. I cannot conceal from myself the conviction that, whoever in this House may be young enough to live to witness the ultimate consequences of this civil war, will see, whenever the waters have subsided, a different America from that which was known to our fathers, and even from that of which this generation has had so much experience. It will be an America of armies, of diplomacy, of rival States and manœuvring Cabinets, of frequent turbulence, and probably of frequent wars.

Two years later, when the Civil War was coming to an end in the victory of the North, Disraeli repeated [1] his warning that America was greatly changing, and acquiring a centralising Government. The balance of power could no longer be confined to Europe, that old Europe to which the United States looked with a want of sympathy. But he held the Americans to be eminently a sagacious people, and he disregarded the violence of their meetings and journals.

[1] March 13, 1865.

I look upon these expressions of opinion as I should look upon those strange and fantastic drinks of which we hear so much, and which are such favourites on the other side of the Atlantic; and I should as soon suppose this rowdy rhetoric was the expression of the real feelings of the American people as that these potations formed the aliment and nutriment of their bodies. . . . The democracy of America must not be confounded with the democracy of the Old World. It is not formed of the scum of turbulent cities, neither is it merely a section of an exhausted middle class, which speculates in stocks, and calls that progress. It is a territorial democracy. Aristotle, who has taught us most of the wise things we know, never said a wiser one than this—that the cultivators of the soil are the least inclined to sedition and to violent courses.

The Civil War has certainly changed America, and produced some of the imperial characteristics, notably a tendency to governmental centralisation, which Disraeli anticipated. But the martial enthusiasm, except in the palmy days of Theodore Roosevelt and the Spanish War, has by no means reached the height which he predicted; though the universal upheaval in Europe after July, 1914, ultimately drove the United States to create for the occasion a vast army and transport it to fight in Europe.

Palmerston's Government proposed in 1863 to get rid of the perpetual difficulties of the administration of the Ionian Islands by yielding to the wishes of the islanders to be incorporated with Greece; provided that Greece, which had just passed through a revolution, should elect a King who might be expected to adopt a constitutional and peaceful policy. Disraeli, whose action in sending Gladstone as High Commissioner in 1858 had undoubtedly precipitated this solution, became alive, when it was too late, to the military importance of the islands to a Mediterranean Power, and protested vigorously against the sentimental grounds on which cession was advocated. He reminded Parliament that the islands originally came into our possession by the right of conquest.

Professors and rhetoricians find a system for every contingency and a principle for every chance; but you are not going, I hope, to leave the destinies of the British Empire to prigs and pedants. The statesmen who construct, and the warriors who achieve, are only influenced by the instinct of power, and animated by the love of country. Those are the feelings and those the methods which form empires. There may be grave questions as to the best mode of obtaining wealth; some may be in favour of protection of domestic and colonial interests, some of unrestricted competition, or some of what I am quite surprised have now become so modish— commercial treaties and reciprocal arrangements for the advantage of commercial exchange, propositions which used to be scouted in this House; but there can be no question either in or out of this House that the best mode of preserving wealth is power. A country, and especially a maritime country, must get possession of the strong places of the world if it wishes to contribute to its power.

There is sound sense in these general principles, stated with a refreshing absence of cant; and undoubtedly Corfu, and some of the other islands, have a military importance of the same kind as that of Malta, Gibraltar, and the Cape of Good Hope, though in different degree. But the difficulties of governing the islands, which had been aggravated by Gladstone's mission and its results, were extreme; the possession of Gibraltar and Malta might well be considered sufficient to secure our Mediterranean position without Corfu; and it was good policy, as well as in accord with liberal and scholarly sentiment, to encourage the rising Greek kingdom, which had shown its anxiety to stand well with England by a practically unanimous offer of the crown to Queen Victoria's second son, Prince Alfred, Duke of Edinburgh. The election— on Prince Alfred's refusal, and the failure of negotiations with Stanley and others—of Prince George of Denmark, brother of the Princess of Wales, tended to insure the friendly interest of both the Court and the people of this country.

To Mrs. Brydges Willyams.

HOUSE OF COMMONS, *Monday, Feb. 23, 1863.*—Nothing thought of but Poland. It recalls the days of Thaddeus of Warsaw, which I dare say you read with a flashing eye and a flushing cheek.

The cards seem most unexpectedly to throw the Rhine into the grasp of Napoleon. How he must regret the disciplined troops that he has sent, upon a Quixote adventure, to the land of yellow fever and black vomit ![1]

Who is to be King of Poland ? That's the question now. Poor Greece has not yet been furnished with a crown. Life becomes like a fairy tale, and our intimate acquaintances turn into Sovereign Princes, who the day before were M.P.'s. and guardsmen, and fox-hunters.

I am content with being leader of the Opposition—at present an office more of thought than action; but the spring will return.

With the coming to the front in 1863 of the Polish and Danish questions, the defects of Russell's foreign policy could not be concealed. Derby expressed the views of many who generally supported the Government when he wrote to Disraeli in the beginning of the year: 'Denmark, Greece, the Ionian Islands, the Maltese scheme for the Pope, are all points in which Johnny has made more blunders than I had thought it possible to crowd into the space of a few months;' and in November: 'Johnny seems to me to have got into such a muddle in every part of the world that I do not see how we are to keep our hands off him. . . . His dealings with Denmark, Poland, and America, have been such as to disgust all parties with whom he has had to do.' A policy of 'meddle and muddle' he afterwards called it in Parliament; while Disraeli was sarcastic over 'the annual harvest of autumnal indiscretions.'

Disraeli entered into the generous feeling of sympathy which pervaded England during this year 1863 on behalf of the Poles, whom the oppression of Russia had goaded into insurrection. But he knew history too well, and was too open-minded, to suppose that the right was all on one side; and he saw no reason why England should engage in war for a cause that was so little hers. He remembered that similar troubles between Poland and Russia had occurred before, and that the settled policy of England had been not to intervene in arms. He said

[1] The ill-fated expedition to Mexico. See below, p. 82.

in the House of Commons that, if the partition of Poland was a great crime, it was a crime shared by the Polish people, as their national existence could not have been destroyed without some faults on their side. But he strongly eulogised Castlereagh for having striven, though in vain, on behalf of Polish independence at the Congress of Vienna; and he desired that Ministers should make use of their treaty rights to forward a policy favourable to the Poles. That, however, did not necessarily mean war, and he trusted that beneficial changes might be effected without an appeal to 'the last arbiter of human destiny.' Polish 'patriots' abroad, however, came in for his scorn. He said:

I always shrink from any expression of political sentimentalism. I do not know any people who have suffered so much from political sentimentalism as the Poles. Year after year there have been people living in Paris and London, some of them in a state of comparative luxury, stimulating their unfortunate countrymen in Poland to fruitless insurrection and to useless revolt; and all this time we have been favoured by them with expressions of feeling which, if expressions of feeling could effect the salvation of nations, have certainly been abundant and profuse.

Russell, ever a friend of human liberty, made drastic demands on the Government of Russia, including a complete amnesty for the insurgents, national representation and administration, and recognition of Polish as the official language. He sought and obtained the co-operation of France and Austria in these demands; but Disraeli sounded in the House a note of caution. The proposals showed no prescience; only a very sanguine politician could believe that Russia would accept them; if accepted, they would raise a phantom of Polish independence, which would lead in due course to a situation similar to the present. But Russell pushed on, and France, which had hitherto shown great reserve, though she was more interested than England in Poland, followed him. Disraeli described the fiasco in a speech in 1864:

What must have been the astonishment of the Emperor of the French when he found the English Government embracing the cause of Poland with extraordinary ardour ? The noble lord the Secretary of State and the noble lord the First Minister, but especially the former, announced this policy as if it were a policy new to the consideration of statesmen and likely to lead to immense results. He absolutely served a notice to quit on the Emperor of Russia. He sent a copy of this despatch to all the Courts of Europe which were signatories of the Treaty of Vienna, and invited them to follow his example. From the King of Portugal down to the King of Sweden, there was not a signatory of that treaty who was not, as it were, clattering at the palace gates of St. Petersburg, and calling the Tsar to account respecting the affairs of Poland. . . . Is it at all remarkable that the French Government and the French people, cautious as they were before, should have responded to such invitations and such stimulating proposals ? We know how the noble lord fooled them to the top of their bent. The House recollects the six propositions to which the attention of the Emperor of Russia was called in the most peremptory manner. . . . An impression pervaded Europe that there was to be a general war, and that England, France, and Austria, were united to restore Poland.

The House remembers the end of all this; it remembers the reply of the Russian Minister,[1] couched in a tone of haughty sarcasm and of indignation that deigned to be ironical. There was then but one step to take, according to the French Government, and that was action. They appealed to that England which had herself thus set the example of agitation on the subject; and England, wisely as I think, recurred to her traditionary policy, the Government confessing that it was a momentary indiscretion which had animated her councils for three or four months; that they never meant anything more than words; and a month afterwards, I believe, they sent to St. Petersburg an obscure despatch which may be described as an apology. But this did not alter the position of the French Government and the French Emperor. The Emperor had been induced by us to hold out promises which he could not fulfil. He was placed in a false position towards both the people of Poland and the people of France.[2]

The vicissitudes of the Polish question were reflected in Disraeli's autumn letters.

[1] The reply was that Russell was not accurately informed of what was passing in Poland, and that Russia was ready to assume the responsibility before God and man.   [2] July 4, 1864.

To Mrs. Brydges Williams.

Confidential. GROSVENOR GATE, *July* 21, 1863. — Just when I was anticipating tranquillity and repose, the affairs of the Continent have assumed so serious a character that the worst may be anticipated. For the last fortnight we have received accounts of the most alarming nature, and they have entirely absorbed the attention both of Lord Derby and myself. Lord Napier, our Ambassador at St. Petersburg, says we are again ' drifting into war.'

A war in the centre of Europe, on the pretext of restoring Poland, is a general war, and a long one. The map of Europe will be much changed when it is concluded, but I doubt whether the name of Poland will appear in it.

All the great questions of the day are still unsolved, and the materials for the infernal cauldron are plentiful.

The Rothschilds, who have contracted two loans this year, one to Russia, and the other to Italy—the latter the largest on record, more than thirty millions, and the Russian fifteen —are naturally very nervous.

The state of affairs is enough to shake anyone, who has any degree of responsibility. It is the reason I have not written to you, and why my letter now is so little gay.

HUGHENDEN, *Aug.* 7, 1863.—. . . Our Government, frightened, seems to be leaving France in the lurch. There will be no war this year. That's something!

Oct. 17.—. . . The troubles and designs of the French Emperor are aggravated and disturbed by the death of Billault, his only Parliamentary debater, and a first-rate one. With for the first time a real opposition to encounter, and formed of the old trained speakers of Louis Philippe's reign, in addition to the young democracy of oratory, which the last revolution has itself produced, the inconveniences, perhaps the injuries, of this untimely decease, are incalculable. It may even force,by way of distraction, the Emperor into war.

Our own Ministry have managed these affairs very badly, acording to their friends. The Polish question is a diplomatic Frankenstein, created, out of cadaverous remnants, by the mystic blundering of Lord Russell.

At present the peace of the world has been preserved, not by statesmen, but by capitalists. For the last three months it has been a struggle between the secret societies and the European millionaires. Rothschild hitherto has won; but the death of Billault may be as fatal for him as the poignard of a Polish patriot: for, I believe, in that part of the world they are called patriots, though in Naples only brigands. . . .

To Lord Derby.

HUGHENDEN MANOR, *Oct.* 30, 1863.—I am very sorry to hear of the gout, but I hope only a light cavalry attack, and that you will be even better, when it has departed. . . .

From what I hear, the Polish affair is virtually extinct— so much for recognising the rights of the insurrectionists as belligerents. The only result of the Polish insurrection has been that Gortchakoff, who, a little more than a year ago, was to have been displaced, in order to secure England and Austria, has become the most popular and powerful Minister of the day. I think John Russell has exposed himself throughout this. Very priggish and pedantic—a policy which was neither flesh, fish, nor fowl, nor etc. . . .

Sir Henry Holland, who has just returned from a visit of six weeks to the Dis-United States, speaks, with wonder, of the splendor and magnificence of life in New York. It is alike glaring and incomprehensible. He has seen nothing like it in any European capital. He was received with equal hospitality. . . .

To Mrs. Brydges Willyams.

HUGHENDEN MANOR, *Nov.* 5, 1863.—. . . The 'great Imperial Sphinx' is at this moment speaking. I shall not know the mysterious utterances until to-morrow, and shall judge of his conduct as much by his silence as his words. The world is very alarmed and very restless. Although England appears to have backed out of the possible war, there are fears that the French ruler has outwitted us, and that by an alliance with Austria, and the aid of the Italian armies, he may cure the partition of Poland by the partition of Prussia !

Austria, in that case, to regain Silesia, which Frederick the Great won, a century ago, from Maria Theresa; France to have the Rhine; and Galicia and Posen to be restored to Poland. If this happen, it will give altogether a new form and color to European politics. The Queen is much alarmed for the future throne of her daughter, the Princess Royal of Prussia; but as the war will be waged for the relief of Poland, of which England has unwisely approved, and to which, in theory, she is pledged, we shall really be checkmated, and scarcely could find an excuse to interfere, even if the nation wished.

So you see there is a good deal on the cards. . . . Adieu ! we shall soon meet.[1]

[1] Disraeli's last letter to Mrs. Willyams, who died Nov. 11. See Vol. I., III., ch. 13.

Napoleon was not the danger to Europe that Disraeli, who always exaggerated his power and ability, conceived him to be. But he was able to exercise a decisive influence on the next important question that engaged the attention of our statesmen. By declining to intervene by force on behalf of Denmark against Austria and Prussia, he nullified the diplomatic efforts of Russell and Palmerston, and left to England only the alternatives of fighting alone or an inglorious retreat.

In a letter to Earle in November, Disraeli made the curiously unfortunate remark that ' Prussia, without nationality, the principle of the day, is clearly the subject for partition.' Under the far-seeing guidance of her newly appointed Minister, Bismarck, Prussia was just about to utilise the principle of nationality in so masterly a fashion as to unite all the German peoples, except those who dwelt in Austria, under her own hegemony. Bismarck had himself, with the frankness that was on some occasions one of his diplomatic weapons as much as was duplicity on others, outlined his policy to Disraeli at a party at Brunnow's in 1862. His words were:

I shall soon be compelled to undertake the conduct of the Prussian Government. My first care will be to reorganise the army, with or without the help of the Landtag. . . . As soon as the army shall have been brought into such a condition as to inspire respect, I shall seize the first best pretext to declare war against Austria, dissolve the German Diet, subdue the minor States, and give national unity to Germany under Prussian leadership. I have come here to say this to the Queen's Ministers.

Disraeli had been so impressed at the moment that, after repeating Bismarck's conversation to Vitzthum, he added: ' Take care of that man ! He means what he says.'[1] The Schleswig-Holstein question gave Bismarck his opportunity. Both duchies were governed by the King of Denmark, though Holstein was wholly, and Schleswig partially, German in population; and Holstein indeed was part of the German Confederation. This somewhat

[1] Vitzthum, Vol. II., p. 172.

artificial arrangement, which had given rise to popular discontent both in Germany and in Holstein, and had led to a German invasion in 1848,[1] was formally ratified, though not guaranteed, by the Treaty of London in 1852 —a treaty concluded by the first Derby-Disraeli Administration, but founded on a protocol signed in 1850 by Palmerston, as Russell's Foreign Minister. The signatories to the treaty were England, France, Austria, Prussia, Russia, Sweden, and Denmark, but not the German Confederation, the body which had taken the lead in agitating for the annexation of the duchies on the ground of nationality. Austria and Prussia not only signed this treaty, confirming the union of the duchies with Denmark, but had of late pointedly dissociated themselves from the nationalist movement in Germany. Then, in 1863, Bismarck intervened, changed the current of Prussian and Austrian policy, and himself took the lead of the German movement. The death of the Danish King, and a disputed succession in the duchies, greatly forwarded his diplomacy. Russell endeavoured to mediate, but found Denmark as obstinate as the German Powers were determined. The German Powers took up arms, and by February, 1864, both Holstein and Schleswig were in the occupation of their troops.

At the close of the session of 1863 Palmerston had stated in Parliament that, if the rights and independence of Denmark were attacked, those who made the attempt would find that 'it would not be Denmark alone with which they would have to contend'; and Russell's despatches abounded in similar menaces. But Russell's diplomacy, under Palmerston's supervision, was so mismanaged as to insure that it was England who would find herself alone if she endeavoured to vindicate in arms the Treaty of London. The tactless treatment of the Polish question had irritated both Russia and France, her co-signatories, without helping the Poles. It had caused Russia to gravitate to Prussia; it had placed

[1] See Vol. I., pp. 1000-1002.

France in a false position. She had been ready to resort
to arms for Poland; England drew back. There, as in
the case of Italy, France would have been fighting for
the cause of nationality. England now invited her to
fight against that cause; Napoleon, whose proposal of
a European Congress had been curtly declined by Russell,
not unnaturally refused. Russell's blunders had reduced
his country to a position of hopeless isolation; and as,
apart from Russell and Palmerston, the prevailing feeling
in the Cabinet was against a rash adventure, an endeavour
was made to settle the matter by compromise at a Conference in London.

Public feeling in England was strongly in favour of
Denmark, as a small State bullied by two of the Great
Powers. The Manchester School were, of course, against
war; but there was a war party among the Whigs, and
a strong current in favour of forcible intervention
throughout the Conservative party. Robert Cecil advocated this course in the *Quarterly Review* for January
and April, 1864. John Manners wrote to Disraeli: ' I
suspect Government will side with Denmark, and, if
Germany persists, enter upon the *most popular*, the
easiest, and the *cheapest* war (for it can be waged by
our navy alone) of the century. Palmerston will then
become a virtual dictator, and we shall not even have
the poor consolation of having forced upon him the policy
which will have restored his popularity.' He was anxious
that the party should announce ' a decided Danish
policy.' Such being the temper of the country and of
the Conservative party, a great responsibility was laid
upon the Tory leaders, whose attitude would turn the
scale. Disraeli, though he strongly approved of diplomatic action on behalf of Denmark, and was keenly alive
to the disadvantage of having the German power established at the mouth of the Elbe, saw no sufficient occasion
for war. He wrote to Sir George Sinclair on January 20,
1864: ' An English Government that, in its wisdom, goes
to war with Germany, must make France the mistress

of Europe'; and Mrs. Disraeli declined to associate
herself in February with a committee to help wounded
Danes, on the ground that Disraeli feared the step might
'be embarrassing, and rather tend to inflame heats, than
allay them, at this moment of excitement.' Derby, less
decidedly, took the same line; being influenced in part
by the Queen, whose sympathies were with Germany,
and who invited her late Prime Minister to Osborne to
impress her views upon him.

While the Conference of London was sitting, Derby
feared that Disraeli's anxiety for peace, and for the
confusion of Ministers, might have led him into unguarded communications with Prussian and Austrian
diplomatists.

To Lord Derby.

Confidential. GROSVENOR GATE, *May* 13, 1864.—Conversations with Bernstorff are, in general, so insignificant
that I have difficulty in reproducing to myself the one to
which you refer, though it was so recent.

On Tuesday night at Apponyi's, just as I was going away,
he seized me, himself in much excitement, though more
stupid than usual, if that be possible.

I can only recall the following remarks on my part, which
formed any exception to the platitudes I usually bestow on
him.

He was evidently in a great fright about war. I said:
'Why, an armistice is the first step to peace.' He reminding
me that it was only for a month, I went on to this effect:
'Depend upon it, if you have a long armistice, and nothing
settled at the end of it, you *will* be in danger of war: you
ought not to lose a moment in solving the real difficulty.
What does the Conference understand by the words "integrity
of Denmark"? England is not very disposed to go to war
with Germany about German territory; Denmark no longer
hopes she will, perhaps does not wish her to do so.

'Therefore the future of Holstein ought to be considered
by the Conference as a secondary point: the first thing to
decide is, "What is Denmark?" If you can agree upon
that—and, if you can, you ought to do it quickly—all the
rest will somehow or other find its level, and settle itself.'

Of course, all this was not said continuously or so crudely,
but this, so far as I can recollect, and I really have racked

my brain this morning about it, is the cream of what I said. . . .

The Conference of London broke up without producing any settlement. But it became clear, during its sittings, that public opinion in England, however favourable to Denmark, would not sanction war; and the German Powers proceeded to enforce in arms their own solution, namely, the cession to themselves of all the King of Denmark's rights in the duchies, including the Danish as well as the German portion of Schleswig. The British Cabinet, in which Palmerston and Russell were finally overruled by their colleagues, had to be content with pro-testing its powerlessness to act without France or Russia, and to explain that, at any rate, neither the independence nor the capital city of Denmark was threatened. No wonder that Disraeli remarked, with sarcasm that was abundantly justified, that, judging from the past, he would have preferred that Cobden and Bright rather than Palmerston had conducted the affairs of the country. The consequences would be almost the same, but our position would have been more consistent and dignified.

At least those honourable gentlemen would threaten nobody; at least they would not tell Denmark that, if she is attacked, she will not find herself alone; at least they would not exasperate Germany by declaiming in the full Parliament of England against the 'aggravated outrages' of her policy; at least they would not lure on Denmark by delusive counsels and fallacious hopes.

Never had an Opposition a clearer case for censuring Ministerial foreign policy; and a motion was made in both Houses regretting that Ministers had failed to uphold the integrity and independence of Denmark, and that their policy had lowered the just influence of England in the councils of Europe, and thereby diminished the securities of peace. Disraeli, in introducing the motion in the Commons,[1] spoke for nearly three hours, quoting the

[1] July 4.

diplomatic correspondence in great detail in order to show the mismanagement of the Government. Had Ministers maintained an understanding with Russia and France, war would not have broken out, and the independence and integrity of Denmark would have been maintained. But they had estranged both Russia and France; and after the latter had adopted a definitely neutral attitude, England should have done the same, and abstained from all interference, menaces, and promises. He mocked at the Conference, which lasted as long as a Carnival, and, like a Carnival, was 'an affair of masks and mystifications.' In the Conference Ministers even proposed the dismemberment of Denmark—so much for its integrity! and the placing of the remainder under the guarantee of the Great Powers, like another Turkey in Europe—so much for its independence ! His peroration was a declaration for peace.

Sir, it is not for any man in this House, on whatever side he sits, to indicate the policy of this country in our foreign relations; it is the duty of no one but the responsible Ministers of the Crown. The most we can do is to tell the noble lord what is not our policy. We will not threaten and then refuse to act. We will not lure on our allies with expectations we do not fulfil. And, sir, if ever it be the lot of myself, or any public men with whom I have the honour to act, to carry on important negotiations on behalf of this country, as the noble lord and his colleagues have done, I trust that we at least shall not carry them on in such a manner that it will be our duty to come to Parliament to announce to the country that we have no allies, and then declare that England can never act alone. Sir, those are words which ought never to have escaped the lips of a British Minister. They are sentiments which ought never to have occurred even to his heart. I repudiate, I reject them. I remember there was a time when England, with not a tithe of her present resources, inspired by a patriotic cause, triumphantly encountered a world in arms. And, sir, I believe now, if the occasion were fitting, if her independence or her honour were assailed, or her empire endangered—I believe that England would rise in the magnificence of her might, and struggle triumphantly for those objects for which men live and nations flourish. But I, for one, will never consent to go to war to extricate Ministers from the consequences of their own mistakes. It

is in this spirit that I have drawn up this Address to the
Crown. . . . I am ready to vindicate the honour of the
country whenever it is necessary, but I have drawn up this
Address in the interest of peace.

The debate was felt to involve the fate of the Government; and it was accordingly prolonged for four nights,
during which most of the leading men of all parties spoke.
Gladstone was indignant that the House of Commons
should be called upon, for the sake of displacing a Government, to record the degradation of its country. Cobden
condemned the meddling of diplomatists with the destinies
of nations. Horsman said that the Government had
made mistakes, but the Opposition had endorsed them,
so he could not support a vote of censure. Bernal
Osborne riddled Palmerston and Russell with the sarcasm
which in old days he reserved for Disraeli. Palmerston
appealed for support to the achievements of his Administration, consisting mainly of Gladstone's Budgets, which
he himself had thwarted in Cabinet. But, fearing to
meet Disraeli's motion with a direct negative, he, the
apostle of universal interference and the unsuccessful advocate of interference on this occasion, accepted
an amendment moved by Kinglake in favour of noninterference between Germany and Denmark. This
was not a frank or straightforward course, said Disraeli
in reply;[1] but it was a successful one. The motion, which
had been carried in the Lords by a majority of nine, was
defeated in the Commons by eighteen, the numbers being
313 to 295. Thus the House secured what the vast
majority desired, the preservation of peace coupled with
the maintenance of Palmerston as Minister; and Disraeli,
though his policy prevailed, failed once more to persuade
the 1859 Parliament to put him and Derby in office to
carry it out.

The following memoranda by Disraeli relating to foreign
affairs in 1864 may be added here:

[1] It was in this reply that Disraeli dubbed Horsman a 'superior
person.'

August 5, 1864.—Long walk in the park with Brunnow:
spoke much of Bismarck.   I reminded him he had introduced
Bis. to me at a ball at his house two years ago; which he
recollected.   We agreed a man of great energy. ' An
Alberoni,' I added.

Brunnow doubted whether circumstances had favored
Alberoni, as they had Bis.   Thought there was no person
whom circumstances had ever so favored.   France holding
back because she was offended with England; English
Government in a state of *impuissance ;* Russia distracted
with conflicting interests; Austria for the first time sincere
in wishing to act with Prussia; then the weak chivalric
character of the King; the enthusiasm of Germany.

' Bismarck made a good book,' I said.

' He made a good book, and, what is most strange, he
backed the worst horse in the lot.   For Prussia is a country
without any bottom, and in my opinion could not maintain
a real war for 6 months.'

I reminded Brunnow of what he had said about L[ouis]
N[apoleon] (the five years).   He accepted it: I gave him
originally 15 years from 1850, I think.   Well, the lease approaches the term.

Gladstone said (1864) that the invasion of Mexico by the
Emperor Napoleon was one of the greatest political blunders
ever perpetrated—certainly the greatest political blunder of
his time.   But note : there never was a political move over
which the Emperor had so long and so deeply brooded: for
many years.   In 1857 he mentioned to me his wish and
willingness to assist in establishing a European dynasty in
Mexico, and said that for his part he would make no opposition to the accession of the Duc d'Aumale to such a throne.
He looked upon its establishment as of high European importance.

It was his custom to say that there were two Powers
who hated old Europe : Russia and the United States of
America.

CHAPTER X.

DISRAELI AND THE CHURCH.

1860–1865.

'There are few great things left in England, and the Church is one.' This was Disraeli's dictum, expressed again and again, with slight variations of phrase, in speech and letter and book; and one of the main objects which he set before himself during the long period of opposition to Palmerston was to strengthen the position of the Church, to secure her from internal disruption and external assault. To a considerable extent, no doubt, he had his eye, as a party leader, on party and political advantage. The tendency of the Church, as a great historic institution, could not fail to be of a conservative character; to establish an active and successful Church party in the House of Commons must benefit the Conservative cause, and help to rally disaffected Conservatives round the leader who raised the ecclesiastical banner.

But it would be a mistake to treat Disraeli's efforts on behalf of the Church, whether in the House of Commons or in the diocesan meetings at which in these years of opposition he frequently appeared and spoke, as mainly adroit electioneering. The Church appealed to him not merely as a great conservative force, not even merely as a majestic historical tradition, but as a conception derived from his own sacred race, and as a living witness on behalf of the spiritual order against the invading materialism of the age.[1] He expounded his view in a draft letter preserved among the Beaconsfield papers —a letter which was obviously addressed to a clergyman,

---

[1] See Vol. I., III., ch. 3.

but which contains nothing to show definitely to whom or when it was written, or whether it was actually sent:

> . . . I entirely participated at the time in the feelings that influenced you in the Oxford Movement, which, I believe, had it been directed with a discretion equal to its energy and talents, would have conquered the heart of the nation and placed the strong religious feeling of the country on a basis of unassailable authority.
>
> But on the desolating secession of Newman and his followers, to me so unexpected and still to me so unaccountable, I withdrew from the disheartening struggle, and only resumed my weapons, much against the feeling of my political friends, though accused of party motives, when the enemy seemed desecrating the hearth.
>
> I have a certain reverence for the Church of Rome, as I have for all churches which recognise the divine mission of the House of Israel; but I confess I was astounded that a man of the calibre of Newman should have fallen into the pitfalls of the 17th century, and in his search for a foundation have stopt short at Rome instead of advancing to Jerusalem.
>
> For myself, I look upon the Church as the only Jewish institution that remains, and, irrespective of its being the depository of divine truth, must ever cling to it as the visible means which embalms the memory of my race, their deeds and thoughts, and connects their blood with the origin of things.
>
> There are few great things left, and the Church is one. No doubt its position at this moment is critical, and, indeed, the whole religious sentiment of the country is in a convulsive state; but I believe the state of affairs is only one of the periodical revolts of the Northern races against Semitic truth, influenced mainly by mortified vanity in never having been the medium of direct communication with the Almighty; and that it will end as in previous instances, after much sorrow and suffering, in their utter discomfiture.

Similarly, in the General Preface to the Novels, 1870, he deplored the fact that no Churchman equal to the occasion had arisen out of the Oxford Movement, but that it had fallen into the hands of ' monks and schoolmen.'

> The secession of Dr. Newman dealt a blow to the Church of England under which it still reels. That extraordinary event has been ' apologised ' for, but has never been explained. It was a mistake and a misfortune. The tradition of the Anglican Church was powerful. Resting on the Church of

Jerusalem, modified by the divine school of Galilee, it would have found that rock of truth which Providence, by the instrumentality of the Semitic race, had promised to St. Peter.   Instead of that, the seceders sought refuge in mediæval superstitions, which are generally only the embodiments of pagan ceremonies and creeds.

The vital importance of religion in the constitution of the State was recognised by Disraeli in his earliest political speculations. 'It is one of the leading principles of the policy of England,' he wrote in the *Vindication* in 1835, 'that the religious discipline and future welfare of our citizens are even of greater importance than their political or present well-being.' Serious interest, however, in the Church and Church questions seems to have been imbibed by him for the first time from the Cambridge men who formed in the 1841 Parliament his 'Young England' following, and particularly from Smythe and Manners. But the Oxford Movement in which they brought him to sympathise developed in the next few years a Romeward tendency which alienated his nascent good-will; and, as we have seen,[1] the part played in *Tancred* by the Church, which was to have been its main theme, is a very poor one. The Protestant outbreak in 1850-51, on the occasion of the Papal Aggression, confirmed Disraeli in his view that Tractarianism had taken a direction in conflict with the permanent bias of the British character. For some years, accordingly, he rather watched, as a critical spectator, the religious tendencies of the Church and the age, than took any active part in guiding them. It was the first Derby-Disraeli Ministry that granted permission to Convocation to meet for the despatch of business, after an interval of 135 years. But this was done by Derby, the Prime Minister, and Walpole, the Home Secretary ; Disraeli was certainly not active in the matter, and in 1870 he expressed his regret that the revival had not placed Convocation ' on a wide basis,' instead of leaving it the representative of ' a priestly section.'[2]   Indeed, his first

[1] Vol. I., III., ch. 3.   [2] General Preface to the novels, 1870.

public utterance relating to Church affairs, after a long period of silence, occurs in his electoral campaign, in 1857, when there was a fear lest the internal quarrels of ecclesiastical parties might be transferred to the political arena and act disadvantageously to the Tories. In his address to his constituents in that year he gave Churchmen the excellent advice that, instead of quarrelling among themselves, they should evince mutual forbearance, ' unite on the common ground of ecclesiastical polity,' and oppose all efforts to impair the integrity of the Church.

Of the parties in the Church, the only one which steadily supported the Conservatives, a support which had persisted since the days of Dr. Sacheverell, was the old High Church or Anglican party. All 'the other parties, secure in the belief that the union of Church and State was regarded as sacred by statesmen of every political colour were quite as much, or more, disposed, for one reason or another, to favour the opposite political connection. The Evangelicals were attracted to the Whigs by Russell's aggressive Protestantism and by Palmerston's Low Church appointments made under Shaftesbury's influence. The rising Broad Church school, represented by Dean Stanley and Jowett, was naturally inclined to enlist under the banner of Progress. And, strange to say, even the Tractarians were being almost insensibly drawn by the Peelite leaders, Sidney Herbert and Gladstone, who were Churchmen before they were politicians, into the ranks of that Liberalism against which Newman's original movement was in its essence an emphatic protest. Meanwhile, within the Liberal party, a movement was springing up hostile to all State establishment of religion. The Dissenters, from being a purely religious, were being organised as a political body; from defence against oppression, they passed to attack on what they regarded as unwarranted privilege; the Society for the Liberation of Religion from State control, founded in 1844, began to exercise serious political influence. The union of Church and State was threatened as it had never been

threatened before. To use the language of a preface to
a collected edition of Disraeli's Church speeches of the
early sixties—a preface which was written by a prominent High Churchman, the sixth Lord Beauchamp, then
Frederick Lygon, but in which we seem to catch the
veritable accents of Lygon's friend and leader :[1]

Measures were astutely devised either to sap some ancient
buttress which supported, or to pull down some stately
pinnacle which adorned, the venerable fabric of the Established
Church.   Distinguished persons in high places, aghast at these
new dangers, counselled surrender; others advocated a
temporising policy; but Mr. Disraeli, with rare sagacity,
surveyed the position and comprehended the full consequences
of yielding at such a crisis.

The principal measure of the kind before Parliament
at this period was Sir John Trelawny's Bill to abolish
Church rates.   The Church rate was no tyrannical or
hierarchical levy.   It was made by a popular body, the
churchwardens and parishioners in vestry assembled,
and it was devoted to the parochial, if not national,
purposes of defraying the expenses of divine service, repairing the fabric of the parish church, and
paying the salaries of church officials.   It was a
personal charge on the occupier, and the majority in
vestry bound the minority.   If, as happened in many
cases spontaneously, and in others as the result of an
engineered agitation, the rate was not paid, there was
great difficulty in applying compulsion.   The grievance
of the conscientious Dissenter appealed to the Liberal
party, and not to the Liberal party alone; and Trelawny's
Bill was carried by sufficient majorities through the
Commons in 1855 and 1856, though the Lords opposed
a barrier to further progress.   The keen Churchmen in
the second Derby-Disraeli Ministry, as we have seen,[2]
wished to introduce a measure of compromise in 1858,
but were prevented by Disraeli.   In 1859 they got their

[1] Disraeli wrote to Lygon about this republication: 'No one but you
could be the editor, as you know my inmost mind, and there is entire
sympathy between us.'   [2] Vol. I., p. 1527.

opportunity, and for the moment Disraeli hoped that their plan, for which Walpole was responsible, would settle the matter. He told the Queen that the Bill had been received with so much favour that he believed it would pass. 'This is very unexpected; and the satisfactory settlement of this long-agitated and agitating question will be a great relief to public life, and tend to restore and augment the good-humour of the country.'[1]

The hope speedily proved delusive: the compromise was rejected, and the majorities in favour of Trelawny's Bill rose to fifty-three in 1858, and even to seventy-four in 1859. Disraeli then began to change the tactics of the party; to organise a more effective resistance to a Bill which, though plausible enough in itself, was in reality the opening move in a campaign for Disestablishment; to discourage the idea of compromise, and to appeal to the latent conservatism of a Parliament which supported so conservative a statesman as Palmerston. In the session of 1860, while not denying the existence of a grievance, he strongly opposed the second reading of the Bill, which he held would revolutionise the parochial constitution of the country. The real issue to be decided was whether there should be an established Church. The majority dropped to twenty-nine; and on the third reading, in answer to a further appeal by Disraeli on behalf of the Church of England as one of the strongest elements of society, one of the most powerful of our institutions, and the best security of our liberties, what he called Trelawny's rash and ruinous proposition was only carried in the Commons by nine, to perish by an overwhelming majority in the Lords. It is no wonder that, writing to the King of the Belgians on August 23,[2] Disraeli noted, as prominent among the causes which contributed to Conservative consolidation during the session, the appearance of a Church party in the House of Commons for the first time since 1840, and the fact of the clergy throughout the country again generally acting with the Conservatives.

---

[1] *Queen Victoria's Letters*, Feb. 21, 1859.   [2] See above, pp. 16, 17.

In Disraeli's correspondence with Mrs. Willyams this year, especially during the late autumn, an ecclesiastical flavour may be discerned.

To Mrs. Brydges Willyams.

NEW YEAR'S DAY, 1860.—. . . Only think of our living to see the Pope on his last legs—and to be betrayed, too, by 'the eldest son of the Church'! A great Roman Catholic lady told me yesterday that the truth was too obvious; mankind would no longer endure clerical authority. She pitied them, but was consoled by the conviction of their eventual misery, and that no other authority could long endure 'As for your Church of England,' she added, 'what are we to think of that? Four theatres hired, every evening, for "divine" service. A Bishop preaching at Sadler's Wells, I believe! If theatres will do, what is the use of churches? And why not one of the usual performers to preach, instead of an ordained priest?'

Do you know, I thought her remarks unanswerable, and did not much care to prove she was wrong, although she thought she was confounding me. . . .

HUGHENDEN, *Oct.* 18, 1860.—. . . This year is the triennial visitation of our Diocesan, and I have to receive the Bishop [Wilberforce] at this place. This is no slight affair, for on these occasions a Bishop is like a Highland chief and moves with a tail. Besides the descendant of the Apostles, I have to extend hospitality to his Chancellor, his Chaplain, his Secretary, and the Archdeacon of Bucks, and all their servants. . . .

Nov. 11, 1860.—. . . On Tuesday Lord John Manners and Lord Stanley come down here, to assist me in my great episcopal reception, which commences on Wednesday. On Thursday Lord Malmesbury and Lord and Lady Salisbury. I hope to clear my house by the end of the week, but I rather doubt it. Sir William Jolliffe and Colonel Taylor, the chief of my staff, arrive on Friday. . . .

Nov. 18, 1860.—You could not have sent us a more acceptable offering to our banquet, and one, I assure you, more appreciated, than the rosy-colored tribute of Torbay, which quite delighted us for their own merits, and their evidence of the kind thoughts of the donor. The Bishop was quite delighted. Prelates love delicacies, and, as he is a wit as well as a priest, he was very playful about Devonian fairies and magic gifts. It certainly arrived most opportune, and was precious from its history; because no one in Bucks would have tasted a prawn from London, whereas direct from the balmy waters of the West they were a delight.

II.   4

Our house has been brimful, and is not yet quite emptied. Sir William Jolliffe and Col. Taylor still linger, and leave us to-morrow; all the rest have departed. It has been a week of great and unceasing bustle; but the greatest effort, the Bishop's charge at Wycombe, which I and Lord John Manners thought it but right to attend, and which, irrespective of divine service, was three hours long! It's rightly called a *Visitation*. . . .

The episcopal visitation and charge in November were speedily eclipsed in interest by a speech which Disraeli, as a layman of the diocese, made at a ruridecanal meeting at Amersham on December 4. It was, he told Rose, well considered, and intended as a manifesto. In it he definitely cast aside the idea of compromise on the Church Rate Bill, and urged Church people to stand boldly on their rights. Great issues, he said, were generally tried in this practical country on collateral points; the question of Church rates involved that of a National Church. Churchmen should therefore put internal parties aside and unite and organise; but what should be their policy? There were two opinions. Some were for compromise. He agreed, if compromise meant improvement in detail in regard to method, but not if it meant exemption of Dissenters from the charge. That was not compromise, but surrender—an acknowledgment that the Church of England is no longer a National Church.

This is a public charge of which all the circumstances are of a popular character. It is ancient; it is for a general, not to say a common purpose; it is levied by public votes. If, in a country where the majority decide everything, the minority are, on the ground of conscientious scruple, to be exempted from a public payment, on what principle can society be held together? Landowners might have a conscientious scruple against paying the public creditor; peace societies might have a conscientious scruple against paying war taxes. What the Dissenter demands is, in fact, an oligarchical privilege; and the principle, if conceded and pursued, may lead to general confusion.[1]

---

[1] A criticism, in advance, of the campaign of 'passive resistance' carried on by some of the Dissenters against the Education Act of 1902.

He felt deeply the responsibility of giving the advice
to refuse to sanction the principle of exemption. He was
opposing the recommendation of the Committee of the
House of Lords in 1859, and what was then the unanimous
opinion of the bench of Bishops. But the Committee
were precipitate: they mistook public humour for public
opinion. What had happened last spring ?

The second reading of Sir John Trelawny's Bill had been
carried by a much reduced majority, and the advocates of
what is fallaciously called compromise were strongly in favour
of what they called seizing the opportunity for a settlement.
I was of a different opinion. I did not think that the advantage the Church had then obtained was only a happy casualty.
I thought it was the break of dawn. I did my utmost to
dissuade my friends from relinquishing the contest, and
ultimately, on my sole responsibility, opposed the third reading
of Sir John Trelawny's Bill. The whole country was agitated
on the occasion by the opponents of the Church to regain
the lost ground. Instead of that, the majority against Church
rates, which had sat like an incubus on the Church for twenty
years, virtually disappeared. We owe to that division our
commanding position.

He recommended the clergy to petition Parliament,
to organise Church Defence associations, and to bring
their influence to bear on their representatives.

'What changes there are in this world !' wrote Rose
on reading the speech. 'Gladstone going to Bradford
with Bright and Cobden and Milner Gibson, and you
leading the Church party throughout the kingdom !'
Derby, good Churchman as he was, was rather aghast at
the pronouncement. 'You will forgive me,' he wrote,
'if I entertain a fear that you have even spoken too
decidedly. . . . The present law is, if not so objectionable
in itself, so difficult of enforcement that, if an amendment could be obtained by some concession, I think it
would be worth the sacrifice.' Disraeli did not reply;
and Derby, when he next wrote—on January 27, 1861,
just before the session—began: 'I hope you were not
displeased at the frankness with which I expressed my

fears as to the effect of your speech on the Church rate question. I have not heard from you since.'

To Lord Derby.

Private. GROSVENOR GATE, *Jan.* 28, 1861.—I was in hopes that twelve years of trying companionship might have assured you that I was ever grateful for criticism, even from my adversaries, and that it was impossible I could resent the gentle comments of one who, though I have committed so many errors, has never reproached me. The only reason of my silence was that I had nothing to write about. The situation, which I intimated in my last letter, never altered.

As for Church rates, I took the step after great inquiry and reflection; and I think if I had not taken it our counties would have slipped away. The moment was more than ripe. The enclosed will give you some idea how it worked in Wales, where the clergy, and the Church generally, are weakest. It will work more powerfully in Wiltshire, and, from the numerous communications which reach me, I think I shall have effected my purpose. All that I am afraid of are the Bishops, acted on by a coterie, who hate us, and have flattered themselves they had a monopoly of Church championship. Most of these people are now out of Parliament: Roundell Palmer, B[eresford] Hope and Co.; but they are unceasingly at work. They can do the Church no good, for they are utterly incapable of managing England, being a finical and fastidious crew, who are more anxious about what they call the Church, than the Church of England. My own Diocesan has left them, and in his triennial charge, this autumn, declared against their projects: the Bishop of Exeter, whom I saw at Torquay, is all right, and will be up for the meeting of Parliament. I have unceasingly worked, since you wrote to me, to counteract any mischief from my movement, and to secure all the good which might accrue from it; and if the Bishops will only be quiet and not commit themselves any further on the subject, leaving the question to the country and the House of Commons, I have no fear whatever of ultimate success. . . .

Disraeli's determined policy led to a marked Parliamentary success in the session of 1861. He took the precaution, when arranging to give Palmerston general support, to neutralise the Government on this special question. Shaftesbury, who acted as go-between in some of the negotiations, wrote of Palmerston on January 17:

' Reserving of course his own opinion and freedom of
action in respect of Church rates, he distinctly said there
was no intention of making it a "Government question." '
Disraeli was also earnest in beating up doubtful Conservative voters. ' It will never do,' he wrote to Malmesbury
on February 22, ' to have our own men run riot. The
fact is, in internal politics there is only one question now,
the maintenance of the Church. There can be no refrain-
ing or false Liberalism on such a subject. They are both
out of fashion, too ! '[1] Accordingly, the second reading of
Trelawny's Bill was only carried by a majority of fifteen,
and on the third reading, in a very full house, the numbers
were equal—274 each side. The Speaker, interpreting
the attitude of the House as one of hesitation, threw his
casting vote against the measure. In his speech against
the second reading Disraeli gave an interesting insight
into his view of the Dissenters' position:

One would almost suppose, from the manner in which the
Dissenter was mentioned, that he was some stranger in the
country or some wild animal. Why, a Dissenter is our friend,
our neighbour, our tenant, our tradesman; he is an Englishman animated by all the feelings and principles of Englishmen. . . . If he finds himself in a majority in any parish
where a rate is proposed, he has a victorious power of self-
defence in that majority, and he can by the votes of himself
and friends shield himself from these grievances of which
you say that he complains. What is the position of a Dissenter
in parishes in which he is in a minority ? In that case, if
he be animated by the same feelings as any other Englishman
—and I know by experience he is so—he yields to the opinion
of the majority, for such he knows is the principle upon
which our social system is established. If the majority is
overwhelming, he yields without a murmur; if it be slight,
he can exercise his influence if he chooses, so that next year
the majority may change into a minority.

To Mrs. Brydges Willyams.

CARLTON CLUB, *Thursday, June 27, 1861.*—I wrote to you,
about a week ago, on the eve of the Church rate division.
I told you how critical it was, and how important success
was to me, considering that the resistance of the Bill had been

[1] *Memoirs of an Ex-Minister*, Vol. II., p. 247.

mainly prompted by my counsel. I was not altogether
without hope, but not over-sanguine. You have seen in the
papers the strange and wonderful triumph ! Such a scene
has not occurred in the House of Commons since the impeachment of Lord Melville, in the days of Mr. Pitt. . . .

In the autumn of 1861 Disraeli repeated his experiment of addressing a diocesan meeting in Bucks. He
took precautions to be properly reported. ' I will endeavour,' he wrote to Delane, ' to make a *précis* of what
I intend to say, which I will give your envoy if he will
see me before the business. This is rather a difficult
thing for me to do, as it is against my grain, being much
influenced by my audience and the impromptu; but I
must make an effort to entirely control myself, as there
must be no mistake.'

To Mrs. Brydges Willyams.

Most private. HUGHENDEN MANOR, *Nov.* 13, 1861.—The
state of the Church is critical, from dissensions and heresy
among its own children. If it were to fall, philosophy would
not profit: we should only be handed over to a narrow-minded
and ignorant fanaticism. I have been in frequent correspondence of late with the Bishop of Oxford, the Bishop of
this diocese—as you know, a first-rate man; and I have
promised to attend a great diocesan meeting to-morrow at
Aylesbury, and try to give a lead to public opinion in the
right direction. It is a nervous business, for what may be
said and done to-morrow may produce very great effects—
like Sacheverell's sermon, which was nothing till it was
preached, and then nearly set the Thames on fire. After all,
it may end to-morrow in smoke, for a speech is like a play—
success seems always a chance. . . . Think of me to-morrow,
a very critical day I can assure you.

The ' heresy ' about which Disraeli was disquieted was
the recent publication of *Essays and Reviews*, a volume of
mildly latitudinarian essays by various Anglican writers.
Disraeli was a rigid maintainer of orthodoxy in belief,
partly, no doubt, from a realisation of the utility of religion
to the civil magistrate, but also, it appears, from intellectual conviction, and from a jealousy on behalf of his
own sacred race, the original recipients and transmitters

of religious truth. He therefore held the speculations of Broad Churchmen in little favour. Five years before, in 1856, we find him writing to Mrs. Willyams about an article in the *Quarterly*[1] on a work by ' a Rev. Mr. Jowett,' which, he tells his correspondent, ' will give you some idea of the rapid and strange advances which German neology, *alias* infidelity, is making in that seat of venerable orthodoxy, the University of Oxford, and especially among clergymen of the Church of England. When the *Quarterly Review* steps forward, it is clear that the plague in the vitals can be no longer concealed.' Accordingly, in his speech at Aylesbury, Disraeli effectively ridiculed the mutually destructive theories put forward by successive schools of German theologians. His criticism has lost none of its point in an age which has witnessed the conservative revolution wrought by Harnack in New Testament criticism. About a century before, he said, German theology, which had been mystical, became critical. A Rationalist school sprang up which explained the supernatural incidents in the sacred narrative by natural causes. After absorbing for half a century the intellect of the country, this school was displaced by one which applied a mythical interpretation to Scripture. But, ' if the mythical theologians triumphantly demonstrated that Rationalism was irrational, so the mythical system itself has become a myth '; and there had been in its place a revival in Germany of pagan pantheism. What had the Church to fear from ' speculations so overreaching, so capricious, and so self-destructive ? ' He was himself in favour of free inquiry on all subjects, but ' free inquiry should be pursued by free inquirers,' and the authors of *Essays and Reviews* ' have entered into engagements with the people of this country quite inconsistent with the views advanced in those prolusions.'

On the general question of the connection of Church and State, Disraeli deprecated the tendency of some

---

[1] ' The Neology of the Cloisters,' *Quarterly Review*, Dec. 1855.

High Churchmen to contemplate disestablishment without alarm. It was a fallacy to suppose that the Church after disestablishment would occupy the position which it held in the Middle Ages. The civil power would never ' submit to a superior authority, or even brook a rival.' There would be ' possible struggle, probable spoliation,' and the Church might ' subside into a fastidious, not to say finical congregation.' The connection between Church and State was in unison with the spirit of the age and the soundest principles of political philosophy. ' The most powerful principle which governs man is the religious principle.'

A wise Government, allying itself with religion, would, as it were, consecrate society and sanctify the State. But how is this to be done ? It is the problem of modern politics which has always most embarrassed statesmen. No solution of the difficulty can be found in salaried priesthoods and complicated concordats. But by the side of the State in England there has gradually arisen a majestic corporation—wealthy, powerful, independent—with the sanctity of a long tradition, yet sympathising with authority, and full of conciliation, even deference, to the civil power. Broadly and deeply planted in the land, mixed up with all our manners and customs, one of the main guarantees of our local government, and therefore one of the prime securities of our common liberties, the Church of England is part of our history, part of our life, part of England itself.

It is said sometimes that the Church of England is hostile to religious liberty. As well might it be said that the monarchy of England is adverse to political freedom. Both are institutions which insure liberty by securing order.

It was a statesmanlike plea for the union of Church and State; and Disraeli naturally proceeded to urge all Churchmen to come together in its defence. The assault might proceed from a minority, but should not on that account be treated lightly; for ' the history of success is the history of minorities.' ' Clever electioneering speech to clergy and church,' was Bishop Wilberforce's comment in his diary. While not disagreeing, we may add that there was sound sense in Disraeli's advice.

The advice at any rate was taken, and in the following

session of 1862 Trelawny's Bill was actually defeated, on second reading in a full House, by one vote (287 to 286), and a year later by the sufficient majority of ten. 'A House of Commons,' to quote once again Lord Beauchamp's preface, 'which had voted the abolition of Church rates with a tumultuous majority of seventy, negatived the abolition by a majority of ten in a House still more crowded. . . . Churchmen began to appreciate the necessity and power of organisation.'

It was a great Parliamentary success for Disraeli, but was it anything more ? That Church rates could not continue indefinitely to be levied compulsorily from Dissenters was as evident to Disraeli as it was to his opponents, or to those of his colleagues who doubted his tactics, and pressed for some form of compromise or arrangement. And, as a matter of fact, the struggle ended by the passage, at Gladstone's instance, in 1868, when Disraeli was himself Prime Minister, of a Bill making the Church rate purely voluntary, and thus remedying the grievance. This was indeed a different thing from the crude surrender proposed by Sir John Trelawny. But Disraeli could claim besides that, when he raised the banner of resistance, the friends of the Church were dispirited and disorganised, seeing one outwork falling after another and despairing of saving even the citadel; and that, owing to the spirit and courage which he breathed into their ranks, they realised that, whatever concession might have to be made on this point or on that, there was good hope of securing for the future all for which they seriously cared. It may well be doubted whether the alternative tactics of hastening to give up every doubtful privilege the moment it was called in question would not have resulted in many unnecessary surrenders, and thus fatally impaired the integrity of the stronghold.

In the autumn of 1862, for the third year in succession, Disraeli delivered an important speech[1] on ecclesiastical

---

[1] Wycombe, Oct. 30. 'I am told by great authorities,' wrote Disraeli to Mrs. Willyams, 'that it was the speech of a statesman without cant.'

policy at a diocesan meeting in Bucks. The immediate
object of the meeting was the augmentation of poor
livings, and Disraeli did not neglect the opportunity of
pointing out the peculiar duty incumbent on Whig
magnates, whose fortunes were founded in historical
times on grants of ecclesiastical property, to be liberal
in their gifts for such an object. But his main theme
was the difficulty of reconciling the existence of an
Established Church with the principle of civil and religious
liberty on which society in England was now based.
That could only be done, he held, by asserting the
nationality of the Church of England. But how could
a Church be national, when there were millions not in
communion with her, part of them Dissenters, but the
great majority indifferent ? He did not think the
Dissenters would be a difficulty, because the tendency
of the age was for Churches to cease internecine hostility.
But what of the indifferent millions ? The late Archbishop Sumner, he said, was anxiously perplexed by the
anomalous position of the Church; and consequently
counselled surrender whenever momentous questions
involving her interests came up, basing his advice on
the undoubted fact that the population had outgrown
the Church. Disraeli drew an opposite conclusion.
These millions not in communion with the Church were,
after all, the English people. And who were the English
people ?

The English people are, without exception, the most enthusiastic people in the world. There are more excitable races.
The French, the Italians, are much more excitable; but for
deep and fervid feeling there is no race in the world at all
equal to the English. And what is the subject, of all others,
upon which the English people have always been most enthusiastic ? Religion. The notes on the gamut of their
feeling are few, but they are deep. Industry, Liberty,
Religion, form the solemn scale. Industry, Liberty, Religion,
—that *is* the history of England.

There was here, therefore, an immense field for the
Church. Disraeli proceeded to point out five methods

in which she might assert her nationality in view of the
indifference of large masses of the population; and he
added three more in his speech at Oxford in 1864. In
the first place, the Church should educate the people.
In that respect she had by her efforts in the last quarter
of a century already obtained a command, which ought
to be increased. Next, there should be 'a moderate
and well-considered extension of the Episcopate.'
Thirdly, there should be a further development of the
lay element in the Church. 'We must erase from the
mind of the country the idea that the Church of England
is a clerical corporation.' It was a national corporation;
'except—a great exception, no doubt—the ministering
to us of sacred things, there is nothing that concerns the
Church in which it is not alike the privilege and the
duty of laymen to take an active part.' Fourthly, the
parochial system should be maintained, especially in the
large towns. Though there had been great changes in
parochial administration, 'so far as the Church is concerned, the parochial constitution is complete and
inviolate.' Fifthly, the clergy must be made more
efficient, by being better paid. The three additional
points of 1864 were the formation of Convocation on a
broader basis, with a fuller representation of the parochial
clergy, and perhaps with a union of the two Provinces;
the establishment of more satisfactory relations between
the Colonial Churches and the Mother Church at home;
and the reconstitution of the final Court of Appeal in
matters spiritual. 'I do believe,' he said, 'that, with
entire deference to the principle of the Royal Supremacy,
which I trust may never be lost sight of for an instant,
it may be possible to reconcile the requirements of the
State with the conscience of the Church.'

These were all temperate and practical reforms, many
of which have since been carried into effect. If they
seem now to be the commonplaces of sensible Churchmen,
we must remember that Disraeli recommended them at
a time when they were questionable novelties—pressed,

many of them, on a reluctant Church by one who was regarded as a fussy Diocesan, and who was suspected, however unfairly, of disloyalty to the Anglican Communion. The Bishop was himself Disraeli's guest at Hughenden for the occasion in 1862, and recorded in his diary that all Disraeli's talk was aimed at Gladstone. 'I and others,' he said, 'kept the Church as [Gladstone's] nest-egg when he became a Whig, till it was almost addled.'

To Mrs. Brydges Willyams.

HUGHENDEN, *Nov.* 23, 1862.—. . . The Church is much agitated by a book disputing the authenticity of the Pentateuch, and written by a Bishop, one Dr. Colenso, a Colonial Bishop. 'Tis a great scandal, and is almost as bad as Kings becoming Republicans. An indignant clerical critic says it is a queer name, Colenso—he supposes Italian, probably a Jesuit. I believe, on the contrary, 'tis good Cornish, and that you Western people are answerable for the heresy, so we must leave the Doctor to your friend, the Bishop of Exeter.

The Palmerston Government, absorbed in foreign affairs, provided no serious programme of domestic legislation for the session of 1863, and ecclesiastical questions occupied much of the attention of Parliament. The defeat of Trelawny's Church Rate Bill by an appreciable majority, which was at length achieved, was largely due to the success which had attended Disraeli's persistent efforts to secure the support of Roman Catholics by generous treatment of their claims.[1] There was a conspicuous instance of this policy during the session. The Government brought in a Bill to provide prisoners, who did not belong to the Church of England, with the attendance of ministers of their own religious persuasion. It was avowedly a Bill mainly for the relief of Roman Catholic prisoners, and the majority of the Conservative party took strong exception to it. But Disraeli in the Commons and Derby in the Lords, with the concurrence

---

[1] Ten Roman Catholic members, who had hitherto supported the Bill, had on this occasion, Disraeli was told, deliberately abstained from voting.

of most of their late colleagues, supported the measure as one of justice, and secured its passage through Parliament. To a Roman Catholic friend Disraeli explained his views and difficulties:

To Lord Campden.[1]

Private. HUGHENDEN MANOR, *April* 10, 1863.—I shall certainly support the Prison Ministers Bill, which is conceived in the spirit of the policy of the late Government, and I shall do all I can to induce friends to act with me. I anticipate, however, in that respect, no little difficulty. What neutralises my efforts in these matters is the systematic hostility always shown by the Catholic members of the House of Commons to the Church of England. This is most unwise. We live in times when Churches should act together.

I do not expect Catholic members, generally, to vote, for instance, for Church rates, though were I a Catholic I would do so, but at least they might keep away from such divisions. There would be no difficulty about Prison Ministers Bills, and many other measures of that description, if men of the position of Mr. Monsell would only act in Church affairs as Montalembert recommended. I mention Mr. Monsell; both by position and talents he is a leading man, and might exercise even a more considerable influence. If the Churches drew more together, the following of the Newdegates and the Whalleys would sink into insignificance.

Peto's Bill comes on next Wednesday; most offensive to the English clergy. It would be wise in the Catholic members, and would greatly assist me in my conscientious efforts on their behalf, if they did not mix themselves up with these Pedo or Peto Baptists, or whatever they may be.

Peto's Bill was one to permit Dissenters to be buried by their own ministers and with their own rites in the graveyards of the Established Church. Much as there was to be said in favour of a proposal which in after-years became law, it was felt to be somewhat grasping to demand new and special rights in the graveyards simultaneously with relief from Church rates; and, although the Bill was unexpectedly supported by Gladstone, it was rejected by a large majority—221 to 96. Disraeli wrote to Mrs. Willyams, April 15: 'A great division in

---

[1] Afterwards second Earl of Gainsborough.

the House of Commons, and a great triumph. I write
to you while the cheers are still ringing in my ears.
Gladstone, to the astonishment of his friends, deserted
the Church, and I replied to him and closed the debate.'

With the active or passive assistance of the Roman
Catholic vote, not only were Trelawny's and Peto's Bills
defeated in this session, but a motion to relax the subscription by the clergy to the Thirty-nine Articles was
shelved by means of the previous question. Here once
more Disraeli championed, in common with Robert Cecil
and Walpole, the cause of orthodoxy. It was suggested, he said, that not only should the creed of the
Church be catholic, but that its communion should be
catholic. The professors of all creeds were to belong to
one Church, but were all to retain their own particular
opinions. But that experiment had been tried on the
Continent, particularly in Germany, with the result that
you had ' what without offence may be called an infidel
Church.'

' What do you mean by a Church ? I say, No creed,
no Church !1 How can you have a Church without a
creed, articles, formularies, and a subscription ?' He
agreed that neither Articles nor Prayer-Book were perfect.
' There may be blots in their composition. The Prayer-
Book may be divine, but it is also human.' But, if there
were to be any change, it should not originate in Parliament, which was no longer a lay synod, but should be
initiated by a Royal Commission, and brought under the
consideration of the revived Convocation, before its
ultimate submission to Parliament. It may be observed
in passing that this was the process adopted by the
Government in 1864 and 1865, when the subscription
was made more general, but without any alteration, such
as Disraeli deprecated, of the formularies of the Church.
Here Disraeli threw out a sensible hint that ' something
of a lay element ' should be introduced into Convocation.

---

1 ' Pray remember, Mr. Dean,' said Disraeli one day playfully to Dean
Stanley, ' no dogma, no Dean.'

' Nor do I doubt that there are lay members of the Church
at the present moment who, from their learning, their
knowledge of men, and their high character, might bring
to Convocation such ability and reputation as Selden
and Chillingworth might have brought in former days.'
Such a lay representation has now for many years been
obtained in the form of ' Houses of Laymen,' to the
considerable advantage of the Church.

They had been warned, Disraeli concluded, against
a sacerdotal despotism. But the sacerdotal despotism
which he feared was not the re-establishment of the
Inquisition or the High Commission Court, but ' that a
minister of the Church of England, who is appointed to
expound doctrine, should deem that he has a right to
invent doctrine.' The motion was one ' in favour of the
priesthood, and not of the laity.' It was the boast of
England that in politics it had reconciled order with
liberty. ' What in religious affairs is a greater triumph
than this ? It has combined orthodoxy with toleration.'
He preferred to stand on the ancient ground.

A memorandum in the Beaconsfield papers discusses
the ecclesiastical situation in 1863:

Bishop of Oxford sent this year to Switzerland; overworked. Certainly no man was ever so busy, preached more
sermons, wrote more letters, attended more platform meetings,
or infused, generally, such a spirit in his diocese.

I think his present illness, however, is from chagrin. He
never recovered the appointment of Dr. Thomson to York.[1]
It was a long time vacant, and he was my guest at Hughenden
during the interval. I never knew a man more agitated.
It was the height of his ambition. I think he would have
preferred it to Canterbury. He was a Yorkshireman; the
son of a great Yorkshireman, who had represented the undivided county of York; and had fairly won it. It was
known that no more Low Church Bishops were to be appointed.
That vein had been overworked. Some of the last appointments in that way had been mean and insignificant. The
death of the Prince had checked the hopes of the Broad
Church, which were once very high. The Prince had managed
to push one in, and had intended to have made the Queen

[1] In the autumn of 1862.

insist on Dr. Temple; but the subsequent publication of *Essays and Reviews*, to which he was the leading contributor, would probably have rendered this impossible. . . . [The Prince] had made Stanley and Kingsley already Chaplains.

As Lord Shaftesbury, the great champion of Low Church and maker of Low Church Bishops, was, it was understood, to lie by a little, and as Broad Church was from public feeling impossible, the Bishop of Oxford thought that Gladstone, who was his greatest friend and for whom he had left his natural political allies, would have insisted upon his appointment to York. If Gladstone had threatened to resign as he did about the paper duty, he must have gained his point. But Gladstone made no sign,[1] and a comparatively young Oxonian, at least fifteen years younger, I should think, than the Bishop of Oxford, and, if of any political opinions, a Tory, was appointed. An excellent appointment, in my opinion, but that does not alter the circumstances.

Of all Disraeli's appearances during these years as defender of the Faith, none was so dramatic as that of which the scene was laid in the Sheldonian Theatre at Oxford, on November 25, 1864. He was present on the direct invitation of Bishop Wilberforce, who wrote on September 29: ' Would you come to me with Mrs. Disraeli about November 24, and make us a great speech at Oxford for our society for endowing small livings ? I would promise you all the Senior University and the undergraduates and the pick of the county.' Disraeli was very willing, and told Earle on November 2: ' I am meditating a great ecclesiastical function at Oxford this month, which would have been *à propos* for the Dissolution, had it come off.'

The ideas about religion current in the residential and intellectual Oxford which Disraeli came to address were in the main no longer those associated with Newman and Pusey, but those of the rising Broad Church school, whose leaders were Stanley and Jowett, and those of the men of science, rightly clamouring for further recognition in the University, and permeated with the spirit of Darwin's *Origin of Species*, published five years before. Both schools

---

[1] Gladstone pressed the appointment upon Palmerston, but did not threaten to resign.

gravitated towards the Liberal party; both latitudi-
narianism, in the shape of the Higher Criticism, and
evolution, in its more extravagant claims, impugned the
tradition of the Semitic Scriptures.   Whether in a political
or in an intellectual and religious aspect, both were
therefore repugnant to Disraeli; and he gladly seized the
opportunity to expose their weaknesses and hold up
these new-fangled lights to scorn and derision.

He turned first to the Broad Church, a party founded,
not like the historical parties of High[1] and Low Church,
on authority, but on the ' singular principle ' of criticism.
Criticism being necessarily sceptical, such a party might
very well reject inspiration and miracles, and, as a logical
consequence, the creeds and articles of faith based on
inspiration and miracles.   But he could not understand
how, after having arrived at these conscientious conclusions, they should still be ' sworn supporters of ecclesiastical establishments, fervent upholders, or dignitaries, of
the Church.'

If it be true, as I am often told it is, that the age of faith
has passed, then the fact of having an opulent hierarchy,
supported by men of high cultivation, brilliant talents and
eloquence, and perhaps some ambition, with no distinctive
opinions, might be a very harmless state of affairs, and it
would certainly not be a very permanent one.   But . . .
when I observe what is passing around us—what is taking
place in this country, and not only in this country, but in
other countries, and even hemispheres—instead of believing
that the age of faith has passed, I hold that the characteristic
of the present age is a craving credulity.   Why, my Lord,
man is a being born to believe.   And if no Church comes
forward with its title-deeds of truth, sustained by the tradition
of sacred ages and by the conviction of countless generations,
to guide him, he will find altars and idols in his own heart
and his own imagination.   But observe this.   What must be
the relations of a powerful Church, without distinctive creeds,
with a being of such a nature ?   Why, of course, the chief
principle of political economy will be observed.   Where
there is a great demand there will be a proportionate supply;

---

[1] Throughout his Church speeches of this period Disraeli, much as he
disliked the extreme developments of Ritualism, made no attempt to distinguish between the different schools of High Churchmen.

and commencing, as the new school may, by rejecting the principle of inspiration, it will end by every priest becoming a prophet; and beginning as they do by repudiating the practice of miracles, before long, rest assured, we shall be living in a flitting scene of spiritual phantasmagoria. There are no tenets however extravagant, and no practices however objectionable, which will not in time develop under such a state of affairs; opinions the most absurd and ceremonies the most revolting—' Qualia demens Ægyptus ˙portenta colat '—perhaps to be followed by the incantations of Canidia and the Corybantian howl.

But consider the country in which all this may take place. Dangerous in all countries, it would be yet more dangerous in England. Our empire is now unrivalled for its extent; but the base—the material base—of that empire is by no means equal to the colossal superstructure. It is not our iron ships; it is not our celebrated regiments; it is not these things which have created, or indeed really maintain, our empire. It is the character of the people. Now, I want to know where that famous character of the English people will be if they are to be influenced and guided by a Church of immense talent, opulence, and power, without any distinctive creed. You have in this country accumulated wealth that never has been equalled, and probably it will still increase. You have a luxury that will some day peradventure rival even your wealth. And the union of such circumstances with a Church without a distinctive creed will lead, I believe, to a dissoluteness of manners and of morals rarely equalled in the history of man, but which prepares the tomb of empires. . . .

Will these opinions succeed ? Is there a possibility of their success ? My conviction is that they will fail . . . for two reasons. In the first place, having examined all their writings, I believe without any exception, whether they consist of fascinating eloquence, diversified learning, and picturesque sensibility—I speak seriously what I feel—and that too exercised by one honoured in this University, and whom to know is to admire and regard;[1] or whether you find them in the cruder conclusions of prelates[2] who appear to have commenced their theological studies after they had grasped the crosier, and who introduce to society their obsolete discoveries with the startling wonder and frank ingenuousness of their own savages; or whether I read the lucubrations of nebulous professors,[3] who seem in their style to have revived chaos, and who if they could only succeed

---

[1] Dean Stanley.   [2] Bishop Colenso.
[3] Frederick Denison Maurice.

in obtaining a perpetual study of their writings would go
far to realise that eternal punishment to which they object;[1]
or, lastly, whether it be the provincial arrogance and the
precipitate self-complacency which flash and flare in an essay
or review,[2] I find that the common characteristic of their
writings is this, that their learning is always second-hand.

The learning was not only second-hand, and therefore
not treated with the caution and circumspection natural to
those who have prosecuted original research; there was
also nothing in it really new. The German scholars
from whom it was derived had been anticipated, Disraeli
maintained, by the great Hebrew scholars, such as
Astruc and Father Simon, who flourished in the eighteenth
and the end of the seventeenth century, and whose labours
'formed the mind and inspired the efforts of the two
most intellectual bodies of men that have existed certainly since the Greek philosophers . . . the free-thinkers
of England and the philosophers of France.'

All that inexorable logic, irresistible rhetoric, bewildering
wit, could avail to popularise those views were set in motion
to impress the new learning on the minds of the two leading
nations of Europe—the people of England and the people of
France. And they produced their effect. . . . Their promulgation largely contributed to that mighty movement
popularly called the French Revolution, which has not yet
ended, and which is certainly the greatest event that has
happened in the history of man. Only the fall of the Roman
Empire can be compared to it. . . . Look at the Europe of
the present day and the Europe of a century ago. It is not
the same Europe. Its very form is changed. Whole nations
and great nations, which then flourished, have disappeared.
There is not a political constitution in Europe existing at the
present time which then existed. The leading community
of the continent of Europe has changed all its landmarks,
altered its boundaries, erased its local names. The whole
jurisprudence of Europe has been subverted. Even the
tenure of land, which of all human institutions most affects
the character of man, has been altered. The feudal system
has been abolished. Not merely laws have been changed—

---

[1] In deference to the representations of Bishop Wilberforce and others,
Disraeli omitted this clause about eternal punishment when he authorised
the republication of the speech.

[2] Jowett and Temple were the most eminent of the authors of *Essays
and Reviews*.

not merely manners have been changed—but customs have been changed. And what happened ? When the turbulence was over—when the shout of triumph and the wail of agony were alike stilled—when, as it were, the waters had subsided, the sacred heights of Sinai and of Calvary were again revealed, and amid the wreck of thrones and tribunals, of extinct nations and abolished laws, mankind, tried by so many sorrows, purified by so much suffering, and wise with such unprecedented experience, bowed again before the Divine truths that Omnipotence in His ineffable wisdom had entrusted to the custody and the promulgation of a chosen people !

In the latter part of his speech Disraeli turned from the Broad Church to the evolutionists, and attracted the attention of the whole world by a pungent phrase.

The discoveries of science are not, we are told, consistent with the teachings of the Church. . . . It is of great importance, when this tattle about science is mentioned, that we should annex to the phrase precise ideas. I hold that the function of science is the interpretation of nature, and the interpretation of the highest nature is the highest science. What is the highest nature ? Man is the highest nature. But I must say that when I compare the interpretation of the highest nature by the most advanced, the most fashionable and modish, school of modern science with some other teachings with which we are familiar, I am not prepared to say that the lecture-room is more scientific than the Church.

What is the question now placed before society with a glib assurance the most astounding ? The question is this—Is man an ape or an angel ? My Lord, I am on the side of the angels.

I repudiate with indignation and abhorrence the contrary view, which is, I believe, foreign to the conscience of humanity: more than that, even in the strictest intellectual point of view, I believe the severest metaphysical analysis is opposed to such a conclusion. But, on the other hand, what does the Church teach us ? What is its interpretation of this highest nature ? It teaches us that man is made in the image of his Creator—a source of inspiration and of solace—a source from which only can flow every right principle of morals and every Divine truth. . . . It is between these two contending interpretations of the nature of man, and their consequences, that society will have to decide. Their rivalry is at the bottom of all human affairs. Upon our acceptance of that Divine interpretation for which we are indebted to the Church, and of which the Church is the guardian, all sound and salutary legislation depends. That truth is the only security for civilisation, and the only guarantee of real progress.

Froude has drawn for us the picture of the orator who claimed to be on the side of the angels, addressing the University dons and country clergy ' in a black velvet shooting coat and wideawake hat, as if he had been accidentally passing through the town.' How absurd it seemed of this fantastic creature, with his apish tricks, to advance such exalted pretensions on behalf of himself and the human race !   The University wits polished their epigrams. A Fellow of Oriel amused the common-rooms with a set of sapphics, beginning:

> Angelo quis te similem putaret
> Esse, vel divis atavis creatum,
> Cum tuas plane referat dolosus
> Simius artes?

Both in the University and outside, people asked, What did Disraeli mean ?   Could he be serious ?   Was it all mere fireworks intended to dazzle and hoodwink the clergy ?

Those who have read and studied *Tancred* and *Lord George Bentinck*, and the speeches and letters on religious and philosophic topics which have been quoted in this biography, know that Disraeli was perfectly serious, and was only concentrating in an unforgettable phrase his most vital convictions. He held that, whatever man may be biologically and physiologically, he is something more; and that this something more, which transcends biological and physiological science, is the most distinctive and essential thing about him.   And even the scientific world is now coming round to this opinion. In order, apparently, to make people understand how entirely in earnest he was in his argument in the Sheldonian Theatre, Disraeli reproduced it in a careful and deliberate form in the General Preface to the Novels, published in 1870. He expressed himself then with less confidence as to the future than he had in 1864; but the course of events has largely justified his hope that ' the Teutonic rebellion against the Divine truths entrusted to the Semites ' would ultimately meet with the fate of ' the Celtic insurrection ' of Voltaire and the Encyclopædists;

while the incapacity of science to take the place of religion is now much more widely recognised than it was in the days when Huxley and Tyndall flourished. The passage in which Disraeli ridiculed the claims of modern scientific men to a monopoly of scientific discovery is very typical of his outlook on the world.

There is no fallacy so flagrant as to suppose that the modern ages have the peculiar privilege of scientific discovery, or that they are distinguished as the epochs of the most illustrious inventions. On the contrary . . . the greatest discoveries are not those of modern ages. No one for a moment can pretend that printing is so great a discovery as writing, or algebra as language. What are the most brilliant of our chemical discoveries compared with the invention of fire and the metals ? It is a vulgar belief that our astronomical knowledge dates only from the recent century, when it was rescued from the monks who imprisoned Galileo; but Hipparchus, who lived before our Divine Master, and who among other sublime achievements discovered the precession of the equinoxes, ranks with the Newtons and the Keplers; and Copernicus, the modern father of our celestial science, avows himself, in his famous work, as only the champion of Pythagoras, whose system he enforces and illustrates. Even the most modish schemes of the day on the origin of things, which captivate as much by their novelty as their truth, may find their precursors in ancient sages, and after a careful analysis of the blended elements of imagination and induction which characterise the new theories, they will be found mainly to rest on the atom of Epicurus and the monad of Thales. . . . We may analyse the sun and penetrate the stars, but man is conscious that he is made in God's own image, and in his perplexity he will ever appeal to our Father which art in Heaven.

The speech in the Sheldonian was Disraeli's last great effort on behalf of the Church before the General Election of 1865. He had this and his other main ecclesiastical speeches of these years collected and republished with a view to influence public opinion; and in his address to his constituents he based the claim of the Conservatives to the confidence of the country, first and foremost, on their defence of the Church. If the response was not quite what he hoped, it was the popularity of Palmerston rather than hostility to the Church that was responsible.

It may be interesting to collect here certain scattered memoranda dealing with religion, written by Disraeli during the sixties:

Sir George [Cornewall] Lewis said to me at Bellamy's, 'If there be anything established, it is that the Semitic nations invented the alphabet, and, after all, that may perhaps be considered the greatest achievement of the human race.' . . . 'Of one Semitic nation, the Jews,' I observed, 'it can be said that they invented alike the Ten Commandments and the Lord's Prayer.'

Sir George Lewis thought the merits of the Lord's Prayer exaggerated.   There were expressions in it which could not be understood by the million, as, for instance, 'Thy kingdom come' and 'Thine is the kingdom,' which, in fact, referred to the impending 'Kingdom of Heaven,' which was the foundation of the School of Galilee and of real Christianity. I observed that these expressions, though doubtless originally limited in the sense he mentioned, were now of general application, and had always been capable of it.   I thought the Lord's Prayer a masterpiece.   It was the most perfect exponent of the purest religious feeling, that had yet appeared.   And while it soothed the cottage, it was difficult to conceive a society so refined that it would not satisfy.

Assuming that the popular idea of inspiration be abandoned, and the difference between sacred and profane history relinquished, what would be the position of the Hebrew race in universal history, viewed with reference to their influence on man?   I thought of advertising, through a medium that would command confidence, £500 or even £1,000 for the best essay on this question—perhaps more precisely expressed.   The judges, perhaps, to be Gladstone, Canon Stanley,[1] and myself. Not bound, however, to award the prize unless satisfied with the performance.

Elmley[2] was always saying, 'What did Jesus do before he was thirty?   My conviction is that he must have had an eventful youth, and that he had travelled a great deal.' This travelling of Jesus was a great point with Elmley.   He frequently recurred to it.   I never could agree with him.   It seemed such an original mind: so completely formed in seclusion, and, with all its Shakespearian genius, so essentially local.   All the illustrations are drawn from inward resources or from surrounding scenery.

[1] Dean Stanley, then Canon of Christ Church, Oxford.
[2] M.P. for Worcestershire W., 1853-1863, then succeeded as fifth Earl Beauchamp; died young in 1866; elder brother of F. Lygon, afterwards sixth Earl.   Both brothers were close friends of Disraeli.

After Derby's fiasco in the beginning of 1855, Disraeli had, through his organ the *Press*, endeavoured to cheer his dispirited party by telling them that they might control, if they did not direct, the course of public affairs.[1] A review of this and the two preceding chapters shows that never was that control so brilliantly and so successfully exercised as during the six years of Palmerston's last Administration.   Whether we look at Reform, at public economy, at ecclesiastical disputes, or at the great issues of peace and war, the decisive influence, which finally determined the course for policy to pursue, was not that of the Ministry, but of the Opposition, and of Disraeli as its leader in the House of Commons.   It was mainly owing to Disraeli's tactics that Russell and Bright were brought to a standstill over Reform; that Palmerston was checked over extravagant expenditure; that the Dissenters and Secularists were stopped in their attacks on the Church; and that Palmerston and Russell were prevented from carrying to the point of military operations their well-meant but ill-managed policy of intervention in the internal affairs of Europe and America.   It is, of course, true that in all these matters the Opposition and their leader had, now one, now another, of the strongest men in the Administration secretly favourable to their cause; but that fact detracts very little from the insight and adroitness which seized and utilised the various occasions. The only sphere in which the Opposition met with partial failure was that over which Gladstone's fiery energy presided.   In the early years of the Administration Gladstone was able, in spite of their protests, to reduce to what they considered a dangerous extent the existing sources of revenue, and to curtail the power and humiliate the pride of the House of Lords.   But, on the other hand, in the last half of the period his Budgets largely followed the lines which Disraeli had recommended from the first —a steady reduction of income tax and of the war duties on tea and sugar.   It enhances Disraeli's reputation to

[1] See Vol. I., p. 1386.

reflect that this successful control of policy was achieved with a party behind him containing an element of active disloyalty, with colleagues seldom in hearty agreement, and in the face of criticism, as often as helpful suggestion, from Derby; and that it was maintained in spite of the fact that, in every pitched battle, faint-heartedness and desertion in his own camp secured for the Government at least a nominal victory.

Throughout the period he was building up his party so as to fit them for office, and keeping constantly before them a national rather than a sectarian or territorial ideal. Take the fine peroration of a speech which he delivered in Parliament at the close of the session of 1862:

Ever since that period of disaster and dismay, when my friends and myself were asked for the first time to sit upon these benches,[1] it has ever been our habit, in counselling the Tory party, to recur gradually but most sincerely to the original elements of that great political connection. To build up a community, not upon Liberal opinions, which anyone may fashion to his fancy, but upon popular principles,[2] which assert equal rights, civil and religious; to uphold the institutions of the country because they are the embodiments of the wants and wishes of the nation, and protect us alike from individual tyranny and popular outrage; equally to resist democracy and oligarchy, and favour that principle of free aristocracy which is the only basis and security for constitutional government; to be vigilant to guard and prompt to vindicate the honour of the country, but to hold aloof from that turbulent diplomacy which only distracts the mind of a people from internal improvement; to lighten taxation; frugally but wisely to administer the public treasure; to favour popular education, because it is the best guarantee for public order; to defend local government, and to be as jealous of the rights of the working man as of the prerogative of the Crown and the privileges of the senate—these were once the principles which regulated Tory statesmen, and I for one have no wish that the Tory party should ever be in power unless they practise them.[3]

Similarly, at a party dinner in 1863, Disraeli summed up the Liberal opinions, to which Conservatives were

[1] 1847.   [2] See Vol. I , p. 838.   [3] Aug. 1, 1862.

opposed, as follows: That the electoral franchise ought
to be democratic, and property deprived of its legitimate
influence; that the union between Church and State
ought to be abolished; that the relations between the
mother-country and the colonies—that national estate
which assured a freehold to Englishmen and an inexhaustible theatre for their energies—should be abrogated;
that the rights of corporations and the privileges of
endowments should be terminated.

The Tory party is only in its proper position when it represents popular principles. Then it is truly irresistible. Then it
can uphold the throne and the altar, the majesty of the empire,
the liberty of the nation, and the rights of the multitude.
There is nothing mean, petty, or exclusive, about the real
character of Toryism. It necessarily depends upon enlarged
sympathies and noble aspirations, because it is essentially
national.

He congratulated the party on their present position
compared with that at the time of Bentinck's death,
when ' we were like a wreck stranded on the beach, and
it was a question who should rifle our stores.'

Contrast that position with our position now! In either
House of Parliament you confront the Ministry with at least
an equal power. You are the advocates of a generous and
a national creed; and as for public men, why, there is not a
subject that can be brought forward in the House of Commons
but I am sure, from every part of the benches on the side on
which I sit, men will come forward who, by the amplitude of
their knowledge, their argumentative power, and their general
ability, will so demean themselves as to command, as they
deserve, the attention of the assembly which they adorn.[1]

Disraeli had a right to be proud of the work which he
had accomplished in resuscitating and nationalising his
party and in imposing their control on the Government.
But office was apparently out of their grasp so long as
Palmerston lived; and on what had been, and must
ultimately be again, the main domestic issue, Parliamentary Reform, there was no fundamental agreement
within the party save to postpone legislation.

[1] June 26, 1863.

CHAPTER XI.

DISRAELI AND THE COURT.

1861–1863.

Queen Victoria, during her long reign, had occasion not infrequently to revise her original opinion of eminent men who rose to be her chief Ministers. In almost every instance, be it said to the credit both of the Sovereign and of the Minister, the change was from distrust to confidence. The only exception was in the case of Gladstone, of whom the Queen and the Prince had thought highly in his middle career, but whose later policies, and perhaps still more the 'pilgrimages of passion '[1] in which he advocated them, caused Her Majesty much disquiet. On the other hand, Peel, as Minister, not only entirely conquered the prejudice raised by the Bedchamber dispute, but even succeeded in inspiring peculiar confidence; and, in a lesser degree, Palmerston, whose conduct as Foreign Secretary had given so much offence, earned Her Majesty's respect during his last Administration. But, of course, the most conspicuous change of all was that which took place in regard to Disraeli. In the forties the Court identified itself completely with Peel and his Free Trade policy; and Peel's assailant and destroyer was regarded by the Queen and Prince with especial aversion. This was lessened, but by no means removed, by the experience of the first Derby-Disraeli Ministry, and of the collaboration then initiated with the Prince in the promotion of science and art. The second Derby-Disraeli Ministry resulted in much more

[1] A phrase used by Disraeli of Gladstone's provincial progresses as early as 1866, more than a dozen years before the first Midlothian campaign.

friendly relations; and in the couple of years between the fall of that Ministry and the death of the Prince, Disraeli, though in opposition, received frequent invitations to the Palace. In January, 1861, he announced with much satisfaction to Mrs. Willyams a forthcoming visit to Windsor in which his wife was included. ' It is Mrs. Disraeli's first visit to Windsor, and it is considered very marked on the part of Her Majesty to ask the wife of the leader of the Opposition, when many Cabinet Ministers have been asked there *without* their wives.' This attention caused comment, and Derby asked Disraeli what had passed. ' They were very gracious and very communicative,' was the reply. In fact, a better knowledge of Disraeli's character had overcome the distrust of the Court before the Prince's death; but it was the sympathetic and appreciative manner in which Disraeli treated that tragic event that converted the Queen's somewhat negative feeling towards him into friendly interest, which was ultimately to develop, during his great Ministry, into unbounded and even affectionate confidence.

It was on December 14, 1861, that this heavy blow fell upon the Queen. Already, in the spring of this year, Her Majesty had lost her mother, the Duchess of Kent. In seconding the address of condolence on the Duchess's death, Disraeli had happily emphasised the commanding part which the domestic affections played in the Queen's life. It was generally supposed, he said, that the anguish of affection was scarcely compatible with the pomp of power; but ' she who reigns over us has elected, amid all the splendour of empire, to establish her life on the principle of domestic love.'

To Frances Anne Lady Londonderry.

Confidential. TORQUAY, *Dec.* 19, 1861.—There is a north post from this place, which tempts me to write to you a hurried line, as my news, received this morning from the fountain-head, may not be stale.

It seems that the departed Prince had lectured the Queen severely about giving way so completely on the death of her mother, and told her to remember that the blow was dealt by the hand of the All-Wise. She remembers this now, and keeps saying, ' Now you see I am calm; I am profiting by his advice, I am doing what he wished.' The Duchess of Sutherland and Lady Augusta Bruce with her.

On the 17th she saw Lord Granville, who brought Palmerston's [box], and she signed several papers of pressing importance.

The Prince of Wales seems anxious to take his place, and, I hear, behaves with great tact and feeling. The funeral strictly private, which I knew before I left town, or should have remained. They wish to move the Queen to Osborne, but she puts it off every day, dreading the sight of the glaring daylight, it being impossible for the yacht to bring up under Osborne after dark. As matters now stand she will go to-day, the Prince of Wales escorting her and returning. . . .

The Prince of Wales wishes not to have the Gren. Guards, and says that they ought to be given to some old General officer

He wrote yesterday to Palmerston by desire of his mother, to say that Lord P. would always find her mindful of her duty and of her people, but that her worldly career was at an end. . . .

From the very outset of his personal knowledge of the Prince Consort, at a time when it was the fashion to belittle him, Disraeli conceived a great admiration both for his abilities and for his character. He told his sister in 1852 that the Prince was the best-educated man he ever met, but not over-educated; and he told Lord Ponsonby in 1854 that his sentiment towards the Prince was 'one of devotion.'[1] Further intercourse only strengthened this feeling. ' With Prince Albert,' he said to Vitzthum just after the death, ' we have buried our Sovereign. This German Prince has governed England for twenty-one years with a wisdom and energy such as none of our Kings have ever shown. . . . If he had outlived some of our " old stagers," he would have given us, while retaining all constitutional guarantees, the blessings of absolute government. Of us younger men who are qualified to enter the Cabinet, there is not one who would not willingly have bowed to his experience. We are now in the midst of a change of government.'[2]

[1] See Vol. I., pp. 1187, 1347.   [2] Vitzthum, Vol. II., p. 176.

Disraeli's public tributes to the Prince's memory were particularly felicitous. On the Address in 1862, when the leaders of parties gave formal expression to the general sorrow, Disraeli described him as the ' prime councillor of a realm the political constitution of which did not even recognise his political existence.' He directed special attention to the Prince's services to culture in England. A want of culture had been a great deficiency in the national character. ' He was not satisfied with detecting a want; he resolved to supply it. His plans were deeply laid; they were maturely prepared; and, notwithstanding the obstacles which he inevitably encountered, I am prepared to say they were eminently successful.' Further,

Prince Albert was not a mere patron; he was not one of those who by their gold or by their smiles reward excellence or stimulate exertion. His contributions to the cause of the State were far more powerful and far more precious. He gave to it his thought, his time, his toil; he gave to it his life. On both sides and in all parts of the House I see many gentlemen who occasionally have acted with the Prince at those council boards, where they conferred and consulted upon the great undertakings with which he was connected. I ask them, without fear of a denial, whether he was not the leading spirit, whether his was not the mind which foresaw the difficulty, his not the resources which supplied the remedy; whether his was not the courage which sustained them under apparently overpowering difficulties; whether everyone who worked with him did not feel that he was the real originator of those plans of improvement which they assisted in carrying into effect.

The Queen expressed her thanks.

From Lord Derby.

St. James's Square, *Saturday night* [*Feb.* 8, 1862].—I have had this afternoon a letter from Charles Phipps, with a complimentary notice from the Queen of my speech of Thursday, ending with the following: ' The Queen would be glad that Mr. Disraeli should also be made aware of H.M.'s grateful sense of his testimony to the worth and character of the Prince— perhaps as discriminating in the characteristics pointed out, and certainly as eloquent in the language employed, as any of those beautiful and glorious orations.' . . .

To Sir Charles Phipps.

GROSVENOR GATE, *Feb.* 9, 1862.—Lord Derby has communicated to me the gracious expressions of Her Majesty, and I should feel obliged to you, if the opportunity offer, to lay before Her Majesty my humble and dutiful acknowledgments.

What I attempted to express on Thursday night I deeply felt. During those conversations with which, of late years, the Prince occasionally honored me, I acquired much, both in knowledge and in feeling, which will ever influence my life.

In further acknowledgment the Queen sent Disraeli what he termed in reply ' a hallowed gift '—two engravings of well-known pictures of herself and the Prince.

In 1863, the year of the Prince of Wales's marriage, Disraeli was specially distinguished by Her Majesty, as he has explained in a long and interesting memorandum written at the time:

I heard at the end of the last, and at the beginning of this, year, more than once, from great personages about the Court, that the Queen had said, and repeated, that ' Mr. Disraeli was the only person who appreciated the Prince.'

When Parliament met, too, Her Majesty had occasion to write personally to Lord Derby respecting the Memorial Monument to the Prince, and some necessary steps that might be taken in Parliament thereon; and she mentioned in the letter that she had no objection to his conferring with Mr. Disraeli, ' towards whom she should always entertain feelings of gratitude for the support which he had always given to the Prince ' in all his undertakings for the refinement of public taste and the improvement of society, or some words to that effect.

Lord Derby was generous enough to read this passage of H.M.'s letter to me.

In March the Royal Wedding took place. The Prince of Wales was married to the Princess of Denmark at Windsor. This alliance made a great sensation and excitement in the country. The long-pent-up feeling of affectionate devotion to the Queen, and of sympathy with her sorrows, came out with that deep and fervid enthusiasm for which the people of England are, I think, remarkable. But the excitement of the nation with their public receptions, and addresses, and processions, and splendid gifts, and the long vista of universal festivity, which was planned, and which lasted the whole season, was quite equalled among the aristocracy, as to who should, or rather would, be invited to the Royal Wedding.

As the beautiful Chapel of St. George was very limited, and as there were a considerable number of royal guests, and as the principal persons of the Household, the Ambassadors, the Knights of the Garter, and the Cabinet Ministers, were as a matter of course to be invited, it became an interesting question where the line was to be drawn. At last it was whispered about that the limit was to be Duchesses. But as time drew on nobody seemed to be asked, and some great persons received suspicious invitations to a breakfast at Windsor Castle *after* the ceremony. At the same time tickets began to circulate in influential quarters, permitting the bearers to places in the cathedral nave, without the chapel, in order to see the processions pass. At last, however, about a fortnight before the ceremony or less, it was announced that, as there were only —— seats in the chapel, and as Sovereigns and Royal Princes, Knights of the Garter and their wives, Cabinet Ministers and Ambassadors and Great Officers of the Household, and their wives, would nearly fill it, there were necessarily few seats for H.M.'s private friends.

The disappointment and excitement equally increased. I have heard that, when the list was finally submitted to her Majesty, there were only four places not, as it were, officially appropriated. Her Majesty named Lord and Lady De la Warr, her earliest friends, and myself and my wife.

There is no language which can describe the rage, envy, and indignation, of the great world. The Duchess of Marlboro' went into hysterics of mortification at the sight of my wife, who was on terms of considerable intimacy with her, and said it was really shameful, after the reception which the Duke had given the Prince of Wales at Blenheim; and as for the Duchess of Manchester, who had been Mistress of the Robes in Lord Derby's Administration, she positively passed me for the season without recognition.

However, we went, and nothing could be more brilliant and effective than the whole affair [1] was. It is the only pageant which never disappointed me. The beautiful chapel, the glittering dresses, the various processions, first the Knights of the Garter, of the Royal Personages, of the Bridegroom, of the Bride: the heralds, the announcing trumpets, the suspense before the procession appeared, the magnificent music, the Queen in widowed garments in her Gothic cabinet, all deeply interesting or effective.

I had never seen the Queen since the catastrophe, and ventured, being near-sighted, to use my glass. I saw H.M.

[1] March 10.

well, and unfortunately caught her glance: perhaps she was
looking to see whether we were there, and triumphing a
little in the decided manner in which she had testified ' her
gratitude.' I did not venture to use my glass again.

The Prince of Wales, who was habited as a Knight of the
Garter, deported himself with great dignity, and conducted
himself at the altar, where he was left an unusual time alone,
from some accident that occurred in the procession of the
bride, with grace and tact: all eyes being upon him.

The way in which the royal personages looked up and
bowed to the royal cabinet was singularly graceful and
imposing: and in this respect the Princess Mary of Cambridge
exceeded them all. Her demeanour was most dignified.

After the ceremony, the festival was very joyous, a great
number of guests who had been invited to the breakfast at
the Castle then appearing. I should say 500 or 600 persons.
The royal personages breakfasted apart: but the mistake
was made of not inviting the Ambassadors and their wives
to this exclusive repast, who took rank above all the royal
guests who were inferior to their Sovereigns whom they
personally represented. Comte Apponyi was wroth on this
head, and certainly the Hungarian dress of Madame Apponyi,
which had only arrived the night before, justified any distinction. It was the most gorgeous and graceful costume ever
worn: bright blue velvet, richly embroidered in gold, and
astounding sables, but the fancy of the dress exceeded its
costly materials.

They had lodgings at Windsor, and the Ambassadress
changed her costume before she left Windsor. This was
fortunate, for the arrangements for departure were bad; the
ladies were mobbed at the station, and, as many of them had
tiaras of diamonds, they were in danger of being plundered.
Madame Apponyi was separated from the Ambassador; I
rescued her, and got her into a railway carriage with my wife
and some other grand dames, who had lost their husbands.
I think I had to sit on my wife's lap. When we got to
Paddington in the rain, there was no ambassadorial carriage:
but ours was there, and so we took home safe this brilliant
and delightful person.

A great lady of the Court, who was my secret friend, and
proved herself on many occasions a real one, told me at the
breakfast that the Queen meant to see me. She repeated
that the Queen said she was determined to see me. From
which, and other things, I inferred that there had been difficulties put in the way. Lord Derby had had an audience
of H.M. before the wedding, on the alleged ground of conferring about the Memorial, but understood as a token of

H.M.'s return to public life, and that she would commence
to see her Ministers socially, and exalted persons who had
been near her person. Lord Derby never mentioned any of
the details of this audience to me, but his son did. The
Queen-received him in her closet sitting; the audience was
by no means brief, and Lord Derby stood the whole time,
although recovering from a severe fit of the gout. The Queen
even alluded to this, and said she feared he would suffer by
standing, but offered no seat. So severe was the etiquette.

Notwithstanding my private intimation, time rolled on,
and I never heard anything of my audience. Weeks, even
months, passed.[1] The Queen had received all her principal
Ministers, Lord Clarendon and Lord Derby, and there it
stopped. I saw my friend occasionally in society, and once
she asked me whether I had heard anything; and when I
replied in the negative, she said, ' Be sure you will, for H.M.
said only the other day she was determined to see Mr. D.'

On —— I received an invitation to Windsor Castle for
April 22, and to stay till the next day.

When I arrived at the Castle, I received a note from Biddulph telling me that the Queen would receive me before
dinner, at a ¼ past seven o'clock. He gave me the hint, that
I might make my toilet early, and so be able to leave the
presence chamber for the banquet, which was about an hour
after. After I was dressed, there came another note to
say that Lord John Russell had arrived from town with important despatches, and that the Queen would be engaged,
and would postpone my audience till the morrow after breakfast.

It was the beginning of the Polish Insurrection, and the
Ministry were much perplexed. The despatches were about
Poland. I was struck at dinner by the contrast with the
somewhat subdued tone that prevailed in former days at
the royal dinners. The Prince and Princess of Wales were
our host and hostess. The party large, though consisting
only of courtiers (there were more than two households
blended), the only guests being Earl Russell and myself.
The Prince of Wales gave me the idea of a young man who
had just come into a large estate and was delighted at entertaining his friends. He took out his sister, the Princess
Helena, and sate opposite the Princess of Wales, who was
taken out by Prince Alfred. On the other side of Prince
Alfred was the Countess of Desart (in waiting), and I sate
between her and Lady Augusta Bruce, sister of Lord Elgin,
whom I had met before at Windsor, when she was in attendance on the Duchess of Kent. I was glad to renew my

---

[1] The delay was just six weeks.

acquaintance with her, for, like all her family, she is clever, and told me in the course of the dinner a great deal.

When the ladies had retired, I was next to Prince Alfred, who invited me to take Lady Desart's vacated seat. I had not seen him since he was a very young and very little midshipman. Though still in his teens, he was much altered, had grown a great deal, a bronzed and manly countenance, with a thoughtful brow; altogether like his father. His brother, the Prince of Wales, was a Guelph, not a Coburg. The Queen said he was exactly like a portrait which they had there of Frederick, Prince of Wales. I thought him very like a portrait also at Windsor of his [great-]grandfather, George the Third, shortly after his accession. Lord Malmesbury said that his general resemblance to his [great-]grandfather was so great that he already was always asking questions and talking loud.

Prince Alfred had just recovered from a severe and dangerous fever, which had prevented (*sic*) being at the wedding. He was detained by it at Malta, and the telegrams, which were constant, were so alarming that one day they feared the wedding could not take place. Alluding to his illness and Malta, we naturally talked of his travels: he had seen a great deal, having been at the Cape, etc.: on all of which he spoke with simplicity and sense. He was glad to be home again. I remember he said, 'What a fine Castle this is! I never saw any one in any country to be compared with it. I love this Castle; I was born in it.'

When we returned to the saloon, the circle was formed as if the Queen were present, but the Prince and Princess did not make the round. She kept apart, and then the Prince came and addressed Lord Russell in the circle, and then led him to the Princess, with whom he conversed for about ten minutes. Then, after a very short space, the Prince came to me, and conversed a little. He asked me whether I thought the Bill for abolishing the City Police would pass? I replied that I had not given any personal attention to the subject, but my impression was not favorable to its success. He said he had heard the same, but it ought to pass; there ought to be only one police for the capital. I perceived from this what I afterwards had proof of, that the passing of the Bill was a capital point with the Court. The opposition to the Bill turned out to be so general throughout the country, that it was eventually withdrawn by the Ministry without a division; not before, however, several courtiers, who had seats in the House of Commons, making (*sic*) speeches against it, which made the discomfiture more flagrant, as well as the particular animus more obvious.

After this, the Prince proposed that he should present me to H.R.H. and I went up accordingly. I had therefore, at last, a good opportunity of forming an opinion of her appearance, which was highly favorable. Her face was delicate and refined; her features regular; her brow well moulded; her mouth beautiful; her hair good and her ears small. She was very thin. She had the accomplishment of being gracious without smiling. She had repose. She spoke English, but not with the fluency I had expected, and I don't think she always comprehended what was said. The Prince hovered about her, and after a few minutes joined the conversation.

I remember nothing very particular about it except that it fell upon nightingales, and I asked H.R.H. whether she knew what nightingales fed upon. While she was confessing her ignorance and her curiosity, the Prince came, and she addressed the question to him, which he could not answer. I told them —upon glow-worms; exactly the food which nightingales should require. The Prince was interested by this, and exclaimed: ' Is that a fact, or is it a myth ?'

' Quite a fact, sir; for my woodman is my authority, for we have a great many nightingales at Hughenden, and a great many glow-worms.'

' We have got one nightingale at Sandringham,' said the Prince, smiling.

I remember now that the conversation got to nightingales in this manner. The Princess told me they were delighted with their London residence; they awoke in the morning, and looked into a garden, and heard the birds sing. I said then, ' I fear, not nightingales, madam.'

After this there was the private band, just the same as if H.M. were present; and at 11 o'clock the Prince and Princess and attendants retired.

On the morrow I breakfasted with the Lady-in-Waiting and the Maids of Honor, and Lord John Russell. We had a merry breakfast, for the ladies wished to make Lord John and myself talk: and I, who was really somewhat nervous from my approaching interview, was glad to take refuge in raillery. Lord John was genial, which, on the whole, he generally has been with me. For, notwithstanding our fierce public struggles for long years, and the crusade I have always preached against High Whiggism, of which he was the incarnate creation, there were really some elements of sympathy between us, being (sic), with all his hauteur and frigid manner, really a man of sentiment, and imagination, and culture.

When breakfast was over we were left together, and I asked him seriously what was the real state of affairs in Poland. He spoke with great frankness on the matter, and among other things that the Cabinet had sent a secret agent to Poland in order to obtain some accurate information (I think Oliphant); ' but I can't say,' he added, ' we are much the wiser. The best opinions seem to hold that it will be put down in the summer: but '—and he shrugged his shoulders —' it may not be: and then——' He went to town, and I was left alone with the newspapers. In about a quarter of an hour I was summoned. The attendant led me down part of the great gallery, and then turned off into a familiar corridor; and then, through an antechamber, I was ushered into Prince Albert's special room: a small cabinet, decorated with all the objects of art he loved, and in which I had frequently had the privilege of conferring, and listening at length to his views on public life and politics; when, throwing off his reserve and shyness, he warmed into eloquence, not unmixed with sarcastic humor, but, on all subjects on which he spoke, distinguished by his perfect knowledge and his thought. The room was quite unchanged. It was in every respect as if he had resided in it yesterday: the writing materials, the books, all the indications of habitual occupation. Only one change I observed: a plate on his accustomed chair, with an inscription: ' This was the Prince Consort's chair from 18— to 1861.'

In less than five minutes from my entry, an opposite door opened, and the Queen appeared.

She was still in widow's mourning, and seemed stouter than when I last saw her, but this was perhaps only from her dress. I bowed deeply when she entered, and raised my head with unusual slowness, that I might have a moment for recovery. Her countenance was grave, but serene and kind, and she said, in a most musical voice: ' It is some time since we met.'

Then to some murmuring words of mine H.M. said: ' You have not had a very busy session this year ?' In assenting to this, I expressed my wish that politics were in general as serene as the House of Commons. Upon this H.M. entered into the state of public affairs with frankness and some animation, which entirely removed the first embarrassment of the audience. It was then like an audience between a Sovereign and a Minister.

H.M. expressed her conviction that, whatever happened, the American Union could not be restored. She spoke fully about Poland, nor was it difficult to recognise that the insurrection alarmed her from its possible consequences on the state of Germany. H.M., however, it was quite clear, was sanguine that the Russians would suppress it by the summer.

She asked me frankly whether I thought the present Ministry

would get through the session. I said they were weak, but
there was no desire to displace them unless a stronger one
could be established. She said she hoped no crisis would be
brought about wantonly, for, in her forlorn condition, she
hardly knew what she could do. I said H.M.'s comfort was
an element in all our considerations, and that no action
would be taken, I felt sure, unless from commanding necessity.

She said ' Lord Palmerston was grown very old.' I replied,
' But his voice in debate, madam, is as loud as ever.'

' Yes !' she exclaimed with animation. ' And his handwriting ! Did you ever see such a handwriting ? So very
clear and strong ! Nevertheless I see in him a great change,
a very great change. His countenance is so changed.'

Then H.M., turning from public affairs, deigned to say
that it had given her great pleasure to observe that I had
been chosen Trustee of the British Museum in the place of
the late Lord Lansdowne: and she spoke for some time on
kindred subjects, alluding to what the Prince had done rather
than directly referring to him herself.

At last she asked after my wife, and hoped she was well,
and then, with a graceful bow, vanished.

On the afternoon of this audience the question of the
memorial to the Prince came up in the House of Commons
on a resolution for a grant of £50,000, in addition to the
£60,000 already collected by voluntary subscriptions.
Disraeli pleaded strongly for a monument rather than a
work of utility—a monument which ' should, as it were,
represent the character of the Prince himself in the
harmony of its proportions, in the beauty of its ornament,
and in its enduring nature. It should be something
direct, significant, and choice, so that those who come
after us may say: :" This is the type and testimony of a
sublime life and a transcendent career, and thus they
were recognised by a grateful and admiring people." '[1]
A monument was decided on, and London knows it well;

---

[1] Disraeli was dissatisfied with the report of this speech, and apparently
sent the Queen a memorandum of his actual words. A draft letter to Her
Majesty, preserved among his papers, explains: ' Ld. P. had judiciously
arranged that the memorial vote should take precedence of other business,
and there were skilled reporters ready who would have faithfully represented what was said on that occasion. But an American debate was
irresistibly forced on, and the skilled reporters exhausted their energies
on its grey proceedings, so that those who spoke afterwards, on the gentler
themes, fell to very rude and uncouth hands.'

whether it entirely carries out Disraeli's aspirations may be doubted.

To Mrs. Willyams, whom he had gratified with an account of his audience in much the same words as in the memorandum, he detailed in a subsequent letter the sequel.

To Mrs. Brydges Willyams.

Confidential. GROSVENOR GATE, *May* 5, 1863.—I must continue, and conclude, my Windsor adventures. When I came up to town on the Thursday, from the Castle, there was a debate in the House of Commons on the vote for a monument to Prince Albert. The Queen, with great delicacy, had not mentioned the subject to me—and of course I did not allude to it.

You probably read the observations which I made on the question in the House of Commons.

That was on Thursday night, and on Saturday morning I received from the Queen her own copy of the speeches of the Prince (the same work which I gave you when first published). The copy was bound in white morocco, and on the fly-leaf, in the Queen's own handwriting, was this inscription:[1]

TO

THE RIGHT HONOURABLE BENJAMIN DISRAELI

IN RECOLLECTION OF THE GREATEST AND BEST OF MEN

FROM THE BELOVED PRINCE'S BROKEN-HEARTED WIDOW

VICTORIA R.

WINDSOR CASTLE,
April 24, 1863.

I think you will agree with me that this is the most remarkable inscription which a Sovereign ever placed in a volume graciously presented to a subject!

But there was also a packet tied with black silk, and that contained a letter! But I must stop, like the Sultana in the Arabian Nights, and I find I cannot conclude as I intended.

This was the Queen's letter:

From Queen Victoria.

WINDSOR CASTLE, *April* 24, 1863.—The Queen cannot resist from expressing, personally, to Mr. Disraeli her deep gratification at the tribute he paid to her adored, beloved,

---

[1] In transcribing the inscription Disraeli made one or two slips, which have been corrected by reference to the original.

and great husband. The perusal of it made her shed many tears, but it was very soothing to her broken heart to see such true appreciation of that spotless and unequalled character.

The Queen asks Mr. Disraeli to accept the accompanying book.

Disraeli, in reply, sent Her Majesty a considered estimate of the Prince's character and career.

To Queen Victoria.

GROSVENOR GATE, *April 25, 1863.*—Mr. Disraeli, with his humble duty to your Majesty, begs permission to express his gratitude to your Majesty, for your Majesty's gracious and affecting condescension, and for the inestimable volume which your Majesty has deigned to present to him.

If, in venturing to touch upon a sacred theme, Mr. Disraeli may have, occasionally, used expressions which your Majesty has been graciously pleased to deem not altogether inadequate to the subject, he has been enabled to do so only because, on that subject, he speaks from the heart, and from long and frequent musing over its ever-living interest.

His acquaintance with the Prince is one of the most satisfactory incidents of his life: full of refined and beautiful memories, and exercising, as he hopes, over his remaining existence, a soothing and exalting influence.

The Prince is the only person, whom Mr. Disraeli has ever known, who realized the Ideal. None with whom he is acquainted have ever approached it. There was in him an union of the manly grace and sublime simplicity, of chivalry with the intellectual splendor of the Attic Academe. The only character in English History that would, in some respects, draw near to him is Sir Philip Sidney: the same high tone, the same universal accomplishment, the same blended tenderness and vigor, the same rare combination of romantic energy and classic repose.

Both left us in their youth. But there is no person in our history who has established such a permanent, and almost mystic, ascendancy over national feeling as Sir Philip Sidney; and the writer of these lines is much mistaken if, as time advances, the thought and sentiment of a progressive age will not cluster round the Prince; his plans will become systems, his suggestions dogmas, and the name of Albert will be accepted as the master-type of a generation of profounder feeling and vaster range than that which he formed and guided with benignant power.

How the Queen was affected by this, it must be confessed, somewhat hyperbolic eulogium may be seen from a letter written to the editor of the Prince's speeches by the lady who afterwards became Dean Stanley's wife.

Lady Augusta Bruce to Arthur Helps.

OSBORNE, *May* 4, 1863.—The Queen knows with what peculiar interest you will read anything from the pen of Mr. Disraeli on the subject which so engrosses Her Majesty; but, independently of this, the Queen has been anxious that you should have an opportunity of perusing the most striking and beautiful letter that Her Majesty has received, and has therefore directed me to send you the enclosed extracts from that in which Mr. Disraeli acknowledges the volume sent to him by the Queen.

I need not tell you how her Majesty has been affected by the depth and delicacy of these touches, or how soothing it is to the Queen to have this inexhaustible theme so treated. . . .

Disraeli failed rather signally this summer in an attempt to help the Court to carry out the Prince Consort's South Kensington schemes. Parliament was asked by the Government, with Disraeli's support, to acquire for the nation both the site and the building of the Exhibition of 1862. There was no difficulty about the site, but the purchase of the building was resented on account of its ugliness and unsuitability. Malmesbury tells us that the scene was extraordinary. 'Disraeli had canvassed his supporters, telling them that he had a letter in his pocket from the Queen. This had a disastrous effect, and when he got up the hooting was so terrific that he could not be heard.' Gladstone had already infuriated the House by using an argument, which was taken as a menace, that the contractors were under no obligation to remove the building. 'So the House,' adds Malmesbury, 'rose *en masse*, and, after a scene of the utmost confusion and excitement, defeated the Government by more than two to one;[1] Gladstone and Disraeli looking equally angry.' Both Disraeli's tact and his knowledge of the House seemed to have deserted him,

[1] July 2.

II.   5*

and he was the more chagrined as he had confidently
assured the Court that success was certain in a matter
which the Queen had much at heart.

Disraeli's letters to Mrs. Willyams during the first
half of 1863 are full of Court functions and other festivities incidental to the royal marriage. Celebrations of
the kind, which most British statesmen in the Victorian
era regarded as a necessary bore, whatever pleasure
their wives may have taken in them, were entered into
by Disraeli with a keen zest. The trappings of royal
and noble life appealed to his sense of fitness; and the
world of to-day has largely come round to his view,
discarding the old Benthamite intolerance of everything
that could not prove its economic utility.

To Mrs. Brydges Willyams.

GROSVENOR GATE, *Jan.* 14, 1863.—The Saxon Minister at
this Court, Comte Vitzthum, told me on Sunday that he was
at Dresden in the autumn, on leave of absence from St.
James's, when the Prince of Wales arrived there, and the
King of Saxony consigned His Royal Highness to his care.
He was the Prince's companion for three days, making Dresden
(and Saxony, too, for they went several excursions) agreeable
to him.

He says the Prince has good talents—not of the high class
of the Princess Royal and Princess Alice, but good. He is
gay, extremely amiable, well informed, and, although simple
and unaffected, quite *grand seigneur*.

The King of Saxony told the Prince not to waste time in
paying state visits of compliment and wearing uniforms,
but to go about in plain clothes and see all that was worth
looking at in Dresden; and ' in the evening we will dine at
a palace in the country where there will be no form, and you
can wear a plain coat.'

After Comte Vitzthum and the Prince had examined the
museums, galleries, etc., the Prince said to him: ' Don't you
think now we might have a little shopping ?'

Agreed: and they went to a great jeweller's, and the Prince
bought some bracelets for his future bride; and to some
porcelain shops, where he purchased many objects for his
brothers and sisters; but he never asked the price of anything, which quite delighted the Saxons, who look upon that
as quite *grand seigneur*.

CARLTON CLUB, *Feb.* 25, 1863.—I went to the Prince of Wales's first levée to-day. He received me very cordially, and shook hands with me. I had not seen His Royal Highness for two years. He looked well, and has grown. Sir Henry Holland says that he is 5 ft. 8 in. high, but, then, Sir Henry is not only a physician, but a courtier. However, the Prince certainly looks taller than I ever expected he would turn out to be. . . .

Nobody talks of anything but of the Princess's entrance into London.

GROSVENOR GATE, *March* 4, 1863.—. . . Summer weather, and the world quite mad; all London is encased with tapestried scaffolding and carpeted galleries, and the streets already swarm.

The Lord Mayor has invited us to view the procession from the Mansion House, Baron Rothschild from Piccadilly, and there are many intermediate invitations between these extremes of East and West.

This is for Saturday, the 7th. Tuesday, the 10th, is the bridal day. . . .

March 21, 1863.—I hope you have not had the influenza: if any of your friends have, avoid them; 'tis infectious. It has raged in London—half the House of Commons are absent from their posts: Gladstone ill, Lord Russell *very*. I have escaped comparatively lightly: that is to say, I have not absolutely knocked up, and during the Court festivities have managed to make my appearance, but that was all. Very weak and without energy, and quite unable to write even a letter, which is the reason I have not troubled you.

The wedding was a fine affair—a thing to remember. A perfect pageant, with that sufficient foundation of sentiment which elevates a mere show. The bridal of a young heir to the throne would have been enough in this sense, but the presence of the imperial and widowed mother in her Gothic pavilion, watching everything with intense interest, seeing everything, though herself almost unseen, was deeply dramatic, and even affecting. . . .

The Queen was very anxious that an old shoe should be thrown at the royal pair on their departure, and the Lord Chamberlain showed me in confidence the weapon with which he had furnished himself. He took out of his pocket a beautiful white satin slipper, which had been given him, for the occasion, by the Duchess of Brabant; alas! when the hour arrived, his courage failed him, and he hustled the fairy slipper into the carriage. This is a genuine anecdote, which you will not find in the *Illustrated News*.

On the Friday following, the Duchess of Cambridge gave

a grand entertainment to the Danish Royal family at her rooms at St. James's. The Danish Minister presented me to the father of the Princess of Wales, the Prince Christian, still a very young man, or looking so. Five-and-twenty years ago he came over to Queen Victoria's Coronation as one of her suitors.

Later in the evening the Duke of Cambridge presented me to the mother of the bride, the Princess Christian: a woman of great vivacity and grace, still pretty, and once famously so.

Last evening, the Prince and Princess of Wales, having returned from Osborne, gave their first evening party at St. James's Palace, which had not been used for such an occasion since the reign of George III.

It was a very brilliant affair, limited to 500 guests of the diplomacy and the *haute noblesse :* all the Dukes and Duchesses with scarcely an exception. The Prince and Princess looked like a young couple in a fairy tale. She had on a crown of diamonds, and walked in procession through the illumined saloons, while the Queen's private band, of the choicest musicians, played triumphantly. . . .

June 14, 1863.—This royal honeymoon, of many months, is perfectly distracting. Nothing but balls and banquets, and receptions, and inaugurations and processions, so that one has not a moment to oneself, and lives only in a glittering bustle. This has been a remarkably busy week. On Monday a marvellous fête given in the Guildhall by the Corporation of London—a very great success, and in its splendor and fine taste quite equalling the similar displays at Paris, which hitherto we have not approached; for though the Hôtel de Ville may yield to us in turtle soup, it has always surpassed our citizens in the elegance and invention of their festivals. But on Monday Gog and Magog triumphed.

On Tuesday I was taken up with the ' Act of Uniformity ' and the House of Commons, but, though kept up late, I was in time on Wednesday to take my place in a procession, when the Prince of Wales inaugurated the uncovering of the statue of his father at Kensington.

Thursday was a tremendous banquet given to the Prince by the Merchant Taylors' Company, where I had to return thanks for the House of Commons: a very grand affair with four Royal Princes and six Dukes present. But everything yielded in splendor, in brilliancy, in gorgeous magnificence, to the fête which the Duke and Duchess of Northumberland gave to the Prince and Princess of Wales on Friday last !

We dined sixty guests of the high nobility in a magnificent gallery, as fine in dimensions, and far more splendid than the Galerie de Diane of the Tuileries. Such plate, such diamonds, so many Duchesses, and Knights of the Garter, were never before assembled together !

To-morrow we go to the glories of Oxford.

June 25, 1863.—Oxford was a Carnival. There was too much crowded into every day. That was the only fault. Every day there were five or six *functions*, as the Spaniards call them. On Wednesday, for example, there was Grand Commemoration; a collation in the Library of All Souls College, which is more than 300 feet long—the noblest of apartments; a bazaar for the Radcliffe Infirmary; a garden fête; a boat race, worthy of the Regattas and Ridottos of Venice; a banquet at Exeter College; and a Christ Church Ball—and the Prince and Princess went to all ! And all this amid endless cheering, and music, and shouts. Too much even for youth and beauty. We had three days of it, and this holiday made such an arrear of business that I have never been able to get right since my return. As Lord Chesterfield said of the old Duke of Newcastle, who was Minister in his time, I am always running after the three days I have lost. . . .

To-morrow the Conservative Association give me a public dinner; and in the evening the Brigade of Guards are to give the Princess of Wales the most gorgeous ball ever produced in any age or any country Mrs. Disraeli will be there, and I if possible.

To Lord Derby.

HUGHENDEN MANOR, *Sept.* 2, 1863.—. . . The Queen returns from a not uneventful German campaign, for not only is Princess Helena to be married, but Prince Alfred, and that, too, early in the spring: the Princess not inferior to the Princess of Wales ! But you know all this.

For my part I think even Princes should sow their wild oats, and not step out paterfamilias from the nursery or the middy's berth. . . .

Mention was made, in Disraeli's account of his audience of the Queen in 1863, of his recent election as a Trustee of the British Museum. Not merely the election itself, but the circumstances in which it took place and the manner in which it was communicated to him, gave Disraeli legitimate satisfaction.

From Lord Palmerston.

94, PICCADILLY, *March* 25, 1863.

MY DEAR MR. DISRAELI,—You will of course receive from the Secretary to the Trustees of the British Museum the

official notification that at a meeting held by them this afternoon you were elected a Trustee in the room of the late Lord
Lansdowne; but it may be agreeable to you to know the
grounds upon which the choice of the Trustees was made.

The Trustees were of opinion that in making choice of a
new colleague they ought to select a person distinguished by
literary eminence; that it would be useful to the interests
of the Museum that he should be in a prominent position in
the House of Commons, so as to be able, when occasions might
arise, to explain with authority to the House any matter
connected with the Museum which might be brought under
discussion ; and, lastly, it was felt that, whereas many of the
existing Trustees belong more or less to one political party,
it was desirable that the choice to be made should show that
party politics are not to be permitted to enter within the
gates of a building dedicated to Learning and to the Arts.
All these considerations seemed to point to you as the proper
object of choice, and accordingly you were unanimously elected.
—Yours faithfully, PALMERSTON.

To Lord Palmerston.

March, 1863.

MY DEAR LORD,—There are few distinctions I should more
highly value than to become a Trustee of the British Museum.

My father was the first man of letters who, much more than
half a century ago, began to turn its MS. wealth to account
in the illustration of our history, and I have been brought
up in a due appreciation of its treasures and a due reverence
for its authorities.

But what I most esteem in the present matter are the mode
and medium by which my election has been communicated
to me.

I hope your Lordship is not quite unaware of the sincere
regard which I have always personally entertained for you
since our first acquaintance, and, notwithstanding the inevitable collisions of public life, I can truly say that perhaps no
one grudges your greatness less than your obliged and faithful
servant, B. DISRAELI.

Disraeli has left a note of his conversation with the
Queen about the Museum:

H.M. asked me what I thought of Panizzi,[1] and whether
he were equal to the post.

I replied that my official experience was too slight to

[1] Principal Librarian, 1856-1866.

permit me to offer a personal opinion, but that he was much
esteemed by my colleagues.

H.M. thought it strange that a foreigner should be at the
head of an institution so peculiarly national.

I observed that the post had been frequently filled by
foreigners; that when I was a boy it was filled by Mr. Planta,[1]
a Swiss, and the father of a gentleman who had served Her
Majesty's uncles as U.S. of State for Foreign Affairs; that
in older days Dr. Maty,[2] who, I believe, was a Frenchman,
had been in high office at the Museum. . . . I mentioned
also that Mr. Hallam thought very highly of Panizzi, and
that my father, a great authority on vernacular literature,
had been astonished by his intimate acquaintance with
English books.

Disraeli attended with assiduity to his duties as Trustee,
and when in office never forgot the interests of the
Museum.   It was mainly due to his clear-sightedness
and promptitude that the wonderful Blacas Collection
in Paris, which, with its wealth of gems and cameos, the
French Emperor was anxious to keep for France, was
secured for England and the British Museum at the
cost of £48,000.   'This purchase,' wrote Disraeli to the
Queen on November 26, 1863, 'will facilitate the plans
of the Chancellor of the Exchequer for the separation
of the National Collections, and the establishment of the
Museum of Natural History at Kensington.'   Another
matter in which he specially interested himself was
the securing for the British Museum, during the 1874
Ministry, of the Castellani Collection, including the fine
bronze head of Venus.   In fact, his record as Trustee
and as Minister is one for which the Museum has reason
to be grateful.

[1] Principal Librarian, 1799–1827.
[2] Principal Librarian, 1772–1776.

CHAPTER XII.

REFORM REVIVED.

1864–1866.

'Rest and be thankful'; that was the cold comfort which Russell, the veteran Reformer, offered to his fellow-Reformers in a speech in Scotland in the autumn of 1863. Reform was certainly in a backwater. Not only were the Prime Minister and Parliament indifferent or hostile; but the apparent disruption of the United States, that ideal democratic community which Bright and his friends had constantly held up for imitation, was taken by the ordinary Englishman as evidence that a democratic suffrage was an unstable basis on which to build a State. In Disraeli's words, the collapse of republican institutions must tell immensely in favour of aristocracy. The argument was pressed home repeatedly in Robert Cecil's articles in the *Quarterly Review*. But the Cabinet contained one restless Minister, who was little disposed to accept his colleague Russell's advice. On a Wednesday afternoon[1] in 1864, while a private member's Bill for lowering the borough franchise was occupying the languid attention of the House, Gladstone, who interposed to state the position of the Government, electrified the torpid audience by a momentous declaration: 'I venture to say that every man who is not presumably incapacitated by some consideration of personal unfitness or of political danger is morally entitled to come within the pale of the Constitution.' No

[1] May 11.

public man, outside of the Radical ranks, had hitherto openly advocated a lowering of the franchise at all comparable in extent to that suggested in these words; and great and widespread was their reverberation. Curiously enough, in substance, and indeed in language, the declaration was hardly distinguishable from the pronouncement of Disraeli's organ, the *Press*, more than ten years before, in an article written by Stanley,[1] which advocated bringing ' within the pale of the Constitution everyone whose admission cannot be proved dangerous.' But Disraeli, who had not seen the article before publication, hastily dropped this sweeping proposition; and in any case neither he nor Stanley would have justified it by an appeal to the moral law.

It was this appeal that constituted the most striking feature of Gladstone's dictum—an appeal which, as Disraeli said, recalled Rousseau's *Social Contract*, and Tom Paine's *Rights of Man*. It was an appeal which was to stand Gladstone in good stead to the end of his career. He could seldom adopt a policy with enthusiasm until he had satisfied himself that to carry it out was a moral, if not a religious, obligation. But, if that were so, opposition must obviously be inspired by the spirit of evil ; and it was too frequently as the incarnation of that spirit that Disraeli was regarded by his great rival. To Disraeli, on the other hand, politics in most of its phases presented itself as what surely it usually is— a choice between the more and the less expedient; and he was naturally disposed to regard as cant an advocacy which was ostentatiously put on the moral plane. A toleration, if not an affection, for cant is, however, unless all our foreign critics are in error, a characteristic of the British people; and undoubtedly the attitude of moral superiority which Gladstone constantly assumed was, in the Britain of the nineteenth century, worth much in votes.

[1] Nov. 5, 1853. See Vol. I., p. 1317.

To Lord Derby.

GROSVENOR GATE, *May* 13, 1864.—. . . Though Gladstone's move was matured, and, indeed, for a considerable time contemplated, I have no doubt the visit and reception of Garibaldi have acted on his impressionable nature, and have betrayed him into a far more extreme position than was at first intended. The consequences must be grave, though I dare say the Cavendishes, Russells, etc., will, in due time, swallow his programme. The smaller Whigs, Beaumonts, Ramsdens, and perhaps Lansdownes and Fitzwilliams, may detach themselves.

Gladstone's declaration, though it disturbed his chief and embarrassed his colleagues, marked him out as the coming Liberal leader, with democratic Reform as a principal feature of his policy; and it was in that capacity that he was welcomed in Lancashire in the following autumn, during an oratorical tour which he made in his native county. But in Parliament, in spite of him, Reform made in 1864 no progress. The ballot was rejected by a majority of 89, and Locke King's County Franchise Bill by 27; while Baines's Borough Franchise Bill was shelved by 56. Finance, foreign affairs, and the Church, were still the topics that occupied men's minds and the attention of Parliament. Disraeli has left a short note describing this session of 1864.

The session a very curious one; I was watching for five months for the proper moment for battle. It was very difficult to restrain our friends. The Government every day more unpopular, and yet it was clear to me that the House would not directly censure them. The tactic was to postpone to the last moment a direct attack, but to defeat them in the interval on some indirect vote, taking advantage of the discontent of the House. Thus, on the Ashantee War[1] we ran them to 6 or 7, and on Stansfeld's affair[2] to 10; on either question they would have resigned. On the direct vote (their Danish policy)[3] their majority was 18, of which

---

[1] A minor expedition in which there had been excessive loss of life by disease.

[2] Stansfeld, at this time a subordinate member of the Government, had allowed letters for Mazzini, the Italian revolutionist, to be sent to his private address under a false name. It was in this debate that Bright quoted the *Revolutionary Epick* against Disraeli. See Vol. I., pp. 245, 246.

[3] See above, Ch. 9.

they affected to be proud, though in old days it would have
been considered a defeat. Sir Robert Peel, on his vote of
want of confidence in 1840, moved by Sir John Buller, was
beaten by 22, but was Minister next year, 1841.

Lord P., after the division, scrambled up a wearying
staircase to the ladies' gallery. My informant, who was
behind him, had the good taste and tact to linger. He saw
the ladies' gallery open, and Lady Palmerston advance, and
they embraced ! An interesting scene, and what pluck !
To mount those dreadful stairs at three o'clock in the morning,
and eighty years of age ! My informant would not disturb
them. It was a great moment.

Disraeli repeated in the session of 1865 the tactics
of reserve which he had practised in 1864, and which
seemed to him particularly prudent in view of the
forthcoming elections.

To Lord Derby.

HUGHENDEN MANOR, *Dec.* 12, 1864.—. . . There is only
one point which I wish to submit to you—to consider whether
it is necessary that the leaders of Opposition in the two
Houses on the first night should make those elaborate and
comprehensive surveys of the public situation which, of
late years, it has become their habit of doing.

The principle, now conveniently assumed by our opponents, that the Opposition is a body prepared to take
office, and therefore bound to give its quasi-official opinion
on the conduct of every department, seems to me to have
no sound foundation, and is very injurious to us. It forces
us to show our cards the first night of the session, and the
Government profits accordingly. They see where the breakers
are ahead, and what perils they have escaped. . . .

Disraeli could not persuade Derby to silence on the
Address; but he was silent himself, and, indeed, did not
for many weeks take an active part in debate. In spite
of pressure from Derby, he refused to speak on the
question of the disestablishment of the Irish Church,
which was brought forward by an independent Radical.
Derby wrote, March 10, 1865: 'Considering the great
stress you have always laid upon Church questions as
our main *cheval de bataille*, I hope that you will yourself

consider it not an unfitting occasion for breaking through (if you should not have done so before) the profound silence which you have maintained during the present session.' Disraeli was, as we know, conscious of the weak points in the position of the Irish Church, and thought it wiser to take no part in a debate in which Gladstone expressed at once his dissatisfaction with the Establishment and his reluctance to take any immediate step. Disraeli exhibited an ostentatious indifference to a motion for the repeal of the malt tax, which Fitzroy Kelly, the principal Law Officer of the last Derby Government, insisted on bringing forward in opposition to his leader's wishes. In a discussion on the subject in the previous session, Disraeli had expressed his agreement as to the objectionable character of the tax, which he had himself endeavoured to reduce in 1852. But the question should be dealt with in a large and comprehensive manner; and, as he had contended over and over again, the war duty on sugar should first be repealed. In 1864 the motion was rejected by more than two to one; in 1865 it was shelved by a majority of 81.

It was colonial policy which drew Disraeli from his reserve. The successful Northerners in the United States appeared to be threatening Canada—Canada, which was now uniting into a confederation under pressure of events, and which might, Disraeli thought, become the 'Russia of the New World.' What was to be the political future of that and our other colonies ? It was the parting of the ways. Disraeli gave a patriotic lead in a speech on March 13. How strong the anti-Imperial drift was in Parliament at the time is shown by the tentative and hypothetical manner in which he handled the question.

We are on the eve of events of very great importance. The question we have to ask ourselves is, Is this country prepared to renounce her American dependencies and colonies, or are we to retain that tie ? Now, if these colonies expressed a wish to separate the connection, and if they preferred to be absorbed by the United States, we might terminate our connection with dignity and without disaster. But if, on the other hand, those views are just which are more generally accepted—if there should be, on the part of Canada and the other North American colonies, a sincere and deep desire to form a considerable State, and develop its resources, and to preserve the patronage and aid of England, until that mature hour when we shall lose our dependency but gain a permanent ally and friend—then it would be the greatest political blunder for us to renounce, relinquish, and avoid, the responsibility of maintaining our interests in Canada at the present moment.

If, from considerations of expense, we were to quit the possessions that we now occupy in North America, it would be ultimately, as regards our resources and wealth, as fatal and disastrous a step as could possibly be taken. Our prosperity would not long remain a consolation to us, and we might then prepare for the invasion of our country and the subjugation of the people. I infer that hon. gentlemen opposite do not express these views, which have, however, found utterance in other quarters; but that they take a truly patriotic and English view of this subject—namely, not to force our connection on any dependency; but if, at a moment of revolution in North America, we find our colonies asserting the principle of their nationality, and if, foreseeing a glorious future, we find them still depending on the faithful and affectionate assistance of England, it would be the most shortsighted and suicidal policy to shrink from the duty that Providence has called upon us to fulfil.

In a subsequent debate on a vote for the defence of Canada, Lowe said that we ought to tell Canada that, if she chose to maintain British connection, it would be at the risk of having to protect herself from American invasion; that it was open to her, if she pleased, to establish herself as an independent republic, or to join the American Republic; and that in any case she should have in England a friend, protector, and ally. Disraeli protested warmly that it was our duty to aid Canada to defend herself in case she were attacked by America. Canada had a great future and all the elements that made a nation. The House ought to cherish the connection with the North American provinces.

The 'mature hour' which Disraeli foresaw has now arrived. From a dependency, Canada—and the statement is true also of Australia, South Africa, and New Zealand—has become 'a permanent ally and friend'; nay more, an integral, self-governing member of the British Empire throughout the world, yielding allegiance to one common Sovereign.

Two deaths in April moved Disraeli to memorable speech. Of his old opponent, Cobden, 'the greatest political character that the pure middle class of this country has yet produced,' he finely said: 'There are some members of Parliament who, though they may not be present, are still members of this House, who are independent of dissolutions, of the caprices of constituencies, and even of the course of time.' When President Lincoln was murdered, he declared that in the character of the victim, and in the accessories of his last moments, there was something so homely and so innocent that it took the subject out of the pomp of history and the ceremonial of diplomacy. It was consolatory to reflect that assassination had never changed the history of the world; and he expressed a fervent hope that from these awful years of trial the various populations of North America might come out elevated and chastened, rich with that accumulated wisdom, and strong in that disciplined energy, which a young nation could only acquire in a protracted and perilous struggle.

But Disraeli's principal effort in the session of 1865 was on the Reform Question; and, strangely enough, though but two years were to elapse before he proposed and carried household suffrage, there is no period in the history of his connection with Reform in which he made a more definite stand against a forward movement. The effect of Gladstone's outburst had been rather to frighten Parliament and the politicians than to attract them. The Parliament of 1859 and the Prime Minister who dominated it became more conservative in this respect as they grew older. The discussion took place on Baines's Borough Franchise Bill, which had been the occasion of Gladstone's pronouncement in 1864. Perhaps

the most outstanding feature of the debate was the
definite emergence of an anti-Reform Liberal section,
of which Lowe and Horsman were the leaders. Lowe,
who had recently resigned office in circumstances which
had left him somewhat sore, spoke as a lifelong Liberal,
but one who had no faith in *a priori* rights of man, and
who would not cast in his lot with that particular form
of government called democracy.   There could, he
thought, be no greater danger for the country than to
transfer power from the hands of property, industry,
and intelligence, to those of men necessarily occupied
in daily struggles for existence. The Government were
careful to be represented, not by the impulsive Gladstone,
but by an old Whig ' stager,' Sir George Grey, who was
ready to read the Bill a second time, but would not
pledge the Government to the £6 franchise which it proposed, or to any large measure of Parliamentary Reform.

Disraeli, ever responsive to the Parliamentary atmosphere in a matter which depended so greatly upon
feeling and opportunity as did Parliamentary Reform,
expressed satisfaction with the general position of the
Government. He proceeded:

All that has occurred, all that I have observed, all the
results of my reflections, lead me to this more and more: that
the principle upon which the constituencies of this country
should be increased is one, not of radical, but, I would say,
of lateral reform—the extension of the franchise, not its
degradation. Although—I do not wish in any way to deny
it—being in the most difficult position when the Parliament
of 1859 met, being anxious to assist the Crown and the
Parliament, by proposing some moderate measure which
men on both sides might support, we did, to a certain extent,
agree to some modification of the £10 franchise, yet I confess
that my present opinion is opposed, as it originally was, to
any course of the kind. I think that it would fail in its
object, that it would not secure the introduction of that
particular class which we all desire to introduce, but that it
would introduce many others who are unworthy of the
suffrage. . . . I think it is possible to increase the electoral
body of the country, if the opportunity were favourable and
the necessity urgent, by the introduction of voters upon

principles in unison with the principles of the Constitution, so that the suffrage should remain a privilege, and not a right; a privilege to be gained by virtue, by intelligence, by industry, by integrity, and to be exercised for the common good. And I think if you quit that ground, if you once admit that a man has a right to vote whom you cannot prove to be disqualified for it, you would change the character of the Constitution, and you would change it in a manner which will tend to lower the importance of this country.

The question at issue was between an aristocratic government in the proper sense of the term—that is, a government by the best men of all classes—and a democracy. The English were a peculiar people.

You have an ancient, powerful, richly-endowed Church, and perfect religious liberty. You have unbroken order and complete freedom. You have landed estates as large as the Romans, combined with commercial enterprise such as Carthage and Venice united never equalled. And you must remember that this peculiar country, with these strong contrasts, is not governed by force; it is not governed by standing armies; it is governed by a most singular series of traditionary influences, which generation after generation cherishes because it knows that they embalm custom and represent law. And, with this, what have you done ? You have created the greatest Empire of modern time. You have amassed a capital of fabulous amount. You have devised and sustained a system of credit still more marvellous. And, above all, you have established and maintained a scheme so vast and complicated of labour and industry, that the history of the world affords no parallel to it. And all these mighty creations are out of all proportion to the essential and indigenous elements and resources of the country. If you destroy that state of society, remember this—England cannot begin again.

The United States and France, with their immense natural resources, could survive great disasters and revolutions; but not England—'the England we know, the England we live in, the England of which we are proud.' 'I do not mean to say that after great troubles England would become a howling wilderness, or doubt that the good sense of the people would, to some degree, prevail, and some fragments of the national character survive; but it would not be Old England—the England of power and tradition, of credit and capital, that now exists.' He hoped the House would 'sanction no step that has a tendency to democracy, but that it will maintain the ordered state of free England in which we live.'[1]

The speech was a recantation, in set terms, of the proposals which Disraeli had been ready to accept in June, 1859; but at the same time it reiterated his desire to see a decided addition to the working-class element in the constituency. It brought him a letter of gratitude and appreciation from an eminent man with whose social work he had sincere sympathy.

From Lord Shaftesbury.

May 10, 1865.—You will not, I hope, be offended that I presume to thank you for your speech on the Baines Bill. The sentiments and the language were worthy of each other, and a masterly protest against any truckling to democracy. I believe that, in proportion as a man is a deep, sincere, and consistent lover of *social*, civil, and religious liberty, he will be a deep, sincere, and consistent hater of pure democracy, as adverse to all three.

You well showed that America, France, Australia, may endure convulsions, and partially recover from them; but England rests entirely on her institutions.

We have, however, made a great advance towards safety and satisfaction, when so many of all classes and opinions seem to agree that the franchise may be largely extended, without being degraded.

The Bill was shelved by the decisive majority of 74, the numbers being 288 against 214—an unmistakable testimony to the conservative disposition of the expiring Parliament. But interest was rapidly shifting from that Parliament to its successor; and in his address to his constituents, issued shortly after this debate, Disraeli claimed the confidence of the country for the Conservative party on the twofold ground of its successful defence of the Church and of its attitude towards Reform. On this latter point, he referred to the Conservative Bill of 1859 as a measure which would have greatly extended the Parliamentary suffrage ' on principles in harmony

[1] May 8.

with the Constitution, which wisely recognises the electoral franchise as a privilege, and not a right.' That Bill was defeated by a majority which insisted that the franchise must be lowered in boroughs, and a new Administration was formed pledged to that principle. But only a few nights before, 'the House of Commons, impatient of protracted mystification, reflected the candour of the community, and declared by a vast majority that the franchise in boroughs should not be lowered, and that the principle on which Lord Derby wished to extend it was the just one.' Public opinion might not, perhaps, be yet ripe enough for legislation; but, when the time for action came, they should legislate 'in the spirit of the English Constitution, which would absorb the best of all classes, and not fall into a democracy, which is the tyranny of one class, and that one the least enlightened.' Disraeli's address obviously contemplated that the Conservatives might be called upon to settle the question; but it certainly led the public to expect that they would favour no solution of which the main feature was an immense lowering of the borough franchise.

Disraeli's attitude in regard to Reform brought down upon his head the wrath of his sometime friend, John Bright, who, indeed, saw little to praise, at this election, in the official leaders of either party. 'The treachery of official statesmen' was the keynote of his speeches. Palmerston had treated the subject with 'contemptuous silence,' not even referring to it in a lengthy address to his constituents. As for the Conservatives, 'Lord Derby, speaking through the mouth of his prophet Disraeli,' offered lateral franchise; in other words, when the working men demanded the vote, he proposed to 'admit—somebody else!' Bright continued: 'Mr. Disraeli is a man of brains, of genius, of a great capacity of action, of a wonderful tenacity of purpose, and of a rare courage. He would have been a statesman if his powers had been directed by any ennobling principle or idea.'

Condemnatory as Bright's speech was, its language showed how greatly Disraeli had advanced in public estimation. When he appealed to the electors of Bucks at the General Election of 1865, he occupied a very different position from that which he had held, eighteen years before, on first seeking their suffrages. Then, indeed, he had accomplished the immense feat of overthrowing Peel, but his future appeared to be uncertain; it was still the fashion, in many circles of distinction, to regard him as a charlatan and to treat him as a pariah. But now he had led his party in the Commons during four Parliaments; had twice led the House, as a Minister of the Crown second only in importance to the Prime Minister; and had won further admiration owing to his masterly conduct of the Opposition during the last six difficult years. There were still, no doubt, exclusive regions, mostly of high Whiggery, in which he was looked at askance, and there was a group of aristocratic Tories in Parliament whose grudging attitude was represented by the cricketer among them who said: 'Our team is the Gentlemen of England, with a Player given.' But in Society as a whole, and among his fellow-statesmen, he had obtained remarkable consideration, and he was regarded with favour at Court. In February of this year one of the last of the social barriers gave way before him; and he was elected a member of Grillion's dining club, a select coterie of which it has been customary to make rising politicians of both parties free, but from which the socially objectionable are rigorously excluded. Not only Derby, who, as was natural, had been elected on his first entry into politics in 1825, but most of Disraeli's past and future Cabinet colleagues, even some of comparatively little account, had been chosen several years before the doors opened to him. Gladstone had been a member since 1840. Save for the recognition which it implied, the election gave Disraeli little satisfaction. The dreariness of men's dinners was one of his favourite themes;

and when, at the close of 1868, he was asked whether he
would be willing to join ' the Club,' an older institution of
a similar kind, he did not conceal from his friend Cairns
that, if he accepted membership, it would be in obedience
to a social tradition rather than of his own inclination.

To Lord Cairns.

Confidential. GROSVENOR GATE, *Dec.* 9, 1868.—*Entre
nous,* I greatly dislike our feeble mimicry of ' the feast
of reason and the flow of soul ' of the eighteenth century.

Lord Stanhope's list of *the* Club seems our friends, the
Grillionites, under another name.

I have not dined with those gentry for three years;[1] but my
recollection of them is extreme dullness; no genuine and
general conversation, but a dozen prigs and bores (generally)
whispering to their next-door neighbors over a bad dinner
in a dingy room. Not a single thing ever said at Grillion's
remains in my memory.

Nevertheless, as you and I are both candidates for the
Consulship, we must not run counter to the social traditions
of the country any more than against any other traditions;
so you can tell Ld. Stanhope, that I shall feel honored in
belonging to so classical and renowned a society as the Club.[2]

The recognition of Disraeli's services and statesmanship
in his own county at the General Election of 1865 was
very marked. Not only was he re-elected without a
contest, but he brought in with him, as on no previous
occasion, two Conservative colleagues, instead of one
Conservative and one Liberal. Gladstone at the same
time was discarded, after long forbearance, by the
University, with the prevailing views of whose graduates
he had for some time ceased to be in harmony; and had
gone ' unmuzzled ' to Lancashire, where he secured with
some difficulty a seat for an industrial constituency, to
which he appealed in the spirit of his declaration on
Baines's Bill and of his popular progresses of the past
two years. Gladstone's defeat at Oxford by a Conserva-

[1] Disraeli's memory was at fault. It appears from the records that he
dined at Grillion's on May 7 and 16, 1866, and March 27, 1867.

[2] In spite, or because, of the disposition shown in this letter, Disraeli
was never elected a member of ' the Club.'

tive, Gathorne Hardy, with a growing reputation for eloquence and practical ability, was naturally welcome to Disraeli. He congratulated Frederick Lygon, who was a Fellow of All Souls, on 'that historical event, which I believe to be mainly, if not entirely, owing to your energy and resolution.' He added: 'G. A. Denison[1] will crow till the end of the year. I am glad we helped him to such an euthanasia.'

But Disraeli had few other grounds for satisfaction in the results of the elections. It proved to be hopeless for the Conservatives to contend against the popular and equally conservative Palmerston. The conditions of the last Parliament were just those which the middle-class electorate desired to reproduce—Palmerston as Prime Minister to sustain and guard the national honour and interests, with Gladstone at the Exchequer to promote the national prosperity; but both faced by a strong Conservative opposition, which would prevent Palmerston from involving the country in war, and Gladstone and the Radicals from committing it to democracy. What little chance of a majority the Conservatives might have had was spoilt by a character-istic indiscretion of Derby, who talked in the House of Lords of the necessity of muzzling Roman Catholics[2]— Roman Catholics whom Disraeli had with infinite patience and adroitness brought to realise that, now that they were emancipated, their political affinities were rather with the Conservative than with the Liberal cause.[3] But in his first letter, after the tendency of the elections was clear, Derby attributed the defeat rather to over-confidence and want of exertion. Disraeli demurred.

---

[1] A combative High Churchman, Archdeacon of Taunton.

[2] On a Bill for modifying the oath required to be taken by Roman Catholic members. Disraeli showed considerable reserve in regard to the Bill in the Commons, but Derby procured its rejection in the Lords.

[3] In a draft letter of 1864 to an anonymous correspondent, preserved among the Beaconsfield papers, Disraeli wrote that he had always looked, from his first entrance into public life, to 'a reconciliation between the Tory party and the Roman Catholic subjects of the Queen. . . . I have never relinquished my purpose, and have now, I hope, accomplished it. If the Tory party is not a national party, it is nothing.'

To Lord Derby.

HUGHENDEN MANOR, *July* 28, 1865.—. . . I have no
doubt there were instances on our side of over-confidence.
There always will be. And I feel sure that, if we had succeeded in forcing a dissolution last year, we should have
done better; but, on the whole, I cannot conceal from myself
that the dissolution took place on fair conditions for the
Opposition. The Ministry had no cry, and we had the
advantage of six years of unceasing preparation, well employed; for, notwithstanding the result, I think the energy,
resource, and general efficiency, of Mr. Spofforth and Lord
Nevill,[1] who, after all, were the real managers, were truly
admirable—not to say unique.

And on paper affairs look well enough. After Lord P.'s
dissolution in 1857 you had 260 followers in the H. of C.
After your own dissolution in 1859, you had 287. At present,
with what we consider a great check, you will top 290.

But beneath the surface things are not so fair. The state
of Scotland alone is most serious. All influence appears to
have slipped away from its proprietors; and if irremediable,
if Scotland and the Metropolitan districts are to be entirely,
and continuously, arrayed against the Conservative cause,
the pull of the table will be too great, and no Conservative
Government, unless the basis be extended, will be possible. . . .

In a later letter Derby admitted that his ' unlucky '
reference to the muzzling metaphor might have lost some
votes. Disraeli took the opportunity of the correspondence to explain his views as to the party leadership.

To Lord Derby.

Private. HUGHENDEN MANOR, *Aug.* 6, 1865.—. . . You
will do me the justice, I hope, to remember that, when some
of your followers, ten years ago, suggested, for the common
cause, you should condescend to take a subordinate office,
I utterly repudiated the scheme. It would then have been
most improper, but perhaps not impossible. Now it would
be equally improper and quite impossible.

With regard to myself, although I am quite aware that
I have had an opportunity in life to which I have not been
adequate, still, having led a portion of the House of Commons
for seventeen years, I am disinclined, in the decline of life,
to serve under anybody in that assembly; and as no one
but yourself would offer me its lead, and as we both agree
that such a combination would not succeed, I look upon

[1] Afterwards fifth Earl and first Marquis of Abergavenny, 1826-1915.

my career in the House of Commons, so far as office is concerned, to have concluded. But I am not at all sure that, at a moment of alarm and embarrassment, an influential body of new adherents might not be disposed to rally round a person who has so considerable a following in the country as yourself. But this can never happen so long as they understand, as a condition precedent of such adhesion, that the leadership in both Houses is to be appropriated by us. And who can blame them ? What, therefore, I wish you to do is to take the fitting opportunity to avail yourself of those confidential connections which you have among the Whigs, and let them clearly understand that you are free and prepared to form an anti-revolutionary Government on a broad basis. But this should be done in time, not delayed till the crisis arrives, and when other persons have been hurried into conduct which, had they been aware of the real state of affairs, they would have avoided. This course involves really no sacrifice on my part. The leadership of hopeless opposition is a gloomy affair, and there is little distinction when your course is not associated with the possibility of future power. My retirement from the post would also assist you in another respect. It would be an unanswerable precedent for relieving you from some embarrassing claims, which now weaken you in the country.

From Lord Derby.

KNOWSLEY, *Aug.* 12, 1865.—The suggestion contained in your letter of the 6th inst. is a very generous one on your part; but I felt instinctively, on receiving it, that the course it indicates would not only be entirely repugnant to my own feelings, but that practically it would be found impossible, and, if possible, highly impolitic; and if I did not at once write to say so, it was because, setting all personal considerations aside, I desired fully and impartially to consider whether, under any circumstances, public duty could impose on me the necessity of making such a sacrifice.

The result is the fullest confirmation of the view which I originally took. Though I say 'putting all personal considerations aside,' I cannot forget that you and I have acted together, with perfect cordiality, and, I believe, mutual confidence, for more than seventeen years. I believe that we have been mutually serviceable to each other; my influence with the party has, I hope, served to strengthen your position in the Commons; and I should have looked in vain for anyone in that House, on either side, who would have seconded me with the same ability, faithfulness, and perseverance, which you have exhibited. But my position would be very different if I had a colleague in your place with whom I was politically associated only by a compromise. Such a state of things would leave me the *nominal* head of a coalition Government, with the lead of the most powerful of the two branches of the legislature in the hands of one entertaining different views, and, not unnaturally, regarding himself less as a colleague than as a rival. Such a position would not be politically tenable, and, personally, it would be intolerable. As I can never hold any office but the first, so neither can I be the head of any but a *bona-fide* Conservative Government.

But even supposing the case which you put, of a sufficient number of moderate Liberals becoming alarmed at the progress of events, and willing to join our ranks, to give us a numerical majority, is there the slightest prospect that among them there could be found one who would be competent to take the lead of the House, or entitled to aspire to it, looking to the proportion between his followers and the party which he joined ? Is there, moreover, any prospect that the old Conservative party would submit to such a leadership ? . . .

I come, therefore, to the conclusion that neither you nor I, certainly not I, can be members of a Government of which the leaders and the principles should not be distinctly and avowedly Conservative; and as I see little chance of such an accession to our strength as would enable us to conduct a Government on such principles, the conclusion is as obvious with regard to one of us as to the other. . . .

After the General Election, the Disraelis paid a round of visits to great country-houses—two of them Whig, two Tory: Raby, Lowther, Ashridge, Woburn. Country-house visiting, as Disraeli explained in a letter in 1863 to Mrs. Willyams,[1] was regarded by him as one of the duties of his position. He met thereby, in undress fashion, all the people of distinction in politics and society, and was enabled ' to feel the pulse of the ablest on all the questions of the day.' But, if he profited, he also suffered. One of his characters in *Lothair* says that life in a country-house is ' a series of meals mitigated by the new dresses of the ladies '; and Mrs. Disraeli confided to Sir William Fraser that ennui and indigestion often cut short her husband's stay. At Raby he saw for the first time a future Prime Minister, Lord Rosebery, then Lord Dalmeny; and also a young man, the son of a

---

[1] See above, p. 65.

colleague, who was destined to be the most intimate
follower and friend of his old age, Montagu Corry.
Disraeli has left a note describing these visits.

August 31, Mary Anne and I went to Raby [1] and stayed a
week. I believe it was the first reception of the Harry
Vanes since their accession. [2] Raby a real castle, and vast,
and, though occasionally altered and 'improved,' not substantially changed in character. The general effect feudal
and Plantagenet. Though the country in the vicinity not
beautiful, the immediate domain well wooded; a herd of
400 deer, and red deer also; but they never blend physically
and socially; they live apart.

The Duchess a brilliant woman—sister of Lord Stanhope;
she has the quickest, and the finest, perception of humor
I know, with extraordinary power of expression, and the
Stanhope wit; her conversation unceasing, but never long or
wearying; a wondrous flow of drollery, information, social
tattle, taste, eloquence; such a ceaseless flow of contemporary
anecdote I never heard. And yet she never repeats.

The Duke makes a very good Duke; tall and dignified,
but very natural, and, though not exactly good-looking, a
good presence and a good expression of countenance, kind
eyes. Affectionate to his step-children—hers by her former
marriage with Lord Dalmeny, eldest son of Earl of Rosebery.
The grandfather yet living.

Her eldest son, Dalmeny, seemed to me very intelligent and
formed for his time of life (not yet of age), and not a prig,
which might be feared. His younger brother, Everard
Primrose, seventeen, very promising. Two sisters: one
handsome, and both pleasing.

Of the meeting with Montagu Corry, Disraeli has left
no account; but a well-authenticated tradition tells how
one wet afternoon the girls of the house-party, on the
look-out for amusement, seized on a young man with
a reputation for gravity, and insisted on his dancing a
breakdown, singing a comic song the while. In the
midst of the frolic, Disraeli, who was supposed to be
letter-writing in his room, looked in at the door, and,
to the confusion of the young man caught playing the
fool, remained steadily regarding the scene for some

---

[1] In the visitors' book at Raby, Disraeli described his profession as
'Patriotism.' Gladstone, a subsequent visitor, called himself 'Apprentice.'
[2] To the dukedom of Cleveland.

minutes Corry very naturally feared he had forfeited
for ever the good opinion of one with whom he particularly wished to stand well, and who had cordially
welcomed him the previous day for his father's sake.
But Disraeli, though his face had worn its usual mask,
had been greatly attracted by the combination of youth,
ability, good looks, good-nature, and social gifts, and,
after dinner that evening, secured the lifelong devotion
of a prince among private secretaries with the gracious
words, ' I think you must be my impresario.' [1]

The note describing the country-house visits proceeds:

Then we went from the ancient to a modern castle, Lowther
—a splendid domain; parks and deer, mountains and lakes.
The house convenient, and handsome in the interior, but the
exterior deplorable, as might be expected from the Gothic
of 1800 and Sir Smirke (sic). As my Lord receives no ladies,
but would receive my wife, a female cousin, Lowther, and her
brother, were present, and the rest a silent, but not scanty,
court of retainers.

Then we returned to the south, to Ashridge Castle, Lord
Brownlow's; also a modern erection by Wyatt, but gorgeous,
and in a vast park of wonderfully sylvan beauty.

Lord Brownlow,[2] a good deal beyond six feet high, slender,
rather bent, with one lung already lost, and obliged to pass
the winter at Madeira; intellectual, highly educated, with
a complete sense of duty, and of a soft and amiable disposition; living, as it were, on sufferance, but struggling to
perform his great part. A devoted mother [3] watches every
glance and every wind; shares his annual exile, where she
actually has not a single companion. . . .

Adalbert Cust,[4] B.'s only brother, has both his lungs;
is as tall; well formed, and one of the handsomest young
fellows in England. . . .

Lady Marian a woman of commanding ability. Above
the common height, a fine figure, but a countenance of
animation and intelligence marred by a red and rough
complexion. She always reminded me of Lady Blessington
in face, when Lady B.'s beauty had departed; the eyes were
the same—extremely speaking. Lady Marian had also, like
Lady Blessington, very pretty hands, which tell particularly in
a large woman; well-shaped, and small, and plump, and white.

---

[1] Meynell's *Disraeli*, Vol. I., pp. 164-166.
[2] The 2nd Earl, who died in 1867.   [3] Lady Marian Alford.
[4] The 3rd and present Earl.

From Ashridge we went to Woburn Abbey, and paid a visit of several days to Hastings Russell [1] and his wife, Lady Elizabeth, sister of Lady Salisbury. The present Duke of Bedford [2] lives in perfect solitude, and fancies himself unable to encounter the world. . . . He detests the country and country life, especially the provincial magnificence of grand seigneurs. 'Let me live always among chimney-pots,' he says. . . . He must be now nearer sixty than fifty; nor is it probable, he will ever marry. . . . The only person in society he ever sees except Hastings Russell is Poodle Byng, who recommended him to marry and get heirs. 'Why should I ?' said the Duke. ' Could I have a better son than Hastings ?'

Hastings is his cousin, and will be, in all probability, the future Duke; a young man, at least he looks young, though he has been married twenty years; good-looking, graceful, though hardly the middle size, very intelligent, well-informed and well-meaning. The Duke gave him Oakley and £6,000 a year, and expressed his wish, also, that he would receive every year his friends at Woburn, which is kept up exactly as if His Grace resided there. Hastings has the entire management of the property; it is a principality. . . .

Woburn is fine from its greatness and completeness, everything that the chief seat of a princely English family requires. The house, though not beautiful in its exterior, is vast; the great quadrangle, when lit up at night, with its numerous and flashing windows, reminded Bright, he said when on a visit there, of a factory. Then there are stables not unworthy of Chantilly, a riding-house, a gallery of sculpture, the finest private one, perhaps, in the world. A mass of choice and rare collections of all kinds which have been accumulating for centuries: splendid books, rare MSS.; some fine, many interesting pictures. A park of 3,000 acres, with great variety, and undulation and wild scenes you would not expect in Bedfordshire; splendid oaks, unrivalled cedars; ornate gardens and wilderness drives. And all this only forty miles from town !

The Salisburys, our dear friends, and the Caringtons, were there, and Comte Pahlen, who gives the results of a life experienced in society with taste and terseness, and Odo Russell [3] just arrived from Rome (where he is our Minister), *via* Paris. He brought the new toy, Pharaoh's serpent. Quite a miracle ! A most agreeable party, which it could not fail to be with such guests and such a host and hostess for Lady Elizabeth is quite worthy of her husband.

[1] Afterwards the 9th Duke of Bedford.   [2] The 8th Duke
[3] Afterwards 1st Lord Ampthill.

The predominant feature and organic deficiency of the Russell family is shyness. Even Hastings is not free from it, though he struggles to cover it with an air of uneasy gaiety.

The General Election, though it weakened the Conservative forces, made no serious change in the political situation. So long as Palmerston lived to lead the nation, the Palmerstonian spirit would prevail. Before the new Parliament, elected to support him, could meet, he had passed away. Though in his eighty-first year, he was still actively carrying on the heavy duties of Prime Minister when he died on October 18. There had been few signs to prepare the world, or even his intimates, for the end. Disraeli jotted down some stories which Speaker Denison told him, to illustrate the old statesman's vigour at the beginning of his last session.

At the meeting of the House this year, when I went up to salute the Speaker, I asked particularly after his health; he had had a severe attack in the autumn. 'I am all right,' said the Speaker, 'but how is your great man ? How is Lord Derby ? I dined with the other [1] yesterday, according to custom, as you know. I have had the honor, too, of dining at your right hand. Well, yesterday there was a young man—he is coming into the House now in scarlet uniform (Hanbury Tracy, who was to second the Address)—who sate on my left, and I said to him at the end of the dinner: "Now, you are a very young man, and if I were you, when I went home to-night, I would make a memorandum of what happened to-day; something in this fashion: Mem.—Dined with the Prime Minister, who was upwards of eighty years of age. He ate for dinner two plates of turtle soup; he was then served very amply to a plate of cod and oyster sauce; he then took a paté; afterwards he was helped to two very greasy-looking entrées; he then despatched a plate of roast mutton; there then appeared before him the largest, and to my mind the hardest, slice of ham that ever figured on the table of a nobleman, yet it disappeared, just in time to answer the inquiry of his butler, 'Snipe, my Lord, or pheasant ?' He instantly replied 'Pheasant,' thus completing his ninth dish of meat at that meal." I need not tell you what is the state of *his* health.' This is a literal report of an anecdote told by the Speaker with much grave humor.

[1] Palmerston.

A few weeks afterwards—it was after his first levée—he said to me: ' I know you remember a little trait or two I gave you of our friend's health on the Treasury Bench, because I believe you have been pleased to mention what I said on that occasion.　Now I will give you another bulletin. He did me the honor of attending my levée last night—which, by the bye, the leader of the Opposition did not do—and was graciously pleased to inquire after my health.　" That," I said, " was really of very little importance; but yours, my Lord, is a national affair.　I venture to hope you have not entirely disregarded my representations to you on that head, and that you take a little more care of yourself than heretofore."　" Oh ! I do indeed," he replied; " I very often take a cab at night, and if you have both windows open it is almost as good as walking home."　Almost as good !' exclaimed the valetudinarian Speaker with a rueful expression.　' A thorough draught and a north-east wind !　And in a hack cab !　What a combination for health !'

Disraeli sincerely regretted his genial opponent's death. As Mrs. Disraeli wrote on October 22 to Lady Cowper: ' Mr. Disraeli had a great regard for Lord Palmerston, and, although circumstances prevented them from acting politically together, there had subsisted between them, for twenty years, a feeling of mutual confidence, which often removed difficulties.'　When Parliament met in February, Disraeli found more than one occasion of expressing his appreciation.　He spoke of the loss to the authority of the House of Commons by the disappearance ' of so much sagacity, of so much experience, and, I may say, of so much fame '; of the happy disposition of the man, his good temper and good sense; of his geniality and his moderating wisdom.　' He combined in the highest degree two qualities which we seldom find united—energy and experience. . . .　I trust that the time may never come when the love of fame shall cease to be the sovereign passion of our public men.[1] But I still think that statesman is peculiarly to be envied who, when he leaves us, leaves not merely the

---

[1] ' We come here for fame,' Disraeli said once at Westminster to Bright, who records the remark in terms which suggest that, in spite of his admiration for Milton, he had scanty tolerance for ' that last infirmity of noble mind.'

memory of great achievements, but also the tender tradition of personal affection and social charm.'

With Palmerston's death the old era passed away. That Russell, who became Prime Minister, and Gladstone, who was to lead the House of Commons, would immediately revive Reform was certain. Disraeli wrote to Lonsdale on October 20: 'If Johnny is the man, there will be a Reform Bill—very distasteful to the country. The truce of parties is over. I foresee tempestuous times, and great vicissitudes in public life.' Stanley wrote to Disraeli on October 23: 'The Reform crisis cannot now be delayed. There are at least fifty Conservatives on the Whig side; the question is, Can we utilise them, and how ?' Stanley was for strengthening the hands of the moderate as opposed to the thoroughgoing Reformers, but Disraeli preferred to maintain his anti-movement attitude of the spring. He talked in this sense to the Whig company whom he met at Wrest in November. He said he thought Russell entirely mistaken in believing a Reform Bill to be necessary for his own position or required by the country. Only the extreme Radicals, some ninety votes, desired it, and they would be counterbalanced by the whole Conservative party, who would resist any demand for Reform.

In fact, Disraeli believed Reform to be still occupying the same position as during the last fifteen or twenty years; to be merely, or mainly, a game to be played on the Parliamentary stage, useful for the purpose of gaining or retaining office, but not seriously meant either by Whigs or by Tories as a party, however earnest some individual politicians might be in its pursuit. He was probably, for the moment, right. The verdict of the country at the elections had been, unquestionably, in a broad sense, conservative. Though the Reformers had had some successes, particularly in the London boroughs, where John Stuart Mill, the philosopher and economist, and Thomas Hughes, the social reformer, had won seats, yet the great bulk of members had been returned to support either Palmerston, whose indifference to Reform almost amounted to active hostility, or the Conservative leaders, who had announced a waiting game. The existing electorate was therefore obviously, on the whole, apathetic on the question; and Bright's crusade had down to the General Election failed to evoke any very clear manifestations on the part of the unenfranchised working men.

Russell tried, as Palmerston had tried in 1855, and with the same lack of success, to persuade Stanley to join his Ministry. Some thought that Stanley himself might be able to form a Government on Liberal-Conservative lines; but Disraeli poured scorn on the idea.

To Ralph A. Earle.

HUGHENDEN, *Nov.* 6, 1865.—Who are the moderate men of all parties who are to form this new Government ? Opposite to us there is, certainly, Mr. Lowe. He could not join us alone, or, if he did, he would be fruitless.

As for the movement in *The Times*, the same organ, and probably the same pen, agitated as vigorously in favor of our Reform Bill, yet all the Whigs voted against us, and Mr. Lowe, then a six-pounder, among them.

So long as the Whig party hold together, nothing can be done.

The name of Stanley would at first produce some excitement, even an appearance of enthusiasm. The great towns would no longer growl; the great employers of labor would smile; Bass would pay us public compliments, and Peto embrace us in the lobby. But when the new Government were formed, if such a thing were possible, ' the great Liberal party ' would, as usual, reconstruct in Opposition, and Stanley after a twelvemonth would be kicked out, like his father, though with a little more respect, and Gladstone installed as first Minister, with a stronger bench of colleagues, and some spoil among the Liberal outsiders, who are now bawling for Stanley.

So long as the Whigs are united, the views you describe are a fairy tale.

Derby, looking ahead, and noting the appointment of Chichester Fortescue to be Chief Secretary for Ireland, scented an attack on the Irish Church. He hoped

Disraeli would agree that with this the Conservatives
must not tamper, and that no member of the English
branch would look on the Irish as 'heavy top-hamper,
which it is wise to throw overboard to lighten the ship.'
Disraeli did not much relish the prospect of fighting on
behalf of the Irish Church, but comforted himself with
the hope of a speedy break-up of the Ministry.

To Lord Derby.

Private. GROSVENOR GATE, *Nov.* 24, 1865.—. . . If the
Government bring forward any specific measure respecting
the Irish Church, it is possible that it may be effectually
resisted, because it would not be difficult to pick holes in it,
and of various kinds and sizes; but I do not think that any
general resolution respecting the Irish Church could be
successfully withstood in the present Parliament. It is a
very unpopular cause, even with many of our best men.

So far as I can learn, the difficulties of the existing Cabinet
are so serious that it would at once break up, if there were
a successor, but there is none—at least, this is the opinion
of Lord Taunton and that class of men. I think, however,
myself, that it will not last very long, and for two reasons:

Firstly, because the Prime Minister and the Foreign
Secretary are both in the House of Lords, which I hold to be
fatal to any Cabinet under any circumstances, and which
is really the proximate cause of the present malaise.

Secondly, because all the younger portion of the Liberal
party, including those in the Ministry, think that, by getting
rid of Lord Russell, they will obtain more, and higher, place
under one whom they deem immediately, or at a short
interval, must be his successor, viz., the present leader of
the House of Commons.

The alternative they contemplate is, that you will decline to
take the reins, or that, if you do, with the ancient régime,
you must speedily fail. I think they would prefer the latter
course, because they could make better terms and arrange
and consolidate their resources better in Opposition. In
either case Gladstone will declare that he never will take the
second post again.

With these views, I cannot refrain from again calling your
attention to the suggestions I made respecting the party and
its prospects at the end of the summer. Some new combination must be formed, or considerable changes will occur
both in Church and State, which neither the necessities of
the country require, nor its feelings really sanction.

The conviction that the Government would be short-lived, and would founder on Reform, and that therefore it was imperative to begin at once to make preparations for its successor, grew upon Disraeli as the session approached.

To Lord Stanley.

GROSVENOR GATE, *Jan.* 23, 1866.—. . . I have been here some days, and, pretty well, know everything. The whole affair is utterly rotten; quite ruined; the blow will be struck from the other side. The appointment of Goschen [1] precipitated the revolution. It was the first nail in their coffin, according to Milner Gibson, but the sound of the undertaker in the house has been heard ever since. But what then ? The present plan, I hear, is to meet the second reading of the Reform Bill adversely. In that case, I should think, it would be wise to meet it by a resolution; but at present I shall leave them to themselves. The other side will do the business.

That knave, Sir Fitzroy [Kelly], is recommencing his mischievous agitation about the malt tax. He has arranged for a monster meeting in London, and then has the impudence to ask for my counsel. I have given him such a duster in reply that he has gone, I believe for his health, to Torquay. I am taking measures to prevent our men unnecessarily going to his meeting, which many did last year, thinking they were aiding us. Far from sanctioning him, I have told him I shall oppose him actively and personally. He may do immense mischief. . . .

Reform was not the only difficulty the Ministry had to face. A Fenian conspiracy of a serious and wide-spread character had been discovered in Ireland; while in England and Scotland the rinderpest had broken out, and was carrying off thousands of valuable cattle every week. Moreover, public opinion in Great Britain was feverishly excited over the conduct of Governor Eyre, who had suppressed in the autumn, with great prompti-tude and equal severity, a negro rising in Jamaica.

[1] G. J. Goschen, then regarded as a Radical, afterwards the distinguished Liberal Unionist statesman, had just been admitted to the Cabinet as Chancellor of the Duchy of Lancaster, in place of Clarendon, who had succeeded Russell as Foreign Secretary. Goschen was only thirty-four, and had sat in Parliament for the City of London less than three years.

Ministers had instituted an inquiry and suspended the Governor. Some members of the Tory party, notably Manners, urged that the Governor's defence should be taken up as a party question; but other leading Tories, such as Northcote and Carnarvon, strongly objected; and Disraeli wisely left the question alone and declined to embarrass the Government. He supported them also when they proposed to suspend the Habeas Corpus Act in Ireland, in order to deal with Fenianism. But, in regard to the cattle disease, he helped to defeat them on an amendment which Ward Hunt, on behalf of the agricultural community, proposed in order to make their Bill more stringent; and he spoke in favour of compensation to owners whose cattle were slaughtered for the public good. Derby thought 'affairs most critical,' and the Government 'at the last extremity,' in the first fortnight of the session.

Considerable as were the other difficulties before Ministers, Reform still remained the most serious of all. The opposition among both Whigs and Liberals, which had taken definite shape in 1865, manifested itself at once in both Houses, on the mere mention of the topic in the Queen's Speech. Lord Grey, the representative of a great Whig family and the son of the Minister who carried the first Reform Act, reproached Russell in the Lords with his desertion of finality; and Lowe, the leader of the anti-Reform Liberals in the Commons, told Adderley that, if the Conservatives would stand firm in opposing the Ministerial proposals, he would undertake to bring sufficient Liberals into the same lobby to insure a majority of fifty against 'any Bill that lowers the borough franchise by one sixpence.'

Here were, obviously, the elements of that extended basis, that new combination, for which Disraeli had vainly urged Derby to arrange. He was ready himself, as he told Northcote as well as Derby, to resign the lead and go below the gangway, in order to promote a durable Administration. But, in spite of some discrepancy in the

language which he used on the subject, he does not appear
to have regarded with much favour the plan that was
most persistently put forward, that Stanley should head
a coalition Government of Conservatives and moderate
Whigs. It is true that he had proposed an arrangement of
the kind himself when the Government of 1858-59 was
in its death agony; and he seems again to have thrown
out the idea in conversation with Stanley in the autumn
of 1865, much to Stanley's horror. But the shrinking
from risk and responsibility which Stanley had so
markedly shown had probably by this time convinced
Disraeli that his friend and pupil, with all his great
qualities, had not the making of a leader. This is the
natural deduction from Disraeli's letter, in November,
to Earle, and from his comment to Northcote, who
reported a wild scheme by which Gladstone, with Stanley
as his right-hand man, was to form a Government mainly
Conservative: 'Lady —— wants Stanley to take a
leading place. It won't do. W. E. G. and S. sound
very well. One is a man of transcendent ability; the
other, though not of transcendent ability, has considerable
power. But neither of them can deal with men. S. is
a mere child in such matters.' None of the other possibilities which were canvassed among the party—the
leadership of Lord Cranborne,[1] or of General Peel, or
of a Whig like the Duke of Somerset or the Duke of
Devonshire—ever had much promise in them. One of
the most curious of the developments of this uneasy
period was the temporary conversion of Cranborne and
Carnarvon to the view that it was Derby who was the
difficulty and who must go. Meanwhile Disraeli kept
his own counsel, showing great reserve in Parliament,
where, once again, he was silent on the Address, but
in private cultivating friendly relations with Lowe, and
even his followers, 'empty fellows' though he thought
them, and promoting Derby's overtures to Whig leaders

---

[1] Lord Robert Cecil had become Lord Cranborne in 1865, on the death
of his elder brother.

such as Lords Westminster and Lansdowne. On one point he was quite emphatic. He had the deepest contempt for the view that it might not be a bad plan to let the Government pass a moderate Reform Bill and so get rid of the question; 'such a course would seat the Whigs for a lifetime.'

It was a comparatively moderate Bill which Gladstone introduced on March 12. It reduced the county franchise to £14—not so low as the £10 of Derby's and Disraeli's own Bill; and the borough franchise to £7, not so low as the £6 which Disraeli had been ready to accept after the General Election of 1859. It also took the savings bank franchise and the lodger franchise of the Derby-Disraeli proposals. But it abolished the rate-paying clauses in boroughs, and diluted the county constituency by giving copyholders and leaseholders in boroughs the county franchise; moreover, it was limited to franchise alone, neither redistribution nor the delimitation of boundaries being dealt with in any way. The Bill had a very unfavourable reception; 'no enthusiasm for it, and sound reason against,' was Gathorne Hardy's entry in his diary. The high Tories, such as Cranborne and Whiteside, denounced it as a democratic measure; but their language was not so forcible as that of Horsman and Lowe. Horsman said the Bill was based on the old stale device of government by numbers; Lowe, that it was of a most dangerous and revolutionary character, leading inevitably to pure democracy. Bright gave it his hearty support, though it did not go nearly so far as he wished. He likened the dissentient Liberals to the discontented who gathered in the Cave of Adullam; and political vocabulary was thereby permanently enriched; 'Cave' and 'Adullamites' becoming rapidly household terms. Disraeli watched the temper of the House narrowly, but did not speak; and the Bill was introduced without a division.

Four days later the Conservative party met to consider their policy, and it fell to Disraeli, in the absence of

Derby from gout, to give them a lead. Northcote tells
us what passed:

Dis. made a capital speech, reciting the history of the
Reform Bills since 1852; throwing all the blame of the present
agitation upon W. E. G.; objecting principally to the county
franchise proposed in this Bill—especially the admission of
copyholders and leaseholders in boroughs to vote for the
counties—and still more to the fragmentary character of
the measure. He said it was obviously our duty unanimously
to oppose the Bill on the second reading, but that we must
leave it to our leaders to decide in what form the opposition
had better be made, having reference especially to the feelings and dispositions of our friends on the other side. The
meeting was most cordial and unanimous.[1]

It was the fragmentary character of the measure which
was seized upon as the point of attack; and notice of an
amendment declining to proceed with the second reading
till the redistribution scheme was before Parliament
was given by a leading Whig dissentient, Lord Grosvenor,
afterwards first Duke of Westminster, distinguished
alike as a philanthropist and as a sportsman. That
this was an eminently reasonable proposal is shown
by the fact that the course it recommended of coupling
franchise and redistribution was pursued, in substance,
in all the three great measures of Reform which passed
through Parliament, in 1832, in 1867, and in 1884, though
in the last instance Gladstone fought desperately till the
eleventh hour against this procedure. The heat which
was engendered in the debates in 1866, and the strenuous-
ness with which the Bill was opposed, were largely due
to the arguments and attitude of its proposer, Gladstone,
which were felt to be such as to justify universal suffrage
and the intimidation of Parliament by popular clamour.
In the House he defended the right of the seven-pounders
to the suffrage on the ground that they were 'our
fellow-Christians, our own flesh and blood'; but so, of
course, were tramps and paupers and lunatics. In the
Easter vacation, before the second reading debate, he

[1] Lang's *Northcote*, p. 154. Northcote's diary for the session of 1866
throws great light on this period.

went down into Lancashire, and there held up to reprobation Lords Grosvenor and Stanley—who were to propose
and second the amendment, and who were the heirs
of great houses honoured in that part of the country—
as aristocrats who were combining to defeat an act of
justice to the general community. He proceeded to
stake the existence of the Government on the measure;
they had passed the Rubicon, broken the bridge, and
burnt the boats behind them. No wonder that Disraeli
should have remarked about this time to Northcote
that 'it was a great advantage to a leader of the House
of Commons that he should be, not unable, but unwilling to speak.'

The second reading debate began on April 12, and
lasted more than a Parliamentary fortnight. It was a
contest of giants. Stanley, Lytton, Mill, Cairns, Bright,
and Cranborne, all made fine speeches, and Disraeli
summed up the case for the Opposition on the last
night.[1] But by common consent the protagonists were
Lowe and Gladstone. Throughout this session the
struggle tended to become a duel between these two,
Lowe, for one short spell in his career, reaching the
political level of the greatest Parliamentarians. Disraeli
was well content to have it so. He was in constant
communication with Lowe and the Whig dissidents,
mainly through Lord Elcho, and pulled the wires in the
background. He could not have taken, either with
sincerity or with consistency, the whole-hearted anti-
democratic attitude of Lowe. He spoke instead with
caution and circumspection. He pointed out that
Russell and Derby had both in the past battled against
piecemeal Reform; yet here was Russell, under the
influence of Gladstone's theory of the rights of man,
introducing just such a piecemeal Reform himself. He
showed in detail the injustice done to the counties by
the arrangements of the Bill, if passed either without
redistribution or with a redistribution that was un-

[1] April 27.

fairly adjusted. Once more he maintained that the choicest members of the working classes should form a part, and no unimportant part, of the estate of the Commons, but that there should not be an undistinguishing reduction of the franchise. You should represent opinion, not numbers; votes should be weighed, not counted. This was a Bill conceived in the spirit of the American rather than the British Constitution. Gathorne Hardy thought the speech 'too long and not lively'; Gladstone, who followed and wound up the debate, was, in his opinion, 'very fine in parts, but . . . absolutely democratic in argument.' Disraeli had chaffed his rival about a Tory speech made at the Oxford Union in 1831. Gladstone, after administering a solemn rebuke, responded in a classical passage about his generous reception by the Liberals when he came among them as the shipwrecked Æneas came to Dido, *ejectum littore, egentem.* The Bill might fail, he said, but

Exoriare aliquis nostris ex ossibus ultor.

'You cannot fight against the future; time is on our side.' The great social forces were marshalled on behalf of Reform; victory was certain and not far distant.

The prophecy was fulfilled; but, owing in large measure to the faulty temper and mismanagement of the prophet, the victory was achieved by other hands. The division showed that both the Ministry and the Bill were in great peril. The second reading was only carried by a majority of 5. Its opponents mustered 313 against the 318 of its supporters. About 30 Liberals voted against the Government.

After some natural hesitation, the Ministry decided to struggle on and produce their redistribution proposals. Of these the most striking feature was a large extension of the system of grouping two or three small boroughs into one constituency. In his speech on the second reading,[1] Disraeli put in a plea for the small boroughs

[1] May 14.

as a means of representation for varied interests, such
as those of the learned professions, and of the Colonial
and Indian Empires—a plea which was felt to be weighty
and which recalled a somewhat similar line of argument
used by Gladstone in 1859. In conclusion, he skilfully
diagnosed the unsatisfactory condition into which the
Government and House had drifted, and showed a more
excellent way.

I am told, as I walk down to the House of Commons,
every day by the man in the street; as I walk down Parliament
Street—'Ibam forte viâ sacrâ'—somebody tells me, 'I
hope you are going to settle the question.' Sir, ignorance
never settles a question. Questions must be settled by
knowledge, and it is not the vexation of an opposition,
from whichever side of the House it may come, that prevents
this Bill from advancing. It is that we none of us see our
way. I say it with a frankness that I trust will be pardoned,
I do not believe the question of Parliamentary Reform is
thoroughly understood by the country, is thoroughly understood by this House; and although I dare only utter it in a
whisper, I do not believe that it is thoroughly understood by
Her Majesty's Government. I often remember with pleasure
a passage in Plato, where the great sage descants upon what
he calls ' double ignorance '—that is, when a man is ignorant
that he is ignorant. But, sir, there is another kind of
ignorance that is fatal. There is in the first place an ignorance
of principles, and in the second place an ignorance of facts.
And that is our position in dealing with this important
question. There is not a majority in this House that can
decide upon the principles upon which we ought to legislate
in regard to this matter; there is not a man in this House
who has at command any reliable facts upon which he can
decide those principles. . . . The country, the House of
Commons, the Ministry, are—although · it may seem an
idiomatic, it is a classical phrase, as it was used by Dean
Swift—' in a scrape.' . . . We must help the Government.
We must forget the last two months. The right honourable
gentleman must recross the Rubicon; we must rebuild his
bridges and supply him with vessels.

Disraeli advised Gladstone to withdraw his present
Bills, to obtain carefully prepared statistics about county
and borough franchise and about boundaries, and then
submit to Parliament in the next session a measure

which might command the sympathies of the country
and the sanction of Parliament. Disraeli's sketch of
the position was undoubtedly accurate, and his advice
thoroughly in harmony with the general feeling of the
House. But the Government determined to go forward;
and their foes of both parties drew closer together in
their resolve that these Bills, at any rate, which were
pressed upon them, as they thought, so unnecessarily
and so high-handedly, should by no means become law.
Disraeli's was largely the guiding hand, and the Whitsuntide recess was utilized to marshal the forces for a serious
fight on the motion to go into Committee. Bouverie,
a Whig of considerable standing, had given notice of an
instruction to refer both Bills to the same Committee.
Captain Hayter,[1] a young Liberal, son of a Liberal Whip,
had a motion on the paper objecting to the system of
grouping adopted. To these, Knightley, on behalf of the
Conservatives, added an instruction to the Committee
to make provision against bribery in elections.

From Lord Elcho.

22, St. James's Place, S.W., *May* 15, 1866.—Let me
congratulate you on your most excellent and convincing speech
—quite unanswerable. It told immensely on both sides of
the House, was much cheered by Liberals, and cannot fail
to make converts to common-sense and statesmanlike views
of a great question. Grosvenor came here last night full
of your speech, and I think, when the time comes, we shall
find him right in action as he is in opinion. Perhaps it is
as well that the debate fell as it did.[2] Your speech thus
goes forth unanswered, or, rather, undiluted by other speeches
on the same side, for answered it cannot be. . . .

To Ralph A. Earle.

Grosvenor Gate, *May* 19, 1866.—Write immediately to
Lord Grosvenor, who lives, I think, at 28, Prince's Gate,

---

[1] Afterwards Sir Arthur, and ultimately Lord Haversham.
[2] Disraeli did not divide against the second reading of the Redistribution
Bill, knowing that he would not secure on that issue a full support of the
Adullamites. Derby was restive under these sound, but not showy tactics,
and wrote gloomily to the Whip about a 'fiasco.'

and place yourself at his disposal. He expects this, and Lord Elcho requests that you will do it.

You will continue to consult with Lord Grosvenor as to the best means to adopt in the present exigency. . . .

HUGHENDEN, *May* 22, 1866.—Yours just received very satisfactory—as it shows that Grosvenor has not got over his original repugnance to the lowering of the franchise, and that, when a final effort is to be made, the whole of the Adullamites may be counted on.

At present I am clearly of opinion that the young H[ayter] must be utilised; and it may do the business if sanctioned by G[rosvenor].

He must give notice of his resolution on Friday, and Lord D. must pledge the party to support it on Monday. If you can discreetly modify the language, well and good. It will, however, be looked upon as his father's, and so gain confidence.

As to the seconder, that is more serious. . . . It should be a popular man; no harm if from our side, though that is not indispensable. Would Anson do it ? . . .

CARLTON CLUB [? *May* 27].—I shan't be able to see you again to-day. Lord D. says that W. Martin comes on before Knightley and Sandford, and also that if it were the reverse, and either of their motions were negatived, we might altogether be shut out, and find ourselves in the Committee in a jiffy.

This is a result which he, most of all, fears. Then he says that, if the veto be exercised (of which, by the bye, he never heard before), Hayter's amendment could not be moved at all, because it does not refer to the Franchise Bill.

This is serious. What we most fear is a general collapse, and Committee, which would be fatal. If Hayter can be brought on *à propos* to Bouverie's resolution, we must contrive a long debate.

The combined Opposition failed to prevent the Bills from going into Committee; but they achieved further successes which materially damaged the Government. Bouverie's instruction to take the two Bills together was accepted without debate; on Knightley's motion about bribery, Ministers were defeated by 10; Hayter's resolution about grouping was withdrawn after an announcement by Gladstone that the Government did not regard the principle as a vital one. 'We have got them, depend upon it, in a fix,' wrote Elcho to Disraeli on June 2, 'out of which there is no escape with both honour and place.

One or other must be abandoned.' He added, after a reference to the wavering and trimming of some of the Adullamites: ' I cannot resist again expressing the real pleasure it has been, in the midst of so much wavering, crookedness, and cowardice, to find myself acting with a man of your frankness, straightforwardness, and resolution. Forgive my saying this, for I really feel it.'

On getting into Committee the onslaught of the Opposition was for the moment checked. A motion by Stanley to postpone the franchise to the redistribution clauses was defeated by 17, and one by Walpole, to fix the county franchise at £20 instead of £14, by 16. Disraeli wrote to his wife on June 8: ' Our troops are a little dispirited after the two battles of yesterday: but I think of you, which always sustains me, and I know we shall find many sources of happiness without politics, if it comes to that.'

But at this stage the combined forces of Adullamites and Conservatives advanced a serious principle on which they could firmly and reasonably take their stand. The occupation franchises in boroughs and counties proposed by the Government were based on rental; it was maintained against them that rating was a much more satisfactory basis, as it would both associate the vote with the performance of civic duty, and also greatly simplify the process of registration. From the point of view of those who desired to lower the franchise as little as possible, the rating basis had the additional advantage of admitting fewer voters, as a house was rated at from four-fifths to nine-tenths of its rental value. Ward Hunt, a Tory, moved an amendment to this effect in regard to the county franchise, and was only beaten by 7—280 to 273. A Whig, Lord Dunkellin, put on the paper a similar motion affecting the borough franchise. On June 12 Disraeli wrote hopefully to his wife: ' Affairs look here pretty well. Lord Clanricarde has quite joined the Opposition, and his son, Lord Dunkellin, has given notice of a motion against the

Government. Grosvenor seems also active, so far as talking and writing to men.'

Dunkellin's motion proved fatal. At the close of a short if warm debate, in which Disraeli took no part, Gladstone protested that the acceptance of the amendment was incompatible with the progress of the Bill. It was nevertheless carried on June 18 against the Government by 11 votes, in a House only slightly less full than that in which Grosvenor's amendment was rejected. The numbers were 315 against 304. The Opposition hailed vociferously a result which, after the repeated blows of the last couple of months, must, they felt, and felt rightly, involve the downfall of the Government. The reluctance of the Queen to change her Ministers while war was impending between Austria and Prussia postponed the final decision for a week; but then the logic of the situation prevailed, and Disraeli's opportunity had come once more. What could he do with it ? The attempt of Russell and Gladstone to rush a Palmerstonian Parliament into Reform had failed disastrously. But they had accomplished a great deal, aided all unwittingly by their foes. By the magnificent speeches and well-sustained debates of the session, and by the uncertainty of the issue throughout several months, Liberals and Conservatives had joined in fixing the attention of the nation upon a subject which it had been wont to put aside, and they had thus given Reform an enormous advertisement. Would it be possible, after all that had happened, even for a Palmerstonian Parliament to trifle with the question any longer ?

CHAPTER XIII.

THE REFORM MINISTRY.

1866–1867.

In the division on Lord Dunkellin's amendment, Taylor, the Conservative Whip, calculated that forty-two Liberals voted with the Opposition. Supposing the Russell Government to resign, the strength and durability of a new Administration must depend to a great extent on the willingness of these seceders to co-operate in forming it. The week that elapsed between the adverse vote and the resignation was largely occupied by meetings of the Adullamite leaders at Elcho's house to decide the terms on which they would join the Conservatives in Government. With characteristic Whig self-sufficiency, they suggested an arrangement which should displace the existing Conservative leaders in both Houses, and give the premiership to a Whig; although the proportion of Adullamites to Conservatives in the House of Commons was as 1 to 7. Ready as Disraeli might be to efface himself, neither he nor Derby could possibly accept such preposterous subordination for their party.

From Lord Derby.

ST. JAMES'S SQUARE, 7.20 *p.m.* [? *June* 22 *or* 23].—Grosvenor writes to Wilton:
'After a long conference the opinion expressed was that we could not guarantee Lord Derby the support (in its strict sense) of the Cave; that a Government under a Whig in the House of Lords, such as Lord Clarendon, would be most desirable on all accounts, with Stanley leader in the House of Commons; that, if such an arrangement could be effected

173

there would be every reason for believing that a very strong Government could be formed under those auspices. Present at the meeting: Lord Lansdowne, Lowe, Elcho, Horsman, Gregory, G. Heathcote, A. Anson.'

So much for Adullamite co-operation !

To Lord Derby.

GROSVENOR GATE, *June* 23, 1866.—The terms intimated by Lord. Grosvenor, in his letter to Lord Wilton, are not consistent with the honor of the Conservative party, and are framed in ignorance, and misconception, of its elements and character.

I am, and, as you know, ever since the last General Election have been, prepared to withdraw from the leadership of that party in the House of Commons, with the view, and the hope, of seeing it reconstructed on a broader personal basis; but I have only been ready so to act on two conditions:

Firstly, that, whether in or out of office, you should be the chief; and, secondly, that, in the event of your declining the post, you should be succeeded by Lord Stanley.

GROSVENOR GATE, *June* 25, 1866.—The amiable and spirited Elcho [1] has played his unconscious part in a long-matured intrigue.

The question is not Adullamite; it is national. You *must* take the Government; the honor of your house and the necessity of the country alike require it.

What is counted on, and intended (not by the Court), is that you should refuse; that a member of the late Government shall then be sent for, and then that an application should be made to a section of your party to join the Administration; which application will be successful, for all will be broken up.

There is only one course with the Queen: to kiss hands.

And the effect will be this: in four-and-twenty hours, all, Lansdowne, Granville (if you want him), Clanricarde, who thought yesterday you would not have an 'application,' but who will think very differently to-morrow, will be at your feet.

Nothing can prevent your winning, if you grasp the helm. . . .

Derby was entirely of Disraeli's opinion; and the other leading men of the party, with hardly an exception, agreed. The resignation of the Russell Ministry was

---

[1] Elcho had told Derby, in conversation, that ' the only mode of obtaining numerical strength from the moderate Liberals would be a junction with some of their present officials.'

announced on Tuesday, June 26. The Queen's summons reached Derby on the following morning; and after consulting Disraeli he called together next day [1] twenty-two of his political friends, who, in Northcote's words, ' were unanimously of opinion that he ought to attempt the formation of an Administration on an enlarged basis, and almost unanimous that, if he failed in that attempt, he should undertake the Government with his own friends alone. Lord Bath alone expressed himself decidedly against the latter course.' Disraeli had written to Earle on the previous day: ' The formation of Lord Derby's Government is *certain ;* but there is a good chance of its being on a broad basis, with elements that will command general approbation and support.' He spoke in the same optimistic sense at the meeting, adding, amidst general cheering, that they must be prepared to make sacrifices for a junction; he himself was prepared to make the greatest sacrifices.

In spite of Disraeli's optimism and the obvious necessities of the situation, Derby found it impossible to secure a Government on a broad basis. There was, perhaps, no great reason for surprise that the two moderate Whigs, Lord Clarendon and the Duke of Somerset, to whom overtures were made, should have declined, in spite of their imperfect sympathy with the Reform policy for which they were responsible. But the behaviour of the Adullamites was less explicable and less defensible. As Derby put it in conversation with Lansdowne: ' I looked with more confidence to those seceders from the Government on the Reform Bill, in consequence of whose secession the Government were defeated and resigned. I thought that, as they had mainly caused the position in which I found myself, I might fairly look to them for assistance.' He offered three seats in the Cabinet, privately intimating that Lansdowne, Grosvenor, and Gregory,[2] were those on whom he chiefly

---

[1] Thursday, June 28.
[2] M.P. for Co. Galway; afterwards Governor of Ceylon.

counted. But Lowe, the most powerful Parliamentarian of the party, was strongly opposed to taking office; and eventually, as they could not obtain their Whig Premier, all the leaders declined, though promising an independent support—Horsman, indeed, boggled even at that promise. Derby had to console himself with the reflection, which he had already uttered in conversation with General Grey, that there was not a man among them, except Lowe, who was of the least value as regarded talent.

There was one other quarter in which, at Disraeli's instance, help was sought; but in vain, as Shaftesbury, the great philanthropist, would not quit his social labours for the restraints of office.[1]

To Lord Derby.

Private. GROSVENOR GATE, *June* 27, 1866.—What do you think of utilising Lord Shaftesbury? The suggestion reaches me from Lord Beauchamp—though a keen partisan, a very high Churchman. Lord Shaftesbury would be a representative of Palmerstonian sympathies and influences; powerful with the religious middle class, etc., etc.

He dined with Lord Lansdowne. The latter, whom you may yet gain in a personal interview, could not join you alone;[2] Lord Shaftesbury would remedy that.

It is an adhesion that, I think, would bring strength at elections.

Derby had to fall back on the resources of his own party, but these, largely owing to Disraeli's skilful leadership, were now considerable both in extent and in ability. In the House of Commons alone, the long period of opposition to Palmerston had developed three new men of exceptional capacity, Northcote, Gathorne Hardy, and Cranborne, while Cairns had more than justi-

---

[1] Though Lord Shaftesbury did not accept office, he exerted himself at first to help Ministers. He writes in his diary, August 9, 1866: 'Have laboured much to put the Government and Derby right with the working classes. . . . Have spoken to Disraeli, whom I found, as I always found him in House of Commons, decided and true to the cause.'

[2] The 4th Marquis of Lansdowne, the son of one distinguished statesman and the father of another, died suddenly on July 5 at the age of fifty, before the new Ministry was completely formed.

fied his early promise. Disraeli had pondered deeply over the proper distribution of men and offices; and there were three arrangements which he was especially anxious to effect. The first, which had been in his mind ever since 1859, was to substitute Stanley for Malmesbury as Foreign Secretary. Malmesbury facilitated this change by a spontaneous withdrawal of his claims; but neither the Queen nor Derby quite approved of Stanley for the post. 'May Lord Stanley not be inclined to go too far in the line of non-interference?' was the Queen's warning. Derby replied that he did not think the office the most suitable for Stanley, but Stanley the best choice available for the office. Stanley's success in the 1866 Ministry justified Disraeli's selection; but the Queen's warning of that year must have often come back to his mind between 1876 and 1878. The second arrangement, in which for the time Disraeli failed, was the strengthening of the Government in the House of Lords by the appointment of a Lord Chancellor more serviceable than Chelmsford in council and debate. The failure was apparently mainly due to the difficulty of finding a suitable substitute, as it was desired to keep Cairns in the Commons; but Derby, in reluctantly reappointing Chelmsford, warned him that he might ask him before long to give way to another.

The third arrangement which Disraeli had specially at heart was to secure the assistance in the Cabinet of his faithful henchman, Northcote. 'I began to say,' writes Northcote in his diary, narrating a conversation with Disraeli on June 29, 'that he might naturally expect me to resume my old place of Financial Secretary, when he stopped me and said that he had told Lord D. that under any circumstances, and whether there were a fusion or not, he must make a point of my having a seat in the Cabinet . . . ; that he must make my admission into the Cabinet a condition of his own taking office, so that the matter was quite settled.' There is reason to believe that Disraeli forwarded also the advancement

of Hardy and Cranborne. He was always eager to enlist
talent in Government service; and, though his close
relations with Hardy only began in office, he had marked
his success in the House, and rejoiced in his overthrow
of Gladstone at Oxford. As for Cranborne, Disraeli
was the last man to think permanently worse of a young
politician who attacked his leader, even when that leader
was himself, provided the attack were brilliantly carried
out. The two men had been in amicable relations,
as leader and follower, at least since 1864; and Disraeli
was not likely to forget that Cranborne, whose independent mind and pungent speech had made him a
power in Parliament, was the son, and now the heir,
of an old friend and colleague. A further appointment
in which we may trace his hand was that of another
old friend and excellent man of business, Lord Chandos,
who had succeeded in 1861 to the dukedom of Buckingham, to the Presidency of the Council; though it is
probable that the introduction into the Cabinet of Lord
Carnarvon, a man of many gifts and much attraction,
but perhaps of too delicate a fibre for the rough work
of politics, was due rather to Derby.

The one serious difficulty in Derby's path proved to be
the Irish administration, which, with Fenianism rife,
was, as he told the Queen, of paramount importance.
There was, indeed, an excellent and experienced Chief
Secretary to his hand in Lord Naas, soon to become
Lord Mayo, of whom Disraeli wrote at this period:
'I have a high opinion of Naas. I think him eminent
for judgment—a quality rare, in any degree, in an
Irishman; and eminent judgment, with a complete
knowledge of Ireland, is a choice combination for a
Chief Secretary.' But the former Conservative Lord
Lieutenant, Lord Eglinton, was dead, and a successor
was very hard to find. After one or two other un-
successful applications, Disraeli tried in vain to persuade
the modest Manners to take the post. Eventually, after
Derby had almost abandoned his task in despair, what

proved to be an admirable selection was made in the person of Lord Abercorn, a much respected landowner in the North of Ireland. The most important appointment outside the Cabinet was that of Cairns to be Attorney-General, a judicial post being found for Fitzroy Kelly. Lytton received that peerage which Derby would not recommend in 1858-59; and a peerage was also bestowed on Jolliffe, the Whip with whom Disraeli's relations had been particularly close.

Lord Derby's third Cabinet was thus composed:

First Lord of the Treasury ..	EARL OF DERBY.
Lord Chancellor	LORD CHELMSFORD.
Lord President	DUKE OF BUCKINGHAM.
Lord Privy Seal	EARL OF MALMESBURY.
Home Secretary	S. H. WALPOLE.
Foreign Secretary	LORD STANLEY.
Colonial Secretary	EARL OF CARNARVON.
War Secretary	GENERAL PEEL.
Indian Secretary ..	VISCOUNT CRANBORNE.
Chancellor of the Exchequer ..	B. DISRAELI.
First Lord of the Admiralty ..	SIR JOHN PAKINGTON.
President of the Board of Trade	SIR STAFFORD NORTHCOTE.
President of the Poor Law Board	GATHORNE HARDY.
First Commissioner of Works ..	LORD JOHN MANNERS.
Chief Secretary for Ireland ..	LORD NAAS.[1]

It was a strong combination with very few weak spots—a proof, in itself alone, of the success with which Disraeli had built up the Conservative party out of the ruins of the late forties, and had attracted to the service of the cause a goodly proportion of the intellect of the country. 'Not a single Scotchman or Irishman among us,' was Northcote's comment after its first meeting;[2] but that defect was speedily remedied by the admission of Naas.

There was one minor appointment which was of more importance to Disraeli, with his temperament and

[1] The Chief Secretary was not taken into the Cabinet until a few weeks after its formation.

[2] Northcote also tells us of an amusing misadventure which befell Disraeli when Ministers went down to Windsor to be sworn in ; how, 'thinking there was a seat at the end of the saloon carriage, he sat down there, and found himself unexpectedly on the floor' (Lang p. 160).

constitution, than that of most of his Cabinet colleagues.
It is not clear whether he expected that Earle, who had
been in his confidence for nine years, who had taken a
large share in the negotiations with the Adullamites, and
whom he had constantly consulted about the arrangements
for the new Administration, would resume his former
position of Private Secretary. But Earle, who had come
back to Parliament at the General Election of 1865,
desired political office; and Rose told Disraeli that the
party expected that Earle's undeniable services should
be rewarded. Disraeli acknowledged the justice of the
claim, and secured for his young friend the secretaryship
of the Poor Law Board, under Hardy. Earle was completely satisfied.

From Ralph A. Earle.

Friday [? *July* 6].—I don't know how to thank you
enough. The Secretary of the Poor Law Board does *not*
vacate. I think it would suit me better than the Admiralty,
perhaps, as a contest would be disagreeable. . . .
As to the Secretaryship, I have been thinking much about
it. Would Cameron of Lochiel do ? He is intelligent and
devoted to you, but I fear shooting and Scotland might
interfere. If it would be any comfort, I will work for you
at the beginning and put the thing in train.

Disraeli did not require Earle's suggestions as to his
successor. He had already had an application from the
young man who had so greatly attracted him at Raby,
and on July 12 Montagu Corry began his duties in
Downing Street as Private Secretary, with a Treasury
Clerk of a Bucks family, who afterwards became Sir
Charles Fremantle, as his colleague.

From Montagu Corry.

72, GROSVENOR STREET, *Friday, June* 29, 1866.—It is with
much hesitation that I write to you, and only your kindness
to me when I met you at Raby last autumn induces me to
do so. I have for three years been practising as a barrister,
and am now most anxious to get a start in political life;
and though I can scarcely presume to ask for the honour
of being Private Secretary to yourself, yet I do venture to
hope that, should you know of some member of the Govern-

ment to whom my services might be acceptable, you would be willing to mention me, as one most desirous to serve in that capacity, and to give all my time and energies to the Conservative cause.

In a very few weeks the relation between the Minister and his principal secretary had become of the most intimate and confidential character, and so remained till Disraeli's death, fifteen years later. Corry never quitted the service of his chief, in office or in opposition; and the bonds between them were knit still more closely by Lady Beaconsfield's death in 1872, which left her husband, whom she had carefully shielded from all domestic worries, peculiarly dependent upon Corry's devotion. On Beaconsfield's final retirement from office in 1880, he shocked the sticklers for precedent by recommending his secretary for a peerage; and by his will he left all his papers, the foundation of the present biography, to that secretary's sole charge, to be dealt with at his absolute discretion. The world, which had always acknowledged Lord Rowton's personal charm, discovered in later years his sterling qualities, when, by starting and directing the system of cheap lodgings for men known as Rowton Houses, he supplied in a practical fashion a serious social need. In *Endymion*,[1] written while Corry was in his service, Disraeli expresses his view of what the relations between Minister and secretary should be, and what in this case they unquestionably were.

The relations between a Minister and his secretary are, or at least should be, among the finest that can subsist between two individuals. Except the married state, there is none in which so great a confidence is involved, in which more forbearance ought to be exercised, or more sympathy ought to exist. There is usually in the relations an identity of interest, and that of the highest kind; and the perpetual difficulties, the alternations of triumph and defeat, develop devotion. A youthful secretary will naturally feel some degree of enthusiasm for his chief, and a wise Minister will never stint his regard for one in whose intelligence and honour he finds he can place confidence.

[1] Ch. 49.

The new Administration was well received; and the
Liberals were for the time so hopelessly broken up
that, in spite of the large majority against it, there was
good hope that it might retain office, provided that
its attitude on Reform was satisfactory to Parliament.
Disraeli grappled with the question in his speech on the
hustings on re-election. He strongly maintained both
the right and the competence of the Government to
effect a settlement, recalling Derby's important share
in carrying the great Reform Bill, and adding with
regard to the only subsequent measure of Reform ever
mentioned with respect, 'Why, I myself brought it
in.' But he declined to give any pledge to introduce
a Reform Bill in the next session, only declaring that,
if Ministers had to legislate, they would not recognise the
rights of man or permit a numerical majority to dictate
to the nation, but would act on the principle that electoral
power should be deposited with the best men of all
classes. This policy, which was echoed in Derby's
statement in the House of Lords, encountered no serious
resistance in Parliament.

The first duty of a Government coming into office in
July was to wind up the necessary Parliamentary
business; and Disraeli's official letters to the Queen give
a lively picture of House of Commons life during the
short remainder of the session.

To Queen Victoria.

DOWNING STREET, *Monday night, July* 16, 1866.—The
Chancellor of the Exchequer, with his humble duty to your
Majesty:

The House of Commons met this evening after a month's
abeyance. Nearly the whole evening has been taken up
by an animated and interesting debate on the charter to
the Queen's University (Ireland); brought on by Sir Robert
Peel. It was, with the exception of a clear but technical
speech on the part of Sir Hugh Cairns, confined to the
Opposition.

It was occasionally rather warm, and Mr. Gladstone
concluded with a vindication of passion and fire; but it

was generally felt and observed that he left the House
in doubt whether he was in favour of mixed education
or not. . . .

July 19.—. . . Lord Cranborne brought forward the
Indian Budget, to-night, in a speech which interested the
House.

The manner was vigorous, and showed a mastery of his
matter which, considering his short experience of office,
evidently surprised the House.   Persons of weight, in private,
of both parties, spoke of the effort with approbation.

The Chancellor of the Exchequer much regrets that, from
want of habit, he omitted to send a report on Tuesday night.
It was not an eventful one; a discussion on the Ballot, very
insipid.   The House recoiled from the subject.

Yesterday the Church Rates, a higher tone, but the House
wearied.

July 20.—. . . An interesting discussion on foreign affairs
opened by Mr. Laing, in a colorless, non-intervention
speech. . . .

A considerable oration from Mr. Gladstone, which covered
the subject.   Though glowing and earnest, it was conciliatory,
and fair and courteous to the Government.

It produced less sensation than it otherwise would have
done, for the House was anxious to hear the new Minister,
and Mr. Gladstone was long and too academical.

The new Secretary of State afforded a great contrast to
him.   Lord Stanley was never more characteristic; at the
same time, clear, cautious, and candid.   He pleased the House,
which evidently gave him, on both sides, its confidence.[1]

HOUSE OF COMMONS, *July* 24, 1866.—. . . The discussion
in the House to-night on the affairs of the Park was highly
and unexpectedly satisfactory.

Though introduced by a speech from Mr. Ayrton, and
from some others, in a very full House, which appealed
rather to the malevolent passions of a popular assembly, the
reply of Mr. Walpole was so dignified, so full of good feeling,
and supported by so much adequate knowledge, that a very
favourable reaction soon was visible.

This was clenched by an animated speech from Sir George
Grey, than which nothing could be more complete, more
gentlemanlike and generous.

When Sir George rose, nearly a dozen members of the

---

[1] The discussion turned on the new situation created in Europe by the
victory of Prussia over Austria at Sadowa.   Stanley said that he could
not see that the establishment of a strong, compact Power in North
Germany would be either a detriment or a menace to Great Britain,
whatever it might be deemed to be by other Powers.

extreme party rose at the same time, but when he sate down the feeling of the House was so decided that none of these gentlemen attempted to follow him. Among these was Mr. Bernal Osborne, who had risen twice.

The Chancellor of the Exchequer hoped that all was over, and over well, but Mr. Cowper would make a speech, chiefly on his flower-beds. This gave breath to the extreme party, and Mr. Mill rose, and delivered a speech hardly worthy of a philosopher, but rather more adapted to Hyde Park.

The Chancellor of the Exchequer ventured to tell him this, and then the matter died off, the general result being that the leading authorities in the House discountenanced entirely the criticism on Mr. Walpole's conduct.

The accounts this evening are that the chief leaders of the mob are now active in their efforts to terminate the disturbances.

July 27.—. . . The general rumor and understanding, in the House to-night, is that all attempts at tumultuous meetings are now definitively relinquished, and that Monday will be quite tranquil.

It is said that no effort will be made to hold a public meeting in Victoria Park any more than in Hyde Park. The principle that they are Royal Parks is to be fully recognised.

If this be true, as the Chancellor of the Exchequer hopes and believes, he ventures to think that the whole question of the localities of public meetings deserves the serious consideration of your Majesty's servants.

Public meetings are the recognised and indispensable organs of a free constitution. They are safety-valves.

It is desirable, it would seem, that, when the occasion offers, some Act should be passed, recognising and regulating the rights and privileges of your Majesty's Parks, enjoyed, through your Majesty's gracious sanction, by all classes of your Majesty's subjects, and, at the same time, that there should be some public places provided, where the great body of the people, like the Comitia of the Romans, should have the right to assemble, and discuss, and express, their opinion.

Your Majesty will perhaps deign to consider these suggestions.

From Queen Victoria.

OSBORNE, *July* 26, 1866.—The Queen thanks Mr. Disraeli for all his interesting reports, but she is especially anxious to express to him her great satisfaction at the manner in which he carried the vote for the gun-metal for her dear, great husband's memorial.[1] She knows how truly he appreciated him !

To Queen Victoria.

DOWNING STREET, *Aug.* 2, 1866.—. . . The evening has been taken up with a dreary debate on the Habeas Corpus Suspension Act in Ireland.[2]

Mr. Bernal Osborne, at one moment, promised some relief in a very elaborate speech and evidently, from several allusions, long matured; but it was old-fashioned and out of tune and time, and fell very flat. . . .

HOUSE OF COMMONS, *Aug.* 16, 1866.—. . . The Extradition Treaty Act passed, but with a limitation to one year.

We defeated all attempts to exclude ' political offences,' which would have included everything, but thought it best to accept the condition of time, as nothing could have prevented the discussion next year; the question must be reproduced, and, under any circumstances, the opinion of the House will be taken. Time brings everything, consolation and catastrophe; and it is hoped it may help your Majesty's servants in this matter.

The House meets again to-morrow, but only for a few minutes. Its pulse is very low; but extreme unction will not be administered, I believe, until Friday.

' The affairs of the Park,' referred to in the letters of July 24 and 27, were the famous Reform riots led by Beales, when the mob, being forbidden to hold a meeting in Hyde Park, broke down the railings near the Marble Arch and worked some havoc in the flower-beds, continuing their demonstrations for three days, July 23, 24, 25. Grosvenor Gate was close to the centre of disturbance; and Disraeli, whose duties kept him at the House of

---

[1] Palmerston had promised the Queen, in the spring of 1863, that, as had commonly been done in the case of other public statues, old guns should be supplied for the statuary of the Albert Memorial. But Gladstone, when application was made to him at the Exchequer, raised the objection that asking for the gun-metal was the same as asking for a fresh vote, and that it was understood, when £50,000 was voted for the memorial, that the vote was to be final. After much correspondence between the Court and Ministers, Palmerston eventually, in July, 1864, expressed his concurrence with Gladstone. But contracts had already been entered into on the faith of the Prime Minister's original promise; and Disraeli, though Gladstone still considered an application to Parliament ' impolitic,' easily secured, in July, 1866, the assent of the House of Commons to the transaction.

[2] The Government renewed the Habeas Corpus Suspension Act, which had been passed for only a limited period by their predecessors.

Commons while the riots were in progress, trusted to
his secretary to secure the safety of his wife.

From Montagu Corry.

GROSVENOR GATE, *July* 24 [? 23], 1866, 6.40 *p.m.*—No
mob outside your house now, the Marble Arch being the
centre of attraction; and even there the police say the
disturbance is lessening. The Inspector in charge at Grosvenor
Gate tells me that while the crowd was at its worst here
your house was never mentioned as obnoxious—though the
houses of Mr. Walpole and Lord Elcho and others have come
in for some threats. The soldiers have moved away to the
Marble Arch, and Mrs. Disraeli wishes me to add that the
people in general seem to be thoroughly enjoying themselves;
and I really believe she sympathises with them. At any
rate, I am glad to say she is not the least alarmed—nor do
I think you need be at all.

The mob broke down more than the railings of the Park;
they broke down the nerve of Walpole, the Home Secretary, who was said to have shed tears when a deputation
visited him on the subject. 'This fiasco of Walpole's,'
to use Derby's phrase in a contemporary letter to Disraeli,
the constant demonstrations in the streets of London,
and the countenance afforded to the agitators by many
of the Radical leaders, such as J. S. Mill and Bright,
made Disraeli anxious. He wrote to his wife on July
26: 'I hope with energy and prudence we may overcome the difficulties, but it is very obvious to me that
the affair is encouraged by our opponents underhand,
with the view of upsetting the Government. I think
they will fail.' One happy thought, which he suggested
ineffectually to Derby, might have profoundly modified
the course of political history, if it had been adopted by
the Prime Minister and the Cabinet.

To Lord Derby.

Confidential. GROSVENOR GATE, *July* 29, 1866.—I would
not trouble you with things when you are dealing with
persons, but things may affect persons.

This is, I think, important; it is the result of my reflections
this day on what Gladstone said yesterday.

Suppose, instead of discharging the order of the day on

the Reform Bill, you took up the measure where it stops: £6 *rating* for boroughs; £20 rating for counties, to be brought up on report; the northern boroughs to be enfranchised; no disfranchisement of any kind.

You could carry this in the present House, and rapidly. It would prevent all agitation in the recess; it would cut the ground entirely from under Gladstone; and it would smash the Bath Cabal, for there would be no dangerous question ahead.

Think of this.

The course proposed was too startling, perhaps, for acceptance. The session came to an end without further Parliamentary action about Reform; and the agitation was transferred from London to the country, where large demonstrations were held and violent language was used, in Birmingham, Manchester, Leeds, Glasgow, and Dublin. It is usually assumed that by these proceedings Disraeli was convinced in the early autumn that the demand for Reform had now become a genuinely popular one, and must be treated comprehensively without further delay by a Conservative Ministry. This is an erroneous assumption. Disraeli's suggestion to take up Gladstone's Bill and carry it to the statute-book in a modified form not having been accepted, he thought it more prudent to postpone further action. It was Derby himself who pushed the matter forward He believed, in his own words, 'that there is a genuine demand *now*, however it may have been excited, but in favour of the acceptance of a moderate and Conservative measure.'

From Lord Derby.

Private. KNOWSLEY, *Sept.* 16, 1866.—. . . I am coming reluctantly to the conclusion that we shall have to deal with the question of Reform. . . . I wish you would consider whether, after all the failures which have taken place, we might not deal with the question in the shape of resolutions, to form the basis of a future Bill. We *need* not make the adoption of any of the resolutions a vital question; while, if we should be beaten on some great leading principle, we should have a definite issue on which to go to the country. This is worth turning in your mind; and I should be glad to hear what you think of it. . . .

Disraeli's reply was not encouraging. 'Observation and reflection,' he wrote on September 24, 'have not yet brought me to your conclusion as to the necessity of bringing in a Bill for Parliamentary Reform; but I hope I say this with becoming diffidence.' Derby, however, immediately received a powerful reinforcement from the highest quarter. He went to Balmoral, where the Queen herself expressed to him her anxiety to have the question settled, and settled by the Conservatives, and her readiness to do anything she could personally to bring opinions together. Accordingly we find him writing to Disraeli on October 9: 'I come myself more and more to the conclusion that in some shape or other we must deal with it, and that immediately'; but he preferred the method of resolutions, which he had previously suggested.

To Lord Derby.

Confidential. HUGHENDEN MANOR, *October 12, 1866.*—I had no idea, when you first wrote to me about 'resolutions,' that you contemplated the possibility of not legislating the session they were passed. If we can succeed in that, we shall indeed be on velvet. This view throws quite a new light on our position, and therefore I will not trouble you now with any remarks on the comparative advantages of Bills or resolutions, in case, as I now conclude, the Cabinet resolves on acting.

It will, I think, be quite unnecessary to have Cabinet Committees of preparation, as of yore; there is so much previous knowledge now, on the main subject, that these preliminary investigations are unnecessary, while they tend to jealousy.

The time for meeting will quite suit me.

I shall endeavour to draw up a series of resolutions in your vein. They must, however, be distinct enough for us to fall back upon, as a clear policy, for the country, in case we are forced to appeal to it, which Heaven forfend ! . . .

I think you have decided wisely about Fitzgerald.[1] The morale of a party is injured when any individual who has been encouraged to take a prominent part is neglected in the hour of triumph. He was also personally popular among the rank and file. Our Stanley never thinks anybody in

[1] Under-Secretary for Foreign Affairs in 1858-59 ; appointed Governor of Bombay in 1866.

the House of Commons is equal to anything; and I am not
sure he is not right.   But the world cannot be governed by
this inexorable estimate of human qualities, and the political
circle generally will agree that a man who, if in Parliament,
would probably have been a Cabinet Minister, is not unfit
to be an E.I[ndian] President.

The suggestion which the Queen had tentatively made
to Derby she pressed again upon Northcote, who was
at Balmoral in October as Minister in attendance.   He
reported what passed both to Derby and to Disraeli.

From Sir Stafford Northcote.

BALMORAL, *Oct.* 17, 1866.—. . . Nothing can exceed Her
Majesty's kindness and friendliness.   She is evidently very
anxious for our success, but particularly so with regard to
the great Reform problems.

A day or two ago General Grey brought me a note in
Her Majesty's handwriting, to the effect that she was most
anxious for a settlement of the question; that she would
gladly render any assistance in her power; that she did not
like to speak to me about it, but that her idea was to offer
Lord Derby her assistance in communicating with Lord
Russell and Gladstone.   The General told me she meant to
speak to me and consult me on the point, and that this note
was a preparatory one.   She did accordingly lead up to the
subject when I saw her in the evening; but I turned the
conversation, and the next morning wrote a note to the
General saying that the question was so difficult, any false
step so dangerous, and my position as a young and unin-
fluential member of the Government so delicate, that I had
been glad that Her Majesty had not asked for my opinion;
that I thought that, if she were to intimate to Lord Derby
her willingness to make such a communication as she spoke
of, if he thought it desirable, at the same time graciously
adding that she did not require any formal answer to the
proposal, it might strengthen his hands to be thus made
aware of her readiness to support him; but that I thought
that a formal offer might be embarrassing, as, if the Cabinet
ultimately decided that it was inexpedient that any communication should be made to the Liberal party leaders,
it might be awkward to have to decline Her Majesty's gracious
proposal.   The General told me afterwards that she quite
understood my difficulty, that he thought she would probably
write to Lord Derby, but would intimate that she did not
desire an immediate answer.   I told the General that I

thought there would be very little practical use in communicating with Lord Russell or Gladstone; that they would
only give vague promises of candid consideration, which would
lead to nothing. . . . I reported what had passed to Lord
Derby.

Last night the Queen renewed the subject with me, saying
that she quite understood my position and could not ask me
for an opinion. She was very anxious that something should
be done, and discussed the question from what I think an
important point of view—the purchasing power of the
nouveaux riches, ' who buy your Totnes.'

The General has been talking the matter over with me
again this morning, and showed me a letter of Lord Grey's,
who is very anxious that the question should be settled,
and that we should be the men to settle it. (By the bye,
the Queen mentioned Lord Grey to me as a person who
would be ready to give his assistance to us. I said I had
always supposed we should find him friendly. She said,
' Yet you didn't ask him to join the Government.' I said
I knew very little of the communications which took place
when the Government was forming. She said, ' Well, none
was made to him.') Lord Grey thinks it would be equally
fatal to us to bring in a Bill, or to abstain from doing anything; and thinks we ought to proceed, as he advised the late
Government to do, by way of resolutions; but his idea of
resolutions appears to be the affirmation of some general
principles, and an Address to the Crown to appoint a Committee of Privy Councillors to draw up a measure.[1] I told
the General that I thought the time was passed (if there ever
had been a time) for that mode of proceeding; and I discussed with him the idea of resolutions of a more definite
character, such as those Lord Derby shadowed out to me at
Knowsley. . . . He seemed to think the plan would, or
might, answer. . . .

Disraeli was somewhat impatient under the royal
suggestion and Grey's scheme, and brushed them both
aside in letters, couched in very similar terms, to Derby
and to Northcote.

To Sir Stafford Northcote.

HUGHENDEN MANOR, *Oct.* 22, 1866.—I was much obliged
to you for your interesting despatch, and appreciate the

---

[1] In his letter to Derby, Northcote adds that he asked General Grey
' if he proposed that we should make Bright a Privy Councillor, or leave
him out altogether.'

entire fidelity which I have always experienced from you, and on which I have ever, rightly, counted. Lord Derby also forwarded to me your letter to him, on Saturday last.

I am much gratified by your successful visit to Balmoral.

I doubt myself whether Lord Grey's scheme, at any time or under any circumstances, would or could have been accepted, but at the present moment, and in the existing state of things, it is the murmuring of children in a dream.

The royal project of gracious interposition with our rivals is a mere phantom. It pleases the vanity of a Court deprived of substantial power, but we know, from the experience of similar sentimental schemes, that there is nothing practical in it, or, rather, that the only practical result is to convey to our rivals that we are at the same time feeble and perplexed.

Our future, and in some degree the future of our country, depends on the course we shall chalk out for ourselves; and that must be the result of anxious, grave, and profound deliberation. . . . The first question for the Cabinet to decide will be, ' Shall we act in the matter of Reform ?' I think the discussion of that question will occupy entirely our first meeting, and will facilitate our subsequent councils, in case we decide on action. . . .

P.S.—I have not room to tell you how entirely I approve and admire the wisdom with which you parried the royal proposition. It was worthy of Hyde, and you tell it as well.

The Queen was in earnest in her resolve to get the Reform question settled at once, and undoubtedly judged the signs of the times better than her Chancellor of the Exchequer. Before the month was over, she wrote to the Prime Minister the letter which Northcote had suggested, emphasising the necessity of an early settlement, and offering her services to bring it about.

Queen Victoria to Lord Derby.

BALMORAL, *Oct.* 28, 1866.—The Queen has been thinking a great deal, ever since Lord Derby left Balmoral, of the subject on which she had some conversation with him while he was here. As she then told him, she is convinced that, if the question of Reform be not taken up in earnest by her Ministers, with a view to its settlement, very serious consequences may ensue.

The Queen is well aware of the great difficulties which her Government must be prepared to meet, in any attempt to effect this object, and if she can in any way help in surmounting them, Lord Derby and his colleagues may reckon confidently on her best support and assistance.

It seems evident to the Queen, after the failure of so many successive Administrations, which have all been overthrown in their attempts to settle this question, that it never can be settled unless adverse parties are prepared to concede something, and to meet each other in a spirit of mutual conciliation. Nothing would gratify the Queen more than to be instrumental in bringing about such a disposition; and if Lord Derby thinks there is any chance of its doing good—indeed, she views the matter so seriously that she hardly thinks she would be justified in not making the attempt under any circumstances —she is ready to make a personal appeal to Lord Russell and Mr. Gladstone, and other leading members of both Houses of Parliament, and to urge them, by every consideration of loyalty and patriotism, to meet her present Ministers fairly, in an honest endeavour to find out terms of agreement as might lead to a measure of Reform being proposed which would conciliate the support of all moderate men, and afford at least a chance of setting a question at rest, which, while it continues to be made a subject of agitation, must act injuriously upon the best interests of the country, and may even threaten the disturbance of its peace and tranquillity.

Lord Derby need not answer this letter at once. He is quite at liberty to consult his colleagues upon it previously, and the Queen relies with confidence upon their patriotism not to allow any feelings of a mere party nature to interfere with their candid consideration of her suggestions. . . .

The Cabinet appears to have taken Disraeli's advice and decided both against Grey's scheme and against utilising, at any rate for the present, the Queen's offer to approach the Liberal leaders. But Her Majesty's impulsion and Derby's own conviction sufficed to make Ministers take in hand at once the drafting of Reform Resolutions to be submitted to Parliament next session. The scheme provisionally adopted was quite general in terms; but it followed the principle of the Grosvenor amendment by dealing with redistribution as well as with franchise, and that of the Dunkellin amendment by adopting a rating and not a rental basis. It involved an increase of the number of electors in both counties and boroughs by a reduction of qualification in the occupation franchise and by the addition of other franchises; more representation for the labouring classes, but without giving any class a preponderating power ; no absolute disfranchisement save for corrupt practices ; revision of county registration, employment of voting papers, and provision of additional polling-places; and the appointment of a Boundary Commission, which 'should also revise and verify the returns laid before Parliament in its last session, with respect to the possession of the franchise; and obtain such further information as may be the ground for well-considered legislation.' The question of the Commission immediately assumed considerable importance. Derby had written to Disraeli on October 19, with reference to Grey's scheme: ' I think a Commission to frame a measure both inexpedient and impracticable. One for information, following up resolutions of principle, I should think very desirable; but with that object we should not require to appoint Privy Councillors.' Disraeli's main design, at this period, was so to delay matters as to avoid having to introduce actual legislation in the approaching session; and he was quick to see that the only method in which this policy could be combined with effective resolutions was to create a Commission with really important work to do, and not merely to rearrange boundaries. He drew up a memorandum in order to place his point of view clearly before Derby and the Cabinet.

To Lord Derby.

Nov. 18, 1866.—. . . We are entirely unpledged upon the subject [of Parliamentary Reform]. But if no notice is taken of it in the Queen's Speech, or no subsequent announcement of measures is made by the leader of the House of Commons, it is probable that an amendment of a general character may be carried, which will replace the question in the hands of the late Government, and they return to power not more embarrassed by the Radicals than before.

II.   7*

It is not probable that a dissolution, even if granted would, under these circumstances, help us.

It would seem therefore we must act.   How ?

1. By the introduction of a Bill ?
2. By resolutions leading to a Bill ?
3. By resolutions leading to inquiry ?

It seems probable that no measure of Parliamentary Reform could be passed by a Conservative Government except in a Parliament where they have essentially a majority.

Resolutions as the basis of a Bill, though not so immediately dangerous as a proposal of direct legislation, would ultimately lead to defeat.

There remains, therefore, to be considered the case of resolutions, which, though laying down a complete scheme, should end in a Royal Commission.

If the difficulty to which in a moment I will advert could be removed, the chances are that this would be a successful course.

It may be assumed that the House of Commons is really opposed to any violent Reform, and to any Reform of any kind which is immediate; and the longer the decision of its opinion can be delayed, the more likely it will be in favor of moderation and postponement.

If the first week of March was fixed for the introduction of the resolutions, the discussion on them need not commence until the first week in April.

If the House then gets involved in the discussion, the Liberal party will probably be broken up.

If, as is more likely, Mr. Gladstone meets the Ministerial motion by a general resolution in favor of immediate legislation, it is not impossible he may be defeated, which will establish the Government.   But if he succeed it will probably be by a narrow majority, and the dissolution would then take place on an issue between Bright's policy and our programme.

But to insure the success of such a campaign one condition is necessary: that there should be substantial grounds for a Royal Commission, and this is the difficulty to which I referred.

I myself am at a loss to find these grounds, and this is the point on which the thought of the Cabinet should be concentrated.

If the resolutions at present in your portfolio were adopted, there would be substantial grounds, in a great degree arising from the necessary resettlement of the boundaries of the smaller boroughs; but reflection persuades me that this proposal would not, on the whole, be a wise one; because one of our leading principles should be to enlist, as far as possible, the sympathies of the small boroughs, and they, perhaps, would deem an alteration of their boundaries only second, as a disaster, to their total disfranchisement.

The settlement of the boundaries of the northern boroughs is not ample enough for a Royal Commission issued under such circumstances. Means to effect such an end might have been adopted in the recess.

It has been suggested that the subject of bribery might be referred to the Royal Commission, and this deserves consideration; but if it were practicable, there is still not a *dignus nodus*.

The substantialness of the Royal Commission is the key of the position, and I therefore bring it under your deep consideration.

After further consultation with the Cabinet and the Prime Minister, who was clear that Ministers, in order to extricate themselves from 'the Reform dilemma,' must have a Commission as a ' buffer,' Disraeli redrafted the Resolutions, suggesting that the proposed Commission might be so comprehensive as to embrace inquiries into the extent to which the wage-paid class already had the vote, and why some were excluded and others admitted; how far changes in the value of money had affected the electoral qualification; and how far the franchise might be beneficially extended without the domination of mere numbers; and that the Commission might also investigate and report on bribery and corruption, and revise the boundaries of boroughs.

To Lord Derby.

Confidential. 11, DOWNING STREET, *Dec.* 29, 1866.—. . . I have been most inconveniently summoned to town, in the midst of Christmas, to be sworn in, to-day, a brother of the Trinity House. Those of my brethren who are also country gentlemen must think such a disturbance of a holy festival, on the part of such a body, very strange, and, indeed, scarcely orthodox.

I should like the Cabinet not to be summoned till Thursday, as there are many points of great importance on which consultation is desirable before we meet in formal council. Work thickens. The army question must be grappled with. Then the Portuguese Treaty of Commerce is assuming a practical shape, and a plan of the Post Office for the purchase of all the private telegraphs of the country demands our decision. These are all heavy affairs, and the latter two fall entirely on the Treasury.

With respect to Reform: I agree with you that it is quite premature to trouble ourselves about the materials[1] of the Royal Commission. . . .

I have not the draft of the Resolutions at hand, but I suspect you will find, on reference to them, that the Resolution pledges the House to ' extension,' not ' reduction,' of the franchise; and ' extension ' would include everything.

We must be careful not to commit ourselves both to reduction and ' fancy ' franchises, if it be true, as I now hear, that the lodger franchise in the way of extension, and especially among the wage-paid class, would produce incredible results. Indeed, I think that particular franchise should be specifically referred to the Commission, and, indeed, I am rather inclined to refer plurality also, and all the cognate expedients for protecting the minority. . . .

It is quite clear that, throughout the autumn and early winter, Disraeli, far from being stimulated into drastic action by the Reform demonstrations throughout the country, was anxious to postpone legislation as long as possible in order to secure a moderate measure. He was confirmed in this policy by his correspondence with friends and supporters. There was, indeed, one significant exception. Spofforth, who had had a large share in the management of the General Election on the Tory side, told Disraeli that a series of visits in the northern counties had converted him into an advocate of ' a wise and moderate measure next session.' But Cranborne informed him of a strong declaration by Lowe that his valuable support was conditional on no Reform Bill being brought forward in February; Manners saw nothing in what had happened to make such a Bill advisable; and reports from Brooks's Club assured Disraeli that the Liberal party had gone to pieces, and that Bright's greatest friends had been earnestly beseeching him to desist from his mad career.

It must not be forgotten that the circumstances in

---

[1] The context, and Derby's letter, show that Disraeli is referring to the persons to be appointed Royal Commissioners.

which this third Derby-Disraeli Ministry took office
were very different from those which prevailed when the
second Ministry of the kind was formed in 1858.   Then
there was an understanding that the Conservatives
should tackle the Reform Question; now they had come
in because Parliament resented having Reform forced
down its throat by Russell and Gladstone.   Moreover,
several members of the 1866 Ministry, notably Cranborne,
were very lukewarm Reformers; and Disraeli himself,
in accordance with what he believed to be the opinion
of the country and of Parliament, had taken up in 1865
and in 1866 a much more pronouncedly anti-movement
attitude than had been at all usual with him.   Always
an opportunist on Reform, he held during this autumn
that the composition of the Ministry and the temper
of the nation necessitated a policy of moderation and
delay.   He was, indeed, for the time, on the question
not of principle, but of tactics, nearer in opinion to his
colleague Cranborne than to his leader Derby.

To Lord Cranborne.

HUGHENDEN MANOR, *Dec.* 26, 1866.—. . . I have throughout been against legislation, and continue so.   Lord Derby,
about the time you were here, thought it inevitable, but, as
you know, his views are now modified.

It's a difficult affair, but I think we shall pull through; the
Whigs are very unanimous in wishing the question ' settled '—
but you and I are not Whigs.

At the same time there must have been lurking at
the back of Disraeli's mind a consciousness that the
Queen might be right in her view, that circumstances
might arise, when Parliament met, to make it desirable,
and indeed necessary, for the Ministry to abandon
the policy of procrastination and deliberation, and to
act—act promptly, thoroughly, and comprehensively.
He published in the winter his collected speeches on
Parliamentary Reform, with a preface asserting that the
views therein expressed were the opinions of the Con-

servative party, and claiming once more for that party
the right, if it thought fit, to take up and settle the
question. The book was nominally edited, and the
preface signed, by his young secretary, Montagu Corry;
its exact genesis and history appear from Disraeli's
letters.

To Montagu Corry.

HUGHENDEN, *Sept.* 2, 1866.—Longmans want me to
publish all my speeches on ' Parliamentary Reform,' in an
8vo vol. They evidently think the subject will revive, and
that it may be, in every respect, expedient and advantageous
that the collected views of one who has taken an active part
in the question should be before the country in a portable
form.

I shall not consent, if I do at all, until I have made further
observations on the public humor with respect to this
question.

But I may eventually have to act with promptitude,
and therefore I wish to be prepared for the occasion.

I wish, therefore (not having ' Hansard ' at Hughenden),
that you would make me a list of my speeches on Parliamentary Reform. . . .

Oct. 4.—. . . Longman is pressing me about the speeches.
Have you confidence in the list you sent me ? For example,
on acceding to office in 1852, I had to speak on a Reform
motion—probably one of Hume's—in which I took occasion
to observe that, in any future change, the claims of the working class ought to be considered. They had been unwisely
dealt with, and neglected, in the measure of 1832. My recollection, faint, is that my observations were brief. They
occasioned much discontent, I remember, and particularly at
Court. Events have proved they were just, and I felt they
were in accordance with true Tory principles. . . .

I think it worth consideration, whether you might not
figure in the title-page as editor. It might assist your
introduction into public life. We can think about
this. . . .

Oct. 16.—I see that Longmans have advertised your
volume; in the *Saturday Review,* I think, I saw it. ' Speeches
on Parliamentary Reform, by Rt. Hon. B. D., M.P., C.
of E., etc.'

A horrid title; it will do for the moment, but when we
advance a little, and real advertising begins, there should
be something more condensed and simpler. . . . I hate

Rt. Hon.'s and M.P.'s and all that. C. of E.'s *must* be R.H.'s and M.P.'s and so on, as a matter of course. . . .

Oct. 30.—I send Gladstone's book, which I found on my arrival at Grosvenor Gate, 'With the Publisher's compliments.'

It is a sorry-looking volume; merely a reprint of the speeches of last year, with no evidence of matured and continuous policy. I hope yours will be much more business-like and impressive, both in matter and in form; but the sooner you get it out the better. . . . .

STRATHFIELDSAYE, *Nov.* 29.—My dear Editor—I send you the two proofs, and begin to see daylight. Herein, also, is a rough sketch of an advertisement, or preface, which you may not only alter in any way you like, but even reconstruct or altogether put aside. . . .

ADVERTISEMENT.

These speeches, commencing at a period even antecedent to the desertion of the principle of finality by Lord John Russell, and ending with the last session, were made by a member of Parliament who, during the whole interval, was either leader of the Opposition or principal Minister of the Queen in the House of Commons.

They represent, therefore, the opinions of a party, and we have the highest authority for stating that, scarcely with an exception, the views, which they represent, were, after due deliberation, adopted by every eminent man, who has since sate in the councils of Lord Derby, and by every leading country gentleman of the time.

So long as the Whig party were firm in upholding the settlement of 1832, the Tory party, though not insensible to some injustice in that measure, resolved to support its authors against all attempts at further change in the constitution of the House of Commons. But when the Whigs yielded their position, their political opponents determined to assert the principles which, in their opinion, should guide any future reconstruction, and which from that time have, consequently, been placed before the country in the following speeches with an amplitude of knowledge, and a vigor and versatility of argument and illustration, which have been acknowledged.

These speeches, then, form a complete and consistent record of the main opinions of a great party in the State during the important period in which a further change of the constitution of the House of Commons has been in agitation; and the country, therefore, will now be enabled to see with what justness it has been asserted that the Tory party are disqualified from dealing with the most difficult of modern political questions in consequence of their constant and unvarying hostility to any attempt to improve our popular representation.—M. C.

The 'Advertisement' was printed as drafted in the above letter, with a few slight verbal alterations, and the volume appeared in January.

Though, in view of the history of the session of 1867, what went on about Reform behind the scenes in the autumn of 1866 is of great interest and importance, it would be a mistake to suppose that Disraeli's energies were at that time exclusively, or even specially, directed to the subject. Indeed, Reform did not occupy nearly so much of his attention as in the autumn of 1858; and no detailed work whatever was done on it either by him or by his colleagues. Whereas, in 1858, Disraeli first elaborated a scheme in conjunction with Stanley, then hammered out the details in a special Cabinet Committee, and finally went over all the ground again in full Cabinet; on the present occasion general resolutions were all with which Ministers concerned themselves, till the session of 1867 had begun. The confusion and mishaps of the early part of that session might well have been avoided if Disraeli's foresight on this occasion had been equal to that of the Queen and of the Prime Minister.

Foreign policy and finance occupied Disraeli at least as much as Reform. He was anxious to set an example in office of the unadventurous and economical administration which he had pressed on Parliament in opposition. Ministers acceded to office while Bismarck was carrying out that attack upon Austria which, he had frankly confessed to Disraeli some years before, was the immediate aim of his policy. The division of the spoils of Schleswig-Holstein was the excuse; and nobody in England wished to interfere in the internecine quarrels of the German Powers who had robbed Denmark. In this matter Ministers only carried on the neutral policy of their

predecessors. Disraeli, in his speech on re-election, laid
down the broad lines on which any British intervention
should rest, giving, after his wont, a philosophical basis
to a practical policy.

The abstention of England from any unnecessary interference in the affairs of Europe is the consequence, not of her
decline of power, but of her increased strength. England
is no longer a mere European Power; she is the metropolis
of a great maritime empire, extending to the boundaries of
the farthest ocean. It is not that England has taken refuge
in a state of apathy, that she now almost systematically
declines to interfere in the affairs of the Continent of Europe.
England is as ready and as willing to interfere as in old days,
when the necessity of her position requires it. There is no
Power, indeed, that interferes more than England. She
interferes in Asia, because she is really more an Asiatic Power
than a European. She interferes in Australia, in Africa, and
New Zealand, where she carries on war often on a great
scale. Therefore, it is not because England does not recognise
her duty to interfere in the affairs of the Continent of Europe
that persons are justified in declaring that she has relinquished
her imperial position, and has taken refuge in the *otium cum
dignitate*, which agrees with the decline of life, of power, and
of prosperity. On the contrary, she has a greater sphere
of action than any European Power, and she has duties
devolving upon her on a much larger scale. Not that we
can ever look with indifference upon what takes place on the
Continent. We are interested in the peace and prosperity of
Europe, and I do not say that there may not be occasions in
which it may be the duty of England to interfere in European
wars.

Though the passage was a plea for non-interference in
European affairs, it was far from being an unconditional
plea; and the right of England to intervene, and her
reserved power to do so with effect, are carefully enforced.
The new Foreign Secretary, Stanley, was indeed a
whole-hearted adherent of the policy of non-intervention.
But Disraeli himself never lost sight of the difference
between meddling with the domestic affairs of European
nations, and intervening in their international relations
when those relations affected British interests or public
law; and the continuous experience of office which he

was now to enjoy for two years and a half, made him
doubt whether the natural reaction from Palmerston's
and Russell's meddlesomeness was not being carried
too far. It was impossible, he felt, to trust either of
the two principal forces on the Continent, Napoleon III.
and Bismarck. There was reason to fear that they
might at any moment combine to the disadvantage of
British interests. Vigilance was all the more necessary,
as Disraeli had a poor opinion of British diplomatists.

To Lord Stanley.

GROSVENOR GATE, *Aug.* 17, 1866.—I have read Cowley's
letters with much interest. Bloomfield's, both handwriting
and matter, are those of a greengrocer; Loftus should be
the foreign editor of the *Morning Herald.* Morier, as
ambassador, is ' high life below stairs.' Elliot a partisan.[1]

Mem.: None of your people address you rightly in their
public despatches. They should be addressed to ' Secretary
the Right Hon. the Lord Stanley, M.P.'

As the Venetians, who were great authorities in their day,
used to say, ' Punctilio is the soul of diplomacy.'

The interests both of the country, and—what Disraeli
never neglected—the party, seemed to point to a more
vigorous assertion of British influence. ' Non-intervention might have been successfully opposed to
Palmerston,' wrote Earle to Disraeli on September 1;
' but it is impossible for us to gain any popularity in this
wise, which could not be obtained in a greater degree by
Gladstone.' Earle feared the Tories might be ' colourless,
neither Cobdenite nor Imperial '; ' a little more expensive
than Gladstone and not a whit more glorious and
national.' The influence of the Queen was strongly
exercised in the same direction, especially in regard to
two questions which the rival intrigues of Napoleon
and Bismarck forced to the front—the independence
of Belgium and of Luxemburg. Disraeli let Stanley see
the drift of his thoughts.

[1] Cowley was at Paris, Bloomfield at Vienna, Loftus at Berlin, Morier
at Frankfort, and Elliot at Florence.

To Lord Stanley.

GROSVENOR GATE, *Dec.* 30, 1866.—I have just heard, from a first-rate quarter, that, at the last Cabinet Council at the Tuileries, a proposition, from Bismarck, suggesting an arrangement by which the Southern States of Germany should blend with Prussia, and that France should take possession of Belgium, was absolutely brought forward, and favored by several of the Ministers, principally by Lavalette. It was opposed by the Minister for Foreign Affairs.

Can this be true? And if so, or if there be any foundation for it, what are Bismarck's relations with us? Have you heard anything from our Goosey Gander at Berlin, a pretty instrument to cope with the Prussian Minister! And Mr. Fane,[1] what does he say? And what shall we say?

The Emperor is like a gambler who has lost half his fortune and restless to recover; likely to make a *coup*, which may be fatally final for himself.

I doubt whether this country would see any further glaring case of public violence and treachery with composure. Reaction is the law of all human affairs; and the reaction from non-intervention must sooner or later set in. I would rather, however, try to prevent mischief—*i.e.*, as long as we can. . . .

The threat to Belgium, the reality of which Bismarck in his own good time revealed to the world, was at the moment treated by Stanley as a *canard*. But the threat to Luxemburg was definitely made in the following spring. The position of Luxemburg largely reproduced the anomalous conditions of Holstein before 1864. It had been a member of the Germanic Confederation, but its ruler, with the title of Grand-Duke, was the King of Holland, from whose Dutch dominions, however, it was separated by many miles. The Germanic Confederation had now been dissolved as a result of Prussia's victory over Austria; but the city and fortress of Luxemburg were still garrisoned by Prussian troops, which, after Prussia's recent aggrandisement, were not unreasonably looked upon by France as a menace on her flank. Napoleon III. opened negotiations with the Dutch Government for the sale of the grand-duchy to France.

[1] First Secretary at Paris.

On April 3, 1867, Disraeli wrote to Stanley: ' Rothschilds have received information that the Emperor has definitely informed Bismarck that the arrangement between himself and the King of Holland is concluded, and that he shall act at once on it.' This transaction was strongly resented in Germany; and for some days war appeared to be imminent, the Emperor telling the Prussian Minister that the possession of Luxemburg involved the question of his own existence. As the grand-duchy had been guaranteed to the King of Holland by a treaty in 1839, to which Great Britain, with the other Great Powers, was a party, this country was directly interested; and the Queen's personal intervention, and Stanley's urgent efforts, prevailed to make both sides reasonable.

To Lord Stanley.

Windsor Castle, *Easter Monday, April 22*, 1867.—My visit here has tumbled me into the midst of the Luxemburg business, and I have had all the despatches, and all the private letters of all the cousins, submitted to me; and you know all the rest.

I assured our Royal Mistress, and most sincerely, that she was quite under a mistake in supposing that you would not act, if necessary, and that, I knew, you have well considered all the eventualities about Belgium; that you would never act without determination and constancy; and that anything you did or said would have double the effect of the old stagers with their mechanical interference—sometimes bluster and sometimes blundering.

I told Her Majesty, also, that we were not really half a Government until the division of last Friday,[1] and that a hint from you could, and would, do more now than reams of despatches a month ago.

I think she understood all this, and I think I did good.

I pointed out also that, so far as matters went, the question of Belgium was really not on the *tapis*. This, after reflection, she agreed to; but still thought that, in confidential conversation, our people might let it be known at Berlin and Paris that the violation of Belgian neutrality should not pass with impunity

At present it seems the pressure should rather be put upon Berlin than on the ancient capital of Julian the Apostate.

[1] On Gladstone's amendment, in Committee, on the Reform Bill, about compound householders See below, Ch. 14.

Two things seem to me clear: that France is not prepared, and that Bismarck lies to everyone. His explanations prove his perfidy.

I think, myself, as old Brunnow says, 'it is time for a little reaction,' and that we might begin to dictate a little to Europe. Gladstonism is at a discount.

It's very lucky, however, we didn't take off any taxes, and that by paying off some debt we shall be able to borrow any amount at a very moderate price. That is to say, in case we want it. Nevertheless, as nothing happens which one expects, I begin to believe you will turn out a regular Chatham. . . .

Stanley replied: 'I am ready to go as far as may be necessary in support of Belgium, short of giving an absolute pledge to fight for its independence. Suppose we gave such a pledge, that France and Prussia came to an understanding, Russia and Austria standing aloof, where should we be ?' It was a prudent rather than a generous or even a statesmanlike view. According to general belief, we had given such a pledge; in any case it was the traditional policy of England not to permit the Low Countries to be controlled by a dominant military Power. With regard to Luxemburg, Stanley rightly saw that its neutralisation was 'the one indispensable condition of peace'; but he was very reluctant to give the guarantee which would alone make neutralisation effective. The Queen could not understand his hesitation. 'We are already parties to the guarantee of Belgian neutrality and independence,' wrote General Grey on her behalf to Disraeli on May 5, 'and to extend the guarantee of neutrality to Luxemburg does not seem to entail upon us any great additional responsibility.' Her Majesty's arguments, which Disraeli reinforced, prevailed; and at a Conference in London in May a treaty was signed by which the duchy was neutralised under the guarantee of the Powers, and the Prussian garrison withdrawn. Stanley was very insistent in the House of Commons, that the guarantee was a collective and not a separate one; that the liability was limited, and amounted rather to a moral sanction than to a contingent liability to go

to war. Derby laboured the same point in the House of
Lords. Under a collective guarantee, he said, if there
was a difference of opinion among the guarantors, no
one party was called upon to undertake the duty of
enforcing it. Both statesmen had in view the contingency which Stanley had discussed in writing to
Disraeli, of France and Prussia combining to violate
the treaty. But their language was unfortunate. The
real point was: Would England assist either France or
Prussia to support the neutrality of Luxemburg if the
other proceeded to violate it ? As the Queen and
Disraeli understood the treaty, the answer was Yes.

Throughout this matter the Queen was constantly
appealing to Disraeli for support for a more vigorous
policy than Stanley, with Derby's adherence, was
disposed to pursue. Disraeli sympathised with Her
Majesty's standpoint, and used his influence to stiffen
Stanley. The Queen warned Disraeli of the bad effect
produced on the Continent by Derby's and Stanley's
language about Luxemburg, and told him that she had
had to explain that, so long as other Powers, especially
France and Prussia, adhered to the engagements they had
entered into, England would never be found unfaithful
to hers. Her Majesty anticipated the impending struggle
between France and Prussia, and was not reconciled to
the adoption by this country of a purely fatalistic and
detached attitude. Was Great Britain to make no
attempt to avert such a calamity ? If those Powers
were bent on quarrelling with each other, it might be
difficult to prevent them. Still, if the aggressor were to
know that, in such a quarrel, the moral, and in certain
cases the material, support of England would be given
to the other side—if, for instance, both Powers were
assured that the violation of Belgium and Luxemburg
would certainly bring England into the field—it might
prevent steps being taken on either side that must lead
to war. To the Queen, as to most contemporary
statesmen, France appeared the most likely violator

of international guarantees, and Disraeli, long as he had clung to the French alliance, could not contradict her when she advocated, in adherence to the Prince Consort's tradition, a good understanding with North Germany; but the principle remained equally good, whoever might be the aggressor. Her Majesty struck a chord to which he responded.

From General the Hon. Charles Grey.

OSBORNE, *July* 29, 1867.—. . . Prussia is not likely to violate either the neutrality of Luxemburg or the independence of Belgium—indeed, she has no interest to do so— *unless she sees reason to believe that England means her guarantee of both these objects to remain a dead letter, in which case she might think it in her interest to come to an agreement with France fatal to the independence of the rest of Europe.* . . . The Queen is confirmed in her opinion of the expediency of our acting firmly on a well-defined and well understood principle of foreign policy, by the result of our intervention on the Luxemburg question. It is not only that peace was preserved chiefly by our means, but that our action on that question went far towards restoring to England the prestige there can be no doubt she had lost. It is neither for our national credit nor for the interest of the world that we should again fall into the state of absolute disregard from which we have now partly recovered. H.M. would therefore strongly urge the necessity of your giving your best attention to our whole system of foreign policy, so as to secure to England the respect and influence due to her as the Power who, above all others, can have no ambitious views of her own, nor any interest but in the preservation of peace. . . .

At the close of the session of 1867 Disraeli assured the Queen that an impression had been made upon Stanley, whose opinions, he thought—but apparently was mistaken in thinking—were undergoing modification

To Queen Victoria.

DOWNING STREET, *Aug.* 16, 1867.—. . . Lord Stanley seems to have increased, and increasing, confidence in the maintenance of European peace; although Lord Stanley is of a reserved and rather morose temper, and will not go out of his way to confess that he has been in error, he is really *au fond* truthful and impartial; and, if convinced that he has erred or miscalculated, is never blind to the result, and, often unavowedly, to a certain degree perhaps unconsciously, will assuredly modify his conduct. So, in the present state of affairs, it is far from improbable that Lord Stanley will, ultimately, be the Minister who will destroy, and shatter to pieces, the decaying theory and system of non-interference.

A consideration of the principal foreign difficulty which had to be dealt with by the new Administration has carried us some way beyond the autumn of 1866. Other questions loomed more largely at first. Portugal proposed a commercial treaty, and there was some hope that Spain also would come in. Disraeli, as Chancellor of the Exchequer, was greatly interested in proposals which might 'increase our markets; and that,' he wrote to Northcote, 'is the main interest of the labouring class.' But the negotiations, after dragging on a long time, proved abortive. The mutterings of trouble with the United States about the *Alabama* Claims, and with Abyssinia over some British prisoners whom King Theodore wrongfully detained, were also beginning at this time to be heard.

Meanwhile Disraeli was urgent in pressing for economy in administration to suit an unaggressive policy; and he made his first attack on the mismanagement of the Admiralty.

To Lord Derby.

Confidential. HUGHENDEN MANOR, *Aug.* 20, 1866.—The maladministration, not to say malversation, of the Admiralty has struck deep into the public mind, and is, at this moment, the predominant feeling of the nation. If dealt with vigorously, it will divert opinion from Parliamentary Reform; if neglected, it may precipitate great political changes.

Some few years ago, when I endeavoured to draw the attention of our party, but not as successfully as I wished, to this subject, I was guided by the information and advice of Mr. Laird, M.P. for Birkenhead.[1] Before I left town, that gentleman requested an interview with me, of which the object was to offer, if I wished it, to resume the reports and counsels that he had previously given me.

Mr. Laird attributes the deplorable administration of the Admiralty, mainly, to two causes:

[1] The shipbuilder and shipowner.

Firstly, the expenditure and waste which are occasioned by the accumulation of stores. . . .

Mr. Laird is of opinion that the surplus stores should be sold, and, consisting mainly of timber, iron, and copper, he believes they may be disposed of at half-price. This would place a large sum at the disposal of the Admiralty.

The second cause of maladministration was pointed out by him to me some years ago, and is now still more enforced, viz., the obstinacy with which the Admiralty has declined building iron ships, and the vast sums which they have vainly expended in cobbling up old wooden vessels.

These are the two principal causes of the present condition of the navy, which, if encountered in a masterly manner, may be a source of strength and reputation to your Government; if neglected, may lead to public disaster.

There increased expenditure will aggravate, not cure, the disease.

I refrain from having any communication with Sir John Pakington on this subject. All extraordinary motion in the great departments should come from you. It confirms your authority and it prevents jealousies. But I earnestly beg you to give your personal attention and energy to this matter. A First Lord is surrounded by the criminals, and it requires intellectual grasp, and a peremptory firmness, to deal with them.

An unexpected military drain was caused by the sudden despatch of troops to Canada to protect the colony against a threatened Fenian raid from the United States. Disraeli was clear that these troops must be recalled directly the danger was past, and that the colony which repudiated any interference from home with her local government should also learn that, in that case, she must provide for her local defence, thus enforcing a doctrine which Adderley had vainly pressed on him a year or two before. The impatience which allowed him to write of the colonies as 'dead-weights' recalls the irritable epithet 'wretched' of fourteen years before; but, as guardian of the public purse, he did well to protest against the one-sided relation which some colonies seemed then to think fair. The Dominions have long since recognised the obligation on which Disraeli insisted. With regard to the somewhat sweeping proposal to abandon our West African settlements, it must be remembered that only a year previously a representative Committee of the House of Commons on West African affairs had unanimously reported against any further extension of territory or assumption of government, and that what is now by far the most valuable and prosperous of British possessions in that quarter, Nigeria, was then unappropriated and practically unknown.

To Lord Derby.

HUGHENDEN MANOR, *Sept.* 30, 1866.—. . . Until the American elections have taken place, there will be no chance of anything like sense or moderation in American politics; but there will be a chance then.

Then, also, we must seriously consider our Canadian position, which is most illegitimate. An army maintained in a country which does not permit us even to govern it ! What an anomaly !

It never can be our pretence, or our policy, to defend the Canadian frontier against the U.S. If the colonists can't, as a general rule, defend themselves against the Fenians, they can do nothing. They ought to be, and must be, strong enough for that. Power and influence we should exercise in Asia; consequently in Eastern Europe, consequently also in Western Europe; but what is the use of these colonial deadweights which *we do not govern ?*

I don't regret what we did the other day about Canada, because the circumstances were very peculiar. A successful raid of the Fenians was not off the cards, which would have upset your untried Ministry, and might have produced an insurrection in Ireland; and it was not fair to the Canadians, when, at the last, they were making some attempts at self-defence, to allow them to be crushed in the bud of their patriotism. But the moment the American elections are over, we should withdraw the great body of our troops, and foster a complete development of self-government.

Leave the Canadians to defend themselves; recall the African squadron; give up the settlements on the west coast of Africa; and we shall make a saving which will, at the same time, enable us to build ships and have a good Budget.

What is more, we shall have accomplished something definite, tangible, for the good of the country. In these

days, more than ever, the people look to results. What we
have done about Canada is perfectly defensible, if it is not
looked upon as a permanent increase of our Canadian
establishments.

According to my accounts from the Continent, Hartington
mentioned at more than one place that our recent despatch
of troops is to be made the great point of attack on the part
of the Opposition. May they long enjoy that venerable
name, which I never yet read, or hear, without thinking
there is something personal ! . . .

Derby had loyally backed his lieutenant in his demands
on Pakington and the Admiralty ; but Disraeli had to
exercise continual pressure to obtain the results he
desired. The circumstances in which Ministers succeeded
to office added weight to Disraeli's representations. The
City of London was then slowly recovering from the
terrible panic caused by the failure in May of the great
discount establishment of Overend and Gurney, the
most striking incident of a crisis due to the excessive
development of speculative companies.

To Sir John Pakington.

HUGHENDEN, *Oct.* 23, 1866.—. . . If your proposition
involves a second naval supplemental estimate, and a consequent charge on the balances of the present financial year,
I must at once express my inability to provide for it.

Our financial position is not satisfactory. I have been
obliged to borrow largely from the bank for the payment of
the recent dividends, and though, by the last return, the 20th
inst., these advances have been satisfied, still, that result
has been accomplished by appropriating the revenue of
nearly three weeks of the new quarter, and our balances in
the bank are under one million. They ought to be between
three and four millions. But that is not all. On these
feeble balances the demands are great and unusual. Claims
for the advances agreed upon in respect to cattle compensation, Irish railways, and Cheshire distress, are now pouring in.

Although, notwithstanding the financial pressure and the
bad harvest, the revenue has wonderfully maintained itself,
it, as yet, scarcely realises the estimate of my predecessor,
and you may remember in that estimate, virtually, no surplus
was provided.

When we acceded to office, the magnificent crop of barley,

then in the fields, gave me reason to believe that the second half of the financial year would have been buoyant from the increased malt tax, then anticipated; but all these hopes have been, since, dashed to the ground.

Under these circumstances, it will be one of my first duties, when the Cabinet reassembles, to call its attention to our financial position, and, discarding every other consideration but that of an inexorable economy, to request its sanction to a proposal that no department of the State shall exceed the amount of the estimates of 1866-67, with a hope that they may not reach them; otherwise we shall get into a scrape.

I ought to observe, with respect to second supplementary estimates—on the ground of good administration alone, so very objectionable—that I have communicated with General Peel on this head; and he has promised me that the increased expenditure for Canadian small arms shall be defrayed out of the supplemental vote of this year. . . .

To Lord Derby.

GROSVENOR GATE, *Feb.* 2, 1867.—The Admiralty is beyond the control of a Chancellor of the Exchequer, or any other subordinate Minister. It is the Prime Minister that can alone deal with that department.

If the Admiralty want more guns, they must proportionately diminish their contract expenditure.

It is useless to attempt to reason with them; you must command. The whole system of administration is palsied by their mutinous spirit. Not another four-and-twenty hours ought to elapse without the estimates being settled. Several acts of great policy—the formation of the army of reserve, and the Portuguese treaty—depend upon the programme on which we agreed, and which, so far as the Admiralty is concerned, gives it more than half a million of excess.

Disraeli's vigorous efforts for economy had their due effect. They gave him an estimated surplus on his 1867 Budget of £1,200,000. This he applied, with general consent, to the reduction of debt, appeasing the indefatigable opponents of the malt tax by the appointment of a Select Committee.

Other subjects of moment which occupied Disraeli's attention during the autumn were the purchase of the telegraphs by the State—'a great affair. but, though difficult, it appears to be sound and solid '; and the local government of London, which he pressed upon Hardy, who remarked that it was a ' very puzzling ' question, and that ' a number of municipalities would hardly vary from the vestries which are the local governments in many cases justly complained of.' The purchase of the telegraphs Disraeli was to carry through before he quitted office; but the local government of London he left to be reconstituted by Conservative successors after his death. A letter to Northcote tells of other anxieties:

To Sir Stafford Northcote.

HUGHENDEN, *Oct.* 14, 1866.—. . . I am anxious, and rather alarmed, about the financial systems of our railway companies. So far as I can judge, from the information that reaches me, nearly the whole of them will collapse; the distress and ruin to many industrial establishments will be great, but the effect on the condition of the working classes, at a moment when there are elements of discontent abroad, would be very serious.

Is it possible for the Government to interfere ? It would be a great affair. Between bonds and debentures we should have to deal with more than a hundred million. This is one of the subjects over which we must talk together. . . .

Our great misfortune at present is the acceptance by Cairns of the Lord Justiceship, vacant by the resignation of Knight Bruce. It is an irreparable loss, and falls with peculiar severity on myself, for in debate he was my right arm.

If Cairns had had only a little heart and a little imagination, he would have been by far the first man in the House of Commons; and if he had had only a little heart and a little imagination, he would not have deserted Lord Derby at such a crisis, which may be historic. . . .

We are victims of patronage. Never was such a shower, especially of legal posts.[1]

Cairns was never a strong man physically, and he found the calls of the Attorney-Generalship on his strength to be excessive. He took the opportunity of a vacancy

[1] Writing to Lord Barrington on Jan. 29, 1868, Disraeli said: ' I wish, almost, it were an *indoctum parliamentum* again, and that we had no lawyers in it.'

in the Court of Appeal to retire to the bench, without much consideration for the feelings of his leader in the House of Commons, who was left to face a critical session without the aid of his most trusted debater. Disraeli's letters of this date are full of laments over this desertion. 'With him I was not afraid to encounter Gladstone and Roundell Palmer,' he wrote to Corry; 'now I have got them both, without the slightest assistance.' He had not then realized to the full the value of Gathorne Hardy, who succeeded to Cairns's place as his 'sword-arm' when the fight was fierce in the House of Commons.

A pleasant picture of Disraeli's methods in dealing with business is sketched for us in his notes written from Hughenden to his secretary during this autumn.

To Montagu Corry.

HUGHENDEN, *Sept.* 2, 1866.—. . . When letters come from my colleagues marked 'Private,' it is unnecessary to open them, as no action can be taken on them until they are forwarded to me. Nothing, therefore, is gained by the process, which is not necessary, and which my correspondents, under such circumstances, dislike.

My hand is by no means so bad as my handwriting would imply; the scrawl is the consequence of the wretched, cheap huckster's ink, supplied by that miserable department, the Stationery Office.

Sept. 5.—I enclose you Lord Stanley's letter.

In the first place, obtain immediately for me the answer of the Board of Trade referred to.[1] Be pleased also to tell the Board of Trade—I suppose it will be Mr. Cave, as Sir Stafford is absent—that I wish copies of all correspondence, etc., that may take place between the Board and the F. O., respecting commercial treaties, to be forwarded immediately to me. The Treasury is the chief, and controlling, department of the State, and it is perfectly absurd that, in matters which cannot be carried into operation without sensibly influencing the revenue, we should not have the best information at the earliest date. . . .

Observe what Lord S. says about the 'compares.'[2] As

---

[1] With reference to the proposed commercial treaty with Portugal.
[2] Weekly revenue returns printed for the use of the Treasury.

there is, and has ever been, an entire alliance between us, I wish particularly that his request should be complied with.

But I don't want it to be known in the office. Do this: tell the office that, in future, I wish *two* copies of the ' compare ' to be sent to me. It will be your duty to send one immediately to Lord Stanley in a packet marked ' Private,' with ' C. of E.' in the corner. . . .

Sept. 9.—. . . I am not surprised B[oard] of T[rade] rather demurs at having to work in September, which is unnatural, but it will give them a lesson, and teach them which department is at the head of the Government.

You, also, have not found the secretariat quite as much of a sinecure as we expected; but you have done your work very well, and it will season you for the impending struggle. . . .

Sept. 11.—. . . Read the enclosed letter from Mr. Wellings, a clergyman of Shropshire. The youth referred to was the godson of the late Mrs. Brydges Willyams, who, about three years ago, made me her heir. She left this lad £3,000, and requested me, if I had the opportunity, of planting him in life. I never saw him, nor wish to see him, but I should like very much to forward his interests—particularly as he does not seem to want much.

The Mr. Lovell referred to is the lawyer to the Brydges Willyams estate, who has communicated with all the legatees, but this matter should not be left to Mr. Lovell any further.

I don't want the boy to be unnecessarily plucked, and therefore I would wish you to write to his uncle, and inquire whether he is prepared to pass the preliminary examination, etc., etc., and generally put things in train. . . .

Sept. 25.—What do you think of the ink they give us ? Is it detestable ? Or is it this fat, woolly paper, which they think so fine ?

The ink is not so bad on my own paper, of which I enclose a specimen; but it soon gets so. I can't think it is the pens. Bad stationery adds much to the labor of life; and whether it be the ink, the pens, or the paper, it seems to me, when in office, I never can write like a gentleman. It's a serious nuisance.

Sept. 26.—We must not make another mistake about our paper. I observe the ' Hughenden ' sheet, which I sent you yesterday, is part of a lot which I did not much approve of at the time. I thought it too austere.

Now I write on some ' Grosvenor Gate ' paper, which I think perfectly satisfied me in town; but whether it be the office ink or the office pens, my caligraphy has a cheesemongerish look. . . . The whole subject will employ your

vacant hours till I return to town, as I shall certainly lose
my temper, when real business commences, if my tools are
not first-rate.

You do your business very well, and I am always glad to
hear from you. . . .

Oct. 2.—What you write about Mr. A—— sending the
' compare ' regularly to Mr. Gladstone is distressing.

It appears to me a proceeding highly irregular, and fraught
with injurious consequences, while at the same time I feel
reluctance in interfering, where Mr. Gladstone is concerned.

If Mr. Gladstone, on the ground alleged,[1] as I understand,
by Mr. A——, had asked me for this privilege, considering
his eminence and services, however reluctant to do so, I
should not have hesitated to have accorded it; but there is
a great difference in such a proceeding sanctioned by me,
and a communication, which has the appearance of being
clandestine, between a permanent officer of the Government
and an ex-head of his department.

I do not know of any precedent for such a course, and Mr.
A—— has certainly no right to make one.

Where is the line to be drawn between communications
between Mr. A—— and a late Chancellor of the Exchequer ?
Why should they not refer to future Budgets as well as to
past ?

Such a proceeding has a tendency to destroy that complete
confidence which ought to exist between me and an officer
in Mr. A——'s position.

I should wish that you should have conferred, on this
matter, with Sir Stafford Northcote, who, from being a
friend of Mr. Gladstone, would have considered the circumstances without prejudice against him, but Sir S. is at
Balmoral.

In the meantime, consult Mr. Hamilton [2] confidentially on
the matter, and report to me. . . .

Oct. 16.—. . . I assume that, after all our experience,
now of many years, of Roman Catholic influences and
interests in Ireland, men like Naas and Taylor, and especially
the former, who is a most able, sensible, and enlightened
man, are taking the right course; and I will not interfere
with them in any way. They know my Irish policy, and
any observations of mine are unnecessary.

---

[1] That it was fair that an outgoing Chancellor of the Exchequer should
be kept informed of the working of his budget till the end of the financial
year.

[2] The permanent head of the office, who immediately ordered the
practice to be discontinued.

As for Hennessy [1] running with us and Cullen [2] and Co. (Cullen is a mere Whig) at the same time, it is plainly impossible that he can succeed in such an adventure.

The Tipperary election will show whether there be any substance in Monsell's views of a national Roman Catholic party in Ireland. I confess I am not sanguine. . . .

Dec. 21.—. . . I think the time has arrived when the Patronage Secretary of the Treasury (of all men in the world !) should at least learn the office which his master fills, and his due title. Give him at the earliest opportunity a gentle educational hint. Somebody has instructed Hunt long ago— I suppose Hamilton. The manners of D[owning] S[treet] are getting quite American. The tradition of the old etiquette must be gradually revived.

We ought to have made the F. O. Press print all their labels over again, and I think you had better order the circular one. I did insist upon it in the case of ' Earl Derby ' ! I dare say Colonel Taylor addresses the Lord Chancellor as Lord Chelmsford !

Disraeli, ever an artist on the national stage, was a great upholder of what he sometimes called the etiquette, and sometimes the punctilio, of office. He made it a practice to address a colleague who was a Secretary of State as ' Secretary So-and-So '[3]; his intimate notes to Stanley, when they were in office together, frequently began ' My dear Secretary '; and he expected, when he was responsible for the national Treasury, to be, as a matter of course, himself officially addressed as ' Chancellor of the Exchequer.'

[1] Sir John Pope-Hennessy, appointed Governor of Labuan in 1867, and eventually Governor of Mauritius.

[2] The Cardinal.

[3] Disraeli, when Prime Minister for the second time, endeavoured to get this nomenclature adopted in the House of Commons; but Speaker Brand and Raikes, then Chairman of Committees, refused their consent. See *Life of Raikes*, pp. 91, 92.

CHAPTER XIV.

DISRAELI'S PARLIAMENTARY TRIUMPH—I.

1867.

' Of all possible hares to start, I do not know a better than the extension to household suffrage, coupled with plurality of voting.' In this light-hearted manner was the idea, on which the great measure of 1867 was based, thrown out in a letter from Derby to Disraeli on December 22, 1866. The sentence occurs among a number of suggestions as to the matters which might be submitted for inquiry to the Commission then contemplated by the Government. 'The advantage,' Derby continued, ' of multiplying such questions is that we do not bind ourselves to the adoption of any, but afford an opportunity for feeling the pulse of Parliament and the country on all.' Of this special suggestion Disraeli in reply took no particular notice, save to say that ' extension ' of the franchise, the word used in the Resolutions, would include everything.

Household suffrage was no new proposal; but it was one that hitherto both Whigs and Tories had united to oppose. Its Parliamentary sponsor had originally been the Radical, Joseph Hume; but of late years it had been revived by Bright, who, in his Reform campaign in the autumn and winter of 1858-59, definitely committed himself to it as the basis of the borough franchise. Disraeli, on behalf of the Government, as definitely rejected it in his speech moving for leave to bring in the Ministerial Bill of 1859. Arguing against the reduction of the £10 borough franchise, he said: ' It certainly would be most injudicious, not to say intolerable, when we are guarding

ourselves against the predominance of a territorial aristocracy and the predominance of a manufacturing and
commercial oligarchy, that we should reform Parliament
by securing the predominance of a household democracy.'
He would have nothing to say to a constituency so monotonous. This was his public language in 1859; but, on
the third reading of the Bill of 1867, he stated that household suffrage was proposed as the principle of the borough
franchise in the Derby-Disraeli Cabinet of 1858-59; though
it was not adopted, on the ground that it would receive
no support from public opinion, which was at that time
against any reduction of the borough franchise whatever.
But he added that the Cabinet were unanimous that, if
they attempted to reduce the borough qualification at
all, recourse to household suffrage was inevitable. Henley
at once disputed the statement, so far, at least, as concerned the Cabinet while he remained a member of it
—that is, down to the introduction of the Bill in the House
of Commons. The explanation probably is that what
had become in 1867 the principle was in 1859 the bogey.
That Disraeli and other members of the 1858 Cabinet
were clear-sighted enough to perceive that, when once you
abandoned the £10 limit, there was no logical or substantial basis short of household suffrage, we can well believe;
but, when we remember the attitude of the Government
and of public opinion at the time to Bright's proposal,
we can only read the unanimity of the Cabinet on the
point as meaning that they must adhere without flinching
to the £10 limit, so as to avoid being ultimately driven
to the very unpalatable alternative of household suffrage.
It was a £6 limit, and not household suffrage, that Disraeli
was ready to accept, in May and June, 1859, as a settlement.[1] Indeed, household suffrage does not appear to
have been mentioned in the correspondence about Reform

---

[1] In his speech on Baines's Bill in 1865, Disraeli said that what the
Government were prepared to propose in June, 1859, was ' not a franchise
of £6, but an arrangement that was to be taken with the rest of the Bill.'
This is vague, and does not affect his readiness to accept Roebuck's terms,
which included a £6 borough franchise. See Vol. I., p. 1643.

between him and Derby down to the winter of 1866-67.
The question is always of £8 or £7 or £6 or £5, even
in July, 1866[1]; and of course these were the figures
actually proposed or suggested by those Whig and Tory
legislators who contemplated the abandonment of the
£10 limit. It must be confessed that Disraeli's statement
about the Cabinet of 1858 and household suffrage can
only be regarded as rather a glaring instance of the besetting sin of Parliamentary statesmen, to make out
that there is no inconsistency between the course they
may be rightly taking under the exigencies of the moment,
and that which they took or recommended in earlier and
different circumstances.

It was as a subject for inquiry that Derby first recommended household suffrage. But the Commission to
inquire into all the conditions and surroundings of Reform, which was to be of so comprehensive a character
as to justify Ministers in postponing legislation for a
year, and was accordingly regarded with satisfaction by
Derby, Disraeli, and Cranborne, never saw the Parliamentary light. The discussions of January killed it.
' The scheme of an inquiry does not seem to find favour
with the public,' wrote that cool observer, Stanley, on
January 2. On the same day Corry told Disraeli: ' I
have been rather surprised at the unanimity with which
all classes, in the provinces where I have been, desire a
Reform Bill—from Lord Shaftesbury[2] to the Shropshire
rustic.' The next day Disraeli wrote urging on Derby
the necessity of coming to an early decision on their
' Reform movements '; ' otherwise I see anarchy ahead.
There are many other great matters pressing, but this
is paramount.'

The first thing on which Ministers decided was to proceed by resolution, and thereby to associate the House
of Commons, as a whole, with the Government in the
shaping of Reform. The decision met with the enthusiastic approval of the Queen. ' It is the course,' she

---

[1] See above. p. 186.   [2] Corry's uncle.

wrote on January 12, 'dictated by common-sense, and
which all who are sincerely desirous of seeing the question
settled, and who do not use it as a mere weapon of party
warfare, are bound to support.' Her Majesty offered once
more to use her good offices with the Opposition, if desired
by the Government. Disraeli was equally clear in favour
of proceeding by resolution.

To Lord Derby.

Private. GROSVENOR GATE, *Jan.* 13, 1867.—. . . The more
I think over it, the more complete seems to me the conclusion,
that proceeding by resolution is the Parliamentary, and constitutional, consequence of the conduct of the House of
Commons itself upon the question of Parliamentary Reform.
The House of Commons first disturbed the settlement of 1832,
and the House of Commons has defeated the measures, taken
in consequence of that disturbance, of *five* Ministries. . . .

But to decide to proceed by way of resolution was,
after all, only to confirm the provisional decision of the
autumn. The vital question was : Were the Resolutions
to lead up to an inquiry, or to immediate legislation ?
On this point Disraeli entirely changed his mind within
a few weeks or even days. On December 26 he expressed
himself as still being opposed to legislation, and not
seeing the necessity for the settlement which the Queen
desired. But January was not far advanced before he
was seeking, in concert with Derby, who had reverted
to his original opinion of the autumn, for an enduring
basis on which a Reform Bill could be founded. Disraeli's papers throw very little light on this change of
attitude. But it was clearly based on a revised estimate
of the state of public opinion. He would not admit in
the autumn that the success of the agitation which
Bright was conducting showed that the country had
determined to obtain Reform; but in January he found
the evidence conclusive. It is, of course, obvious that
evidence of the kind is cumulative, and that, as it grows,
there comes a point when the most reluctant must give
way to facts. As soon as Disraeli reached that point,

he acted with promptitude and decision. If the Resolutions were to lead to an immediate Bill, and that Bill was to be a settlement, the Cabinet could not rest in the generalities of the autumn, but, loth as they might be to adventure upon the slippery surface of the details of Reform, must make the attempt at once, so as not to be taken absolutely unawares when Parliament met.

Accordingly Disraeli and Derby both addressed themselves to the question, and before the end of the month had both arrived at the conclusion that rating household suffrage, duly hedged in by securities, was the one safe basis for the borough reduction. It is not difficult to see how the two leaders, who were Reformers as well as Conservatives, reached this conclusion. If they were to effect a settlement of the controversy, some logical basis must be found, other than the mere reduction of the limit by a few pounds; and a householder, who was also a ratepayer, had that stake in the prosperity and good government of the country which, from a Conservative point of view, might reasonably be held to qualify him for the franchise. Besides, ' household suffrage ' was, as Gladstone called it, a ' great phrase,' and the creator of Taper and Tadpole knew well the political value of a sonorous cry. The idea was apparently first broached tentatively in Cabinet by Disraeli in the last week of January. Cranborne was at once disquieted, perceiving that the safeguards which all the Cabinet were at that time agreed in maintaining might easily be swept away in debate. Carnarvon, who was shortly to follow Cranborne into retirement on this very question, was quite prepared for household suffrage, provided distinct checks were insisted upon.

From Lord Cranborne.

Confidential. INDIA OFFICE, *Feb.* 1, 1867.—. . . What alarmed me in the programme you sketched on Wednesday was the introduction into the resolutions of very specific suffrage—such as household suffrage, which you named. Such a course would make it easy for the other side to frame an amendment that should drive the waverers into their lobby, and would deprive your concession of all neutralising safeguards. Such a result would be more dangerous in a resolution than in a Bill. I think resolutions are only safe so long as they are general.

From Lord Carnarvon.

Private. GROSVENOR STREET, *Feb.* 2, 1867.—. . . 1. I understand that we are generally agreed upon an attempt at legislation, provided that no unforeseen circumstances arise. In this I quite agree; I see no alternative.

2. My own view is to carry the borough franchise down to a considerable depth in order to get a ledge on which to rest. I believe an arbitrary reduction of £1, £2, or £3 to be of all measures the most fatal. For this reason, I do not—as far as I understand the conditions of the problem to be solved—object to household franchise.

3. But such a reduction needs some very distinct checks. A residential qualification of three years, with the payment of rates and taxes, is excellent: but I feel some fear of depending on one single safeguard. I assume that any plan that we propose will—so far as the leading features of it are concerned—be proposed as a whole: but must we not expect that the moment that the measure is passed agitation against the restrictive portions of it will commence; and, if so, is it not probable that that agitation will have a fairer chance of success if the restrictions upon the freedom of the franchise are narrowed to one single, tangible, very definite point of opposition ? . . .

The checks upon which Carnarvon insisted so strongly, and about the maintenance of which Cranborne was so sceptical, were also regarded at this period as indispensable by the Prime Minister.

From Lord Derby.

Confidential. ST. JAMES'S SQUARE, *Feb.* 2, 1867.—I return the papers you left with me. They are conclusive, to my mind, that without plurality of voting we cannot propose household suffrage, which would give the working classes a majority of nearly 2 : 1. Even Gladstone repudiated the idea of giving them *any* majority; and our friends would not, and I think ought not, to listen to it for a moment. . . .

From the first the idea of household suffrage attracted many of the Cabinet, besides Carnarvon. One of the earliest to entertain it was Malmesbury, who suggested it in conversation to Carnarvon in the previous summer. Pakington wrote to Disraeli on February 1 that he inclined more and more to the belief that the boldest course would be the safest, and that, if they must adopt a novelty, it would be better to take that which was ' simple and effective, rather than one which is complicated, invidious, and incomplete.' Disraeli, moreover, found that a settlement based on rating household suffrage would unite Walpole, who stood for Church and State Conservatism, and Graves, member for Liverpool, a representative of the Tory democracy of that great port, and a man who played a considerable, though unobtrusive, part in determining the event.

To Lord Derby.

Confidential. 11, DOWNING STREET, *Feb.* 4, 1867.—Walpole is very much against ' plural voting.' He says he has only heard but one opinion of it since Horsman's suggestion, ' And is this all the Adullamites have invented !'

He says there is but only one course, if we legislate; household suffrage, founded on residence and rating, which he is convinced is most conservative—no compound householders on any account.

So far as he has spoken with our friends, he has heard no difference on the point; that fighting about £1 or £2 is ridiculous, and probably will give us a worse constituency.

Mr. Graves, the M.P. for Liverpool, has just left me. He was delighted with the Reform par. in the Speech : an immense relief to him: only one opinion out of doors: settlement of the question.   But what settlement ?

' Oh ! a moderate settlement.'

' But what do you call moderate '?

' Oh ! I should say, for myself, household suffrage founded on rating. That's the real thing; rating is better than any money qualification. There are 10,000 Parliamentary voters now in Liverpool who do not pay their rates—and never will. It is the distribution of seats that is the difficulty; not the franchise.'

The Reform paragraph of the Queen's Speech, which gave Graves, who was to second the Address, so much satisfaction, ran as follows:

Your attention will be again called to the state of the representation of the people in Parliament; and I trust that your deliberations, conducted in a spirit of moderation and mutual forbearance, may lead to the adoption of measures which, without unduly disturbing the balance of political power, shall freely extend the elective franchise.

This paragraph occupied the forefront of the part of the Speech devoted to projects of domestic legislation; and by it the Cabinet committed themselves to a ' free ' extension of the suffrage.   In the debate Gladstone insisted, without contradiction, and amid general approval, that the question of Reform stopped the way to all other legislation, and should be promptly dealt with and disposed of.   As Derby wrote to Disraeli, Parliament was ' very hot on Reform without delay.'

Ministers showed no lack of promptitude in opening the matter to the House.   Parliament met on Tuesday, February 5, and on the following Monday Disraeli introduced the Reform Resolutions.   But, in the short interval, the Cabinet had already passed through its first crisis.   ' Household suffrage,' which had only been thrown out as a possible idea by Disraeli in the previous week, was, after the Queen's Speech, definitely proposed to the Cabinet by Derby.   His suggestion was that the Resolution which referred to borough franchise might recommend that, if plural voting were adopted, it would be safe to introduce household suffrage on a rating basis. Though no details were mentioned, the principle was apparently accepted by the Cabinet.   But General Peel at once objected, and threatened resignation if the Resolution were not altered.   Disraeli was full of expedients to meet the situation; and for the moment his efforts were successful.

To Lord Derby.

Confidential.   11, DOWNING STREET, *Feb.* 7, 1867.—Besides urging all the considerations, to which you so properly referred, as to the impossibility of carrying on affairs if mutual concessions are not made, and so on, this suggestion might relieve us.

Our great anxiety not to lose his services would make you agree to recast, and modify, the Resolution in question, which

II.   8*

you also might take the occasion of making him understand
was your own particular policy, and which you had deeply
and carefully considered.

' That the principle of plural voting, if adopted by Parliament, might lead to the adjustment of the borough franchise
on a safe and permanent basis.'

The House, and the country (more important) would understand this. If the Resolution be adopted, we could do without
Peel. If rejected, we should have to fall back on a moderate
reduction of the franchise, coupled with fancy safety valves for
the working class. With such a Resolution, Peel could honorably remain until we attempted to carry it into action
according to our interpretation of it; and if the House did not
sanction our doing so, then, of course, he need not budge.

But you ought to make him understand that it is your personal appreciation of his value, etc., that makes you consent
to a change which, in your opinion, enfeebles your policy. It
would be a great thing if the resignation could be postponed.

Pardon these crude suggestions of a much-vexed, but faithful, colleague.

HOUSE OF COMMONS, *Thursday* [*Feb.* 7, 1867].—. . . I have
sent you a note to House of Lords, telling you of my interview
with Peel, and of its general success. The words I gave you
would entirely satisfy him, but I have not committed *you* to
them: and if you can devise, with him, more suitable ones for
your purpose, you can.

You will find him very placable, except on the phrase
' household suffrage,' when his eye lights up with insanity.
He evidently annexes no definite idea to the phrase, but told
me that the whole of our back benches would rise and leave
us, as one man, if the phrase remained. I believe in three
months' time they will unanimously call for it.

But I soothed him, *and it is all right*. You will give the
finishing touch.

Though internal dissension had begun, important external support had been already received in the world
of journalism. Early in February, Derby wrote to Disraeli: ' It will be a crumb of comfort to you to know that
I have had a most satisfactory interview with Delane.
He is cordially with us, and will do all in his power to
carry us through. He listened most attentively to the
whole of our programme, and pronounced oracularly,
" I think it will do." ' The precedent of the India Bill,
introduced in the first instance by Resolutions, and ulti-

mately passed by consent, was quoted to justify the procedure on which Government had resolved. Accordingly, in
spite of Cabinet troubles, it was with a good heart that
Disraeli rose on Monday, February 11, to introduce the Reform Resolutions, and to endeavour to persuade the House
of Commons to take the reasonable course of settling this
vexed question by mutual concession and consent. It
was, no doubt, a convenient doctrine for himself and his
colleagues that, as he began by maintaining, Parliamentary Reform should no longer be a question which
should decide the fate of Ministries. But his reason was
incontrovertible, that all parties had attempted to deal
with it, in 1852, 1854, 1859, 1860, and 1866, and had
failed. Ministers therefore proposed to proceed by
resolution, in order to obtain the views of the House
before introducing a Bill. The main principles of the
Resolutions, as he explained them, were the rating basis;
a reduction of both county and borough franchise; a
dealing with redistribution, boundaries, and bribery, as
well as with franchise. Ministers were not angling
for a policy; they had distinct principles of their
own; but they desired the co-operation of the House.
The course of the Government was not one flattering to
themselves, but it was more honourable to assist, however humbly, in effecting a settlement for the public good,
than to bring forward mock measures which the spirit
of party would not allow to pass. Gladstone made the
obvious comment that everything would depend on
whether the Resolutions were sufficiently precise to form
the basis of a settlement. He should strongly object
to mere vague preliminary declarations, as the duty of
the House was to extend the franchise and get the question out of the way.

When the Resolutions appeared, their vagueness was
immediately commented on and condemned. They were
substantially as drafted in the autumn; but the one about
the borough franchise had been watered down, in order to
retain Peel, to the very general formula, ' that the prin-

ciple of plurality of votes, if adopted by Parliament, would facilitate the settlement of the borough franchise '; and the proposed Royal Commission was only to deal with borough boundaries. The Opposition were at once up in arms, demanding greater precision and definite proposals, and the prospect of Reform by general consent apparently disappeared.

Queen Victoria to Lord Derby.

OSBORNE, *Feb.* 13, 1867.—The Queen cannot help feeling a good deal of fear as to the prospects of a settlement of the Reform question. Mr. Disraeli, in a short account of what passed in the House on Monday, says the Opposition will probably be forced to ' join issue ' on the Resolutions.

Thus, then, the party contest, which the Queen had *hoped* and *understood* it was the object of this mode of proceeding to avoid, is to recommence. And though Mr. Disraeli antici- pates the defeat of the Opposition, and that the future conduct of the question will then be comparatively easy, this does not by any means reassure the Queen, who had been led to believe (as she is herself firmly convinced) that the question could *only* be settled by mutual concession. . . .

Disraeli refused to give the House any further details as to the Government proposals before he rose on the 25th to move the resolutions; and for the best of all reasons, that the Cabinet were not agreed. When he said that Ministers were not angling for a policy, but had one of their own, he was, no doubt, partly using the brave words which the situation demanded, but mainly thinking of the policy of household suffrage, which the Cabinet, with the exception of Peel, had apparently, in general terms, accepted.[1] But, with a view to retain Peel, he spent the next few days in elaborating a modified scheme em- bodying a much smaller reduction of the borough fran- chise. This scheme was explained to the Cabinet on Saturday, the 16th; but entirely failed in its object, as Peel refused to accept even this proposal, and once more

[1] Hardy, when reasoning a few days later with the dissentients, used the argument ' that our personal honour, in allowing our chiefs to state that we were prepared with a Bill, was at stake, and that we must present one in concert ' (Gathorne Hardy, Vol. I., p. 199).

tendered his resignation.   Disraeli reported and explained
the whole situation to the Queen at Osborne next day,
and the Beaconsfield papers contain some rough notes
for a letter to Her Majesty recording the conversation.

On February 16, the Cabinet having been summoned to
sanction the definitive propositions to be made on the subject of P[arliamentary] R[eform] to the House of Commons
by the Chancellor of the Exchequer on Monday, the 25th inst.,
General Peel, after the propositions had been unanimously
adopted by his colleagues, and after they had been modified
in the interval since the preceding Cabinet to meet his views,
announced his inability to sanction any reduction of the franchise, and his intended resignation.

The confusion and embarrassment of such a proceeding
at such a moment were extreme, and as, by a fortunate chance,
the Chancellor of the Exchequer had received Her Majesty's
gracious commands to repair to Osborne on the next day,
Lord Derby was of opinion that it was an occasion to appeal
to Her Majesty for her aid and influence, and authorised the
Chancellor of the Exchequer to confer fully and freely with
Her Majesty on the subject.

The Chancellor of the Exchequer arrived at Osborne on
Sunday, the 17th, and had an audience of Her Majesty on the
same day at 7 o'clock.

Her Majesty, who had been apprised of the resignation,
expressed her regret [at the] loss of Peel: he was a faithful
servant, an able Minister, and one personally very acceptable
to her; but the Reform Bill, she added, was more important
than General Peel.

Rumours had reached her of the probability of some event
of the kind; but not confined to one—Lord Cranborne, and
perhaps Mr. Hardy.

[Chancellor of the Exchequer] assured [Her Majesty] that
Lord Cranborne and Mr. Hardy had made the most earnest
appeals in the Cabinet to Peel. Then described General
Peel's conduct during the various phases of the policy of the
Cabinet until the present moment. At the outset, in November, when Lord Derby proposed to proceed by Resolutions,
pledging the House in the first [place] to reduction of franchise, and ending with address to the Crown for inquiry [two
or three illegible words]; his conduct at the resumption of the
Cabinet after Christmas, when gradually it developed that
the country expected legislation and settlement, not inquiry;
the final giving up of the plan of inquiry, and proposing
resolutions by way of basis of Bill ; and passage in the

Queen's Speech: throughout all this time Peel's conduct dogged silence. After the Queen's Speech Lord Derby called the attention of the Cabinet to the final revision of the Resolutions, and proposed that, if the principle of plural voting were conceded, we should recommend borough franchise on a rating basis. The Cabinet universally adopted this, but Peel requested that a copy of the Resolutions should be sent to him, which Chancellor of the Exchequer did, and the next morning Peel resigned. The Chancellor of the Exchequer saw him at the House, and, after an interview, proposed a modification of the Resolutions as it now appears, and Peel said he was perfectly satisfied and would remain.

On Saturday, the 16th, Lord Derby requested the Chancellor of the Exchequer to state in detail to the Cabinet the application of the principles which he proposed to make on February 25, and Mr. Disraeli, with regard to the borough franchise, proposed that if the securities were conceded it should rest on a £5 [basis], modifying Lord Derby's original plan in order to conciliate the General.

The Cabinet adopted this view, and when all had spoken, the General, who seemed very sullen, spoke and said that he was not prepared to support any reduction of the franchise. Every argument was used and every appeal was made to him, but in vain. Lord Derby reminded the General that for many months he had repeatedly sanctioned their first Resolution, which pledged them to reduction.

After the Cabinet the Chancellor of the Exchequer received Lord Derby's instructions to lay the matter before Her Majesty, and, as a last resource, to invite Her Majesty's aid.

Her Majesty seemed to intimate that the retirement of General Peel alone might not, perhaps, be injurious to the Cabinet on this particular question of Reform (and that after that was settled), but graciously invited the Chancellor of the Exchequer to enter into discussion as to the best course.

The Chancellor of the Exchequer, encouraged by Her Majesty's kindness, put the opposite views before Her Majesty: on one side the greater chance of success with the Reform Bill; on the other that of a homogeneous Cabinet, and the weakness and injury which, generally speaking, secessions at critical moments occasion; and he humbly offered his opinion that, on the whole, it was more prudent, if possible, to retain him.

Her Majesty then most graciously said she was willing and prepared to do anything in her power to support the Administration, as she desired above all things that the Reform question should be settled, and added, if Lord Derby wished it, she would certainly write to Peel.

Chancellor of the Exchequer said that he might presume

to answer for Lord Derby's wishes, as there was entire confidence between them, and at the time of the first resignation
Chancellor of the Exchequer had suggested to Lord Derby
to appeal to Her Majesty; but Lord Derby said he was reluctant to press too much upon the Queen, whose personal interference should be reserved for other questions, and he thought
he ought to keep his colleagues in order.

Her Majesty then entered into the inquiry as to the sort
of letter she should write, and encouraged the Chancellor of
the Exchequer to give his views.

Chancellor of the Exchequer said it was not a case for argument or reference to details of measures; it should rather be
an expression of Her Majesty's deep interest in the question, a
declaration of Her Majesty's personal desire that a measure
should be passed, but mainly an appeal to the personal devotion of the General, which was, no doubt, very great to Her
Majesty.

Her Majesty deigned to listen to these suggestions, and
mused as they were made.

Her Majesty then with great frankness opened the delicate
question as to what was to be done in case of his persistence.
What would Lord Derby do ?

The Chancellor of the Exchequer said that he probably
might try to gain some additional strength, and, as he was
in communication with Lord Grosvenor, might perhaps appeal
to—— [The rest is missing]. [1]

This draft seems to prove that Disraeli, however he
may have decided in his own mind in favour of household
suffrage, was still drifting as to the best immediate policy
for the Cabinet to adopt.   One of the points that comes out
most strongly from a study of his papers is his constant
anxiety to keep colleagues from resigning, even at the cost
of modifying his own cherished policies.   As in the winter
of 1858-59, and during the anxious times of 1876-78, far
from assuming an uncompromising attitude, he showed
himself ready to go even to extreme lengths in order to
preserve the harmony of the Cabinet unbroken.   Peel,
as he was the only dissentient, gave way for the moment
to the representations of the Queen and of his colleagues;
but as his hostility was rather to the general principle
than to the extent of borough franchise reduction, there

[1] The remainder is printed in *Queen Victoria's Letters*, Second Series, I.,
396-399.

was no object in proceeding with the modified scheme. From this time, therefore, Disraeli, and Derby, too, must have taken a definite resolve to press forward with a Bill on the basis of household suffrage, with residence, personal payment of rates, and perhaps dual voting, as checks. Disraeli brought the scheme in detail before the Cabinet on Tuesday, February 19. 'All was smooth,' recorded Hardy in his diary; and even Cranborne, doubtful as he was about what he regarded as a 'very dangerous experiment,' which demanded all the securities that could be got, was still prepared to go forward. Only he urged, in a letter to Derby on Friday, February 22, in anticipation of the final Cabinet discussion on the Saturday, that the limit of the direct taxation franchise, which was to give a second vote, should be ten instead of twenty shillings. That would bring in, he calculated, the great bulk of the payers both of house tax and of income tax. 'You propose to take in every ratepayer. It will only be making your system complete and avoiding needless anomalies to take in every direct taxpayer.'

All remained smooth on the surface during the week, and on the Saturday, February 23, the comprehensive scheme was adopted, apparently by general consent, with the understanding that Disraeli should explain it to the House of Commons on the following Monday. 'The Cabinet unanimous for the great plan. Baxter [who was acting as draftsman] must stop to see me,' scribbled Disraeli to his private secretary. But Sunday, as all politicians know, is, or was, till the week-end habit greatly diminished its critical importance, often a day of political heart-searching and caballing; and never with more fatal effect than on this occasion. On the Monday morning Disraeli was greeted, before he rose, by a hurried note from Derby, written at 8.45 a.m., saying: 'The enclosed, just received, is utter ruin. What on earth are we to do ? ' The enclosure was Cranborne's threat of resignation, endorsed by Carnarvon.

Lord Cranborne to Lord Derby.

INDIA OFFICE, *Sunday evening* [*Feb.* 24, 1867].—I trust you will believe that it gives me great pain to have to say what I am going to say.

I find, on closely examining the scheme which Mr. Disraeli brought to the notice of the Cabinet five days ago, that its effect will be to throw the small boroughs almost, and many of them entirely, into the hands of the voter whose qualification is lower than £10. I do not think such a proceeding is for the interest of the country. I am sure it is not in accordance with the hopes which those of us who took an active part in resisting Mr. Gladstone's Bill last year raised in those whom we induced to vote with us. I find that, in almost every case, those of our friends who sit for boroughs with less than 25,000 inhabitants (a majority of the boroughs) will be in a much worse condition in consequence of our Bill than they would have been in consequence of Mr. Gladstone's.

Under ordinary circumstances I should apologise to you for not having discovered this difficulty before. But in the present case I cannot blame myself on this account. This proposition was made on Tuesday last—to my extreme surprise; and though, since that day, I have devoted every spare moment to the study of the statistics, it was not till to-day that I could obtain the leisure, from heavy departmental work, in order to go through them, borough by borough. Mr. Baxter's error has been that he has made the calculation *in a lump,* and has assumed that the effect would be distributed equally over all boroughs. This assumption is unfounded: for while in small boroughs the addition is large and the counterpoise small, in the large boroughs, where we are hopelessly overmatched, the counterpoise is large and the addition small. I hope by to-morrow morning to have a statement ready which will show this fact in detail.

Unable, therefore, to concur in this scheme, I have to ask you to be good enough to summon a meeting of the Cabinet before the meeting of the party to-morrow. Lord Carnarvon, to whom this evening I showed the figures, concurs with me in this request.

At the same time I am bound in candour to say that I do not see my way to an alternative proposal. The error of attempting to frame a Reform Bill during the week previous to its production is one that, in my opinion, cannot be redeemed.

I need not say how deeply grieved I am by any act of mine to cause inconvenience to you. Though I think the abandonment of the policy under which the Queen's Speech was framed was a disastrous step, I would gladly have gone as far as I could possibly do to prevent any embarrassment to the Cabinet. But if I assented to this scheme, now that I know what its effect will be, I could not look in the face those whom last year I urged to resist Mr. Gladstone. I am convinced that it will, if passed, be the ruin of the Conservative party. . . .

Disraeli's comment to Derby was: ' This is stabbing in the back ! I will come to you as soon as possible, but I am not up, being indisposed; but I shall rally immediately in such dangers. It seems like treachery.' Hardy, whom Cranborne and Carnarvon had vainly endeavoured to seduce from his allegiance on the Sunday night, bears witness that Derby and Disraeli, though much mortified, ' took the sudden and trying emergency well.' How sudden and trying the emergency was, was made clear by an indiscreet speech which Pakington delivered on the hustings when he sought re-election on change of office. Ministers had thought that everything was settled on the Saturday, and so were all dispersed and could not be collected till half-past one. They were then informed that Cranborne and Carnarvon had seceded, objecting to the details of the Bill which they all believed had been unanimously adopted. Here was a pretty business ! It was now two o'clock; at half-past two Derby had to address the party in Downing Street, and at half-past four Disraeli had to explain the Reform scheme in the House. Literally, the Cabinet had not more than *ten minutes*, said Pakington, to make up their minds on their course. In order to retain their colleagues, they hurriedly determined, apparently on Stanley's suggestion, to recur, in substance, to the milder scheme of the previous Saturday week, which had been drawn up in the hope of placating Peel. This, therefore, was the scheme, known to history by the nickname of the ' Ten Minutes ' Bill, that Derby explained to the party meeting, and Disraeli to the House of Commons.

' I am going down to the House. The ship floats; that is all,' was the note Disraeli sent to his wife. It was a strange scene in Parliament that afternoon: a House packed in every corner, with members even sitting on the floor, the galleries and the bar crowded with peers, ambassadors, and other distinguished strangers, headed by the Prince of Wales; and a calm, passionless orator recommending, in a very unenthusiastic fashion, to the attention of members, proposals for which he had no particular affection, and which were very similar in kind to those which Gladstone had unsuccessfully offered a year before, save that the borough franchise was to be £6 rating instead of £7 rental, and the county franchise £20 rating instead of £14 rental. Various fancy franchises were mentioned; but, on the other hand, the principle of plurality, adopted in the Resolutions, was given up. The redistribution proposed was to apply to thirty seats. Such were the main features of the Bill which the Government would introduce on the passing of the Resolutions; but Disraeli asked the House to pass the Resolutions first.

When Disraeli sat down, a storm of indignation burst on his head. Lowe, who had never really shared the friendliness generally felt by the Adullamites for the Government, poured scorn on the attitude of Ministers, whom he described as coming to the House with the cry, 'Say what you like to us, only, for God's sake, leave us our places.' Why were Ministers to have the mark of Cain set upon them, that nobody might kill them? Let the two parties give up this Dutch auction in which the country was to be knocked down to the one who proposed the swiftest element for its destruction. Government should withdraw the Resolutions and bring in a Bill. 'Touch the nettle timidly, and it will sting you; but grasp it firmly, you are unhurt, and can tear it at your leisure.' Bright also urged the withdrawal of the Resolutions, and derided the detailed proposals made that afternoon. He demanded, and promised not factiously to oppose, 'a substantial and satisfactory Bill,' which should settle the question. The support that Ministers got from their own friends was slight, and cries of 'Withdraw!' and 'Bring in a Bill!' assailed the Chancellor during his reply to critics.

Montagu Corry to Mrs. Disraeli.

HOUSE OF COMMONS, *Monday, Feb. 25, 1867, 9.20.*—
Clouds always pass away at last, and that terrible one of
to-day already looks less dense. In spite of the unexampled
trial he has gone through, the Ch. of the Exch. made an
admirably clear and forcible statement, which on the whole
was well received. . . .

I have seen him since the debate, decidedly in better spirits,
while at this moment he is at dinner with Lord Stanley, and
by the time you see him, depend upon it, he will be himself
again. Only one person in the world sympathises with him
to-day as you do, and I can only say that even *my* veneration
has been increased by the noble way in which he has borne
himself.

If Disraeli was in better spirits after the debate, it was
probably for quite another reason than that assumed
by his admiring young secretary. He certainly was under
no illusion as to the popularity of the scheme he had perforce introduced. If not that evening, then undoubtedly
the next day, he realised that events were working in
favour of the bolder course which he and Derby desired,
and that the only safety of the Government would lie in
a reversion to it. Lowe had a premonition of what was
coming. It was said at one time, he remarked, on the
question of Reform, that they were within twenty-four
hours of a revolution. He believed that they had been
within much fewer hours than that of household suffrage,
which he himself held in great dread. The arguments in
favour of household suffrage were winning converts
rapidly, not only within the Cabinet, but in the party
outside. The veteran Henley, who stood out from the
Cabinet, was known to hold this view. The smaller
Bill, which was to preserve the harmony of the Cabinet,
had no special attraction for its followers. They perceived at once that it contained no hope of a final settlement. Accordingly that Monday evening, in the inner
sanctum of Toryism, the smoking-room of the Carlton
Club, Graves, who had already expounded his views to
Disraeli, strongly urged on his fellow-members, who had
met there after the debate, that the municipal suffrage

was the only basis on which a successful Reform Bill could rest. He found a willing audience and immediate support.

The movement thus started in the club gained fresh impetus next morning, not merely among county members, who would not be affected by a great lowering of the borough franchise, but among the borough members themselves, who would suffer if the lowering proved, from a Conservative point of view, to be a mistake. Four of these—Laird, the shipbuilder, who sat for Birkenhead; Goldney, M.P. for Chippenham; Jervis, M.P. for Harwich; and Graves himself, who represented Liverpool—were deputed to convey to Disraeli the intensity of the feeling. Graves, in a statement drawn up a year and a half later for Montagu Corry, thus describes what happened:

I met the Chancellor [of the Exchequer] in the lobby of the House and explained the object of the desired interview. He said it was too late. I inquired if it was too late for a friendly amendment. He replied it was, adding we should certainly upset the Government; to which I ventured to reply that our anxiety was rather for the country and our party, and assured him the feeling was so strong it would find vent in some embarrassing way. Once more I urged the reception of the deputation, when the Chancellor, throwing off the reserve which had thus far marked our interview, said it was no use to discuss the matter with any deputation, as he was free to admit he had long been of the opinion that rating and residence were the true principles for a Reform Bill, and added: 'Lord Derby was also of this opinion.' I simply replied: ' In that case I would undertake to give him proof of the strength of the feeling amongst the borough members on the subject.' That night I obtained two-and-twenty signatures in favour of the principle of municipal suffrage. . . . A greater instance of loyalty to colleagues has rarely been met with than Mr. Disraeli displayed in his interview with me.

This talk with Graves was not the only important political development of the day. The Liberals met to the number of 289 under Gladstone's leadership, and determined to demand the setting aside of the Resolutions and the production of a Bill; but Disraeli anticipated them by an announcement to that effect when the House met. 'What must be done is best done without the appearance of compulsion,' wrote Stanléy, and the Cabinet agreed. Disraeli gracefully covered his retreat by acknowledging a disposition on the part of the House to afford the Ministerial proposals a fair and candid consideration, to secure which was the main object of proceeding by resolution.

To Lord Derby.

Confidential. HOUSE OF COMMONS, *Feb.* 26, 1867.—I have requested Taylor to furnish you, without loss of time, with two reports:

1. The general result of the effect, on the small boroughs, of your plan.

2. A special report, from every member of a small borough, on our side, of his individual feelings and wishes.

Sir Henry Edwards and Mr. Waterhouse, for example, who have just been with me, are members for small boroughs. They are absolutely for the great plan.   Is that feeling general or universal ?

I dined alone with Walpole, who thinks that our fall now is only an affair of a little time, assuming that, in our present feeble position, all the sections will reunite for a vote against which it would be absurd to appeal to the country.   *That*, he thinks, is Gladstone's tactic: to play with us until we are contemptible.   As Sir Lawrence Palk says, 'Till he comes in with household suffrage, which is getting riper every moment.' At present the House expects ' compensation.'

' I tried Walpole hard as to regaining our position.   He thought if certain persons left, and you reorganized your Ministry, that it would not be looked upon as changing our front, but that, with a frank and obvious explanation, it would do us good and strengthen us in the country.   It was evident that he was contemplating the old story of a reconstruction with the Adullamites.   I don't think that can be brought about: what we must think of is the country, not the House of Commons.   But it would never have done, as Pakington proposed, to have thrown ourselves on the House of Commons with three Secretaries of State in abeyance.   A policy must be supported by a *complete* Cabinet.

Rather than die in a ditch, think of this, if the worst comes— The Duke of Buckingham *vice* Carnarvon; the Duke of Richmond *vice* Buckingham; Pakington *vice* Peel; Corry *vice* Pakington; Northcote *vice* Cranborne; Cave without Cabinet *vice* Northcote.

At the same time, I must tell you that I have since heard from Noel that a meeting at the Carlton will probably take place, and some memorial will be signed by the party to Cranborne, Peel, etc., to show them they have completely misapprehended the feeling and spirit of the party. This, of course, would be good.

Next day, Wednesday, February 27, Disraeli, following Derby, had an audience of the Queen. The nature of the conversation that then passed is apparent from the following letters:

To Lord Derby.

[*Feb.* 27.]—I had my audience, which was long and animated. She said she did not like to see you dispirited. I replied you were, naturally, chagrined at such incidents, but I saw a marked improvement in your countenance since your audience to-day. She said, and repeated, she would do anything.

Still more important was my interview with Stanley, who exhausted the subject in the most logical manner, and concluded there was only one thing to be done, and that was to recur to our original position; but how was that to be done? He added, ' Only by the pressure of the party. . . .'

From General the Hon. Charles Grey.

WINDSOR CASTLE, *Feb.* 28, 1867.—Immediately on my return to Windsor yesterday evening, I wrote you a very hasty line, by the Queen's command[1]; for Her Majesty was anxious to give you every support in the opinion you had yourself expressed in your interview with her, that nothing should be done in a hurry, and that it would be far better not to summon any Cabinet before the usual day of its meeting.

Her Majesty was sorry to see that both you and Lord Derby seemed to take a gloomy view of the prospects of the Government in its endeavours to settle this question; for which, as far as Her Majesty can judge from the accounts of what passed on Monday night in the House of Commons, and from the tone of the Press, she can see no sufficient reason.

It is true that the numbers who attended Mr. Gladstone's meeting are formidable, if they could be united in opposition to the Government. But it is reasonable to suppose that a large proportion of those who attended went there sincerely anxious for a settlement of the question, and only desirous

[1] Grey had written, on Her Majesty's instructions : ' A bold front, and cheery language, will go a great way in securing victory.'

of hearing what course Mr. Gladstone would recommend, with that view. . . . The pinching point, as Mr. Bright says, is the amount of the franchise, and you stand upon firm and intelligible ground when you take the sense of the House upon a £6 rating as the lowest point to which a Conservative Government can go. But there is nothing, as you say, to prevent your stating an alternative plan of a simple rating franchise, with the provision against the undue preponderance of mere numbers afforded by your proposed second vote, and, if beat upon the first proposal, taking the sense of the House on the second. But there seems every advantage in your adhering in the first instance to the £6 rating. In the first place, it will probably avert further unpleasant discussions in the Cabinet; and in the next it will avoid the appearance of weakness, to which I have already alluded, inseparable from frequent changes of plan. Nor does it seem at all certain that you will be beat on the £6 franchise. . . . Her Majesty wishes me to add to this that, if Lord Derby should think it more advisable to take the bolder course, which, on the first impulse of the moment, the Queen recommended to him, he may depend, as she then assured him, on her best support. But, on further consideration, Her Majesty is inclined to think, unless the disposition shown in the Cabinet should make the more decided line necessary, that it would be better to avoid the appearance of disunion, and consequent weakness, which would be occasioned by the retirement of the three Ministers. . . .

Meanwhile Disraeli kept up a steady pressure on Derby to accept the resignations, reconstruct the Cabinet, and revert to the large scheme.

To Lord Derby.

GROSVENOR GATE, *Feb.* 27, 1867.—I think Gladstone's position, and even tone, seemed changed since the declaration of our definite policy. Although there may not be, probably is not, any compact alliance yet, he has nevertheless succeeded in getting the party together, and even in combining them in an united action: the assault on the Resolutions. Lord Russell, Bright, Grosvenor, all under the same roof !

He will proceed slowly, and feel his way: but I little doubt that, by the time we get into Committee on our Bill, he will be prepared to try five against six, and probably succeed. What shall we do then? He will count on our giving up the Bill, with nothing to go to the country on. I will not, however, trouble you now with all these various considerations, but, if you wish it, will call upon you anywhere after the Court. If

Gladstone have these views, it would hardly seem that the Queen could interpose with any advantage. The most he would offer would be that you should go on with the Bill as amended by the House; but even if, from a sense of duty, you might be inclined to do this, the malcontents in the Cabinet would leave you, and therefore you would be forced to resign, or reconstruct. If there is to be reconstruction, I think it should be at once.

I could not see Northcote yesterday—a wise head: and Stanley was away. . . .

Confidential [*Feb.* 27].—I had not read *The Times* when I wrote early this morning. If you follow the course there indicated, they will censure your Government immediately the Bill is passed, and you will not be able to appeal to the country, as the new constituency will not be registered.

It appears to me that Gladstone has committed himself in a manner which may extricate you. He is for £5 rating; you can truly say that is no better settlement than £6—worse; and therefore you can revert to your original scheme in preference. If they throw out the Bill on the second reading, or defeat your boro' qualification, you could dissolve with honor, and a prospect of success, and meet Parliament, at any rate, with a powerful party.

I conceive that Gladstone has weakened and embarrassed his position by his programme. But, no doubt, with this prospect, you must reconstruct at once if the malcontent colleagues will not, on reflection, see they are only cutting the throat of the party by not supporting you.

The pressure from the party which Stanley, and no doubt Disraeli too, was hoping for, was duly applied. The ardour of Graves and his friends who sat for boroughs was naturally stimulated by Disraeli's avowal, and Wednesday saw a great extension of the Carlton movement. The county members joined hands with the borough members, and on the Thursday a meeting, at which some 150 were present, was held in the club, under Sir Matthew White Ridley's presidency. Laird and Graves had drafted resolutions, but, as the meeting was not unanimous, they were not pressed. A decided majority, however, proved to be in favour of household suffrage in boroughs, with three years' residence and personal payment of rates. There was a minority who protested; but Derby and Disraeli

were told that if the leaders were willing to go that
length—as the best means of resisting further changes
and obtaining a lasting settlement—they would be supported by a majority of the Conservatives, and by sufficient Liberals to carry the Bill.   Ridley, Banks Stanhope,
Laird, Graves, H. Baillie, and Barttelot, were the principal speakers for the majority; and Beresford Hope, James
Lowther, and George Bentinck, for the minority.   Fraser,
in *Disraeli and his Day*, calls the meeting a 'county
caucus,' selfishly prepared to sacrifice the interests of
borough members.   But this is a serious misrepresenta-
tion.   The movement began with the borough members,
though influential county members subsequently adhered
to it; and the meeting was generally representative of
the party in the House of Commons.   The feeling that a
thorough settlement should be made, and made by the
Tory party, was rapidly growing; and it must never be
forgotten that Tories had no special reason for wishing
to preserve a constituency which, like that created in 1832,
had, with few exceptions, steadily supported the Whigs
who created it.   A generous extension to a new and
respectable class, the rate-paying householders, might
well inure to the benefit of a party which claimed to be
national, and dethrone one which was still largely
oligarchical.   Feelings of this kind, which were powerful
with Disraeli, were widely shared in influential quarters
among the party.

Disraeli's spirits steadily rose as this critical week wore
on.   The Adullamites also met on the Thursday, eighty in
number, Disraeli was told, and declared for household
suffrage and plurality.   'All I hear and observe,' he wrote
to Derby on that evening, 'more and more convinces me
that the bold line is the safer one, and, moreover, that
it will be successful.'   The Queen, indeed, still expressed
a preference for the Ten Minutes Bill, but, with that
loyalty to her servants which always distinguished Her
Majesty, was quite ready to yield her view and hearten
her Ministers, in order that a settlement might be effected.

To Lord Derby.

Confidential.　Mar. 1, 1867.—General Grey, *au fond*, is trying to carry Gladstone's Franchise Bill of last year.　He thinks
it the best way to settle the question: it will settle you and
your party.　He has unceasingly impressed the Queen, since
Wednesday, with the expediency of your not receding from
your £6 position, and, therefore, you will find a change in the
Queen's mind, for which it is well that you should be prepared.
She will not, however, recede a jot from her engagements to
you if she finds you firm and confident. . . .

From Lord Derby.

Friday morning [*Mar.* 1].—There is no doubt that Grey has
been working on the Queen in favour of the £6; but the enclosed, received last night, will show you how fully we may
rely on her support.

[Enclosure.]

Queen Victoria to Lord Derby.

WINDSOR CASTLE, *Feb.* 28, 1867.—Though General Grey
has written fully in *her* name to Mr. Disraeli, she wishes to
add a few lines herself to express her earnest hope that Lord
Derby will *not* be too much discouraged, and that, *on reflection*,
she is inclined to think that it might be wisest and best, *if
possible*, to *adhere* to the measure as announced by Mr. Disraeli to the House.　He may, however, be sure of her support
in whatever course he will, after *due consideration*, propose to
her to pursue.　The Queen feels *sure* a *bold* front must be
shown, and the country will then see that the Government
is sincere in trying to settle this *vexed* and *vital* question of
Reform.　She hopes to find Lord Derby in better spirits and
less worried when she sees him to-morrow.

The support of the bulk of the Tories, of the main body
of the Adullamites, and of the Queen, was secured for
Derby's and Disraeli's policy.　What about the keen
Reformers, led by Disraeli's friendly foe, John Bright?
A conversation in the lobby on Friday, March 1, which
Bright has recorded in his journal, and which is quoted
in Trevelyan's *Life*, gave him assurance of their disposition.　Disraeli told Bright that he meant to do this thing,
if it could possibly be done, and then extracted from him
the information and advice which he desired.　Bright
writes:

I told him of a conversation with three of his party in the smoking-room, how far they were willing to go, and that at the pace they were moving I should soon have to hold them back. He thought they were fair specimens of a considerable section of the party. I advised him to advance his offers so far in regard to the suffrage that he would not be driven to accept defeat on every proposition; that £5 rating franchise or household suffrage would save him in the boroughs, and that £10 or £12 would do for the counties.[1] He said he did not care much for the counties. The working-class question was the real question, and that was the thing that demanded to be settled. He had once proposed a £10 franchise for the counties. He said: ' You will attack me whatever I propose.' I said: ' No, I will not. I will do all I can fairly to help a Bill through, if you will do the right thing. I am against faction, and if our leaders do as you did last year I shall openly denounce them. . . .'

As we were talking, Mr. Brand, the Opposition ' Whip,' went by, and Disraeli said: ' He will think it is a Coalition,' that he and I should be seen in conversation at such a crisis as this. At parting he pressed my hand with an apparent earnestness of feeling, saying: ' Well, whatever happens, you and I will always be friends.'

It was necessary for the Cabinet to come at once to a fateful decision. Everything pointed to a bold policy. The ill reception of the Ten Minutes Bill, the Carlton meeting, the Adullamite meeting, Bright's advice and support, that spirit of the age which rarely found Disraeli unresponsive—all urged advance. What public feeling was at the moment is depicted for us by an acute and impartial onlooker, Matthew Arnold, who wrote to his mother on the day of the Cabinet Council: ' I am in hopes that Lord Derby and Disraeli will take heart of grace, bring in a good measure of Reform, and let Cranborne and others leave them if they like. . . . Quite a passionate desire to get the question done with is springing up, and is gaining all the better Conservatives themselves.'[2]

Even colleagues supposed to be least affected by Disraeli's progressive ideas, such as Walpole and Hardy,

---

[1] Bright sent Disraeli a few days later a confidential memorandum, making this proposal, which corresponded with the Bill as finally passed, in more detail. See Trevelyan's *Bright*, pp. 381, 382.

[2] M. Arnold's *Letters*, Vol. I., p. 353.

pointedly dissociated themselves from the Cranborne group; and Malmesbury, who was detained at Heron Court by Lady Malmesbury's serious illness, wrote decisively to the same effect.

Lord Malmesbury to Lord Derby.

Private. HERON COURT, *Mar.* 1, 1867.—. . . Perhaps away from the scene of our distracted councils I may see a little more clearly than others what our position is.

I do not hesitate to say that the only course that can save our credit before the country is for your master mind to determine what is the best Bill, and, in spite of secession, of a menacing Press, and of all plausible intrigues whatever, to adhere to that Bill. Nor have I any doubt as to which is the best. I always preferred household suffrage (properly counterpoised) to any halfway resting-place, and I believe the whole country is of that opinion. If it is yours also, as it seemed to be when I last met you in Cabinet, I would urge you to act upon it. The loss of three able and honourable men is a great one, but far greater would be the loss of reputation which a vacillating and subservient policy would inevitably bring upon us personally, and upon our party. No colleagues can be worth that sacrifice.

Accordingly on Saturday, March 2, the Cabinet decided to revert to their original plan, and Cranborne, Carnarvon, and Peel resigned. Peel, who had been the first to feel alarm, was the most reluctant to take the final step, and called out, we are told, after the others as they were leaving the room: ' I will waive my objections if you will.' The conduct of the three seceders has been variously judged. What is and what is not a principle in a matter so essentially of detail as Parliamentary Reform is very difficult to determine. But, undoubtedly, continuance in the Cabinet at this period involved consent to two main propositions: first, that the suffrage, in the language of the Queen's Speech, should be ' freely ' extended; secondly, that in the provisions of the Bill the co-operation of the House, in which the Government were in a minority, should be willingly accepted, so that the settlement might be of a permanent and agreed character. The seceders were not prepared to make such large additions to the electorate as these propositions involved; and in those circumstances they were right to withdraw.

Of the manner of the withdrawal, and of the *animus* shown by the principal seceder, Cranborne, there is more to be said. Hardy, a witness friendly to both sides, wrote in his diary on February 26: 'Clearly Cranborne will not long act with Disraeli; that is at the bottom of it.' As we have seen, Cranborne, through all the early years of his Parliamentary life, profoundly distrusted Disraeli, and attacked him violently in the Press. He did not put off his suspicions when he joined him as a colleague; nor did Disraeli's friendly behaviour to him, and frequent consultation with him since they took office together,[1] remove his prejudice. His treatment of Derby and Disraeli and the rest of his colleagues in this matter was very inconsiderate. He had had warning that household suffrage was in his leaders' minds before the Queen's Speech, and had assented to it in general terms just after the session had opened. Reform was a subject with which he had been familiar at least ever since he wrote a philosophical essay on it in 1858; and, therefore, what was notice sufficient to make Peel resign ought to have been sufficient to make Cranborne begin those upsetting calculations which he delayed until after the Cabinet had accepted the larger measure, and had notified the Queen of their decision.

The postponement of action to the eleventh hour, the endeavour to embarrass his colleagues by inducing others to accompany him, and the virulence with which, after resignation, he attacked and denounced his leaders, require a good deal of justification. His plea is understood to have been that those leaders, Derby and Disraeli, had made, behind the backs of their colleagues, a secret agreement, certainly at the time of the formation of the 1866 Government, prob-

---

[1] The late Sir Charles Fremantle, who was Disraeli's secretary at the time, told me that Disraeli's desire to keep in touch with, and consult, Cranborne between July, 1866, and February, 1867, was very marked. See above. p. 197.

ably ever since 1859, that household suffrage should be adopted by the Conservatives as their principle of Reform. The facts which have been brought out in this biography show how ill-founded and unworthy was this suspicion, though some unguarded remarks of Derby's, and Disraeli's attempt on the third reading to connect his present policy with his policy in 1859, gave a colourable pretext for entertaining it. The Reform Bill of 1867 was an improvisation by Derby and Disraeli, and its inception dates back no farther than the January of 1867. The guiding principle, which led to such surprising results, was the willing acceptance of the co-operation of the House of Commons. The truth is that Cranborne, having adopted, from his first entry into Parliament, a jaundiced view of his leaders, and especially of Disraeli, refused to open his mind to the plain evidences, under his eyes as a Minister, of Disraeli's loyalty to colleagues, to the interests of the Conservative party, and to the great institutions of the country.

On the Monday, Derby gave a full account in the Lords of the Cabinet crisis and of the resignations, but in the Commons Disraeli merely said that the Government had determined ' to revert to their original policy ' in regard to the franchise, and in consequence three Cabinet Ministers had resigned. The House was naturally very restive under this treatment.

To Lord Derby.

GROSVENOR GATE, *Monday, Mar.* 4.—We have had a bad night in the House of Commons. They would let Peel do nothing. He has put off his business [1] till Thursday; they will let him do nothing then. Nothing can be more insolent, bullying, and defiant, than they are. I am confident they will not let Pakington move the estimates, and he himself says it is not of the slightest importance.

The sooner we get out of this mess, the better. If we had moved the writs, they would have been daunted.

The House, too, is sulky now, because there has been an explanation in the Lords, and not in the Commons.

[1] The Army Estimates.

The proposal for the introduction of the Bill for the 18th passed without comment, but I shall be surprised if, to-morrow, some adverse move is not hatched by them. The fear of a dissolution may check them, but that is all. . . .

The explanations to the Commons were tendered on the following night, when Disraeli pointed out that the Ten Minutes Bill, which had been introduced in order to preserve the integrity of the Cabinet, had given satisfaction to no party. 'It seemed to us, therefore, that we were fast sinking into that unsatisfactory state which distinguished last session, when one proposition was met by another not materially differing from it, and that the attempt to bring this great question to a solution would have been fruitless in the present, as it had been in preceding sessions. But, sir, we are conscious that there is some difference between this and the preceding session; and we did believe and hold that, if the question were not seriously and earnestly and vigorously grappled with, it would not be for the honour of Parliament or the advantage of the country.' Lord Derby had therefore advised reversion to the original course in order to provide a solution of the problem. Disraeli deplored the resulting loss of three colleagues. 'If my resignation of office could have prevented that unfortunate result, that resignation was at the command of my noble friend. It was at his command, then, as it has always been. . . . But the state of affairs would not have been bettered by my retiring from office.' He paid a special tribute to Cranborne, 'whose commanding talents, clear intelligence, capacity for labour, and power of expression, will always, I am sure, qualify him for taking a leading part in the affairs of this country.' He had already written him a graceful letter about his forthcoming explanation—an explanation which followed the lines of the letter of February 24 to Derby. It is impossible to avoid the reflection that Disraeli's treatment of Cranborne contrasts very favourably with Cranborne's treatment of Disraeli.

To Lord Cranborne.

DOWNING STREET, *Mar.* 5, 1867.—Lord Derby has written to me what has taken place between you. I shall say something when the House meets. It will not displease you, tho' it will only feebly express my sense of your services and loss, and I hope it will disembarrass us all of the difficulties inseparable from our position.

Lord Derby says you are to consult with me what you are to say, I mean as to Cabinet secrets, but I have such confidence in you, in every respect, that such previous communication is quite unnecessary.

Disraeli's vague language and Cranborne's criticisms suggested that household suffrage was to be the basis of the Bill; and Lowe and Horsman denounced, while Bright welcomed, the prospect. Both Cranborne and Peel treated the proposed checks and securities as worthless. Stanley, in reply, indignantly repudiated the notion that the Conservatives would outbid any party, or adopt Bright's policy in their Bill.

The whole discussion was, of course, in advance of detailed knowledge, and Ministers immediately set to work, under Disraeli's guidance, to reduce the measure into shape. The offices vacated by the resignations had been filled up very much in the way suggested by Disraeli. Northcote succeeded Cranborne, Pakington Peel, and the Duke of Buckingham Carnarvon. The resulting vacancies at the Board of Trade, the Admiralty, and the Council, were made good by the appointment of the Duke of Richmond,[1] Henry Corry (Montagu Corry's father), and the Duke of Marlborough. That the Cabinet difficulties should have been solved by the promotion of three Dukes provoked many a smile, and the reflection that the arrangement was characteristic of Disraeli.

The place of authority in the Cabinet which was vacant by Cranborne's resignation was occupied by Hardy. The wreckers had failed to inveigle him; and Disraeli and Derby immediately took him into their special confidence on Reform, and he became Disraeli's lieutenant in

---

[1] The sixth Duke. See Vol. I., p. 1019.

carrying the Bill through the Commons. His diary contains the following: ' *March* 5.—Disraeli had a long talk with me, going through the heads of our proposed Reform, and said he and I must do it, but there must be full and early explanation with the Cabinet, and no putting off. *March* 7.—I had more talk with Disraeli, whose fault is that he is always looking for what will suit others, rather than what is sound in itself. . . . I am to go to Lord Derby to-day on the same subject.'[1] The main troubles of the reconstructed Cabinet naturally occurred about the checks and securities. The principal checks under discussion were residence for a substantial period, personal payment of rates, and dual voting—that is, giving property a second vote so as to balance numbers. For dual voting Disraeli never had any particular affection; and he felt sure the House of Commons would not accept it. He therefore tried to persuade the Cabinet not to commit themselves to it at all; and Derby, on the whole, took the same view. The Beaconsfield papers contain a note in Derby's handwriting: ' If we do not take care, we shall have another break-up. Duality will defeat us; abandonment of it will destroy us.' This note is endorsed: ' Written by Ld. D. in Cabinet Sat. March 9, 1867, to the C. of E., who was pressing Mr. H[ardy] and Mr. W[alpole] to give up the dual vote.' The Duke of Buckingham declared that he could not support the Bill if the dual vote was withdrawn, and Malmesbury kept writing from Heron Court: ' I hope one of the conditions is that we stick through thick and thin and in full to our counterpoises or to some certainly equivalent;' . ' we ought to resign rather than carry or suffer to be carried household suffrage *pur et simple.*' ' We must watch and hope,' wrote Disraeli on March 11 to Northcote; ' things are not so dark as they seemed.' Dual voting, in consequence of the obstinacy of some Ministers, made its appearance in the Bill, but in a very half-hearted fashion. The Queen, to whom the

[1] Gathorne Hardy, Vol. I., p. 203.

Bill was sent as soon as the Cabinet had passed it, fixed
on this point at once, and was greatly reassured when
Disraeli told her confidentially in reply that Derby did
not intend to make the second vote a vital question.
'H.M. wishes me,' Grey added, 'again to repeat the
expression of her sincere and anxious hope that this Bill
may pass the ordeal of the two Houses in a shape that
the Government will accept, and that it may settle this
important question for many years to come.'

How the new situation was regarded in the enemy's
camp was explained to Disraeli in an interesting letter on
March 8 from a friend in their midst, relating the conversation at a Liberal dinner-party.   Milner Gibson thought
that Government could not pass any Bill, and that Russell
would be back in office in a few weeks.   Horsman dilated
on the profligacy of the Ministry—they were like Peel in
1846.   'To which Ayrton and others replied that there
was this difference, that you are strictly consistent; that
you are carrying out your leading political idea of restoring the Tory party to popularity, and vindicating
their claims to be the champions of real popular rights.'
Seely said he and many other Liberals would support
the Government on the ground that it was better to have
the question settled by Derby rather than by Beales
and Potter.   'They all admitted that no Minister was
placed in a more difficult position, in our times, than you
were put into by the conduct of the three deserters in not
having deserted earlier.'

The Bill had been drafted by Dudley Baxter, a partner
of Philip Rose in the firm of Baxter, Rose and Norton.
But it was obviously desirable to have the first expert
assistance before submitting it to the scrutiny of a critical
House of Commons.   There was no regular Treasury
draftsman at that date, the tradition, largely created
by Gladstone, that the Treasury was the proper source
of legislation, not having yet grown up.   But there was a
notable expert at the Home Office, who afterwards became Lord Thring, and he was consulted, and reported

unfavourably on the amateur draft. Baxter resented this criticism, and refused to communicate with Thring. What was to be done ? It was now Thursday afternoon, March 14. The Bill was to be finally revised by the Cabinet on the Saturday, introduced by Disraeli on the Monday, and circulated in print to members of Parliament on the Tuesday morning. 'What have you done *re* Thring *v.* Baxter ?' wrote Derby on this Thursday. 'The defendant has done all the work, and the plaintiff has all the real knowledge and experience on his side.'

To Lord Derby.

HOUSE OF COMMONS, *Thursday, Mar.* 14, 1867.—It was painful, but decision was absolutely necessary. I decided for Thring. He will sit up all night,[1] and, I believe, we shall have the Bill printed for the Cabinet on Saturday. I have written myself to Baxter.

Much depends on to-morrow.

Grosvenor has established a newspaper—the *Day*—and has engaged Kebbel, an Oxford man, well acquainted with the Press, but a fine writer, and a scholar, for editor. Grosvenor and Elcho were with Kebbel to-day, giving him his final instructions: he asked them, for his general government, to let him know what they really thought would be the result. Grosvenor said that if our policy was what he understood it to be, household suffrage, absolute rate-paying, and compensatory arrangement against compound householders, they had ascertained they could pull the Government through, *provided our men went straight.*

That is the question. Banks Stanhope has written to Taylor that real rating will unite the party to a man, or something like it. But there is Hotham, Cecil, and Co. Gladstone's great fight is against real rating—that is ascertained.

At dinner Stanley said he thought we had a good chance, at any rate a policy, and no Minister was ever more justified in going to the country.

'Much depends on to-morrow.' The Government took the unprecedented, but, in the circumstances, honest and straightforward, course of calling their Parliamentary followers together, explaining the terms of their Bill to them three days before its production in Parlia-

---

[1] Thring worked on the Friday with two shorthand writers from ten to six, and completed the draft, which was printed during the night.

ment, and asking for their confidence and support. It was a large meeting, 195 members of Parliament attending, and 43, who were unable to be present, sending letters of adhesion to the Government. Derby was perfectly candid. Household rating suffrage was to be the basis of the borough franchise, and the only conditions which he pronounced to be essential were payment of rates and two years' residence; he explained that compound householders, or those whose landlords paid a composition for the rates and charged the amount in the rent, would be permitted to obtain the vote by assuming personal payment themselves. The dual vote would be proposed, but he admitted that the Government were not strongly wedded to it. If necessary, they would be prepared to recommend dissolution. This frank treatment of the party, which contrasted, as was pointed out at the meeting, so favourably with Peel's behaviour over Roman Catholic Emancipation and Free Trade, had an admirable effect. Henley, the most respected Conservative leader outside the Government, expressed his full adhesion. He held that household suffrage, with payment of rates, was the true basis of the right to vote according to the principles of the Constitution. These sentiments were echoed by others. The seceders kept quiet, the only expression of dissent coming from Heathcote, the senior member for Oxford University, who believed that the measure would destroy the influence of rank, property, and education, by the force of numbers.

Once again there was a crowded House, on Monday, March 18, to hear Disraeli introduce the Government Reform Bill—this time no makeshift, but the Bill which, after emendation by the co-operation of the House, Ministers hoped to pass into law. But the interest had, to a large extent, been discounted by Derby's speech to his party on the Friday. Everyone knew that the basis of the new borough franchise was to be household suffrage, qualified by personal rating and by two years' residence; that the payment of twenty shillings in direct taxes

would also give a vote over and above the vote already
obtained as a householder; that there would be an educational franchise, and that £50 in the funds or in the savings
bank would give a vote.   It was known, moreover, that
the county franchise would be reduced from £50 to £15
rating, and that the redistribution would be on the same
scale as in the previous Bill.   No surprises as to the provisions were, therefore, to be looked for; interest would
lie in the manner in which Disraeli would present the
scheme to the House, and in the reception which the different sections would accord to it.

At the outset Disraeli claimed that the object of the
Bill was to establish the character and functions of the
House ' on a broad, popular basis '; to concede a liberal
measure of popular privileges, but by no means to confer
democratic rights.   Hitherto the proposals which had
been made to alter the borough franchise, right down to
the Bill of 1866, had all been in the nature of a diminution in the £10 value fixed by the great Reform Act.
But last year a most important principle was asserted,
the principle of rating; it was carried against the then
Government, and caused their retirement.   ' A great
decision was arrived at by the unerring instinct of the
House.'   It meant that ' the being rated to the poor, and
the paying of the rates, constituted a fair assurance that
the man who fulfilled those conditions was one likely to
be characterised by regularity of life and general trustworthiness of conduct.'   It was found to be unsatisfactory to connect this principle of rating with value.
So the Government considered the principle without
reference to value, and found that it would admit 237,000.
There were 486,000 compound householders.   These, not
having the qualification of personal rating, should not
have the vote; but every facility would be given to them
to enter their names on the rate-book, and thus acquire
the qualification.   Household rating was the only solid
foundation for the borough franchise: the only possible
settlement.   The alternative was a £5 rating; but that

would be a Serbonian bog, and would inevitably lead to manhood suffrage.

It was said that this new basis of household rating suffrage was an assault on the power of the middle classes. But the twenty shillings direct taxation franchise would largely give the middle classes a second vote. This would probably add 200,000 votes. The fancy franchises altogether would add 100,000. The £15 rating county franchise would add 171,000; and, taking the other franchises, there would be a general addition to the county franchise of 300,000. Disraeli defended the moderate nature of the redistribution scheme, which was based on the principle of no absolute disfranchisement of boroughs, by saying that, unless you were prepared to reconstruct the electoral map of England, you must be prudent and practical.

He referred shortly to the very great difficulties and sacrifices which had been involved in the preparation of the Bill, and his own chagrin and mortification. But he had done his duty. 'In attempting to bring the question to this point we have lost those whose absence from our councils we more than regret; we have had to appeal to a high-spirited party to make what, no doubt, to some was, to a certain extent, a sacrifice of principle, much sacrifice of sentiment, and much sacrifice of interest. But we have not appealed in vain.' The party, he declared, felt the time had come for an extensive and complete settlement. If there were checks or counterpoises in this scheme, so there were in the British Constitution. They wished to prevent a preponderance of any class, and to give a representation to the nation.

No sooner had the Chancellor sat down than Gladstone rose, and fell tooth and nail upon the Bill. It was both too wide and too full of checks. It would only admit 140,000 new voters. He opposed the reduction to household suffrage; but he opposed equally the restrictions on household suffrage—personal rating and the dual vote. He demanded a lodger franchise. He foreshadowed a

vehement opposition. The general reception was uncertain, but Henley for the Conservatives, and Roebuck
and Bernal Osborne for the Independent Liberals, urged
that the Bill should go to Committee for amendment.
Almost all the speakers, whether Conservative or Liberal,
showed hostility to the dual vote. The small knot of
Conservative malcontents, Cranborne, Heathcote, Beresford Hope, and Sandford, sounded at once a note of
bitter antagonism; Cranborne predicting that the checks
would all be swept away, and household suffrage pure
and simple be the result. Disraeli, in reply, declared
with much emphasis that the Government would never
introduce household suffrage pure and simple. He was
as yet insufficiently acquainted with those intricacies of
compound householding, which ultimately drove him, in
pursuit of a settlement, into something hardly distinguishable from the solution which he deprecated.

The reception was not good enough to augur favourably
for the future of the Bill. The principal Ministers, such as
Hardy, were despondent; the Liberal leaders thought the
enemy who had overthrown them was delivered into
their hands. Gladstone gathered his followers together,
anxious to dispose of both Bill and Ministers on the second
reading; but he found, to his discomfiture, that wrecking
tactics would not be supported, and that at least a second
reading must be accorded to his rival's Bill. His recalcitrant following might not be prepared to beard him to
his face; but they made it sufficiently clear that they
would not all follow him into the ' No ' division lobby.

To Lord Derby.

Confidential. GROSVENOR GATE, *Mar.* 24, 1867.—It is very
trying, and no doubt we shall, both of us, always remember
the year 1867.

But there is more than hope. . . . I must tell you that
there are 100 men on the other side against Gladstone, but they
are *moutons ;* there is nobody who can speak against him.

At the meeting, there was no one, though the feeling was
so strong, that by murmuring, round robins, and scuffling of
feet, they controlled ' iracundus Achilles.' . . .

In truth, Gladstone made the astounding mistake of supposing that, after a definite and final basis, such as household rating, had been proposed by the Government for borough franchise, it would be possible to get the Liberal party to follow him in restricting extension to a £5 value. Though he was no longer in a position to divide, he yet took up this attitude with great keenness in his speech on the second reading, a week later, Monday, March 25, laying down dogmatically what was and what was not to be done. But several Liberals who were enthusiasts for Reform, among whom Fawcett, the blind economist, was conspicuous, saw that they were getting a great and sufficient principle established, and refused to support their leader. Bright, indeed, backed Gladstone up, because he fixed his eyes rather upon the limitations than upon the main principle, and so regarded the Bill as a deception. Hardy made an effective speech in which he insisted that it was a rating franchise Bill, rather than a household suffrage Bill, but at the same time expressed the readiness of the Government for mutual concession and forbearance. Several independent Liberals came to the help of Ministers; and it was felt that the general upshot of the debate would be mainly determined by the character of the Chancellor's speech in reply at the close of the second night.

Derby, who was deeply involved in the policy of the Bill, wrote to Disraeli as the debate drew to an end:

From Lord Derby.

St. James's Square, 9.30 [*Mar.* 26].—I am anxious for reports from your House. . . .

Last night was excellent. Hardy has quite vindicated our selection of him, and has placed himself in the front rank as a debater. The Sol.-Gen. seems to have done very well also, and Roebuck's was a most useful speech, and full of sound sense. P. Talbot sat by Delane all through the debate, and the latter said: ' Gladstone has done you more good than all your Cabinet put together.'

Shall you close to-night? If so, excuse me for saying that I hope you will be as short and pithy as possible, striking the keynote which I understand to have been agreed upon between us, of willingness to consult the opinion of *the House*, but refusal to submit to the dictation of *one assumed* leader of a party. If you are going to speak, don't trouble yourself to answer, but depute somebody to write or to come up.

Disraeli received this note just as he was about to rise to deliver one of his most memorable and successful speeches; and brilliantly did he carry out the policy of Derby's last sentences—refusal to submit to Gladstone's dictation, coupled with ready deference to the general feeling of the House. He had to defend, he said, what was called one night a revolutionary measure, and then, on the next, a measure of extreme restriction. He strongly maintained, on the contrary, that it was a Bill founded on a popular and a rational principle. Yet it was attacked with violent excitement by Gladstone.

The right hon. gentleman gets up and addresses me in a tone which, I must say, is very unusual in this House. Not that I at all care for the heat he displays, although really his manner is sometimes so very excited and so alarming that one might almost feel thankful that gentlemen in this House, who sit on opposite sides of this table, are divided by a good broad piece of furniture.

Gladstone had peremptorily demanded a lodger franchise. Well, as Disraeli had proposed it in 1859, he could hardly be supposed to have a prejudice against it; but his colleagues, when he suggested it in Cabinet, had naturally said that it was inconsistent with the principle of rating. Moreover, last year Gladstone had spoken of lodger franchise as a very insignificant affair. It was a question for Committee.

Disraeli went in detail through Gladstone's demands and menaces, showing the inconsistencies in which the Opposition leader had involved himself in his resolve at all hazards to destroy the Government and the Bill. He scoffed at his exaggerated fears of the corruption of the new voters; apparently he thought the great body of the people were not to be trusted. Gladstone had fulminated against a two years' residence—the very provision which

he had himself laid down in 1866 for his lodger franchise.
Rating and residence, said Disraeli, were essential, and
the House would make a great error if it reduced the term
of residence.   A franchise based on direct taxation,
which Gladstone had condemned, had been proposed
by Russell in 1852 and 1854. He twitted Gladstone
with his demand in general terms that redistribution
must be enlarged, without specifying which of his friends'
seats he meant to disfranchise.   As to the county franchise, Ministers had made a very large reduction from £50
to £15, but the exact figure was of secondary importance,
and should be left to Committee.   In deference to the
general opinion of all parties, the dual vote, which had
been introduced as a protection to the middle classes,
would be abandoned.

Disraeli dilated on the governing inconsistency of
Gladstone's opposition, which wished at one and the
same time to have a more restricted suffrage and to do
away with the checks proposed for household suffrage.
That was blowing hot and cold at once.   One of the
most pregnant passages in the speech was that in which
he dealt with the calculations as to the number of persons
to be enfranchised under the Bill.

Our Bill is not framed, as was the one of last session, to
enfranchise a specific number of persons.   We do not attempt
that.   We lay down a principle, and let that principle work;
but if you ask us what will be the result of its working, we say
—although we do not wish to found our policy upon it—that
we do not apprehend the number that will be admitted to the
enjoyment of the franchise will exceed the number contemplated by the Bill of last session.   But there is this difference
between our proposition and the proposition made by the
right hon. gentleman.   The proposition of the right hon.
gentleman was founded upon a state of things which was
liable to be changed the next year, when the question might
possibly have to be raised again, while the proposition that
we make is founded upon a principle that is not liable to alteration.

In his final sentences, Disraeli laid down broadly,
and in the most unmistakable terms, the desire of the

Government for the co-operation of the House, and their readiness to defer to it.

One word before I conclude. I hear much of the struggle of parties in this House, and I hear much of combinations that may occur, and courses that may be taken, which may affect the fate of this Bill. All I can say on the part of my colleagues and myself is that we have no other wish at the present moment than, with the co-operation of this House, to bring the question of Parliamentary Reform to a settlement. I know the Parliamentary incredulity with which many will receive avowals that we are only influenced in the course we are taking by a sense of duty; but I do assure the House—if they need such assurances after what we have gone through, after the sacrifices we have made, after having surrendered our political connection with men whom we more than re- garded—I can assure them no other principle animates us but a conviction that we ought not to desert our posts until this question has been settled. Rest assured that it is not for the weal of England that this settlement should be delayed. You may think that the horizon is not disturbed at the pres- ent juncture. You may think that surrounding circumstances may be favourable to dilatory action. Some of you may think, in the excitement of the moment, that ambition may be grati- fied, and that the country may look favourably upon those who prevent the passing of this Bill. Do not believe it. There is a deep responsibility with regard to this question, resting, not on the Government merely, but upon the whole House of Commons. We are prepared, as I think I have shown, to act in all sincerity in this matter. Act with us cordially and candidly: assist us to carry this measure. We will not shrink from deferring to your suggestions so long as they are con- sistent with the main object of this Bill, which we have never concealed from you, and which is to preserve the represen- tative character of the House of Commons. Act with us, I say, cordially and candidly; you will find on our side com- plete reciprocity of feeling. Pass the Bill, and then change the Ministry if you like.

With this reasonable and attractive appeal ringing in their ears, the House passed the second reading without a division. There is an almost universal consensus of opinion that the speech was the turning-point of the session; that it practically secured the carrying of a Reform Bill under the conduct of the Government. A young journalist, then on the threshold of a distinguished career, who was no friend to Disraeli, wrote of it at the time: ' Its exuberance caught the House. Its bold caricature of Mr. Gladstone's cloud-compelling manner placed an obstacle such as ridicule can rarely raise in the path of the official Opposition. The whole House seemed tickled too much ever seriously to fall out with Mr. Disraeli on this subject again. . . . Men who have heard Mr. Disraeli throughout his career agree that never did he show such mastery over his audience, such boundless histrionic resource.' [1] Liberals such as Lord Enfield and Hastings Russell, Manners reported, were as loud in praise of the speech as Conservatives; and Disraeli's colleagues were unanimous. ' Masterly ' is Malmesbury's epithet, ' brilliant ' Hardy's. Manners heard on all sides nothing but admiration and satisfaction. Even the unenthusiastic Stanley wrote: ' The speech of last night has pleased all our friends. I think it one of the best you have ever made; and, after our troubles, it has come like the warm weather after frost and snow.' Derby was entirely satisfied.

From Lord Derby.

ST. JAMES'S SQUARE, *Mar.* 27, 1867.—I cannot let the day pass over without offering you my cordial congratulations on your splendid achievement of last night. I hear from all quarters that it was the finest speech you ever made; and you seem to have carried the House bodily away with you. In fact, you have won our game for us; and in writing to the Queen this morning, to announce your ' triumphant success,' I told H.M. that I now, for the first time, entertained a sanguine hope of carrying a Bill through in the course of the present session. . . .

There was one episode connected with the reversion of the Cabinet to the larger Bill which caused a small public scandal, and much personal pain to Disraeli. When Earle, at his own wish, exchanged his private secretaryship to Disraeli for public office in the new Ministry, he did not realise that he necessarily cut himself off from the intimate intercourse and admission to the arcana of politics

---

[1] Article by Sir Edward Russell in *Belgravia*, Sept., 1867.

which he had previously enjoyed. But it would be very imprudent of a Minister to admit more than his actual secretaries to the privilege of confidential information; and, when Earle manifested a tendency to frequent the secretaries' room and expect to be treated as if he were still one of them, Disraeli gave Corry and Fremantle distinct instructions that matters of confidence should not be imparted to him. Earle marked Corry's rapid advance to a degree of intimacy to which he had never himself attained; his feelings were deeply wounded; he brooded over what he regarded as slights and humiliations; and in February poured out his heart to Rose, accusing Disraeli of altered demeanour, of snubbing him before subordinates, and of excluding him, in spite of ten years of devotion, from his confidence. Finally, when the Household Suffrage Bill was introduced, he determined to follow the three seceding Ministers, resigned his office, and from his place in Parliament attacked the Bill and the Minister who introduced it. 'A more painful exhibition,' says Fraser, 'never was witnessed.' It appeared to be an act of unprovoked ingratitude, and Earle had no power of speaking which could render his criticism of his late chief palatable to the House. A letter to a friend gives a glimpse into Disraeli's feelings on this outburst.

To Lord Beauchamp.

HUGHENDEN, *April* 18, 1867.—. . . There are, no doubt, breakers yet ahead, but I feel great hope of overcoming them, and of realising the dream of my life and re-establishing Toryism on a national foundation.

The only black spot in this great business, and which I would not notice to anyone but yourself, is the treason of Earle! I have known him for ten years, and, tho' warned from the first by the Cowleys, whom he had treated as he has treated me, I utterly disregarded their intimations, and ascribed them all to prejudice and misapprehension.

I have worked for his welfare more earnestly than for my own, and do not believe that I ever, even in the most trying times, gave him a hasty or unkind word. I loaded him with favors, and among them introduced him to you. I am ashamed of my want of discrimination. . . .

We may sympathise with Disraeli's grief at Earle's ingratitude; but it is impossible not to remember, when he refers to Earle's misbehaviour to Cowley, the British Ambassador in Paris, that Disraeli himself had profited by it.[1] Earle not only quitted office, but, in a short time, Parliament and English politics; and, for the rest of what was not destined to be a long life, engaged in a successful financial career in the Near East.

In spite of Disraeli's appeal for general co-operation, and the large amount of response which it elicited, Gladstone obstinately persisted in his attempt to substitute a £5 value in the place of rating household suffrage as the basis of the borough franchise. He called his followers together on Friday, April 5, and his ardour and insistence obtained a general assent to the proposal that, on the following Monday, an instruction to that effect should be moved by Coleridge, afterwards Lord Chief Justice. But, though cowed, the household suffrage Liberals were not convinced. They met subsequently in the tea-room of the House of Commons, and determined not to support the official policy of the Opposition. Disraeli wrote what he heard to Derby, who at this crisis in his party's fate was once more absent from Cabinet councils owing to gout.

To Lord Derby.

Confidential. GROSVENOR GATE, *Sunday* [? *April* 7].— Gladstone is more violent than ever, and the Independents who baffled him the other day have had a council, at which it was discussed whether some communication should not be opened with Mr. Henley and Colonel Wilson Patten, in order to assist the Government and pass the Bill: the names even were mentioned of managers of the conference on the part of the Independent Liberals—Mr. Whitbread and Mr. Clay. It is said that, whatever statement is made by us, Gladstone means to propose to his party an abstract resolution on the Speaker leaving the chair, to the effect that no settlement, etc., can be satisfactory which recognises in electoral rights a distinction between rich and poor. . . .

[1] See Vol. I., p. 1468.

The tea-room revolt spiked Gladstone's guns. 'The House met,' wrote Hardy on April 8; 'rumours rife that a large meeting of Liberals had thrown over Gladstone, and that his instruction, so far as it was hostile, was to be withdrawn. Locke asked Disraeli if he would accept the change. His answer was admirable. Gladstone lowering and gloomy, full of mortification, no doubt. A desultory talk, and we were in Committee, but reported progress at once. . . . The disunion on the other side seems complete.' 'Disraeli's insolent triumph' was the entry of a fervent Gladstonite in his diary.

From General the Hon. Charles Grey.

WINDSOR CASTLE, *April* 9, 1867.—The Queen desires me to write in her name to say how much pleased she is by the result of last night's proceedings in the House of Commons. . . . It was, in all probability, the suspicion that Gladstone was seeking the means of destroying the measure altogether that caused the defection from him, and any want of conciliation on the part of the Government might operate equally injuriously against them. . . .

But Gladstone had not yet learnt his lesson. There was a real and serious difficulty in the compound householders, which was not met by Disraeli's plan of facilitating direct payment of rates by this class. Gladstone determined to make this question the ground for one more attempt to oust Disraeli and the Government from the control of the Reform question, and to retransfer it to his own hands. He accordingly gave notice of drastic amendments dispensing with personal rating and recurring to the £5 value; and before the debate came on there were negotiations between the tea-room Liberals and the Government, at which an attempt was made to find some compromise which should eliminate the compound householder. A 'secret' Cabinet was held, on Malmesbury's suggestion, at Lord Barrington's house, but Hardy and Walpole appear to have resisted concessions which Disraeli was prepared to make, and no arrangement was effected.   The upshot of the division was therefore very doubtful, as Cranborne and his friends proposed to vote with Gladstone.   Beresford Hope, who was of Dutch extraction, enlivened the debate with a vehement attack upon the 'Asian mystery.'   His heavy and clumsy figure was typical of his racial descent; so Disraeli lightly retorted that there was a 'Batavian grace' in his invectives which took the sting out of what he said.   A vigorous speech by Hardy had a great effect. Disraeli had given him sagacious advice which he had followed.   'Permit me to intimate that, without in the slightest degree compromising your convictions, it is expedient not to make an unnecessarily uncompromising speech to-night; and with regard to the question on which the Cabinet was so divided this morning, it seems to me unnecessary to touch on it.'   Bright once more rallied to Gladstone's side, supporting the £5, or it might be £4 or £3, value against his own policy of household suffrage.   Disraeli, when he came to wind up the debate, went straight to the point.   It was really a question between Gladstone's hard-and-fast line and his own logical position.   Gladstone's amendment was merely one more attempt to overthrow Disraeli and reseat himself in power.

The right hon. gentleman opposite is a candidate for power, and no man has a greater right to be a candidate for power. The right hon. gentleman is an opponent with whom any man may be proud to have to contend.   I know nothing more legitimate than the ambition of such a man, and I am sure I bear the right hon. gentleman no ill-will, or as little ill-will as a man can bear, for the efforts which he may make to change his position and to cross from one side of the House to the other.   But I am sure the right hon. gentleman will not be offended if I, without passion, but, I am sure, clearly, express to the House what I believe to be his position with regard to the Government, and this question.   I can quite understand how the right hon. gentleman should be so very emulous to deal with this important question with which Her Majesty's Government have felt it their duty to grapple; but the right hon. gentleman seems to forget what he ought to remember.   The right hon. gentleman has had his innings.   He has dealt with

the subject of Parliamentary Reform very recently, and in
this House—in this House elected under the auspices of a
Government of which he was a member; and he introduced
a measure with the advantage, which we have never had, of
being supported by a large majority. I do not begrudge the
right hon. gentleman those advantages, but I may still remind
him of them; and I say, under these circumstances, we have
a right that there should be no great eagerness to make party
attacks. I cannot but view the amendments proposed by
the right hon. gentleman in this light. They are not amendments to our Bill. They are counter-propositions. . . . I
acknowledge the right hon. gentleman's position and talents—
that he is perfectly justified in attacking the Government;
but do not let us misunderstand the motion or the conduct
of the right hon. gentleman. Nothing can be more legitimate. It is a party attack; and the endeavour to parry it
as a party attack is in accordance with the tactics which
were understood to be adopted in the House on this subject.

But as regards the House of Commons, generally speaking,
I wish, on the part of Her Majesty's Government, whatever
may be the decision to-night, whatever may be the consequences of this division, to say that in dealing with this question Her Majesty's Government have never for a moment
swerved from those sentiments which, with the full concurrence and desire of my colleagues, I have often expressed in
this House—namely, that we are most anxious to co-operate
with the House in bringing this question of Parliamentary
Reform to a satisfactory settlement; and although we could
not swerve with respect to the borough franchise from those
principles which we regarded as vital—namely, personal payment of rates and residence—still, with regard to almost
every other point which has been mentioned in our discussion,
we are most anxious, in Committee, after a fair deliberation,
and after an interchange of opinion, to adopt that course
which the House in its wisdom may think most expedient
and desirable.

Gladstone, in reply, affected to be unable to understand
how Disraeli could be ready to consult the House, and
yet unwilling to accept amendments from the Opposition
leader. But the House realised that Gladstone's was a
wrecking amendment, and the first division on the
Reform Bill of 1867, taken on the night of Friday, April
12, gave a majority of twenty-one for the Government.
The result had been throughout uncertain, and Gladstone

had to the last expected a victory. He felt it to be 'a
smash, perhaps, without example.' The Conservative
cheering was loud and long, and, as Mr. Kebbel writes,
'none rushed to shake hands with the Chancellor of the
Exchequer more enthusiastically than those Tory country
gentlemen whom he was absurdly said to have betrayed.'
The enthusiasm was not all expended at Westminster.
A quarter of an hour or so later, there was a number of
excited Conservative members collected for supper at
the Carlton Club. Disraeli looked in at the club on his
way home, and as he entered the large, crowded dining-
room the cheers rang out again and again, and Sir Matthew
Ridley interpreted the feeling of the party by proposing a
toast: 'Here's the man who rode the race, who took the
time, who kept the time, and who did the trick!' They
crowded round their leader, and pressed him to stay and
sup with them. Mr. Kebbel gives us the sequel.

As Lady Beaconsfield told me afterwards, with manifest
pride and joy, 'Dizzy came home to me.' And she then proceeded to describe the supper: 'I had got him a raised pie
from Fortnum and Mason's, and a bottle of champagne, and he
ate half the pie and drank all the champagne, and then he
said: "Why, my dear, you are more like a mistress than a
wife."' And I could see that she took it as a very high compliment indeed.[1]

Gladstone and Bright were as much cast down as the
Conservatives were elated. The story ran that Bright
said that night at the Reform Club to Bernal Osborne:
'You may do what you like, Osborne, but you will never
manage to put salt on Dizzy's tail.' Gladstone was so
chagrined at his desertion by the tea-room party that
he appeared for a while to contemplate retirement to a
back bench. But the House adjourned after the division
for the Easter recess, and there was a quiet opportunity
for the reconsideration of rash impulses.

[1] *Lord Beaconsfield, and Other Tory Memories*, p. 40.

CHAPTER XV.

DISRAELI'S PARLIAMENTARY TRIUMPH—II.

1867.

Disraeli retired to Hughenden for the Easter recess in high spirits after the unexpectedly satisfactory campaign of the early spring. Corry wrote to tell him the vivid impression which had been made in the depths of the English countryside; his old friend Vitzthum—now no longer Saxon Minister in London, owing to Prussia's victory over the German Confederation—forwarded from Dresden a thoughtful appreciation of the situation as it looked to a well-informed foreigner who knew England.

From Montagu Corry.

ROWTON CASTLE, SHREWSBURY, *Easter Sunday, April* 21, 1867.—. . . Your name is in the mouth of every labourer, who, without knowing what 'Reform' means, or caring, hears that Mr. —— has won a great victory. I leave the blank, as it is impossible to express the Protean variety which a name, revered and cherished by me, here assumes. My private opinion is that my aunt's carpenter, who 'heard say that Mr. Disraeli had laid Mr. Gladstone on his back,' thinks that you really knocked that godly man down. I have too much jealousy for your fair fame to undeceive him.

From Count Vitzthum.

HÔTEL DE SAXE, DRESDEN, *April* 21, 1867.—. . . I never regretted my absence from England so much. I need not to tell you the joy I felt at your victory. I was sure of it. May I tell you frankly why? Looking on, without party bias, during fourteen years, I could not help being struck by the fact that you appeared the only man in England working for posterity. Your genius bore, to my eyes, always the historical stamp, and I never listened to a speech of yours without thinking, this word, this sentence, will be remembered a hundred years hence. . . .

268

If I understand right your present position, you are the Œdipus who solved the Sphinx's riddle; you have thrown in the chasm worn-out prejudices, and you put the good ship in order before the great storm which may blow over for a moment, but which soon will shake Europe from one end to the other. At the eve of such a crisis, what are ten-pounders and lodgers? The great point was to settle and to subdue this internal agitation, and I think you paved the way for a settlement which will last until the resettlement of Europe. . . .

But, though the Bill was well begun, the thorny questions ahead pressed upon Disraeli at Hughenden, and followed him to Windsor, where he was asked to spend Easter. ' I am sorry to say,' he writes to Corry on Good Friday, ' the Compound Householder has found his way to Hughenden, introduced by Lord Cairns.' [1] At Windsor it was the Lodger who was troubling him.

To Lord Stanley.

WINDSOR CASTLE, *Easter Monday, April 22, 1867.*—. . . As for domestic affairs, we ought to carry our Reform now in a canter, if all I hear be true.

We can't take Torrens's lodger, and I doubt whether the House will take him at any rate or rent.

I wish, in the interval of settling the affairs of Europe, you would get up an anti-lodger speech, or a speech on the subject either way; as I think our debates want a little variety, and the House will get tired of the eternal partridge of your affectionate colleague, THE CHANCELLOR OF THE EXCHEQUER. [2]

' Or a speech on the subject either way ! ' How the old Disraeli comes out in a flash ! Detail, even important detail, was almost as nothing; lodger franchise had been one of his own proposals in former years, and he regarded it now as a pure question of tactics; but the Bill, with or without lodger franchise, was to pass in a canter ! That was what mattered. Stanley was in favour of lodger franchise, and may have decided Disraeli's course. ' I am so deeply pledged to the principle,' he replied, ' that I cannot speak against it; but we may fix the limit where we please.

---

[1] Cairns, who was now a Lord Justice of Appeal, had been made a peer, and was resuming his political activity.
[2] This is the latter part of the letter printed above on pp. 204, 205.

I think £15 would do no harm. It would swamp only constituencies which are already as radical as they well can be. I think our Bill, or at least a Bill, is safe.' Stanley, it will be seen, entered with grim humour into the situation. ' Or at least a Bill ' is the apt retort to Disraeli's fling.

᾽ Before Easter Disraeli had resisted, and successfully resisted, Gladstone's repeated attempts to take the Reform question out of his hands and substitute a £5 value with all its logical consequences. After Easter he showed the readiness which he had frequently pro-claimed to co-operate with the House and to accept the amendments which the general sense of Parliament desired. Gladstone and the official Liberals, and Bright, who acted generally with them, did not even yet desist from occasional attempts to impose their own scheme, but these efforts signally failed. During the Easter recess they had countenanced or instigated great popular gatherings which, strangely enough, treated a Bill establishing rating household suffrage as a virtual denial of working men's rights. Gladstone received and en-couraged a deputation from a society engaged in pro-moting this movement, and was amusingly chaffed in the House of Commons by Disraeli.

I regret very much that these spouters of stale sedition, these obsolete incendiaries, should have come forward to pay their homage to one who, wherever he may sit, must always be the pride and ornament of the House:

> Who but must laugh if such a man there be,
> Who would not weep if Atticus were he ?

Nothing has surprised me more in the ebullitions which have recently occurred than their extremely intolerant character. Everybody who does not agree with somebody else is looked upon as a fool, or as being merely influenced by a total want of principle in conducting public affairs. But, sir, I cannot bring myself to believe that that is the temper of the House of Commons or the temper of the country.

On the whole, however, Gladstone was content, after Easter, to take a less conspicuous part in debate; and

amendments, which came from private members in all
quarters of the House, were frequently offered, and accepted, modified, or rejected, without his intervention at
all. No doubt the general nature of these amendments was
to widen the proposed enfranchisement, as was inevitable,
seeing that the Liberals had a majority of sixty or seventy
in the House, and the tea-room party and many of the
Adullamites were some of the most convinced supporters
of the principle of the Bill. But many of the enfranchising
amendments had strong Conservative support, from
Henley and others; the forward section of the Conservative
party being as resolved as the Government that the outcome of this legislation should be a real settlement that
would stand for many years. Malmesbury's diary bears
witness to this tendency. For May he writes: ' Cabinets
all May on Reform Bill. The *laissez-aller* system followed
by the Government trying to make the best they could
of it, but constantly yielding something. The Conservative members seem disposed to adopt anything, and
to think that it is " in for a penny, in for a pound." '

The first important amendment which was discussed
after Easter was one by Ayrton, an Independent Radical,
reducing the two years' residence proposed for the new
voter to the one year which was all that was required of
the ten-pounder. The Government resisted, but were
badly beaten by eighty-one votes; and they promptly
put in practice the readiness to defer to the opinion of
the House which they had repeatedly announced.

From General the Hon. Charles Grey.

OSBORNE, *May* 4, 1867.—The Queen desires me to thank
you for your letter of the night before last. She was very
sorry to hear of the defeat of the Government by so large a
majority, though rejoiced to find that you did not consider
the points on which you were beat vital.

Her Majesty now desires me to express her earnest hope
that you will avoid, as far as possible, the mistake made by
the late Government, and should further amendments be
carried against you, in a way to show that they are in accordance with the feeling of the House and of the country, that

you will not refuse to accept them, and thus again postpone
the settlement of this question, as Lord Russell did, the Queen
thinks, so unnecessarily last year.

The Queen was thus entirely at one with the course
which Disraeli had marked out and was steadfastly
following. The question of lodgers was the next to which
it was applied. It was found that there was a general
feeling in the House that it would be unfair to exclude
lodgers, who were really in exactly similar circumstances
to the householders who were to be admitted, save in the
nature of their occupation. Two or three families of
precisely the same status often lived in one house; while
the head of one only would rank as a householder. Disraeli could have no insuperable objection to a franchise
which he had once proposed himself; and it was agreed
to admit lodgers down to a £10 limit.

The troublesome question of the compound householder
had now to be faced. The difficulty was that the new
system would apply so irregularly. The Small Tenements
Act and local Acts with the same object affected some
boroughs only; others were entirely innocent of the compound householder. Half a million votes were in question. To the timid Whig or Tory it seemed most important not to swamp the constituencies with this swarm of
what he fancied to be barbarian invaders; to the Radical
the Bill was hopelessly incomplete without their inclusion. For Disraeli and the bulk of the Conservative for-
wards who believed in the efficacy of personal rating,
the principle of the Bill was involved. 'We lay down a
principle,' he had said on the second reading, 'and let
that principle work.' If these half-million could be rated
personally, they ought to have the vote as they would
have the responsibility; otherwise they had no claim to
it. This view is the clue to Disraeli's attitude on the
various attempts to solve the question. His own
plan had been to grant special facilities for placing the
compound householder's name on the rate-book. But
that offered many difficulties; and as General Grey wrote

on the Queen's behalf: ' She fears that you are preparing
for yourself a probable, if not a certain, defeat.'   But he
could not well accept Hibbert's amendment, which gave
the householder a vote on paying his composition, without being directly rated.   That would be to surrender
the principle on which the Bill was founded.   Gladstone
came vehemently to Hibbert's aid, and accused the
Government of 'fraud and dissimulation,' or at least of
taking care that the apparent extension of the franchise
should not be realised.   ' I prefer the invective of Tor-
quemada to the insinuation of Loyola,' replied Disraeli.
The amendment was defeated by sixty-six votes.

In asking the House to reject Hibbert's amendment,
Disraeli expressed a strong desire to find a solution of
the difficulty, commended the matter to the consideration of the Committee, and trusted that with their aid
the Government might still conduct it to a happy termination.   An amendment was immediately proposed by
Hodgkinson, M.P. for Newark, which was open to none
of the previous objections, but which would enfranchise
at one blow the whole of the half-million whose advent
moderate Reformers dreaded.   This amendment swept
away the Small Tenements Act and other local Acts, and
made the occupier alone the person responsible for local
rates.   Bright, his biographer tells us,[1] was the author of
the proposal, and Gladstone spoke in its favour, though
treating it as a forlorn hope.   But here was Disraeli's
principle of personal rating conceded.   What was he to
do ?   His leading colleague in the Commons, Hardy,
was not by his side, but seeking re-election on change
of office.   Hardy had been, with general approval, appointed to take over the Home Secretaryship from
Walpole, who had once again had to deal with Reform
meetings in the parks, and, having once again failed to
do so with success, had resigned his office, though remaining in the Cabinet without portfolio.   Disraeli, left
alone, acted up to the principle of personal rating, and,

---

[1] Trevelyan's *Bright*, p. 376.

to the astonishment of a thin House, announced at the dinner-hour his acceptance of the amendment. He was naturally eager to get his principal lieutenant's approval.

To Gathorne Hardy.

GROSVENOR GATE, *May* 18, 1867.—I have had great difficulties about the Reform Bill since we parted, and have terribly missed your aid and counsel.

On Thursday night, Dalgleish gave notice of a motion for Committee on Compound Householders, which, if carried, would have ' hung up ' the Bill, and which, as it was to be supported by all the Independent Liberals and many of our own men, would certainly have been carried. I prevailed on him, yesterday morning, to give this intention up, but he informed us at the same time that he, and all his friends, and many of ours, as we knew, must support Hodgkinson's amendment for repeal of Small Tenements Act.

I sent off to you, but you had gone to Osborne: Lord Barrington told me, however, that you had mentioned to him that you were not unfavorable to the repeal in itself. I sent for Lambert, who, after long consultation with myself and Thring, said, if required, he could effect the repeal of the Rating Bill in five clauses, and was in favor of it. Two months ago such a repeal was impossible: but a very great change had occurred in the public mind on this matter. Two months ago Gladstone would have placed himself at the head of the Vestries and ' Civilisation ': now, we were secretly informed, he intended to reorganise on the principle of repeal of Local Acts.

In this state of doubt and difficulty I went down to the House; and about nine o'clock, being quite alone on our bench, and only forty-five men on our side, some of whom were going to vote for Hodgkinson, the amendment was moved, and, as I had been led somewhat to believe, Gladstone got up (his benches with about a hundred men) and made his meditated *coup*, which you will read.

I tried to get up some debate, or, rather, I waited for it, for I could do no more, but it was impossible. His ' appeal ' to me prevented anyone but Bass and Co. speaking, and they were for Hodgkinson. I waited until the question was put, when, having revolved everything in my mind, I felt that the critical moment had arrived, and when, without in the slightest degree receding from our principle and position of a rating and residential franchise, we might take a step which would destroy the present agitation and extinguish Gladstone and Co. I therefore accepted the spirit of H.'s amendment.

It was most painful, truly grievous and annoying, to act in

such a matter without your personal and immediate countenance; and I can't conceal from myself, tho' I felt the pulse
of many in the course of the morning, feeling that some crisis
which required decision might arrive—I say I cannot conceal
from myself that this course may excite some discontent;
but if you stand by me all will go right.

I have no reason to doubt the adhesion of the Cabinet, with
the exception of the Duke of Bucks, whom I have not seen.
If the Cabinet is united to-day, all will go right, and no further
opposition to the Reform Bill will take place.

I had always, from our frequent conversations on the subject, inferred that, in theory, you were opposed to the Rating
Bills, but were of opinion, as I was myself, that it was unwise,
not to say impossible, for us to touch them.   But if the Opposition originated the move, that was a great difference.   I
inferred also, from what Barrington impressed on me, that
you were not insensible to the change of public opinion on
this subject.

I have written all this off to you, *curr. cal.*, that you might
fully understand all I feel at this moment.   It is a critical one
which requires alike courage and conciliation for all.   I hope
you may, on the whole, not disapprove of my course; but I
feel confident that, if you do not entirely, you will for the sake
of the party, and perhaps a little for mine, support a colleague
who has endeavoured to do his best in great difficulties.

Hardy, on consideration, agreed.   In retrospect he
wrote : ' We had so far stepped in that we could not, on
such a point, draw back; but it was a new proof that a
great measure ought not to be in the hands of a minority,
but with those who can mould and resist the moulding
of others.'   To Disraeli, at the time, he wrote that the
course taken was logical and consistent.   ' We have never
treated compounding as a check which we insisted on, but,
finding it so prevalent, did our best to open a way out of
it, to those who desired to be voters. . . .   Though the
change may now be more rapid than we anticipated, I do
not see upon what principle we can object to enabling all
who pay their rates to come upon the register.' [1]

Disraeli put a bold face on the change in the House.
The amendment, he said, would carry out the principle
of the Bill; the Government had originally introduced a

[1] Gathorne Hardy, Vol. I., pp. 207-211.

similar provision, and had only withdrawn it to avoid overloading the ship. But the word flew round from the half-empty House to the lobbies and the clubs that Disraeli had now conceded what amounted to pure household suffrage,[1] in spite of the previous protestations made by his colleagues and by himself; and Cranborne and Lowe, looking merely at the great numbers added to the constituency, both poured forth copious jeremiads, which from their strongly anti-democratic point of view were well justified. On the other hand, that unimpeachable old Tory, Henley, entirely backed up the Government. They were carrying out, he said, their fundamental principle; it was the most Conservative thing in the Bill. Disraeli fully realised the enormous numerical addition that would be made to the constituency, and, till he had received Hardy's consent, was most anxious. The morning after the concession, he sent an early note to his wife: ' Dearest, come to me when you are up and breakfasted, as it is necessary to confer on affairs before you go into the world '; and he was greatly relieved to receive the reply: ' All right; Mr. Hardy highly approves.'

The concession of the lodger franchise and the abolition of compounding opened the borough franchise so widely that the *raison d'être* of the direct tax franchise and the ' fancy franchises ' was taken away. Practically everyone who would be enfranchised under those clauses must be either a rate-paying householder or a lodger; and Disraeli, naturally, made no serious opposition to their elimination. With regard to the county franchise, the original proposal of the Government was to fix it at £15 rating. Locke King, in pursuance of his constant policy, to which Disraeli and his colleagues had been temporarily converted in 1859, moved to substitute £10. There was a meeting of county members, which urged the Government to fix

---

[1] Gladstone's Government, in 1869, on the plea of administrative convenience, restored compounding for local rates without electoral disqualification, thus eliminating the rating principle and establishing in boroughs household suffrage pure and simple.

a lower rate than £15; and, when a moderate Liberal
suggested £12 as a compromise, Disraeli adopted it as
such.

To Queen Victoria.

House of Commons, *May* 27, 1867.—The Chancellor of
the Exchequer, with his humble duty to your Majesty.

The Reform Bill makes good, and even great, progress.
We have had a most important and successful night, and the
feeling of the House is excellent.

We meet again to-morrow morning, and shall, at the least,
have four sittings per week.

The Chancellor of the Exchequer takes even a sanguine
view of affairs, and counts on sending the Bill up to the Lords
in the earlier part of July.

The House received the announcement of the remission of
the capital punishments of the traitor-convicts with dignified
satisfaction.

As the proposed measure of enfranchisement had been
enlarged, enormously in the boroughs, slightly in the
counties, so the Government scheme of redistribution,
which was originally of a somewhat limited character,
was considerably extended in Committee; though the
extension was on the same lines, and did not involve any
absolute disfranchisement of boroughs, save for electoral
corruption. The Government had proposed to take
away one member from boroughs below 7,000 population,
and, of the thirty seats obtained in this manner and by
disfranchisement of corrupt places, to give fourteen to
new boroughs, fifteen to counties, and one to London
University. On the ground that this scheme did not go
far enough to give reasonable hope of a permanent settlement, Laing, an independent Liberal member, proposed
that the limit below which the second member should be
taken away from boroughs should be 10,000 instead of
7,000 population. He had an elaborate scheme for disposing of the extra seats thus obtained, which involved
giving a second member to towns over 50,000 population,
and a third member to both towns and counties over
150,000. Disraeli resisted the enlargement on behalf of
the Government; but seventy-two Conservatives voted

against their leaders, and the amendment was carried by
the great majority of 127. Once again the party had
forced the hands of the Government. Whether on this
occasion Disraeli wished to have pressure put upon him,
as he had over the Ten Minutes Bill, it is difficult to
say; but there is a curious letter from Lennox on the
circumstances of the division:

From Lord Henry Lennox.

June 2.—While you, as organ of the Government, were
speaking against Mr. Laing's amendment, W. Spofforth, the
paid agent of the party, was diligently whipping in favour of
it, and, with considerable audacity, asserting that the Government wished to be beaten on the point.

For the truth of this, incredible as it seems, I am ready to
vouch; and even more, that his whipping was enforced upon
our men by a list which he held in his hand, and which professed to give the statistics why Laing's amendment ought to be
carried, and why the Government wished to be beaten. . . .

Laing's motion was, at most, merely an extension of the
principle on which redistribution was dealt with in the
Bill. When another Liberal endeavoured to introduce
the principle of total disfranchisement with regard to
all boroughs under 5,000 population, Disraeli successfully
resisted the change by the considerable majority of fifty-
two. But he was ready to remodel and enlarge his
scheme in accordance with the vote on Laing's amendment. 'Several Cabinets during this month on the Reform Bill, which each time becomes more radical,' wrote
Malmesbury in June. On the 13th, Disraeli explained
the new plan of redistribution of the forty-five seats
given by the adoption of the 10,000 population limit.
Nineteen were to go to towns, mostly new boroughs, and
twenty-five to counties, and there was one University
seat. As the small boroughs represented the rural population, it was fair that the extra seats taken from them
should go mainly to the counties But a strenuous
attempt was made to get a third member for the largest
towns. One such amendment by Laing was beaten by
eight votes; but subsequently Disraeli consented to a

compromise by which Liverpool, Manchester, Birmingham, and Leeds, were each given a third member, the seats being obtained by withdrawing proposed new boroughs from the schedule.   This compromise, which in no way altered the balance as between county and town, and which was therefore eminently reasonable, gave Disraeli a bad quarter of an hour, both in Cabinet and in the House. Hardy wrote in his diary : ' Our course about the large boroughs is, to my mind, unsatisfactory, and again and again I long to be out of the bother.   General Peel attacked us vehemently, and the House sneered at Disraeli's surrender.   Odious work ! '   Peel's attack, on this occasion particularly undeserved, was indeed bitter ; he seemed to be avenging Disraeli's treatment of his brother.   The proceedings on the Bill, he said, had taught him three things—first, that nothing had so little vitality as a ' vital point ' ; secondly, that nothing was so insecure as a ' security ' ; and, thirdly, that nothing was so elastic as the conscience of a Cabinet Minister.

Thus Disraeli had consented to allow the House to enlarge both the enfranchisement and the redistribution proposed in the Bill ; but he had preserved the principles on which he had based each, rating and residence in one case, no disfranchisement and no entire reconstruction in the other.   It remains to notice how he dealt with a few incidental questions.   On voting papers, he was beaten on a division by thirty-eight ; it was a mere matter of machinery, and the Government accepted the decision of the House.   To all proposals of minority voting and minority representation, he showed a determined hostility.   J. S. Mill brought forward Hare's plan, which has in later days received so much favour.   The House generally thought the scheme was impracticable, and Disraeli was merely its mouthpiece in recommending withdrawal.   A motion by Lowe in favour of cumulative voting, that is, permission to the voter in all cases of three- or four-member seats to cast all his votes for one of the candidates, met with much more support, not only

J. S. Mill, but Fawcett, one of the tea-room party, as
well as Cranborne, speaking for it. Though rejected at
first on Bright's and Disraeli's advice, the scheme was
revived in another form by the Lords. On a proposal
by Mill to enable women to vote, which was defeated by
196 to 73, Disraeli took no part; he did not even vote.

The carrying of the Reform Bill through Committee in
the House of Commons was the work of Disraeli, and of
Disraeli alone. He was always in his place, never
at a loss, but always armed with facts and arguments;
full of tact and conciliation where these were required,
or of retort and sarcasm when a wrecking amendment
was persisted in ; but on indifferent points of detail,
no one in the House so indifferent as he. It was
estimated that he spoke on the Bill more than 300
times. It was what in modern slang is called a ' one-
man show,' as was pointed out in quaint, but forcible,
language by Bernal Osborne. He bade the House rely
on the Chancellor of the Exchequer, who had ' lugged up
that great omnibus-full of stupid, heavy country gentlemen,' and converted them into Radical Reformers. ' In
fact, the Chancellor of the Exchequer is the Ministry by
himself, for it could not exist a day without him, and all
the rest who sit near him are the most respectable pawns
on the board, their opinion being not worth a pin.'

One shrewd observer insisted that Disraeli's capacity
for silence, even more than his power of speech, was the
principal agent in carrying the Bill.

But for this power to hold his tongue, Mr. Disraeli would
never have got this Bill through the House. Moreover, he
seems to be able to silence his colleagues' tongues, either by
positive and inexorable command or by the mesmeric power
of example. In reviewing the course of this Bill, it is astonishing to find how little speaking came from the Treasury Bench.
. . . The Chancellor of the Exchequer has ruled his Ministry
with despotic power. ' You must speak,' he seemed to say
to one, and he spoke. To others he issued no commands,
and they were silent. . . . Further, it has been remarked
that, whatever may have been done in the Cabinet, in the
House the leader appeared to consult none of his colleagues.

. . . In short, Disraeli has steered this Bill through himself; alone he did it; and with what wonderful skill none but those who watched him from night to night can know.[1]

This observer adds that there was generally no one present with Disraeli in his private room during the progress of the Bill except his secretary Corry, and Lambert, of the Poor Law Board, who was greatly consulted as a statistician. There was also, no doubt, almost always Thring, the draftsman, who has recorded that Disraeli 'seemed to have an intuitive perception of what would pass the House of Commons; but he cared nothing for the details of a Bill, and, once satisfied with the principle, he troubled comparatively little about its arrangements and construction.' Thring added:

It was in course of preparing this Reform Bill of 1867, and watching every night its passage through Parliament, that I had ample means, for the first and last time, of judging of Mr. D.'s characteristics. I was constantly struck by his great skill in overcoming difficulties as they arose in Parliament, and his tact in meeting, by judicious compromises, the objections of his opponents. His courtesy to me never failed, even under the most trying circumstances.

By the middle of July the long labour of Committee and Report was over, and the Bill was set down for third reading on the 15th. The debate resolved itself into a violent attack on Disraeli and the Government, conducted by Cranborne and Lowe. Cranborne said that when the Bill was read a second time it bristled with securities which had all now disappeared. He attributed the parentage of the measure, in the shape in which it emerged from Committee, to Gladstone, whose demands, he said, had all been conceded. He omitted, by the way, to mention that Gladstone's principal demand had been for a £5 value for the borough franchise, and that this had been successfully resisted. If the concession of Gladstone's demands and the adoption of Bright's principles were a triumph, then the Conservative party had never won so signal a triumph as this. The party had been misled by

[1] W. White's *Inner Life of the House of Commons*, Vol. II., pp. 76, 77.

the mystery and reticence of its leaders. There had been a political betrayal without a parallel in our annals. Lowe said they were entering upon an epoch of revolution. We must educate our new masters in order to avert the consequences of a measure which every honest and educated Englishman regarded with shame, scorn, and indignation. Bright hailed the Bill as giving the best permanent foundation for the suffrage, though he would have agreed to a more limited measure; and Elcho, as a leading Adullamite, accepted the Bill as a satisfactory settlement, and said the course of events had justified the action his party had taken last year. He especially selected for praise Disraeli's management of the question as contrasted with Gladstone's.

Disraeli's speech was naturally, in form, an answer to the diatribes of Cranborne and Lowe. He was easily able to show that he himself for the last twenty years had steadily spoken in favour of increasing the representation of the working classes; and he added that statement about the discussion of household suffrage in the Cabinet of 1858-59 on which we have already commented. The Government did not believe in the enfranchisement of a favoured portion of the working classes, a sort of Pretorian Guard. That would have been the result of setting up a limit of an £8, £7, £6, or £5 value, such as Gladstone's proposal of the present year. It was better to appeal to the sympathies of the great body of the people. He gave the following interesting account of the evolution of the Bill.

We acceded to power last year, and we found it was absolutely necessary to deal with this question; we came into power unpledged, and I have heard, with some astonishment, reproaches in regard to our change of opinion. I am not here to defend, to vindicate, or even to mitigate, every expression I may have used on this subject during the course of many years, but I can appeal to the general tenor of the policy we have recommended. I have always said that the question of Parliamentary Reform was one which it was quite open to the Conservative party to deal with. I have said so in this House, and on the hustings, in the presence of my countrymen, a hundred times. I have always said, and I say so now, that, when you come to a settlement of this question, you cannot be bound to any particular scheme, as if you were settling the duties on sugar; but dealing with the question on great constitutional principles, and which I hope to show have not been deviated from, you must deal with it also with a due regard to the spirit of the time and the requirements of the country. . . . Believing that another failure would be fatal, not merely to the Conservative party, but most dangerous to the country, we resolved to settle it if we could. . . . Knowing the majority was against us, and knowing the difficulties we had to deal with, being in a minority—and even with a majority our predecessors had not succeeded—after due deliberation we were of opinion that the only mode of arriving at a settlement was to take the House into council with us, and by our united efforts, and the frank communication of ideas, to attain a satisfactory solution. . . . It was in harmony with these views that I placed resolutions on the table. It is very true that at that time—in the month of March or February, it may be—you derided those resolutions and ridiculed the appeal; but reflection proved the policy was just, and you have adopted it. . . . You have all co-operated with us, and it is by that frank and cordial co-operation that we have arrived at a third reading.

Disraeli had no difficulty in exposing the inaccuracy of Cranborne's statement that the securities in the original Bill had been ' obsequiously ' yielded to Gladstone's ' imperious dictation.' The preceding narrative has shown in how many cases it was the feeling, sometimes the almost unanimous feeling, of the Conservative party itself which determined the action of the Government, so that Disraeli could plead that ' the party on this question has always been in advance of the Government. There is not a security that we have proposed that has not been objected to by the Conservative party.' If the policy of the Bill of 1859, retaining the £10 limit, could no longer be upheld, then there was no safe resting-place till rating household suffrage. In regard to redistribution, there had been no disfranchisement, but there had been a very considerable attempt to do justice to the inadequately represented millions of dwellers in the counties. He ridiculed Lowe's speech, with its classical tags, as that of ' some inspired schoolboy,' and poured contempt upon its ' doleful vaticinations.'

For my part, I do not believe that the country is in danger.
I think England is safe in the race of men who inhabit her;
that she is safe in something much more precious than her
accumulated capital—her accumulated experience; she is safe
in her national character, in her fame, in the traditions of a
thousand years, and in that glorious future which I believe
awaits her.

The Bill passed the third reading in the Commons
without a division; it had yet to run the gauntlet of the
House of Lords. Undoubtedly the vast extension which
it had received in Committee had alarmed even some of
the most convinced friends of a real settlement; and it
was thought that the Lords might reasonably reduce its
proportions. The Queen wrote to Derby that she did
not wish to say anything that could embarrass the Government, and that she felt it would be impossible to
recede from the concessions already made to popular
feeling; but that she hoped Ministers would give a fair
consideration to any amendments which might be proposed in the House of Lords ' with a view to avert the
danger which many people apprehend from the great
increase of democratic power.'   Derby, however, as well
as Disraeli, realised that it was essential there should be
no narrowing of the scope of the Bill; and the thorough
fashion in which, after its transmogrification in the Commons, it was adopted by the most powerful man in
the Lords, made its acceptance there fairly safe, unless
the great Whig peers could bring themselves to play over
again, in concert with the Tory seceders, the game in
which Gladstone had, not without humiliation, failed.
Derby called his followers in the Upper House together,
and urgently requested their support for a Bill which,
he said, notwithstanding Gladstone's factiousness, the
Government had, by making fair concessions and owing
to the inimitable tact and temper of the Chancellor of
the Exchequer, passed with the practically unanimous
consent of the House of Commons. The high Tory peers
grumbled, but came to heel. The threatened Whig opposition collapsed; as Disraeli wrote to Derby, ' the younger

generation, Granville, Argyll, and Co., shrank from the too ridiculous climax—of a Reform Bill in 1867 opposed by Lord Grey and the Whigs.' Accordingly, in spite of an inopportune fit of gout which deprived the House for a while of Derby's leadership, the Bill passed through all its stages with comparatively small amendment.

The most notable incidents of its passage through the Lords were a speech of dark foreboding by Shaftesbury, the emergence of Cairns as a strong defender of the scheme, and two characteristic sayings by Derby, one related by Granville, but not denied, the other uttered on the third reading by Derby himself. Granville's story was that Derby's answer to a Conservative friend, who reproached him with his revolutionary proposals, was merely, 'Don't you see how we have dished the Whigs ?' The third reading speech admitted and defended the experimental character of the Bill : ' No doubt we are making a great experiment and taking a leap in the dark, but I have the greatest confidence in the sound sense of my fellow-countrymen, and I entertain a strong hope that the extended franchise which we are now conferring upon them will be the means of placing the institutions of this country on a firmer basis.'

The amendments of the Lords caused very little difficulty. The contentious ones, though perfunctorily supported by Disraeli, were all rejected, with the exception of one proposed and carried by Cairns, giving a certain representation to minorities, by enacting that in the three-member constituencies, which were about a dozen in number, each elector should only have two votes, and in the one four-member constituency, the City, only three votes. Disraeli did not himself approve this system any more than Gladstone and Bright, who strongly opposed it; but, in spite of having helped to defeat a somewhat similar amendment by Lowe, he was not sorry to try an experiment which proceeded from his friend Cairns, and to secure the acceptance of at least one of the Lords' contentious amendments. His sense of humour was, no doubt, tickled by the fact that it would certainly give the third seat in his own constituency of Bucks to the Liberals—that third seat which, in the present Parliament, for the first time since his own first return in 1847, was filled by a Conservative. With this and a few other minor alterations, the Bill, which only dealt with England, became law on August 15, progress with the corresponding Bills for Scotland and Ireland being perforce postponed till the following session.

Ministers were, naturally, in the highest spirits at the Greenwich whitebait dinner. Stanley is said to have been the only Minister present who wore evening dress; so he was dubbed ' the Reverend Mr. Stanley,' called to the chair, and asked to say grace. Gordon, the Lord Advocate, sang a jovial Scotch song written for the occasion by Lord Neaves, the Judge, called ' The Ministerial Cogie ' —'cogie' meaning literally a small wooden drinking vessel, and metaphorically any pleasant mixture. ' The Bill is safe, the Bill is passed,' it began, and went on to celebrate the ' dishing ' of the Whigs and the triumph of the Tories.

> Now from this day the country's sway
> Belongs to no Whig fogie;
> And none can now of Tories say
> They scrimped the people's cogie.

Gordon's demeanour was usually grave and austere, and it was noticed that the incongruity of the man and the song moved Disraeli to one of his very rare bursts of hearty laughter.

In a speech at the customary Mansion House banquet to Ministers just before the close of the session, Disraeli reviewed his great achievement, and related it to what had been his life-work in politics, the restoration of the Tory party to its due place in the government of the country. The claim to have terminated the monopoly of Liberalism is a repetition of the sentiments of his speech at Liverpool in the autumn of 1859; the vindication of Toryism as the national and popular party pervades all his political writings and speeches from first to last.

I have seen in my time several monopolies terminated, and recently I have seen the termination of the monopoly of Liberalism. Nor are we to be surprised when we see that certain persons who believed that they had an hereditary right, whenever it was necessary, to renovate the institutions of their country, should be somewhat displeased that any other persons should presume to interfere with those changes which, I hope in the spirit of true patriotism, they believed the requirements of the State rendered necessary. But I am sure that when the hubbub has subsided, when the shrieks and screams which were heard some time ago, and which have already subsided into sobs and sighs, shall be thoroughly appeased, nothing more terrible will be discovered to have occurred than that the Tory party has resumed its natural functions in the government of the country. For what is the Tory party unless it represents national feeling ? If it do not represent national feeling, Toryism is nothing. It does not depend upon hereditary coteries of exclusive nobles. It does not attempt power by attracting to itself the spurious force which may accidentally arise from advocating cosmopolitan principles or talking cosmopolitan jargon. The Tory party is nothing unless it represent and uphold the institutions of the country. . . . I cannot help believing that, because my Lord Derby and his colleagues have taken a happy opportunity to enlarge the privileges of the people of England, we have not done anything but strengthen the institutions of the country, the essence of whose force is that they represent the interests and guard the rights of the people.

The party as a whole, though some were vindictive and many more bewildered over the great transformation scene of the year, were not unappreciative of the magnitude of their leaders' performance; and several demonstrations, especially in the great urban centres, were arranged in their honour, and in celebration of the passing of the Bill. The chief of these were in Lancashire, where Derby was naturally the principal figure, and in Edinburgh, where Disraeli was invited by his Scottish admirers to a banquet such as Edinburgh in former days had offered to statesmen of the calibre of Grey and Peel.

To Lord Derby.

CHANCELLOR OF THE EXCHEQUER, *Oct.* 18, 1867.—I congratulate you on the Manchester demonstration. It will do great good, especially at this moment. . . .

And I thank you for the kind manner in which you spoke of myself, and which you invariably do.[1]

I came up to town for change of air, for when the leaf falls I fall. I never can escape: luckily my attack is as regular as the trade winds, and occurs at a time when it little signifies, and can be kept secret. Unfortunately, this year I have something to do—the Edinburgh banquet. How I am to get there I know not, but I feel I shall. I think of troops that have marched thirty miles, and then, on empty stomachs, too, have to fight. They do fight, and often conquer.

Unfortunately, the Queen, I am sure entirely from kindness, and to do me honor at this particular moment, has asked me to pay a visit to Balmoral before the dinner, and to fix my time. This, I feel sure, would quite finish me, and I have written to General Grey, and have a hope his friendliness may extricate me from this overwhelming honor.[2] . . .

Disraeli's visit to Scotland was a memorable one. He had apparently never been in that country since the autumn of 1825, when, as a boy of twenty, he went north on two occasions to see Scott and Lockhart on Murray's behalf in connection with the founding of the *Representative*.[3] The miscarriage of that undertaking had probably given him rather a distaste for Scotland, which the ingrained Liberalism of the Scotch, especially of the working classes among them, did nothing to remove; and he was, moreover, throughout his life, wont to jar upon the feelings of ultra-patriotic Scotsmen by almost invariably using ' England ' as a short term to express the United Kingdom of Great Britain and Ireland, in that respect erring—if it be an error—in company, it is only fair to say, with most of the leading statesmen of the time. But his democratic Toryism had met with a ready response from the younger generation of Scottish Conservatives, represented by men like Bannerman-Robertson and Stormonth-Darling, both eventually law officers and Judges; and, despite the ridicule of the leading Scottish journal, the *Scotsman*, and the lukewarmness or opposi-

---

[1] Derby said that it was mainly due to Disraeli's tact, temper, and judgment, that the arduous undertaking in which they were engaged had not resulted, instead of a triumphant success, in disastrous failure.

[2] The Queen excused Disraeli from attendance at Balmoral.

[3] See Vol. I., I., ch. 5.

tion of certain influential Conservatives, such as the Duke
of Buccleuch and Disraeli's old friend Sir George Sinclair, the banquet, which was presided over by Sir William
Stirling Maxwell, was an enormous success.

Disraeli, in his speech, vindicated the historical title of
the Tories to deal with Reform, from the first efforts of
Bolingbroke and Wyndham, through the policy of the
younger Pitt, down to his own and Derby's action.　Dealing with the most recent history, he said:

> I had to prepare the mind of the country, and to educate—
> if it be not arrogant to use such a phrase—to educate our
> party.　It is a large party, and requires its attention to be
> called to questions of this kind with some pressure.　I had to
> prepare the mind of Parliament and the country on this ques-
> tion of Reform.　This was not only with the concurrence of
> Lord Derby, but of my colleagues.

The points on which Disraeli claimed to have educated
his party were certain principles of Reform, including
the necessity of comprehensiveness, of increased county
representation, and of the rating basis; not, however, of
household suffrage, as has often been wrongly asserted.
But he doubtless meant to hint, and the world at once
acknowledged, that the educating process had not been
confined to Reform.　The phrase aptly described the
whole course of his leadership of the party out of the
narrow policies of the late forties into the broad and
national programme of the 1866 Administration.

Two striking passages followed, the first on the principle of the Bill:

> When you try to settle any great question, there are two
> considerations which statesmen ought not to forget.　First
> of all, let your plan be founded upon some principle.　But that
> is not enough.　Let it also be a principle that is in harmony
> with the manners and customs of the people you are attempt-
> ing to legislate for.　Now I say, when you come to this question
> of the suffrage for boroughs, there is a principle in saying a
> man shall have a vote who has, by his residence and his con-
> tribution to local taxation, proved that he is interested in the
> welfare of his community.　That man is a man whom you may
> trust in preference to a migratory pauper.　That is a prin-

ciple; and then, if you can apply that principle in harmony
with the manners and customs of your country, then I say
that you have the chance of a solution—a happy solution—
of a great question.   When you find it was an old custom of
the country that the householder should possess this suffrage
—that the man who, by his residence and his rate, proved he
was one who, on an average, might fairly be looked upon as a
responsible and trustworthy individual—you had your principle, and you had your traditionary practice to consecrate
your principle.   A rating and residential borough franchise
was not new even in modern times.   It had been tried in
the Municipal Act.

The acceptance of the Hodgkinson amendment, he
maintained, was the logical consequence of this principle:

We had insisted that no man should vote who did not pay
rates.   We had sympathised with the compound householder
by having prepared clauses by which his vote might be facilitated, and if he chose to come forward and commit suicide,
and say, ' I will no longer be a compound householder, but I
will give up these privileges and pay rates,' what was our
duty ?   It would have been most inconsistent in us to resist
such a proposal.   I say that the compound householder bowing down, and giving up his peculiar position, and saying,
' In order to exercise the suffrage I will pay the rate,' was the
very triumph of the principle of our Bill.

These plain statements, Disraeli proceeded, disposed
of the ' enormous nonsense ' which had been circulated
through the country by Liberals and by Conservative
seceders.   If the principle of the Bill was thus maintained,
what became of the talk of the unprincipled withdrawal
of checks and securities, ' the betrayal of our friends, who
insisted upon being betrayed ' ?   The two great quarter-
lies, Whig and Tory, had just published articles, both
harping on this same string, the article in the *Quarterly
Review* being Cranborne's famous philippic, ' The Conservative Surrender.'   The nature of the argument is sufficiently indicated by the title; the pungency of the writing
rivalled the writer's first attack on Disraeli in the same
review seven years before.   Disraeli's comment was conceived in his happiest vein.

He who has written the summary of the session in the
Edinburgh is not mounted on the fiery barb of Francis Jeffrey;

he is rather placed upon a prancing hearse horse, with which
he consummates the entombment of Whig principles. The
'Conservative Surrender' . . . is what one would call a *replica*.
You have had the subject treated in speeches, in articles, in
reviews, and sometimes in manifestoes. The colouring is not
without charm, but the drawing is inaccurate, the perspective
is false, the subject is monotonous. . . . I should say that
article was written by a very clever man who has made a very
great mistake. The leaders of the Conservative party are
false; the Conservative party are false. They do not know
that they have been abused; they have not recognised that
their confidence has been betrayed and outraged. I see many
gentlemen here who have been, no doubt, inspectors, like myself, as magistrates, of peculiar asylums, who meet there some
cases which I have always thought at the same time the most
absurd and the most distressing; it is when the lunatic believes
all the world is mad, and that he himself is sane.

But to pass from such gloomy imagery: really these *Edinburgh* and *Quarterly Reviews*, no man admires them more than
myself. But I admire them as I do first-rate, first-class post-
houses, which in old days, for half a century or so—to use a
Manchester phrase—carried on a roaring trade. Then there
comes some revolution or progress which no person can ever
have contemplated. They find things are altered. They do
not understand them, and, instead of that intense competition
and mutual vindictiveness which before distinguished them,
they suddenly quite agree. The boots of the 'Blue Boar' and
the chambermaid of the 'Red Lion' embrace, and are quite
in accord in this—in denouncing the infamy of railroads.

Towards the close of his speech Disraeli looked to the
future:

In a progressive country change is constant; and the great
question is, not whether you should resist change which is inevitable, but whether that change should be carried out in
deference to the manners, the customs, the laws, the traditions of the people, or in deference to abstract principles and
arbitrary and general doctrines. The one is a national system;
the other, to give it an epithet, a noble epithet which perhaps
it may deserve, is a philosophic system. Both have great
advantages; the national party is supported by the fervour
of patriotism; the philosophical party has a singular exemption from the force of prejudice.

Disraeli concluded by recalling the 'three master influences which have at all times guided and controlled
all other powers and passions.' These were, as he had

said in a speech[1] in Bucks in 1863, Industry, Liberty, and Religion. ' So long as this sacred combination influences the destiny of this country, it will not die.'

The Edinburgh functions included the conferment of the freedom of the city by the Corporation, and of the honorary degree of LL.D. by the University, and also an evening meeting of working men in the Music Hall. A Conservative open meeting in Scotland was at that time an entirely new experiment, but Disraeli fairly captivated his audience.

From Mrs. Dundas of Arniston.

ARNISTON, GOREBRIDGE, N.B., Nov. 7, 1867.—. . . Mr. Dundas . . . returned from the meeting of working men, much pleased with the enthusiastic reception you met with.

I was much amused a few days afterwards at hearing a very Radical servant in Edinburgh say he had gone to the meeting, and he said he knew plenty of fellows went there to make a row. ' But,' quoth my friend, ' I came back *almost* a Tory. I was prejudeeced against the Chancellor; but you know he jist showed sich tack (? tact) that he made us all think like him. I never saw sich tack before in my life.' . . .

The Dundases of Arniston had entertained the Disraelis for the first few days of the Scottish expedition; for the remainder the visitors were the guests of Lord Advocate Gordon at his house in Edinburgh. There they met the young Lord Bute, whose story suggested the novel of *Lothair*, on which Disraeli was engaged less than two years later; and there he and his wife came under the friendly but critical inspection of a leading Scottish literary man of the day, Sir John Skelton, who, in the *Table Talk of Shirley*,[2] has given us a vivid and penetrating sketch of the Disraeli of 1867, ' clari giganteo triumpho.'

Old Lady Ruthven was there—a miraculous old woman. She and Mrs. Disraeli, sitting over the fire with their feet on the fender, making between them the funniest pair—the witches in *Macbeth*, or what you will. And the potent wizard himself, with his olive complexion and coal-black eyes, and the mighty dome of his forehead (no Christian temple, be sure), is unlike any living creature one has met. I had never

[1] See above, p. 98. [2] P. 247.

seen him in the daylight before, and the daylight accentuates
his strangeness. The face is more like a mask than ever, and
the division between him and mere mortals more marked. I
would as soon have thought of sitting down at table with
Hamlet, or Lear, or the Wandering Jew. He was indeed more
than cordial; especially appreciative of the Scottish allies—'rari
nantes in gurgite vasto '—who had stood by him through thick
and thin. 'I fancied, indeed, till last night, that north of the
border I was not loved; but last night made amends for much.
We were so delighted with our reception, Mrs. Disraeli and I,
that after we got home we actually danced a jig (or was it a
hornpipe ?) in our bedroom.'

They say, and say truly enough, What an actor the man is !
and yet the ultimate impression is of absolute sincerity and
unreserve. Grant Duff will have it that he is an alien.
What's England to him, or he to England ? There is just
where they are wrong. Whig or Radical or Tory don't matter
much, perhaps; but this mightier Venice—this Imperial
Republic on which the sun never sets—that vision fascinates
him, or I am much mistaken. England is the Israel of his
imagination, and he will be the Imperial Minister before he
dies—if he gets the chance.

Skelton had a real insight into Disraeli's character and
policy; but greater literary men showed less discernment.
Carlyle prophesied woe in his ' Shooting Niagara.' A
Conservative English poet, Coventry Patmore, was horrified. He dubbed 1867

> The year of the great crime,
> When the false English nobles, and their Jew,
> By God demented, slew
> The trust they stood twice pledged to keep from wrong.

Patmore, at any rate, realised that ' the Jew ' could not
have carried the Reform Bill without the ' English nobles.'
Speaking broadly, the party went with Disraeli ; and
Derby's own class followed the leader whom they trusted.
The landed aristocracy, no doubt, regarded with considerable misgiving the policy which they nevertheless accepted; by the urban Tories of the rank and file, the backbone of the Tory democracy, it was welcomed, in many
quarters with enthusiasm. The active dissentients were
very few in number; but they included the most incisive
writer of the party, and were supported by its most

weighty organ. Posterity has been asked to look at the conduct of the Conservative leaders through the spectacles either of Lord Salisbury and the *Quarterly*, or of the Whigs and Liberals who were 'dished,' or of idolaters of the middle class, like Lowe. What Disraeli did in 1867 has been treated, accordingly, with the same unfairness as what he did in 1846 and 1852.

What is the trust the leaders are charged with betraying ? The Conservatives certainly had no trust to resist Reform. Disraeli had preached the doctrine that Reform was no Whig preserve for twenty years, and the party had definitely accepted it in 1859. Where the leaders are vulnerable is on the score of surrendering the government of the country to the control of mere numbers. They had protested against any policy which should entrust power to a single class; they had advocated admitting freely the more educated and skilled members of the working classes, but not the working classes in bulk. Disraeli's speeches and addresses, especially during the Palmerston régime, at the General Election of 1865, and when the 1866 Bill was before the House, abounded, as we have seen, in this sense. Reform should be lateral; there should be extension, not degradation; the choicest members of the working class should be freely admitted, but there should be no undistinguishing reduction of the franchise; opinion, not numbers, should be represented; votes should be weighed, not counted. In fact, the policy of the Pretorian guard of working men, which Disraeli deprecated and ridiculed in his speech on the third reading in 1867, was apparently his own policy, from the days when he first suggested fancy franchises in 1848 down to the debates on the Bill of 1866; fancy franchises were even introduced into the Bill of 1867 as originally explained to the House of Commons. It was a policy for which there was much to be said; so thorough and consistent a friend of the working men as Shaftesbury held to it throughout, and denounced the Bill of 1867 for its departure from it.

But no policy of the kind could be a permanent settlement; and in all his previous efforts at Reform, particularly in the Bill of 1859, Disraeli did not aim at a permanent settlement, but at a temporary expedient, which
should merely satisfy the immediate demand. The aim of
all Russell's various Bills since 1852 had been the same;
there was no pretence of laying down a final principle.
But this time the question was to be settled. The great
debates of 1866 and the continued agitation in the country
had prepared men's minds to expect a definite solution.
The Republicans of the Northern States, whose apparent
failure had so long discredited democratic government,
had at length emerged triumphant, and thereby re-established the reputation of their institutions. The British
artisan, with manhood suffrage prevalent in the two
countries, America and France, which most influenced
him, would insist before long upon a like enfranchisement,
unless a broad and satisfactory basis were conceded.
There is a passage in ' The Conservative Surrender,'
where the writer is contrasting the general opposition to
household suffrage in 1866 with its general acceptance in
1867, which has a significance hardly perceived by himself. When household suffrage was openly proposed by
the Ministry, he writes, ' it was received with much murmuring indeed in private, but externally with almost
universal acceptance. Only a few scattered men here and
there in Parliament ventured to oppose it.' He rejects
the simple and obvious explanation that it was generally
recognised to be the settlement which the situation
required.

The credit for first recognising that the hour had come
for a real settlement is due, as we have seen, primarily to
the Queen, and next to Derby. Disraeli was reluctant
to admit the weight of the accumulating evidence. His
attitude in the autumn of 1866 makes indeed a serious
deduction from his reputation for foresight; and many
of his difficulties in the session of 1867, and of the inconsistencies into which he and his colleagues were betrayed

in debate, sprang from what Cranborne deservedly called
' the error of attempting to frame a Reform Bill during
the week previous to its production.' But, when Disraeli did finally acknowledge that decisive action was
necessary, he was prompt, in conjunction with Derby,
in sweeping aside temporary expedients, and founding himself upon an abiding principle. There is no
evidence to show whether the definite acceptance of
rating household suffrage is due rather to Disraeli or
to Derby; both based themselves upon it in January,
1867. Both, too, cordially accepted the only method by
which a settlement could be effected—the policy of welcoming, and deferring to, the co-operation of the House
of Commons in the application of the principle adopted.
But Derby was not so quick as Disraeli to see that the
frank acceptance of this method could hardly fail to involve the disappearance of checks and securities to which
he originally attached importance. The actual determination of what amendments should be accepted and
what resisted necessarily devolved mainly on the leader
of the House of Commons; and for the shape in which the
Bill emerged from Committee—for the fact, indeed, that
it emerged with safety at all—Disraeli was almost solely
responsible. But that he had Derby's support throughout is clear from the whole-hearted fashion in which the
Prime Minister urged his followers in the Lords to pass
the Bill substantially as it stood.

When it was a question of a permanent settlement,
numbers necessarily became a secondary consideration.
A principle had to be found that would not be disturbed:
if possible, a principle that would work automatically by
admitting gradually all desirable citizens. Rating household suffrage, in the actual state of the community, admirably fulfilled the conditions. The extensive use of the
system of compound householding would apparently prevent the immediate swamping of the ten-pounders by the
swarm of new voters; while the provisions for enabling
the compound householder to get upon the rate-book

would, it was hoped, prevent a feeling of grievance and
enable all the more responsible among them to acquire
the franchise sooner or later. Unfortunately neither Derby
nor Disraeli, owing to the hurry in which their Bill was
improvised, realised at first how very local and capricious
the distribution of the compound householding system
was; how the application of their principle would enfranchise practically the whole of one community and leave
another, whose circumstances were in every other respect
similar, as completely unenfranchised as before. As the
discussion proceeded, it became clear that the facilities
provided in the Bill would not meet the grievance; and
Disraeli was faced with the alternatives of either accepting the domination of numbers, which he deprecated, or
abandoning the idea of a permanent settlement. When
the first alternative was presented in such a form as to
preserve the principle of the Bill, and subject the compound householder to the steadying and conservative
influence of personal payment of rates, he could not
hesitate; and his prompt action, taken on his own responsibility, carried not only Derby's assent, but that of the
whole Cabinet.

Undoubtedly the upshot of the Act was, roughly
speaking, to double the constituency by adding about a
million new voters, mostly of one class—a result which
neither Derby nor Disraeli had originally contemplated,
but which they had reached by a perfectly open and
honourable road. Disraeli, at any rate, was confident
of the ultimate benefit both to the country and to the
party. He wrote to a working men's club about this
time: ' None are so interested in maintaining the institutions of the country as the working classes. The rich
and the powerful will not find much difficulty under any
circumstances in maintaining their rights, but the privileges of the people can only be defended and secured by
popular institutions.' He kept ever before his eyes the
establishment of the Conservative party on a national and
popular basis. Some weeks before the acceptance of the

Hodgkinson amendment he told his friend Beauchamp that he now began to see his way to realise the dream of his life. Ever since the reactionary proceedings of the Liverpool Administration, the Tory party had been associated in the popular mind with a policy [of exclusion and restriction. Peel had endeavoured to remove the reproach, but he had gone too fast and too far for his party; and the Whigs regained and held the allegiance of the middle-class electorate. Since 1846 all Disraeli's efforts and combinations had been unavailing to obtain a majority at the polls. Now was the supreme moment to show that, however much Conservatism revered our institutions, it did not distrust the people. Events have largely justified Disraeli's policy. The constituency which the Reform Act of 1867 created, and which was logically completed by the extension of household franchise to the counties in 1884, gave the Conservative party, either alone or in alliance with the Unionist Liberals, majorities at four General Elections— 1874, 1886, 1895, and 1900; insuring a fair spell of power to Disraeli himself, and a much longer tenure, by one of the caprices of fortune, to the statesman who worked his hardest against Disraeli to prevent that constituency from coming into being—Lord Salisbury. The existence, in considerable numbers, of the Conservative working man, whom it was the fashion of the Liberals of the sixties to treat as a myth, has been shown over and over again by the immense polls cast for the party in the largest urban constituencies. If the association of aristocracy and democracy which Disraeli brought about has given Conservative, as well as national, policy a strong bias in the direction of social reform, that is a result which would have been thoroughly acceptable to the author of *Sybil*.

Whatever might be thought of the Bill, there was no doubt or question of the personal triumph of Disraeli. In a cartoon labelled 'D'Israel-i in Triumph,' *Punch* depicted him as the Egyptian Sphinx being dragged in state to

the Temple of Reform by a straining team of eminent
politicians of all parties, some pulling willingly, some
under fear of Derby's whip. What were the facts? Every
Government of the last fifteen years had taken the Reform question in hand; and every Government had failed
with more or less of discredit. Disraeli, with a majority of
seventy against him, had carried his Bill; a Bill, moreover,
that was no temporary makeshift, but established the
borough franchise on a basis which was not altered in
essentials till the Great War opened the floodgates
without distinction of sex. Disraeli and Gladstone
had definitely measured their strength against each
other over this issue; and victory had rested unmistakably with Disraeli. 'Why is Gladstone like a tele-
scope ?' was a riddle which had a great vogue in Tory
circles. 'Because Disraeli draws him out, looks through
him, and shuts him up.' Gladstone's miscarriage in
1866 served brilliantly to set off Disraeli's achievement in 1867. If any contemporary was a good judge of
success, it was Bishop Wilberforce. Writing in August
at the end of the session, he declared: 'The most wonderful thing is the rise of Disraeli. It is not the mere
assertion of talent, as you hear so many say. It seems
to me quite beside that. He has been able to teach
the House of Commons almost to ignore Gladstone;
and at present lords it over him.' Gladstone talked to
his own friends of 'the diabolical cleverness of Dizzy.'
But, as the Bishop saw, there was more than cleverness.
There was even more than wit, humour, sarcasm, and
irony. There were good temper, patience, tact, resource,
judgment, resolution, courage, and loyalty; in fact—in
spite of the violent and unfounded reproaches of tricki-
ness and of (in Gladstone's phrase) 'revolting cynicism '—
there was what is summed up in one word, character.

Gigantic as was the task of carrying a comprehensive
Reform Bill through a Parliament in which Ministers
had a large majority against them, it by no means represented their sole achievement for the session. As in 1852

and in 1858, Disraeli's judicious management of the House
and the energy of his colleagues succeeded in putting on
the statute-book several useful measures besides. The
social reform which Disraeli's preaching and practice had
made an integral part of Conservative policy was forwarded by legislation materially extending the operation of the Factory Acts, and by establishing proper
provision in London for the sick and insane poor; and a
Trades Union Commission was appointed. But by far
the most important measure, after the Reform Bill, was
a Bill which Carnarvon prepared and introduced in the
House of Lords, though he had ceased to be Minister
when it became law, to federate the North American
Colonies into one Dominion. In connection with the
federation, Parliament also guaranteed a loan for a railway from Quebec to Halifax. The policy of these Canadian measures was one in which both front benches
concurred; Carnarvon was carrying through what Cardwell had initiated. But Radicals and economists, Bright
and Lowe, sniffed at the proposals, and suggested that
these Colonies should rather be encouraged either to join
the United States, or to set up for themselves. Disraeli
and the Government, on the other hand, were patrioti-
cally carrying to a further stage the policy which, after
the establishment of British Columbia, they had announced in the Queen's Speech in the summer of 1858—
that British North America should be occupied 'in an
unbroken chain, from the Atlantic to the Pacific, by a
loyal and industrious population of subjects of the British
Crown.'[1]

There was, however, at least one important measure
which Government failed to pass, in circumstances explained by Disraeli to the Queen:

To Queen Victoria.

DOWNING STREET, *Aug.* 16, 1867.—The Chancellor of the
Exchequer, with his humble duty to your Majesty.

He has now virtually brought the business of the House of

---

[1] See Vol. I., p. 1570.

Commons to a conclusion, and it will only meet on Monday to complete the business of the House of Lords.

He regrets that H.M.'s Government were obliged to relinquish the Parks Bill yesterday, after a division which showed that the House was desirous of legislation on the subject, but it was impossible to proceed with the Bill without considerably lengthening the session.

The truth is that the whole dealing with this subject, from the commencement, has been a series of errors, originating in a fundamental one. The matter was originally treated by your Majesty's Government without sufficient knowledge and sufficient thought. . . . It will require great tact and temper to bring all this right, but it will be done. . . .

Disraeli found time, in this busy session, to explain to his peer colleagues the constitutionality of the use of proxies in the Upper House; but the common-sense view prevailed that lords who wished to record their votes ought to come and hear the arguments, and the practice was discontinued.

To Lord Malmesbury.

July 10, 1867.—The Constitution of this country is a monarchy, modified in its action by the co-ordinate authority of the Estates of the Realm. An Estate is a political order invested with privilege for a public purpose.

There are three Estates: the Lords Spiritual, the Lords Temporal, and the Commons. The Estates of the Lords Spiritual and Temporal being very limited in number, their members can easily meet in their own chamber. The Estate of the Commons, being, on the contrary, very numerous, choose, for convenience, representatives instead of holding general meetings, like the Polish Diets.

The House of Commons is not an Estate of the Realm; its members are only the proxies of an Estate. The Lords, in using proxies, possess and exercise the same privilege as the Commons, no more; and if it is not convenient for them to attend the meetings of their orders, they have the right to choose their representatives.[1] . . .

To Sir Stafford Northcote.

July 20, 1867.—I can't refrain from congratulating you on the brilliant success of your fête,[2] one of the most striking

---

[1] *Memoirs of an Ex-Minister*, under date.
[2] A ball at the India Office in honour of the Sultan of Turkey, who paid a visit this summer to England

festivals of the century—if, indeed, ever exceeded at any time. The space, the proportion, beauty of form and color, and the glittering guests, produced a *coup d'œil* unrivalled; heightened by the occasion so strange and picturesque.

The admirable arrangements, so perfect and so unusual, and which put everyone at their ease, were worthy of the historic scene.

The long session did not close till August 21, and after his Herculean exertions Disraeli was glad indeed to escape to the repose of Hughenden. But the repose was rudely broken before many days had passed. The Queen's Speech had contained an ominous paragraph about the British captives detained by King Theodore of Abyssinia. Her Majesty was advised to express regret that her efforts to obtain their release had, so far, proved ineffectual, and to add that she had found it necessary to address to Theodore ' a peremptory demand for their immediate liberation, and to take measures for supporting that demand, should it ultimately be found necessary to resort to force.' By the beginning of September it became clear that Theodore would not yield, and preparations were in progress for an expedition from India.

To Lord Derby.

Confidential. HUGHENDEN, *Sept.* 8, 1867.—So long as there was a wild chance of the captives being released, I would not trouble you; but now, when that hope seems over, I must call your consideration to the difficult and dangerous position to which, it seems to me, your Government is drifting.

We are carrying on a war, and an expensive war, without the sanction of Parliament.

I feel persuaded that this is exactly a condition of affairs which, in February next, the whole ' Liberal ' party will resent; and they will do it under the leadership of Gladstone, who, from the line which he pursued in the instance of the Persian War, will advance, in this case, with additional authority.

I see only one mode of extricating ourselves from this impending peril, and that is a very disagreeable one. Parliament ought, in my opinion, to be called together as soon as practicable.

The refusal of the ultimatum, and the act of war consequent thereon, would be the logical occasion.

The earlier the Houses are summoned, the more anxious they will be to get away again.

At present the contemplated expedition is popular with the country, and the expenditure already incurred would not only be condoned, but might, under the peculiar circumstances, be justified.

From Lord Derby.

Confidential. KNOWSLEY, *Sept.* 10, 1867.—. . . One of the severest and most painful attacks of gout that I have had for years. In point of fact, it has been long due, and my London doctor only succeeded in patching me up for the exigencies of the session, in which, however, he was happily successful. But if the increasing frequency of these attacks is to continue, I feel that the time cannot be far distant when I must seek for restoration to health in absolute withdrawal from the public service. In the meantime, while I remain in it, I will not shrink from any possible performance of its duties.

To Lord Derby.

HUGHENDEN, *Sept.* 14, 1867.—. . . I am selfish in hoping you will not quit public life, as my career will terminate with yours: but it is not for that reason that I beg you will let me know how you are getting on, by the ' ready and confidential pen ' to which I offer my sympathies and kindest regards.

Unfortunately the next news which the ' ready and confidential pen ' of Lady Derby had to send Disraeli, on September 26, was that Derby had been once again attacked by ' the worst fit of gout he has had for a very long time,' and had no hope of leaving his bed for many days. Most of the arrangements for the November session had to be made, therefore, by Disraeli. As it was clear that Parliament could not have its attention confined to the single question of Abyssinia, it was decided that the form the sitting should assume should be that of the commencement of the session of 1868, and therefore a regular Queen's Speech would be necessary, with a programme of legislation. ' You cannot introduce great changes,' as Stanley wrote on September 24, ' dependent on the decision of the legislature, because that legislature is itself about to be superseded;' ' measures of practical utility and second-rate importance are those which seem most likely to succeed, and most suitable to the circumstances.'

The session was to open on Tuesday, November 19 ; and, the week before, Mrs. Disraeli, who was now seventy-five, and who had just been through all the excitements of the Scottish expedition, was struck down by serious illness. Her condition grew worse, and Disraeli appealed to Stanley 'as a comrade in arms, and the friend of my public life,' to take his place at the official dinner of the leader of the House on the eve of the session. 'This has been,' he added, 'a critical day in my wife's life, but not a bad one. There seems a favorable turn, and I count almost on being in my place to-morrow.' His hopes were justified, and he was able to attend the debate on the Address, and to hear and respond, with tears (it was noted) in his eyes, to the sympathetic allusion which Gladstone made to Mrs. Disraeli's condition. There was a strong mutual regard between Mrs. Disraeli and Gladstone, which often exercised a mollifying influence at a crisis. She told Mr. Kebbel that, after a sharp encounter in the House of Commons, Gladstone would frequently come round to Grosvenor Gate just to show he bore no malice. Mindful of this, Disraeli feared that his words in the House had been an insufficient expression of gratitude for sympathy, and he wrote to amplify them, adding: ' My wife had always a strong personal regard for you, and being of a vivid and original character, she could comprehend and value your great gifts and qualities.'[1] Gladstone replied with grace and feeling: ' I have always been grateful for, and have sincerely reciprocated, Mrs. Disraeli's regard, and during the recent crisis I was naturally mindful of it; but, even if I had not had the honour and pleasure of knowing her, it would have been impossible not to sympathise with you at a moment when the fortitude necessary to bear the labours and trials of your station was subjected to a new burden of a character so crushing and peculiar.'

[1] *Gladstone*, Book VII., ch. 3.

To Queen Victoria.

DOWNING STREET, *Nov.* 19, 1867.—The Chancellor of the Exchequer, with his humble duty to your Majesty.

The address to your Majesty's Speech was moved this evening by Mr. Hart Dyke, with grace and great ability: a young man, good-looking and very popular. He gained the whole House. M.P. for W. Kent.

Mr. Gladstone rose immediately, and made a very fair and just speech, and very kind and considerate to the Chancellor of the Exchequer, who was much touched by it.

And he begs leave to offer to your Majesty his very grateful thanks for all your Majesty's sympathy and gracious kindness in his great sorrow.

Your Majesty is too good. This morning all seemed dark, and he was told to hope no more; but within three hours of this there was a change, and everything became hopeful: a state of complete composure, but accompanied by increased strength.

Mrs. Disraeli got slowly better, but the anxiety, coupled with the pressure of public business, was too much for her husband, and after moving and carrying, in spite of Lowe's acrid opposition, the vote of credit of £2,000,000 for the Abyssinian Expedition, he collapsed himself. ' When I got home on Wednesday morning,' he wrote on November 30 to Stanley, ' in the cab in which you kindly tumbled me, I could not get out, and the driver, I fancy, thought I was drunk.' He had to get his Secretary to the Treasury, Ward Hunt, to move the supplementary Budget.

To Sir Stafford Northcote.

(*In pencil.*) GROSVENOR GATE. I am obliged to write to you on my back, and can't move, though I am otherwise well enough. I am clear that nothing should be postponed.

Hunt will find no difficulty. If he do, which is impossible, the House, I am sure, will take the division on a subsequent stage.

With regard to India, you are quite sufficient to fight the battle. You know the case thoroughly, can speak as often as you like, and will win.

Sooner than have the business postponed, I will come down and be carried into the House. I am serious in this, and beg, therefore, that you will let me know, that I may prepare.

Disraeli's illness was first diagnosed as sciatica, ' which frightens me,' he wrote humorously in pencil to Corry. ' James, my man, says his mother has the *sciatics*, and they last a year at least.   But, though depressed, I have still faith in my star.   I think it would be a ridiculous conclusion of my career; and, after all, ridicule settles nothing and nobody.'   It was, however, not sciatica, but the statesman's foe, gout, which had attacked Disraeli.   He and his wife were ill simultaneously in the Grosvenor Gate house, and she preserved the pencilled notes she received from him in a bundle labelled, ' Notes from dear Dizzy during our illness, when we could not leave our rooms.   At the end of the month (Dec. 1867), we were both quite well.'   Here are some specimens:

To Mrs. Disraeli.

Being on my back, pardon the pencil.
You have sent me the most amusing and charming letter I ever had.   It beats Horace Walpole and Mme. de Sévigné.

Grosvenor Gate has become a hospital, but a hospital with you is worth a palace with anybody else.—Your own D.

I have had a sleepless night, and in agony the whole time. This morning the pain in the foot became greatly mitigated, and I dozed a little from 6 to 8.   I have been nearly a week in bed, and am much worse than when I took to it. . . .   My only consolation is that you are better and stronger.   I never felt worse or more desponding.   I am so irritated at the blundering manner in which I have been treated.

We have been separated four days, and under the same roof ! How very strange !

To Sir Stafford Northcote.

(*In pencil.*) GROSVENOR GATE, *Dec.* 7, 1867.—My dinner, consisting, I am sorry to say, of a tapioca pudding, need not have prevented us meeting yesterday; but my butler is a pompous booby. . . .
We shall remain in town at present.   Mrs. Disraeli must not leave her room, tho' getting on well.

Disraeli had hardly recovered from his somewhat serious attack when he was called upon to deal with an acute stage of the Fenian Conspiracy. The policy of outrage was transferred this autumn from Ireland to England, and culminated in two grave crimes—the murder of Police-Sergeant Brett at Manchester on September 18, and the blowing up of Clerkenwell Prison on December 13. Hitherto the measures for meeting the conspiracy had been left, in the main, to the very efficient Home Secretary, Gathorne Hardy. When the Clerkenwell explosion occurred, Derby was at Knowsley, and Disraeli, who was still in London, took the lead.

To Lord Derby.

Confidential. Dec. 14, 1867. Affairs here are very serious. I have contrived to get Colonel Fielding [1] over, though after inexpressible difficulties, and even now doubt whether I shall be able to set him to work, so great are the obstacles at every step; but it must be done. I have not been able to see Hardy until to-day, and, unfortunately, he has gone out of town again, but will be here on Monday.

It is my opinion that nothing effective can be done, in any way, in these dangers, if we don't get rid of Mayne.[2] I have spoken to Hardy, who says he 'wishes to God he would resign'; but surely, when even the safety of the State is at stake, there ought to be no false delicacy on such a point ? I am too harassed to go into detail, which would require a volume on these matters. I think you ought to interfere.

I took upon myself to send Government aid to the Clerkenwell sufferers.

Confidential. Dec. 16, 1867. I will not trouble you with all the schemes, conferences, hopes, and disappointments, of this busy day. The result is that Colonel Fielding, who has just left my room, has undertaken to ascertain, if possible, the relation between the Fenians in England and the revolutionary societies abroad. . . .

There is no doubt that there is a system of organised incendiarism afloat, and we credibly hear of men coming from America, who are to take empty houses in various parts of London, and set them on fire, probably simultaneously. Colonel Fielding would have wished to have grappled with these impending calamities.

---

[1] He was brought from Ireland and put in charge of a special detective department to cope with Fenianism in England.

[2] Sir Richard Mayne, Commissioner of Police. He was seventy-one years old.

Many of the miscreants who are to perpetrate these crimes are now here, and are known—and we can't touch them. I think the Habeas Corpus ought to be suspended. However, the Colonel undertakes the original purpose. . . .

Most secret. Dec. 16, 1867.—. . . You remember Mrs. Montgomery and her strange, but now not improbable, information a year ago.

She now informs me that, on Saturday morning last, a dying Irishman in one of the London hospitals confessed that, early in the session, there was a plot, quite matured, to blow up the Houses of Parliament by gunpowder introduced through the gas-pipes; but it failed through the House being too well watched. They are going, however, to blow up another prison, but which, though pressed, he refrained from declaring.

I have sent this information to Hardy, though silent as to the source. Gunpowder through gas-pipes is a new idea, and worth attention. . . .

Confidential. Dec. 17, 1867.—Affairs appear to be so serious that last night the Cabinet in town (seven strong) agreed to meet and confer, mainly on the critical condition of the Metropolis. Four Secretaries of State (Northcote away), myself, the Lord Chancellor, and Corry.

Hardy's bulletins, some received this morning, were of a most anxious and menacing character: but the chief feature was a telegram from Lord Monck, informing the Duke of Bucks that, some eight days past, a Danish brigantine left New York with a band of thirty men sworn to assassinate H.M. and her Ministers. Lord Monck is not an alarmist, and particularly deprecates the expense of Trans-Atlantic telegrams; but in this instance he requests a telegram of receipt.

We have no powers to cope with such circumstances as these, and others which are taking place under our nose.

The Duke of Bucks has ascertained that on the day named such a vessel did leave New York, and, with the prevailing westerly wind, may be expected to arrive in four or five days. Ostensibly chartered for Dieppe, it is to land its passengers in the Bristol Channel. What are we to do ? If they land, and are seized, Habeas Corpus will immediately release them. If stopped on the high seas, we may be involved in a war with America.

For my part, I should not hesitate advising seizure, and trusting to a Parliamentary indemnity; but it seems that Habeas Corpus is too strong even for such daring, and that we should violate the law without gaining our purpose. If we call Parliament together, the object will be apprehended by these miscreants and their like, and, during the interval that

must elapse before the meeting of Parliament, every crime
and plot will be stimulated and encouraged to avail themselves
of the vanishing opportunity. . . .

The Canadian story turned out to be a hoax, and the
Queen chaffed the Cabinet and Hardy for paying any
attention to it. The Government aid to the Clerkenwell
sufferers was distributed by Disraeli through Montagu
Corry, who thus probably obtained his first initiation into
the work of practical philanthropy. Henry Matthews,
afterwards Lord Llandaff, wrote to Corry on December 18
that his beneficent exertions in Clerkenwell did the
utmost honour to his chief and himself. 'It reads quite
like an oriental story; as though you were secretary to
a Vizier of Haroun-al-Raschid, rather than to a Minister
of Queen Victoria.'

The Clerkenwell outrage was a turning-point in Irish
politics. Six days after the explosion Gladstone announced at Southport that the time had come for an
Irish policy on Irish lines which should deal with Church,
land, and college in turn. The first effect, even on some
who were to be his colleagues within a year, of this acceptance of crime as a legitimate ground for concession, was
hardly what he wished. Lowe, wrote Lennox, who met
him at dinner at Christmas-time, 'denounced Gladstone's
speech as disgraceful'; and added, 'Several of our party
want to bid for Fenian support, and, if they do, the
country will administer them a sound chastisement.' But
Gladstone had better gauged the temper of the new voters;
and was preparing to trump Disraeli's Irish policy of
firm administration, patience, and conciliation with more
spectacular and drastic methods.

CHAPTER XVI.

PRIME MINISTER.

1868.

The great Parliamentary triumph which Disraeli enjoyed in 1867 was appropriately followed by his succession, early in 1868, to the first place among the servants of the Crown. But, when the year opened, no immediate change was anticipated.

To Lord Derby.

DOWNING STREET, *New Year's Day*, 1868.—I send you the compliments of the season. It is the first time that you have been Premier for three continuous years—1866, 1867, and 1868. I hope a good omen.

You have done also very well for your friends: 3 Garters, 4 Bishoprics, 8 Lord Lieutenancies, and almost the whole Bench in the three kingdoms.

European affairs are not satisfactory. The Emperor of the French has to choose between what are called Liberal institutions and war—and does not like either. But a war will be a war of Louis Quinze, and such slow and balanced successes will soon weary the great nation. I think he feels this.

Stanley seems a little nervous about the *Alabama* claims. The Americans are reckless partisans, and will do much for the Irish vote, though, except the Irish, nobody in America wants to go to war with us. Nevertheless, I doubt whether the Irish vote is yet strong enough to insure such a catastrophe. At present all that the Fenians have done is to strengthen your Government. . . .

While Derby remained at Knowsley, Disraeli was busily occupied in London with preparations for the session, but in constant correspondence with his chief. Though this Parliament had received sentence of death through the Reform Act, and was therefore hardly com-

petent to cope with new party issues, there was a large
programme before the Government, partly consisting of
supplementary Reform measures—Irish and Scottish
Reform Bills and a Corrupt Practices Bill; and partly of
important administrative and departmental measures,
affecting bankruptcy, railways, and the transfer of the
telegraphs to the State. To these there was added
the thorny Education problem, which Russell had
again raised in the Lords before Christmas; and Disraeli's special attention was claimed by Admiralty administration—a constant preoccupation of his during his
periods of rule at the Exchequer. Moreover, Ireland,
which Stanley called this January in a speech at Bristol
' the question of the hour,' and which certainly proved to
be the question of the session, was always in the background. Besides the Irish Reform Bill, a further suspension of habeas corpus in the island was inevitable, and
Roman Catholic University Education was also under
consideration. When the time came in mid-January for
the Cabinet to resume its meetings and get its programme
into shape, Derby had once more succumbed to gout, and
Disraeli was in despair.

To Lord Stanley.

Confidential. DOWNING STREET, ½ *past* 4 *o'clock, Jan.* 17,
1868.—Your box just come in. I'm in despair about the gout.
The Cabinet ought to have met after Epiphany. There is
work enough now for *de die in diem.*

This is the urgency. Lord Derby entirely disapproved of
my suggestion as to the treatment of the Education question
by the establishment of an Education Minister, and legislation for 1869. I won't give you his reasons here, being pressed
for time, and wishing you to see him at once. Enough that I
don't contest his decision, and believe that we must deal with
the question at once.

To deal with the question in a moonshiny way won't do.
The D. of Marlboro' has been with me all this afternoon, and
has unfolded the project of the Council Office. I think it
excellent: large, I would almost say complete, and yet moderate and prudent. But it is a scheme which would require frequent Cabinets and minute discussion.

Question is Shall the Cabinet, under these circumstances

meet on Tuesday, and again on Thursday, when you will all have returned from Bristol, and so on ? I think it best. We can rough-hew and prepare the way, like Merewether and Phayre, and, when your father takes the field, can proceed to action.

But I can't advise such a course without the chief's sanction, and even wish. Obtain his sentiments upon this head.

I confess, if the Cabinet is postponed till Tuesday week, and perhaps even later, I should tremble for consequences.

I hope you will be able to make this out, but my hand is palsied with pencraft all day.

A small selection from Disraeli's frequent and copious letters during the next two or three weeks to the Prime Minister and to the Queen will give some idea of the difficulties he had to surmount, and of his energy and versatility in dealing with them.

To Lord Derby.

Confidential. DOWNING STREET, *Jan.* 28, 1868.—. . . The state of our finances will not permit any increase in our expenditure; but if the state of our finances would do so, the requisitions of the Admiralty are unwise and unnecessary. Last year there was the same pressure, on the ground of the great increase of the American navy. We successfully resisted the appeal, and it now turns out that the Americans have no navy, and not an ironclad except for coast defence. Now it is the old bugbear of the French navy. The American panic is now a French panic. The Admiralty wants a large increase of our ironclad fleet; but it offers no plan how this increase is to be effected, except by the vulgar expedient of a large increase of the navy estimates. Let them spend less money annually on small unarmored wooden ships. Why do they maintain up to their present strength the numerous squadrons of small unarmored ships that we have scattered over the world ? This is the keystone of the position. We spend an enormous sum annually for building and repairing these vessels for their three-yearly reliefs. Why ? First, for old-fashioned notions, that we should not otherwise have employment for our officers and men. Second, for our colonists and merchants, etc. There is no answer to the first reason, except the question, Why should we keep up more men and officers than we have employment for ? As to the second reason, suppose an insult were offered, or an injury inflicted, on some of our merchants in Peru, or the Brazils, or the River Plate. Would any naval officer, in this age of telegraphs, take upon himself to redress these insults and injuries ? He would send home for orders. But this commodore of sloops could not exact reparation, even if he would. The smallest South American State has an ironclad at command that could destroy his whole force. The Americans have flying squadrons, and we must imitate them.

I have not seen the second paper of the Admiralty, which, very improperly, has not been sent to me (as the first was); but if it be full of the battle of Lissa, I can only say that, in that instance, the Italian guns and gunnery were notoriously deficient, and that Tegethoff secured his wooden walls by covering them over with chain cables. A naval administration that wants to increase our ironclads, and at the same time wants to keep up a large reserve of wooden ships as well, and the old-fashioned distribution of that force, wants what is impossible with the present navy estimates, which were largely increased last year.

As for the Admiralty view of the present condition of the French navy, I believe it is marked by the usual exaggeration and false coloring which always accompanies these estimates. Five of the French ironclads mentioned only mount the old weak armament, while we have only one labouring under that grave disability.

Let the Admiralty build ironclads, but they must adapt their naval policy to the changed circumstances which the introduction of naval armor has introduced. Two wooden line-of-battle ships could be built for the cost of one ironclad, and the armament of the present day costs 50 per cent. more than in the days of ' the wooden walls of old England.'

Irrespective of all I have said, the management of the Admiralty, with regard to ship-building, is at this moment so decried and distrusted that, if the House of Commons wished to increase its naval expenditure, it would not entrust the office to a department constituted as at present.

But what is the state of our finances—and that with a costly war ? I have directed the heads of the financial departments to prepare provisional estimates of the revenue of next year. I received them last night, and result is most unsatisfactory. We must prepare for an increase of taxation, which can no longer be limited to an additional twopence to the income tax. When a Chancellor of the Exchequer has to contemplate increasing the duties on tea and malt, the wild suggestions of these ignorant and narrow-minded Admirals are doubly distressing. . . .

Confidential. DOWNING STREET, *Jan.* 30, 1868.—I am in receipt of your letter on the Education measure. . . . Any forced decisions, at this moment, on conscience clauses and rating, and boards of managers, would break up the Cabinet.

What the Cabinet decided on, I may say unanimously, was that legislation was necessary; that it should be preliminary, not definitive; that, to be preliminary and not insignificant, the institution of an Education Minister was necessary, whose duties should be very large—no longer confined to the application of the Revised Code, but harmonising the system of lower class with pauper education; dealing with the distribution of endowments, which the forthcoming Report on Middle Class Education will render necessary; supervising all the departments of art and science, and, as proposed by Lord Stanley, and much approved, controlling generally Irish education. It was felt that, if our Bill were limited to census and incorporation, the Opposition would successfully start Mr. Bruce's[1] Bill, and the question of the day would be taken out of our hands. It was felt that, if our action was limited to extending aid to the poor schools, a minute to be laid on the table would be sufficient, and that in the present temper of Parliament and the country that would not suffice.

I have seen to-day several of our most influential colleagues, and *separately*, on this matter. I have no hesitation in saying that the project of a measure preliminary, but of magnitude, is the only scheme by which unanimity in counsel can be obtained. I think myself that success in Parliament might thus also be secured.

If we gain a year, the public mind, now in a state of effervescent inquiry on these matters, will ripen on such subjects as conscience clauses and rating, and especially on the non-interference of the State with the religious element in schools, which might render conscience clauses unnecessary. But time is required.

It is sad work to have to write on such matters, and not confer together. But I am sure you will pardon every uncouth and imperfect phrase. I only wish to be a faithful steward to you in your troubles, to give you the best information I can, and counsel to which the advantage of being on the scene of action may give some value. . . .

To Queen Victoria.

DOWNING STREET, *Feb.* 4, 1868. *Six o'clock.*—. . . The Cabinet concluded the discussion of all the principles (not many) involved in the new Education Bill, and appointed a Committee—Lord President, Duke of Bucks, Mr. Walpole, and Lord John Manners—to finish some details.

[1] Home Secretary, Dec., 1868; afterwards 1st Lord Aberdare.

The Cabinet is unanimous on all points of principle, but the Duke of Marlboro' wishes the Lord President to be the *ex-officio* Education Minister on a great scale, which is not an arrangement which would be popular in the House of Commons, as it would seem to close the House of Commons to the Minister for Education: for the precedent of Lord John Russell sitting in the Lower House is not a very strong one. He sate so only a few months, and was no ordinary man: had led the House of Commons twelve years, six of which he was Prime Minister, and was himself of ducal birth. . . .

To Lord Derby.

DOWNING STREET, ½ *past six, Feb.* 6, 1868.—A very busy, but tranquil, Cabinet. Scotch Bill gone through, and waiting, for finish, the Lord Advocate on Tuesday—our last Cabinet. Irish Bill discussed.

Letter from the Lord Chief Justice of England in the name, and with the unanimous authority, of all the Judges, protesting against the Parliamentary Elections Bill as ' an impossibility.'[1] In short, the Judges have struck ! As I am to bring in the Bill the first night, this was awkward. However, we set to work like men. We must fall back on our original proposition, which the S[elect] Committee of the House of Commons very conceitedly altered.

All going on very right with the Duke of Marlboro'. Duke of Richmond of great assistance to me in this matter. I have gained time and mollified him. He will do whatever you decide on.

But, so far as I can judge, the Education flame is more bright than lasting, and in a month's time I am not sure the Lord President may not bring in a strictly preparatory measure in the House of Lords, and keep the great question for the next Parliament. But it must be in the Lords now; at any rate, we want education discussed by Dukes and Bishops. It will have a beneficial effect on all. . . .

To Queen Victoria.

DOWNING STREET, *Feb.* 15, 1868.—The Chancellor of the Exchequer, with his humble duty to your Majesty.

In the Cabinet to-day he brought forward the condition of your Majesty's navy, with reference to the navy estimates, and in consequence of some observations of your Majesty on the subject, when he was last at Osborne.

He has, since that period, been unceasingly working to effect some change in our system of naval expenditure, and to adapt

---

[1] The Bill put upon the Judges the trial of election petitions.

it more to modern requirements; and he has the utmost gratification in informing your Majesty that he has induced the Cabinet, this day, unanimously to adopt his views; that the naval estimates have been reconstructed; and, without any material increase of expenditure, your Majesty will now have a real and, he hopes, rapidly increasing naval reserve.

The Cabinet determined to-day to lay down immediately three more ironclads.

He calculates that your Majesty will have at the end of this year a reserve of seven ironclads, irrespective of these three, which will take two years to finish. . . .

It was only by correspondence that Derby had been able to participate in these decisions and arrangements. The gout had this time obtained a complete mastery over him, and the resumption of the session on February 13 found him still incapacitated, with no prospect of early return to health and work. An article in *The Times* of February 11 urged the necessity, in view of Derby's condition, for reconstruction of the Government, and two days later Derby told Disraeli that he contemplated resignation.

From Lord Derby.

Confidential. KNOWSLEY, *Feb.* 13, 1868.—Parliament sitting, and I still lying here, like a useless log! You may imagine how much this annoys me, and the more so as, although I hope that I have turned the corner within the last day or two, after a slight relapse of three or four days, my doctors (for I have two in attendance) will not venture to name any time for my probable removal. . . .

I have for some time been aware that the increased frequency of my attacks of illness would, at no distant period, incapacitate me for the discharge of my public duties. During the past year I have hardly ever been really well, and the steps which I have been obliged to take for patching myself up for particular occasions have not been without their effect on my general health; and I am warned that there are symptoms which will require constant vigilance, probably for the remainder of my life, if I wish to guard against a sudden and complete break-up. To no one except the Queen have I communicated upon this subject, on which it is due to you that you should receive the earliest intelligence. What I have said, however, to H.M. is simply this: that while, on the one hand, my increasing infirmities hold out little expectation of my being

able for any long period to serve Her Majesty, I hoped she
would do me the justice to believe that I would not willingly
desert her service during a period of difficulty: but that, if
the appearance of political affairs should be smooth, I hoped
that H.M. would bear in mind my anxious desire to be relieved
from duties to which I should shortly find myself unequal.
I added that I thought it was right that H.M. should be the
first person to receive an intimation of my views, in order that
she might have full time to consider the course which it might
be necessary for her to pursue.

Nothing could be kinder and more considerate than the
answer which I received, in which, after some gratifying expressions of her personal feeling, and the assurance that she
shrank from the idea of being deprived of my services, she
added that she had no right to place her own wishes in opposition to the considerations of health, and even of life, which I
brought before her. She hoped, however, at all events, that
my resignation would not be tendered during the course of
the present session; and to this I have no hesitation in agreeing, so long as my colleagues are willing to overlook the probably inefficient manner in which I shall be able to discharge my
duties. To no other member of the Cabinet, not even to
Stanley, have I made my intentions known. But what particularly pleased me in the Queen's answer was that she by no
means contemplated the break-up of the present Government
as the result of my retirement. And I am sure that, so far as
she is concerned, you, with the aid of the majority of our present colleagues, will receive the same cordial support which I
have enjoyed.

I am very much annoyed that the Chancellor should not
have been ready with his Bankruptcy Bill. Not only was it
distinctly understood in November that that measure should
be brought forward in the House of Lords, but I wrote some
weeks since to press it upon his particular attention. . . .

To Lord Derby.

Confidential. DOWNING STREET, *Feb.* 14, 1868.—I received
your letter this morning, and learn, with deep regret, that
there is no immediate prospect of the Cabinet having the advantage of your guidance and authority.

I cannot shut my eyes to the danger of the present state of
affairs, but, after twenty years of confidential co-operation,
scarcely with a cloud, I need not, I feel convinced, assure you,
at this critical moment, that all shall be done on my part
which perfect devotion can accomplish, to maintain, unimpaired and unsullied, your interests and influence.

The plan of delaying the resignation till the close of
the session proved quite impracticable. There was so
serious a relapse on February 16 that Stanley was telegraphed for to Knowsley.

From Lord Derby.

Confidential. KNOWSLEY, *Feb.* 19, 1868.—Stanley will have
given you a full account of the state in which he found me,
and will have prepared you for the communication which I
should not be justified in delaying, of the absolute necessity
of my resigning my present office. I am certainly better,
and I hope in a fair way towards recovery; but that recovery
must be very slow, and my doctors not only do not encourage
me to hope to move from hence much under a month, but are
unanimous in their opinion that, if I hope to regain a moderate
degree of health, absolute repose of mind and body for some
months to come is indispensable. I had hoped that I might
have been enabled to struggle through the present session;
but, as matters stand, my attempt to do so would not only
be a certain failure, but would involve a risk of life which I am
not justified in incurring.

I have not yet written positively to the Queen, nor will I
do so until I hear from you; but I ought not to delay making
this announcement to H.M. longer than is absolutely necessary.
I am not insensible of the public inconvenience which may be
caused by my resignation at this moment, nor of the increased
difficulties in which it will place you. I trust, however, that,
if H.M. should send for you, which, under the circumstances,
I should think most probable, you will not shrink from the
heavy additional responsibility. You may be assured of receiving from me all the support which, out of office, it is in my
power to give; and, so far as I can, I shall urge upon our friends
to extend to you, separately, the same generous confidence
which, for twenty years, they have reposed in us jointly.
And I cannot make this communication without gratefully
acknowledging your cordial and loyal co-operation with me,
in good times and bad, throughout that long period: nor,
above all, the courage, skill, and judgment, with which you
triumphantly carried the Government through all the difficulties and dangers of the last year.

I think I ought not to resign without asking the Queen, if
she desires to mark her approval of my services, to allow me
to recommend some five or six names for the honour of the
peerage. . . . My intention of resigning has been already
surmised, and will, no doubt, be very generally anticipated:
but I should be obliged by your not announcing it as an

irrevocable decision, even to our colleagues, until I shall have had an opportunity of submitting it to, and having it accepted by, the Queen.

Derby, it will be seen, had no doubt as to who ought to be, and would be, his successor; and it is pleasant to read the cordial and thoroughly merited tribute which the retiring chief pays to his tried lieutenant.

To Lord Derby.

Confidential.   DOWNING STREET, *Feb.* 20, 1868.

MY DEAREST LORD,—I have not sufficient command of myself at this moment to express what I feel about what has happened, and, after all, has happened so rapidly and so unexpectedly !

All I will say is that I never contemplated nor desired it. I was entirely content with my position, and all that I aspired to was that, after a Government of tolerable length, and, at least, fair repute, my retirement from public affairs should have accompanied your own; satisfied that I had enjoyed my opportunity in life, and proud that I had been long confidentially connected with one of the most eminent men of my time, and for whom I entertain profound respect and affection.

I will not shrink from the situation, but I do not underrate its gravity, and mainly count, when you are convalescent, on your guidance and support.

I have talked over affairs with Stanley. Our difficulty will be our more than debating weakness in the House of Lords. If, when you were present there, you felt the necessity of some support, what must be the state of things now, with Lord Chelmsford and Lord Malmesbury for the managers ? Such a condition is impossible; and it appears to me most desirable, as you once contemplated, and once formally mentioned to Lord Chelmsford, that Lord Cairns should be induced to take the Great Seal.

After him, I think the Duke of Marlborough the most competent man in our ranks to address a senate. He has culture, intellectual grasp, and moral energy—great qualities, though in him they may have been developed, perhaps, in too contracted a sphere. . . .

I hope Lady Derby has not suffered from all her anxieties and labors. I am, hers and yours ever,—D.

Derby, on receipt of this letter, at once forwarded his resignation to the Queen, who was at Osborne. An extract from his letter will show the exact terms of his resignation, and what he wrote about his successor.

Lord Derby to Queen Victoria.

Feb. 21, 1868.—. . . Lord Derby greatly regrets the inconvenience to which he knows that his retirement must subject the public service, and the additional trouble which it must entail upon your Majesty. But he has reason to believe that, the fact of his retirement being once understood, there would be no pressure from any quarter for the immediate and formal resignation of his office—perhaps not until he should be enabled to surrender it to your Majesty in person. In the meantime, if he may be permitted to offer any suggestion to your Majesty as to his successor, he would venture to submit that, as there is no question of any political change, your Majesty should apply to the Chancellor of the Exchequer, who has held the most important and, next to his own, the most prominent post in the present Government. Lord Derby believes that, although with a deep sense of the responsibility attaching to it, he would not shrink from undertaking the duty; and that he, and he only, could command the cordial support, *en masse*, of his present colleagues. . . .

Disraeli already knew that, on Derby's resignation, the Queen would entrust the fortunes of the Ministry to his hands. A month earlier he had been specially invited for a couple of days to Osborne. His letters to his wife were discreet, but they suggested that what had passed was momentous and gratifying. In the first letter he said that Her Majesty was ' most gracious and agreeable '; the second ran as follows:

To Mrs. Disraeli.

[*Jan.* 25, 1868].—The most successful visit I ever had: all that I could wish and hope. I was with the Queen an hour yesterday. She spoke of everything without reserve or formality.

A brilliant day here.

The Queen ordered a vessel at Portsmouth to be at my disposal, as there was some difficulty about going.

M. Corry a lucky fellow. He had to come down here yesterday on some business, and Her Majesty, hearing of it, invited him to dine with the household and sleep here !

' All that I could wish and hope.' The words are strong, but they were justified. A note by Corry, himself at

Osborne at the time, explains that before Disraeli's audience ' General Grey came to his room to inform Mr. D. that the Queen intended to make him her First Minister on Lord D.'s resignation.   Mr. D. was much struck by the fact that his old rival at Wycombe should become the bearer of such a message.'[1]   The Queen had already been warned by Derby that his resignation could not be long deferred, and thus graciously herself intimated to Disraeli his approaching elevation and her own satisfaction at the prospect.

The hour had now come, and Grey arrived in London with the expected message from the Queen, and with instructions to place himself at Disraeli's disposal in case of any difficulty with his colleagues.   But Grey brought also Derby's letter of resignation, and on reading it Disraeli, in view of the ambiguity of its terms, and the suggestion that the formal but necessary steps might be indefinitely postponed, hesitated to proceed with his task. He consulted Stanley, and Stanley both wrote and telegraphed to his father.

Lord Stanley to Lord Derby.

Feb. 24, 1868.—Disraeli sent for me, very anxious and agitated, about 12 o'clock to-day; explained that all was going well, the Queen had been most gracious, would give him every support, and, if any of his colleagues objected to the new arrangement, she would see what her personal influence could effect in securing their adhesion. . . .   She wished him to go down to Osborne to-morrow to kiss hands.

But . . . a letter of yours to the Queen, shown him by Grey, seemed to imply that you did not contemplate the immediate formation of a new Ministry under him.   Under these circumstances he thought it would be indelicate, and might hurt your feelings, if he were to consider the matter as settled.

I combated these scruples. . . .   The end of it was, we agreed to telegraph down for your sanction.

Derby's telegram in reply was as mysterious as his letter.   ' Glad there are no difficulties,' it ran.   ' Will write by post.   Do nothing formal till you hear.   A few days indispensable to me.'   This, as Disraeli wrote to

---

[1] See Vol. I., pp. 215-226.

Lord Barrington, made things more confused than ever; and the result of letter and telegram was entirely to paralyse action on this Monday, February 24, which should have seen the arrangements for the reconstituted Ministry well on the road to completion. Happily, the next morning brought another letter from Derby, making it clear that he had no desire to delay the formation of a new Administration, but merely wished to settle the peerages and a few minor matters before taking the formal final step.

From Lord Derby.

Confidential. KNOWSLEY, *Feb.* 24, 1868.—I was about to write to you, when I received Stanley's telegram, from which I am glad to find that you have no serious difficulties in the way of forming a Government.

I hope that neither you nor he will have misunderstood the purport of my telegraphic answer. You will not for a moment suppose that I wish to retain nominal office for an hour longer than is absolutely necessary; on the contrary, the sooner the new arrangements can be made, the better it would be for all parties, and the more agreeable to me, nor can there be the slightest objection to its being publicly known that my resignation has been tendered and accepted, and that you have been charged with the duty of forming a new Administration. But I have only this morning heard, by a few lines from the Queen, Her Majesty's acceptance of my resignation, and I am promised a fuller answer, probably by to-morrow's post.

Her Majesty has said nothing as yet upon the subject of the peerages, and I have consequently been unable to write to any of those to whom I propose to offer them. I require, therefore, a few days for the disposal of this subject, and of other minor matters which I shall have to wind up, and which I shall have no power of doing after you have once formally kissed hands as Minister. This final and formal step is the only one for which I think it necessary to ask for a short delay.

You have my best wishes for the success of your endeavour to form your Government, and if I can be in any way of service to you, you may entirely command me. I will not trouble you with speculations as to your probable arrangements. Your main difficulties, as it seems to me, will be the Exchequer and the lead in the Lords. Could you not, to avoid extensive changes, continue for the present session to hold the former in conjunction with the office of First Lord of the Treasury ?

I know the work will be tremendous, but such a combination in former times was not unusual. As to the Lords, Cairns would undoubtedly be a great acquisition to your Government; but Stanley, who suggested him as a possible leader, forgot that it would be impossible for a Lord Chancellor to hold that office. I shall be most anxious to hear your contemplated arrangements, and that you have every prospect of success in the arduous task which you have undertaken.

By the receipt of this letter on the Tuesday morning Disraeli's scruples were removed, and in the course of the day he was able to make most of his arrangements; but before going down to Osborne to kiss hands he waited Derby's pleasure.

To General the Hon. Charles Grey.

2, GROSVENOR GATE, *Feb.* 25, 1868.—I have not written to the Queen, because I thought you could keep Her Majesty *au fait,* and that it would be better for me to be silent till I could give H.M. a digested account.

Lord Cairns has accepted the Great Seal, and all my colleagues have placed themselves at my disposal, except Walpole, who, I fear, is still at Ealing.

I am deeply considering the question of the Chancellor of Exchequer, but have done nothing: the more so, as about two hours ago I received a mysterious intimation not to precipitate affairs in this direction, as ' a most important and influential adhesion ' was possible. I conclude it can't be Gladstone ! . .

To Lord Derby.

GROSVENOR GATE, *Feb.* 25, 1868.—I remain in London, though supposed to be at Osborne: if I be forced to go down, I shall not kiss hands, nor shall I until I have your sanction. . . .

From Lord Derby.

(*Telegram.*)   *Feb.* 25, 5 p.m.—I have heard from H.M. My formal resignation is sent in.

Confidential. Feb. 26, 1868.—I feel very sensibly your kindness in postponing, to suit my convenience, your formal acceptance of office. My chief object in asking for a short delay was that I might be enabled as Minister to communicate to a few of our friends H.M.'s consent to my recommendation of their promotion to the peerage. This I have now received, and if there should be any trifling matter which I ought to wind up before leaving office, I am sure I may rely upon you to afford every facility for having it done. . . .

To Lord Derby.

GROSVENOR GATE, *Feb.* 27, 1868.—I duly received your telegram of yesterday and your letter this morning. I have, therefore, arranged to go down to-day by 3 o'clock train, and therefore, I suppose, in four-and-twenty hours the thing will be done. . . . I think Hunt must be the Chancellor of the Exchequer, and I have prepared the Queen for it. . . .

With respect to some intimation in your letter of your wishes being attended to in some slight matters, permit me to say very distinctly, once and for ever, that, in the position in which I am so unexpectedly placed, I consider myself, and shall always consider myself, only your deputy. Your wishes will always be commands to me, and commands that will be heartily obeyed. I shall never take any step of importance in public life without apprising you of it before it is decided on, and without at least seeking the counsel which, I trust, will never be refused.

And I do, even solemnly, entreat you never to permit any sentiment of estrangement to arise between us, but to extend to me for ever that complete confidence which has subsisted so long between us; which has been the pride and honor of my life, and which it will ever be my constant effort to cherish and deserve.

From Lord Derby.

Private. Feb. 28, 1868.—One line to thank you for your very kind letter of yesterday, and to assure you that, so far as I am concerned, there is no danger of any sentiment of estrangement arising between us, who for more than twenty years have worked together with unreserved and unbroken confidence. But I cannot accept for you the position which you are willing to accept for yourself, of being considered as my deputy. You have fairly and most honourably won your way to the highest round of the political ladder, and long may you continue to retain your position ! At the same time, whenever you are inclined to consult me or ask for my opinion, I shall be most happy to give it you frankly and unreservedly. But I shall not be so unreasonable as to expect that it shall always be adopted, or be surprised, still less affronted, if upon any ground you find yourself unable to act upon it. . . .

Before concluding, let me beg of you to offer my congratulations to Mrs. Disraeli upon your having attained a post your pre-eminent fitness for which she will not be inclined to dispute.

Disraeli's behaviour to Derby throughout this crisis was a model of delicacy and good feeling, and, if Derby may have seemed a little inconsiderate and dilatory, the serious state of his health is a sufficient excuse.

Disraeli had now become the Queen's First Minister, and was necessarily about to enter into a much more intimate relation with Her Majesty than he had ever enjoyed before. At the outset he struck, both in letter and audience, the note of chivalrous devotion, as of one who, while he reverenced his Sovereign, never forgot that she was a woman—a note which was to characterise all his intercourse with Her Majesty, and was to help to win for him a unique place in her esteem and confidence.

To Queen Victoria.

DOWNING STREET, 12 o'clock, Feb. 26, 1868.—Mr. Disraeli with his humble duty to your Majesty.

He ventures to express his sense of your Majesty's most gracious kindness to him, and of the high honor which your Majesty has been graciously pleased to confer on him.

He can only offer devotion.

It will be his delight and duty to render the transaction of affairs as easy to your Majesty as possible: and in smaller matters he hopes he may succeed in this; but he ventures to trust that, in the great affairs of state, your Majesty will deign not to withhold from him the benefit of your Majesty's guidance.

Your Majesty's life has been passed in constant communion with great men, and the knowledge and management of important transactions. Even if your Majesty were not gifted with those great abilities, which all now acknowledge, this rare and choice experience must give your Majesty an advantage in judgment which few living persons, and probably no living prince, can rival.

He whom your Majesty has so highly preferred presumes to trust to your Majesty's condescension in this behalf.

Mr. Disraeli proposes to have the honor of waiting on your Majesty to-morrow (Thursday) afternoon. . . .

From Queen Victoria.

OSBORNE, Feb. 27, 1868.—The Queen thanks Mr. Disraeli very much for his kind letter received to-day, and can assure him of her cordial support in the arduous task which he has undertaken.

It must be a proud moment for him to feel that his own

talent and successful labours in the service of his Sovereign
and country have earned for him the high and influential position in which he is now placed.

The Queen has ever found Mr. Disraeli most zealous in her
service, and most ready to meet her wishes, and she only wishes
her beloved husband were here now to assist him with his
guidance !

The Queen rejoices to see how much unanimity he has found
amongst his colleagues. She will be glad to see Mr. Disraeli
to-morrow, but does not ask him to stay overnight, as she
knows how precious every moment must be to him. . . .

To Mrs. Disraeli.

OSBORNE, *Feb.* 28, 1868.—I arrived here yesterday at seven
o'clock, and had an audience about half an hour afterwards.
The Queen came into her closet with a very radiant face,
holding out her hand, and saying, ' You must kiss hands,'
which I did immediately, and very heartily, falling on my
knee. Then she sate down, which she never used to do, and
only does to her First Minister, and talked over affairs for half
an hour (I standing), so that I had scarcely time to dress for
dinner. . . .

Disraeli, in writing to Corry, added that he said to the
Queen that he ' kissed her hand in faith and loving
loyalty.' He was frankly and unaffectedly happy. ' All
is sunshine here,' he wrote to more than one correspondent,
' moral and material.'

All the old colleagues to whom he applied rallied round
Disraeli, with the exception of Walpole, who had remained
reluctantly in the Cabinet for some months without any
office, and who now, in spite of remonstrances from the
Queen, took the opportunity of retiring. One colleague,
we have seen, Disraeli felt bound to leave out. The
Government, with Derby gone, was peculiarly weak in
the House of Lords, and one of its weakest members was
the Lord Chancellor, Chelmsford. He had been a distinguished and successful advocate, but he was neither a
great lawyer nor a very skilful debater; and a complaint
of his dilatoriness appears in Derby's first letter to Disraeli
about resignation. Disraeli had always thought him an
inefficient Chancellor, and had been opposed to his re-

appointment in 1866 [1]; nor had he ever been at all sympathetic with one who was among the bitterest and most persistent opponents of the Jewish cause. Chelmsford's dislike and distrust of Disraeli had been markedly shown in a short correspondence in this very month of February. On a vacancy occurring among the Judges, Disraeli, as leader of the Commons, expressed a hope that the Chancellor would not treat with indifference the claims of the Conservative lawyers in Parliament [2]—a not unreasonable request, which has been made by many leaders of the House, and complied with, perhaps too often, by many Chancellors. Chelmsford immediately suspected a job, and mounted the high horse; his trust was a sacred one, his choice would be governed by fitness, not politics, and he would not suffer the smallest interference with his judicial appointments.[3]

Disraeli applied the test of fitness to the Chancellor himself, and found him wanting. Derby had expressly intimated to Chelmsford more than once that he contemplated asking him, after a time, to make way upon the Woolsack for Cairns, who was not only a lawyer of the highest class, but a statesman excelling in debate. That arrangement Disraeli considered it to be imperative now to carry out.[4] He has been accused by Chelmsford and Chelmsford's friends of a want of tact and delicacy in his manner of opening the subject to him; but the letter which he actually wrote seems hardly to warrant this reproach. It should be remembered that, with the resignation of its head, the Derby Cabinet became *ipso facto* dissolved, and that no Minister had a right to his post save on the direct invitation of the new Prime Minister.

---

[1] See above, p. 177.

[2] In a note to Derby during 1867, Disraeli had written: ' I can't speak to the Lord Chancellor, for I lose my temper with him. With prodigious patronage, he does nothing for the party, and is so insensible of his great obligations to you and his own demerits.'

[3] Atlay's *Victorian Chancellors*, Vol. II., pp. 121-125, where Chelmsford's own version of the controversy is given at length.

[4] It was a ' painful but necessary ' change, wrote Hardy in his diary.

PRIME MINISTER [4, xvi

To Lord Chelmsford.

11, DOWNING STREET [*Feb.* 25].

DEAR LORD CHANCELLOR,—The announcement in Parliament has informed you of the accepted resignation of Lord Derby, and of the office which the Queen has graciously confided to me of forming a new Government.

My first wish is to recall to the management of affairs my former colleagues, but there are some obstacles to this course, and the principal one is found in the House over which you preside. If Lord Derby in his time was so sensible of the weakness of our party in debate in the House of Lords that he was constrained to submit to yourself an arrangement which, though delayed, he still contemplated, I am sure you will feel that, without Lord Derby, I have no option but in having recourse to his plan, among others, of strengthening Her Majesty's Government in the Upper House of Parliament. If, therefore, for this reason, and for no other, it is not in my power to submit your name for the custody of the Great Seal to the Queen in the list of the new Government, I can assure you it would afford me sincere gratification if you could suggest to me some other mode by which Her Majesty might testify her sense of your services.

Chelmsford answered hotly and angrily, expressing his disbelief in Derby's still contemplating a change on the Woolsack, and declining to suggest any other mode in which his own services might be recognised. He appealed from Disraeli to Derby; he took the Press into his confidence over his grievance. Three days later he had to confess that Derby confirmed Disraeli's statement; but he complained that Disraeli had not recalled to his recollection the particulars of the arrangement; and he talked of his ' dismissal,'and of the slur upon his reputation which only some mark of Her Majesty's gracious approval could remove. Disraeli's reply was justifiably short.

To Lord Chelmsford.

OSBORNE, *Feb.* 29, 1868.—I received your letter this morning. I only alluded to your understanding with Lord Derby because I thought it must be impressed on your memory, and did not wish to dwell in detail on circumstances necessarily of a character not agreeable.

After the allusion to that understanding, and the necessity

of my acting on it, the rest of my letter invited communication. You could have arranged with me any cause for your retirement most to your liking, and you could have responded to my inquiry. Instead of that, from a total misapprehension of my communication, which was really influenced by delicacy, the public have been invited to our confidential communications, with the usual consequence under such circumstances.

I shall do nothing to add to the controversy, but shall be always ready to show the great respect I entertain for you.

It was not found possible to come to an understanding as to the distinction to be conferred by Her Majesty on the outgoing Chancellor. The Grand Cross of the Bath, which Disraeli offered, Chelmsford declined, suggesting in his turn that he might be advanced to the dignity of an earldom, as were Loughborough, Eldon, and Cottenham, a suggestion which it is not surprising that Disraeli could not accept. Accordingly, Chelmsford retired in dudgeon; and society and the clubs were entertained by stories of his bitter jokes and of Disraeli's pungent retort. It was said that the ex-Chancellor talked of premature elevation making some people *dizzy*, and that he distinguished the old and new Administrations as the ' Derby ' and the ' Hoax '; while the new Prime Minister was declared to have curtly summed up his former colleague in the biting words, ' Useless in council, feeble in debate, and—a jester !'

Disraeli's wise resolve not to inflict too heavy a strain on his own strength created a vacancy at the Exchequer, which he quitted to become First Lord of the Treasury. The natural successor would have been Northcote, who had been his lieutenant in all his financial combats with Gladstone in the past decade. But Northcote could not very well be spared from the India Office during the Abyssinian War, and Disraeli determined, somewhat to the public surprise, to promote Ward Hunt, the Secretary to the Treasury, whose good work he had often noticed and commended.[1] The appointment was well received. ' It

---

[1] The changes consequent on this promotion enabled Disraeli to offer subordinate office to Sir Michael Hicks Beach, who became ultimately Lord St. Aldwyn.

was, of course, my own suggestion,' Disraeli wrote to
Delane, whose approval had been ascertained at the
dinner-table; 'but it was carped at by commonplace
minds, who seemed shocked at the sudden elevation,
and talked of other people as being "looked up to" in
the city. Your clear and sagacious judgment came to
my aid opportunely, which should teach both of us the
advantage of dining out.' [1]

The Whips and the party managers urged that overtures
should be made to Cranborne and to Peel. One of them
thought he discerned a change of tone on Cranborne's
part; another wrote, 'He would not accept, but it would
please the party.' In deference to these representations
Disraeli, always placable, sounded Cranborne through
Northcote. The refusal was immediate and uncompromising. The time for reconciliation in office had not
come, though the rank and file of the recalcitrants were
reported to be less disaffected than before. At any rate,
Corry wrote, February 27: 'Taylor, Noel, and Barrington, are well pleased with the feeling at the Carlton.
Even Sandford tells me that he feels less hostility to a
Government with you at the head, than to one led by
Lord D. What you did last session might have been
expected of you from your known opinions, but Lord
Derby's conduct was unpardonable.'

Cairns, though the most powerful member of the Ministry in the House of Lords, could not, as Derby pointed
out, lead that House from the Woolsack; and Disraeli
had therefore to appoint a leader from among his other
peer colleagues. He turned first to the Duke of Marlborough, who was himself a friend of some years' standing,
and who had married the daughter of one of his most
intimate friends, Frances Anne Lady Londonderry. In
him he discerned 'culture, intellectual grasp, and moral
energy.' But the Duke told Disraeli that Malmesbury,
who had filled the place in Derby's frequent absences,
had a prior claim, and Disraeli accepted the suggestion.

---

[1] Dasent's *Delane*, Vol. II., pp. 222, 223.

Malmesbury was, naturally, anxious that his utterances in the Lords should be kept duly in accord with those of his new chief. 'When I lived at Whitehall Gardens during Peel's Government,' he wrote, 'I used to see the Duke [of Wellington] ride into [Peel's] garden every morning at eleven and stay a quarter of an hour. This was to go over the minutes of the day together for the House of Lords. God forbid we should follow exactly this military routine, but whenever I think your direction desirable I want a general *lascia passare* to you about that hour.'

'A great triumph of intellect and courage and patience and unscrupulousness employed in the service of a party full of prejudices and selfishness and wanting in brains. The Tories have hired Disraeli, and he has his reward from them.' That was the grudging tribute paid to Disraeli by Bright in his diary. Intellect, courage, and patience, were undoubtedly leading elements in Disraeli's composition. A certain lack of scruple on some occasions may be laid to his charge, as to that of almost all vigorous personalities in the field of politics; but the persistent faithfulness of his career as Conservative leader sufficiently rebuts the accusation that unscrupulousness was in any sense a note of his political character. The suggestion that his relation to his party was that of a hired bravo is ridiculous. There was a revolutionary side to his character, which was, of course, most conspicuous in youth; but there was a much stronger vein in him of historic and aristocratic sentiment, which naturally inclined him, as it had his father before him, to espouse the Tory cause.

Intellect, courage, and patience, carried to a high pitch, constitute genius; and it was the due recognition and just elevation of genius which Lord Houghton rightly hailed in Disraeli's accession to the Premiership.

From Lord Houghton.

ROME, *Mar.* 12, 1868.—The days of our familiar intercourse lie so far away that I hardly know whether personal interest would justify me in writing to you on the event which, after

all, is only the natural sequence of your political work, did I
not feel such earnest satisfaction in the recognition of your
intellectual worth and in the fair reward of industrious mental
power.

When one looks back on many years of political life, one is,
no doubt, more conscious of the unjust elevation of poor
abilities and common characters than of the depression of any
remarkable faculties or real desert. But there is assuredly
a tendency in the English mind to dislike and distrust original
individuality as such, and to do its worst to limit the scope
and effect of the talents it does not entirely comprehend.
When, therefore, genius makes its own way in public life, there
is a good beyond the momentary gain and a true national
advantage. . . .

From Odilon Barrot.

Paris, 1 *mars*, 1868.—Laissez-moi vous offrir toutes mes
félicitations pour votre avènement à un rang qui, on peut le
dire, est le plus élevé auquel un homme, qui n'est pas assis sur
un grand trône, puisse aspirer—Premier Ministre d'Angleterre !

Though there had been an anticipation in some quarters
that the Tories might look once again to the great houses ·
for a successor to Derby, and the names both of Stanley
and of Richmond were mentioned, the public at large
and the Press recognised that Disraeli was the rightful heir, and his promotion was favourably received.
The party, as a whole, knowing well that the choice
was Derby's as well as the Queen's, tendered Disraeli
loyal adherence; and the dissentients over the Reform
Bill made no protest. The House of Commons, as
might be expected, gave a generous welcome to its foremost gladiator. Westminster Hall and the lobbies were
packed to see him pass and to cheer him, while his reception in the Chamber itself was all but enthusiastic.
His statement was brief, as its keynote was that he would
continue Lord Derby's policy. In foreign affairs the
Government would pursue peace, without selfish isolation;
in domestic affairs, ' a liberal policy.' Disraeli paused
to give effect to the unexpected phrase, and then
continued, ' a truly liberal policy—a policy that will
not shrink from any changes which are required by

the wants of the age that we live in, but will never
forget that it is our happy lot to dwell in an ancient
and historic country.' Critics naturally interpreted
this oracular sentence as meaning that the Government
would resist where resistance was possible, but consent
to all such changes as Parliamentary exigencies made
inevitable. There was no debate, and little comment,
in the House. Bouverie admitted that Disraeli had
fairly earned his promotion, but added that the position
of the Government in the House was weak; as for the
Liberals, they had leaders who could not lead and followers
who would not follow.

Mrs. Disraeli to Lady de Rothschild.

Feb. 25, 1868.

MY VERY DEAR LADY DE ROTHSCHILD,—By the time this
reaches you, Dizzy will be Prime Minister of England! Lord
Stanley is to announce this at the House of Commons to-day.
Yours affectionately,—M. A. DISRAELI.

It is pleasant to think of the pride and happiness of
Mrs. Disraeli in the elevation of the husband whose coming greatness she had prophesied from the first, and whose
ambitions her own self-sacrificing affection had so eminently forwarded. An occasion for the display of her
triumph and for the congratulations of the world was
speedily provided. ' Will you lend your reception-rooms
to my wife for a couple of nights or so ?' wrote Disraeli
to Stanley early in March. 'According to the Whips,
there must be some high festivals on a very extensive
scale; and she can do nothing with D[owning] S[treet],
it is so dingy and decaying.' So the fine rooms of the
still unfinished Foreign Office were thrown open on Wednesday, March 26, in order that Mrs. Disraeli, as the
Prime Minister's wife, might hold a grand reception. It
was a miserable night, with a storm of wind and sleet
sweeping over the town; but nevertheless there was an
immense gathering both of society and of the Conservative party, with a sprinkling of Liberal friends such as

the Gladstones.   Bishop Wilberforce, one of the guests, wrote in his diary: ' Dizzy in his glory, leading about the Princess of Wales; the Prince of Wales, Mrs. Dizzy —she looking very ill and haggard. The impenetrable man low.'   It was such a party as the author of *Coningsby* and *Lothair* loved to describe, with half enthusiasm and half satire; and this time the author himself and his wife were the leading figures in the show.

' Yes, I have climbed to the top of the greasy pole,' was the Prime Minister's jaunty reply to congratulations. No one realised better than he how difficult it would be to maintain himself in that precarious elevation.   With the shield of Derby gone, he would have to justify himself afresh to his own party; and his opponents, and more particularly their discomfited chief, would be all the more eager to pull him down.   Even assuming that he could command the ungrudging support of the whole of the Conservatives, he would still, if the other sections of the House of Commons could effectively combine, be in a minority of sixty or seventy.   If, however, a strict party fight could be avoided, he might hope to keep his power and place comparatively undisturbed down to the impending General Election, and to appeal, with a fair possibility of success, to the new electors as the man who had enfranchised them.   But Gladstone was as capable of a bold, dramatic stroke as was Disraeli; and the new Prime Minister, who had so recently dominated the scene, was to find, in the moment of his elevation, that authority over the expiring House of Commons had largely passed once again to his rival, and that the election was to be fought on a novel and most embarrassing issue of that rival's choice.

V

1868–1876

BY GEORGE EARLE BUCKLE

PREFACE TO V. AND VI.

It was originally intended that the story of the last phase of Disraeli's life should be completed in one volume. This would only have been possible if his management of the Eastern Question, the most outstanding feature of his great Administration, were treated merely in general terms; a course which, however unsatisfactory in itself, appeared to be discreet and judicious, so long as Russia was our faithful ally in the war, and was governed by a friendly Sovereign, the grandson of that Emperor Alexander who was in antagonism in the later seventies to Queen Victoria and to her Minister. But the Revolution in Russia, the repudiation of the Alliance, and the murder of the Tsar have entirely changed the conditions. There can be now no reasons of international delicacy to prevent a full disclosure of Disraeli's Eastern policy; without which disclosure, indeed, the record of his life and accomplishment would be seriously imperfect. While the course of history has thus tended to promote an extension of plan, there has also been placed unexpectedly at my disposal a great mass of important new material for the final eight years, 1873 to 1881. It has, therefore, become inevitable to expand the single last volume originally contemplated into the two volumes now submitted to the public.

During more than half the period, 1868 to 1881, covered by these volumes, Disraeli was the First Minister of the Crown; and the principal documents not hitherto accessible to the world, bearing on his public policy, must necessarily be his correspondence with Queen

Victoria. His Majesty the King has graciously permitted me to make an extensive selection from these royal papers, and thus to illustrate and elucidate in an ample manner both the policy of the Minister and his relations to his Sovereign. I am deeply sensible of the magnitude of the benefit that the book has received through His Majesty's kindness, for which I desire to tender very dutiful acknowledgments.

O ly second to my obligations to the King are my indebtedness and my gratitude to those who have afforded me access to the new material mentioned above. By the courtesy of the Bridgeman family, and, in particular, of the Dowager Lady Bradford, of Commander the Hon. Richard Orlando Beaconsfield Bridgeman, D.S.O., R.N., Beaconsfield's godson and namesake, a gallant officer who has since given his life for his country, and of Lady Beatrice Pretyman, the present owner, I have been enabled to make copious use of the voluminous correspondence which Disraeli in his last years carried on with two sisters, Selina Lady Bradford and Anne Lady Chesterfield. The character of Disraeli's letters and of the intimacy between him and these ladies is fully explained in Volume V., chapter 7; and every subsequent chapter in both volumes bears witness to the vital importance of the contribution thus made to Disraelian biography. Attention may perhaps be drawn here to one feature of this familiar correspondence: the highest in the land are often playfully alluded to in it under fanciful names. Thus Queen Victoria appears frequently as the Faery or Fairy, Disraeli's imagination conceiving of Her Majesty as a modern Queen Elizabeth, a nineteenth-century Faery Queen, so that he could write of and to her somewhat in the same romantic fashion as Spenser or Raleigh employed in describing and addressing their magnificent mistress.

I desire to thank the Proprietors of *The Times*, to whose enterprise the inception and completion of this biography are due, for the great consideration and

generosity with which they have treated Mr. Monypenny and me throughout. I have also to thank the
Beaconsfield trustees for the continuance of their confidence and encouragement; and to lament that death
has again been busy in their ranks. Mr. Leopold de
Rothschild, whose marriage reception in January, 1881,
was among the last social functions which Beaconsfield
attended, and Sir Philip Frederick Rose, of Rayners,
Penn, the son of Disraeli's confidential agent, have both
passed away since Volume IV. was published. There are
many others to whom I owe gratitude either for permission to use letters, or for more direct assistance in the
preparation of these final volumes. I would especially
mention Lord Derby, Lord Sanderson, Lord Salisbury,
Lord Iddesleigh, the Bishop of Worcester, Major
Coningsby Disraeli, Mr. Norton Longman, Mr. Murray,
and my wife.

It is with a sense of thankfulness and relief that I
bring to a conclusion a biography, the publication of
which has suffered so much through death and delay.
Lord Rowton, Beaconsfield's literary executor; Nathaniel
Lord Rothschild and Sir Philip Rose, the original trustees
of the Beaconsfield estate, and two of their successors;
Mr. Moberly Bell, who, at the request of the trustees,
undertook, on behalf of *The Times*, to arrange for
the publication and to supply a biographer; and
Mr. Monypenny, who projected the work and completed
the first two volumes—are all dead; and further delay
has been caused by illness and the war. The fact
that two writers have been successively engaged upon
the book has necessarily impaired its unity; though
I have not consciously departed from the lines upon
which Mr. Monypenny worked, save perhaps in making
an even more extensive use of the wealth of Disraeli's
letters at my command. Wherever possible, I have
preferred to let Disraeli tell his own story, rather than
to tell it for him. It is, I hope, a fair claim to make for

these six volumes that, whatever their imperfections, they largely enable the reader to realise Disraeli's life from the inside, through the evidence of his familiar letters to wife, sister, and friends, as well as of his political and personal letters to his Sovereign and his colleagues.

This method of biography, of course, precludes brevity. But a large canvas is required to display with anything like justice the character and achievement of one who did so much, and who was so much; who held the attention of the world, as man, author, Parliamentarian, and statesman, for between fifty and sixty years, from the publication of *Vivian Grey* till the last day of his life; whose career his rival Gladstone pronounced to be the most remarkable, with the possible exception of that of the younger Pitt, in our long Parliamentary history; who, apart from his political eminence, won a definite and distinguished place in literature; and who, to borrow the apt words of a reviewer of the fourth of these volumes, was also 'one of the most original, interesting, and interested human beings who ever walked through the pageant of life.' Unlike as Disraeli was in most respects to the great Tory of a hundred years before him, Dr. Johnson, he resembled him in being a unique figure of extraordinary and, I would fain believe, perennial human interest; one of those men about whose personality and performance the curiosity of the world remains ever active. It has been my aim, as it was Mr. Monypenny's, from the mass of papers bequeathed to Lord Rowton, and from an abundance of other original sources, to satisfy that legitimate curiosity.

G. E. B.

LONDON,
    Christmas, 1919.

CHAPTER I.

The Irish Church.

1868.

From February, 1868, till his death thirteen years later, Disraeli was the titular head, as he had long been the most vital force, of the Conservative party. But until after his victory at the polls in 1874 his authority was of an imperfect character, liable to question and dispute. Lord Derby lived for a year and a half after his resignation; and throughout that period many of his old followers still looked upon him as their leader, with Disraeli as acting deputy; a position which, indeed, Disraeli himself had gracefully volunteered to accept, though Derby's common sense and good feeling had repudiated the suggestion.[1] Derby's death, in 1869, converted Disraeli's regency over the party into actual sovereignty; but the ill-fortune which had attended the Conservatives at the General Election in November, 1868, continued to discredit the foresight and diminish the prestige of the new Chief until the by-elections from 1871 onwards showed that the tide had turned. With success came general and unstinted confidence; and during the Administration of 1874–1880, Disraeli exercised as undisputed a sway over his followers, and as complete a control over Parliament, as ever was attained in this country by Minister or party-leader. The confidence of his party was not seriously shaken by the crushing defeat of 1880; he retained it in almost undiminished measure to the last day of his life.

The nine months of his first Administration were, how-

[1] See p. 324.

ever, a troubled and unsatisfactory time.   Not that the unfavourable turn of events was due to the deficiencies of the Cabinet, which was constituted as follows:

First Lord of the Treasury	B. DISRAELI.
Lord Chancellor	LORD CAIRNS.
Lord President	DUKE OF MARLBOROUGH.
Lord Privy Seal	EARL OF MALMESBURY.
Home Secretary	GATHORNE HARDY.
Foreign Secretary	LORD STANLEY.
Colonial Secretary	DUKE OF BUCKINGHAM.
War Secretary	SIR JOHN PAKINGTON.
Indian Secretary	SIR STAFFORD NORTHCOTE.
Chancellor of the Exchequer	G. WARD HUNT.
First Lord of the Admiralty	HENRY J. L. CORRY.
President of the Board of Trade	DUKE OF RICHMOND.
First Commissioner of Works	LORD JOHN MANNERS.
Chief Secretary for Ireland	EARL OF MAYO.

Though not so powerful as Derby's original Cabinet in July, 1866, it was still a formidable combination, containing half a dozen members who were real statesmen, and several more who were experienced and competent administrators.   If it had lost Cranborne, it had gained Cairns; and its principal loss, that of Derby himself, did not affect the Chamber in which the battle was immediately to be fought, though it undoubtedly affected the ultimate tribunal, the electorate, who had regarded him with respect, though not with enthusiasm, for nearly forty years.   But the most efficient Cabinet is of no avail in the face of an adverse, and united, Parliamentary majority.   In Parliament Whigs, Liberals, Radicals, and Irish, taken all together, had a majority of sixty or seventy over the Conservatives; and, with the settlement of the Reform question which had divided them, they would, however sore with one another, have a disposition to reunite in order to regain office.

One aspect of the Parliamentary situation demands especial notice.   As Derby had been obliged by ill-health to give way to Disraeli, so Russell, owing to his increasing years, had retired this winter in favour of Gladstone. With the session of 1868 the protagonists of the two

parties in the House of Commons stood out as the party
leaders. Each admired and respected the great Parliamentary qualities of his rival; but Gladstone's respect
was combined with an alloy of deep moral disapprobation
—a frame of mind which was fostered by what Disraeli
had called the ' finical and fastidious crew ' of high
Anglicans among whom Gladstone familiarly moved.
To them and to him Disraeli's elevation was an offence.
A brilliant journalist shrewdly diagnosed the Gladstonian
temper of the moment:

One of the most grievous and constant puzzles of King
David was the prosperity of the wicked and the scornful,
and the same tremendous moral enigma has come down to our
own days. . . . Like the Psalmist, the Liberal leader may
well protest that verily he has cleansed his heart in vain and
washed his hands in innocency; all day long he has been
plagued by Whig Lords and chastened every morning by
Radical manufacturers; as blamelessly as any curate he has
written about *Ecce Homo ;* and he has never made a speech,
even in the smallest country town, without calling out with
David, How foolish am I, and how ignorant ! For all this,
what does he see ? The scorner who shot out the lip and shook
the head at him across the table of the House of Commons last
session has now more than heart could wish; his eyes, speaking
in an Oriental manner, stand out with fatness, he speaketh
loftily, and pride compasseth him about as a chain. . . . That
the writer of frivolous stories about *Vivian Grey* and *Coningsby*
should grasp the sceptre before the writer of beautiful and
serious things about *Ecce Homo*—the man who is epigrammatic, flashy, arrogant, before the man who never perpetrated
an epigram in his life, is always fervid, and would as soon die
as admit that he had a shade more brain than his footman—
the Radical corrupted into a Tory before the Tory purified
and elevated into a Radical—is not this enough to make an
honest man rend his mantle and shave his head and sit down
among the ashes inconsolable ? [1]

But inaction in face of such a moral paradox would
have been wholly out of keeping with Gladstone's vigorous
character. His ' teeth were set on edge,' as Gathorne
Hardy wrote, ' and he prepared to bite.' [2] It might be

[1] *Pall Mall Gazette,* March 3, 1868.
[2] Gathorne Hardy's *Life of Lord Cranbrook,* Vol. I., p. 264. Hardy's
diaries are most valuable evidence as regards the proceedings of Disraeli's

thought that the last session of an expiring Parliament—
a session which must be devoted mainly to the corollaries
of Reform and to necessary administrative work—would
afford him little opportunity. There was, however, a
weapon to his hand, but it was one which he had hitherto
hesitated to grasp, so completely would its employment
mark his severance from the most cherished of the ideas
with which he entered public life. On the other side,
nothing could recommend him so strongly to the party
which he had now finally adopted as to brandish the
sword of religious equality, even if only in Ireland. Gladstone's Church views had been the one great stumbling-
block to complete sympathy with his new party; and
hitherto he had declined to associate himself with that
attack on the Irish Establishment which had united
Whigs (when in opposition), Radicals, and the Irish
brigade ever since the days of Russell's motion in
1835 about the Appropriation Clause. He had, indeed,
he has told us, regarded the position of the Irish Church
as indefensible since 1863; but both in 1865 and in 1866 he
had, as Minister, resisted motions against it, and when he
was seeking re-election at Oxford in 1865 had informed a
clerical voter that he regarded the question as ' remote
and apparently out of all bearing on the practical politics
of the day.' At that time, so far as public declarations
went, it seemed even more unlikely that Gladstone would
effect Irish disestablishment than that Disraeli would
carry household suffrage.

But the Fenian conspiracy had forcibly directed public
attention to the defects of British government in Ireland,
and the leaders of both parties were preoccupied with
Irish policy. The object at which both aimed was the
reconciliation with England of the leaders of Roman
Catholic opinion in Ireland. With Roman Catholic
opinion in England Disraeli had established a *modus
vivendi* during Palmerston's Government, though, owing

two Governments; and the following pages will show how great are my
obligations to the admirable biography of the father by the son.

to an indiscretion of Derby's, its effect had been impaired
at the last General Election.   In regard to Ireland he had
advocated conciliation, but conciliation through the
action of a powerful and vigorous executive, from his
early days in Parliament.   In a famous speech[1] in 1844
he had said that it was the duty of an English Minister to
effect in Ireland by policy all those changes which a
revolution would effect by force; in 1847 he had urged the
liberal outlay of English gold to forward Irish economic
development; in the first Derby-Disraeli Government he
had endeavoured to pass into law a comprehensive reform
of Irish land tenure in favour of the tenant; and in the
second Derby-Disraeli Government he had contemplated
the grant of a charter to a Roman Catholic University in
Dublin, but had lacked the time to carry the policy into
act.   It was this last scheme which he took up once more
in the years 1867 and 1868, being much encouraged by
Manning, who had recently become Roman Catholic
Archbishop of Westminster, and who was eager to assume
the lead in all movements for the benefit of his adopted
co-religionists.   From May, 1867, to March, 1868, Disraeli
was in regular communication with the Archbishop, who
represented himself as fully acquainted with the views of
Cardinal Cullen and the other leaders of Irish Roman
Catholic opinion.   After an informal conversation on an
early Sunday in May, Manning brought the Rector of
the existing Roman Catholic University in Dublin to
see Disraeli.   In a letter arranging for the interview
Manning wrote, on May 21: ' I am able to say, of my
own knowledge, that any favourable proposal from
Government on the subject of the Catholic University
would not only encounter no opposition, but would be
assisted.   I believe I may say that this includes the granting of a charter.   What I write is not from second-hand.
I can add that the " Chief " I conferred with is in the
front, and he fully recognises the need of removing the
Catholic education of Ireland from the turbulent region

of politics.' He urged Disraeli to disregard certain expressions of Irish members of Parliament, hostile to chartering a Catholic University. ' I am now able to state,' he wrote on August 20, ' that they do not represent the sense and desire of Cardinal Cullen or of the Irish Bishops.' He warned Disraeli of the importance of securing the co-operation of the Irish Bishops.

In the winter months the conversations were resumed. On December 22 Manning wrote that he had just received a letter from Cardinal Cullen ' on the subject of our last conversation,' and requested a further appointment, which apparently took effect on December 28. On January 15, 1868, he suggested another talk, stating in his letter that he had been reading ' with great assent ' Disraeli's speech on Irish affairs in 1844. Again, on February 19, he accepted an appointment for the following day. This was just after the reopening of Parliament, when the grave news of Derby's relapse was turning all eyes upon his Chancellor of the Exchequer. ' I fully understood your silence,' Manning wrote, ' knowing how much and anxiously you must be pressed. The present moment is truly a crisis, but I trust that all may issue in good.' Throughout these weeks Manning was lending his assistance in maturing the Ministerial plan, and he hailed Disraeli's elevation to the Premiership in terms which showed not obscurely that he was looking forward to co-operation with him in a policy of Roman Catholic amelioration—a policy which involved, besides University education, a reform of the Irish land laws, and an ultimate vision of concurrent endowment in Ireland for the Roman Church.

From Archbishop Manning.

8, YORK PLACE, *Feb.* 26, 1868.—The kindness and consideration I have received from you impels me to convey to you my sympathy at this great crisis of your public life.

It is my privilege to stand neutral between political parties, and I have been united, for nearly forty years, in close personal friendship with Mr. Gladstone; nevertheless it is a happiness

to me to see you where your public services have justly placed
you as first Minister of the Crown, and to add an expression of
my best wishes.   I trust you may have health and life to carry
out the legislation which, as you one day told me, you thought
yourself too old to see realised.   That is not so; and the
season has set in sooner than you then looked for.

This letter needs no reply, but I could not let the moment
pass without assuring you of my sympathy.

There was undoubtedly a certain disposition to look to
Disraeli—a statesman who had always regarded Ireland
in a spirit alike of detachment and of sympathy—for a
settlement of the Irish question.   Early in the session of
1866 Bright had adjured both leaders, Gladstone and
Disraeli, to lay aside their Parliamentary rivalry and
combine with this object; and Bernal Osborne, shortly
after the formation of the 1866 Government, had recalled
the speech of 1844 and urged that now was the moment
for Disraeli to put in force the policy then proclaimed.
The successful settlement of the Reform difficulty by the
method of taking the House as a whole into council
suggested that the same man and the same method might
solve the still more intractable problem of Ireland.
A voice reached Disraeli in that sense from Australia.
Gavan Duffy wrote from Melbourne on November 26,
1867, congratulating him on his success in his Herculean
task of Reform, and urging that there was a ' crowning
work' for him still to do.   ' You could give Ireland peace,
and, after a little, prosperity.'   It was too late for half-
measures.

A statesman must offer the agricultural classes terms which
a reasonable man may regard as fairly competing with the
terms upon which he can obtain land if he emigrates to
America or Australia. . . .   If the State will buy up at a
reasonable valuation the waste lands now unproductive,
and let them at a rent yielding 3 per cent. on the purchase
money, and will further enable the more intelligent and
industrious Irish tenants on ordinary estates to purchase
the fee simple of their farms by a series of annual payments
representing the actual value, you will have tranquillised
Ireland for this generation.   The Church question and the
education question will remain to be dealt with, no doubt,

but these are the questions of the educated minority; the uneasy class *are* uneasy because of the perpetual uncertainty of tenure.

Subsequent history has shown that Gavan Duffy was right; that—putting the national question aside—the tenure of land was the crux of the Irish problem, and could only be solved by an extensive system of purchase. But the ' educated minority ' of Roman Catholics in Ireland were more vocal than the farmers and peasants; accordingly it was the Church question and the educa-tion question which were taken in hand at this time by leaders and parties in Parliament, the one by Gladstone and the other by Disraeli; though Disraeli had recognised in the past, and Gladstone, as his Irish researches pro-ceeded, was to discover in the future, the supreme impor-tance of a satisfactory settlement of the land question.

The idea of Disraeli and the Government was to establish in Dublin an institution which should stand in relation to Roman Catholics somewhat in the same position that Trinity College does to Protestants. The governing body should entirely consist of Roman Catho-lics, and the teaching be mainly conducted by them; but full security should be taken that no religious influence should be brought to bear on students who belonged to another faith. Five prelates, together with the President of Maynooth, were to be put on the governing body, the senate; but there was to be a strong lay element in its constitution, and the Govern-ment contemplated the appointment of a layman as the first Chancellor. The State would pay the establish-ment charges of the new University, but the general question of State endowment would be postponed. This scheme, in general terms, had Manning's approval; and, from his assurances, Disraeli had reason to hope that it would be accepted in substance by the Irish Bishops. Accordingly, after its promulgation on March 10 by Mayo in the House of Commons—where, though scoffed at by Bright as a pill good against the earthquake, it was

received with benignity both by Chichester Fortescue on
behalf of the official Liberals and by Monsell on behalf of
the Roman Catholic laity—it was submitted to Archbishop
Leahy and Bishop Derry, the appointed representatives
of the hierarchy. Unfortunately, their attitude was
widely different from what the Government had been led
to expect. They demanded the submission of the new
University to episcopal guidance. The Chancellor, they
claimed, must always be a prelate, and Cardinal Cullen
ought to be the first Chancellor. General control must
not rest with the senate as a whole, a preponderatingly
lay body, but with its episcopal members. These prelates
must have an absolute veto on the books included in the
University programme, and on the first nomination of the
professors, lecturers, and other officers; and must also
have the power of depriving such teachers of their
offices, should they be judged by their Bishops to have
done anything contrary to faith and morals.

Claims of this kind were so preposterous that the whole
scheme had to be relinquished. Dr. Leahy and Dr.
Derry were not men of affairs, and it has been suggested
—and may well be true—that they asked for twice as
much as they were prepared to take, and were astonished
when the Government abandoned the negotiation as
hopeless. But it is difficult not to connect the extremist
attitude of the Irish negotiators with the development
of Gladstone's policy of disestablishment. The preliminary reply of the Bishops was dated March 19, three
days after Gladstone's announcement that the Irish
Church, 'as a State Church, must cease to exist.' The
final reply, expressing the episcopal views in detail, was
dated March 31, after Gladstone had tabled his famous
Resolutions, and while the debate on them in the House
of Commons was in progress. Until Gladstone's announcement Manning was still active on behalf of the
scheme; but his last letter to Disraeli was dated on the
very day (March 16) when the announcement was made.
From that moment he ceased all communication with

the Prime Minister till the close of the Government in
December, when he excused himself as follows:

From Archbishop Manning.

8, YORK PLACE, W., *Dec.* 2, 1868.—. . . I have felt that a
ravine, I will not say a gulf, opened between us when the
Resolutions on the Irish Church were laid upon the Table
of the House. I regretted this, as I had hoped to see the
scheme of the Catholic University happily matured; but with
my inevitable conviction as to the Irish Church I felt that I
ought not to trespass upon your kindness, which I can assure
you I shall remember with much pleasure. . . .

It is not unnatural that Disraeli should have felt that
he had been treated shabbily by the representatives of
the Roman Catholics, and especially by Manning. He
said on more than one occasion to Roman Catholic friends
that he had been stabbed in the back. Manning's defence,
when he heard the accusation, was that the University
negotiations ' were entirely taken out of my hands by
the Bishops who corresponded with you, and in a sense
at variance with my judgment and advice.' Had he
been left free to act, he maintained that he would have
been successful; and he averred that he had never ceased
to regret the failure of his efforts.[1]

Whatever the degree of Manning's responsibility, the
facts and dates suggest that the Roman Catholic
authorities were diverted from adhesion to Disraeli's
programme by Gladstone's superior bid. It was impossible to resist the temptation of wreaking vengeance on
the Anglican Church, though in the result they got
nothing of the Church revenues, nor even, till after forty
years, the Catholic University which was within their
grasp; and the temporal power of the Pope, the importance of which to Roman Catholics Disraeli alone among
British statesmen appreciated, perished a couple of years
later, in 1870.

[1] Letter from Manning to Disraeli, dated Rome, May 7, 1870. Manning
cited, as a witness to the accuracy of his account, Cashel Hoey, a well-
known Irish journalist.

Gladstone allowed the new Government no close time, but, like a capable general, took the offensive at once. Derby's resignation and Disraeli's appointment as his successor were announced in both Houses on Tuesday, February 25; on Thursday, March 5, after nine days' adjournment, Disraeli and his colleagues presented themselves to Parliament and made their Ministerial profession of faith; only five days later, on Tuesday, March 10, came a debate on the Irish question initiated by an Irish member, and the Chief Secretary's exposition of policy; and on the last night of that debate, Monday, March 16, less than three weeks after Disraeli's acceptance of office, Gladstone launched the new policy of the Liberal party, the immediate disestablishment and disendowment of the Irish Church. It was Gladstone's most brilliant and successful stroke as a party leader. The settlement of the Reform question by Disraeli's statesmanship had deprived the Liberals of the popular cry which they had for long utilised at elections, if they forgot it in Parliament. If no new cry were raised, there was a fear lest the working man might be disposed to vote, not for those who had often promised but failed to perform, but for those who had actually given him the franchise. The Irish Church was in a very weak position, and could not long be left untouched; it was, at this very time, undergoing investigation by a Commission which the Government had appointed in the previous year. It claimed, indeed, to be, like the Church of England, the historical representative of the ancient Church of the country; and its maintenance, as an establishment united to its sister Church, was one of the provisions by which the assent of the then dominant Protestants in Ireland was secured for the Act of Union. But, though it was the Church of the ruling classes, it had failed to win the affections of the people. More than three-quarters of the total population were Roman Catholics, and of the remainder nearly a half were Presbyterians. The Church of Ireland ministered to only about one-eighth of the people of Ireland. More-

over, it was Evangelical in its tendencies, and had been
very little affected by the Tractarian development.   Here
was an institution the attack upon which would rally to
the Liberal banner Roman Catholics, Liberal Anglicans,
Dissenters and Secularists, Whigs jealous of ecclesiastical
power, and Radicals hostile to corporate property.   Besides, a policy of disestablishment and disendowment gave
a great opportunity for specious electioneering cries
calculated to attract the new voter: ' religious equality,'
' justice to Ireland.'

How were the Government, how were the Conservative
party, to meet it ?   The Prime Minister, nearly a quarter
of a century before, had declared that an ' alien Church '
was one of Ireland's legitimate grievances.   He had
refused to respond to Derby's urgent requests that he
should speak on its behalf in Parliament, and had written
to him shortly after the General Election: ' I do not think
that any general resolution respecting the Irish Church
could be successfully withstood in the present Parliament.
It is a very unpopular cause, even with many of our best
men.' [1]   On the other hand, the party which Disraeli led
was essentially the defender of the Church of England,
and had been especially mobilised by himself in its defence.
Moreover, any loosening of the bond between religion
and the State was repugnant to all his theocratic ideas.
One section of the Cabinet, headed by Hardy, and powerfully supported by Derby from without, desired that high
ground should be taken and the proposal denounced as
sacrilege; or, if unity could not be preserved on those
lines, at least that a strong passive resistance should be
offered to change.   Another section, in which Stanley and
Pakington were conspicuous, was ready to accept disestablishment as inevitable, and desired to concentrate on
liberal treatment of the disestablished Church together
with a utilisation of surplus revenues for the benefit of
Roman Catholics.

[1] See pp. 139, 140, 159, 160.

From Lord Derby.

Confidential. KNOWSLEY, *March* 3, 1868.—Anxious as I
am for the permanence of your Government, I cannot refrain
from expressing my apprehensions as to the forthcoming
discussions upon the Irish questions. . . .

Your real difficulty will arise when you come to deal with
the Established Church. You know that I have always
entertained a very strong opinion adverse to the right of
Parliament to alienate any part of the property of that or of
any other corporation, and this was the main ground of our
successful opposition to the Appropriation Clause, the object
of which was to convert to secular purposes any surplus, over
and above what might be deemed requisite for the maintenance of the establishment. It seems to be generally assumed
that this principle is no longer tenable; but the moment you
depart from it, you will find yourself involved in inextricable
difficulty. The obvious course would appear to be, at all
events, to wait for the report of the Commission which we
issued last year; but Stanley says, though I do not agree with
him, that Parliament will not, and Gladstone says that it shall
not, admit that ground for postponement of legislation. In
my opinion, however, the safest course for the Government will
be to abstain from making any proposition whatever. . . .
The difficulties of this question are such that I am convinced
your safety is to sit still, and, instead of showing your hand, to
compel your adversaries to exhibit theirs, with all their
discrepancies and contradictions. . . .

To Lord Derby.

10, DOWNING STREET, *March* 4, 1868.—. . . We have discussed our Irish policy for two days, and have arrived at
conclusions which are very much in unison with your suggestions—to bring in a Land Bill, which will deal with all those
points of the controversy on which there begins to be a concurrence of opinion; and with respect to the others, to propose
another Devon Commission.

The famine and State emigration have happened since the
labors of that inquiry, and we think that such a body of evidence will be collected as to the present improved state of the
country that a great effect may be produced on public opinion.

The Cabinet adopted unanimously the University scheme
which you had approved.

With regard to the great difficulty and the real danger, the
Church, although there was great difference of opinion in the
Cabinet on the merits of the question, there was unanimity

II.   12*

that it ought not to be treated except in a new Parliament; and also that no pledge should be given of maintaining absolutely unchanged the present state of ecclesiastical affairs. . . .

Disraeli was not likely to overlook one obvious method of contributing to the tranquillisation of Ireland—the presence of royalty in that country. Like other Ministers, before and after his time, he was hampered by the unfortunate reluctance of Queen Victoria either to go to Ireland herself or to permit members of her family to go. No doubt the disturbed state of the country gave some reason for anxiety in case of a royal visit, but both the Lord-Lieutenant and the Chief Secretary, Abercorn and Mayo, each of them an Irishman with a wide knowledge of Irish feeling, urged the great advantage of a visit from the Prince of Wales; and the representations of Disraeli at length prevailed to secure Her Majesty's consent.

To Lord Derby.

Confidential. 10, DOWNING STREET, *March* 9, 1868.— . . . The Prince of Wales is to pay a visit to Ireland at Easter. This affair has given me much trouble. They invited the Prince without the previous consent of Her Majesty, and the occasion chosen for eliciting the loyal feeling of Ireland was a princely visit to some races at a place with the unfortunate title of Punchestown, or something like it. The Queen did not approve of the occasion, or a state visit agreed to without her authority; and the matter appeared to me, at one time, more serious than the Irish Church, but with much correspondence and the loyal assistance of General Grey, whose conduct is really admirable, I think we have got all right. Lords Abercorn and Mayo are pardoned, and, I hope, the Prince; and, if my humble suggestion be adopted, the inauguration of H.R.H. as a Knight of St. Patrick, in the renovated cathedral, will be an adequate occasion for the royal visit, and a more suitable and stately cause than a race, however national.

Stanley did more than well about *Alabama;* strengthened the Government. He gives me daily good accounts of you, which are agreeable to your devoted D.

The Irish Government would have liked to follow up the Prince's visit by the establishment of a permanent royal residence in Ireland.   But on this point the resistance of the Queen could not be overcome.

From Sir John Pakington.

Confidential.   52, GROSVENOR PLACE, S.W., *March* 14, 1868.
—Is it not still possible that you may suggest in your speech a compromise on the Church question, which may at least diminish the effect of any move on the opposite side ?   It is clear that a state of affairs which no one ventures to defend cannot be maintained.

I think we may consent to disestablishment, but we cannot consent to disendowment.   Hardy hinted that any surplus may be dealt with.   May not this hint be pushed further, and an outline be sketched for (1) disestablishing; (2) insuring a surplus by reducing the provision for the Church to the minimum of her real requirements; (3) devoting the surplus to providing glebes, parsonages, and good churches for the R.Cs.; (4) extending the powers of the Commission, if necessary, to arrange the details of such a plan ?

You will excuse the zeal which offers a suggestion to one who so little needs it.

The opinions expressed in the Irish debate, which asted four days,[1] were very various, but the Liberals, Radicals, and Irish brigade all united in demanding the disestablishment of the Church as the first step.   This policy united Lowe and Bright, Mill and Chichester Fortescue, Horsman and Monsell.   The Government speakers ridiculed the idea that confiscation could be the proper way to start a healing policy.   But the Chief Secretary disclaimed a merely negative attitude on the part of Irish Protestants, and hinted that levelling upwards and not downwards was the proper course.   Gladstone dismissed the Government policy for Ireland as inadequate, though he agreed that the Roman Catholic grievance about University education ought to be remedied.   But the Irish Church must first be dealt with, and must, as an establishment, cease to exist.   He brushed aside the idea of waiting till the Commission then sitting had reported. If the Government would not move, the Opposition must

---

[1] March 10, 12, 13, and 16.

not be content with an empty declaration of opinion, but must proceed to act.

Disraeli began happily by contrasting the apathy and indifference on this question shown by Gladstone and his friends when in office, and their discovery of its instant importance when in opposition. 'I could not but feel,' he said, ' that I was the most unfortunate of Ministers, since at the moment when I arrived, by Her Majesty's gracious favour, at the position I now fill, a controversy which had lasted for 700 years had reached its culminating point, and I was immediately called upon with my colleagues to produce measures equal to such a supernatural exigency.' He defended the Irish policy of the Government as being one of dealing with all such points as were by general agreement sufficiently advanced for legislation, and referring to Commissions only those matters which were not ripe for decision. To suggest that the object was delay was ' the lees and refuse of factious insinuation.' He admitted that the Irish Church was not in the condition in which he could wish to see a national Church; but he dwelt earnestly on the importance of connecting the principle of religion with government, otherwise political authority would become a mere affair of police. If religion and government were to be associated, endowment was inevitable. The Irish, whether Presbyterian, Anglican, or Roman, were essentially a religious people, and therefore in favour of ecclesiastical endowments. This great principle was at stake, and Parliament had no moral competence to deal with it till after an appeal to the nation —an appeal which the Government were prepared to hasten. He pointed, as Mayo had, to some form of concurrent endowment. The moment had arrived, he said, when there must be a considerable change in the condition of the unendowed clergy of Ireland which would elevate their influence. But he did not mean what was vulgarly called ' paying the priests,' and so making them stipendiaries of the State, of which he strongly disapproved.

He did not shrink from meeting the challenge which had been thrown down to him to reconcile his present attitude with his famous dictum in 1844 about a starving population, an absentee aristocracy, and an alien Church.

With reference to that passage which has been quoted from a speech made by me, I may remark that it appeared to me at the time I made it that nobody listened to it. It seemed to me that I was pouring water upon sand, but it seems now that the water came from a golden goblet. With regard to the passage from that speech there are many remarks which, if I wanted to vindicate or defend myself, I might legitimately make. I might remind the House that that speech was made before the famine and the emigration from Ireland, and the whole of that passage about the starving people and the amount of population to the square mile no longer applies. I might remark that that speech was made before the change in locomotion and the sale of a large portion of the soil of Ireland, which has established a resident proprietary instead of an absentee aristocracy, though, so far as I can collect, the absentee aristocracy seems more popular than the resident proprietary. All this I might say, but I do not care to say it, and I do not wish to say it, because in my conscience the sentiment of that speech was right. It may have been expressed with the heedless rhetoric which, I suppose, is the appanage of all who sit below the gangway; but in my historical conscience the sentiment of that speech was right.

Disraeli's speech pleased his colleagues and impressed the House of Commons. Hardy was struck by its skill and humorousness as opposed to Gladstone's extravagant violence. Cairns wrote: ' I doubt if anything, at once so difficult and so perfect, was accomplished even by yourself. The issue on which you have placed our policy with Gladstone is excellent.' Lennox reported Lowe and Henry Cowper as being both decidedly of opinion that Disraeli had the best of it in his duel with Gladstone. But the speech, in view both of the divisions in the Cabinet and of Disraeli's strong feeling, in his ' historical conscience,' of the anomalous position of the Irish Church, was rather a debating answer to Gladstone than a definite statement of policy; and the Prime Minister felt the necessity of deciding promptly on some line of action on which he could hope to secure the united support of his colleagues. He accordingly outlined during the next few days to Cairns, who as an Irish Protestant was specially interested in the question, the policy which, with certain modifications, was eventually adopted by the Cabinet.

To Lord Cairns.

Secret. 10, DOWNING STREET, *March* 19, 1868.—I wish very much to confer with you, but as that is, I suppose, impossible, I must endeavor, without loss of time, to convey to you my present impressions as to the critical position at which not only the Cabinet, but the country, has now arrived.

I assume, from what reaches me, that Gladstone and his party will now propose the disestablishment of the Irish Church.

He seems to me to have raised a clear and distinct issue. I don't think we could wish it better put.

I think we ought to hold that the whole question of national establishments is now raised; that the Irish Church is but a small portion of the question; and that those who wish to demolish it must be held to desire the abolition of national establishments in the three kingdoms.

But we must detach the Irish Church as much as possible from the prominent portion of the subject, for, there is no doubt, it is not popular.

I think, if the principle that the State should adopt and uphold religion as an essential portion of the Constitution be broadly raised, a great number of members from the north of England and Scotland, called Liberals, would be obliged to leave the philosophic standard.

I am, therefore, at present inclined to an amendment which, while it admitted that the present condition of the Church in Ireland was susceptible of improvement, while it might be desirable to elevate the status of the unendowed clergy of that country, still declared it was the first duty of the State to acknowledge and maintain the religious principle in an established form, etc.

All this is very rough writing, and the amendment would require the utmost thought and precision. What I want at present to do is to call your immediate thought to the situation. It has come on us like a thief in the night. It is useless to launch such thoughts, as I suggest, in an unprepared Cabinet. You and I must settle all this together, and then speak to one or two leading spirits; but it is quite on the cards that we may have to take our course on Saturday in Cabinet.

There ought to be no faltering on my part in that case; therefore I beg your earnest and devoted attention to all this. We are on the eve of great events, and we ought to show ourselves equal to them.

To Sir Anthony de Rothschild.

10, DOWNING STREET, *March* 19, 1868.—You sent me some good stuff to keep up my spirits in the great battles at hand; so, if I beat my enemies, the ' great Liberal party ' will owe their discomfiture to your burgundy !

Would you like to be Lord Lieutenant of the county ? If so, you must return me at least six members. That's the quota for such a distinction. My love to your wife.

To Lord Derby.

10, DOWNING STREET, *March* 21, 1868.—I have been intending, and expecting, to write to you every day announcing the hostile motion, and requesting your advice on it; but it has been delayed so long that I am almost in hopes you may reach London before it is made public. We had anticipated considering it in Cabinet to-day, but, as you have observed, it was postponed last night, and the House was favored only with a notice that a notice would be given. Something new in Parliament ! We have, however, spent two hours and a half in the old room, from which I have just escaped to send you this line to let you know how we all were. We did a good deal of business, but nothing very striking except settling our Bill for the purchase of the telegraphs of the United Kingdom.

A person of authority, and a social friend of Gladstone's, told me yesterday that his present violent courses are entirely to be attributed to the paralytic stroke of the Bishop of Winchester.[1] Until that happened G. was quiet and temperate, and resisted all the anti-Church overtures of the advanced party. But when this calamity happened to the worthy prelate Gladstone became disturbed and restless, and finally adopted a more violent course even than his friends had originally suggested. Strange that a desire to make Bishops should lead a man to destroy Churches !

I hope Lady Derby is well, and that your followers will soon see you. Your very tired but devoted D.

Gladstone's Resolutions, though they were not ready so soon as Disraeli anticipated, were not delayed beyond

---

[1] Sumner.

a week, being laid on the table of the House on Monday,
March 23. They were three in number. The first
affirmed the necessity of immediate disestablishment; the
second the desirability of preventing the creation of fresh
interests in the Irish Church; the third proposed an
address to the Queen asking her to place her interest in
the temporalities of the Church at the disposal of Parliament. Disraeli immediately put forth his reply in the
shape of a letter to Lord Dartmouth, who had forwarded
to him a Conservative memorial expressing confidence
in his leadership. In it he followed the line laid down
in the letter to Cairns, insisting that there was a ' crisis in
England ' rather than in Ireland; ' for the purpose is now
avowed, and that by a powerful party, of destroying that
sacred union between Church and State which has hitherto
been the chief means of our civilisation and is the only
security of our religious liberty.'

The Queen was greatly disturbed by Gladstone's proceedings, but with true statesmanship was very anxious
to avoid raising a religious issue.

From Queen Victoria.

WINDSOR CASTLE, *March* 24, 1868.—The Queen has read
Mr. Disraeli's account of Mr. Gladstone's proposed Resolutions with the deepest concern. She fears there is but too
much truth in what Mr. Disraeli says of the spirit that may
possibly be excited amongst the Protestants of the three
kingdoms, and of the danger that exists of those old cries
being revived which, in the name of religion, have worked
evils which successive Governments have so long tried in vain
to remedy. Mr. Gladstone must be aware that the chief
difficulty in governing Ireland has always been to restrain
the mutual violence of the old Orange party on the one side,
and of the Roman Catholics on the other; and he might, the
Queen thinks, to say the least, have paused before he made a
declaration, of which the only effect will certainly be to revive
and influence the old sectarian feuds and to render the administration of Ireland more difficult.

The Queen trusts, however, to her Government, and
especially to Mr. Disraeli, *carefully to avoid* saying *anything*,
however great the provocation may be to act otherwise,
that can tend to encourage a spirit of retaliation amongst

the Protestants or to revive old religious animosities. It seems to her essentially a state of things in which her Ministers will deserve and receive the support of all who look to what is really for the good of the country if they show moderation and forbearance in meeting this attack, and studiously avoid taking a course which, though it might give them a party advantage for the moment, would surely be injurious to the permanent interests of the Empire.

In view of their internal disagreement, the Cabinet determined to meet Gladstone's motion to go into Committee on his Resolutions by a temporising amendment to be moved by Stanley, which, while admitting that considerable modifications in Irish Church temporalities might be expedient, declared that the decision of the question should be left to a new Parliament. It was an eminently reasonable proposition, but naturally, as it avoided the issue of principle, was not combative enough to satisfy Derby, who wrote to Disraeli on March 25: 'It seems to me in the right sense, but it implies rather more of concession than pleases *me*; for the expression "without prejudging the question of *considerable* modifications, etc.," appears practically to prejudge the question to an extent which will not satisfy your Protestant friends, and I shall be rather nervous as to Stanley's mode of handling the subject.' Derby's nervousness was justified; Stanley's mode of handling his subject dismayed and disorganised his party. Even Cairns found him 'colourless and chilling,' while Hardy in his diary pungently described his speech as 'the cry of a whipped hound.' Cranborne seized the opportunity to make an attack, in Hardy's words, 'sneering as regards us all; venomous and remorseless against Disraeli.' He went so far as to suggest that, having betrayed the party over household suffrage, Disraeli was preparing to betray them once more over the Irish Church, Stanley's 'Delphic' amendment being the first step in a policy of disestablishment. Hardy made a spirited reply to this malicious outburst, quoted recent letters and speeches to show the suddenness of Glad-

stone's conversion, and defended the Irish Church and
the principle of establishment and endowment in eloquent terms.   All the leaders took part in the debate.[1]
Gladstone endeavoured to vindicate his consistency, and
asserted that the Church of England would be benefited
and not injured by being severed from a communion with
what was politically dangerous and socially unjust.
Lowe gave Liberals the catchword, ' Cut it down; why
cumbereth it the ground ?'

Disraeli had no difficulty, in his reply, in vindicating
the reasonableness of Stanley's amendment.   The
Government could not meet Gladstone's motion with a
direct negative, as they thought some modification
would be necessary.   They held, moreover, that, when
a fundamental law of the country was attacked, Parliament was not morally competent to decide the question,
unless some intimation had been given to the constituency which elected it.   Once again, as on the third reading of the Reform Bill, Disraeli dealt with the virulent
attacks made on him by Cranborne and Lowe.   The
former he let off comparatively lightly.   He recognised
the vigour and vindictiveness of his invective, but thought,
as a critic, that, in spite of all the study which Cranborne
had given to the subject, it lacked finish.[2]   He turned
to Lowe, Cranborne's ' echo ' from the Liberal side.

When the bark is heard on this side, the right hon. member
for Calne emerges, I will not say from his cave, but perhaps
from a more cynical habitation.   He joins immediately in
the chorus of reciprocal malignity, and ' hails with horrid
melody the moon.'   . . .   The right hon. member for Calne
is a very remarkable man.   He is a learned man, though he
despises history.   He can chop logic like Dean Aldrich;
but what is more remarkable than his learning and his logic
is that power of spontaneous aversion which particularises

---

[1] March 30 and 31, April 2 and 3.
[2] This was the last encounter between Cranborne and Disraeli in the
Commons.   During the Easter recess Disraeli's old colleague, Salisbury,
died, and Cranborne succeeded to the title.   Father and son had been
reconciled, and Salisbury had even espoused Cranborne's quarrel with
Disraeli, who, however, was able to write to Stanley on April 15: ' I am
glad that Lord Salisbury shook hands with me cordially before he died.'

him. There is nothing that he likes, and almost everything
that he hates. He hates the working classes of England.
He hates the Roman Catholics of Ireland. He hates the
Protestants of Ireland. He hates His Majesty's Ministers.
And until the right hon. gentleman the member for South
Lancashire [Gladstone] placed his hand upon the ark, he
almost seemed to hate the right hon. gentleman.

Disraeli maintained that there had been a great improvement in the state of Ireland since the Union, due
to the steady policy of conciliation which had been for
many years pursued by England, and especially by his
own party. They had acted on the principle that in
Ireland it was wise to create and not to destroy, and to
strengthen Protestant institutions by being just to Roman
Catholics, as in the University proposals then before
Parliament. But Gladstone's policy would revive the
acrimony of which they had hoped to get rid, place
classes and creeds in antagonism, and indefinitely defer
the restoration of political tranquillity. He strongly
objected to disendowment. ' I view with great jealousy
the plunder of a Church, because, so far as history can
guide me, I have never found that Churches are plundered except to establish or enrich oligarchies.' There
might be some palliation if there were a question of restitution to the Roman Catholics, but he could not in any
circumstances agree that the endowments should be
applied to what Liberals called secular purposes. ' A
secular purpose is always a job.'

Towards the close of his speech Disraeli developed the
argument on which he had touched in the previous
debate, which he had pressed in his letter to Cairns, and
which was especially congenial to one whose Jewish
traditions gave a theocratic bent to his mind. He
insisted on the vital importance of the union of
Church and State; by which he meant ' that authority
is to be not merely political, that government is to be
not merely an affair of force, but is to recognise its responsibility to the Divine Power.' The divine right of
Kings had properly been discarded, ' but an intelligent

age will never discard the divine right of Government.
If government is not divine, it is nothing. It is a mere
affair of the police office, of the tax-gatherer, of the
guardroom.'[1] If the Church in Ireland fell, he foresaw
attacks on the Church in Scotland and on the Church in
Wales; and the crisis in England, as he had said in his
letter to Lord Dartmouth, was fast arriving. 'High
Church Ritualists and the Irish followers of the Pope
have been long in secret combination, and are now in
open confederacy. . . . They have combined to destroy
that great blessing of conciliation which both parties in
the State for the last quarter of a century have laboured
to effect.'

Gladstone, in reply, deduced from Ministers' speeches
that their policy was some form of endowment for the
Roman Catholic Church, and condemned this alternative
as 'too late.' Gladstone's tone was the assured one of
a leader who knows that he has found a cause which
unites and inspires his party, and the division lobbies
justified him. Stanley's amendment was defeated by
sixty votes, and the motion to go into Committee was
carried by fifty-six.

From Lord Cairns.

Confidential. 5, CROMWELL HOUSES, W., *April* 4, 1868.—
. . . The division is larger than I expected, and yet I cannot
but hope that the numbers, together with the views which
Gladstone's supporters have expressed, will during the recess
make the country awake to the gravity of the position. The
issue, as you have placed it, is excellent, and I cannot express
my admiration of the whole of your magnificent speech.[2]

It was as an outwork of the Church of England that the
Church of Ireland especially appealed to Disraeli. The
same forces of Whiggery, Rationalism, and Dissent that

---

[1] In the General Preface to the novels, 1870, he reaffirmed this doctrine:
'The divine right of Kings may have been a plea for feeble tyrants, but
the divine right of Government is the keystone of human progress, and
without it government sinks into police, and a nation is degraded into a
mob.'

[2] On the other hand, to Hardy, the High Churchman, the speech appeared
'obscure, flippant, and imprudent.'

had gathered to the attack on Church rates were once
more mobilised; and they were on this occasion reinforced
by the Roman Catholics and by some of the High
Churchmen and Ritualists, who were closely allied
with Gladstone and dreaded Erastianism more than
disestablishment. It was to this danger that Disraeli
called attention in the last words of his speech. His
statement was widely challenged, but he unhesitatingly defended it in a letter to a correspondent.

To the Rev. Arthur Baker.

HUGHENDEN MANOR, *Maundy Thursday*,[1] 1868.—. . . You
are under a misapprehension if you suppose that I intended
to cast any slur upon the High Church party. I have the
highest respect for the High Church party; I believe there is no
body of men in this country to which we have been more
indebted, from the days of Queen Anne to the days of Queen
Victoria, for the maintenance of the orthodox faith, the rights
of the Crown, and the liberties of the people. . . .

When I spoke I referred to an extreme faction in the
Church, of very modern date, that does not conceal its ambition to destroy the connection between Church and State,
and which I have reason to believe has been for some time in
secret combination, and is now in open confederacy, with the
Irish Romanists for the purpose. The Liberation Society,
with its shallow and short-sighted fanaticism, is a mere instrument in the hands of this confederacy, and will probably be
the first victim of the spiritual despotism the Liberation
Society is now blindly working to establish. As I hold that
the dissolution of the union between Church and State will
cause permanently a greater revolution in this country than
foreign conquest, I shall use my utmost energies to defeat
these fatal machinations.

It was, therefore, in Disraeli's view, essential that
the Church of England should collect her powers for
resistance. As a layman who had taken an active part
in diocesan affairs, he appealed to his Bishop, the
energetic Samuel Wilberforce, to give a lead to the clergy.
'What is the *mot d'ordre* to the diocese?' he asked on

---

[1] The exaggerated ecclesiasticism of this method of dating his letter
exposed Disraeli to deserved criticism. Always an artist on the public
stage, he sometimes over-dressed his part.

April 15.   It would be very unwise of the High Church clergy, he maintained, to let their imperfect sympathy with ' a Calvinistic branch of the establishment ' neutralise their action, as ' the fate of the Established Church will depend upon the opinion of the country as it is directed, formed, and organised during the next eight months.'[1]   The Bishop had been much discomposed at his friend Gladstone's new move, which he attributed to ' the unconscious influence of his restlessness in being out of office '; and, in response to Disraeli's appeal, he set himself vigorously to work both in his diocese and in the Church at large, and took a prominent part in a great Church meeting of protest in St. James's Hall in May. In this Churchmen of all parties joined: Archbishop Longley with Dean Stanley, Bishop Tait with Bishop Wilberforce.   Spofforth, the Conservative organiser, told Disraeli that the meeting was an unmeasured success, and would rouse the Protestant party throughout the country; but Shaftesbury, with more discernment, warned him that it was a failure.   ' It was one mass of clergy with a sprinkling of peers. . . .   The time is gone by when the country could be be-bishoped and be-duked on public matters.   Unless you can get a mighty body of laity, bankers, lawyers, merchants, shipbuilders, etc.'   The Liberal party, seldom behindhand in agitation, had taken the lead in organising great gatherings throughout the country in Gladstone's support, beginning with a meeting in London over which Russell presided; and it was manifest that the new policy had an increasing volume of public opinion behind it.

The large majority by which Gladstone had carried his motion against the resistance of the Government placed Ministers in a difficult situation.   If that majority were maintained when the Resolutions were moved in detail, resignation or dissolution would in ordinary circumstances be inevitable.   The circumstances, however, were not ordinary.   Parliament had passed sentence of death upon

[1] *Life of Bishop Wilberforce*, Vol. III., p. 245.

itself by accepting a policy of Reform; but the policy was as yet incompletely carried out, as only the English Bill had become law, and the Irish and Scottish Bills were still under consideration. Moreover, when they were passed, some months would be required to draw up the new registers and bring them into operation. It was not reasonable to permit a moribund Parliament to decide without reference to the country a question of vital importance unexpectedly thrust upon its attention. On the other hand, it was absurd to dissolve at once and appeal to the old constituencies; and it was doubtful whether the new constituencies could be properly created before 1869. Strong influences were at work to prevent what apparently most of the Liberals expected and desired—namely, resignation. Derby advised against it. The Queen would not hear of it, and expressed herself strongly in that sense in a private talk with Derby on the very morning of the initial vote.

From Lord Derby.

Most Confidential. ST. JAMES'S SQUARE, *April* 3, 1868.— I would not have troubled you with a letter when I know how much your thoughts must be engaged, had I not thought that you would like to hear that the Queen, who has honoured me this morning with a visit of near an hour, spoke in most unreserved terms of condemnation of Gladstone's motion and conduct; and on my venturing to refer to the precedent of 1835, and the corresponding motion, and saying that its only result had been to turn out the Government, H.M. exclaimed with great emphasis, 'It shall not have that effect now !' I took on myself to say that I had strongly urged you, in the event of defeat, not to think of resigning, to which H.M. answered ' Quite right.' . . .

Disraeli, ever a fighter, agreed with Derby and the Queen; but several members of the Cabinet, of whom Hardy was the most prominent, were reluctant to sanction a course which would involve Ministers, in Hardy's words, ' in inextricable difficulties. The Opposition,' he wrote in his diary, ' has tasted blood, and will bully and endeavour to control us, so as to place us in minorities con-

stantly, and impede any legislation in our own sense.'
During the Easter recess the Queen entertained at Windsor
not only Disraeli, but also Hardy and Cairns, and impressed
her view very strongly upon them all. Hardy wrote to
Disraeli, April 5: ' I have been much struck by the dread
which the Queen expresses of Gladstone and his scheme.
The Coronation Oath weighs upon her mind. She thinks
she should be relieved of it legislatively with her own
consent, before being called upon to agree to the destruction of the Church of Ireland. . . . The Queen is, as you
say, extraordinarily friendly, and anxious not to have a
change.' Disraeli, after his visit, wrote to Cairns on April
8: ' The Queen is in a state of considerable excitement and
determination about the present state of affairs, which
she looks upon as very grave, tho' sanguine that the
country will rally to sound views.'

Before the recess concluded Disraeli had another
audience of Her Majesty on the question, and on the
resumption of Parliament, in anticipation of the forthcoming debate on the first Resolution, obtained the
general sanction of the Cabinet to a policy of dissolution
in preference to resignation.

To Lord Cairns.

Secret. 10, DOWNING STREET, *April* 22, 1868.—I shall open
the Cabinet to-day by giving the result of my audience last
Thursday at Windsor.

I shall indicate what I think is the duty of the Cabinet as
regards themselves and their party, and then, by Her Majesty's
especial desire and command, I shall refer to their duty, under
the circumstances, to the Queen personally.

When I have finished I shall request your opinion, and the
Queen hopes that you will confirm, from your personal
experience, the accuracy of my statement as to Her Majesty's
views. She expects the same from Mr. Secy. Hardy, and for
the same reason; but I shall appeal to you first, not only
because you are my principal colleague, but because there is
only one black sheep in the Cabinet, the Duke of M[arlborough],
and as he sits far from you, he will be governed by the
numerous opinions that will precede his own.

From Queen Victoria.

OSBORNE, *April 22*, 1868.—The Queen received yesterday Mr. Disraeli's letter, and thanks him very much for his full explanation of the course which the Government propose to recommend to her when Mr. Gladstone's first Resolution shall be affirmed.

The Queen has always believed that that question, which has been so unseasonably raised, cannot be settled without an appeal to the country, and her Government may depend upon her support in any measures which may appear to her calculated to effect that settlement in a satisfactory manner.

But as Mr. Disraeli postpones any specific recommendation till the division on Mr. Gladstone's motion shall have taken place, the Queen will only say now that any recommendation she may then receive from her Government shall have her careful and anxious consideration. She would, however, press upon Mr. Disraeli the importance of his *not* 'feeling,' as he expresses it, ' for the opinion of the House,' as to the proper time for appealing to the country, but that her Government should consider this for themselves, and announce the decision which they may think it right to submit to the Queen in a manner that shall show no hesitation or doubt as to the policy they mean to pursue.

Disraeli had some reason for thinking that, in spite of the violent outcry of many Liberals and the Liberal press for an immediate change of Government, Gladstone and the more responsible leaders recognised the advisability of waiting for the result of the appeal to the new constituencies. He wrote to Hardy on the 23rd: ' Gladstone, instead of wishing to upset us, has no Cabinet ready, and, tho' sanguine as to his future, is, at present, greatly embarrassed. He wishes to build us a golden bridge, and if we announce a *bona fide* attempt to wind up, he would support Bills to extend the time of registration, which would be necessitated by the passing of the Scotch and Irish Bills.' He added that ' the commercial Liberals . . . look with the greatest alarm to Lord Russell's return to the F.O., or even that of Ld. Clarendon. They think the peace of Europe depends upon Stanley's remaining. I am assured that there never was a moment in which a want of confidence vote had a worse chance.'

The debate on Gladstone's first and main Resolution, that the Irish Church should cease to exist as an establishment, was carried over three nights,[1] but added little to the exhaustive arguments urged during the preliminary stage. Gladstone was able to show that the policy of joint endowment tentatively advanced by Disraeli was repudiated by other leading Conservatives, and that accordingly the only alternative to disestablishment was a course of procrastination. Disraeli's main point was that to carry the Resolution would, on the one hand, shake the principle of property throughout the kingdom, and, on the other, impair our security for religious liberty and civil rights by tampering with the royal supremacy.

The absence of a practicable alternative made a strong impression, and the majority increased to 65, 330 voting for the Resolution and only 265 against. Disraeli immediately moved the adjournment on the ground that the vote had altered the relation between the Government and the House; and proceeded on the next morning[2] to Osborne to tender to the Queen the advice which, in general terms, the Cabinet had agreed upon in the previous week. As the course to be followed had already been concerted with Her Majesty, there was no difficulty in obtaining her consent; but she very properly desired that her Minister's advice and her own answer should be formally recorded in writing.

To Queen Victoria.

[*May* 1, 1868.]—The division of this morning in the House of Commons, by which at half-past two o'clock a.m. Mr. Gladstone carried a Resolution for the disestablishment of the Irish Church by a majority of sixty-five, renders it necessary to call your Majesty's attention to the position of your Majesty's Government.

About two years ago Lord Derby undertook the management of your Majesty's affairs in a Parliament elected under the influence of his opponents, and in which there was a Liberal majority certainly exceeding seventy.

In the spirit of the Constitution he might have advised your

---

[1] April 27, 28, and 30.   [2] Friday, May 1.

Majesty to dissolve this Parliament, and, in the broken state of the Liberal party at that moment, perhaps not without success. But considering that the Parliament had been so recently elected he resolved to attempt to conduct affairs without that appeal. In the following year he had to encounter the Reform question under peculiar difficulties, and he succeeded in carrying a large measure on a subject which had for a long series of years baffled all statesmen and all parties.

Lord Derby would naturally have advised your Majesty to dissolve Parliament at the close of last year, had there not been some Bills supplementary to the Reform Bill, which time prevented carrying, but the principle of all which had been sanctioned by the House of Commons.

Was there anything in the general conduct of affairs by your Majesty's present Government which should have deterred them from this appeal to the opinion of the nation ?

The conduct of affairs has never been impugned during these two years in any department; on the contrary, in every department it has been commended by their opponents. On the grounds, therefore, that they assumed office in a large and avowed minority in a House of Commons elected by their opponents; that they succeeded in passing the Reform Act; that their policy has been never impugned, but has been entirely accepted, they would be acting only in the spirit of the Constitution, were they to advise your Majesty to dissolve Parliament.

In this state of affairs, while attempting to wind up the session and pass the supplementary Reform Bills, Mr. Gladstone at a few days' notice introduces a policy to disestablish the Church in Ireland.

The objections of your Majesty's Government to this measure are very grave.

1. It is a retrograde policy, and would destroy the effect of thirty years of conciliation.

2. It shakes property to the centre.

3. It dissolves for the first time the connection between Government and religion.

And fourthly and chiefly in their opinion it introduces a principle which must sooner or later, and perhaps much sooner than is anticipated, be applied to England, where the effects must be of a most serious consequence.

The Church will become either an *Imperium in Imperio* more powerful than the State, or it will break into sects and schisms and ultimately be absorbed by the tradition and discipline of the Church of Rome; and the consequence will be that the Queen's supremacy, the security for our religious liberty, and, in no slight degree, for our civil rights, will be destroyed. In fact, this will be a revolution, and an entire subversion of the English Constitution.

Is the fact that this policy has been sanctioned, perhaps heedlessly, by the House of Commons a reason for not appealing to the nation ? Your Majesty's Ministers humbly think not, and that no satisfactory settlement can be arrived at without such an appeal.

Under these circumstances the advice they would humbly offer your Majesty is to dissolve this Parliament as soon as the public interests will permit, and that an earnest endeavor should be made by the Government that such appeal should be made to the new constituency.

In offering your Majesty this advice your Majesty's Ministers would most dutifully state that if your Majesty thought the question could be more satisfactorily settled, and the public interest best consulted, by the immediate retirement of your Majesty's present Ministers from your Majesty's service, they would at once place their resignations in your Majesty's hands, with only one feeling of gratitude to your Majesty for your Majesty's constant support to them in their arduous duties, which has always encouraged and often assisted them.

From Queen Victoria.

OSBORNE, *May* 2, 1868.—The Queen has given her most serious consideration to Mr. Disraeli's letter, and cannot hesitate, as she has already verbally informed him, to sanction the dissolution of Parliament, under the circumstances stated by him, in order that the opinion of the country may be deliberately expressed on the important question which has been brought into discussion.

The Queen admits the correctness of Mr. Disraeli's statement of the circumstances under which Lord Derby undertook the Government in the first instance, and Mr. Disraeli has since continued to carry it on.

She has frequently had occasion to express her satisfaction at the zeal and ability with which the several departments of her Government have been administered; and while her Ministers have done nothing to forfeit the confidence she has hitherto reposed in them, she cannot think of having recourse to the alternative which Mr. Disraeli has placed before her, of accepting their resignations, till the sense of the country shall have been taken on a question which, [it] is admitted on all hands, cannot be settled in the present Parliament.

It will be seen that, while an alternative tender was made of resignation, the advice given to the Queen was to dissolve Parliament ' as soon as the public interests will permit,' coupled with a suggestion that, in the event of dissolution, Ministers should make ' an earnest endeavor ' to ensure that the appeal should be made to the new constituency; and that the Queen's reply was to refuse to accept resignation, but ' to sanction the dissolution of Parliament, under the circumstances stated,' without making any distinction between the old constituency and the new.

Disraeli had gone to the Queen without calling a Cabinet, relying on the general assent which his colleagues had given ten days before to a policy of dissolution rather than resignation. This somewhat highhanded departure from precedent was naturally resented. ' Disraeli has communicated with none of us, which is strange,' wrote Hardy mildly in his diary. Malmesbury, more roundly, noted: ' The Ministers are very angry with Disraeli for going to the Queen without calling a Cabinet, and the Duke of Marlborough wants to resign, but I have done all I could to dissuade him from this course.' The Duke, it will be remembered, was described by Disraeli, in writing to Cairns, as a ' black sheep ' on this question. It is evident from the entries in Hardy's diary, and especially one on May 6 (' A Cabinet before Osborne would have altered everything, but now ?'), that Disraeli avoided a preliminary Cabinet because he had good reason to fear that his colleagues would weaken in their resolution now that the moment for action had arrived, but might be trusted to accept a *fait accompli*. He returned from Osborne on the Saturday evening, May 2, saw on the Sunday two of the colleagues upon whom he principally relied, Cairns and Hardy, and perhaps others, and explained to them what had passed with the Queen. Hardy greatly doubted, and had a strong personal longing for resignation;[1] Cairns expressed agreement with his chief; and the Cabinet next day endorsed, though with

---

[1] In 1889, on reconsideration of the whole position, Hardy wrote: ' Looking back, I doubt if we could have done otherwise than we did ' (Gathorne Hardy, Vol. I., p. 273).

considerable hesitation, the bill which the Prime Minister
had drawn upon its confidence.

A course which had only with difficulty been accepted
by Disraeli's colleagues could hardly be expected to commend itself offhand to the Liberal majority in the House
of Commons.   Disraeli's recital of the successful conduct
of affairs by Ministers since 1866, his justification by
precedent of the constitutionality of government by a
minority, his withdrawal of protracted opposition to the
remaining Resolutions, and his promise to expedite
public business so that the dissolution might take place
in the autumn, did not prevent the Opposition from using,
in Hardy's words, ' plenty of unpleasant language ' about
the advice which Ministers had tendered to the Queen.
Gladstone protested angrily against a penal dissolution,
though, in view of Disraeli's readiness to facilitate debate
on the remaining Resolutions, he did not persist in his
announced motion to take the conduct of public business
into his own hands.   Lowe said that Parliament was
asked to give a ten months' lease of office to Ministers
whom it did not trust; Ayrton and Bouverie denounced
Disraeli for bringing the Crown into conflict with the
Commons; Bright said that it was merely for the sake of
prolonging his own term of office that Disraeli was making
this outrageous demand on the indulgence of Parliament.
Disraeli, in reply, pointed out that, while he was ready to
make all arrangements for an appeal to the new constituency in November, the Queen's permission to dissolve
was unqualified, without any reference to old or new
constituencies; and he challenged the Opposition to give
Parliamentary effect to their taunts by moving a vote
of want of confidence.

The challenge, as Disraeli expected, was not taken up.
However ready the Liberal leaders might be to insult
and to bluster, and their followers to annoy Ministers by
putting them in a minority on this question and on that,
the general sense of the House was that the Government
which had passed Reform should remain in office to com-

plete its work, and to pass the supplementary measures necessary to secure at the earliest possible date an appeal to the new constituency.   The very reasonableness of this view only served to exasperate Gladstone and his friends; and for several days they kept recurring to Disraeli's statements about his audiences of the Queen and the advice he had given her, suggesting supposed discrepancies and denouncing supposed improprieties. One such occasion is described in the following letter:

To the Duke of Richmond.

CARLTON CLUB, *May* 5, 1868.—Mr. Gladstone,[1] to-night, without giving me any notice whatever, called on me to explain what he described as a discrepancy in our statements as to the Queen's declaration in my audience at Osborne.

Had he been courteous enough to give me the usual notice, I could have had the opportunity of conferring with your Grace, and learning from yourself what you had stated, instead of being referred to the mere extract of an alleged report in a newspaper.

All that I could do, therefore, was to repeat what Her Majesty had been pleased to declare, and to add, that if there were any discrepancy in our statements, as I was the Minister, who had waited on Her Majesty, it seemed to me, that the inquiry ought rather to be made in the House of Lords, than to myself.

I write this note, that your Grace should not suppose, that I hesitated to defend, or support, an absent colleague: but under the circumstances of the case, having had no notice from Mr. Gladstone, and having no evidence that the alleged quotation was authentic, I thought it best to take a course wh. suspended all judgment on the question.

Another occasion arose on the motion of a Liberal member condemning the policy of making any public grants whatever in Ireland to religious bodies, such as the *Regium Donum* to Presbyterians, or the Maynooth grant and the proposed University endowment for Roman Catholics.   A warm discussion sprang up, chiefly among Liberal members themselves; and Ayrton, whose unconciliatory and overbearing demeanour in office was subse-

---

[1] ' In a white heat,' noted Hardy in his diary.

quently to bring discredit upon Gladstone's first Administration, commented severely upon the absence of the
Leader of the House during the debate.   Disraeli, who
arrived during Ayrton's lecture, made the characteristic
excuse that there had been, as he anticipated, a quarrel
among gentlemen opposite over the plunder of the Irish
Church, and that it was not his duty to give an opinion
on the subject.   This sneer seems to have caused Bright
to lose all command over himself, and to use language
which necessarily brought to an end the unconventional
but undoubted private friendship which had existed
between him and Disraeli for twenty years.   Bright had
been falling under the spell of Gladstone's influence, and
apparently was ready now to regard Disraeli through his
rival's eyes.   This is what he permitted himself to say:

The right hon. gentleman the other night, with a mixture
of pompousness and sometimes of servility, talked at large
of the interviews which he had had with his Sovereign.   I
venture to say that a Minister who deceives his Sovereign
is as guilty as the conspirator who would dethrone her.   I do
not charge the right hon. gentleman with deceiving his
Sovereign.   But if he has not changed the opinions which
he held twenty-five years ago, and which in the main he said,
only a few weeks ago, were right, then I fear he has not stated
all that it was his duty to state in the interviews which he
had with his Sovereign.   Let me tell hon. gentlemen opposite,
and the right hon. gentleman in particular, that any man in
this country who puts the Sovereign in the front of a great
struggle like this into which it may be we are about to enter—
who points to the Irish people and says from the floor of this
House, ' your Queen holds the flag under which we, the
enemies of religious equality and justice to Ireland, are
marshalled '—I say the Minister who does that is guilty of a
very high crime and a great misdemeanour against his Sovereign and against his country; and there is no honour, there
is no reputation, there is no glory, there is no future name that
any Minister can gain by conduct like this, which will acquit
him to posterity of one of the most grievous offences against
his country which a Prime Minister can possibly commit.

It was an outrageous attack, and was suitably answered
by Disraeli.   Observers differed as to whether he was
deeply moved or whether he merely spoke with quiet

scorn. Lord Ronald Gower tells us that 'Dizzy quite
lost his temper and shook his fist at Bright'; but Malmesbury's record is that the Prime Minister 'replied in the
most gentlemanlike manner, and was cheered by both
sides of the House.'

I shall not condescend to notice at length the observations
of the hon. member for Birmingham. He says that, when
it was my duty to make a communication to the House, of
the greatest importance, and which I certainly wished to
make—as I hope I did make it—in a manner not unbecoming
the occasion, I was at once pompous and servile. Well, sir,
if it suits the heat of party acrimony to impute such qualities
to me, any gentleman may do so; but I am in the memory
and in the feeling of gentlemen on both sides of the House—
and fortunately there are gentlemen on both sides of this
House; they will judge of the accuracy of this representation
of my conduct. It is to their feeling and to their sentiment
on both sides of the House that I must appeal; and no words
of mine, if the charge be true, can vindicate me. The hon.
gentleman says that he will make no charge against me; and
then he makes insinuations which, if he believes them, he
ought to bring forth boldly as charges. I defy the hon.
member for Birmingham, notwithstanding his stale invective,
to come down to the House and substantiate any charge of
the kind which he has presumed only to insinuate. Let him
prefer those charges; I will meet him; and I will appeal to
the verdict only of gentlemen who sit on the same side of
the House as himself.

This challenge, it need hardly be added, was not met,
any more than the challenge to bring forward a vote of
censure had been met. But the stream of calumny in
the House, on the platform, and in the press, flowed on
unabated. It was the cue of many Liberals to treat
Disraeli as being capable of any trickery and of any
breach of constitutional usage. When therefore Gladstone's second and third Resolutions had passed, the one
suspending Irish ecclesiastical appointments, the other
praying the Queen to place her interest in the temporalities at the disposal of Parliament, the absurd suggestion
was made that Disraeli was likely to advise the Queen to
set herself in antagonism to the House of Commons by
returning an unfavourable answer to the third Resolution.

From General the Hon. Charles Grey.

OSBORNE, *May* 5, 1868.—. . . Her Majesty hears with much satisfaction what you say of the favourable prospects in the House of Commons; and trusts that your expectation of being able to surmount the difficulties still before you may be realised. She is very anxious to hear what you propose to advise her as to the answer to the Address which is the object of the third Resolution. *The Times* assumes that the ' Suspensory Bill ' which the Address will ask the Queen to allow to be introduced, will certainly be thrown out in the House of Lords. This would place the H. of Lords in a position of antagonism to the House of Commons from which, in H.M.'s opinion, they ought, if possible, to be saved. Yet, after all that has passed, it seems difficult for the Govt. to advise the Queen to refuse the request of the Commons.

Could Her Majesty, without refusing it (on the contrary, expressing her anxiety to act with her *Parliament* in any measures calculated to give satisfaction to her Irish subjects), not require that, in a matter which cannot be settled without the concurrence of the House of Lords, the Address should be agreed to by both Houses ? . . .

Disraeli was too shrewd even to endorse this not un-reasonable suggestion to withhold an answer to the Address till it had been adopted by both Houses; and the answer which, after special consultation with Cairns and Hardy, he settled in Cabinet stated that Her Majesty desired that her interest in the Irish temporalities should not stand in the way of the consideration by Parliament of legislation in the current session. Gladstone promptly introduced his Suspensory Bill, and the second reading was carried on May 22 by a majority of fifty-four, after a debate in which the Opposition leader insisted that the choice lay between a system of concurrent endowment such as had been hinted at by the Government and the general disendowment which he himself proposed to effect by repealing the Maynooth Act and discontinuing the *Regium Donum* to Presbyterians, as well as by dis-establishing and disendowing the Church of Ireland. Disraeli was hampered, in his reply, by the disfavour with which the policy of concurrent endowment had been received by his own party and by the country. He accordingly minimised the extent to which the Government had committed themselves to it. He denied that their University proposals amounted to endowment, or that they contemplated paying the Roman Catholic clergy or increasing the *Regium Donum*. The logical position of Disraeli and his Government was necessarily much weakened by this public deprecation of the only alternative policy; a policy, moreover, which he favoured himself and which had the historical support of a succession of British statesmen from Pitt and Castlereagh down to Russell, who had only abandoned it that year. He had to fall back, as his main argument, on the resulting danger to the Church of England. ' I say this act is the first step to the disestablishment of the English Church.' The correctness of this view subsequently received unexpected confirmation from Mr. Birrell, Chief Secretary for Ireland for many years and no friend of the Church of England, who deplored in an important State paper that the Irish Church was disestablished rather from a desire to please the Dissenters in England than to do justice to Ireland. But a practical people like the English will never be deterred from dealing with a practical and admitted grievance by apprehension of possible but remote consequences.

The Suspensory Bill had been pushed forward rather to show that Gladstone and the Liberals were in earnest than with any expectation that it would pass into law. Disraeli having once registered his opposition to it, facilitated its speedy passage to the Lords, where it was promptly rejected by a majority of two to one, on the ground that the whole question should be left without prejudice to the judgment of the electorate.

From Lord Derby.

St. James's Square, *May* 29, 1868.—. . . I think . . . I may congratulate you on being master of the position for the remainder of the Session, which I presume you will close as soon as you can. Will you allow me to suggest that, partly to promote that object, it would be well to let it be understood that you do not mean further to oppose Gladstone's Suspension Bill. . . . Our object should be to get it disposed of in the Lords as soon, and as summarily, as possible. I suggest this for your consideration as a matter of tactics, of which however you are too great a master to stand in need of any hint from me. . . .

To Lord Derby.

10, DOWNING STREET, *May* 30, 1868.—I must thank you for your kind letter, and for your invaluable counsel. I had moved a little in the direction you advise, and will still further prosecute that course. . . .

To Charles N. Newdegate.

Confidential. 10, DOWNING ST., *May* 31, '68.—I think it would be well to consider whether it may not be desirable to place no further impediments to the passing of the Suspension Bill in the House of Commons, so that the decision of the House of Lords may be taken as speedily as possible.

It is probable that the Church Commission will report towards the end of next month, and if they recommend any modification of appointments it will be difficult for the Lords to oppose the Suspension Bill and they will be driven to define and limit its objects, instead of opposing the second reading: and this the country will never understand.

No doubt Gladstone sees this chance and will not be in a hurry to carry his Bill through our House, whereas, in my opinion, our object should be to get it disposed of in the Lords as soon, and as summarily, as possible.

I wish you would think over this and give me your opinion.

These letters were written during the Whitsuntide recess, which roughly corresponded with the close of the great party struggle of the session. If Disraeli was, as Derby suggested, ' master of the position ' from that time till the prorogation, it was largely because he had not only evaded the snares of his foes, but had also brought his somewhat distracted Cabinet into harmony and subordination

To Mrs. Disraeli.

HOUSE OF COMMONS, *May* 14, '68.—I think we have got out of our danger, but it has been very ticklish.

May 19, '68.—The Cabinet was very satisfactory, and they signed a paper, projected and headed by the Duke of Richmond, to stand by me in any advice I should give the Queen on the great subject. This puts an end to one source of wearing disquietude, namely, the fear that the Cabinet might not stand firm and united.

The reunited Cabinet utilised the recess to come to an agreement as to the measure to expedite the new register so as to make possible a General Election in November and the summoning of the new Parliament in December. Disraeli was justifiably anxious that the acceleration should not be such as to arouse a suspicion in the new constituency ' that there is any design to neutralise the large franchises with which they have been wisely invested, by hurrying and hustling them in the establishment of their electoral privileges.' [1] But Cairns and Hardy were particularly urgent in pressing for an early date, to maintain the honour of the Government and to save them from any possible charge of bad faith; and their scheme was accepted first by the Cabinet and then, amid general satisfaction, by Parliament.

This Registration of Voters Bill was one of five measures which Disraeli carried during this session to complete the work of Parliamentary Reform. The factiousness of the Opposition made the progress of the Irish and Scottish Reform Bills through the House of Commons a tedious and aggravating business, and Disraeli had need of all his tact and good temper to bring them safely into port. On the Scottish Bill, particularly, he was subjected to some annoying defeats; but, in pursuance of his acknowledged principle of acting, in regard to Reform, in co-operation with the general sense of the House, he accepted the amendments of the majority with a good grace. The Boundary Bill was the occasion of further worries. The decisions of the Commission appointed by the Government in 1867 were not accepted in the House, and were submitted for revision to a Select Committee presided over by Walpole. The Commission

[1] Letter to Cairns, dated May 29.

enlarged the Parliamentary boundaries of many big towns, but the Committee restored the old limits; and Government and Opposition, Lords and Commons, were set by the ears over the somewhat trivial questions as to which tribunal's decisions were to be followed, and whether a compromise accepted by the Prime Minister in the Commons was binding on the majority in the Lords. Disraeli repudiated the interpretation put by the Opposition on his words; but, after the Liberal Peers had adopted the childish expedient of leaving the House of Lords in a body, Malmesbury and the majority gave way.

To Lord Malmesbury.

10, DOWNING STREET, *July* 3, 1868.—I have learnt your proceedings in the House of Lords, last night, with astonishment. The interpretation placed on my words, when speaking of the progress of business in the House of Commons, is one painfully distorted. I was answering an enquiry as to the prospects of business in that House, and in estimating them, I mentioned, that certain measures, tho' they had not formally passed the House of Commons, might be considered virtually settled: that is to say, would lead, in the House of Commons, to no further debate or division.

A much more important reform was effected by the Corrupt Practices Bill; and it is to the lasting credit of Disraeli that he removed the trial of election petitions from the jurisdiction of a partisan Committee of the House of Commons and transferred it to an impartial tribunal consisting of His Majesty's Judges. In order to carry this simple and desirable reform he had to overcome many obstacles, in particular the united protest of the Judges themselves against the new duties it was proposed to put upon them. The Bill underwent several changes and, in order to pass, had to be made experimental in form and duration; but the principle was firmly established that irregularities committed in political elections, like other breaches of the law, should be investigated and punished by a legal tribunal and not by a committee of active politicians. A great purification

of public life has resulted from the firm determination of
Disraeli and his Government to associate the proper trial
and due punishment of corrupt practices at elections
with the extension of the Parliamentary suffrage.

If Disraeli's Parliamentary course was troubled, the
principal external venture of his Government was brilliantly conducted. At the beginning of the very week which
witnessed the decisive defeat of Ministers on Gladstone's
first Resolution, there came news of the complete success
of the Abyssinian expedition under the command of Sir
Robert Napier. It was on the morning of Sunday,
April 26, and about 11 o'clock, the present Lord Iddesleigh, on behalf of his father Northcote, the Secretary of
State for India, brought the intelligence to Disraeli. He
found him ' gorgeously arrayed in a dressing-gown and in
imposing headgear,' and, as might be expected, ' opulent
in compliment.'[1] The Queen told her Prime Minister that
she was ' truly delighted at the glorious and satisfactory
news from Abyssinia, which she thinks must have a
favourable effect on the general position of the Government.' There was, indeed, universal satisfaction; and
Gladstone joined in the compliments paid, not only to the
commander and his gallant force, but to the Government,
and especially the Indian Secretary, for their prudent
conduct of a difficult affair.

For it was a very difficult affair to rescue a British
envoy and a British consul, who with other captives were
imprisoned in an impregnable fortress, far inland in a
wild and inhospitable country, by a half-mad and only
half-civilised potentate. Ministers had only with great
reluctance accepted the necessity of sending an expedition,
Stanley characteristically writing to Disraeli in the autumn
of 1866, ' I sincerely hope the W[ar] O[ffice] will find the
country inaccessible. I think they will.' But, as Disraeli
explained when moving the credit of £2,000,000 in November, 1867, they felt that the honour of the Crown and the
duty of the country were involved; that magnanimity

[1] Lang's *Northcote*, p. 194.

and forbearance had been pushed to extreme limits; that justice could only be had by recourse to arms. None of the numerous little expeditions which England has sent out was ever more completely successful. The difficult country was safely penetrated, King Theodore's army was defeated with insignificant casualties on our side, his citadel Magdala was stormed, he himself committed suicide, and the prisoners were duly brought away. Disraeli may be forgiven the slight touch of pomposity with which, in moving Parliament to thank the commander and his forces, he dilated on the difficulties overcome and the success attained. Napier, he said, had to form a base on a desolate shore, to create a road through a wall of mountains, and to guide his army across a barren and lofty tableland, intersected with high ranges and unfathomable ravines; leading ' the elephants of Asia, bearing the artillery of Europe, over African passes which might have startled the trapper and appalled the hunter of the Alps.' Finally our troops ' had to scale a mountain fortress, of which the intrinsic strength was such that it may be fairly said it would have been impregnable to the whole world had it been defended by the man by whom it was assailed.' Thus it was, said Disraeli, linking modern achievement with Johnsonian romance, that ' the standard of St. George was hoisted on the mountains of Rasselas.'

It was not merely for its conduct that the expedition was remarkable, but for its character. Disraeli pointed out in November, 1867, that the country was going to war, ' not to obtain territory, not to secure commercial advantages, but for high moral causes and for high moral causes alone.' Accordingly, when the prisoners had been released and Theodore's capital destroyed, the British force, having accomplished its object, completely evacuated, by the orders of the Ministry, the country which it had successfully invaded. Disraeli naturally congratulated the House and the country on so unique a spectacle.

When it was first announced that England was about to embark on a most costly and perilous expedition, merely to vindicate the honour of our Sovereign, and to rescue from an unjust but remote captivity a few of our fellow-subjects, the announcement was received in more than one country with something like mocking incredulity. But we have asserted the purity of our purpose. In an age accused, and perhaps not unjustly, of selfishness, and a too great regard for material interests, it is something, in so striking and significant a manner, for a great nation to have vindicated the higher principles of humanity. It is a privilege to belong to a country which has done such deeds.

Disraeli has been charged with lowering the standard of British foreign policy by basing it upon British interests rather than upon public right and justice. The Abyssinian expedition, which his detractors prefer to ignore, is incontestable evidence that he placed public right and justice high among British interests. The only criticism to which his policy on this occasion is fairly open is that he underrated the cost. Ward Hunt, in his Budget speech, estimated the total at £5,000,000, and raised the income tax from fourpence to sixpence in order to meet the expense; but it turned out that nearly as much again was required, and Gladstone's Chancellor of the Exchequer had in 1869 to provide for meeting the balance of an ascertained total of £9,000,000. The fault seems to have lain mainly with the Indian Government, who supplied the General and the troops; but the miscalculation must necessarily detract somewhat from the credit otherwise due to Disraeli and his Government. Disraeli himself, in retrospect, treated the cost as a trifling matter in comparison with the successful result.

To Lady Bradford.

2, WHITEHALL GARDENS, *Oct.* 2, 1875.— . . . I do not look back to the Abyssinian [war] with regret: quite the reverse. It was a noble feat of arms, and highly raised our prestige in the East. It certainly cost double what was contemplated, and that is likely to be the case in all wars for wh. I may be responsible. Money is not to be considered in such matters: success alone is to be thought of. Abyss.

cost 9 mills. or so, instead of 4 or 5 anticipated; but by that expenditure we secured the business being accomplished in one campaign. Had there been a second campaign, it wd. probably have been 19 mill. and perhaps failed—from climate, or an abler and more prepared military resistance. . . .

Though Parliament was prorogued at the comparatively early date of July 31, yet once more, in spite of the time necessarily devoted to the corollaries of Reform, and of the many days spent on the Irish problem and Gladstone's new policy, there was a good harvest of other legislation. The Queen's Speech enumerated as having passed ' Bills for the better government of public schools, the regulation of railways, the amendment of the law relating to British sea fisheries, and for the acquisition and maintenance of electric telegraphs by the Postmaster-General, and several important measures having for their object the improvement of the law and of the civil and criminal procedure in Scotland.' A small measure, which was not mentioned, was the Act which abolished, none too soon, the degrading practice of public execution. The purchase of the telegraphs was a question to which Disraeli had given special attention. To transfer the working of so essential a public service to the State was undoubtedly a great public benefit; but the price paid to the telegraph companies was so high, and popular pressure for cheap messages so persistent, that the transaction has never yielded the profit to the State which those who effected it contemplated. The educational bill upon which the Cabinet had been closely engaged at the beginning of the year [1] did not get beyond a second reading in the House of Lords, where it was introduced by the Lord President, the Duke of Marlborough. It had the great merit of recognising the importance and dignity of education by constituting a comprehensive education department under a Cabinet Minister, a reform which Disraeli had advocated in 1855 [2] but which Parliament did not accept till 1899, and it provided an effective con-

[1] See IV., ch. 16. [2] See Vol. I., IV., ch. 2.

science clause; but Ministers hesitated to introduce the principle of a rate, without which a general system could hardly be established. It was a measure, in Disraeli's words, ' preliminary, but of magnitude '; but there was no time to consider it, and the whole question, as he antici- pated, was left over to the next Parliament.

Through all the troubles and worries of this spring and summer Disraeli was greatly cheered and supported by the constant sympathy and encouragement of the Queen. Her Majesty considered that her Minister's conduct and the advice he had given her at the time of the crisis were perfectly correct and constitutional; and she was disgusted with what she held to be the factious and unworthy treat- ment which he received at the hands of the Opposition. The relations between Sovereign and Minister, which were eventually to become so intimate, were drawn very per- ceptibly closer during this May and June. The Queen began that practice of sending Disraeli spring flowers, which was a constant mark of their later relationship, and which has resulted in the permanent association of his name and memory with the primrose; and he, whose official letters to his Sovereign had always sounded a strongly individual and personal note, was encouraged to develop this tendency and entertain Her Majesty by such correspond- ence as he alone was able to write. Lady Augusta Stanley told Clarendon at this time that ' Dizzy writes daily letters to the Queen in his best novel style, telling her every scrap of political news dressed up to serve his own purpose, and every scrap of social gossip cooked to amuse her. She declares that she has never had such letters in her life, which is probably true, and that she never before knew *everything !* ' [1]

Princess Christian to Mrs. Disraeli.

May 12.—Mama desires me to . . . send you the accom- panying flowers in her name for Mr. Disraeli. She heard him say one day that he was so fond of may and of all those

[1] Letter from Clarendon to Lady Salisbury. Maxwell's *Clarendon* Vol. II., p. 346.

lovely spring flowers that she has ventured to send him
these, as they will make his rooms look so bright. The
flowers come from Windsor.

Mrs. Disraeli to Princess Christian.

. . . I performed the most pleasing office which I ever had
to fulfil in obeying Her Majesty's commands. Mr. Disraeli is
passionately fond of flowers, and their lustre and perfume
were enhanced by the condescending hand which had showered
upon him all the treasures of spring.

From Queen Victoria.

May 14.—The Queen was glad to hear how very warmly
Mr. Disraeli was received yesterday. It is very significant.
The Queen trusts that the debate to-night[1] will be satisfac-
tory, tho' Mr. Disraeli told her he had anticipated the worst.

WINDSOR CASTLE, *May* 16, 1868.—The Queen is most
thankful to Mr. Disraeli for his very kind and feeling letter.
She feels most deeply when others *do* sympathise as he does
with her; Mr. Disraeli has at all times shown the greatest
consideration for her feelings. . . .

The Queen sends by this evening's messenger a few more
flowers for Mr. Disraeli.

BALMORAL, *May* 21.—The Queen was very sorry to hear
from Mr. Disraeli what an unsatisfactory night they had
on Monday.[2]

She feels very anxious to hear what course they intend to
pursue, but trusts that this as well as other difficulties will be
got over, and this annoying Session soon be brought to an
end. . . .

May 23.—. . . Really there never was such conduct as
that of the Opposition.

May 25.—The Queen thanks Mr. Disraeli for several kind
letters. . . .

The Queen is really shocked at the way in which the House
of Commons go on; they really bring discredit on Constitutional Government. The Queen hopes and trusts, however,
that to-day's division will be satisfactory and then there will
be quiet.

The sooner the Dissolution can take place the better. . . .

June 6.—The Queen thanks Mr. Disraeli very much for his
kind, long letter. She hopes all will go smoothly. She
regrets however the acrimonious discussion respecting the

---

[1] On the Boundary Bill.

[2] When the Government were defeated in important divisions on the
Scotch Reform Bill.

letter[1] which she wishes could have been avoided. This personal bitterness in politics is a bad thing, and if possible should be prevented. But alas! it is often *impossible*.

The Queen trusts the Session will speedily be got to an end, for it is sure to be disagreeable as long as it lasts. . . .

June 21.—. . . Most grateful to Mr. Disraeli for the gift of his novels, which she values much.

It was particularly tactful and appropriate of Disraeli to present the Queen with his novels, as Her Majesty had herself entered the ranks of authorship in the beginning of the year by publishing *Leaves from the Journal of our Life in the Highlands*. There was thus a fresh link between the Minister and his royal mistress, which so accomplished a courtier could hardly fail to turn to good account. There is no reason to doubt the story which represents him as using more than once, in conversation with Her Majesty on literary subjects, the words: 'We authors, Ma'am.'

To Arthur Helps.

[*January*, 1868].—I am most obliged to you for sending me a copy, and an early one, of the royal volume.

I read it last night and with unaffected interest. Its vein is innocent and vivid; happy in picture and touched with what I ever think is the characteristic of our royal mistress —grace.

There is a freshness and fragrance about the book like the heather amid which it was written.

They say that truth and tact are not easily combined: I never believed so; and you have proved the contrary; for you have combined them in your preface, and that's why I like it.

The Queen was far from well in the spring of 1868. She informed Disraeli in May that the anxiety and worry of the last two or three years were beginning to tell on her health and nerves; that she often feared she would be unable physically to go on; and that she felt the necessity of rest in a pure and bracing air. A visit to Switzerland was accordingly arranged; and the Queen, travelling as Countess of Kent, left England at the beginning of

[1] Gladstone had written a letter imputing to the Government a policy of concurrent endowment.

August. She passed through Paris, where a slight *contretemps* occurred which gave Disraeli an opportunity of showing how tactfully he could offer somewhat unwelcome advice.

To Lord Cairns.

Private. HUGHENDEN, *August* 11, 1868.—. . . I heard from Lucerne to-day. Our Peeress is very happy and, as yet, quite delighted. Her house is on a high hill, above the town, with a splendid view over the lake; the air fine, the rooms large, lofty, cool. There has been rain and there is a grim world.

The gentlemen of the suite don't like the hill; *facilis descensus*, but the getting back will be awful. Stanley has not yet arrived, but he likes hills; a member of your Alpine Club.

There was a sort of Fenian outrage at Paris; one O'Brien, a teacher of languages, shook his stick at Princess Louise, and shouted ' A bas les Anglais,' and some other stuff. The Queen was not there.

I fear, between ourselves, the greater outrage was that our dear Peeress did not return the visit of the Empress. This is to be deplored, particularly as they had named a Boulevard after her, and she went to see it ! . . .

To Queen Victoria.

10, DOWNING STREET [*August*, 1868].—. . . There is no doubt that your Majesty acted quite rightly in declining to return the visit of the Empress at Paris. Such an act on your Majesty's part would have been quite inconsistent with the incognito assumed by your Majesty, for a return visit to a Sovereign is an act of high etiquette: which incognito is invented to guard against.

Nevertheless there is, Mr. Disraeli would ask permission to observe, perhaps no doubt that your Majesty was scarcely well advised in receiving the visit, as such a reception was equally inconsistent with incognito.

Certain persons, M. de Fleury notably among them, made a great grievance of the visit not being returned, but Mr. Disraeli hoped the matter would have blown over and been forgotten. The Empress, who is far from irrational, was not at first by any means disposed to take M. de Fleury's view, but everybody persists in impressing on her she has been treated with incivility; and there is no doubt that it has ended by the French Court being sore.

Mr. Disraeli thought it his duty to lay this matter before

your Majesty; as your Majesty perhaps on your return, with your Majesty's happy judgment, might by some slight act gracefully dissipate this malaise.

It was not found possible to arrange to make the return visit as the Countess of Kent passed through Paris on her way back to England; but Lady Ely wrote to Disraeli: 'The Queen desires me to tell you that H.M. has written to the Empress herself to express all her regrets, but to say H.M. has given up paying visits now and had declined going to her own relations, but hoped at some future time when she passed through Paris to call and see the Empress.'

Immediately upon her return to this country, Her Majesty commanded Disraeli's presence for ten days at Balmoral, where he had never before been Minister in attendance. Mrs. Disraeli did not accompany him, and he kept her fully informed of his doings and experiences.

To Mrs. Disraeli.

PERTH, *Sept.* 18, '68.

MY DARLING WIFE,—I telegraphed to you this morning, that all was well. Within an hour of this place, where we ought to have arrived a little after eleven o'clock, it was signalled that something had gone wrong with a goods train, and that the road was blocked up: and we had to sit in the dark for two hours and more ! However, this was better than being smashed. Everything, otherwise, has gone very well.

You provided for me so admirably and so judiciously, that I had two sumptuous meals: a partridge breakfast, and a chicken and tongue dinner: and plenty of good wine ! I did not slumber on the road, but had a very good night here, and have got up early, quite refreshed, to send you a telegram, and write a few letters, this particularly, which you will get to-morrow.

There was a great mob at Carlisle who cheered me very much, but I profited by our experience during our Edinbro' visit, and would not get out: so they assembled on the platform round the carriage. It was an ordeal of ten minutes: I bowed to them and went on reading; but was glad when the train moved.

I was greatly distressed at our separation, and when I

woke this morning, did not know where I was. Nothing but the gravity of public life sustains me under a great trial, which no one can understand except those who live on the terms of entire affection and companionship like ourselves: and, I believe, they are very few.

Write to me every day, if it is only a line to tell me how you are; but you, with your lively mind and life, will be able to tell me a great deal more. Montagu [Corry] will have discovered by this time the best mode of communication. The Queen's messenger goes every day by the same train I did—10 o'clock Euston. Adieu, with a thousand embraces, my dearest, dearest wife. D.

BALMORAL CASTLE, *Sept.* 19, '68.—Arrived here last night, ½ past nine; the household at dinner. The Queen sent a considerate message, that I need not dress, but I thought it best, as I was tired and dusty, not to appear: particularly as I found some important letters from Stanley on my table. They served me a capital little dinner in my room, and I had a very good night. . . . I thought it right to appear at breakfast to-day, as I had not presented myself last night.

Lady Churchill in attendance and Miss Lascelles, and Lord Bridport, etc., etc.

Bridport told me that I need not wear frock coats, ' which, as a country gentleman, I know in the country you must abominate.'

Sept. 20.—I write to you whenever I can snatch an opportunity, and they are so frequent here, but so hurried, that I hardly know when I wrote to you last, or what I said. Yesterday, I dined with the Queen, a party of eight. H.M., the Prince and Princess Xtian, Princess Louise, the Duke of Edinburgh, and myself, Lord Bridport and Lady Churchill.

We dined in the Library, a small, square room, with good books—very cosy; like dining with a bachelor in very good rooms in the Albany.

Conversation lively, though not memorable. The Duke of Edinburgh talked much of foreign fruits, and talked well.

Although my diet has been severe, and I have not tasted anything but sherry since we parted, I have suffered much from biliary derangement, which weakens and depresses me. . . . Yesterday morning I went out walking with Lord Bridport, and made a tour of the place: so I quite understand the situation, and general features: I much admire it. Mountains not too high: of graceful outline and well wooded, and sometimes a vast expanse of what they call forest, but which is, in fact, only wild moor, where the red deer congregate. The Duke of Edinbro' came from the Prince of Wales' place with his keepers, and dogs, and guns. . . . He wears the tartan and dined in it: and so did Prince Xtian, but it was for the first time; and the Duke told me he was an hour getting it on, and only succeeded in getting it all right by the aid of his wife and his affectionate brother-in-law. . . .

Sept. 21.—The Queen sent for me yesterday afternoon.

Her rooms are upstairs: not on the ground floor. Nothing can be more exquisite, than the view from her window. An expanse of green and shaven lawn more extensive than that from the terrace of Clifden, and singularly striking in a land of mountains: but H.M. told me, that it was all artificial, and they had levelled a rugged and undulating soil. In short, our garden at Hughenden on a great scale: except this was a broad, green glade, the flower garden being at the other side of the Castle. I dined with the household, and, between ourselves, was struck, as I have been before, by the contrast between the Queen's somewhat simple, but sufficient, dinner, and the banquet of our humbler friends.

Sept. 22.—The weather here, instead of being cold as they predicted, has been wet and warm: and my room every day too hot; so I have written always with a fire, and the window open. It is now, under these circumstances, 63: but my fire nearly out.

Yesterday, after a hard morning's work—for the messenger goes at 12 o'clock, and I rise exactly at seven; so I get four hours' work—Lord Bridport drove me to see some famous falls—of Garrawalt: and though the day was misty and the mountains veiled, the cataract was heightened by the rain. I never in my life saw anything more magnificent: much grander falls often, as in Switzerland, but none with such lovely accessories; such banks of birchen woods, and boulders of colossal granite.

I dined with the Queen again yesterday. . . .

Sept. 23.—Yesterday we went one of those expeditions you read of in the Queen's book. Two carriages posting and changing horses. We went to the Castle of Braemar, where, every year, the contiguous clans assemble, and have Highland games. The castle was most picturesque, and is complete and inhabited, and in old days must have been formidable, as it commands all the passes of the valleys. I was very glad that there were no games. The drive to it sublime, or rather nobly beautiful. Then we went on to the Linn of Dee—a fall of the Dee River; and on the bank we lunched. One might take many hints for country luncheons from this day, for our friends have great experience in these matters: and nothing could be more compact and complete than the whole arrangements. The party was very merry: all the courtiers had a holiday. Lady Churchill said that, when she asked the Queen, through the Princess Louise, whether she was wanted this morning, the Queen replied 'No: all the ladies are to go, to make it amusing to Mr. Disraeli.'

Returning we went to Mar Lodge, and took tea with Lady Fife. There we found Sylvia Doyle, looking more absurd than any human being I can well remember. The highlanders call her 'The colored Lady.' Her cheeks were like a clown's in a pantomime, and she had a pile of golden hair as high as some of the neighbouring hills. However, she smiled and cracked her jokes as usual, and gave me, as usual, a long list of all the places she was going to.

Lord Bridport gave me the enclosed photographs for you. I saw the Queen on my return home—on business. We left Balmoral at ½ past 12 and got home by 7: a very fine day: no clouds on the mountains and the outlines all precise: while we lunched, sunshine; and not a drop of rain the whole day.

Sept. 24.—The Queen gives her Minister plenty to do: but I will write every day, however briefly. . . .

Sept. 25.—Only a line to keep up the chain. . . .

The Queen has got a photographer and insists upon my being *done*. This gave me an opportunity to give your collection to Lord Bridport. I said you had sent them for the Queen, but I would not give them, etc., etc.: but he did; and the Queen was delighted . . . 'and said many kind things about Mrs. Disraeli.' I shall try to find them out.

Sept. 26.—The bag has brought me no letter from you this morning, which greatly distresses me: for although all goes on well here, I am extremely nervous, my health being very unsatisfactory. . . . I have never tasted one of your dear peaches, which I much wished to do for your sake, and have drunk nothing but sherry. However, the attack never continues in the day, but then I am in a miserable state in these morning hours, when I have to do the main work, and the work is very heavy. . . .

I leave this on Monday, and get to Perth to sleep, and the next morning to Knowsley, as I must see Lord Derby. On Thursday, I propose to be at Grosvenor Gate, after an absence of a fortnight ! . . .

This morning, the Queen has sent me two volumes of views of Balmoral: a box full of family photographs, a very fine whole-length portrait of the Prince, and 'a Scotch shawl for Mrs. Disraeli, which H.M. hopes you will find warm in the cold weather.' To-day, I am resolved to keep in my room.

Adieu, my dearest love; though greatly suffering, I am sustained by the speedy prospect of our being again together, and talking over a 1,000 things.

Sept. 27.—The Queen sent for me yesterday after she came home from her ride: but said, when I left H.M., ' This is not your audience before leaving.'

Sept. 28.—A very rapid letter before departure. The joy at our soon meeting again is inexpressible.

Princess Christian said yesterday, that they were all very sorry I was going, but she knew who was glad, and that was Mrs. Disraeli. . . .

I had a long audience of the Queen at four o'clock, and shortly afterwards was invited to dine with H. Majesty again.

Disraeli's visit to Balmoral coincided with a great pressure of public work, and he realised the serious inconvenience caused to public interests by a ten days' sojourn of the Prime Minister in the remote Highlands. ' Carrying on the Government of a country six hundred miles from the metropolis doubles the labour,' he wrote to Bishop Wilberforce. He only repeated the experiment once, in 1874; for the rest of his second Administration he prevailed on Her Majesty to excuse him from taking his turn of Ministerial attendance at Balmoral.

CHAPTER II.

Defeat and Resignation.

1868.

The fate of the Irish Church and of the Conservative Ministry and party would be decided by the result of the General Election in November. To one competent observer it appeared a fairly matched fight. Clarendon wrote in June: ' Confidence in Gladstone seems on the increase thro'out the country, though it remains feeble and stationary in the H. of C. On the other hand a demoralised nation admires the audacity, the tricks, and the success of the Jew.' Disraeli realised the powerful effect that organisation might produce; and with his well-known disregard of money was ready to take a liberal lead in supplying the necessary funds. ' What we want,' he wrote to Stanley, ' is to raise one hundred thousand, which, it is believed, will secure the result. It can be done if the Cabinet sets a good example.'

To Lord Beauchamp.

10, Downing St., *June* 22, '68.—The impending General Election is the most important since 1832, and will, probably, decide the political situation for a long period. The party that is best organised will be successful. No seat, where there is a fair prospect, should be unchallenged. To effect this, and to operate on a class of seats hitherto unassailed, it is necessary that a fund, to aid the legitimate expenses of candidates, should be raised, and that upon a scale not inferior to the range which democratic associations have, on more than one occasion, realised, in order to advance their views.

As it is natural that the success of such an effort must depend upon the example set by Her Majesty's Government, I have induced my colleagues in the Cabinet to subscribe a minimum sum of ten thousand pounds, tho', if they follow my example, it will reach a greater amount.

May I hope that you will support me in this enterprise ? Some more formal application may, possibly, be made to you; but, to so intimate a friend, I prefer to appeal myself.

One thing was clear to Disraeli, namely, that, in determining the result of the General Election, the Church of England, if united and resolved, must play a considerable, perhaps a preponderant, part. To secure her active support for a cause, in which, to his mind, her own ultimate fate was involved, he bent his energies; and it was with that temporal end largely in view that he distributed the ecclesiastical patronage of the Crown, which happened to be of a peculiarly momentous character in his nine months' premiership. Five sees had to be filled in that short period, including those of Canterbury and London; three or four deaneries, including that of St. Paul's; besides canonries, a divinity professorship, and important parochial cures. Both Low Churchmen and High Churchmen were restive. The former marked with alarm the rapid advance of Tractarianism and the resulting Ritualism, and many of them were disposed to quit for Dissent a Church which seemed to them to be heading straight for Rome; the latter were inclined to regard themselves as the only true inheritors of the Anglican tradition, to resent the want of recognition under which their leaders suffered, and to magnify the episcopal character of the Church at the expense of its national aspect. To Disraeli, who never forgot the popular outburst at the time of the Papal aggression, the political danger, at least, appeared to be greatest from the Low Church side; and, though he desired to make a fair distribution among all loyal schools, it was to placate the Evangelicals that he mainly set himself.

In this whole question of Church patronage he laboured

under two serious disadvantages: personal ignorance of the leading clergy, and a multiplicity of divergent counsellors, eager to enlighten that ignorance. Keenly interested as he was in the ultimate issues of religion, and considerable as had been his study of the historical claims and present needs of the Church of England, Disraeli had never moved in ecclesiastical or even academical circles, and knew only such clergy as he met in society; moreover, though he regularly attended his parish church, he did not go about to hear preachers of renown. In Dean Stanley's *Life*[1] there is a story of the Dean's meeting Beaconsfield in the street, on the last Sunday in 1876, and taking him to hear for the first time F. W. Farrar, whom he had just made a Canon, preach in Westminster Abbey. To Gladstone it would have been an ordinary experience; to Beaconsfield it was a ' Haroun-al-Raschid expedition ' to be piloted into the north transept of the Abbey to hear a popular preacher. The Dean and the Premier listened, unnoticed, for a few minutes, and then came out. 'I would not have missed the sight for anything,' said Beaconsfield; ' the darkness, the lights, the marvellous windows, the vast crowd, the courtesy, the respect, the devotion—and fifty years ago there would not have been fifty persons there.' It was the comment of an artist and not of an informed churchgoer. 'Send me down to-morrow the clergy list. I don't know the names and descriptions of the persons I am recommending for deaneries and mitres,' Disraeli wrote to Corry in August, 1868, from Hughenden; and again from Balmoral in September, ' Ecclesiastical affairs rage here. Send me Crockford's directory; I must be armed.' ' He showed an ignorance about all Church matters, men, opinions, that was astonishing,' said Wellesley, Dean of Windsor, in November. One leading Churchman Disraeli did know well, his own Bishop, Samuel Wilberforce. But much as he admired his gifts both of oratory and of organisation, he did not trust one who had been for years hand in

---

[1] Vol. II., p. 447.

glove with Gladstone; and he was convinced that the
great mass of his countrymen distrusted him still more.

The Bishop was one of those who were eager to direct
the disposal of the Crown patronage. He and Hardy and
Beauchamp[1] plied Disraeli with recommendations on the
High Church side; while Cairns, on the Low Church side,
aspired to play the same part in Disraeli's ecclesiastical
appointments as Shaftesbury had in Palmerston's.
Derby's advice also was sought and given on every
important occasion. Last, but by no means least, the
Queen had strong views of her own, founded partly on the
Broad Church traditions of the Prince Consort, but
largely on personal experience of distinguished divines.
Her Majesty, moreover, had naturally no political bias,
such as, consciously or unconsciously, swayed Disraeli
himself and most of his other counsellors; but was guided
solely by the good of the Church, as she saw it.

Disraeli's first important appointment was to the
Bishopric of Hereford. There he disregarded both
his Low Church and his High Church advisers, and
nominated a hard-working parish clergyman of moderate
opinions, Atlay, the Vicar of Leeds. This was in
May. It was in August that he made his great bid
for Protestant support by appointing to the Deanery of
Ripon Canon McNeile of Liverpool; 'a regular Lord
Lyndhurst in the Church,' as an Evangelical correspondent
wrote, who would make 'the Protestant party fight like
dragons for the Government.' Cairns was naturally
'satisfied that nothing more politic could occur at the
present time.' It would stop the feeling that was abroad
that the Bishop of Oxford was interfering and influencing
Church patronage—a feeling which was due, no doubt,
to the appointment of Wilberforce's chaplain, Woodford,
to succeed Atlay at Leeds. Derby was startled;

---

[1] Beauchamp had endeavoured to influence ecclesiastical appointments
while Derby was Prime Minister. Disraeli wrote to him on Nov. 24, 1866:
'I will do my utmost, and immediately, to forward your wishes; but,
entre nous, I don't think my interference, in matters of that kind, is much
affected: at least, I fancy so. I asked for a deanery the other day, for
Mansel, but he is not a Dean.'

McNeile's nomination seemed to him 'rather a hazardous bid for the extreme Low Church.' Disraeli did not disguise from his leading colleague his electioneering aim.

To Lord Stanley.

HUGHENDEN, *Aug.* 16, 1868.—. . . No human being can give anything like a precise estimate of the elections until the Registration is over. All that is certain at present is, that we have our men better planted than our opponents; more numerous candidates, and stronger ones. The enemy also have no electioneering fund. It is a fact that both the Duke of Devon[shir]e and D. of Bedford refused to subscribe. We, on the contrary, have a fund, tho' not ½ large enough: but sufficient to stimulate and secure contests, where there is a good chance, and which, otherwise, would not have been engaged in.

What we want at this moment is a strong Protestant appointment in the Church. I have been expecting a Bishop to die every day, but there is hardly a 'good Protestant' strong enough to make a Bishop. I thought, however, of recommending Dean Goode, an Evangelical, but really an ecclesiastical scholar, and equal in Patristic lore to any Puseyite father.

Strange to say, instead of being made a Bishop, he has suddenly died: and I have recommended the Queen to make McNeile of Liverpool, Dean of Ripon, which is a Protestant diocese. I believe the effect of this will be very advantageous to us. . . .

Aug. 21.—. . . Things are rapidly maturing here: the country, I am convinced, is, almost to a man, against the High Ch. party. It is not the townspeople merely, but the farmers universally, the greater portion of the gentry, all the professional classes: nay ! I don't know who is for them, except some University dons, some youthful priests and some women; a great many, perhaps, of the latter. But *they* have not votes yet.

It's still a quarter of a year to the dissolution, and that's a long time for this rapid age: but I have little doubt it will end in a great Protestant struggle. The feeling in England is getting higher and higher every day: but it is Protestant, not Church, feeling at present. The problem to solve is, how this Protestant feeling should be enlisted on the side of existing institutions. I think it can be done: but it will require the greatest adroitness and courage.

Not a Cath. will be with us: not even Gerard. They can't. . . .

The Queen, like Derby, was startled at the nomination of McNeile, and only consented with reluctance. But Disraeli was so satisfied with what he had done that he was anxious, when the Bishopric of Peterborough presently fell vacant, to proceed with another strongly Evangelical appointment. Here he met with decided resistance from the Queen, to whom he explained at length his view of the ecclesiastical and political situation.

To Queen Victoria.

[*End of Aug.*, 1868].— . . . The appointment of the new Dean of Ripon has quite realised Mr. Disraeli's expectations: it has done great good, has rallied the Protestant party and has been received by the other sections with no disfavor or cavil.

Since Mr. Disraeli wrote last a long impending vacancy on the Episcopal Bench has occurred. There is no necessity to precipitate the appointment and the final decision can await your Majesty's return. Perhaps Mr. Disraeli may be permitted to wait on your Majesty at Windsor on your Majesty's return, before he attends your Majesty in Scotland, to which he looks forward with much interest.

On the nomination to the See of Peterboro' in the present temper of the country much depends. The new prelate should be one of unquestionably Protestant principles, but must combine with them learning, personal piety, administrative ability, and what is not much heeded by the world but which is vital to the Church, a general pastoral experience.

Mr. Disraeli after the most careful enquiries and the most anxious thought is strongly inclined to recommend to your Majesty Canon Champneys of St. Paul's and Vicar of Pancras. . . .

Affairs at this moment ripen so rapidly in England, that he must lay before your Majesty the result of his reflexions on a mass of data, that for amount and authenticity was probably never before possessed by a Minister. He receives every day regular reports and casual communications from every part of the United Kingdom. . . .

There is no sort of doubt that the great feature of national opinion at this moment is an utter repudiation by all classes of the High Church party. It is not only general: it is universal.

If the Irish Church fall it will be owing entirely to the High Church party—and the prejudice which they have raised against ecclesiastical establishment.

Mr. Disraeli speaks entirely without prejudice. The bias of his mind from education, being brought up in a fear of fanaticism, is certainly towards the High Church, but he has no sort of doubt as to the justness of his present conclusions and it is his highest duty to tell your Majesty this.

Nevertheless the Church as an institution is so rooted, and the doctrine of the royal supremacy so wonderfully popular, that if the feeling of the country be guided with wisdom Mr. Disraeli believes that the result of the impending struggle may be very advantageous and even triumphant to the existing constitution of the country. . . .

From Queen Victoria.

LUCERNE, *Sept.* 7, 1868.—The Queen thanks Mr. Disraeli for his two letters. She is glad that Mr. Disraeli has not pressed for an answer relative to the new Bishop, as the appointments are of such importance, not only for the present but for the future good of the Church in general, that it will *not* do merely to encourage the ultra-Evangelical party, than wh. there is none more narrow-minded, and thereby destructive to the well-being and permanence of the Church of England. Dr. McNeile's appointment was *not* liked by *moderate* men, but still, this having been done, it is not necessary or advisable to make more of a similar nature, and the Queen, with the greatest wish to support the Government and the Protestant feeling in the country, feels bound to ask for moderate, sensible, clever men, neither Evangelical or Ritualistic in their views, to be appointed to the high offices in the Church.

The Church of England has suffered from its great exclusiveness and narrow-mindedness, and, in these days of danger to her, *all* the liberal-minded men should be rallied round her and pressed into her service to support her and not to make her more and more a mere Party Church, which will alienate all the others from her. This is the more important as we are threatened with the loss of several more Bishops and of one most eminent man—the Dean of St. Paul's. . . .[1]

To Queen Victoria.

[*Sept.*, 1868].—. . . If, when the verdict is given, the Church of England is associated in the minds of the people with the extreme High Church school, the country will deal to that Church a serious, if not a deadly, blow.

Your Majesty justly observes that the appointment of Dr. McNeile did not satisfy moderate men. With becoming

[1] Milman, the ecclesiastical historian.

humility Mr. Disraeli would venture to observe it was not intended to do so. But it satisfied some millions of your Majesty's subjects and acted as a safety valve to such an extent, that while, before that appointment, an extreme pressure on your Majesty's advisers existed to appoint to the vacant see some professor of very decided opinions, from the moment of the preferment of Dr. McNeile that pressure was greatly mitigated, and almost ceased.

With humility Mr. Disraeli would presume to observe, that he knows not, in his long political experience, any happier instance of seizing the *à propos*.

The country was on the eve of a series of public meetings on the Church, held by Churchmen, to protest against the imputed designs of the Crown and the Crown's Ministers in favour of Ritualism and Rationalism, when this preferment was decided on. Twenty preferments of clergymen of the same type as McNeile but not of his strong individuality would not have produced the effect.

And what did he receive ? A mock deanery which your Majesty could not have offered to some of the great scholars who sigh for such, etc.

The appointment of Dr. McNeile already allows your Majesty greater latitude in the selection of a Bishop.

Again, if a wise selection be made in this instance of Peterboro' your Majesty will find still more freedom in the impending vacancies which your Majesty is obliged to contem-plate but which it is trusted may be at least postponed.

Your Majesty very properly wishes to appoint to the Bench ' moderate, sensible, and clever men ' neither Ritualist nor Evangelical. But Mr. Disraeli humbly asks, Where are they to be found ? The time is not come, at least certainly not the hour, when Deans of St. Paul and Westminster, and men of that class of refined thought, however gifted, can be submitted to your Majesty's consideration. It is not ripe for that; tho' with prudence it may be sooner than some suspect. The consequences of such a step at this particular moment would be disastrous. And, as for men, qualified as your Majesty wishes, without the pale of that school, why your Majesty has already been obliged to go to New Zealand for a Prelate,[1] and even Dr. Atlay, whom Mr. Disraeli recommended to your Majesty as almost *ultimus Romanorum*, is denounced, tho' erroneously, as a creature of the Bishop of Oxford, a prelate, who, tho' Mr. Disraeli's diocesan, he is bound to see is absolutely in this country more odious than Laud.

As a matter of civil prudence, he would presume to say wisdom, Mr. Disraeli is of opinion, that the wisest course at

[1] Selwyn.

this conjuncture is to seek among the Evangelical school some man of learning, piety, administrative capacity, and of views, tho' inevitably decided, temperate and conciliatory in their application. He thinks that, with the more ardent satisfied by the tardy recognition of McNeile and the calmer portion, now alarmed and irritated, encouraged and soothed and solaced by such an appointment as that which he indicates, we might get over the General Election without any violent ebullition: and even if another vacancy were to occur in the interval, a man more conformable with your Majesty's views might be advanced, if Your Majesty could fix upon one.

The names which Mr. Disraeli, after the most anxious and painful investigation, places before your Majesty's consideration, are both of, as he believes, admirable men: and who by their standing, compass of mind, and tact in their intercourse with their fellow-clergy, are qualified for the office of a Bishop.

They are Canon Champneys of St. Paul's and Vicar of Pancras, Archdeacon Hone of Worcester.[1]

Doubtless neither of these appointments would please the sacerdotal school nor even satisfy the philosophic: that is not to be expected: but they would be received with respect alike by Ritualist or Rationalist; and with confidence and joy by the great body of your Majesty's subjects.

From Queen Victoria.

BALMORAL, *Sept.* 18, 1868.—Tho' the Queen will have an opportunity of seeing and conversing with Mr. Disraeli on this important and difficult subject, viz. the Church appointments, she thinks it as well to put down in writing the result of much reflection on her part.

First of all—it is to be remembered that any ultra-Protestant appointment, or at least any extreme Evangelical one, will only alienate the other party and not please the really moderate men—while it is bringing into the Church those who by their natural illiberality will render the Church itself more and more unpopular. . . .

The deanery of St. Paul's, which the Queen fears will soon be vacant, she thinks ought certainly to be given for eminence only—either as a *preacher or a writer*—irrespective of party, and she trusts that, should we lose the valuable, distinguished and excellent present Dean of St. Paul's, Mr. Disraeli will concur in this. Another very clever man, and the finest preacher the Queen has ever heard out of Scotland, and whom she would much wish to see promoted—is the Dean of Cork (Dr. Magee).

---

[1] 1805–1881: Rect r of Halesowen, and Archdeacon of Worcester: a respected but hardly outstanding Evangelical.

To Lord Derby.

Private. PERTH, *Sept.* 18, '68.—. . . I wish I could consult you about the Bishop, but it would require a volume instead of a letter. These questions, within the last few months, have become so critical and complicated. They were always difficult enough. I have begun to write to you several times on this subject, but have given it up in despair from the utter inability of conveying to you my view of the circumstances in a letter.

I think the deanery of Ripon has been a *coup.* I was really surrounded by hungry lions and bulls of Bashan till that took place, but, since, there has been a lull, and an easier feeling in all quarters—strange to say—among all parties. Probably they were all astounded.

Oh ! for an hour of confidential talk in St. James' Square ! There are priests now, and men of abilities, who are as perverse as Laud, and some as wild as Hugh Peters ! . . . I am, as I always am, to you, most faithful, D.

The High Church party were deeply affronted by McNeile's appointment. Even so moderate and representative a Churchman as Hook, Dean of Chichester, came out against the Conservative cause. Disraeli complained to the Bishop of Oxford that ' in the great struggle in which I am embarked, it is a matter of great mortification to me that I am daily crossed, and generally opposed, by the High Church party.' The Bishop replied on September 11: ' The vast body of sound Churchmen are entirely with you on the great question of the day. But I should not tell you all that I believe to be the truth if I did not add that there is at this moment a jealous and alarmed watchfulness of your administration of Church patronage. Those who through the long period of Palmerston's Administration held their fidelity in an ostracised position are in danger of being alienated.' The Bishop assisted Disraeli by explaining to Hook that McNeile's appointment only meant that no allowed party in the Church would be excluded from promotion; but he repeatedly urged Disraeli to placate what he called ' the strong middle party of orthodox English Churchmen,' who alone could give him the support he wanted. Disraeli rejoined emphatically from Balmoral on September 28:

> There can be no doubt that every wise man on our side should attract the Protestant feeling, as much as practicable, to the Church of England. It has been diverted from the Church of England in Scotland. There the Protestant feeling is absolutely enlisted against us. If we let it escape from us in England, all is over. It appears to me that, if we act in the spirit of the Dean of Chichester, we may all live to see the great Church of England subside into an Episcopalian sect. I will struggle against this with my utmost energy.[1]

Disraeli, apparently, knew little or nothing of Magee, the great orator of the Irish Church, till his name was suggested by the Queen. But soon recommendations came from many quarters in his favour; and before the end of the month he attracted widespread attention as the preacher of a famous sermon of appeal from the Irish Church to her English sister, on the text: ' They beckoned unto their partners, which were in the other ship, that they should come and help them.'[2]

To Montagu Corry.

BALMORAL, *Sept.* 21, '68.—. . . The Queen, I found, very desirous to make Magee (Dean of Cork) the Bishop. I waived all this by saying he must be an Oxford man, and she suggested the Dean might be one: but I had no book to refer to, and I am not sure whether Crockford, shortsighted Crockford, biographises the Irish clergy. Generally speaking, I also discouraged the idea: but to my intense surprise I received yesterday a letter from John Manners, the highest Churchman in the Cabinet, proposing Magee himself for my consideration, as an appointment which would satisfy all parties. We should then, he said, by this, and the instance of Selwyn, prove our recognition of the *unity* of the Church: colonial and I. .h, etc.

One objection to Magee is, that his appointment would give us nothing, and that is a great objection.

---

[1] *Life of Bishop Wilberforce*, Vol. III., pp. 266, 267.
[2] St. Luke v. 7.

The Queen prevailed, and Magee was appointed Bishop,[1] Champneys being preferred to the Deanery of Lichfield. For the Deanery of St. Paul's, Disraeli had a very suitable man of his own, Mansel, the distinguished Oxford meta-physician, who had been associated with him on the *Press*, and who shared and powerfully expressed the scepticism which Disraeli entertained of the value of the conclusions of German professors and theologians. The author of *Phrontisterion* was a congenial spirit with the orator of the Sheldonian theatre.

The appointments of Magee and Mansel gave very general satisfaction, approval being expressed by Derby, Hardy, and even Wilberforce. The latter's favourite candidate, Leighton, the Warden of All Souls, though disappointed of a Bishopric, was made a Canon of Westminster; and the High Churchmen were further placated by the appointment of the energetic Gregory to a Canonry at St. Paul's, and of the scholarly Bright to Mansel's chair at Oxford—the latter appointment pressed by Beauchamp, who warned Disraeli that the High Church party other than 'the old port-winers' were holding aloof from the political contest. But a much more difficult and delicate selection was now laid upon Disraeli. In the end of October the Archbishop of Canterbury, Dr. Longley, died.

To Lord Derby.

Secret. 10, DOWNING STREET, *Nov.* 2, 1868.—Returning from Balmoral, I was disappointed in the opportunity of consulting you on two important matters : the Church appoint-ments then pending, and my address, of which I would have brought you the draft. However, I got through those diffi-culties, and pretty well.

Now comes a greater one : the Archbishop.

[1] Magee, at the time Dean of Cork, had written to the Prime Minister, 'asking him, when filling up the deanery of St. Paul's, to give him one of the appointments that might be vacant in so doing.' Magee's biographer notes the touch of humour in Disraeli's reply, 'beginning with a refusal of the Dean's modest request on the first page, and then making the offer of the bishopric when he turned over the leaf.' MacDonnell's *Magee*, Vol. I., p. 197.

My Church policy was this: to induce, if possible, the two great and legitimate parties to cease their internecine strife, and to combine against the common enemies: Rits and Rats. This could only be done by a fair division of the patronage, and though at first beset by great difficulties, arising from party jealousy and suspicion, I think I have now succeeded in getting them well to work together. . . .

As I did not want a very High Churchman, or an Evangelist, for Archbishop, the materials from which I could select were very few. I was disposed in favour of the Bishop of Gloucester,[1] whom I don't personally know, but was pleased by his general career since your accession to office, and also by a correspondence which he held, subsequently, with me, arising out of the Ritual Commission. It seemed to me very desirable that the new Primate should not be mixed up with all the recent controversies, and clerical fracas, which have damaged all concerned in them. I sent my proposal, with well digested reasons: the boxes crossed, and one came to me saying that there could be no doubt what was to be done, as there was *only one* man fit for the position: the Bishop of London.[2] Then came another box, mine having been received, still more decided, if that could be. Now I think the Bishop of London an appointment which will please neither of the great parties—and only a few clerical freethinkers, who think, and perhaps justly, he may be their tool, and some Romanisers—for he supports sisterhoods as strongly as Oxford or Sarum.[3] I wrote in reply, acknowledging the two letters, and saying merely they should have my most serious attention, and I have been employed all this morning in drawing up a statement touching the whole case, which will be received, by the person to whom it is addressed, on her arrival on Thursday. That will be followed, probably, by an audience on Saturday, and before that time I should be deeply obliged if you would give me, through the ever faithful secretary,[4] some hints, and your general impressions. . . .

From Lord Derby.

Confidential. KNOWSLEY, *Nov.* 3, 1868.—. . . I am afraid that I can do but little towards relieving you from the difficulty in which you are now placed. . . . I agree in your general principle of dealing, in respect to patronage, with the rival parties in the Church; and you have been fortunate in having at your disposal a succession of appointments which has enabled you to distribute your favours with some appearance of impartiality. But the appropriation of the highest

---

[1] Ellicott.   [2] Tait.   [3] W. K. Hamilton.   [4] Lady Derby.

prize of all can hardly be hoped to give general satisfaction, and you must be satisfied if it does not produce general discontent. Your range of choice is limited, and your materials by no means first-rate. I cannot agree with H.M. that the Bishop of London would be either a popular or a judicious selection. I am perhaps prejudiced against the man, but I must confess that I have no confidence in his judgment. If you should be finally driven to promote him, which I hope will not be the case, the Bishop of Oxford, though ineligible for the Primacy, would make a very good and useful Bishop of London.

With the Bishop of Gloucester, whom you name, my acquaintance is only slight. He is undoubtedly a learned man, and I believe a sound Churchman, rather inclining to the High School. But I should doubt his having much strength of character, and he has a foolish voice and manner which make him appear weaker than I believe he really is. He is said, and I believe with reason, to be entirely under the influence of the Bishop of Oxford. Of the other Bishops, has the name ever occurred to you of my Bishop of Rochester, Claughton? If his opinions are not too High Church, he has many qualifications for the office—and I think that you might do worse. Harold Browne, the Bishop of Ely, is a man of very high reputation—but I do not know him personally, even by sight . . .

To Lord Derby.

Secret. 10, DOWNING STREET, *Nov.* 12, 1868.—Harold Browne is offered as a compromise. But what do I gain by Harold Browne ? While H.M. will only be annoyed. I could win, if I had a man. I don't know personally the Bishop of Gloucester—and you can't fight for a person you don't know. I proposed him as one appointed by Palmerston, and yet not an Evangelical, and certainly, from his correspondence, not a follower of the Bishop of Oxford. The Bishop of Oxford is quite out of the running, so great is the distrust of him by the country. That is the great fact, that has come out of the canvass of England. I thought, last night, of taking the Bishop of London, and countervailing his neological tendencies, which I think form the great objection to him, and, of course, his great recommendation in the eyes of H.M., by raising Jackson[1] to London. He is orthodox and Protestant. . . .

Tait was a Liberal and a Broad Churchman, unacceptable to Disraeli on the score both of politics and of

---

[1] Bishop of Lincoln.

theology. Accordingly Disraeli fought with passion against his appointment, coming out of the royal closet, it was noticed, in great excitement, and telling Malmesbury ' Don't bring any more bothers before me; I have enough already to drive a man mad.' But, having no really satisfactory candidate of his own, he had to give way in the end; and the Church thereby gained a statesman on the throne of Canterbury, but one whose want of sympathy with the Oxford school impaired his usefulness in the troubled times which followed. Tait, in his diary, described with a dry humour his interview with the Prime Minister after the nomination.

He harangued me on the state of the Church; spoke of rationalists, explained that those now so called did not follow Paulus. He spoke at large of his desire to rally a Church party, which, omitting the extremes of rationalism and ritualism, should unite all other sections of the Church; alluded to his Church appointments as aiming at this— Champneys, Merivale,[1] Wordsworth, Gregory, Leighton, myself, Jackson. He promised to support a Church Discipline Bill, but deprecated its being brought in by Lord Shaftesbury. Remarked that, whether in office or out, he had a large Church party. . . . I stated my views shortly, and we separated.[2]

For the see of London Dean Wellesley told Wilberforce that Disraeli proposed Christopher Wordsworth, the nephew of the poet, the learned Canon of Westminster. ' The Queen objected strongly; no experience; passing over Bishops, etc.; then she suggested Jackson, and two others, not you, because of Disraeli's expressed hostility; and Disraeli chose Jackson.' Though Jackson made a good Bishop of London, Disraeli had better have taken Derby's advice and proposed Wilberforce, whom the Queen would have accepted. Wilberforce's energy and organising power, his knowledge of the world and of society, his high reputation and influence in the Church, would have made him almost an ideal Bishop for

[1] The historian, appointed Dean of Ely.
[2] Tait's *Life*, Vol. I., p. 536.

London. Manners, writing to Disraeli two years later about the lament in the General Preface to the novels that no Churchman equal to the occasion had arisen from the Oxford movement, says: 'I doubt whether a Churchman was not produced by the Oxford move-ment—sufficiently a statesman, with all his faults, to have helped you greatly; and I have never under-stood why, when, for reasons I can appreciate, you sent Tait to Lambeth, you did not transfer Wilber-force to London.' The reason was that, as appears in letter after letter, Disraeli was told, from the most divergent quarters, that public opinion throughout the country would resent the appointment, and visit its displeasure at the polls on the Government responsible for it. It must be borne in mind that, though the world knows now how carefully and loyally the Bishop kept the *via media* of Anglicanism, he was still in 1868 outside his diocese widely suspected of Romeward tendencies, which had operated with fatal effect in his own family. Since he became Bishop all three of his brothers, and two brothers-in-law, of whom Manning was one, had joined the Roman Church; and in this very year the example was followed by his daughter and her husband. Disraeli can hardly be blamed for not facing the threatened storm; but, had he shown his wonted courage here, he would not have lost a useful ally or alienated a powerful party.

For the appointment of Wordsworth to the Bishopric of Lincoln, of Bright to a professorship, and of Leighton and Gregory to canonries, did not console the High Church party for the slight to their principal champion; and Wilberforce himself could not hide the bitterness of his disappointment. He wrote in his diary, ' I am trying to discipline myself, but feeling the affront,' and to a friend, ' In myself I really thank God; it very little disturbs me. I in my reason apprehend that by the common rule in such matters I had no right to be so treated; but I am really thankful in feeling so cool about it.' He had resented Gladstone's new policy and had been working cordially with Disraeli to save the Irish Church. But now he resumed his former intimate association with Gladstone, who became Prime Minister next month; and he was unsparing in condemnation of his rival. He immediately began to contrast the two men greatly to Disraeli's disadvantage, 'Gladstone as ever: great, earnest, and honest; as unlike the tricky Disraeli as possible'; and to smooth the way for Gladstone's Irish policy, by writing to Archbishop Trench, of Dublin, urging him to arrange a compromise. Trench had suggested delay, till Gladstone had realised the difficulties before him. The Bishop replied that this would be a wise course if they were dealing with 'a master of selfish cunning and unprincipled trickery,' 'a mere mystery-man like Disraeli,' whose whole idea was 'to use the Church to keep himself in office'; but happily in Gladstone they had 'a man of the highest and noblest principle.'[1] And when *Lothair* was published, in which he himself was pertrayed, the Bishop wrote: 'My wrath against D. has burnt before this so fiercely that it seems to have burnt up all the materials for burning and to be like an exhausted prairie-fire—full of black stumps, burnt grass, and all abominations.' Fortunately the Bishop was translated in 1869, on Gladstone's motion, from Oxford to Winchester, so that he no longer had among his flock the statesman with whom he had for a time so zealously co-operated, but of whom, since his disregard of his diocesan's claims to promotion, he had come to think so meanly.

In the general result, with the conspicuous exception of the neglect of Wilberforce, the appointments for which Disraeli was responsible were not unsatisfactory; and his policy of fair division and of a clear insistence on the national character of the Church was a right policy. But it cannot be denied that in its application he pursued a seesaw and zigzag course, and laid himself open to Dean Wellesley's criticism that 'he rode the Protestant horse

---

[1] *Wilberforce*, Vol. III., pp. 277-279.

one day; then got frightened it had gone too far and was injuring the county elections, so he went right round.' The result was that, so far as his object was a political one, he did not succeed in it; there was no such union at the General Election, as he hoped for, of all parties in the Church to resist Gladstone's Irish policy. ' Bishoprics, once so much prized, are really graceless patronage now,' he wrote ruefully during the year to Derby; ' they bring no power.' The Crown had intervened in Church patronage in a decisive way, largely owing to the Minister's ignorance; had carried the Archbishop of its choice directly in his teeth, and had proved the determining factor in other appointments, including the striking nomination of Magee. Both in the principles which Her Majesty laid down, and in the divines whom she recommended, the Queen's intervention must command respect, and it attained, as well as deserved, success.

Disraeli maintained intimate and confidential relations with his predecessor Derby throughout this Government, and had constant recourse in all difficulties to his counsel. He even submitted the Queen's Speech to be delivered on the prorogation of Parliament to his revision. Derby made considerable alterations in the form, though not in the substance, of the draft; but only advanced these as suggestions, and hoped Disraeli would not think he had taken too great liberties with his ' skeleton.' Sensible as he was of his obligations to Derby and the house of Stanley, Disraeli sought, as Prime Minister, for opportunities of showing his gratitude and friendship. Early in the spring he paid his old chief the graceful compliment of placing at his disposal the lord-lieutenancy of Middlesex; and at the close of the session he found an official vacancy for Frederick Stanley, Derby's younger son, afterwards War Secretary, Governor-General of Canada, and the sixteenth earl. Derby declined the lord-lieutenancy, as he had no local connection with the county, and no local interest; but he was gratified by the political opening afforded to his son.

To Lord Derby.

Private. 10, DOWNING STREET, *July* 31, 1868.—Parliament being prorogued, I have had the pleasure of offering the Civil Lordship of the Admiralty to Frederick, and shall be gratified if he accept it. At any rate, it is an introduction to official life, and his tenure of office may last longer than some imagine.

We work at the elections with ceaseless energy. I have got the matter out of the hands of Spofforth, and placed in those of a limited, but influential, Committee of gentlemen, and it seems to work very well.

Lord Abercorn is to be an Irish Duke, and Mayo our Indian Viceroy: so the Irish Government may be satisfied. What the Irish title is to be I can't tell you. The Prince of Wales wants it to be Ulster, of which he is Earl,[1] but as I would not countenance this, H.R.H. is to go to the Queen to-morrow anent. I should think the regal brow would be clouded, and that our friend must be content with being Duke of Abercorn. He is very happy, and six inches taller.

I had thought of offering the Irish Secretaryship to Elcho, a friend of Lord Abercorn, but His Excellency seems to think that the political connection might disturb the fervor of the friendship. If so, I think it must be John Manners, who is sensible, conciliatory, and very painstaking, and certainly will not 'override' Abercorn, or quarrel with anybody. Then Elcho might have J.M.'s place. But would he take it without the Cabinet ? And Henry Lennox will resign if he be not promoted ! Nothing seems to satisfy him, and if he had Henry Corry's place, he would soon want mine.[2]

The Cabinet to-day was very tranquil, a great contrast to three or four months ago. Cairns is a great success at the Council Board.

Short as was Disraeli's term of office, he had not merely to give an Archbishop to Canterbury, but a Governor-General both to Canada and to India. The first of these two posts was offered in succession to Mayo and to Manners, but was eventually filled by a seasoned administrator, Sir John Young, afterwards Lord Lisgar, who had been High Commissioner for the Ionian Islands and Governor of New South Wales. Mayo, who had done

---

[1] Derby pointed out in reply that it was the Duke of Edinburgh, and not the Prince of Wales, who was Earl of Ulster.

[2] Wilson Patten, created at the close of the Government Lord Winmarleigh, was ultimately appointed Irish Secretary.

yeoman service for his country and his party as thrice
Chief Secretary for Ireland, was sent to India.

From Lord John Manners.

April 30, '68.—In spite of all your encouraging kindness,
for which I shall never cease to be grateful, I have finally decided—mainly on private and family grounds—to decline the
great post offered to me last week; and have written to the
Duke of Buckingham to that effect.

Though private considerations have determined this decision,
I own I derive satisfaction from thinking that it will enable
me to remain by your side to the end of the most eventful
chapter in our political life.

Let it terminate as it may, it will always be to me a source
of unalloyed pleasure to have seen you at the summit of power,
and to have had my humbler fortunes linked—unbrokenly—
to yours.

To Sir Stafford Northcote.

10, DOWNING STREET, *June* 9, 1868.—I could have wished
to have replied to your letter [1] instantly, but every moment,
yesterday, was taken up.   Although your loss to me would be
not easily calculable, I don't think I could allow it to weigh
against your personal interests, for which, I trust, I have
always shown a due regard.   But the Indian V. Royalty has
always been destined for Lord Mayo, who did not wish to
return to Ireland, and I spoke to Lord Derby, with that view,
when his Government was formed, and when you did not
occupy that great office of State,[2] which you have since administered with so much satisfaction to the country, and with
so much credit to yourself.   Certainly, Lord Mayo's administration of Ireland affords no reason for disturbing the prospect
in which, for a considerable time, he has been permitted to
indulge, and, being myself now at the head of affairs, it would
hardly become me to shrink from the fulfilment of expectations, which I sanctioned and supported as a subordinate
member of the Ministry.

I could not speak to you on this matter before, because,
when the prospects of the Ministry were not as bright as they
are at present, Lord Mayo had nearly made up his mind to
go to Canada, when the next mail brought the news, that the

---

[1] Northcote's name had been canvassed, among others, as that of a
possible Viceroy; and he wrote to say that, while he would very much like
to go to India, he did not put himself forward as a candidate, and would
most cheerfully accept Disraeli's decision. Only, for family reasons, he
should like to know, as soon as might be convenient, what the decision was.

[2] Indian Secretary.

wise Parliament of the Dominion had reduced the salary of
the Governor-General from £10,000 to £6,000 per annum,
thereby depriving themselves of ever having the benefit of
the services of a first-class man.[1]

You did quite right in addressing me directly and frankly,
and I reply to you in the same spirit. I should be more than
sorry to occasion you disappointment, because I highly esteem
and regard you, and am anxious, so far as it is in my power,
to advance, and secure, your fortunes.

How well Mayo justified Disraeli's choice is recorded in
English and Indian history. But the Liberals, indignant
at the wealth of patronage that had fallen to a Ministry
which they maintained to have no constitutional claim to
remain in office, raised a loud outcry at the appointment
in their press, and intimated in no uncertain fashion
that, if they got a majority in the election, they would
cancel it. This was no mere journalistic bravado, as
has sometimes been asserted since. The correspondence
of the Liberal leaders shows that cancellation was
seriously contemplated. ' If you cancel Mayo's appointment,' Granville wrote to Gladstone on September 28,
' what do you think of Salisbury ? It would be a teat
taken away from our pigs, but it would weaken the
Opposition.' ' I think the suggestion an excellent one,'
Gladstone replied.[2] If Mayo was after all left undisturbed, and the Duke of Argyll, Gladstone's Indian
Secretary, was able to assert that no advice to remove
him was given to the Crown or contemplated by the
Gladstone Government, the reason may be found in the
following letters:

From Lord Stanley.

Private. F.O., *Sept.* 17, 1868.—I hear from more than
one quarter, and in a manner that leaves no doubt on my
mind as to the truth of the report, that the Opposition have
decided, in the event of their coming in before the end of the
year, to remove Mayo, even if he should have sailed, from the
Gov.-Gen.ship. . . .

---

[1] The Queen was advised to withhold her assent to the bill reducing the
salary, which accordingly remains £10,000 per annum.

[2] Fitzmaurice's *Granville*, Vol. I., p. 541.

I think this worth naming, as you may be able to stop it *in limine* by getting the Queen to express her disapproval. The step is an extremely unusual one—the only precedent being the removal of Lord Heytesbury to make way for Lord Auckland, which caused the Afghan War. . .

To Lord Stanley.

BALMORAL, *Sept.* 21, 1868.— . . . Your hint about Mayo was *à propos,* for our Mistress herself touched upon the business. She thinks the contemplated recall of her representative will weaken her name and authority in India: as if she were a mere pageant ! This is the Constitutional view, and I confirmed it. There is a material difference in recalling a Govr.-Genl. of the Company and the Vice-Roy of the Sovereign. Clearly.

H.M. recurs to her hope, that, whatever happens, we shall gain a material accession of strength. I told her the truth—that all the stories about, respecting the result of the General Election, were alike untrustworthy: that the great body of the new constituency in towns were unpledged: that the new electors in the counties were reported as singularly conservative; and the victory, at the last moment, would be to the party, which was wealthiest, and best organised.

She does not conceal, from me at least, her personal wishes. . . .

Magnanimity to foes and gratitude to friends were among Disraeli's most notable qualities; and in both respects power revealed the man. In all the early stages of his career he had been held up to ridicule by John Leech in *Punch* with a mercilessness which was far removed from the *bonhomie* with which the artist and the journal treated other public men. But when his attention was called in 1868 to the fact that Leech's widow, who had been granted a pension by the Liberal Government, was dead, and that his two children were more than ever in want of assistance, he had no hesitation in continuing the pension to the family, remembering only the dead artist's genius and disregarding the persistent animosity of his pencil. His enduring gratitude to a benefactor was manifested in a still more striking manner.

For many years after the caprice of the Duke of Portland, in calling in the money advanced by the Bentincks

for the purchase of Hughenden, had thrown Disraeli back
upon the moneylenders,[1] his private affairs were in an
unsatisfactory condition and he was greatly hampered by
the exorbitant interest on his apparently still accumulating debts.   In the winter of 1862–1863 fortune sent him
a much-needed relief.   The Conservative cause in the
North had a strong supporter in a Yorkshire squire,
Andrew Montagu, of Melton, Yorks, and Papplewick,
Notts; son of Fountayne Wilson, who had sat in Parliament for the undivided county of York; and representative, in the female line, of the famous Charles Montagu,
Earl of Halifax, the Finance Minister of William III.
Andrew Montagu was a bachelor of great wealth and of
somewhat eccentric habits.   The story runs that he made
inquiries in that winter of the Conservative headquarters
as to how best he could use his wealth to promote the
success of his party.   Among other suggestions he was
told that a rich man could render no more acceptable
service to the cause than by buying up the debts of the
leader in the Commons, and charging him only a reasonable interest in the place of the exactions under which
he was suffering.   He showed himself disposed to
entertain the idea, and was put by Rose, through whom
the negotiation was carried on, into communication with
Disraeli's friend, Baron Lionel de Rothschild, who was
himself ready to help Disraeli pecuniarily, but who, as
Disraeli wrote, preferred to give, not lend, to his friends.
Rothschild and Montagu met, with the result that, in
return for a mortgage on Hughenden, accompanied, it
may be, by some guarantee or assurance from Rothschild,
Montagu assumed the whole responsibility for Disraeli's
debts, charging him apparently merely the 3 per cent.
which was then the interest on Consols instead of the
10 per cent. or more that he was previously paying.   The
immensity of the service thus rendered to Disraeli may be
gauged by the fact that he estimated the resulting increase
in his annual income, in one letter at £4,200, and in

---

[1] See Vol. I., p. 968.

another at £5,000. His gross income in 1866 appears to have been nearly £9,000 a year; but by that time he had received £30,000 as Mrs. Brydges Willyams's residuary legatee.[1]

Disraeli was anxious to show his gratitude by recommending his benefactor for a peerage. It was perhaps rather a hazardous step; but Rose, who encouraged his chief, quoted as a precedent in its favour the Carrington peerage, conferred at Pitt's instance on Robert Smith, the banker, to whom the Minister was under great personal and pecuniary obligations. He advised Disraeli to disregard an anonymous letter of warning. He pointed out that this was no case of an obscure man of recently acquired wealth. Montagu's father had formerly refused a peerage, and he himself, though eccentric, was a man of great possessions, good family, and political influence in the county of York. Thus reassured, Disraeli made the offer.

To Andrew Montagu.

BALMORAL CASTLE, *Sept.* 20, 1868.—It is my intention, if agreeable to you, to recommend Her Majesty to confer on you the dignity of the Peerage.

Altho', unlike your father, who was the last representative of the undivided county of York, you have not chosen to avail yourself of a seat in the House of Commons, your vast possessions, noble lineage, and devotion to the Conservative party, fully authorise this act on the part of the Queen, as one in entire conformity with the social custom, and the Constitutional practice, of the Realm.

Montagu declined the honour, mainly on the ground that his usefulness to Disraeli and to the Conservative party in the forthcoming elections would be seriously impaired if he accepted a title. His friends in Yorkshire, where he was a leading worker for the Conservative cause, would think he wanted to save himself from a sinking ship. In other circumstances he might accept a favour from his ' best friend and benefactor,' but not in the autumn of 1868.

[1] See Vol. I., III., ch. 13.

The election was to be fought upon domestic issues, and it would avail Disraeli little with the new electors that he was able to boast, with good reason, that a great improvement had supervened in our foreign relations by the substitution of Stanley for Russell in the direction of our policy. He dwelt on this improvement on more than one occasion, but especially in a speech at Merchant Taylors' Hall in June.

When we acceded to office the name of England was a name of suspicion and distrust in every Court and Cabinet. There was no possibility of that cordial action with any of the Great Powers which is the only security for peace; and, in consequence of that want of cordiality, wars were frequently occurring. But since we entered upon office, and public affairs were administered by my noble friend [Stanley] . . . I say that all this has changed; that there never existed between England and foreign Powers a feeling of greater cordiality and confidence than now prevails; that while we have shrunk from bustling and arrogant intermeddling, we have never taken refuge in selfish isolation; and the result has been that there never was a Government in this country which has been more frequently appealed to for its friendly offices than the one which now exists.

The Liberals could only reply that a considerable improvement had been effected in Clarendon's few months of office after Palmerston's death, and reproach Disraeli, in Gladstone's words, with his language of 'inflated and exaggerated eulogy.' That Stanley's conduct of foreign affairs was eminently satisfactory was the general opinion of all parties.

It looked at one time as if Disraeli would have the good fortune of settling the acute questions which separated this country from America. His constant yet dignified friendliness to the United States throughout the troubled period of the Civil War merited such a success. The difficulty mainly arose from the negligence, in the observance of neutrality during that period, of the Palmerston Administration, and especially of Russell its Foreign Secretary, who had permitted the *Alabama* to escape from a British port to prey on American commerce. Russell had obstinately maintained the correctness of his action, or rather inaction, and refused to refer the questions at issue to arbitration in any form. Stanley, as Foreign Minister, had adopted a more reasonable course. He was prepared to accept arbitration; but he resisted, with practically universal approval here, an attempt by the American Secretary of State to include in the reference the question of the recognition by this country of the belligerent rights of the Confederate States—a recognition which the Federals had themselves made in proclaiming a blockade. But the speech in which Stanley announced his policy in March, 1868, was so conciliatory as well as firm that public opinion in America was favourably impressed; and, as a result, when a vacancy arose in the summer in the United States Ministry in London, a notable man, Senator Reverdy Johnson, was appointed Minister, with, as Stanley understood, 'very conciliatory instructions.' When Johnson arrived, Stanley was in Switzerland in attendance on the Queen; and so it fell to Disraeli to show the appreciation of the British Government. He immediately asked the newcomer down to Hughenden to meet a distinguished party, including the hero of the hour, Sir Robert Napier, just created Lord Napier of Magdala, and the historian Lord Stanhope.

To Lord Stanley.

HUGHENDEN, *Aug.* 16, 1868.—. . . Reverdy J. has not arrived. I will send a Secy. the moment he does, and ask him down here. The hero of Magdala is coming on the 24th. I should like to kill them with the same stone.

I have given orders for the new Adm[iralt]y Patent to be prepared, as I hear there is no danger, now, of any election being precipitated at Preston, so Fred. will be soon at work: Sir M. Hicks Beach to be U. Secy. Home, and Jem Lowther to have his place in the Poor Law Board, which he will represent in the Commons. Thus we get the young ones, who promise, into the firm, and they will sit on the front bench, wherever that may be.

To Montagu Corry.

HUGHENDEN, *Aug.* 21.—. . . Understand the Minister of the Un: States comes on Tuesday. . . . Remember, if you can, the venison: and oh ! don't forget some work of the illustrious and noble author,[1] bound, and let me have it in time to put book plate in: otherwise, enemy for life. . . .

Aug. 23.—. . . I count on your punctuality to-morrow: as I hear to-day, there is to be a triumphal arch at the entrance of the Park, and Mr. Coates and the tenantry on horseback to escort the hero ! I entirely rely on your being the Master of the Ceremonies. . . .

To Lord Stanley.

HUGHENDEN, *Aug.* 26, '68.—You sent me a most amusing letter. Do you know, I think you an excellent letter writer; terse and picturesque; seizing the chief points, and a sense of humor.

Reverdy Johnson is here, and gets on very well. The ladies like him. He has eleven children, and 33 grand-children: so they call him Grandpapa. He has only one eye, and that a very ugly one; and, yet, at a distance, looks something like old Lord Lansdowne, after a somewhat serious illness. His manners, tho', at first, rather abrupt and harsh, are good; he is self-possessed, and turns out genial.

Stanhope, who is here, seems to delight in him, and thinks it a *coup de maître* to have asked him here, and that the *Alabama* and all other claims will be settled forthwith. His visit to Hughenden is to our joint credit.

They all like Napier of Magdala very much: he is interesting and graceful, and tells even a story—but not too long: Chinese or Abyssinian.

Stanley, in his speech in March, had expressed his readiness to consider a suggestion which Seward, the American Secretary of State, had thrown out, of a General Commission to which the claims of both countries might be referred. On these lines a convention was arranged in the autumn with Reverdy Johnson, with a special proviso for the reference of the *Alabama* claims to a neutral Sovereign, in case the Commission should not agree. Though the American Minister at the Lord Mayor's banquet in November spoke of the matter as settled,

[1] Lord Stanhope.

the good work was not actually completed when the Government went out of office; but Clarendon, the new Foreign Secretary, took it up and brought it to formal signature in January. Internal politics in the United States, however, caused the convention to miscarry. It had to pass the Senate, then in antagonism to President Johnson and his executive; and the electors in the autumn had chosen a new President, who would wish to have his hands free when he assumed office in March. More also might be hoped from England under a Liberal than under a Conservative Administration. All these considerations determined the Senate to reject the convention; and the difficulty was left to be settled in a costly and less satisfactory fashion by the Gladstone Government a few years later.

It is natural to search Disraeli's correspondence during this period of office, to see how far he realised the catastrophe which was impending over France and over Europe, owing to the rapid rise of Prussian power and the jealousy with which it was regarded to the west of the Rhine. In obedience to his own inclinations and the Queen's command,[1] he kept a watchful eye on the situation abroad; but it cannot be maintained that he saw much farther than his neighbours. In the August of 1867 the French Emperor and Empress had paid a visit to the Emperor of Austria at Salzburg, ostensibly to condole with him on the tragic fate in Mexico in the previous June of the Emperor Maximilian, Francis Joseph's kinsman. But the visit also signified a certain drawing together of two Powers, of which one had been defeated, and the other was threatened, by the growing might of Prussia. Disraeli's letters of that date show how he viewed the European kaleidoscope.

To Lord Stanley.

HUGHENDEN, *Sept.* 1, 1867.—. . . I have heard nothing from the R[othschild]s. I observe, they never write, and

[1] See p. 207.

only speak, indeed, on these matters in a corner, and a whisper.

To form a judgment of the present state of affairs, one must be greatly guided by our knowledge of the personal character of the chief actors.

The Emperor will never act alone; Bismarck wants quiet; and Beust,[1] tho' vain, is shrewd and prudent.

Gortc[hako]ff[2] is the only man, who could, and would, act with the Emperor, in order to gain his own ends, on which he is much set, but if the Emperor combines with him, he will so alarm, and agonise, Austria, that she will throw herself into the arms of Prussia, in order that an united Germany may save her from the destruction of all her Danubian dreams.

I think affairs will trail on, at least for a time, and the longer the time, the stronger will be your position. In such a balanced state of circumstances, you will be master. . . .

GROSVENOR GATE, *Oct.* 14, 1867.—I thought it wise to reconnoitre, and called on our friend[3] yesterday.

He said the Emperor was no longer master of the position, and repeated this rather significantly.

In time, I extracted from him, that they had information from Paris, that there was a secret treaty between Prussia and Italy.

I rather expressed doubts about this, and hinted that it seemed inconsistent with what had reached us, that there was an understanding between France and Italy, that the Emperor should give notice of his course, etc.

He was up to all this, and showed, or rather read, me a telegram, I should think of yesterday, in precisely the same words as you expressed, so I inferred the same person had given the news to Fane and his correspondent. Probably Nigra[4] himself.

The information of the secret treaty had arrived subsequently, and he stuck to it, and evidently believed it. . . .

The Berlin Ministry have consulted another member of the family about ironclads. They are going to expend 1½ mill. sterling immediately thereon, and told him they thought of having the order executed in America, as, in case of war with France, the ships would not be allowed to depart if they were constructed in England. . . .

In the spring of 1868 one of those pretended reductions of Prussian armament, which have occasionally been advertised since, was understood to be in progress at

---

[1] Austrian Foreign Minister.   [2] Russian Chancellor.
[3] Baron Lionel de Rothschild.   [4] Italian Minister in Paris.

Berlin; and Disraeli, who should have had enough experience to disbelieve, was caught by a story which was rightly treated by Stanley as not worth serious attention.

To Lord Stanley.

GROSVENOR GATE, *April* 23, '68.—This appears to me important: Charles [Rothschild] is virtually Bismarck.[1]

A few days ago, B. was all fury against France, and declared that France was resolved on war, etc.: but on Monday the Rs. wrote to Berlin, that they understood England was so satisfied with Prussia, so convinced, that she really wished peace, etc., that England would take no step, at the instance of France, which would imply doubt of Prussia, etc.

This is the answer. I can't help thinking, that you have another grand opportunity of securing the peace of Europe and establishing your fame. . . .

[ENCLOSURE.]

Charles Rothschild to Baron Rothschild.

(*Telegram.*) BERLIN, *April* 23, 9.45 a.m. — Tell your friend that from the 1st of May army reduction here has been decided upon, and will be continued on a larger scale if same system is adopted elsewhere. Details by post.

To Lord Stanley.

10, DOWNING STREET, *April* 24, '68.—Bernstorff never knows anything.[2] I am sure there is something on the tapis, and I want you to have the credit of it. Vide Reuter's Tels: in *Times* of to-day: ' Berlin, Ap: 23,' rumor on the Bourse, etc.

What I should do would be to telegraph to Loftus, and bring things to a point, and then act.

I feel sure it will be done without you, if you don't look sharp. You risk nothing, and may gain everything.

April 25, 4 o'c.—I feel persuaded it's all true. They have a letter this morning in detail, explaining the telegram, and enforcing it. The writer, fresh from Bismarck himself, does not speak as if doubt were possible: gives all the details of the military reductions to commence on 1st May, and the larger ones, which will be immediately set afoot, if France responds.

How can you explain all this ? What of Loftus ?

[1] 'They see one another daily,' was Stanley's note on the letter. To avoid misunderstanding, it should be added that there has not been, since 1901, any branch of the house of Rothschild in the German Empire.

[2] Stanley had replied that the Ambassador knew nothing of intended reductions.

From Lord Stanley.

Private. *Sat.,* **6** p.m. [*April* 25, 1868].—The telegram confirms your friend's expectations. I spoke to La Tour [d'Auvergne][1] in anticipation of it, 'Supposing the news were true, what would you do ?' His answer was discouraging He says (and indeed the tel. confirms him in that respect) that Prussian reductions mean nothing. 'What security do they give, when it is admitted that the men can be brought back in a week's time, if not in 24 hours ?' I am compelled to own there is some force in the reply. Still, with the facts actually before us, we may press them a little.

Throughout the summer and early autumn Disraeli remained sanguine of success at the polls. Derby, however, told him in August that 'Stanley's language as to the result of the elections is absolute despondency—he hardly seems to think the battle worth fighting.'

To Lord Derby.

Private. HUGHENDEN, *August* 23, 1868.—. . . I heard from Stanley[2] to-day, who seems rather jolly, and wonderfully well. He makes excursions in the mountains, and takes very long walks. He confesses he is 'enjoying himself.' He has not seen much of his Royal Mistress, but he says that, on Sunday last, she was looking very well, and in high good humor—does not talk much politics, but highly disapproves of the Opposition, praises her Ministers, and is very anxious that the elections should go right. According to your last, she did not get hold of the right man to encourage her on that subject; but the fact is Stanley does not know anything about it; he reads newspapers and believes in them; and as they are all written by the same clique, or coteries almost identical in thought, feeling, life and manners, they harp on the same string. It is very difficult to say, in this rapid age, what may occur in a General Election, which will not now happen for nearly a quarter of a year, but I myself should not be surprised if the result might astonish, yet, the Bob Lowes, Higgins, Delanes, and all that class of Pall Mall journal intellect. . . .

The newspapers, and Stanley, who, like the newspapers, had a shrewd instinct for average opinion, saw more clearly

---

[1] Of the French Embassy in London.
[2] At Lucerne in attendance on the Queen.

than the Conservative leader and his advisers what was going to happen. The party Committee to whom was entrusted the duty of conducting the elections assured Disraeli that there was reason to expect that the Conservatives would make sufficient gains to give them more than half the House of Commons: 266 from England, 51 from Ireland, and 13 from Scotland; 330 in all out of a House of 658. With this report before him Disraeli, absorbed in the heavy and responsible work of Government, was apparently content to wait in comparative passivity for the country's verdict. He had given the vote to a hitherto unenfranchised million of his fellow-countrymen, belonging in the great majority to the working classes; but so absolutely incapable was he of demagogic arts that he neglected, almost to a culpable degree, to endeavour to utilise his great legislative achievement to secure their support for himself and his party. The Liberals went up and down the country explaining that, though the Conservatives had passed the Reform Bill, the thanks of the new voters for the boon were really due to Gladstone and Bright; and Gladstone and several of his colleagues undertook impassioned electoral campaigns in which the new Irish policy of their party was eloquently expounded. But Disraeli contented himself with issuing an address, undoubtedly of some length and elaboration, to the electors of Bucks; and, as there was no contest in his constituency, with one speech on the hustings on re-election—a speech which was not even delivered till after the verdict of the boroughs had been largely given against his Ministry.

The address was drafted early in September, and during the remainder of the month was submitted to his principal colleagues for criticism and emendation; particularly to Cairns, on whose judgment Disraeli had come very thoroughly to rely, and whom he begged ' to give his whole mind to the affair, and, if necessary, to rewrite it.' No serious alteration was suggested by Cairns or others, and at the beginning of October the document was

issued. In the forefront Disraeli claimed the confidence
of the party and the country as Derby's political heir,
who had pursued his old chief's policy ' without deviation.'
The settlement of the Reform question on broad lines,
a foreign policy which established the just influence
of England, the successful expedition to Abyssinia, and
the strengthening of the naval and military forces, were
all put forward as grounds for support. But, owing to
the tactics of the Liberal party, Ireland had necessarily
to be the main subject of the address. He claimed that
Ministers had, by vigilance and firmness, baffled the
Fenian conspiracy, and had also pursued a wise policy
of sympathy and conciliation. But Gladstone had
suddenly proposed ' a change of the fundamental laws
of the realm ' and ' a dissolution of the union between
Church and State.' To that policy Ministers had offered,
and would offer, ' an uncompromising resistance. The
connection of religion with the exercise of political
authority is one of the main safeguards of the civilisation
of man.' No doubt the new policy was only to be partially
applied in the first instance, but the religious integrity of
the community would be frittered away. Confiscation,
too, was contagious. Finally the religious security
which was the result of the royal supremacy would
be endangered, and Rome alone would profit.

Amid the discordant activity of many factions there moves
the supreme purpose of one Power. The philosopher may
flatter himself he is advancing the cause of enlightened progress; the sectarian may be roused to exertion by anticipations
of the downfall of ecclesiastical systems. These are transient
efforts; vain and passing aspirations. The ultimate triumph,
were our Church to fall, would be to that Power which would
substitute for the authority of our Sovereign the supremacy
of a foreign Prince; to that Power with whose tradition,
learning, discipline, and organisation our Church alone has,
hitherto, been able to cope, and that, too, only when supported
by a determined and devoted people.

In this address Disraeli made his main appeal for
confidence to the Protestantism of the nation. There

is no doubt that, misled by the violent outbreak at the time of the Papal aggression, by the suspicions arising out of the Roman missionary propaganda in society during the sixties, and by the popular dislike of the developments of Ritualism, he overrated the electoral strength of a feeling which undoubtedly was widely spread.

As the election drew near, the signs of Liberal victory became more evident, though Disraeli, still sanguine, tried to explain them away. Derby, surveying the field now from an outside standpoint, anticipated unsatisfactory results generally, save in his own county of Lancashire. ' I am afraid,' he wrote on October 29, ' that, where it has any operation, the minority clause will operate unfavourably for us in almost every instance, and there appears to be a lamentable apathy on the part of the Conservatives in abandoning seats which might fairly be contested, or even of availing ourselves of the rival pretensions of Liberal candidates for a single seat.'

To Montagu Corry.

Private. 10, DOWNING STREET, *Nov*. 3, '68.—Might not these two queries lead to a solution of the difficulty—perhaps the fallacy—of yesterday's speculations on the General Election ?

1 : Was there ever a General Election in which half the seats were not uncontested ?

2 : Is it not a fact, that the winning side always, or generally, gains ⅔rds of the contests ?

For illustration, examine Palmerston's two dissolutions: China—and 1865. And then Peel's in 1834 when he gained 100 seats : and dissolution of 1841 when he gained 80.

These are materials from which an expert might deduce instructive results.

If I could have them before my audience I should be glad.

Nov. 10.—Send me a line of news. Our men seem to be running away. . . .

On the very eve of the dissolution came the celebration of Lord Mayor's Day, and Disraeli at the Guildhall banquet gaily affected to entertain a confident expectation that he would be the Lord Mayor's guest in the following November, and chaffed the Liberals over their boastful and braggart methods of conducting the campaign.

I think I have read somewhere that it is the custom of undisciplined hosts on the eve of a battle to anticipate and celebrate their triumph by horrid sounds and hideous yells, the sounding of cymbals, the beating of terrible drums, the shrieks and screams of barbaric horns. But when the struggle comes, and the fight takes place, it is sometimes found that the victory is not to them, but to those who are calm and collected: the victory is to those who have arms of precision, though they may make no noise—to those who have the breechloaders, the rocket brigade, and the Armstrong artillery.

One of the most frequent and most telling weapons which the Opposition used in their campaign was the assertion that the Government were quite as ready to disestablish the Irish Church as they were themselves. ' There is as much chance,' wrote Disraeli in the vain hope of silencing this slander, ' of the Tory party proposing to disestablish the Protestant Church in Ireland as there is of their proposing to abrogate the Monarchy.' It was a great misfortune that Disraeli could not bring his colleagues to agree to concurrent endowment; but, that being so, Ministers, however ready for reform, could hardly for the election take up any other position than that of simple resistance to Gladstone's plan of destruction. This was naturally distasteful to the reforming section of the Cabinet, and especially to Stanley. He pressed his views again on Disraeli in the autumn, and Disraeli replied, on September 26, from Balmoral: ' I highly appreciate your criticisms, as you well know; but I think your views about the Irish Church are of a school of thought that has passed. Excuse my presumption. I don't think compromise is now practicable.' Both Derby and Disraeli feared that Stanley, when he gave, according to promise, a full explanation of his views to the electors of Lynn, might seriously embarrass the future of the Conservative party; and the father, now as on previous occasions, relied upon

Disraeli to keep the son straight. It was an immense relief to both chiefs to find from the next morning's paper that the Foreign Secretary had been cautious and discreet.

To Lord Stanley.

10, DOWNING STREET, *Nov.* 10, '68.—I should like to have seen you, for a moment, before you departed. I shall have sleepless nights, until I have read your Lynn words.

Pray don't stab me in the back after all the incredible exertions I am making for the good cause.

And don't believe newspapers, and newspaper writers, too much. The result of the General Election, rest assured, will surprise all the students of that literature.

Nov. 14.—Perfect !

I am told our own party are enthusiastic: but all praise it. It must do us great good.

Stanley's speech was at the opening of the polls. By the time that the county returns were beginning, and that Disraeli was elected unopposed for Bucks, it was clear that Ministers would be defeated;[1] and the Prime Minister, in marked contrast to Gladstone's bellicose utterances, felt himself justified in taking a detached and impartial view of the situation on the hustings at Aylesbury. To this happy contingency we owe a priceless appreciation of the Irish character.

The Irishman is an imaginative being. He lives on an island in a damp climate, and contiguous to the melancholy ocean. He has no variety of pursuit. There is no nation in the world that leads so monotonous a life as the Irish, because their only occupation is the cultivation of the soil before them. These men are discontented because they are not amused. The Irishman in other countries, when he has a fair field for his talents in various occupations, is equal, if not superior, to most races; and it is not the fault of the Government that there is not that variety of occupation in Ireland. I may say with frankness that I think it is the fault of the Irish. If they led that kind of life which would invite the introduction of capital into the country, all this ability might be utilised; and instead of those feelings which they acquire by brooding over the history of their country, a great

[1] 'Our shadows seem to grow very long,' Disraeli wrote on the day of the election to Northcote.

part of which is merely traditionary, you would find men acquiring fortunes, and arriving at conclusions on politics entirely different from those which they now offer.[1]

Derby, while singing the praises of his own county of Lancashire, gave Disraeli a gloomy exposition of the general upshot of the elections.

From Lord Derby.

Confidential. KNOWSLEY, *Nov.* 22, 1868.—On looking over the returns, which are now nearly completed, I am sorry to see that our numbers will not only greatly disappoint your sanguine hopes, but will fall considerably below even my more modest anticipations. Even taking the most favourable view of the elections which are yet to take place, I cannot make out that Gladstone's majority will be less, and probably more, than a hundred. I am happy to think however that my county at least has done its duty. I told you I hoped to secure 18 out of the 32 seats[2]—we have done that already, if, as I have every reason to believe, we have carried both seats in the North-East. There are four seats remaining, out of which I have every hope of carrying three, including this division, in which we shall defeat Gladstone by not less than a thousand. We have lost Wigan by sheer mismanagement, and Warrington temporarily by rascality; the Mayor's poll clerk, who has absconded, having omitted 50 or 60 of Greenall's supporters, whose votes appear on the books of both parties. . . .

In the midst of our disasters, let me congratulate you, which I do very sincerely, on your speech at your nomination. It was perfectly suited to the occasion, calm, temperate, and dignified, and a striking contrast to the balderdash and braggadocio in which Gladstone has been indulging on his stumping tour—and which, I am happy to say, has done him more harm than good. The fate of the Government however is, I apprehend, decided.

Household suffrage, on its first experiment, produced results which were very unfavourable to its authors. The working men accepted the Liberal contention as to the real giver of their franchise; and were seduced by the captivating cries of religious equality and justice to Ireland. Accordingly, the boroughs, save in Lancashire,

[1] Aylesbury, Nov. 19, 1868.
[2] The final result for Lancashire showed 19 Conservatives to 13 Liberals.

declared with considerable unanimity against the Government; but the reduction of the occupation franchise in the counties operated favourably to the Conservatives, and enabled them to appear in Parliament as a considerable and coherent, if a reduced, minority. Unsatisfactory as was the general result, which, roughly speaking, doubled the majority of sixty which the Liberals had held in the last Parliament, there were several individual returns which were calculated, in some measure, to console the losers. Gladstone, in spite of a campaign of copious oratory, was rejected by the Lancastrian constituency which had come to his rescue after his defeat at Oxford; and he would sit in the new Parliament as the junior member for the metropolitan borough of Greenwich. Lancashire further gratified the Tory party and the house of Stanley by returning Frederick Stanley in the place of Lord Hartington; and in two important metropolitan constituencies victories were won for the party by two men who were to be among the ablest of Disraeli's younger colleagues in his last Administration—William Henry Smith ousted John Stuart Mill from Westminster, and Lord George Hamilton, then a young guardsman, came in at the top of the poll for Middlesex. If there was considerable slaughter among Tory lawyers, the failure of Roebuck, Milner-Gibson, H. Austin Bruce, Bernal Osborne, and Horsman—to name the more conspicuous of the Liberal notabilities who fell—must have brought some balm to Disraeli's spirit. By the operation of the minority clause a Conservative was returned also with three Liberals for the City of London, and Disraeli's Liberal friend, Baron Lionel de Rothschild, whom he had done so much to seat in the House, was rejected.

The country had registered a decisive verdict against Ministers. What ought they to do? According to the old precedents, they ought to meet Parliament as if nothing had happened, and wait to be defeated either on the election of Speaker or on an amendment to the

Address. This was the course pursued by Melbourne's
Government in 1841; but Disraeli had condemned it
then as a policy resting on constitutional fictions and not
on facts, and so causing harmful and unnecessary delay.[1]
Ministers, now as then, had been defeated in Parliament,
had thereupon appealed from Parliament to the country,
and had had at the polls their defeat confirmed and
emphasised. It was advisable, he thought, to acknowledge the fact and resign at once. As was his frequent
custom in this Government, he first talked the matter
over with Stanley, who had independently come to
the same conclusion. Disraeli's two other most important colleagues, Hardy and Cairns, agreed; and the Queen
threw the weight of her influence into the scale. Apart
from her invariable preference for realities and readiness
to accept political facts even if unpalatable to her, Her
Majesty was naturally anxious to have the political
changes completed, so far as possible, before the recurrence
of the sad anniversary of her loss on December 14.

While the concurrence of the Queen and of Disraeli's
principal colleagues made it probable that the assent of the
Cabinet would be secured for immediate resignation, it
was certain that the country would be surprised, and it
was possible that the party might be offended. Accordingly, it was necessary, as Disraeli wrote to Derby, to
accompany resignation 'by some simultaneous act
which should reassure and satisfy the party'; 'some
proceeding,' as he wrote to Hardy, 'which leaves no doubt
in the minds of our friends, in Parliament and the country,
of our determination to stand by our policy of [? on] disestablishment.' As Parliament was not sitting, this was
difficult. At first Disraeli thought of effecting his purpose
by an open letter to Derby; but finally decided to send
a circular to all Conservative peers and members of
Parliament. The Cabinet accepted the advice of the
Prime Minister, backed by his most influential colleagues,
in spite of a strong letter from Derby in the contrary sense,

---

[1] See Vol. I., p. 514.

written to Stanley, and read, at the writer's request, both to Disraeli and apparently also to the Cabinet. 'It does not alter my opinion,' Disraeli told Stanley. 'However, the Cabinet will consider and decide. If you think it expedient to read it, postpone its reading till we have ascertained the unbiassed sentiments of our colleagues.'

To Queen Victoria.

10, DOWNING STREET, *Nov.* 28, 1868.—Mr. Disraeli with his humble duty to your Majesty.

The Cabinet is over, and has arrived at the conclusion he wished, though after much criticism, and great apprehension, that the Conservative party, not only in Parliament, may be offended and alienated.

Assisted by Lord Stanley, and by the Lord Chancellor, Mr. Disraeli successfully combated these fears, and adopted several suggestions, which were made, sensible and ingenious, which are calculated to prevent their occurrence. . . .

From General the Hon. Charles Grey.

WINDSOR CASTLE, *Nov.* 30, 1868.—The Queen commands me to return Lord Derby's letter. H.M. is still of opinion that you have taken the course which was most honourable and straightforward as regards the character of the Govt., and certainly best for the public interest. . . .

To Lord Derby.

10, DOWNING STREET, *Dec.* 2, 1868.—The Cabinet were unanimous on the subject of resignation, not so much from any sentimental feeling of personal honor, which would not bear discussion, but from a conviction that the course was more advantageous to the party.

I enclose you a copy of the circular, which I propose to forward to every member of the party in both Houses, and which will, of course, appear in all the newspapers.

I tendered my resignation yesterday.

In the circular Ministers explained that they had not modified their opinion that Gladstone's policy of Irish disestablishment and disendowment was 'wrong in principle, probably impracticable in application, and if practicable would be disastrous in its effects.' But they justified their immediate resignation in the following terms :

Although the General Election has elicited in the decision of numerous and vast constituencies an expression of feeling which in a remarkable degree has justified their anticipations and which in dealing with the question in controversy no wise statesman would disregard, it is now clear that the present Administration cannot expect to command the confidence of the newly elected House of Commons. Under these circumstances Her Majesty's Ministers have felt it due to their own honour and to the policy they support not to retain office unnecessarily for a single day. They hold it to be more consistent with the attitude they have assumed and with the convenience of public business at this season, as well as more conducive to the just influence of the Conservative party, at once to tender the resignation of their offices to Her Majesty rather than wait for the assembling of a Parliament in which in the present aspect of affairs they are sensible they must be in a minority.

The precedent thus wisely set has been followed on every subsequent occasion when the circumstances have been at all similar; by Gladstone after the General Elections of 1874 and 1886, by Beaconsfield himself after that of 1880, and by Mr. Ramsay MacDonald after that of 1924. In 1885 and in 1892 Salisbury, and in 1923 Mr. Baldwin, took a different course on the reasonable ground that, though there was apparently a majority against Ministers, it was not a homogeneous majority and might fairly be tested in Parliament; but on none of these occasions did the Government survive the Address. For the moment in 1868 there was some doubt as to the constitutionality of the proceeding; but the press and the party were in general favourable.[1] Disraeli was able to report to Grey, for the Queen's information, on December 4: 'Montagu Corry tells me that he went into the Carlton Club yesterday, which was crammed and crowded, as it always is during a Ministerial crisis, and that there was only one, and even enthusiastic, opinion as to the propriety of the course

[1] Even Derby changed his mind; and ' on further consideration of all the circumstances,' told Disraeli he was satisfied that the decision of the Government was right.

which I had taken.   This is a great relief to me; even the
malignant *Times*, on second thoughts, finds it wise to
approve.'   Public opinion, on the whole, endorsed Grey's
verdict in a letter to the Queen: ' Nothing more proper
or manly than [Disraeli's] way of taking defeat.'   Many
Liberal journals paid a similar tribute.   ' Mr. Disraeli's
conduct,' said the *Spectator*, ' although astute, is still
manly and straightforward.   He is a gamester in politics,
but having lost the rubber he pays the stakes without a
squabble.'   He knew how to lose like a gentleman.

When Disraeli quitted office he was just completing his
sixty-fourth year and his wife had reached the advanced
age of seventy-six.   Considering the size and enthusiasm
of the Liberal majority, it was most improbable that she
at any rate would live to share office once more with her
husband.   Was it even worth *his* while to resume the toil
of apparently hopeless Opposition ?   He had reached the
goal of his ambition, had become what he told Melbourne
he meant to be, Prime Minister.   Might he not reasonably
now retire from the active fight, accept the honours to
which his long service had given him a claim, and settle
down to enjoy them with his wife in the few years during
which he might yet keep her with him ?   The vision
attracted him; but, even if he could bring himself to
forgo the joy of battle in the Commons, he must have
felt the honourable obligation, so long as his health permitted, of remaining to rebuild the party from the ruin
into which, according to his busy detractors in the ranks,
it was his reckless Reform policy that had plunged them.
If, however, he remained, he might still secure for his
wife the honours which she would value the more highly as
coming through him and on his account.   In his audience
of the Queen after the elections he broached the suggestion
that Mrs. Disraeli might be created a peeress in her own
right; and was encouraged to submit his exact proposal
in writing to Her Majesty.   It will be noticed that, in his
memorandum, Disraeli treats the party which was about
to go into opposition as in no mere conventional
language but in a very real sense ' Her Majesty's Oppo-

sition,' to be directed not only with a view to the promotion of its own principles but with constant regard to the Queen's comfort, welfare, and advantage.

To Queen Victoria.

Nov. 23, 1868.—Mr. Disraeli with his humble duty to your Majesty. Pursuant to your Majesty's gracious intimation he will endeavour to succinctly state what passed in audience with reference to the condition of the Conservative party after the General Election and his personal relations to it.

It was to be considered, 1st, whether it was for your Majesty's comfort and advantage to keep the party together—and, 2ndly, whether if kept together it was expedient that Mr. Disraeli should continue to attempt the task or leave the effort to younger hands. It seemed desirable that the party should be kept together because, although not numerically stronger, its moral influence appeared to be increased from the remarkably popular elements of which the Conservative party was now formed under the influence of the new Reform Act. Viewing England only, the Conservative party in the House of Commons will represent the majority of the population of that country.

This is a strange and most unforeseen result. It did not appear after great deliberation that any person could guide this party for your Majesty's comfort and welfare with the same advantage as Mr. Disraeli, as no one could be so intimately acquainted with your Majesty's wishes and objects as himself.

It had been the original intention of Mr. Disraeli on the termination of this Ministry to have closed his political career and to have humbly solicited your Majesty to have bestowed upon him some mark of your Majesty's favor, not altogether unusual under the circumstances.

When the Leader or Speaker of the House of Commons has been elevated by the Sovereign to the peerage, the rank accorded to him hitherto has been that of Viscount. And on this ground, that otherwise his inferiors in political position, who had been elevated often by his advice while he held either of these great posts, would take precedence of him who had been the chief in the Commons or who had presided over and controlled the debates. This was felt so strongly by Lord Russell, that when Sir C. Wood was elevated, who tho' an eminent was still a subordinate Minister, Lord Russell counselled your Majesty to make him a Viscount,[1] otherwise in the House of Lords he would have been in an inferior position

[1] Halifax.

to Sir B. Hall,[1] Mr. V. Smith,[2] and others who in the House of
Commons were immeasurably his inferiors both in political
rank and public reputation.

Mr. Disraeli might say that, at his time of life and with the
present prospects, it is a dreary career again to lead and form
an Opposition party: but he does not say so, because in truth,
if in that post he could really serve your Majesty and your
Majesty really felt that, it would be a sufficient object and
excitement in public life, and he should be quite content even
if he were never Minister again.

But next to your Majesty there is one to whom he owes
everything, and who has looked forward to this period of their
long united lives as one of comparative repose and of recognised honor.   Might Mr. Disraeli therefore, after 31 years of
Parliamentary toil, and after having served your Majesty
on more than one occasion, if not with prolonged success at
least with unfaltering devotion, humbly solicit your Majesty
to grant those honors to his wife which perhaps under ordinary
circumstances your Majesty would have deigned to bestow
on him ?

It would be an entire reward to him, and would give spirit
and cheerfulness to the remainder of his public life, when
he should be quite content to be your Majesty's servant if
not your Majesty's Minister.   He would humbly observe that
no precedents are necessary for such a course, but there are
several.

When his friends on the formation of a new Govt. wished
that the elder Pitt, who only filled a subordinate office, should
not leave the House of Commons, his wife was created a peeress
in her own right as Baroness Chatham.   When in very modern
times—indeed in your Majesty's own reign—Lord Melbourne
wished to induce Sir John Campbell to remain in the House of
Commons, and only as Attorney-General, his wife was created
Baroness Stratheden.

Mr. Disraeli is ashamed to trouble your Majesty on such
personal matters, but he has confidence in your Majesty's
gracious indulgence and in some condescending sympathy
on your Majesty's part with the feelings which prompt this
letter.

Mrs. Disraeli has a fortune of her own adequate to any position in which your Majesty might deign to place her.   Might
her husband then hope that your Majesty would be graciously
pleased to create her Viscountess Beaconsfield, a town with
which Mr. Disraeli has been long connected and which is the
nearest town to his estate in Bucks which is not yet ennobled ?

[1] Created Lord Llanover.   [2] Created Lord Lyveden.

From Queen Victoria.

WINDSOR CASTLE, *Nov.* 24, 1868.—The Queen has received Mr. Disraeli's letter, and has much pleasure in complying with his request that she should confer a peerage on Mrs. Disraeli, as a mark of her sense of his services. The Queen thinks that Mr. Disraeli, with whom she will part with much regret, can render her most useful service even when not in office; and she would have been very sorry if he had insisted on retiring from public life.

The Queen can indeed truly sympathise with his devotion to Mrs. Disraeli, who in her turn is so deeply attached to him, and she hopes they may yet enjoy many years of happiness together.

The Queen will gladly confer the title of Viscountess Beaconsfield on Mrs. Disraeli.

The Queen cannot conclude without expressing her deep sense of Mr. Disraeli's great kindness and consideration towards her, not only in what concerned her personally, but in listening to her wishes—which were however always prompted by the sole desire to promote the good of her country.

To Queen Victoria.

Nov. 25, 1868.—Mr. Disraeli at your Majesty's feet offers to your Majesty his deep gratitude for your Majesty's inestimable favor and for the terms—so gracious and so graceful—in which your Majesty has deigned to speak of his efforts when working under a Sovereign whom it is really a delight to serve.

Though there was some ill-mannered comment in a portion of the Radical press, public opinion in general accepted Mrs. Disraeli's peerage as a graceful and appropriate recognition of her husband's eminence and her own devotion. Derby wrote: ' Pray let me be among the first to congratulate " Lady Beaconsfield " on her new honour. She will, I am sure, receive it as a graceful acknowledgment, on the part of the Crown, of *your* public services, unaccompanied by the drawback of removing you from the House in which (*pace* Sir R. Knightley) your presence is indispensable.' And Gladstone concluded a formal letter to Disraeli about the Speakership with a pleasant reference: ' I also beg of you to present my best compliments on her coming patent to (I suppose I must

Viscountess Beaconsfield
from the portrait at Hughenden
painted in 1873 by G. F. Middleton

still say, and never can use the name for the last time
without regret) Mrs. Disraeli.' By a happy thought,
or a happy chance, the Secretary of State, who signed
the warrant for the issue of the patent of the new peeress,
was an old friend, Stanley.

To Lord Stanley.

10, DOWNING STREET, *Nov.* 27, '68.—She was very much
pleased with your note; and still more, that you were destined
to be the Secretary of State, who performed the function.

There seemed a dramatic unity and completeness in the
incident; bringing her memory back to old days, wanderings
over Buckinghamshire commons, when, instead of a great
statesman, you were only a young Under-Secy.

CHAPTER III.

RESERVE IN OPPOSITION.

1868–1871.

The concentration of the Liberal party, which had been a marked feature of the elections, was reflected in the composition of the new Government. Gladstone was able to combine in his Cabinet both Whigs and Radicals, Reformers and anti-Reformers, Clarendon and Goschen, Bright and Lowe. Clarendon went to the Foreign Office as of right; Lowe was very infelicitously placed at the Exchequer; Granville was of course restored to that leadership of the Lords which he had held with general acceptance under Palmerston. No sooner was the Ministry constituted than the Prime Minister set himself to work out in detail and reduce to legislative form his Irish Church policy; with such success that he was in a position to introduce his measure within a fortnight of the reassembling of Parliament in February.

Meanwhile Disraeli's attention, almost immediately after his retirement from office, was claimed by a family loss. His youngest brother James, whose health had been failing for some time, died very suddenly. He had been for ten years a Commissioner of Excise. Disraeli described him to Corry as ' a man of vigorous and original mind and great taste,' and mentioned that he had left ' a collection of French pictures of Louis Quinze period, and bricbracquerie, very remarkable; and of drawings by modern artists of the highest class.' Disraeli inherited a substantial sum, about £5,000, from his brother; but he did not enjoy the duties of executor.

To Lord Beauchamp.

GROSVENOR GATE, *Dec.* 24, '68.—I was most distressed at missing to write to you by yesterday's post: but the death was so sudden, everything so unprepared, everybody away, I finding myself executor without having had the slightest hint of such an office devolving on me, and having to give orders about everything, and things which I least understand, and most dislike—that I was really half distracted, and lost the post.

Amid sorrow, and such sorrow, one ought not to dwell upon personal disappointments, but it is a great one to Lady Beaconsfield and myself, not to pass our Xmas with friends we so dearly love, as Lady Beauchamp and her lord.

To Lord Stanley.

GROSVENOR GATE, *Jan.* 11, 1869.—Your letter was very welcome, and very interesting, as your letters generally are. Events affect the course of time so sensibly, that it came to me like a communication from some one I had known in another life, perhaps another planet. It seemed such long ages, since we used to see each other every day, and communicate almost every hour.

Here I have remained; and probably shall until the end of the month, when we shall re-enter life by going to Burghley. I have seen no one, and been nowhere, not even to a club: I have in fact realised perfect solitude: but I have found enough to do, and regular hours are the secret of health. . . .

The General Election of 1868 sent Disraeli back once more to that seat facing the box on the Speaker's left, in which he had already spent so much of his Parliamentary life. He had no doubt as to what must be the immediate course of the Opposition. Just before the session was resumed, he wrote to Stanley, declining an invitation to a public dinner in Lancashire, and giving as his reason, ' I think on our part there should be, at the present, the utmost reserve and quietness.' Even when, in opposition to Palmerston, he commanded a formidable minority not much short, in voting strength, of the forces of the Government, he often practised tactics of the kind. Now that he was facing a Minister who had behind him a large and enthusiastic majority such as Parliament had not seen since the fall of Peel, reserve was all the more imperative. Kicking against the pricks was neither dignified nor useful. Plenty of rope, to vary the metaphor, was what a wise Opposition would extend to a Premier of boundless eagerness and activity.

Accordingly the resistance which Disraeli offered to Gladstone's Irish Church Bill, though strenuous, was not prolonged. Nor was his speech on the second reading a very successful effort. Salisbury in retrospect described it as much below the orator's usual level; Hardy at the time characterised it as ' sparkling and brilliant, but far from earnest.' Perhaps the most interesting passage in it was one protesting against the confiscation by the State of corporate property, and especially of Church property, which was ' to a certain degree an intellectual tenure; in a greater degree a moral and spiritual tenure. It is the fluctuating patrimony of the great body of the people.' The constant sense of the anomalous position of the Irish Church rather paralysed Disraeli's efforts in its defence; and in this second reading debate the Opposition speaker who roused the enthusiasm which can only be produced by conviction as well as eloquence was Gathorne Hardy.

But no conviction and no eloquence were of any avail against a majority returned by the newly created constituency to deal with this very question, and against a Minister who conceived himself to be entrusted with a mission to pacify Ireland. The second reading was carried by 118. Though Disraeli told Archbishop Tait that it was ' a mechanical majority,' which ' created no enthusiasm,' and gave the Archbishop the impression that he hoped to be able to set the Liberal party by the ears, he realised that it was impossible to resist the Bill with effect in the Commons. He discouraged blind opposition to every clause in Committee, urged his followers to concentrate on a few vital amendments, and made no attempt at delay. The Bill, therefore, in spite of its complexity, passed easily through its various stages with the support

of an undiminished majority, and on the last day of
May was read a third time by 114. Disraeli's speech on
that occasion, though Hardy was again dissatisfied and
called it 'wretched,' contains at least one passage which
was highly prophetic. All who remember what the state
of Ireland was at the moment of the outbreak of the
Great War in August, 1914, will realise that Disraeli
had grasped the essentials of the Irish position, which
Gladstone and his followers glozed over with optimistic
sentimentalism. 'It is very possible,' he said, 'that
after a period of great disquietude, doubt, and passion,
events may occur which may complete that severance
of the Union [between England and Ireland] which to-
night we are commencing.'

What I fear in the policy of the right hon. gentleman [Glad-
stone] is that its tendency is to civil war. I am not surprised
that hon. gentlemen should for a moment be startled by such
an expression. Let them think a little. Is it natural and
probable that the Papal power in Ireland will attempt to
attain ascendancy and predominance ? I say it is natural;
and, what is more, it ought to do it. Is it natural that the
Protestants of Ireland should submit without a struggle
to such a state of things ? You know they will not; that is
settled. Is England to interfere ? Are we again to conquer
Ireland ? Are we to have a repetition of the direful history
which on both sides now we wish to forget ? Is there to be
another Battle of the Boyne, another Siege of Derry, another
Treaty of Limerick ? These things are not only possible,
but probable. You are commencing a policy which will
inevitably lead to such results.

Disraeli looked to the Lords to secure better terms for
the Irish Church than Gladstone and the Commons were
disposed to accord. Directly the second reading was
carried he had written to the Archbishop urging him to
call a meeting at Lambeth of leading peers of various
shades of opinion, in order that the Upper House, whatever it might ultimately decide to do, should not act on
party lines or under party leaders. 'Every day,' he
added, 'will make us comprehend more clearly what is
the real feeling of England. It is on a just appreciation

of that that the right decision will depend.' The Archbishop, who had already at the Queen's instance accepted
a mediatory position, was only too glad to do what he
was asked. ' I saw the Archbishop of Canterbury to-day,'
wrote Disraeli to Cairns on April 10, ' a long interview.
He is in favour of reading the Bill a second time, I think,
tho' he does not wish to decide on that prematurely; and
he accedes to my suggestion of summoning a preliminary
meeting of peers at Lambeth to consult.' There is reason
to believe that Disraeli agreed with the Archbishop's
tactics. But he was in a difficult position, as his authority
with the Conservative peers was very far short of what it
ultimately became, and Derby, to whom they looked,
absolutely refused to attend the Lambeth meeting, on
the ground that ' no consideration on earth ' would
induce him to enter into any compromise on a measure
of the kind. The meeting was accordingly a failure,
Cairns, the leader in the Lords, showing, in view of Derby's
attitude, great reserve, though Salisbury and one or two
others agreed with the Archbishop. The Conservative
peers met at the Duke of Marlborough's house, and
disregarded the hesitations of their leaders. It was
resolved to oppose the second reading, in spite of the
certainty that the rejection of the Bill, immediately after
a decisive General Election, would provoke a constitutional crisis of the first magnitude. Happily some of the
leaders, acting we may well believe with Disraeli's
sympathy, were able, in conjunction with the Archbishop, to effect by influence behind the scenes what
they had failed to carry at the party meeting; so the
Bill, owing to many abstentions and thirty-six Tory
votes in its favour, was carried on second reading by the
respectable majority of thirty-three.

There followed a series of somewhat drastic amendments
making ampler pecuniary provision than the Bill allowed
for the Church about to be disestablished, and inserting
the principle of concurrent endowment by applying some
of the surplus to the needs of Roman Catholic priests

and Presbyterian ministers instead of converting it altogether to secular use. Concurrent endowment still, as in the previous year, divided the friends of the Church; for Disraeli and the majority of his colleagues were in favour, and Cairns and some others strongly against. It is unnecessary here to describe the game of battledore and shuttlecock which was played over these amendments during June and July between Lords and Commons, Ministers and ex-Ministers, as the whole story has been set out in full in the *Life of Archbishop Tait*, ch. 19, and Lord Morley's *Gladstone*, Book VI., ch. 1, and Disraeli was hardly a protagonist. That an arrangement, by which the Church obtained a considerable slice of what her friends thought to be her right, was finally arrived at was due mainly to the tireless efforts of the Queen and the Archbishop, maintained in spite of Gladstone's unconciliatory attitude, and to the willingness of Cairns to assume at the last moment, without possibility of due consultation, an onerous responsibility. Disraeli's letters to Cairns show that it was the question of concurrent endowment which gave him most trouble.

To Lord Cairns.

Confidential. GROSVENOR GATE, *June* 27, 1869.—. . . What I hear of the state of your House and of the Cabinet alarms me; both conditions seem to me rather anarchical.

Your followers want a meeting, that they should be advised, according to custom, as to what amendments they should support. But this I apprehend, might be embarrassing to you, from your hesitation as to your course respecting the appropriation of the surplus. The Government's truly idiotic scheme on that head will not hold water. It is universally condemned, while the general principle of some concurrent endowment seems to gain ground, in both Houses, daily. It is thought that many would support a liberal treatment of our own Church, if something were simultaneously done for presbyter and priest.

There can be little doubt I conceive, abstractedly, of the wisdom of such an arrangement. But what alarms me is the possibility of your being put in the situation of supporting the Government with a fraction of your followers, and that not the most influential, and dividing against the bulk of your friends. This would be serious.

July 12.—What I originally apprehended occurred last night, and it will be now necessary to arrange our course with respect to ‘concurrent endowment’ in the House of Commons. With all our late colleagues there favorable to it, except perhaps Hardy, this will not be a very easy business, looking to future consequences as well as present results. . . .

Concurrent endowment was eventually abandoned. Disraeli sent his wife early intelligence of Cairns's arrangement:

To Lady Beaconsfield.

July 22, '69.—The Irish Church Bill is settled. Cairns has made a compromise with Lord Granville; which saves the honor of the Lords, and will satisfy all moderate men I don't think the more decided spirits on either side will like it as much.

I am obliged to hold my tongue even to my colleagues, as Cairns is to announce the terms. They may be known soon after this reaches you, but it will be prudent not to send the news to anyone.

Perhaps the Archbishop's comment in his diary best sums up the net result:

We have made the best terms we could, and, thanks to the Queen, a collision between the two Houses has been averted; but a great occasion has been poorly used, and the Irish Church has been greatly injured, without any benefit to the Roman Catholics.

The most strenuous opponent of the Irish Church Bill in the Lords was the old Tory leader, Derby; it was he who made the most stirring speech in the debate on the second reading; and, when the compromise over the Lords' amendments was announced, he was so angry, Malmesbury tells us, that he left the House.[1] It was the final scene of his political life, and his natural life lasted only three months longer. But, though his strength was failing, he was for some weeks without actual illness, and

[1] Mr. Alfred Gathorne Hardy, in *Cranbrook*, Vol. I., p. 271, records ‘on Lord Cairns's authority’ that Lord Derby, though at first startled and annoyed, ultimately expressed satisfaction with what was done.

Disraeli's last letter to his old 'chief' was apparently written without any premonition of the approaching end.

To Lord Derby.

HUGHENDEN MANOR, *Sep.* 15, 1869.

MY DEAR CHIEF,—I was delighted at hearing from Knowsley, which recalled old times: not that I mean to say I was insensible to the charms of your red venison, which I particularly appreciate.

We have been here three weeks, and have literally not seen a human being, beyond the dwellers on the soil. After the session we visited for a few days some of our friends, and among other places we found ourselves at Alton Towers. It pleased me very much. Though in Staffordshire, it is on the Derbyshire border, and combines the character of both counties: the scenery is romantic and rich. As for the house, it is the only thing I have ever seen that gave me an idea of the castle of Barbe Bleu in Madame D'Aulnois's wondrous tale. It is so various and fantastic.

We are now literally stepping into the carriage to pay a visit of a couple of days to Bulstrode. The late Duke of Somerset bought the park from the Minister Portland, who pulled down the mansion where lived Judge Jeffreys, and began building a castle, but, being turned out of office, he fancied he was ruined, and sold the place. The present Duke of Somerset has built a fair and convenient dwelling, in the Tudor style, in the park, which is undulating and well-timbered: but I dare say you may remember it when you were at Eton.

Pray make our kindest remembrances to Lady Derby. I shall take the liberty of writing to you sometimes, if I have anything to say, and you, perhaps, will not entirely forget Your devoted D.

Early in October the last illness began, and on the 23rd the end came. To Disraeli Derby's death was the severance of the most momentous political connection of his life, a connection which had survived Derby's resignation and his own succession to the first place. The long and intimate association with one of a social position so much higher, and a political reputation so much longer and at first so much greater, had tended to habituate Disraeli to the part of inspirer of measures and policies for which Derby bore the main public responsibility; and there is probably some truth in Fraser's assertion that Disraeli's ' fixed idea ' was ' that he was to be the mysterious wirepuller; the voice behind the throne; unseen, but suspected. That he should rise to be the absolute monarch, which he was at last, does not seem to have been anticipated by him.' So far as Fraser's view is correct, Derby's death was the emancipation of Disraeli.

To Lord Stanley.

HUGHENDEN, *Oct.* 25, '69.—It is with reluctance, that I intrude on you at this moment, overwhelmed, as you must be, with sorrows, cares, and duties; the memory of the past and the responsibility of the future. But I cannot refrain from expressing to you the sympathy of friendship.

As for the great departed, there existed, between him and myself, relations wh. have rarely been maintained between two human beings; twenty years, and more, of confidential public life, tried by as searching incidents as can well test men. I remember at this moment, not without solace, that there never was any estrangement between us; and that I have to associate with his memory no other feelings, than those of respect and regard.

How well justified was Disraeli's claim, in spite of occasional misunderstandings, has been shown throughout this biography. Lennox wrote to him from Paris: ' I fear you will have felt Lord Derby's death much. He was, with all his peculiarities, very true to you.' Disraeli, too, for his part, was ' very true ' to Derby; even in the deferential manner with which he used, as his secretaries noticed, to clinch disputed matters when in office by the phrase, ' Lord Derby wishes it.' He paid a worthy tribute to his old chief when, as Prime Minister, he unveiled in 1874 the statue of the ' Rupert of debate ' in Parliament Square; but he observed on that occasion a dignified reticence as to their personal relations. The qualities which he singled out for eulogy were ' his fiery eloquence, his haughty courage, the rapidity of his intellectual grasp '; ' his capacity for labour and his mastery of detail, which never were sufficiently appreciated because the world was astonished by the celerity

with which he despatched public affairs.' He summed
up Derby's share in the great transactions of the previous
fifty years in a noteworthy sentence: ' He abolished
slavery, he educated Ireland, and he reformed Parliament.' [1] It was not for him to say what history records,
that one of Derby's claims to the interest of posterity
was his intimate association with the career of Benjamin
Disraeli.

Derby's death sensibly affected the evolution of a
question which, during the first year and more of opposition, caused Disraeli some trouble—the leadership of the
party in the House of Lords. Malmesbury, who had
filled the post during 1868, was indisposed to continue
after the General Election. In Disraeli's view, Cairns,
the ablest man on the Conservative front bench in that
House, ought to be the successor. But so great was the
impression that Salisbury's character and abilities had
created that, in spite of his secession from, and denunciation of, his colleagues over the Reform Bill, there
was a movement among the peers to choose him; and
even Cairns sounded him on the subject. Disraeli
promptly made it clear that he could concur in no such
arrangement.

To Lord Cairns.

Confidential. GROSVENOR GATE, *Dec.* 14, 1868.—Taylor
came to me yesterday, much perplexed and alarmed about
a conversation, between Colville and yourself, as to the leading
in the Lords. I told him I had seen you on the matter, and
would see you again, if necessary. He thinks, unless we act
with some decision, we may injure our position.

The Leader in the Lords must be one who shares my entire
confidence, and must act in complete concert with myself.
I do not know whether Lord Salisbury and myself are even
on speaking terms.

You contemplate making a man leader of a party of which
he is not even a member. If we show strength in Parliament
and the country, it is probable, in due time and course, he
will join us. If we try to force the result, we shall only subject
ourselves to humiliation.

[1] ' Every word of your admirable speech went to my heart, you understood my dearest husband so well,' wrote the widowed Lady Derby.

Parliament will not virtually meet till the middle of February, and you ought to meet it as the leader of the party in the Lords.

Salisbury himself realised the impropriety of the suggestion, urged Cairns to accept, and promised him cordial and earnest support. Accordingly Cairns, though very reluctant owing to his semi-judicial position as ex-Chancellor and his recent creation as a peer, consented, and was elected unanimously. One session, however—but that session an exceptionally trying one, owing to the controversy over the Irish Church Bill—convinced him that his objections were sound and should prevail; and he wrote to Disraeli on September 27 that he had made up his mind to resign. Not only was he anxious to devote considerable time to the judicial business of the House of Lords, but he had felt in the recent debates that his authority had not been duly regarded by the party. 'The more anxious part of the labours of the session has been, not the resisting the measures of our opponents, but the endeavouring to avoid the appearance of disunion among our friends. I have little capacity for either operation, but for the latter I have absolutely none.' The state of Lady Cairns's health, he added, had made it necessary for him to pass the entire winter abroad, so that in any case there would be a temporary interruption of his leadership; and he considered this a fitting opportunity for his permanent withdrawal from it.

To Lord Cairns.

Private. HUGHENDEN MANOR, *Sep.* 29, 1869.—The receipt of a letter, like yours, ought immediately to be acknowledged. At present, I can only say, that I have read it with consternation. When I recover from its contents, if I ever do, I will endeavor to consider the perplexities of our sad situation now so much aggravated, and will communicate with you.

There was no need to come to any decision in the early months of the recess; and the death of Derby, by transfer-

ring Disraeli's friend and political pupil, Stanley, to the
Lords, seemed to open out a satisfactory solution. But
the new head of the house of Stanley was slow to move
and to take risks; and friends and colleagues found it
impossible to obtain any definite promise during the
autumn.

To Lord Derby.

CARLTON CLUB, *Nov.* 20, 1869.—We came up from Strathfieldsaye yesterday, and I found your kind recollection of
your old comrade.

Never was a present more opportune; and I dined off a
Knowsley hare yesterday, and breakfasted off a Knowsley
pheasant this morning: both first-rate.

I am sorry to hear, that the House of Lords is to meet,
so far as our friends are concerned, as *acephali*. It will, of
course, at first, produce great scandal; but I have witnessed
so many ' breaks-up ' of the party, that I have come to view
them as Talleyrand did his ' revolutions '—with sanguine
indifference.

To Lord Cairns.

Private. HUGHENDEN MANOR, *Dec.* 12, 1869.—. . . I
saw Stanley when in town, and he is coming to stay here on
our return from Blenheim, which I suppose will be about the
sixteenth or so.

Nothing could be more cordial or more satisfactory, than
the expression of his relations towards myself, but I could
not expect any man to walk into a House of Parliament for the
first time, and at once offer to take the conduct of affairs.
Certainly I could not expect such a course from a man of the
cautious and usually reserved habit of the present Lord
Derby.

The arrangement you have decided on,[1] tho' I regret the
personal inconvenience it may entail, appears to me the
most judicious to be pursued; at once prudent and conciliatory.

I trust that all will develop satisfactorily, and I count on
your continued counsel and support. . . .

To Lord Derby.

HUGHENDEN MANOR, *Dec.* 16, 1869.—. . . We shall be
delighted to receive you next Tuesday, the 21st. Although
the shortest day, it is my birthday, wh: will be a sort of hedge,
and I shall look out, in consequence, for a bottle of the best
Falernian.

[1] To come over from Mentone for the meeting of Parliament, hold the
usual Peers' dinner, and then formally resign.

I met Hardy at B[lenheim] and had much gossip about the H. of Lords with the Duke, but this and many other things will keep. Excuse a frozen hand.

The choice of a leader in the Lords did not, of course, rest with the party chief who sat in the Commons or even with the party as a whole, but with the Conservative peers themselves; as Disraeli explained to a correspondent who suggested a joint meeting of the Conservatives in both Houses to make the election.

To William Johnston of Ballykilbeg.

HUGHENDEN MANOR, *Dec.* 8, 1869.—The leader of a party in a House of Parliament is never nominated: the selection is always the spontaneous act of the party in the House in which he sits. It was so in the case of Lord Cairns, who yielded most unwillingly to the general wish, Lord Salisbury being one of the warmest of his solicitors. It was so in my own case. Lord Derby never appointed me to the leadership, but the party chose to follow me and the rest ensued.

The same jealousy of interference with an arrangement in which their own feelings and even tastes should pre-eminently be consulted would no doubt be felt, if the leadership of a House was to be decided by the votes of those who did not sit in it.

I make no doubt our friends in the House of Lords will in due season find their becoming chief; but our interposition will not aid them, they will be better helped to a decision by events. . . .

The claims of Salisbury were once more advocated by a section, but there was a general feeling that the man best able to unite the party would be Derby. Would he accept ? Hardy described him in his diary in December as ' not quite willing, but showing symptoms of persuada-bility.' He was elected unanimously at the beginning of the session of 1870, Salisbury seconding the nomina-tion, which was proposed by the Duke of Richmond. He took a day to consider, and then declined; as Hardy in retrospect wrote, ' He knew himself better than he was known.' Thereupon Carnarvon put forward the impracticable plan that Salisbury should take an independent lead in and for the Lords, without holding any confidential communication with the leader in the Commons, who happened also to be the leader of the party. The plan was not merely impracticable; it would also have been not far short of an insult to Disraeli. This absurdity was avoided, and finally Richmond, who had joined the Cabinet in 1867 when the three seceded, accepted the 'uncoveted position,'[1] being proposed by Salisbury and seconded by Derby. Salisbury manifested throughout a disposition to resume friendly working relations with his old friends—except with Disraeli.

How unchanged was his attitude to Disraeli had been shown in an article which he wrote in the *Quarterly Review* in the autumn of 1869, on ' The Past and the Future of Conservative Policy.' This renewed attack formed the logical sequel of the articles in 1860 and 1867,[2] and like them condemned severely the tactics of selecting the Whigs for hostility and the Radicals for alliances. In the Reform Act the party had committed a ' great Parliamentary suicide.' A lurid picture was drawn of the degradation and danger of office without power, as revealed in past history. Though Disraeli's name was never mentioned, it required only the most superficial knowledge of politics to understand that it was he who was portrayed as the ' dishonest man,' the ' mere political gamester,' to whom office in a minority afforded too tempting a field; that it was his ' baseness ' and ' perpetual political mendicancy ' that the writer was chastising; that he was the parliamentary leader whose conduct was described as worthy of unmitigated contempt.

To Sir Anthony de Rothschild.

HUGHENDEN MANOR, *Dec.* 30, 1869.—A battalion of pheasants, and some hares, arrived here yesterday, without any label, but the porter said, that, tho' it had been lost,

---

[1] See Gathorne Hardy, Vol. I., pp. 294, 295.
[2] See pp. 19-27, 290, 291.

there was no doubt that the game was for Hughenden and that it had come from Aylesbury.

No one in that direction cd. be so magnificent except yourself. You not only send many pheasants, but you send pheasants worth eating; nothing could be finer than those wh. preceded the last arrivals.

There is no middle state in this bird. A pheasant is ' aut Cæsar, aut nihil.' . . .

To Lord Derby.

GROSVENOR GATE, *Feb.* 1, 1870.—Will you come and dine at a large House of Commons dinner—forty—here on Wednesday the 16th ?

And if you will, wh. will please them much, shall I ask some swells to meet you, K.G.'s and that sort of thing—or would you prefer being the sole swell, like a big boy to the old school for a day ? I think that would be more characteristic, but just as you please.[1]

The disestablishment of the Irish Church did less than nothing for the moment to promote that pacification of Ireland towards which it was to be the first step; a tempest of sedition and crime swept in 1869 over the island which Abercorn and Mayo, the Tory Viceroy and Chief Secretary, had brought into comparative order. Gladstone, though he admitted, in the language of the Queen's Speech of 1870, that ' the recent extension of agrarian crime in several parts of Ireland ' had caused the Government ' painful concern,' held it to be all the more imperative to proceed with his second Irish measure, a Land Bill; and Disraeli, in his speech on the Address, promised a candid consideration for Ministerial proposals, though he pointed out that the tenure of land in Ireland was an old grievance, and could not possibly be the immediate cause of the present disorder. That disorder he attributed mainly to the extravagant hopes which the policy of the Government and the language of their supporters had encouraged. The Irish people reasoned: ' Is it not a natural consequence that if you settle the

---

[1] Derby accepted the second alternative; but the dinner had to be abandoned, as Disraeli, when the time came, was confined to his room by illness.

question of the Irish Church by depriving the bishops and rectors of their property, you will settle the question of the land by depriving the landlords of their property?' Disraeli called attention to a recent election for Tipperary in which the Government candidate, who had been Law Adviser at Dublin Castle, pledged himself to an extreme policy, and yet was beaten by a convicted Fenian, O'Donovan Rossa. 'The people of Ireland had to choose between a sham Fenian and a real Fenian, and it is astonishing what a preference is always given to the genuine article.' Then the Government, long so tolerant of disorder, at last took action.

Horrible scenes of violence had been occurring in Ireland, but the Government would never move. Landlords were shot down like game, respectable farmers were beaten to death with sticks by masked men; bailiffs were shot in the back; policemen were stabbed; the High Sheriff of a county going to swear in the grand jury was fired at in his carriage and dangerously wounded; households were blown up, and firearms surreptitiously obtained. All this time the Government would not move; but the moment the Government candidate was defeated at the hustings—a Government candidate pledged to confiscation, pledged to a course of action which would destroy all civil government—the moment that occurred there was panic in the Castle, there was confusion in the Council; the wires of Aldershot were agitated; troops were put in motion, sent across from Liverpool to Dublin, and concentrated in Waterford, Tipperary, and Cork.... I remember one of Her Majesty's Ministers [Bright] saying, I think last year, 'Anyone can govern Ireland with troops and artillery.' So it seems; even that right honourable gentleman.

The speech appears to have been generally admired. Malmesbury wrote to Cairns: ' Lady Tankerville says that at the opening of the session Bright had become dizzy, and Dizzy had become bright.'

To Sir Joseph Napier.

Confidential. GROSVENOR GATE, *Feb.* 21, 1870.—It is eighteen years since you and I first conferred together about an Irish Land Bill. It was a great thing then for me to have such an adviser, and it would have been a wise thing if our friends had adopted the result of our labors.

Now I am in a very different situation. Not a single Irish lawyer in the H. of Commons, at least on our benches, except Ball, who is of course in the diocese of Armagh; even Cairns has departed for Mentone. On the 7th I have to express my views on the Government Bill. What a situation for the leader of a party; as Bright says, ' still a great party !'

Under these circumstances I write to you, my old confederate. Can you find time from your ecumenical council to give me the results of your reflections on the Government scheme, and such materials as may be opportune and profitable to me ?

I don't even know whether the Ulster right can be enforced in a court of law, and there is nobody here to tell me ! I must therefore summon ' Napier to the rescue.'

Gladstone's Bill was directed to the security of the Irish tenant, who, contrary to the usual practice in England, had generally received his land in a prairie condition from the landlord, and had done all the draining, reclaiming, fencing, farm-building, and other improvement himself. By custom in Ulster and in some other parts of Ireland, so long as the tenant paid his rent he could not be evicted; and on giving up his farm he could claim compensation for unexhausted improvements and sell the goodwill for what it would fetch in the market. Where no custom prevailed, the landlord was at liberty to raise the rent in proportion as the tenant improved the land, and to evict him at will without compensation. Roughly speaking, Gladstone's Bill turned the Ulster custom into law and extended it throughout Ireland, thus giving the Irish tenant an estate in the land he farmed. So far as the measure provided for compensation, and retrospective compensation, to the tenant, Disraeli was heartily in its favour, as this was one main principle of the Bills which Napier prepared under his auspices in 1852; and he therefore announced on the second reading that some legislation was necessary and that he should support the Bill in principle. But he had his doubts about the wisdom of turning custom into law.

The moment you legalise a custom you fix its particular character; but the value of a custom is its flexibility, and that it adapts itself to all the circumstances of the moment and of the locality. All these qualities are lost the moment you crystallise a custom into legislation. Customs may not be as wise as laws, but they are always more popular. They array upon their side alike the convictions and the prejudices of men. They are spontaneous. They grow out of man's necessities and invention; and, as circumstances change and alter and die off, the custom falls into desuetude and we get rid of it. But if you make it into law, circumstances alter, but the law remains, and becomes part of that obsolete legislation which haunts our statute-book and harasses society.

Disraeli deplored the interference with freedom of contract effected by the Bill; but Gladstone asked with some force whether Disraeli would allow the tenant to contract himself out of its benefits. By far Disraeli's shrewdest and most incisive criticism was that the Bill terminated 'at one fell swoop all moral relations between the owner and occupier,' and endeavoured to establish a purely commercial relation between them. Yet, if ever there was a state of society where the relations should be paternal, where forbearance should be shown to the tenant who from vicissitudes of seasons is in arrear with his rent, it was Ireland, where there were farmers holding only one acre. Hitherto small tenants had not appealed in vain 'to the distinguished facility and good nature of the Irish landlord.' But why should forbearance be shown when the tenant in arrear is a co-partner, in getting rid of whom the landlord has a direct interest, and when the payment of rent is the only bond? Disraeli developed this point in Committee, when he reduced the majority of the Government to seventy-six on an amendment limiting compensation to unexhausted improvements. The landlord would say to the tenant in future, argued Disraeli, ' We must both stand upon our rights. This new-fangled law, which has given you a contingent remainder to the third of my freehold, has at least given me this security, that if you do not pay me your rent I may get rid of you.' Evictions would naturally follow; there would be a new grievance, the payment of rent; and the non-payment of rent would become a principle asserted by the same rural logic which had produced the crimes and horrors of the past year. There would be great complaints of vexatious and tyrannical evictions, and the occupiers would assert their supposed rights by the most violent means. ' So far from the improvement of the country terminating all these misunderstandings and heartburnings, which we seem now so anxious on both sides of the House to bring to a close, you will have the same controversies still raging, only with increased acerbity, and under circumstances and conditions which must inevitably lead to increased bitterness and increased perils to society.'

It was a speech of extraordinary prescience, predicting with exactness the course which the agrarian movement followed in Ireland during the next ten or fifteen years. In painful contrast was Gladstone's optimistic reply, insisting that the measure was an exceptional one to meet a temporary need, and expressing the hope that the time would come when it would be no longer necessary and freedom of contract would be restored. Though he anticipated the failure of Gladstone's scheme, Disraeli did not realise, any more than Gladstone, that the creation by the aid of the State of a peasant proprietary was, as Bright with real vision maintained, and subsequent history has shown, the true remedy for agrarian discontent in Ireland. To placate Bright, Gladstone did indeed frame some inadequate clauses with this object, but he laid no stress on them, and Disraeli even singled out these clauses for disapproval. However, having recognised the necessity of legislation, Disraeli discouraged divisions on both second and third readings; and, the Opposition in the Lords following the example of the Commons, the experiment which Gladstone sanguinely advocated was duly tried— and proved so inadequate that in ten years its author had, with unabated optimism, to set his hand once more to the same task.

The other great measure of the session, the one whose passage was perhaps the foremost distinction of Gladstone's Ministry, Forster's Education Bill, was actively assisted by the Conservative party, under Disraeli's direction. He had claimed at Edinburgh, in the autumn of 1867, that from his entry into public life he had done his best to promote the cause of popular education. He had given it a prominent place in his address when first elected for Bucks in 1847; one of the outstanding features of his scheme for administrative reform in 1855 was the constitution of education as a separate Ministry with a Secretary of State as its head; the Derby - Disraeli Government of 1858 appointed the Newcastle Commission on the subject; and, while the last Palmerston Government had persistently neglected to take any steps in consequence of the Commission's Report, save to enforce the very questionable recommendation of payment by results, Disraeli's first Ministry in 1868 prepared and submitted, through the Duke of Marlborough, to the House of Lords, a comprehensive scheme which, at least in the importance attached to the Education Department, was even in advance of Forster's measure. But Forster introduced the principle of a local rate which Disraeli's Ministry had shirked, and his scheme, while increasing the Government grants to denominational schools, mainly belonging to the Church of England, already in existence, provided for supplementing their deficiencies by the creation of school boards all over the country, which should establish and conduct rate-aided schools, so that elementary education should be ultimately provided for every English child. The great difficulty, then as subsequently, proved to be the religious teaching. The general sense of the House and of the country was that the Bible should be read and that there should be religious education in all schools, guarded by a conscience clause; but the Radicals and the bulk of the Dissenters pressed for an entirely secular system. This the Government could not concede; but they ultimately accepted a compromise, proposed by Cowper Temple, a Whig, providing that, while the Bible should be read and explained, no catechism or other distinctive formulary should be taught in a board school. Disraeli immediately fastened on the weakness of this arrangement. The schoolmaster could not, he pointed out, teach, enforce, and explain the Bible without drawing some conclusions, and what could those be but dogmas ?

You will not entrust the priest or the presbyter,' he said, ' with the privilege of expounding the Holy Scripture to the scholars; but for that purpose you are inventing and establishing a new sacerdotal class. The schoolmaster who will exercise these functions . . . will in the future exercise an extraordinary influence upon the history of England and upon the conduct of Englishmen.' In a speech in the autumn at a Bucks diocesan meeting he described the new Act, though it was a step in advance, as but a measure of transition, with which the English people would not be satisfied in the long run. They would require richer and more various elementary education, and, when they obtained that, they would require a religious education, because as their intelligence expanded and was cultivated they would require information as to the most interesting of all knowledge—the relations which exist between God and man. The various subsequent modifications in our education policy, culminating in Mr. Balfour's Act of 1902, and in Mr. Fisher's Act of 1918, testify to Disraeli's foresight. With one immediate result of Forster's policy he must have been well content—the opening of a rift between the Gladstone Ministry and its erstwhile devoted supporters, the political Dissenters. He was careful to avoid inconsiderate attacks which might draw his opponents together.

Not merely the policy of reserve which he had deliberately adopted, but ill-health of a continued character greatly restricted Disraeli's activities during the session; and on several occasions he had to rely upon Hardy, his

' sword-arm,' to take his place. Writing to Lennox in
July he said: ' I have been unwell all this year, and am
afraid I have thought too much of myself. Illness
makes one selfish and disgusts one's friends.' A letter
to Northcote, who had gone to Canada, as Chairman of
the Hudson Bay Company, in connection with disputes
between the company and the Canadian Government,
gives a picture of the work of the session up to May.

To Sir Stafford Northcote.

GROSVENOR GATE, *May* 14, 1870.—. . . The Land Bill
after Easter moved; and then, like a ship on the stocks, moved
rapidly. I think the Lords will certainly have it before Whitsun. It has been greatly modified in Committee—much by
the Govt. yielding to Roundell Palmer and Co.; and much
by our friend Ball, who has shown as much resource and knowledge as on the Irish Church Bill, and with a happier result.
We must be cautious in not over-altering it in the Lords. . . .

There is a hitch about the Education Bill. Gladstone,
I apprehend, is prepared to secularise, if he were only convinced he could keep his majority together by that process.
But the elements of the calculation are various and discordant, and every possible result, therefore, doubtful.

The Ballot bothers me. Cross and the Lancashire men are
all in favor of it, and say that at this moment we should carry
every great town in the North, were it adopted. But I apprehend the great body of our friends would not like to see it
applied to counties; and then there are Ireland and Scotland
and Wales also to be remembered. We are going to have a
council in a day or two; the leading members of both Houses,
and some representative men. I miss you sadly on these
occasions, and indeed always.

The great social event is Derby's approaching marriage.
He is radiant with happiness. Literally you would not know
him.

I can't say much for myself. I have been to the seaside;
but it has brought me no relief, and I still suffer, which is
disheartening. . . .

Derby was about to marry Salisbury's stepmother,
who had long been a friend of Disraeli's, and had frequently entertained him at Hatfield during the last
twenty years. To his sister he described her in 1851 as

' an admirable hostess and a very pleasing woman; great simplicity, quite a Sackville.'[1]

To Lord Derby.

GROSVENOR GATE, *May* 7, 1870.—Next to yourself, by what you tell me, no man, perhaps, will be happier, than I am. Under this roof, we have long, and fondly, wished, that this shd. happen. The lady I have ever loved; and if fine intelligence, a thoughtful mind, the sweetest temper in the world, and many charms, can make a man happy, your felicity is secured.

Marriage is the happiest state in the world, when there is, on each side, a complete knowledge of the characters united. That you have secured—and to all the many blessings wh. distinguish you in life, rank, wealth, and, above all, great abilities, you have had the wisdom to add the only element, wh. was wanting to complete the spell.

Lady Beaconsfield sends you her congratulations thro' her tears—of joy.

To Gathorne Hardy.

GROSVENOR GATE, *May* 22, '70.—I am sorry—very—to say, that you must not count on me to-morrow to support and assist you in the debate on University Tests, as was my hope, and firm intention. My medicos declare that I must not attempt anything like public speaking at present, and refrain, indeed, as much as possible, from private.

Tho' I hope I shall get it all straight, my right lung is seriously affected, and it is no use any longer to tamper with it. Remedies, and quiet, and this hot weather, may put all to rights, and in a short time, but I must try them.

It pains me to leave a faithful colleague to struggle alone with a difficult question—but you will do all that man can do, which is my consolation, tho' not a sufficient one.

Hardy's own account of Disraeli's health and views is given in his diary for May 22: ' Called on Disraeli, who remains poorly and dreads the east wind. He is desponding, but looks forward to Gladstone becoming useless to the Radicals, and a disruption. Gives two years or more.'

[1] See Vol. I., p. 1152.

To Lord Stanhope.

GROSVENOR GATE, *July* 17, '70.— . . . I quite agree with
you about the division in the House of Lords:[1] avowedly to
regulate that assembly by the prejudices, or convictions,
of the University of Oxford, cannot be wise. Some think,
however, that the great event of the last eight and forty hours
may bring about a state of affairs more suitable to a policy
of resistance, tho' that was not contemplated by the instigator
in the present instance.

I dined at York House, Twickenham, yesterday: a curious
and interesting moment to be a guest there. It was not
wonderful, that my host[2] should be somewhat excited. It is
an important break in the existence of himself and his brother
colonists. One of the guests, however, did not think so;
and said they were forgotten, and had done nothing to make
themselves remembered. We shall see! They may be
wanted. Nobody is forgotten, when it is convenient to
remember him.

'The great event of the last eight and forty hours '
was indeed calculated to alter men's views and affect their
policies. The relations of France and Prussia had caused
the statesmen of Europe, and Disraeli among them, grave
anxiety ever since 1866; and when he wrote this letter to
Stanhope a sudden dispute between the two countries
over the offer of the Spanish throne to a Hohenzollern
prince had, in spite of the prince's withdrawal, been
aggravated, by Bismarck's unscrupulous manipulation
and Napoleon's fatal folly, into a quarrel which only the
sword could decide. A despatch from Ems, describing the
diplomatic proceedings between Benedetti, the French
Minister, and the King of Prussia, had been so dexterously
edited by Bismarck as to prove, as he hoped and expected,
a red rag to the Gallic bull. French mobilisation had been
ordered ; the Parisians were shouting 'To Berlin '; a
declaration of war was inevitable within a few days.
Bismarck's share in provoking the explosion was not then
known; and Disraeli was at one with public opinion in

---

[1] On a motion by Salisbury, the recently elected Chancellor of the
University of Oxford, which defeated the second reading of the University
Tests Bill.

[2] The Comte de Paris.

England in casting all the blame on Napoleon's ambition
and French recklessness. Moreover, in expressing the
view that a Sovereign who trusted to melodramatic
catastrophes, such as military surprises and the capture
of capitals, would have to meet ' a more powerful force
than any military array,' namely, ' the outraged opinion
of an enlightened world,' he showed that he was not
himself entirely emancipated from the sentimental
optimism about international relations which was rampant among his political opponents.

For a quarter of a century Disraeli had preached that
a good understanding with France should be the basis of
British foreign policy; and when in office, both in 1852
and in 1858-1859, had acted throughout in the spirit of
that creed. It was not without great reluctance, and only
after mature consideration and the experience of Napoleon's ambition and instability gained during his two
years and a half of office in 1866-1868, that, like Palmerston in his latter days, he abandoned the theory as no
longer practicable; and, in spite of a profound distrust
of Bismarck's policy, began to incline rather to the Court
view that the more natural affinity of Great Britain was
with the Germans, who had often been our allies and never
our enemies. The behaviour of the French Government
and people in July, 1870, confirmed him in his new faith;
and so too did the calculated revelation, by Bismarck,
at this critical moment, of the overtures made to (and
perhaps perfidiously provoked by) him, in 1866 and
subsequently, to abet a French conquest of Belgium in
return for compensations to Prussia in South Germany.

But, though Disraeli considered that the orientation of
our European policy must be changed, he was as determined as the Government that Great Britain must preserve a strict neutrality in the war. Only he insisted,
in a speech on August 1, that it must be an armed
neutrality, a neutrality which on the right occasion might
speak with authority to the belligerents. In such a
neutrality he hoped we might be able to secure the co-

operation of Russia.   But, he asked, were our armaments
in a condition to enable us to adopt this policy ?   This,
though he omitted to claim the credit, was a question he
had every right to put, as the additions to the navy and
army estimates which his own Government had wisely
sanctioned were fiercely denounced by the Liberals during
the General Election of 1868; and the Gladstone Ministry,
in spite of the unstable European equilibrium, had
boasted of the economies and reductions they had effected
during their two years of office.   Disraeli had made careful inquiries, as the Beaconsfield correspondence shows,
into the actual condition of our armed forces, and
warned the Government that there were defects urgently
requiring to be supplied.   Let them remember the
humiliation the country suffered at the time of the
Crimean War, because of the failure of the Aberdeen
Government to come to a decision in time.   Let them
speak to foreign Powers with that clearness and firmness
which could only arise from a due conception of their
duties and a determination to fulfil them.

In this speech Disraeli dwelt upon the vital importance
of securing the neutrality and independence of Belgium,
guaranteed by the Treaty of 1839.   Here he was forcing
an open door, as Ministers, moved by Bismarck's revelation, negotiated a fresh treaty with France and Prussia,
by which, in the event of the violation of Belgian neutrality by either of the belligerent Powers, England bound
herself to co-operate with the other to ensure its observance.   This satisfied public opinion both in England and
in Belgium; and, though Disraeli expressed a doubt
whether a fresh treaty was required and whether a notice
of England's firm determination to uphold the Treaty of
1839 would not have been sufficient, he accepted the
resolve to maintain the independence of Belgium as a
wise and spirited policy.   ' It is of the highest importance
to this country that the whole coast from Ostend to the
North Sea should be in the possession of flourishing
communities, from whose ambition, liberty, or independ-

ence neither England nor any other country can be menaced.'

From Disraeli's correspondence of the autumn we can obtain glimpses into his feelings as to the rapid and startling German victories; the announcement of the impending marriage of a daughter of the Sovereign to a subject, Lord Lorne; and the progress of Con- servatism among the electorate.

To Lord Derby.

GROSVENOR GATE, *Aug.* 17, 1870.—I am here, the focus of all intelligence, and where we get news sooner, than at Berlin or Paris.

I do not much believe in the great battle, wh. they say is going on. The French are in full retreat on their whole line, and the Prussians, as is usual under such circumstances, are following them up and harassing them. Being strong in cavalry, the Germans have an additional advantage.

This collapse of France has all come from the Emperor's policy of nationality. That has created Italy and Germany; wh. has destroyed the French monopoly of Continental com- pactness. The Emperor started this hare in order that he might ultimately get Belgium. Belgium is safe and France is smashed ! . . .

England is busy at mediation, but Prussia thinks the Gauls are not yet sufficiently humiliated. Russia jealous of Prussia, yet hating France—England strong in words, but a mediation of phrases won't do.

P.S.—I never was better: quite, quite myself.

To Lord Cairns.

Oct. 9, 1870.—. . . I have entirely cured mine [gout] by giving up sugar, burgundy, and champagne—almost as great a surrender as Sedan !

To Montagu Corry.

HUGHENDEN, *Oct.* 9, '70.—We go to-morrow to Lord Bathurst's, and I expect to be in town on Friday night and on the following Monday to Knowsley. We have refused almost every invitation this year, and particularly those at a distance : but found it impossible to say *no* to Lord and Lady Derby: the first gathering of their friends. I look forward to the journey with fear and trembling: having scarcely ever left this delicious place in this delicious weather. . . .

To Queen Victoria.

[*Oct.*, 1870.] Mr. Disraeli with his humble duty thanks your Majesty for your gracious kindness in communicating to him through Lady Ely the very happy news of the approaching marriage of the Princess Louise.

The engaging demeanor of Her Royal Highness, her beauty her sensibility and refined taste had always interested him in her career and made him desirous that her lot should not be unworthy of a nature so full of sweetness and promise.

What is about to happen seems to him as wise as it is romantic. Your Majesty has decided with deep discrimination that the time was ripe for terminating an etiquette which has become sterile, and the change will be effected under every circumstance that can command the sympathy of the country.

Mr. Disraeli has the pleasure of knowing Lord Lorne. The gentleness of his disposition and the goodness of his temper are impressed upon his countenance, which, while it is bright with cultivated intelligence, could not, he feels sure, express an evil passion.

Knowing the depths of your Majesty's domestic affection, which the cares of State and the splendor of existence have never for a moment diminished or disturbed, Mr. Disraeli feels that he will be pardoned if he presumes to offer your Majesty his sincere congratulations on an event which will consolidate the happiness of your hearth.

There is no greater risk perhaps than matrimony, but there is nothing happier than a happy marriage.

Though your Majesty must at first inevitably feel the absence of the Princess from the accustomed scene, the pang will soften under the recollection that she is near you and by the spell of frequent intercourse. You will miss her, Madam, only like the stars: that return in their constant season and with all their brightness.

Lady Beaconsfield thanks your Majesty for your Majesty's gracious enquiries after her. She is, I am happy to say, quite well and singularly interested in the subject of your Majesty's communication.

To Lord John Manners.

HUGHENDEN MANOR, *Oct.* 30, 1870.—. . . France can neither make peace or war. No country in modern times has been placed in such a predicament, nor she herself at any time except under Charles the 7th, whose reign she is fast reproducing. She has no men now, as then. Will she have a maiden ?[1]

[1] The reference is, of course, to Joan of Arc.

I am glad to hear of your working-man's meeting. My hope in them hourly increases. How well for the country that we settled the suffrage question ! The trading agitators have nothing to say, or, if they open their mouths, are obliged to have recourse to European Jacobinism. . . .

The Franco-German War had two by-products, both distasteful to Disraeli. The Italian Government seized the opportunity offered by the withdrawal of the French garrison and the serious plight of the French armies to enter and occupy Rome, the last remnant of the Papal States, and to restrict the Pope's temporal jurisdiction to St. Peter's and the Vatican. Disraeli regretted the abasement of anything that represented, as the Pope did, the spiritual order; but Protestant and Italophil England rejoiced. The country, however, was as disturbed as was Disraeli when Russia—instead of combining, as he had hoped, with Great Britain in a watchful and armed neutrality to impose peace at a suitable moment on the belligerents—took advantage of France's critical position and of Britain's comparative helplessness to notify the European Powers, that she would no longer hold herself bound by the Black Sea neutralisation clauses of that Treaty of Paris, which France and Britain, as victorious allies in the Crimean War, had forced her to accept. Granville, who on Clarendon's death in the summer had succeeded him as Foreign Secretary, strongly protested; and the Government, by allowing their agent to threaten a war with Russia which the Prime Minister never seriously contemplated, obtained Bismarck's aid in getting Russia to submit her claim to a Conference of the Powers in London, with the understanding that the modifications she desired would receive European assent.

To Lord Derby.

HUGHENDEN MANOR, *Nov.* 27, 1870.—. . . The Govt. appear to be in trouble, and probably will continue to be so. What[eve]r their ultimate decision, these matters take time. But, no doubt, how[eve]r they may act, their embarrassment must be great, for they can hardly avoid proposing increased armaments.

Gladstone wished a paragraph to be inserted in *The Times* intimating, in dark and involved sentences, that he was not the writer, only the inspirer, of the *Edin. Rev.* Art.—that is to say, I suppose, dictated it to Mr. W. H. Gladstone or, perhaps, to dr. Catherine herself—but Delane refused his columns to the *communiqué* and suggested a distinct letter from the Premier himself, wh. never came.[1]

Dorothy Nevill says that Lowe impressed on her to preach the only gospel, ' Peace at any price,' and that she goes about society preaching accordingly.

Lorne, who has been here for a couple of days, is for cross benches in the House of Commons: significant. . . .

To the Hon. Algernon Egerton.

[? *Dec.* 27, 1870.]—I am honored by the wish of my Lancashire friends that I should pay them a visit and very proud of it.   But in the present critical state of public affairs I doubt the expediency of political gatherings.

I regret that Her Majesty's Ministers did not feel it consistent with their duty to advise the summoning of Parliament before Christmas, but that meeting cannot now be long delayed and our position will then be ascertained from authority, and we shall be better enabled to consider our prospects.   Unquestionably they are serious, and I fear not likely to diminish in gravity: but the people of Lancashire will be more qualified to form an opinion upon them after the Speech from the Throne; and if at a fitting season in the course of next year they continue to care to hear my views of the condition of the country I shall feel it a great and gratifying distinction to be their guest.

To Lord Stanhope.

HUGHENDEN, *Jan.* 22, '71.—. . . I think the avoidance of Parliament, at such a crisis, is highly to be condemned: but I doubt, whether delays will mend their position.

Next to Gambetta, the most wonderful man of the day is John Russell, who raises armies by a stroke of his pen, and

---

[1] Lord Morley writes in *Gladstone*, Bk. VI., ch. 5: ' It was about this time that Mr. Gladstone took what was, for a Prime Minister, the rather curious step of volunteering an anonymous article in a review, upon these great affairs in which his personal responsibility was both heavy and direct.   The precedent can hardly be called a good one, for, as anybody might have known, the veil was torn asunder in a few hours. . . .   The article . . . was calculated to console his countrymen for seeing a colossal European conflict going on, without the privilege of a share in it.   One passage about happy England—happy especially that the wise dispensation of Providence had cut her off by the streak of silver sea from Continental dangers—rather irritated than convinced.'

encourages the country almost in ' Cambyses' vein.' What energy ! At least in imagination.

To Lord Derby.

GROSVENOR GATE, *Jan.* 25, 1871.—My views respecting French affairs are the same as expressed in our talks at Knowsley in the autumn, except that they are stronger. I can conceive nothing more fatal, than our entering into the contest, or assuming an anti-German position; and I deeply regret the inveterate manner in wh. Ld. Salisbury works the Q[*uarterly*] R[*eview*], and inspires the *Standard,* in that direction. No one has recognised his powers more readily than I have done at all times, but he is always wrong.

It is unnecessary for me, therefore, to say, that I entirely agree with all you have written about France, and I shall be careful to use no word in a contrary spirit.

I am not, however, sorry to see the country fairly frightened about foreign affairs. 1st, because it is well, that the mind of the nation should be diverted from that morbid spirit of domestic change and criticism, which has ruled us too much for the last forty years, and that the reign of priggism should terminate. It has done its work, and in its generation very well, but there is another spirit abroad now, and it is time that there shd. be.

2nd, because I am persuaded that any reconstruction of our naval and military systems, that is practicable, will, on the whole, be favorable to the aristocracy, by wh. I mean particularly the proprietors of land: and 3rdly because I do not think the present party in power are well qualified to deal with the external difficulties wh. await them.

I cannot believe, that the conference, tho' peaceable, will be satisfactory, because I understand we are to relinquish all we fought for, and because I am persuaded that Russia will make another move on the board in about six months' time.

Moreover, tho' I do not believe in an American war, I think the U.S. are going to worry us. Their reduction of their over-moderate armaments means nothing. Were there hostilities bet[wee]n U.K. and U.S., they trust to privateering mainly for their naval offence, and their military institutions are of such a character, that they can create a powerful army as quickly as Germany. The Militia system of U.S. was always first-rate, or, in the revolt, our Generals would not have been beaten by a Militia Colonel !

I think the Government, with the information wh. they possessed, were not justified in their reductions; that they completely blundered the business when the crisis arrived; and that they do not comprehend our present position. On all these points I shall attack them, and I shall not discourage the country. And I hope you will not. With all your admirable prudence, I always maintain you were really the boldest Minister that ever managed our external affairs. Witness the Luxemburg guarantee ! the way in wh. you baffled Russia about Crete, when you were left alone; and the Abyssinian expedition—all successful and eminently successful, but daring. *Macte tuâ virtute !*

When Parliament met, Disraeli attacked the Government on the lines of his letter to Derby. While he promised full support for any measures they might propose to increase our military strength, he repeated that an armed neutrality might have prevented war and would certainly shorten it. But how could such a policy be adopted by a country without armaments ? An armed neutrality was a very serious thing for a nation that for a year and a half had been disbanding its veterans; a nation with skeleton battalions and attenuated squadrons, batteries without sufficient guns, and yet more guns than gunners; a nation without a military reserve; a nation, moreover, which had left off shipbuilding, reduced its crews and its stores, and failed to furnish artillery for its men-of-war. This was our plight when we were faced with an upheaval, the magnitude of which was fully realised by Disraeli's vivid imagination.

Let me impress upon the attention of the House the character of this war between France and Germany. It is no common war, like the war between Prussia and Austria, or like the Italian war in which France was engaged some years ago; nor is it like the Crimean War. This war represents the German revolution, a greater political event than the French revolution of last century. I don't say a greater, or as great a social event. What its social consequences may be are in the future. Not a single principle in the management of our foreign affairs, accepted by all statesmen for guidance up to six months ago, any longer exists. There is not a diplomatic tradition which has not been swept away. You have a new world, new influences at work, new and unknown objects and dangers with which to cope, at present involved in that obscurity incident to novelty in such affairs.

We used to have discussions in this House about the balance of power. Lord Palmerston, eminently a practical man, trimmed the ship of State and shaped its policy with a view to preserve an equilibrium in Europe. . . . But what has really come to pass ?   The balance of power has been entirely destroyed, and the country which suffers most, and feels the effects of this great change most, is England.

The result of this destruction of the balance of power was Russia's repudiation of the Treaty of 1856.   Russia had a policy which, if inevitably disturbing, was legitimate and not blameworthy.   She wished to get to the sea.   Disraeli maintained that she had already accomplished her object, and had admirable harbours.   But her further policy, to obtain Constantinople, he pronounced to be illegitimate, like the French claim to have the Rhine.   She had no moral claim to Constantinople; she did not represent the race to which it once belonged; she had two capitals already, and a third would produce a dislocation of the general arrangement of her population. This was the policy which we fought the Crimean War to frustrate; and now the object for which we made serious sacrifices of valuable lives and treasure was to be treated as moonshine and given up in the Conference.

The line which Gladstone and the Government took in answer to this argument was to assert that Palmerston and Clarendon never believed that the neutralisation of the Black Sea could last long, that they said so at the time to diplomatists and in private conversation with friends, and that in consequence they did not attach serious value or importance to that part of the treaty. Lord Morley seems to accept these stories as credible and conclusive.   Disraeli, however, powerfully pointed out in a subsequent debate[1] that England could have obtained all the other stipulations of the Treaty of Paris at the Conference of Vienna in the spring of 1855; but that Palmerston and Clarendon, supported by the country, did not hesitate to fight for another year rather than make peace without

[1] Feb. 24.

obtaining the neutrality of the Black Sea. And yet
Ministers were prepared ' to impute to statesmen of great
eminence, and now unfortunately departed, opinions
not only which they did not hold, but which were contrary to their convictions, which contradicted their
whole policy, and which would intimate that public
men of the highest distinction who proposed a policy,
in enforcing which the treasure of the country was
expended without stint, and the most precious lives of
the country were sacrificed, were laughing in their
sleeves at the excitement of the nation.' Disraeli suggested that those who took Palmerston's private remarks
about public affairs too seriously forgot that that eminent
man was a master of banter, and disliked discussions of
grave matters when not in his cabinet or in the House of
Commons.

Gladstone, with a deplorable lack of humour, had
adduced the fact that he had himself expressed in the
House in 1856 the confident conviction that it was impossible to maintain the neutralisation of the Black Sea,
as evidence of the view taken by the country at the
time. Disraeli reminded him that he was then not a
Minister, nor even leader of Opposition, but the most
unpopular member of ' a minute coterie of distinguished
men who had no following in the country,' and whose
lukewarmness and hesitation were supposed to have been
responsible for the Crimean War. It is no wonder that
Gladstone winced under this attack. ' The Premier
was like a cat on hot bricks,' wrote a looker-on, ' and
presented a striking contrast to Disraeli; for Disraeli cuts
up a Minister with as much *sang-froid* as an anatomist cuts
up a frog. Gladstone could hardly keep his seat. He
fidgeted, took a quire of notes, sent for blue books and
water, turned down corners, and " hear-heared " ironically,
or interrupted his assailant to make a denial of one of his
statements, or to ask the page of a quotation so frequently
that Disraeli had to protest once or twice by raising his
eyebrows or shrugging his shoulders. And when Glad-

stone rose, you could see that every stroke of Disraeli's
had gone home. He was in a white passion, and almost
choked with words, frequently pausing to select the
harshest to be found.'

Disraeli satisfactorily vindicated Palmerston and
Clarendon, and the *bona fides* of British policy in 1855 and
1856, but he observed a discreet silence about his own
personal opinion at the time, which he did not indeed ob-
trude in those years in debate, but to which he had given
frequent vent in the *Press*. As may be remembered [1]
he, like Gladstone, then thought that too much stress
was laid on Black Sea neutralisation, and that restrictions
on the amount of naval force to be maintained by a
Sovereign Power were illusory guarantees. So they had
proved in this case to be, and the Conference of London
buried them decently to the accompaniment of a special
protocol recording that it was ' an essential principle of
the law of nations that no Power can liberate itself from
the engagements of a treaty, nor modify the stipulations
thereof, unless with the consent of the contracting Powers
by means of an amicable arrangement.' But the example
of Russia's success proved more powerful than a paper
protocol. In 1908 Austria, one of the signatories of the
protocol, repudiated an integral portion of the Treaty of
Berlin, just as Russia in 1870 had repudiated an integral
portion of the Treaty of Paris; and, under the threat of
Germany in shining armour, Russia, the Power disregarded in 1908, and Europe acquiesced, without even
providing a conference to give the repudiated clauses
decent burial. It was but a short step from 1908 to 1914.

What Disraeli said in the debate on the Address about
America was almost as noteworthy as what he said about
the Franco-Prussian War and the Russian thunderbolt.
The claims of the United States against Great Britain,
arising out of the American Civil War, were still unsettled; and, in consequence, the then customary licence
of American public men in speaking of this country had

[1] See Vol. I., IV., ch. 1.

exceeded all bounds, even the President himself and the
Chairman of the Foreign Affairs Committee of the Senate
having joined in it. As Gladstone gracefully confessed
in the debate, ' the course of forbearance and prudence '
that Disraeli pursued during the Civil War entitled him,
if any man, to be a critic in this matter without offence;
and his criticism was very plain and timely. The American tone towards Great Britain, he said, was not, as he
once thought, an instance of ' the rude simplicity of Republican manners '; because the American Government
could be courteous enough to other Powers, such as
Russia or Germany. It was only to Great Britain that
they were insolent and offensive; and it was because
they believed that they could adopt this attitude with
impunity. It might be a mere electioneering game;
but Disraeli uttered an impressive warning.

> The danger is this—they habitually excite the passions of
> millions, and some unfortunate thing happens, or something
> unfortunate is said in either country ; the fire lights up, it is
> beyond their control, and the two nations are landed in a
> contest which they can no longer control or prevent. . . .
> Though I should look upon it as the darkest hour of my life
> if I were to counsel or even support in this House a war with
> the United States, still the United States should know that
> they are not an exception to the other countries of the world;
> that we do not permit ourselves to be insulted by any other
> country in the world, and that they cannot be an exception.
> If once . . . it is known that Her Majesty's dominions
> cannot be assaulted without being adequately defended,
> all this rowdy rhetoric, which is addressed to irresponsible
> millions, and as it is supposed with impunity, will cease.

Gladstone had come triumphantly through the first two
sessions of the 1868 Parliament, and had carried three
great Acts—the Irish Church Act, the Irish Land Act, and
the Education Act—in such a manner as to enhance
even his Parliamentary reputation, and to confirm the
position of his Government. The session of 1871
saw a change. Russia's high-handed action appeared
to show that Great Britain under Gladstone enjoyed
no particular consideration in Europe, and his acqui-

escence in Russian demands, thinly disguised under the paraphernalia of a conference, hurt British self-respect and disposed people to look critically upon the other proceedings of his Government. And partly through ill-luck, but mainly through Ministerial ineptitude, there was much to criticise. Disraeli accordingly became more active, and began those mordant and deftly aimed attacks which were eventually to bring the Ministry to the ground.

First of all, the Minister who had persuaded Parliament to discard the principles it cherished for England in order to pacify Ireland, and who had in the winter testified to his belief in the success of his policy by releasing the Fenians still in prison, came nevertheless to Parliament, for the third year in succession, for repressive legislation. The motion which the Chief Secretary made was for a secret Committee to inquire into the condition of an Irish county, Westmeath, where life was rendered intolerable by gross and constant outrages. Disraeli's taunts went home.

The right hon. gentleman [Gladstone] persuaded the people of England that with regard to Irish politics he was in possession of the philosopher's stone. Well, Sir, he has been returned to this House with an immense majority, with the object of securing the tranquillity and content of Ireland. Has anything been grudged him ? Time, labour, devotion— whatever has been demanded has been accorded, whatever has been proposed has been carried. Under his influence and at his instance we have legalised confiscation, consecrated sacrilege, condoned high treason; we have destroyed churches, we have shaken property to its foundation, and we have emptied gaols; and now he cannot govern a county without coming to a Parliamentary Committee ! The right hon. gentleman, after all his heroic exploits, and at the head of his great majority, is making government ridiculous.

To Sir Stafford Northcote.[1]

GROSVENOR GATE, *Mar.* 10, '71.—We have had some disquietude since you left us, and nearly a ministerial crisis.

[1] Who was at Washington, as one of the Commissioners to negotiate the *Alabama* treaty.

Gladstone astonished us all by proposing a secret Committee on some Irish counties, where anarchy is rampant and spreading. It seemed, for four and twenty hours, that the Government must have been beaten: and I was obliged to leave the House with Hardy and between 50 and 60 of our friends to prevent a catastrophe, or something approaching one. However, affairs now are calm again, tho' the unpopularity of the Government, both in and out of the House, [is] daily increasing. If we only had fifty more votes, I could and would turn them out, but in the present state of affairs, they must remain.

Politics seem also interesting in your part of the world, and the expulsion of Sumner [1] from the seat of his ceaseless mischief and malice seems to promise for the success of your mission.

If U.S. would give in their adhesion to the Paris Declaration,[2] my objections to that unwise document would certainly be mitigated, tho' I shall always regret that shallow surrender to waning Cobdenism. I could not however sanction the principle of private property at sea, and I do not believe, in the present state of the public mind, it would go down. There is a rising feeling that stringent maritime rights are the best, perhaps only, check and counterpoise against the military monarchies of the Continent. . . .

The Army Bill does not get on; the Radicals begin to think that, after doing away with purchase, they will have as aristocratic an army as before.

In the next place Lowe, whose Budgets Disraeli scornfully qualified as 'harum-scarum,' produced his most harum-scarum Budget of all. Having an estimated deficit, due to additional military expenditure, of £2,700,000, Lowe proposed to meet it by a tax on matches, an increase of the succession duties, and an increase of 10s. 8d. per cent. (slightly over 1¼d. in the pound) in the income tax. Rich and poor were alike disgusted. Popular discontent compelled the Government incontinently to drop the match-tax; the Whigs brought pressure to bear to prevent the increase of the succession duties; and finally Gladstone announced that Ministers would put the whole burden on the income tax, which would be increased by 2d. On 'the

[1] Sumner was deposed this spring from the chairmanship of the Committee of the Senate on Foreign Relations.
[2] The Declaration of Paris in 1856 about maritime war.

sweet simplicity' of this proposal Disraeli was justifiably severe, and in many felicitous speeches held up
the Budget, the Chancellor of the Exchequer, and the
Government, to scorn and ridicule. The income tax was
essentially an emergency or war tax; it was monstrous,
when your proposed indirect taxes had proved unpopular,
to fall back on direct taxation for the whole amount of
the deficiency. It was equally monstrous to charge the
Opposition, who had the support of only one newspaper
in London, with 'hounding on' the country, and to
attribute to their machinations the pecuniary difficulties
in which the Government were involved.

The mortality among Government Bills was prodigious.
Out of more than 130, the chronicler in the *Annual
Register* tells us, the University Tests Bill alone, with
some trifling exceptions, passed into law in its original
shape. Two Bills of first-class importance—Bruce's
Licensing Bill and Goschen's Local Government Bill—
proved so unpopular, the one in the boroughs, the
other in the counties, that they were withdrawn before second reading. Confidence in the administration of the navy was shaken by the capsizing of our
newest battleship, the *Captain*, and in that of the
army by the postponement of manœuvres owing to the
anticipation of rainy weather! Important business
was thrust aside in order to push forward a Ballot Bill,
to which Gladstone was a very recent convert. 'Why,'
asked Disraeli, 'is all this old stuff brought before us?
Only because the Prime Minister has been suddenly
converted to an expiring faith, and has passionately
embraced a corpse.' It was all, he said, part of a system,
the object of which was to oppress and alarm the public
mind by constant changes. New methods of Government, new principles of property, every subject that could
agitate the mind of nations, had been brought forward
and patronised until the country, anxious and harassed,
knew not what to expect. There might have been a
plausible case, he maintained, for the ballot in the past,

in the days of Old Sarum and Gatton. But now that
the franchise was recognised to be a privilege and not
a trust, it was a retrograde step to divorce political life
from publicity. The Bill, obstructed by Conservative
free-lances—Beresford Hope, James Lowther, and the
Bentincks—in the Commons, was defeated in the Lords.

The principal measure of the session, Cardwell's Army
Regulation Bill, was indeed passed into law in a truncated
form; but not until the Prime Minister, irritated by a
dilatory resolution in the Lords, had invoked the prerogative to effect the main alteration proposed, the abolition of
the system by which officers purchased their promotion.
The system had grown up under Royal Warrant, and the
Queen was in the end advised to terminate it by Royal
Warrant, but only after the greater part of the session
had been occupied in the effort to terminate it by the
clauses of a Bill. So far as Cardwell's measure was
calculated to effect a reorganisation of all our military
forces, and to create a reserve by short service, Disraeli
supported it; and he did not even oppose the abolition of
purchase; though he rather doubted whether there was a
really strong feeling on the subject in the country, and
whether a system of selection would give us the officers
we wanted. But he unhesitatingly disapproved the *coup
d'état* by which Ministers attained their object. It was
part of 'an avowed and shameful conspiracy against the
privileges' of the House of Lords. He did not dispute
the prerogative of the Crown; but the prerogative should
not be used to cut the Gordian knots that have to be
encountered in dealing with popular assemblies. 'No
Minister acts in a wise manner who, finding himself
baffled in passing a measure, . . . comes forward and
tells the House that he will defy the opinion of Parliament,
and appeals to the prerogative of the Crown to assist
him in the difficulties which he himself has created.'
Public opinion supported Disraeli in this protest against
the manner in which an otherwise popular reform was
carried.

To Montagu Corry.

HUGHENDEN, *Sept.* 17, '71.—. . . I am sorry to find we shall not have you for our harvest home, which is on the 26th. Lancashire hangs fire. They themselves only propose the end of January, or the first week in February. I would not, under any circumstances, involve myself in such distant engagements, and I am still very doubtful, whether affairs are yet ripe enough for the move: in spite of Truro.[1] I have answered Lancashire in your name, not extinguishing all hope.

We have never left Hughenden for a moment. Enjoying a summer of unbroken brilliancy: Miladi very well indeed. . . .

Meyer de Rothschild continues his year of triumphs,[2] and Bucks is proud of having the first stable in the country. . . . Lord Russell is going abroad for a year, and shall not return for Parliament 'unless,' he adds, 'Mr. Gladstone attempts to abolish the House of Lords.' He has become quite deaf, but my informant tells me most agreeable and entertaining, because, as he can hear no one talk, he never ceases to talk himself. But when he is exhausted, he is bored, and you must go. . . .

In the course of this year 1871, as Lord Morley tells us, ' a wave of critical feeling began to run upon the throne.' [3] The seclusion which the Queen had practised since the death of her husband was not unnaturally resented by her people; and her Prime Minister repeatedly pressed her to increase the number of her public appearances. Neither Minister nor people quite realised the physical weakness which at this period made it impossible for Her Majesty to add, to the unceasing and laborious duties which she was bound to perform of government behind the scenes, those ceremonial displays which make much more demand upon the strength than can be easily understood by private individuals, whose modest position exempts them from the tiring experience. Disraeli had the knowledge and insight which others lacked; and he took the opportunity of the harvest festival at Hughenden to explain what the state of the Queen's health was, and how conscientiously in spite of weakness she carried on the most material part of her work.

---

[1] The Conservatives won a seat at Truro in a by-election this month.
[2] On the turf.   [3] *Gladstone*, Bk. VI., ch. 10.

The health of the Queen has for several years been a subject of anxiety to those about her, but it is only within the last year that the country generally has become acquainted with the gravity of that condition. I believe I may say that there is some improvement in Her Majesty's health, but I fear a long time must elapse before it will reach that average condition which she has for some time enjoyed, and I do not think we can conceal from ourselves that a still longer time must elapse before Her Majesty will be able to resume the performance of those public and active duties which it was once her pride and pleasure to fulfil, because they brought her into constant and immediate contact with her people. The fact is we cannot conceal from ourselves that Her Majesty is physically incapacitated from performing those duties, but it is some consolation to Her Majesty's subjects to know that, in the performance of those much higher duties which Her Majesty is called upon to perform she is still remarkable for a punctuality and a precision which have never been surpassed, and rarely equalled, by any monarch of these realms.

A very erroneous impression is prevalent respecting the duties of the Sovereign of this country. Those duties are multifarious; they are weighty, and they are unceasing. I will venture to say that no head of any department in the State performs more laborious duties than fall to the Sovereign of this country. There is not a despatch received from abroad nor one sent from this country which is not submitted to the Queen. The whole internal administration of this country greatly depends upon the sign manual; and of our present Sovereign it may be said that her signature has never been placed to any public document of which she did not know the purport and of which she did not approve. Those Cabinet Councils of which you all hear, and which are necessarily the scene of anxious and important deliberations, are reported and communicated on their termination by the Minister to the Sovereign, and they often call from her critical remarks, necessarily requiring considerable attention. And I will venture to add that no person likely to administer the affairs of this country would treat the suggestions of Her Majesty with indifference, for at this moment there is probably no person living in this country who has such complete control over the political traditions of England as the Sovereign herself. The last generation of statesmen have all, or almost all, disappeared: the Sir Robert Peels, the Lord Derbys, the Lord Palmerstons have gone; and there is no person who can advise Her Majesty, or is likely to advise Her Majesty in the times in which we live, who can have such a complete mastery of what has occurred in this country, and of all the

great and important affairs of State, foreign and domestic, for
the last thirty-four years, as the Queen herself. He, therefore,
would not be a wise man who would not profit by Her Majesty's
judgment and experience. . . .

I would venture, in conclusion, to remind those whom I
address that, although Her Majesty may be, and often is, of
great service and assistance to her servants, there never was
a more Constitutional Sovereign than our present Queen.
All who have served her would admit that, when Ministers
have been selected by her in deference to what she believed
to be the highest interests of the State in the opinion of the
country, she gives to them a complete confidence and un-
deviating support. But although there never was a Sovereign who would more carefully avoid arrogating to herself
any power or prerogative which the Constitution does not
authorise, so I would add there never was a Sovereign more
jealous, or more wisely jealous, of the prerogatives which the
Constitution has allotted to her, because she believes they
are for the welfare of her people.

The effect of Disraeli's words was unfortunately marred
by a slip which he made in speaking—a slip which party
malice magnified and distorted. He said that the Queen
was 'physically *and morally* incapacitated' from performing her duties of ceremonial and pageant. It was not a
happy phrase and he immediately recalled it; but it gave
no real foundation for the legend that was promptly
circulated, to the effect that the Opposition leader had
declared the Queen to be mentally incapacitated for
her work. Even the Queen herself was disturbed, and
Disraeli had to explain.

To Sir William [Jenner].[1]

[*Oct.*, 1871.]—. . . I need not assure you that the
epithet *moral* involves *mental* no more than the epithet
physical does. What I meant to convey was that neither
Her Majesty's frame nor feelings could at present bear the
strain and burthen of the pageantry of State.

After I had used the word it was suggested to me that it
might be misinterpreted by the simple, and I requested the
reporters to omit it. I understood they willingly agreed to

---

[1] The letter is printed from a draft, but it is fairly clear that Jenner,
Her Majesty's physician, is the 'Sir William' to whom it was addressed.

do so; but it seems the *Daily Telegraph* could not resist the opportunity of attempting a sensation.

The whole Press of authority, *Times, Post, Standard, Pall Mall, Daily News, Spectator, Saturday Review, Echo,* have denounced, or utterly disregarded, the interpretation of the *Telegraph,* which the country have not accepted and have felt to be quite inconsistent with the whole tenor of my observations.

I need not say how deeply I regret that any expression of mine should have occasioned pain to Her Majesty, especially when my only object in speaking was an humble endeavor to assist the Queen. . . .

A selection from Disraeli's letters throws some light on his interests during the autumn and winter of this year, the later weeks of which were a period of acute anxiety, owing to the dangerous illness of the Prince of Wales from typhoid fever.

To the Duke of Wellington.

[? *Oct.*, 1871.]—. . .   I was detained in town for three days with my time greatly to myself, and I spent it in examining and then partly perusing these 3 volumes [of the Wellington Despatches and Memoranda]—with such keen interest, with so much delight, I may say, that I cannot refrain from expressing to you, however imperfectly, my sense of their inestimable value.   They form out-and-out much the most interesting political book that has been published in this century.   Indeed I know of no memoirs of a great leading character, either in civil or military life, in any age or language, that I can place above them.   The importance of the subjects treated, their immense variety, the striking events, the marked and historic character of the correspondents, the towering greatness of the chief actor, make a whole, so far as my knowledge can guide me, unrivalled.

It would be useless to select portions or passages, yet if I had to name a composition which, alike in conception and execution, may vie with anything in classic pages, it is the letter of the Duke recommending the appointment of Mr. Canning to the King.   Nothing more noble and nothing more skilful was ever penned by man, and one feels, as one reads it, that it must have raised and re-established, at least for the moment, the lax and shattered moral tone of the individual to whom it was addressed.

All about Canning subsequently, all about poor Castlereagh's sad and I fear disgraceful end, are most dramatic

That is the character of the volumes. They are full of life, and stirring life. The papers on the campaign, on the state of Spain and so on, all beyond praise.

The effect of reading these volumes on me is this: that although my time for the past is now very limited, I shall certainly read the whole of your great father's works: a volume will always be at hand when I have time to recur to what has gone before us.

The country owes you a debt of gratitude not easily to be repaid for the publication of this book.

To Lord Henry Lennox.

GROSVENOR GATE, *Nov.* 3, '71.—I thought your speech thoroughly capital: out-and-out, the star of the recess. I have not read Gladstone's.[1] I tried, but I could not get on with it: not a ray of intellect or a gleam of eloquence. They tell me that, if I had persevered, I should have been repaid, by encountering a quotation from the Hyde Park Litany; either a burlesque of the Athanasian Creed or of the National Anthem; equally appropriate in the mouth of our most religious and loyal ruler. . . .

To Montagu Corry.

HUGHENDEN, *Dec.* 4, '71.—. . . . Our camp is struck, and, probably in 8 and 40 hours, we shall be settled permanently at G.G. The stable goes up to-morrow. The severe and savage weather, that prevents all outdoor employment, quite sickened my lady, who had trusted to planting and marking trees to amuse her. Now she sighs for Park Lane, and twilight talk and tea. The Canford party rather precipitated her resolve, but the prospect even of that being put off will not now change affairs here. . . .

We have received telegrams from Sandringham every morning, and generally speaking Francis Knollys[2] has written by post with details which telegrams cannot convey. Our telegram this morning the most favorable we have yet received, and the second post, which brought your letter, brought also one from F. K.

They are still very nervous at Sandringham, and very cautious in their language, but it is evident to me, that they think they have turned the corner. . . .

---

[1] Gladstone's famous speech of two hours in the open air at Blackheath in the course of which he quoted, with approval, from a republican and secularist book of poems, a parody of the National Anthem.

[2] Private Secretary to the Prince of Wales, and subsequently to King Edward and King George; now Viscount Knollys.

To Gathorne Hardy.

GROSVENOR GATE, *Dec.* 23, 1871.—I had seen Noel[1] before I received your letter, and had given him the same answer as you had done. Great wits, etc.

The proposition is absurd. We cannot modify the position we have taken up on the Ballot, tho' many of our friends may wish to do so. It wd. break up the party, which is in a tolerably robust state at present.

What we shd. do, is to get the Bill thro' our House with as much promptitude as decency permits. The Govt. wd. like to keep it there and distract attention from other matters. Our policy is the reverse.

There must be a discussion on the principle, but it need not be a prolonged one, and, in Comm[itt]ee, we shd. confine ourselves to *bona fide* improvements of its machinery, wh. may be the foundation, if fortune favored us, of a future compromise.

We are here rather unexpectedly, having been stopped in our progress to country houses by the impending calamity, and being too anxious to return to Hughenden; and now, in a few days, we shall have to fulfil some of these engagements, so I don't think we shall return to Bucks. . . .

[1] One of the Whips.

CHAPTER IV.

LOTHAIR.

1869–1870.

In 1869 Disraeli had some real leisure, for the first time for many years. When he led the Opposition against Russell, Aberdeen, and Palmerston, it had been in Parliaments where parties were fairly balanced, and a change of Government was always a possibility. In these circumstances the labours of leadership were nearly as onerous in opposition as in office. But, with the large and compact majority of 1868, Gladstone's Government was for the time impregnable; and Disraeli's mind therefore naturally turned to his early love, literature. It was more than twenty years since the publication of his last novel, *Tancred*, in March, 1847; it was nearly twenty years since his last book, *Lord George Bentinck*, in December, 1851; it was more than a dozen years since he had ceased active journalism in the *Press*, in February, 1856. *Tancred* and *Lord George Bentinck* and the articles in the *Press* had still breathed, though not to the extent of his earlier political writing, the spirit of combat and propaganda; they had been the work of one who, though he had risen high, was still fighting for his ideas and for his place. Now he had arrived; he had carried a great historical measure; he had held the highest position under the Crown; his ambition was largely satisfied; and when he began to write again, in his sixty-fifth year, it was in a somewhat different vein. He surveyed the great world of his day, now intimately known by him, and he drew a picture of aristocratic and political society, and of the

ideas animating it, together with the currents of thought
and action which were moulding the history of Europe.
Like the great trilogy of *Coningsby*, *Sybil*, and *Tancred*,
Lothair was a political novel, and a political novel dealing
with the events of the day; unlike them, its underlying
purpose seems to have been subordinated to a desire to
mirror and satirise the passing show.   Unlike them, too,
it observes a reticence, becoming in an ex-Premier, with
regard to the leading figures in the political arena and to
the immediate subjects of acute political dissension.

Different as it was from the trilogy in its outlook, it
was different also in the secrecy in which it was conceived
and written.   ' I make it a rule never to breathe a word
on such matters to anyone,' Disraeli told a literary friend
in 1872.   'My private secretary, Mr. Montagu Corry,
who possesses my entire confidence in political matters,
who opens all my letters, and enters my cabinet and deals,
as he likes, with all my papers in my absence, never knew
anything about *Lothair* until he read the advertisement
in the journals.'   This was a new practice for Disraeli, as
in regard to the trilogy and to *Lord George Bentinck* he
made confidences about his progress from time to time
to his sister, and to his close friends such as Manners,
Smythe, and Lady Londonderry.   No such sources of
information are available in regard to the composition of
Lothair.   But the incident which suggested the main
action of the story, the reception of the third Marquis of
Bute into the Church of Rome, only took place in
December, 1868.   Disraeli had then just resigned office;
and we may therefore confidently look upon the book as
the firstfruits of his retirement.   The stimulus to write
it may well have been provided by the offer of £10,000
for a novel, which was made to him by a publisher
immediately on his resignation, but declined with
thanks.   The book was finished in the spring of 1870.
The arrangement with Longmans for its publication was
made in February of that year, and it appeared at the
beginning of May.

The story of *Lothair* covers almost exactly the period
of Disraeli's third tenure of office; it is all comprised
between the August of 1866 and the August of 1868; and
yet, though a great number of his English characters are
more or less politicians, there is no reference to the Reform
struggles or to the passage of the Reform Bill, or (save as
a matter involving urgent whips) to the debates on the
Irish Church; nor is there any personal allusion to the
Prime Ministers of the time, first Derby and then Disraeli
himself.   The political and social movements, the intellectual and spiritual problems, which form the background
of Disraeli's story, had in truth little relation with actual
proceedings in Westminster Palace.   Secret societies and
their international energies, the Church of Rome and her
claims and methods, the eternal conflict between science
and faith: these are the forces shown to be at work beneath
the surface of that splendid pageant of English aristocracy
in which most of Disraeli's characters move, and which he
never described with more brilliance and gusto than in
Lothair.   So brilliant is that description that Froude
even asks us to see the true value of the book in its
perfect representation of patrician society in England
flourishing in its fullest bloom, but, like a flower, opening fully only to fade.

   The plot is simple.   The hero, one of those fortunate
beings whom he loved to paint, an orphan peer—apparently
a marquis—of fabulous wealth, brought up and educated
quietly in Presbyterian fashion in Scotland, is thrown,
as he reaches adolescence, fresh upon the world, first
of Oxford, and then of London and the great country
houses.   The priggishness born of his early education
leads him at the outset to say, ' My opinions are already
formed on every subject; that is to say, every subject of
importance; and, what is more, they will never change.'
But he is in reality very impressionable, and anxious to
discover, like Tancred, what he ought to do and what he
ought to believe.   All the influences and all the teachers
of the day are naturally concentrated upon one whose

adhesion might be expected so materially to benefit any
cause which he espoused. The main struggle is between
three forces, represented by three women, with all of
whom Lothair falls successively in love.   These forces are,
first, the Church of Rome; secondly, the international
revolution and what may be called free religion; and
thirdly, the Church of England and the round of duties
and occupations natural to Lothair's birth and station.
Clare Arundel, the representative of the first force, is an
attractive and ardent saint; Theodora Campian, the representative of the second force, has great personal charm,
lofty character, and high purpose. But Theodora dies and
Clare enters a convent; and the victory is won in the end
by the Lady Corisande, the representative of the third
force, whose principles are indeed immaculate but who is
a somewhat uninteresting heroine. The action takes
place mainly in London and in three English country
houses; but the autumn and winter of 1867 are occupied
with Lothair's experiences in Rome and the neighbourhood; and the spring of 1868 finds him in those scenes
of the Mediterranean and the Holy Land which Disraeli
visited as a young man and afterwards lovingly reproduced in so many of his novels.

Nothing in the book is more carefully drawn or more
delicately finished than the chapters which deal with the
Roman Catholic group of priests and laymen who conspire
—the word is hardly too strong—to entrap Lothair into
the Roman Church. The old Catholic English family—
Lord St. Jerome, devout and easy in his temper, but an
English gentleman to the backbone, who gave at his ball
suppers the same champagne that he gave at his dinners;
Lady St. Jerome, an enthusiastic convert, ' a woman to
inspire crusaders,' who received Lothair at a party ' with
extreme unction'; and their beautiful niece, Clare Arundel,
who could only be weaned from the convent in which
her hopes had centred by the vision of attracting
Lothair through marriage into the true fold: and then the
priests—Father Coleman, whose devotion to gardening

masked his skill as a controversialist; Monsignore Catesby, the aristocratic and fashionable missionary of the Church to convert the upper classes; Monsignore Berwick, the priest as statesman, the favourite pupil of Antonelli; and Cardinal Grandison, a wonderful study of asceticism, devotion, high breeding, tact, delicacy, and unscrupulousness, whose appearance and manner were copied from Manning, though some of his mental and moral characteristics may be referred to Wiseman. ' It seemed that the soul never had so frail and fragile a tenement' as his attenuated form; ' I never eat and I never drink,' he said in refusing an invitation to dinner. One marked feature in his character was that he was ' an entire believer in female influence, and a considerable believer in his influence over females.'

Disraeli was at once attracted and repelled by Rome. Her historical tradition and her sensuous and ceremonial worship appealed strongly to one side of his nature; but he was even more keenly alive to the bondage which she imposed upon the spirit of man, and he had been of late particularly impressed by the stealthy and indirect methods which her propaganda in England had assumed. He had had a personal experience of a disagreeable but revealing character in the ' stab in the back ' which Manning and the Roman party had given him over the question of University education. Both the attraction and the repulsion are brought out in *Lothair*. The description of the service of *Tenebræ* in Holy Week at Vauxe, the St. Jeromes' country house, is such as to satisfy the emotions of a devout Roman Catholic; the St. Jerome family life and Clare's aspirations are sympathetically treated; and there is no lack of appreciation of the enormous support the Roman Church affords to that religious element in man which he held it to be essential to foster.

On the other hand, a large portion of the book is occupied by a merciless dissection of the various arts employed by Cardinals and Monsignori to entangle

Lothair so deeply in the meshes of Roman influence that conversion might appear to him to be the only honourable outcome. Begun in London and at Vauxe, continued during the coming-of-age festivities at Muriel Towers, and brought to a climax at Rome after the battle of Mentana, these machinations were so cleverly contrived that their object was within an ace of accomplishment. Moved by the overpowering personality of Theodora, Lothair had temporarily thrown off their trammels, and had even ranged himself by Garibaldi's side in the advance on Rome in the autumn of 1867. The return of the French garrison had wrecked the hopes of the enterprise; Theodora was killed; and Lothair himself fell, badly wounded, at Mentana. A kindly Italian peasant woman of handsome mien brought news of his plight to Clare Arundel, who was in Rome for the winter and occupied in caring for the faithful wounded. She found him all unconscious in a hospital and nursed him back to life. During his illness a pious legend was evolved; the peasant woman was discovered to be the Virgin Mary, recognised as such by the halo round her head; and it was claimed that Lothair had been fighting, when he fell, on behalf of the Pope instead of against him. He was induced in his weak state to support Clare in an ecclesiastical function which he believed to be merely one of thanksgiving for recovery, but which the official Papal journal treated as a solemn recognition on his part of the special favour shown by the Mother of God to her chivalrous defender. The mendacities of the official account drove Lothair, still suffering, and almost a prisoner of the Church in a Roman palace, to a mixture of indignation and despair; but he thought he might rely on Cardinal Grandison as an English gentleman and a man of honour to put the matter right. He was mistaken; and the description of the conversation between the two is inimitable.

To Lothair's protestations against ' a tissue of falsehood and imposture,' the Cardinal opposed confidence in an ' official journal ' drawn up by ' truly pious men.' It

was, he said, the ' authentic ' story of what happened at
Mentana; Lothair's own statement, he airily suggested,
had neither confirmation nor probability; ' you have been
very ill, my dear young friend, and labouring under much
excitement.' Such hallucinations were not uncommon,
and would wear off with returning health.

King George IV. believed that he was at the Battle of
Waterloo, and indeed commanded there; and his friends
were at one time a little alarmed; but Knighton, who was a
sensible man, said, ' His Majesty has only to leave off curaçao,
and rest assured he will gain no more victories.'

Lothair must remember, the Cardinal continued, that he
was in the centre of Christendom, the abode of truth.
' Divine authority has perused this paper and approved
it. . . . It records the most memorable event of the
century.' The appearance of the Virgin in Rome had
given the deathblow to atheism and the secret societies;
Lothair must return to England and reconquer it for
Rome. The eye of Christendom was upon him. He
might be bewildered like St. Thomas, but like him
he would become an apostle. The Holy Father would
personally receive him next day into the bosom of the
Church.

In spite of all the Cardinal's arts, a vision of Theodora
at night in the Coliseum—Disraeli was partial to visions
as a melodramatic resource—saved Lothair from the
priests; and the Cardinal, when he met him afterwards
in London, affected complete unconsciousness as to the
intrigue in Rome, and even suggested to him that he
should attend the approaching Ecumenical Council as an
Anglican !

The revolutionary characters in *Lothair* are almost as
closely studied, in themselves, and in their setting, as the
Roman. With the Revolution as with Rome Disraeli,
who claimed once that he had a revolutionary mind, had
a certain sympathy, which, though it did not blind him to
the impossible nature of the creed, enabled him to understand it. Theodora herself is certainly his most elabor-

ately conceived heroine. Seen by Lothair first at an
evening party, her face is thus described: ' It was the face
of a matron, apparently of not many summers, for her
shapely figure was still slender, though her mien was
stately. . . . The countenance . . . pale, but perfectly
Attic in outline, with the short upper lip and the round
chin, and a profusion of dark chestnut hair bound by a
Grecian fillet, and on her brow a star.' She had sat for
the head of ' La République Française ' in 1850, as a girl
of seventeen, and was therefore well over thirty when she
met Lothair in the autumn of 1866. She was the wife of
an American Colonel, with a villa at Putney. An Italian
by birth, she was an ardent sympathiser with movements
for freedom throughout the world; but for the unity of
her native country and the destruction of Papal government in Rome she was prepared to give her life. Dr.
Garnett has happily observed that ' she impersonates all
the traits which Shelley especially valued in woman,' and
that she was also her creator's ideal. ' There is not a
single touch of satire in the portrait; it plainly represents
the artist's highest conception of woman.' A hater of
priests and priestcraft, Theodora is yet strongly religious
in her idealistic way. Orthodoxy, she holds, has very
little to do with religion; ' I worship,' she tells Lothair,
' in a church where I believe God dwells, and dwells for
my guidance and my good: my conscience.' The romantic
adoration, free from all sensual taint, with which she
inspires Lothair is drawn with great delicacy. Indeed
' the exquisite and even sublime friendship, which had
so strongly and beautifully arisen, like a palace in a dream,
and absorbed his being,' was a sentiment of which the
author was himself capable, at all stages of his life.

As Theodora represents the ideal side of the revolutionary movement, so Captain Bruges embodies the
practical side. His career corresponds to, and may have
been copied from, that of General Cluseret, the military
commander who was so prominent in the Paris Commune.
Bruges's common sense and resolution shine amid the

mouthings of the revolutionary council in Soho and the
turmoil of the Fenian meeting in Hoxton; and when he
takes command of the camp in the Apennines he appears
as a true leader of men, bold, wary, and unscrupulous.
His mission is to be the sword-arm of the secret societies,
Mary Anne of France and Madre Natura of Italy.

From a very early date, Disraeli had been deeply
impressed by the widespread activities of the secret
societies in Europe. He drew special attention to the
danger in *Lord George Bentinck* and in his speeches in the
House of Commons on the Italian question. During his
recent term of office, Irish and Irish-American Fenianism
had to be met and defeated; and the information that
then poured in upon the Government confirmed and
extended his previous knowledge of revolutionary conspiracies. Of all this he made full use in *Lothair*.
Reviewers accused him of gross exaggeration, of conjuring
up imaginary perils; Mary Anne, though referred to in the
protocols of Paris in 1856, was treated as a bogey. But
within a year the outbreak of the Paris Commune, with
its revelation of the malign workings of the International
Society, showed how thoroughly well justified were the
apprehensions of Disraeli's Monsignori and diplomatists,
and the boasts of his revolutionaries. Catesby says of the
secret societies: 'They have declared war against the
Church, the State, and the domestic principle. All the
great truths and laws on which the family reposes are
denounced. Their religion is the religion of science.'
The French Ambassador declares that the Mary Anne
associations in France were all alive and astir. 'Mary
Anne,' he explains, ' was the real name for the Republic
years ago, and there always was a sort of myth that these
societies had been founded by a woman. . . . The word
has gone out to all these societies that Mary Anne has
returned, and will issue her orders, which must be obeyed.'
And Bruges, the revolutionary general, confirms the
representatives of authority. 'There are more secret
societies at this moment than at any period since '85,

though you hear nothing of them; and they believe in
Mary Anne, and in nothing else.' He anticipates, moreover, and defends the policy of arson which the Commune
employed, to the world's horror, in Paris in the spring of
1871. He is speaking of Rome. 'Those priests! I
fluttered them once. Why did I spare any ? Why did
I not burn down St. Peter's ? I proposed it.' There was
something to be said for Monsignore Berwick's ejacula-
tion: ' It is the Church against the secret societies. They
are the only two strong things in Europe, and will
survive kings, emperors, or parliaments.'

When Disraeli dealt with his third set of influences, those
springing from English society and the Anglican Communion, he painted with some boldness from people he knew
and personal and family circumstances which had come
directly under his observation. The plot was suggested by
Lord Bute's recent conversion to Rome; and Bute's history was faithfully followed in Lothair's vast fortune and
long minority, in his elaborate coming-of-age festivities,
in his relations with Monsignore Capel (called in the book
Catesby, but ' Capel ' appeared by a slip in one passage
in the original issue), and even in the ducal family where
he went to seek a bride. But Lothair was not received
into the Church of Rome, and Bute in the end married a
lady who was not a daughter of ' the duke ' of the novel.
Nor did Lothair resemble Bute in appearance, character,
or tastes. Indeed Lothair is given so little character,
save that of general candour, openness, and desire to do
right, coupled with a trifle of priggishness, that Sir Leslie
Stephen is almost justified in his remark that ' Lothair
reduces himself so completely to a mere " passive bucket "
to be pumped into by every variety of teacher, that he is
unpleasantly like a fool.'

If the hero's circumstances almost directly reproduced
Bute's, there is a still closer resemblance between ' the
duke ' of *Lothair* and his family, and a duke and his
family who were numbered among Disraeli's friends.
' Lord Abercorn has thirteen children,' wrote Disraeli in

1863 to Mrs. Willyams after meeting the Abercorns at Hatfield; 'and looks as young as his son who is an M.P. . . . His daughters are so singularly pretty that they always marry during their first season, and always make the most splendid matches.' So of the ducal family described in the early pages of *Lothair* we are told that the sons and daughters reproduced the appearance and character of their parents, and the daughters 'all met the same fate. After seventeen years of a delicious home, they were presented and immediately married.' The Duke of Abercorn, who obtained his dukedom on Disraeli's recommendation, was one of the handsomest men of the day; and society enjoyed the gentle raillery which wrote of ' the duke ': ' Every day when he looked into the glass, and gave the last touch to his consummate toilette,[1] he offered his grateful thanks to Providence that his family was not unworthy of him.' That the family so graciously characterised by Disraeli was not unworthy has since been abundantly shown by the distinguished place its members have occupied in the political and social world. But Disraeli has dowered the dukedom of Abercorn with all, and more than all, the then possessions of that of Sutherland. Brentham must be Trentham, and Crecy House in London Stafford House (now the London Museum).

From Montagu Corry.

ADMIRALTY, *Sept.* 22, 1868.—. . . He (Lord Bute) is going to Baronscourt next month, it is evident rather as a claimant of his bride than as a suitor. Evidently the whole matter is already arranged. But still, I fear, that his joining himself to the ' scarlet woman '—and soon too—is equally certain.

Fergusson says that no ingenuity can counteract the influence which certain priests and prelates have over him, chief among them being Monsignore Capel. The speedy result is inevitable, and the consummation is only delayed till he has won his bride. . . .

[1] Disraeli seldom committed the artistic mistake of reproducing the character and habits of his original in every detail. The Duke of Abercorn was careless about the fit of his clothes.

The Anglican Bishop is clearly taken from Wilberforce; and, considering the licence which the Bishop since the autumn of 1868 had permitted himself to use in speaking and writing of Disraeli, it is a not unflattering portrait. The Bishop in *Lothair* is described as ' polished and plausible, well-lettered, yet quite a man of the world. He was fond of society, and justified his taste in this respect by the flattering belief that by his presence he was extending the power of the Church; certainly favouring an ambition which could not be described as being moderate.' We are told of his ' gracious mien,' his ' honeyed expressions '; that he was a ' man of contrivance and resolution '; while in his lighter moments he was capable of ' seraphic raillery,' ' angelic jokes,' and ' lambent flashes.' It was when he had made some particularly deadly lunge or adroit parry, in the secret duel for Lothair's soul which was carried on between him and the Cardinal at Muriel Towers, that these playful characteristics were displayed.

The minor characters are as distinctive and amusing as they are wont to be in Disraeli's novels. There is St. Aldegonde, heir to the wealthiest dukedom in the kingdom, but ' a republican of the reddest dye. He was opposed to all privilege, and indeed to all orders of men, except dukes, who were a necessity. He was also strongly in favour of the equal division of all property, except land. Liberty depended upon land, and the greater the landowners the greater the liberty of a country.' He comes down to breakfast in a country house on Sunday morning in a ' shooting jacket of brown velvet and a pink shirt and no cravat,' and, in the presence of the Bishop of the diocese, exclaims ' in a loud voice, and with the groan of a rebellious Titan, " How I hate Sunday !" '

Then there is Mr. Phœbus, the painter, who belongs rather to the revolutionary group than to the panorama of society; a descendant of Gascon nobles, and brilliant, brave, and boastful as they; the prophet of Aryan art against Semitism. ' When Leo the Tenth was Pope,' he says, ' popery was pagan; popery is now Christian, and

art is extinct.' What he admires about the aristocracy
is that they 'live in the air, that they excel in athletic
sports; that they can only speak one language; and that
they never read.' It was the highest education since the
Greek. Nothing could induce him to use paper money;
but he carried about with him on his travels 'several
velvet bags, one full of pearls, another of rubies, another
of Venetian sequins, Napoleons, and golden piastres. "I
like to look at them," said Mr. Phœbus, "and find life
more inténse when they are about my person. But bank
notes, so cold and thin, they give me an ague."' He
rented an island in the Ægean where, in the company of his
beautiful Greek wife and her equally attractive sister, he
'pursued a life partly feudal, partly Oriental, partly
Venetian, and partly idiosyncratic'; but, in spite of his
Aryanism, he consented to go to the Holy Land on a commission from the Russian Government to paint Semitic
subjects, moved partly by the reflection, 'They say no one
can draw a camel. If I went to Jerusalem a camel would
at last be drawn.' It was Phœbus who refurbished and
launched the ancient gibe at the critics, as 'the men who
have failed in literature and art.'

Mr. Pinto is another capital sketch; the middle-aged,
oily Portuguese who was one of the marvels of society.
'Instead of being a parasite, everybody flattered him; and
instead of being a hanger-on of society, society hung on
Pinto.' 'He was not an intellectual Crœsus, but his
pockets were full of sixpences.' Here is one of his 'sixpences' in conversation with St. Aldegonde. 'English
is an expressive language, but not difficult to master. Its
range is limited. It consists, as far as I can observe, of
four words: "nice," "jolly," "charming," and "bore."'

Then we have Lord and Lady Clanmorne, 'so good-
looking and agreeable that they were as good at a dinner-
party as a couple of first-rate entrées'; and Apollonia, the
wife of Putney Giles, the prosperous solicitor, whose
principal mission it was to destroy the Papacy and her
lesser impulses to become acquainted with the aristocracy

and to be surrounded by celebrities. Sir William Stirling Maxwell, in congratulating Disraeli, happily singled out 'your remarkable power of painting a character by a single stroke.'

Nor must we forget Mr. Ruby, the Bond Street jeweller, whose conversation with his eminent clients is delightful. He holds forth to Lothair on pearls.

Pearls are troublesome property, my Lord. They require great care; they want both air and exercise; they must be worn frequently; you cannot lock them up. The Duchess of Havant has the finest pearls in the country, and I told her Grace, 'Wear them whenever you can, wear them at break-fast;' and her Grace follows my advice, she does wear them at breakfast. I go down to Havant Castle every year to see her Grace's pearls, and I wipe every one of them myself, and let them lie on a sunny bank in the garden, in a westerly wind, for hours and days together. Their complexion would have been ruined had it not been for this treatment.

Visitors to Hughenden in the latter years of Lady Beaconsfield's life remember how faithfully Disraeli followed Mr. Ruby's advice; how he was wont himself, on sunny days, to bring out his wife's pearls and lay them carefully on the grass by the terrace, so that they might not fail to get the 'air' which was so important for their complexion.

Scattered here and there throughout the book are many shrewd political appreciations. Take this, of Scotland: 'The Establishment and the Free Kirk are mutually sighing for some compromise which may bring them together again; and if the proprietors would give up their petty patronage, some flatter themselves that it might be arranged.' Disraeli himself was to abolish the 'petty patronage,' and now for several years Presbyterian reunion has been drawing visibly nearer. About Ireland there is naturally more. A revolutionary leader says of the Irish: 'Their treason is a fairy tale, and their sedition a child talking in its sleep'; while a Roman Monsignore tells us that 'the difficulty of Ireland is that the priests and the people will consider everything in a purely Irish point of

view.   To gain some local object, they will encourage the
principles of the most lawless Liberalism, which naturally
land them in Fenianism and atheism.'   The aspirations of
Germany after a fleet are again noted.   In the revolutionary meeting in London the German delegate says: ' The
peoples will never succeed till they have a fleet. . . .   To
have a fleet we rose against Denmark in my country. . . .
The future mistress of the seas is the land of the Viking '—
an odd paraphrase for Germany.   Of Austria Monsignore Berwick says: ' Poor Austria !   Two things made
her a nation : she was German and she was Catholic, and
now she is neither.'   A French diplomatist suggests
to the Monsignore the very settlement of the Roman
question which was actually effected in a few months :
' I wish I could induce you to consider more favourably
that suggestion, that His Holiness should content himself with the ancient city, and, in possession of St.
Peter's and the Vatican, leave the rest of Rome to the
vulgar cares and the mundane anxieties of the transient
generation.'   And the Disraeli of *Sybil* and of the Artisans'
Dwellings Acts speaks through the mouth of Lothair
when he says: ' It seems to me that pauperism is not an
affair so much of wages as of dwellings.   If the working
classes were properly lodged, at their present rate of wages,
they would be richer.   They would be healthier and
happier at the same cost.'

There are of course the oddities of grammar, absurdities
of expression, and exaggerations of fact and of phrase,
which no novel of Disraeli's is without; and in *Lothair*
some readers are put off by the occurrence of a large
proportion of these in the early pages.   But we have also,
what is more to the purpose, an abundance of those apt
phrases, half aphorism half paradox, into which Disraeli
distilled his worldly and other-worldly wisdom.   The
hansom is ' the gondola of London '; Pantheism is
' atheism in domino '; a member of the Church of England
appears to a Roman convert to be ' a Parliamentary
Christian '; an agreeable person is ' a person who agrees

with ' you; at the end of the season ' the baffled hopes
must go to Cowes, and the broken hearts to Baden '; ' the
originality of a subject is in its treatment '; ' the world,
where the future is concerned, is generally wrong ';
' patriotism was a boast and now it is a controversy ';
' to revive faith is more difficult than to create it.'

The joy which Disraeli evinces in the material world, in
natural and artistic beauty, in the dignity and even in the
gauds and tinsel of wealthy and aristocratic life, should
never blind the reader to the fact that the story of the
book is a spiritual conflict, and that the author puts here,
as in *Tancred* and all his more serious writing, the soul
above the body.   It is Lothair's soul for which the various
forces have been contending.   The somewhat shadowy
Syrian Christian, Paraclete, whom Lothair meets towards
the end of his wanderings, seems to speak the author's real
mind.   What is his teaching ?   ' Science may prove the
insignificance of this globe in the scale of creation, but it
cannot prove the insignificance of man. . . .   There is no
relation between the faculties of man and the scale in
creation of the planet which he inherits.'   ' There must
be design, or all we see would be without sense, and I
do not believe in the unmeaning.'   ' A monad of pure
intelligence, is that more philosophical than the truth . . .
that God made man in his own image ?'   Science can no
more satisfy the soul than superstition or revolt.   But
Disraeli's practical advice is that which the revolutionary
General gave as his parting word to Lothair.   ' Whatever
you do, give up dreams. . . .   Action may not always
be happiness, but there is no happiness without action.'
These are the things in the knowledge of which Disraeli
declares the salvation of our youth to consist.   ' Nôsse
omnia hæc salus est adolescentulis ' is the motto from
Terence prefixed to the book.

Beyond this motto, Disraeli, who revealed in the
General Preface to the novels in the autumn the origin
and intention of his earlier romances, declined to give any
hint about the purport of *Lothair*.   But Longmans, his

publishers, circulated, presumably with his consent, as an
advertisement of the new edition, a letter which Professor
John Stuart Blackie had addressed to the *Scotsman* on
the significance of the work.   It was undoubtedly, Blackie
maintained, ' what the Germans call a *tendenz-roman*,'
showing how certain intellectual agencies, prominent in
the world at the time, act upon a hero of the Wilhelm
Meister type, and how the illusions of Romanism may be
dispelled in favour of rational liberty and rational piety.
Count Vitzthum, Disraeli's old friend in the diplomatic
world, also noted the resemblance to *Wilhelm Meister*,
both novels treating of ' the development of a human
being by the working of life and experience.'   But he
thought Goethe's hero looked 'pale, narrow-minded, little,
a poor bourgeois,' by the side of Lothair, 'a real prince,
a citizen of the world.'   Vitzthum, moreover, selected
for praise the facility of giving the formulas of all the
philosophical schools of the age so that a child might
understand them.   But perhaps the appreciation of
James Clay, a friend from the days of the Mediterranean
wanderings, pleased Disraeli most: ' You are a wonderful
fellow to have retained the freshness and buoyancy of
twenty-five.'

Seldom has a book been anticipated with such interest
or produced such a sensation on its first appearance.
There was no occasion for Longman to employ the puffing
tactics by which Colburn in Disraeli's youthful days had
heralded the publication of *Vivian Grey*.   A novel by an
ex-Premier, and an ex-Premier of so strange and fascinating a type, was enough in itself to set the town, if not the
world, agog.   ' There is immense and most malevolent
curiosity about Disraeli's novel,' wrote Houghton.   ' His
wisest friends think that it must be a mistake, and his
enemies hope that it will be his ruin.'   The book was
actually published, in three volumes, on Monday, May 2.
But the advance demand had already kept Longman's
printers busy.   On April 22, he told Disraeli that the
subscription list would be about 2,000, and that a third

thousand was ready; on the 27th that 3,000 were bespoken
and a fourth in hand; and on the 29th, three days before
publication, that they had gone to press with a fifth.
Four days after publication he humorously described to
Disraeli the run upon his ' bankers in Paternoster Row.'

From Thomas Longman.

FARNBOROUGH HILL, HANTS, *May* 6, 1870.—There has
been a run upon your bankers in Paternoster Row, and our
last thousand is nearly gone ! We shall have another thousand in hand on Wednesday next. This will be the *sixth*
thousand, and I do not feel quite certain we shall not be
broken before Wednesday ! I am not sure that it would not
do good, now we have nearly 5,000 in circulation. On Monday
morning Mr. Mudie's house was, I am told, in a state of siege.
At an early hour his supply was sent in two carts. But real
subscribers, and representative footmen, in large masses were
there before them. Mr. Mudie has had 700 more copies. . . .

All the world read the book; every journal reviewed it.
It was the principal topic of polite conversation during the
London season: a pretty woman was even heard to bet a
copy of *Lothair* on a race at Ascot. Horses, songs, and
ships were named after the hero and heroine; a scrap in
Disraeli's handwriting gives the following list:

Lothair. Mr. Stevens' colt, Mr. Molloy's song by Mme.
Sherrington, Greenwich ship, Lothair Galloppe, Lothair Perfume, Lothair Street.
Corisande. Baron Rothschild's filly,[1] Mr. Martin's song
by Mme. Montserrat, Durham ship, Corisande Valtz.

Edition followed edition. The circulation was greatly
helped by the publication of an abusive letter from one
who conceived himself to be the original of the Oxford
professor described in the book as ' of advanced opinions
on all subjects, religious, social, and political '; ' clever,
extremely well-informed,' but with ' a restless vanity and
overflowing conceit '; 'gifted with a great command of

[1] Lady Beaconsfield preserved among the Beaconsfield papers the telegram by which Baron Meyer de Rothschild announced to her and Disraeli
the victory of the famous filly Corisande in the Cesarewitch.

II.   17

words, which took the form of endless expos'tion, varied by sarcasm and passages of ornate jargon'; and—unkindest cut of all—' like sedentary men of extreme opinions, . . . a social parasite.'

From Goldwin Smith.

CORNELL UNIVERSITY, ITHACA, STATE OF NEW YORK, *May* 25, 1870.—In your *Lothair* you introduce an Oxford professor, who is about to emigrate to America, and you describe him as a social parasite. You well know that if you had ventured openly to accuse me of any social baseness, you would have had to answer for your words; but when, sheltering yourself under the literary form of a work of fiction, you seek to traduce with impunity the social character of a political opponent, your expressions can touch no man's honour; they are the stingless insults of a coward.

This was, indeed, as a journalist said, ' 'Ercles' vein '; and it is ño wonder that Longman could write on June 9: ' The Oxford Professor's letter is doing its work well. So much so that we shall print again as soon as I have your corrections.' Disraeli never answered Goldwin Smith; but in a letter to an American literary friend he threw an interesting sidelight on the outburst.

To Robert Carter.

Confidential. HUGHENDEN MANOR, *Aug.* 13, 1870.— . . . I know nothing personally of Mr. Goldwin Smith. I never saw him. More than twenty years ago, the Peelite party, who had purchased the *Morning Chronicle*, mainly to decry me and my friends, engaged a new hand who distinguished himself by a series of invectives against myself, wh. far passed the bounds of legitimate political hostility. I cared nothing, and have never cared anything, about these personal attacks, to which I have been subject all my life and wh. have never, in the least, arrested my career; but the writer, I found out many years afterwards, was Mr. Goldwin Smith, who was well paid for his pains. I don't, and never did, grudge him that; but this is hardly the person to inveigh against personalities and anonymous writing. I have sometimes brushed him aside, as I would a mosquito, but am always too much occupied to bear him, or any other insect, any ill-will. . . .[1]

[1] Disraeli once said to the present Lord Esher, 'I never trouble to be avenged, but, when a man injures me, I put his name on a slip of paper

The outbreak of the Franco-German War caused the demand, for the moment, somewhat to slacken; but with the appearance in November of a collected edition of Disraeli's novels, at 6s. a volume, having *Lothair* as the first volume, the 'Lothair-mania,' as Longman wrote, broke out again 'with all its virulence. Twice we have printed 5,000 copies, and now we have another 5,000 = 15,000, at press.' The book was translated into every European language, and the demand in Germany so far exceeded expectation that Baron Tauchnitz, the publisher, as Longman noted, 'doubled, *more suo*, his tribute-money.' In America the sale was even greater than in England. Messrs. Appleton began by printing 25,000 copies, which were sold out in three days; and in July the demand was still a thousand copies a day. By October 80,000 copies had been sold there. Disraeli proudly claimed, in the General Preface which he wrote for the collected edition, that the book had been 'more extensively read both by the people of the United Kingdom and the United States than any work that has appeared for the last half-century.'

But if the public devoured the novel, the reviewers for the more critical journals and magazines were, as a rule, unfavourable. *The Times* was, indeed, highly appreciative; and the *Pall Mall Gazette* called it an 'admirable novel' which 'must have cost the author, we cannot help fancying, no effort whatever; it was as easy and delightful for him to write as for us to read.' But the *Saturday Review* was captious, and the *Edinburgh* patronising; the *Athenæum* maintained that the book would have passed unnoticed if written by anyone else; while both *Blackwood*, a representative of Scottish Conservatism, and the *Quarterly*, true as ever to its anti-Disraeli attitude, condemned it with the utmost severity. The latter dubbed it a 'failure,' an 'outrage,' 'a sin

and lock it up in a drawer. It is marvellous how men I have thus labelled have a knack of disappearing.' See article by Lord Esher on *Lord Beaconsfield* in the *Quarterly Review*, July, 1920.

against good taste and justice,' ' a vast mass of verbiage
which can seldom be called English '; and even had the
hardihood to call a book which contains some of Disraeli's
liveliest and most satirical writing, ' as dull as ditchwater
and as flat as a flounder.'   Abraham Hayward, always a
malignant critic of Disraeli, wrote the *Quarterly* article;
Houghton, a ' good-natured ' friend, the *Edinburgh ;* the
Blackwood attack was from the incisive pen of the
soldier-critic, Hamley.   In the General Preface Disraeli
hit some shrewd blows back; and one can recognise
at least Houghton and Hayward in the following
passage:

One could hardly expect at home the judicial impartiality
of a foreign land. Personal influences inevitably mingle in
some degree with such productions. There are critics who,
abstractedly, do not approve of successful books, particularly
if they have failed in the same style; social acquaintances also
of lettered taste, and especially cotemporaries whose public
life has not exactly realised the vain dreams of their fussy
existence, would seize the accustomed opportunity of welcoming with affected discrimination about nothing, and
elaborate controversy about trifles, the production of a friend;
and there is always, both in politics and literature, the race
of the Dennises, the Oldmixons, and Curls, who flatter themselves that, by systematically libelling some eminent personage
of their times, they have a chance of descending to posterity.

At least one later critic of undoubted competence has
endorsed the condemnation of the contemporary reviewers.
Sir Leslie Stephen, who showed much appreciation of the
earlier novels, has left on record the opinion that the
easiest assumption to make about *Lothair* is ' that it is a
practical joke on a large scale, or a prolonged burlesque
upon Mr. Disraeli's own youthful performances.'   Nevertheless, the judgment of the world is decisive against
Stephen, and holds that *Lothair* is among the best, if not
the absolute best, of Disraeli's novels.   Mr. George
Russell expressed a growing opinion when he declared it
the author's masterpiece; ' a profound study of spiritual
and political forces at a supremely important moment in
the history of modern Europe.'   Lord Russell saw deep

significance beneath the gaudy trappings, and held it to be the work of a political seer. Froude regarded it as ' immeasurably superior ' to anything of the kind which Disraeli had previously produced; adding, ' *Lothair* opens a window into Disraeli's mind, revealing the inner workings of it more completely than anything else which he wrote or said.' This last appreciation is, perhaps, excessive; *Tancred* and *Lord George Bentinck* are more self-revealing, if only because of their insistence on the Jewish standpoint, which is not obtruded in *Lothair ;* but *Lothair* takes rank beside *Coningsby*, and these two are the novels on which Disraeli's literary reputation rests with the general reader of to-day.

The pecuniary return of *Lothair* was considerable. For the original edition of 2,000 copies Longmans paid Disraeli £1,000; and together with royalties on subsequent copies and on the one-volume edition, and with the foreign rights of the book, he had received in all by the end of 1876 over £6,000. The large sales of *Lothair* increased the demand for its predecessors, from *Vivian Grey* to *Tancred*. On these in the new edition Disraeli had already received over £1,000 in royalties, when, in 1877, he came to a new arrangement with his publishers by which they paid him a further sum of £2,100 for the copyright of the whole ten volumes of novels. He was so much encouraged by his success that he soon made a start upon a new novel, *Endymion ;* which, however, owing to the renewal of his political activity and his subsequent return to office, was not completed and published till ten years later.

The publication of *Lothair*, like that of *Tancred*, w s politically a hindrance rather than a help to Disraeli. The serious politician, like Gladstone in the *Punch* cartoon, pronounced it flippant. How could Parliamentarians be expected to trust an ex-Premier who, when halfway between sixty and seventy, instead of occupying his leisure, in accordance with the British convention, in classical, historical, or constitutional studies, pro-

duced a gaudy romance of the peerage, so written as
to make it almost impossible to say how much was
ironical or satirical, and how much soberly intended ?
It may be taken for granted that Disraeli's old colleagues
did not know what to think of the book, as among the
congratulatory letters preserved in the Beaconsfield
correspondence their handwriting is markedly absent.
This political distrust was increased by the resuscitation,
in the General Preface in the autumn, of all the peculiar
doctrines about English history and politics, about
Christianity and Judaism, and about religion and science,
which the English people had found difficult of assimila-
tion when propounded in *Coningsby, Sybil,* and *Tancred,*
in *Lord George Bentinck* and in the Sheldonian speech,
and many of which were even now *caviare* to the general.
The whole literary performance of the year made Disraeli,
the man, a more interesting figure than ever; but it only
deepened the doubts about Disraeli, the statesman, which
the heavy defeat of 1868, and the apparent hopelessness
of the Conservative cause in opposition, had aroused.

CHAPTER V.

The Turn of the Tide.

1872–1873.

'There are few positions less inspiriting than that of the leader of a discomfited party.' The words are Disraeli's own, from the first chapter of *Lord George Bentinck*, and they were written in reference to Russell's position in the Peel Parliament of 1841. But they apply with at least equal force to the situation which Disraeli had himself occupied since the General Election of 1868. Opposite him there had sat an overwhelming and enthusiastic majority, who, with few exceptions, had steadily acted on the principle that it was their duty ' to say ditto to Mr. Gladstone ' as the Prime Minister pursued his strenuous career; and though in the session of 1871 there had been many Ministerial mishaps, with the corollary of some Opposition victories in by-elections, yet all the efforts of the Conservative party and the adroitness of their leader had hitherto been unavailing materially to improve their position and prospects. *The Times*, in a judicial leading article towards the close of 1871,[1] pronounced that anything like a permanent tenure of office for the Conservatives was impossible. ' The leaders of the party do not believe in it. The country gives them no confidence. The majority is against them. All the forces of the time are strained in an opposite direction.' It was as true of Disraeli from 1869 to 1872, as of Russell from 1841 to 1845, that

he who in the Parliamentary field watches over the fortunes of routed troops must be prepared to sit often alone. Few care to share the labour which is doomed to be fruitless, and

[1] Nov. 20.

none are eager to diminish the responsibility of him whose
course, however adroit, must necessarily be ineffectual. . . .
A disheartened Opposition will be querulous and captious. A
discouraged multitude have no future; too depressed to indulge in a large and often hopeful horizon of contemplation,
they busy themselves in peevish detail, and by a natural
train of sentiment associate their own conviction of ill-luck,
incapacity, and failure, with the most responsible member of
their confederation.[1]

The discontent reached a climax in the winter of 1871–
1872. The policy of reserve in opposition which Disraeli
had on the whole maintained, and which had produced
satisfactory results in alluring Ministers into indiscretions, was galling to eager and impetuous spirits; and in
the previous session the ' Colonels ' had got out of hand
in their violent opposition to the Army Bill, and the anti-
Disraeli clique in their obstruction of the Ballot Bill.
Complaint was made that, in spite of tempting opportunities afforded by Ministerial blunders, Disraeli had
avoided political speaking during the recesses, putting off
from year to year the demonstration in Manchester which
his Lancashire friends pressed him to accept. His own
excuse to Matthew Arnold, who met him at a country
house party at Latimer in January, 1872, was that ' the
Ministers were so busy going about apologising for
their failures that he thought it a pity to distract
public attention from the proceeding.' Further, the
publication of *Lothair* and of the General Preface to
the novels had revived all the former doubts as to whether
a Jewish literary man, so dowered with imagination,
and so unconventional in his outlook, was the proper
person to lead a Conservative party to victory. Would
it not be better to go into battle under the old Stanley
banner ? Derby had gained golden opinions as Foreign
Secretary, and had that plain common sense, love of
peace, and moderation of political faith which appealed
to the middle classes in the rapidly growing urban
communities, and which might be expected, were he

[1] *Lord George Bentinck*, ch. 1.

the party leader, to attract considerable Liberal support
to the Conservative cause. The rival claims of Disraeli
and Derby were widely discussed by politicians throughout the party and the country, in newspapers, clubs, and
debating societies; though Derby made no sign whatever,
and there is not the smallest reason to suppose that he
would have consented to play the part his admirers
allotted to him.

Even Disraeli's colleagues were infected with the rising
spirit of dissatisfaction; and no less intimate a friend than
Cairns was the first to give it expression at a gathering of
Conservative leaders at Burghley just before the session;
from which gathering not only Disraeli himself, but also
Derby, Richmond, and Malmesbury were absent. Hardy's
diary is our authority for what took place.

At our meeting (February 1) Cairns boldly broached the
subject of Lord Derby's lead, and the importance of Disraeli
knowing the general feeling. We all felt that none of his old
colleagues could, or would, undertake such a task as informing
him. John Manners alone professed ignorance of the feeling
in or out of doors. I expressed my view that D. has been
loyal to his friends, and that personally I would not say that
I preferred Lord D., but that it was idle to ignore the general
opinion. Noel [1] said that from his own knowledge he could
say that the name of Lord Derby as leader would affect 40
or 50 seats. . . . For my own part I do not look forward with
hope to Derby, but I cannot but admit that Disraeli, as far
as appears, has not the position in House and country to
enable him to do what the other might. [2]

Northcote is not mentioned in this account; but he
has recorded in his diary under a subsequent date that
he and Manners were the only two present who were
stanch to their chief, and that he wondered if Disraeli
knew of their loyalty. It may be taken for granted that
none of Disraeli's colleagues informed him of the opinions
expressed at Burghley. Apparently, however, some representation of the discontent of a section of his followers in
the House of Commons was conveyed to him, and in

---

[1] One of the Whips.   [2] Gathorne Hardy, Vol. I., p. 305.

reply he intimated that he would be quite ready to give place to Derby if the party wished it, but in that case he would himself retire below the gangway—a contingency which the most recalcitrant follower would hardly face.

In any case so shrewd a judge of party feeling could not fail to be aware of the prevailing uneasiness; accordingly, while his lieutenants were discussing his shortcomings at Burghley, he, as his correspondence shows, was gathering in his hands all the strands of a complicated political situation, and preparing to demonstrate that he was as indispensable as he had ever been since he had imposed himself on his party in 1849. A rap over the knuckles for his colleague, the duke who led the Opposition in the Lords, was a clear reminder of his claims as leader— especially if the censure was, as Hardy thought, unjust. Incidentally the high tone he takes shows how little disposed he was to that adulation of dukes, which some who misread *Lothair* have attributed to him. 'Talk not to me of dukes,' he burst out on one occasion when a duke had disappointed him; 'dukes can be made!' He had made one himself.

To the Duke of Richmond.

Confidential. BURGHLEY HOUSE, STAMFORD, *Jan.* 11, 1872. —I have been much engaged during the last six weeks, in correspondence with our supporters in the Ho. of Commons, as to their course, in the next session, respecting the ballot. The Lancashire members, our most powerful friends, are particularly embarrassed by this question: the members for the boro[ugh]s, in some instances, being hard pressed by their constituents to support it, while, on the other hand, Mr. Cross, the M.P. for South Lancashire, who defeated Mr. Gladstone, moved, at his own request, the absolute rejection of the Bill during the last session.

This gentleman, uneasy on the matter, and requesting my advice, informed me, some time ago, that Lord Skelmersdale had assured him, that he might depend on the Whig peers giving the measure an uncompromising opposition. Not being myself certain of this, I advised him, in our perplexity, not to change his front, but not unnecessarily to dwell on the subject.

In this state of affairs, I took advantage of being in the West to arrange to meet Lord Cairns at Ld. Malmesbury's, and to confer with him on matters in general, wh. daily assume a more critical character. To my astonishment, I learned from Lord Cairns, that your Grace had received a communication from Lord Russell, that our party in the House of Lords must no longer count on him, the Duke of Somerset, and others, as opponents to the ballot. Lord Cairns naturally assumed that your Grace had immediately apprised me of this information, so necessary to me for the satisfactory conduct of business.[1]

I am sure your Grace will not misconceive my·meaning, when I express my deep regret at the habitual want of communication, which now subsists between the leaders of our party in the two Houses. If my individual feelings only were concerned, I should not touch upon the matter, but, with the responsibility of conducting difficult affairs for the common good, it is my duty to remark on circumstances, wh., I am sure, are fraught with injurious consequences to the cause wh. we are anxious to uphold.

From the Duke of Richmond.

GOODWOOD, CHICHESTER, *Jan.* 12, 1872.—I hope that ere this you will have recd. a letter which I wrote a few days ago, and directed to Hughenden. I enclosed a letter from Lord Russell.

I will not conceal from you how very much annoyed I am to find from your letter that you consider there has been habitual want of communication subsisting between the leaders of our party in the two Houses.

This wd. imply that I had studiously avoided acting with you. If this was so I should have been justly liable to censure, for I quite concur that, unless the leaders in both Houses act in concert and with cordiality, it is quite impossible that the business can be carried on in a satisfactory manner.

I think, if you reflect, you will recollect that I was in constant communication with you during the last session of Parliament. You will recollect Cairns and I met you in the Carlton to discuss the American question. I also saw you frequently about the Army Bill and the ballot, and communicated to you at once all the negotiations which were then pending between me and Lord Russell.

I did not think it necessary to trouble you with the letter I recd. fr. Lord Russell after I got to Scotland, but always

[1] 'I shall certainly tell the Duke of R.,' wrote Malmesbury to Disraeli on Jan. 8, 'my opinion as to his want of concert with you.'

intended to do so before the meeting of Parliament. It is possible that it would have been better had I sent it to you sooner, but for some time past I have been very busy with my own affairs.

I have deemed it right to enter into these details, because I am most anxious that you should be satisfied that I have not been guilty of any want of courtesy towards you. Indeed I should have hoped that our long acquaintance would have been sufficient to have prevented you from imagining such a thing. I quite appreciate the responsibility and difficulty of your position, and always wish to assist you by all means in my power.

To the Duke of Richmond.

LATIMER, CHESHAM, *Jan.* 16, 1872.—I have received both your letters, and have read the last in the spirit in wh. it is written.

I return herewith the letter of Lord Russell, and the copy of his letter to Lord Lyveden. They do not appear to me to bear altogether the interpretation, wh. Lord Cairns placed upon them, or, rather, wh. I apprehended he placed upon them.

The intimations of Lord Russell seem to me to be altogether hypothetical, and to rest upon a basis, wh. he contemplated as probable, but wh. has not occurred, viz., ' That the country would support the House of Commons in asking for the ballot.'

The country during the recess has been silent on the subject, and tho' many important elections have happened, and are about to take place, the question of the ballot seems to have no influence upon their result.

Lord Russell and his friends, therefore, on the reassembling of Parliament, are free to recur to their old grounds of opposition to the measure, and may even do so.

Whether such a course on their part should regulate ours, is another question, and wh. I would rather leave to personal deliberations when we are better acquainted with the exact propositions of the Ministry.

We must not conceal from ourselves, that the Tory party in the Ho. of Commons is not united on the question, and tho' I am not myself prepared, under any circumstances, to concede the principle of secret voting, as at present advised, I fear our ranks may be broken.

I wish I could see the practical elements of that compromise wh. Lord Russell seems to contemplate. Any provision to secure scrutiny and prevent personation, will, according to the Radical view, destroy the Bill.

Richmond showed this correspondence to his principal colleagues, who, while they gave him their sympathy, could not fail to draw their own conclusions as to the disposition of their chief. Cairns's comment was that after two years of apathy Disraeli was beginning to wake up, and fancy all beside were asleep. What Cairns called apathy might perhaps be more truly described as calculated and successful reserve; but at any rate there is no doubt that Disraeli was awake now.

The public question which gave him and his political friends at the moment most concern was the difficulty with the United States over the *Alabama* question. Disraeli and his Foreign Secretary, Derby, had been the first British statesmen in office to admit the principle of arbitration; and accordingly Northcote, as a leading Conservative statesman, had consented to take a share in negotiating in the previous year the Treaty of Washington which carried the principle into practical effect.[1] Disraeli was not satisfied with the conduct of the negotiations; but, at any rate, the terms of the treaty were so limited by the British Commissioners as to render it in their opinion *ultra vires* for the tribunal to admit and adjudicate upon those indirect claims, making this country responsible for the prolongation of the Civil War, which spread-eagle politicians in America like Sumner put forward, but which Derby had expressly excluded in 1868. Great was the shock, therefore, when it was discovered that the American case to be submitted to the arbitrators embraced and insisted upon these very far-reaching claims as well as those specifically ' growing out of the acts committed ' by certain vessels.

[1] Lord George Hamilton in his *Reminiscences* says that Northcote accepted the task without consulting Disraeli; but this is a mistake. Lord Morley in his *Gladstone*, Bk. VI., ch. 9, quotes a contemporary letter from Granville, then Foreign Secretary, to Gladstone: ' I asked Northcote. . . . He said he must ask Lady Northcote, and requested permission to consult Dizzy. The former consented, ditto Dizzy '; and the Beaconsfield papers contain another letter from Granville, dated April 24, 1871, to Disraeli himself, which speaks of 'your encouragement to Northcote to undertake a share in the work' of the British Commission at Washington.

To Lord Cairns.

Private. GROSVENOR GATE, *Jan.* 27, 1872.—. . . Affairs here are most critical and anxious. All is absorbed in the *Alabama* question. Hayward told Exmouth yesterday, that unless they withdraw from the arbitration, the Cabinet must break up. Would that they would withdraw! But can they? After having advised their Sovereign to ratify the treaty—and in such haste!

I have not seen the foreign case, nor has Lord Derby, but we know its scope from those who have—Cockburn, Delane, Ld. Stanhope and others speak of it as most masterly. Northcote, who has it, speaks of it disparagingly: can easily be answered, crushingly, and all that. But this is not the point. Our complaint is, that it opens the indirect issue, the relinquishment of which by U.S. was our consideration for consenting to express regret, and dealing with the law of nations *ex post facto.* In the initiated quarters, there is no confidence in, at least two of, the arbitrators. They are supposed to be manageable by an unscrupulous Government. Altogether I never knew public feeling so disturbed and dark.

I am most anxious to see you Tuesday at 12. Perhaps Northcote may be here. It was impossible for me to go to Burghley, as I had previously declined Belvoir. At this moment I must be at headquarters.

To Sir Stafford Northcote.

Private. GROSVENOR GATE, *Jan.* 30, '72.—. . . Cairns has been with me this morning. A long, but not a satisfactory, visit. He holds, in this with me, that the Government scheme of protesting to the arbitrators, and awaiting their judgment on the protest, [is] quite futile.

They are not bound to adjudicate on the point and they will decline. Arbitrators, he says, always avoid unnecessary decisions, and details; and he is quite prepared, if the arbitration is concluded, that they will give their verdict for a sum without apportioning the amount.

2. He holds withdrawal from the arbitration, a clear *casus belli.*

3. He is of opinion that the treaty justifies the American demand, and, he says, he said as much in House of Lords last year.

In such a mess of difficulties all I can see at present, is to counsel direct and friendly application to the Government of Washington. This will not be a *casus belli*, but I fear must end in that.

The Americans will not go to war—at least at present—for there are many reasons to deter them, but they will keep the question open, and we shall still, after our sacrifices, have the *Alabama* claims, but in a worse form. . . .

When Parliament met, Disraeli described the indirect claims as ' preposterous and wild,' and equivalent to ' the tribute of a conquered people.' If the Government held that there was no doubt that the treaty excluded these claims, they must speak out calmly, frankly, and firmly, avoiding ' the Serbonian bog of diplomacy,' and tell the United States Government plainly that it was impossible to accept their interpretation, and that, if they maintained it, the treaty must be cancelled. Gladstone responded in a like spirit, acknowledging Disraeli's patriotic and discreet treatment of American questions, and insisting first that the terms of the treaty were absolutely clear, and secondly that no nation with any spirit could submit to the American demands. There is no doubt that the strong support which Disraeli gave to the Government materially contributed to the cause of arbitration by convincing the American people that Great Britain was in earnest. The United States, however, made it a point of honour not to waive the indirect claims; and the British Government on its side determined to adjourn the arbitration until these were abandoned. But what the United States would not do as a Government their arbitrator, Charles Francis Adams, did for them. He persuaded his colleagues summarily to rule these claims out; and the arbitration accordingly proceeded. Disraeli raised himself decidedly in public estimation by his con- duct of this question. It was seen that there had been serious mismanagement by the Government to bring matters to such a pass, and that it was highly patriotic of Disraeli to dwell but lightly on these shortcomings, and to strengthen Gladstone's hands at a critical moment.

In other respects he did not spare the failures of Ministers. They had lived, he said in the debate on the Address, during the last six months ' in a blaze of apology.'

They would have further opportunities for defending themselves in the House. ' If it is in the power of the Government to prove to the country that our naval administration is such as befits a great naval power, they will soon have an occasion for doing so; and if they are desirous of showing that one of the transcendental privileges of a strong Government is to evade Acts of Parliament which they have themselves passed, I believe, from what caught my ear this evening, that that opportunity will also be furnished them.' The last sentence referred to two pieces of the Prime Minister's patronage, one legal, the other clerical, which required a good deal of apology. In one case, Sir Robert Collier, the Attorney-General, had been appointed a paid member of the Judicial Committee of the Privy Council, although by statute such appointments were limited to those who had held judicial positions in the superior courts. A technical compliance with the law was effected by making Collier a Judge of the Common Pleas for a couple of days. In the other case, the rectory of Ewelme, which by statute could only be held by a member of Oxford Convocation, had been conferred upon a Cambridge graduate, who was thereupon technically qualified by being admitted to an *ad eundem* degree at Oxford. There was no suggestion in either case that an unfit person had been appointed; but the evasion of the plain meaning of the law was rendered all the more flagrant by the fact that the statutes regulating the two appointments had both been passed at the instance of Gladstone's Government in the preceding session of Parliament. Disraeli, who seldom in his maturer years mixed himself up in personal squabbles, took no part in the angry debates which were raised in both Houses on these strange proceedings; though he noted with satisfaction that the Collier appointment only escaped condemnation in the Commons by twenty-seven votes—a number almost exactly corresponding with the number of Ministers voting—while in the Lords the rescue had to be effected by the Chancellor's own vote.

To Montagu Corry.

H. OF C., *Feb.* 16, '72.—. . . On Wednesday, the Government had not even made a whip in the H. of C. for next Monday, and last night, the Ministers thinking they were going to be beaten by a whacking majority, like damned fools, did nothing but abuse the House of Lords, and deride their judgment and influence.

The old Whigs, without an exception almost, came to their rescue on this occasion, there having been a meeting at Brooks's anent, and either our men purposely stayed away from fear of disturbing the Ministry or were shockingly whipped, as is the commoner opinion: the abuse of Skelmersdale being very rife.

He told me, the day before, the majority would be 60. Yesterday evening, about 8 o'clock, that it would be between 30 and 40, and at 12 o'clock, that it would be only ten. At ½ past 12 he was beaten apparently by two: but there was an error of one in the counting, and the majority was only an unit: described really by the Lord Chancellor, who voted for himself ! Our friends are chapfallen, but, for myself, I think the affair was well enough. . . .

Disraeli's resolute and ambitious character was not the only thing with which the dissatisfied pundits of the party, whether colleagues, members of Parliament, or wire-pullers, forgot to reckon; there was also the profound impression which his personality had made among the British people. For the goodwill of the democracy he had never laid himself out, even when enormously extending their privileges. No British statesman of recent years was ever less of a demagogue. With few, if striking, exceptions, it was only in Parliament and in Bucks that he opened his lips. ' I have never in the course of my life,' he said at Manchester in April, ' obtruded myself upon any meeting of my fellow-countrymen unless I was locally connected with them, or there were peculiar circumstances which might vindicate me from the imputation of thrusting myself unnecessarily on their attention.' But the admiration and confidence which he had never courted came to him spontaneously, and even for a while unperceived. Gladstone had been extraordinarily popular in 1868 with an electorate which had been taught to believe that they owed to him that which they had received from Disraeli. His inexhaustible and lofty eloquence, his insistence on the moral law in politics, the specious cries with which he garnished his electoral campaign, took captive an inexperienced constituency. But the frequently destructive nature of their favourite's energies, his arrogant demeanour, his apparent indifference to his country's prestige, the un-English casuistry which was inwoven in his moral texture, and the inexplicable vagaries of some of his colleagues, had alienated public sympathy; and that enthusiastic nature of the English people, on which it was Disraeli's wont to insist, led them to seek another object for their trust, as different as might be from him who had so failed them. Disraeli had for years excited an amused curiosity and interest; but it was as often an interest of repulsion as of attraction. There was now an awakening to the fact that his patience, his courage, his genius, his experience, and his patriotism constituted a character round which popular feeling, disappointed in its idol, might safely rally.

The first outward sign of this development of opinion was shown in the autumn of 1871, when the youth of Liberal Scotland recognised Disraeli's eminence by electing him, in preference to Ruskin, as the Lord Rector of Glasgow University. But London politicians, and probably Disraeli himself, first realised how strong was the popular interest in him, on February 27, 1872, when the Prince of Wales went to St. Paul's to return thanks for his recovery from typhoid fever, and when the people had in consequence an unusual opportunity of singling out its favourites as they passed in succession along the streets. The reception of Gladstone was indifferent or hostile;[1] but that of Disraeli was so enthusiastic that Sir William Fraser maintains that it changed his destiny. Fraser writes:

On returning from St. Paul's, Disraeli met with an over-powering ' ovation '; I should say ' triumph,' for he was in

[1] See *Life of Dean Church*, p. 291.

his chariot. This not only continued from the City to Waterloo Place; but his carriage, ascending Regent Street, turning to the right[1] along Oxford Street, and thence back to the Carlton Club, the cheers which greeted him from all classes convinced him that, for the day at least, a more popular man did not exist in England. Soon after his return I happened to pass into the morning room of the Carlton Club. Disraeli was leaning against the table immediately opposite to the glass door, wearing the curious white coat which he had for years occasionally put on over his usual dress. Familiar as I was with his looks and expression, I never saw him with such a countenance as he had at that moment. I have heard it said by one who spoke to Napoleon I. at Orange in France, that his face was as that of one who looks into another world: that is the only description I can give of Disraeli's look at the moment I speak of. He seemed more like a statue than a human being: never before nor since have I seen anything approaching it: he was ostensibly listening to Mr. Sclater Booth, now Lord Basing. In the afternoon I said to the latter, ' What was Disraeli talking about when I came into the room ?' He replied, ' About some county business; I wanted his opinion.' I said, ' I will tell you what he was thinking about: he was thinking that he will be Prime Minister again !' I had no doubt at the time; nor have I ever doubted since.[2]

The principal demonstration of Disraeli's popularity with the masses and of the reviving power of Conservatism was made at Manchester at Easter, when he and his wife paid that visit to his Lancashire friends which was so long overdue. It was, as Disraeli wrote, a ' wondrous week.' It opened on Easter Monday with a rousing reception by a holiday crowd of workers who promptly extemporised a human team to draw the visitors' carriage. But perhaps its most striking feature was an immense parade next day, undaunted by pitiless rain, of deputations from all the Conservative Associations of the county, between two and three hundred in number. For each deputation the leader had an apt word, as one after another, with banners flying and laudatory addresses in their

---

[1] ' Right' is apparently a mistake for ' left.' The carriage was presumably going to drop Lady Beaconsfield at Grosvenor Gate before taking Disraeli to the Carlton Club.

[2] Fraser, pp. 374-376.

hands, they defiled before Disraeli and Lady Beaconsfield, filling the vast dancing hall of the Pomona Gardens, a building reckoned to hold thirty or forty thousand people.

Well might Disraeli be proud of the show, as it was the direct result of his own labours behind the scenes. During these years of reserve in opposition, when he appeared to colleagues and followers to be apathetic, he had been quietly working at Conservative reorganisation, and creating a machine which was to lead to the victory of 1874, and to be the forerunner of the great party organisations of to-day. The arrangements for party management which he had originally made in the early fifties with Rose, his lawyer and confidential agent, and which had been continued, after Rose's withdrawal, with Spofforth, a member of Rose's firm, had been a great improvement on the chaos which existed before Disraeli's accession to the leadership. But, even with the assistance of that shrewd politician the fifth Earl and first Marquis of Abergavenny, and of a special committee appointed *ad hoc* in 1868, they were wholly insufficient, as had been shown in the last election, for an age of household suffrage and large popular constituencies. An entirely new system must be set up; and Disraeli looked about for a young and ambitious Conservative who would be ready to devote the best years of his life to working out a scheme. His choice fell upon John Eldon Gorst,[1] a barrister, who had had a distinguished career at Cambridge, and had sat for a year or two in Parliament, but was now no longer a member. An authentic statement of what was done by Disraeli in this important sphere is furnished in a short political life of him written by Gorst's son.[2] What was most wanted, Disraeli told his new manager, was that every constituency should have a suitable candidate ready in advance. To secure this desirable object a Central Conservative Office was established in Whitehall under the party manager and furnished with a capable

[1] Afterwards Sir John Gorst, Q.C., Solicitor-General, and subsequently Under-Secretary for India.
[2] See Harold Gorst's *Earl of Beaconsfield*, ch. 13.

staff. Then the influential Conservatives in each constituency were persuaded to form local associations on a substantially democratic basis; the interest and co-operation were sought and obtained, not merely of the aristocratic and professional and trading classes, but also of the local artisans. In Lancashire, where several Conservative working men's societies already existed, the idea was taken up with special enthusiasm. Communication was regularly maintained between the central office and the provincial associations. The central office kept a register of approved candidates; but instead of supplying these at its discretion to the constituencies, it endeavoured to get the local people to make their own selection. ' In registering candidates care was taken to note down their peculiar qualifications. . . . A constituency, in applying for a candidate, was asked to state the kind of man wanted. The party manager declined to make the selection himself, but requested some of the leading men in the constituency to come up and make their own choice. Meanwhile a list of likely men was compiled from the register; and, if desirable, personal interviews were arranged. By this means each place was provided with a candidate suitable to its political needs.' Finally, mainly at the suggestion of Henry Cecil Raikes, a coping stone was put on the edifice by the affiliation of all these Conservative associations to a comprehensive National Union.

Though, in entrusting the business to Gorst, Disraeli left him a free hand, he paid nevertheless constant personal attention to all that was being done, and was ready to give his manager the benefit of his sagacity and experience at every stage. And when the machine was established and was proving its utility by the satisfactory results of the by-elections from 1871 onwards, he kept a careful watch on its working in each particular instance. Writing to a friend in October, 1873, he mentioned that ' after every borough election, an expert visits the scene of action, and prepares a confidential despatch for me, that, so far as is possible, I may be thoroughly acquainted with the facts.' One point he made clear from the outset, as might be anticipated from his insistence on accompanying his great measure of Reform by a Corrupt Practices Act. He was resolved that no countenance whatever should be given by his new organisation to the practice on which both parties had too often relied in the past, the winning of elections by bribery.

Disraeli was thus responsible for starting the first great party machine, and he reaped the harvest in the victory of 1874. But, though experience here and elsewhere seems to prove that party organisations are essential to democratic government, Disraeli's judicious admirers are hardly likely to claim much credit for him on the score of this feat. As might have been expected, the Liberals bettered the Conservative example by perfecting the Birmingham caucus, and extending its operations to the whole country; and the machine soon became so highly organised on both sides as to make increasingly difficult the entry into the House of Commons, and the continuance there, of those independent politicians to secure whose adhesion it was necessary for Governments in the past to look beyond party. Hence there has come a serious decline of Parliamentary control over Ministers; and a great accession of power to the statesman or the party committee who may happen to have commanded at the preceding election the support of a majority in the con-stituencies.

The full importance of the parade of Conservative associations at Manchester was hardly realised at the time; and attention was mainly fixed on the great meeting on the Wednesday evening[1] in the Free Trade Hall, where, with Derby by his side and the numerous Conservative members for the county on the platform, Disraeli spoke to an enthusiastic audience with unflagging spirit for three hours and a quarter. In this effort, so tremendous for a man never very robust and in his sixty-eighth year,

[1] April 3.

he was sustained, H. C. Raikes tells us, by two bottles of white brandy, indistinguishable by onlookers from the water taken with it, which he drank in doses of ever-increasing strength till he had consumed the whole !

The speech was an answer to the Liberal taunt that the Conservatives had no programme. Their programme, said Disraeli, was to maintain the Constitution of the country, because political institutions were the embodied experience of race. It was the cue of his critics to say that our great institutions, such as the Monarchy, the House of Lords, and the Church were as dear to Gladstone and the Liberals as to the Conservatives, and so their defence could not be appropriated by any one party. But the left wing of the Liberal party was in full cry both against the Church and against the House of Lords; and individual Radicals, who could not be dismissed as nobodies, Dilke and Auberon Herbert, were declaiming against the heavy cost of Monarchy, and comparing it unfavourably with the supposed cheapness of a republic. Moreover, on all these questions, as Disraeli pointed out, Gladstone sent forth an uncertain sound, avoiding, as far as might be, a distinct breach with even extreme followers. On each of the three threatened institutions Disraeli had something to say which arrested attention. He maintained that the continuous prosperity of the country and its advance in civilisation were very largely due to the Throne.

Since the settlement of [the] Constitution, now nearly two centuries ago, England has never experienced a revolution, though there is no country in which there has been so continuous and such considerable change. How is this ? Because the wisdom of your forefathers placed the prize of supreme power without the sphere of human passions. Whatever the struggle of parties, whatever the strife of factions, whatever the excitement and exaltation of the public mind, there has always been something in this country round which all classes and parties could rally, representing the majesty of the law, the administration of justice, and involving, at the same time, the security for every man's rights and the fountain of honour.

Disraeli proceeded to explain, in language which, though of course general, recalled his speech about the Queen in the autumn, that it was a mistake to suppose that the personal influence of the Sovereign was absorbed in the responsibility of the Minister: and that such influence must increase, the longer the reign and the greater the experience of the Sovereign. That, it may be added, was certainly, in the opinion of competent statesmen, the case with Queen Victoria, whose influence, in spite of the increasing democratisation of the country, was never greater than in the twenty years by which she survived her favourite Minister. As to the cost of Monarchy, Disraeli pointed out how cheap it was, compared with the Continental scale; and even compared with America, when you added together the salaries of the Federal Legislature and those of all the sovereign legislatures of the different states that went to form that greatest of republics—an argument, by the way, which has been weakened since members of Parliament here have accepted payment.

With regard to the House of Lords, experience showed a Second Chamber to be necessary; but with the exception of the American Senate, composed of materials not possessed by other States, no other country had solved successfully the problem of its constitution, whereas the House of Lords had developed historically, and periodically adapted itself to the necessities of the times. That House had the first quality of a Second Chamber, independence, based on the firmest foundation, responsible property. Would life peerages be as satisfactory ? A peer for life could exercise the power entrusted to him according to his own will; and nobody could call him to account. But a peer whose dignities descend to his children had every inducement to study public opinion, ' because he naturally feels that if the order to which he belongs is in constant collision with public opinion, the chances are that his dignities will not descend to his posterity.'

There are some philosophers who believe that the best
substitute for the House of Lords would be an assembly formed
of ex-Governors of Colonies. . . . When the Muse of Comedy
threw her frolic grace over society, a retired governor was
generally one of the characters in every comedy; and the last
of our great actors . . ., Mr. Farren, was celebrated for his
delineation of the character in question. Whether it be the
recollection of that performance or not, I confess I am inclined to believe that an English gentleman—born to business,
managing his own estate, administering the affairs of his
county, mixing with all classes of his fellowmen, now in the
hunting field, now in the railway direction, unaffected, un-
ostentatious, proud of his ancestors, if they have contributed
to the greatness of our common country—is, on the whole,
more likely to form a senator agreeable to English opinion
and English taste than any substitute that has yet been produced.

Disraeli's defence of the Church followed the lines which
he had adopted in the sixties. He dwelt on the vital
importance of connecting authority with religion, and
maintained that ' to have secured a national profession of
faith with the unlimited enjoyment of private judgment in
matters spiritual is the solution of the most difficult problem, and one of the triumphs, of civilisation.' As a practical answer to the disestablishers he pointed out how
powerful and highly organised and wealthy a corporation
the Church was, and must remain, whatever the conditions
of disestablishment; and asked whether the severance of
the controlling tie which bound such a body to the State
could be favourable to the cause of civil and religious
liberty. He had a great respect for the Nonconformists, and expressed his mortification that, from a
feeling of envy or pique, they should have become the
partisans of secular education, instead of working with
the Church for religious education, which was ' demanded
by the nation generally and by the instincts of human
nature.'

While expressing his belief that the working classes both
in town and country had shared in that advance of national
prosperity which had been favoured by the stability of
our political institutions, he pointed to social reform as

a sphere in which no inconsiderable results might be
obtained, and gave his party a famous catchword.

A great scholar and a great wit, 300 years ago, said that,
in his opinion, there was a great mistake in the Vulgate,
which as you all know is the Latin translation of the Holy
Scriptures, and that, instead of saying ' Vanity of vanities,
all is vanity '—*Vanitas vanitatum, omnia vanitas*—the wise
and witty King really said, *Sanitas sanitatum, omnia sanitas.*[1]
Gentlemen, it is impossible to overrate the importance of the
subject.   After all, the first consideration of a Minister should
be the health of the people.

So far Disraeli's discourse had been rather a constitutional lecture[2] than a party speech.   But now he turned
on the Government and in biting words summed up the
pith of his charges against their proceedings.   It was an
Administration avowedly formed on a principle of violence.
Their specific for the peace and prosperity of Ireland
was to despoil churches and plunder landlords, with the
result of sedition rampant, treason thinly veiled, and the
steady return to Parliament of Home Rulers ' pledged to
the   disruption   of   the   realm.'   ' Her   Majesty's   new
Ministers proceeded in their career like a body of men
under the influence of some deleterious drug.   Not
satiated with the spoliation and anarchy of Ireland, they
began to attack every institution and every interest,
every class and calling in the country.'   After giving
some instances he proceeded in a passage which Lord
Morley calls ' one of the few pieces of classic oratory of
the century.'

As time advanced it was not difficult to perceive that
extravagance was being substituted for energy by the Government.   The unnatural stimulus was subsiding.   Their par-
oxysms ended in prostration.   Some took refuge in melancholy, and their eminent chief alternated between a menace
and a sigh.   As I sat opposite the Treasury Bench the Ministers

---

[1] Disraeli had given this watchword of *Sanitas*, etc., at Aylesbury on
September 21, 1864, without much notice being taken of it.

[2] Cairns, in congratulating Disraeli on the speech, wrote: ' It will live
and be read, not only for its sparkling vigour, but also for the deep strata
of constitutional thought and reasoning which pervade it.'

reminded me of one of those marine landscapes not very un-usual on the coasts of South America. You behold a range of exhausted volcanoes. Not a flame flickers on a single pallid crest But the situation is still dangerous. There are occasional earthquakes, and ever and anon the dark rumbling of the sea.

Before concluding, Disraeli turned to foreign affairs, prefacing what he had to say with a few introductory sentences whose truth will be more generally acknow-ledged now than they were in the early seventies, in spite of the then recent lesson of the Franco-German War.

I know the difficulty of addressing a body of Englishmen on these topics. The very phrase ' foreign affairs ' makes an Englishman convinced that I am about to treat of subjects with which he has no concern. Unhappily the relations of England with the rest of the world, which are ' foreign affairs,' are the matters which most influence his lot. Upon them depends the increase or reduction of taxation. Upon them depends the enjoyment or the embarrassment of his industry. And yet, though so momentous are the consequences of the mismanagement of our foreign relations, no one thinks of them till the mischief occurs, and then it is found how the most vital consequences have been occasioned by mere in-advertence.

Disraeli proceeded to condemn the weakness of the Government in its dealings with Russia over the Black Sea, and its negligence and blundering in regard to the difficulties with the United States over the indirect claims; and he finished on the imperial note.

Don't suppose, because I counsel firmness and decision at the right moment, that I am of that school of statesmen who are favourable to a turbulent and aggressive diplomacy. I have resisted it during a great part of my life. I am not unaware that the relations of England to Europe have under-gone a vast change during the century that has just elapsed. The relations of England to Europe are not the same as they were in the days of Lord Chatham or Frederick the Great. The Queen of England has become the Sovereign of the most powerful of Oriental States. On the other side of the globe there are new establishments belonging to her, teeming with wealth and population, which will, in due time, exercise their influence over the distribution of power. The old establish-

ments of this country, now the United States of America,
throw their lengthening shades over the Atlantic, which mix
with European waters.   These are vast and novel elements
in the distribution of power.   I acknowledge that the policy
of England with respect to Europe should be a policy of
reserve, but proud reserve; and in answer to those statesmen,
those mistaken statesmen, who have intimated the decay of
the power of England and the decline of her resources, I express here my confident conviction that there never was a
moment in our history when the power of England was so
great and her resources so vast and inexhaustible.   And yet,
gentlemen, it is not merely our fleets and armies, our powerful
artillery, our accumulated capital, and our unlimited credit
on which I so much depend, as upon that unbroken spirit of
her people, which I believe was never prouder of the Imperial
country to which they belong.

The speech and the Manchester reception at once placed
Disraeli's leadership beyond question, and proved the
reality of Conservative reaction.   Sidonia's familiar words
—' The age of ruins is past.   Have you seen Manchester ?'
—had acquired a fresh significance.   That Conservatism
should have taken such a hold of Lancashire and that
Manchester should welcome Disraeli with such enthusiasm
was indeed a portent.   There was no more industrial
district in England, and none where the working man was
more independent.   Manchester was the home of Free
Trade, and the hall in which Disraeli spoke was the
favourite platform of Cobden and Bright during the
struggle against the Corn Laws.   Lancashire was the
native county of both Gladstone and Bright, the pillars
of Liberalism at this period; and Gladstone, by political
progresses through its towns in the sixties, had made an
impassioned bid for its support.   Both Gladstone and
Bright had sat for a while for Lancashire seats; but both
had been defeated and gone elsewhere.   The great
territorial Conservative influence in Lancashire was that
of the house of Stanley, whose present head was designated
by the discontented as Disraeli's supplanter.   But even
in Lancashire Derby was ready to yield Disraeli place,
to speak of him not merely as his ' old political colleague '
and ' a personal friend of more than twenty years' stand-

ing,' but as his ' chief,' and to bear striking testimony to his high qualities. ' Few leaders of men have ever been more successful in securing the personal confidence and sympathy and goodwill of those with whom they act, and no one has ever shown himself more faithful both to the obligation of private friendship and to the honourable tie of party connection.' Another passage in Derby's speech at the meeting in the Free Trade Hall showed that the Conservative leaders were determined not to snatch prematurely at power, but to wait till the disgust of the country with Gladstonian policy was complete. It might be the tactics of the Radical party to put a Conservative Government in office in a minority; ' but just because it is their game it ought not to be ours.' The course which Disraeli took when Gladstone resigned over his defeat in the following spring on the Irish University Bill was clearly foreshadowed in this sagacious advice.

To W. Romaine Callender, jun.[1]

GROSVENOR GATE, *April* 6, 1872.—I am sure you and kind Mrs. Callender will be glad to hear of our safe and agreeable arrival at Grosvenor Gate; cheered, as far as the Potteries, by your enthusiastic population, which calmed, by degrees, as we entered less busy lands, and which, when we traversed my own country, was as still as became a true prophet.

One is little disposed to do anything to-day, but it is impossible to refrain expressing to you our sense of all your kindness, delicate attentions, and munificent hospitality.

We have talked of them ever since, and shall often do so; and, from all I hear, this wondrous week will have no ordinary influence on public opinion and future history. . . .

Disraeli took another opportunity in June to review and inspirit his new party machine and to elaborate the policy which he proposed to the country. This time the body which he addressed was the National Union, the central society to which the Conservative and Constitutional associations throughout the country were affiliated.

---

[1] Disraeli's host at Manchester and chairman of the Free Trade Hall meeting. He won a seat at Manchester in 1874, was selected by Disraeli to second the Address, and was offered by him a baronetcy at the close of 1875; but he died, prematurely, early in 1876, before the baronetcy had been gazetted.

Speaking, on June 24, to this representative audience at a banquet at the Crystal Palace he laid it down that the Tory party had three great objects: to maintain our institutions, to uphold the Empire, and to elevate the condition of the people. On the first he had dwelt at considerable length at Manchester, and he added little that was fresh at the Crystal Palace. With regard to social reform, Liberals had scoffed at his proposals as a 'policy of sewage'; but to a working man, Disraeli maintained, it was a policy of life and death. It was, he said, a large subject, with many branches.

It involves the state of the dwellings of the people, the moral consequences of which are not less considerable than the physical. It involves their enjoyment of some of the chief elements of nature—air, light, and water. It involves the regulation of their industry, the inspection of their toil. It involves the purity of their provisions, and it touches upon all the means by which you may wean them from habits of excess and of brutality.

But the part of his speech which struck the highest note was that which associated Conservatism with the maintenance of Empire. His Reform Act of 1867, he said, was founded on the confidence that the great body of the people were conservative in the purest and loftiest sense; that the working classes were proud of belonging to a great country, and wished to maintain its greatness; that they were proud of belonging to an Imperial country, and resolved to maintain their Empire. What was the record of Liberalism in regard to Empire, and what ought to be Conservative policy?

If you look to the history of this country since the advent of Liberalism—forty years ago—you will find that there has been no effort so continuous, so subtle, supported by so much energy, and carried on with so much ability and acumen, as the attempts of Liberalism to effect the disintegration of the Empire of England. And, gentlemen, of all its efforts, this is the one which has been the nearest to success. Statesmen of the highest character, writers of the most distinguished ability, the most organised and efficient means, have been employed in this endeavour. It has been proved to all of

us that we have lost money by our Colonies. It has been
shown with precise, with mathematical demonstration, that
there never was a jewel in the Crown of England that was so
truly costly as the possession of India. How often has it
been suggested that we should at once emancipate ourselves
from this incubus! Well, that result was nearly accomplished.
When those subtle views were adopted by the country under
the plausible plea of granting self-government to the Colonies,
I confess that I myself thought that the tie was broken. Not
that I for one object to self-government; I cannot conceive
how our distant Colonies can have their affairs administered
except by self-government.

But self-government, in my opinion, when it was conceded,
ought to have been conceded as part of a great policy of
Imperial consolidation. It ought to have been accompanied
by an Imperial tariff, by securities for the people of England
for the enjoyment of the unappropriated lands which belonged
to the Sovereign as their trustee, and by a military code
which should have precisely defined the means and the responsibilities by which the Colonies should be defended, and by
which, if necessary, this country should call for aid from the
Colonies themselves. It ought, further, to have been accompanied by the institution of some representative council
in the metropolis, which would have brought the Colonies
into constant and continuous relations with the Home Government. All this, however, was omitted because those who
advised that policy—and I believe their convictions were
sincere—looked upon the Colonies of England, looked even
upon our connection with India, as a burden upon this country;
viewing everything in a financial aspect, and totally passing
by those moral and political considerations which make nations
great, and by the influence of which alone men are distinguished from animals.

Well, what has been the result of this attempt during the
reign of Liberalism for the disintegration of the Empire?
It has entirely failed. But how has it failed? Through
the sympathy of the Colonies for the Mother Country. They
have decided that the Empire shall not be destroyed; and
in my opinion no Minister in this country will do his duty
who neglects any opportunity of reconstructing as much as
possible our Colonial Empire, and of responding to those
distant sympathies which may become the source of incalculable strength and happiness to this land.

That is the famous declaration from which the modern
conception of the British Empire largely takes its rise.
In it Disraeli struck a chord that immediately echoed

round the Colonies, India, and the Dependencies; and the reverberation has never ceased. The time could not be far distant, he prophetically told his hearers, when England would have to decide between national and cosmopolitan principles. In their fight against Liberalism or the Continental system Conservatives would have against them those who had enjoyed power for nearly half a century; but still they could rely, he said in sonorous Disraelian language, on ' the sublime instincts of an ancient people.'

The issue is not a mean one. It is whether you will be content to be a comfortable England, modelled and moulded upon Continental principles and meeting in due course an inevitable fate, or whether you will be a great country, an Imperial country, a country where your sons, when they rise, rise to paramount positions, and obtain not merely the esteem of their countrymen, but command the respect of the world.

Lord Morley remarks of Disraeli's watchwords of Empire and Social Reform, that ' when power fell into his hands he made no single move of solid effect for either social reform or imperial unity,'[1] whereas it was Gladstone's wont to embody policy in Parliamentary Bills. The statement is very far from being accurate, and subsequent chapters of this biography will show what a material contribution both to social welfare and to imperial con-solidation was made by the Beaconsfield Government of 1874. But it is, of course, true that many of Disraeli's most fertile ideas did not issue in Bills; and as a practical politician he must in this respect yield place to Gladstone. It is, however, precisely the fact that Gladstone seldom or never played with political ideas which could not be enclosed within the compass of a Bill that marks his inferiority as a statesman and explains his diminishing hold on the present generation; and it is precisely the fact that Disraeli did allow his mind such free play that is his greatest praise in our eyes and that will insure his fame with those who come after us.

[1] *Gladstone*, Bk. VI., ch. 8.

Between Manchester and the Crystal Palace Disraeli had another proof of his growing popularity. He attended, along with a crowd of distinguished personages, the Literary Fund dinner, in order to support a reigning Sovereign in the chair, Leopold II., King of the Belgians. Writing to Corry a day or two afterwards, he said: ' The demonstration at the Literary Fund meeting was equal to Manchester. The mob consisting of Princes, Ambassadors, wits, artists—and critics !' His speech in proposing the King's health was one of his happiest. It was a charming and delightful inconsistency, he said, that the republic of letters should be presided over by a monarch; let them meet it by an inconsistency as amiably flagrant, and give their Sovereign Chairman a right royal welcome. His description of Belgium, and of the policy which guaranteed its independence and neutrality, has a special interest to-day.

Forty years ago a portion of Europe, and one not the least fair, seemed doomed by an inexorable fate to permanent dependence and periodical devastation. And yet the conditions of that country were favourable to civilisation and human happiness; a fertile soil skilfully cultivated, a land covered with beautiful cities and occupied by a race prone alike to liberty and religion, and always excelling in the fine arts. In the midst of a European convulsion, a great statesman resolved to terminate that deplorable destiny, and conceived the idea of establishing the independence of Belgium on the principle of political neutrality. The idea was welcomed at first with sceptical contempt. But we who live in the after generation can bear witness to its triumphant success, and can take the opportunity of congratulating that noble policy which consecrated to perpetual peace the battle-field of Europe.

Disraeli's political activities in this spring of 1872 were almost entirely confined to his two great extra-Parliamentary appearances. He was much shocked in February to receive the news of the murder of his friend Mayo, the Viceroy of India, in the Andaman Islands.

To Lady Beaconsfield.

Feb. 12, '72.—Horrible news from India! Lord Mayo assassinated and dead! The enclosed telegram is from Robert Bourke!

Shall be home pretty early.

Quite shaken to the centre. Gladstone announced it: I said a few words.

G. GATE, *April* 26, '72.—Last night was very damaging to the Government:[1] a family quarrel, in which we did not interfere, except on the part of Ball, who could scarcely be silent. Bouverie in fierce opposition; and though the affair ended without a vote, as was inevitable, the Government most unnecessarily blundered into a signal defeat at the end of the night. . . .

May 7.—Last night the Government received a great, and unexpected, blow: Gordon's resolution[2] having been carried to the surprise of both sides! The cheering exceeded even that on the Ballot Clause. . . .

To Lord Derby.

GROSVENOR GATE, *May* 3, 1872.—My suggestion of identical subscriptions from [Mayo's] colleagues found no favor. It was thought to be an idea, perhaps, suited to colleagues in a Ministry, who then can frame a tariff according to their salaries, but was not deemed applicable to existing circumstances. Our late colleagues are like Martial's epigrams—some rich, some poor, some moderate; so they prefer subscribing according to their means, or their inclination. . . .

The ballot was again seriously damaged in Ho. of Comm. last night, and we supported the Govt. and the Whigs against an infuriated Mountain. . . .

The Ballot Bill was the main occupation of the session; and as Disraeli's object, in view of divided opinions in his party, was to get the question settled, he maintained a rigorous silence while it was running a troubled course through the House. His policy was to take care that the Liberals should not have a popular grievance to exploit, a popular cry on which to dissolve, either through the

---

[1] A debate on a University Tests (Dublin) Bill, in which independent Liberals like Fawcett, Playfair, and Bouverie strongly attacked the Government.

[2] On the Scottish Education Bill. The Government was defeated by 7; 216 to 209.

failure of the Bill in the Commons owing to Tory obstruction or through its rejection on second reading by the Lords. But he hoped that amendments making the Bill optional would be secured in the Lords by the pressure of a unanimous Tory party aided by Russell and the old Whigs. This programme was duly carried out, and when the Bill was returned amended to the Commons Disraeli broke his silence to defend the fantastic plan of optional secrecy. But the Commons would have none of it; and in the Lords, the Duke of Northumberland, at the head of a body of independent Conservatives, averted a struggle between the two Houses by supporting the motion not to insist upon the amendment. Disraeli was rather put out at the way in which the matter had been bungled.

To Lord Derby.

GROSVENOR GATE, *June 20*, 1872.—I was in hopes I might have met you somewhere yesterday, and had a few minutes' conversation with you *re* Ballot Bill (H. of Lords) wh. seems to me in an unsatisfactory position.

When the Duke of Richmond called on me to confer on his alternative propositions—to throw out the Bill on the 2nd reading, or to make it permissive in Committee, I assented to the latter scheme on the very distinct conditions that it shd. be sanctioned by the unanimous assent of the party, and especially of yourself. The Duke subsequently wrote to me, that he had conferred with you, Ld. Salisbury, and others, and that you had unanimously adopted the latter scheme.

But it seems there must have been some terrible mistake on this head, as I observe you did not vote on the occasion, and it is now rumored, that you disapprove of the proposal.

Unless the Duke is supported, the Ballot Bill will pass, wh. neither the House of Comm. nor the country desire. It is impossible for the Duke to recede from his position; it would make him ridiculous and totally unable in future to pretend to control affairs. Lord Russell sanctioned the move, and still is of opinion, that we shd. not recede from the ground we have, after deliberation, occupied. Whether the Duke is beaten or not, his character and the repute of the party demand that he shall be firm. All that important and influential section who were in favor of throwing out the Bill on the 2nd reading, at least on our side, would be outraged, if there were any transaction or compromise, wh. secured the virtual passing of the Government measure.

I hope, therefore, you will gravely consider these critical circumstances, for, tho' the Duke of Richmond, publicly and privately, must make every effort to rally his forces for the occasion, there is no doubt those exertions will be considerably neutralised if you are the avowed opponent of his proceedings.

July 12.—Thanks for your letter, wh. is full of good stuff; I think we may raise a flame, wh. will well occupy the lieges during the recess, and sustain the unpopularity of the Ministry.

The ballot in your house was a sad business. Nothing but unanimity could justify our course. I think it was the right one, and that throwing out the Bill on the second reading (even if it cd. be done) would have raised an agitation against the House of Lords on the ground of their purely obstructive policy.

The Duke of Northumberland shd. be asked why, after having attended the two meetings at D. of Richmond's in silence, interpreted as assent, he shd. have led the defection ? Had he spoken out at the meetings and been supported, the course might have been changed.

The truth is, I fancy, he, and his following, and all others, were satisfied enough at the time, but got frightened afterwards by the articles in *The Times*, wh. laughed at them the next day for their pains.

However, the mischief is done, and our only consolation must be, that the Government wh. first appeals to the country on the secret suffrage will, in all probability, be cashiered.

One serious rebuff which the Government received in this session must have given Disraeli peculiar satisfaction. When he had assumed the leadership in the spring of 1849 he had made it his principal object to endeavour to convince Parliament of the injustice suffered by the landed interest in having charged upon it the whole of the local rates. Rates, he had pointed out, were raised for national as well as for local objects, and benefited the whole community and not merely the owners and occupiers of real property. Now that the State had withdrawn protection from the landed interest, they had a right, he had argued, to have this injustice redressed. The argument impressed the House at the time, and the majorities against Disraeli's motions became smaller with succeeding years. But little or nothing had been actually done in this direction in Parliaments where Disraeli never had a majority; and fresh charges had been constantly put upon the rates, while the actual administration was largely withdrawn from local control. Sir Massey Lopes, a substantial county member who had made a special study of the question, carried this session against the Government, by a majority of no less than a hundred, a motion that £2,000,000 worth of these charges, dealing with the administration of justice, police, and lunatics, should be placed on the Consolidated Fund. Disraeli strongly urged that the reform was five and twenty years overdue, while the burdens on real property had greatly increased, and, with the urgent claims of public education and public health, must increase still further. In spite of the adverse vote, the Government shirked their responsibility; accordingly, the relief which Disraeli had pleaded for in his first days of leadership he was himself to be the Minister to grant.

The Government were damaged less by their defeat on Lopes's motion than by their success in carrying a much-needed measure, the Licensing Act, which irritated a powerful trade and interfered with the habits of countless individuals. Their unpopularity was increased in the autumn by the blow to British pride involved in the swingeing damages awarded to the United States by the Geneva arbitrators in respect of the *Alabama* dispute. The loss of Ministerial seats at by-elections continued. Consequently, though Disraeli, absorbed by domestic sorrow,[1] did not resume his pungent attacks between the close of the 1872 session and the opening of the next, Ministers met Parliament in February, 1873, with a tarnished reputation and clouded prospects, and promptly received a stunning blow from which they never pro-

[1] See below, ch. 6.

perly recovered. The task before them in the session was obviously a perilous one. Gladstone, who had already carried, with the full force of an unimpaired majority, two great Irish Bills, was about to venture, with his majority much less under control, on a third. This time he was to deal with that University question which his rival had in hand when he himself overtrumped him with disestablishment. Once again Manning was deep in the counsels of a British Premier hopeful of finding a solution; and he was to mislead Gladstone as he had misled Disraeli. Disraeli's letters show us the hopes and fears of the Opposition.

To Montagu Corry.

H. OF C., *Feb.* 10, '73.—Lord Derby on Saturday seemed to think a crisis was at hand, and rather regretted going away (which, by the bye, Cairns is also doing). D. said ' You can telegraph for me.' . . .

Feb. 11.—I wrote you a wretched scrawl yesterday from H. of C. in a miserable state, and am not much better to-day.

From what I gathered from Robert Montagu, coached by Manning, I should think Gladstone's scheme will do. I infer something like this. Trinity Coll. to be no longer a University, but to retain a considerable endowment. The Romans not to be endowed. The Peel Colleges to be abolished. An Examining Board $\frac{1}{2}$ Catholic and $\frac{1}{2}$ Protestant; but Cath. under-grads. to be examined only on those subjects and in that manner the priesthood approves and, of course, by the Cath. moiety of examiners.

They say G. is to make the greatest speech to-morrow he has yet accomplished. . . .

Feb. 15.—I have been in a state of coma for the last few days—and have been unable to write. Indeed, it is only the recollection that it is Saturday, which forces me to this feebleness. Everything seems to have calmed down again, and I see no movement for the next fortnight. . . .

I conclude there will be no attempt to oppose the 2nd reading of the Bill, though there will be a considerable debate thereon: and in Committee, though nothing ever succeeds in Committee, there will be an effort to establish the Professorships of Philosophy and History, and perhaps to reconstruct the Governing Council. . . .

Feb. 18.—There is to be a council at my rooms on Saturday *re* Ir. Univ. Bill. . . .

Feb. 22.—We had our meeting this morning; it was very long and very troublesome. We came to a conclusion, as a Home Ruler has given notice of opposing 2nd reading, to encourage and carry on a great debate—for three nights, if possible, and, in the course of it, to announce, that we should move resolutions on going into Committee.

I should not be surprised if Fawcett gives notice of resolutions at once in much the same spirit, speculating on the Home Ruler relinquishing his purpose. . . .

Feb. 25.—. . . There is a feeling in the air, that the 3rd branch of the Upas-tree will still blast Celtic society. As Ball says, if the Bill is got rid of, no party in the country, and neither side of the House, will ever hear of the question again: for, in fact, it is all humbug. . . .

12, GEORGE ST., *Feb.* 27.—I had an interesting letter from Lord Derby yesterday, anxious about the Irish Bill, and impressing upon me, that, if wanted, he could be here in 4 and 20 hours. He dined with Thiers, whom he found very old, feeble, with a cracked voice, but warming up into animation as he talked on; never alluding even to domestic affairs, but expatiating on every point of foreign. . . . He seemed to think dissensions must soon break out between Prussia and Bavaria, and repeatedly said that the first and, indeed, only object for France was the reorganisation of her army: ' not that we wanted war, etc., but nobody knew what might happen, and we must be prepared.' . . .

I am now going down to the House, walking; as the air is clear and the wind westerly. . . .

March 1.—. . . There is no news, except a general impression that Gladstone will withdraw his Bill. So Lord Stanhope told me this morning at British Museum: but I doubt it. He will not like losing the opportunity of self-vindication in many speeches.

To Gathorne Hardy.

Saturday, March 8, 1873.—I thought your speech excellent' and so, I observe, does the *Spectator* to-day; no mean Parliamentary critic.

It was a hard trial to get up at midnight, as I know from experience—but all the things you omitted to say will come into another speech, and had you not demonstrated, the effect wd. have been most injurious.

I was very glad that you alluded to a Gladstone dissolution as ultimately inevitable, and that you spoke out to Knightley.[1]

[1] Sir Rainald Knightley (afterwards Lord Knightley), of Fawsley, M.P. for South Northants, a squire of long descent, high honour, many prejudices, and some Parliamentary capacity, was an irreconcilable member of the

He belongs to a clique, who think we have no single object in the world but place and patronage; little suspecting, that for four years we have, for the sake of the country, and especially for the Tory party, unceasingly labored to prevent a premature change.

The fever of my attack seems to have subsided, but I am very feeble.

As the letters suggest, Gladstone's scheme sounded very plausible when set forth by himself in one of those exegetical discourses in which no other Parliamentarian could compare with him; but it would not stand critical examination. Protestant feeling was offended by the constitution of the governing body of the new University, which was such that, in Lord Morley's euphemistic words, ' it did not make clerical predominance ultimately impossible.' In spite of this prospect, the Irish Bishops were offended by the maintenance of the principle of mixed education, in which Protestant colleges and students were to stand side by side with Roman Catholic colleges and students; and ultimately Cardinal Cullen refused and denounced the offer. Those who realised what a University meant and cared for the interests of higher education, of whom Fawcett was the most prominent representative, were disgusted by the prohibition of any University teacher in theology, modern history, or mental and moral philosophy; and by the liability of all teachers to suspension or deprivation for giving offence to religious convictions.

---

anti-Disraeli Tory clique, and only supported the Opposition leaders by his vote on this occasion because he was satisfied from Hardy's speech and conversation that they would not take office till after a dissolution. A story which Lady Knightley tells, in her *Journals*, p. 240, of the origin of her husband's feeling towards Disraeli, suggests that a plentiful lack of humour had much to do with Tory mistrust of their witty and sardonic chief. ' I asked Rainald to-day,' writes Lady Knightley on March 15, 1873, ' when he first began to distrust [Disraeli].' He said, "Very soon after I came into Parliament, I was desired by the Whip to do all I could to get our men to vote against the Government on some question—not a very important one—on which they seemed to me to be in the right. However, I trusted our leader, and thought he probably knew more about it than I did, so I did as I was bid. When we got into the lobby, we found ourselves in a minority, upon which Disraeli said, 'There! we've sacrificed our characters, and voted wrong, and haven't beat the Government after all!'" Comment, I think,' adds Lady Knightley, ' is superfluous.' It is indeed.

The impracticability of the scheme as it stood was so patent that Ministers were reduced to endeavouring to obtain support by suggesting that large amendments could be made in Committee, and by dwelling on the threat that they would treat the second reading as a vital matter.

Disraeli in his speech on the last night of the debate declined to put any confidence in these unconfirmed hints of Committee amendments, and protested against the threat of resignation. No one wished to disturb Gladstone in his place, but it was the duty of members to say distinctly whether they could approve this particular measure. It proposed to found a University which was not universal, and in an age when young men prattled about protoplasm and young ladies in gilded saloons unconsciously talked atheism, to prohibit the teaching of philosophy ! He chaffed Gladstone about the 'anonymous persons' who were to constitute the council of the new University. He vindicated his own policy of concurrent endowment in 1868, a policy which had been steadily pursued by statesmen of all parties down to that date, but had then been killed by Gladstone. 'The right hon. gentleman says I burnt my fingers on that occasion, but,' said Disraeli, holding out his hands across the floor of the House amid general amusement, 'I see no scars.' He continued:

The right hon. gentleman, suddenly—I impute no motive, that is quite unnecessary—changed his mind, and threw over the policy of concurrent endowment, mistaking the clamour of the Nonconformists[1] for the voice of the nation. The Roman Catholics fell into the trap. They forgot the cause of University education in the prospect of destroying the Protestant Church. The right hon. gentleman succeeded in his object. He became Prime Minister of England. . . . The Roman Catholics had the satisfaction of destroying the Protestant Church—of disestablishing the Protestant Church. They had the satisfaction before the year was over of witnessing the disestablishment of the Roman Catholic Church at

---

[1] Another reading has 'the *Nonconformist*'—the newspaper organ of the Dissenters.

Rome. As certain as that we are in this House, the policy that caused the one led to the other. . . . The Roman Catholics, having reduced Ireland to a spiritual desert, are discontented and have a grievance; and they come to Parliament in order that it may create for them a blooming Garden of Eden.

And then Disraeli proceeded to one of those attacks on the general tendency of Gladstonian policy which were beginning to sink deeply into the national mind. Gladstone, he said, had substituted a policy of confiscation for the policy of concurrent endowment:

You have had four years of it. You have despoiled churches. You have threatened every corporation and endowment in the country. You have examined into everybody's affairs. You have criticised every profession and vexed every trade. No one is certain of his property and nobody knows what duties he may have to perform to-morrow.

Gladstone, in reply, urged Parliament to go on in its work of bringing justice to Ireland in spite of the perverseness of those whom it was attempting to assist; but the House realised the absurdity of proceeding with proposals repudiated by Catholics as well as by Protestants. The division was taken after two o'clock on the morning of Wednesday, March 12. Ministers were beaten by 3 votes, the numbers being 287 to 284. They had a small majority among the English members, and a large majority among the Scotch; but the Irish voted 68 to 15 against them. ' The Irish Romans,' wrote Hardy in his diary, ' voted against Gladstone in a body, but it was utterly wrong of Gladstone to taunt us, for our opposition long preceded theirs, and there was no compact whatever. And now what will follow ? I doubt not Gladstone will try to. force us in, but in vain. It is neither our duty nor our interest to dissolve Parliament for him, and I cannot admit the right of any Government to make any question they please vital, and, if a combination negatives, to force upon one portion of it all the responsibility.'

Hardy's opinion, thus recorded decisively at the first

moment in his diary, was the one which prevailed with
Disraeli and his colleagues. In truth the situation had
been anticipated; and, though two of Disraeli's most
important colleagues, Derby and Cairns, were abroad, he
had ascertained from them before they went their unwillingness to accept office in the event of such a contingency as had occurred. The Beaconsfield papers contain
the following scrap in Derby's handwriting:

If it is only contended that Mr. D. before announcing his
decision, ought to have maturely considered the circumstances
and consulted with his friends, the answer is that he had done
so already in anticipation of what for the last six weeks was
a possible and not improbable contingency.

Hardy and Richmond went to see their chief on the
morrow of the division, and there was an agreement between them all in this sense, though apparently Disraeli's
Socratic method suggested to Hardy that he had a doubt
on the subject. The upshot of the talk of the three
colleagues was that the impracticability of office was
so clear that Disraeli might decline without further consultation.

Meanwhile there was some hesitation in the Ministerial
camp, and it required a couple of Cabinet Councils,
one on the Wednesday and one on the Thursday, to bring
them to resignation.

To Lord Beauchamp.

Thursday, March 13.—I have had a good night, except disturbed too much by my cough, which must be again attended
to. I neglected remedies in the anarchy of yesterday.

What is going to take place ? And what is the 2nd Cabinet
about ? Our friend cannot even resign in the usual manner,
I was in hopes yesterday that the Q. had not accepted his
resignation as in my case, which would have solved many
knots, and that we should have an early dissolution on his
part; but the ambiguous voices of the oracles this morning
perplex me.

The second Cabinet, however, decided for resignation;
Gladstone saw the Queen in the early afternoon of the
Thursday, and announced the fact in Parliament at 4.30.

Disraeli was stopped in the lobby, as he was entering the House of Commons, by a message from the Palace.

From Queen Victoria.

BUCKINGHAM PALACE, *March* 13, 1873.—Mr. Gladstone has just been here and has tendered his resignation and that of all his colleagues in consequence of the vote of the House of Commons on Tuesday night—which the Queen has accepted. She therefore writes to Mr. Disraeli to ask him whether he will undertake to form a Government.

The Queen would like to see Mr. Disraeli at 6 or as soon after as possible.

She sends this letter by her private secretary, Colonel Ponsonby, who can be the bearer of any written or verbal answer from Mr Disraeli.

The Queen herself drew up a memorandum to describe what passed at the audience which followed.

Memorandum by Queen Victoria.

BUCKINGHAM PALACE, *March* 13, 1873.—Mr. Disraeli came at a little after 6. After expressing my feeling for him in his sorrow and shaking hands with him, I said I had sent for him in consequence of last night's vote; and he asked whether I wished him to give a categorical answer, or to say a few words on the present state of affairs. I said I should willingly hear what he had to say.

He then went on to say that he had not expected the vote; he had thought, after Mr. Cardwell's speech, the Government would have a majority. That the Conservative party never was more compact or more united; that there was the most perfect understanding between him and all those who had served with him, and especially named Ld. Derby, Ld. Cairns, Mr. Hardy, and Sir S. Northcote. That he was perfectly able to form a Government at once, perfectly fit to carry on the administration of the country to my entire satisfaction; that he could command 280 votes; that since, as he said, ' I had left your Majesty's *immediate* service, for I never consider myself out of your Majesty's service,' the party had gained considerably, about thirty seats; that he had laboured to keep the party as much together and in as efficient a state as possible; but that it would be useless to attempt to carry on the Government with a minority in the House of Commons, and that he must therefore state his inability to undertake to form a Government in the present Parliament.

What was then to be done ? I asked. 'Mr. Gladstone ought
to remain in and continue to carry on the Government.'
This, I said, I thought he very likely would object to, having
declared his views so strongly on this measure. This was a
mistake, Mr. Disraeli replied, and he ought never to have
done so. That might be so or not, I said, but anyhow Mr.
Gladstone *did* feel this, and did not ask for a dissolution,
therefore I thought it doubtful whether he would consent
to resume or continue in office, feeling he could not submit
to this vote. ' But he has *condoned* for it by his resignation
and readiness to give up power,' was the answer; that he
should not throw up office merely for this vote; it would not
be a good return to the present Parliament, which had supported him so warmly, and in which he had carried 3 great
measures, for so he must call them, though he might not agree
with them. I again asked him what I was to say to Mr.
Gladstone, and he repeated that ' I decline to form a Government in the present Parliament, and I do not ask for a dissolution.'

Of course, he said, there were instances where a Sovereign
had been left without a Government, and in such a case he
would, of course, be ready to serve me. I said that I would
at once let Mr. Gladstone know, but that I might have to
call upon him again.

Disraeli, in giving Hardy afterwards an account of his
audience, added that the Queen's ' cordiality was *marked*,'
and that ' she manifested, as he thought, a repugnance
to her present Government.' To Beauchamp he wrote:
' I had a more than gracious reception; and, if Her
Majesty were leader of the Opposition, I believe this
morning she would be First Lord of her own Treasury.'
The Queen at once sent Ponsonby to Gladstone with
an account of what had passed, adding, ' She considers
this as sending for you anew.' But Gladstone suspected
a trick and told Ponsonby that he ' thought Mr. Disraeli
was endeavouring, by at once throwing back on me an
offer which it was impossible for me at the time and under
the circumstances to accept, to get up a case of absolute
necessity founded upon this refusal of mine, and thus,
becoming the indispensable man and party, to have in his
hands a lever wherewith to overcome the reluctance and
resistance of his friends, who would not be able to deny

that the Queen must have a Government.' To Gladstone Disraeli was the wily mystery-man, and the simple reasoning which had led his rival to decline did not appear at all adequate to one who was determined to find some deep calculation in all that rival did. Accordingly, Gladstone asked, through Ponsonby, that Disraeli's reply might be put in writing.

Memorandum in Colonel Ponsonby's Handwriting.

March 13, 1873.—Colonel Ponsonby called on Mr. Disraeli in the evening with a message from the Queen, asking him to give Her Majesty, in writing, the substance of his conversation with the Queen.

Mr. Disraeli willingly complied with Her Majesty's wishes, and wrote down roughly the chief points on which he had spoken.

Colonel Ponsonby asked Mr. Disraeli if he might assume that this meant an unconditional refusal. Mr. Disraeli replied that such was the meaning in the present state of affairs.

Colonel Ponsonby asked, if the Queen was ready to sanction a dissolution as soon as possible, whether Mr. Disraeli could then accept office, taking, of course, the responsibility of giving the advice to Her Majesty to dissolve.

Mr. Disraeli replied that he could not accept office with such an understanding, and that his refusal was absolute.

He hoped in some future day, when another Parliament assembled, to find an opportunity of serving the Queen, but with the present House of Commons with a large majority opposed to him, he could not undertake the Government.

Such was the official report, certified by Disraeli to be correct, which Ponsonby made to the Queen. But Ponsonby drew up a longer and more detailed account of what took place, which shows more clearly Disraeli's position, while it also amusingly brings out the secretary's Whig distrust of the Tory leader.[1]

---

[1] Disraeli, subsequently, during his great Ministry, bore striking testimony to the absolute impartiality with which Ponsonby carried out his duties as private secretary to the Queen. He said to a political friend: 'I believe that General Ponsonby used to be a Whig, but, whatever his politics may once have been, I can only say that I could not wish my case better stated to the Queen than the private secretary does it. Perhaps I am a gainer by his Whiggishness, as it makes him more scrupulously on his guard to be always absolutely fair and lucid.' See article on 'The Character of Queen Victoria,' *Quarterly Review*, April, 1901.

Her Majesty sent me to see Mr. Disraeli in Edwards's Hotel, George Street, Hanover Square.[1]   He at once acceded to the Queen's wish, and getting pens and ink said, ' There, let me see, I can easi y put down what is wanted; that is very nearly what I said.'   I observed that I did not quite understand it, and hoped he would forgive me if I asked him whether he meant it as a refusal to take office while this Parliament sat, or whether he refused entirely, whether the Queen consented to dissolve or not.   He said he meant it as a refusal, that he could not carry on the Government in a Parliament where there were 80 votes of majority against him.   ' But,' I said, ' would you take office and dissolve ?'   He said, ' I thought the Queen would not agree to this.'   I replied I thought she would not object, in fact, I felt certain she would not.   ' But,' he said, ' there is an idea that this, being my Parliament, cannot be dissolved by me.'   ' But,' I remarked, ' the Queen could offer you a dissolution, though, of course, you would be responsible for advising her to do so.'   ' Of course,' he said, ' I well understand that; but I decline altogether to accept office.'

He went on, ' How could I proceed ?   For two months at least Parliament must continue, while the regular estimates, Mutiny Act, etc., are passed.   The Conservatives are gaining favour in the country, but these two months would ruin them.   They would be exposed in a hostile House to every insult which the Opposition might choose to fling at them, and the party would be seriously damaged, while the business of the country would suffer.   The only possibility of carrying any measure would be by allying myself to the Irish lot, whom I detest and disagree with, and who would throw me over whenever it suited their purpose.'   I said, ' You have defeated the Government; ought you not therefore to undertake the responsibility of forming one ?'   ' No,' he replied; ' we did not defeat the Government.   We threw out a stupid, blundering Bill, which Gladstone, in his *tête montée* way, tried to make a vote of confidence.   It was a foolish mistake of his; but he has condoned for it by resigning.   He can now resume office with perfect freedom.'

During the first part of the interview Disraeli sat at a table, and as he spoke with eagerness, there was something in his over-civil expressions about the Queen or ' my dear Colonel,' which made me think he was playing with me, and I felt once or twice a difficulty in not laughing; but when he developed the reasons of his policy he rose and stood much more upright than I have ever seen him, spoke in a most frank and straightforward manner, and with a sharpness and decision which

[1] See below, p. 573.

was different from his early words. Yet probably he had measured the length of my foot, and had been more sincere and honest in his message to the Queen than when he made me believe in his frank exposition of policy.

He was far easier to speak to than Gladstone, who forces you into his groove, while Disraeli apparently follows yours and is genial, almost too genial, in his sentiments. . . .

In accordance with Her Majesty's desire, Disraeli embodied in a couple of sentences the reply which he had already given:

In answer to the gracious inquiry, whether he would undertake to form a Government, Mr. Disraeli said he was prepared to form an Administration which he believed would carry on Her Majesty's affairs with efficiency, and would possess her confidence, but he could not undertake to carry on Her Majesty's Government in the present House of Commons.

Subsequently, Her Majesty having remarked that Mr. Gladstone was not inclined to recommend a dissolution of Parliament, Mr. Disraeli stated, that he himself would not advise Her Majesty to take that step.

The language was perhaps not as categorical as it might have been, and Gladstone's ingenious mind found a discrepancy between the two sentences, which led him on the Friday to make a further inquiry of the Queen. To Her Majesty's common sense it was clear that, if Disraeli would neither take office in the existing Parliament nor advise a dissolution, his attitude amounted, as Ponsonby put it in his memorandum, to an ' absolute refusal '; and she accordingly answered that Disraeli had unconditionally declined to form a Government. After such a reply, it might have been thought that a Minister who still possessed for the ordinary purposes of government a majority of eighty or ninety would have considered the immediate resumption of office, with or without the intention of an early dissolution, to be his obvious duty. But Gladstone, indignant at Disraeli's avoidance of responsibility, embarrassed the Queen by discovering an alternative course—the drafting of a detailed memorandum to show that Disraeli's action was neither justifiable in itself nor in accordance with precedent. He urged that the proceeding between the Queen and Disraeli could not be regarded as complete, as the vote had been the result of concerted action by the Opposition on a matter declared to be vital by Ministers; and therefore Disraeli ought by counsel and inquiry among his friends to have exhausted all practicable means to form a Government. He recited the history of previous Parliamentary crises to show that there was no precedent for Disraeli's summary refusal. He could not call his colleagues together and ask them to resume their offices were he not able ' to prove to them that according to usage every means had been exhausted on the part of the Opposition for providing for the government of the country, or at least that nothing more was to be expected from that quarter.'[1]

It was a lame conclusion. Gladstone had already been told that nothing more was to be expected from that quarter. The Queen felt this strongly, when the memorandum was presented to her on the Saturday. But as her constitutional duty was to obtain a Government, and as it was plain that the only way in which this could be done was to persuade Gladstone to return, she consented to humour him so far as to become the medium of communication for the rival leaders. Her secretary put on paper an explanation of her views.

Memorandum in Colonel Ponsonby's Handwriting.

BUCKINGHAM PALACE, *March* 15.—The unusual course followed by Mr. Gladstone of asking the Queen for further explanations before he could call the Cabinet together, made it necessary for Her Majesty to consider how she could meet his request.

The Queen could not refuse to take any notice of it, as this would have retarded the progress of the negotiations which Her Majesty was anxious to bring to a satisfactory termination. Besides which, Her Majesty desired there should be no misunderstanding.

The Queen could not assure Mr. Gladstone that Mr. Dis-

[1] The text is given in Lord Morley's *Gladstone*, Book VI., ch. 12, where the crisis is narrated and examined at length.

raeli's refusal to accept office was complete, as Her Majesty would then have undertaken the responsibility of answering for the Opposition party.

The Queen could not herself have called on Mr. Disraeli for further explanations, as Her Majesty would then have assumed the view taken by Mr. Gladstone of Mr. Disraeli's conduct.

The Queen therefore, with Mr. Gladstone's knowledge and consent, forwarded his letter entire to Mr. Disraeli.

From Queen Victoria.

BUCKINGHAM PALACE, *March* 15, '73.—The Queen communicated, as Mr. Disraeli is aware, the substance of his refusal to undertake to form a Government in the present Parliament, to Mr. Gladstone, and she thinks it due to Mr. Disraeli to send him the accompanying letter (with Mr. Gladstone's knowledge), and will be glad to receive a reply from Mr. Disraeli which she can show Mr. Gladstone.

The Queen allows this communication to be made through her in order to prevent as much as possible any misunderstanding.

On receipt of this letter on Saturday afternoon, Disraeli told Ponsonby that he could easily write a short reply at once, but he ' felt sure it would meet with your Majesty's wishes and his own inclinations if he consulted Lord Derby and other members of his party before writing to your Majesty.' Derby had returned on the Friday, but Cairns remained abroad. Disraeli's memorandum was not ready till the middle of Sunday, and he sent it down in the afternoon to the Queen, who had retired to Windsor.

To Queen Victoria.

GEORGE STREET, HANOVER SQUARE, *March* 16, 1873.— Mr. Disraeli with his humble duty to your Majesty.

He thanks your Majesty for communicating to him Mr. Gladstone's letter, with Mr. Gladstone's knowledge.

He is grateful to your Majesty for deigning to allow these communications to be made through your Majesty, and humbly agrees with your Majesty that it is a mode which may tend to prevent misunderstanding.

The observations of Mr. Gladstone, generally considered, may be ranged under two heads: an impeachment of the conduct of the Opposition in contributing to the vote against the Government measure, when they were not prepared, in the event of success, to take office; and a charge against the Leader of the Opposition, that, when honored by the commands of your Majesty, he gave a 'summary refusal' to undertake your Majesty's Government, without exhausting all practicable means of aiding the country in its exigency.

The argument of Mr. Gladstone, in the first instance, is that the Opposition, having, by 'deliberate and concerted action,' thrown out a Bill, which the Government had declared to be 'vital to their existence,' is bound to use all means to form a Government of its own, in order to replace that which it must be held to have intentionally overthrown.

It is humbly submitted to your Majesty, that though, as a general rule, this doctrine may be sound, it cannot be laid down unconditionally, nor otherwise than subject to many exceptions.

It is undoubtedly sound so far as this: that for an Opposition to use its strength for the express purpose of throwing out a Government, which it is at the time aware that it cannot replace—having that object in view, and no other—would be an act of recklessness and faction, which could not be too strongly condemned. But it may be safely affirmed that no conduct of this kind can be imputed to the Conservative Opposition of 1873.

If the doctrine in question is carried further; if it be contended that, whenever, from any circumstances, a Minister is so situated that it is in his power to prevent any other Parliamentary leader from forming an Administration which is likely to stand, he acquires, thereby, the right to call upon Parliament to pass whatever measures he and his colleagues think fit, and is entitled to denounce as factious the resistance to such measures—then the claim is one not warranted by usage, or reconcilable with the freedom of the Legislature.

It amounts to this: that he tells the House of Commons, 'Unless you are prepared to put some one in my place, your duty is to do whatever I bid you.'

To no House of Commons has language of this kind ever been addressed: by no House of Commons would it be tolerated.

In the present instance, the Bill which has been the cause of the crisis, was, from the first, strongly objected to by a large section of the Liberal party, and that on the same grounds which led the Conservative Opposition to resist it, namely, that it seemed calculated to sacrifice the interests of Irish education to those of the Roman Catholic hierarchy.

A protracted discussion strengthened the general feeling of the House of Commons as to the defects of the measure: the party whom it was, apparently, intended to propitiate,

rejected it as inadequate; and, probably, if the sense of the
House had been taken on the Bill, irrespective of considerations as to the political result of the division, not one-fourth of
the House would have voted for it. From first to last, it was
unpopular, both inside and outside Parliament, and was
disliked quite as much by Liberals as by Conservatives.

It is humbly submitted to your Majesty that no Minister
has a right to say to Parliament, ' You must take such a Bill,
whether you think it a good one or not, because, without
passing it, I will not hold office, and my numerical strength
in the present House is too great to allow of any other
effective Administration being formed.'

The charge against the Leader of the Opposition personally,
that, by his ' summary refusal ' to undertake your Majesty's
Government, he was failing in his duty to your Majesty and
the country, is founded altogether on a gratuitous assumption
by Mr. Gladstone, which pervades his letter, that the means
of Mr. Disraeli to carry on the Government were not ' exhausted.'   A brief statement of facts will at once dispose
of this charge.

Before Mr. Disraeli, with due deference, offered his decision
to your Majesty, he had enjoyed the opportunity of consulting
those gentlemen, with whom he acts in public life; and they
were unanimously of opinion, that it would be prejudicial to
the interests of the country for a Conservative Administration
to attempt to conduct your Majesty's affairs, in the present
House of Commons.   What other means were at Mr. Disraeli's disposal ?   Was he to open negotiations with a section
of the late Ministry, and waste days in barren interviews,
vain applications, and the device of impossible combinations ?
Was he to make overtures to the considerable section of the
Liberal party who had voted against the Government, namely,
the Irish Roman Catholic gentlemen ?   Surely Mr. Gladstone
is not serious in such a suggestion.   Impressed by experience,
obtained in those very instances to which Mr. Gladstone
refers, of the detrimental influence upon Government of a
' crisis ' unnecessarily prolonged by hollow negotiations,
Mr. Disraeli humbly conceived that he was taking a course
at once advantageous to the public interests and tending
to spare your Majesty unnecessary anxiety, by at once
laying before your Majesty the real position of affairs.

There are many observations in Mr. Gladstone's letter
which Mr. Disraeli, for convenience, refrains from noticing.
Some of them are involved in an ambiguity not easy to
encounter in a brief space: some of them, with reference to
Mr. Disraeli's conduct in the House of Commons, Mr. Disraeli
would fain hope are not entirely divested of some degree of

exaggeration. 'The deliberate and concerted action of the Opposition' would subside, Mr. Disraeli believes, on impartial investigation, into the exercise of that ordinary, and even daily, discipline of a political party, without which a popular assembly would soon degenerate into a mob, and become divested of all practical influence. In the present instance, Mr. Disraeli believes he is correct in affirming, that his friends were not even formally summoned to vote against the Government measure, but to support an amendment by an honorable gentleman, which was seconded from the Liberal benches, and which could only by a violent abuse of terms be described as a party move.

Then, again, much is made of the circumstance that the existence of the Government was staked on this measure. Mr. Disraeli has already treated of this subject generally. But what are the particular facts ? No doubt, more than a month ago, the Prime Minister, in a devoted House of Commons, had, in an unusual, not to say unprecedented, manner, commenced his exposition of an abstruse measure by stating that the existence of the Government was staked on its success. But inasmuch as, in the course of time, it was understood that the Government were prepared to modify, or even to withdraw, most of the clauses of this measure, these words were forgotten or condoned, and could not be seriously held as exercising a practical influence on the ultimate decision.

From Queen Victoria.

WINDSOR CASTLE, *March* 16, 1873.—The Queen thanks Mr. Disraeli for his letter. She has sent it to Mr. Gladstone, and asked him whether he will undertake to resume office.

Gladstone was at last convinced, to use his own language, that no 'further effort' was to be expected from the Opposition 'towards meeting the present necessity.' He and his colleagues accordingly resumed their offices. But in writing to the Queen he recognised that the political position had been 'seriously unhinged by the shock,' and that neither the Administration nor the Parliament could again be what they were; and he did not disguise in his explanation to Parliament the damage that had been sustained, and the disadvantages necessarily attaching to a returning or resuming Government.

The best opinion, both of the public and of the Conserva-

tive party, approved of Disraeli's decision. *The Times*
had advised that course throughout. Its editor's view
was sent to Disraeli by Lennox.

From Lord Henry Lennox.

Private. 19, GROSVENOR GARDENS, S.W., *March* 16,
1873.—Delane dined with me last evening, and I cannot for-
bear letting you know what he said.

First, that you now stand in the highest position in which
any statesman has stood for many years past; that you had
by your decision given proof of the very highest order of
statesmanship, both unselfish and patriotic; that he is convinced your statement of to-morrow will produce the very
best effect throughout the country, and will earn for you the
gratitude of your followers and the respect and admiration
of your opponents; and lastly that in this matter you have
displayed a judgment and a spirit of which Gladstone would
be utterly incapable.

I need not tell you with what pleasure I heard his remarks,
especially as they were made in presence of the P. of Wales,
the Duke of Edinburgh, and many others.

So strong a party man and competent a manager as
Lord Abergavenny held that 'Dizzy has acted most
wisely in refusing to form a Government.' But there was
of course a disappointed section of the party, who
clamoured for the bold policy of forcing a dissolution and
forming a Government, and maintained that any hesitation
to seize the helm would have as discouraging and dispiriting an effect as Derby's refusal in 1855. It was mainly
to the satisfaction of these impatient partisans that
Disraeli addressed himself in his Parliamentary explanation on March 30. Some parts of an unnecessarily
elaborate speech were not very happy; and Hardy rightly
criticised his chief's remarks about the impossibility of
a matured and complete policy in opposition. But there
was a large amount of necessary financial and other
business which a new Government would have had to get
through before the session could be wound up and dissolution accomplished, and there was no answer to the
passage in which Disraeli pointed out what would during

the intervening period be the certain lot of an Administration with a majority of ninety against them.

I know well—and those who are around me know well—what will occur when a Ministry takes office and attempts to carry on the Government with a minority during the session, with a view of ultimately appealing to the people. We should have what is called ' fair play.' That is to say, no vote of want of confidence would be proposed, and chiefly because it would be of no use. There would be no wholesale censure, but retail humiliation. A right hon. gentleman will come down here, he will arrange his thumbscrews and other instruments of torture on this table. We shall never ask for a vote without a lecture; we shall never perform the most ordinary routine office of Government without there being annexed to it some pedantic and ignominious condition. . . . In a certain time we should enter into the paradise of abstract resolutions. One day hon. gentlemen cannot withstand the golden opportunity of asking the House to affirm that the income tax should no longer form one of the features of our Ways and Means. Of course a proposition of that kind would be scouted by the right hon. gentleman and all his colleagues; but, then, they might dine out that day, and the Resolution might be carried, as Resolutions of that kind have been. Then another hon. gentleman, distinguished for his knowledge of men and things, would move that the diplomatic service be abolished. While hon. gentlemen opposite were laughing in their sleeves at the mover, they would vote for the motion in order to put the Government into a minority. For this reason. ' Why should men,' they would say, ' govern the country who are in a minority ?' totally forgetting that we had acceded to office in the spirit of the Constitution, quite oblivious of the fountain and origin of the position we occupied. And it would go very hard if on some sultry afternoon, some hon. member should not ' rush in where angels fear to tread,' and successfully assimilate the borough and the county franchise. And so things would go on until the bitter end—until at last even the Appropriation Bill has passed, Parliament is dissolved, and we appeal to those millions, who, perhaps, six months before, might have looked upon us as the vindicators of intolerable grievances, but who now receive us as a defeated, discredited, and degraded ministry, whose services can neither be of value to the Crown nor a credit to the nation.

The Tory party, Disraeli maintained, occupied a most satisfactory position. It had divested itself of excrescences and emerged from the fiscal period. In order to deal with the more fundamental questions which were rapidly coming to the front, it was of the utmost importance that there should be ' a great Constitutional party, distinguished for its intelligence as well as for its organisation, which shall be competent to lead the people and direct the public mind.' That there might be no obstacle to its future triumph, he, as the trustee of its honour and interests, declined to form a weak and discredited Administration.

To the Duke of Richmond.

Friday, March 21, 1873.—I thought what you said was most judicious and *à propos*, and will have a good effect, and encourage the country. You spoke too highly of your colleague and correspondent, but it proved our union; and I must try to deserve your praise.

I don't think the Prime Minister greatly distinguished himself in our House.

We shall all of us be glad to see Cairns again. How much has happened in his absence, and ripe, I think, with the seeds of the future.

The seeds of the future were indeed germinating. To an Opposition which, little more than a year before, was discredited, discontented, factious, and hopeless, Disraeli had given organisation, policy, popular respect, the assurance of high and unselfish leadership, and the expectation of early and definitive success.

CHAPTER VI.

BEREAVEMENT.

1872–1873.

While Disraeli's political prospects grew daily brighter, a heavy cloud fell upon his domestic life. After thirty-three years of unbroken happiness and affection, he lost the wife who was in very deed his chosen helpmate,[1] to whom he attributed, in a speech at Edinburgh in 1867, all the successes of his life, 'because she has supported me by her counsel and consoled me by the sweetness of her mind and disposition.' The world might laugh at her queernesses and *gaucheries*, which became more marked with age; might find it difficult to decide which were the odder, her looks or her sayings, the clothes she wore or the stories she told. In externals, she might seem a strange wife for a statesman. But, besides the obvious kindness and genuineness of her nature, and the shrewd judgment which underlay her inconsequent words, she had qualities peculiarly becoming in her place : absolute trustworthiness and discretion in political secrets, which Disraeli never seems to have hid from her; a constancy and heroism which matched his own, and which, on one notable occasion, enabled her to bear the jamming of her finger in a carriage door in smiling silence so that his equanimity on the way to an important debate might not be disturbed.

Lady Beaconsfield was now an old woman of eighty, and of late years had experienced much ill-health; on one occasion, in 1868, her life was for some days in

[1] See Vol. I., II., ch. 2.

peril. In the spring of 1872, after the fatigue and excitement of the Manchester demonstrations, she once more showed signs of breaking down; but for a time performed, and was encouraged by her physician to perform, her social duties as usual.

To Montagu Corry.

G. GATE, *May* 7, 1872 —Sir William [Gull] examined me this morning and has decided that though one of the bronchial tubes is clogged, there is nothing organically wrong, or which may not soon be put right.

Miladi is suffering less. She went to Lady Waldegrave's last night, but was obliged to come home almost immediately. But, as she boastfully says, her illness was not found out. She delighted Fortescue[1] by telling him that she had heard him very much praised. He pressed her very much when and where. She replied, ' It was in bed.'

Sir William gives a good account of her to-day, and seems to think he has remedied the pain, which is all we can hope for, and has sanctioned, and even advised, her to go to Court : but I don't think he allows enough for her extreme weakness. However, I shall be with her to-day; last night she was alone, which I think fearful.

H. OF C. *May* 9, '72.—The visit to Court was not successful. She was suffering as she went, and was taken so unwell there, that we had to retreat precipitately; but without much observation. Knowing the haunts of the palace a little, I got hold of some female attendants who were very serviceable. . . .

CARLTON CLUB, *May* 14, '72.—I have been, and am, so harassed, that I have been quite unable to write a line—and this will be sad stuff.

Nothing encouraging at home. To see her every day weaker and weaker is heartrending. I have had, like all of us, some sorrows of this kind : but in every case, the fatal illness has been apparently sudden, and comparatively short. The shock is great under such circumstances no doubt, but there is a rebound in the nature of things. But to witness this gradual death of one, who has shared so long, and so completely, my life, entirely unmans me.

For herself, she still makes an effort to enter society : and Sir William approves and even counsels it : but it is impossible the effort can be maintained.

---

[1] Chichester Fortescue, afterwards Lord Carlingford, was Lady Waldegrave's husband.

I know not what are our movements. If the weather were genial, I think she is disposed to try Hughenden, but I leave everything of this sort to her fancy and wish. She once talked of going down on Thursday. I can't believe that after her return, she will attempt society any more: the break of a fortnight will produce some effect in this way. . . .

Lady Beaconsfield was taken to Hughenden for the Whitsuntide recess; but the malady did not yield to the change and country air.

To Montagu Corry.

HUGHENDEN, *May* 22, 1872.—. . . I have no good news. Her sufferings have been great here: but the change of weather has brought a ray of distraction.

She moves with great difficulty and cannot bear the slightest roughness in the road, which sadly limits our travels. She enjoyed yesterday going to the German Forest, ascending from the Lady's Walk, but suffered afterwards. Antonelli pushes her about in a perambulator a little, and seems to amuse her. He heard a nightingale ' whistling ' about the house. She thinks ' whistling ' a capital term for bird noises. . . .

With indomitable pluck, Lady Beaconsfield, after her return to town, refused to accept the confinement of an invalid; but resumed her social life, until on July 17, at a party at Lady Loudoun's house to meet the Duchess of Cambridge, she suddenly became very seriously ill and had to be taken home at once. The hostess and the guests were struck by her wonderful courage, ' and indeed heroism,' and by the unselfishness with which she seemed to think more of the inconvenience which her illness might cause her hostess than of her own acute pain. She was never able to go out in London society again.

To Lady Beaconsfield.

July 25, 1872.—I have nothing to tell you, except that I love you, which, I fear, you will think rather dull. . . .

Natty[1] was very affectionate about you, and wanted me to come home and dine with him; quite alone; but I told him that

[1] The late Lord Rothschild, at this time M.P. for Aylesbury.

you were the only person now, whom I could dine with; and only relinquished you to-night for my country.

My country, I fear, will be very late; but I hope to find you in a sweet sleep.

From Lady Beaconsfield.

July 26.

MY OWN DEAREST,—I miss you sadly. I feel so grateful for your constant tender love and kindness. I certainly feel better this evening. . . . Your own devoted BEACONSFIELD.

This is the last letter of his wife's which Disraeli preserved—probably the last she wrote him. She was not able to be moved to Hughenden until the end of September; so he and she passed, as he expressed it, their 'first summer in London.'

To Lord Cairns.

Private. GROSVENOR GATE, *Aug*. 17, 1872.—Many, many thanks. The birds were capital and pleased the fastidious palate of my invalid.

The prospect of reaching Hughenden seems every day fainter. Lady Beaconsfield has had more than one return of her hemorrhage, and, sometimes, I feel, and fear, that even her buoyant and gallant spirit will hardly baffle so many causes of exhaustion.

We have not been separated for three and thirty years, and, during all that time, in her society I never have had a moment of dullness. It tears the heart to see such a spirit suffer, and suffer so much! May you, my dear Cairns, never experience my present feelings ! . . . .

From the Duchess of Cleveland.

RABY CASTLE, DARLINGTON, *Sept*. 12, '72.—. . . One privilege you have which is not granted to all. No two people surely can look back upon a life of such loving and perfect companionship. One of my sons once spoke to Lady Beaconsfield in wonder of the youthful energy and high spirits she preserved, and said something of the courage and force of character it showed. 'No,' she said, 'it is not that. It is that my life has been such a happy one. I have had so much affection, and no troubles—no contradictions: that is what has kept me so young and well.' . . .

To Gathorne Hardy.

Private. GROSVENOR GATE, *Sept.* 16, 1872.—We are much touched by yr. kind letter, which I mentioned to my wife. She sends her very kindest regards to Mrs. Hardy and yourself, but she does not see this letter, so I will say that her condition occasions me the greatest disquietude, tho' they tell me there is some improvement. Her illness, under wh. she has, to some degree, been suffering for many months, is a total inability to take any sustenance, and it is to me perfectly marvellous how she exists, and shows even great buoyancy of life.

We have never left Grosvenor Gate, tho' as everything has been tried in vain, Lady Beaconsfield now talks of trying change of air, and endeavouring to get down to Hughenden. As for myself, I have never been into the town during the whole of August and the present month, so, when business commences, Pall Mall and Whitehall shall be as fresh to me as to my happier comrades, who are shooting in Scotland or climbing the Alps. One has the advantage here, when we wake, of looking upon trees, and bowery vistas, and we try to forget, that the Park is called Hyde, and that the bowers are the bowers of Kensington.

We take drives in the counties of Middx. and Surrey, and discover beautiful retreats of wh. we had never heard; so we have the excitement of travel. What surprises me, more than anything, is the immensity and variety of London, and the miles of villas wh. are throwing out their antennæ in every suburban direction. . . . I should like to hear from you again as to your own health. All depends on you. I am only holding the reins during a period of transition, and more from a feeling of not deserting the helm at a moment of supposed difficulty and danger, than any other. . . .

A note in Disraeli's handwriting, apparently intended for the Queen, gives some further particulars of these drives round London.

What miles of villas! and of all sorts of architecture! What beautiful churches! What gorgeous palaces of Geneva![1]
One day we came upon a real feudal castle, with a donjon keep high in the air. It turned out to be the new City prison in Camden Road, but it deserves a visit; I mean externally

[1] In letters to friends written at this time the 'gorgeous palaces of Geneva' became more prosaically 'gin-palaces.'

Of all the kingdoms ruled over by our gracious mistress, the most remarkable is her *royaume de Cockaigne*, and perhaps the one the Queen has least visited. Her faithful servants in question, preparing their expeditions with a map, investigated all parts of it from Essex to Surrey, and Lady Beaconsfield calculated that from the 1st of August to the end of September she travelled 220 miles.

To Lord Cairns.

GROSVENOR GATE, *Sept.* 26, 1872.—You have expressed so much sympathy for us, and it has been so highly appreciated, that I must tell you that, to-day, we hope to reach Hughenden. There has been, within the last week, a decided, and, I hope now, a permanent improvement in my wife's health, and she is resolved to try change of air. I am a little sorry, that we go home in the fall of the leaf, and that too in a sylvan land, but home only can insure her the comforts and the ease, which an invalid requires.

If she could only regain—not appetite—but even a desire for sustenance, I should be confident of the future, the buoyancy of her spirit is so very remarkable. However, there is a streak of dawn. . . .

What Disraeli called ' our hegira from Grosvenor Gate ' proved at first a success; and on October 3 he could write more cheerfully to Corry: ' Lady Beaconsfield has been here a week, and has improved daily; there seems a sustained revival of appetite, which had altogether ceased.' In answer to the Queen's sympathetic inquiries through Lady Ely he was able to report ' continuous improvement. You know her buoyancy of spirit. She says she is now convinced that everybody eats too much; still at the same time she would like to be able to eat a little.'

The improvement was fallacious; and though Lady Beaconsfield occasionally received visitors and even apparently paid a call on near neighbours, her husband's letters show that her strength was waning during the following two months, till the final attack came upon her in the second week of December.

To Montagu Corry.

HUGHENDEN, *Oct.* 13, '72.—. . . Things here very bad.

Nov. 8.—. . . Affairs have been going very badly: so badly, that I telegraphed, yesterday, for Leggatt and he came down immediately: but he took a different view from us, I am glad to say: and persisted that, if sustenance could be taken, no immediate danger was to be apprehended. But how to manage that ? The truth is, she never has even tasted any of the dishes, that the Rothschilds used to send her in London, and anxious as she was to partake of the delicacies you so kindly provided for her, and which touched her much, it has ended with them as with the feats of Lionel's *chef !*

Shall you be disengaged for three or four days on the 21st ? The John Manners are to come here on that day, if all goes well. A party is impossible, but perhaps we might manage a couple of men.

Nov. 13.—Things go on here much the same: some improvement which I ascribe to the weather—not in the appetite, but in continued absence of pain, and consequently enjoyment of life. . . .

To Philip Rose.

HUGHENDEN MANOR, *Nov.* 13, 1872.—. . . Lady Beaconsfield intended to have called at Rayners to-day, and to have hoped that Mrs. Rose and yourself would be able to dine with us on Friday the 22nd. I trust we shall find you disengaged. The snow frightened me, tho' my wife was inclined to face it.

The temporary improvement lasted long enough to enable the patient to enjoy her little party from November 21 to 25, including, besides the John Manners, Lord Rosebery for the first two days, and Harcourt and Lord Ronald Gower for the last two; and to justify one of those guests in writing her a jocular letter of thanks.

William Vernon Harcourt to Lady Beaconsfield.

TRIN. COLL., CAMBRIDGE, *Nov.* 26, 1872.—I have all my life made efforts (apparently destined to be unsuccessful) to appear what Falstaff, or is it Touchstone ?, calls ' moderate honest.' But here I am actually a felon *malgré moi.* Joseph's butler was not more alarmed and shocked than I was when, on opening my sack, the first thing I discovered in its mouth was the French novel you had provided for my entertainment in my charming bedroom at Hughenden. Whether the act

was one of accidental larceny by my servant or whether it
was insidiously effected by Lord J. Manners in order to ruin
my public and private reputation, I do not feel sure. I did
however return it by this morning's post before I left London,
and so I hope to be forgiven.

I have already taken measures to secure a consignment to
you of Trinity audit ale. Delicious as it is, I doubt whether
there really exists anyone except a Cambridge man who can
drink it with impunity. . . .

And now a truce to nonsense. I must offer you one word
of serious and sincere thanks for the true and genuine kindness
which I have received at your hands and those of Mr. Disraeli.
It was no language of compliment but of simple truth which
I spoke when I told you that, of all visits which it was possible
to pay, there was none of which I should have been more
ambitious than that which I owed to your hospitality last
Sunday. There are things in the world which one not only
enjoys at the time but which one remembers always—and
these are of them. . . .

Disraeli told Harcourt that a glass of the Trinity audit
ale was almost the last thing which passed Lady Beaconsfield's lips before she died. Lord Ronald Gower, writing
of this visit in his *Reminiscences*, vividly depicts Disraeli's
distress in talking of his wife's sufferings. ' His face,
generally so emotionless, was filled with a look of suffering
and woe that nothing but the sorrow of her whom he so
truly loves would cause on that impassive countenance.'

To Montagu Corry.

Nov. 29.—. . . My lady's appetite has been sustained;
indeed I think I may say it is restored: but her sufferings are
increased, and I have just been obliged to send to Leggatt
to beg him to come down to-morrow.

She got over her visit and visitors, notwithstanding this,
with success and great tact: showing little, but always to
effect. . . .

To Philip Rose.

HUGHENDEN, *Dec.* 6, 1872.—Affairs are most dark here—
I tremble for the result, and even an immediate one. My
poor wife has got (it matters not by what means) congestion
on her lungs, and with her shattered state, it seems to me
almost hopeless, that, even with her constitution, we should
again escape. I entirely trust to your coming to me, if anything happens. *I am totally unable to meet the catastrophe.* . . .

The last stage was mercifully not prolonged. She died on December 15, after a week's acute illness, during which her husband seldom left her room. A note which he sent out to Corry on one of these days is preserved: ' She says she must see you. Calm, but the delusions stronger than ever. She will not let me go out to fetch you. Come. D.'

There was a great outpouring of public and private sympathy with Disraeli in this severe trial. The terms of close affection on which he had lived with his wife, long familiar to his intimates, had of late years become widely known to the country. Letters of condolence poured in, not merely from friends and colleagues, but from perfect strangers of all classes and parties; and the public journals manifested appreciation and respect. The Queen, whose telegrams and messages of inquiry had been constant throughout the illness, wrote:

From Queen Victoria.

WINDSOR CASTLE, *Dec.* 15, 1872.—The Queen well knows that Mr. Disraeli will *not* consider the expression of her heartfelt sympathy an intrusion in this his first hour of desolation and overwhelming grief, and therefore she at once attempts to express what she feels. The Queen knew and admired as well as appreciated the unbounded devotion and affection which united him to the dear partner of his life, whose only thought was him. And therefore the Queen knows also *what* Mr. Disraeli has lost and what he must suffer. The only consolation to be found is in *her* present peace and freedom from suffering, in the recollection of their life of happiness and in the blessed certainty of eternal reunion.

May God support and sustain him is the Queen's sincere prayer.

Her children are all anxious to express their sympathy. *Yesterday* was the anniversary of her great loss.

The Prince and Princess of Wales and other members of the Royal Family were among the first to send their sympathy. Queen Sophia of the Netherlands wrote: ' It is given to few to have a character like hers '; the King of the Belgians, on behalf of the Queen and himself: ' Toute notre sympathie est avec vous dans ce cruel

moment'; the Duc D'Aumale: 'Personne mieux que moi
ne comprend pas l'étendue de votre douleur. . . . Mon
cœur est tout avec le vôtre'; and the Empress of Austria,
through Count Bernstorff: 'She knows how deeply Lady
Beaconsfield was devoted to you and how you returned
her devotion by touching affection and gratitude.' Her
great personal kindness was what the old Whig leader,
Russell, among many others, dwelt on in a sympathetic
note. Lord Rosebery, who had been one of the last
visitors at Hughenden, wrote: 'I can hardly now realise
that my kind hostess whom I saw full of life and spirit a
few days ago has passed away. . . . I suppose no one
ever came near her without admiring her goodness, her
unselfishness, and her magnificent devotion.' The
Prime Minister's letter and an American tribute may be
given more at length:

From William Ewart Gladstone.

10, DOWNING STREET, WHITEHALL, *Jan.* 19, 1873.—. . .
You and I were, as I believe, married in the same year. It
has been permitted to both of us to enjoy a priceless boon
through a third of a century. Spared myself the blow which
has fallen on you, I can form some conception of what it
must have been and be. I do not presume to offer you the
consolation which you will seek from another and higher
quarter. I offer only the assurance which all who know you,
all who knew Lady Beaconsfield, and especially those among
them who like myself enjoyed for a length of time her marked
though unmerited regard, may perhaps render without impropriety; the assurance that in this trying hour they feel
deeply for you, and with you. . . .

To William Ewart Gladstone.

HUGHENDEN MANOR *Jan.* 21, 1873.—I am much touched
by your kind words in my great sorrow. I trust, I earnestly
trust, that you may be spared a similar affliction. Marriage
is the greatest earthly happiness, when founded on complete
sympathy. That hallowed lot was mine, and for a moiety
of my existence; and I know it is yours.

From John Lothrop Motley.

MENTMORE, LEIGHTON BUZZARD, *Feb.* 21 '73 —. . . I shall never forget the most agreeable visit which my wife and I enjoyed at Hughenden a little before we left England nor any of Lady Beaconsfield's acts of charming and graceful hospitality united to your own. I always admired her ready wit, her facility and charm in social intercourse, her quick perception of character and events, and it was impossible not to be deeply touched by her boundless devotion to yourself, which anyone, allowed the privilege of your acquaintance, could see was most generously and loyally repaid. . . .

I never met her in society without being greeted by a kindly smile and a sympathetic word, and I have frequently enjoyed long and to me most agreeable conversations with her. She knew well how thoroughly I appreciated and shared in her admiration for the one great object of her existence. . . .

Disraeli was, for the time, overwhelmed by his loss. Two of his letters will show his feeling. He used the same or very similar expressions to all his friends. That she had appreciated them was their great merit in his eyes. ' Of character,' he wrote to one of them, ' she was no mean judge. I must ever regard those who remember her with tenderness and respect.'

To the Prince of Wales.

HUGHENDEN MANOR,
Dec. 22, 1872.

SIR AND DEAR PRINCE,— I will attempt to thank Her Royal Highness and yourself for the sympathy which you have shown to me in my great sorrow, a grief for which I was unprepared, and which seems to me overwhelming.

A few days before her death, she spoke to me of the Princess and yourself, Sir, in terms of deep regard, and, if I may presume to say so, of affection. I took, therefore, the occasion of mentioning the invitation she had received to Sandringham, and she was gratified. She said ' It would have been a happy incident in a happy life, now about to close. I liked his society, I delighted in the merriment of his kind heart.'

I shall always remember with gratitude the invariable kindness shewn by Her Royal Highness and yourself, Sir, to one who for 33 years was the inseparable and ever interesting companion of my life.

To Lord Cairns.

GROSVENOR GATE, *Dec.* 28, '72.—Kind and much loved friend! I thank you for all your sympathy in my great sorrow, and for all your goodness to one, who was my inseparable, and ever-interesting companion for a moiety of my existence. She always appreciated you, and thought me fortunate in having such a friend.

Altho' you are the one, whom I should wish first, and most, to see, I will not precipitate our interview, for I have not yet subdued the anguish of the supreme sorrow of my life.

I am obliged to be here on business, and shall remain here till Friday, when I go out of town for a day or two, but not to Hughenden. On Monday, *i.e.*, to-morrow, week, I must return here. It will be my last visit to a house, where I have passed exactly half my days, and, so far as my interior life was concerned, in unbroken happiness. . . .

Among Lady Beaconsfield's papers was found a touching letter of farewell to her husband, written many years before, in view of the high probability that she, who was the elder by twelve years, would be the first to die.

June 6, 1856.

MY OWN DEAR HUSBAND,—If I should depart this life before you, leave orders that we may be buried in the same grave at whatever distance you may die from England.[1] And now, God bless you, my kindest, dearest! You have been a perfect husband to me. Be put by my side in the same grave. And now, farewell, my dear Dizzy. Do not live alone, dearest. Some one I earnestly hope you may find as attached to you as your own devoted MARY ANNE.

Accordingly, Lady Beaconsfield was buried in Hughenden churchyard in the vault in which her husband was himself to be laid, and by the side of their benefactress, Mrs. Brydges Willyams. Directly the simple funeral was over, Disraeli, as appears from his letter to Cairns, was plunged in business. His wife's death made a vast change in his circumstances; he lost thereby £5,000 a year and a house in town; though his generous friend, Andrew

---

[1] This was written shortly before Disraeli and his wife were about to leave England for a cure at a Continental watering-place on account of his health. See Vol. I., p. 1451.

Montagu, gave him material assistance by reducing the interest on his debts from 3 to 2 per cent. He had to move all his possessions from Grosvenor Gate, and find a new abiding-place in London. 'Corry seems his factotum,' wrote Hardy in his diary, 'and he needs one, for he is quite unfit for that sort of business.' He took refuge for a time in an hotel—Edwards's Hotel, in George Street, Hanover Square. 'It was, in the days of my youth,' he told Northcote, 'the famous house of Lady Palmerston, then Lady Cowper; and at least I shall labour in rooms where a great statesman has been inspired.'

There had been some fear amongst his colleagues, whom the events of the past year had quite converted from their heresies on the leadership, lest the loss of one so intimately associated with the triumphs of his political career should incline Disraeli to withdraw from active politics. On the contrary, he turned to them as a welcome distraction. He asked two of his leading colleagues, Cairns and Hardy, to come to him at Hughenden in the middle of January. Their presence, he wrote, would be 'a source of strength and consolation,' and would make him 'much more capable of re-entering public life.' With them he discussed the political situation and the vagaries of the Government; and to them he declared his intention of being present and speaking when the session began.

When he went up to town he was deprived of the comfort of Corry's presence, owing to the serious illness of Corry's father.

To Montagu Corry.

EDWARDS'S HOTEL, *Feb.* 4, '73.—I left you with a bleeding heart yesterday, amid all the sorrows, which seemed to accumulate around our heads: but your telegram has a little lifted me out of the slough of despond. I had just energy enough to send a paragraph to the papers, and messages to Northcote and Derby. The former was with me at 11 o'clock, and has undertaken to communicate with Gladstone about the speech, and the latter has just left me. . . . Barrington has also paid me a long visit. Hardy is to be with me to-morrow morning, and has sent me a memorandum from Cairns, which

contains all I required.   Hardy gives a dinner to the party
to-morrow : Cairns to-day to Lords and Commons.

Give my kind regards to your father and sister. I hope
every hour to have another telegram that his amendment
has become convalescence.

All my friends admire my rooms.   I cannot say I agree
with them, but things may mend.

Fortunately for Disraeli the political crisis which
resulted in Gladstone's abortive resignation immediately
supervened.   He had something therefore to distract his
thoughts; but his loneliness in his hotel weighed heavily
upon him, and in his letters to Corry he constantly harped
on his ' miserable state,' his ' melancholy,' ' the heaviness
and misery ' of his life.   Corry could not return to him,
as the elder Corry's illness became increasingly serious and
ended fatally in March.   Disraeli said to Malmesbury
with tears in his eyes, ' I hope some of my friends will
take notice of me now in my great misfortune, for I have
no home, and when I tell my coachman to drive home I
feel it is a mockery.'   His friends responded to his appeal,
and did their best to cheer him up by asking him to dine
with them quietly.

To Montagu Corry.

HOUSE OF COMMONS, *Feb.* 10, 1873.—. . . All yesterday,
rumors of a crisis were in the air.   At Lionel's[1] where I was
asked to a family circle I found, to my annoyance, not merely
Charles Villiers and Osborne, whom I look upon as the family,
but Lords Cork and Houghton.   The political excitement
was great, and not favorable to the position of Ministers:
but Lionel told me afterwards, that he had seen the Bill
(Delane had shown it him).   Would you believe it, I was so
distrait, and altogether embarrassed, that I never asked him
a question about it?

This morning I was obliged to go to Middleton's about
the picture,[2] which is virtually finished.   He has altered the
expression, but not hit the mark.   I have made some suggestions, but am not sanguine about them. . . .

Adieu ! *mon très cher.*   I never wanted you more, but it
is selfish to say so.

Feb. 17.—. . . I was much pleased with the portrait,

---

[1] Baron Lionel de Rothschild.
[2] Of Lady Beaconsfield; see opposite p. 562.

and the frame, which is exquisite. He has succeeded in giving to the countenance an expression of sweet gravity, which is characteristic. . . .

Feb. 18.—. . . I dined yesterday at the Carlton: latish and was not annoyed. The John Manners asked me again for to-morrow, but I declined. On Thursday I am to dine with the Cairns and meet the Hardys, and on Friday alone with the Stanhopes: Saturday alone with my Countess:[1] so all my plans of absolute retirement are futile. I regret this, for every visit makes me more melancholy—though hotel life in an evening is a cave of despair.

I was with Brunnow an hour to-day—and Madame would come down, and kiss me !

March 1.—Your letter greatly distressed me, and I have been in hopes of receiving a telegram.

I have been dining out every day, but only with my host and hostess alone—and sometimes a very friendly fourth. Yesterday, at the John Manners', with Duke of Rutland; and on Thursday at the Stanhopes' with dear Henry,[2] who received two despatches from Marlboro' House, during the dinner. I dine with dear Henry to-day to meet B. Osborne alone: and to-morrow with the Malmesburys; it is better than dining here alone, which is intolerable, or at a club, which, even with a book, is not very genial. . . .

March 7.—Your silence, my best and dearest Montagu, was ominous of your impending woe. What can I say to you, but express my infinite affection ? Death has tried you hard during the last few months, but you have shown, in the severe proof, admirable qualities, which all must admire and love.

I should be glad to hear some tidings of your sister: as for myself, I am a prisoner, and almost prostrate, with one of those atmospheric attacks which the English persist in calling ' colds,' and, for the first time in my life, am absent from House of Commons in the midst of a pitched battle.

But these are nothings compared to your sorrows. Though I cannot soften, let me share, them.

April 4.—. . . To-day I went by appointment to New Court, expecting to do business: nothing done. Lionel there, but not well: a terrible luncheon of oysters and turtle prepared, and after that nothing settled. This was disgusting. I dine with the Stanhopes to-day. On Wednesday last a rather full party at Grillion's: the last dinner at the bankrupt Clarendon [hotel]. Salisbury was there, and Lowe. . . .

[1] Apparently Lady Chesterfield, or perhaps Lady Cardigan.
[2] Lord Henry Lennox.

To the Duchess of Abercorn.

12, GEORGE STREET, HANOVER SQUARE, *May* 18, '73.—
It is most kind of you, and of his Grace, to remember me :
but I am, really, living in seclusion, so far as general society
is concerned, and therefore, I am sure you will permit me to
decline your obliging invitation for the 24th.

Your ' boys ' deserve kindness and encouragement, because they are clever and, above all, industrious, and perhaps,
also, because they inherit the agreeable qualities of their
parents.

CHAPTER VII.

Lady Bradford and Lady Chesterfield.

1873–1875.

To Disraeli the rupture of a union so complete as was that between him and his wife meant more than it would have meant to most affectionate husbands. His temperament was such that he could not be happy, and could not bring out the best work of which he was capable, without intimate female association and sympathy. ' My nature demands that my life should be perpetual love,' had been a glowing outburst of his youth; and that love, for all his wealth of men friends and the affection which he lavished on them, must be the love of woman. In *Henrietta Temple* he wrote: ' A female friend, amiable, clever, and devoted, is a possession more valuable than parks and palaces; and, without such a muse, few men can succeed in life, none be content.' Throughout his whole life he had been blessed with devotion and sympathy of this kind in ample measure. Two women, first his sister and then his wife, had made him and his ambitions the centre of their existence; to both of them his own affection and devotion had been unstinted; there had been between him and them a constant communion of thoughts and hopes and sympathies. In a lesser degree Mrs. Brydges Willyams, in her later years, shared in this close intimacy. There were, moreover, other ladies whose sympathetic appreciation had cheered and helped his career — such as Lady Blessington and Frances Anne Lady Londonderry. ' I feel fortunate,'

he wrote[1] in 1874, ' in serving a female Sovereign. I
owe everything to woman; and if, in the sunset of life,
I have still a young heart, it is due to that influence.'
With all the women who influenced him he kept up a
constant correspondence of a romantic and sentimental
kind, in which he revealed, not merely his doings,
but his thoughts and his character. ' A she-corre-
spondent for my money,' was the exclamation of one of
his exuberant youthful heroes; and it is to the fact that
he carried on throughout his life a copious correspondence
with women that our knowledge of the real Disraeli is
largely due.

With Lady Beaconsfield's death the last of the women
with whom he had hitherto enjoyed this sympathetic
intercourse passed away; and he was left for the time
widowed indeed. Few men at his age—sixty-eight—
would have had the freshness of heart to form new attachments, and to resume with others the sentimental and
romantic intimacy which had proved so stimulating an
influence; and of those who still possessed sufficient youth-
fulness for the adventure, most would have been prevented, especially if public men, by the fear of incurring
censure and ridicule. But Disraeli's affections were still
warm, and craved sympathetic understanding; nor was
he to be deterred by possible ridicule from following their
dictates. He spoke for himself when he wrote a few
years earlier in Lothair:[2] ' Threescore and ten, at the
present day, is the period of romantic passions. As for
our enamoured sexagenarians, they avenge the theories
of our cold-hearted youth.'

Among those who showed him special kindness in his
early months of loneliness and desolation were two sisters,
whom he had long known in society, Lady Chesterfield
and Lady Bradford. Anne Countess of Chesterfield was
the eldest, and Selina Countess of Bradford was the
youngest, of five sisters, daughters of the first Lord
Forester, the head of an ancient Shropshire family. Of

[1] To Lady Bradford.   [2] Ch. 35.

the other sisters one married Lord Carrington's eldest
son, Robert John Smith, and died young in 1832, before
her husband succeeded to the title.   She was of course a
neighbour of the Disraelis after they established themselves at Bradenham in 1829; and it was at Wycombe
Abbey, but apparently after Mrs. Smith's death, that
Disraeli first met Lady Bradford. 'Mr. D. will tell you,'
wrote Lady Bradford to Mrs. Disraeli in March, 1868, ' that
our first acquaintance was 100 years ago in poor Lord Carrington's house, before he [Disraeli] knew you.'   Another
sister married General Anson, who was Commander-in-
Chief in India when the Mutiny broke out ;[1] and the
remaining sister married Lord Albert Conyngham, afterwards the first Lord Londesborough.   In their youth the
five sisters were prominent in the world of fashion, gaiety,
and sport—the world that revolved round Almack's,
of which their mother Lady Forester was an eminent
patroness; and at least Lady Chesterfield, Mrs. Anson,
and Lady Bradford had been reigning beauties.   Disraeli,
in his days of dandyism, was naturally thrown in their
company.   In 1835 he went to a specially gorgeous fancy
dress ball with a party which included the Chesterfields
and the Ansons, and told his sister that ' Lady Chesterfield was a sultana.'[2]   In 1838 he met at Wycombe
Abbey a whole family party of the Foresters—' rather
noisy, but very gay '—' Lady Chesterfield, George and
Mrs. Anson, the Albert Conynghams, Forester,' and
' made the greatest friends with all of them,' he told Mrs.
Wyndham Lewis.[3]   The second brother, General ' Cis '
Forester, who sat for Wenlock in Parliament for nearly
half a century and succeeded to the title in 1874, had
been a friend of Disraeli's from early years.

Of the five sisters only Lady Chesterfield and Lady
Bradford were still living.   Lady Chesterfield, who was a
couple of years older than Disraeli, was the widow of the
sixth Earl of Chesterfield who had died seven years before.

[1] See Vol. I., p. 1487.   [2] See Vol. I., pp. 306, 307.
[3] See Vol. I., p. 447.

Her daughter had married one of the Reform Bill dissentients, Carnarvon. Lady Bradford was the wife of
the third Earl of Bradford, a sporting peer, and a man of
character and consideration, who had been Disraeli's
colleague as Lord Chamberlain from 1866 to 1868, and
was again to be his colleague as Master of the Horse from
1874 to 1880. She was seventeen years younger than
her sister; but both ladies were by this time grandmothers.
When Lady Bradford's eldest son, Lord Newport, was
married in 1869, Disraeli had written him what his mother
called, we learn from a note of Corry's of that date, ' the
nicest letter in the world, and *such* a clever one.'

  With both these sisters Disraeli became, during the
spring and summer of 1873, on terms of intimate friendship. In them he found that female sympathy and
companionship without which life was for him an incomplete thing. That they were ladies influential in the
fashionable and aristocratic Tory society which had shown
some reluctance to admit his undisputed sway as leader
counted, no doubt, for something with him. That they
recalled the memories and attachments of his youth, when
to be taken up by Lady Forester and the bright particular
stars of Almack's was of importance to him, counted for
more with one whose gratitude was lifelong. But, over
and above all these considerations, his personal affection
for, and devotion to, both ladies were quite unmistakable.
Of the circumstances in which the intimacy arose he
wrote to Lady Chesterfield in the autumn, ' Altho', from
paramount duty, I attended Parliament this session, I
have never been in society, except that delightful week
when, somehow or other, I found myself in the heart of
your agreeable family.' The first letter to Lady Chesterfield which has been preserved was written in June, 1873,
and he was already on such terms with her that he
addressed her as ' Dearest Lady Ches.' and subscribed
himself, ' Your most affectionate D.' The first letter of
the series to Lady Bradford was written in July, and in
the second, in August, she too was ' Dearest Lady Brad-

ford.' He went to stay in the autumn with the one at
Bretby and with the other at Weston; and these visits
were constantly repeated to the close of his life, and were
returned by the ladies and by Lord Bradford at Hughenden. There have been preserved some 500 letters to
Lady Chesterfield in these eight years, and no fewer than
1,100 to Lady Bradford; while the twelve years of his
acquaintance with Mrs. Brydges Willyams only produced about 250. This Bradford-Chesterfield correspondence is absolutely invaluable for a due understanding of Disraeli's final period; like the letters in
earlier times to his sister and his wife, it both reveals
his intimate hopes and feelings, and also describes
in brilliant fashion, from day to day, at times almost
from hour to hour, his political and social experiences.[1]
The ladies' letters were destroyed, by their desire, after
his death.

So necessary to Disraeli's life was the intimacy thus
established—'the delightful society,' as he told Lady
Chesterfield in March, 1874, 'of the two persons I love
most in the world'—that he endeavoured to make it
permanent by asking Lady Chesterfield to marry him, so
that he might grapple one lady to his heart as his wife,
and the other as his sister. She not unnaturally refused.
Even had she been willing, when she had passed her
seventieth birthday, to marry once more, she must have
speedily realised that she did not occupy the first place
in Disraeli's affections. For though it was to Lady
Chesterfield, as the only sister who was free, that he
proposed marriage, it was to Lady Bradford that he was
most tenderly attached. He wrote to her more than
twice as many letters as he did to her sister, sometimes, when in office, sending her two, or even three,
in one day, by special messengers from Downing Street
or from the Treasury bench. Such messengers, he
wrote, ' may wait at your house the whole day, and are

---

[1] The Duke of Richmond told Cairns on July 27, 1876, that Lady Bradford ' seems to know everything, down to the most minute details of everything that passes.'

the slaves of your will.   A messenger from a Prime Minister to a Mistress of the Horse cannot say his soul is his own.'   Romantic devotion breathes in Disraeli's language to both sisters; but the Oriental extravagance of his sentiments is beyond a doubt more marked when he is addressing Lady Bradford.   The correspondence with Lady Chesterfield, in spite of the offer and refusal, preserves on the whole an even tone of deeply affectionate friendship.   But Lady Bradford was often taken aback by Disraeli's septuagenarian ardour, and embarrassed by his incessant calls at her house in Belgrave Square and his unending demands on her time; though she, as well as her sister, could not but be flattered by the assiduous attentions of one who was for the greater part of the last eight years of his life the most famous and admired man in the country.

The relation between Disraeli and these sisters can hardly fail to recall the relation between Horace Walpole, in the last decade of his long life, and the two Miss Berrys. There was the same affection in each case for two sisters; the same desire to marry one, in order to insure the constant society of both.   The Miss Berrys, however, were in the twenties when Horace Walpole made their acquaintance; whereas Lady Chesterfield was over seventy and Lady Bradford was in her fifty-fifth year when Disraeli's attachment began.   But Disraeli's chivalrous devotion to women was independent of physical attraction and the appeal of youth.   Otherwise his elderly wife—not to speak of Mrs. Willyams and others—would hardly have influenced him as she did to the day of her death.   Though the Russian Ambassador might sneer at the society which Disraeli in his latter years affected as *toutes grand'mères*, it is a most honourable feature in his composition that, in his relation to women, as in his relation to the problems of life and eternity, he rejected absolutely any physical or sensuous standard, and poured out his devotion before an ideal, regardless of the ravages of care and time.

Selina Countess of Bradford
from the portrait after Sir Francis Grant
at Hughenden

The characters of the two sisters were complementary; Lady Chesterfield had more strength and constancy, Lady Bradford more sweetness and gaiety ; both were sympathetic in a high degree. Lady Bradford, as befitted the mother of marriageable daughters, was in the full whirl of society, a constant attendant at the functions of the London season, and at the principal race meetings, moving in the autumn from one country house party to another. Lady Chesterfield, a much older woman, though taking a fair share of social pleasures, was more often to be found, surrounded by friends, in her own home at Bretby. Lady Bradford had perhaps a quicker appreciation of Disraeli's moods and aspirations, but was by no means so certain to respond to them as her sister. Writing to Lady Bradford, in January, 1874, he said of Lady Chesterfield that ' the secret of her charm is the union of grace and energy; a union very rare, but in her case most felicitous.' Of Lady Bradford's own character he wrote to herself in May of that year: ' A sweet simplicity, blended with high breeding; an intellect not over-drilled, but lively, acute, and picturesque; a seraphic temper, and a disposition infinitely sympathetic—these are some of the many charms that make you beloved of D.'

The fervid nature of Disraeli's devotion will be realised from a letter which he wrote to Lady Bradford three weeks after becoming Prime Minister for the second time. She and Lady Chesterfield were leaving London for the country; and a separation which was only to last from the middle of March till the first week of April filled him with consternation.

To Lady Bradford.

10, Downing Street, Whitehall, *March* 13, 1874.—The most fascinating of women was never more delightful than this afternoon. I could have sat for ever, watching every movement that was grace, and listening to her sparkling words—but alas ! the horrid thought, ever and anon, came over me—' It is a farewell visit.' It seemed too cruel ! I might have truly said,

> Pleased to the last, I cropped the flowery food,
> And kissed the hand just raised to shed my blood.

Constant separations ! Will they never cease ? If anything could make me love your delightful sister more than I do, it is her plans for Easter, which realise a dream !

I am certain there is no greater misfortune, than to have a heart that will not grow old. It requires all the sternness of public life to sustain one. If we have to govern a great country, we ought not to be *distrait*, and feel the restlessness of love. Such things should be the appanage of the youthful heroes I have so often painted, but alas ! I always drew from my own experience, and were I to write again to-morrow, I fear I should be able to do justice to the most agitating, tho' the most amiable, weakness of humanity.

Writing to Lady Chesterfield of the same farewell visit Disraeli said : ' The matchless sisters, as I always call them, were never so delightful as yesterday afternoon,' and he proceeded to use to her much the same language as to Lady Bradford. Lady Chesterfield, the widow, accepted the compliment without demur : but Lady Bradford, the wife, was offended by the extravagance of his expressions. Disraeli assumed, in return, the airs of a despairing lover.

To Lady Bradford.

10, DOWNING STREET, *March* 17, 1874.—I sent you a hurried line this morning, as I thought it my only opportunity of writing, and I did not wish you to think I was silent, because I was ' tetchy.' I have just come back from W[indsor], and I send you this, because I think it may prevent misapprehension.

Your view of correspondence, apparently, is that it should be confined to facts, and not admit feelings. Mine is the reverse; and I could as soon keep a journal, wh. I never could do, as maintain a correspondence of that kind.

The other day you said it was wonderful that I cd. write to you, with all the work and care I have to encounter. It is because my feelings impel me to write to you. It was my duty and my delight: the duty of my heart and the delight of my life.

I do not think I was very unreasonable. I have never asked anything from you but your society. When I have that, I am content, which I may well be, for its delight is ineffable. When we were separated, the loneliness of my life found some relief in what might have been a too fond idolatry.

The menace of perpetual estrangement seemed a severe punishment for what might have been a weakness, but scarcely an unpardonable one. However you shall have no cause to inflict it. I awake from a dream of baffled sympathy, and pour forth my feelings, however precious, from a golden goblet, on the sand.

' I thought all was over between us,' he wrote in his next letter; but two days afterwards the difference was made up; ' I found a letter, which took a load off my heart, and I pressed it to my lips.' This lovers' comedy was repeated with Lady Bradford over and over again during the early years of the 1874 Administration. The septuagenarian, who had the governance of the Empire and the conduct of the Commons on his shoulders, and who necessarily was leading a public life of incessant and laborious occupation, nevertheless traversed in his private life the whole gamut of half-requited love—passionate devotion, rebuff, despair, resignation, renewed hope, reconciliation, ecstasy; and then traversed it *da capo*. One such crisis occurred in connection with a masked ball in the height of the season of 1874.

To Lady Bradford.

H. OF C., *June* 29, 1874.—I am distressed at the relations which have arisen between us, and, after two days' reflection, I have resolved to write once more.

I went to Montagu House on Friday with great difficulty, to see you, and to speak to you on a matter of interest to me. I thought your manner was chilling: you appeared to avoid me, and when—perhaps somewhat intrusively, but I had no other chance, for I saw you were on the point of quitting me— I suggested some mode by which we might recognise each other at the ball, you only advised me not to go !

Your feelings to me are not the same as mine have been to you. That is natural and reasonable Mine make me sensitive and perhaps *exigeant*, and render my society in public embarrassing to you, and therefore not agreeable. Unfortunately for me, my imagination did not desert me with my youth. I have always felt this a great misfortune It would have involved me in calamities, had not nature bestowed on me, and in a large degree, another quality—the sense of the ridiculous.

That has given me many intimations, during some months; but, in the turbulence of my heart, I was deaf to them Re-

flection, however, is irresistible; and I cannot resist certainly
the conviction that much in my conduct to you, during this
year, has been absurd.

On Friday night, I had written to you to forget it, and
to forget me. But I linger round the tie on which I had
staked my happiness. You may deride my weakness, but
I wished you to know my inward thoughts, and that you
should not think of me as one who was ungrateful or capricious.

2, WHITEHALL GARDENS, *Wedy* [? *July* 1].—Your note
has just reached me. It was unexpected and delightful.
I am touched by your writing so spontaneously, for my stupid
words did not deserve a response. . . . I am glad you think
I am ' better and wiser of late.' I feel I am changed, but
I am much happier.

Thursday [*July* 2, 1874].—. . . I regret to tell you that
my enemy attacked me in the night, and I am obliged to go
down to the Ho. of C. in a black velvet shoe, of Venetian
fashion, part of my dress for that unhappy masqued ball,
my absence from wh. causes such endless inquiries wh. exhaust even my imagination for replies. . . .

Lady Chesterfield was in the secret of this misunderstanding, and to her Disraeli humorously explained how
he had obtained a pleasant revenge for Lady Bradford's
treatment of him.

To Anne Lady Chesterfield.

2, WHITEHALL GARDENS, *Thursday* [*July* 9, 1874].—. . .
Yesterday was very agreeable at the Palace. I found a seat
next to Selina, and I took her to supper. She was standing
by me in the royal circle, when the P. of Wales, Princess,
Princess Mary, and others, came up in turn, and asked why I
had not been at the masqued ball. I said to some, ' It was a
secret, and that I was bound not to tell.' I said to the Princess
of Wales, that I was dressed in my domino and about to go,
when a fair Venetian gave me a goblet of aqua tofana, and I
sank to the ground in a state of asphyxia. Selina heard all
this ! . . .

Here is another self-revealing letter after a rebuff :

To Lady Bradford.

2, WHITEHALL GARDENS, *Aug.* 3, 1874.—. . . To love as
I love, and rarely to see the being one adores, whose constant society is absolutely necessary to my life; to be pre-

cluded even from the only shadowy compensation for such a torturing doom—the privilege of relieving my heart by expressing its affection—is a lot which I never could endure, and cannot.

But for my strange position, wh. enslaves, while it elevates, me, I would fly for ever, as I often contemplate, to some beautiful solitude, and relieve, in ideal creation, the burthen of such a dark and harassing existence. But the iron laws of a stern necessity seem to control our lives, and with all the daring and all the imagination in the world, conscious or unconscious, we are slaves. . . .

This is rather a long scribblement: pardon that, for it is probably one of the last letters I shall ever send you. My mind is greatly disturbed and dissatisfied. I require perfect solitude or perfect sympathy. My present life gives me neither of these ineffable blessings. It may be brilliant, but it is too fragmentary. It is not a complete existence. It gives me neither the highest development of the intellect or the heart; neither Poetry nor Love.

And here, from the correspondence of 1875, are letters betraying various moods of jealous and unsatisfied affection:

To Lady Bradford.

2, WHITEHALL GARDENS, *Feb.* 24, 1875.—I should grieve if the being to whom I am entirely devoted shd. believe for a moment that I am unreasonable and capricious. Therefore I will condense in a few lines a remark or two on a topic to which I hope never to recur.

You have said that I prefer your letters to your society. On the contrary, a single interview with you is worth a hundred even of your letters, tho' they have been, for more than a year, the charm and consolation of my life. But I confess I have found a contrast between yr. letters and yr. general demeanor to me, which has often perplexed, and sometimes pained, me: and it is only in recurring to those letters that I have found solace.

Something happened a little while ago, wh., according to my sad interpretation, threw a light over this contrariety; but it was a light wh. revealed, at the same time, the ruin of my heart and hopes. I will not tell you how much I have suffered. I became quite dejected, and could scarcely carry on public affairs.

But the sweetness of your appeal to me yesterday, and the radiant innocence of yr. countenance, entirely overcame me; and convinced me that I had misapprehended the past, and that the mutual affection, on wh. I had staked the happiness of my remaining days, was not a dream.

March 21.—. . . It [a letter Disraeli wished to show Lady Bradford] will keep till my next visit after yr. return from France, if you ever do return, and if ever I pay you another visit. These things much depend on habit, unless there is a very strong feeling such as sincerely actuated me when, last year, I said I cd. not contemplate life without seeing you every day. I feel very much like poor King Lear with his knights; half my retinue was cut down before you went to Kimbolton: 'three times a week' was then accorded me. When you return from your foreign travel, wh. wonderfully clears the brain of former impressions, there will be a further reduction of my days; till, at last, the dreary and inevitable question comes, ' Why one ?'

Don't misunderstand this. This is not what you call a ' scolding.' It is misery: that horrible desolation wh. the lonely alone can feel. . . .

I have given this morning the Constableship of the Tower to General Sir Chas. Yorke, G.C.B. I keep the Isle of Man still open: open till you have quite broken my heart.

July 4.—. . . I hardly had a word with you to-day, and cd. not talk of to-morrrow ! I wonder if I shall see you to-morrow ! Not to see you is a world without a sun. . . .

I wonder whom you will sit bet[wee]n to-day, and talk to, and delight and fascinate. I am always afraid of your dining at houses like Gerard's, in my absence. I feel horribly jeal[ous]; I cannot help it.

In such moods I sometimes read what was written to me only a year ago—tho' that's a long time—words written by a sylph, ' Have confidence in me, believe in me, believe that I am true—oh ! how true !'

Even if one cannot believe these words, it is something to have them to read—and to bless the being who wrote them.

Make what discount we may for Disraeli's tendency to extravagance and exaggeration, especially in his address to women, it is impossible, after reading his letters to Lady Bradford, to doubt the reality and depth of his attachment. During one year, 1874, we find such expressions as the following: ' To see you, or at least to hear from you, every day, is absolutely necessary to my existence.' ' I have lived to know the twilight of love has its splendor and its richness.' ' To see you in society is a pleasure peculiar to itself; but different from

that of seeing you alone; both are enchanting, like moonlight and sunshine.' 'It is not "a slice of the moon"
I want; I want it all.' Playful references of this kind
to the meaning in Greek of Lady Bradford's Christian
name Selina—'the moon'—are plentiful in the correspondence. In one letter Disraeli explained the different
nature of his feelings towards the two sisters.

To Lady Bradford.

2, WHITEHALL GARDENS, *Nov.* 3, 1874.—. . . I am sorry
your sister is coming to town. She will arrive when I am
absorbed with affairs, and will apparently be neglected and
will probably think so. This will add to my annoyances,
for I have a great regard for her. I love her, not only because
she is your sister and a link between us, but because she
has many charming qualities. But when you have the government of a country on your shoulders, to *love* a person and to
be *in love* with a person makes all the difference. In the first
case, everything that distracts your mind from yr. great
purpose, weakens and wearies you. In the second instance,
the difficulty of seeing your beloved, or communicating with
her, only animates and excites you. I have devised schemes
of seeing, or writing to, you in the midst of stately councils,
and the thought and memory of you, instead of being an
obstacle, has been to me an inspiration.

You said in one of yr. letters that I complained that you did
not appreciate me. Never! Such a remark, on my part, wd.
have been, in the highest degree, conceited and coxcombical.
What I said was: You did not appreciate my love; that is to
say, you did not justly estimate either its fervor or its depth.

The affection between Disraeli and Lady Chesterfield
had none of the alternations of hot and cold that marked
his relation with her sister. Here there was steady
warmth and steady devotion; and he could always count
upon consolation from her when, as often happened, he
was rebuffed by what he called Lady Bradford's 'irresistible, but cold, control.' Though his passion was less,
yet in his method of address he was more ardent to Lady
Chesterfield than to the other. The letters to Lady
Bradford generally start without any prefatory endear-
ments; but Lady Chesterfield was 'dearest, dearest Lady
Ches.,' 'dearest of women,' 'charming playfellow,' and

finally, in most of the letters after the first year or two,
' dear darling '; and we find such expressions as ' whatever happens to me in the world I shall always love you ';
and after an attack of gout at Bretby, ' Adieu, dear and
darling friend, I have no language to express to you my
entire affection.' It might not always suit Lady Bradford
to have him at Weston or Castle Bromwich; but Bretby
was constantly open to him, and his table in London and
at Hughenden was regularly furnished with the produce
of its gardens, its dairy, its poultry farm, and its coverts.
'My dearest, darling friend,' he wrote on one occasion
to Lady Chesterfield, ' you literally scatter flowers and
fruit over my existence.'

To Anne Lady Chesterfield.

2, WHITEHALL GARDENS, *March* 6, 1875.—. . . It is a long
time since [*Contarini Fleming*] was born—some years before
I had the pleasure of meeting you at Wycombe Abbey, and
fell in love with your brilliant eyes flashing with grace and
triumph—and wh. cd. hardly spare a glance, then, to poor
me. But now I am rewarded for my early homage, and, amid
the cares of empire, can find solace in cherishing your sweet
affections. . . .

Such was the nature of the attachments that gave
brightness and colour to the last eight years of Disraeli's
life. It must not be supposed that there was in them any
unfaithfulness to the memory of a wife who had herself
laid on him her injunction to find consolation in others.
He never forgot her and his happiness with her; his
poignant regret and his loneliness without her are the
frequent theme of his letters. On one Queen's birthday
during his great Ministry he was looking with Lord
Redesdale at the elaborate preparations for his official
banquet, ' when all of a sudden,' his companion tells us,
' he turned round, his eyes were dim, and his voice husky,
as he said, " Ah ! my dear fellow, you are happy, you have
a wife." ' He always maintained the signs of mourning;
the whole of his correspondence with the sisters, as with
others, save on a few occasions when, being away from

home, he had to fall back on local stationery, was written
on paper with a deep black edging; nor did he feel that
there was any incongruity in inscribing protestations of
devotion to the living on pages which recalled by their
very appearance the memory of the dead.

To Lady Bradford.

HUGHENDEN MANOR, *Sept.* 27, 1875.—. . . You said you
were glad to see ' white paper ' the other day. It is strange,
but I always used to think that the Queen, persisting in these
emblems of woe, indulged in a morbid sentiment; and yet it
has become my lot, and seemingly an irresistible one.   I lost
one who was literally devoted to me, tho' I was not alto-
g[ethe]r worthy of her devotion; and when I have been on
the point sometimes of terminating this emblem of my
bereavement, the thought that there was no longer any being
in the world to whom I was an object of concentrated feeling
overcame me, and the sign remained.

Once—perhaps twice—during the last two years, I have
indulged in a wild thought it might be otherwise; and then
something has always occurred, wh. has dashed me to the
earth. . . .

These new sentimental relations were springing up
during the second portion of the session of 1873, after the
reluctant return of the discredited Ministers to their
places.   In the House of Commons Disraeli continued on
the whole his policy of reserve, assured that his opportunity must come before long.   His main political activity
was behind the scenes, preparing with his whips and his
party manager for a dissolution which could hardly be
postponed beyond the next year, rather than in the House
itself where there was not much contentious business.

To Montagu Corry

April 5, '73.—It will be impossible to get a Tory majority,
if lukewarmness, or selfishness of those who have a safe seat,
prevent contests.   There are more than 30 seats in this predicament, and I have appointed a small committee of men of
social influence to take them in hand: Lord J. Manners,
Barrington, Chaplin or Mahon.

I hope you are better.   I am well enough, but wretchedly
low-spirited. . .

To William Hart Dyke.

HUGHENDEN MANOR, *April* 15, 1873.—. . . Lady Derby writes to me this morning, that she means to give assemblies on 29th inst. and 6th May, and if somebody could send her a list of names to St. Jas. Sqre., marked to be forwarded, she would work at the list. If, therefore, you could forward her a catalogue of the M.P.s, their wives and dau[ghte]rs, that ' she would do well to invite,' business wd. be advanced.

I think, from what Miladi said to me when I last saw her, that she wished a little discretion to be exercised in the transaction. An overplus of quizzes neutralises the distinction, and it is better that she shd. be encouraged to give more parties than to swamp her good intentions and make her feel her receptions are a failure.

To Montagu Corry.

May 17, '73.—The Government continues in a discredited state, but we have not availed ourselves, as much as we ought to have done, of several recent opportunities. The causes, or probable causes, of this, I must keep till we meet. It seems that the Ministry will totter through the session, though at present, the decomposition of ' the great Liberal party ' is complete. It still keeps, on the surface, together, from the hope, I think a vain one, that ' something will turn up ' for them: the last resource of imbecility and exhaustion.

I am not particularly well, and sent for Leggatt to-day, and am now a prisoner, besieged by this scathing easterly wind. . . .

Such incursions as Disraeli made in debate had a distinctly electioneering flavour. When the Budget was discussed, he delivered a lively attack on Lowe's finance, partly with a view to deride that eminent anti-Reformer's pose as the friend of the working man, and partly in the interest of that relief of local taxation which the party had championed with success in the previous year. But his most interesting speech was made in opposition to Osborne Morgan's Burials Bill, which proposed to open the parish churchyards to Dissenting funerals. His view was that by refusing to pay church rates the Dissenters had publicly recognised that the churches and churchyards belonged to churchmen; and therefore if they wished to use the parish churchyards, that use must be, by every principle of law and equity, upon the conditions imposed by those to whom they belonged. He ended his speech by some earnest words of advice to his Nonconformist fellow-countrymen. Lord Grey's Reform Act, he said, had given them great power, which in many cases they had used wisely.

So long as they maintained toleration, so long as they favoured religious liberty, so long as they checked sacerdotal arrogance, they acted according to their traditions, and those traditions are not the least noble in the history of England. But they have changed their position. They now make war, and avowedly make war, upon the ecclesiastical institutions of this country.[1] I think they are in error in pursuing that course. I believe it not to be for their own interest. However ambiguous and discursive may be the superficial aspects of the religious life of this country, the English are essentially a religious people. . . . They look upon [the Church] instinctively as an institution which vindicates the spiritual nature of man, and as a city of refuge in the strife and sorrows of existence.

I want my Nonconformist friends to remember that another Act of Parliament has been passed affecting the circumstances of England since the Act of 1832. It appeals to the heart of the country. It aims at emancipation from undue sectarian influence; and I do not think that the Nonconformist body will for the future exercise that undue influence upon the returns to this House, which they have now for forty years employed. . . . Let them not be misled by the last General Election. The vast majority arrayed against us was not returned by the new constituencies. It was the traditional and admirable organisation of the Dissenters of England that effected the triumph of the right hon. gentleman. They were animated by a great motive to enthusiasm. They saw before them the destruction of a church. I do not think that, at the next appeal to the people, the Nonconformist body will find that the same result can be obtained. I say not this by way of taunt, certainly not in a spirit of anticipated triumph. I say it because I wish the Nonconformist body to pause and think, and to feel that for the future it may be better for them, instead of assailing the Church, to find in it a faithful and sound ally. There is a common enemy abroad to all churches and to all religious bodies. Their opinions rage on the Continent. Their poisonous distillations have entered even into this isle.

[1] Miall, the Nonconformist spokesman in Parliament, regularly introduced motions for the disestablishment of the English Church.

The Dissenters, distracted by the controversies over the Education Act, were not a determining force in the 1874 election. But their enthusiastic support of Gladstone's bag and baggage policy went far to settle the result in 1880, and, a quarter of a century later, their campaign of passive resistance was certainly one of the causes which helped in the decisive overthrow of the Unionists under Mr. Balfour. On the other hand, the life seems to have gone out of the disestablishment movement, save in regard to Wales; and it is noteworthy that the Dissenters have never been able to secure, during many years of Parliaments in which their friends have always had a considerable majority, that educational arrangement with a view to which they exerted themselves so strenuously in 1906.

As the session drew to a close there was a painful out-crop of administrative scandals mainly affecting mail contracts and telegraphic extension. Disraeli, true to his practice of avoiding personal squabbles, took little or no part in the discussion of matters which reflected seriously on three important members of the Government. The principal achievement of Ministers was the Judicature Act for the reorganisation of the Courts of Law and Equity. A curious question of privilege arose during the passage of this measure. The Commons made an amendment which no less an authority than Cairns declared to be a breach of the Lords' privileges. It was rather a storm in a teacup, but it gave Disraeli an opportunity to show his quality.

To Lord Cairns.

12, GEORGE STREET, HANOVER SQUARE, *July* 15.—Misled by Gladstone, who bewildered me in the most Jesuitical manner, I dined at Grillion's, and lingered there, and was going home when I heard Frdk. Cavendish, G.'s private secretary, say to Hardy ' about this time the privilege is on.' Hardy seemed astonished, and maintained it was impossible. However I thought I would go down to the House. I found it on. and nearly finished, and G. was concluding when I entered, with my wits scarcely collected. However, I went at it, and tho' I should have spoken much better, if I had remained at the House, and went almost breathless into battle, I still got the materials of the case fairly out, and am now going down to the House to resume the fight if G. chooses.

From Lord Cairns.

5, CROMWELL HOUSES, W., *July* 15, 1873.—I think the dinner at Grillion's must have been a most happy preparation for the speech: at all events, nothing could, in my opinion, have been more successful in at once putting before the House the substance and truth of the precedents; in maintaining the proper attitude of the House of Commons on such an occasion; and in covering the Govt. with ridicule for their terror-stricken and undignified attitude.

As soon as the session was over Gladstone effected a very considerable reconstruction of his Government. The Ministers chiefly concerned in the Post Office irregularities, of whom Lowe was one, could not remain longer in their existing places; and, in the course of the shuffle, Gladstone took himself the Chancellorship of the Exchequer in addition to his previous office, and Bright, who had a year or two before left the Cabinet owing to ill-health, re-entered it as Chancellor of the Duchy. But nothing could stem the unpopularity of the Government. They continued during the autumn to lose seat after seat at by-elections: in August, at Shaftesbury, East Staffordshire, and Greenwich; in September, at Dover and in Renfrewshire; in October, at Hull; and in December, at Exeter. Many of the vacancies were caused by Ministerial promotions, so that the verdict of public opinion was particularly marked and particularly galling.

Disraeli went down to Hughenden before the end of July, and spent a quiet time in examining and sorting his own papers and his wife's; burrowing among those treasures which have formed the basis of this biography. His letters to old and new friends show both how he felt his loneliness in the country home of his wedded life, and the way in which he regarded the political scene, in which, for many weeks, he refused to take an active part.

To Montagu Corry.

HUGHENDEN, *July* 30.—I came down here with a resolve to get the house in complete order, and worked yesterday to my satisfaction. This morning I determined, with all the keys, to grapple with the bird's nest imbroglio. The first thing I wanted were her private papers, etc., which I thought were stowed in one of the new tin boxes. I have opened four, all there, but cannot find them: nothing, apparently, but scraps and chaos. I am now exhausted, and have given up the task, for the day at least.

Can you throw any light on the matter ? . . .

Aug. 1.—. . . The Government really seems on its last legs. They can gain no laurels in the recess. That must be spent in apologies, and explanations; especially of the discomfitures and imbroglios of the last fortnight of the session They will, probably, also lose every election, that occurs before the reassembling of Parliament.

The weather here is delicious, and I have also plenty to amuse me in the house, in trying to get the library into perfect order, arranging pictures and so on; but my great business must be the papers, and I am about to set at them again forthwith. I shall not be content until the house is in perfect order. . . .

Aug. 3.—. . . I found the missing papers, and continue at work at their companions between two and three hours each day. I cannot manage more. The progress is not encouraging, but I feel, if I missed this opportunity in my life, I should probably never have another.

She does not appear to have destroyed a single scrap I ever wrote to her, before or after marriage, and never to have cut my hair, which she did every two or three weeks for 33 years, without garnering the harvest; so, as you once asked for some of an early date, I send you a packet, of which I could not break the seal.

There are missing at present two Russian sabres, which Lord Strangford left me, and a long yataghan in a crimson velvet scabbard. These arms were too long to be packed up with the other daggers. Can you throw any light on them ? You can on most things.

Aug. 10.—Hardy writes ' What does it all mean ? Dissolution, or a more radical policy ?'

My opinion is, that instead of dissolution, it is merely a

diversion to escape dissolution, which was inevitable, had they not done something. But their reconstruction is only a sham, and the idea of being saved by the return of that hysterical old spouter, Bright, is absurd. As for a policy, they are much too flustered to have any.

These great events are exciting, especially the elections, and one wants something. The business of my life is a most melancholy one. I only finished arranging her personal papers yesterday: and she has died for me 100 times in the heartrending, but absolutely inevitable, process.

To Lord John Manners.

HUGHENDEN MANOR, *Aug.* 28, '73.—A letter from a friend is like the sight of a sail to one on a desert isle; but when it comes from the best and dearest of friends, it is cheering indeed.

I have been here since the last days of July, and have never been out of the grounds. With one or two casual exceptions, I have never spoken to a human being. Among the casuals, between ourselves, was Sir Arthur Helps, on his way to Balmoral: a royal reconnaissance. It is a dreary life, but I find society, without sympathy, drearier.

As for my health, it is perfect. I have been often told, and I have sometimes thought, that the bronchial disturbance from which I suffered, was a gouty symptom: and so, two years ago, I left off sugar, and with advantage. For a month and more I have now lived without wine, and my cure seems complete. Some stimulus is requisite, but the Lord Rector of a Scotch University has not far to seek for the necessary restorative, tho' it must be kept a secret from the more delicate Southrons.

I am greatly amused with the fast-drifting incidents of the political scene, and so, I suspect, are some others of higher mettle. I don't suppose, that Gladstone, at present, has decided on any course whatever, but he will not go out without attempting something. I hear he is deeply mortified by the utter destruction of the prestige of his Administration, and that his only thought now is to, what they call, re-habilitate it, before it disappears. He will find this a hard task. . . .

To Lady Bradford.

HUGHENDEN MANOR, *Aug.* 29, 1873.—. . . I hope your visit to Windermere has been enchanting. They say the weather has been fitful in England generally, but here we have had a summer of romance. . . .

On Wednesday last, I received from the lady an announcement of the immediately impending event,[1] 'as you have always taken so kind an interest in my welfare.' One can scarcely congratulate, but may sincerely wish her every happiness. It sounds very bad. . . .

To Anne Lady Chesterfield.

HUGHENDEN MANOR, *Sept.* 8, 1873.—. . . I expected, when I saw the Queen in March, the decomposition of the Ministry, but it has been more complete than I contemplated. Had Gladstone then gone out, uncommitted on either Church or education, and the squabbles of his colleagues unknown, he would have gone out with almost undiminished prestige, and would soon have rallied. The firm is now insolvent, and will soon be bankrupt. When the Tories return, it will be their own fault if their reign be not long and glorious. . . .

To Sir Stafford Northcote.

Confidential. HUGHENDEN MANOR, *Sept.* 11, 1873.—You cannot take too decided a line about Ashantee, barring prophecies, like Lowe, of the indubitable failure of the expedition. The great point to insist on, after indicating the dangers and the chances of failure, is the want of analogy between the Ashantee and the Abyssinian cases. What is the cause of quarrel ? If the Ash. want commercial access to the coast, wh. they always used to have, their claim does not seem unreasonable : a matter certainly that ought to admit of arrangement. . . .

The country is deadly to Europeans. Black troops may

---

[1] Lady Cardigan's marriage to the Count de Lancastre. Lady Cardigan's story in her *Recollections* that Disraeli himself made her an offer of marriage may safely be disregarded. Apart from the improbability of a statesman in Disraeli's position desiring to marry a woman of a somewhat equivocal reputation, there were only eight months—between December, 1872, when he became a widower, and August, 1873, when she married a second time—in which a proposal of marriage was possible from him to her; and these were months when he was forming other attachments. She narrows the time still more by placing the occurrence in the hunting season—in other words, very shortly indeed after Lady Beaconsfield's death. By way of corroboration she states that she asked and obtained the advice of the then Prince of Wales, whom she encountered at a meet at Belvoir, whether she should accept; but, when the book was published, King Edward told his personal friends that she had seriously misrepresented the purport of the conversation. It is, of course, possible that there was a question of marriage between Lady Cardigan and Disraeli in the sense that she proposed to him and he declined. There is, certainly, in the *Recollections* a striking exhibition of spite against Lady Bradford, as well as a tendency to disparage Disraeli. Moreover, there is reason to believe that there were other ladies of wealth and position who gave Disraeli to understand, at this period, that they were ready to unite their lot with his.

live in it, but, then, they won't fight. But above all there
are no prisoners to rescue. If we get there, what is the gain?
If we are beaten by the climate, wh. is on the cards, are we
to sit down with a defeat, or is there to be another expedition;
more lives thrown away and more money?

There cannot be a more unprofitable, and more inglorious
quarrel. All the motives of the Abyssinian expedition are
wanting, and all the circumstances are different. Lord Derby
writes me that he met Lowe, who made no scruple of saying
that he had not been consulted, and did not know what his
colleagues were about! So much for Ash.!

As to general politics, I think it highly desirable that you
should notice the misconception of my expression of the
necessity of our knowing the situation and engagements of
the Govt. before we could decide on our policy on several
foreign subjects of pressing importance. Nothing can be
better than what you propose to say on this head. As to
our general policy, it is to uphold the institutions of the country,
and to arrest that course of feverish criticism and unnecessary
change, too long in vogue. I would not too much insist on
our policy being essentially defensive, because they always
make out that means being stationary. If pressed about
reduction of county suffrage, or unable to avoid it, take the
ground that constant change in the distribution of power
is in itself an evil; that the measure of 1868 is only just digested;
that it has been followed by the ballot, hardly yet tried;
that we have no reason to fear extension of the franchise to
properly qualified classes, but that any large increase of either
the boro' or the county constituency cannot be considered
alone; that the latter must lead to a considerable disfranchisement of the towns from 30,[000] to 10,000 inhab.; that,
tho' this may not be immediately unfavorable to the Cons.
cause, you are not prepared, without deep consideration and
clear necessity, to diminish, to a great extent, the influence
of urban populations in our system of Govt., being one favorable to public liberty and enlightenment. . . .

For the last month, I have not interchanged a word with a
human being. It is a dreary life, but I find society drearier.
I have realised what are the feelings of a prisoner of State
of a high class: the fellow in the Iron Masque, and so on.
I have parks and gardens, and pictures and books, and everything to charm and amuse, except the human face and voice
divine. I really have never been out of my own grounds.
However, my imprisonment is nearly at an end, for towards
the close of this month I am going to the Bradfords in Shropshire. I hope I shall be able to behave myself in civilised
society. . .

To Montagu Corry.

HUGHENDEN, *Sept.* 14, 1873.—. . . All that we have seen, or I have told you, of the correspondence, is nothing to what has since transpired. I am amazed! I should think at least 5,000 letters in addition to all I had examined: and apparently, more important and interesting than any. Nothing seems to have escaped her. Many letters of Metternich, Thiers, Brougham. I should say 100 of Bulwer: as many of Stanley, beginning with Trinity College, Cambridge; enough of George Smythe for three volumes, and I dare say not a line in them not as good as Horace Walpole. The whole of Lady Londonderry's correspondence—I dare say 100 letters! Among them, I saw a packet—more than a doz.—from Butt. Many of D'Orsay: his last letter written in pencil, just before his death, on hearing that I was C. of E[xcheque]r and leader of the H. of C. The last letter received from Lady Blessington—a most interesting one. It is the only one I have read: if I had once indulged in reading them, I never should have licked them into any form.

To Lady Bradford.

BEDFORD, BRIGHTON, *Sept.* 24, 1873.—. . . You will be a little surprised at my date; but after two months of solitude, with everything to charm except the greatest of charms, the human face and voice divine, I thought London might be a relief. It was intolerable, so I came down here. It might have succeeded, for I found our friends, the Sturts,[1] here, and in the same hotel. She is ever pleasing, and his wondrous rattle is as good as champaign [*sic*]; but alas! she fell ill, and fancied it was the fault of Brighton, and they went off at a moment's notice.

Yesterday the Brunnows found me out, and took me home to dine with them, quite alone. I sate between the Ambassador and Madame. No other guest, not even a *sous-secrétaire* of embassy. We had six servants in the room, and a wondrous repast, which, as I live on a ' spare radish,' was rather embarrassing. They were kind but it was not lively, tho' I was amused by the great excitement of Brunnow as to English politics, which he flattered himself he concealed. He was always recurring to the Dover election which made a great sensation here. We had telegraphs of the poll every hour, and at ten o'ck. they gave me a serenade, or a chorale, the most beautiful thing I ever heard. No one knows who were the serenaders; they say a private musical society. Not, certainly, the Christie [*sic*] minstrels, who all take off

---

[1] Afterwards Lord and Lady Alington.

their hats to me when I pass: which is awkward, as I was told I should be as unnoticed here in September, as in the woods of Hughenden.

My kind remembrances to Lord Bradford.

I cannot express to you the delight I anticipate from seeing you again. It seems to me that the only happy hours I have had in this melancholy year are due to your charming society.

The visits to Lord and Lady Bradford at Weston and to Lady Chesterfield at Bretby followed, and confirmed him in his devotion to both ladies, though he protested to a friend that he did not really enjoy this country-house visiting.

To Lord Henry Lennox.

WESTON, SHIFNAL, *Oct.* 2, '73.— . . . I hope you have not given up your Bretby visit, and that we shall meet on Monday. I am not very much inclined to it, and rather count on your help. The fact is, visiting does not suit me, and I have pretty well made up my mind, after this year, to give up what is called society, and confine myself solely to public life. The only consolation I have is, that my health is good; as, doubtless, we have some coming scenes, that will try both our nerves and muscle.

I linger on here, boring and bored, notwithstanding a charming hostess, on whom I feel myself a tax. I could not make my other visits[1] fit in without postponing my arrival at Bretby for a couple of days. And this, I thought, under all circumstances, would be too great a liberty.

The Weston visit was notable for Disraeli's last experiment in riding to hounds. He never rode at all at Hughenden, and, indeed, is only recorded to have crossed a horse twice in the past quarter of a century: once when Lord Galway's guest at Serlby in 1853, and again when Lord Wilton showed him the Belvoir hounds in 1869.[2] In these circumstances it argued great pluck in a man nearly sixty-nine to accept an invitation to go cub-hunting at Chillington, five miles from Weston. He rode a little chestnut hack, remained in the saddle three or four hours, and was so exhausted that he actually reeled against the stable wall when he dismounted.

While Disraeli was at Weston, there was an election

---

[1] One of these was to Knowsley.
[2] See Meynell's *Disraeli*, Vol. I., p. 177.

contest proceeding at Bath, the third in the course of the year. At the beginning of the Parliament Bath had been represented by two Liberals. Both had died, one after the other, this spring, and each seat in turn had been won for the Conservatives. Now one of the new members, Lord Chelsea, had succeeded to the peerage; and to Lord Grey de Wilton, the Conservative candidate for the vacancy, a personal friend of his own, Disraeli wrote for publication from Weston on October 3:

For nearly five years the present Ministers have harassed every trade, worried every profe sion, and assailed or menaced every class, institution, and species of property in the country. Occa ionally they have varied this state of civil warfare by perpetrating some job which outraged public opinion, or by stumbling into mistakes which have been always discreditable, and sometimes ruinous. All this they call a policy, and seem quite proud of it; but the country has, I think, made up its mind to close this career of plundering and blundering.[1]

It was a full-blooded letter, conceived in the hustings spirit, but it only restated, in pointed fashion, charges which Disraeli had often brought against Ministers in public speeches and across the table of the House of Commons. A vehement outcry was, however, raised against its tone and language; and even many of his own party attributed to this indiscretion Grey de Wilton's failure by a small majority to retain the seat which Chelsea had won by a majority somewhat similar. Disraeli, at any rate, was quite impenitent.

To Anne Lady Chesterfield.

HUGHENDEN MANOR, *Oct.* 24, 1873.—. . . The storm against my letter to Grey was quite factitious; got up by a knot of clever Liberal journalists, who had, they thought, an opportunity. It has quite evaporated, and from the number of letters I daily receive about it, from all parts of the country, and from the quotations from it daily cropping up in the press, I have no doubt it will effect the purpose for which it was written.

---

[1] Disraeli had used the phrase before, in *Coningsby*, Bk. II., ch. 4.

I wished to give a condensed, but strictly accurate, summary of the career of the Gladstone Ministry. There is not an expression which was not well weighed, and which I could not justify by ample, and even abounding, evidence. Lord Salisbury,[1] and the Hull election, together, will effectively silence my critics. . . .

Disraeli went in the following month to Glasgow, and there defended himself in detail. Ministers might sigh, he said, and newspapers might scream, but the question was, Was the statement a true one ? It was no answer to say ' Oh, fie ! how very rude !' He maintained that he had written the history of a Ministry that had lasted five years and had immortalised the spirit of their policy in five lines.

The occasion of Disraeli's visit to Glasgow was that he might be installed Lord Rector of the University, and might thereupon deliver his address to the students who had elected him two years before, but who had been deprived of the treat of seeing and hearing him in the previous autumn by Lady Beaconsfield's last illness. Many other functions, however, were planned to welcome the man of the hour to the Clyde. Writing to Lord Barrington a few days beforehand he said the expedition was ' assuming colossal proportions. . . . My plans assume that I shall return to England alive; when I see the programme of the Glasgow week, it seems doubtful. Nothing can be more inhuman; and if there were a society to protect public men, as there is to protect donkeys, some interference would undoubtedly take place.'

Few statesmen were more qualified by sympathy and experience to give advice to youth. He had never ceased to be young in feeling, and to feel for the young; and he himself was a dazzling example of what resolute and aspiring youth could achieve. He impressed upon his hearers at Glasgow the necessity, in order to succeed in life, for two kinds of knowledge—first self-knowledge, and then knowledge of the spirit of the age. Self-know-

[1] Who had written an article in the current number of the *Quarterly Review*, strongly criticising ' The programme of the Radicals.'

ledge, he told them, could not be obtained with certainty either in the family circle, or from the judgment of one's fellows, or from that of one's tutors; but from self-communion. The young would make many errors and experience much self-deception; it was their business to learn the lesson of their mistakes, and to accept the consequences with courage and candour. Only by severe introspection could they obtain the self-knowledge they required and make their failures the foundation of their ultimate success.

But self-knowledge was not enough. Without a knowledge of the spirit of the age life might prove a blunder; a man might embrace a profession doomed to grow obsolete, or embark his capital in a decaying trade. It did not follow that the spirit of the age should be adopted; it might be necessary to resist it; but it was essential to understand it. He considered the spirit of the mid-Victorian age in which he spoke to be one of equality. So far as the word stood for civil equality—equality of all subjects before the law—it was the only foundation of a perfect commonwealth, and had been largely responsible for British patriotism and security. But there was also social equality, which had been established by the Revolution in France, but which recent events, in 1870 and 1871, showed not to be a principle on which a nation could safely rely in the hour of trial. And, further, there was the demand of a new school for physical and material equality. 'The leading principle of this new school is that there is no happiness which is not material, and that every living being has a right to share in that physical welfare.' The school substituted the rights of labour for the rights of property, and recognised no such limitation of employment as resulted from the division of the world into states or nations. 'As civil equality would abolish privilege and social equality would destroy classes; so material and physical equality strikes at the principle of patriotism, and is prepared to abrogate countries.' Against this theory he appealed to the

traditional patriotism of his Scottish audience, and proceeded, in a peroration which sums up his teaching on
spiritual matters in *Tancred*, *Lord George Bentinck*, the
Sheldonian speech, and *Lothair:*

It is not true that the only real happiness is physical happiness; it is not true that physical happiness is the highest happiness; it is not true that physical happiness is a principle on
which you can build up a flourishing and enduring commonwealth. A civilised community must rest on a large realised
capital of thought and sentiment; there must be a reserved fund
of public morality to draw upon in the exigencies of national
life. Society has a soul as well as a body. The traditions
of a nation are part of its existence. Its valour and its discipline, its venerable laws, its science and erudition, its
poetry, its art, its eloquence and its scholarship are as much
portions of its life as its agriculture, its commerce, and its
engineering skill. . . .

If it be true, as I believe, that an aristocracy distinguished
merely by wealth must perish from satiety, so I hold it equally
true that a people who recognise no higher aim than physical
enjoyment must become selfish and enervated. Under such
circumstances, the supremacy of race, which is the key of history, will assert itself. Some human progeny, distinguished
by their bodily vigour or their masculine intelligence, or by
both qualities, will assert their superiority, and conquer
a world which deserves to be enslaved. It will then be found
that our boasted progress has only been an advancement in
a circle, and that our new philosophy has brought us back to
that old serfdom which it has taken ages to extirpate.[1]

But the still more powerful, indeed the insurmountable,
obstacle to the establishment of the new opinions will be
furnished by the essential elements of the human mind.
Our idiosyncrasy is not bounded by the planet which we
inhabit. We can investigate space, and we can comprehend
eternity. No considerations limited to this sphere have
hitherto furnished the excitement which man requires, or the
sanctions for his conduct which his nature imperatively
demands. The spiritual nature of man is stronger than codes
or constitutions. No Government can endure which does not
recognise that for its foundation, and no legislation last
which does not flow from that fountain. The principle may
develop itself in manifold forms, in the shape of many creeds
and many churches; but the principle is divine. As time

[1] A profound passage, which the history of the world since 1914 enables
the men of to-day to appreciate.

is divided into day and night, so religion rests upon the Providence of God and the responsibility of man. One is manifest, the other mysterious; but both are facts. Nor is there, as some would teach you, anything in these convictions which tends to contract our intelligence or our sympathies. On the contrary, religion invigorates the intellect and expands the heart. He who has a due sense of his relations to God is best qualified to fulfil his duties to man.

Disraeli brought to a close an address which had contained many references to Greek and Latin authors by a quotation, in the original Greek, of four lines from the *Ajax* of Sophocles, containing the poet's acknowledgment of Divine Providence. Other quotations from Greek plays are found in *Lord George Bentinck*. Disraeli has been accused of pretending, in these and other passages, to a classical erudition which he did not possess. But, as was shown early in Vol. I., he had attained while at school, and in the year or more of private study which followed, to a wide knowledge of Latin and a moderate acquaintance with Greek; and it is reasonable to assume that a man of letters who, like Disraeli, rather ignored contemporary literature, wou'd refresh his mind throughout life by recurring to his favourite authors of antiquity. He was at any rate sufficiently familiar with classical literature, Greek as well as Latin, to sustain an evening's conversation on the subject in the summer of 1880 with Northcote, a lifelong scholar, upon whom he could not hope to impose with sham knowledge, and who records the talk in his diary without a suggestion that his chief was discussing matters which he did not understand. Sophocles, in particular, he told Northcote, he used at one time to carry about in his pocket.

So satisfied were the Glasgow students with the brilliancy of their Rector's address and the lustre of his career that, having originally elected him in 1871 by a large majority in each of the four 'nations' into which they were divided, they paid him the unusual compliment of re-electing him in 1874, in the same handsome fashion, for a second term.

The Glasgow festivities included, besides the Uni-

versity function, a municipal banquet with the Lord
Provost in the chair, the conferment of the freedom
of the city, and the presentation of an address by the
local Conservative association. Every mark of respect
and consideration was shown Disraeli; and the warmth
of the popular reception was unmistakable. He told
Rose that ' Glasgow, without exaggeration, was the
greatest reception ever offered to a public man : far beyond
Lancashire even !' At the banquet he touched with
some grace on the question of the leadership, now a
purely academic one. He had led his party in the Commons, he said, for twenty-five years, the longest period
of leadership on record. Peel had led the Conservative
party there for eighteen years, though unfortunately
it twice broke asunder; and Russell's leadership of the
Liberals had lasted seventeen years, till at last it slipped
out of his hands.

Do not suppose for a moment that I am making these
observations in a vain spirit of boasting. The reason that
I have been able to lead a party for so long a period, and
under some circumstances of difficulty and discouragement,
is that the party that I lead is really the most generous and
most indulgent party that ever existed. I cannot help smiling
sometimes when I hear the constant intimations that are given,
by those who know all the secrets of the political world, of
the extreme anxiety of the Conservative party to get rid of
my services. The fact is, the Conservative party can get
rid of my services whenever they give me an intimation that
they wish it. Whenever I have desired to leave the leadership of the party they have too kindly requested me to remain
where I was; and if I make a mistake the only difference in
their conduct to me is that they are more indulgent and more
kind.

A declaration at once modest, generous, and politic,
but giving perhaps a somewhat idealised version of the
relationship between leader and party. His political
address to the local Conservatives was largely occupied
with the defence of the Bath letter; but in his peroration
he sounded a warning note as to the contest that was
proceeding in Europe between the spiritual and the temporal power. It would be the greatest danger to civili-

sation if in this struggle the only representatives of the two sides should be the Papacy and the Red Republic. England could hardly stand apart. ' Our connection with Ireland will be brought painfully to our consciousness; and I should not be at all surprised if the visor of Home Rule should fall off some day, and you beheld a very different countenance.' It might be the proud destiny of England to guard civilisation ' alike from the withering blast of atheism and from the simoom of sacerdotal usurpation.' Finally he adjured Scotsmen to ' leave off mumbling the dry bones of political economy, and munching the remainder biscuit of an effete Liberalism.'

From Montagu Corry.

WESTON, SHIFNAL, *Nov* 28, '73.—The Duke of Richmond tells me that nothing but regard for your time has prevented his obeying his impulse to write to you his warm appreciation of the great speech of Saturday. He asked me to tell you this at our next meeting, and also that all his correspondents agree in declaring the satisfaction which it has given the party.

He further told me that none of your words at Glasgow had afforded him so much pleasure as your remarks on your leadership, which he thought well timed and in excellent taste. He hopes the mouths may now be shut of those who, ' whenever Lord Derby goes about starring at Mechanics' Institutes, etc.,' . . . cry out ' Here is *the* man !' With such the Duke does not agree, nor seems to deem the Earl better qualified to lead in his own Chamber ! . . .

To Lady Bradford.

KEIR, DUNBLANE, N.B., *Nov.* 26, 1873.—You were right in supposing that your letter was more precious to me than ' loud huzzas.'

It has been a great week—without exaggeration.

What pleased me, personally, most was the opportunity, *forced* on me, of shattering all the hypocritical trash about my letter to Grey. I call it the Weston manifesto, for it was written under the roof that you inspire and adorn.

I rather long for rest, but have no prospect of it. I live on the railroad and am now going to Cochrane's for a day, for I could not resist his reproachful countenance any more. . . .

To Gathorne Hardy.

BLENHEIM PALACE, WOODSTOCK, *Dec.* 12, 1873.—. . . We have a very gay and gorgeous party here, but the frost has stopped all the hunting, and the fog has marred the shooting.

I attended the Princess yesterday on a visit to yr. constituents, but the fog was so great, that we could neither see, nor be seen.

We lunched at the Dean of Xchurch, and I saw in the flesh Jowett, M. Müller, and Ruskin![1] That was something. M. Bernard was also there, tho' I wonder he had an appetite for any meal, even luncheon, after the quantity of dirt he has eaten.[2]

The Whigs here did not like Exeter. . . .

To Anne Lady Chesterfield.

HUGHENDEN MANOR, *Dec.* 15, 1873.—. . . What with Glasgow, Keir, Lamington, Gunnersbury, Ashridge, Sandringham and Blenheim, I have lived in such a whirl during the last month, that I can hardly distinguish the places where I met persons, and attribute the wrong sayings to the wrong folk.

I think the Government has quite relapsed into the miserable condition they were in at the end of the session, and from which the accession of Mr. Bright, and his sham programme, had, for a moment, a little lifted them out. There will be no measures about reform, or land, or education, and I continue of the opinion I expressed when I was at Bretby, that they will have to dissolve in March. . . .

I was agreeably disappointed with Sandringham. It is not commonplace; both wild and stately. I fancied I was paying a visit to some of the Dukes and Princes of the Baltic; a vigorous marine air, stunted fir forests, but sufficiently extensive; the roads and all the appurtenances on a great scale, and the splendor of Scandinavian sunsets.

Disraeli interrupted his merely social visits to attend a gathering of the party chiefs just before Christmas, at Hardy's house in Kent. ' It is a meeting,' he told Lady Chesterfield, ' that usually takes place at Hughenden,

---

[1] In a letter of the same date to Sir Arthur Helps, Disraeli wrote of these three eminent men: "The first does not look like a man who could de ise or destroy a creed, but benignant; the second all fire, and the third all fanta-y" (*Correspondence of Sir Arthur Helps*, p. 360).

[2] Professor Mountague Bernard had been one of the British Commissioners at Washington.

but I am not equal to the affair this year, with a broken household, and with no organising spirit;' to Lady Bradford he protested, ' It is the sort of thing I abhor.'   The date originally suggested was December 15, but Disraeli wrote to his ' dearest Hardy ': ' Pardon me all the trouble I am giving you, but, as far as I am concerned, it must be the 16th.   The preceding day is the anniversary of my great sorrow.' Besides Disraeli and Hardy, Cairns, Northcote, Manners, Ward Hunt, Taylor (the Whip), and Montagu Corry were present.   No definite conclusions were come to, Hardy tells us; and indeed the next move must necessarily be with the Government.   But there was, no doubt, much interchange of opinion on a subject which had for months formed the topic of Conservative correspondence; namely, how to deal, when the session opened, with the question whether the Prime Minister, since his acceptance of the additional office of Chancellor of the Exchequer, was any longer a Member of Parliament, seeing that he had not, in compliance with the statute of Anne, submitted himself to his constituents for re-election.   It is a question on which much can be, and has been, said on both sides; but which was deprived of all actuality by the unexpected course which Gladstone took before Parliament could meet.

To Lady Bradford.

HEMSTED PARK, STAPLEHURST, Dec. 19, 1873.— . . [Corry] leaves me, I am sorry to say, on Monday for Savernake, so I shall pass my Xmas alone.   That is, however, not a great grief to me beyond losing his society, as I never was a great admirer of a merrie Xmas, even when a boy.   I always hated factitious merriment, in the form of unnecessary guzzlement, and those awful inventions, round games, worse even than forfeits, if that be possible ! . . .

HUGHENDEN MANOR, Dec. 28, 1873.— . . . I passed my Xmas at Trentham in the enemy's camp, where I was taken captive; but they treated me with great humanity, and spared my life, which was valuable to me, as I had a prospect of seeing you.   They wished me to remain a week, but I gave them only two days.   I do not stay a week, except with those I love.   The page of human life is quickly read, and one does not care to dwell upon it, unless it touches the heart.

CHAPTER VIII.

POWER.

1874.

The opening of the New Year found Disraeli still pursuing a round of visits in country-houses, Crichel, Heron Court, and Bretby; strengthening the ties which bound him to Lady Chesterfield and Lady Bradford; and busying himself apparently almost as much about securing a permanent residence in London as over the favourable political outlook. By-elections continued to herald the doom of the Government. Stroud and Newcastle-on-Tyne, both with a long record of Liberal representation, polled in the early days of the year, with the result that a Conservative took the place of a Liberal at Stroud by a substantial margin, while the Liberal majority at Newcastle sank from 4,000 to 1,000.

To Anne Lady Chesterfield.

CRICHEL, WIMBORNE, *Jan.* 10, 1874.—Lady Bradford gave me your congratulatory message on the Stroud election; much the most important event of the kind that has yet occurred. I observe even the *Spectator* acknowledges that to deny the ' reaction ' now is impossible and absurd.

I enclose you a letter on the subject from Sir Michael Beach, a very able and rising man, and who threw himself into the Stroud contest as Sir Stafford Northcote did into that of Exeter. I agree with Sir Michael that, after Stroud, nothing ought to astonish us. . . .

To Lady Bradford.

BRETBY PARK, BURTON-ON-TRENT, *Jan.* 20, 1874.—. . . I arrived here yesterday at tea twilight, and the first words I heard were ' Selina is ill, and they are going to Bournemouth.' This so knocked me up that I could scarcely perform

the offices of civility to my delightful hostess, and her guests
who loomed in the chamber, of ambiguous light, in the shapes of
Wilton, the Dick Curzons, and your friend the great General.[1]
I ought not to forget Carnarvon, whom I absolutely did not
recognise. . . .

I have not yet received an answer about Duchess[2] Eleanor's
house. What do you think of your sister's house in Hill
St.? She wants to let it. Would that do for me ? They
seem to think that Whitehall Gardens has such a strong
recommendation in being near the Ho. of Commons. I doubt
that. Hill St. would secure a walk, which is something.
Certainly I might find a substitute, if in Whitehall, by walking
to the House of C. *via* Belgrave Square,[3] which would not only
secure health, but also happiness, which is something also.

To-day's post informs me that I have succeeded in getting
rooms at Edwards's Hotel from Friday next, and I shall keep
them on till my plans for the season are matured. They are
miserable; merely a couple of rooms on the ground floor, but
they are a sort of headquarters, until I get a house, or commit
some other folly. . . .

Accordingly on Friday, January 23, Disraeli came up
from Bretby to his London hotel with the view of attending on the Saturday a meeting of the trustees of the
British Museum, and also of deciding finally on his future
house. It still wanted nearly a fortnight to the date
fixed for the opening of the session; and his intention
was to return after a week-end in town to his home at
Hughenden. When, however, he woke on the Saturday morning, he was greeted by the momentous news
that the Queen had been advised to dissolve Parliament
immediately, and that Gladstone, in appealing to the
electors to give him a new lease of power, had dangled
before their eyes a surplus of several millions, and promised therewith to abolish the income tax. ' I saw
the necessity,' Disraeli told Lady Bradford, ' of immediately accepting the challenge of Gladstone, which of
course he counted on my not being able to do. But a
political manifesto is the most responsible of all undertakings, and I had not a human being to share that
responsibility.' It was a Saturday in the recess;

---

[1] J. Macdonald.						[2] Of Northumberland.
[3] Where the Bradfords lived.

he had only such conveniences at his disposal as two 'miserable' hotel rooms provided; he was without secretary, papers, or books; and his colleagues were all scattered. But, in spite of these disabilities, his indomitable resolution and industry enabled him to issue his reply to Gladstone's appeal on the following Monday morning. A letter to Lady Chesterfield tells how it was done.

To Anne Lady Chesterfield.

EDWARDS'S HOTEL, *Jan.* 27, 1874.—I was quite taken by surprise. Luckily, I was in London: as you perhaps remember, I curtailed my visit to dear Bretby, and lost a day of your charming society, in order to attend a meeting of the Trustees of the Brit. Museum, whom the Government threatened with some harassing legislation.

I was not up when my servant brought me *The Times.* Be sure I did not go to the Brit. Museum, but, after carefully studying the manifesto, instantly commenced a draft of answer, as I felt everything depended on an immediate reply. Then, I telegraphed to my secretary, Montagu Corry, who was at his uncle's, Lord Shaftesbury, in Dorsetshire ! to Ld. Derby, Lord Cairns, Mr. Hardy, and Sir Stafford Northcote. Lord Cairns and Mr. Hardy[1] soon appeared, my secretary at night; and working hard all the next day we got copies prepared for *all* the Monday morning's papers. Our friends are much pleased with my reply, and are full of courage.

It is too soon to speak with confidence either of details, or probable result, of the election; but, generally speaking, we are well prepared, for there had been, during the last six months, two occasions when dissolution seemed inevitable, so, with the exception of five or six men abroad, all our candidates are at work.

I have never had three days of such hard work in my life as the three last; writing, talking, seeing hundreds of people, encouraging the timid and enlightening the perplexed.

I will let you know, however roughly, how things go on. But be of good heart !

The Derbys arrived on Sunday night, too late to assist me with his counsel with my address. I dined with them yesterday alone. . . .

---

[1] Hardy did not arrive till after the address had been settled by Disraeli in conjunction with Cairns. 'I only had the advantage,' Disraeli told Lady Bradford, 'of the critical counsel of my Lord Chancellor, but he is a host.' Hardy suggested a few changes 'rather verbal than of substance' which Disraeli accepted. See Gathorne Hardy, Vol. I., p. 334.

Think of me, and write to me, whenever you can, for I like, in this great struggle, to feel I have friends whom I love.

Mem. I agree with Carnarvon that G[ladstone]'s manifesto is very ill-written, but I do not agree with Carnarvon that it is not in his usual style. I think his usual style the worst I know of any public man; and that it is marvellous how so consummate an orator should, the moment he takes the pen, be so involved, and cumbersome, and infelicitous in expression.

Many considerations had converged to drive Gladstone to dissolution, of which the almost unbroken series of defeats in by-elections was perhaps the most operative, though the outside world, and especially the Opposition, were disposed to attribute most importance to the difficulty about his seat in Parliament. But the immediate occasion was a serious difference of opinion with Cardwell and Goschen, the Ministers responsible for the defence of the country. To realise his grandiose scheme of total abolition of income tax Gladstone wanted, he told Granville, from three-quarters of a million to a million off the naval and military estimates jointly; and the two Ministers concerned sturdily resisted his demands. There was no way out of the deadlock save by dissolution; but in the *verbosa et grandis epistola*, occupying more than three columns of *The Times*, which Gladstone issued to the electors of Greenwich, the country was never told that, in order to realise the promised boon, it would be necessary not merely to have an 'adjustment,' which Disraeli interpreted to mean an increase of taxes, but also to cut down the naval and military estimates seriously below what the Admiralty and the War Office thought requisite for national safety.

If Gladstone's manifesto was, as Disraeli said, ' a prolix narrative,' Disraeli's answering address to the electors of Bucks was rather of a negative character. Remission of taxation, he observed, would be the course of any party or any Ministry in possession of a large surplus; and as for Gladstone's principal measures of relief, the diminution of local taxation and the abolition of the income tax, these were 'measures which the Conservative party have always favoured and which the Prime Minister and his friends have always opposed.' For the rest, the improvement of the condition of the people had been Disraeli's aim throughout, in or out of office, but not by 'incessant and harassing legislation.' It would have been better if, during the last five years, 'there had been a little more energy in our foreign policy, and a little less in our domestic legislation.' After blaming the Ministry for their diplomatic action in regard to the Straits of Malacca—an obscure and intricate matter, of little serious importance, which loomed largely in election speeches and then disappeared—and deprecating further extension of the suffrage at the moment, Disraeli repeated his charge that our national institutions were not safe in Liberal hands, and ended on the imperial note.

Gentlemen, the impending General Election is one of no mean importance for the future character of this Kingdom. There is reason to hope, from the address of the Prime Minister, putting aside some ominous suggestions which it contains as to the expediency of a local and subordinate Legislature, that he is not, certainly at present, opposed to our national institutions or to the maintenance of the integrity of the Empire. But, unfortunately, among his adherents, some assail the Monarchy, others impugn the independence of the House of Lords, while there are those who would relieve Parliament altogether from any share in the government of one portion of the United Kingdom. Others, again, urge him to pursue his peculiar policy by disestablishing the Anglican as he has despoiled the Irish Church; while trusted colleagues in his Cabinet openly concur with them in their desire altogether to thrust religion from the place which it ought to occupy in national education.

These, Gentlemen, are solemn issues, and the impending General Election must decide them. Their solution must be arrived at when Europe is more deeply stirred than at any period since the Reformation, and when the cause of civil liberty and religious freedom mainly depends upon the strength and stability of England. I ask you to return me to the House of Commons to resist every proposal which may impair that strength and to support by every means her imperial sway.

There is no doubt that Disraeli was well advised in basing his main appeal on the desire of the electorate for rest, and on their sense of wounded pride at the disrepute of their country abroad. Great sections of the community were in arms against the Government, moved either by resentment at past treatment, or by fears for the future; not merely the landed interest, always Conservative in tendency, but also, on the one hand, the clergy and an overwhelming proportion of the laity of the Church of England, together with those outside her pale who desired religious education in elementary schools, and, on the other hand, the brewers and the licensed victuallers, whom Ministers had threatened with even more stringent regulation than that which they had carried through; a fortuitous but powerful combination, which Liberals might deride as ' beer and the Bible,' but which they realised would be very difficult to defeat. Moreover, some of the classes upon which the Liberals usually relied were far from enthusiastic for the cause; the Dissenters were sore over the Education Bill, and the working men were inclined to believe that their social aspirations would meet with at least as much sympathy from a democratic Tory Government as from a politico-economic Liberal Administration. In external affairs, the disregard with which British representations had been treated in 1870 by France and Prussia, Russia's contemptuous repudiation of treaty obligations, and the humiliations of the *Alabama* negotiations and award, had sunk deeply into the mind of the country, and made men of different opinions unite in a resolve to have a Government which should insure respect for Britain among the nations of the world. The bait of abolition of income tax was offered in vain to the classes who would mainly benefit by it, as they were the very classes who had most reason to be dissatisfied with Ministers, and they did not believe that abolition could be secured without readjustments of taxation which would hit them equally hard. To many even among the Liberals the mere offer of such a bait seemed a discreditable electioneering manœuvre; and the supporters of the Government, as a body, were irritated by what appeared to them to be a capricious and premature dissolution. The Conservatives had the advantage both in organisation and in leadership; Gorst's machine was in full working order, while the Liberal caucus had not yet been developed; the popularity of the ' People's William '[1] had temporarily waned, and the eyes of the country were fixed on his rival, who had given utterance at Manchester, the Crystal Palace, and Glasgow to the ideas which were beginning to stir the nation's heart.

It seemed probable, therefore, that the General Election would follow the lines of the by-elections and result in a Conservative success. But the best judges on that side dared not, in view of the long predominance of the Liberals at the polls, place their expectations very high. Gorst's estimate just gave them a majority, but so small a majority as to have left a Conservative Government at the mercy of any malcontent section.

From John Eldon Gorst.

CARLTON CLUB, *Jan.* 30, 1874.—Our estimate is as follows:

	Cons.	Rad.
England ..	271	189
Wales ..	10	20
Scotland ..	12	48
Ireland ..	35	68
	328	325

Thompson thinks this is fair and reasonable: Taylor says we have underestimated. We have been rather hard upon the boroughs, but we have taken a sanguine view of the counties.

One feature of the elections, which disturbed the calculations of wirepullers, was the introduction of the ballot; but Disraeli's prediction in 1872 was absolutely verified that ' the Government which first appeals to

---

[1] This was the popular sobriquet for Gladstone in the early seventies; afterwards superseded by the ' Grand Old Man,' or ' G.O.M.'

the country on the secret suffrage, will, in all probability, be cashiered.' Disraeli's expectations during the contest appear from his letters to Lady Bradford.

To Lady Bradford.

CARLTON CLUB, *Jan.* 27, 1874.—. . . It is impossible to form any opinion at present of the result of a General Election. There has not yet been time to learn the feeling of the country. But I see no signs of enthusiasm on the part of the Liberals, and their press is hesitating and dispirited.

So far as the surprise is concerned, we are as prepared as our opponents. There is no possible seat without a candidate. . . .

Wednesday [*Jan.* 28]—. . . I think things look well. What sustains me is the enthusiasm among the great constituencies. This was never known before. I shall be disappointed if we do not carry both seats for Westminster and two for the City. Chelsea even looks promising, and there are absolutely spontaneous fights in Finsbury and Hackney. Nothing like this ever occurred before.

I am making no sacrifice in writing to you. It relieves my heart; and is the most agreeable thing to me, next to receiving a letter from you. Yours, this morning, gave me the greatest pleasure. In the greatest trials of life, it sustains one to feel that you are remembered by those whom you love.

I can truly say that, amid all this whirl, you are never, for a moment, absent from my thoughts or feelings.

Thursday.—. . . With two sons candidates, you certainly ought to write to their chief every day. . . .

HUGHENDEN MANOR, *Feb.* 1.—Yesterday was a complete success; to my content—and you know that, as regards my own doings, I am very rarely content. I think the Malacca Straits will now be pretty well understood by all England—and Mr. Gladstone too.

I found on my table on my return at night tels. telling me of three seats *gained*—Guildford, Andover, Kidderminster; and two, which I thought *lost*, *saved*—Eye and Lymington. That looks well; but I will not indulge in hopes till I have more information: much must be known which is not known to me, for the telegraph will not work on Sunday.

Thursday [*Feb.* 5].—. . . This morning, I hear from the Managing Committee that they now absolutely contemplate obtaining a majority. I think it must greatly depend on this day, which was always the critical one. If London and West[minste]r follow Mary[le]bone, the situation will be grave. . . .

Polling began at the end of the last week in January; and before the close of the first week in February the borough returns were known and were decisive of the general result. The grant of household suffrage in boroughs, which Salisbury had condemned as ' Parliamentary suicide ' for the Conservatives, had been justified, as Disraeli always maintained that it would be justified, even from a party point of view. Gorst reported on February 6: ' If all the elections were to go as we estimated at the time when we made out a majority of 3, we should have a majority of 27.' The city of London swung over to the Conservatives, Goschen only coming in as the minority member, and Disraeli's Liberal friend Rothschild suffering a final defeat; Westminster followed the City; and seats were won at Chelsea, Greenwich, Marylebone, Southwark, and Tower Hamlets. At Greenwich Gladstone was only returned second on the poll, below a Conservative; ' more like a defeat than a victory,' he wrote. Striking Conservative victories were recorded in the great manufacturing towns, such as Manchester, Leeds, Bradford, Oldham, Newcastle-on-Tyne, Nottingham, Stoke-on-Trent. Wakefield, Wigan, Warrington, Stalybridge, and Northampton. In the English boroughs as a whole there was a net Conservative gain of over thirty seats. No wonder the Liberals were in despair at this revelation of the impression produced on the working man by five years of Gladstonian government.

From Montagu Corry

CARLTON CLUB, *Feb.* 6, '74.—. . . There is a panic, I am told at Brooks's: there *was*, I should say, for all is now bitterness and despair. Wolverton[1] has fled from town in horror, and the cry is ' They are in for years.' Gladstone is prostrate and astounded, and his colleagues (in two cases at least which have come to my knowledge) announce in their offices that the next is their last week of power.

Wolverton's advice has caused the whole catastrophe, which has caught a Cabinet in a fool's paradise.

---

[1] The Liberal Whip.

The Carlton is crowded till midnight: all the dear ' old lot ' whom we know so well—all the *frondeurs* and the cynics, professors, *now*, of a common faith—cry for ' The Chief,' as young hounds bay for the huntsman the day after the frost has broken up.

You will have to come, next week.

We meet so soon that I say no more—except to record what I hear on every side, that the Newport Pagnell speech has immeasurably influenced the events of the last 48 hours.

During the elections there was an oratorical duel between Greenwich and Bucks; and little attention was paid to any other speeches save to the thrusts and parries of the rival leaders. These orations were not in themselves very remarkable; though Disraeli's at least served their purpose of heartening his party, and received cordial praise from that one of his colleagues on whose judgment he most depended. ' A splendid effort,' Cairns wrote of the first; of another, ' your Newport Pagnell oration must certainly stand at the head of all the election speeches of this, and perhaps of any, crisis '; and the last he described as ' the fitting topstone of the series.' One passage may be rescued in which Disraeli distinguished between true and false economy.

All Ministers of all parties are in favour of economy, but a great deal depends upon what you mean by economy. I venture to say, that I do not believe you can have economical government in any country in which the chief Minister piques himself upon disregarding the interests of this country abroad, because such neglect must inevitably lead us into expenditure, and an expenditure of the kind over which we have the least control. We are in the habit of hearing it said (and nothing is more true) that the most economical Government we ever had was the Duke of Wellington's—and why was it ? It was because the Duke of Wellington paid the greatest possible attention, more than any Minister who ever ruled in this country, to the interests and position of England abroad. . . .

But Mr. Gladstone's view of economy, or rather the view of his own party and of the school which he represents, is of another kind. He says—' The English people do not care for their affairs abroad. I don't much care for them myself, but I must have economy. I must discharge dock-yard workmen. I must reduce clerks. I must sell the Queen's stores. I must starve the Queen's services. I must sell the accumulations of timber in the dockyards and arsenals. I must sell all the anchors belonging to the navy. I must sell '—which we were selling for the first year or two— ' half the ships in the navy.' And this is economy !

The county elections emphasised the tendency of the borough returns. The home counties followed the lead of London; the Liberals were swept out of Middlesex, Surrey, Essex, and Sussex, where the representation had hitherto been divided. In the whole of this area, including, besides the four counties already mentioned, Kent, Herts, Bucks, and Berks, there were only three Liberal candidates returned for county seats, the minority members for Herts, Bucks, and Berks. Disraeli was for the first time at the head of the poll, his old colleague Du Pré having retired. The figures were: Disraeli (C) 3004, Harvey (C) 2902, Lambert (L) 1720— all these elected, and Talley (LC) 151. Though the verdict of the metropolitan area was perhaps the most outstanding feature of the elections, victories were reported from counties in all parts of England, despite the fact that the Conservatives already held the majority of the county seats.

The Conservative majority in England was over 110; and substantial gains were even made in Liberal Scotland (9) and in Liberal Wales (2). In Ireland a new situation arose, more disquieting for the Liberals than for the Conservatives, though it involved the nominal loss of a few seats to the latter. The first response of Ireland to Gladstone's remedial legislation had been a violent recrudescence of crime; the second, a revival in a more specious form of the Repeal agitation, on the plea that the British Parliament was incompetent to remedy Irish grievances. This movement was started by Isaac Butt, a distinguished Irish lawyer, who had won popularity by his exertions in defending Fenian prisoners. He christened his new policy ' Home Rule,' and invited all

Irishmen, independently of party, to join him. He had sat himself at Westminster in past years as a Conservative, and had been one of the original writers in Disraeli's *Press ;* and Disraeli, at first, mistaking the movement as merely one for local government, expressed a wish to have in Parliament Conservative, as well as Liberal, Home Rulers. The rapid spread of Butt's organisation, and the disintegrating doctrines which it preached, speedily enlightened him as to its tendency, and he offered it a strong opposition. Butt returned to Parliament at a by-election in 1871 as a Home Ruler; and the new party, under his guidance, took a material share in the rejection of Gladstone's Irish University Bill. When the General Election came, they won seats all over Ireland, heavily defeating Chichester Fortescue, who had been Gladstone's Chief Secretary and right-hand man in Irish policy; and at a meeting in Dublin they formally severed themselves from connection with any British party. Ireland, which in 1868 had sent to Parliament 67 Liberals and 38 Conservatives, was represented in 1874 by only 12 Liberals and 34 Conservatives, while there were 57 Home Rulers, constituting an actual majority of the Irish representation. The final figures of the whole election were: Conservatives, 350; Liberals (including two representatives of Labour), 245; Home Rulers (among whom an appreciable minority claimed to be Conservative), 57: While the Conservatives, therefore, had a majority of about fifty over all other parties, they could boast, as compared with the Liberals alone, of a balance of over a hundred: a position of extraordinary strength and security.

As the returns came in, Disraeli's letters naturally became more jubilant, in spite of his disgust at being forced into an unnecessary contest in Bucks.

To Lady Bradford.

HUGHENDEN MANOR, *Friday* [*Feb.* 6, 1874].—Amid 1000 affairs, I write to you one line. I have written to Lady Ches: I am detained here by my *contested ! !* election. No danger, but great trouble when I have so much to think of and do, and great and vexatious expense, for nothing.[1]

My last accounts are that we have gained 40 seats, equal to 80 on a division, and have now a majority of 14 over Gladstone. That majority will increase.

Amid all this, I continually think of you and of your grief, and should like to wipe the tears from your eyes, for I feel they flow. Bear up! Francis[2] is young, and if we prosper he will soon have his way.

I think of going up to town on Monday, but on Tuesday or Wednesday I must be at Buckingham and speak.[3] This is horrid!

Feb. 8.—. . . Myself, I do not think the crisis so near as the world does. I think he will meet Parliament, if only not to imitate me. . . .

Our gains up to last night were 46 = 92; more than Peel gained in 1841, and more than Gladstone gained in 1868.

I am very well, but sigh for moonlight. I think I could live, and love, in that light for ever!

Thursday [*Feb.* 12].—. . . I hear from high authority that the crisis is at hand, and that G.'s colleagues will not support him in his first idea of meeting Parliament.

The Fairy[4] will be here on the 17th.

We shall have 50 majority; the strongest Government since Pitt. . . .

If Ministers were about to follow the precedent of 1868 and resign at once without meeting Parliament, and if a strong and representative Conservative Administration was to be ready to take their place, no time must be lost on the Opposition side in healing the breach caused by the Reform policy of 1867. General Peel had retired from Parliament and public life in 1868, and so had no longer to be reckoned with. With Carnarvon Disraeli had just re-established amicable relations through the

[1] The expenses were subsequently met by a spontaneous movement among Disraeli's constituents, anxious to show their 'pride and gratification' at the eminent position which their representative had attained.

[2] The Hon. F. Bridgeman, afterwards General Bridgeman (1846-1917), was defeated at Stafford.

[3] It was in this speech that Disraeli, with office looming in the immediate future, congratulated Bucks on having supplied four, or (in some reports) five, Prime Ministers out of thirty in all. They were George Grenville, Lord Shelburne, Duke of Portland (twice), and Lord Grenville. Disraeli was himself a Bucks man by adoption.

[4] Disraeli's romantic imagination conceived of his Royal Mistress as the Faerie Queene of Spenser; and to his intimates he wrote of her as 'the Fairy,' or 'Faery.' See VI., ch. 12.

good offices of Lady Chesterfield, Carnarvon's mother-in-law.   There remained Salisbury, at once the most distinguished and powerful, and the most bitter, of the secessionists.   He had, indeed, been working in general harmony with his old colleagues in the House of Lords throughout the Gladstone Administration; and had given cordial support to Disraeli's lieutenant there, the Duke of Richmond.   But his distrust of Disraeli himself had apparently not abated.   No direct communication whatever had passed between them since they parted in March, 1867; the overture about office in February, 1868, having been made through Northcote, and rejected in so summary a fashion as to close the door upon amicable intercourse.   Disraeli, who had been ready throughout for reconciliation, had taken advantage of his visit in December to Hardy's house in Kent to pay a friendly call on Salisbury's sister, Lady Mildred Beresford-Hope, whose husband's antagonism to him rivalled Salisbury's; and, for a final healing of the breach, he now made use of the kindly offices of the lady who was at once Derby's wife and Salisbury's stepmother.   Salisbury's main objections of a public character had been met by Disraeli's refusal to take office in a minority in 1873, and by the fact that a Conservative Government in 1874 would have a secure majority.   Nevertheless, before consenting even to meet Disraeli, Salisbury, we are told, went through a severe mental struggle; but public spirit and a noble ambition prevailed.   Disraeli was so well aware both of the strength of Salisbury's distrust and of his vital importance as a colleague in office that until the meeting, which was at first accidentally delayed, had been satisfactorily effected and agreement reached, he did not disguise his anxiety.

To Lord Salisbury.

2, WHITEHALL GARDENS, *Feb.* 16, 1874.—Lady Derby tells me, that she thinks it very desirable, and that you do not, altogether, disagree with her, that you and myself should have some conversation on the state of public affairs.

The high opinion which, you well know, I always had of your abilities, and the personal regard which, from the first, I entertained for you, and which is unchanged, would render such a conversation interesting to me, and, I think, not disadvantageous to either of us, or to the public interests.

I should be very happy to see you here, at your convenience, or I would call on you, or I would meet you at a third place, if you thought it more desirable.

From Lord Salisbury.

BEDGEBURY PARK, CRANBROOK, *Feb.* 16, 1874.—It would certainly be satisfactory to me to hear your views upon some of the subjects which must at present be occupying your attention—the more so that I do not anticipate that they would be materially in disaccord with my own. I am much obliged to you for proposing to give me the opportunity of doing so. In conformity with your suggestion I called on you this afternoon; but I was not fortunate enough to find you at home. . . .

Just in the nick of time Disraeli found a house to suit him in Whitehall Gardens,[1] within a short walk both of Downing Street and of Westminster Palace; and so he was able to escape the inconveniences of an hotel, and, as he told Lady Bradford, 'live again like a gentleman.' To Whitehall Gardens he came up before the close of the second week in February, and in private conferences with his principal counsellors, Derby, Cairns, Northcote, and Hardy, settled the general plan of his Ministry, so that he was fully prepared when General Ponsonby arrived with the expected message on the evening of Tuesday, the 17th. Ponsonby found him 'much more open, lively, and joyous' than at the crisis in the preceding year; not concealing his delight at the astonishing majority, which had shown, he claimed, how correct was the information on which he wrote the Bath letter.

From Queen Victoria.

WINDSOR CASTLE, *Feb.* 17, '74.—The Queen has just seen Mr. Gladstone, who has tendered his resignation and that of

---

[1] No 2, Whitehall Gardens in recent years became, very appropriately, the office, first, of the Committee of Imperial Defence, and, afterwards, of Mr. Lloyd George's War Cabinet.

his colleagues, which she has accepted. She therefore writes to Mr. Disraeli to ask him to undertake to form a Government.

The Queen would wish to see Mr. Disraeli here at ½ past 12 to-morrow morning.

To Lady Bradford.

¼ to 7 o'ck., *Tuesday, Feb.* 17.—General Ponsonby, who brought me a letter from the Queen, has just left me. I go down to Windsor to-morrow morning at 11 o'ck.

I have seen Lord Salisbury, who joins the Government.

Disraeli knew that a cordial welcome awaited him at Windsor. Lady Ely had written to him on the Monday: ' My dear mistress will be very happy to see you again, and I know how careful and gentle you are about all that concerns her. I think you understand her so well, besides appreciating her noble fine qualities.' The Queen was in sympathy with the country in desiring a less harassing time in domestic legislation, and a prouder outlook in foreign affairs; and she had a pleasant recollection of the care for her wishes and her honour which had marked Disraeli's short Administration in 1868.

Memorandum by Queen Victoria.

Feb. 18.—Mr. Disraeli came at ½ p. 12. He expressed great surprise at the result of the elections. He had thought there might have been a very small majority for them; but nothing like this had been anticipated, and no party organisation cd. have caused this result of a majority of nearly 64. Not since the time of Pitt and Fox had there been anything like it. Even in '41 when such a large majority had been returned for Sir R. Peel, it had not been so extraordinary, because he had had a small majority. It justified, he said, the course he had pursued last March in declining to take office. . . . Sir J. Pakington Providence had disposed of,[1] as he amusingly said. . . . He was anxious to bring as much new talent and blood into the Govt. as possible. . . . He repeatedly said whatever I wished shd. be done—whatever his difficulties might be !

Disraeli returned from his audience of the Queen with his Cabinet fully matured and provisionally approved,

[1] Pakington was defeated at Droitwich, and raised to the peerage as Lord Hampton.

and he gave an account of his arrangements to the colleague who had now for four years led the Conservative party in the Lords.

To the Duke of Richmond.

Private. WHITEHALL GARDENS, *Feb.* 18, 1874.—I had an audience of the Queen to-day at Windsor, from which I have this moment returned, when Her Majesty directed me to form an Administration and invited my views, how the Cabinet was to be constructed.

I said, that I thought it ought not to be too large, that it should not exceed 12 members and that they might be divided equally between the two Houses.

I proposed that your Grace should take the lead and management of the House of Lords, in which you have been successful, with the post of Lord President, supported by the Lord Chancellor, and three Secretaries of State, namely Foreign, Indian, and Colonial, filled by Lords Derby, Salisbury, and Carnarvon respectively; that these secretaryships, not being departments connected with the great branches of expenditure, might fairly be placed in the Lords : and, with the Privy Seal, that would account for a moiety of the Cabinet.

In the Commons, [that] the Treasury would be represented by myself, and Sir Stafford Northcote as Chancellor of Exchequer, and that the two great spending departments of Army and Navy I proposed to entrust to Mr. Hardy and Mr. Hunt, as it was impossible to sustain debate in the Commons, if these great offices were represented by little men.

It would be necessary to introduce a stranger to public, or rather official, life for the office of Home Secretary, and I mentioned for Her Majesty's consideration the name of Mr. Cross, the Member for Lancashire.

Lord John Manners would, as Postmaster-General, complete the other moiety.

The Queen will consider all this, and I shall hear from her probably this evening, but Her Majesty viewed the scheme favorably, and I am now going to communicate it to my contemplated colleagues. I earnestly hope that you, and they, may also favorably receive it, as I count much upon your support. . . .

This is rather a rough epistle, but I have had rather a rough day. Excuse its shortcomings, and believe me, that it is written with a sincere and anxious desire, to secure for the Queen a valuable servant, and for us all a colleague, whom we greatly regard, and highly respect and esteem.

The formation of the Cabinet proceeded without friction amongst Disraeli's colleagues. Malmesbury, who became Privy Seal, expressed a very general feeling in his letter of acceptance. ' In the almost unexampled importance of your present position you *must*, at any sacrifice of your personal predilections, look, not to the past services, but to the future usefulness of your colleagues.' The Cabinet accordingly was constituted as follows:

First Lord of the Treasury	B. DISRAELI.
Lord Chancellor	LORD CAIRNS.
Lord President	DUKE OF RICHMOND.
Lord Privy Seal	EARL OF MALMESBURY.
Home Secretary	RICHARD A. CROSS.
Foreign Secretary	EARL OF DERBY.
Colonial Secretary	EARL OF CARNARVON
War Secretary	GATHORNE HARDY.
Indian Secretary	MARQUIS OF SALISBURY.
Chancellor of the Exchequer	SIR STAFFORD NORTHCOTE.
First Lord of the Admiralty	G. WARD HUNT.
Postmaster-General	LORD JOHN MANNERS.

Wisely restricted to the very manageable number of twelve persons,[1] it was as strong and capable a Cabinet as has ever taken over the government of this country. In its chief it had the most arresting figure in politics since the death of Pitt; in Salisbury a man who was destined to hold in the future a place in history little less than his chief, and who was even then recognised as of unlimited promise. Besides these two there were four statesmen, not unequal to the first place if fortune should accord it to them—Cairns, Derby, Hardy, and Northcote; five more who had given proofs, either of character or of cleverness or of administrative ability beyond the common—Richmond, Malmesbury, Carnarvon, Hunt, and Manners; and one new man—Cross, who was to administer the Home Office in such fashion as to set a shining example to future Governments. Little difficulty was found in allotting the departments. Cairns, Malmesbury, Derby, Carnarvon, and Salisbury went

---

[1] Gladstone's Cabinet had numbered fifteen.

naturally back to the offices which they had filled in one or other of the Cabinets of 1866-68, and where Cairns and Derby at least had served with much distinction. For Richmond, as leader of the Lords, the Presidency of the Council was a suitable post. Northcote, the only financier in the Commons capable of coping with Gladstone, was in his right place at the Exchequer, where, but for the Abyssinian War, he would have been sent in 1868; and it was wise to allot to Hardy, perhaps the most successful administrator as well as the most fervid orator of the party, the delicate task of conducting the military forces of the Crown through the transition period inaugurated by the Cardwell reforms, with a view to their transformation into an army of modern type. There was, indeed, no particular reason why Ward Hunt, whose reputation had been gained at the Treasury, should have been sent to administer the Admiralty; and there may be some who, remembering Hunt's enormous size and physical weight, will suspect Disraeli of having had a double meaning when he wrote to Richmond that a great office like that of First Lord should not be represented by a little man. Manners, too, was perhaps a square peg in a round hole with a business department like the Post Office; and he told Disraeli he was 'rather apprehensive' of not fulfilling expectations. Cross's appointment was the natural outcome of the substantial support given by his native Lancashire to the Conservative cause; his qualifications, as lawyer and man of affairs, were vouched for by the Lancashire magnate, Derby, and had been recognised by Disraeli on his Manchester excursion.

A galaxy of ability in a Cabinet does not always promote efficiency. Unless Ministers are deeply imbued with loyalty to a cause or a chief, their individual cleverness may indeed tend to resolve them into a chaos of jarring atoms. But this Cabinet was bound together by strong confidence in its chief. There were only two men, Salisbury and Carnarvon, who entered it with any misgiving; and there is evidence that Salisbury, at any rate, having once, though with difficulty, brought himself to come in, sought loyally from the first for points of agreement rather than of difference, and did his utmost to make the combination a success. For the rest of the Cabinet, four of them—Derby, Manners, Malmesbury, and Northcote—were bound to Disraeli by ties of long-standing personal friendship and political companionship; and though the intimacy with Cairns and Hardy was more recent, the friendship and mutual confidence were almost equally strong. With Richmond as leader in the Lords there had been four years of harmonious working; and Hunt and Cross owed their promotion to their chief's appreciation of their ability.

If the Cabinet was capable and united, there were men of note in responsible positions outside. The most rising of the new men, Sir Michael Hicks Beach, whose exclusion from the Cabinet was almost accidental, became Chief Secretary for Ireland. A first-class man of business, William Henry Smith, was appointed Secretary of the Treasury; and in Lord George Hamilton Disraeli discovered a young man who justified his discernment, and who proved adequate to the heavy task of representing India in the House of Commons. Lord George had been offered the Under-Secretaryship for Foreign Affairs, but had been doubtful of his French: Disraeli assured him that at the India Office there would be no necessity of speaking either Hindustani or Persian. Sir John Karslake and Sir Richard Baggallay were the law officers; not perhaps quite so admirable a combination as that which succeeded them in the later years of the Government, Sir John Holker and Sir Hardinge Giffard. In Hart Dyke Disraeli had a most efficient Chief Whip. The Lord-Lieutenancy of Ireland proved a difficulty, as often before and since. The Duke of Abercorn, who had filled the post with such distinction from 1866 to 1868, at first refused it; but after ineffectual attempts had been made to obtain the services first of the Duke of Marlborough, and then of the Duke of Northumberland, he was pressed to reconsider his decision and ultimately consented. The government of Scotland was placed in the capable hands of Lord-Advocate Gordon, whose mettle Disraeli had already proved.

No statesman ever succeeded in forming a Ministry without giving more or less serious offence in some quarter. There was a clever friend of Disraeli's, who as a young man had been one of his discoveries, but who, owing to a certain instability of character, had hardly fulfilled anticipations. Him Disraeli approached in the most tactful and conciliatory manner, making him an offer somewhat above his deserts, but decidedly below his hopes.

To Lord Henry Lennox.

WHITEHALL GDNS., *Feb.* 19, '74.—The Queen said to me yesterday, that there was one office which she was always anxious about, and that was the President of the Board of Works: it touched her more personally than most.

When I told Her Majesty, that I contemplated recommending her to appoint you, she appeared relieved, and pleased.

It is an office with a great deal of work; but agreeable work. It gives room for the exercise of your taste and energy. The parks, the palaces, and the public buildings of London, under your rule, will become an ornament to the nation, and a credit to the Government, of which, I trust, you will thus become a member.

Lennox, who had set his heart on Cabinet rank—very unreasonably, considering that his brother, the Duke of Richmond, was bound to be of the number—was deeply hurt. Though he accepted the post and kept up the forms of the old affectionate friendship with Disraeli, he ' never forgave the indignity,' and spoke of his chief to others with ' venomous acerbity.' Such is the testimony of Lord Redesdale, who, as Bertram Mitford, served as Secretary to the Board of Works under Lennox's presidency, and who was himself deeply attached to Disraeli. Lennox's administration was not a success, caused Disraeli frequent worry, and came to a premature end.

' The first thing after the Cabinet is formed is the
Household,' remarked a magnate in *Coningsby*. To this
delicate part of his task, so interesting to the great
people among whom he moved, Disraeli's mind was
directed on his very first audience of the Queen; as he
hoped by a Household appointment to gratify the wishes
of his dearest friend.

To Lady Bradford.

WINDSOR CASTLE, *Feb.* 18, 1874.—It is doubtful whether
I shall see you to-day, for a tremendous pressure awaits me
when I get back to town; which I think may be about ½ past
4 or 5; but I hope to try in the evening.

What you suggested in your note of this morning had already
occurred to me some days ago; but the difficulties are immense,
as you will see when we meet. Yet they will, I trust, be overcome, for I am influenced in this matter by a stronger feeling
even than ambition.

To Anne Lady Chesterfield.

2, WHITEHALL GARDENS, *Feb.* 21.—Yesterday I kissed
hands, and to-day I take down Carnarvon to Windsor and
make him a Secy. of State, which, I hope, will please you.

Bradford is Master of the Horse, and Selina will ride in
royal carriages, break the line even in the entrée, and gallop
over all Her Majesty's lieges. I see a difference already in
her demeanor. . . .

It was in the course of the formation of the Household that Disraeli was first brought face to face with a
thorny problem, which was to divide his Cabinet in their
first session, and to range against the Government a
section of the community who should have been among
the firmest upholders of Conservatism. The spread of
Ritualism was a marked feature of the day, and one
specially repugnant to the Queen; who refused to admit
advanced High Churchmen into that personal service to
herself which the Household involved unless they undertook not to take a prominent part in Church politics.
Disraeli turned in this difficulty to the leading High
Churchman in his Cabinet.

To Lord Salisbury.

2, WHITEHALL GARDENS, *Feb.* 22, 1874.—You were very right in saying, that the only obvious difficulties we should have in our Govt. would, or rather might, be religious ones.

Last night, the Queen, while accepting the appointment of Beauchamp as a favor to myself, requires that there shall be an undertaking from him, that he will take no prominent part in Ch. politics.

It is very desirable, Her Majesty adds, that this condition should be clearly understood, as she looks upon the views of the Ch. party with wh. Ld. B. is connected, as detrimental to the interests of the Ch. of England, and dangerous to the Protestant religion.

The Queen, therefore, could give no countenance to that party by admitting a prominent member of it into the Royal Household.

This morning comes another letter. She hears with regret, that Lord Bath is as bad, as Lord Beauchamp: consequently, the same restrictions must be put upon him as on Lord Beau., etc., etc.

I shall say nothing to Beauchamp myself, lest he throw up his appointment in an ecclesiastical pet, wh. would be only cutting his own throat, and whatever may be his faults of manner and temper, he is a thorough good fellow, as, I believe, we both feel.

But I wish you would consider all this, and give me your advice. You might perhaps say things as a friend to him, wh. might be harder to bear from an official chief. I think with tact, and a thorough understanding between you and myself, the ship may be steered thro' all these Church and religious sandbanks and shallows, but I see that vigilance is requisite. Greater trials will arise than the appointment of a Lord Steward or a Lord Chamberlain.

From Lord Salisbury.

Confidential. 20, ARLINGTON STREET, S.W., *Feb.* 22, '74.— I will speak, if you think it desirable, to both Bath and Beauchamp on this point. I am sure they will feel it a matter of duty not to put themselves forward in Church matters in a sense disapproved of by the Queen, so long as they are so closely connected with her immediate service. The argument —if I may venture to suggest it—which will weigh with her most strongly, I believe, against too decided measures, is that this Ritualist party, though not preponderant in numbers, is numerous enough, if it goes against the Establishment, to turn the scale. It is earnest, to fanaticism: it sits loosely to the Establishment, as matters stand: and if driven by any act of serious aggression, will listen to its most reckless advisers and throw itself on the Free Church side. A disruption in England will not perhaps take place for so light a matter as that which took place in Scotland. But, if it does take place, it will bring the whole fabric of the Church down about our ears.

Of course this applies to graver matters than Household places. Mere discountenance will do little harm: but I should look with the gravest alarm to any action on the part of the Legislature. The Bishops are at some work which may be dangerous—moved by Ellicott,[1] who is an unsafe guide. I hope in such matters you will take counsel with the Bishops whom you and Lord Derby placed upon the Bench. They are all I think sound men.

Salisbury's advice was in the main judicious, and for the moment Disraeli was apparently disposed to accept it, as he passed it on to his royal mistress, to whom it was extremely unpalatable.

To Queen Victoria.

2, WHITEHALL GARDENS, *Feb.* 23, 1874.—Mr. Disraeli with his humble duty to your Majesty:

Your Majesty may rest assured, that your Ministry will do everything in their power to discountenance the Ritualist party. Much may be done in that way, particularly if done by a Ministry that is believed to be permanent. Any aggressive act of a legislative character will only make martyrs and probably play the game of the more violent members of the party. . . .

Feb. 28.—. . . Your Majesty's Household is now complete and need not fear competition with the Royal Household formed by any Ministry, either in your Majesty's happy reign, or in those of your royal predecessors.

Mr. Disraeli thinks it of importance, that the high nobility should be encouraged to cluster round the throne

'To change back the oligarchy into a generous aristocracy round a real throne' had been one of the aims of 'Young England'; and Disraeli no doubt felt he was fulfilling at least part of his earlier aspirations when he

---

[1] Bishop of Gloucester and Bristol.

placed round the person of his Sovereign the heads of
the houses of Cecil (elder branch), Seymour (younger
branch), Bridgeman, and Lygon, the heir of the Percies,
a Wellesley, and a Somerset; while in the Cabinet and in
important positions outside there were the representatives of the Stanleys, Hamiltons, Lennoxes, Herberts, and
Cecils (younger branch), besides a Manners, a Lowther, a
Bentinck, and a Bourke; the house of Churchill failing
to be represented only because its head had declined for
family reasons the Lord-Lieutenancy of Ireland.

Hardy describes Disraeli during the process of Ministry-
making as ' in a whirl, much excited and tired of all his
disagreeable duty.'　But though the business tired him,
and drove him at its close to Brighton to recruit his
strength, there can be no doubt that he took a keen and
justifiable pleasure in his first uncontrolled exercise of
the patronage of the Crown,[1] and especially in the opportunity it gave him of finding suitable positions for those
of his friends whom he knew to be competent.

To Lady Bradford.

2, WHITEHALL GARDENS, S.W., *Feb.* 27, 1874.—What with
the drawing-room yesterday and a crowd of interviews
afterwards in Downing St., and endless letters, I could not
find time to write the only lines which really interested me—
to her, who is rarely absent from my thoughts and never from
my heart.

It has been an awful affair altogether, but it is now done,
and on Monday next there will be a Council at Windsor,
when we shall appoint the Lord Lieut[enan]t of Ireland, and
swear in, and sanction, all the remaining members of the Govt.
The Queen did not settle about the Chamberlainship till
midnight on Wednesday.　I had retired when the box arrived,
but was roused at 6 o'ck. a.m. with the news of the capture of
Coomassie,[2] which I sent on to H.M. immediately with three

---

[1] ' After all,' he wrote to Lady Bradford on Oct. 23, 1875, it is affectation
to talk of the bore and bother of patronage and all that.　The sense of
power is delightful.　It is amusing to receive the letters I do. . . . I had
no idea I was the object of so much esteem, confidence, public and private,
and respectful affection; and as nobody in the world, were I to die to-morrow,
would give up even a dinner party, one is sensible of the form of life,'

[2] The Ashantee capital.

dashes under the word ' Important ' on the label. She had been very low the night before about the first news.

The Government is a very strong Government, and gives much satisfaction. I have contrived, in the minor and working places, to include every ' representative ' man, that is to say every one who might be troublesome. Clare Read and Sir Massey Lopes have enchanted the farmers, and I have placed Selwin Ibbetson, Jem Lowther, Cavendish Bentinck, and all those sort of men who would have made a Tory cave. There are some terrible disappointments, but I have written soothing letters, which on the whole have not been without success. . . .

Montagu [Corry] is with me here as much as he can, but, be-tween dead and living sisters, not as much as I wish. Since you left town, I have never dined out. There is plenty to occupy me in the evening, for my table is covered with despatch boxes, all of which must be attended to. In ordinary affairs, these can be managed, even with a Ho. of Commons, but there is nothing so exhausting as the management of men—my present life—except perhaps the management of women; and I make little progress at night.

I shall always consider it most unfortunate, I would almost say unkind, that you quitted town at this conjuncture—the greatest of my life. I do not think I could have deserted you; but I will only say, Adieu.

March 1.—The Queen is delighted with the Household appointments in the Commons, . . .

I am a prisoner to-day, but I hope I shall be all right to-morrow and get to Windsor: then my indisposition will not transpire. I have had a great many visitors to-day, among them the Master of the Horse.

I have been writing consolation letters all the morning—among them to Cochrane.[1]

I should not be surprised were the Und. Secy. of War to be—the Earl of Pembroke !² but this is a *real* secret, known only to me, himself, and you.

Tuesday night [*March* 3].—. . . I am not as well as I could wish to be. The truth is forming a Government is a very severe trial, moral and material. I have never, until to-day, had air or exercise, tho' I have had to make five journeys to Windsor.

I was thinking of getting to Brighton for a couple of days after the Cabinet to-morrow, but I shall come up if I hear of your arrival.

---

¹ The first Lord Lamington.
² Son of Disraeli's old opponent, Sidney Herbert. The appointment was made.

The P. of Wales has written me a most affectionate letter from St. Petersburg; he was so touched by my note telling him that the Queen had sent for me ! You know all about that. . . .

The Countess of Cardigan and Lancastre called here the other day, and has since written—a wondrous letter ! These are some of the things that have happened to D.

BEDFORD HOT[EL], BRIGHTON, *March* 8.—. . . How very unlucky I should have left town—but for the first time in this great affair I felt dead beat ; always, almost, in the same room, unceasing correspondence or endless interviews. But to have seen you would have been a much better and more beneficial change, than even these soft breezes and azure waters. . . .

H.R.H. paid me a visit on Friday morning, before noon— a very long one; and he asked me to dine with him *en petite* [*sic*] *comité* on Sunday. I was obliged to decline and gave him the reason. . . .

If affairs were not at this moment so *pressing*—the Queen's Speech to prepare, and frequent Cabinets, I should come down to Bournemouth. I cannot do that, tho' my thoughts will be ever there. . . .

To Anne Lady Chesterfield.

WHITEHALL GARDENS, *Mar.* 16, 1874.—I was interrupted while writing to you late yesterday, by the unexpected call of the Duc d'Aumale. . . . Next to Lord Orford, the Duc d'Aumale is my greatest friend—I dedicated *Lothair* to him. I do not know his equal. Such natural ability, such extreme accomplishment, and so truly princely a mind and bearing. Between the Comte de Chambord and the Comte de Paris, he has been ' sat upon ' in life, and has had no opportunity. He looks extremely well and says he is, ' tho',' he added with much melancholy, ' I am now alone in the world.' . . .

Corry, of course, resumed his position of principal private secretary to the new Prime Minister—with two Treasury clerks to assist him: Algernon Turnor, after- wards Financial Secretary to the Post Office, and James Daly, who succeeded later to the peerage of Dunsandle. There was no suitable place on Disraeli's staff for Rose, who was intimately associated with his private fortunes; and who had long been in the closest touch with his political career, until the work of agent to the Conserva- tive party outgrew the capacities of a busy firm of solicitors. But Disraeli was never ungrateful; and one of his earliest recommendations for honours was that of Rose for a baronetcy.

Philip Rose to Montagu Corry.

Feb. 21, 1874.—What a pleasure it is to see D. so really great ! You can understand some of my feelings at witnessing the complete realisation of my early predictions, attributed at that time to boyish enthusiasm,but which only strengthened as time went on, and which I have never let go even in the darkest times. You will not wonder that at times it cost me a pang at being shut out from all share in those triumphs of political life with which at one time I was actively asso- ciated, and for the main object of which I have toiled and striven for 30 years, and with which my life has been identified; but in the lottery of life some are destined to climb the ladder, and others to remain obscure.

To Queen Victoria.

10, DOWNING STREET, *April* 17, 1874.—. . . Mr. Philip Rose is the son of a burgher family of Bucks, which has existed in repute for more than two centuries. Mr. Rose is now the possessor of a fine estate in that county, of which he is a magistrate. He is a man of education, but entirely the creator of his own fortune. His life has been one of singular prosperity; mainly owing to his combined energy and in- tegrity, and to a brilliant quickness of perception.

Disraeli, from first to last, regarded his life as a brightly tinted romance, with himself as hero. Now the third volume[1] had been opened. By genius and resolution, in spite of a thousand obstacles, the ' Jew boy,' the despised adventurer, the Oriental mystery-man, had reached the summit of place and power. Not only was he once again the First Minister of what Englishmen may be forgiven for thinking the leading nation in the modern world, but his countrymen had unmistakably expressed their desire to be governed by him; he was supported by a large majority in both Houses of Parliament, all signs of dis- affection in the party to his leadership having dis-

---

[1] The present generation may need to be reminded that, in mid-Vic- torian days, novels—and Disraeli's among them—were wont to appear in three volumes.

appeared ; he was surrounded by a capable and unusually homogeneous band of colleagues ; he was
regarded with peculiar favour by his Sovereign; and he
rapidly came to hold in society, strictly so called, a place
of distinction such as few Prime Ministers have aspired
to and fewer attained.

It was a triumph of romance, but it was also a tragedy.
The hero had all that he had played for; but fruition had
been delayed till he was in his seventieth year and had
lost the partner of his life and of his ambition. Even
on his first attainment of the Premiership in 1868, he
had said to W. F. Haydon in reply to congratulations,
' For me it is twenty years too late. Give me your age
and your health.' How much more fervently did he
echo that cry of ' Too late ' to those who congratulated
him six years afterwards ! ' Power !' he was heard once
to mutter in his triumphal year of 1878; ' it has come
to me too late. There were days when, on waking, I
felt I could move dynasties and governments; but that
has passed away.' That youth was the period for action;
that to be granted adequate scope for your genius when
young was the supreme gift of Heaven, had always been
his creed. Now, however much he might call in art to
assist nature, he was indubitably becoming old; though
he might still be fresh in spirit, he was not physically
comparable to Palmerston when he reached the Premiership at a similar age in 1855, or to Gladstone when he
took up the burden a second time at the age of seventy
in 1880. Tough as Disraeli's fibre had proved through the
struggles of nearly fifty years, he had never been really
robust, and indeed in early manhood had undergone a
prolonged period of grave debility. His intimate notes
to his wife from the House of Commons form a constant
record of indisposition, and of requests for pills and
other remedies or prophylactics. Then in 1867 he had
had a serious attack of gout, and he had suffered in-
termittently since, notably from bronchial trouble in
1870. The labours of the Premiership in the Commons

almost immediately brought on renewed attacks; first in the spring and then in the autumn of 1874 he was pursued by gout, gouty bronchitis, and asthma; and finally in 1876 he was driven to choose between definite retirement and a retreat to the House of Lords. Even the relief afforded by the conduct of business in the less laborious House, though great, was not sufficient; and the unwearied service which he rendered to his country was accompanied by a persistent undercurrent of pain and physical debility, down to his last illness in 1881.

Without the stimulus given not merely by his honourable ambition but by the intimate and endearing relations which he had established with Lady Bradford and Lady Chesterfield, he could hardly have borne the principal burden of government during years of difficulty and danger. But even the intimacy with his new friends could not dull the sense of loneliness and desolation caused by the absence of the wife to whom, as Hardy noted in his diary, the ' long reign ' of 1874-1880 would have been a ' true joy.' Had Lady Chesterfield accepted him, or had it been possible for him to marry Lady Bradford, the vacancy by his hearth, which so keenly affected him, would have been filled. But, as things were, he experienced only too vividly through all his last eight years that melancholy which prompted the bitter cry of his friend the Duc d'Aumale, ' I am now alone in the world.' Sir William Fraser's fussy obtrusiveness and misplaced egotism often mar the effect of his Disraelian stories; but he was inspired by a true discernment in the message which he sent to his chief in the beginning of the 1874 Administration.

The only communication which I made to Disraeli at the time of his last Premiership was one which I was told he felt deeply. I asked a common friend to tell him that I was sure that the feeling in his heart which dominated all others was, that one who had believed in him from the first, whose whole life and soul had been devoted to him, who had longed and prayed for his ultimate success, was, now that his success had come, no more—his wife.[1]

[1] Fraser, pp. 270, 271.

CHAPTER IX.

POLITICAL SUCCESS AND PHYSICAL FAILURE.

1874.

'I am only truly great in action. If ever I am placed
in a truly eminent position I shall prove this.' So in a
moment of exaltation wrote Disraeli in his thirtieth year;
now, in his seventieth, at long last, he was to show that
he had not misjudged his own capacity. Social improvement at home and the enhancement and consolidation of
our imperial position abroad were to be the task of the
Ministry under his guidance; but in both respects Ministers proceeded with caution and deliberation, with the
unexpected result that the interest of their first session
was predominantly ecclesiastical. On the domestic side,
in compliance with the general desire for a respite from
incessant legislation, they determined to do no more than
lay this year a foundation for their policy. They appointed a Royal Commission to investigate the subject
of the relations of master and servant; and proposed to
deal at once with only a few minor matters, including
an amendment of the Factory Act and certain modifications of the new licensing law. On the imperial
side, in order to show that the new Government hoped
to infuse some spirit and dignity into foreign policy,
Disraeli suggested to Derby the introduction into the
Queen's Speech of ' a phrase which, without alarming,
might a little mark out our policy from our unpopular
predecessors'.' The phrase actually used was: ' I shall
not fail to exercise the influence arising from these cordial
relations [with foreign Powers] for the maintenance of

European peace, and the faithful observance of international obligations.'

To Queen Victoria.

10, Downing Street, *March* 14, 1874.—Mr. Disraeli with
his humble duty to your Majesty:

He encloses a draft of the Royal Speech for your Majesty's
consideration.

Your Majesty will observe, that he has somewhat deviated
from the routine paragraph respecting foreign affairs. He
thought the accession to office of a new Ministry was not a
bad occasion to call the attention of Europe to that respect
for treaties which your Majesty's present advisers, with your
approbation, are resolved to observe.

In case news of the treaty being signed do not arrive, the
paragraph respecting the Ashantee War will require modification.

Parliament will open on Thursday the 19th. Whether your
Majesty will be graciously pleased to open it, shall be a matter,
always, for your Majesty alone to decide.

Mr. Disraeli has too high, and genuine, an opinion of your
Majesty's judgment, and too sincere an appreciation of your
Majesty's vast political experience, to doubt that, whatever
your Majesty's decision on this important subject, it will be a
correct one. He will not, therefore, presume to dwell [on], only
to glance at, the peculiar circumstances of the present occasion:
a new Parliament; a ballot Parliament; a new Ministry;
a Ministry recommended to your Majesty by an extraordinary
expression of Conservative opinion; the great and deep popularity of the Royal House at the present moment, and the
especial, and even affectionate, reverence for your Majesty's
person; the presence of illustrious strangers, at this moment,
at your Majesty's Court, and the most interesting cause of
that presence [1]—all these considerations, Mr. Disraeli feels
sure, will be duly weighed by your Majesty, and decided upon
with dignified discretion.

Disraeli's insinuating pleading did not prevail to
secure the Queen's presence at the opening of Parliament;
and accordingly there was nothing dramatic about the
first public appearance of his Ministry. He had the
wisdom and magnanimity to suggest the re-election of
the Liberal Speaker chosen towards the close of the last

[1] The recent marriage of the Duke of Edinburgh to a daughter of the
Emperor of Russia.

Parliament, Henry Brand. The depression of the beaten Liberals was augmented by Gladstone's announcement that he only proposed to attend occasionally during the present session, and reserved to himself the right to resign absolutely the leadership of the Opposition in the following spring. It was, Disraeli said on one of the occasions when he met his rival on the neutral ground of Marlborough House, ' the wrath, the inexorable wrath, of Achilles.'

To Anne Lady Chesterfield.

WHITEHALL, *March* 17, 1874.—. . . Yesterday we had a grand banquet at Marlboro' House, which was agreeable enough. I had not very lively neighbours at dinner. . . . However, I do not dislike what Macaulay called some ' flashes of silence,' and unless I sit next to you, or somebody as interesting and charming, I find a pleasant repose in a silent banquet, particularly with a good band.

After dinner we had conversation enough, and I could amuse you for hours, if we were walking together alone at Bretby, but alas ! the pressure of business, wh. is now getting intense, can only spare time for a snatch.

The Dss. of Edinburgh was lively as a bird. She does not like our habit in England of all standing after dinner, and I must say I find it exhausting. In Russia the Court all sit.

She asked me who a certain person was, talking to a lady. I replied, ' That is my rival.' ' What a strange state society is in here,' she said. ' Wherever I go, there is a *double*. Two Prime Ministers, two Secretaries of State, two Lord Chamberlains, and two Lord Chancellors.' . . .

To Lady Bradford.

WHITEHALL, *March* 19, 1874.—. . . I had a very hard day yesterday. A great personage,[1] a favourite of yours and of mine, was with me all the morning at this house with difficult and delicate affairs; then without luncheon, I had to run to D[owning] S[treet] to keep my appointments with the mover and seconder of the Address, each of whom I had to see separately; then a long Cabinet, and then the banquets ! Mine was most successful, and I believe also Derby's. Everybody said they never saw a more brilliant table. I gave Gunter *carte blanche*, and he deserved it. He had a new service of plate. Baroness Rothschild sent me six large baskets of English strawberries, 200 head of gigantic Parisian

[1] The Prince of Wales.

asperges, and the largest and finest Strasburg *foie gras* that ever was seen. All agreed that the change of nationality had not deprived Alsace of its skill. . . .

To-day I am to take my seat at four o'ck., introduced by *Cis*[1] and Mr. Henley. . . .

'Things went off very quietly in the House,' was Disraeli's description of the opening day to Lady Bradford. ' Gladstone made a queer dispiriting speech, and, in short, told his party that the country had decided against them, and that they were thoroughly beaten.' The one urgent topic was the famine in India; and the vigorous measures which, in spite of Anglo-Indian opposition, the Liberal Viceroy, Northbrook, was taking to cope with it received warm support from Salisbury and the new Government. The occasion gave Lord George Hamilton an opportunity to show that Disraeli had not been mistaken in singling him out for responsible office. ' This is a triumph for me,' he wrote to Lady Bradford.[2]

To Queen Victoria.

HOUSE OF COMMONS, *March* 20, 1874.—Mr. Disraeli with his humble duty to your Majesty: . . .

Mr. Disraeli was very inadvertent in not reporting the proceedings of the House of Commons last night to your Majesty. He will to-night *ab initio*, so that your Majesty's record of the new Parliament shall be complete.

He is now writing hurriedly in his place, in the midst of business and not wishing to keep the Windsor messenger.

10, DOWNING STREET, *March* 20, 1874.—. . . An interesting evening in the House of Commons. The Home Rule debate was actively, but not forcibly, sustained by the Irish members. Mr. Gladstone spoke early in the debate, and well. Sir Michael Beach with great force and success.

The night was favourable to the young Ministers. Lord George Hamilton greatly distinguished himself in his Indian statement. Both sides of the House were delighted with him: with his thorough knowledge of his subject; his fine voice; his calmness, dignity, and grace. He spoke for exactly

---

[1] General Forester, Lady Bradford's brother, who shortly afterwards succeeded as 3rd Lord Forester, was in March, 1874, Father of the House of Commons.

[2] Lord George, in his interesting *Parliamentary Reminiscences*, has given in full the flattering description of his speech in the letter to Lady Bradford.

an hour.   Mr. Disraeli has rarely witnessed so great a success
—and, what is better, a promise of greater.

There were only ten days of the Parliamentary session
before the Easter recess; and the new Minister had a vast
amount both of work and of society to pack into his
early days of power.

To Anne Lady Chesterfield.

WHITEHALL, *March* 24, 1874.—. . . Yesterday was a gal-
loping day. . . .

I had to see Sir Garnet Wolseley[1] at one, and find out what
he expected, or wished, as a reward : not a very easy or pleasing
task.   It often happens, in such cases, that Governments
put themselves much out of the way to devise fitting recognition of merit, and then find they have decided on exactly
the very thing that was not wanted.

Then I had a great deputation in D.S. at $\frac{1}{2}$ past 2 o'ck.;
then the Ho. of Comm. at $\frac{1}{2}$ past four, and then, keeping my
brougham ready, I managed to steal away to Belgrave Sqre.
at $\frac{1}{2}$ past 6, and see somebody I love as much as I do yourself.
Then I had to get home to dress for one of the great wedding
banquets; at Gloster House: all the royalties there—Marlboro'
House, Clarence House, and Kensington Palace; and a host of
Abercorns, Ailesburys, Baths, Barringtons, etc., etc., not
forgetting the hero of the hour, Sir Garnet again.

He is a little man, but with a good presence, and a bright
blue eye, holds his head well, and has a lithe figure: he is only
40; so has a great career before him. . . .

I am very well, altho' the work is increasing and it seems
a dream.   I told *somebody* that I was well because I was
happy, and she said ' Of course you are, because you have got
all you wished.'

But I assure you, as I assured her, it is not that.   I am
happy in yr. friendship and your sister's.   They are the charm
and consolation of a life that would otherwise be lonely.
You are always something to think about; something that
soothes and enlivens amid vexation and care. . . .

5 *o'ck., March* 29.—. . . We have had a busy week, social
and otherwise: a drawing-room and a levée.   Selina presented
her daughter, Lady Mabel,[2] as you know.   Selina was in mourning, but it particularly becomes her, and, in my opinion, she

---

[1] Who had commanded the Ashantee expedition and taken Coomassie;
afterwards F.M. Viscount Wolseley.

[2] Now Lady Mabel Kenyon-Slaney.

was much the most distinguished person at the Palace. I dined in Belgrave Sqre. aft[erwar]ds and met the Baths, and one or two agreeable people: a little round table; not more than the Muses and not less than the Graces. . . .

10, Downing St., *March* 31.—I have just adjourned the Ho. of Commons for a fortnight. I begin to feel the reality of power. . . .

To Lady Bradford.

10, Downing Street, *March* 31.—. . . I spoke last night[1] quite to my own satisfaction, which I rarely do, but did not produce any great effect on the House, which expected something of a more inflammatory kind in all probability. I gave them something Attic. Your friend *The Times* again assailed me, wh. I disregard and' shd. not notice if you did not. . . .

Disraeli spent the Easter recess at Bretby. Two sentences, one from a letter to Corry, and the other from a letter to Lady Bradford, give us pictures of his afternoon drives and his evening relaxations. 'We came home in an open carriage—a break—in pelting rain; but my fascinating hostess covered me with her umbrella, so that I was as comfortable as in a tent, and wished the storm to last.' 'We play whist every evening, and I have never once revoked; more than that, Lady Ches. says I play a "really good game."'

The immediate business before the Government was the Budget—a particularly crucial issue, as it was on the financial cry of abolishing the income tax that Gladstone had gone to the country. From Bretby, in answer to an appeal from Northcote, who had kept him fully informed of the development of his schemes, he wrote a decisive letter.

To Sir Stafford Northcote.

Bretby Park, *April* 4, 1874.—If we don't take care, we shall make a muddle of the Budget. It is indispensable that we should take 1d. off the income tax. . . .

I was always in favour of introducing a rating bill, provided we could deal largely with local taxation. If you pass a rating bill, relieve the ratepayers from police and lunatics, and

---

[1] In moving the vote of thanks to the General and the troops for the Ashantee expedition.

abolish the Government exemptions, I consider the local
taxation question virtually settled. The rating bill would
run pretty easily with such adjuncts. You will have, by this
mode, satisfied a large party in the House, and largely consisting of our friends.

The repeal of the sugar duties will satisfy the free traders
and the democracy.

The reduction of one penny in the income tax will be a
golden bridge for all anti-income tax men in our own ranks.
They will grumble, but they will support us.

With these three great objects accomplished, I think you
may count on success.

If you can do more, do it, but that would not be necessary.
The repeal of the horse duty was necessary, when you contemplated dealing so partially, and, comparatively speaking,
slightly, with the local burthens. Now it will range itself
if necessary with the taxes on locomotion, the consideration
of which may keep. It seems to me, however, that you
might repeal the horse duty in addition; and I am clear
that you had better not recede in any considerable degree
from the original estimates. . . .

I hope I have made my views pretty clear. I send this by
messenger, as I don't like the post as a means of conveyance,
when the repeal of taxes is concerned.

It pleased the Opposition to describe a Budget drawn
on these large lines as frittering away the Liberal surplus
of over five millions; but subsequent history has shown
how utterly impracticable was Gladstone's showy policy
of complete abolition of the income tax. Had he prevailed for the moment, the increasing demands of armaments on the one hand, and of social legislation on the
other, must have led to its reimposition within a very
few years; and it is creditable to Disraeli, that, though
he dallied long with the hope of abolition, yet when he
attained power in 1874 he declined, with the prospect
of progressive expenditure, to abandon so powerful an
engine of revenue. He was able, in this halcyon period
of abounding trade and political quietude, to reduce the
rate to twopence, to abolish the sugar duties and the
horse tax, and to relieve local rates of the burden of
police and lunatics; boons which, save in comparison
with total relief from income tax, would have been

regarded as eminently praiseworthy, and which were accepted by Parliament as satisfactory.

Within a few days of his return from Bretby Disraeli was seized by the first of a series of attacks of gout which crippled him, at intervals, for the remainder of the year.

To Anne Lady Chesterfield.

WHITEHALL GARDENS, *April* 16, 1874.—. . . After five years' truce, the gout attacked my left hand on Monday last. I have borne up against it as well as I could, for I don't think the world likes sick Ministers, but I am afraid it has beaten me. After a long Cabinet yesterday, I was obliged to send my excuses to the Speaker, to decline dining with him; and tho' I must manage to appear in the H. of C. to-day for the Budget, I fear my arm must be in a sling. . . .

WHITEHALL, *April* 18.—. . . I have seen my hand to-day for the first time for a week, and tho' not exactly fit for a Lord Chamberlain, it would do for a morganatic marriage, wh. is always rather an ugly affair. . . .

To Lady Bradford.

W[HITEHALL GARDENS], *April* 18, 1874.—. . . The Budget is very successful.[1] . . .

If I can I must go to the Salisbury banquet to-day, but I will not decide till six o'ck. . . . I was in the House last night till midnight, and only left because I was assured there cd. be no more divisions. There was one, however, and Mr. Secy. Cross talked, I see, of the Prime Minister's absence on account of the *state of his health ! ! !* What language! . . .

April 19.—. . . It won't do for me to go down to Brighton, and give up the dinners I have accepted, or they wd. make out I was very ill and all that. I have refused every invitation that has arrived since I returned to town. I mean to fashion and frame my life into two divisions: the public life, wh. speaks for itself; and the inner, or social life, wh., so far as I can arrange, shall be confined to the society of those I love and those who love them.

Life, at least so much of it as may remain to me, is far too valuable to ' waste its fragrance on the desert air.' I live for Power and the Affections; and one may enjoy both without being bored and wearied with all the dull demands of conventional intercourse. . .

[1] In reporting to the Queen Disraeli wrote that 'the Budget was extremely well received by the House. The speech was artistically conceived and the interest skilfully sustained till the end.'

Yesterday was one of those cumbrous banquets wh. I abhor, and wh. in my present condition was oppressive—French Ambassadors, and Dukes and Duchesses of Marlboro' and Cleveland, and all that. It did me no harm, however, for I was resolved and firm, asked for seltzer water, did not pretend to drink wine, or to eat. I had the honor to sit by the great lady of the mansion, so long, and so recently, my bitter foe. She feasted me with, sometimes skilful, adulation. If I were not really indifferent to it, wh. I think I am, I certainly appeared to be so yesterday, for with the depression of my complaint, and the want of all artificial stimulus, I felt I was singularly dull and flat. I could scarcely keep up the battle-dore; the shuttlecock indeed frequently fell.

I am told by another great lady, that all this homage is sincere. It is the expression of '*gratitude*'; not so much for the offices I have showered on them,[1] as for the delicate manner in which I spare them the sense of ' humiliation.'

April 25.—. . . Last night[2] was most amusing. Gladstone stagey, overdone, and full of false feeling and false taste; trying to assume the position of Scipio Africanus, accused by a country which he had saved.

But, between Smollett and Whalley, it was a provincial *Hamlet* bet[wee]n clown and pantaloon.

To Anne Lady Chesterfield.

W.G., *May* 6.—Yesterday was the first party division of the session, and the Ministry won triumphantly.[3] The battle came off on a different issue from that which I had appre-hended when I dined out, wh. was almost as rash as the Duke of Wellington's ball at Brussels. But I had made all my preparations, tho' I had contemplated a different point of attack.

The majority of 63 may be looked upon as our working majority—to be raised to 80 on very critical occasions. Our friends are in high spirits and have quite forgotten the mis-

---

[1] Besides Lord Salisbury, his brother, Lord Eustace Cecil, held office in Disraeli's Administration; as well, of course, as Lord Exeter, the head of the elder branch of the Cecils.

[2] Smollett (C.) moved and Whalley (L.) seconded an abortive vote of censure on Gladstone for advising the recent dissolution. On the debate on the Address, Disraeli had generously said: 'If I had been a follower of a parliamentary chief as eminent, even if I thought he had erred, I should have been disposed rather to exhibit sympathy than to offer criticism. I should remember the great victories which he had fought and won; I should remember his illustrious career; its continuous success and splendour, not its accidental or even disastrous mistakes.'

[3] The question at issue was the educational standard to be reached by the children of out-door paupers.

adventure of the other night.[1]   Forster, Lowe, Goschen, and
Co. looked dreadfully crestfallen. . . .   All the Home Rulers
voted against us.

The humdrum course of hardly contentious Government
business was little to the taste of eager spirits on the Opposition benches.   Mr. (afterwards Sir George) Trevelyan,
accordingly, pushed into the foreground the question of
the county franchise.   But a newly elected Conservative
Parliament could hardly be expected to welcome an
immediate prospect of further constitutional change, and
Mr. Trevelyan's motion was decisively rejected.

To Anne Lady Chesterfield.

W. Gardens, *May* 14, 1874.—We had a capital division
on a capital subject—the extension of the household franchise to counties.   There were rumors that the Liberal
party was to be reorganised on this ' platform,' and amazing
whips were made by both sides.   The result surprised both.
Lord Hartington . . . and other Whigs left the House without
voting; and Mr. Lowe actually voted with us !   There were
five hundred, and more, in the House during the debate, and
we had a purely Conservative majority, with the exception
of Mr. Lowe, of 114 ! . . .

Disraeli's opposition to the motion was of an opportunist character.[2]   While pointing out that the distribution of political power in the community was an affair
of convention, and not of moral or abstract right, he
expressly disclaimed any objection in principle to the
enfranchisement of the county householder.

I have no doubt that the rated householder in the county
is just as competent to exercise the franchise with advantage
to the country as the rated householder in the town.   I have
not the slightest doubt whatever that he possesses all those
virtues which generally characterise the British people.   And
I have as little doubt that, if he possessed the franchise, he
would exercise it with the same prudence and the same benefit
to the community as the rated householder in the town.

---

[1] When the Government was beaten during the dinner hour on an
Irish question by two votes.

[2] ' The measure will not be passed for ten years; and when ten years are
over it will be harmless.'—*Letter from Corry for Beaconsfield to C. S. Read.*
Dec. 27, 1877.

But, as the enfranchisement would enormously increase the county electors, causing them considerably to outnumber the borough electors, it would be necessary to have a great redistribution of seats at the same time, with the result of the erasure from the Parliamentary map of the important class of boroughs of 20,000 or 25,000 inhabitants. He was not prepared to strike a fatal blow at the borough constitution of the United Kingdom. It was an unwise thing for an old country to be always speculating on organic change. In that matter their course of late years had been very rapid and decisive. He was confident in the good sense of the people. But they had had a great meal to digest, and he was not sure that it had as yet been entirely assimilated. The mind of the agricultural class was occupied not with political change, but rather with the elevation of their social condition. 'When the disposition of the country is favourable, beyond any preceding time that I can recall, to a successful consideration of the social wants of the great body of the people, I think it would be most unwise to encourage this fever for organic change.'[1] Here was sounded clearly the note of social reform, which honourably distinguished all the domestic legislation of the Government.

To Anne Lady Chesterfield.

2, WHITEHALL GARDENS, May 19, 1874.—. . . Last night was critical. Gladstone reappeared with all his marshals, Lowe and Childers and Goschen, and others of the gang. They were to make an attack on our Supplementary Estimates for the navy. But a traitor had apprised me of their purpose, and my benches were full to overflowing. They dared not attack the master of 100 legions, and they took refuge in a feeble reconnaissance by Childers, who was snuffed out by the Chanr. of the Excr.

The elections continue to go well for the Ministry, wh. shows that the Conservative reaction was not a momentary feeling. . . .

---

[1] This was Disraeli's last statement of policy on Parliamentary Reform. He had, it may be added, when still in opposition, announced his adhesion in principle to the extension of the suffrage to women.

To Queen Victoria.

2, WHITEHALL GARDENS, *May* 22, 1874.—. . . To-night, there was an amusing debate respecting making Oxford a military centre. Mr. Hall, the new Conservative member or Oxford City, made a maiden speech of considerable power and promise: a fine voice, a natural manner, and much improvisation. While he was sitting down, amid many cheers, Lord Randolph Churchill rose, and, though sitting on the same side of the House, upheld the cause of the University against the City, and answered Mr. Hall.

Lord Randolph said many imprudent things, which is not very important in the maiden speech of a young member and a young man; but the House was surprised, and then captivated, by his energy, and natural flow, and his impressive manner. With self-control and study, he might mount. It was a speech of great promise. . . .

The Whitsuntide recess was a period of great refreshment to Disraeli, as he had the Bradfords to stay with him at Hughenden, the party to meet them comprising Maria Lady Ailesbury, the Wharncliffes, and Pembroke. It was ' the fulness of spring,' he wrote to Lady Chesterfield, while awaiting their arrival: ' thorns and chestnuts and lilacs and acacia, all in bloom, and the air still and balmy. . . . I am as restless as if I were as young as the spring.' Unfortunately he came back to town with a suspicion of trouble in his throat; and the remedies given him to restore his voice brought out the gout once more. ' I left the H. of C. on Monday night at 10 o'ck.,' he wrote to Lady Bradford on June 10, ' all the difficulties about the Licensing Bill being triumphantly over, with the view of going to Montagu House; but when I began to dress I found I hobbled, and a P. Minister hobbling wd. never do, so I gave it wisely up.' ' The enemy has entirely overpowered me,' he wrote in another note. ' After a night of unceasing suffering I have been obliged to send to Hardy to take the reins, as it is physically impossible for me to reach the Ho. of C.'

To Lady Bradford.

2, WHITEHALL GARDENS, *June* 12.—. . . . Yesterday, about six o'ck., I was invaded by the Cr. of the Exr., John Manners, Barrington, with pale faces and distracted air, bearing me a paper signed by all the Irish members of both sides announcing that they must vote against the Ministry on the Factory Bill, unless Ireland was excluded from its provisions. In their alarm, they seemed inclined to yield.

I said that such a representation, if it were a just one, ought to have been made to me long ago, not when my Secy. of State was moving the 2nd reading of this Bill. 2ndly that the representation was unjust and absurd. That to exempt the flax spinners of Belfast from the restrictions on labor placed on the flax spinners of Yorkshire would be in fact establishing a system of Protection in favor of Ireland.

My friends were much alarmed, but I was clear as to our course; and that it was better to be beaten than to yield to such remonstrances.

You see the result. We had 200 majority. . . .

To Anne Lady Chesterfield.

2, WHITEHALL GARDENS, *June* 16.—. . . It was a very rash venture yesterday, but it was successful. The House was cordial, they cheered me when I rose, and I knocked up the terrible Lyon Playfair in no time, tho' a few days ago it was said that, on the question of a Minister of Education, the Opposition would certainly beat us.

I got away by eight o'ck., not materially injured by the exertion: but I am now to be quiet for 8 and 40 hours, and then I shall be more than quite well. . . .

Last Sunday Bradford came on a social visit, and was so shocked at finding me knocked up, that he directed Selina to pay me a visit, wh. she did yesterday before her departure. . . .

Handicapped in this way by illness, Disraeli had to face, in the last portion of the session, the most critical stage of a delicate and difficult question. 'There is not a rock ahead or a cloud,' he told Lady Chesterfield; but, as he remembered when writing to Lady Bradford, there was one exception, 'the Church Bill, which is not our child, and of which the fortunes are very obscure.' It was an unmerited misfortune for Disraeli that his accession to

power should have coincided with the transference of the
Ritualistic controversy from the stage of public discussion to that of legislative action.   He had been a party
to the appointment of a Royal Commission in 1867 to
investigate the problem, and might reasonably have
hoped that it would have been taken in hand by Parliament before 1874.   The Commission had been issued after
a condemnation of Ritualistic excesses by Convocation; it
contained a full representation of the High Church party,
Bishop Wilberforce, Beauchamp, Beresford-Hope, J. G.
Hubbard, Canon Gregory, and Sir Robert Phillimore;
and in August of 1867 it issued its first and practically
unanimous report, affirming the expediency of restrain-
ing variations of vestments, and pronouncing that this
should be done by providing aggrieved parishioners with
easy and effectual process for complaint and redress.
Gladstone, a devoted son of the Church of England, had
held office, with a large majority at his back, for five
subsequent years; and yet, beyond expressing strongly in
the House of Commons in 1872 his belief that there was an
urgent case for legislation, he had taken no step whatever
to deal with the extravagance which he deplored.   Shaftesbury, as Evangelical as he was philanthropic, had endeavoured year after year to obtain support in the Lords
for a drastic Bill of his own; but a man of his extreme
views could hardly expect support from the bench of
Bishops.   Meanwhile the situation had become worse,
owing to the rapid extension of the Ritualistic party on
the one hand, and, on the other, to a striking discrepancy
among the oracles of the law.   In the Purchas case the
use of Eucharistic vestments, of the eastward position by
the celebrant, of wafer-bread, and of the mixed Chalice
—the four points to which most importance was attached
by both the contending parties—had first been affirmed
to be lawful by the Dean of Arches and then, on appeal
to the Privy Council, had been condemned as unlawful.
By these judgments each party in turn was exalted and
depressed; and the reversal of the first by the second

rallied to the Ritualistic side no small following among the moderate High Churchmen. In these circumstances the Bishops, under the guidance of Archbishop Tait, came to the conclusion that legislation must be promoted to prevent the further spread of anarchy and the possible disruption of the Church. But they concerned themselves solely with the machinery for enforcing the law, ignoring the patent fact, which the Purchas judgments advertised, that that law was capable of very different interpretations.

When, in January, 1874, the episcopal decision was taken, Gladstone was in power; before the session opened, there was a new Government, and one in which both High and Low Church had eminent representatives— Salisbury, Hardy, and Carnarvon on one side, and Cairns on the other. Disraeli himself, much impressed, as *Lothair* showed, by the recent successes of Roman propaganda in England, and believing also, as he wrote in the General Preface to the Novels, that the ' medieval superstitions,' which Ritualism revived, were ' generally only the embodiment of pagan ceremonies and creeds,' was averse from the new development; in private letters he disrespectfully referred to Ritualistic practices as ' high jinks.' But, with a vivid recollection of the Ecclesiastical Titles fiasco in 1850-51, he was much too shrewd to wish to embark on ecclesiastical legislation; and in his correspondence over Beauchamp's appointment to the Household had been quite ready to accept Salisbury's standpoint.

But hardly was he installed in office before pressure was applied to him. Within the first week he received, along with the Archbishop's congratulations, a notification that the Bishops were contemplating a Bill and looked to the Government for advice and support.

From Archbishop Tait.

Pirvate and Confidential. ADDINGTON PARK, *Feb.* 23, '74.— First let me express my congratulations, if indeed it be a subject of congratulation to have won the most influential post in Europe by a most honorable manifestation of the regard of a great people, even though that post brings the heaviest burden that any one man can be called to bear. May God sustain you and help you to use all your influence for the best interests of the country !

Secondly will you allow me in my own department to proceed to add to your burden ? May I ask you to read the enclosed memorandum ? It has been drawn up after full consultation with the Queen. Her Majesty is much interested in it, thinking, I believe rightly, that, unless something of the kind indicated is done, the Church of England will go on the breakers. The Bishops also have almost unanimously approved.

If, after talking over the matter with the Queen, you see your way to help us with the force of Government in some necessary legislation, I shall feel very grateful for your advice.

The great body of moderate persons will I think approve, unless some cannonade is opened against us in the newspapers and they are frightened from their guns.

Lords Salisbury and Carnarvon, B[eresford] Hope and Hubbard must be persuaded that we do not mean to persecute their friends, only to make them act reasonably. Lord Shaftesbury and his following must be convinced that there is no danger of weapons intended for other purposes rebounding against themselves, unless in such cases as are obvious violations of the law.

I trust you may be able and willing to help us. I am sure there is a well-grounded alarm caused by the lawlessness which has sprung up of late, and which is sure to go on and increase, if we wait for a general amendment of the administration of the ecclesiastical law, which may I fear be expected to be accomplished about the Greek Kalends. . . .

The Archbishop of York is thoroughly with me in the matter on which I write.

The Queen had already shown her antipathy to the Ritualistic movement by her protest against receiving extreme High Churchmen into her Household; and before the end of February she talked earnestly to Derby about ' the duty of the Government to discourage Ritualism in the Church.' The Archbishop's memorandum dwelt on the lawlessness of selfwilled incumbents, the complicated and cumbrous proceedings of the ecclesiastical courts, and the necessity for ' some simple, summary, and inexpensive process, for securing obedience to the law.'

The Bishops, Disraeli was told, suggested that summary effect should be given to a monition issued by the Ordinary, the Bishop, on the advice of a diocesan board, half clergy, half laity, to be enforced by sequestration, subject to an appeal to the Archbishop of the Province. Disraeli at once, as on the Household difficulty, consulted Salisbury, who put the capital objection in a nutshell: ' I sympathise with you sincerely in having this trouble put upon you. The Archbishop is asking for an impossibility: that it shall be as easy to apply a much-disputed law, as if it were undisputed.' Salisbury proceeded to detail his criticism in a note.

Note by Lord Salisbury.

March 2, 1874.—Most people will sympathise with the Archbishop's desire to prevent ' rash innovations which destroy the peace of parishes.' The difficulty is to devise the legislation that will do this without producing a civil war in the Church of England. The memorandum is vague: and upon the most essential point ambiguous. I cannot help thinking that the acquiescence of the Bishops is due to that cardinal ambiguity.

It proposes to give to a Bishop, acting with a council of clergy and churchwardens, a power of forbidding under pain of sequestration—*something*—but what ? May they forbid anything they please ? or only anything illegal ? The distinction is vital: but there is nothing in the memorandum to indicate which kind of power they are to have. I must therefore, examine both alternatives.

1. Let us assume that they are to have the power of forbidding anything they please. I cannot conceive that so despotic a proposal would pass. . . .

I pass to the second alternative. Let us assume that the Bishop and his council are, by the new legislation, to have power of forbidding, not what they please, but what is illegal. I cannot see what advantage such an enactment would bring. Its object is to avoid costly litigation. But the question would still remain—what is illegal: and that question can only be decided in a court of justice. . . .

I conclude therefore that the proposals of the memorandum, if understood one way, would be contrary to the whole tenor of English law, and would certainly break up the Establishment: if understood the other way, they would not attain the cheapness and the simplicity they have in view.

Disraeli was very reluctant to meddle with a thorny question which must necessarily divide his Cabinet. But events rapidly forced his hand. Within a few weeks an indiscretion of the press revealed the intentions of the Bishops, whereupon public feeling began to kindle, the Protestant party demanded legislation of an even more stringent kind, and Pusey in a series of letters to *The Times* marshalled High Churchmen in general to take their stand by the Ritualists. It was clear that a hornets' nest was being stirred; and the Queen seized the occasion to bring strong pressure to bear on Disraeli to support the Archbishop.

From Queen Victoria.

WINDSOR, *March* 20, '74.—Mr. Disraeli is aware, the Queen believes, that the Archbishop of Canterbury intends to introduce a Bill after Easter to check the prevalence of Ritualism in the Church of England, which is becoming very alarming.

No measure so important affecting the Established Church should be treated as an open question, but should have the full support of the Government.

As far as the Bill may be directed against practices so lately declared illegal, little difficulty can arise. But the Queen wishes to express further that she warmly sympathises with the laity in general and with those of the clergy, who wish to carry on the service according to long-established usage.

The Queen therefore earnestly hopes that her Government may equally support any dispensing powers in the Bill that may be added for their protection or suggest others to meet the same object. Her *earnest* wish is that Mr. Disraeli should *go as far as he can without embarrassment* to the Government, in *satisfying* the *Protestant* feeling of the country in relation to this measure.

The Queen's proposal, which was in effect that those clergy who erred on the side of excess of ceremony should be restrained and punished, but those who erred on the side of defect should be protected, provoked very naturally a strong protest to Disraeli from Salisbury.

From Lord Salisbury.

INDIA OFFICE (*Undated*).—A very unpleasant state of things. Of course I cannot—and I suspect other members of the Cabinet could not—support such a Bill as is here sketched out

But I hope that no serious difficulty is really impending. I saw the Bishop of Peterborough on Thursday. He assured me that the Bishops had as a body approved of no Bill; and that the majority of them were opposed to any Bill giving them despotic powers. All he wanted was power to stop practices which he thought illegal, *pending* the decision of the proper court.

This is a perfectly reasonable proposal—and at the same time it might be made to satisfy the Queen.

Such a unilateral Bill as she proposes would be simply impossible to draw. If you gave a dispensing power to Bishops they would use it on both sides; and you cannot name the excepted practices in an Act of Parliament.

I have seen Liddon. He was very moderate: promised me that he and Pusey would write to the chief Ritualists in the most earnest terms to warn them of the danger of their proceedings. This has been done. But he told me that he was being treated as a renegade by a large section of his party. . . .

Salisbury further pointed out that the procedure suggested by the Archbishop's Bill involved a fundamental change in the status of the clergy. At present the beneficed clergy were freeholders so long as they obeyed known conditions; under the Archbishop's scheme they would be subjected to a purely discretionary power. But Salisbury was anxious to find a *modus vivendi;* and had various talks with Cairns to that end. Cairns was as little disposed to accept the Archbishop's proposal as Salisbury.

From Lord Cairns.

5, CROMWELL HOUSES, S.W., *March* 25, 1874.—This is a very embarrassing question.

I have a strong opinion that if it were attempted to carry or support a Bill like this, *as a Government*, it would lead to a secession of several members of the Cabinet.

I doubt much whether the Evangelical and 'Protestant' division of the Church would be willing to give to Bishops and Archbishops as much power and discretion as this Bill does.

The Bill is full of crudities and unworkable provisions, and the alterations in some of its leading features shew that its framers are not decided as to what they mean.

By the Bill the Archbishop and his Vicar-General could decide the most knotty point of law as to ecclesiastical ritual or practice without appeal.

I should, individually, much prefer an enactment by which six household parishioners (without any fantastic council), declaring themselves members of the Church, might, on giving security for costs, complain of any breach of the law . . .; the complaint to be made in a summary way to the Bishop, and an appeal from him to the Queen in Council, to be referred to the Appellate Court, with ecclesiastical assessors, under the Act of last year.

Something like this passed a select committee of the H. of L. a few years ago, and was assented to by, *inter alios*, Lord Salisbury.

With Cairns's help Disraeli set himself to make the Archbishop's Bill a more workable and practicable measure; substituting for the brand-new diocesan board the assessors provided under the Church Discipline Act, and providing that the ultimate appeal should be to the Privy Council instead of the Archbishop. Disraeli was well aware of the pitfalls, and therefore, while lending his aid to the Archbishop, was careful to do so as a layman of influence rather than as Prime Minister.

To Lady Bradford.

WHITEHALL, *March* 26, 1874.—. . . At twelve to-day, the Archbishop comes. There falls to me the *hardest nut* to crack, that ever was the lot of a Minister. A headstrong step, and it is not only Ministries that wd. be broken up, but political parties altogether, even the Anglican Church itself.

I have no one really to consult with. I can listen to my colleagues, and all they say is worth attention, but they are all prejudiced, one way or other. . . .

To Queen Victoria.

2, WHITEHALL GARDENS, *April* 18, 1874.—Mr. Disraeli with his humble duty to your Majesty:

He has just had an interview with the Archbishops of Canterbury and York.

They informed him of the result of the meeting of the Bishops yesterday at Lambeth, when they submitted to them the new Bill, framed on the lines suggested by Mr. Disraeli and the Lord Chancellor. These new propositions have at least secured unanimity on the part of the Bench of prelates: the High Church Bishops, especially Salisbury[1] and Oxford,[2] though still expressing their opinion that legislation

---

[1] Moberly.   [2] Mackarness.

is unnecessary, assenting to the proposed measures. This is something.

It is clearly understood, that the Prime Minister, and the Lord Chancellor, have assisted in these deliberations, and in this correspondence, only as two Churchmen, not without influence, but in no way or degree binding on your Majesty's Government.

The only object of Lord Cairns and Mr. Disraeli has been to further your Majesty's wishes in this matter, which will always be with them a paramount object.

After the statement of the Archbishop of Canterbury in the House of Lords next Monday, and the first reading of the Bill, Mr. Disraeli will summon a Cabinet, probably on Wednesday, for its consideration.

Mr. Disraeli refrains from being sanguine as to this appeal, but he is supported by the conviction, that his efforts, which have been unceasing, have at least prevented some mischief from occurring, and he can only assure your Majesty, that in this, as he hopes in all things, your Majesty may rely on his efforts for the advantage of your realm and Church.

So strong was the public feeling of the necessity for legislation to prevent anarchy that, in spite of the growing opposition of High Churchmen and of the doubts as to the machinery suggested, the Bill passed both its first and its second reading in the Lords without a division; and Salisbury appeared as the Government mouthpiece on the latter occasion. The Government, he said, occupied an independent position. He admitted that a check to lawlessness was desirable; but he dwelt strongly on the danger of jeopardising the spirit of toleration on which the stately fabric of the Establishment reposed. The three great schools in the Church, the Sacramental, the Emotional, and the Philosophical, must be frankly accepted; no attempt must be made to drive any of them into secession. Cairns grumbled to Disraeli that he should be sorry if this speech ' was to continue to be the expression of the manner in which, as a Cabinet, we looked at questions of this kind.' But Disraeli was manœuvring with great skill to preserve the unity of his Cabinet in a difficult position. Here is his account of a critical moment in the Committee stage in the Lords.

To Lady Bradford.

2, WHITEHALL GARDENS, *June* 5, 1874.—The proceedings of yesterday in the H. of Lords were the most important in the history of the present Government. You saw, then, the result of all my anxious deliberations with the Archbishops for the last three months and more; of my long counsels with Lord Cairns; and of the anxious discussions of many Cabinets.

Nothing could be more triumphant: the Archbishops deferring entirely to the Ministry; and Ld. Salisbury himself supporting the masterly, and commanding, exposition of the Lord Chancellor. Every arrangement was brought about, and every calculation succeeded.

You were in the secret which even the Fairy[1] was not, tho' I shall now tell her all; but the admirable *sangfroid* with which our amendments were divided between Ld. Shaftesbury and the Bp. of Peterboro' must have been amusing to you. I think the whole affair, in conception and execution, one of the most successful, as it certainly is one of the most important, events in modern political history. I don't think Bismarck really could have done better; and I believe the Church will be immensely strengthened, notwithstanding Beauchamp will probably resign and, I fear, our friend Bath is furious. I fear, too, we are doomed not to meet at Longleat.

I cannot give you a good account of myself. I was well yesterday, and in good spirits considering I had not had the solace of seeing you; I looked after affairs in both Houses, guided the Licensing Bill in the Commons thro' some quicksands, and frequently visited the Lords, conferring with D. of Richmond, Bishops of Peterboro' and Winchester, Ld. Derby, and Beauchamp during the crisis. The latter came to me twice while under the Throne, to assure me the Lord Chancellor had ruined everything, and when I mildly mentioned that Ld. Salisbury approved, he said 'the High Ch. thought nothing of Lord Salisbury.' But, as Derby said, ' if Beauchamp disapproves, we must be right.'

Our House sate till two o'ck.; and it was critical to the last, so I cd. not leave my place. And then I had to write to the Fairy on the proceedings of both Houses, as I had promised her. I did it in my room in the H. of C., but when I rose from my seat, I found the enemy had attacked my left foot. I was obliged to send a policeman, over half our quarter of the town, to find me a cab: and here I am with the D. of Manchester, Ld. Fitzwalter, and Andrew Montagu, with three different appointments bet[wee]n 12 and 2, and the absolute necessity of being in the H. of C. at ½ past 4. . . .

[1] Queen Victoria. See above, p. 623, and VI., ch. 12.

[*Same date*].—. . . I look upon the affair in the Lords as the greatest thing I have ever done. . . .

Shaftesbury's amendment, which was supported by the High Churchmen Salisbury, Selborne, and Bath, and inserted in the Bill, was the vital one which established a single lay judge, to be appointed by the two Archbishops, as the sole tribunal of first instance. The Bishop of Peterborough's proposal was to constitute a ' neutral zone ' of practices—some affected by High Church, some by Low, some by Broad—which should not be liable to prosecution. Its exact value in the tactics of the campaign is shown by a sentence in a letter from Cairns to Disraeli on June 12:

You may be interested to know that the Bishop of Peterborough's clause seems to have perfectly done its work as a ' red herring ' across the scent; and the probability is that with the thankful approval of both Archbishops, most of the Bishops, Shaftesbury, Salisbury, Harrowby, Beauchamp and the Ritualists, it will be withdrawn on Monday, and the remodelled Bill pass out of Committee with universal consent, if not applause !

Cairns's expectation was fulfilled. So adroitly had Disraeli pulled the wires behind the scenes that the Bill was read a third time in its amended form without a division and sent down to the Commons. Neither the Government nor the Prime Minister had as yet taken any overt responsibility for it; and it was a respected private member, Russell Gurney, the Recorder of London, who moved the second reading on Thursday, July 9. On the eve of the debate the Archbishop of Canterbury wrote to Disraeli to urge, in the Queen's name, as well as in his own, that it would be highly inexpedient to allow the Bill to fail, and so to encourage a perilous agitation in the autumn. Its progress was at once seriously threatened by the greatest orator in the House. Gladstone emerged, by no means for the first time, from his retirement, delivered an impassioned speech of strong opposition on the broad ground of liberty, and announced that he would move six voluminous Resolutions defining the whole

position of the Established Church. For the moment
he carried his hearers away, but a powerful argument from Harcourt, who reminded the House that
the Church was based on successive Acts of Uniformity,
broke the spell of the great enchanter; and when Hardy
appeared to support Gladstone's case, he was met by
noisy demonstrations of disapproval. Disraeli watched
the rising temper of the House and of the public, and drew
the conclusion that his own sentiments about Ritualism
were shared by the great body of his countrymen, and
that therefore it was now the moment to come into the
open and associate himself and the Government with
the national resolve. He was no doubt confirmed in his
decision by the insistence of his Sovereign.

From Queen Victoria.

WINDSOR, *July* 10, '74.—. . . She [the Queen] is deeply
grieved to see the want of Protestant feeling in the Cabinet;
Mr. Gladstone's conduct is much to be regretted though it is
not surprising: but she wrote to him in the strongest terms of
the danger to the Church and of the intention of the Archbishop
to bring forward a measure to try and regulate the shameful
practices of the Ritualists.

He [Disraeli] should state to the Cabinet how strongly the
Queen feels and how faithful she is to the Protestant faith,
to defend and maintain which, her family was placed upon
the Throne ! She owns she often asks herself what has become of the Protestant feeling of Englishmen. . . .

July 11.—The Queen thanks Mr. Disraeli for his letter
which is very reassuring. It is a *most* important question.
Mr. Disraeli must have managed his refractory Cabinet most
skilfully.

(*Telegram in cypher*) *July* 13.—Pray show that you are in
earnest and determined to pass this Bill and not to be deterred
by threats of delay.

Accordingly Disraeli announced that Gladstone's Resolutions amounted to a challenge of the whole Reformation
settlement, and must be brought to an early issue; and
on the resumption of the second reading debate, he
urged that the Bill should be passed, and passed during
the current session. Its object was, he said—adopting
a phrase from Gladstone's speech which has ever since

been fathered on himself—'to put down Ritualism.'
He protested that he considered all three parties in the
Church, characterised respectively by ceremony, enthusiasm and free speculation, to be perfectly legitimate;
but he wished to discourage 'practices by a portion of
the clergy, avowedly symbolic of doctrines which the
same clergy are bound, in the most solemn manner, to
refute and repudiate.' He was prepared to treat with
reverence Roman Catholic doctrines and ceremonies,
when held and practised by Roman Catholics; what he
did object to was the 'Mass in masquerade.' The speech
elicited the sympathy of the whole House with insignificant exceptions. The second reading, in spite of Gladstone's vehement opposition, was carried without a
division; and a Gladstonian of proved fidelity urged his
leader to withdraw Resolutions for which not twenty
men in his own party would vote—a suggestion which
Gladstone was too experienced a Parliamentarian to
disregard. 'An immense triumph: Gladstone ran away,'
was Disraeli's complacent report to Lady Chesterfield.
The enthusiasm which carried the second reading without a division was prolonged throughout the Committee;
the members were 'mad,' said the protesting Hardy;
and all the important clauses were passed by vast majorities. Only one point of detail needs notice. The
Archbishops had been careful to give the Bishop a veto
so as to prevent frivolous and irresponsible prosecutions
of devoted clergymen. In the teeth of Gladstone's remonstrances there was inserted a clause permitting
appeal against the veto to the Archbishop of the Province,
and, in spite of Gladstone's renewed assault, and of a
plea from both front benches against disturbing the
settlement reached in the Lords, the House maintained
its amendment by a majority of twenty-three.

The right of a Bishop to uncontrolled rule in his diocese
at once became the war-cry of High Churchmen, and
was warmly taken up by Salisbury and their other representatives in the Cabinet. 'Affairs are very critical,
and I believe that wrongheaded Marquis will bolt after

all,' wrote Disraeli late in July to Lady Bradford. In the first days of August it looked as if the Bill would fail and the Cabinet might be broken up. Disraeli was urgent with the Archbishop to get the Lords to acquiesce in the Commons' amendment, without which, in his opinion, the Commons would refuse to proceed with the Bill. The Archbishop himself was inclined to share Disraeli's fears, but could not persuade his suffragans to surrender what they held to be their unquestionable episcopal rights. Salisbury urged the House of Lords to disregard the kind of bluster which was always used when the Peers showed a disposition to insist on a disputed point. He for himself repudiated the bugbear of a majority in the House of Commons. The Lords accordingly struck out the appeal to the Archbishop of the Province; and Disraeli was in despair.

To Anne Lady Chesterfield.

Private. 2, WHITEHALL GARDENS, *Aug.* 5.—Things are as bad as possible: I think the Bill is lost, but worse things will happen in its train.

I found Carnarvon at the Carlton, dining in a tumultuous crowd of starving senators. He not only voted against the Archbishops, Ld. Chanr., and D. of Richmond, but spoke against them; and did as much harm as Salisbury: more, they say. . . .

Eventually, however, owing largely to the Archbishop's unwearied diligence in bringing his personal influence to bear, Disraeli managed to induce the Commons to surrender the amendment rather than lose the Bill; and to be content with a little strong language in the place of destructive action. The Bill, therefore, passed; but the final stage, on Wednesday, August 5, just before prorogation, was of dramatic quality. Salisbury's stinging phrase about bluster provoked an outbreak. Harcourt, long Disraeli's friend in private, made from the front Opposition bench his most notable approximation to him in public. Amid general cheers, he appealed to him, as ' a leader who is proud of the House of Commons and

of whom the House of Commons is proud,' to vindicate
its dignity 'against the ill-advised railing of a rash and
rancorous tongue, even though it be the tongue of a Cabinet Minister, a Secretary of State, and a colleague.' The
speech provoked a satirical rebuke from Harcourt's
leader, Gladstone; but Disraeli responded sympathetically.
The necessity of putting down a 'small but pernicious
sect' was, he said, urgent. The House, therefore, would
do wisely to pass the Bill, even without the amendment;
and members should not be diverted from the course
which, as wise and grave men, they thought it right to
follow, by any allusions to a speech in the other House of
Parliament.

My noble friend was long a member of this House, and is
well known to many of the members even of this Parliament.
He is a great master of gibes and flouts and jeers; but I do
not suppose there is anyone who is prejudiced against a Member
of Parliament on account of such qualifications. My noble
friend knows the House of Commons well, and he is not
perhaps superior to the consideration that by making a speech
of this kind, and taunting respectable men like ourselves with
being 'a blustering majority' he might probably stimulate
the *amour propre* of some individuals to take the course which
he wants, and to defeat the Bill. Now I hope we shall not fall
into that trap. I hope we shall show my noble friend that
we remember some of his manœuvres when he was a simple
member of this House, and that we are not to be taunted into
taking a very indiscreet step, a step ruinous to all our own
wishes and expectations, merely to show that we resent the
contemptuous phrases of one of our colleagues.

It was no doubt chaff, but it was chaff with a sting in
it; nevertheless Disraeli, having conspicuously asserted
himself, and vindicated the Commons, was anxious that
a public difference should not degenerate into a private
quarrel.

To Lord Salisbury.

2, WHITEHALL GARDENS, *Aug.* 5, 1874.—Harcourt attacked
your speech in H. of Lords last night. I conceived a playful
reply to his invective, but what was not perhaps ill conceived was, I fear, ill executed, and knowing what figure that
style of rhetoric makes in 'reports,' I write this line to

express my hope, that you will not misconceive what I may have been represented as saying, or believe, for a moment, that I have any other feelings towards you but those of respect and regard.

Salisbury wrote a good-humoured reply, and took an opportunity before the prorogation to explain in the Lords that he had never used the expression ' blustering majority,' and that when he talked of ' bluster ' he was referring to the argument that, when there was a difference of opinion between the two Houses, it was the privilege of the Commons to insist and the duty of the Lords to yield. There was accordingly no lasting soreness between Disraeli and his colleague—a happy result, creditable to both men, which many of the public and some even of their friends were slow to believe.

From Lady Derby.

Private. 23, St. James's Square, S.W., *Aug.* 7, 1874.— . . . I thought you might like to have some private report of the wild man of your team.[1] I have just seen him, and all is right for the moment; he seems much pleased with a letter he has had from you; he was hard at work at his chemistry and experiments, which the state of the atmosphere was interfering with, and he will be off to Dieppe to-night. I have had some anxious moments this week, and dread a recurrence of difficulties from that quarter in November when Cabinets recommence.

To Lord Carnarvon.

Longleat, *Aug.* 8.—. . . I had never seen the newspapers, and of course took it for granted that Harcourt was strictly accurate in his quotation of Lord Salisbury's speech, particularly as Cairns had complained to me, the night before, of S.'s violent speech. It was a mess; but Salisbury has behaved like a gentleman, and I earnestly trust that we shall all manage to keep together. No effort, for that object, will be spared on my side. . . .

For the moment, and from the Parliamentary standpoint, Disraeli's championship of the Public Worship Regulation Bill was an enormous success, and riveted his

[1] Here Lady Derby was almost certainly quoting a playful phrase of Disraeli's own coinage.

hold on his Sovereign, the legislature, and public opinion,
without even dislocating seriously his hesitating Cabinet.
But subsequent experience of the scandals of imprisoned
clergymen—men of high character if doubtful judgment—
has shown that he would have done better, in the interest
both of the Church and of his party, to adhere to his
original position, and to discourage and postpone legislation which certainly brought to the Church not peace
but a sword. No one could blame an ordinary Prime
Minister for fixing his attention almost exclusively on
a growing lawlessness which seemed to demand prompt
abatement, and ignoring delicate points of Church tendency and feeling to which Archbishops and Bishops and
a large number of High Church laymen were equally
blind. But a deeper insight might have been expected
from Disraeli, who never failed to recognise the profound
importance of the spiritual in human nature, whose
historical studies had made him thoroughly familiar
with the inflammability of High Churchmen, as shown
in Dr. Sacheverell's case, and who had had personal
experience, in the Irish Church controversy, both of
their detachment from political party, and of their electoral weight. He had warnings both from ecclesiastics
and from wirepullers. The Bishop of Brechin (Alexander
Forbes) told him in June that three-fourths of the clergy
—a class whom the Bishop called ' proverbially vindictive '
—regarded the Bill with extreme discontent. ' That the
great mass of the clergy, who have no sympathy with the
effrenata licentia of the younger men, should make common
cause with them against the Bill shows how strongly they
feel, and I put it to you whether 15,000 discontented
men of education scattered thro' the country is not a
thing to be dreaded by any Government.' The gross
exaggeration of this statement probably blinded Disraeli
to the substratum of truth which it contained. But
his party manager, Gorst, reported in the same general
sense. ' The potential electoral strength of the High
Church party,' he wrote on July 29, ' is generally under-

estimated on our side. If they became actively hostile, as the Dissenters were to Gladstone before the dissolution, we should lose many seats both in the counties and boroughs.' It has always been the opinion of some of the shrewdest judges that resentment at Disraeli's action on the Public Worship Regulation Bill counted for much in the readiness of the High Church leaders to think evil of his policy on the Eastern Question and to throw themselves ardently into the support of Gladstone's whirlwind propaganda.

In one of his letters to Archbishop Tait at a critical moment in the history of the Bill,[1] Disraeli described himself as ' one who, from the first, has loyally helped you, and under immense difficulties.' There is no reason to doubt that, over and above the political game, Disraeli was, in his conduct of this awkward business, sincerely anxious to promote the interests of religion in the Church. It is a shallow cynicism that refuses to see earnestness as well as insight—coupled unfortunately with an inadequate sense of the historic continuity of the Church—in such a passage as the following from his second reading speech in the House of Commons.

I have never addressed any body of my countrymen for the last three years without having taken the opportunity of intimating to them that a great change was occurring in the politics of the world, that it would be well for them to prepare for that change, and that it was impossible to conceal from ourselves that the great struggle between the temporal and the spiritual power, which had stamped such indelible features upon the history of the past, was reviving in our own time. . . . . I spoke from strong conviction and from a sense of duty. . . . When I addressed a large body of my countrymen as lately as autumn last, I said then, as I say now— looking to what is occurring in Europe, looking at the great struggle between the temporal and spiritual power which has been precipitated by those changes of which many in this House are so proud, and of which, while they may triumph in their accomplishment, they ought not to shut their eyes to the inevitable consequences—I said then, and say now, that

---

[1] For a detailed history of the controversy on this measure, see chapters 21 and 24 of the *Life of Archbishop Tait*.

in the disasters, or rather in the disturbance and possible disasters which must affect Europe, and which must to a certain degree sympathetically affect England, it would be wise for us to rally on the broad platform of the Reformation. Believing as I do that those principles were never so completely and so powerfully represented as by the Church of England; believing that without the learning, the authority, the wealth, and the independence of the Church of England, the various sects of the Reformation would by this time have dwindled into nothing, I called the attention of the country, so far as I could, to the importance of rallying round the institution of the Church of England, based upon those principles of the Reformation which the Church was called into being to represent.

A private letter in the autumn provoked by a magazine article of Gladstone's on Ritualism further elucidates Disraeli's position.

To Lady Bradford.

2, WHITEHALL GARDENS, *Oct.* 5.—. . . I have read G., but with difficulty. He is a cumbrous writer. Now for the substance, however. Nothing. He does not meet the great question, wh. every instant is becoming greater.

All—at least all civilised beings—must be for the ' beauty of holiness.' No one stronger than myself. In ecclesiastical affairs I require order, taste, ceremony. But these are quite compatible with a sincere profession of the estab[lishe]d religion of the country. What I object to is the introduction of a peculiar set of ceremonies, wh. are avowedly symbolical of doctrines wh. that Established Church was instituted, and is supported, to refute and to repudiate. This is what the people of England are thinking of. His article is mere ' leather and prunella.' . . . .

If Disraeli's well-intentioned efforts had not materially contributed to strengthen the Church of England, he had the satisfaction this session of settling the affairs of the Church of Scotland on a generally acceptable basis. The question of patronage had agitated Scottish churchmen for 300 years. There was a strong feeling in Presbyterian Scotland, thoroughly conformable to its special type of Christianity, that the congregation was the proper authority to select the minister; and it was largely because this privilege was denied in the Establishment and the patronage rested to a great extent in the Crown and in the hands of laymen that there had been the momentous secession of the Free Kirk in the forties.   But even in the Establishment there had been several variations of custom, and on the advice of Lord-Advocate Gordon on the one hand, and of the Duke of Richmond, a great lay patron, on the other, Disraeli determined to settle the vexed question by a universal transfer of lay patronage to the congregations.   The Bill passed the Lords with ease, being blessed by that eminent Presbyterian Liberal, the Duke of Argyll; but Gladstone, enticed by the lure of ecclesiastical controversy, appeared in the Commons to make a vigorous protest, mainly on the strange ground that it would be an injustice to the Free Kirk to remedy a grievance in the conditions of establishment which caused them to secede !   He further expressed a fear lest the measure should hasten on disestablishment, a policy of which he professed himself ' no idolater,' though he was willing that his memory should be judged by his dealings with the Church of Ireland.   Disraeli, in reply, naturally expressed the hope that upon Gladstone's tombstone there would not be inscribed the destruction of another Church.   It was not Gladstone's fault that his epitaph lacked this additional embellishment.   In later years he gave in his adhesion to the policy of disestablishment for Scotland which in 1874 he professed to dread; but the removal of the grievance of patronage, which had been effected in his despite by Disraeli's prudence, had by that time so strengthened the Church of Scotland in the affections of the Scottish people that the assault was repulsed without serious difficulty; and the whole current of Scottish opinion has now for many years set in the direction, not of disestablishment, but of reunion of all Presbyterians in one national Church.   Now that this desirable consummation is apparently on the point of being reached, Scotsmen should not forget Disraeli's important share in creating the predisposing conditions.

There was one other ecclesiastical measure, introduced
by Ministers in July, which gave Disraeli some trouble,
and did not enhance the reputation of the Government.
This was an endowed Schools Bill, which modified the
policy of Gladstonian legislation, by restoring to the
Church of England certain schools on which their founder
had impressed a specially Church character, but which
had been thrown open indiscriminately by the last Parliament. However theoretically defensible, it was hardly
an act of wisdom to disturb an arrangement accepted by
Parliament and already in force; and the Liberals, under
Gladstone's lead, came together with some animation to
protest. Disraeli saw that it was desirable to abandon
a course which Salisbury had pressed upon his colleagues;
so he amusingly assured the House that the clauses of
the Government Bill were so obscure as to be unintelligible to him, and he must therefore withdraw them for
reconsideration. The Bill was accordingly reduced to a
measure merely to substitute Charity Commissioners
appointed by the Tory Government for Endowed Commissioners appointed by their predecessors.

To Queen Victoria.

House of Commons, *Wednesday*, 1 a.m. [*July* 25, 1874].—
Mr. Disraeli with his humble duty to your Majesty:

The debate on endowed schools has ended with a good
majority for the Government; between 60 and 70.

What is of equal importance, with a much better tone in
the House: everything good-tempered and conciliatory.

The Cabinet agreed to many concessions yesterday, though
with difficulty: Lord Salisbury stood almost alone, but he was
very unmanageable. It is entirely his Bill, but had Mr.
Disraeli refused to sanction it, which he only did after many
great alterations by himself and Lord Derby, Lord Salisbury
would never have consented to your Majesty's Government
passing the 'Public Worship Bill'; and that was all-important.

From Queen Victoria.

Confidential. Osborne, *July* 27, '74.—The Queen has
received Mr. Disraeli's letter of yesterday. She sees *all* the
difficulties and herself has regretted that the Church Regula-

tion Bill could not have been delayed till next year, on account of the inconvenience and difficulty it caused to the new Government: but it was impossible.

As however Mr. Disraeli always likes to have the Queen's opinion, she will state to him openly what she thinks it most important for him and his government to avoid, in order to enable them to carry on the government for a length of time, and thus to save the country from frequent crisises.

He will recollect that when he left office in '68 the Queen urged upon him the importance of keeping the Conservative party to what it really ought to be, viz.: *Conservative*, and not to attempt to be *more liberal* than the Liberal party, which the passing of the Reform Bill (which was forced no doubt upon the late Lord Derby) rather led them to appear to be.

Now, while being decidedly still of this opinion, which the Queen considers to be essential to the wellbeing of the British Constitution and safety of the Crown, it is at the same time equally important that there should be no attempt at a *retrograde* policy which would alarm the country and injure the present Government. The country has great confidence in Mr. Disraeli, but not so much in those of his adherents, not to say colleagues, who show a disposition to urge such a policy as she has named above. This would be, the Queen need not say to Mr. Disraeli, *very* dangerous; and while improvements, modifications and alterations may no doubt in many cases—where new systems have not worked well—be very desirable and even necessary, any reversal of principle ought to be avoided, even for the sake of precedent. The Queen feels sure that, with Mr. Disraeli's very enlightened views, he would be as much against this as any one; still this Endowed Schools Bill has been by many looked at in this light and she trusts that Mr. Disraeli will take any opportunity he may have to show that this is *not* the policy of the Government.

Disraeli's letters to his intimate friends give a kaleidoscopic view of the ups and downs of the Parliamentary session at its height. Here, first of all, are some extracts which show his own personal exertions in order to augment the art treasures of the nation.

To Lady Bradford.

H. OF COMM., *June* 2, 1874.—. . . I mean to rise early to-morrow and go to Christie's. If the Barker pictures are as raer and wondrous as I hear, it shall go hard if the nation does not possess them. I always remember with delight that in

1867-8, on my own responsibility, I bought for the nation the Blacas collection of gems—£50,000 !

If I could give our gallery some pictures of equal quality, one wd. not have lived in vain.

2, WHITEHALL GARDENS, *June* 4.—. . . I have been closeted the whole morning with Mr. Burton, the Director of the National Gallery, concocting my plans for Saturday's sale. I believe it will end in the H. of Comm. repudiating my purchase, and I shall have to appeal to Rothschild, Lord Bradford, and some other great friends, to take the treasures off my hands, and relieve me, by a raffle, from my æsthetical embarrassments. We must be very silent till Saturday, as I don't want any one to know the Government is a purchaser. . . .

10, DOWNING STREET, *June* 17.—. . . When the debate over the pictures comes off, there will be some fun. . . .

July 28.—. . . After all, the great attack, so long threatened, about my pictures, ended in vapor. I thought once the vote wd. have passed unchallenged, and in silence; but Mr. Hankey forced me up, and the purchase[1] was sanctioned amid cheers from both sides. . . .

To Anne Lady Chesterfield

H. OF COMM., *June* 20, 1874.—A hurried line. Yesterday was a very hard day in the House. The Opposition got so irritated at all our new proposals in the Licensing Bill, which are very popular, that they waxed factious, and resolved to delay business, and throw over the Bill till next Monday. I had a great force and beat them throughout the night by large majorities.

My new troops got blooded, and begged me to sit up dividing till 5 o'ck. in the morning; and I am not sure I shd. not have done so, had I not found out that I could appoint a morning sitting without notice. This quite turned their flank. We met this morning accordingly, and have carried the Bill through. A great triumph ! . . .

To Lady Bradford.

2, WHITEHALL GARDENS, *July* 3.—. . . Yesterday's debate was satisfactory. I think Home Rule received its *coup de grâce*.

Hartington had spoken in a manner worthy of the subject, and his own position, on the previous night. Yesterday Beach quite confirmed his rising reputation in the House,

---

[1] The pictures bought included a Piero della Francesca, a Pinturicchio, a Luca Signorelli, and two Botticellis.

and the public confidence in my discrimination of character and capacity.   Lowe was very good; terse, logical, and severely humorous; and your friend was not displeased with himself, wh., for him, you know is saying a great deal. . . . The most effective passage in my speech was the reference to the three Irish Prime Ministers I had known, *the three Irish Viceroys*, etc., etc.   All this in the synopsis in *The Times* appears; but in the report it is a hash, and the 3 Irish Viceroys are turned into three judges.   A curious piece of ignorance is ' morbid sentiment ' turned into a ' mere bit of sentiment,' [1] wh. is a feeble vulgarism. . . .

Disraeli's speech in the Home Rule debate was one of his very happiest performances.   Its keynote was a bantering protest against the absurd insistence of the Irish in proclaiming to the world that they were a subjugated people, a conquered race.   The House seized the point with immediate sympathy and punctuated the sentences in which he elaborated it with frequent cheers. ' I have always been surprised,' he said, ' that a people gifted with so much genius, so much sentiment, such winning qualities, should be—I am sure they will pardon my saying it; my remark is an abstract and not a personal one—so deficient in self-respect.'   He denied that the Irish were conquered; ' they are proud of it; I deny that they have any ground for that pride.'   England had been subjugated quite as much, but never boasted of it.   Both the Normans and Cromwell had conquered England, before they conquered Ireland.   He was opposed to Home Rule in the interests of the Irish themselves. ' I am opposed to it because I wish to see at this important crisis of the world—that perhaps is nearer arriving than some of us suppose—a united people welded in one great nationality; and because I feel that, if we sanction this policy, if we do not cleanse the Parliamentary bosom of this perilous stuff, we shall bring about the disintegration of the Kingdom and the destruction of the Empire.'

[1] A natural, almost excusable, mistake.   In the shorthand note ' morbid ' would be written ' mrbd,' and ' mere bit ' ' mr bt '—a difference of only one letter and a space.

To Lady Bradford.

2, WHITEHALL GARDENS, *July* 31.—A most severe day yesterday, the Irish members having announced their determination, whatever might happen, not to allow the continuance of what are called their ' Coercion Acts ' to pass; and their success was inevitable with an adequate quantity of staying power.

I was in my seat 12 hours—from 4 to 4 ![1] a most exciting scene, with many phases of character. At first they were in serried rank, and very firm and resolute: our men the same, and Dyke ordered, in the great dining-room, a grilled bone and champagne supper at 2 o'ck. to be ready for the Tories.

As the evening advanced, the Liberal party, who had ostentatiously informed us that nothing in the world wd. induce them to act with the Home Rulers, could no longer resist the opportunity of embarrassing, or defeating, the Government, and joined the rebels in force; but were defeated —our smallest majority being 61.

Then about two, the Irishry began quarrelling among themselves, the more respectable, Butt himself, Sullivan, a clever fellow, who wants to be the leader, and Mitchell Henry, an English millionaire tho' an Irish member, and who supplies the funds of the party, getting ashamed of the orgies of faction in wh. they found themselves being steeped; and about three o'ck., when they left the House, when the factious divisions took place, they were absolutely hissed by their own assumed creatures. And a little before 4 o'ck. we tired out, or shamed, even these rapscallions, and the Bill went thro' Committee amid loud cheers.

I broke their ranks by keeping my temper and treating Butt and his intimate colleagues as gentlemen, wh. they certainly are not; but their vanity is insatiable, and these fierce rebels did nothing but pay me compliments. . . .

10, DOWNING STREET, *Aug.* 1.—. . . We have had a long Cabinet, and I have had many deputations and interviews; business gets thick the last days, and gentlemen get audiences wh. they asked for months ago. You wd. have been amused if you had seen and heard all I have done since the Cabinet closed at three o'ck.: Sir Henry Rawlinson and the President of the Royal Society and Admiral Sherard Osborn, who want a new polar expedition; and Owens College, with a *posse* of professors and M.P.'s, who want 100 thousand pounds and to become a University; and Mr. —— who says his brother (late M.P.) is low-spirited that, after 40 years of

---

[1] ' The hardest life I ever went thro',' Disraeli told Lady Chesterfield.

Parly. service, ' there is nothing now attached to his name '—
would like to be a Privy Councillor, or baronet, and wd.
not refuse an Irish peerage, and so on. . . .

The tone of complacency which Disraeli adopts with
reference to his achievements during the session is fully
justified by the comments of the chief Parliamentary
observer of the day.

Foremost in official position, as in personal success, is the
Premier. Never did the peculiar genius of Disraeli (it is a
sublime sort of tact) shine more transcendently than during
the past session. He has at no period of his career risen higher
as a Parliamentary speaker, while his management of the House
is equalled only by that of Lord Palmerston. Not in the
zenith of his popularity after the election of 1868 did Gladstone
come near his great rival in personal hold upon the House
of Commons. . . . Disraeli's slow, deliberate rising in the
course of a debate is always the signal for an instant filling up
of the House and a steady settling down to the point of attention, the highest compliments that can be paid to a speaker.
At the outset of his current Premiership, Disraeli fixed upon
a policy of polite consideration, to which he was the more
drawn as certain members of the Ministry he succeeded
were notorious for the brusqueness of their manner. The
addition of a bit of banter and of a dash of serio-comicality
lent a spiciness to his speech which was always relished, and
was never allowed to reach the proportion at which the
mixture left an unpleasant taste upon the Parliamentary
palate. . . . Suffering acutely from gout, Disraeli has
stuck to his post with Spartan-like patience; and one of his
most successful speeches, if not, on the whole, his best speech
of the session—that on the Home Rule question—was delivered
after he had been sitting for four hours with folded arms on
the Treasury Bench, visibly tortured by twinges from his
slippered and swollen feet.[1]

The somewhat acute difference which had arisen between Disraeli and the High Churchmen did not prevent
him from fulfilling an engagement to pay a visit to his
friend, Lord Bath, a conspicuous member of that party,
at Longleat, immediately after the close of the session.
He came direct from Osborne, experiencing on the journey
the embarrassing attentions which await popular states-

[1] Sir Henry Lucy's *Diary of Two Parliaments*, Vol. I., p. 40.

men at the hands of their admirers.   Bath told Mr. George
Russell that Disraeli was the dullest guest he ever entertained at Longleat; and Disraeli's own accounts suggest
that he did not find himself in congenial society.

To Lady Bradford.

LONGLEAT, WARMINSTER, *Aug.* 7.— . . . Osborne was
lovely, its green shades refreshing after the fervent glare of
the voyage, and its blue bay full of white sails.   The Faery
sent for me the instant I arrived.   I can only describe my
reception by telling you that I really thought she was going
to embrace me.   She was wreathed with smiles, and as she
tattled, glided about the room like a bird.   She told me it
was ' all owing to my courage and tact,' and then she said
' To think of your having the gout all the time !   How you
must have suffered !   And you ought not to stand now
You shall have a chair !'

Only think of that !   I remember that *feu* Ld. Derby,
after one of his severest illnesses, had an audience of Her
Majesty, and he mentioned it to me, as a proof of the Queen's
favor, that Her Majesty had remarked to him ' how sorry she
was she cd. not ask him to be seated.'   The etiquette was so
severe.

I remembered all this as she spoke, so I humbly declined the
privilege, saying I was quite well, but wd. avail myself of her
gracious kindness if I ever had another attack. . . .

I have very bad stationery here,[1] but I have sent for some
official stores from D.S. to-day, and shall then get on better.
If you find this a stupid epistle, it is the stationery.   Their
paper, muddy ink, and pens, wh. are made from the geese
on a common, entirely destroy any little genius I have, and
literally annihilate my power of expression. . . .

My travelling from S.hampton to Warminster was very
fatiguing.   I had to wait at S. and also at Salisbury; an hour
at each place.   They had telegraphed along the line to keep
compartments for me, so wherever I stopped there was an
enthusiastic group—' Here he is ' being the common expression,
followed by three times three, and little boys running after
me.   You know how really distressed I am at all this. . And
I had a headache, and wanted a cup of tea, and made fruitless
efforts to get one.   I always found outside of my chamber,
wh. had been lent me by the manager, a watchful band.   I
got a cup of tea at Salisbury, however, from apparently a most
haughty young lady; but I did not do her justice.   She not
only asked me for an autograph, but to write it in her favorite

[1] At Longleat.

work, *Henrietta Temple !* I could have refused the Duchess of Manchester, but absolutely had not pluck to disobey this Sultana. I never felt more ashamed of myself in my life.

At Salisbury, I found Lady Paget, who was going to Longleat with her son, a very young Etonian. Sir Augustus had travelled by an earlier train with the luggage. I cd. not avoid giving her a place in my compartment, and she talked, and with her usual cleverness, the whole way: an hour of prattle on all subjects. . . .

We did not get to L. till 9, and tho' we dressed in ten minutes, people who dine at 8 don't like dining at 9. We were seven at table. . . . I sate by Lady B. but with a racking headache, rare with me, and not in very good spirits, for if Bath was rather furious for your defalcation, I cannot say it added to my happiness. A more insipid, and stupid, and gloomy dinner I never assisted at, and I felt conscious I added my ample quota to the insipidity and the stupidity and the gloom. Lady P[aget] tried to rally the scene, but she had exhausted her resources bet[wee]n Salisbury and Warm[inste]r.

It was only two hours before we all retired, and had I been younger, and still in the days of poetry, I shd. have gone away in the night, wh. I used to do in my youth, when I was disgusted.

This morning things are a little brighter. The Baths are appeased. . . .

Perhaps, and probably, I ought to be pleased. I can only tell you the truth, wh. I always do, tho' to no one else. I am wearied to extinction and profoundly unhappy.

Aug. 8.—. . . Of all the people here, I like best the *châtelaine.* She is very kind and has offered more than once, and unaffectedly, to be my secretary, and copy things for me. Bath says she writes an illegible hand. I rather admire it. It reminds me somewhat of missals and illuminated MSS. . . .

Aug. 11.—. . . Monday (yesterday) Lady Bath drove me to Frome to see Bennett's famous church, with a sanctuary where ' lay people ' are requested not to place their feet, and among other spiritual pageantry, absolutely a Calvary—and of good sculpture. The church is marvellous; exquisitely beautiful, and with the exception of some tawdriness about the high altar, in admirable taste. . . .

The priest, or sacristan, or whatever he was, who showed us over the church, and exhibited the sacred plate, etc., looked rather grimly upon me after my anti-ritualistic speeches; and, as Lady Bath observed, refrained from exhibiting the ' vestments.' But I praised everything, and quite sincerely; and we parted, if not fair friends, at least fair foes. The world found out who was there, and crowded into the church. They evidently were not Bennett's congregation; however, they capped me very much, wh. pleased Lady Bath, who would drive me, in consequence, round the town in triumph. . . .

After leaving Longleat and spending a couple of days at Fonthill and one in London, Disraeli passed most of the early part of the autumn, with the exception of a week at Balmoral, as the guest of Lady Chesterfield at Bretby; though he made a short excursion to the Bradfords at their villa on Lake Windermere, and would have visited them at Weston in October but for the death of Lord Forester, the brother of the two ladies. Although he was seemingly not attacked by gout till the middle of September, his letters suggest that he was in poor health and in poor spirits.

To Lady Bradford.

10, DOWNING STREET, *Aug.* 14.—. . . You seem surprised I went to Fonthill. I went for distraction. I cannot bear being alone, and when I join others, I am wearied. I do not think there is really any person much unhappier than I am, and not fantastically so. Fortune, fashion, fame, even power, may increase, and do heighten, happiness, but they cannot create it. Happiness can only spring from the affections. I am alone, with nothing to sustain me, but, occasionally, a little sympathy on paper, and that grudgingly. It is a terrible lot, almost intolerable. . . .

BRETBY PARK, *Aug.* 20.—. . . I came down here very much out of sorts, but the kindly methodical life here—the regular hours, the tranquillity of the sylvan scene, and a delightful companion, who has the sweetness and simplicity of a flower, have combined much to restore me. And increased tone brings that serenity of mind, wh. ought to content one, instead of those romantic thoughts that tear the heart and spirit, wh. ought to vanish with youth, and certainly ought not to be cherished by any being who pays rates and taxes.

Southey wrote a very remarkable poem on the falls of Lodore, wh. imitates the rush and crash and splashing and hissing of the waters. It is difficult to find his poems anywhere nowadays, but, if they can be found, I should think it must be at Windermere. Consult John Manners anent.

Southey was a poet, but he could not condense or finish. He was gifted with a fatal facility. He was in fact an improvisatore. And this is strange, because as a prose writer he is almost without a rival, and has none superior to him in polish and precision. . . .

BRETBY PARK, *Aug.* 21.—[My letters] are weak, inconsistent, incoherent, and, without meaning it, insincere: the reflex of a restless, perplexed, hampered, and most unhappy spirit. . . . Your sister has thrice, in five days, drawn me aside, to ask if anything had happened, I looked so unhappy. . . .[1]

To Anne Lady Chesterfield.

ST. CATHERINE'S, WINDERMERE, *Aug.* 30.—. . . I visited with interest, the scene of Wordsworth's life and poetry. I shall recur to his, perhaps, not hitherto sufficiently appreciated volumes with much interest after gazing on the mountains, the woods, and waterfalls of Rydal.

All has gone here, on the whole, pretty well: Selina charming, tho' fitful, and my Lord absolutely friendly.

Whatever happens to me in the world I shall always love you.

To Lady Bradford.

BRETBY, *Sept.* 1.—My journey was not very successful, for my train was always too late to fit in with Bradshaw, so I had to wait an hour at Staff[ord] and at Lichfield. But after all, this is not a mischance that ever much disturbs me: one can always think. I got in good time, and they were congratulating me on having a quiet dinner (wh. by the bye I wanted), . . . when, lo and behold, as we were about to sit down to table, Mr. Scott[2] in an affected whisper, audible to everybody, and looking very pompous, announced a messenger from the foreign office on very urgent business. I was obliged to go out; and found matters as he described. Had I been at Weston or Windermere I don't know whether the secret wd. have been kept exactly, for I have told you one or two before this, and I know the Master of the Horse to be very discreet; but here things are different. I read the despatch, and found it utterly impossible to reply to it offhand: it required, however urgent, much deliberation. So I made up my mind to sleep upon it, and send a telegram for the moment. But then I had to telegraph in cypher, and you know what that is, from George Paget, who was a whole morning over one line. However I managed it at last, and tried to return with a smiling and easy mien to my dinner. But, hungry as I was, having touched nothing but my St. Catherine's

---

[1] In answer to this letter, it appears that Lady Bradford called Disraeli 'a humbug.'

[2] Lady Chesterfield's servant.

sandwich, and that before noon, my appetite was nothing to the ravenous eyes of Lady A.,[1] who exhausted all her manœuvres to obtain an inkling of what had occurred.

I had a good dinner all the same, and indulged in some good claret, convincing myself it was a wine favorable to judgment: then we had a rubber which I lost as usual, and my wits were so woolgathering that it was fortunate I did not revoke, as I did at Weston.

I slept very well till five o'ck., when I woke, but with my mind quite clear, and what, at night, had seemed difficulties were all removed; so I opened my shutters and wrote my despatch in pencil in bed. By the time my fire was lit, it was done, and I had nothing left to do but to write it in ink with very few alterations; and the messenger was off by the very earliest train. . . .

You will say ' Here is much ado about nothing. Who cares for his despatches and his telegrams ?'

That is true in a certain sense; but everything interests, if you are interested in a person. I assure you I like to know very much how you are all getting on. You need never want matter in writing to me if you will only give me a bulletin of the sayings and doings of your circle—the one, after all, wh. interests me more than any other family in England. . . .

To Anne Lady Chesterfield.

[AT BRETBY] *Sept.* 2.—A piece of great social news ! Don't tell them directly, but make them guess a little. A member of the late Government, of high rank, and great wealth, has gone over to the Holy Father !

Who is it ? No less a personage than the Marq. of Ripon, K.G. ! ! !

Shall not be able to come down to breakfast, as bag very heavy, and if I don't work now, I shall not get my walk with my dear companion.

From Bretby Disraeli went for his second and final visit to Balmoral, stopping for a week-end with the John Manners at Birnam on the way.

To Lady Bradford.

BALMORAL CASTLE. *Sept.* 10.—. . . The Faery here is more than kind; she opens her heart to me on all subjects, and shows me her most secret and most interesting corre-

[1] Maria Lady Ailesbury, a friend both of Lady Chesterfield's and of Disraeli's, was generally known in society as ' Lady A.'

spondence. She asked me here for a week, but she sent to-day to say that she hoped I wd. not so limit my visit, and that I would remain at least to the end of next week, and so on. . . .

The Derbys dined here yesterday, and with Princess Beatrice and Lady Churchill made up the 8[1]. . . . The Dss. [of Edinburgh] was full of life,[2] asked the Queen at dinner whether she had read *Lothair*. The Queen answered, I thought, with happy promptitude, that she was the first person who had read it. Then the Duchess asked her Gracious Majesty, whether she did not think Theodora a divine character; the Queen looked a little perplexed and grave. It wd. have been embarrassing, had the Dss. not gone on, rattling away, and begun about Mr. Phœbus and the 'two Greek ladies,' saying that for her part she shd. like to live in a Greek isle. . . .

Sept. 12.—. . . I have not been well here, and had it not been for Sir William Jenner, might have been very ill. All is ascribed to my posting in an open carriage from Dunkeld to Balmoral, but the day was delicious, and I was warmly clothed and never apprehended danger. I felt queer on Wednesday, tho' I dined with the Queen on that day. Thursday Sir William kept me to my room. I have never left the Castle once. On Friday I paid Prince Leopold a visit, who wanted to see me, and, later in the day, the Queen sent for me, and I had a very long and most interesting audience. She told me that Sir Wm. had reported to her that I had no fever, and therefore she had sent for me; otherwise she wd. have paid me a visit. She opened all her heart and mind to me, and rose immensely in my intellectual estimation. Free from all shyness, she spoke with great animation and happy expression, showed not only perception, but discrimination, of character, and was most interesting and amusing. She said I looked so well that she thought I cd. dine with her.

But when Sir William came home from his drive with P. Leopold and paid me his afternoon visit, he said the symptoms were not at all good; put me on a mustard poultice on the upper part of my back, gave me some other remedies and said I must not think of dining, or of leaving my room. The remedies have been most successful; an incipient congestion of the lung seems quite removed, and he does not doubt of my being able to travel on Tuesday.

[1] The other four being the Queen, the Duke and Duchess of Edinburgh and Disraeli.

[2] Writing to Lady Chesterfield, Disraeli described the Duchess at dinner on the previous day as 'most lively,' and as breaking through 'all the etiquette of courtly conversation. Even the Queen joined in her vivacity, and evidently is much influenced by her.'

This morning the Queen paid me a visit in my bedchamber. What do you think of that ?[1]

The G. Duchess[2] is in despair at not seeing me: she is reading Froude, and wanted to talk it over with me   The Derbys also came to see me to-day. . . .

You will understand from all this that I am a sort of prisoner of state, in the tower of a castle; royal servants come in and silently bring me my meals; a royal physician two or three times a day to feel my pulse, etc., and see whether I can possibly endure the tortures that await me.   I am, in short, the man in the Iron Masque. . . .

To Lord Salisbury.

BALMORAL CASTLE, *Sept.* 13.—Being here, I attended to your business at once. . . .

Our royal mistress is well, and looks extremely so. She takes the greatest interest in the Ripon incident, and is most curious to ascertain, who was the artist, who cooked so dainty a dish. H.M. believes neither Manning, nor Capel. . . .

The Ld. Chan[cello]r is only a short distance from me, as the crow flies, but a day's journey, from the mountainous ranges.   He wants to see me before I return to the South, but it is difficult.

The Derbys seem quite delighted with Abergeldie and its birchen groves.   Not that the Court see much of them—' they are so devoted to each other.' . . .

From Balmoral Disraeli went back, still unwell, to Bretby, and there on Saturday, September 19, to use his own words, ' fell into the gout, and that very badly.' The attack came in time to prevent his committing a great imprudence.   Zealous to perform his high duties with efficiency, and realising the importance to the Prime Minister of having some first-hand knowledge of a country which, like Ireland, was necessarily so constantly in his mind, he had proposed to spend part of his first vacation after accepting office in a visit to the island.   The arrangement was that he was to arrive in Dublin as the Viceroy's guest on Saturday, October 24, and then visit Killarney, Cork, Waterford, Derry, Giant's Causeway, and Belfast, delivering speeches in the three capital cities,

---

[1] ' What do you think,' Disraeli wrote to Lady Chesterfield, ' of receiving your Sovereign in slippers and a dressing-gown ?'

[2] The Duchess of Edinburgh, who was a Russian Grand Duchess.

and only returning to England just in time for the autumn
Cabinets in the middle of November. It was an anxious
undertaking for a man in his seventieth year, full of gout,
and therefore needing rest between two arduous sessions
instead of a wearisome progress of this kind; and the
nearer the date approached, the more serious the difficulties appeared. 'What am I to speak about, as
politics are out of the question ?' he wrote to Corry on
September 10 from Balmoral. A few days later Derby,
with sound common sense, wrote to dissuade his friend
and leader from carrying the mad scheme through.

From Lord Derby.

ABERGELDIE, ABERDEEN, *Sept.* 15, 1874.—More I think of
your Irish tour, less I like it: and for various reasons.

First you are overdoing yourself. No man can go through
two years of such work as yours, leading the H. of C. and all
the rest of it, without an interval of complete repose. You
are depriving yourself of yours without any strong reason
for so doing that I can see: and in the interest of the party
and the public, I think you are wrong. We ought to be in
for 3 or 4 years, and neither you nor anyone else can keep up
the pace at which you have started for that length of time.

Everybody would understand the case and nobody would
consider you as either invalided or indolent if you put off
your Irish expedition on that ground alone. Indeed a quiet
interval is in your position almost necessary in order to consider what shall be proposed to the Cabinet. When Cabinets
begin it is too late for any other work than discussion of details.

But, apart from personal reasons, what are you to say to
the Irish ? Every question in Ireland whether of the past,
present or future, is a party question. It is not in the power
of man to deal with topics of public interest in such a way as
to please Ultramontanes and Orangemen. The moderates
are few and feeble—what the press is you know. You must
be pressed to do local jobs which you must refuse—to release
political prisoners—to give fixity of tenure in land—and to
receive deputations suggesting, with the utmost loyalty,
some perfectly impracticable modification of Home Rule.
You cannot be decently civil to Catholics without offending
Protestants, and *vice versa*. The only point upon which both
parties agree is the duty of spending more English money on
Irish soil.

Your knowledge will fill up the rough outline which I am

drawing of your difficulties.   And why incur them ?   We are
doing very well.   A moderately extensive programme of well-
considered measures will satisfy Parliament for next year.
There is absolutely not a cry of any kind that has attracted
the least public attention of late.   The only strong feeling that
I can trace in the public mind is anti-Catholic feeling: and that
you cannot gratify and may possibly have to run against in
the course of an Irish progress.

Pray excuse unasked advice: though in fact you did partly
ask for it when we met.   If you modify the large programme
which has been marked out for you, is it not worth considering
whether the postponement of the whole affair, leaving hopes
for another year, will not give less offence than the curtailment of parts ?

Derby's reasoning may have shaken Disraeli's purpose;
in any case the gouty attack at Bretby put the Irish
visit out of the question.   The Queen expressed a hope
that he might ' some other year be able to go there, when
he is quite well, for it would do good '; but the opportunity never recurred.   Consequently Disraeli never set
foot in Ireland; Gladstone was once there, for three
weeks, in October, 1877.   To those who reflect upon the
prolonged contentions of the rivals over Irish policy and
the dominating hold which Ireland obtained over Gladstone's later career, these facts must seem incredible,
were they not true.

To Lady Bradford.

(*In pencil.*)   BRETBY PARK, *Monday* [*Sept.* 21].—I am too
ill to write even to you.   A severe attack of gout has been
the culmination of my trials, and tho' it has removed, or
greatly mitigated, dangerous symptoms, it adds to my suffering
and my prostration.   The dear angel here is more than kindness, but that only makes me more feel what an enormous
outrage on her hospitality is the whole affair. . . .

I sit in silence quite unable to read, musing over the wondrous 12 months that have elapsed since this time last year.
I have had at least my dream.   And if my shattered energies
never rally, wh. considering that these attacks, more or less,
have been going on for 6 months, is what I must be prepared
for, I have at any rate reached the pinnacle of power, and
gauged the sweetest and deepest affections of the heart.
Adieu !

It was nearly a fortnight before Disraeli was able to be moved, and then, after passing through town to consult Sir William Gull, he went home to remain quietly at Hughenden till the November Cabinets were approaching.

To Anne Lady Chesterfield.

HUGHENDEN MANOR, *Oct.* 23.—. . . There is no repose. The Court is a department in itself.

However the Ministry are in great favor. The adieu of the Queen, after the Council, to the Duke of Richmond, was ' I wish you to remain in as long as you possibly can.' He had quickness eno' to reply ' That is exactly, Madam, what I and my colleagues intend to do.'

This letter *really* must be for your own eye and ear. . . .

To Lady Bradford.

HUGHENDEN MANOR, *Oct.* 26.—. . . I like him [M. Corry] very much, better than any man: but, as a rule and except upon business, male society is not much to my taste. Indeed I want to see only one person, whom I never see, and I want to see her always. Otherwise I would rather be alone. Solitude has no terrors for me, and when I am well, has many delights. But one can't be always reading and thinking; one wants sympathy, and the inspiration of the heart. . . .

I have not seen Chas. Greville's book, but have read a good deal of it. It is a social outrage. And committed by one who was always talking of what he called ' perfect gentlemen.' I don't think he can figure now in that category. I knew him intimately. He was the vainest being—I don't limit myself to man—that ever existed; and I don't forget Cicero and Lytton Bulwer; [1] but Greville wd. swallow garbage, and required it. Offended selflove is a key to most of his observations. He lent me a volume of his MS. once to read; more modern than these; I found, when he was not scandalous, he was prolix and prosy—a clumsy, wordy writer. The loan was made *à propos* of the character of Peel, which I drew in George Bentinck's *Life*, and which, I will presume to say, tho' you may think me as vain as Greville for saying so, is the only thing written about Peel wh. has any truth or stuff in it. Greville was not displeased with it, and as a reward,

---

[1] In the corresponding letter of the same date to Lady Chesterfield this phrase takes the more clear-cut form: ' I have read Cicero, and was intimate with Lytton Bulwer.'

and a treat, told me that he wd. confide to me his character
of Peel, and he gave me the sacred volume, wh. I bore with
me, with trembling awe, from Bruton St. to Gros[veno]r Gate.
If ever it appears, you, who have taste for style and expression,
will, I am sure, agree with me that, as a portrait painter,
Greville is not a literary Vandyke or Reynolds: a more
verbose, indefinite, unwieldy affair, without a happy expression, never issued from the pen of a fagged subordinate of the
daily press.[1]

With regard to myself, what I am suffering from is not
gout, but incipient affection in my throat, tho' I doubt not
real gout is at the bottom of it all. I have more confidence
in Leggatt than the other gentlemen you mention. L. says
I ought to go to Buxton, or at least to the sea, and so on, and
not live, as I am doing, among decomposing woods. That
is very true, and I have generally managed to avoid the fall
of the leaf. But the total absence of all comfort or comforts,
that one encounters at an hotel, countervails the happier
atmosphere. One must be at home; and I am going to town,
where I am not surrounded by mighty beeches brown with
impending fate, and limes of amber light, and chestnuts of
green and gold—and every now and then an awful sou'-wester
that brings, in whirling myriads, their beauties to the ground.

In the meantime, I am like Crusoe on his isle, taking infinite
delight in many silent companions. My mittens are a ceaseless charm. I fear they will wear out sooner than you expected,
for they are never off my hands. They keep the hand warm
and yet free. My aneroid is at my side at this moment; not on
my dressing-table, as originally projected, but my writing-
table. I manage it now with the same facility, as Herschel
or Ld. Rosse did their colossal telescopes. If, in my loneliness,
one is tempted sometimes to feel or fancy that some characters
and things we remember are merely a dream, my pencil case
in my waistcoat pocket proves their reality, and if I still
doubted, something is singing, all day long, which is called
' Selina.' [2]

Disraeli's verdict on the Greville Memoirs was endorsed
with great vigour from Balmoral. It is not surprising
that the Queen should have been horrified at the relentless

---

[1] Greville's character of Peel appears in Part II., Vol. III., ch. 31, of the
Memoirs : Disraeli's character of Peel appears in *Lord George Bentinck,*
ch. 17, and is quoted in Vol. I., II., ch. 11, of this biography. The loan of
part of Greville's MS. to Disraeli is mentioned in *Memoirs,* Part II.,
Vol. III., ch. 32.

[2] The mittens, aneroid, pencil case, and singing bird were, of course, all
presents from Lady Bradford.

exposure of the vices and foibles of her royal uncles contained in the first part, which was all that was published in 1874. But Reeve, the editor, was quite impenitent under royal and Ministerial displeasure. Sir Arthur Helps, Disraeli told Lady Bradford, read to Reeve some passages of a letter from the Queen. ' The Queen said, " the book degraded royalty." " Not at all," rejoined Reeve, " it elevates it, by the contrast it offers between the present and the defunct state of affairs," and so on, fighting every point with smiling impudence !'

From Queen Victoria.

BALMORAL, *Nov.* 12,[1] '74.—The Queen thanks Mr. Disraeli for his letters received to-day. She hopes that he is quite well and taking care of himself. But she would strongly advise him not to accustom himself to very hot rooms, for nothing gives people more cold than sitting over a large fire and then going out.

The Queen omitted in her last letter saying how *horrified* and *indignant* she is at this dreadful and really scandalous book of Mr. C. Greville's, who seems to have put down all the gossip which he collected and which, as we well know from the experience of the present day, is totally unreliable. His indiscretion, indelicacy, ingratitude towards friends, betrayal of confidence and shameful disloyalty towards his Sovereign make it *very important* that the book should be severely censured and discredited. The tone in which he speaks of royalty, is unlike anything which one sees in history even, of people hundreds of years ago, and is most reprehensible.

Mr. Reeve however is almost as much to blame considering that he is a servant of the Crown and ought never to have consented to publish such an abominable book.

To Queen Victoria.

WHITEHALL GARDENS, *Nov.* 10,[1] 1874.—Mr. Disraeli with his humble duty to your Majesty:

He thinks your Majesty's critique on the Greville publication, ought to be printed. It condenses the whole case— no, not the whole—' indiscretion, indelicacy, ingratitude.' The book is a social outrage, but what is most flagrant is, that it should be prepared, and published, by two servants of the Crown !

[1] There must be some mistake in the dates of these letters. The second is clearly the answer to the first.

Mr. Disraeli has been revolving in his mind, how some public reprobation of such conduct could be manifested. For this purpose he has wanted to confer with various people—and, unhappily, he has never been able to leave his house since he arrived in town, so he has not been able to go to clubs, or talk with men, who, as Dr. Johnson used to describe them, are ' clubable.' . . .

Mr. Disraeli humbly thanks your Majesty for your Majesty's ever gracious interest in his health.

He assures your Majesty he endeavors to obey all your Majesty's commands in this respect. He never sits over a fire, and he has a thermometer in every room, with instructions never to exceed 63. He fears he is suffering from a gouty habit, which has broken out late in life, but which, now understood, may be conquered with care and diet.

What details for a servant of the Crown to place before a too gracious mistress! His cheek burns with shame. It seems almost to amount to petty treason.

Disraeli had a further attack of gout in Whitehall Gardens in the early part of November, and it was with considerable difficulty that he managed to appear at the Guildhall banquet and to hold the autumn Cabinets. At Guildhall he vindicated, against Gladstone's scepticism, the existence and indeed inevitability of the Conservative working man.

I have been alarmed recently by learning, from what I suppose is the highest Liberal authority, that a Conservative Government cannot endure, because it has been returned by Conservative working men, and a Conservative working man is an anomaly. We have been told that a working man cannot be Conservative, because he has nothing to conserve—he has neither land nor capital; as if there were not other things in the world as precious as land and capital! . . . There are things in my opinion even more precious than land and capital, and without which land and capital themselves would be of little worth. What, for instance is land without liberty ? And what is capital without justice ? The working classes of this country have inherited personal rights which the nobility of other nations do not yet possess. Their persons and their homes are sacred. They have no fear of arbitrary arrests or domiciliary visits.[1] They know that the adminis-

---

[1] It was suggested that Disraeli was indirectly reflecting upon Bismarck, who was employing methods of this kind in his quarrel with Count Arnim, German Ambassador in Paris. Disraeli thought it worth while to dis-

tration of law in this country is pure, and that it is no respecter
of individuals or classes.   They know very well that their
industry is unfettered, and that by the law of this country they
may combine to protect the interests of labour; and they know
that though it is open to all of them to serve their Sovereign
by land or sea, no one can be dragged from his craft or his
hearth to enter a military service which is repugnant to him.
Surely these are privileges worthy of being preserved !   Can
we therefore be surprised that a nation which possesses such
rights should wish to preserve them ?   And if that be the case,
is it wonderful that the working classes are Conservative ?

The exertion of holding the Cabinets was too much
for Disraeli, and in the end of November he had another
attack, almost as severe as that which had prostrated him
at Bretby.

To Lady Bradford.

2, WHITEHALL GARDENS, *Nov.* 23. —. . . I called in
Jenner on Saturday, suffering much in my chest, I believe
from the fogs, wh. have been very bad here.   He insisted on
Bournemouth, but I had intended first to pay a little visit to
you all, wh. wd. have been a consolation in my loneliness;
but last night attacked by gout in my right foot, and cannot
move.

If you write to me sometimes, when you have time or
inclination, I shall be grateful: but I do not press it or expect
it—hardly think it reasonable to wish it.   I can make no
return.   Long suffering—for this has gone on more or less for
many months—and exhaustion, and some chagrin of the heart,
have done their work on me.   Our correspondence has always
been so essentially spontaneous, that I do not wish it to degenerate into forced sentences or the bulletins of an invalid,
which, I know, you do not like, and there we resemble each
other   I cannot write; all my spring is gone. . . .

(*In pencil.*)   *Dec.* 1.—Amid my daily reveries and nightly
dreams, it seemed to me I had only one purpose—to write to
you, and try to convey to you some conclusions, at wh. I had
arrived, as to this strange illness, wh. has harassed me, more
or less, for nine months, and now has reached its climax.   But
when I take up my pencil (your pencil), my mind deserts
me, and I am utterly incapable of expressing thought or

---

claim this interpretation by a *communiqué* in *The Times :* whereupon he
was absurdly accused by the Liberals of subservieacy to Bismarck.   ' No
man in his senses,' wrote Delane to Corry, ' will blame the Premier for
removing a cause for irritation he had not intended to excite.'

feeling when, only a moment before, the thoughts seemed so deep, and the feelings so just and vivid.

But I can be silent no more, if I write only to thank you for your letters. They have always had for me an ineffable charm; being both gay and affectionate, like yr. own happy disposition.

Mine have been different: unreasonable, morose, exacting, discontented. I feel all this now. I will not defend them. I wd. rather leave their vindication to your seraphic idiosyncrasy.

What is exactly to become of me, I don't know. Whether I can rally must be doubtful. To get out of this *repaire* is a necessity, but how I can bear travelling for hours when writing this makes me fall back exhausted on my pillow, I cannot comprehend.

After this last attack Disraeli went, on the recommendation of the Queen as well as of his physicians, to try what Her Majesty called ' the very salubrious air of Bournemouth' for the midwinter weeks. The physicians declared that the sea-air would gradually ' burn the gout poison ' out of his blood. Unfortunately, it was a particularly bitter season. ' How damnable,' wrote Corry on December 19, ' that we should be having the most inclement winter of the decade !' ' The cold is intense here,' Disraeli replied: ' deep snow, and I can't get my rooms up to 60.' Nevertheless the change was successful. He was decidedly better when he left Bournemouth early in January for Crichel; and he was able to tell Rose on January 15: ' I am pretty well; not quite; but much better than I was any day last year.'

To Queen Victoria

B-mouth, *Dec.* 10, 1874.—Mr. Disraeli with his humble duty to your Majesty:

He cannot refrain from thanking your Majesty for your gracious inquiries as to his health.

It is difficult to decide on atmospherical influences under a week, but he thinks he can venture to say, that the visit to this place, which your Majesty yourself deigned to recommend, will turn out a great success.

The weather has been too variable; one day it was like the Corniche, so soft and sunny, the Isle of Wight looming, and

yet not distant, and the waters glittering in the bay-like coast.
But storm has prevailed, and nothing but the bending pines
could have withstood its violence. Mr. Disraeli is on the cliff,
which is a great advantage to him.

He has received the Prince's *Life*,[1] which he is reading with
much interest, particularly as it reaches a period, when he
himself began to take some part in public affairs. Much
of the earlier part he was familiar with from General Grey's
volume. This, however, will be all fresh to the public, and
Mr. Disraeli has no doubt the work will produce a deep, a
pleasing, and an enduring impression. . . .

Dec. 18, 1874.— . . . He began the *Life* towards the
end, being interested in the new matter; then he turned to
other parts to compare the different treatment in the
present, and in the volume compiled by General Grey.
Then he got so interested in the treatment of the subject,
that he began the work regularly from the beginning, and he
can truly say, that it is a most able book, and one that will
endure. There is in the general treatment of the theme an
amenity worthy of the subject. Your Majesty most truly
and justly observes, that the contrast between Mr. Martin's
volume and a too notorious publication is striking; but it is
also beneficial. This book will rally the public tone. After
the turbulent and callous malignity of the Greville Memoirs,
one feels as if an angel had passed through the chamber.
He may be invisible, but one feels, as it were the rustling of
his wings.

To Lady Bradford.

2, WHITEHALL GARDENS, *Jan.* 30, 1875.— . . . I am going
to Hughenden to-day with Monty; and on Tuesday I am going
to Osborne, and to stay there till the Council is held on the
4th. The *Alberta* is to be placed at my disposal, wh. can go
alongside the pier, so I am not to get into an open boat, and
there is a cabin closed in on the deck, where I am to sit during
the passage.

Mr. Corry is to accompany me, and I am forbidden to make
any change in my usual evening costume, as it might give
me cold.

Everything is to be made comfortable for me, and it is hoped
I may stay for two days, in order that I may rest, and, having
the *Alberta*, I may choose my own time.

What do you think of this ? And when will you be so
kind to me ? Fancy Monty a recognised courtier ! The
first private secretary whose existence has been acknowledged
by royal lips. . . .

---

[1] Sir Theodore Martin's *Life of the Prince Consort.*

It was while he was at Bournemouth that Disraeli completed the arrangement for one of the most picturesque features of his first year of office—the offer to Thomas Carlyle of the G.C.B. and a pension. He had been corresponding with Derby in the autumn as to what could be done to honour men of science. 'I wish,' he wrote on October 9, 'we had some comprehensive order like the Legion of Honor. I am sorry that society persists in cheapening a simple knighthood. It satisfied Sir Isaac Newton and Sir Walter Raleigh. Would it satisfy Stokes?'[1] The Government gratified the scientific world by promoting the Arctic Expedition under Sir George Nares. 'Can we do anything for Literature?' wrote Derby on November 28. He suggested that Tennyson and Carlyle were the only conspicuous names; and in pressing Carlyle's claims mentioned that he was, 'for whatever reason, most vehement against Gladstone. . . . Anything that could be done for him would be a really good political investment. What it should be you know best.' Disraeli caught at the idea; he realised the splendour of Carlyle's genius and the reproach of its total neglect by the State; and his imagination supplied the unique distinction[2] which might not unfitly be offered to the *doyen* of English letters.

To Queen Victoria.

B-mouth, *Dec.* 12, 1874.—Mr. Disraeli with his humble duty to your Majesty:

As your Majesty was graciously pleased to say, that your Majesty would sometimes aid him with your advice, he presumes to lay before your Majesty a subject on which he should much like to be favored with your Majesty's judgment.

Your Majesty's Government is now in favor with the scientific world. The Arctic Expedition, and some small grants which may be made to their favorite institutions, will secure their sympathy, which is not to be despised.

Can nothing be done for Literature?

Eminent literary men are so few, that there would be no

---

[1] Professor George Gabriel Stokes, the mathematician and physicist, 1819–1903. He was created a baronet in 1889.

[2] The Order of Merit was not founded until the Coronation of King Edward VII.

trouble as to choice, if any compliment in the way of honor was contemplated. Mr. Disraeli knows only of two authors, who are especially conspicuous at this moment: Tennyson and Carlyle. He has no personal knowledge of either, and their political views are, he apprehends, opposed to those of your Majesty's Government, but that is not to be considered for a moment.

He has an impression, that Mr. Tennyson could sustain a baronetcy, and would like it. Sir Robert Peel offered that distinction to Southey.

Mr. Carlyle is old, and childless, and poor; but he is very popular and respected by the nation. There is no K.C.B. vacant. Would a G.C.B. be too much ? It might be combined with a pension, perhaps, not less than your Majesty's royal grandfather conferred on Dr. Johnson, and which that great man cheerfully accepted, and much enjoyed.

These thoughts are humbly submitted to the consideration of your Majesty, with, Mr. Disraeli hopes, not too much freedom.

The Queen, in Disraeli's words, 'entered into the spirit of the affair'; and he conveyed the offer to Carlyle in a letter conceived in the grand manner, to the composition of which, it is evident from the interlined draft found among his papers, he had devoted considerable labour. As a proffer of State recognition by a literary man in power to a literary man in (so to speak) permanent opposition, it would be difficult to excel it either in delicacy or in dignity. Fully to appreciate its magnanimity, it must be remembered that Carlyle had always treated Disraeli as a ' conscious juggler,' ' a superlative Hebrew conjurer.' ' He is the only man,' Carlyle wrote to John Carlyle, ' I almost never spoke of except with contempt; and if there is anything of scurrility anywhere chargeable against me, he is the subject of it; and yet see, here he comes with a pan of hot coals for my guilty head.'

To Thomas Carlyle.

Confidential. BOURNEMOUTH, *Dec.* 27, 1874.—A Government should recognise intellect. It elevates and sustains the tone of a nation. But it is an office which, adequately to fulfil, requires both courage and discrimination, as there is a chance of falling into favoritism and patronising mediocrity, which, instead of elevating the national feeling, would eventually degrade and debase it.

In recommending Her Majesty to fit out an Arctic expedition, and in suggesting other measures of that class, her Government have shown their sympathy with science. I wish that the position of high letters should be equally acknowledged; but this is not so easy, because it is in the necessity of things that the test of merit cannot be so precise in literature as in science.

When I consider the literary world, I see only two living names which, I would fain believe, will be remembered; and they stand out in uncontested superiority. One is that of a poet; if not a great poet, a real one; and the other is your own.

I have advised the Queen to offer to confer a baronetcy on Mr. Tennyson, and the same distinction should be at your command, if you liked it. But I have remembered that, like myself, you are childless, and may not care for hereditary honors. I have therefore made up my mind, if agreeable to yourself, to recommend Her Majesty to confer on you the highest distinction for merit at her command, and which, I believe, has never yet been conferred by her except for direct services to the State. And that is the Grand Cross of the Bath.

I will speak with frankness on another point. It is not well that, in the sunset of life, you should be disturbed by common cares. I see no reason why a great author should not receive from the nation a pension as well as a lawyer and a statesman. Unfortunately the personal power of Her Majesty in this respect is limited; but still it is in the Queen's capacity to settle on an individual an amount equal to a good fellowship, and which was cheerfully accepted and enjoyed by the great spirit of Johnson, and the pure integrity of Southey.

Have the goodness to let me know your feelings on these subjects.

The letter to Tennyson reproduced the phraseology of the early portion of that to Carlyle, though it naturally did not draw a distinction between a 'real' poet and a 'great' one. Both authors refused. Tennyson had had a similar offer from Gladstone nearly a year before, and explained to both Prime Ministers in succession that he could not accept a baronetcy for himself, but would be grateful if such an honour could be secured for his son. Nine years later the poet was raised to the peerage on Gladstone's recommendation. Carlyle's answer was reported to Derby by Disraeli.

II.   23

To Lord Derby.

B-MOUTH, *Jan.* 1, '75.—. . . Alas! the Philosopher of Chelsea, tho' evidently delighted with the proposal, and grateful in wondrous sentences, will accept of nothing— 'Titles of honor, of all degrees, are out of keeping with the tenor of my poor life,' and as for money—' after years of rigorous and frugal, but, thank God, never degrading poverty,' it has become 'amply abundant, even super-abundant in this later time.'

Nevertheless the proposal is 'magnanimous and noble, without example in the history of governing persons with men of letters' and a great deal more in the same highly-sublimated Teutonic vein.

I have not received any reply from Tennyson, but this is a secondary affair.

I think of getting away from this on the 4th and shall stay a week at Crichel and then to Westminster. Northcote is with me for a day or two, preparing for the Cabinets; and the Ld. Chan[cello]r is a great assistance to me. . . .

For the moment Carlyle recognised that he had misjudged Disraeli. Lady Derby, whom Carlyle credited, perhaps rightly, with the origination of the idea, wrote to Disraeli on January 15: 'I saw old Mr. Carlyle to-day, and he scarcely knew how to be grateful enough for the mark of attention you had paid him. I assure you it was quite touching to see and hear his high appreciation of the offer.' But, save that he continued to prefer Disraeli to Gladstone, the feeling was transient; and when, a few years later, he dissented from Ministerial policy in the East, he reverted once again to his earlier language, and was not ashamed to talk of the Prime Minister as 'a cursed old Jew, not worth his weight in cold bacon,'[1] 'an accursed being, the worst man who ever lived.'[2]

[1] *Life of James Macdonell*, p. 379.
[2] *Some Hawarden Letters*, p. 15.

CHAPTER X.

SOCIAL REFORM.

1874-1875.

The main Government programme of Social Reform was definitely entered upon in the second session of the Parliament. ' In legislation,' wrote Disraeli to Hicks Beach in December, 1874, ' it is not merely reason and propriety which are to be considered, but the temper of the time.' The time was propitious. Though there were disquieting symptoms underlying the situation abroad, the surface was undisturbed, and there was no immediate reason to anticipate any foreign complication; while at home the defeated Opposition showed as yet no sign of cohesion or recovery. Social improvement and not revolutionary change was what people demanded; and, to give effect to this desire, Labour members, Alexander Macdonald and Thomas Burt, the forerunners of a mighty political force, had been returned for the first time to Parliament. The general tendency of the projected legislation was settled, on Disraeli's initiative, early in the history of the Government; and as the autumn Cabinets of 1874 approached, the Prime Minister asked his principal colleagues for further suggestions. The letter which he wrote to Salisbury is typical.

To Lord Salisbury.

HUGHENDEN MANOR, *Oct.* 12, 1874.—I hardly know, whether you have left your *château sur la Manche*,[1] but doubt not this will reach you, somehow or other.

[1] Salisbury had a villa at Dieppe, where he spent the autumn

In about a month we ought to commence our November Cabinets. It would be of great service to me, and very agreeable also, if you would favor me, some time previously, and confidentially, with your general views as to our situation, and any suggestions you can make as to our future course.

I saw the French Ambassador,[1] as I passed thro' town—an intimate acquaintance, and more, of forty years. He is, as you know, experienced in English politics. He said, ' In your internal situation, I do not see a single difficulty.' I trust he is correct.

The position of affairs in Ireland must, however, demand our attention. The group of laws, called the Coercion Acts, are on the eve of expiring—but we could scarcely arrive at a definite resolution on the subject until the meeting of Parliament.

Is there any question connected with home affairs that occurs to you, wh. has not been touched on in our councils ? I believe, that Mr. Secy. X[2] is working at a Dwellings Bill. . . .

The Cabinets were very harmonious, the only measure, a *remanet* from the past session, which might have caused friction being judiciously shelved in a manner which showed that Salisbury bore no lasting grudge against either chief or colleagues.

To Queen Victoria.

2, WHITEHALL GARDENS, *Nov.* 12, 1874.—Mr. Disraeli with his humble duty to your Majesty :

The Cabinet met to-day, and sate two hours, and did a great deal of work, and all satisfactory.

In the first place, not in order, but in importance, the question of the endowed schools was brought forward, so that there might be no future misconception on the subject.

Lord Salisbury spoke with much moderation and said, that he would be satisfied with a compromise, which Mr. Hardy had suggested in the Cabinet at the end of the session. This was conciliatory, but not satisfactory to those, who deprecated any further legislation at all.

To our great surprise and relief, Mr. Hardy said that he thought it, on the whole, best, not to take any further action in the matter, particularly as there was a new Commission, whose views we ought to become acquainted with.

The Lord Chancellor strongly supported Mr. Hardy, and,

---

[1] The Comte de Jarnac. See Vol. I., p. 988.
[2] R. A. Cross, the Home Secretary.

no one then speaking, Lord Salisbury said, that neither in this, nor any subject, did he wish to urge his views against a majority of the Cabinet, and one apparently unanimous. He was prepared, therefore, to do nothing.

Upon which Lord Derby exclaimed ' Thank God, we have got rid of the only rock a-head !' . . .

Nov 15.—. . . The Cabinet was engaged yesterday in considering the measure for the Improvement of the Dwellings of the People.   This is likely to be a very popular and beneficial measure, but will require great care.   Your Majesty's Ministers must be cautious not to embark in any building speculation: but nothing of this kind is contemplated.   This, and some other measures completing the code of sanitary legislation, took up the whole sitting. . . .

These meetings have been eminently satisfactory: unanimous and friendly, and never the slightest indication of there being two parties in the Cabinet.

The path of the Government was still further smoothed, as the session approached, by Gladstone's definite retirement from the Opposition leadership, and the choice in his place, as leader of the Liberal party in the House of Commons, of a politician of weight and judgment rather than of aggressive force—Lord Hartington, the heir of the Whig house of Cavendish.   Disraeli told Lady Chesterfield ' the new joke about the Whigs. . .   You know Ld. Derby, *père*, said the Whigs were *dished;* they say now they are Caven*dished.*'

To Lady Bradford.

2, WHITEHALL GARDENS, *Feb.* 2.—. . . The political world was never more amusing: I am glad that Harty-Tarty has won the day.   Never was a party in such a position, and, tho' I never would confess it to anybody but yourself, never was a man in a prouder position than myself.   It never happened before, and is not likely to happen again.   Only those who are acquainted with the malignity of Glad[stone] to me thro' a rivalry of 5 and 20 years, can understand this. . .

To Queen Victoria.

2, WHITEHALL GARDENS, *Feb.* 5, 1875, *Friday night.*— Mr. Disraeli with his humble duty to your Majesty:

The House of Commons reassembled to-day, in unusual numbers, the benches on both sides being thronged.

Lord Hartington took his seat at the last moment; ½ past four; and was cheered by both sides. Mr. Forster[1] and your Majesty's humble correspondent were also received by their friends with great cordiality.

The Address was moved by Hon. Edward Stanhope in a speech of striking ability. Instead of a mechanical comment on each paragraph of the Royal Speech, Mr. Stanhope generalised on two great subjects, your Majesty's Colonial Empire, and the Health of your People. He produced a great effect. He commenced by an allusion to the illness of H.R.H. Prince Leopold, and to your Majesty's anxiety, than which few things could be more graceful and felicitous.

The Member for Glasgow, who seconded the Address, unfortunately spoke in the language of his country, and, so, soon lost the House; but all his observations were sensible and acute, and worthy of a descendant of Bailie Nicol Jarvie. The new houses in Glasgow for the artisans, and the polluted state of the famous Clyde, gave him a becoming position in the business of the evening.

Lord Hartington, well-prepared and thoughtful, made a reputable appearance, and the general impression on both sides was favorable to the effort.

Mr. Disraeli closed the debate, as no one would rise, though there had been rumors that Mr. Fitzgerald was about to call the consideration of the House to the contemplated invasion of Holland by Prince Bismarck. The House was in good spirits and good temper, and there seems the prospect of an active, but serene session.

Writing to Lady Chesterfield, Disraeli described Hartington's *début* as leader more familiarly. ' Harty-Tarty did very well; exactly as I expected he would; sensible, dullish, and gentlemanlike. Lowe said, " At last I have heard a proper leader's speech; all good sense, and no earnest nonsense." '

In the favourable atmosphere thus created, the Ministerial programme of social legislation was auspiciously launched. *Sanitas sanitatum, omnia sanitas* had been Disraeli's watchword. ' A policy of sewage,' the Liberals had sniffed in reply. Even if limited to sewage, such a policy was praiseworthy; but, as Disraeli pointed out

[1] W. E. Forster, afterwards Chief Secretary for Ireland, had refused to let his name be submitted in competition with Hartington's for the Liberal leadership.

at the close of the session, sanitary reform, ' that phrase so little understood,' included ' most of the civilising influences of humanity.' Disraeli had given the artisans the vote in 1867. Gladstone had prevailed on them to use it in effecting great political changes in the institutions of the country, and particularly of Ireland. What they really wanted, in Disraeli's opinion, and what in the General Election of 1874 they set themselves to obtain, were better, healthier, more humanising conditions in their own daily life. They wanted sanitary and commodious homes; they wanted regulation of their occupations so as to minimise risk to life and health and to prevent excessive toil for their women and children; they wanted freedom of contract and equality before the law with their employers; they wanted encouragement and security for their savings; they wanted easy access to light and air and all the beneficent influences of nature. These were their principal wants in the sphere of material sanitation; but they had no less need of what may perhaps be called mental and spiritual sanitation—a sphere which Disraeli was little likely to overlook; they wanted the provision of sound education and the enlargement of religious opportunity.

In regard to elementary education and local government, Gladstone's Ministry had done good work; but otherwise the direct and obvious needs of the working population had been neglected by the Liberals, still dominated as a party by the doctrines of *laisser faire*. Indeed, Forster's great Education Bill would never have passed into law, in view of the bitter hostility of Radicals and Dissenters, had it not received the general support of Disraeli and the Conservatives. Another working-class problem which Gladstone's Ministry had touched, that of the relations between employers and workmen, they had conspicuously failed to solve. In one single session, 1875, Disraeli and his colleagues vigorously attacked the ' condition of the people ' question in three main branches, housing, savings, and relations of master and man, effecting in each case a striking improvement in the law; and there was none of the working-class needs enumerated above that was not to a large extent supplied before the Tory Government were expelled from office.

The Minister chiefly responsible for this social legislation was the Home Secretary, Richard Cross, the shrewd Lancashire lawyer and man of business who frequently figures in Disraeli's correspondence as ' Mr. Secy. X '; and, after him, Northcote, the Chancellor of the Exchequer. The homes of the poor were dealt with first of all; and an entirely new departure was made in the Artisans' Dwellings Bill, which for the first time called in public authorities to remedy the defects of private dwelling-houses. By its provisions local authorities in large towns were empowered to remove existing buildings for sanitary reasons and replace them by others, the new buildings to be devoted to the use of artisans. True to his rigid economic doctrine, the eminent Radical, Fawcett, scoffed at the proposal; and asked why Parliament should facilitate the housing of working men and not that of dukes ? But the artisans themselves and the public at large welcomed this honest attempt to deal with the rookeries which disgraced our urban civilisation, and which made decent life almost impossible for those who dwelt in them. When excessive demands for compensation impeded the working of the scheme, the Government passed in 1879 an Amending Bill providing that, if overcrowding had created a nuisance, compensation should be fixed on the value of the house after abatement of the nuisance, so that grasping and callous owners should not profit by their misdeeds.

Savings were promoted and secured by a Friendly Societies Bill, in Northcote's charge. This struck a mean between the extremes of too great State interference and of insufficient protection. It left the Societies a wide measure of self-management, but insured the adoption of sound rules, effective audit, and rates of payment sufficient to maintain solvency. It established

the Friendly Societies, and with them the people's savings
on a satisfactory basis.

But the most important legislation of the session
dealt with the relation of master and man. Hitherto
the workman had been severely handicapped in his contentions with his employer about wages and conditions
of service by two rules of law coming down from a state
of society antecedent to the industrial epoch. In the
first place, breach of contract by the workman was regarded, and punished, as a criminal offence, while the
employer in a like case was only liable in the civil courts;
and, in the second place, the doctrine of ' conspiracy '
among workmen was applied in such a way as to cover
the normal actions of trade unions, and to bring their
promoters within reach of the criminal law. By two Bills
which Cross introduced, in pursuance of the report of
the Royal Commission of the previous year, both these
wrongs were righted. The one made employers and
workmen equal before the law as regards labour contracts, constituting breach of contract merely a civil
offence on the part of a workman as it had always been
on the part of an employer. The other made ' conspiracy ' as applied to trade disputes no longer a crime,
except when it was for the purpose of committing what
would be a crime if done by one person. These two Acts,
said a Trade Union Manual of Labour Laws of the day,
were the charter of the social and industrial freedom of
the working classes; and the Labour member, Alexander
Macdonald, in the House, and the Labour Congress
formally in the autumn, thanked the Government
warmly for passing them.

The Acts already described were by no means the
whole crop garnered by the Government in this fertile
session of constructive social legislation. The interests
of agricultural tenants were not forgotten, but Disraeli
himself advocated and secured the passage through the
House of Commons of a Bill by which the tenant obtained
compensation for unexhausted improvements, a presump-

tion of law being created in his favour, while at the same
time freedom of contract between landlord and tenant was
preserved. Moreover, the protection of merchant seamen
from the dangers of unseaworthy ships was undertaken in
circumstances to which we shall recur. Finally, the Government, completing in this field their predecessors' work, consolidated the whole sanitary code in the Public Health Act—
the starting-point for all subsequent amendment in detail.

After 1875 there was never again, during the lifetime
of the Government, a session untroubled by serious
foreign or imperial complications; but, though the pace
was necessarily slower, steady progress was made throughout with social reform. The greatest and most important
work of all was to put the coping-stone on that edifice
of factory legislation which Shaftesbury had gradually
reared, with the steady support of Disraeli and of ' Young
England,' in the teeth of the bitter opposition of Bright
and the Manchester School. In their very first session,
1874, the Government had remedied the wrong done
in 1850, when the ten hours' day which Parliament had
decreed in 1847 for women and children was for administrative reasons enlarged, in face of strong opposition
by Disraeli and John Manners, to a ten-and-a-half hours'
day.[1] Fifty-six hours a week, or ten hours on five week-
days and six on Saturday, was the total allowed by the Act
of 1874; and even this modification was opposed by the
individualist Fawcett, and, in the division lobby, by 79
Liberals. Then in 1878 the whole intricate series of
factory laws were brought under review, improved, and
codified by a Consolidation Act, of which Shaftesbury
spoke in the Lords with unbounded satisfaction. He
said that he was lost in wonder at the amount of toil,
of close investigation, and of perseverance involved in its
preparation; two millions of people in this country
would bless the day when Cross was appointed Home
Secretary. Nor were the Factory Acts the only measures
passed by this Government ameliorating the circum-

[1] See Vol. I., p. 1070.

stances of labour. Hosiery manufacture was brought under the Truck Acts in 1874; provision for inspecting and regulating canal boats was made in 1877; and in 1876 permanent and humane conditions were laid down for merchant shipping.

In these ways the Government effected a notable improvement in the conditions of labour; but it was on the old lines of Shaftesbury's movement. In another field they broke new ground. They reversed the old policy of the Enclosure Acts, which encouraged the conversion of common land into private and therefore presumably productive occupation; and, in view of the rapid development of the urban population and the necessity of securing for it the enjoyment of grass and light and air, prevented by an Act of 1876 any further enclosure save where it would be a public as well as a private benefit, and promoted free access to commons and their use as public playgrounds. In a similar spirit, in 1878, Ministers secured, by the Epping Forest Act, the unenclosed portion of that wild tract on the verge of East London to the use of the public for ever. In these acts they were putting into effect a policy in which George John Shaw-Lefevre, afterwards Lord Eversley, and Henry Fawcett, so often a foe to Disraeli's social legislation, were pioneers; but both these reformers opposed the Enclosure Bill, because it was not, in their opinion, sufficiently drastic. With the like object of preserving the bounty of nature free and uncontaminated for the people's enjoyment Ministers passed in 1876 the Rivers Pollution Act, absolutely prohibiting the introduction of solid matter into rivers, securing them from further pollution by sewage, and imposing upon manufacturers the liability to render harmless the liquid flowing from their works. Here, as so often in their sanitary legislation, the strongest opposition with which Ministers met was from an eminent Radical—in this instance Dilke.

While passing these measures of material sanitation,

the Government in no way neglected the mental and spiritual health of the people. Indeed, their record in the promotion of education was a substantial one. In 1876 they widely extended the benefit of elementary educa-. tion by a Bill amending Forster's Act of 1870; in 1877 they reformed by the agency of statutory commission the Universities of Oxford and Cambridge, making the revenues of the Colleges more available for educational purposes: while in 1878 and 1879 they materially improved Irish education—university, secondary, and elementary— first, by establishing an examining and degree-giving Royal University to meet in some degree the claims of the Roman Catholics; next, by taking a million from the Irish Church fund to encourage secondary education by means of exhibitions to successful students and of grants to managers of efficient schools; and finally by establish- ing out of the same fund a proper system of pensions for national school teachers. In the sphere of spiritual sanitation, besides the respect for the religious needs of the people which a critical body of Dissenters and secularists in Parliament found only too clearly expressed in the terms of the English educational Bills, the Govern- ment encouraged the Church of England to extend her usefulness by extending her episcopate as advocated by Disraeli himself in 1864; passing Bills for the creation of new dioceses of St. Albans and Truro in 1875 and 1876, and a more general Bill in 1878, under which no fewer than four additional sees, Liverpool, Newcastle, Wake- field, and Southwell, were authorised. It was the greatest ecclesiastical reform since the Reformation, said Tait, the Archbishop of Canterbury, in the House of Lords.

Such in general scope was the code of social and sanitary legislation which Disraeli's great Ministry established for the people of this country. It took the practical pressing needs of the working population one by one, and found a remedy for them, without inflicting hardship on any other class, or affecting our historical institutions in any way, save to strengthen their hold on popular affections.

' The palace is not safe, when the cottage is not happy,'
Disraeli had said at a Wynyard Horticultural Show in
1848; and he did his best in the 1874-1880 Ministry to
make the one safe by making the other happy. Well
might Alexander Macdonald tell his constituents in 1879,
' The Conservative party have done more for the working
classes in five years than the Liberals have in fifty.'
The work then done has had of course to be extended
and supplemented in many respects, but in its main outlines it has stood the test of time. The aspirations of
Sybil and ' Young England,' the doctrines in which
Disraeli had ' educated ' his party for thirty years, the
principles laid down in the great speeches of 1872, were
translated into legislative form; it was Tory democracy
in action. Gorst, who, owing to his position as party
organiser, was in close touch with Disraeli during these
years, has expounded in an impressive passage[1] what he
understood the domestic policy of his ' ancient master '
to be.

The principle of Tory democracy is that all government
exists solely for the good of the governed; that Church and
King, Lords and Commons, and all other public institutions
are to be maintained so far, and so far only, as they promote
the happiness and welfare of the common people; that all
who are entrusted with any public function are trustees, not
for their own class, but for the nation at large; and that the
mass of the people may be trusted so to use electoral power,
which should be freely conceded to them, as to support those
who are promoting their interests. It is democratic because
the welfare of the people is its supreme end; it is Tory because
the institutions of the country are the means by which the end
is to be attained.

It is a proof of Disraeli's greatness, and of the soundness of his conception, that the stamp printed by him
on Tory policy has persisted, though it has at times
been obscured by accretions of class and party interest.
Gorst, indeed, whose relations with his party became
increasingly uncomfortable until he finally quitted it,

[1] In a letter in *The Times* of Feb. 6, 1907.

held that only Randolph Churchill and his immediate comrades carried on the Tory democratic tradition. This tradition was perhaps not the aspect of Disraeli's work that specially appealed to his successor, Salisbury. But circumstances drove Salisbury into a close alliance with Chamberlain and Chamberlain's school of social reformers, and thus powerfully reinforced all the progressive elements of the Tory party. The result has been, to take only a few conspicuous instances, that it is to that party that the people of this country owe the popular reconstitution of county government and of London government, the freeing of elementary education, the consolidation of the Factory Acts in 1901, the enormous educational advance of Mr. Balfour's Act of 1902, and the large and varied programme of social legislation carried through by Mr. Baldwin's 1924 Government. It may be added that the intimate association of Tory leaders with Labour representatives in Mr. Lloyd George's Ministry of 1916 was an arrangement which largely carried into effect the ideals of *Sybil*.

It has sometimes been suggested that because Disraeli left the conduct of the Ministerial measures of social reform mainly in the very competent hands of Cross and Northcote, therefore his own share in this beneficent legislation was little or none, and all the credit should be given to his lieutenants. In view of the facts, this is an untenable theory. Disraeli was no *roi fainéant* in his Cabinet; on the contrary, by the testimony both of colleagues and of opponents, he was, in matters which interested him, himself the Government. But from his first experience of Ministerial leadership in 1852 he had adopted the practice of leaving his colleagues to manage by themselves the conduct of Bills affecting their own departments, and of not intervening himself save at critical moments. A system of Ministerial devolution, deliberately adopted when he was in the prime of manhood, would be all the more strictly followed at a time when approaching old age and recurrent gout made it imperative for him to husband his physical resources. His correspondence with the Queen and with his friends confirms in detail what was already sufficiently apparent from his public speeches, especially those at the close of the 1875 session: that the carrying into effect of the programme of social policy outlined in 1872 was not less his work than the programme itself.

We have seen how he wrote of the Artisans' Dwellings Bill to the Queen; to Lady Bradford he boasted of his social reforms as 'a policy round which the country can rally.' He showed his personal interest in housing problems by attending, as Prime Minister, in June, 1874, the opening by Shaftesbury of a 'workmen's city,' at Lavender Hill, built by a limited company having shareholders of all ranks from dukes to bricklayers; and then he had said that the best security for civilisation was the dwelling. 'It is the real nursery of all domestic virtues, and without a becoming home the exercise of those virtues is impossible.' He had added that the experience gained at Lavender Hill might 'guide the councils of the nation in that enterprise which I believe is impending in this country on a great scale, of attempting to improve the dwellings of the great body of the people.' With the labour legislation of the 1875 session his personal connection was especially close. He had been studying the labour laws at Hughenden in the autumn of 1873, and had asked Hardy at that time for a memorandum on the law of conspiracy as being a subject that 'will press us.' We have his own definite statement that on this subject he converted to his policy a hesitating Cabinet.

To Lady Bradford.

2, WHITEHALL GARDENS, *June* 29.—. . . I cannot express to you the importance of last night. It is one of those measures, that root and consolidate a party. We have settled the long and vexatious contest bet[wee]n capital and labor. It will have the same effect on the great industrial population 'on the other side Trent' wh. the Short Time Bill had in the West Riding and Lancashire.

I must tell you what I will tell to no other being, not even the Faery, to whom I am now going to write a report of the

memorable night, that when Secy. X explained his plan to
the Cabinet, many were agst. it, and none for it but myself;
and it was only in deference to the P. Min[iste]r that a decision was postponed to another day.　In the interval the thing
was better understood and managed.

To Queen Victoria.

2, WHITEHALL GARDENS, *June* 29, 1875.—Mr. Disraeli with
his humble duty to your Majesty:

The proceedings in the House of Commons were so important
last night, that he feels it his duty to furnish your Majesty
with a memorandum of them.

The ' Labor Laws ' of the Government, contained in two
bills, were read a second time with not only approbation, but
with general enthusiasm.　The representative working men,
like Macdonald, and the great employers of labor, represented
by Mr. Tennant, the member for Leeds, and othe s, equally
hailed these measures as a complete and satisfactory solution
of the greatest question of the day; the relations between
Capital and Labor.

Mr. Lowe and Mr. Forster spoke in the warmest terms of
the measures, and the latter said that, after passing such
Bills, Her Majesty's Government need have no apprehension
of their reception during the recess, and that all their opponents must join in the general commendation of the country.

Mr. Disraeli believes, that this measure, settling all the long
and long-envenomed disputes between ' master and servant,'
is the most important of the class, that has been carried in
your Majesty's long and eventful reign: more important, he
thinks, because of more extensive and general application,
than even the Short Time Acts, which have had so beneficial
an effect in softening the feelings of the working multitude.

He is glad, too, that this measure was virtually passed on
your Majesty's Coronation Day. . . .

As the Prime Minister took little personal part in
recommending to the House of Commons the social
legislation which owed so much to his initiative, the
dramatic scenes of the session were few, and were mostly
concerned with issues of very secondary importance.
Questions of privilege, in lieu of more vital matters,
loomed large, and the Opposition coquetted with the
discontented Irish in raising difficulties where Disraeli's
strong sense of the dignity of the House of Commons led

him to hold a straight course. The House supported him
in refusing to allow John Mitchel, an unpurged felon,
elected for an Irish constituency, to take his seat; in
allowing Kenealy, the counsel whose outrageous methods
in conducting the defence of the Tichborne claimant
had caused his profession to cast him out, to advance,
as a duly elected and unconvicted member, to the table
of the House and take the oath—in spite of his inability
to get any fellow-member to introduce him; in condemning Kenealy's unworthy agitation against the judges who
decided against him, and in declining to pay the smallest
attention to his ridiculous contention that a private jest
of Lord Chief Justice Cockburn's at a dinner-table was
evidence of a fixed determination to condemn the plaintiff;
and, further, in refusing to abandon offhand, because of
an indiscreet enforcement of privilege claims, the ancient
privilege of Parliament, as against the press. His letters
to the Queen and his friends give some idea of the vicissitudes of the session.

To Lady Bradford.

2, WHITEHALL GARDENS, *Feb.* 17, 1875.—. . . Yesterday,
when I could well have been spared such trifling trouble, was
taken up with a struggle betn. Parliamentary privilege and
semi-royal prerogative.

I was engaged to dine with the Speaker, whom I threw over,
as the phrase is, for the P. of W., alleging *command.* The
Speaker wd. not take my excuse, alleging that there was no
' command ' except from the Sovereign; that a dinner to the
Ministry without the P.M. was a mockery, and that he must
vindicate the authority of the Chair.

The Prince behaved very well. I was rather afraid, and
prepared he wd. be annoyed. Monty, who was pretty well,
was of great use to me. He saw Knollys and explained the
painful situation, and after saw the Prince, who had been
hunting. The Prince said it was a grand party; all the Ambassadors and the Derbys, etc., and that he wanted the Prime
Minister; that he thought the Speaker always dined on Saturday (in wh. he was right; this is an innovation) but he felt
the importance of the occasion and so released me. Monty
was with him twenty minutes or so, and he was amiable
and agreeable. In the evening came a large card, and a note

from Knollys, saying the Prince thought I cd. be represented
at the dinner by no one better than by my faithful Secy.
Monty is quite in his stirrups, and has no doubt that all
the Prince's banditti, at the Marlboro' Club, will be very
jeal[ous]. . . .

To Anne Lady Chesterfield.

2, WHITEHALL GARDENS, *Feb*. 19.—. . . I could not
write yesterday, for it was a day of great trouble and anxiety.
The Opposition chiefs had signified their intention to support
my resolution against the rebel, Mitchel; but only just before
the meeting of the House I heard that Harcourt and Lowe
had got round Ld. Hartington, and persuaded him to support,
as an amendment, a committee to inquire. This, if carried,
would have been a great blow, and it was supposed, that there
was a chance, and not a bad one, of its being carried.

If I had accepted the amendment, in lieu of my own uncompromising Resolutions, the humiliation of the Government would have been very great.

The result showed that I had not miscalculated the spirit
of the Ho. of Commons, and the Opposition chiefs, while taking
an unpatriotic course to please the Irish rebels, sustained an
ignominious overthrow. There has seldom been a greater
triumph for a Minister than yesterday. After dividing on
the pretence of adjourning the debate, and getting beaten by a
majority of more than 160, they allowed my Resolutions to
pass *nemine contradicente*. . . .

To Lady Bradford.

W[HITEHALL], *Feb*. 26.—. . . We did well in the House
last night, and carried the second reading of our Friendly
Societies Bill. That, with the Artisans' Dwellings Bill, is the
second measure of social improvement that I think we shall
now certainly pass. It is important, because they indicate
a policy round wh. the country can rally.

The question who shall be Serg[ean]t-at-Arms in the House
of Commons, is agitating political society, and is in a strange
quandary. . . . In brief, Ld. Hertford nominated his son-
in-law (Erskine[1] I think), and sent in his name to the Queen.
The House of Commons signed a Memorial to Her Majesty,
praying the Queen to bestow the office on Gosset,[2] wh.
they intended the Speaker to present. He disapproved the
Memorial, as an interference with the prerogative, but said

---

[1] Sir H. D. Erskine, Sergeant-at-Arms from 1885 to 1915.
[2] Then the Deputy-Sergeant, who was, Disraeli told Lady Chesterfield,
'a great favorite with all parties,' and had served for thirty-five years.

he wd. represent the unanimous feeling of the House to the Primo, etc., etc.

So I wrote to the Queen and put the matter before her, never anticipating what wd. happen. Last night, I received her reply. She has thrown over Ld. Hertford, and leaves me to communicate her gracious favor to the Commons, the son-in-law of Ld. Hertford to have the deputy place. I have not told a human being except you, as I wish, if possible, to spare Ld. H. and give him a golden occasion to be gracious. . . .

To Queen Victoria.

2, WHITEHALL GARDENS, *March* 5, 1875.—Mr. Disraeli with his humble duty to your Majesty:

The large majority of your Majesty's Government, on the Army Exchange Bill, was sustained last night, and it is rumored, that the future opposition will be slight.

There is a strong party, in both Houses, which desires the restoration to the House of Lords of their position as Court of Ultimate Appeal.

An Act to abolish this function, so far as England is concerned, has already passed, but does not come into force until next November.

The House of Lords is still the Court of Ultimate Appeal for Ireland and Scotland, and it is not probable that the Bills introduced, to assimilate those countries to England, will pass.

The anomaly, then, will be established of separate Courts of Final Appeal for different parts of your Majesty's dominions.

To remove this anomaly, it is understood that Mr. Walpole will bring the matter before the House of Commons, with the view of practically rescinding the English Act, that comes into play in November. The circumstances are rather critical.

Mr. Disraeli attended, yesterday, a meeting of the peers, at the Duke of Richmond's, and succeeded so far as to induce them to take a prudent and moderate course for the moment, but their spirit was high and somewhat unmanageable. Peers, who, two years ago, showed the greatest apathy on the subject, have become quite headstrong. . . .

March 17.—. . . Yesterday was a great day in the House of Commons. In consequence of the tactics of delay on the part of the Opposition, Mr. Disraeli was obliged to have recourse to a morning sitting; unprecedented before Easter— so yesterday the House was sitting all day.

But the greater event was—the return from Elba: Mr. Gladstone not only appeared, but rushed into the debate. The House, very full, was breathless. The new members

trembled and fluttered like small birds when a hawk is in the
air. As the attack was made on Mr. Secretary Hardy and his
department, Mr. Disraeli was sorry not to be able to accept
the challenge, but he had nothing to regret. Mr. Hardy, who,
suffering under a great sorrow,[1] has been languid this session,
was inspired by the great occasion, and never spoke with more
force and fire. The Bill[2] was carried through Committee
by large majorities, and without alteration. . . .

To Anne Lady Chesterfield.

HUGHENDEN MANOR,[3] *March* 30.—I returned here yesterday
with a cold, notwithstanding all my care: but I had to pace
the corridor at Windsor, wh. I think can't be less than 1,000
feet long, five times a day (that was exercise) with blasts from
every opening in my progress (that was air).

I did not return smothered with flowers, tho' the Faery
was most gracious, and is going to give me her portrait for
Hughenden. For a long time I wrote, almost every day, to
three ladies: one of them has given me her portrait; another
has promised me her portrait; the third has not only not given
me her portrait, but has prevented another person from
giving it to me. I shd. have placed the two sisters in the
aloon, each on one side of our Sovereign. . . .

Confidential. 2, WHITEHALL GARDENS, *May* 5.—Public
affairs are so grave and pressing that I can hardly command
my mind to write a private letter—even to you.

I am now going to the Faery, who has much to make her
disquieted. Bismarck is playing the game of the old Buonaparte.[4]

Then I must go to the Ho. of Commons, and blow into the
air the conspiracy of the Liberals, the Fenians, and *The Times*
newspaper, their organ, to discredit, and eventually to destroy,
H.M. Government. They will find both results a little more
difficult than they imagine. I have no doubt I shall baffle
and beat them down, but I have got a little gout, wh. is not
very agreeable under such circumstances. . . .

To Lady Bradford.

2, WHITEHALL GARDENS, *May* 7, 1875.—. . . We got
on capitally last night in the House of C. after my lecture.
The Irish withdrew all their opposition, and we nearly got

[1] Hardy's eldest daughter died on Jan. 8.
[2] Regimental Exchanges Bill.
[3] Disraeli spent the Easter Recess at Hughenden, with the exception of
a short visit to Windsor.
[4] See below, ch. 11.

thro' Committee with one of our sanitary Bills, all of wh. I am resolved to carry.

Gladstone, I am told, is furious, tho' a greater bully than himself never ruled the Ho. of Comm. The plot was to waste the sess[ion] and then hold the Government up to scorn, for their imbecility, during the recess.

Late at night on Tuesday, without anybody being aware of it, we passed the 3rd reading of the Artisans' Dwellings Bill, our chief measure, wh. now goes to the Lords. They have got the Army Exchange Bill already, and before many days they will have the Irish Bill;[1] so we have not done so very badly.

The Agricultural Holdings Bill, which has passed the Lords, I intend to bring in myself; nor shall they have a moment's rest. . . .

Northcote's Budget for 1875 raised the reputation of the Government. He established a new sinking fund, setting aside for the service of the National Debt a fixed annual sum, in excess of what was required for payment of interest; an admirable plan, under which more than 150 millions of debt were paid off in the last quarter of the nineteenth century. Gladstone once more rushed out of his retirement into the fray, but, says a Liberal historian,[2] ' did not even succeed in dispelling the notioh that if he had been in office he would have done mucn the same thing himself.'

---

[1] Irish Peace Preservation Bill. Disraeli's speech on the second reading contained a well-known passage: ' There was once a member of this House, one of its greatest ornaments, who sat opposite this box, or an identical one, and indeed occupied the place which I unworthily fill. That was Mr. Canning. In his time, besides the discovery of a new world, dry champagne was invented. Hearing everybody talking of dry champagne, Mr. Canning had a great desire to taste it, and Charles Ellis, afterwards Lord Seaford, got up a little dinner for him, care of course being taken that there should be some dry champagne. Mr. Canning took a glass, and after drinking it and thinking for a moment, exclaimed, " The man who says he likes dry champagne will say anything." Now I do not want to enter into rude controversy with any of my hon. friends opposite who doubt the existence of Ribbonism; but this I will say, that the man who maintains that Ribbonism does not exist is a man who—ought to drink dry champagne.' Ribbonism was the form that Irish conspiracy had assumed for the time.

[2] Mr. Herbert Paul in his *History of Modern England.*

To Lady Bradford.

2, WHITEHALL GARDENS, S.W., *May* 8, 1875.—Last night was to have witnessed the destruction of the Govt: an attack on our whole line, led on by Achilles himself. Never were assailants so completely overthrown.

There was really a flutter of fear along our benches, which were crowded, when Gladstone rose. We have many new members, and they had heard so much of G. that they trembled.

The great man spoke for two hours, but it was the return from Elba. The Chancellor of the Exr. our little Northcote, originally G.'s private secretary, followed him, and I can truly say annihilated him, in one of the most vigorous speeches that ever was made by a man master of his subject.

Lowe tried to rally the affair, and I put up Hunt to answer him. It did not require great gifts to do that, for Lowe made a stammering affair of it—a dead failure.

Then the most curious part of all—every finance authority on the Liberal side spoke for the Government, and by the time I had intended to rise to sum up the question, the House had nearly vanished. Enough members however remained to help us to get thro' a great deal of business; and, whether it be what I said in the House or not, all I know is that we have done more business during the last 8 and 40 hours than for the last fortnight. . . .

HUGHENDEN MANOR, *May* 19.—. . . I have been here nearly a week,[1] and have not interchanged a syllable with any human being. My personal attendant (Baum), tho' sedulous, and, sometimes I believe, even honest, is of a sullen and supercilious temperament, and never unnecessarily opens his mouth. This I think a recommendation. Work has been brisk, especially foreign. . . .

I am very much like Robinson Crusoe on his island, before he found Friday. Talking of which immortal work reminds me how I have passed my evenings here: in reading *Gil Blas*. What a production! It is human life. I read it when a child, and was charmed with its unceasing adventure; but could not realise its real meaning. I read it now with a very large experience of existence, and I relish every line.

HOUSE OF COMMONS, 6 *o'ck.* [? *May* 27, 1875].—Gladstone has come down like the Dragon of Wantley breathing fire and fury on some of our financial Bills. . . .

---

[1] For the Whitsuntide recess.

To Queen Victoria.

HOUSE OF COMMONS, *May* 31, 1875.—Mr. Disraeli with his humble duty to your Majesty:

He has, generally speaking, been a little remiss, this session, in reporting the operations of the House of Commons to your Majesty, but there have been more interesting topics to trouble your Majesty about.

To-night, however, has been one of a signal character.

For nearly a month, the Opposition, by every means the press could afford, have endeavoured to impress upon the country, that your Majesty's Government have made a great mistake in their management of the ' privilege question '; that they have lost a golden opportunity of settling these difficulties; and have given that opportunity to Lord Hartington to establish himself in the confidence of the country.

Mr. Disraeli was perfectly aware, that the whole of the representation was a delusion, and knew that the advice he had given to his party, on the subject, was the sound and right one: that which had been adopted, or followed, on similar occasions, by all the great leaders and members, who preceded him: Peel, Lord Russell, Graham, Lords Eversley and Ossington, Sir George Grey, Bouverie.

To-day and to-night, after many delays, the great occasion arrived, ' one of the decisive battles ' not of the world, but of the session.

There was a meeting of the supporters of the Ministry in the morning in Downing Street, when [? whom] Mr. Disraeli addressed. There were 248 present. The hour, in consequence of the levée, was changed from two to noon: otherwise, as the telegrams showed, there would have been 333 members present. Sir Robert Peel never could assemble such a number, even in his palmiest day.

The battle commenced at five o'clock; at $\frac{1}{2}$ past seven the House divided on Lord Hartington's chief resolution, when he was beaten by a majority of *107 :* then he threw up his cards, and said he would leave it to Mr. Disraeli to do what he thought best. And he did it.

This immense victory will have an incalculably beneficial effect on the progress of public business.

To Anne Lady Chesterfield.

2, WHITEHALL GARDENS, *June* 1, 1875.—Before you get this you will have known the result of the great Opposition plot, scheme, confederacy, of wh. poor Hartington was the tool, and the victim.

For more than a month, there has been an organised agitation, to subvert the privileges of the House of Commons, showing that I was totally incapable of dealing with these great questions, self-confessedly incompetent, and ought to be deprived of the leadership, not only because I was of opinion that no change was desirable, but had also given my rival such a golden opportunity of distinguishing himself and his party. They had engaged every newspaper in the plot; even the *World*, and of course Carnarvon's favorite, the *Spectator*. *The Times* began it before Whitsun with announcing in a series of articles that the Ho. of Commons was in a state of chaos from my disinclination, or inability, to settle these inevitable changes. Even 4 and 20 hours ago, they said the Cabinet Council of Saturday was to receive my resignation, and to listen to the address in wh. it was to be communicated to the House of Commons.

Yesterday morning I held a meeting of the party in Downing St., and soon saw they were troops with wh., as the D. of Wellington sd. of his Peninsular legions, that they were men with whom he cd. march anywhere [*sic*]. I addressed them in a speech of 55 minutes, and spoke to my satisfaction.

Then, after a long levée, I went to the House of C.; and at ½ past seven Ld. Hartington, 'the coming man,' was beaten by a majority of 107 ! ! ! threw up the reins, and begged me to settle the matter as I liked; wh. I did. There never was such a smashing defeat. The House in the most signal manner confirmed my policy, that no change in our privileges shd. take place, and it was only owing to my personal influence that I cd. get them to assent to a slight alteration in one of our rules,[1] wh. will keep the Irish ruffians in order. . . .

I can't get rid of my cough; but I am stronger, and Sir William [Jenner] maintains every day that I am better. He says he has to write to the Queen every day he sees me: but that her great anxiety about my health is occasioned, he thinks, not so much from love of me, as dread of somebody else. . . .

To Queen Victoria.

HOUSE OF COMMONS, *June* 11, 1875.—. . . With respect to compulsory education, it was defeated on Wednesday by a majority of more than 90, and though the majority was even much larger last year, Mr. Disraeli attributes this diminution only to casual and social causes; principally Ascot races, always perilous to the Tories.

---

[1] At that period strangers, including reporters, were ordered to withdraw whenever any individual member called attention to their presence; and the Irish Extremists had made use of the rule to obstruct business. The alteration provided that a division should first be taken, without debate.

Mr. Disraeli had scores of supporters away: the Opposition only their leader, the Marquess of Hartington.

Lord Henry Somerset, the Controller of your Majesty's Household, was absent, and entertaining his friends; among them, several of your Majesty's Government. Mr. Disraeli was, however, ruthless; he kept the wires of the telegraph vibrating alternately with menaces and entreaties, and exactly five minutes before the division, a special train arrived with the Controller of the Household, and all his wassailers.

Lord Sandon spoke well: and was completely master of his subject.

To Lady Bradford.

2, WHITEHALL GARDENS, *June* 13, 1875.—. . . I had a Cabinet at 12, and I gave them a good 'wigging,' I believe that is the word, for the treatment of the Sultaun of Zanzibar at Ascot. They sate still and silent, like schoolboys; but my observations told, for, in the course of the afternoon I received the enclosed letter from one of the most powerful of our daimios. You know what those animals are in Japan ?

About four o'ck. by appointment, I paid my visit to the Sultaun myself. He received me at the door, or rather in the hall, of his hotel, with all his chiefs. They were not goodlooking, but he himself is an Arab with a well-favored mien, good manners, a pleasing countenance, and the peculiar repose of an Oriental gentleman. Being used, from my travels, to these interviews and gentry, I addressed him directly, looking in his face as I spoke, and never turning to the interpreter. This greatly pleases them, but it is very difficult to do. The audience was successful. I took Monty (just arrived) with me, and Mr. Bourke the Under Sec. for For. Affairs. . . .

The article is certainly Gladstone's; I have not seen it, but I never read anything he writes. His style is so involved, so wanting both in melody and harmony, that it always gives me a headache.

Tho most dramatic moments of the session arose out of the Merchant Shipping Bill, an apparently prosaic measure, which, however, resulted in an explosion, dangerous to the existence of the Government. For some years there had been a growing movement, headed by Plimsoll, member for Derby, in favour of legislation to bring merchant shipping under further control, so as to minimise loss of life among seamen. The movement was in accord with the social policy of the Government;

and accordingly, the Board of Trade prepared a Bill. But the subject was a thorny one, and the Government found it difficult to steer a middle course between shipowners and humanitarians; while the difficulties were increased by the inadequacy of Adderley, the President of the Board of Trade, and his uneasy relations with the permanent officials of the Board. Disraeli's interference became necessary at an early stage.

To Lady Bradford.

2, WHITEHALL GARDENS, *April* 10.—. . . This has been a week of immense labor, and some anxiety, tho' of more excitement. . . . The Mercht. Shipping Bill, a measure necessarily of great importance, was the cause. Before I left town, I was confidentially informed that there were rocks ahead, that Adderley had quarrelled with all his office, that he was disliked by his own party in the House, that they wd. not support the Government measure but Plimsoll, who is a Moody and Sankey in politics: half rogue and half enthusiast — that is to say, one of those characters who live by pandering to passion, and fall into an enthusiastic love and admiration of themselves. I took certain measures to put things right before I left town, and delegated the rest to Northcote, who generally succeeds. But alas ! not in this case.

I had a bad despatch at Hughenden, and when I got to town—the Bill being fixed for 2nd reading on Thursday ensuing—I found perfect anarchy. . . . I was obliged to undertake the management of the whole case : a vast and most complicated case, and of wh. then I knew little. Besides this I have had to give constant interviews to the confused, the refractory and the vacillating. After the Cab. on Wednesday, I was obliged to give myself to this work, instead of writing to the Queen as I had promised; and I did not get things really right—in order—until 4 o'ck. on Thursday afternoon, so that they were painting the scenes as the curtain drew up.

But the result was most triumphant. Adderley, who is after all a gentleman, and who has been, and may be yet, the victim of a cabal, behaved very well, and made a discreet opening address. We not only carried the second reading, but carried it without a division, and Plimsoll had to leave the House, being desperately ill, probably from chagrin. Then the enemy, finding they cd. not successfully oppose the Bill, tried to adjourn the debate, wh. wd. have been most injurious to us, but I coaxed the House into carrying my point. . . .

It is perhaps not surprising that, after this troublesome experience, Disraeli and the Cabinet should have preferred, when a choice had to be made late in July, to drop the Merchant Shipping Bill in order to proceed with the Agricultural Holdings Bill. But when Disraeli made the announcement, on July 22, Plimsoll lost patience, moved the adjournment in order to protest against the abandonment of the shipping measure, vehemently denounced 'shipknackers,' shouted that he would unmask the 'villains' who sent seamen to their graves, pirouetted in the middle of the floor, shook his fist at Disraeli, and, defying the authority of the Speaker, flung himself out of the House. Disraeli, as leader of the House, moved that Plimsoll should be reprimanded; but he eventually accepted the plea of the offender's friends that he was in a state of intense excitement and would, when he was calmer, express regret for his conduct; and substituted a motion merely requesting him to attend in his place on that day week.

The Opposition, who had been on the lookout for a cry against the Government, thought that they had now found an excellent opportunity for working upon the humanitarian feelings of the people. Disraeli's private letters give a highly coloured story of the proceedings of the next few days, and show how he turned his difficulties to good account and finally passed a Shipping Bill after all.

To Lady Bradford.

2, WHITEHALL GARDENS, *July* 27.—I was up till 3 o'ck., and have a terrible day (days!) before me, but I have risen early, that, if possible, I might write to you.

The ——[1] was an anxious one. A certain person violent, treating the whole agitation with contempt—would not sacrifice our dignity as a Government, wh. he saw wd. be the result.

Strange to say, he was supported by one of a totally different temperament, who had proved by inexpugnable logic on

---

[1] The dash appears in the original letter. The word omitted is obviously 'Cabinet.'

a previous occasion that the course then adopted was 'the only one,' and he stuck to it.

At one moment I thought nothing cd. be effected; but at last, and *with unanimity*, there was a decision.

That has had immediate effect—at least in the H. of C. There was ' a meeting ' in the morning of yesterday, as last year, of an expectant Cabinet. Gladstone was brought up, and Carlingford, who had been President of the B. of Trade, and then a great opponent of Plimsoll, was consulted. There was to have been a fierce attack on the Government on the order of the day, but Sir C. Adderley's announcement stopped all this, and we went quietly into Committee on the Agri-[cultura]l Bill, and made immense progress, so that I really expect to conclude the Committee to-day, for I have got the whole morning late from 2 to 7, and then from 9 till the usual hour.

I *entreat* you not to breathe a word of what I have written above to any human being. I don't mean Bradford, of course, from whom I have no secrets, and who is a Privy Councillor, and whom I wd. trust were he not a P.C.

The Cabinet meets in an hour. We have to settle our measure; and what is of not less importance my answer this morning at 2 o'ck. to Dillwyn, as to whether we will give a day immediately to P[limsoll]'s Bill. I think as much depends on my reply as on our measure. . . .

I sadly miss you all, tho' I could not go and see dear Ida,[1] even if she cd. receive me. I had a talk with Newport in the lobby, who seems now my only link to domestic life and private happiness. . . .

J[ohn] M[anners], who has just come from O[sborne], says that the Faery only talked on one subject, and that was her Primo. According to him, it was her gracious opinion that the Govt. shd. make my health a Cabinet question. Dear John seemed quite surprised at what she said; but you are more used to these ebullitions. . . .

A certain person, the great logician, made, among many other sharp remarks, a good one yesterday. He said he had not only not changed his opinion, but believed that the withdrawment of the Mercht. Ship. Bill wd. have passed without notice by the country, had it not been for two unexpected incidents—wh. we cd. not have counted on—the Plimsoll scene, and the verdict against a wicked shipowner in the Irish Courts.

The first showed, he said, what a dangerous man P. was to trust to in legislation, and the second proved that the

---

[1] Then Lady Newport, now the Countess Dowager of Bradford.

existing law was an efficient one; and yet these two incidents,
fanned of course by faction, have agitated the country. . . .

P.S.—What do you think of yr. new friend, Delane ? I
believe he was at the meeting of the new Cabinet. . . .

July 28, 6 *o'ck.*—I send a rapid line after a morning of
great excitement, of endless and terrific rumors, and all
possible events and combinations—Plimsoll, to-morrow, not
to appear; Plimsoll, to-morrow, to appear and re-defy the
House; to get into the custody of the Sergt.-at-Arms at
all events, but to come down first with four brass bands,
open carriage with four white horses, and twenty thousand
retainers !

Then our Bill to-day was not to be permitted to be brought
in, and other mischances and difficulties and humiliations.
However, our Bill *has been* brought in, and I have fixed its
second reading for Friday morning—and remain, ostensibly
at least, perfectly calm, amidst a sea and storm of panic and
confusion. My position is difficult in one respect, for the
Queen, devoted to me, can't help me; for if I were defeated in
the House, I cd. not dissolve, for, in the present fever, I shd.
probably get worsted; and I can't prorogue, for I have not
got my money, the Estimates not yet being concluded.

All I have got to look to are my friends. If they stand by
me, I shall overcome everything, and greatly triumph, but
does friendship exist in August ? Does it not fly to Scotland,
and Norway, and the Antipodes—or Goodwood ? I have
seen some wonderful long faces, that used to smile on me.
I neither love them more nor less. The only beings in the
world I care for are away—and Heaven knows even if they
spare a thought to me and my agitated fortunes.

July 29, 10 *o'ck.*—I got your letter an hour ago; a great
consolation to me in my fierce life. . . .

Now I know exactly what a General must feel in a great
battle—like Waterloo for example — with aide-de-camps
flying up every moment with contrary news; and spies, and
secret agents, and secret intelligence, and all sorts of proposals
and schemes.

The Plimsollites, in and out of Parliament, are at me; now
cajoling, now the reign of terror. Their great object is to get
Plimsoll into the custody of the Sergt.-at-Arms, and on my
motion. That, they consider, from what they have been
told, is inevitable if he does not appear to-day; and they are
right according to precedent. But I am the person to make
the motion, and I will make a precedent too. After the declarations of his authorised friend in the House, that ' he was
off his head,' etc., I shall hold him as a man not responsible
for his conduct, and move the adjournment of his case for a

month. This will sell them if they try the scheme of his absence—*i.e.*, disobedience to the commands of the House.

I shd. not be surprised if, after all his bluster, he gives in and makes an unconditional apology. Every intriguer is trying to make some fortune by the crisis. Plimsoll has a wonderful number of enthusiastic friends, very suddenly. I only wish they had supported our Bill when it was before them, instead of throwing every obstacle in its way. Horsman is very busy; asked Monty to luncheon yesterday, told him it was all over with the Government, tho' he once thought he cd. save them; advised, as a last resource, that I should deliver a panegyric to-day in favour of P. and accept his Bill *pure et simple*.

My own judgment of the House of Commons is that a considerable, and the most reputable, section of the Opposition is against Plimsoll, and believes, wh. is the truth, that his Bill wd. injure, not to say destroy, our mercantile marine, and that, if my friends are firm to me, I shall certainly triumph.

As far as I can hear, I have no reason to doubt their devotion. Many of our most considerable men have told me that they are prepared, if necessary, to alter all their plans and remain by my side. . . .

Tell Bradford I was greatly disappointed that his horse came in second. I cannot understand why a great noble, with his brains and knowledge of horses, does not command the turf. I don't want him to have a great stable, but I want him to have a famous one; that he shd., at any rate, obtain some first-rate blood, and then carefully, and sedulously, breed from it, as Rothschild did with King Tom. I saw the beginning of his plan at Mentmore, and people turned up their noses at his scheme and his sire for a while; and yet eventually that blood gave him the Derby, the Oaks, and the St. Leger in one year. I shd. like to see that done at dear Weston.

For aught I know, while I write of these pleasant things, the mob may be assembling wh. is to massacre me. I have several letters threatening assassination. I shall take no precautions, but walk down alone with Monty, and meet my fate, whatever comes I feel sure, at least almost, that there will be one family in England who will cherish my memory with kindness and indulgence.

July 30.—Everything went off quietly yesterday out of doors, and triumphantly inside.

Mr. Secy. X, who is naturally a brave and firm man, got so frightened about his chief, that I believe there were 1000 constables hid in the bowers of Whitehall Gardens and about. But I had no fear, and principally from this, that Monty, who has been everywhere and doing everything, ascertained that

Bradlaugh and Co. had completely failed in getting up a Clerkenwell mob, as the people said they wd. not go agst. me, who had passed the Labor Laws for them.

All the meetings in the provinces were held by tel. orders from the Reform Club; but before they cd. hold their meetings, at least generally speaking, the announcement of the Govt. measure had taken the wind out of their sails.

Plimsoll also got restive and did not like the brass bands and flags, etc., and said he wd. not be made a party tool, and that he had received more support from the Tories than the Whigs. The consequence of all this was very much fiasco.

The papers will tell you what took place in the House. The campaign opened unfortunately for the foe. They tried to stop public business and failed ignominiously. Adam, the Whig Whip, who is a gentleman, told Dyke that ' the Plimsoll business was a flash in the pan.' They did not think so 8 and 40 hours ago.

Then after the failure I got into Committee on my Bill, and absolutely at one o'ck. concluded it amid loud cheers. I never had more continuous, and greater, majorities than thro'-out this Bill.

I am very glad Harry C[haplin] was not at Goodwood. He has never left my side, and his aid has been invaluable. He is a natural orator, and a debater too. He is the best speaker in the H. of C., or will be. Mark my words.

I have a Cabinet at noon: the H. of C. at two, when we have the 2nd reading of our Ship. Bill. I shd. not be surprised if it passed without a division. The battle of Armageddon, howr., will be on Monday, when in Committee they will try to substitute Plimsolliana for our proposals. I am sending all over the world for votes. Chaplin has a house full for Brighton races, but remains here. *O ! si sic omnia !* or rather, *omnes*.

Aug. 3.—We pulled thro', but not triumphantly; had the Opposition had a leader adequate to the opportunity, we might have been much humiliated. As it was, it needed much tact and vigilance to mitigate, or conceal, our concessions; but the enemy made so many mistakes, and played their cards so ill, that it all ended better than was once hoped.

Adderley committed an awful blunder ! . . .

These political excursions and alarums did not prevent Disraeli from making frequent appearances in society. He always set a high value on social influences in con-solidating a political connection, and often lamented the backwardness of Tory magnificoes and great ladies in providing counter-attractions to Whig hospitalities. He was determined to do his own part as Prime Minister; and accordingly, in the spring of 1875, when he had for a while thrown off his gout, he gave a series of political and Parliamentary dinners, mixing Royal Princes and Ambassadors with his peers and Members of Parliament. In this experiment he was following the counsels of his own Vivian Grey, uttered fifty years earlier: 'I think a course of Parliamentary dinners would produce a good effect. It gives a tone to a political party. The science of political gastronomy has never been sufficiently studied.' The dinner-parties proved a great success; and, when Granville started a somewhat similar series, Disraeli flattered himself that this time it was the Whigs who were the imitators.

To Anne Lady Chesterfield.

WHITEHALL GARDENS, *Feb.* 24.—. . . I have asked an Ambassador to each of my dinners, a new feature. . . . Ct. Schouvaloff [1] is a most agreeable man, and very good-looking, and very clever. When he had his first audience of me in the spring on his arrival, he cd. not speak or comprehend a word of English. Yesterday at the levée he said to me, 'I want to have the honor of another interview some day, but *here* I will not talk shop.' And so I found that he now not only speaks English, but English slang, quite idiomatic. . . .

To Lady Bradford.

H. OF COMM., *Feb.* 25, 1875.—. . . The dinner, wh. I expected to be a failure, turned out to be a great success. The physical part was good. It was really a dinner of high calibre and quite hot, which is wonderful when you have to feed forty. I sate betn. the German Ambassador and D. of Manchester, who is silly, but not dull. Next to him was Lothair,[2] who had travelled up from the wilds of Scotland to show his gratitude for his Thistle. He had other hardships to endure, for it is Lent! and, of course, he could eat nothing but fish. He managed pretty well, for he instructed his attendant to secure for him a large dish of well-sauced salmon, and that sustained him during all the courses. Claud Hamilton sate next to Lothair, and talked well, and made him

---

talk. But everybody talked. I think it was the most noisy party, without being boisterous, I well recollect. These affairs, generally, are solemn, not to say dull. To make up for the lack of brilliant furniture, I gave them *carte blanche* for plants and flowers; and they certainly effected marvels. . . .

I found Münster a very capable man, with great conversational powers. The cold proud Duke of Northumberland sate next to him, but was grim and acid. . . .

2, WHITEHALL GARDENS, *March* 15.—. . . My new dean preached: Monty liked him, he never charmed me. What was good was his length; twenty minutes, tho' a charity sermon. The plate brought to me was disgraceful: there were so many sixpences, that it looked like a dish of whitebait. . . .

It is mentioned to me, and it is true (look in the newspapers) that Granville, my rival in more senses than one, has copied my scheme and system of banquets, wh. was quite original. He started on Saturday, with an Ambassador or two, ½ a dozen peers (with one Duke at least) and a batch of commoners, tho' he can only manage ' covers for 26.' I can 42. . . .

To Anne Lady Chesterfield.

2, WHITEHALL GARDENS, *April* 17.—. . . Affairs are very heavy—in weight, I mean, not in spirit, for there is no want of that in external affairs; but I hope to prevent war. It is a proud position for England if she can do this.[1] . . .

I have got a banquet to-day, and H.R.H. the Duke of Cambridge comes to me: the Duke of Edinburgh on the 28th, and the Prince of Wales, I believe, on the Birthday. I have now dined 242 members of the House of Commons and sixty peers. I had hoped to have finished this campaign by the end of April; but I shall hardly be able to do it, as there are 112 members of the Commons to be invited, and they are not contented unless they meet a certain portion of swells. . . .

Besides giving many dinners himself, Disraeli constantly dined out, often attended evening parties, and even sometimes, until he was scolded out of his imprudence by Lady Chesterfield, finished up his night at a ball. If the dinner or the party involved a meeting and a talk with Lady Bradford, it counted with him as a success.

To Anne Lady Chesterfield.

2, WHITEHALL GARDENS, *July* 3.—. . . On Wednesday I dined at the Malmesburys'—a Duke of Cambridge banquet,

---

[1] See below, ch. 11.

good company. I took down Lady Tankerville, who is joyous. On my other side an Australian, who has beguiled foolish and very young Ld. —— into marrying her, on the pretence she is a great beauty. All the relations are by way of vowing she is so now, tho' they were very squeamish about the match at first. I thought her an underbred minx, affecting artlessness, and trying it on me ! I cd. only see Selina at a distance, but after dinner, when the D. of Cambridge had done with her, I got my turn, and she was delightful—made a rather dull dinner a success. Lady A. was there. Three great houses were open that night, Grosvenor, Apsley, and Stafford. But I was firm and went home at once. This getting to bed before midnight answers very well. . .

Yesterday I dined at 43, Bel. Square—a brilliant and amusing party. I took down the Dss. of Westminster to dinner and sate next to Pss. Mary. The Duchess said as we walked in, ' You are going to sit between the two fattest women in London.' That might be true; and yet they have both grand countenances, and are agreeable and extremely intelligent. Indeed Princess Mary has wit. The Abercorns were there also: the beautiful Viceroy in goggles ! having been struck on his eyes by a cricket ball. He excels in the game, as in everything. I never saw such roses as S. had on her dinner-table. I suppose other people have as good, but she arranges them, or inspires their arrangement, with peculiar taste. Her party was very successful, the guests wd. not go, but stayed till nearly midnight, the test of an agreeable dinner party.

I wd. not go to Dorchester House, where there was a great festival. I told S. I shd. tell you this, and it wd. please you. She also was prudent and did not go either.

July 25.—. . . Yesterday I dined at Holland House; a banquet, 4 and 20 at least. As they were all grandees, I went out, as usual, last, and feared I shd. be as badly off as at Lady A.'s, and dine, as I did there, between two men; but, as I entered, a faithful groom of the chamber took me under his care, and deposited me, by the instructions of the lady of the house, next to—S. ! She had been taken out by Lord Stanhope. It was a most delightful dinner, and a most charming evening. We had Mr. Corney Grain to amuse us, with his songs and mimicry, and some were quaint and good. S. immensely enjoyed them The Grand Mecklenburgs were there, the blind Duke in fits of laughter; Duke of Sutherland; the Ilchesters who, by an arrangement, accede to Holland House on the demise of its present genial lady; the Malmesburys; some distinguished foreigners, of course, who knew me years ago.

I had a dreadful accident to my brougham in the evening, and I fear I shall lose my beautiful horse, the Baron, for whom I gave 300 gu[ine]as, four years ago, and who has never been ill a single hour.

Bradford was most kind, as, I must say, he always is to me, and took me home with S. and Mabel. It was such a happy day that I did not care much for any accident.

I have 8 and 40 hours' distraction from heavy and anxious affairs. I shall manage them, but they are hard.

I meet S. at dinner to-day at the Sturts, her great friends; and then the curtain falls.

July 28.—I can't write letters, not even tels. I live in a storm—at the House morning and night; glad to get off for 12 hours a day; Cabinets early in the morning; called out for ceaseless interviews: much fright and confusion—but I am cool and have no fear.

I see, as from a tower, the end of all.

Never mind *The Times;* it will soon change. I will beat even your *Times*, wh. I know you are always afraid of; so is dear S.

Amid all this, the servant perpetually comes in, and announces, ' fruit from Bretby,' ' flowers from B.', ' butter from B.' Blessed Bretby ! and I can only send you in return my love.

It was the cue of the Opposition to represent the legislation of the session as petty and valueless, because in two of the principal measures, the Artisans' Dwellings Bill and the Agricultural Holdings Bill, the principle of compulsion was not admitted. In both cases a new departure was made in English legislation, and Disraeli strenuously upheld the wisdom of proceeding at first by way of permission, rather than of compulsion. ' Permissive legislation,' he said on the Agricultural Bill, ' is the character of a free people. It is easy to adopt compulsory legislation when you have to deal with those who only exist to obey; but in a free country, and especially in a country like England, you must trust to persuasion and example as the two great elements, if you wish to effect any considerable changes in the manners of the people.' And again, in the House at the close of the session : ' It is only by persuasion—the finest persuasion in the world, which is example—persuasion in action, that you can influence, and modify, and mitigate habits which you disapprove.' The other charge against Government, which resounded through the Liberal press, and was even echoed by *The Times*, was one of Parliamentary mismanagement, largely based on Disraeli's refusal to accept the press view of Parliamentary privilege. Sir Henry Lucy draws a strong contrast between Disraeli's success in the Commons in the early part of the session, and what he considers his failure and feebleness after the privilege question had been raised. It is possible that Disraeli's regular participation in the social events of the season may to some extent have exhausted the energy which should have been directed to Parliamentary management; it is also possible that Sir Henry, whose contrast on this point is too much heightened to be convincing, was biassed both by his Liberalism and by his sympathy with the press. In any case a great mass of beneficent social legislation was enacted amid the plaudits of the working classes; what Disraeli called a ' crucial session ' was successfully surmounted; and the attempt of the Opposition just before the prorogation to enforce their apocryphal version of events was easily repelled. Disraeli himself, in replying to Hartington, was, says Hardy, ' full of fire, force, and energy, and wound up our sessional career admirably.'

To Lady Bradford.

2, WHITEHALL GARDENS, *Aug.* 7, 1875.—. . . I was indeed sorry I cd. not reach Bel. Sqre. last night, but Harty-Tarty could not rise till nearly eleven. Had he given me 10,000 pounds he cd. not have done me a greater service than making his attack. I am rarely satisfied with myself, but I was last night—almost as much as my friends, who were literally in a state of enthusiasm. I think I left Harty-Tarty in a state of syncope. He sate quite opposite to me, and I cd. see his face—the look of wooden amazement and the blush of proud confusion. Gladstone was by him, having been kept in town for the occasion; but the bottleholder was Lowe, who made copious notes to answer me, but did not dare to rise! They all deserted him. *The Times* has not even a leading article ' to cover his retreat '!

Aug. 8.—. . . You will be rather pleased to hear that when we met yesterday[1] Derby said, ' Our first act ought to be to thank our chief for closing the campaign by a victory.'

Aug. 9.—. . . N. Rothschild, who knows everything, told me yesterday about the coming art. in *The Times*. It was written by Lowe, and shd. have been his answer to me.

Aug. 10.—. . . Notwithstanding the House of C. I ventured in trembling, for a division was impending, to call on Lady Holland, whom I had not seen since the very happy day when she called me ' naughty boy.'

The servant informed me that her L[adyshi]p had ' gone to town '; she always went on Monday, the only day in the week she did not receive. ' I thought you wd. know that, Sir,' he added. ' I did not,' I replied, ' nor did I know this was Monday.' And I left him staring.

But my disappointment was fortunate, for the division came on instantly on my arrival, and I had the pleasure of supporting Geordie Hamilton, who is deservedly a great favorite of mine, and who, yesterday, as usual, much distinguished himself. . . .

We have done capital business, both in Lords and Commons, these few last days; and several most important measures, wh. they pressed me so eagerly to give up a month ago, have been passed.

Some capital measures of the Chr. of the Exr. wh. Harty-Tarty taunted me with having to give up, and wh. I thought then were virtually surrendered, have been carried: but above all, the Trade Marks Bill, a measure of the utmost gravity and importance, a subject wh. Parlt. has been hammering at for years, and no Govt. cd. settle, has been passed triumphantly and will give profound satisfaction to the whole manufacturing and commercial world. After the approval of the Speech by the Queen this has happened, and I have been obliged this morning to insert a fresh paragraph in tho great document,

The Times may scold; it may rave and rant; but it will not daunt me. I know it greatly influences you, and it rules Anne, and that the confidence of you both in me is greatly shaken: but you will see that I am right, and very soon see it, and that public opinion will decide in my favor. The Queen's Speech is a document of such weight and authenticity, dealing only with facts, that the nation is always influenced by this sovereign summary. . . .

---

[1] In Cabinet.

Ministers, at any rate, were satisfied with themselves, and celebrated their successful session with a more than usually hilarious fish dinner at Greenwich.

To Lady Bradford.

OSBORNE, *Aug.* 13, 1875.—Bradford has told you all about the fish dinner; therefore I need not dwell on it. I put Geordie Hamilton in the chair, the youngest member of the Ministry. They were all astonished and charmed by him: I was not astonished, but charmed. I knew my man. It was a perpetual flow of wit, and playful humor, and grace; a due mixture of the aplomb of the statesman and the impertinence of the page.

You know he is authorised by me, while he is in the chair, to do anything he likes, and say anything he chooses. He is a sort of Abbot of Misrule; 'tis a carnival, a saturnalia; the Roman slave freely criticising his masters; and Cabinet Ministers trembled in their shoes before the audacious sallies of this brilliant stripling and subordinate. Part of the hilarious ceremony is the investiture of an illustrious order. The decoration is a wooden spoon of rather gigantic and pantomimic size. It is strictly to be given to the member of the Ministry who has been in the least number of Ho. of Commons divisions; practically it ought to be the appanage of our stupidest member. Geordie had the impudence to award it to me, who sate on his right hand! his lord and master, and who had helped him a little in his wonderful summary of the session. Ungrateful youth!

In bygone days, I remember this decoration being awarded to an eminent gentleman, who has filled great posts, and is now a member of the Upper House: he was so indignant that he could not smother his rage and mortification, and actually rose from his seat and left the room. I was not quite such a fool as that, but wore my decoration, suspended round my neck by a piece of cord for the whole evening, and even dared to vindicate, as well as I cd., the order of Spooneys.

I expected to find that the remaining one of the three ladies, to whom hitherto I have written for some time every day of my life, had also lost her confidence in me; but that was not so. She looks extremely well; ten years younger than when I saw her last. She almost deigned to say the same of me, and I tried to cough, lest I shd. be commanded to Balmoral, but could not. . . .

The Queen, I ought to tell you, had ordered the *Fairy* for my special use, in order that I shd. not get into boats; but

Monty, by tel. to Ponsonby, declined this, as I think it makes an injudicious distinction from my colleagues, who have been to me faithful and devoted colleagues

It is decided that Adderley shd. leave the Board of Trade, and be succeeded by Sir Michael Beach, and that H. Chaplin shall succeed Beach and go to Ireland as Secretary. Little George Bentinck also must leave the Board of Trade, but I have been able, I think, to provide for him. These are great secrets, unknown to any of my colleagues, and perhaps will not be announced for a month. I need not impress upon you the most profound secrecy, always excepting Bradford of course. . . .

The changes which Disraeli foreshadowed to Lady Bradford as imminent at the Board of Trade were never carried out, save for the removal of Bentinck from the Parliamentary Secretaryship. Both Disraeli and his principal colleagues, especially Cairns and Northcote, felt, after the experience of the session, the advisability of strengthening the Board, but serious difficulties arose in the way of the suggested shuffle of offices. Northcote, with characteristic unselfishness, offered to step down from the Exchequer and take the Presidency himself, but Disraeli would not hear of the idea. 'I think your proposition monstrous,' he wrote on August 3. 'You are, and ever have been, my right hand, my most trusty counsellor; and I look to your filling a higher post than that which you admirably discharge.' The discussions occupied several months of the autumn; and finally Adderley was left in possession of his post, but the Board was strengthened by the appointment, as Parliamentary Secretary, of Edward Stanhope, the historian's son, one of the most promising of the younger Tories, whose death some years later in the prime of manhood was a real loss to his country.

To Sir Stafford Northcote.

2, WHITEHALL GARDENS, *Sept.* 23, 1875.—. . . Adderley has mistaken a letter, which I thought was clear. I lost no time, after seeing the Queen, in informing him of my intentions, because I thought, if they reached him from any other source, he might think himself the victim of an intrigue, which he certainly is not.

But I have done nothing in the matter, tho' I have labored much. I have conferred greatly about it with the Lord Chancellor, and with Dyke and Sclater Booth, and the result has been nothing.

There are great objections to our increasing the number of the Cabinet. It is thought, that Adderley might remain, if George Bentinck were removed, and Ibbetson, who has studied the railway question, were put in his place, and there is a great objection to any great change of any kind.

The difficulty about an Irish Secretary is immense. George Hamilton could not go there with his father V.Roy. Chaplin, whom I thought of, is not experienced enough for this nest of corruption, intrigue, and trickery.

I did write to Beach, but after corresponding with the Lord Chancellor and conferring with Sclater Booth, the letter remains in my red box, six weeks old, and I will break the seal when we meet. . . .

To Lady Bradford.

2, WHITEHALL GARDENS, *Nov.* 12.—. . . Adderley's business still teases me, tho' I have sent word to-day that all must be settled in 4 and 20 hours, or everybody concerned shall go out. Monty is of use to me, being resolute as well as sharp; but his interference is *my* interference, and I don't want to appear unnecessarily in these matters. The Cr. of the Exchequer, to whom I look to arrange these things, tho' very clever, is a complete Jesuit, and proceeds always by innuendo, wh. coarse natures do not understand. . . .

It was during this autumn of 1875 that events occurred —the insurrection in Herzegovina, the visit of the Prince of Wales to India, the purchase of the Suez Canal shares—which made, in ever-increasing measure, the foreign policy and the imperial position of Great Britain the dominating considerations in the mind of the Prime Minister and in the counsels of the Government. But Disraeli was also not without worries in domestic affairs. The Admiralty, after consultation with the Foreign Office, issued a fugitive slave circular, drafted by the Law Officers, which roused public indignation by its apparent reversal of British anti-slavery policy; it directed the surrender on demand, within territorial limits, of a fugitive slave who had sought the protection of a British ship. When the storm arose, Disraeli acted with promptitude and decision. Derby was about to speak at a banquet at Liverpool, and his chief telegraphed his wishes.

To Lord Derby.

(*Telegram*) *Oct.* 6, 1875.—The affair is grave. Many letters to-day. It should be stated that there is not the slightest change in our policy, that the instructions have been referred to the Law Officers, who do not agree in the public interpretation, but that as there should be no ambiguity on such a subject the instructions are at present suspended. Answer if you agree.

Derby replied that he entirely agreed, and he made an announcement in the sense of Disraeli's telegram. Disraeli called the Cabinet together a few days earlier than had been intended, to take action.

To Queen Victoria.

Confidential. HUGHENDEN MANOR, *Oct.* 28, 1875.—Mr. Disraeli with his humble duty to your Majesty:

He finds it necessary to call the Cabinet together on the 4th November. The immediate cause is the Admiralty Resolutions, respecting slavery.

Although the expressions of Lord Derby at Liverpool, and the suspension of the instructions—and Mr. Disraeli is responsible both for the expressions and the suspension—arrested mischief, they have not terminated a state of public opinion, with reference to this unfortunate affair, which may be dangerous. It has got hold of the public mind more than the newspapers would convey, of which, indeed, your Majesty is aware, for your Majesty has already called Mr. Disraeli's serious attention to the subject. . . .

2, WHITEHALL GARDENS, *Nov.* 5.—. . . The consideration of the Cabinet yesterday was entirely confined to the slave circular and Admiralty circumstances. The Lord Chancellor, as arranged with Mr. Disraeli, put the whole question of the instructions before the Cabinet, and showed, that they were as wrong in law as in policy. The Cabinet came to an unanimous resolution to cancel immediately the already suspended instructions, and requested the Lord Chancellor himself to draw up those, which are to be substituted for them.

II. 24*

A strange affair altogether! That all the Law Officers should blunder, and that the indiscretion in policy should have been committed by the Earl of Derby ! ! ! . . .

After this muddle, it is not surprising to find Disraeli writing next day to the Queen that he ' suffers terribly from the want of capable law officers. The unfortunate break-up of Sir John Karslake's health broke the chain, and we have never been able to find an adequate link.' Within a fortnight, however, he had secured a team on which he could rest with much greater confidence.

To Queen Victoria.

2, WHITEHALL GARDENS, Nov. 17, 1875.—. . . In conse-quence of the promotion of Sir R. Baggallay, it would be desirable, that your Majesty should sanction that of Sir John Holker to the Attorney Generalship.

As high legal talent is wanted in the House of Commons, Mr. Disraeli recommends your Majesty to appoint Mr. Har-dinge Giffard [1] to the office of your Majesty's Solicitor-General. Mr. Giffard is not at present in Parliament, but Mr. Disraeli can arrange to bring that about.[2] There is no lawyer in the Ministerial benches, at present, equal to the post. . . .

To Lady Bradford.

2, WHITEHALL GARDENS, Nov. 17.—. . . Hardinge Giffard is Solicitor-General. . . . I don't know whether he will turn out as strong a man as his friends suppose, but at any rate I shall have a lawyer of high reputation, who will be able to state his opinions with effect. . . .

Further worry was entailed on Disraeli, and much correspondence with the Court and with the Admiralty, by a misadventure in the Solent in August. The royal yacht *Alberta*, when crossing from the Isle of Wight with the Queen on board, had the ill-fortune to run down the sailing yacht *Mistletoe* with fatal results. Her Majesty was immensely distressed by the accident, and was dis-satisfied both with the public comments and with the

---

[1] Afterwards Earl of Halsbury.

[2] The arrangement did not prove easy to bring about, and the Solicitor-General did not appear in Parliament till the spring of 1877, when he was elected for Launceston.

incidents and outcome of the various inquiries which
were instituted.   But, with all his burdens and responsibilities, Disraeli was able to enjoy a number of country
visits, and even to attend the Doncaster St. Leger, where
he betted and lost his money.   When he went subsequently to Sandringham, he had to put up with plenty of
chaff on this adventure from the Prince of Wales.   He
told Lady Bradford that he denied his losses at first,
' having really forgotten that I had been so unlucky and
so foolish.'   ' Sir,' he protested, ' a sweepstakes with some
ladies.'   ' Oh no,' replied the Prince, ' I hear a good round
sum; paid in bank notes, a rouleau.   I always thought
Bunny was sharp, but I never thought he would top all
by putting the Prime Minister on a dead horse !'

To Lord Bradford.

HUGHENDEN MANOR, *Aug.* 18.—I am most obliged to you
for your kind proposal.   If I might, I would offer to come at
once, I mean next Monday the 23rd, for several reasons—
1st I shd. be glad to see Weston with unshrivelled leaf; 2nd
because I am never happier than under your roof, and with
you and yours; and 3rdly because it would save me some
terrible local functions, opening a Cottage Hospital for the
hundred of Desborough, and wh. I wish to foist on the
shoulders of Charley Carington,[1] etc., etc., the impending
sense of wh., I believe, is the cause of my horrible despondency, wh. does not become a Minister, who has, I believe,
less cause for care and anxiety than any man, who ever had
his hand upon the helm.

You will never see *The Times* go wrong for any length of
time, tho' it is managed by those who are personally our foes.
It is managed in this way.   They receive daily, I am well
informed, about 300 letters from all parts of the country, and
it is from these spontaneous, unpaid and unsolicited, correspondents that they, after due reflection, derive their cue.
The Times thought it had caught us napping, and attacked
us, animated by their own personal feeling, and the passions
of their social patrons, but the 300 letters have poured in
since, and they find, wh. I believe is a fact, that the present
Ministry is popular with the country.   This is the explanation wh. was given to me by Baron Rothschild, who is a
Liberal and who knows everything.

[1] Now the Marquis of Lincolnshire.

Here our harvest is *splendid !* Nothing less, after all our
fears and trials; wages high and rising; our local manufacture,
the chair trade, exporting everywhere, to 'China and Peru'!
I get 2s. per foot for my beech, and can't supply them with
the raw material. My father got 6d. . . .

To Montagu Corry.

HUGHENDEN, *Sept.* 30, '75.—. . . After a short, but satisfactory, visit to Osborne, leaving my royal mistress in the
highest health and spirits, little anticipating the months of
mortification and anxiety that were then impending over
her, I went to this place for a week. I crossed the Solent in
the now too celebrated yacht, which was accorded to me as a
particular attention, and it was commanded by Welsh !

From Hughenden, I went to Weston for a week or so, and,
they[1] then going to Longshawe, I made my visit to Bretby,
and joined them again at Wortley, where I passed two or
three agreeable days, and then I went with the Bs. to Sandbeck, where I had a long engagement for the Race week.
I left Sandbeck and S. on the 18th, when our party broke
up, and then I went to Duncombe, a place of high calibre.
Returning, I passed a day with Harlowe[2] at Gopsal ! S.
was jeal.

I am well, and the old attack once menacing me, I treated
it, determinately, on my own system, and completely baffled it.
I have not had much repose: foreign affairs are troublesome, and between them and ' the collision,' it has rained telegrams, sometimes, as the diplomatic phrase is, ' in figures.'
S. helped me in this, and is very clever at it. She says ' it is
immense fun.' H.M., I think, has written to me every day,
until she went to Inverary. You really must put the royal
correspondence in some order.

I have had a function to open my new church, and on the
whole, I got through it with less annoyance, than I expected.
I got the Cheshams, without the prize ox himself, and Carington
and Harcourt and N. Sturt to meet the Bishop. Lady Ely
was to have been with us, but continual, and contradictory,
telegrams about her departure for Balmoral prevented her,
to her and our great vexation, for now she does not depart
until to-night.

I shall see her this afternoon, for I am now going to London,
preliminarily to a visit to-morrow to Sandringham, a farewell
visit previous to his departure for India : and I am asked ill
the 6th, but this is too long. I was about to enjoy some

---

[1] The Bradfords.   [2] Lady Howe.

repose, when this command arrived, and on the 9th, the Northcotes come here.

There is a great deal of business, official and personal,
rather pressing, to attend to, and he is the best of my colleagues
for that sort of work.   He can put his hand to anything. . . .

The prodigality of contributions for my local entertainments
was remarkable.   Bretby and Weston vied with each other
in cases of roses and nectarines, and peaches and grapes:
haunches of venison, and mighty hams.   When I had got all
this, the Rothschilds must have stripped one of the glasshouses at Gunnersbury, and all their gifts provided a public
dessert.   But what will surprise, and please, you was a cargo
of grapes from Rowton !

The restoration of Hughenden Church had been taken
in hand by Disraeli's new vicar, the Rev. Henry Blagden,
a young and eager High Churchman, whom he had
nominated in 1869. Mr. Blagden had not been the patron's
first choice when the vacancy occurred. Disraeli had
begun by offering the living to a Devonshire friend whose
acquaintance he may have made in his visits to Mrs.
Brydges Willyams at Torquay, the Rev. Reginald Barnes,
father of the accomplished ladies known on the stage as
Violet and Irene Vanbrugh. The offer was at first
accepted, and the presentation was even made out on
December 14, 1868; but Mr. Barnes never actually entered
upon the living, apparently because he found that the
highlands of Bucks would not suit a delicate man who
had long basked in the more genial climate of Devonshire. Mr. Blagden's energy, and the generosity of
Mrs. Blagden's father, accomplished what Disraeli had
long desired. The Church was a picturesque building,
mainly Early English in style, with a massive tower
containing Norman, if not Saxon, work; but the roof
was unsound, the tower had a crack extending nearly
from top to bottom, and the walls were so much out of
the perpendicular as not to be safe. Blomfield, the archi-
tect, recommended a new roof, a new aisle with the tower
rebuilt at its west end, thorough repair of the walls, and a
remodelling of the chancel. The patron took the alterations to the chancel as his share.   The work was carried

out, but not without friction, especially about the manorial right to a seat in the chancel, which Disraeli successfully asserted. Lady Beaconsfield was dead, and her husband was too much occupied as leader of Opposition and Prime Minister to exercise any personal superintendence over the operations.

To the Rev. Reginald Barnes.

GEORGE STREET, HANOVER SQUARE, *Wednesday, June* 11 [1873].—I am much touched by your letter, and shall, with satisfaction, insert your name in the list of our restorers; but as the accomplishment of my wishes is not so near, as I had hoped, you will, I am sure, not misinterpret my returning to you, for a time, your obliging cheque.

Hughenden, in a parochial sense, is no longer the Paradise it was, for nearly twenty years, under the gentleman[1] to whom I wished you to succeed. Parties have arisen among us, the unhappy Education Act[2] has brought affairs to a crisis, and, among other evils, it delays, and may even prevent, my consolatory intention of connecting the restoration of the church with the memory of her, whom I have lost. I thought at Whitsun I had settled these differences, but, since my return to town, they have broken out afresh; and having a great pressure of public affairs on me, and being deprived of the wise and skilful energy, that used to regulate my home interests, I sometimes almost despair of accomplishing my wishes.

I trust your health is good in the Favonian atmosphere of your lovely county. I always remember Devon with delight and affection.

Neither the difficulties hinted at in this letter, nor the fact that the new vicar felt it to be his duty to protest to his patron and principal parishioner against the policy of the Public Worship Regulation Bill, prevented the steady maintenance of friendly relations between the manor-house and the vicarage or the cordial encouragement by the squire of the parochial activities of the vicar and his wife. But Disraeli wrote of his parson to Lady Bradford, half in jest and half in earnest, as a ' rebellious priest,' and he was by no means pleased with the elaborate

---

[1] The Rev. C. W. Clubbe.   [2] Mr. Forster's Act of 1870.

ceremonial with which the restored church was opened. In his speech at the subsequent luncheon, after expressing his satisfaction that it could no longer be said of Hughenden that the house least honoured in the parish was the house of God, he significantly added: 'I trust that we shall show to the country that it is possible to combine the " beauty of holiness " with the profession of the pure Protestant faith of the Church of England.'

To Lady Bradford.

HUGHENDEN MANOR, *Sept.* 30, 1875.—. . . The sacerdotal procession was tremendous; not only a banner, but the Bishop's crosier, borne, and certainly nearer a 100 than 50 clergymen in surplices and particolored scarves. I was resolved not to be betrayed into a speech, and especially an ecclesiastical speech; but I was obliged to bring in a Protestant sentiment by way of protest. Everything was intoned, and the high altar and its rich work absolutely emblazoned with jewels. One lady in Warwickshire absolutely sent a string of pearls, and not mean ones, to enrich the altar cloth.

Nothing cd. be more stupid and misapprehensive than *The Times* remark on Harcourt's speech; wh. was perfectly playful and goodhumored, and very happy. It helped us on; he was so goodtempered that he wd. not allude to the rather ritualistic display, tho' he was glad of my Protestant phrase, wh. saved us. . . .

Disraeli had hoped for the pleasure of a visit from Lady Bradford at Hughenden in October; but she disappointed him at the last moment, and Bradford came alone.

To Anne Lady Chesterfield.

HUGHENDEN MANOR, *Oct.* 14, 1875.—I have been very busy, in many ways, and out of sorts a little, wh. is awkward when people are in the house. So I was not in a vein to write—even to you.

The Northcotes came here on Saturday, and depart tomorrow: a long visit, but there was much to do. There never was such an indefatigable worker as the Chanr. of the Exr.[1] Yesterday he went up to town, to clear up some points, but returned for dinner.

Bradford arrived on Monday, in a very good humor. By

---

[1] ' He is quite " a little busy bee," ' Disraeli wrote to Lady Bradford.

dining late, and retiring early, the day dies. We also managed a couple of rubbers. I can't, myself, get beyond that. In the third rubber my wits are woolgathering; in Downing St., Pekin, the Herzegovina, and the Admiralty. . . .

Your picture at Hughenden was much admired. Bradford admired it, and said he wd. have one of S. copied for me, and offered me his own. I accepted everything, but as S. wd. not come here, I do not know whether she wd. care to have her portrait here; or rather I do believe that she cares nothing about the matter.

I was very busy the morning of Tuesday, and have been so all the time, but we managed pretty well. . . . B[ernal] O[sborne] came down for dinner, and was, of course, immensely amusing, and Bradford seemed really pleased. They played whist in the evening, I sitting out, and Brad[for]d went off to Weston yesterday morning. B. O. departed this [morning], and the Ns. go to-morrow. . . .

The portraits which Bradford promised reached Hughenden early in the New Year.

To Lord Bradford.

Private. HUGHENDEN MANOR, *Jan.* 11, '76.—Lady Bradford arrived at Hughenden last night; a most charming picture; and you have signally added to the many kindnesses for which I am indebted to you and to your house.

It will be the greatest, and most treasured, ornament of my Gallery of Affection; for I shall have no portraits in it, except Byron, but of those who have personally influenced my heart and life. Those [? that] of Her Majesty, after her favorite and famous new painter, Herr von Angeli, and that of yourself, will soon arr've, and you will find them, I trust, on your next visit to Hughenden.

Here is a pleasant picture of Disraeli's working day, when alone, as Prime Minister, at Hughenden:

To Lady Bradford.

HUGHENDEN MANOR, *Oct.* 18, 1875.—. . . I do not breakfast in public: I only did that, in the summer, to see you, as I thought it was perhaps the only opportunity (and it often was) of seeing you in the course of the day, or of speaking to you, wh. you always seemed to grudge me.

I always rise at ½ pt. 7, go thro' my bag, and after my

toilette, saunter on the terrace, if the sun shines, **and review**
the peacocks; then I go up to my little room (my cabinet),
for my correspondence, and work at that till one.   Then
déjeûner; and at ½ past one, the messenger arrives, and as now
I am not at home to any human being, I change the scene
after *déjeûner*, and work at my boxes in the library.   It is a
favorite room of mine, and I like to watch the sunbeams on
the bindings of the books.

Now that you are more knowing in such things, I shd.
like to show you some of my Renaissance books.   My
Guicciardini and my Machiavelli are, as becomes such writers,
modern editions; but there are many volumes, of less use no
doubt, but of more rarity, wh. wd. charm your eye and taste.

Some day when I have time, wh. I really have not now,
for only to you cd. I write this, I will tell you about *Scmnium
Poliphili*, the dream of Poliphilus, one of the most beautiful
volumes in the world, and illustrated throughout by Giovanni
Bellini, as only in the Renaissance they could illustrate.   But
I was delighted yesterday, as I have been delighted before
and after, by a thin folio of the sacred time   It is a letter from
Cardinal Bembo to Giulio de' Medici, opening the Cardinal's
grand scheme for the nation to renounce writing in Latin and
dead languages, and dare to form a popular style in their own
beautiful vernacular.   The subject, the author, the beautiful
printing, the pages, 400 years old but without a stain—all
these are interesting circumstances; but then the exquisite
binding with the tiara and the keys, and the arms of the
Medici, boldly tooled on the side of the book—for Giulio had,
in the interval, become Pope Clement 7!   This was his
own copy, and must have been captured and secured in the
famous sack of Rome by the Constable of Bourbon. . . .

2, WHITEHALL GARDENS, *Nov.* 20.—. . . I agree with you
in liking him [Lord Hartington].   Indeed, I think he is
exactly the man to suit you; having all he qualities you
require and appreciate; a certain distinction, only made up
of fashion, rank, intelligence, and personal influence, and
none of that imagination and surplus sensitiveness, wh.
disturb the cr am of existence, and wh., tho' for a moment
interesting from novelty, are ultimately found to harass and
embarras life.   'He is easy to et on with because he is not
spoilt.'   We know who is constantly said to be 'spoilt,' tho'
perhaps most unjustly, and who, therefore, is not easy to get
on with. . .

CHAPTER XI.

An Imperial Foreign Policy.

1874–1875.

It was as an ' imperial country ' that Disraeli, when laying down his programme in 1872, invited his hearers to regard Great Britain; to maintain and heighten its imperial character was the special work at which he laboured as Minister. During the early months of his Administration the process was mainly silent and almost unperceived, though the diplomatic world soon began to realise that the atmosphere of British diplomacy under the inspiration of Disraeli was different from that to which they had grown accustomed since 1869; that observance of European treaties, respect for British rights, and consideration for British opinion in matters of European concern, were expected and would, if necessary, be enforced. The veil was a little lifted in May, 1875, when it was discovered that a wanton renewal by Germany of her attack on France would be resented not only by Russia but, under Disraeli, by England also; that England, with Disraeli Prime Minister, was not prepared to regard with indifference Continental complications which, though they might not affect her directly, yet would grievously upset the European balance. A sudden opportunity in November, 1875, revealed in a flash the new spirit, and immediately arrested the attention of the world.

The situation of Great Britain when Disraeli was called to power was in many ways unsatisfactory. There was, indeed, great prosperity at home. Though the social improvement of the mass of the people had not kept pace with the increase of wealth, and though there had been so

746

many years of abounding trade and good harvests that, in the normal cycle, bad times were nearly due, still the immediate prospect was good. Abroad, however, the reputation of the country had sunk. Looked up to for half a century as the leading power in Europe, she had been treated as a negligible quantity at the time of the Franco-German War; she had permitted Russia to tear up, no doubt under the guise of due diplomatic formalities, the Black Sea clauses of the Treaty of Paris; she had so mismanaged her relations with the United States as to have to put up with a judgment which condemned her to pay preposterously exaggerated damages for her negligence during the Civil War. Germany under Bismarck dominated the European field; but for the moment a more serious domination for the British Empire was that of Russia in the Near Eastern and Asiatic field. While Russian influence in this sphere extended from year to year, the direct connection of England with her great Asiatic dependency of India and with her Australasian dominions had been rendered less secure. Since the discovery of the Cape of Good Hope, the main route from Europe to India, and, indeed, the only one, with the exception of tedious caravan tracks across deserts and mountains under Turkish control, had been for generations by the open sea round Africa. In the middle of the nineteenth century competition had been set up by the establishment of the overland route across Egypt from Alexandria to Suez; this involved breaking bulk and was only suitable for passengers, mails, and light wares. But in 1869 the journey had been absolutely revolutionisedby the opening of the Suez Canal, which provided the means of a short, and uninterrupted, sea voyage from England and Europe to India, Australia, and the East. Palmerston had realised what a change the Canal would make in the defensive position of the British Empire, and had therefore opposed the project from the first. Disraeli also had opposed it, relying, however, mainly on what he believed to be its engineering impracticability. Gladstone had supported it in the name of progress, ridiculing the possibility of danger arising from it to British interests. As the English followed Palmerston's lead and refused co-operation, the Canal had been built by French enterprise and French money; it was managed by a French company, whose head office was in Paris; and the shares were held, roughly speaking, half by Frenchmen, and half by the Khedive of Egypt, the ruler of the country through which it passed, who was himself a more or less independent feudatory of the Sultan of Turkey. The Eastern trade was diverted at once to the new route, and, from the first, 75 or 80 per cent. of the shipping which used the Canal was British. Accordingly what became, as soon as it was completed, a vital link in British imperial communications was under the control of a foreign company and at the mercy of a foreign ruler. Gladstone, who held office during the first five years of the Canal's existence, omitted, in spite of several opportunities and of the representations of some of his colleagues, to take any steps to remedy this unsatisfactory position and to secure British interests in the new waterway.

Meanwhile Russia was pressing on, both in Europe and in Asia. In Europe she had restored her power in the Black Sea, had started a menacing Pan-Slavonic propaganda, and was becoming as formidable as ever to the Sublime Porte. In Asia, in spite of repeated assurances from the Tsar and his Ministers to the contrary, her proconsuls were rapidly advancing her frontiers by annexing, one after another, the decadent Tartar and Turcoman States which occupied the country between Siberia on the north, and Persia, Afghanistan, and India on the south. General Kaufmann, who became Governor of Turkestan in 1867, captured Samarkand and subdued Bokhara in 1868, and reduced Khiva in 1873, proceeding in 1875 to the conquest of Khokand north of the Syr Darya. In 1870 he opened friendly communications with the Ameer of Afghanistan, into whose immediate neighbourhood Russian power had now penetrated. The Indian Government, to whom the Ameer referred this new development, treated it with indifference, relying on the assurances of the St. Petersburg Government that they regarded Afghanistan, the frontier State across which an invader from the north-west must advance to attack India, as completely outside the sphere of Russian influence. Kaufmann was therefore able to proceed without interference in a persistent policy of tampering with the Ameer's fidelity to the British connection. After the fall of Khiva, Sher Ali, the Ameer, felt that the advance of Russia made it indispensable for him to know where he stood between the two great European forces in Asia. He asked for a definite promise of aid from the British Government in case of Russian attack; and one of the last acts of Gladstone's Ministry was to refuse, in adherence to the Lawrence policy of avoiding all inter-meddling with Afghanistan, any definite engagement beyond vague assurances of support. From this time Sher Ali steadily gravitated to the Russian side.

For dealing with difficulties of this kind Disraeli was especially fitted by the bent of his mind and the experiences of his career. It was the fortune of Great Britain, at a time when the British Empire in Asia and the highway to the East were threatened, to have a Prime Minister of Oriental extraction and imagination, whose whole outlook had been coloured at the most impressionable period of his life by his travels in the Levant, and who had played a large and decisive part in the affairs of India in the troubled fifties. Disraeli's personal and anxious attention to the problem was therefore assured; but he necessarily relied much on two colleagues, his Foreign Secretary and his Indian Secretary, Derby and Salisbury. The intimate political and personal relations which had bound him to Derby from the first made their confidential co-operation, in spite of serious differences of temperament, easy and natural; but with Salisbury, just converted from critic into colleague, the beginnings of mutual trust had to be created. Disraeli, guided by good feeling no less than by his knowledge of men, set himself to win confidence by giving it; showing abundantly the reliance he felt on his colleague's capacity to administer rightly the great affairs entrusted to his care, and his own anxiety to help and support him in all difficulties; and recurring, as we have seen, to his advice on many important matters outside departmental work. Approximation was aided by the mutual realisation of a great community of aim in imperial affairs, and of a considerable similarity of temper and method in dealing with them. A lover of peace, Salisbury was never afraid on fitting occasion to assume serious responsibilities which might lead to war; resembling in this respect his chief, and having none of that tendency to hesitation and procrastination which often afflicted Derby at a critical moment.

In the very first days of the Government we find Disraeli making arrangements for combined working with Derby and Salisbury, and following with keenness the Russian advance in Central Asia.

To Lord Salisbury.

BRIGHTON, *March* 7, 1874.—Lord Northbrook's letter is dated Feb. 5th.   He had then received Sir Henry Rawlinson's mem. but does not seem to have received a copy of Lord Granville's despatch to Ld. A. Loftus dated Jan. 7th; but wh. as I learn, was not sent off till the 17th.

Lord Northbrook cd., therefore, know nothing of the subsequent assurances of the Russian Government; that no such expedition, as he referred to, was to take place.

The despatches of Lord A. Loftus in consequence of Lord Granville's despatch, and the concluding despatch of Prince Gortchakoff to Comte Brunnow, of wh. a copy was left with H.M.'s Government (communicated to Granville by Brunnow on the 17th Feb.), contain, on the part of the Russian Govt., a complete disclaimer of the intentions, wh. it was supposed to entertain at the time when Lord Northbrook's letter was written; this information is, therefore, superseded by what we have since heard.

The Russians may be lying, but we cannot do more, so far

as diplomacy is concerned, than obtain from them such
pledges as they have given.

But the question arises, have you seen these despatches ?
I have in MS.; and they are, now, in that form, I believe,
circulating thro' the Cabinet—but it strikes me, that the
system of communicating such information among ourselves
is not a very convenient one.

The whole correspondence is in print at the F.O. by this
time, and a copy will, of course, be sent to each Cab. Minister.
This by the way.

It seems to me, that a private communication to you from
the Viceroy should be treated as a private letter from an
Ambassador to the For. Secy. of State.   It is always forwarded
to the P. Minister, but not circulated, unless it leads to questions of instant business and responsibility.

In the instance of Northbrook's letter, had it been sent
on to me immediately, I should have requested you and Lord
Derby to have met me at D. S. and then we would have
ascertained exactly how we stood.   There ought to be some
system, especially in these times, when the Secretaries of
State for F.O. and India should be able to communicate
with more promptitude, and, if necessary, reserve, than at
present seems the habit.   I do not, at this moment, see any
better system, than that which I have intimated—but we
will talk the matter over together, and I doubt not will arrive
at a sound conclusion.

I question, also, the expediency of sending despatches,
like Lord Northbrook's, in a common circulation box, except
marked ' strictly confidential.'   In these days, every private
secy. has a Cabinet key, I believe—perhaps I might add,
I fear; and we should encourage some processes of reserve.

I feel confident you will not be offended by the frankness
of these remarks.   They are literally *currente calamo*, and are
jotted down rather for our future joint consideration, than in
any spirit of pedantic over-regulation. . . .

Not merely the Central Asian question, but also that of
the Suez Canal, was forced on Disraeli's attention immediately on assuming office.   Ferdinand de Lesseps, the great
Frenchman who had conceived and executed the work,
had hitherto failed to make it remunerative, and had
in consequence given the Gladstone Government those
opportunities of securing British interests in the Canal
which they had neglected to utilise.   His latest resource
had been to increase the tonnage duties from which the

company derived its revenue by levying them on a novel
basis which the maritime nations, and especially Great
Britain, considered not to be warranted by the terms of
the concession, and which, early in 1874, had been
condemned as illegal by an International Commission.
Lesseps defied the Commission and the British Admiralty,
insisted that no ship should be let through the Canal
which did not pay on the higher scale, and was only
reduced to reason by the mobilisation by the Khedive
of 10,000 men to evict the company.

To Lord Derby.

WHITEHALL G., *April* 23, 1874.—The Lesseps affair is
getting serious ; he has gone to Jerusalem to get out of the
way, but there is little doubt he intends mischief, at least
what we call mischief, for, so far as I can judge, the law is on
his side.

I do not like to contemplate the Canal being shut up for
months, wh. will probably be the case.

Could we advise the Porte to postpone the enforcement of
their regulations for one month; and, in the interval, make an
arrangement ?   Lesseps is ' toujours prêt de negocier sur la
base du droit.'   His self-love would be spared and soothed,
if you took the matter in hand, and you would gain European
glory.

My own opinion is that the ultimate and proper solution
would be an International Commission, like that of the
mouths of the Danube.

From Lord Derby.

Private.   F.O., *April* 24, 1874.—Read Col. Stokes's mem.
on the Suez Canal. . . .   You will see in this the true explanation of Lesseps's conduct.   The surtax question is little more
than a pretext.   Our engineers were right as to the difficulty
of keeping up the Canal when made.   Port Said is silting up,
and cannot be maintained in a state of efficiency without an
outlay greater than the company can afford, except at an
absolute sacrifice of profit for years to come.   In fact, the
undertaking is all but bankrupt: and M. L[esseps] is probably
well pleased at having an excuse to get out of it.

We cannot let the Canal go to ruin: it is too useful to us.
Stokes suggests buying out the shareholders, by guaranteeing
them a fixed dividend, and working the Canal through the
agency of an International Commission.   There are difficulties

in the way, obvious and grave; but things really look as if
this were the only way out of the scrape. . . .

Our course is plain. Lesseps has put himself in the wrong,
all the Powers are agreed in saying so (even France): and we
must maintain our decision. That does not preclude his
being fairly, and even generously, treated. But you must
bear in mind, in considering his recent sayings and doings,
that the thing is a commercial failure, utter and hopeless, and
that he knows it.

Disraeli did not rest content with solving the immediate
difficulty. He made up his mind to secure British
interests in the new waterway by obtaining some control
over the company, whose ' bankrupt ' state seemed to
provide an opportunity. He went to work, not through
the regular diplomatic agency, but by the private methods
which he had used in the Government of 1858–1859, when
he had sent Earle on a mission to Napoleon III. It was,
on one side, a financial matter, and he invited in May the
aid of the prince of financiers, his old friend Baron Lionel
de Rothschild; with the result that Rothschild's eldest
son, M.P. for Aylesbury, and afterwards Lord Rothschild,
went over to Paris to intimate to Lesseps that the British
Government were prepared to purchase the Canal if
suitable terms could be arranged. The mission was a
failure. French patriotic feeling, then reviving after the
disasters of the war of 1870, was not disposed to tolerate
any surrender of French rights over a French canal; and
Lesseps, after his repeated rebuffs by England in past
years, and his quarrel with the British Government and
British shipowners over the tonnage question, was in no
mood to renew his previous offers. Disraeli was disappointed, but bided his time, keeping constantly in
touch with the Canal authorities. ' On more than one
occasion,' he told the House of Commons in 1876, ' M. de
Lesseps came over here himself, and entered into communication with us as he had before with our predecessors,
but there was no possible means of coming to any settlement which would be satisfactory to the proprietary.'

In the comparative calm of the first eighteen months

of the Disraeli Administration, a few episodes in foreign
affairs attract attention, and may serve to indicate the
Prime Minister's aims and methods.   A visit to London,
during the first session, of the Tsar Alexander, whose
daughter had just been married to Queen Victoria's
second son, the Duke of Edinburgh, was the occasion of
a difficulty with the Court, which Disraeli was able to
settle in such a fashion as to command the admiration
of his colleagues, and to contribute materially to the
maintenance of friendly relations with Russia.   The
Emperor's visit was to be prolonged for a couple of days
beyond the date fixed by the Queen for entering upon
that spring sojourn at Balmoral which her physicians
prescribed for her health; and Her Majesty refused at
first to modify her plans.

From Lord Derby.

Private.   F.O., *May* 4, 1874.—The more I think of the
matter, and the more I hear what is said, the stronger becomes
my conviction that the Queen's going away during her guest's
stay in England will really make a serious trouble.   It will
be talked of everywhere as an instance of incivility so marked
as to appear intentional: it will be resented by the Russians,
who are as touchy as Yankees, and for the same reason: it
will entirely destroy whatever good result may be expected
from the marriage and the visit: in India it will be taken up
by the native press—much of which is nearly as seditious as
that of Ireland—as a proof that the two countries are not
really on good terms; and what possible excuse can we make ?
Not health, for if the great lady can bear 5 days of ceremonies
she can bear 7: not public business, for what has she to do at
Balmoral ?   It is . . . the less excusable because, of all
persons connected with the reception, she will have the least
personal trouble.

As a rule, I try always to keep matters which concern the
Government, and matters which concern the Court, as far
apart as possible : but it is not always possible: and if there
is a row, part of the blame will fall on us.

Do try what you can to set this business right.   Nobody
can have managed the lady better than you have; but is
there not just a risk of encouraging her in too large ideas of
her personal power, and too great indifference to what the
public expects ?   I only ask: it is for you to judge.

To Lady Bradford.

Ho. of Comm., *May 5.*—My head is still on my shoulders. The great lady has absolutely postponed her departure! Everybody had failed, even the Prince of Wales; but she averted her head from me—at least I fancied so—at the drawing room to-day, and I have no doubt I am not in favor. I can't help it. Salisbury says I have saved an Afghan War, and Derby compliments me on my unrivalled triumph. . . .

From Queen Victoria.

May 7.—. . . [The Queen] feels much the kindness of Mr. Disraeli as expressed to herself and Sir William Jenner on the occasion of the delay of her departure for Scotland. . . . It is for Mr. Disraeli's sake and as a return for his great kindness that she will stop till the 20th. . . . The Queen thinks Lord Derby and Lord Salisbury have little knowledge of what is the etiquette between Sovereigns.

Disraeli took his full share in the festivities held in honour of the Russian visit.

To Anne Lady Chesterfield.

2, Whitehall Gardens, *May 15, 1874.*—. . . Yesterday was the great festival at Windsor, and really not unworthy of the Crown of England. St. George's Hall was a truly grand scene, and cd. not be easily surpassed: at least I have never seen it equalled, tho' I have dined, in the great days of France, in the Gallery of Diana. . . .

The Emperor is high-bred: dignified, but soft in his manners, not that *ton de garnison* wh. offends me sometimes in the Russian Princes, particularly the Cesarevitch, and the Grand Duke Constantine.

I only arrived from Windsor to-day at noon. At 3 o'ck. I am to have an audience of the Emperor at Buckingham Palace. I dine at Marlboro' House to meet him; and I close with a ball at Stafford House in his honor! And at ½ past four I must be at the House of Commons! It is difficult to get thro' such a day, and I have to change my dress as often as an actor! . . .

May 16.—. . . At three o'ck. the Emperor held a levée of the Diplomatic Body and our Ministry at Buckingham Palace. There I had an audience, which was an audience rather of phrases, but nothing but friendliness to England and hopes that my Government wd. cherish and confirm those

feelings. His mien and manners are gracious and graceful,
but the expression of his countenance, wh. I now could very
closely examine, is sad.

Whether it is satiety, or the loneliness of despotism, or the
fear of violent death, I know not, but it was a visage of, I
should think, habitual mournfulness. . . .

The Government and the Queen did not miss the
opportunity to strengthen the bonds of amity between
England and Russia. Under Derby's advice the Queen
expressed to the Emperor on his departure her desire for
a frank and free exchange of ideas at all times, so as to
avoid misunderstandings between the two countries—
a desire which Alexander reciprocated. Disraeli, however, did not believe that in existing circumstances
complete agreement was possible. He wrote to Salisbury
on June 2: ' I have no great faith in a real " understanding
with Russia " as to our Eastern possessions, but much
faith, at this moment, in a supposed understanding,
wh. will permit us to avail ourselves of the present
opportunity of settling and strengthening our frontiers.'

Early in 1875 differences about the proper treatment
of the Spanish Government brought out in high relief the
characters of four individuals who were shortly to have
a large share in moulding that Eastern policy by which
the Beaconsfield Government is mainly remembered. The
chaos of Republican administration in Spain had culminated towards the close of 1874 in a strong movement for
a Bourbon restoration; and in January, 1875, the young
Alphonso, son of the ex-Queen Isabella, was proclaimed
King. Queen Victoria, attracted by the romance of
a youthful Prince restored by an unexpected turn of
Fortune's wheel to his hereditary throne, and anxious
to support the cause of Constitutional Monarchy in
Europe, pressed for his immediate recognition, and
for the observance by the British Government of a
very sympathetic attitude to the new régime. Derby,
the Queen complained, was ' so terribly impartial that
he will never express interest one way or the other ';
but it was surely wise, in regard to a country which

had gone through so many revolutions in the past
six years, to use the caution and circumspection by
which the Foreign Secretary was, above all men,
distinguished. Derby was confirmed in his waiting
attitude by the British Minister at the Spanish Court.
This was Austen Henry Layard, the excavator of Nineveh,
an old acquaintance of Disraeli's, nephew of the Austens
who had befriended the young author of *Vivian Grey*.
Layard, a Palmerstonian Liberal, had been Foreign Under-
Secretary in Palmerston's last Administration; and was
therefore more in sympathy with the Republican Government which had fallen than with the Conservative
Administration which Alphonso established and which
necessarily relied on Catholic support. But in any case
he was right in advising the Home Government to be
cautious, as a formidable Carlist insurrection on the one
hand and the discontent of the Republicans on the other
rendered Alphonso's prospects doubtful. The Queen was
impatient of these arguments, which Derby pressed on
her with more logic than sympathy, and wrote of him to
Disraeli as 'that very peculiar person Lord D.,' who was
'very difficult to manage.' It needed all Disraeli's tact,
and his loyalty to his Sovereign on the one hand, and to
his colleague and his colleague's agent on the other, to
steer through the difficulties. He was less disposed than
Derby to trust Layard entirely, and wrote to Derby on
January 12: 'It is unfortunate, at this crisis, we have
such a man as Layard there. Tho' of unquestionable
talents, he is prejudiced and passionate, and always—I
will not say misleads—but certainly misinforms us';
on February 20, 'his tone is not diplomatic'; and on
March 2, he deprecated 'the exaggerated view Mr.
Layard takes of the Protestant party and interests in
Spain. They really are nothing,' Disraeli shrewdly
added, 'and tho', when the Republican and infidel
party is in power, the Protestants are permitted to hold
up their heads in order to mortify the Church, their
number and influence are alike contemptible.' But, as

he told Derby, 'I make it a rule to support everything which you have well considered,' and therefore sustained his policy against the royal remonstrances.

He was, however, especially anxious to promote a cordial and sympathetic feeling between his royal mistress and his colleague, and succeeded at any rate for the moment. The artist, the diplomatist, and the courtier in Disraeli are all brilliantly displayed in a letter which he wrote to the Queen describing his management of his uncourtly friend.

To Queen Victoria.

2, WHITEHALL GARDENS, *March* 21, 1875.—Mr. Disraeli with his humble duty to your Majesty:

He is grateful to your Majesty for your Majesty, amid all the cares and pressure of public business, graciously making him acquainted with the result of the audience of the Secretary of State. It much relieved Mr. Disraeli, for the disquietude of your Majesty on this matter has often greatly distressed him.

He had an interview with Lord Derby after the Cabinet, which was at 12 o'clock and lasted two hours. Mr. Disraeli spoke to him very seriously and earnestly about affairs, and adjured him, in the approaching audience, to do justice to himself, and step out of his icy panoply.

The necessary gulf, between a Sovereign and her Ministers, is no bar to confidence and sympathy, and, without these qualities, it is difficult to see how public affairs in England can be satisfactorily carried on.

Lord Derby did not speak a single word, but, when Mr. Disraeli closed the interview, he would accompany Mr. Disraeli, and when they reached the street door in Downing Street, instead of going into the Foreign Office, he offered Mr. Disraeli his arm, and would walk home with him, but in silence.

Mr. Disraeli invited him to enter his house, and lunch. He replied he never lunched; it prevented work. And, then, even with softness, he gave Mr. Disraeli his hand, which is not his habit, and said 'Good-bye, old friend.' 'Dear friend' Mr. Disraeli assumes Lord Derby would say to no one, but Mr. Disraeli had hopes, from this moment, that the impending audience might happily bear fruit. . . .

The points of view of the Queen and the Foreign Secretary were, however, too divergent to be permanently reconciled. The Queen pressed for the removal of Layard to some other post, and Derby definitely appealed to his chief for support. ' The question really is,' he wrote on April 22, ' whether our representatives abroad are to send statements of fact which seem to them true, or to colour them and dress them up to suit what they suppose to be the prevailing ideas at home. . . . I cannot agree to any proposal for [Layard's] removal, unless it were to give him a better post; and even then I do not think this would be a convenient time.' Disraeli at once (April 24) rallied to his colleague's side. ' As I do not think you ought to bear all the brunt of the fray, I have written to the great lady, I think, conclusively on the matter: telling her that, in the opinion of her Govt., L. is substantially correct in his views; that he cannot be removed, as it would be a triumph to the *Parti Prêtre*.'

The Queen, according to her sound constitutional practice, yielded to her Prime Minister and Foreign Minister; but her instinct was right as against Derby's caution and Layard's prejudice. Alphonso XII. established his position, to the advantage of Spain and of Europe, and his son occupies his throne to-day with a granddaughter of Queen Victoria as his royal consort. Layard was retained at Madrid till he was promoted in 1877 to be the convinced instrument, at the embassy at Constantinople, of that Eastern policy which Beaconsfield forwarded with the Queen's support, but which Derby resigned rather than pursue at the risk of war.

The outstanding fact of the international situation in Europe, as Disraeli found it on his return to power, was the dominance of Germany, and of Germany's masterful Chancellor, Bismarck. He had consolidated the German people into a strong Empire under the Prussian kingship; he had bound Austria to his chariot, though as yet only informally; he had humbled and crippled France; he was in friendly relation with Russia; and he was now, by legislation subjecting the churches to the State, trying a fall with the Pope. His experience of the Gladstone Ministry inclined him to regard England as a negligible factor in European affairs; but, until he had better assurances of the temper of the new Government, he showed them a benevolent friendliness, proffering them in particular his good offices in regard to the Eastern Question. ' I begin to think Bismarck means business,' wrote Disraeli to Derby on January 6, 1875, after reading a despatch from Lord Odo Russell, British Ambassador in Berlin; ' and, if so, the future may be less difficult.'

German policy in the spring made the position not less but more difficult. Catholic Belgium was stirred to its depths by the progress of Bismarck's campaign against the Pope, and things were said and done there by bishops and others which were made the excuse for grave warnings by the German Government. Belgium was told that, while it was incumbent upon every State not to allow its territory to be the basis of attacks against the peace of neighbouring States and against the security of their subjects, the doctrine applied with special force to a State enjoying the privilege of neutrality; that the perfect fulfilment of that duty was a tacitly presumed condition of its neutrality. Belgium promptly amended its penal laws in response to this threat to its neutrality and independence; but Disraeli began to realise that it would be necessary to stand up to Bismarck, if life in Europe for other, and particularly smaller, nations was to be tolerable. On reading the despatches from Brussels, he wrote on April 18 to Derby: ' We shall have no more quiet times in diplomacy, but shall be kept in a state of unrest for a long time: probably till the beginning of the next thirty years' war.' He gave a hint in the House of Commons.

To Queen Victoria.

HOUSE OF COMMONS, *April 12*, 1875.— . . . Mr. Disraeli has answered a question to-night about Germany and Belgium, which he hopes may do good, and will not displease your Majesty.

He endeavored to convey the impression, that cordial and confidential relations existed between your Majesty's Govern-

ment and that of Germany, which is flattering to Prince
Bismarck, and which he wishes to be believed, but at the same
time, struck a clear note about Belgium, which the House
understood, and cheered. A county member said to him
when he sate down, ' It was trust in God, and keep your powder
dry.'

From warning Belgium Germany passed to menacing
France. The German press was mobilised to call attention
to the rapid resurrection of French military power and
preparation, German diplomatists held language of a
similar character in the various European capitals,
Bismarck himself spoke serious words to Odo Russell;
and it looked as if he were endeavouring to force a
quarrel upon his recent victim before her recovery was
complete, in order to crush her once for all. France
turned for support to Russia and England, and her
Foreign Minister appealed to public opinion by communicating the facts to Blowitz, the famous Paris correspondent
of *The Times*. But even before Blowitz's article appeared
on May 6 and horrified a world desirous of peace, the
Tsar Alexander, who was about to pay a visit to the
German Emperor at Berlin, seems to have interposed
and sent an urgent message to his expectant host deprecating a hasty decision; and Derby was able on May 2 to
write, perhaps prematurely, to Disraeli: 'I believe the
alarm is over now, but nobody will answer for next year.'

Disraeli was fully alive to the danger, and resolved to
show Bismarck and Europe that England was to be
reckoned with; ' Bismarck is really another old Bonaparte
again, and he must be bridled,' he wrote to Lady Chesterfield. His former tendency to a political friendship with
France was revived. ' I had a rather long conversation
about French politics with Mr. Disraeli,' wrote Lord
Lyons, British Ambassador in Paris, on April 21, ' and
I found him thoroughly well up in the subject. He
wishes to encourage confidence and goodwill on the part
of France towards England, but sees the danger to
France herself of any such appearance of a special and
separate understanding as would arouse the jealousy of

Bismarck.'[1] Disraeli was entirely in accord with the Queen, who wrote on May 5, that 'every means should be used to prevent such a monstrous iniquity as a war'; and Derby gave formal assurances in this sense to the French Government.

To Lord Derby.

2, WHITEHALL GDNS., *May 6*, 1875.—I had an audience yesterday: she was very gracious, and, speaking entirely on foreign affairs, I thought very sagacious and intelligent.

She is much pleased with your letter which she praised highly; 'clear and full,' she said. She was ready to do anything, that you and I wished her to do in these matters; would write, if we wished it, to the Emperor of Russia, etc., etc. She said the Emperors met at Berlin on Monday, and they would be there two days. Then she threw out the idea, that Ld. Cowley might be sent there by you—and so on.

My own impression is that we shd. construct some concerted movement to preserve the peace of Europe, like Pam did when he baffled France and expelled the Egyptians from Syria.

There might be an alliance between Russia and ourself for this special purpose; and other powers, as Austria, and perhaps Italy, might be invited to accede. . . .

May 8.—I replied, that in all probability, Schou[valoff][2] was with you at this moment, and that I wd. write to her at Windsor after I had seen you: also, that there was a Cabinet to-day at three, and, if necessary, I wd. write after that.

I have just got Odo's letter. It only makes me more anxious to pursue the course we contemplated yesterday. . . .

It was on a Saturday that the Cabinet was held, and the Tsar and his Chancellor, Gortchakoff, were due for the Berlin visit on the following Monday. Odo Russell was instructed by telegraph strongly to support the Tsar's movement for peace; and the Queen wrote to that Emperor herself[3] in the same sense. Ministers felt fairly confident because, as Derby wrote to Disraeli on May 10, 'we know what the [Russian] Emperor is prepared to say and that it is in the sense we desire.' The next day they learnt that the British Ambassador had received all the requisite assurances.

---

[1] Lord Newton's *Lord Lyons*, Vol. II., p. 73.

[2] Russian Ambassador in London, who had just returned from St. Petersburg to his post, *via* Berlin.

[3] The correspondence is printed in *The Letters of Queen Victoria*, Second Series, Vol. II., pp. 396 and 398.

Lord Odo Russell to Lord Derby.

(*Cypher telegram*.) BERLIN, *May* 11, 1875.—I have had a most satisfactory interview with Prince Gortchakoff at Prince Bismarck's house. They are both agreed that the peace of Europe shall not be disturbed, and co-operate for the maintenance of peace.

Confidential. Prince Gortchakoff has since called to tell me that he is so perfectly satisfied with the result we have achieved and the assurances given that he thinks we had better say no more for the present and allow the subject to drop.

To Anne Lady Chesterfield.

2, WHITEHALL GARDENS, *May* 12.—We shall have peace. . . . The news from Berlin came in the middle of the night on Monday, but they wisely did not wake me. However, it gave me an appetite for breakfast. . . .

The measures taken, first by Russia, and then by Great Britain, had been successful. Peace was for the time assured; and both the German Emperor and Bismarck strongly protested that Germany had never for a moment entertained the intentions attributed to her. The world, however, has made up its mind that the menace was real; the only question still in doubt is whether it proceeded from Bismarck himself, or from the military party forcing his hand. As England did not take action until after the Emperor of Russia had intimated to Berlin his strong disapproval, British intervention on this occasion has often been treated as of little account. In accordance with his temperament, the Foreign Secretary himself was one of the principal minimisers.

To Lord Derby.

HUGHENDEN MANOR, *May* 18, '75.—Your policy seems to be very popular, and very successful—I congratulate you heartily. It is encouraging. We must not be afraid of saying ' Bo to a goose.'

But we must get our forces in trim. We shall be able to do that next year. The revenue is coming in well.

From Lord Derby.

KNOWSLEY, *May* 20.—. . . We have been lucky in our foreign policy; for what we did involved no risk and cost no trouble, while it has given us the appearance of having helped, more than we really did, to bring about the result.

To Lord Derby.

2, WHITEHALL GARDENS, *May* 30, '75.—Let me earnestly impress upon you, in case Granville enquires or pushes you at all, to adhere to what I said in H. of C.: that it would not be expedient that our 'representation' shd. be produced at present. And I don't want it to be produced this sess. It is working well: *omne ignotum, etc.*

However Derby might seek to minimise what he and Disraeli had done, public opinion, both at home and abroad, recognised that England had reverted in a striking manner to the traditions of her foreign policy before Gladstone's premiership. The French Government expressed its gratitude; and Bismarck at once realised that he had to deal now in England with people who could make up their minds and act.

To Lady Bradford.

2, WHITEHALL GARDENS, *May* 14.—. . . P. Bis[marck] has sent a message to me and Derby, thanking us for our interference, and glad to see Eng[land] taking an interest in Cont[inental] affairs again. I believe, since Pam, we have never been so energetic, and in a year's time we shall be more.

Bismarck's compliments veiled a feeling of resentment at having unexpectedly to reckon once more with an international factor which he had come to think might be left out of account. A letter from the Crown Princess of Prussia, which her mother Queen Victoria forwarded to Disraeli, throws much light on the Chancellor's real views and position.

The Crown Princess to Queen Victoria.

POTSDAM, *June* 5, '75.—The Crown Prince saw the Great Man yesterday evening, who is going away into the country for some time. He assured him that he sees no cause any-

where for alarm on the political horizon—that he had never
wished for war, nor intended it—that it was all the fault of
the Berlin press, etc., etc. He said he deeply regretted
England being so unfriendly towards us, and the violent
articles in *The Times* against us. He could not imagine why
England suddenly took up a position against us. That you
had been much excited and worked upon against us, etc.
He even named the Empress Eugénie ! ! ! This seems so
foolish to me ! Certain it is that he did not intend (as you
will read in the little German *aperçu*) to alarm the world to
the extent he has done, and is now very much annoyed at the
consequences. He also fancies that in England there is yet
anxiety about India, and that England must therefore try
to make friends with Russia (*à nos dépens*). The P. of W.'s
journey to India is mentioned as a symptom ! This seems
to *me* very absurd, but that is what he thinks ! Lord Derby's
speech has also offended him, which I cannot understand.
I feel sure that all this irritation will blow over, but to us,
and to many quiet and reflecting Germans, it is very sad,
and appears very hard, to be made an object of universal
distrust and suspicion, which we naturally are, as long as
Prince Bismarck remains the sole and omnipotent ruler of our
destinies. His will alone is law here, and on his good or bad
humour depend our chances of safety and peace. . . .

Disraeli realised that the representations of the country
would not command respect abroad without a sufficient
backing of force. The Cabinet had already sanctioned
in the Budget of the current year additional expenditure
on the Navy and Army, and, after the anxious days of
April and May, even Derby reluctantly agreed that a
further increase was inevitable.

To Queen Victoria.

10, DOWNING STREET, *Jan.* 14, 1875.—Mr. Disraeli with
his humble duty to your Majesty :
Mr. Hardy was able to attend the Cabinet, which sate two
hours, and discussed the military expenditure. There must
be an increase, probably between £5[00,000] and £600,000, on
the Army and Navy. It is to be regretted, that it should
take place this year, as a Conservative Ministry, according
to their opponents, always increases expenditure. But it
cannot be helped, and Mr. Disraeli will be satisfied if the
expenditure, though increased, is not accompanied by fresh
taxation. But the government of the country becomes more

expensive every year. A great portion of the expenditure,
too, is automatic, self-acting, as education for example, the
amount claimed for which is this year enormous, but cannot
be refused. . . .

From Lord Derby.

F.O. [*June*, 1875].—I should be more impressed by these
papers if I could remember a time when the C.-in-Chief had
not been seriously alarmed at the state of our armaments.

No doubt the Continent is arming; but with Germany and
France watching one another, both are more likely to be
civil to us than if they were on good terms.

It is a question, too, how long these enormous armaments
will be endured by the masses who are compelled to serve.

But I do not suppose you want the question argued on
abstract and general grounds. What we have to consider is
what we can do.

The discussions in Cabinet left on my mind an impression
that an increase of £300,000 or £400,000 is justifiable, because
inevitable—I mean taking Army and Navy together. Beyond
that we must not go. . . .

It should not be overlooked that during the crisis of
May, 1875, as during the Tsar's visit to London in May,
1874, Disraeli's intervention was directed to the promotion
of friendlier relations between Great Britain and Russia, an
object which, in spite of acute antagonism at one period,
he pursued throughout his career. While recognising
that the interests of the two countries might well clash,
he recognised also that it was the duty of statesmanship,
so far as might be, to prevent such a clashing as would
lead to war. Hence his anxiety during all these early
months of his Ministry with regard to the position of
Afghanistan, where he held that a system of drift would
be fatal. Salisbury was convinced, and Disraeli agreed
with him, that, with Russian emissaries at the ear of the
Ameer, it was highly desirable that the Indian Government on its side should have a duly established agent at his
court. This policy Salisbury pressed upon Northbrook,
the Viceroy; but was met by strong representations of its
inexpediency in view of the certain unwillingness, and
probable refusal, of the Ameer to accept such an agent.

To Lord Salisbury.

HUGHENDEN MANOR, *Oct.* 15, 1874.—. . . Persia and Afghan[ista]n are broken reeds—and I am sorry to see an inclination, on the part of Northbrook, to lean on them.

Our man in Persia, Thompson, the same. He is restless for arms, ammunition, officers, and, of course, subsidies, for the Shah !

Utterly useless for our object; indeed pernicious, as they would, and rightly, offend Russia. But the arms, the ammunition, discipline, and treasure, if used at all, would probably be used against us—at least, against the Turks.

Oct. 17.—The telegrams I receive from China this morning are very menacing; and I more than fear that war between that country and Japan is inevitable. This will increase your difficulties, for the East hangs together, and is wonderfully mesmeric.

You have a critical time before you in your department. I am sorry to hear that Northbrook disdains the only means by wh. safe intelligence can be obtained in Asia. This is a very serious point. However, I have the utmost confidence in your judgment, firmness, and resource.

CRICHEL, WIMBORNE, *Jan.* 6, 1875.—I had been thinking, for more than a month past, that it would be very satisfactory to me, were I, the moment I got to town, to have a full conversation with you on Indian affairs. They occasion me some disquietude, and would occasion me more, were it not for my firm, I might say unlimited, confidence in the colleague to whom those affairs are intrusted.

And now I receive your confidential and interesting despatch. . . .

I have always been strongly in favor of our Government being represented in Afghanistan, tho' not unaware of the difficulties and dangers. The necessity, however, outweighs everything. It is a question, whether we should not have an agent both at Candahar and Herat. . . .

To Lady Bradford.

10, DOWNING ST., *Jan.* 13, 7 *o'clock.*—. . . Ld. Salisbury called on me this morning at 12, and we had an interesting hour over Central Asia, and all its mysterious fortunes and perils. It is impossible for anyone to be more cordial ! . . .

While the question of the external security of India on its north-west frontier hung fire, Disraeli was deeply engaged in promoting its internal consolidation and

contentment by arranging for a personal visit of the heir
to the Throne. The original idea appears not to have
been his, but to have come from the Prince of Wales
himself, who had already visited the principal Colonies
and rightly thought it his duty now to proceed to India.
The Queen gave her assent; but, on reconsideration of
the many personal and political difficulties involved,
would gladly have recalled it. Her Prime Minister and
Indian Secretary, however, recognised the immense
political importance of establishing those personal relations between the British Throne and the princes and
peoples of India, on which Disraeli had insisted at the
time of the Mutiny. Disraeli, at the Queen's request,
undertook the management of the affair, with Salisbury's
assistance; and a thorny and anxious business he found
it. There was the critical question of expense. ' A
Prince of Wales must not move in India in a *mesquin*
manner. Everything must be done on an Imperial
scale,' as the Queen and her Minister agreed. ' The
simplicity of arrangement which might suit a visit to
our own fellow-subjects in the Colonies,' Disraeli said in
the House of Commons, would not equally apply in the
case of India. There was that remarkable and deeply
rooted characteristic of Oriental manners—the exchange
of presents between visitors and their hosts. Presents
of ceremonial could rightly be discouraged; but the Prince
would visit immense populations and be the guest, or
make the acquaintance, of many chiefs and rulers, and
he ' must be placed in a position to exercise those spontaneous feelings, characteristic of his nature, of generosity
and splendour, which his own character, and the character
of the country likewise, requires to be gratified.' Disraeli
accordingly proposed a vote, in addition to the charge
for the cost of the journey, of £60,000 for the Prince's
personal expenses during the visit.

The sum was felt by the country to be moderate; and
many of the Prince's personal friends and even some of
his Anglo-Indian counsellors advised him that he was not

being treated generously. The Prince himself was too amiable to bear any grudge—'the most amiable of mortals,' Disraeli wrote of him this year to Lady Chesterfield, but 'a thoroughly spoilt child,' who 'can't bear being bored. I don't much myself,' he added. Still, between the indignation of the Prince's entourage and the Queen's dislike of the whole expedition and desire to curtail it, Disraeli's social and official steering during the summer of the year 1875 was a delicate matter requiring a dexterous touch. He was justified in the end, as his estimate proved to be within the mark; and yet the Prince's progress was on a sufficiently imperial scale.

Disraeli's letters illustrate various phases of the controversy.

To Lord Salisbury.

2, WHITEHALL GARDENS, *June* 13, 1875.—I think you had better not report, to H.R.H., the Queen's approval.

One of his present grievances, is that Her Majesty does not communicate with him directly, but by her Ministers. . . .

I am now going to write to him fully on all the matters; worse than 'gathering samphire'; and to Her Majesty. . . .

To Lady Bradford.

2, WHITEHALL GARDENS, *July* 7.—. . . General Probyn and Mr. Ellis came to me about the eternal business and its ever-recurring difficulties. The Prince is at Newmarket.

I have had ceaseless correspondence with the Faery, who had refused Prince and Secy. of State, to permit H.R.H. to hold an investiture of the Star of India, and things looked very black indeed. I had to interfere. . . . She writes: 'As you recommend me to do it I consent, but I don't like it.' This is not pleasant. Then she summons me again for Sunday to the Château, wh. is most inconvenient. . . .

July 17, *Friday.*—All went well last night, but it was a very hard one. I made clear to the House and the country the *two* sorts of visits wh. the P. might make to India, and showed, I hope without offending him, how, after the second programme had been adopted by the Govt., his thoughtless parasites had substituted for it the first.

The letter in *The Times* signed 'A Conservative M.P.', was written by Randolph Churchill, under the dictation of Blandford and Bartle Frere. Under their inspiration he had

prepared a Marlboro' House manifesto, and utterly broke
down, destroying a rather rising reputation. The letter is a
mass of absurdities. It assumes the P. is to make presents
to the 95 reigning Princes. If he visited them all, his tour
wd. be six years, not six months. He will visit only about
five. . . .

Do you think I ought to dine at Stafford House on Tuesday
to meet the P. of Wales ? or wd. it be better for me to write
to the Duchess and get off ? Advise me. . . .

July 19.—. . . Yesterday, after work and church, I called
on Sir Anthony de R[othschild], whom I cd. not see, and doubt
wh[ethe]r I shall see again.[1] I saw, however, his wife. . . .
I am sorry—very—for Sir Anthony; a thoro[ugh]ly good
fellow, the most genial being I ever knew, the most kind-
hearted, and the most generous. The P. of W. had called
and would see him, and said he had seen one of the prettiest
women in London that morning, and when he said he was
going to call on Sir A., she replied, ' Then give him my dearest
love.' Poor Sir A. was *intrigué*, and, pleased and perplexed,
could not find out that the lady was the Pss. of Wales. . . .

Then I dined at Piccadilly Terrace[2] where I had invited
myself (the day before), and where they then said, on Saturday,
they were quite alone exc[ep]t Neilson. But I found a most
amusing party, wh. they had scrambled up—Louise,[3] who
was delightful tho' a little noisy, too shrieking in her merriment, and Harty-Tarty, and Count Corti, whom I had not
seen for ten years, and the Peels, and B[ernal] O[sborne] and
Chas. Villiers. . . . I took in to dinner Neilson, who pleased
me, for she did not sing.

Did you hear how the Prince intrigued the Dss. of Sutherland at the masqued ball ? He addressed her, ' How do you
do, Mrs. Sankey ? How is Mr. Moody ?' Very good, I
think.

I dread my Stafford House dinner to-morrow. There was a
Greenwich dinner on Friday or Saturday; the Prince there.
The D. of Sutherland arrived, and said, ' What a shabby
concern this vote is ! If I were you, Sir, I would not take it.
I wd. borrow the money of some friends at five pr. ct.' ' Well,
will you lend it me ?' sd. the Prince, wh. shut the Duke up.

If H.R.H. knew I had so successfully proved he was a
wit, perhaps he wd. pardon me. . . .

Disraeli's apprehensions were, of course, rather of a
mock-heroic character. At any rate, early in October

---

[1] Sir Anthony died in January, 1876.
[2] Baron Lionel de Rothschild's house.
[3] Duchess of Manchester.

the Prince, on the eve of departure, invited him to Sandringham for a long week-end visit, and treated his guest with high consideration.

To Lady Bradford.

HUGHENDEN MANOR, *Oct*. 13, 1875.—. . . I was so utterly overwhelmed by the disappointment of not seeing you[1] that I found it impossible on Sunday to write to the Prince (and cd. scarcely converse with my guests). I quite gave it up—I mean the letter; but I had a feeling of remorse at the last moment on Monday, at not following yr. suggestions, wh. I always wish to do, and sent a few lines, wh. he cd. not have received till past seven o'ck. on the eve of his departure. Nevertheless he found time to write me a touching letter and to send me his photograph with his signature, and the fatal date of his departure. . . .

From the Prince of Wales.

MARLBOROUGH HOUSE, *Oct*. 11, '75.

MY DEAR MR. DISRAELI,—I am much touched by your kind letter and good wishes on my long journey, and I thank you for your advice which I shall always be most ready to accept at your hands. I am fully alive to the importance of my visit to India and hope that neither you or any one else in my land will have cause to regret that the honour of my country has been placed in my hands whilst in India. Am I saying too much in stating this ? It will always give me the greatest pleasure to hear from you, and I know that you will always be a good friend to me.

Please accept the accompanying photograph and—Believe me, Yours most sincerely, ALBERT EDWARD.

The Prince's visit, which occupied the cold weather of 1875–1876, was eminently successful. In the midst of his progress, he wrote on January 9, with becoming modesty, to Disraeli: ' My tour through India continues to interest me in the highest possible degree. The work has been hard at times, but the reception from all classes of the natives has been most gratifying, and if on my return home I shall have met with the approval of the Queen and my countrymen, I shall have every reason to

---

[1] Lady Bradford had failed to fulfil her engagement to stay at Hughenden. See above, p. 743.

look back to my visit to this splendid country with the
feelings of the greatest possible satisfaction.' Apart from
his success in introducing the personal note into the
relationship between the Sovereign in England and the
subject in India, the Prince's good feeling and sense of
right led him to make, on one vital topic, generous and
fruitful representations.

To Lord Salisbury.

2, WHITEHALL GARDENS, *Dec.* 13, 1875.—I have just
returned from Windsor. . . . Read extract from letter of
P. of W. to the Queen; and a passage I have marked in pencil.
Frequently I hear of this. Nothing is more disgusting, than
the habit of our officers speaking always of the inhabitants
of India—many of them descended from the great races—
as ' niggers.'
It is ignorant, and brutal—and surely most mischievous.
We ought to do something. If you be in town, I should be
glad to see you. . . .

It was natural that Disraeli should warmly welcome
and enforce representations so entirely in harmony with
what he had laid down in the fifties as the proper policy
of the British Government in India. 'Something' was
done at once. Salisbury took the opportunity of an
address at Cooper's Hill, the Indian engineering college,
to warn the students against treating natives with
contumely and violence, or exhibiting race-arrogance in
any form. And Lytton, who succeeded Northbrook as
Viceroy in the spring of 1876, made the first case of native
ill-treatment and official condonation, which occurred
after his arrival in India, the occasion of a drastic minute,
which, though issued in defiance of current Anglo-Indian
opinion, had a far-reaching effect.

It was while the final preparations were being made for
the Prince's departure from England that Disraeli learnt
that Northbrook, for private reasons, proposed to resign.
He was not entirely surprised, for he had written to
Salisbury on June 8: ' My own impression is that, somehow or other, Northbrook's reign will soon terminate,

and you and I must look out for the right man.'　For the moment it was an awkward complication; but it provided an opportunity for bringing the Government of India into harmony with the Cabinet by placing at its head someone who would receive in a more sympathetic manner than the retiring Viceroy the anxious suggestions of Disraeli and Salisbury for the strengthening of the British position on the north-west frontier.

To Lord Salisbury.

HUGHENDEN MANOR, *Oct.* 15, 1875.—I think it unfortunate, that Northbrook wishes not to fulfil his term.

If his intended resignation be announced at once, the public mind, agitated at this moment about India, will impute his withdrawal to any motive except the private one alleged, and wh. indeed, under no circumstances, will ever be credited. . . .

But, if the resignation be announced during the Prince's visit, it will be still worse, for it will then certainly be imputed to a misunderstanding with His Royal Highness.

I don't think he deserves an earldom—but you deserve anything—and, therefore, if, on reflection, you wish it, he shall have five balls.　Hardinge was only a viscount, and he fought battles and gained victories.　Consider this.

Water, I trust, will not prove fatal to the Government. Between Plimsoll, the *Vanguard*,[1] and the Admiralty Instructions and Minute, we seem in a leaky state: but it is only October, and there is time, I hope, to caulk. . . .

Oct. 28.—I have called the Cabinet together, for the 4th Novr., to confer, and decide, upon our course respecting these accursed Admiralty Instructions. . . .

There is none of my coll. whose opinion I more value, than your own.

Here I was going to end, but I can't resist telling you, that I am anxious, and a little disquieted, about Central Asian affairs.　Before you bring them, even indirectly, under the consideration of the Cabinet, I think it would be better, that we should confer together.

I am quite prepared for acting with energy and promptitude in the direction of Herat, if we could only come to a *bona fide* understanding with Afghanistan.　But can we? If a movement on our part, wh. is not only to secure our

---

[1] H.M.S. *Vanguard* had sunk in Irish waters after collision in a fog with H.M.S. *Iron Duke*.

Empire, but to preserve their independence, is actually used by Russia to create ill-feeling between us and Afghan[ista]n, that would be a deplorable result.

However, I have great confidence in you and a little in myself, and I trust, therefore, we may be equal to a critical occasion.

Can you suggest a good High Ch. Dean, who is not a damned fool, and won't make himself ridiculous ?

From Lord Salisbury.

Confidential. INDIA OFFICE, *Oct.* 31, 1875.—. . . Touching Central Asia: I should much like to talk the matter over with you: for the decision is one of great responsibility. The dilemma is simply this. It concerns us much to have an agent in Afghanistan. We want to guide the Ameer, and to watch; for there is the double danger that he may play us false, or, remaining true, may blunder into operations which will bring him into collision with Russia. It would also be a great security for peace, if we were able to keep the Czar, who wishes for peace, informed of the intrigues of his frontier officers, who do not. But on the other hand it is of great importance—I quite admit it—not to irritate the Ameer. But this is a sort of difficulty which the Indian Government has had constantly to meet. Diplomacy has been a real power in Indian history—because of the moral ascendancy which British officers have acquired over the Princes at whose Courts they were placed. I do not propose to send a mission to Afghanistan against the Ameer's wishes: but I propose to tell the Government of India to make the Ameer wish it. It cannot of course be done straight off—by return of post: but by the exercise of tact in the choice of the moment and the argument I feel sure that it can be done. The Ameer is genuinely frightened of the Russians: and every advance they make will make him more pliable, *until* their power on his frontier seems to him so great, and he is so convinced of our timidity, that he thinks safer to tie himself to them than to us. But on all this I should much like to talk to you.

The Queen has written to Lord Northbrook asking him to keep the secret till the close of the Prince's visit. I have telegraphed to him a similar message from her.

She told me that you proposed to make Lord Powis Viceroy. The intelligence rather startled me: for he has no experience of affairs, and I have noted in him no trace of practical ability. Your own judgment must of course guide you: but I hope you will not decide hastily, as there is plenty of time. The post is terribly important: a feeble occupant might bring about a great disaster.

I have put down in a separate note all that I know about possible High Church Deans—'who are not damned fools' —a formidable restriction !

Though the Queen, as well as Salisbury, was startled by the suggestion, Disraeli had excellent reasons for fixing on the third Earl of Powis [1] as his first choice for Viceroy. If Lord Powis never took a very active part in political life and so came little under the Queen's or Salisbury's notice, he was nevertheless an exceptionally able and well-read man, of sound judgment and tact, and of great reputation in local affairs in North Wales and Shropshire. Disraeli knew him in the House of Commons as one of the eager spirits attracted by 'Young England'; and he conceived that India would welcome as Viceroy the great-grandson, in the direct line, of Lord Clive.

To Queen Victoria.

2, WHITEHALL GARDENS, *Nov.* 5, 1875.—. . . The Cabinet meets again to-day, when Mr. Disraeli hopes to lay before them a general view of the probable business of next session.

After the Cabinet yesterday, at four o'clock, Mr. Disraeli had a long interview with Lord Salisbury.

There is no question now about Lord Powis. He had been sounded by Mr. Disraeli, without any unnecessary confidence, but said his health was too delicate for foreign service, and though he should have liked to have served the Crown earlier in life, he felt, now, it was too late for him to begin.

He is modest, for in presiding, somewhat recently, over the Royal Commission on Irish Education, he showed administrative powers of a high character.

The person whom Mr. Disraeli had fixed upon, for your Majesty's consideration, was Lord John Manners, a man of many admirable qualities, and unjustly under-rated by the public.

He is a statesman; with a large practical experience of public affairs; a student, as well as a practical statesman;

[1] 1818-1891: M.P. for North Shropshire, 1843-1848; High Steward of Cambridge University; first President of the University College of North Wales at Bangor; Lord-Lieutenant of Montgomeryshire and Chairman of Quarter Sessions.

thoroughly versed in all the great political questions of
Eastern and European politics; an admirable administrator
with a great capacity of labor; a facile pen; brave, firm, and
a thorough gentleman.   But Mr. Disraeli fears Lord John's
health is breaking up.

Lord Salisbury and Mr. Disraeli agreed, that the resignation
of Lord Northbrook should be kept quite close and confined
to themselves and your Majesty.   If imparted to the Cabinet,
it will soon be babbled about by the wives.   Indeed, the
rumor is in the air, and has been more or less for a year.
Yesterday Lady Derby mentioned it to Mr. Disraeli, who
said ' That is an old story,' but anxious to find out whether
it was the old story with her, he extracted, after a little while,
her authority—Mrs. Morier.

Mr. Disraeli hopes your Majesty will approve of the Deanery
of Chichester being conferred on Mr. Burgon.   It will not
be displeasing to the High Church party, who are very much
offended with Mr. Disraeli, while Mr. Burgon is thoroughly
sound on the great questions, being one of the ablest defenders
of the union of the Church with the State: now the key-note
of ecclesiastical politics, and which the pure Sacerdotalists
are attempting to abolish.

Mr. Burgon is one of the most eminent of the resident
Oxford clergy; eminent as a scholar, a writer, and a preacher:
and a man of original and interesting character.

Mr. Disraeli will keep your Majesty perfectly informed of
all that occurs; probably every day.

John Manners, as Disraeli feared when he wrote to the
Queen, declined the Viceroyalty because he believed he
had not sufficient health and strength for the post;
Carnarvon, another colleague, to whom his chief next
applied, declined because he was a widower with young
children.   After this refusal Disraeli was rather at a loss,
and Salisbury, who was ' in despair at the barrenness of
the Tory land,' could only suggest names that seemed to
him just ' tolerable.'   The Queen mentioned the name of
a man who was afterwards a most successful Viceroy—
Dufferin; but put it aside as ' he, she is afraid, has not
health, and too large a " small family," as the Highlanders say, to enable him to accept it.'   He was also a
Whig.   Of another suggestion which Her Majesty made
Salisbury wrote to Disraeli: ' The appearance of Derby's
name is a charming touch of nature.   It reveals a world

of untold suffering—and desperate hope.' Finally, Disraeli turned, with Salisbury's entire approval, to the son of an old friend and colleague, the second Lord Lytton, then British Minister at Lisbon, who combined the practised deftness of a diplomatist with the imagination of a poet. 'The critical state of affairs in Central Asia demands a statesman,' wrote Disraeli on November 23, 'and I believe if you will accept this high post you will have an opportunity, not only of serving your country, but of obtaining an enduring fame.' Lytton, who was a delicate man, had more claim than others who had pleaded ill-health to exemption on that ground; but, after stating the facts, he submitted to the decision of the Cabinet, and, in Disraeli's words, accepted 'the superb but awful post.' Derby was ready to release him at once from his service under the Foreign Office, observing cheerfully that he would die in India, but that to die Viceroy was something.

To Lady Bradford.

HUGHENDEN MANOR, *Jan.* 5, 1876.—. . . We have been obliged to announce the great Indian change somewhat sooner than we intended, and rather suddenly, but it was leaking out. There is always a traitor—except in the Suez Canal business.[1] . . .

2, WHITEHALL GARDENS, ½ *past* 6 [*Jan.* 20, 1876].—. . . I got from the Cab. at ½ pt. 5, and found Lytton waiting for me; and now he has just gone. I knew him really before he was born—a few months; and now I see him here, and a Viceroy.

He told me his first remembrance of me was calling on him at a little school he was at—at Twickenham, and I 'tipped' him. It was the first tip he ever had; and now I have tipped him again, and put a crown on his head! It's like meeting the first characters of a play in the last scene! . . .

The Far East, as well as the Near East and India, demanded Ministerial attention in 1875. There were anxious negotiations with China arising out of the murder of a British Consular official, A. R. Margary. A letter

---

[1] See below, ch. 12.

to Lady Bradford shows with what imaginative insight
Disraeli had grasped the essentials of Far Eastern development.

To Lady Bradford.

HUGHENDEN MANOR, *Sept.* 27, 1875.—. . . I have taken a
step in diplomacy, wh. I am sure never was taken before.   I
have induced the Japanese Minister in England to telegraph
to his Government, urging them to offer their mediation in
the event of serious difficulty arising bet[wee]n China and
England, and to declare that if China will not accept that
mediation, and act upon it, Japan will join England against
her, and place a Japanese contingent under the orders of
any British forces employed by us against the Celestial
Empire.   I know not why Japan shd. not become the Sardinia
of the Mongolian East.   They are by far the cleverest of the
Mongol race.   Now you know one of the greatest secrets of
State going !

Hence it appears that, only ten years after Japan had
definitely started on the path of progress, Disraeli
recognised her great qualities and possibilities, anticipated
that she would become 'the Sardinia of the Mongolian
East,' and proposed common action between her and
Great Britain on behalf of their common interests in that
region, thus initiating a policy which culminated, thirty
years later, in the Anglo-Japanese Alliance.

CHAPTER XII.

Suez Canal and Royal Title.

1875–1876.

It was while Disraeli's mind was full, on the one hand, of the Indian problems involved in the Russian advance in Asia, in the Prince of Wales's visit, and in the selection of a new Viceroy, and, on the other hand, of the threatened revival of the Eastern question owing to the outbreak in Herzegovina, that the opportunity came, for which he had been waiting, of striking an effective and resounding blow for the security of our imperial communications, and for the strengthening of the British position in the whole Eastern world. On Monday, November 15, 1875, Frederick Greenwood, a journalist of high distinction, who, as editor of the *Pall Mall Gazette*, gave Disraeli and his Government strong but independent support, called on Derby at the Foreign Office to tell him that the Khedive of Egypt, who held some 177,000 out of the 400,000 ordinary shares of the Suez Canal, was negotiating for their transfer to a syndicate of French capitalists, and to urge that the British Government should step in and purchase the shares itself. Greenwood's information was the result of meeting at dinner Henry Oppenheim, a financier largely interested in Egypt, and his political insight and enlightened patriotism prompted his mission to the Foreign Office.

It was a startling suggestion, and was naturally not at first welcomed by the cautious Derby. But Disraeli's imagination discerned at once the high political value of the purchase, and, while the Foreign Secretary

reluctantly yielded to the necessity of preventing the
great highway of British traffic with British India and
British Australasia from passing into wholly French
hands, the Prime Minister was eager for a transaction which should demonstrate the importance England
attached to her Eastern Empire and sanguine of the
immense benefit which would result. It is possible
that Disraeli had got wind of the Khedive's negotiations from another quarter. Baron Lionel de Rothschild, to whose good offices Disraeli had already had
recourse in connection with the Canal, was, like Disraeli
himself and at Disraeli's request, on the lookout for
an opportunity; and he may well have got early news
from Paris or Cairo of what was in progress. It was
Disraeli's frequent habit, when in town on official business out of the season, to offer himself to the Baron
and Baroness for dinner, especially on Sunday evenings.
At their house, he told Lady Bradford in a letter dated
November 20—during the very week whose events we
are describing—'there is ever something to learn, and
somebody distinguished to meet.' M. Gavard, Chargé
d'Affaires of France in London at this time, tells a story
of a dinner at Rothschild's at which some such communication passed. As there was also a tradition in the
Foreign Office that the information reached the Government from more sources than one,[1] it may well be that
Disraeli heard on Sunday night from Rothschild something of what Derby was told by Greenwood on the
Monday morning. This may explain the strange omission
of Greenwood's name in the private correspondence of
leading Ministers during the negotiations; unless indeed
we are to attribute the omission to that dislike and
contempt of newspapers and editors which have often
underlain the outward flattery and deference exhibited
by statesmen, but which could hardly be felt by one who,

---

[1] A short memorandum respecting the negotiations of the Khedive with
a French group is understood to have reached the Foreign Office from
Northcote at the Treasury on the day on which Greenwood called.

like Disraeli, had boasted in Parliament that he was himself a 'gentleman of the press.'

The information reached the Government only just in time. Turkey, the Empire of which Egypt was a semi-independent province, had gone bankrupt in the previous month; the effect had immediately been felt at Alexandria; and the Khedive Ismail, after many years of more than Oriental extravagance, found his credit on the point of collapse. By December 1, little more than a fortnight later, he had to meet the coupons on the Egyptian public debt, or else follow his Sovereign's example and default. From three to four millions sterling were wanted, and he was at the end of his resources. He was in negotiation with competing syndicates of French financiers, prepared, but on onerous terms, to furnish the needful funds. The principal asset he had to offer were these 177,000[1] shares in the Canal; the coupons on which, it should be added, he had already alienated in 1869 for twenty-five years. The proposals made to him involved either the mortgage of the shares or their sale outright. On the previous Friday, three days before Greenwood's call at the Foreign Office, he had consented to sell them for 92,000,000 francs, or £3,680,000, paying interest on them at 8 (afterwards changed to 11) per cent. till 1894, when the dividends would once again be payable by the Canal Company; the option to remain open till the following Tuesday. The holders of the option found serious difficulties in raising the money in Paris, owing to the opposition of the rival syndicate, and asked for, and obtained, an extension of time till the following Friday.

When, therefore, General Stanton, the British agent in Egypt, made, in consequence of orders from home,

---

[1] The number of shares was presumed throughout the negotiations to be 177,642; but on completion of the contract with the British Government they were found to be actually 176,602, or 1,040 less; and a corresponding deduction was made from the purchase price.

For the detailed history of the whole transaction, see *L'Achat des Actions de Suez*, by Charles Lesage, and an article in *The Times* of Dec. 26, 1905, by Mr. Lucien Wolf, with subsequent correspondence on Dec. 27, 28, and 29, 1905, and Jan. 13, 18, 26, 29, and 30, and Feb. 10, 1906.

inquiries on the Tuesday of Nubar Pasha, the Prime Minister, and of the Khedive himself, the sale had already been conditionally arranged, though Ismail characteristically protested that he had never thought seriously of the proposal of purchase, and had no present intention of disposing of his shares. But the intention to mortgage was admitted, as three or four millions must be obtained at once; and Nubar hinted that even by mortgage the shares might be lost, as the Egyptian Government might not be able to redeem their pledge. General Stanton told both Nubar and Ismail that the British Government could not view with indifference the transfer of the Khedive's interests in the Canal, and insisted on a suspension of negotiations in order to give that Government an opportunity of making a proposal —a suggestion which the Khedive welcomed.

Disraeli, on hearing Stanton's report, lost no time. The next day, Wednesday, November 17, the Cabinet, which was holding its usual autumnal sittings, took the matter into consideration, and determined in principle that England should acquire the shares. It is clear from Disraeli's reports to the Queen and from his private letters that the initiative was his, and that the Cabinet, though in the end unanimous, contained influential members who were reluctant to take such a very new departure. These included not only Derby, but Disraeli's special henchman, the Chancellor of the Exchequer, who loyally forwarded at the Treasury his chief's plans, but, even after they had been carried through, registered a protest, on November 26, against what he considered to be a policy wanting in magnanimity, adding emphatically, ' I don't like it.' Reconsideration, however, seems to have modified his views; and before the matter came to be debated in Parliament, he was able to write to Disraeli (January 25): ' So far as the purchase of the Suez Canal shares is in question, I think our case is perfect. Subsequent events have strengthened, rather than weakened, the arguments which induced us to decide on it.'

To Queen Victoria.

Confidential.   2, WHITEHALL GARDENS, *Nov.* 18, 1875.—Mr.
Disraeli with his humble duty to your Majesty:

The Khedive, on the eve of bankruptcy, appears desirous
of parting with his shares in the Suez Canal, and has communicated, confidentially, with General Stanton.   There is a
French company in negotiation with His Highness, but they
purpose only to make an advance with complicated stipulations.

'Tis an affair of millions; about four at least; but would give
the possessor an immense, not to say preponderating, influence
in the management of the Canal.

It is vital to your Majesty's authority and power at this
critical moment, that the Canal should belong to England,
and I was so decided and absolute with Lord Derby on this
head, that he ultimately adopted my views and brought the
matter before the Cabinet yesterday.   The Cabinet was unanimous in their decision, that the interest of the Khedive
should, if possible, be obtained, and we telegraphed accordingly.

Last night, there was another telegram from General
Stanton (not in reply), which indicated some new difficulties,
but the Cabinet meets again to-day (at two o'clock) and we
shall consider them.

The Khedive now says, that it is absolutely necessary that
he should have between three and four millions sterling by
the 30th of this month !

Scarcely breathing time !   But the thing must be done.

Mr. Disraeli perceives, that, in his hurry, he has not expressed
himself according to etiquette.   Your Majesty will be graciously pleased to pardon him !   There is no time to rewrite
it.   The messenger for Balmoral is waiting.   He thought
your Majesty should know all this, and could not write last
night, as fresh intelligence was hourly expected.

Nov. 19.—. . . The Cabinet considered the affairs of the
Khedive yesterday for one hour and ½, and had, before them,
Lord Tenterden and Colonel Stokes, who has been engaged
by your Majesty's Government on the affairs of the Suez
Canal.

The pecuniary embarrassments of the Khedive appear to be
very serious, and it is doubtful whether a financial catastrophe
can be avoided.   The business is difficult, but it is as important
as difficult, and must not be relinquished.   We received
telegrams from General Stanton, who had personally seen the
Khedive, and we also returned telegrams.

The Khedive voluntarily pledged himself, that, whatever

happened, your Majesty's Government should have the refusal of his interest in the Canal. All that can be done now, is to keep the business well in hand. . . .

From Queen Victoria.

BALMORAL, *Nov.* 19, '75.—The Queen thanks Mr. Disraeli for his letters. She has telegraphed her approval of the course he intends pursuing respecting the Suez Canal, but fears it will be difficult to arrange. . . .

To Queen Victoria.

2, WHITEHALL GARDENS, *Nov.* 20, 1875.—Mr. Disraeli with his humble duty to your Majesty:

Received the telegram yesterday, which was most encouraging. Nothing very significant has happened on the subject during the last four and twenty hours—but communications between your Majesty's Government and Cairo are brisk. The affair will take time, but it must not be lost sight of for a moment; and can now be worked without the Cabinet, as they are unanimous as to the policy, and have given *carte blanche* to Mr. Disraeli to carry it into effect. Your Majesty's approbation greatly strengthens him. . . .

Stanton received the Cabinet decision of Wednesday in time to notify the Khedive the same night [1] that the British Government was ready, if satisfactory terms could be arranged, to purchase the shares. The Khedive expressed his contentment, but continued to protest that he had no present intention of disposing of them. He added that he was obliged to proceed with the mortgage, but, if he changed his views about sale, he would give the British Government the option of purchase. He immediately carried his project of mortgage into effect by signing next day a fresh contract with the owners of the previous option. British opposition and the difficulty of raising in Paris the money for purchase had put an end to the first negotiation. The present arrangement was an advance of 85,000,000 francs (£3,400,000) for three months at the exorbitant rate of 18 per cent. per

---

[1] The dates given in Stanton's despatch of Nov. 18 are not quite clear; and M. Lesage, apparently wrongly, places this notification on Thursday, Nov. 18, instead of Wednesday, Nov. 17.

annum. For this the Khedive pledged not merely the 177,000 shares but his right to 15 per cent. in the annual profits of the Canal. In default of payment, the shares and the 15 per cent. were to become the property of the syndicate, and the Khedive promised to pay 10 per cent. in lieu of the alienated coupons. The contract was to be ratified by November 26.

Presumably the Khedive was reluctant to place himself in the hands of the British Government; otherwise it is difficult to understand how he ever consented to a transaction so unfavourable to himself. It was called a mortgage, but the terms were so onerous that it was, in fact, a disguised sale. This was fully realised by the syndicate, and by Lesseps himself, who entered eagerly into the campaign in Paris to raise the money which should assure French domination over the Canal. Making use of this argument, he urgently prayed the French Government to interpose and remove all financial obstacles to the negotiation. But the Duc Decazes, the French Foreign Minister, was anxious to do nothing to alienate the British Government, who had intervened in a friendly and decisive manner on behalf of France at Berlin in the spring; and he must have realised that the great maritime Powers, and England at their head, could not view with indifference any arrangement by which the control of the main waterway between Europe and Asia would pass entirely into French hands. He sent the Chargé d'Affaires in London to sound Derby, and received the answer he must have expected. Derby pointed out that, as the Canal was our highway to India, and as nearly four-fifths of the shipping which used it was British, our interest in its maintenance and proper management was greater than that of any other European nation; that the possession by the Khedive of a large interest in the company was one of our main safeguards in dealing with Lesseps; and that ' we should certainly be opposed to these shares falling into the hands of another French company, so as to make the property in the Canal more French than it already was.' There possibly might not, he added, be the same objections to a mortgage, provided the Khedive had full power to redeem at any moment.

This categorical answer, which showed that Derby's initial hesitation had now given place to firm resolve, effectually prevented the French Government, though Disraeli seems still to have suspected them, from rendering any assistance to the French syndicates, and so brought the negotiations for a mortgage to naught. It was given on Saturday, November 20, and on the Tuesday, the Khedive, having learnt the failure of his negotiations with Paris financiers, and being encouraged by Derby's friendly assurances of anxiety to help him on reasonable terms, offered the 177,000 shares to the British Government for £4,000,000, with interest at 5 per cent. till the coupons were liberated. The offer was considered by the Cabinet on Wednesday, November 24, and accepted. On November 25 the contract was signed at Cairo, and on November 26 the shares were deposited there in the British Consulate. The whole transaction had been completed in ten days.

When once the policy of purchase had been accepted in principle, as it was at the Cabinet of November 17, it was essential to discover at once whether the £4,000,000 could be procured in time. Parliament was not sitting, and the affair would not wait. 'I am sure,' wrote Northcote to Disraeli on November 22, 'that there is no way by which we can raise the money without the consent of Parliament, and that the utmost we could do would be to enter into a treaty engaging to ask Parliament for the money, and then let the K[hedive] get it in advance from some capitalist who is willing to trust to our power of getting Parliamentary authority.' In these circumstances Disraeli's mind had naturally turned to his friends the Rothschilds, the magnitude of whose resources he knew, and whose aid he had already sought and obtained in connection with his Egyptian policy. Corry used to tell a story that Disraeli had arranged with him that he

should be in attendance—as was indeed his duty as
principal private secretary—just outside the Cabinet room
and, when his chief put out his head and said 'Yes,'
should take immediate action. On this signal being
given he went off to New Court and told Rothschild in
confidence that the Prime Minister wanted £4,000,000
'to-morrow.' Rothschild, Corry was wont to declare,
picked up a muscatel grape, ate it, threw out the skin,
and said deliberately, 'What is your security?' 'The
British Government.' 'You shall have it.' We need not
take as gospel the whole of this picturesque detail; but
it is certain that at an early stage, the 17th or 18th of
November, Corry applied to Rothschild on Disraeli's
behalf, and obtained a promise of his co-operation. The
terms were finally settled with the Treasury at the beginning of the following week. 'I find,' wrote Northcote
to Disraeli on November 24, 'Smith and Welby a good
deal startled by the largeness of Rothschild's commission.
It will, I suppose, be criticised, but, if the business goes
right, a matter of that kind will not signify much.' Lowe
in the House of Commons was maladroit enough to base
his objections to the transaction largely on this point.
When it is considered that two millions were provided
by the firm for the Khedive on December 1, another
million on December 16, and the last million on January 5, the commission of 2½ per cent. will seem moderate
for so vast and prompt an accommodation. The withdrawal of four millions for a considerable period from the
resources even of so commanding a firm as that of the
Rothschilds necessarily entailed a large derangement of
the routine of its business; and they had obviously to
protect themselves against possible fluctuations in the
value of money, and against the conceivable, though
remote, risk that Parliament would refuse to vali-
date the purchase. It was a transaction entirely without precedent, as Rothschild pointed out to Corry in a
conversation at the time of the debates in Parliament.
In the same conversation Rothschild met another

criticism, often urged, that Ministers should have used the Bank of England, and not a private firm, as their agents.

. . . As to the question whether the Government should not have applied to the Bank of England, Baron Rothschild —giving no opinion as to the Bank's *power*—says that he understands the authorities to be about equally divided (even now) on the point of their *willingness* to have acted as the agents of the Government in this transaction. It is a point, moreover, which could only have been determined by the full Board, at the obvious sacrifice of despatch and secrecy. Mr. Hubbard, for one, is clear that the Bank could not, and would not, have acted (Mr. Hubbard tells me that he is prepared to say this in Parliament.—M. C.), while Mr. Gibbs and Mr. Thomson Hankey take the other view. Baron Rothschild imagines that the Government might, possibly, have *compelled* the Bank to find the four millions (and at a lower rate of commission). But this would have been a violent act, before the commission of which, he maintains, they were bound to use every endeavour to obtain the money from independent firms. He declares, too, without hesitation, that the Bank of England could not have found the required sum without grave disturbance of the money market.

It is upon the entire absence of such disturbance, under his operations, that he from a public point of view, rests his vindication of the commission charged, and is content that the matter should be judged by the results. . . .—M. C., *Feb.* 19, 1876.

It is no wonder that in his letters to the Queen and Lady Bradford after the final decision Disraeli should have sounded loudly the note of triumph.

To Queen Victoria.

2, WHITEHALL GARDENS, *Nov.* 24, 1875.—Mr. Disraeli with his humble duty to your Majesty:

It is just settled: you have it, Madam. The French Government has been out-generaled. They tried too much, offering loans at an usurious rate, and with conditions, which would have virtually given them the government of Egypt.

The Khedive, in despair and disgust, offered your Majesty's Government to purchase his shares outright. He never would listen to such a proposition before.

Four millions sterling! and almost immediately. There

was only one firm that could do it—Rothschilds. They behaved admirably; advanced the money at a low rate, and the entire interest of the Khedive is now yours, Madam.

Yesterday the Cabinet sate four hours and more on this, and Mr. Disraeli has not had one moment's rest to-day; therefore this despatch must be pardoned, as his head is rather weak. He will tell the whole wondrous tale to-morrow.

He was in Cabinet to-day, when your Majesty's second telegram arrived, which must be his excuse for his brief and stupid answer: but it was ' the crisis.'

The Government and Rothschilds agreed to keep it secret, but there is little doubt it will be known to-morrow from Cairo.

From Queen Victoria.

WINDSOR CASTLE, *Nov.* 25, '75.—This is indeed a great and important event, which, when known, will, the Queen feels sure, be most popular in the country. The great sum is the only disadvantage.

The Queen will be curious to hear all about it from Mr. Disraeli, when she sees him to-day.

To Lady Bradford.

2, WHITEHALL GARDENS, *Nov.* 25, 1875.—As you complain sometimes, tho' I think unjustly, that I tell you nothing, I will now tell you a great State secret, tho' it may not be one in 4 and 20 hours (still you will like to know it 4 and 20 hours sooner than the newspapers can tell it, you)—a State secret, certainly the most important of this year, and not one of the least events of our generation.

After a fortnight of the most unceasing labor and anxiety, I (for between ourselves, and ourselves only, I may be egotistical in this matter)—I have purchased for England the Khedive of Egypt's interest in the Suez Canal.

We have had all the gamblers, capitalists, financiers of the world, organised and platooned in bands of plunderers, arrayed against us, and secret emissaries in every corner, and have baffled them all, and have never been suspected. The day before yesterday, Lesseps, whose company has the remaining shares, backed by the French Government, whose agent he was, made a great offer. Had it succeeded, the whole of the Suez Canal wd. have belonged to France, and they might have shut it up !

We have given the Khedive 4 millions sterling for his interest, and run the chance of Parliament supporting us

We cd. not call them together for the matter, for that wd. have blown everything to the skies, or to Hades.

The Faery is in ecstasies about ' this great and important event.' . . .

I have rarely been thro' a week like the last, and am to-day in a state of prostration—coma. . . .

WINDSOR CASTLE, *Nov.* 26, 1875.—A most hurried line to tell you that nothing cd. be more successful—I might say triumphant—than my visit. The Faery was most excited about Suez, said ' what she liked most was, it was a blow at Bismarck,' referring, I apprehend, to his insolent declarations that England had ceased to be a political power. This remark she frequently made, showing it was the leading idea of her mind.

I got here at ¼ to 6, and was summoned to the presence exactly at 6. . . . When I cd. get to general business, tho' I had an awful catalogue of demands and suggestions, they were comparatively soon exhausted: no difficulties made, everything granted, nothing but smiles and infinite *agaceries*. . . .

There were only courtiers at dinner. After din., altho' I had been in audience till ½ pt. 7, the Faery came up to me again, and was not only most gracious, but most interesting and amusing: all about domestic affairs. She shewed me, by the bye, at dinner, a couple of tels. she had received that morning from P. of W., and she wished me to write to him about Suez and all that. ' I wish it,' she sd., ' because he likes you.'

Lady Biddulph said after dinner she shd. resign if the Primo dined often there, as she cd. not stand while the Faery was talking to me. . . .

The Times has only got half the news, and very inaccurate, but it is evidently staggered. I believe the whole country will be with me. The Faery thinks so. . . .

Nov. 30.—. . . The Faery was in the 10th heaven, having received a letter of felicitations from the King of the Belges on ' the greatest event of modern politics.' ' Europe breathes again,' etc., etc.

It seems that P. Gortchakoff had arranged to call at Berlin on his way home and just catch P. Bismarck after his five months' retirement, and then confer together, and settle, or seem to settle, the Eastern question. It must have been during this meeting, or the day before it took place, that the great news arrived, wh., as it is supposed they were going to settle everything without consulting England, was amusing ! Bismarck called on Odo Russell, but the latter unhappily was not at home. Odo called at the For. Office and saw Bülow, who handed him a tel. from Münster, saying ' the purchase of the Suez Canal has been received by the whole English nation with enthusiasm'; but not a word cd. be got out of Bülow himself. . . .

I go this morning to Longleat. . . .

To Queen Victoria.

2, WHITEHALL GARDENS, *Nov.* 27, 1875.—. . . He thanks your Majesty for the gracious note of last night.

He is assured, that there was only one opinion in the City yesterday, and the accounts, from all the great centres of your Majesty's kingdom, this morning, re-echo the same feeling.

He believes it may, now, be looked on as a great, perhaps unparalleled success.

But your Majesty predicted this when no one had given an opinion, and when many great judges looked demure.

Sir Philip Rose to Montagu Corry.

1, CROMWELL ROAD, S.W., *Dec.* 1, 1875.—. . . Is it not curious that the arrangement which I was urging upon Mr. D. 18 months ago, to secure the Suez Canal for the English Govt., should have been brought about, tho' in a much better way, as my plan contemplated an arrangement with Lesseps and his company, whereas they have now got a title from the Sovereign, and have helped that Sovereign at the same time ?

Disraeli did not exaggerate when he said that the Ministerial stroke had been an unparalleled success. Public opinion declared itself strongly on his side; and even among leading Liberals there were many who followed Hartington and Goschen in open or tacit approval rather than Gladstone in indignant opposition. Though there was naturally a little soreness in France, Lesseps, having failed in his passionate attempts to prevent the transaction, had the cleverness and good sense promptly to welcome in a letter to his shareholders the acceptance by England of that share in the company which she might have had at the first, and to point out that the co-operation of the British Government was a fortunate occurrence for the commercial success of the Canal. From almost every European country except Russia there came congratulations. Derby, after his fashion, gave at Edinburgh in December a minimising account of what he had done; we had merely acted, he said, in order to prevent the great highway, over which we had three-fourths of the traffic, from being 'exclusively in the hands of the foreign shareholders of a foreign company.' This may have reassured some doubters, and certainly veiled, for some eyes at home, the vital significance of the Ministerial action; but in Berlin they were under no illusions.

From Queen Victoria.

WINDSOR CASTLE, *Dec.* 3, '75.—The Queen sends Mr. Disraeli the extract from a letter from her daughter the Crown Princess, which she thinks will gratify him. But Lord Derby tried to pour as much cold water as he could on the great success of the affair of the Suez Canal, though he seemed pleased at the feeling shown everywhere about it.

[ENCLOSURE.]
The Crown Princess to Queen Victoria.

BERLIN, *Nov.* 30, 1875.—. . . I must congratulate you on the newest deed of your Government, the buying of half the shares of the Suez Canal; it sent a thrill of pleasure and pride, almost of exultation, through me! It is a delightful thing to see the *right thing*, done at the *right moment*. Everybody is pleased here, and wishes it may bring England good; even the great man B[ismarck] expressed himself to Fritz in this sense yesterday evening! Willy[1] writes from Cassel, 'Dear Mama, I must write you a line, because I know you will be so delighted that England has bought the Suez Canal. How jolly ! !'

The newspapers on the subject have been a pleasure to read (the English ones). The French and the Russians will be much annoyed it seems, but that will blow over, and they have no real cause to complain, so I fancy their irritation will not last.

This will rank in history among the many great, good and useful things done in your reign, and that makes me so proud and happy. I am sure Mr. Disraeli and Lord Derby must be quite delighted at the accomplishment of so important a measure, and at its popularity. The wisdom of it is so self-evident, that it *can* only be popular. . . .

---

[1] The German Emperor William II.

To Queen Victoria.

CRICHEL, WIMBORNE, *Dec.* 5, 1875.—Mr. Disraeli with his humble duty to your Majesty:

He thanks your Majesty for your Majesty's most gracious letter, and the gratifying and very interesting extract which accompanied it.

He felt the shock of the ' cold water ' himself, though he had endeavoured to guard against it, and had forwarded, also, a letter from Lord Carnarvon, very well written, and in the same vein.

Our consolation must be, that the deed is done, and it must be an additional solace to your Majesty, that it was greatly owing to the sympathy and support which Mr. Disraeli received from your Majesty, and to the clear-sightedness, which your Majesty evinced in the affair from the outset. . . .

Derby protested, no doubt with perfect sincerity, that nothing was further from his thoughts than the establishment of English authority in Egypt; that we merely wanted a free passage for ourselves and for the rest of the world, and nothing more. Disraeli's imagination cannot have been so limited; but he used none but vague phrases. Anyhow, immediately after the conclusion of the bargain, in response however, no doubt, to a request from the Khedive made before it, the British Government took the first step towards intervention in Egypt by sending a British statesman, Stephen Cave, to inquire into the tangled financial situation of the country. Thence we came, as Mr. Lucien Wolf has well put it, ' by successive stages, to the Dual Control, the bombardment of Alexandria, the " stricken field " of Omdurman, the dramatic crisis of Fashoda, . . . the poetic *dénouement* of the Lansdowne-Cambon Convention,' and, we may add, finally to the establishment of a British Protectorate, with a Sultan entirely independent of Turkey on the throne.[1] But Disraeli himself, having secured the British hold on the Canal, was always careful of French interests in Egypt, and sought French co-operation.

[1] Written in 1919, before the recognition, with reservations safeguarding British interests, of Egyptian independence.

Accordingly, he never advanced throughout his administration beyond the stage of Dual Control, resisting all suggestions to oust France from her share. The withdrawal of France was her own act, when, after Beaconsfield's death, she refused to join in the military operations which put down Arabi's revolt.

Disraeli well understood the kind of spirit in which British statesmen should attack Egyptian problems—the spirit afterwards displayed in such perfection by Lord Cromer.

To Lord Derby.

2, WHITEHALL GARDENS, *Nov.* 26, '75.—I can't approve of the employment of Mr. Lowe, and for this, among others, main reason. Throughout life, he has quarrelled with everybody. We want a calm, conciliatory spirit to deal with Egypt; not to oppose their first impressions and suggestions, but to correct, and change, them, in due time.

I think, that Cave, who has great financial and commercial knowledge, who, tho' ' an Oxford scholar,' has been a Bank director, and a Minister of State, is capable, under our guidance and instructions, of the office.

I think there ought to be no delay in the appointment of some one. . . .

The purchase of the Suez Canal shares promoted materially a better understanding between Disraeli and Salisbury, as what Derby regarded as an unfortunate necessity Salisbury, who, like his leader, possessed imagination, advocated as a stroke of high imperial statesmanship; and a visit to Hatfield in December contributed to the same end.

To Lady Bradford.

2, WHITEHALL GARDENS, *Nov.* 13.—. . . I went yesterday with ' Mary Derby,' whom I continue to call to her face ' Lady Salisbury '—most unfortunate—to Mr. Liebricht,[1] an oculist in Alb[emarl]e St., a famous man, who has only been here two years. I have seen double with my left eye for years, but wd. consult no one, for I assumed it was cat[arac]t, wh. my father and grandfather had, and did not wish to be convinced of the inevitable. But it was no such thing: a change in the focus of my eye, wh. a particular glass cured. Lady

---

[1] The proper spelling of the name seems to have been ' Liebreich.'

Derby had suffered from the same malady and he had cured her. That was why I went. . . .

Dec. 17.—I go . . . to Hatfield. Go I must, or there will be all sorts of misunderstandings; but I would almost as lief go to my execution.

Disraeli had the pleasantest recollections, extending over many years of the fifties and sixties, of visits to Hatfield during the time that his friend, who had now become Lady Derby, was the gracious hostess. It was natural that he should be apprehensive of his first visit under the new régime, considering how bitter had been Salisbury's criticism and how recent the reconciliation. Nor is it to be wondered at that, while he wrote afterwards to Salisbury, ' I remember my visit to H. with great pleasure, and beg to be remembered to miladi and Jem and Fish,' he should have told Derby at the time, and through him Lady Derby, that he found it ' extremely dull, strange people at dinner, and a great many little boys of various families,' though paying in the same letter a tribute to the ' ancient nobility ' and ' first-rate intellect ' of his host. Of the two descriptions of his feelings, that given to Derby was probably for the moment the more sincere; but the awkwardness and inappreciation on both sides soon passed away; and long before the close of the Ministry Disraeli was thoroughly at home at Hatfield, and in very friendly relations not only with his host, but with his hostess and the family; while, to his poignant regret, the intimate political and personal ties which had bound him for thirty years to the Derbys had been completely severed.

To Anne Lady Chesterfield.

2, WHITEHALL GARDENS, *Dec.* 18, 1875.—. . . We had a large and gay party at Ashridge, but I think the Pss. Mary beat them all for her vigor and vivacity. . . . There was a concert to the county on Friday. It was well done. . . . Mme. Neruda played divinely—like an angel with a fiddle in an old picture. I witnessed her début at Orleans House, 9 years ago, and aft[erwar]ds sketched her in *Lothair*, for wh.

she was very grateful, and always reminds me of it. I dare
say you remember the scene, as you have read all my works,
and often remind me of them. S[elina] has read very few,
and does not remember a line she has read.

To Lady Bradford.

HUGHENDEN MANOR, *Dec.* 23, 1875.—. . . You revive the
controversy about reading my books. . . . Those volumes
contain a multiplicity of characters and opinions, and yet I
don't remember your ever having referred to a single one in
all our frequent interviews. *Prima facie* therefore I had a
right to assume you were unacquainted with them. If you
had read the books, the result is still more mortifying, as
their impression must have been very transient. You will
exclaim ' Oh ! the vanity of authors !' I dare say all authors
are vain, even if they be Ministers of State; but I don't think
it is entirely that. I often feel my writing days are not over,
and there is nothing in life I so much appreciate as a female
critic. Her taste, and tact, and feeling, and judgment are
invaluable and inspiring. Therefore I confess I was grieved,
when I found one important and interesting tie between us
cd. not exist—and that, too, when our sources of sympathy
are, I often feel, not too numerous. . . .

From Montagu Corry.

EASTON, *Dec.* 29, '75.—. . . Münster says that we must
expect severe criticism of the Suez Canal affair, or rather
depreciation of the importance of the act. He knows, he
tells me, that the game of the front bench opposite will be to
represent it to the nation at Lord D[erby]'s valuation. They
expect that you will make the matter wear a different complexion, so (to quote Münster), ' they will uphold Lord D.
as the trumpet of common sense, and call Mr. D. a reckless
poet.'

The conferences at Hatfield were largely concerned
with the project of an addition to the Royal Title to
denote the new relation in which India, since the transference of its government, by the Act of 1858, from the
company to the Crown, had stood towards the Sovereign.
Disraeli had insisted at the time on the vital importance of
acting upon the Indian imagination by establishing personal contact between the Sovereign and the people; but it
was not thought, after consideration, that the morrow of the

Mutiny was an auspicious moment for Her Majesty to assume a new Indian title. The idea, however, had persisted both in Disraeli's mind and in the Queen's. Very shortly after assuming office he referred to it in a letter to her.

To Queen Victoria.

HOUSE OF COMMONS, *April* 14, 1874.—. . . The official intelligence of the contemplated cession of the Fiji Islands has not yet arrived, and the Cabinet has not considered the question, but Mr. Disraeli must confess his impression, that your Majesty will feel it necessary to accept the sovereignty of this southern archipelago—as well as the Empire of India.

The Queen thought the present a suitable time for carrying the project through, and impressed her view upon her Minister. Disraeli, with the reopened Eastern question upon his shoulders, and the Suez Canal transaction as yet unsanctioned by Parliament, would gladly have postponed this particular undertaking to a later day; but could not resist Her Majesty's pressure to accomplish, as a pendant to the Prince of Wales's visit, what he considered to be in itself eminently desirable.

To Lord Cairns.

Confidential. HUGHENDEN MANOR, *Jan.* 7, 1876.—The Empress-Queen demands her Imperial Crown. Since our conference at Hatfield, I have avoided touching on the matter, but can do so no longer. Pray let me hear from you, and let me know how it is to be done. . . .

Turn in your mind the paragraph in the Speech from the Throne, which announces the Suez purchase. I have no wish to leave it to the tender mercies of Derby.

To Lord Salisbury.

WESTON, SHIFNAL, *Jan.* 11, 1876.—. . . I am pressed much by the Empress about her Crown, and wrote to Cairns on it a few days back, but his answer, received here on my arrival yesterday, tells me nothing, wh. was not said in our conferences at Hatfield, and, in fact, he refers me to yourself, and, so, you came very *à propos.*

I doubt, whether it can be delayed or avoided, if practicable; and in that case, I would rather have the announcement in the Royal Speech after the Indian Visit paragraph. What then might have been looked upon as an ebullition of indivi- dual vanity, may bear the semblance of deep and organised policy: connected, as it will be, with other things.

I have told her that I have mentioned the Imperial matter only to the Ld. Chancellor and yourself: so you can speak to her on it, if you like.

From Lord Derby.

Private. Feb. 10, 1876.—. . . I wanted to mention to you at our last meeting, but had not an opportunity, that Delane has been making very friendly, and even pressing, overtures to Lady Derby; wanting information, and ready to back us up—as he says. You have many means of getting at him, but I think this worth your knowing.

To Lady Bradford.

2, WHITEHALL GARDENS, *Jan.* 28, 1876.—A most busy day, but I have written the Queen's Speech. . . .

There is to be war to the knife when the Houses meet—at least the Flea[1] told me so whom I met yesterday morn. Glad- stone is to rush in to the arena; but Lowe is to be awful— crushing, overwhelming: a great invective agst. a stock- jobbing Ministry.

I told the Flea that I doubted not that there wd. be a great deal of noise, but that he might bet there wd. be no division. So he will say that all about town. . . .

Disraeli succeeded this year in persuading the Queen to open Parliament in person. Since the Prince Consort's death, she had only nerved herself to undertake three times, in 1866, 1867, and 1871, the task which she had regularly performed during all the earlier years of her reign. For some years after 1868, ill-health had made it necessary for Her Majesty to husband her resources; but that period of physical weakness was now happily over. Sympathetic as Disraeli was with the womanly feelings which made resumption of her public functions distasteful to the Queen, he was convinced that a Monarchy which was not seen could not continue to hold its place in the hearts of the people. Especially was it in his view

---

[1] Mr. Fleming, a man then well known in London society.

important, in order that the Crown might preserve its due weight in the British Constitution, that the Sovereign should show regularly, by personal association year by year, that the Legislature consists of King, Lords, and Commons, and not of Lords and Commons only. He was moreover, of course, not insensible to the political advantage which might accrue to him and his Government from the proof of confidence in her existing Ministers which the Queen's emergence from retirement on their advice and in their support would give. One of his first official recommendations in 1874 was to suggest delicately to Her Majesty the resumption of this ceremonial; and though he did not prevail then, his tactful pleading would, but for the unexpected illness of Prince Leopold, have been successful in 1875, as is shown by the following letter:

To Queen Victoria.

B[OURNE]MOUTH, *Dec.* 10, 1874.—. . . He shall not breathe, even to his colleagues, a word as to the gracious contingency referred to in Lady Ely's note. However interesting to Mr. Disraeli, it is a subject on which he had made up his mind never to press your Majesty, as he knows a long and impending engagement harasses and disquiets. The gracious act, if it occur, should be quite spontaneous.

It was, of course, peculiarly becoming for the Queen to appear in person at Westminster at the commencement of a session which would have to deal with a Bill augmenting Her Majesty's style and title. The royal ceremonial proved to be so attractive that Disraeli, who had compassed it, narrowly escaped serious maltreatment in the press of loyal members of Parliament struggling to get into their Sovereign's presence.

To Queen Victoria.

2, WHITEHALL GARDENS, *Feb.* 9, 1876.—Mr. Disraeli with his humble duty to your Majesty:

He offers his congratulations to your Majesty on yesterday: without sun, without joy-bells, everybody seemed excited and happy. He himself followed the Speaker to the House of Lords, that he might have the satisfaction of seeing your

Majesty in your State, but the throng was so tumultuous, and so violent, that he could not enter the House, and, in attempting to guard the Speaker, who was at one moment nearly overcome, Mr. Disraeli himself was nearly borne down, when he must have been trampled on. He believes that the mob, which he never saw equalled in violence since the old Westminster elections, was, if not entirely, mainly of members of the House of Commons. He saw the respectable Mr. Bass absolutely fighting with a Conservative giant, the member for Plymouth. And yet all this turmoil was, in a certain sense, satisfactory; for it was occasioned by a desire to see your Majesty, and indicates what an immense influence your Majesty's occasional presence can produce.

Mr. Disraeli believes that, in both Houses, the proceedings were eminently satisfactory.

In the Commons, the Address was moved, and seconded, with rare, yet equal ability.

Lord Hartington made an elaborate criticism on the general conduct of the Government, to which Mr. Disraeli replied: on all the main points of coming struggle, especially the Suez Canal, apparently to the satisfaction of a large majority in a crowded house. As he found himself, necessarily, involved in a sharp controversial speech, Mr. Disraeli thought it best not to touch on the Indian visit and the intended alteration of Imperial style, but reserve his remarks for the Bill, which he is going to introduce, but, so far as he could collect from the sympathy of the House with the observations on these subjects which were made by the Mover and Seconder, under his instructions, and from the general tone of the press this morning, he feels persuaded that the Imperial assumption will be most popular in the country.

Disraeli's prediction that there would be a great deal of noise but no division on the Suez Canal purchase came true. The four millions were voted, without challenge in the lobbies, in the second week of the session, but it was the prudence of Hartington which avoided a division, in spite of carping and captious attacks by Gladstone and Lowe. Disraeli defended the purchase as an act of ' high policy.' Why should we not wait, it was said, till the French proprietary put obstacles in our way, as we could always, in the last resort, obtain satisfaction by the use of our naval force ? His answer was fine and dignified.

If the government of the world was a mere alternation between abstract right and overwhelming force, I agree there is a good deal in that observation; but that is not the way in which the world is governed. The world is governed by conciliation, compromise, influence, varied interests, the recognition of the rights of others, coupled with the assertion of one's own; and in addition, a general conviction, resulting from explanation and good understanding, that it is for the interest of all parties that matters should be conducted in a satisfactory and peaceful manner.

England, Disraeli pointed out, was a great Mediterranean power, with strongholds upon those waters which she would never relinquish. But her policy was not one of aggression, and she would not interest herself in the redistribution of territory in that quarter, so long as the freedom of the seas and the dominion which she legitimately exercised were not imperilled. The Suez Canal would form a link in the chain of fortresses which we possess on the road to India; by the purchase we gained a great additional security, which we should prize, for the free intercourse of navigation. Disraeli left it to Northcote to justify the prudence of the investment of British money; but that has been amply vindicated by time. What, forty years ago, was bought for £4,000,000 was officially estimated, shortly before the great war, to be worth over £40,000,000.

To Queen Victoria.

2, WHITEHALL GARDENS, *Feb.* 22, 1876.—Mr. Disraeli with his humble duty to your Majesty:

He has had the honor to receive your Majesty's letter of yesterday. The subjects referred to, occupy his constant attention—but are full of difficulties; he means as regards the *Mistletoe ;*[1] every effort will be made to fulfil your Majesty's wishes.

The great *Suez* business ended last night, and very satisfactorily. The House of Commons proved, that the opinion of the country on the measure was unchanged, and Mr. Gladstone produced no effect, though he spoke with more than his usual ability.

A fiercer struggle commences to-night, and will not terminate till Thursday.

[1] See above, p. 738.

The fierce struggle which this letter anticipated was on the Slave Circular;[1] a matter in which Disraeli had been the victim of departmental blundering. So strong and general was the anti-slavery feeling that the Government were only saved by a majority of forty-five. Disraeli had wisely deprecated a philanthropic agitation in regard to a delicate question of international law.

To the Lord Mayor of London (Alderman Cotton, M.P.).

Confidential. 2, WHITEHALL GARDENS, *Jan.* 20, '76.—It is of importance for the public interest, that there shd. be as little agitation as possible on the slavery question before the meeting of Parliamt.—otherwise, men get committed to views, which, if attempted to be put in practice, only aggravate the evils, wh. it is our common purpose to prevent.

Slavery is not a party question, and can't be made one. All parties, and all statesmen, have, upon it, the same policy. But we must remember, that resolutions at public meetings, and even Acts of Parliament, can't alter the law of nations. To that we must all bow, and the only consequences of our attempt to defy its omnipotence is, that our naval commanders are cast in damages, and the State itself suffers in the comity of nations.

A public meeting in the city of London, presided over by its chief magistrate, always produces an effect on opinion, and there is no doubt, that, if you can, without too great personal inconvenience, prevent, or postpone for a time, the proposed meeting at the Mansion House, it would be of public advantage.

The purpose of the meeting is wide and wild. It is not the criticism of an act of the Government that is contemplated, which wd. be a limited issue, and might be encountered; but it is to change the whole law of England on the most difficult of all subjects. There will be, as Lord Derby would say, a fine field for 'rant and cant.'

I shd. be glad, therefore, to hear, that the contemplated meeting, by your prudence and discretion, did not take place, and that the citizens will not be favored with the opinion and sentiments of the Lord Mayor on this interesting and difficult subject, until he expresses them as their representative in the House of Commons.

Over the Royal Titles Bill Ministers were much more successful than over the Slave Circular, though they were

---

[1] See above, pp. 736-738.

met at every stage by the devices of faction. A curious omission on Disraeli's part contributed to inflame his opponents. In matters affecting the dignity of the Crown, it had been the practice for the responsible Minister, in order to minimise controversy, to enter into communication with the leaders of Opposition. But Disraeli, in spite of the easy social relations which he enjoyed with both the official Liberal leaders, Granville and Hartington, neglected this customary and courteous precaution until the measure was already labouring heavily amid storms of parliamentary criticism. The Queen took the blame on herself. She wrote to Disraeli on February 10: ' She is provoked at the conduct of the Opposition about the Indian title, but thinks perhaps she ought (as was done in the case of the Prince's title of Prince Consort) to have *herself informed* Lord Granville of it, and thus have prevented the disagreeable remarks. She could still do this, and state how much *she* had urged this herself, if Mr. Disraeli is of the same opinion.'[1] Her Majesty also accepted the responsibility for a further omission, which led the Prince of Wales to write to Disraeli from Seville on April 22: ' As the Queen's eldest son, I think I have some right to feel annoyed that . . . the announcement of the addition to the Queen's title should have been read by me in the newspapers, instead of having received some intimation on the subject from the Prime Minister.' Ponsonby wrote on the Queen's behalf to Disraeli on May 3: ' She blames herself for not having written to [the Prince] about the Titles Bill, adding, however, that she certainly thought sho had done so.'

The Bill was one to enable Her Majesty to add to the royal style and title in order to mark the new relation in which since 1858 she had stood towards India, its sovereign Princes, and its many and various races. When he introduced it, Disraeli did not say what the new title would be; Her Majesty, he told the House of Commons, would exercise her prerogative and assume that addition

[1] For the correspondence between the Queen and Granville, see Fitzmaurice, Vol. II., pp. 161-163.

to her style and title which she deemed expedient and
proper.   But he used the words ' Empire ' and ' imperial '
throughout his speech.   The Prince of Wales's demeanour
in India had qualified him, he said, for an ' imperial '
post; the new style would set the seal to the unanimous
determination of the people of this country to retain our
Indian ' Empire '; the House, by passing the Bill, would
show their pride that India was a part of Her Majesty's
' Empire,' and was governed by her ' imperial ' throne.
The public and Parliament at once assumed that 'Empress'
was the title intended; and there was much indignation,
partly real, partly affected, at what was described as
tarnishing the grand old title of King or Queen, and
introducing the associations of force, violence, and even
debauchery which were alleged to attach to Emperor and
Empress.

It was not until the debate on the second reading that
Disraeli revealed what the new title was to be; and, in an
adroit speech, he skilfully led up to the announcement
by pointing out the remarkable circumstance that, to
those desirous of objecting to the policy, one title alone
had occurred; ' which *prima facie* is rather in favour of
its being an apposite title.'   It was not difficult to
dispose of objections which can hardly be read with
patience now.   As for the ' bad associations ' of the
title of Emperor, Gibbon had laid it down in an immortal
passage that the happiness of mankind was never so
completely assured or so long maintained as in the age
of the Antonines—who were Emperors.   Nor could the
assumption of the title locally at all impair the title of
King or Queen of Great Britain.   Our Kings had always
asserted an equality with Emperors, and the claim had
been allowed.   Nor was the title un-English; it was used
of Queen Elizabeth in Spenser's dedication to her of the
Faery Queen.   The style of Empress of India so completely
corresponded with notorious fact that, as Disraeli showed,
to the amusement of the House, in a subsequent speech,
it had been already attributed to Queen Victoria in a
popular school geography of the day.

Disraeli justified the policy of the Bill in a weighty sentence. ' It is only by the amplification of titles that you can often touch and satisfy the imagination of nations; and that is an element which Governments must not despise.' In this and other speeches on the Bill he asked the House to turn from these paltry objections and look at the effect in India. There the Bill was anxiously expected. There the Princes and peoples knew exactly what it meant, and they knew that what it meant was what they wished. The Russian advance in Central Asia made the assumption of the new title peculiarly appropriate.

There is a country of vast extent which has been known hitherto only by its having sent forth hordes to conquer the world. That country has at last been vanquished; and the frontiers of Russia . . . are only a few days' march from those of Her Majesty's dominions in India. I venture to speak on this subject with some frankness, because I am not of that school who view the advances of Russia in Asia with those deep misgivings that some do. I think that Asia is large enough for the destinies of both Russia and England. But, whatever may be my confidence in the destiny of England, I know that empires are only maintained by vigilance, by firmness, by courage, by understanding the temper of the times in which we live, and by watching those significant indications that may easily be observed.

The population of India is not the population it was when we carried the Bill of 1858. There has been a great change in the habits of the people. That which the press could not do, that which our influence had failed in doing, the introduction of railroads has done; and the people of India move about in a manner which could never have been anticipated, and are influenced by ideas and knowledge which never before reached or touched them. What was the gossip of bazaars is now the conversation of villages. You think they are ignorant of what is going on in Central Asia ? You think they are unaware that Tartary, that great conquering power of former times, is now at last conquered? No; not only do they know what has occurred, not only are they well acquainted with the power which has accomplished this great change, but they know well the title of the great Prince who has brought about so wonderful a revolution. I have listened with surprise night after night to hon. gentlemen, on both

sides of the House, translating the title of Empress into all
sorts of languages, and indicating to us what name would
at last be adopted. The nations and populations that can
pronounce the word Emperor, and that habitually use it,
will not be slow to accept the title of Empress. That is the
word which will be adopted by the nations and populations
of India; and in announcing, as Her Majesty will do by
proclamation, that she adopts that title, confidence will be
given to her Empire in that part of the world, and it will be
spoken, in language which cannot be mistaken, that the
Parliament of England have resolved to uphold the Empire
of India.

The only objection to the measure of any real weight
was that the Colonies had as valid a claim as India to be
recognised in the royal title. To meet this point, the
propriety of creating the Prince of Wales Prince Imperial
of India, and his second and third brothers Princes of
Canada and Australia, was canvassed between Ministers
and the Queen. But it was a clumsy expedient, and was
very wisely dropped without ever being submitted to
Parliament; the Prince of Wales expressing strong
repugnance to the suggested addition to his style. It
was pointed out by Disraeli in debate that the constant
intercourse and interchange of people between the Colonies
and the Mother Country entirely differentiated their case
from that of India; that the colonists were Englishmen
with relations to the Sovereign comparable to those of
Englishmen who remained at home. India had a special
claim. There was, at any rate, good reason for doing
one thing at a time; and the Dominions and Colonies
received their due when King Edward VII., on his accession, acting under the advice of Disraeli's colleague and
successor, Salisbury, and of the Imperial-minded Colonial
Secretary, Chamberlain, assumed the style of *Britan-
niarum Omnium Rex*, thus recognising the 'British
Dominions beyond the seas' as part of his realm.

Hartington's disposition was to leave the responsibility to the Government and let the Bill pass after a
moderate protest; and accordingly the second reading,
being resisted in the lobby by only a handful of Radicals,

was carried by 284 votes to 31, in spite of a speech of vehement opposition by Gladstone.

To Lady Bradford.

2, WHITEHALL GARDENS, *March* 10.—I am well satisfied with last night. When a crowded House ends in a dissolving view, and the Opposition, when the division is called, don't know what to do—run into holes and corners, rush out of the House, or vote against themselves, a Ministry is safe.

I had everything to make me nervous, for I had heard nothing for days but the danger of the situation, and that our own men cd. not be trusted, etc., etc., etc. When I got home from my dinner on Wednesday, I found a box, marked ' secret,' from a colleague on whom I mainly depend, counselling ' surrender.' It rather disturbed my night, I assure you, and I wanted a good one, instead of rising with shattered nerves.

This made me alter my tactics, and I resolved to open the ball with some remarks wh. might conciliate the House generally, and reanimate my friends. I think I succeeded. because I was told, when I sate down, that certain members on the other side of influence and independence, thought that there ought to be now no division, and the Speaker afterwards told me that Ld. Hartington was of that opinion too. But that wd. not satisfy Mr. G., who was brimful, took the reins in his own hands, and after a speech of vituperative casuistry, imagining every combination wh. cd. never happen, fled from his own motion, and left his party in a ditch. . . .

March 13.—. . . Gladstone is quite mad and I have no doubt that, by next Thursday, he will have prepared blowing up materials equal to Guy Faux. I understand it is to be something dreadful, but my friends are firm, and Harry Chaplin is going to give us a speech, out of love for me, and hatred of G. . . .

The measure was disliked by London society, and it had a bad press, *The Times* taking the lead in criticism and ridicule. Thus encouraged, Gladstone and Lowe, on the one hand, and Fawcett and the Radicals on the other, forced Hartington's hand; and the Opposition divided both against the motion to go into Committee and against the third reading, being beaten, however, in each case, by a large majority. This factious resistance puzzled and incensed the Queen. She lavished her sympathy on her harassed Minister, and was fertile in suggesting explanations which should smooth his path and meet all reasonable objections to the policy.

From Queen Victoria.

WINDSOR CASTLE, *March* 11, '76.—The Queen thanks Mr. Disraeli for his letter received yesterday and greatly rejoiced at the successful 2nd reading of the Titles Bill, the opposition to which still remains quite inexplicable to her ! . . .

March 15.—The Queen thanks Mr. Disraeli for his letter and for all he said to General Ponsonby. She has no fear for the result, but is sorry for the trouble it causes Mr. Disraeli and for the ill-advised and mistaken conduct of the Opposition, which will not redound to the credit of the House of Commons abroad.

There is clearly no feeling in the country against it and delay might do much harm.

The Queen is really not worrying herself about it, for she never wished anything that could impair her own old Unionist title; and therefore her conscience is clear.

March 16.—. . . Pray let telegrams be sent this evening. Don't be anxious; all is sure to do well.

March 17.—The Queen is greatly rejoiced at the majority last night, which she learnt on getting up this morning. She heard twice during the evening. She cannot but regret the extraordinary and to her incomprehensible and mistaken course of the Opposition. She concludes that in the House of Lords there will be little trouble.

The Queen cannot help taking this opportunity of impressing on Mr. Disraeli the importance of securing *some* newspaper as an organ for the Government. The *Globe* and *John Bull* are very badly written and the latter so ultra and extreme in its religious views as to prevent the Queen from taking it in any longer, the last 3 years.

She hopes Mr. Disraeli is not the worse for all this excitement and annoyance.

March 18.—The Queen thinks, now that the Government have so triumphantly carried the Titles Bill in the House of Commons, it would be of great importance (as many really excellent, loyal people will not understand it, and are full of apprehension) if Mr. Disraeli, at the last stage of the Bill in the House of Commons, would state strongly and clearly that it was, and always had been, the Queen's wish that the title of Empress of India which had been constantly colloquially used, should apply *only* to *India* and that the title of

Sovereign of the British Empire was *always* to remain what it was now, viz., Queen (or in future times King) of ' Great Britain and Ireland,' the other being added on at the end.

The Queen is very anxious that this should be done, for else she fears people (not the Opposition but the best disposed and ignorant ones) will continue to misinterpret the title, and she may be exposed to annoyance and misapprehension. She would also be glad if it were more generally known that it was *her* wish, as people *will* have it, that it has been *forced upon her !* If all this were once for all clearly put on record the Queen thinks there will be nothing more said about it and it will be completely understood. She would be glad if Mr. Disraeli would bring the purport of this letter before the Cabinet.

(*Same date.*)—The Queen has just received Mr. Disraeli's bag and hastens to answer it, that she fully authorises him to say that there never had been the *slightest intention* of giving the title of Imperial Highness to any of her children, or of making any change in the name of the Sovereign of Great Britain, which will remain precisely the same for all ages, but merely to legalise the name which had been colloquially always used—of Empress of her great Eastern Empire, and adding it on at the end. . . .

From Lady Ely.

WINDSOR CASTLE, *March* 21, '76.—. . . The Queen, quite *entre nous,* has been much upset by this debate, and has taken the opposition very badly to her title, personally, and for the sake of you, as the Queen says, ' her kind, good and considerate friend ';—she fears you have been much annoyed, but her displeasure is very great with those who have opposed it. . . .

For the moment, the royal explanations gave pause to the Opposition; and Disraeli became prematurely sanguine.

To Lady Bradford.

2, WHITEHALL GARDENS, *March* 21.—. . . My interview with Harty-T. was satisfactory, tho' of course he could not answer for Gladstone, who gave us as much trouble as he could, being all the night in one of his white rages, and glancing looks at me, wh. wd. have annihilated any man who had not a good majority and a determination to use it.

Never was such a triumphant evening. I carried the Bill thro' Committee without a single amendment, tho' many

were tried, and more threatened. This is a most unusual
feat. When a Bill is carried thro' Committee without amendments, there is no ' Report ' as it is termed—that is to say,
a stage when all the old objections may be revived and
repeated again; and you go to the 3rd reading and passing it,
on the next stage, wh. we shall do on Thursday. I don't
think there will be any attempt at a division then, and so
I believe [the Bill] will after all pass unanimously. . . .

I look upon the Titles Bill to have proved more than anything the strength of the Ministry. I see no rocks ahead
now; and I am going down to the House for the first time
this session, without that tension of the nervous system, wh.
I have had since Parlt. met. Never was a Government so
unfortunate as we were during the recess, and we yet have
extricated ourselves out of all our mischances !

To Anne Lady Chesterfield.

2, WHITEHALL GARDENS, *March* 22.—. . . . All the hopes
and schemes of the Opposition have now failed: Suez Canal,
Slave Circular, *Vanguard* Minute, and royal titles. I begin
to feel as if it were the end of the session, but I suppose
the fires may yet burst out again. March is too early for
despair, even for the desperate. . . .

The objectors pursued the Bill even in the House of
Lords, where a formidable opposition developed under
the lead of the independent Shaftesbury; but the attack
was repelled, though not without difficulty. Nor did the
outcry cease with the passage of the measure into law.
Fawcett and the Radicals concentrated against the
Proclamation which was to carry it into effect. In order
to disable criticism, Ministers promised that that document should show on its face that the title would not be
used in the United Kingdom. Accordingly it was therein
set out that ' all charters, commissions, letters patent,
grants, writs, appointments, and other like instruments
not extending in their operation beyond the United
Kingdom ' should be excepted from the general use of
the new title. This did not satisfy the objectors.
Ministers were accused of a breach of faith, and Henry
James moved on behalf of the Opposition a vote of censure,
which, largely owing to a brilliant reply from Hardy,

proved as great a fiasco as previous assaults on the new policy. Disraeli explained once more that the Queen would only assume the title of Empress externally; but for the whole internal Government of the United Kingdom it would not be used. It was really a very simple arrangement, and has worked excellently. The Sovereign's signature is decorated with an ' I ' in addition to the familiar ' R '; in public proclamations ' Emperor of India ' follows ' Defender of the Faith '; and the legend on our coins ends with ' Ind. Imp.' But the King has been King and nothing more in official and in ordinary use in these his Kingdoms; only in India, where the change has been heartily welcomed, is he King-Emperor. The fears of the Opposition of 1876 have proved to be chimeras. But the world understood that a new pledge had been given of the determination of the British Crown to cherish India; and her Princes and peoples understood that their Sovereign had assumed towards them a nearer and more personal relation.

' Greater nonsense was, I think, never spoken in both Houses of Parliament '; such was the Prince of Wales's terse and just appreciation, in a letter to the Queen, of the objections of the Opposition. But, nonsensical as it was, the factious controversy none the less bore heavily on the ageing Disraeli, as his private correspondence shows.

To Lady Bradford.

2, WHITEHALL GARDENS, *March* 30.—How is Juliet ? Our factions are not quite as fierce as the Montacutes and Capulets, but Shaftesbury, I really believe, wd. do anything. . . . He was invited to dine [at Windsor], and his denunciations of unutterable woe were his amusing small talk in the circle after dinner ! . . .

To Anne Lady Chesterfield.

10, DOWNING STREET, *March* 31, 1876.—. . . I am living in a fiery furnace. There never was such a factious Opposition. However, the Bill was read for the second time yesterday in the Lords without a division. The great struggle is on Monday, and I hope the faction will be overthrown.

The insolence of the D[uke] of —— surpasses belief. I will, some day, greatly chastise him. When I thought in the autumn that there would be a vacancy in the Cabinet, I recommended the Queen to appoint him ! I won't do that again in a hurry.

The weather is delicious: the spring of Ausonian lands. I walked to Selina in the morning and lunched at 43 [Belgrave Square]. In my walk, strolling up the shadowy walks of the Green Park, and lost in thought, somebody seized my hand, which was on my back. I started, and turned round—and it was S. !

2, WHITEHALL GARDENS, *April* 2.—To-morrow is the great Battle of Armageddon, when it will be decided, who governs England, I or the newspapers.[1] So far as I can judge, my friends will rally well. . . ..

Some want us, if we have a good majority, to give up the title ' Empress.' They are the same people who wanted us, after the Slavery division, to give up our Circular and ' prevent agitation.' It would not; it wd. have been an act of weakness, not of conciliation. And now, whoever hears a word about the ' Circular' ? Perfectly dead. If you want to govern the world you must know how to say ' Bo ' to a goose. And what is the use of power, if you don't make people do what they don't like ?

To Lady Bradford.

2, WHITEHALL GARDENS, *April* 4.—It was a substantial majority[2]—but with decent whipping might easily have been 60. . . .

April 6.—. . . Harty-Tarty has much disappointed me, for he lends himself to every device of faction—even when they are palpably violent and injudicious. After a council at Ld. Granville's on Tuesday, Gladstone present, they resolved to take up Fawcett, who was to move an Address to the Crown before the Proclamation cd. be issued, and they wished me to pledge myself that no Proclamation shd. be issued until the Address had been moved in the H. of C. Harty and Co. counted on the motion coming on after the recess, and the country being agitated during the holidays. I would not stand this and offered Fawcett Monday the 10th, wh. he pretended gratefully to accept; but I heard last night that there is disorder, and some discontent, in their camp, and that they will not fight on Monday. I think of giving the Commons as long a holiday as the Lords, for they have been much worked these two months. That would be to the

---

[1] Or, as Disraeli put the question in a letter to Lady Bradford, ' who shall rule the country, the Queen's Minister, or Printing House Square.'
[2] 137 to 91.

27th. In that, or indeed in any case, a Council could easily be held before Parliament reassembles, the Proclamation wd. be issued, and the affair finished. At present, the only apparent result of all this faction is that H.-T. has doubled my majority in the House of Commons, and ascertained that I have a majority, wh. I rather doubted, in the House of Lords. . . .

I dined in the evening at the Somers. . . . There were the Randolph Churchills; he glaring like one possessed of a devil, and quite uncivil when I addressed [him] rather cordially. Why? I thought at first it was something about the mysterious correspondence—but, perhaps, a simpler cause, that I gave the lordship of the Treasury to Crichton instead of himself. . . .

In the evening there was a reception, which is now a rare performance to me, but in which I distinguished more than one strata of society. While I was observing the world, the most impudent of women in it, a Mrs. —— of ——, addressed me. I never was introduced to her, and she once came to my house without an invitation. Now she said, ' It is delightful to meet an old friend,' and expatiated on her unhappiness in seeing so little of me. I escaped as soon as possible, and, this morning, she has asked me to dinner with her and her daughter next Sunday, *sans façon ! ! !* As Mr. Daly has not yet arrived from Belvoir, Mr. Turnor will have to reply to this impudence. . . .

April 7.—. . . Things have turned out well. The Liberal party—or a good section of them—rebelled agst. Harty-Tarty's alliance with Fawcett, and fairly wd. not march thro' Coventry, so he had to make yesterday an ignominious retreat, with many confused reasons. Then, their attack on the Budget entirely failed. They were beaten in preliminary divisions, and then they conveniently postponed their announced attack until after Easter, altho' Gladstone, and all his clerks, had come down arrayed with Hansards and blue books.

If I can only manage to mitigate the *Mistletoe* business on Monday, we shall have risen 50 per cent. There is good news from Egypt. . . .

I have had some touching letters from the Faery. She says ' The worry and annoyance to wh. Mr. D. is exposed by this unfortunate, and most harmless, Titles Bill, grieves the Queen deeply, as she fears she is the cause of it,' and so on. . . .

I hope to get down to Hughenden on Tuesday, when I shall be alone—but not more lonely than I feel here, since you and yours have gone. It was no doubt quite visionary—a mere delusion; but Belgravia had become to me a sort of home, a link between me and the domestic principle. Now life seems quite inhuman—nothing to soften or distract it: nothing but Parliaments, and Councils, and despatches, without a gentle thought or graceful deed ! Alas ! there was the daily letter always, and the little visit, to charm away cares and sometimes to solve difficulties; for in talking to those in whom we can confide, the knot often falls to pieces. Remember me to Bradford.

April 11.—. . . At four I go to Hughenden. . . .

The Faery has been greatly distressed about the *Mistletoe* business, but it was impossible to prevent its being brought forward, and it ended yesterday very well. She cannot understand that Captain Welsh is not merely her servant, but also an officer of the British Navy, who receives his pay and appointments from the House of Commons, who grant these in the Navy Estimates, wh. depend entirely on their vote. Altho' you say I spoil her, it has fallen to my lot to tell her these grave truths; but how they will be borne I do not know—very badly, I suspect. . . .

Carnarvon will find [the Queen] in great excitement about Captain Welsh, which she says is much more important to her than the ' Royal Titles.' I feel like a Minister disgraced, and as if I were going to be imprisoned in Hampton Court or Claremont.

HUGHENDEN MANOR,[1] *April* 12.—. . . I cannot read Whyte Melville, or anything of the kind; I cannot read now what are called ' works of fiction.' Such compositions entirely with me depend on their style; and that seems a quality quite unknown to the present generation of critics. Something very fine like *Wilhelm Meister*, or the earlier works of George Sand, might not only attract, but absorb, me: but I require nothing short of those great masters. Fiction must be first-rate or it is nothing. Second-rate histories and essays may go down, but when a self-announced magician waves the wand, we expect miracles.

April 13.—Snow, snow, snow ! never-ceasing snow ! A lonely house, and never-ceasing snow ! and no letter from Weston—my solitary joy ! . . .

April 15.—. . . It is a spring day again: the birds sing, and the peacocks, that were screaming all yesterday, and perched upon the pergola with their draggled trains, are magnificent again, reposing at full length on the terrace, or couched in the marble vases, glittering white against their purple gorges and their green and golden tails.

---

[1] Where Disraeli had gone for the Easter recess.

And in ½ an hour I shall leave them, in no very high spirits I can assure you, for the messenger, who has just arrived, brings me nothing but cares. I sometimes wish that they were at the bottom of the Red Sea, with the Suez Canal shares. I really am too old for ambition, and, except that I shall rarely see you again when my reign is over, the loss of my sceptre would not break my heart, I can assure you. But to you I am always the same.

2, WHITEHALL GARDENS, *April* 26.—. . . This inconvenient dying of the Dowager of Derby at this moment is sad. I have not seen the Sec. of F.O. yet ! and so much going on, and the French Ambassador coming to me at ½ pt. 12 !

It is also most injurious to the party. I quite counted on a series of F.O. receptions. With forty years of political experience, I never knew a party so deserted by all social influences as ours. I wonder how they are kept together—not a solitary dinner or a single drum !

If it were not for the mysterious letting of the house of my friend Lady Waldegrave, I think we must fall to pieces. It seems to me we have not a woman with the slightest ambition. All female movement seemed to have died out with poor Lady Carnarvon.[1] What is the use of the fine house of the Lonsdales ? They might try something. It wd. not be fashionable, but it might be grand.

Talking of Carnarvon, I am extremely amused that, while all the Government are attacked in the metrop. papers for their blundering, etc., little Carnarvon, who feeds the Radical press, is always spared, and really he is the only one who has made mistakes, and committed a series of blunders.

(1) The Cape and Mr. Froude's agitation, and (2) the diplomatic mistake about the Gambia, and (3) the war in Malay-land, and now (4) the mysterious Barbados affair ![2]

I had the satisfaction, last night, of extinguishing, I think, Mr. Fawcett and his faction, and forcing Harty-Tarty to throw him over. . . . Talking of Fawcett, yesterday morning all the papers had the most terrific leading articles on the subject of his impending motion, and you wd. have supposed the Govt. were already out. As for the *Daily Tel.*, or rather the *Delirium Tremens*, you wd. have supposed that I was the most abject and discomfited of men. I said ' Bo ' to the goose, however, and this morning not a word ! I mention this, as I know you and yours are ruled by newspapers, and believe every word that is written agst. me; you, I will admit, or hope so, with some pain, but still you believe. I shall say ' Bo ' to a great many more geese before the session is over. . . .

[1] Carnarvon's first wife, Lady Chesterfield's daughter, died on Jan. 25, 1875.   [2] See VI.

April 29.—I could not write yesterday, as it was an urgent
and anxious day: that wretched Fawcett having given notice,
on Monday night, tho' rather at 2 o'ck. on Tuesday morning,
that, at the meeting of the Ho., on going into supply, he wd.
bring forward a vote of censure on the Govt. As there was,
so far as the order of business was concerned, a probability
that he might have the opportunity, I had to make all the
arrangements requisite, telegraph for absent members, etc., etc.
—while I had myself to go to Windsor, instead of preparing
for the combat. He did not, eventually, bring it on, but I
had all the toil and anxiety.

The Prince has not exceeded his £60,000; which is rather
a triumph, tho' a petty one, for me.

I have had a heavy Cabinet to-day, and many toilsome
affairs, and can scarcely write this, and have to go to that
most damnable ceremony, the Academy dinner, where 150
critics of the ' first water ' expect me to give utterance to
Attic sayings, when my brain has no Attic salt left in it. . . .

The only person whom you seem neither to care to see nor
to please, is myself. And when you come to town, it will
only, I fear, be to tell me, as you usually do, that you are
going again into the country on some visit, or still more
probably, even abroad. I fear our romance is over, if indeed
it ever existed except in my imagination; but still I sometimes
dreamed that the dream might last until I slumbered for ever.

2, WHITEHALL GARDENS, *May* 2, 1876.—. . . There is
some chance that the answers in our House, and the full
reply of the Ld. Chan[cello]r, may check the hostile advance;
and if checked, it may die, for the world is anxious, I rather
feel, for a new subject. If the sun wd. only shine, and put
the world in a better humor, we might have a chance, but
gentlemen begin to despair of getting their rents. The
farmers are really sulky, and vent their spite, not on nature,
but the Ministry.

In the House of C. last night a round robin was in secret
circulation among the Liberal party requesting a meeting
of the party to consider the Royal Proclamation and do
something. They are discontented with their chiefs, and
Harcourt and Henry James and Fawcett want to force Harty-
Tarty's hand. . . .

The Academy dinner was an hour shorter in consequence
of F. Grant's health, and therefore was much improved.

May 5.—. . . I am tired and sad ! The session has been
one of extraordinary exhaustion and anxiety, and the burthen
has fallen on myself. . . . I dined at Sir N. Rothschild's
on Wednesday: said to be the best dinner in London and
always charming society. . . .

M[*ay*] 12.—Yesterday, as Cromwell said of the Battle of Worcester, was 'a crowning mercy.' Such a discomfiture has rarely been experienced by a party; and what is most delightful is that the numbers[1] were almost all our own. I don't think a Whig voted with us. The speech of Kenealy, wh. will be read by every rough in Britain, and wh. was well delivered, was *à propos*. Peel[2] spoke some time, and with great effect: without a thought or an argument. Such were the magic of a great name and a splendid voice! I rose, past midnight, with a racking headache, and ought to have disgraced myself, but did not. . . .

In the debates on the Suez Canal purchase and on the Royal Titles Bill the most acrimonious, as well as the most petty, criticism had emanated from Lowe. He had dilated on the enormity of the Rothschild commission as a sufficient ground for rejecting the high policy of purchase; and he had deprecated the introduction of India into the royal style and title on the ground that we ought to contemplate the contingency of losing our dominion there! 'The right honourable gentleman is a prophet,' said Disraeli, 'but he is always a prophet of evil.' In a speech at East Retford during the Easter recess Lowe's recklessness and aversion to Disraeli led him to make a virulent personal attack both on the Queen and on the Minister. Her Majesty had frankly avowed to the Opposition leaders her personal interest and even initiative in the Royal Titles Bill. Hardy wrote to Disraeli from Windsor Castle on February 20: 'The Queen desired me to tell you that she had written to Lord Granville on the title; and that Forster, who had sent a corrected copy of his speech to General Ponsonby for her, had been told that she herself had initiated the proposal, which she thought would rather surprise him.' Lowe responded to Her Majesty's frankness by malicious insinuation. 'I strongly suspect,' he said, 'that this is not brought forward for the first time. I violate no confidence, because I have received none; but I am under a conviction that at least two previous Ministers have entirely refused

---

[1] 334 to 226.   [2] The 3rd Baronet, the Prime Minister's eldest son.

to have anything to do with such a change. More pliant persons have now been found, and I have no doubt the thing will be done.'

This was a very serious accusation for a Privy Councillor, a former Chancellor of the Exchequer and Secretary of State, to make; and Gladstone, Lowe's chief, felt that a peculiar obligation lay upon him to repudiate, as he did in the public press, the natural implication that he was one of the previous Ministers referred to. But even this repudiation did not recall Lowe to a sense of what he had done; and when, on May 2, the attention of Parliament was directed by a private member to the astonishing utterance, he treated the whole matter as trivial, entirely declined to offer any explanation, and denied the right of the House of Commons to call him to account for words spoken out of doors, in a case where no breach of privilege was involved. Disraeli saw that his adversary had been delivered into his hand. 'One of those occasions,' he wrote next day to Lady Bradford, 'which rarely, and yet in a certain sense always, come to the vigilant, came to me, and I smashed that wretched Lowe.' He spoke, on his Sovereign's behalf and his own, with a passion which, if rhetorically heightened, was yet very real, and produced an electrical effect on the House. Lowe's statements, he said, were monstrous if they were true, and, if they were not true, must be described ' by an epithet which I cannot find in my vocabulary.'

Sir, did the right hon. gentleman or did he not—not merely intimate, not insinuate, but I say broadly state to the people of this country, that the Royal Titles measure was introduced to the notice of Parliament by the unconstitutional and personal influence of the Sovereign ? Did he or did he not take that occasion to hold up to public prejudice, and I will say public infamy, the chief Minister, asserting, under circumstances detailed by the right hon. gentleman with minuteness, that after that gracious Sovereign had been balked and baffled in her appeals to previous Ministers she had found a pliant and a servile instrument who was now ready to do her will ?

The words 'pliant Minister,' Fraser tells us, seemed literally to choke Disraeli.[1] Of previous Ministers, Gladstone, he proceeded, had already characterised the allegation as 'false'; he himself could answer for Derby; there only remained the venerable Russell and the honoured Palmerston. To make the proof complete, and stop the calumnies for ever, he asked and obtained leave of the House to introduce the Sovereign's name in debate. It was a short but conclusive message which he gave from the Queen:

It is merely this statement on the part of Her Majesty, that there is not the slightest foundation for the statement that was made, that proposals, such as were described in the Retford speech, were ever made to any Minister at any time. Sir, the whole thing is utterly unfounded; merely that sort of calumnious gossip which unfortunately, I suppose, must always prevail, but which one certainly did not suppose would come from the mouth of a Privy Councillor, and one of Her Majesty's late Cabinet Ministers.

Nothing was left for Lowe but complete retractation and apology. On May 5 Disraeli told Lady Bradford: 'Lowe appeared in a white sheet last night, holding a taper of repentance. He was abject.' It was the last blow to a Parliamentary reputation, which had attained a great height during the Reform debates of 1867, and had been rapidly sinking since. Never again did Lowe count as a serious political force. 'He is in the mud,' wrote Disraeli to Lady Chesterfield, 'and there I leave him.'

It was in this session of 1876 that Joseph Chamberlain entered Parliament as member for Birmingham. Though in later life he was to maintain the same imperial cause and use much the same imperial language as Disraeli, he was regarded by the public then as an extreme Radical, and in a speech at Birmingham in the spring made a bitter attack on the Prime Minister's veracity. A journalist who was present at Chamberlain's *début* in the House writes: 'From the Gallery I saw the two great

[1] Fraser, p. 31.

imperial statesmen meet. Chamberlain had said that
Disraeli never opened his mouth without telling a falsehood. He stood, carefully groomed, eyeglass in eye,
recommending the Gothenburg system.[1] Disraeli was
fetched, sat down, and put up *his* glass, which he seemed
to hold encircled with his forefinger, so that he might be
quizzing; and so the two surveyed each other, doubtless
exchanging telepathic defiance.'

Disraeli himself alluded to Chamberlain's attack, in a
letter addressed to Lady Chesterfield. The letter was preserved among his papers, but was never sent, probably
because he thought better of the disparaging reflections
which it contained on Lady Bradford. She, owing to the
proximity of Castle Bromwich to Birmingham, knew
something of the great qualities of the new member,
to which the crudity of his abuse of Disraeli did little
justice.

To Anne Lady Chesterfield (not sent).

2, WHITEHALL GARDENS, *June 22, 1876.*—. . . I dined at
Marlboro' House on Monday: a banquet given to the unfortunate Sir Salar Jung, who appeared, but in a wheeled chair:
I was amused, sitting next to the Duchess of Manchester,
who is an extremely clever woman, and very agreeable.
To-day, I meet the Prince and Princess at Stafford House:
and yesterday, I went to the concert at Buckingham Palace,
and sate next to S.; but she seemed very bored, and would
have preferred, probably, Mr. Chamberlain.

I thought his attack on me was one of the coarsest, and
stupidest, assaults I well remember. No intellect, or sarcasm,
or satire, or even invective: coarse and commonplace abuse,
such as you might expect from the cad of an omnibus. However, S., I believe, very much admired it, and seemed to be
rather glad, that I was attacked. The House of Commons
were enraged, and I had the greatest difficulty in preventing
it being brought forward as a breach of privilege. The
Speaker was evidently in favor of that course, but deferred
to me.

Are you aware, that Mr. Chamberlain recanted in a letter
to *The Times*—I think of Monday? A most abject apology:

---

[1] This is a mistake. Chamberlain's maiden speech, to which the writer
was referring, was made on the Report stage of the Elementary Education
Bill on Aug. 4, just a week before Disraeli's last appearance in the
Commons.

I would sooner have made the speech than have written the letter, and that is saying a good deal. I said something like this to S., who fired up, admired the letter, and called him ' a great man '! Pleasant ! . . .

As appears from the above letter, the return of the Prince of Wales from his Indian tour was the occasion of much festivity in London society; and the Prime Minister himself, though without a hostess to do the honours, gave a great dinner and reception to the Prince and Princess.

To Anne Lady Chesterfield.

2, WHITEHALL GARDENS, *June* 25.—Most dear, all your beautiful and bountiful presents came safe, and in good time, and added much to the lustre of my banquet. We sate down 42: I had the Princess on my right, and the Dss. of Sutherland on my left; the Prince was opposite to me, with the Dss. of Beaufort, whom he took out, on his right, and the Dss. of Manchester on his left. Everybody was well placed, and, I think, everybody was pleased, as the party was rather noisy; and indeed, with plenty of music, flowers, and light, it is difficult to have a failure. A gentleman sent to me a bouquet for the Pss. wh. quite delighted. It was immense, but of graceful form; wondrous roses, with rare orchids, bright, sweet, and pendulous; and every now and then, studded with butterflies and humming birds. The Princess took one of the butterflies, and put it in her hair.

After dinner was the monster reception, where no one received. The Princess stood in a gallery overlooking the great staircase, surrounded by her Duchesses, and some other *grandes dames* who were equally an ornament, Lady Dudley, and I am glad to say also—S., who looked very well.

I never saw anyone more amused than the Princess watching the guests. She said it was better than a play, and it was so long since she had been out that it made it doubly diverting. I was obliged to trouble Her Royal Highness to make the tour of the apartments, that everybody might see her. But she always resisted a little, and asked for a few minutes more of her gallery. . . .

It was a fruitful session. Not only was the purchase of the Suez Canal shares sanctioned, and the royal title amplified; but, in spite of the time occupied with discussions on a situation in the Near East which grew daily more perplexing, the appellate jurisdiction of the

House of Lords was placed on a proper footing by the addition to the tribunal of paid members, and the vivisection of animals for purposes of scientific experiment was subjected to due regulation; moreover, the social programme of the Government was further advanced by a comprehensive Elementary Education Bill, a Merchant Shipping Bill, and Bills putting a limit to the enclosure of commons and the pollution of rivers. A hope that Disraeli expressed to Lady Bradford on June 13 that ' our domestic reputation, at the end of July, will be equal to our foreign' was fulfilled. A selection from his correspondence with the Queen enables us to regard the progress of this legislation through his eyes. Her Majesty, it may be explained, was especially anxious for the Vivisection Bill, which, she wrote to Disraeli on June 13, 'must be passed if the nation is not to be disgraced by cruelty under the shameful plea of humanity.'

To Queen Victoria.

2, WHITEHALL GARDENS, *July* 2, 1876.—Mr. Disraeli with his humble duty to your Majesty:

The progress of the House of Commons, during the last week, has on the whole been satisfactory. The necessity of giving a Government night to the Irish Land Debate, has rendered that progress less advanced, but it was absolutely necessary, that the opinion of Parliament should be given in an unmistakable manner on these schemes, in order to prevent autumnal agitation, and to commit the leaders of the Opposition to a public expression of sound views.

The prospect of the ensuing week looks well.

The debate on the government of Ireland, in the form of Home Rule, on Friday, was highly interesting, from the speech, in reply to Mr. Butt's motion, by Mr. Smyth, member for the County of Westmeath, an avowed Repealer, and something more.

The House of Commons has not witnessed, for many years, a happier effort, combining, as it did, many of the higher qualities of oratory: close reasoning, fine illustration, wit and graceful sarcasm, in a style natural, though imaginative, and highly finished. It tore up the banner of Home Rule to shreds, and Mr. Disraeli does not believe that it will ever be unfurled again in the House of Commons.

This speech of Mr. Smyth recalled to Mr. Disraeli what he

had read, and often fancied, of the style of the Irish House of Commons; the House of Grattan and of Flood.

It was curious to see both sides cheering a member, who avowed himself a Repealer, and once was a rebel.

It is a pity that this great oration was barely reported. The Parliamentary reporters, who are mere machines, never discovered till too late that a considerable Parliamentary event was occurring. . . .

July 22.—. . . Mr. Disraeli was absent from the House on Thursday night, and he regrets to say that the Ministry fell into one of those messes of ecclesiastical weakness, which seem inevitable, every now and then, for the Conservative party. The whole of yesterday was consequently wasted on an idle Education Clause, which conveyed a petty assault on the Nonconformists.

Mr. Disraeli has called a Cabinet to-morrow morning again on the winding up of the session, and he hopes he may rectify this mistake. . . .

(*Same date.*)—. . . Mr. Disraeli proposed to Lord H. Lennox[1] to move for a Committee of Inquiry and offered not to accept Lord Henry's resignation unless the Committee decided against him; but Lord Henry would not avail himself of this offer. Mr. Disraeli could do no more with any regard to public propriety and the character of your Majesty's Government.

July 25.—. . . Mr. Disraeli deplores the mischance of Lord H. Lennox, whom Mr. Disraeli had known intimately for 30 years, and whose very faults were not disagreeable.

July 29.—. . . There has been an agitating and anxious week in the House of Commons with respect to the new Educational Bill, which is a considerable measure; but all has ended well. After a great struggle, by blended conciliation and firmness, the measure will be carried and the House is now sitting (Saturday) to conclude the Committee. . . .

Mr. Disraeli made a strong appeal for Vivisection, and he is still sanguine of carrying it. The great opponent is Mr. Lowe, and if he persists in his opposition, it will be impossible to attempt it: but there are good reasons to hope, that some compromise may be effected. The great thing is to pass some Act, and give evidence of the determination of the Legislature to control this horrible practice. . . .

Aug. 3.—Mr. Disraeli . . . thanks your Majesty for your Majesty's gracious letters, which always encourage, and, not unfrequently, guide him. . . .

---

[1] Lord Henry Lennox resigned the office of First Commissioner of Works owing to judicial animadversions on the conduct of the directors of the Lisbon Steam Tramways Company, of whom he had been one.

Affairs have gone on rapidly in the House of Commons, and he thinks that the 12th will be the most convenient for the Council, though he will not speak positively till tomorrow.

The Education Bill may yet occasion a day's delay, but he more than hopes not.

It is no use attempting to conciliate the Dissenters. They take all you offer, and, the very next minute, will fly at your throat. The Education Bill, as introduced by the Government, was liberally conceived, and we made, in the course of discussion, several important further concessions to the Opposition. We could only induce our own friends to yield these on our promise that their amendments, or proposals, should also be considered; but the moment we granted anything to our own friends, there was a fierce cry of ' reaction,' which, under the conditions which Mr. Disraeli ultimately suggested, was not really well founded.

There was a stormy Cabinet one day, which required all Mr. Disraeli's experience to guide and assuage. And Lord Salisbury wrote to Mr. Disraeli a letter, which Mr. Disraeli intended to have forwarded to your Majesty, that your Majesty might comprehend the difficulties he had to contend against, which was really alarming. It was long and well written, and said : ' The men I was called upon to desert, were the very men who had stood by me on the Titles Bill'; an appeal difficult to withstand.

This letter has mysteriously disappeared, but when discovered, shall be forwarded to your Majesty.

The Nonconformist party in the country has been weakened by the last Reform Bill.

Mr. Disraeli encloses your Majesty a letter of a different kind from Mr. Secretary Hardy. It is a generous letter. All difficulties, on the subject to which it refers, are now removed, and there will be no unpleasant feeling in the Cabinet of any kind.[1] . . .

HOUSE OF COMMONS, *Aug.* 5.—. . . Vivisection seems quite safe.

The Education struggle has terminated by strengthening the Ministry, and by signally demonstrating the utter disintegration of the Opposition. What was really a point of administrative detail was so magnified and exaggerated by the Opposition, that it was elevated into a discussion, whether the primary education of the country should be religious or secular. . . .

[1] See VI., ch. 1.

To Lady Bradford.

2, WHITEHALL GARDENS, *Saturday, Aug.* 5, 1876.—. . . I knew the storm that was brewing on Thursday night, a storm wh. periodically appears, and suddenly, like a white squall in the Mediterranean. I have had, in older and more factious days, some experience wh. guided me—so I left before one.

The Chanr. of the Exr., and Ld. Sandon, and Sir Willie Dyke, and Mr. Smith, and Monty, were with me next morning at eleven, for counsel, tho' they had not, what the *M. Post* calls, 'retired to their couches till past five.' They looked pretty fresh. I was, naturally, quite so, and had had time to consider their case. So we were all in our places at twelve for the renewed combat. Being an older hand than they, I did not expect one, and I was right. Our new moves all succeeded, and we carried the report of the Bill in its entirety by sitting last night also. Not that I was there for the final and easy stages. It is to be read a third time this morning. I don't think we have lost 4 and 20 hours by this burst of factious fight, and it has shown the utter demoralisation and rancorous breaking up of the Liberal party. It seems split into fragments: all working against each other. One night the whole of the Home Rulers deserted to us, and next day the Scotch Presbyterians joined them. Then Goschen answered Forster, and Rylands Mundella. Sullivan, the fiercest Ultramontanist, declared that he wd. sooner send his children to a Ch. of England school than to a secular. Whereupon Mr. Greene, the fiercest Protestant in the House, vowed that, in preference to a secular, he wd. certainly send his children to a Roman Catholic school: and then there was mutual cheering and embracing, always ending in increased majorities for Government. . . .

In spite of the pressure of the Eastern question, Disraeli followed during the summer and autumn with sustained interest the preparations made by the new Viceroy to celebrate worthily in India the assumption of the imperial title. 'All Lytton's proclamation schemes,' he wrote on September 3 to Salisbury, 'tho' they read like the 1,000 and one nights, I believe are judicious, and will be successful and beneficial—not only in India.' Not all of the imaginative Viceroy's schemes were accepted, but, even so, the effect was sufficiently striking. For the chiefs there were honours and decorations, increases in

salary and pension; for the army increased pay and
allowances; a new order was created for Anglo-Indians;
food and clothing were distributed to the poor; there
was a generous amnesty for prisoners; and a great
Assemblage, collected from all parts of India and from
the neighbouring East, and lasting fourteen days, from
before Christmas till after the New Year, was held at
Delhi. There, on January 1, 1877, with Lytton, the Viceroy, presiding in state, and in the presence of the heads
of all the Indian governments, of envoys from Siam,
Burma, and Khelat, of representatives of the great
Civil Service, of a picked force of British and native
troops, of over seventy ruling chiefs and princes, of some
three hundred native noblemen and gentlemen, and of a
vast concourse of the Indian peoples, Queen Victoria was
proclaimed, with all due solemnity and pomp, Kaisar-i-
Hind, Empress of India, and was saluted by the Maharajah Scindia on behalf of the Indian princes as Shah-in-
Shah Padshah, Monarch of Monarchs.[1] The Queen herself
celebrated the occasion by asking her Minister to dine at
Windsor.

To Lady Bradford.

HUGHENDEN MANOR, *Dec.* 28.—. . . On Monday I go to
Windsor to dine with the Empress of India. It is New
Year's Day, when she is proclaimed in Hindustan, and she
wishes the day to be celebrated, and ' marked,' hereafter. . . .
The Faery is much excited about the doings at Delhi. They
have produced great effect in India, and indeed throughout
the world, and vindicate triumphantly the policy of the
measure wh. was so virulently, but so fruitlessly, opposed.
It has no doubt consolidated our empire there. Our poetical
Viceroy is doing justice to the occasion. The Faery is so
full of the great incident, and feels everything about it so
keenly that she sent me a Xmas card and signed her good
wishes *Victoria Regina et Imperatrix.*

Beaconsfield, as he had then become, took down with
him to Windsor Lord George Hamilton, Under-Secretary
for India, who was responsible for the office while
Salisbury, the Secretary of State, was attending the

[1] See *Lord Lytton's Indian Administration*, ch. 4.

Constantinople Conference. Lord George tells us[1] that, with a fine dramatic sense, the Queen, usually so homely in attire, appeared at dinner that night 'a mass of Oriental jewellery, mostly consisting of very large uncut stones and pearls,' gifts from the reigning Princes of India in 1858 when the Crown took over the government from the Company. After dinner, on the proposal of the Duke of Connaught, Her Majesty was toasted as ' Queen and Empress of India ' in the presence of the statesman responsible for this enrichment of title.[2] Queen and Minister knew what Parliament and English society had not sufficient imagination to realise, that by the measure of the last session, translated into act at that day's Durbar, the British *raj* in India had received a significant accession of internal and external strength; that a new and durable link had been forged between the crowned democracy of the West and the immemorial Empire of the Middle East.

[1] *Reminiscences*, p. 120.
[2] See *Letters of Queen Victoria*, Second Series, Vol. II., p. 514. In the original publication I wrongly, but I hope not inexcusably, assumed that this, rather than some indeterminate later date, was the occasion when (as we were told in the well-informed article on ' The character of Queen Victoria ' in the *Quarterly Review* for April, 1901) Lord Beaconsfield broke through all etiquette by rising and proposing the health of the Empress of India, ' with a little speech as flowery as the oration of a Maharajah,' to which the Queen responded with a ' pretty smiling bow, half a curtsey.'

CHAPTER XIII.

From the Commons to the Lords.

1876–1877.

On Friday, August 11, 1876, a day or two before
the prorogation of Parliament, Disraeli replied, late in
the evening, to an attack on the Government for their
inaction over Bulgarian atrocities.[1] The speech was not
specially remarkable, though it contained a sly hit at the
Herodian, or (according to some reports) Rhodian, oratory
of his friendly opponent Harcourt, and though it closed
upon a thoroughly Disraelian note: 'What our duty
is at this critical moment is to maintain the Empire
of England.' The debate over, Disraeli walked slowly
down the House to the bar; there turned, and
stood for a minute carefully surveying the familiar
scene, galleries and all; and then, retracing his steps,
passed the Treasury bench and went quietly out behind
the Speaker's chair,[2] pausing to chat with Lord George
Hamilton on the prospects of a Liberal 'atrocity'
campaign in the autumn. He was noticed afterwards
in the lobby, 'in a long white overcoat and dandified
lavender kid gloves, leaning on his secretary's arm,' and
shaking hands with a good many people.[3] After that
night, he never entered the House of Commons again,
save as a visitor to the gallery. Unknown to all but one
or two present, he had made his last appearance in the
theatre of the labours and triumphs of nearly forty years.
The next morning it was announced that the Queen had

[1] See VI., ch. 2.
[2] For these details I was indebted to the late Right Hon. T. Burt, who
was present, and noted Disraeli's unusual procedure.
[3] See Dilke's *Life*, Vol. I., p. 211.

been pleased to create her Prime Minister an Earl. Some critics, notably Fraser, have expressed surprise that the supreme artist on the political stage should not have contrived a more spectacular exit. But here surely Disraeli showed a truer taste and a finer instinct than his critics. No formal leavetaking could have been more impressive than this silent withdrawal, which, without warning and without advertisement, transferred at a stroke the centre of political interest from the Commons to the Lords.

Disraeli's action was determined, of course, by considerations of health. Though during 1875 he had been on the whole free from the serious illnesses which had so frequently prostrated him in 1874, the respite proved to be only temporary. He spent the second week of January, 1876, at Weston, and on his return to town and work had an acute seizure. A pencil note from Whitehall Gardens to Lady Bradford, dated January 18, 12.30, says: 'I have had a very sharp attack, and nothing but remedies as sharp cd. have brought me to time—as I hope they have, for in an hour and ½ I must be at the Cab. It wd. not do to hold it here, it wd. be such a bad start; and the day is bland, and one must run risks in life, or else it wd. be as dull as death.' At half-past four the same afternoon, he reports, in ink: 'I have just come from the Cabinet. . . . I have been, and am, a great sufferer. I have had the illness of a month crammed and compressed into 8 and 40 hours.' His colleagues found him greatly pulled down: 'I judge,' he wrote two days later, 'from their expression and general mien, that they thought the Burials Bill, wh. we were discussing, was rather a fitting subject for their chief.'

This was a bad introduction to a session of worry and late hours. 'I wish the H. of C. was counted out oftener,' he wrote pathetically to Lady Bradford on March 1, 'that I might sometimes dine in the family circle. I think I shall retreat to the Elysian fields, where Bradford listened yesterday to Sandhurst and Cadogan, and then I might

a little more enjoy the society of my dear friends.' The
factious opposition to the Royal Titles Bill, and the
increasing gravity of the situation in the Near East, once
more strained the Minister's health almost to breaking-
point in the middle of May.

To Lady Bradford.

2, WHITEHALL GARDENS, [? *May* 16].—I could not call
yesterday and was very unwell with my throat. . . . I sate
through the debate in great suffering, scarcely mitigated by
our triumphant majority, and went home very late and rather
hopeless: but a compress has worked wonders, and if I cd.
have stayed at home, I shd. have been all right. But that
is impossible. Affairs are very grave. . . .

May 18.—The medico said I had a feverish catarrh—the
old story; and the remedies have already done me some good,
so far as the fever is concerned—but I am dreadfully weak
and out of cue. . . . The Faery keeps telegraphing for bulletins
with injunctions to see Jenner, who is going down to Windsor,
and will tell her exactly how I am, etc., etc. ' She is very
anxious.' . . .

[? *May* 19].—I shan't go into the City to-day, or to the H.
of Commons—but I ought to drive a little, or I shall become
a confirmed invalid. . . . I shd. like to know whether I might
call. . . .

May 25.—. . . Of all the duties and occupations wh.
devolve on me, letter-writing is that for wh. the sort of attack
I am now suffering from most unfits me. One can read, and
one can listen, and judge, and talk; but writing requires a
degree of energy and precision of wh. I am now quite incapable.
I am out of all pain this morning, and shd. have publicly
appeared—and may even yet—but the N.E. blast has returned,
and this is my direst foe. . .

I was obliged to hold the Cabinet yesterday under this roof.

May 26.—I can't give a good account of myself, as I had
a fresh attack last night. . . .

May 27.—The Cabinet is just over and under this roof !
I have had a good night and am quite free from pain. . . .

HUGHENDEN MANOR, *June* 3.—A senseless line from the
solitary—you cannot expect much. This place is bright with
bloom; thorns pink and white, and lilac and chestnut; soft
showers in the night and the grass growing all day. Nothing
wrong except they steal the swans' eggs, so that family
does not increase. I had hoped by this time they might have
rivalled the peacocks. . . .

This attack convinced Disraeli that action could no longer be postponed. The Queen herself gave him an opening by a spontaneous offer to call him to the House of Lords.

From Queen Victoria.

BALMORAL, *June* 5, 1876.—The Queen hopes Mr. Disraeli is feeling rested and better.

She was sorry to hear from General Ponsonby that he was feeling the fatigue of his work.

She knows how valuable he is to herself and the country. Should he still feel this, and that the fatigue of the House of Commons is too great, she would be happy to call him up to the other House, where the fatigue would be *far less* and where he would be able to *direct* everything. *No* one, no doubt, can replace him in the House of Commons; still if he felt it too much for his health something must be done, and he has some excellent men—especially Sir S. Northcote— who could no doubt work under him.

The Queen throws this out, as she feels the immense *importance* he is to the Throne and country and how—more than ever now—she wishes and hopes his Govt. may be long maintained.

Everyone agrees that it has gained in strength since the beginning of the Session, as he himself assured her.

Disraeli told the Queen that his physical condition would not permit him to carry on the Government, as Prime Minister in the Commons, after the existing session; but he demurred to Her Majesty's suggestion, and expressed a preference for retirement. He has himself placed on record, in a communication addressed in nearly identical terms to his principal colleagues, the negotiations which followed.

To the Duke of Richmond.

Confidential. 10, DOWNING STREET, *July* 24, 1876.—Some little time ago, when we had extricated ourselves from our difficulties, and the Government was not less popular and strong than at present, I was obliged to inform the Queen, that it would not be possible for me to carry on Her Majesty's affairs after the present Session.

Although, being well acquainted with the Queen's sensitiveness, or perhaps I ought to say Constitutional convictions, on the subject, I did not presume to recommend my successor, I ventured to observe, that, if Her Majesty wished to retain her present Cabinet, I thought there would be no difficulty in keeping them together under an individual, whose fitness would be generally admitted by themselves and the country.

Her Majesty did not seem to believe in this, or to approve of my communication, and wrote to me from Scotland to propose, that I should continue in my present post, and go to the House of Lords, which, she was graciously pleased to say, she had always contemplated since my illness at Balmoral two years ago.

As I have no heir, I was unwilling, in the decline of life, to commence a new career in a House of Parliament of which I had no experience, and where I should be looked upon as an intruder, and I requested Her Majesty's permission to adhere to my original feeling and to make some confidential inquiries on the subject.

I found, to my great surprise, that the Queen had judged the situation more accurately than myself, and that my secession might lead to serious consequences.

Altho' my continuing in the House of Commons for another Session would shorten my remaining life, I was prepared to make such a sacrifice, if, at the end of the year, I could have found the difficulties, occasioned by my withdrawal, removed: but I see no prospect of that.   The identical difficulties would reappear.

Under these circumstances, I have had to reconsider the Queen's proposal, and to bring myself to contemplate, as an act of duty to Her Majesty and my colleagues, the possibility of my going to the Upper House as a Minister, a condition which I had never foreseen.

I invite you as a colleague, whom I greatly value, and with whose Parliamentary position such a step on my part would necessarily, in some degree, interfere, to speak to me frankly on this subject: clearly understanding, that my only motive now is the maintenance of the Ministry and the party, and to secure these, I am ready still to try to serve them, or cheerfully altogether to disappear.

From the Duke of Richmond.

Confidential. GOODWOOD, CHICHESTER, *July* 26, 1876.—I received your letter late yesterday, and hasten to reply to it. I can conceive nothing more fatal to the party and the Cabinet than your retirement from office.   A party strong and united under you, to whom they have looked up so long as leader, might not be at all willing to follow another, and the result might be jealousies and differences which could not fail to be hurtful.

I regret most sincerely that the state of your health is such as to cause you to wish to retire from the House of Commons. I can well understand how very trying to a person suffering from bronchitis must be the attendance in the House of Commons during the early part of the Session. It seems to me that the course advised by Her Majesty, that you should have a peerage conferred upon you, is by far the best arrangement that can be made.

It is a proper recognition of the long and valuable services you have rendered to the country, and will enable you to continue to lead the party. I speak with all sincerity when I say there is no one who will more cordially welcome you in the House of Lords than I shall. I shall be only too happy to serve under you there as I have now done for so many years in the Cabinet and H. of Commons.

I shall most gladly give you all the assistance in my power upon all occasions. . . .

The replies of Derby and Salisbury to a similar communication from Disraeli illustrate the general feeling among his colleagues that his retirement would be a public misfortune, and their consequent approval of his transference to the Lords.

From Lord Derby.

Confidential. FOREIGN OFFICE, *July* 26, '76.—I was prepared for your communication, and have not the slightest doubt or hesitation in saying that I think you have chosen the right course. You can still lead us in Cabinet: and in the Lords your Parliamentary duties will be almost nominal. Your continuance as you were was a sacrifice which could not be asked of you: your total retirement would have been a misfortune to your friends, and to the public. Only this alternative remained, and it really seems to me open to as few objections as any step you could have taken under the circumstances.

From Lord Salisbury.

Confidential. INDIA OFFICE, *July* 27, '76.—Your letter took me so completely by surprise that I thought I might take 48 hours to think over it. Your health had so manifestly improved that I had banished all apprehensions of any probable change

II.   27*

The two alternatives you put are—your absolute retire-ment, or a retreat to the House of Lords.

I have no doubt whatever that your absolute retirement would be a most serious blow to the Ministry and the party, especially at this juncture. Foreign affairs are the absorbing topic of the day. It is quite evident, from the quiescence of Parliament and the country on the subject, that very general confidence is felt in the present conduct of our foreign policy: and in the shaping of that policy the largest share is generally, and justly, attributed to you. If you were to withdraw, the most essential element in the public confidence would be taken away. Of future possible combinations you do not speak hopefully: of course I do not know what was suggested; but no arrangement that seems to me likely would be nearly as acceptable as that which exists now.

If therefore you feel yourself driven to choose between the two alternatives—retirement or the House of Lords—I advise, in the interests of the party and the Ministry, that you should go to the House of Lords.

But I feel it is a choice of evils. You would be very heartily welcomed by the House of Lords: and you would give life to the dullest assembly in the world. But the command of the House of Lords would be a poor exchange for the singular influence you now exercise in the Commons. The experience of those who, having held a first place in the Commons, by choice or necessity went to the Lords, is not encouraging: Walpole, Pulteney, the elder Pitt, Castlereagh, Brougham. In this case it is *facilis ascensus*. As one of the shades who is on the wrong side of the stream, I must honestly say that I think you will regret the irrevocable step when you have taken it.

However, this is a question of health and feeling, and perhaps hardly the subject of advice. We shall be very glad to see you among us if you do resolve to come. In the public interest it would be very desirable that you should so arrange the charge of business that it should be possible for you to remain in the House of Commons. But if this is *not* possible, it is then infinitely better that you should come to the House of Lords than that you should retire.

It will be seen that Derby was prepared for the com-munication, and that Salisbury was not. Derby, Dis-raeli's close ally and politically the most important of his colleagues, and Cairns, whose judgment he had come to value above that of all others, were early taken into confidence: and to them was added, shortly afterwards,

Hardy, who had repeatedly acted as his deputy in the Commons and was after himself the protagonist there of the Government. The arrangement which Disraeli had in his mind when he told the Queen that there would be no difficulty in keeping the Cabinet together was that Derby should succeed him as Prime Minister,[1] with Hardy as the leader in the Commons. When, however, he sounded Derby—making use apparently of Lady Derby for the purpose—he found the scheme quite impracticable. Derby 'utterly scouted the idea of his being Premier. That he could never manage H.M., that he did not think he could lead his colleagues on Church questions: in short that nothing on earth would make him take the post. Added to this, he threw out that he would not act with anyone else.'[2] This was decisive. If Derby would neither take command himself, nor serve under any other chief but Disraeli, there was no alternative to a complete break-up except Disraeli's removal to the Lords. To this course, therefore, whether willingly or reluctantly, he was driven. Though to Salisbury his health appeared to be 'manifestly improved,' he had had another warning in this month of July that he could no longer trifle with it.

To Lady Bradford.

2, WHITEHALL GARDENS, *July* 3, 1876.—I could not write yesterday, being so very ill and quite incapable of thought and expression. What irritates me is that Gull, who has now been tinkering me for a week and making a series of conceited mistakes—ordering me, for example, to drink port wine, wh. I have not done for ten years, and wh. has nearly killed me— keeps telling Monty that I am better, who tells of course the same to you and the Queen, altho' I warn him to the reverse; but as he, very plausibly, contends, he is bound to report what Gull says.

Yesterday I drove out for an hour—to try to accustom myself to life again; but the port wine regimen afterwards brought things to a crisis, and I really thought, and not for the first time, that it was all over. . . .

---

[1] In the letter to Derby announcing his decision, Disraeli calls him 'My principal colleague, and whom I wished to be my successor.'
[2] Hardy's Diary, July 12; Gathorne Hardy, Vol II., p. 4.

July 4.—. . . I had a very hard night, and did not retire till three o'ck. in the morn[in]g. Too hard a life for me now —and there is a prospect of a month of it ! It was, however, softened by colossal majorities on a most important measure,[1] and on wh., a fortnight ago, I was told Govt. was to be defeated. . . .

It is difficult to believe that Disraeli did not foresee and desire the issue of the crisis. With his strong ambition, and his keen interest in India and the East, he can hardly, save in moments of deep physical depression, have seriously contemplated, so long as life and power of work were left to him and he had the confidence of Parliament, the abandonment to others of that forceful Eastern policy which was taking shape under his immediate direction but which was as yet only an outline. He must have anticipated, and thought it politic to provoke, the urgency of his Sovereign and his colleagues which sent him to the Lords. On this point there was no division of opinion. The Queen 'absolutely protested' against the idea of his retirement. The sentiments of Richmond, Derby, and Salisbury on the subject were shared by Ministers generally. Cairns and Hardy, from the first, were in favour of a retreat to the Lords. Malmesbury wrote of the 'chaos your retirement from any cause whatever would create in our party. If I know anything of men there are some excellent heads and hearts in the Cabinet, but only one backbone.' When Disraeli yielded to the general wish, John Manners wrote emphatically, August 8: 'You have acted in this supreme crisis as you have ever acted in public affairs: rightly, wisely, dutifully. I am confident the Queen, your colleagues, and the country will appreciate and approve the decision at which you have arrived.'

There was that general chorus of approval from press and public which Manners anticipated. But in one place there was universal regret and sorrow. If it cost Disraeli,

---

[1] The Prisons Bill, which was eventually withdrawn for this Session, and passed with amendments in 1877.

as he told the Speaker, a ' pang '[1] to separate himself
from the House of Commons, the sense of loss and
bereavement in the House was acute. 'Small groups
are dotted about here and there,' wrote Barrington
picturesquely on the morning of the announcement,
'talking with bated breath, as though there were a
coffin within the precincts of the House.'

From Sir William Hart Dyke.

HOUSE OF COMMONS, *Aug.* 12.—When the news came out
in the early hours here this morning, there was much surprise,
and, amongst our friends, general consternation: Taylor was
frantic, and as to poor Edmonstone, he has done nothing but
cry, and swear, alternately ever since. The deep feeling of
regret is quite universal throughout every corner of the House.
I had no idea, until I heard you make your last speech in the
House, how great the change would prove. All the real
chivalry and delight of party politics, seem to have departed;
nothing remains but routine. . . .
Your constant kindness, assistance, and advice to me here
I shall never forget; always the kind word, when mistakes
have been made: and work which might have been dull and
laborious has been made ever bright and pleasant.

Speaker Brand wrote to Disraeli to say 'on my own
behalf how much I shall miss you, and how much I regret
the cause which has obliged you to leave this House; a
sentiment which is universal throughout the House '—
that ' great assembly ' which was ' the scene of your early
struggles and final triumphs.' There is a real sense of
personal loss in the notes written by colleagues in the
Commons. Manners felt especially forlorn. 'It terminates for me all personal interest in House of Commons
life;' 'I cannot bear to think of the future: the change
will be so mournful, the conditions of service in our
House so altered.' Barrington struck the same note.
'My individual interest in the House of Commons is from
this day gone, and nothing will remain but duty—a very
poor substitute indeed.' Northcote's heart was so full

---

[1] On the night of Disraeli's last speech in the Commons, his colleague,
Frederick Stanley, afterwards sixteenth Lord Derby, saw him shedding tears.

that he could not trust himself to express in detail the sadness which he felt. Lord George Hamilton was the exponent of the feelings of those rising young men whom Disraeli had encouraged and cheered when they had difficult work to do. 'I am not the only Under-Secretary who will miss your kindly advice and will feel that he is in a different place now that you are no longer in it.' The feeling of generous opponents in the House was expressed in happy phrase by the eminent Parliamentarian whom Disraeli had answered in his final speech.

From Sir William Harcourt.

NAWORTH CASTLE, BRAMPTON, CUMB, *Aug.* 14, '76.

DEAR MR. DISRAELI,—If I am to call you so for the last time. It is impossible for anyone, and least of all for one who has had so large an experience of your kindness, to hear without emotion that you have sat for the last time in the great scene of your fame. You have made the House of Lords much too rich and you have left the House of Commons by far too poor. Henceforth the game will be like a chessboard when the queen is gone—a petty struggle of pawns.

I little thought when you touched me so deftly with the blunted point of your spear on Friday night that it was to be your last speech in a place where your fame will always live: a fame not only for genius and eloquence but for a kindness to the small quite as uncommon as your force against the great.

I am sure the feeling on our side of the House will be one of universal regret, for the reason which I remember Julian Fane telling me Metternich expressed to him with regard to Napoleon. He said: 'You will perhaps think that when I heard of his death I felt a satisfaction at the removal of the great adversary of my country and my policy. It was just the reverse. I experienced only "un sentiment de regret que je ne devais jamais encore m'entretenir avec cette grande intelligence."' That you should yearn for repose from the weariness of the petty details of the House of Commons I do not wonder. I have felt sad sometimes to see you jaded by them. I hope the *otium cum dignitate* will add long years to a life which is the admiration of Englishmen and is dear to those who have tasted of your friendship. To the imagination of the younger generation your life will always have a special fascination. For them you have enlarged the horizon of the possibilities of the future.

I am sure you will not think this letter an impertinent intrusion. Your constant kindness has given me the right to rejoice in all that concerns you, and yet to regret the great change which will leave an irreparable blank in my House of Commons life. . . .

'Alas! Alas! for the House of Commons and the country. We shall never see your like again. The days of the giants are over. Ichabod! Ichabod!' wrote Sir Philip Rose. Disraeli's career of nearly forty years in the House of Commons exactly coincided with its best days. His entrance followed hard upon the accession of the first Sovereign in English history who accepted its complete ascendancy. Queen Victoria's immediate predecessor had summarily dismissed a Ministry which enjoyed the confidence of Parliament; but King William's failure to secure the endorsement of the country left the supremacy of the House of Commons undisputed. The year after Disraeli quitted it, Parnell, who had been elected in 1875, organised the systematic obstruction of Parliamentary business; and on the Prisons Bill, the Army Estimates, and the South Africa Bill, showed how powerless under its existing rules the House was in face of members determined to discredit and degrade it. To meet the menace, freedom of debate was steadily curtailed, till now the closure and other hampering restrictions are part of the daily machinery of the Mother of Parliaments. But while Disraeli was numbered among its members the House of Commons was at the height of its power and reputation and preserved all its traditional liberties. The place which it then held in the mind and esteem of the country may be gauged by the amount of space which the newspapers accorded to the reports of debates. Those who search the files of *The Times* during these years will find that, in the session, the Parliamentary reports not only occupied the most conspicuous pages, but filled, day after day, half or three-quarters of the total news columns, crowding most other matter into short paragraphs and obscure corners. The luminaries of the cricket-field and the river, of the stage and the

turf, had not then risen to the rank of popular heroes;
and an oration by Macaulay or Bright, a tussle between
Disraeli and Peel, or a serious debate in which Palmerston,
Russell, Cobden, and Gladstone put forth all their powers,
excited the universal interest among newspaper readers
which has subsequently, in times of peace, only been
secured by the visits of Australian cricketers or the
successes of royal horses at Epsom. It was on this wide
and universal theatre and among these Parliamentary
giants that Disraeli played his striking part, battling with
spirit and distinction against succeeding generations of
orators and statesmen from O'Connell and the elder
Stanley at the beginning to Hartington and Harcourt at
the close.

The secret of his astonishing success—the 'singular
influence,' to use Salisbury's phrase, which he exercised
in the House—may be difficult to probe and to analyse,
but undoubtedly one main element was that he was
always there. 'The House of Commons,' he wrote in
the last year of his life in an unpublished novel,[1] 'is a
jealous mistress, and will not grant success without due
attention. The greatest compliment you can pay to a
woman is to give to her your time, and it is the same with
our senate. A man who is always in his place becomes
a sort of favourite.' More particularly did he feel it
incumbent on him to be always in his place when he
became a Parliamentary leader. 'Unless you are always
there,' he was wont to say, ' how can you lead the House
of Commons ?   How can you feel their pulse ?   How can
you know the men ?' While business was in progress,
however dull and irksome it might be, Disraeli would
neither leave the bench himself, nor, when in office,
permit his colleagues to leave unless they could allege
amply sufficient reason. When the House, as was its
usual practice in his time, sat through the dinner hour,
he remained and took a hasty dinner at the Cabinet table;
or sometimes joined his wife in her brougham drawn up

---

[1] Printed as an appendix on p. 1521.

in one of the courts at St. Stephen's, and there in the carriage ate with her a daintier meal which her solicitude had brought down for him. In either case, the interval was short, and he was back in his place almost before he had been missed.

Being always there, he had a keen perception of all that was going on; of the tone of the House on this question and on that; of the nice gradations of feeling in the course of any important debate. He noted with constant interest the progress of rising young men, especially in his own party; and regarded with particular attention, and a careful scrutiny through his eyeglass, any new member who rose for the first time to address the House. To his immediate neighbour on the bench he would, now and again, drop a caustic reflection on the newcomer. Thus of the philosopher John Stuart Mill, whose manner was at once authoritative and ladylike, he said, 'Ah! I see; the finishing governess!' On catching sight for the first time of the uncouth figure of J. G. Biggar, Parnell's precursor, and lieutenant, in obstruction, he exclaimed, 'What is that?' adding after a closer examination, 'He seems to be what in Ireland you call a Leprechaun.' Fawcett, the blind economist, who deservedly in later years became a favourite of the House, in his earlier appearances bored and depressed it by his pedagogic manner and thunderous tones. 'If this fellow had eyes,' murmured Disraeli during one of these harangues, 'how we should damn them!' When a respected leader of the commercial classes was returned to Parliament by an Irish constituency, Disraeli, after listening to the new member for awhile, turned to Lord Rathmore, then sitting, as David Plunket, by his side, and said impressively: 'My dear David, you usually send us here from Ireland either gentlemen or blackguards; but this is neither!'

Observant and alert as both his private asides to colleagues and his public replies in debate showed Disraeli to have been, nobody would have guessed it from his appearance in the House. He was naturally somewhat restless in manner as, during his days of adolescence, he was flamboyant in costume; but there was no sign of extravagance in demeanour or dress as he sat on the front bench. His clothes were neat and careful, but quiet and subdued. In place of the gaudy raiment and chains and rings of earlier days, he wore a dark frockcoat in winter with a double-breasted plush waistcoat of tabby colour; and in summer a thin blue frockcoat, tightly buttoned, with (says Fraser[1]) 'an unquestionable pair of stays' to be seen through it from the back.[2] His manner was as quiet as his dress. He had cultivated early in his Parliamentary career, and he sedulously matured as leader, an absolutely impassive bearing which served him admirably as a mask till it eventually became second nature. Here is a contemporary description of his appearance in the year 1847 when he first took his seat on the front bench.

You never see him gazing around him, or lolling back in his seat, or seeking to take his ease as other men do in the intervals of political excitement. He sits with his head rigid, his body contracted, his arms closely pinned to his side, as though he were an automaton. He looks like one of those stone figures of ancient Egypt that embody the idea of motionless quiescence for ever.[3]

So an observer in 1854 depicts him as sitting 'sunk into his seat,' his eyes appearing 'to be fixed on the ground or staring at vacancy,' and 'his whole attitude that of the most rigid repose.'[4] Fraser, who watched him, off and on, in the House from 1852 to 1876, writes of his 'studied behaviour':

[1] P. 149.
[2] Disraeli was extremely reluctant to disturb the neat precision of his apparel. A Conservative M.P. was once talking to his leader in the House on a complicated public question, and, fearing to detain and bore him, tendered him some bulky explanatory papers to be put in his pocket and read at his leisure. Disraeli firmly waved them aside. 'I never,' he said 'put papers in my pocket. Give them to Monty Corry; he puts papers in his pocket.' To realise the full flavour of the reply, it must be borne in mind that Corry was at least as much point-device in his attire as his chief.
[3] *Fraser's Magazine*, Feb., 1847.   [4] Ewald's *Beaconsfield*, ch. 11.

He invariably sat with one knee over the other, his arms folded across his breast, leaning against the back of his seat, his hat slightly over his brows. The more vehement the attack of his adversary became, the more he affected somnolence; when it waxed very hot indeed, he, without removing the pendent leg, brought his body round towards the west; placing his eyeglass, with the forefinger of his right hand curved over it, to his right eye, he glanced for about three seconds at the clock over the entrance door; replacing the glass in the breast of his coat, he again relapsed into simulated sleep.[1]

In other passages Fraser adds that he had himself observed Disraeli, when an attack really touched him, shift the pendent leg two or three times, and then curve the foot upwards; and that a colleague had noticed, in similar circumstances, a slight pulling forward of the wrist of his shirt. These were the only signs of feeling that a minute inspection could discover. Disraeli carried this impassiveness and apparent self-absorption into all his actions in the House. 'Observe him anywhere about the House, in the lobbies or in the committee rooms; you never see him in confidential communication with anyone,' wrote the 1847 eyewitness; and he continues: 'See him where you will, he glides past you noiselessly, without being apparently conscious of the existence of externals, and more like the shadow than the substance of a man.' All the accounts of his middle period represent him, when in the purlieus of the House, as quite unapproachable by the ordinary member, whether foe or friend. Towards the close of his career, this unapproachableness in the lobbies was greatly modified, mainly owing to his interest in, and desire to keep in touch with, the promising young men of his party. He liked them, Lord George Hamilton, who entered Parliament in 1868, tells us, 'to come up and talk to him in the lobby during divisions. He nearly always stood with his back to a fireplace, and he was interested in any little piece of gossip or rumour relating to current events, as he wished to know what was going on outside Parliament.'[2]

[1] Fraser, pp. 400, 401.
[2] Lord G. Hamilton's *Parliamentary Reminiscences*, p. 60.

When he rose to speak, though his delivery by no means lacked animation, he did not discard the same general reserve, and he eschewed all extravagance of gesture. He never 'let himself go,' never, like the born orator, allowed himself to be carried away on an impetuous torrent of words; but always kept his powers in hand, prepared to make his points when and how he had originally designed.   Here is Fraser's careful observation of his method.

He rose with his coat buttoned across his breast; he usually moved his open hands downwards above his hips; he then pulled his coat down in front, and threw his shoulders back. He began slowly and very deliberately.   Whenever he was about to produce a good thing, and his good things were very good, anyone in the habit of watching him knew precisely when they were coming.   Before producing the point, he would always pause, and give a nervous cough: the action of his hands was remarkable.   He carried a cambric handkerchief, of spotless whiteness, in his left skirt pocket.   He would place both hands in both pockets behind him; then bring out the white handkerchief, and hold it in his left hand before him for a few seconds; pass it to his right hand: then with his right hand pass the handkerchief lightly under his nose, hardly touching it; and then with his left hand replace the handkerchief in his pocket; still holding his hand, with the handkerchief in it, in his pocket, until a fresh topic.[1]

The picture which this eyewitness draws, of tricks and mannerisms, none of them on the grand scale, gives no suggestion or indication of the mighty power which his hero wielded for thirty years over the House of Commons.   Fraser himself despairs of making his readers understand it.   Very few persons, as he has pointed out, could ever have had an opportunity of hearing Disraeli speak.   Gladstone, in his day, owing to his many popular progresses, must have been heard by hundreds of thousands of his countrymen; and the same is true of the generation of politicians who have swayed men's minds in the last thirty or forty years.   But Disraeli, in the nineteenth century, practised the reserve of an eighteenth-century

[1] Fraser, pp. 401, 402.

statesman, and was rarely tempted to speak away from
St. Stephen's. His oratory was therefore familiar only
to Members of Parliament, officials of the House of
Commons, and newspaper reporters, and to the few
hundreds of the public whom the extremely limited space
allotted to visitors in the House could accommodate.
Those favoured individuals, however, who did hear him
are in general agreement with Fraser's verdict that

> No one, who has not done so, can form any idea of his
> powers. His speeches when read give no adequate idea of
> their effect. The impression made on an emotional assembly
> like the House of Commons can never be put in print. The
> varying sensations, fluctuating like the breast of the ocean;
> the minute rhetorical effects, which moved his audience so
> powerfully; the alterations of voice; the pauses; the grand
> gestures, which he occasionally, but not frequently, used:
> all these are utterly lost upon the reader of a debate. Dis-
> raeli had a perfectly melodious voice; and, what is rare, a voice
> increasing in beauty of tone the more loudly that he spoke:
> he had the proud consciousness of having a master-mind;
> and a masterly power of influencing men. . . . To the reader
> who has read and admired his speeches I say, ' Quid si tonan-
> tem ipsum audivisses !'[1]

An imperfect attempt must be made, by the collation
of the evidence of many witnesses, to describe and explain
the indescribable and inexplicable. In the first place, as
Fraser says, Disraeli was endowed with a magnificent
organ—a voice which was singularly pure and attractive
in tone, without any accent such as Gladstone's northern
burr, and which carried easily to the farthest corners of
the House, even, in his last years, proving thoroughly
audible in the most unacoustic of chambers, the House
of Lords. It is well characterised in a Parliamentary
sketch of 1854 as at once clear, powerful, and penetrating;
and completely under its owner's control. ' It is not a
sea of sound, in which the language and articulation of
the speaker are drowned and dissolved; but a pure,
gushing stream, which, at the will of the orator, expands
so as to fill the spacious hall, and contracts so as to

[1] Fraser, pp. 292, 293.

concentrate upon a single individual the full force of his invective, or the scathing sarcasm of his irony.'[1] Writing of the manner in which this splendid instrument was used, a *Quarterly Reviewer*[2]—an unfriendly witness—testifies in the same year to Disraeli's ' masterly, passionless, finished delivery.' 'Perhaps the art of compelling a hearer to listen to every word spoken by an orator was never carried to higher perfection.' The tone, though very distinct, would usually at the beginning be low and quiet. 'Towards the end of his speeches Mr. Disraeli gets very loud, but his voice takes a purely artistic tone—passion has nothing to do with it—and he drops from an angry clamour to a smooth colloquialism.' Then would come ' a capitally constructed closing sentence, of which the last syllable rings as distinctly in the ear as the first.' Not a little of his impressiveness was due to the clearness of his enunciation and the care with which he gave their full value to words usually slurred over. When Disraeli spoke, says Fraser, the listener could hear the four syllables in ' Parliament,' and the three in ' business.' John Stuart Mill, a candid opponent, said that it was a real pleasure to him when Disraeli rose ; his voice and manner were so satisfying after an overdose of the voices and manners that prevailed in the House of Commons.

Besides a fine voice and skill in managing it, Disraeli, owing to his long apprenticeship to literature, had a great and varied command of language; knew how to select the suggestive epithet, how to turn the appropriate phrase. It is true that literary qualities, though they may preserve speeches for the delectation of succeeding generations, are often useless, as in the case of Burke, to render them impressive at the moment; and that some of the greatest orators, such as Chatham, have produced their effects without much aid from literary form. Still, Demosthenes and Cicero among the ancients, Canning

[1] *Reynolds' Newspaper*, Feb. 26, 1854.
[2] *Quarterly Review*, June, 1854.

and Macaulay among the moderns, show what a powerful reinforcement literary graces may bring to argument,
invective, and exhortation. Disraeli's most marked
literary quality was the power of phrase-making and
phrase-adaptation, of illuminating collocations of words,
now in the shape of ironical aphorism, now of convincing
epigram, now of audacious paradox, now of stinging
satire. This quality was pre-eminent in his speeches.
They seldom lacked these

> jewels, five words long,
> Which on the stretched forefinger of all Time
> Sparkle for ever.[1]

The diamonds may sometimes have been paste, and the
setting sometimes rococo, but the brilliance of all was
undoubted; and again and again the phrases were of the
happiest and aptest kind, and have become part and
parcel of Victorian history.

But voice and language are the mere externals of
public speaking ; 'the foundation of eloquence,' as
Disraeli was wont to say and to write, is to be ' completely
master of the subject.' That foundation Disraeli had
well and truly laid. From the time when his return to
Parliament had definitely settled in favour of politics the
contest which had been waged within him for some years
between that engrossing mistress and his other love,
literature, he had given himself wholeheartedly to
master the subject-matter of what was to be his life's
work. He was unremitting in his study of political
history, domestic and foreign, of political and economic
science, and of Parliamentary papers and bluebooks.
Even when he turned for a relief to letters, there was
always—in the famous trilogy, in *Lord George Bentinck*, in
his newspaper activity, and in *Lothair*—either a political
object to be advanced or a political background to his
story. He not only read and wrote on politics; but, in
spite of his enjoyment of country sights and sounds, of

---

[1] Tennyson's *Princess*, Sec. 2.

trees and flowers and birds, he pondered long and deeply
over political questions in his Bucks retreat. ' Ah ! now
we shall be obliged to talk politics ' was the rather rueful
observation of his old chief, Derby, on learning that a
shooting party at Heron Court was to be joined by
Disraeli. When he was in office, he kept, as Chancellor
of the Exchequer and Leader of the House, thoroughly
in touch with the main business of the principal departments, and encouraged his colleagues to come to him
in any difficulty. He studied political men, as well as
political matters. He was, as we have seen, always in
his place when the House was sitting; he went much
into society in London and in country houses. He was
a regular attendant at Quarter Sessions and agricultural
meetings in his county; and he made due use behind
the scenes of the Rigbys and Tapers and Tadpoles of
politics. Few Parliamentary questions or situations
could find him unprepared. When, therefore, he rose
to speak, he had a full mind; he was master of his
subject.

Disraeli was also gifted with a marvellously retentive
memory, which often indeed betrayed him into plagiar-
isms of a sustained character in speech and writing, but
which, at any rate, enabled him altogether to dispense,
in his ordinary practice, with the use of notes. Not only
did his memory register faithfully the points on which
he meant to dwell and the choice phrases with which
he meant to drive them home, but also the statements
and arguments of the opponents whom he set himself to
answer or to ridicule, and the very words and tones
which they had employed. At the same time he was,
in Fraser's words, ' a chivalrously fair ' speaker; though
he turned his opponent's words into absurdity, he never
altered them, or pretended to mistake what had been said.
Once, when speaking in Parliament, he was observed to
pull a scrap of paper out of his waistcoat pocket and
make great play with it; he held it up in front of his
eyes, and, fixing his eyeglass, seemed to read from it,

with deliberation and emphasis, some statement of Gladstone's which he was controverting; then he tore it up and threw the pieces on the floor. An eyewitness, who was curious enough, when the House rose, to pick them up, found them without any writing on them whatever. Hardy preserved in his diary, as a unique specimen, a sheet of paper on which Disraeli, then in Opposition, had jotted down during a speech of Gladstone's the three words 'at another time'—the sole text for an effective reply delivered on the instant.[1] He did not escape from the inevitable consequence of depriving himself of all artificial means of reminder, namely, the occasional omission of good things which he had intended to use; as his letters to wife and friends after speeches prove. But he justified his practice to Fraser by saying, 'If I once used notes, I should lean upon them; and that would never do.'[2] Like all orators who really move men, though not to the same extent as his rival Gladstone, he depended in some degree on catching inspiration from his hearers; he told Delane, he was 'much influenced by my audience and the impromptu.'[3] This does not, of course, mean that there was not careful preparation before any great effort, or that, in particular, the biting phrases by which he will always be remembered were not deeply studied in his mind and assiduously polished, before they were launched, apparently at random, upon the world. In preparing the few speeches of importance which he delivered outside Parliament he often made use of a highly original method; he privately rehearsed them, either in whole or in part, to an experienced reporter of *The Times*, J. F. Neilson, in whom he placed especial trust.[4]

Above all, Disraeli was armed, in addressing the House of Commons, with a superb self-confidence. Four years before he became a member, he watched its proceedings as a visitor, hearing, among others, orators so renowned

---

[1] Gathorne Hardy, Vol. I., p. 299.   [2] Fraser, p. 206.
[3] See p. 94.   [4] See Vol. I., p. 821.

as Bulwer Lytton and Sheil, and 'Macaulay's best speech,' that in which he denounced O'Connell's ingratitude to Lord Grey and the Whigs; and then told his sister: 'Between ourselves, I could floor them all. This *entre nous;* I was never more confident of anything than that I could carry everything before me in that House. The time will come.'[1] That confidence never left him. It carried him through his initial failure, and enabled him to retrieve that failure almost immediately; it buoyed him up through the years of mediocre success which followed; it nerved him for the titanic struggle against Peel which established his fame. Neither he nor the House ever forgot that he was the man who had overthrown 'the greatest Member of Parliament that ever lived.' He thereby made good his claim to be, as Froude has pointed out, the strongest Member of Parliament in his day; a position which, as early as 1854, was so well recognised that the *Quarterly Reviewer*, whom we have already quoted, remarks that, though Disraeli was assailed, out of the House, with exceeding ferocity, 'in the House it is rare for anyone but Mr. Gladstone to meddle with him.' Absolute unanimity of opinion has not yet been reached as to who had the better in the long rivalry of these two famous men in the House of Commons; but the prevailing judgment seems to be that, while, in individual debates, at one time the glowing eloquence of Gladstone, at another the pungent sarcasm of Disraeli, secured the victory, Gladstone never attained the general mastery of the House in all its moods which Disraeli gained, and kept for years, by patience, self-control, force of will, command of phrase, and unvarying attendance in his place.

A notable tribute to Disraeli's powers in debate was published a few years ago by George W. E. Russell. The Whigs, among whom George Russell was brought up, despised Disraeli and would not take him seriously; but Russell had the opportunity, as the son of the Sergeant-

[1] See Vol. I., p. 227.

at-Arms, of attending as a boy the great Reform debates and there judging for himself. He heard all the famous speakers, Gladstone and Bright and Lowe and Cranborne. 'But one figure appeared to me to tower head and shoulders above the rest, and that was the leader of the Conservative party, the ridiculed and preposterous " Dizzy." His mastery of the House, on both sides, seemed absolute. Compared to him Gladstone played a secondary and an ambiguous part.' The debates, he adds, ' displayed, in the contrast between Disraeli and those who surrounded him, the difference between genius and talent.'[1] Except Gladstone, nobody in the later days, when Peel and his generation had passed away, could challenge Disraeli with success; and that may explain why good judges have been disposed to consider that his high-water mark in oratory was reached in the fighting years between the opening of the attack on Peel and the fall of the Coalition Government. Certainly a review of the marvellous series of speeches during these years chronicled and commented on in this biography, tends to confirm this verdict.

Writing in 1851, during this period, Disraeli told the world that ' what Lord George Bentinck appreciated most in a Parliamentary speaker was brilliancy: quickness of perception, promptness of repartee, clear and concise argument, a fresh and felicitous quotation, wit and picture, and, if necessary, a passionate appeal that should never pass the line of high-bred sentiment.'[2] We know that there was no speaker whom Bentinck more appreciated than Disraeli himself; and we can hardly be wrong in assuming that we have in this summary the qualities which Disraeli believed his own oratory to possess. He could gauge his own powers pretty accurately. The description closely fits the speeches of that time, the late forties and the early fifties, beginning with the philippics against Peel. As Disraeli became an

---

[1] *Portraits of the Seventies—Lord Beaconsfield.*
[2] *Lord George Bentinck*, ch. 10.

old Parliamentary hand of undisputed eminence, the
brilliancy suffered some diminution; the crisp literary
style became, through bad association, diluted with the
verbiage and tautologies familiar to every student of
Parliamentary eloquence in *Hansard;* but, in compensation, there was a steady increase, especially when he
held office, in conscious power and authoritative
weight.

So far as print and description can reproduce the effect
of speeches, the readers of this biography have had ample
opportunity of forming a judgment of Disraeli's oratory.
They will have noticed that in one great quality he was
deficient. There was no fiery impetuosity, no whirlwind of passion, no rush of torrential words, the speaker
seeming, as it were, to be taken out of himself and inspired;
to heights of this kind Disraeli never soared. He never
assumed in the House of Commons the part of a
prophet revealing the eternal verities, but rather that
of the man of the world, no better or more intelligent
than his hearers, who would state facts and arguments as plainly as possible, confident that the intelligent persons whom he addressed would recognise
that there was only one conclusion possible. If he
ever attempted to sound the note of passion, he did
not, in his own somewhat frigid words, 'pass the line
of high-bred sentiment.' But practically all the other
resources of oratory were at his command; and the
reflection may be hazarded that the missing quality has
as often been used to mislead as to enforce reason. He
was a master of the lofty, grave, and authoritative
rhetoric of the statesman and patriot; he could elaborate
a close and consecutive argument; he could expound a
complicated Budget or Bill, so as to carry the intelligence,
if not the sympathy, of his hearers with him; he could
pile up a convincing case by quotation and analysis of
public documents; he could make deadly use of that
'ornament of debate,' invective. The perorations of
most of his great speeches afford admirable examples

of statesmanlike rhetoric; take some of those on Agricultural Depression in his first year of leadership, 1849, or the Manchester and Crystal Palace speeches of 1872. Disraeli's faculty of careful and connected argument may be well illustrated by his speech on going into committee on Peel's Corn Law Bill in 1846; his capacity for exposition was shown in his Budget of 1852 and his Reform Bills of 1867; for powerful analysis of a bluebook there is no better example than the impeachment in 1864 of the Schleswig-Holstein diplomacy of Palmerston and Russell; while the sustained invective of his denunciations of Peel will never be forgotten.

In all these respects, however, other men have been as great, or greater than he. Where he was unsurpassed was in the wit and humour that illuminated his utterances. He was a complete master of all the arts of irony, sarcasm, satire, and ridicule; and he employed these, sometimes in long and elaborate passages, sometimes in concentrated phrases and epigrams. These passages and phrases are the ' good things ' to which Fraser is so fond of referring; of which he truly says that Disraeli's good things were very good. To the reader these need no introduction; they are scattered all over these volumes. The more sustained passages are, indeed, too long to quote, and often too dependent on topics of the moment to be readily understood. Referring to the ' matchless strain of irony ' in which Disraeli loved to address the Coalition Ministry, T. E. Kebbel[1] has acutely pointed out that ' the effect is often not produced by felicitous images or pungent epigrams, but by one continuous flow of elaborate mockery which does not admit of being broken up, and which cannot be appreciated even as it stands without a minute acquaintance with the political and Parliamentary circumstances to which it is addressed.' These weapons are more suited to the attack than to the defence; and it is partly owing to his mastery of them that Disraeli was such an incomparable leader of Opposition. To the

[1] *Life of Lord Beaconsfield*, p. 185.

'good things' which he had prepared he would lead up in the most artistic fashion, with all the by-play which Fraser has preserved for us. The moment arrived, and the audience duly warned (writes the *Quarterly Review* of June, 1854), 'not a blow misses; not a platitude irritates; not a sarcasm is impeded by a weakening phrase. The arrow, stripped of all plumage except that which aids and steadies its flight, strikes within a hair's breadth of the archer's aim.' Disraeli's strong dramatic sense enabled him to get the last ounce of value out of situations thus created. But he was a generous opponent. He never put forth his strength against small men. Great Ministers such as Peel, Russell, Palmerston, and Gladstone were his quarry, or men such as Graham, Charles Wood, and Lowe, who, though not in the first flight, loomed large in the eyes of the House.

With regard to quotation, Disraeli has left a note, written apparently in the sixties, stating what he understood to be the recognised custom of Parliament, and what had been his own practice.

There used to be well understood rules in the House of Commons in old days (before the Reform), respecting quotations. No English poet to be quoted, who had not completed his century. Greek and French never under any circumstances. Latin as you liked: Horace and Virgil by preference; then Juvenal.[1]

Now quotation (in the House of Commons) is what we are most deficient in. Very few will venture on Latin. But it is not that the House has relinquished quotation, but the new elements find their illustrations and exponents in illegitimate means. It is not merely, that they quote Byron and Tennyson before they have completed their quarantine: but Bright and Cobden, and all those sort of people, are always quoting Dickens and *Punch*, etc. Our quotations are either tawdry or trashy. The privilege of quotation should not be too easy. It should be fenced in. When I took the lead of the Opposition, I, temperately and discreetly, somewhat revived the habit of classic quotation. (I had done it before

---

[1] In *Endymion*, ch. 76, Beaconsfield quotes Charles Fox as laying down, in almost identical terms, the unwritten rules about quotation in Parliament.

to some degree, when I had got the ear of the House.)   Applied with discretion, it was not unsuccessful; and I was rather amused in course of time to find Lord John Russell, who was then Prime Minister and Leader of the House, brushing up his classical reminiscences and coming down frequently with Virgilian passages, so that he might keep up the credit of his party.   If it were worth while to examine Hansard for such trifles, this would be found to be accurate.

Disraeli was not copious in quotation, save of inconvenient expressions of opinion which his opponents had incautiously used and had hoped were forgotten; these he often quoted with telling effect.   But every now and then, as his note intimates, he introduced in a felicitous way a few lines from the Latin poets; instances have been given in previous volumes of this biography.[1]   His most famous collocation of Latin words, which he employed both at the beginning of his leadership[2] and at the height of his power[3] to denote his view of the rightful aim of British policy—*Imperium et Libertas*—was a misquotation, into which he was betrayed by the authority of Bolingbroke and Bacon.   Bolingbroke wrote in the *Patriot King:* 'A King, in the temper of whose Government, like that of Nerva, things so seldom allied as Empire and Liberty are intimately mixed.'   So Bacon in his *Advancement of Learning*, Book I., had written: 'Nerva, the excellent temper of whose Government is by a glance in Cornelius Tacitus touched to the life: "Postquam divus Nerva res olim insociabiles miscuisset, imperium et libertatem." ' But both Bolingbroke and Bacon were quoting from memory; Bolingbroke, indeed, was perhaps quoting from Bacon.   The actual words of Tacitus in the *Agricola*, sec. 3, are: 'Quamquam . . . Nerva Cæsar res olim dissociabiles miscuerit, *principatum ac libertatem*.'   Though there is little difference of meaning, undoubtedly *Imperium et Libertas*, Empire and Liberty, is for the modern world the more impressive phrase.

In his management of the House of Commons, Disraeli kept a light, if firm, hand upon the reins.   Here his

---

[1] See Vol. I., pp. 782, 917.   [2] See Vol. I., p. 1099.
[3] See p. 1367.

complete command of temper served him well. Where Gladstone would have fulminated and insisted, he was content to allure and persuade. A timely jest or a mirth-provoking epigram would often conjure the storm-cloud away. At question-time, though ready if necessary to administer a crushing snub, he adopted in general the attitude of polite and welcoming consideration. But, both at this stage and in debate, he intervened very rarely; he allowed no one to draw him; the tactics by which, in the 1880 Parliament, Randolph Churchill contrived to make Gladstone himself occupy in explanatory and exculpatory speech the time which should have been devoted to forwarding Government business, would have had no success with Disraeli. He seldom made any attempt to drive the House, when it was in a recalcitrant mood. There was in those days, of course, no closure, and in order to get business through the choice often lay solely between threatening and humouring a stubborn minority. Gladstone, in the strenuous times of 1869-1873, had frequently endeavoured to extort the passage of his measures by insisting that the House should not rise for the night till some particular stage had been taken, should not be prorogued for the vacation till certain Bills had been passed. Tactics of this sort were distasteful to Disraeli. Much as he deprecated and discouraged obstruction, from whatever quarter it might proceed, yet, when he found that late at night a determined minority would not give way, he would often, after one division, accept the adjournment with a good grace; with the frequent result that the clause, or the measure, which was to have been resisted to the death at one in the morning, was passed after a few minutes' good-humoured discussion in the early hours of the following afternoon. Whether methods of this character would have had any effect upon the organised obstruction started by Parnell in 1877 may perhaps be doubted. Happily for Disraeli's comfort he had then quitted the Commons.

The dignity of the House was very dear to him. 'Let

us remember we are a senate, not a vestry,' he was wont to say. His attitude towards its traditional rules was almost one of veneration, and it was only with the greatest reluctance that he assented to the slightest modification of them. But he insisted that 'the rules were made for *gentlemen*,' and must be observed in that spirit. For his colleagues he was a strict disciplinarian. He required, as we have seen, steady attendance on the bench and in divisions; and the reproof he administered by word of mouth or by letter to absentees was such that they did not court a second. He strongly disapproved of interruptions during speeches in debate. He would neither interpose himself, save on a very special occasion, nor permit a colleague to interrupt, when an opponent was speaking; and, if interruptions proceeded from any of the benches behind him, he would turn and frown the offender down. To interrupt, he would say, was not merely bad manners, but it did not pay; it only gave the speaker an opportunity for an apt retort. He often profited himself in this way by the unmannerly interruptions of the other side. But he would not allow members of his Government to call an opponent their honourable or right honourable 'friend.' Ostentatious intimacy of that sort would make the struggle a mere game.

No wonder a magnanimous and generous figure of the kind we have tried to depict, a unique and magical personality, exotic in appearance, masterful in quality, was sorely missed when he left the House. After little more than a couple of months' experience of the next Session Sir Henry Lucy bitterly lamented the dulness of the place without Disraeli. 'He was not only brilliant himself, but the cause of brilliancy in others. He wound up the House of Commons to a certain pitch, at which it was constantly kept going. His mere presence supplied a focus towards which the minds of speakers were bent.'[1]

Disraeli's final act as a commoner was to bid farewell

---

[1] *Diary of Two Parliaments,* Vol. I., p. 218.

to the constituency, the fidelity of whose feelings, as he gracefully said, had given him an assured position at Westminster. In his short but dignified address to the electors of Bucks, he summed up in one sentence the two chief objects at which he had aimed throughout his public life.

Not insensible to the principle of progress, I have endeavoured to reconcile change with that respect for tradition which is one of the main elements of our social strength; and in external affairs I have endeavoured to develop and strengthen our Empire, believing that combination of achievement and responsibility elevates the character and condition of a people.

In the titles which Disraeli took—Earl of Beaconsfield and Viscount Hughenden of Hughenden—he was faithful to the memory of his wife and to the country home which they both loved. He based himself on a great historical precedent. 'He would prefer,' he wrote to the Queen, 'following the precedent of Lord Chatham, suggested by your Majesty, and take the same title as his wife, with a step.' Moreover, he was not, we may be sure, insensible to the association of the name of Beaconsfield with so eminent a pillar of the British Constitution as Edmund Burke. Disraeli was somewhat annoyed by a disposition on the part of the public to pronounce the first syllable of his new title with a short vowel sound. When Granville and Bradford used this fashion, basing themselves on the recollections of schooldays spent forty years before in the town of Beaconsfield, he humorously said he was not going to be dictated to by two aristocratic schoolboys.[1] 'It is like the Whigs,' he said, on another occasion, 'to call me out of my name.' He told a lady who asked for information, 'My name is Beaconsfield—not "Becc";' and a foreign inquirer that it meant 'the field of the beacon.' It may be added that the Queen expressed her willingness to settle any part of Disraeli's titles on his nephew and heir, Coningsby Disraeli; but the offer was for family reasons declined.

[1] Fitzmaurice's *Granville*, Vol. I., p. 12.

To Queen Victoria.

CASTLE BROMWICH, *Aug.* 20, 1876.—. . . Lord Beaconsfield asks leave to take this opportunity of again thanking
your Majesty for all the honors your Majesty has graciously
conferred on him.   They would not be mean distinctions,
even for the most exalted, but what enhances them to him
beyond all price, is that your Majesty has condescended to
express your Majesty's personal gratification in rewarding a
servant who, whatever his deficiencies, is, he hopes, from his
very heart, devoted to your Majesty.

If there was nothing dramatic about Benjamin Disraeli's
manner of leaving the House of Commons, the first
appearance of the Earl of Beaconsfield in the House of
Lords had a certain piquancy of its own.   When, on
February 8, 1877, the Queen opened Parliament in state,
all eyes were turned on 'a familiar face, but a strangely
disguised figure,'[1] at Her Majesty's left hand as she sat on
the Throne.   It was the Prime Minister, in scarlet and
ermine, bearing aloft the Sword of State; standing mute
and motionless, with all the dignity of pose, and lack
of facial expression, that distinguished him on great
occasions.   He was but lately risen from a bed of sickness,
and the Queen had offered to release him from the 'cumbersome' burden; but he was resolved, once at least, to
play in due form the Minister's part in the historic
pageant.   'He quite counts,' he wrote on January 28,
'on the honor of carrying the Sword of State and standing
next to your Majesty.   He would not like to miss so
great an incident.   It is a chapter in life!'

The brilliant throng of peeresses who attended the
function returned a couple of hours later to see the Prime
Minister of Society take his seat as a peer.   According to
the practice of the Lords a newcomer has to be introduced
by two members of that order of the peerage to which he
has been raised.   The earls whom Beaconsfield chose as
sponsors were Derby and Bradford; the one the son of
his old chief and himself his leading colleague in the

---

[1] *Diary of Two Parliaments*, Vol. I., p. 172.

Ministry, the other the husband of his intimate friend. Conducted by them, and preceded by Garter and other high officers of state, he and they all duly robed, he went through the bowings and handshakings, the peregrinations to various benches, the liftings of the three-cornered hat, that constitute the quaint old-fashioned ceremony of introduction, with the same stateliness and dignity which had marked his manipulation of the great Sword. The notes that passed with reference to Derby's sponsorship have a pathetic interest in view of subsequent events.

To Lord Derby.

2, WHITEHALL G'DNS, *Jan.* 24, '77.—What do you think of introducing me to H. of L. ?   I know it would bore you, and I, always, try to save you from being bored.   But one has a feeling, that it would be the proper thing.   Perhaps the feeling may have no foundation, and there are 1,000 reasons why you should [not] be trespassed on at this somewhat anxious moment.   That chivalric being, the premier earl, is a candidate for the office, but I ventured to observe, that I thought it was the custom to appeal, in such a situation, to one's colleagues.

Bradford would be the second, and if you thought, on the whole, it was more convenient for you not to join him, there is, at least, Beauchamp.

From Lord Derby

FOREIGN OFFICE, *J[an]*. 24.—I am not disposed to be sensitive on such matters as that to which your note refers; but I should have felt sorry, though not aggrieved, if you had applied to anyone but me on the occasion of your introduction to the H. of Lds.   Considering that we have pulled together for nearly 30 years, I think that office of friendship is mine by right; and I accept it with real pleasure.

The old familiar friendship of the two men was still strong; but the coming twelve months, with their searching trial of character, were to sunder the relations of thirty years; and the willing sponsor of the early days of 1877 was to become the deserter of 1878, and, for the remaining few years of Beaconsfield's life, his declared opponent and severe critic.

Edward Henry Fifteenth Earl of Derby
from the portrait of him as Lord Stanley
after Sir Francis Grant at Hughenden

It was by Derby's side, between him and Richmond, that Beaconsfield took his seat as leader; assuming the leadership here, as in the other House, under unprecedented conditions. He had become Leader of the Commons without ever having been in office, or even sworn in as a Privy Councillor; he now became Leader of the Lords directly he entered their House. That historic assembly, to which so notable a figure had been added, then included, among those regularly taking part in its business, many men eminent in the public life of the country. On the woolsack sat a Chancellor, Cairns, hardly inferior to any of his great predecessors in legal acumen and judicial weight, and superior to most of them in statesmanlike wisdom and oratorical power. As colleagues on Beaconsfield's own bench, besides Derby, the mainstay of the sober middle classes, and Richmond, who had proved an acceptable interim leader, there were Salisbury, who after Beaconsfield's death was to exercise undisputed sway in the House for twenty years, and the scholarly and idealistic Carnarvon. A renowned personality, only occasionally present in his place, was the veteran Whig chief, Russell, who had welcomed Beaconsfield in a short but graceful note, written in a trembling hand: 'Let me congratulate the House of Lords that you are one of its members, and that a man of genius and literary fame has been added to its roll.' The actual Liberal leader was the urbane and adroit Granville, who had efficient lieutenants in men like Kimberley, Cardwell, Aberdare, Selborne, Spencer, and Northbrook. The day of Lord Rosebery, still under thirty, and of the late Lord Lansdowne, just over that age, was not yet, though both had begun to interest the House. But the great Opposition orator, whose duels with Beaconsfield were the only episodes that gave the debates of the next few years anything of the animation to which the newcomer had been accustomed in the Commons, was the proud and fiery Duke of Argyll. Others in an independent position, who contributed weight or distinction to the proceedings, were Shaftesbury, still at

the height of his philanthropic renown; Grey, who represented the Whig traditions of his father, the Reform Premier;
and, on the episcopal bench, the statesmanlike Tait, of
Canterbury, and the eloquent Magee, of Peterborough.

Distinguished as were the *élite* of the peers, there was
none among them to give pause to one who had successfully encountered in debate Peel and Palmerston, O'Connell and Cobden, Gladstone and Bright. Beaconsfield
spoke for ten minutes the very first evening on the
Address, and Fraser, who was present, notes that he
seemed at once to be at home in his new surroundings.

I was particularly struck with the perfect ease with which
he leaned forward, glanced at the Chancellor, and moved the
adjournment of the House. One could have thought that he
had passed his life there: this was always his demeanour in
the House of Lords.

In not one of his speeches in the House of Lords was there
the slightest trace either of too much self-consciousness,
too much familiarity, illness of ease, nor indeed of any quality
that a gentleman would not show under the circumstances.
Having been for many years used to address the Speaker as
' Sir,' he never made the mistake of substituting that word
for ' my Lords ': he adapted himself to the new situation ' as
to the manner born.'[1]

' I am dead; dead, but in the Elysian fields,' was
Beaconsfield's reply to an acquaintance among the peers,
who, when welcoming him to the Lords, expressed a fear
lest he should miss the excitement of the Commons. The
shortness and comparative rarity of the sittings, the
chilliness of the atmosphere, the abstinence from noisy
demonstration, may have sometimes caused the Parliamentary gladiator to sigh for the strenuous triumphs of
the past. But one who was a Jewish aristocrat at
heart felt himself naturally at home in an assembly
of aristocrats, where business was conducted with dignity
and manners were urbane; and the leisure of the new
Parliamentary conditions enabled him both to satisfy the
claims of private friendship, and to concentrate his

[1] Fraser, pp. 414, 415.

attention more fully and exclusively on foreign affairs. Far from being dead, in regard to the higher direction of policy he was never more alive and active.

In the *Young Duke* Disraeli had laid it down, with the assurance of youth, that two distinct styles were requisite for speaking in the two Houses of Parliament, and that he meant, if he had time, to give a specimen of both; taking *Don Juan* as his model in the Commons, and *Paradise Lost* in the Lords. In actual fact there was no great difference in his manner in the two Houses; though *Paradise Lost* certainly contains some lines, taken from the great debate—not in the Elysian fields—of Book II., which admirably describe the Minister's appearance, as he was wont to rise to address the Peers.

> With grave
> Aspect he rose, and in his rising seemed
> A pillar of State.   Deep on his front engraven
> Deliberation sat, and public care.[1]

But, though such was Beaconsfield's manner as Leader of the Lords, it was only a continuation of the later and authoritative manner of Disraeli, the Leader of the Commons. Moreover, the good things in his speeches were heralded with just the same play of the handkerchief. Fraser gives an amusing instance;

I was fortunately in the House of Lords, shortly before his departure with Lord Salisbury for the Berlin Conference. Lord Granville had spoken, and had expressed real or affected regret that Lord Beaconsfield and Lord Salisbury should both be absent at the same time from the councils of the Queen. Disraeli replied, ' The noble earl has expressed his regret that my noble friend sitting on my right and myself should be abroad at the same time: he has been pleased to add that he considers that the absence of the noble marquis and of myself from the Cabinet will diminish the personal importance of those that remain.   My Lords;' here out came the handkerchief; ' I can conceive no circumstance, ahem ! more calculated to add to it !' [2]

---

[1] My attention was called to this apt quotation by an article on ' Disraeli's Meridian ' in the *Fortnightly Review* for June, 1916, by Mr. A. A. Baumann.

[2] Fraser, pp. 402, 403.

If there was no serious difference in Disraeli's manner in addressing the two Houses, there was also no difference in the ascendancy which he exercised over both. He assumed in the Lords, at once, as of right, that dominance which he had after years of combat established in the Commons. Before his elevation to their ranks, the Lords had not shown any particular complaisance to his wishes, whether he was Leader of Opposition or Prime Minister. Conservative as they might be in general political complexion, they had acknowledged no special allegiance to any Conservative leader since the death of the fourteenth Lord Derby. They had forced Disraeli's Government to remodel its judicature scheme, and had, even in the last Session, come near, under Shaftesbury's inspiration, to a revolt against Disraeli over the Royal Titles Bill. But as soon as they experienced the personal influence of his genius, they willingly submitted to his claims; and what has been described as the most independent and unenthusiastic assembly in the world accorded, again and again, to the ennobled Jew the loud cheers which few other members of their House have been able to elicit.

By the transfer of the Prime Minister to the Lords the balance of the Cabinet between the two Houses of Parliament was disturbed. It was restored by the retirement of Malmesbury, who was in indifferent health, from the post of Privy Seal, which Beaconsfield himself assumed in addition to the First Lordship of the Treasury, and by the promotion to Cabinet rank of Hicks Beach, the Chief Secretary for Ireland—'without question,' wrote Beaconsfield, 'our most competent man' outside. This rearrangement presented no difficulty. It was otherwise with the vacancy in the commanding position of Leader of the House of Commons. In many respects the natural choice would have been Gathorne Hardy, and Disraeli's thoughts undoubtedly turned to him in the first place. Ever since Cairns had gone to the Lords ten years before, Disraeli had regarded Hardy as his 'sword-arm' in debate; and he had constituted him his deputy in his absence, always when in opposition, and occasionally since the Tory return to office. Hardy, after his chief, was without a doubt the member of the Cabinet whose intervention exercised most influence in the House. Neither Cross, Manners, nor Ward Hunt carried heavy guns; and even Northcote, though always ready, well-informed and persuasive, had none of the sacred fire which moves an audience. Nevertheless, Disraeli came reluctantly to the conclusion that North-cote would be the more suitable successor. Recognising that Hardy had every right to anticipate that the choice would fall upon himself, he took him into his confidence as to the difficulties of the situation at an early stage; and, while leaving him in no doubt as to his anxiety to meet his wishes, appreciation of his services and deep respect for his character, prepared him gradually for a disappointment of his hopes. Finally, when formally communicating to him on August 2 his own resolve to go to the Lords but to remain Prime Minister, in words similar to those which he had used to Richmond and other colleagues, he added the following significant paragraphs, intimating not obscurely what would be the solution of the problem of leadership.

To Gathorne Hardy.

10, Downing St., *Aug.* 2, 1876.—. . . Of the many anxious points connected with this subject, there is none more grave, than the management of the House of Commons after my departure. The choice can only be between yourself and the Chancellor of the Exchequer. You both entered the Privy Council, and the Cabinet, on the same day, and, almost at the same time, you were both promoted to Secretaryships of State. In commanding eloquence, your superiority is quite acknowledged, while, in transacting the various business of the House, the fact of his having no heavy department to engross him, and the miscellaneous character of his duties, have necessarily placed him during this Ministry in more frequent communication with the members.

In mentioning your name to the Queen, I observed, that

the heavy duties of your office might be incompatible with the
management of the House of Commons, and I said that some
arrangement might be made to meet, perhaps, this difficulty;
but the Queen expressed herself very strongly as to her personal wish, that you should not leave the Army, saying that
you possessed her entire confidence, and that there was no
person, in that respect, to whom she could extend equal
trust.

I feel much the responsibility of life in the step which I
am probably about to take, and I regret that my original
purpose has not been practicable; but I am going to Osborne
in a few days, and I must go there with a definite plan.

I speak to you without the slightest reserve, and an anxiety
to meet your wishes in every practicable way. I acknowledge your claim to that consideration on public grounds,
but believe me, I also extend it from a deep respect for your
character, and from a strong personal regard.

Oblige me, then, by communicating to me in the same
spirit, and assist me by your advice in one of the most difficult
passages of my life.

Hardy, while confessing to a pang of disappointment,
accepted the decision with a loyalty beyond praise, and
a generosity which Disraeli fully appreciated. Only he
expressed a wish that he might be allowed before long
to follow his chief 'into a more tranquil sphere'; and
received the immediate promise that 'every wish of
yours, so far as I am concerned, will be gratified, and I
shall rejoice in their gratification.'[1] Beaconsfield, the
most grateful of men, never forgot the fine loyalty and
self-sacrifice which Hardy exhibited at this juncture;
and at the next vacancy, in August, 1877, in a Cabinet
post, he marked his high consideration for him by saying,
in Hardy's own words, 'that I must consider it a standing order that an offer was made first to me in case of
any change: the choice was always open to me, so great
were my services to the party and to him '[2]—an assurance
subsequently repeated on similar occasions.

[1] The correspondence is fully set out in Gathorne Hardy, Vol. II., ch. 19.
[2] Ibid., Vol. II., p. 28.

From Sir Stafford Northcote.

Confidential.   86, HARLEY ST., *Aug.* 2, 1876.—Hardy will probably have told you that he spoke to me after receiving your letter to-day. Nothing could be kinder or more handsome than his language, and I hope there may be no diminution of cordiality between us. Working together, as I think we shall do, we may be able to serve the party.

I cannot write to you all that is in my mind; but I console myself with the reflection that you have a wonderful power of reading men's thoughts, so I hope you know mine, and that it is unnecessary for me to tell you how much the story of the long years of kindness I have received, and of lessons that I have learnt, is filling my heart, or how much of sadness mingles with it.

> Multa ferunt anni venientes:
> Multa recedentes adimunt;

and how much is receding now !

I trust you may find strength and happiness in the change, and there is much consolation in the thought that it will preserve you to us the longer.

But I must not trust myself to say more.

Though the reasons which Disraeli gave to Hardy undoubtedly counted for much in the decision taken, they were not the whole, probably not even the weightier part, of the motives which actuated him. It was perfectly true that Northcote's relations to Members of Parliament, and his more frequent communication with them in regard to public business, when contrasted with Hardy's immersion in the work of a great spending department from which both the Queen and the Prime Minister would be loth to spare him, seemed to mark out Northcote as more qualified to succeed. But many other considerations pointed in the same direction. Remonstrances against the selection of Hardy were made in two important quarters. The Whips, whose opinion could not be neglected, were afraid lest Hardy's quick temper should land the party in difficulties. Derby, who in spite of his reluctance might be forced by a sudden failure of Beaconsfield's health into the first place, recognised in Hardy a temperament and standpoint much less congenial than

Northcote's to his own.   Moreover, Hardy did not come
up to Disraeli's strict standard in the matter of constant
attendance at the House; and he incurred more than
once the reproof of his chief for missing a critical
division owing to his otherwise praiseworthy habit of
going home, whenever possible, to dine with his wife.
Lastly, Northcote was Disraeli's man in a sense in which
Hardy never had been.   He had entered Ministerial life
as Disraeli's immediate subordinate at the Treasury, and
was never quite able to sink the lieutenant in the colleague;
always, for example, addressing his chief in writing as
' Mr.' Disraeli or ' Lord ' Beaconsfield, a formal mode
used by no other colleague occupying a position at all
comparable to that of Chancellor of the Exchequer.
Considering the many possibilities of friction and misunderstanding between a Prime Minister in the Lords
and his deputy in the prerogative House, we can well
understand the preference which Beaconsfield showed
for a leader who combined an immense capacity for
Parliamentary business with an attitude of peculiar
deference to himself.

The leadership of the Commons has often made, or
marred, British Governments; witness the crisis in 1834
caused by the succession of Lord Althorp to the earldom
of Spencer.   And critics have attributed some of the
troubles which befell the Conservatives between 1877 and
1885 to the selection by Beaconsfield of Northcote as
leader instead of Hardy.   Beaconsfield himself, in later
years, came to think that he had made a mistake, and
had presumed too much on the prospects of a period of
political calm, during which the vagaries of Gladstone's
occasional interventions would be controlled by the
abundant common sense of Hartington as Opposition
leader.   To the demands of such a period he felt sure
that Northcote would be adequate.   Had he anticipated
the new crusade which Gladstone was about to launch,
he might have preferred the more combative leader.   It
is, however, only fair to recognise that, in spite of Glad-

stone's impetuous return, Northcote was not unequal to the calls which the Parliament of 1874 made upon him, and was able, by the sweet reasonableness of his expositions of Ministerial policy, to maintain the majorities of the Government at a satisfactory figure. It was not until the period of opposition after 1880, when dashing and harassing tactics were demanded, and when his own health was failing, that Northcote came to be regarded as too yielding and conciliatory for the chief of a fighting confederacy. And, whether in office or in opposition, his readiness, experience, candour, and courtesy won him the respect and affection not only of his own followers but of the House of Commons as a whole.

stone, a important reform. Northcote was not unequal
to the calls which the Parliament of 1874 made upon
him, and was able, by the sweet reasonableness of his
expositions of his ministerial policy, to maintain the majorities
of the Government at a satisfactory figure. It was not
until the period of opposition after 1880, when dashing
and harassing tactics were demanded, and when his own
health was failing, that Northcote came to be regarded
as too yielding and conciliatory for the chief of a fighting
confederacy. And, whether in office or in opposition,
his readiness, experience, candour, and courtesy, won him
the respect and affection not only of his own followers
but of the House of Commons as a whole.

VI
1876–1881

BY GEORGE EARLE BUCKLE

Beaconsfield.

CHAPTER I.

REOPENING OF THE EASTERN QUESTION.

1875–1876.

The change of name corresponded closely with a change in the dominant theme of the life of Benjamin Disraeli, Earl of Beaconsfield. The name Disraeli suggests, in the political sphere, the consummate Parliamentarian, who was proud of the House of Commons and of whom the House of Commons was proud; the destroyer of Peel, the re-creator of the Conservative party, the reformer of the borough suffrage, the promoter of Tory Democracy. The name Beaconsfield has quite other associations, far removed from domestic party politics and gladiatorial combats in Parliament. It recalls the imperial and European statesman, the faithful custodian of his country's interests at a critical epoch in international politics, the leading figure at a European Congress presided over by Bismarck and containing Gortchakoff, Andrassy, and Salisbury among its members. It is for ever associated with the maintenance, and presentation to the external world, of England's ' magnificent and awful cause.' When Beaconsfield died, Salisbury finely said of him that ' zeal for the greatness of England was the passion of his life.' That was generally accepted in 1881 as a natural and, in the main, a just appreciation; but, had it been said in 1874 of the Disraeli who then became Prime Minister for the second time, it would rather have provoked criticism and denial than have obtained general acceptance.

And yet the ardent patriotism, the high imperial spirit, which dominated Beaconsfield, had always been latent in

Disraeli, and had given frequent signs of its presence to those who looked for them. His youthful novel, the *Young Duke*, contains this fervid apostrophe to his country: ' Few can love thee better than he who traces these idle lines. . . . If ever the hour shall call, my brain and life are thine';[1] and in the tract, *Gallomania*, of the same period, he describes his politics as comprised in one word— England.[2] So, in the days of the struggle between Free Trade and Protection, what he strove for was the union of all classes to promote the greatness and prosperity of the whole country; the agriculture, the commerce, and the manufactures working together as co-mates and partners.[3] In the Crimean War he declared that it was the duty of the Opposition, which he led, to support the Sovereign and maintain the honour of the country.[4] And, when combating the policy of universal intermeddling pursued by Palmerston and Russell, he was careful to insist that Britain would never tolerate aggression on its independence or empire; that, when it entered on a just quarrel, it would never cease its efforts till it had accomplished its aim; that, on fitting occasion, it would even be prepared, without allies, to encounter a world in arms.[5] Skelton saw, and pointed out in 1867, that the vision of ' this mightier Venice, this imperial republic on which the sun never sets,' fascinated Disraeli; that England was ' the Israel of his imagination'; and that, if he had his chance, he would be the imperial Minister before he died.[6] So the imperialism of the 1872 programme, of the firm remonstrance with Berlin in May, 1875, of the Suez Canal purchase, and of the Royal Titles Bill, was but a natural development; and with the reopening of the Eastern Question, and the escape from the detail of domestic politics provided by the transfer to the Lords, foreign policy, which from first to last he maintained to be of primary, of paramount importance.[7]

1 See Vol. I., p. 136.   2 See Vol. I., p. 214.
3 See Vol. I., p. 1016.   4 See Vol. I., p. 1353.
5 See Vol. I., p. 1660; and above, pp. 44 and 80.
6 See p. 293.   7 See Vol. I., p. 212; and above, p. 531.

overshadowed and dwarfed in Beaconsfield's mind all other issues.

When Disraeli left the Commons, the Eastern Question had been occupying the increasing attention of the Government for a year; but only in the last few weeks had it become at all matter of controversy, Hartington, the Opposition leader, having deliberately said, when raising the subject in the House, so recently as June 9, ' I do not believe there exists in the country any distrust of the proceedings of Her Majesty's Government.' No sooner, however, had the Prime Minister quitted the arena where he could answer his chief accuser face to face, than the heather was set on fire by Gladstone with a pamphlet on *Bulgarian Horrors*, and a controversy was kindled which was never suffered to die down so long as Beaconsfield remained in office.

The Eastern Question, as it presented itself to Disraeli in the seventies, was one side of the great problem, how to safeguard the British Empire, with its immense commercial and territorial interests in the Levant, in the Persian Gulf, in India, in Australasia, and in the Far East, in face of a simultaneous and sweeping advance of Russian power and propaganda, both in Europe and in Asia, towards the south and the sea. We know now that the Colossus had feet of clay; but then it seemed a reasonable fear that, unless sharply checked, he might bestride at any rate the Eastern world. While in Asia the crumbling Tartar kingdoms were falling one after another under Russian sway, in Europe the Ottoman Empire, which had long barred Russian progress to that key of Mediterranean dominion, Constantinople, had been stricken with a sickness which was for a while arrested by the Crimean War, but which, if not carefully tended, might well prove mortal.

It was nearly five hundred years since, in the battle of Kossovo and in subsequent campaigns in the Balkans and in Greece, the Ottoman Turks, a martial Asian tribe of Mohammedan faith, had submerged the Serbs, the

Bulgars, and the Greeks; it was more than four hundred
years since they had extinguished the Eastern Empire,
that lingering remnant of the Roman State, by the capture
of Constantinople.   All the subjected races were Christian,
after, in the main, the Eastern rite; but many landowners
and others accepted the religion of the conquerors.   The
Greeks were the representatives of the foremost civilisation of the ancient world, a civilisation which had
flourished more than two thousand years before Disraeli's
day, and which under Alexander of Macedon first, and
afterwards under Constantine and his successors, had commanded an empire in three continents.   Both Serbs and
Bulgars were, in world history, like the Turks themselves,
comparative late-comers, the one from a north-east European, the other from an Asiatic, home, and both, also like
the Turks, were only partially civilised; but both races, one
pure Slav, the other mixed Slav and Tartar, at one time
exercised imperial sway in the Balkans.   During a couple
of periods from the ninth to the thirteenth century the
Bulgars had enjoyed an empire stretching from the
Black Sea to the Adriatic, including most of the peninsula
except the part south of Thessaly and Epirus, and except
the immediate neighbourhood of Constantinople.   To
them succeeded the Serbs, who, in the fourteenth century,
included in their kingdom the whole upper portion of
the peninsula from the Save and Danube almost to the
Ægean, and from the Adriatic to the Lower Maritza,
having, moreover, a lordship over Bulgaria proper which
carried their dominion to the Black Sea.   Both these
medieval empires had perished as though they had never
been; but highlanders have long memories.

The Ottoman Empire, based upon these ruins, and
embracing large tracts of Asia and Africa as well as of
Europe, had a period of great magnificence and renown
in the fifteenth and sixteenth centuries; it was feared
and courted by European potentates of every degree.
The flood of Ottoman conquest had indeed twice carried
the Turks to the gates of Vienna; but since the beginning

of the eighteenth century their dominion in Europe had been restricted to the Balkan peninsula; and the nineteenth century had seen a serious inroad made even there on their authority.   While the Ottomans were still a conquering race, the empire was well administered, taxation was light, and the subject races had little cause of complaint.   But the Turkish conquests were never thoroughly consolidated.   There was little or no inter-marriage between the ruling race and the ruled; Turks, Slavs, and Greeks dwelt together side by side but were never fused into a nation.   Accordingly, when the heritage of Solyman the Magnificent passed in 1566 to a series of incompetent successors, there was rapid decay. Corruption and inefficiency at the centre of government produced corruption and oppression throughout the provinces.   Misgovernment rekindled the national spirit of the oppressed peoples, and insurrections and revolutionary wars, often successful, were the inevitable outcome.

Since about 1830, three great peninsular communities had escaped from the effective control of the Turks. Greece, south of Thessaly and Epirus, had become absolutely independent.   Moldavia and Wallachia, the principalities between the Danube and the Carpathians, after receiving local autonomy in 1830, had become practically independent by the Treaty of Paris in 1856, and had subsequently been united into a single state, Rumania, in 1861.   Serbia, under Prince Milosh, had definitely achieved autonomy in 1830, and ecclesiastical independence in 1831; and the Turks had evacuated in 1867 the fortified places which they held under the earlier arrangements, thus giving Serbia virtual, if not technical, independence.   Even Bulgaria, which had seemed the most hopelessly submerged of all the nationalities, had shown signs of reviving national consciousness, and had secured recognition of her Church in a Bulgarian ex-archate in 1870, though her political subjection remained unmodified   Montenegro, the little Slav State in the fastnesses of the Dinaric Alps, had never submitted to the Turkish invader. Thus, in 1875, the effective Turkish Empire in Europe had dwindled to the Slav provinces of Bosnia and Herzegovina in the north-west of the peninsula, between the Save and Austrian Dalmatia, the adjoining sanjak of Novi Bazar, Bulgaria on the Danube and the Black Sea, Albania and Epirus on the Adriatic, Thessaly and Macedonia on the Ægean, and Thrace and the district immediately around Constantinople, commanding the Sea of Marmora and the Straits. Turkey in Europe could hardly suffer much further territorial diminution, and yet remain a real make-weight in Near Eastern politics.

While the Turkish power, largely owing to a succession of incapable Sultans, was waning through the eighteenth and the early nineteenth centuries, the power of Russia, directed by energetic rulers, from Peter through Catherine to Nicholas, was steadily increasing, and was more and more applied to acquiring control over Turkish policy. Of the same or a similar Slav race, and professing the same type of Christianity, as the principal subject peoples of Turkey in Europe, the Russians were also spurred on by the economic necessity of keeping the Bosphorus and the Dardanelles open for their Black Sea trade. Constantinople, accordingly, with its command of both waterways, and its tenure of the keys of two continents, became their inevitable aim. By two treaties, that of Kutchuk-Kainardji in 1774, and that of Unkiar-Skelessi in 1833, Russia obtained, at any rate for the time, that exclusive right to champion the Christian subject races which she recognised as the most efficient lever for making her will prevail with the Sublime Porte.

It took Great Britain long to comprehend its interests in the Near East. William Pitt the younger, indeed, even before the war with France, endeavoured, but in vain, to rouse his countrymen to a sense of the dangers involved in a Russian advance to the Mediterranean. In spite of Napoleon's boast that Egypt was the place where he would strike a mortal blow at the British Empire,

it was not until the nineteenth century was past its
infancy that British diplomacy came to realise how important the Near East and the Caliphate at Constantinople were to a Power which was established in India
and ruled over a large and increasing number of Mohammedan subjects. Canning, while forwarding Greek
independence, had successfully combated Russian claims
to exclusive or even preponderant rights in Turkey; but
it was Palmerston who, by his insistence in tearing up
the Treaty of Unkiar-Skelessi in 1841 and by his successful prosecution of the Crimean War, had finally erased
from the diplomatic map all trace of special Russian
influence over the Sublime Porte. The Treaty of Paris,
which concluded that war, made the support of the
integrity and independence of the Turkish Empire a
principle, not merely of British, but of European policy.

Russia had never acquiesced in this defeat of her
claims in Turkey. For a time she turned her energies
rather in the direction of Asiatic expansion; but her
Government carefully watched European developments
that might favour a resumption of her Balkan pretensions.
Turkey did little or nothing to utilise the breathing-space
afforded her by the Crimean War. In spite of fair
professions and paper edicts, misgovernment and oppression were rife, so that there was a promising field for the
spread of propaganda, secret societies, and conspiracies.
A movement, known as Pan-Slavism, perhaps scientific
in origin, but speedily diverted to political ends, sprang
up in Russia and in neighbouring Slav countries, with
the object of promoting the racial feeling and unity of
the Slav peoples; an ideal which could at that period
only be realised in practice under Russian hegemony.
Though the Russian Government looked somewhat
askance at the revolutionary aspects of the movement,
they made adroit use of it for undermining Turkish
dominion in Europe. They sent as Ambassador to
Constantinople in 1864 a Pan-Slavonic enthusiast, Count
Ignatieff, who made it his chief aim, during the thirteen

years of his mission, to bring under Russian influence all
the Christian nationalities of Turkey and especially the
Bulgarians, and to teach them to look to Russia as their
eventual liberator from the Turkish yoke. It was an
aim which could, of course, only be pursued in a semi-
official and secret manner, so that it might always be
disavowed when inconvenient by the Russian Foreign
Office; but it was steadily kept in view not merely by
the embassy at Constantinople but by the whole Russian
consular staff throughout the peninsula. Hence, owing
to oppression on the one hand and intrigue on the other,
the Balkans became honeycombed with conspiracies and
secret societies, connived at, if not fostered by, Russian
diplomacy; a state of things which a statesman like
Disraeli, only too sensible of the importance of such
underground workings in international politics, was little
likely to disregard.

While the ground was thus being quietly prepared
by a long course of subterranean intrigue, the Franco-
German War provided, as we have seen, an opportunity
for an open advance. In return for the benevolent
neutrality which Russia had extended to Germany in her
hour of danger, Bismarck was quite ready to encourage
his Eastern neighbour to re-establish her naval power
in the Black Sea. With his connivance, Gortchakoff,
in October, 1870, denounced the Black Sea clauses of
the Treaty of Paris, and proclaimed that the Tsar would
resume his ' sovereign rights ' in those waters; pleading,
in defence of this repudiation of solemn obligations, that,
owing to recent infringements of European treaties, it
would be difficult to maintain that the written law
' retains the moral validity which it may have possessed
at other times.' This was a cynical adaptation to
Russia's case of the principles on which Bismarck's
foreign policy had been based, and a direct defiance to
the Powers who had, actively or passively, imposed their
will upon her in the Crimean War. But with France
under Germany's heel, Italy occupied with taking posses-

sion of Rome, and Austria indisposed, after her lesson
in 1866, to adventure, Great Britain could find no effective support in maintaining the sanctity of the written
European law, and had to accept, at the Conference of
London in 1871, a revision of the Treaty of Paris in the
sense desired by Russia. It should, however, be noted
that, in all other respects, save that of naval force in
the Black Sea, the Treaty of London upheld and reaffirmed the provisions of the Treaty of Paris.

It was on the Treaty of Paris, thus revised and re-
established only four years previously by the Treaty of
London, that Disraeli took his stand when the Eastern
Question was reopened in 1875. The maintenance of
the faith of public treaties was always a leading feature
in his political system; and in this case the recent reversion, through the opening of the Suez Canal, of almost
the whole Eastern trade to the Mediterranean route
made it, to his mind, more than ever necessary for
England to support her traditional policy. He obtained
a control of the Canal itself by the purchase of the
Khedive's shares; he looked to the integrity and independence of Turkey, solemnly recognised by Europe, and
especially guaranteed at Paris in 1856 by a tripartite treaty
between England, France, and Austria, to guard the imperial route against a flank attack. In this way European
peace and British interests would be alike secured.

The Treaty of Paris recited that it was the Sultan's
intention to introduce reforms for the benefit of his
Christian subjects. Disraeli acknowledged the obligation
imposed on England, as a leader among the Powers who
had ousted Russia from her protectorate of Christians
in Turkey, to use her influence at Constantinople to
secure for them tolerable government; and he was the
more ready to fulfil this obligation as he realised that
without tolerable government it must be difficult to
ensure either integrity or independence. But he could
not admit that individual signatory Powers had any
right of armed interference, probably leading to occupa-

tion, in order to enforce reform; still less that the non-fulfilment of reform dispensed the signatories from observing their guarantee

There was one element, however, in the problem which Disraeli took insufficiently into account. A fervent believer in race, he had not been converted, even by the success of the Italian Risorgimento and by the establishment of the German Empire, to any sympathy with the cognate idea of nationality. His belief in race as a principle was in its essence a belief in his own race: and the aims of the Jews, whatever they may have been before and since, were, in his day, largely divorced from the assertion of political nationality in any form. Though some leading Jews, such as Sir Moses Montefiore, were already promoting Jewish colonies in Palestine, the modern Zionist movement for the restoration of Jewish population and power in their ancient land had not yet begun; and Jewish aspirations were still mainly directed to the attainment first of equality of status, and next of a leading position in business, art, and politics, among the several nations where they were settled. As individual Jews had thus won fame and power among the Christian peoples of the West, so individual Greeks and Slavs, Arabs and Armenians had risen to influence and authority in the Turkish State. With permeation of this kind he had every sympathy; but, convinced as he was of the benefits derived from the blending of diverse elements into strong centralised Powers like France and Great Britain, he distrusted movements which would break up existing Empires with no likelihood of anything but chaos to take their place. To apply the principle of nationality in the Balkans was obviously a difficult matter. Greek, Roman, Greco-Roman, Bulgarian, Serbian, and Ottoman empires had each in turn dominated practically the whole region. Consequently, in many districts, notably in Macedonia and along the coasts, Greeks, Bulgars, Serbs, and Turks were inextricably intermingled; and the mutual antagonisms of the subject races, with their irreconcilable historical claims and their different stages of civilisation, often prevailed over their common dislike of the governing Turk.

Of these grave difficulties Gladstone took little heed. In regard to nationality he was, as Disraeli was not, responsive to the spirit of the age. Starting from a lively appreciation of the aspirations of unemancipated Italy and half-emancipated Greece, he welcomed similar stirrings among the Slav peoples. In later life he developed so active a sympathy with the real or pretended nationalist movements in various parts of the world that he could recognise a 'people rightly struggling to be free' even in the dervish fanatics of the Sudan. In the present case he had the insight to discern the makings of a nation in downtrodden Bulgaria. He was ready even to accept and applaud invading Russian armies as fitting liberators of the Christian subjects of Turkey.

But what claim had Russia to pose as a crusader in the cause of humanity ? Did Christian Russia compare so very favourably with Mohammedan Turkey? She had indeed recently emancipated her serfs, but she had done little else to raise her backward peoples in the social scale; and the knout and Siberia were among her ordinary instruments of government. Poland was a warning as to her treatment of a subject nationality; for mercilessness and outrage the Cossacks had already acquired in her Asian wars a terrible reputation which the deeds of the Bashi-bazouks by no means obliterated. These were not reflections that Beaconsfield and his colleagues could utter in public about a professedly friendly nation; but they had a large share in determining their policy, and, after a while, in steadying the country.

In July, 1875, the torch was applied to the combustible elements in the Turkish Emp re by a partial revolt in Herzegovina, which did not appear at first to have more than local consequence. But such was the inefficiency of Turkish administration that the Porte was unable to cope, in an outlying province, with even so paltry a disturbance as this; and the fire, as the autumn advanced, spread till it embraced the whole of Bosnia as well as Herzegovina. Disraeli was anxious from the first, especially as the attitude of Austria, the neighbouring Great Power to the disturbed countries, with many Slav subjects of its own, was ambiguous. He desired that Turkey should herself deal with the situation, free from outside interference; and only consented reluctantly, as the revolt spread, to joint mediation by the consuls of the Great Powers on the spot. 'There is no alternative,' he telegraphed to Derby from Weston on August 24; 'but I don't like it.' Subsequent reflection confirmed him in this opinion. He wrote to Derby on June 13, 1876 : 'The fact is, the original interference by the consuls was premature, and all the subsequent failures have been the consequence of that unripe interference.' Nothing, as might be expected, came of the consular efforts, save a profusion of paper promises by the Porte; and the insurgents continued to defeat the inadequate forces sent against them.

To Lady Bradford.

HUGHENDEN MANOR, *Aug.* 20, 1875.— . . . The affairs in European Turkey are anxious: I had four telegrams this morning. I do not think, however, matters are as serious as the newspapers make out. Now that Parliament is up, they want a sensation subject, and a little stock-jobbing is always welcome.

The moment I heard of the outbreak at all making head (I think it was the day before I went to Osborne; yes, the day of the last Cabinet and before the Fish Dinner) I conferred with Derby, and telegraphed to our Minister at Vienna to see Andrassy instantly and ascertain, if possible, his *real* wishes. Nothing cd. be more satisfactory than his reply, and if we were dealing with any one but the Turks, the failure of the insurrection wd. not only be certain, but immediate. If Austria is really neutral, or, as she professes, anxious to assist Turkey, it ought not to last, but the want of energy at Constantinople is superhuman. Tho' ruined in **their** finance, we have been always told that the Turks had,

at least, created an army and a fleet, and both of a high class;
but I only hear, after repeated appeals, from our Ambassador,
that they have scraped together less than 2,000 men, and
are sending them in slow-sailing merchant transports.   They
cd. not reach the scene of war, were it not for Austria. . . .

To Anne Lady Chesterfield.

HUGHENDEN MANOR, *Aug.* 21.—. . . This dreadful Herzegovina affair, wh. had there been common energy, or perhaps
pocket-money even, among the Turks, might have been
settled in a week.

To Lady Bradford.

BRETBY PARK, *Aug.* [*Sept.*] 6.—. . . The Herz. affair,
and Danubian politics in general, are in a very unsatisfactory state.   Andrassy is quite undecided, or playing a double
game: perhaps both.

It is curious, but since the fall of France, who used to give
us so much alarm and so much trouble, the conduct of foreign
affairs for England has become infinitely more difficult.
There is no balance, and unless we go out of our way to act
with the three Northern Powers, they can act without us,
wh. is not agreeable for a State like England.   Nor do I see,
as I have told you before, any prospect of the revival of
France as a military puissance.   She is more likely to be
partitioned than to conquer Europe again.

When I entered political life, there were three Great Powers
in danger—the Grand Signior of the Ottomans, the Pope of
Rome, and the Lord Mayor of London.   The last will survive
a long time: but the fall of France has destroyed the Pope,
and will, ultimately, drive the Turk from Europe. . . .

10, DOWNING STREET, *Sept.* 10.—. . . It is a strange thing
that, at this moment, when so much is at stake, there is not
a single Ambassador in England, and throughout the whole
of the Danubian troubles, not one of Her Majesty's Ambassadors has been at his post.   Sir A. Buchanan returned to
Vienna only two days: the rest are at God knows what waters
—probably Lethe. . . .

2, WHITEHALL GARDENS, *Friday* [*Oct.* 1].—. . . Ct.
Andrassy says that, had it not been for *The Times* leaders,
Herz. wd. have been settled.   They think they indicate the
English policy !   They indicate the policy of stock-jobbers
and idiots.

Fancy autonomy for Bosnia, with a mixed population:
autonomy for Ireland wd. be less absurd, for there are more
Turks in proportion to Xtians in Bosnia than Ulster *v.* the
three other provinces. . . .

The mixture of population and of creeds in these provinces rendered the problem, as Disraeli wrote, a most perplexing one. No part of the Balkan peninsula except Stamboul itself was more Turkish. Not only were there the customary horde of Turkish officials, but the owners of the soil, though Slav by race, were Moslems in religion and Turkish in political feeling. At the time of the Turkish conquest their ancestors, to save their property and privileges, ' abandoned their faith and embraced Mohammedanism, not only with discretion, but with zeal.'[1] Out of a population of some 1,100,000 nearly 400,000 seem to have been Mohammedans; and among the remainder, the Christian Slav population, the bulk of whom were peasants, there was an acute religious division, a quarter being Roman Catholics, and three-quarters belonging to the Orthodox Church. It was not a hopeful field for an experiment in autonomy.

Even the feeble efforts which the Porte had made to grapple with the insurrection had overtaxed finances weakened by a persistent course of misgovernment; and in October the situation was rendered immensely more complex and difficult by the Sultan's announcement that he could no longer pay the full interest on the public debt. Disraeli began to realise that the Eastern Question was reopened and that his opportunity in foreign affairs had come; and he girded up his loins to play, as the Prime Minister of Great Britain, a chief part on the international stage.

To Lady Bradford.

2, WHITEHALL GARDENS, *Nov.* 3, 1875.—. . . Matters are large and pressing. Five weeks ago Russia, and indeed all the Great Powers, agreed ' the Herz. question was settled.' The Prince of Servia changed his Ministry, at their dictation, to ensure that result. But this extraordinary, and quite unforeseen, bankruptcy of the Porte has set everything again in flame, and I really believe ' the Eastern Question,' that has haunted Europe for a century, and wh. I thought the Crimean War had adjourned for half another, will fall to my lot to encounter—dare I say to settle ?

[1] Marriott's *Eastern Question*, p. 282.

Fortunately R. Bourke, Und.-Secy. for For. Affairs, is in town, and he comes and works with me.[1] I find him most intelligent, extremely well informed, and if not up in every-thing, knowing how to set about getting what is wanted. I have seen the Ambassadors: they know nothing, and flatter themselves that I believe they exercise only a wise reserve. The fact is their Governments don't inform them, and these Governments themselves are very puzzled. Beust is fantas-tical and dreamy, and keeps saying ' my only, and last, instructions from Andrassy were to co-operate with you.' I know privately that Andrassy changes his mind every week or day, and has half a doz. intrigues at work, wh. will defeat each other. As for the charming Schou[valoff], I am perfectly convinced that, instead of being a deep and *rusé* diplomat, he does not know the A.B.C. of his business, and is perfectly sincere in his frequent asseverations to that effect.

But the most amusing thing is the mystery of that tall Münster, while a confidl. despatch from Odo Russell this morning informs us that Bismarck remains in sullen solitude, and will see no one, or write or speak. The Emperor is so afraid of him that he dare not remonstrate with him; the Crown Prince has given up speaking to him on public matters, from pure weariness, while the great mass of the Court officials only dare mention the ineffable name in a whisper, and then look round, tho' Bis. is 100 miles away. The truth is, I have no doubt, he is watching for some misunderstanding betn. Russia and Austria, and then he will be communicative enough. . . .

Nov. 4, ½ *pt.* 6 *p.m.*—. . . Ld. Derby arrived last night at five o'ck., and came on to me immediately. He was with me two hours. We resolved not to bring the Turkish affairs at present before the Cabinet, but conduct them together.

The Cab. to-day was entirely on the Admy. scrapes.[2] I am satisfied with what we have done. . . .

At three o'ck. the King of Denmark came, and paid me a visit. It was rather inopportune, as I was rather tired and had to see Lord Saly. at four o'ck. on the affairs of Central Asia. . . .

Ld. Salisbury has just gone. And we have agreed to do, with respect to Central Asia, exactly as Lord Derby and myself had previously agreed to do about Turkey.

[1] Derby was at Knowsley, and Disraeli was seeing the foreign diplomatists, and dealing with urgent telegrams, on his behalf.
[2] See pp. 736-738.

To Queen Victoria.

Nov. 6, 1875.—. . . Affairs in European Turkey, and in Central Asia, require constant thought and vigilance, but Mr. Disraeli has able colleagues in these matters, and thinks he knows well the tone which your Majesty would expect, and approve, that your Ministers should adopt. On Lord Mayor's Day Mr. Disraeli must say something, that will give the note of your Majesty's policy on these great matters. He will be cautious—but not timid. . . .

What Disraeli said at Guildhall was that, now that the financial catastrophe in Turkey had revived the struggle in Bosnia, it could not be denied that circumstances were critical. The Great Powers immediately interested, however, had exercised, and he believed would continue to exercise, a wise forbearance; and he was therefore convinced that peace would be maintained and the public opinion of Europe satisfied. But he significantly added that, though the interests of the Imperial Powers in this question were more direct, they were not more considerable than those of Great Britain; and ' those to whom the conduct of your affairs is now entrusted are deeply conscious of the nature and magnitude of those ' British interests, and those British interests they are resolved to guard and maintain.' The speech was well received at home and abroad.

To Lady Bradford.

2, WHITEHALL GARDENS, *Nov.* 10, 1875.—. . . I think yesterday was very successful; at least everyone seems to think so. I had a great reception, and spoke pretty well. Wonderful how one can speak at all, after sitting for hours in a great glaring hall, amid the wassailing of a 1,000 guests, and seated between existing and ex-Lady Mayoresses ! . . .

Nov. 13.—. . . You will be glad to hear that the Guildhall speech really effected all my purpose, and has been hailed by all parties: in short by the country.

In the hunting field yesterday—Vale of Aylesbury—the great Mr. Horsman, my ' superior person,' who always decries everything and everybody, gave it as his opinion that ' it was the greatest speech since Mr. Pitt.' But after all, what is to come ? My speech is only *point de jour :* the day has

hardly broken, and we shall probably have a flaming sun
and a sultry sky. I hope our sixty years of peace have not
been a Capua to us, and that the English people have yet
some spirit. ' Live in a blaze and in a blaze expire !' wd.
content me, but I won't be snuffed out. . . .

This Guildhall speech deserves especial attention.
Disraeli, as we have seen, based the whole of his Near
Eastern policy on the Treaty of Paris as modified by the
Treaty of London; an absolutely impregnable position
from the diplomatic standpoint. Now the history of
both instruments shows that, internationally, this
country, owing to her undoubted interests, had constantly asserted, and had been as constantly conceded,
a powerful voice in any modification of the Eastern
settlement. Yet when the question was reopened in
1875, the three Imperial Powers, Russia, Austria, and
Germany—two of them, certainly, Turkey's nearest
neighbours, and the third the dominant State in Europe
—assumed from the first the right to take the lead in
shaping European policy, in drafting international instruments. Neither Austria nor Prussia had fought when
the matter was last brought, in the Crimean War, to the
decision of arms, but Austria, though deeply interested,
had then played an ambiguous, and Prussia an indifferent
(or possibly treacherous) part. Nevertheless, these two
Powers now affected to be the natural representatives,
over against Russia, of the interests of Europe and
of Turkey; not seeking, until after they had formulated their conclusions, for the adhesion of France,
England, and Italy, who had poured out blood and
treasure in the cause. It was, perhaps, reasonable to
assume that Italy, whose participation in the Crimean
War had been an astute move by Cavour to forward the
unity of his country, had lost interest in the Eastern
Question since that unity had been achieved; and unfortunately France, owing to the events of 1870 and
1871, was in no position to assert a claim to a leading
voice. But the disregard of England was flagrant, and

II.   29

showed how, after a five years' experience of Gladstone, the estimate of her international weight had declined. Disraeli was not the man to put up with slighting treatment for his country; especially in a matter which, in his judgment, was of vital concern to her.

The Imperial Powers paid no attention this winter to Disraeli's hint that Great Britain's interests in the solution of the Eastern Question were as considerable as theirs. They had, as he admitted, a more 'immediate' and 'direct' interest; and, in view of the spread of the revolt and the increasing unrest in the neighbouring Slav provinces of Turkey, they consulted together, and made the Austrian Foreign Minister, Count Andrassy, the mouthpiece of their demands on the Porte. The Andrassy note pressed upon the Sultan a series of reforms, some of which he had already promised on paper to grant and of which others were, as a rule, in themselves desirable, and urged their immediate concession in act; otherwise the Powers could not continue to assist in the pacification of the disturbed districts. The note was despatched on December 30 to France, Italy, and Great Britain, with a request for their adherence. That adherence Disraeli hesitated to give.

To Lord Derby.

(*Telegram.*) HUGHENDEN, *Jan.* 9, 1876. 2.15.—Three considerations first strike me—

Firstly. Is Austria justified in sending a note advising measures which the Porte has, generally speaking, announced, with the exception of one or two points which are extremely vague, and which, so far as they are intelligible, would appear to be erroneous in principle and pernicious in practice ?

Secondly. This would seem an act of imbecility or of treachery. It may begin in one and end in the other. In all probability it will have no effect upon existing circumstances; then Austria and Russia, who probably contemplate an ulterior policy or should do so, will turn round upon the other Powers and say, 'The advice you gave has been rejected, you are bound to see that it is carried into effect.'

Thirdly. Whether in the advice which we are asked to give Turkey, we are not committing ourselves to principles which are, or which may be soon, matter of controversy in our own country: for instance, the apportionment of local taxation to local purposes and the right of the peasantry to the soil.

These are three suggestions which occur to me, which should make us hesitate, but there are others. . . .

Confidential. (*Same day.*) I sent you, this morning, a figured telegram, conveying some of my impressions respecting the Austrian note. . . . I cannot resist expressing to you, by letter as well, my strong conviction, that we should pause before assenting to the Austrian proposal.

You know how great is my confidence in your judgment, and, therefore, you can better appreciate the hesitation wh. I feel in differing from the course wh. you recommend.

I think it will land us in a false position, and it would be preferable to appear isolated, wh. I usually deprecate, than, for the sake of a simulated union, wh. will not last many months, embarrass ourselves, when independent action may be necessary.

In declining to identify ourselves, as requested, with the note, is it necessary to appear as Turkish, or more Turkish, than the Turks ? Could we not devise a course wh. might avoid that ?

P.S.—I forgot to say, that the Great Lady wishes to see you, whom she rarely sees. Is this a complaint or a compliment ?

Disraeli's hesitations were overcome, not by Derby's arguments, but by the direct request of the Porte, eager no doubt to agree with its adversaries quickly, and also glad to have a sincere friend to its independence and integrity sitting on the European Areopagus assembled for its reform.

To Lady Bradford.

2, WHITEHALL GARDENS, *Jan.* 18.—. . . Our delay so alarmed Austria, who is afraid of Hungary, that Andrassy had offered all sorts of concessions to the Porte, provided the Porte wd. signify to England that the Porte wished us to join the other Powers. And, the day I was with D[erby], he expected this: and sure enough, yesterday Musurus brought it. We can't be more Turkish than the Sultan—*plus Arabe que l'Arabie.*

I think they have only postponed the crisis; wh. will happen in spring, I fancy. . . .

The Government, accordingly, in the words put into Her Majesty's mouth at the opening of Parliament in

1876, considered it to be their duty ' not to stand aloof '
from the action of the Imperial Powers; but they made
it clear that, if they ' joined in urging on the Sultan the
expediency of adopting such measures of administrative
reform as may remove all reasonable cause of discontent
on the part of his Christian subjects,' they intended to
' respect the independence of the Porte.'   There was a
general acceptance of the policy; but public opinion was
as yet apathetic on the Turkish question, being concentrated on the Suez Canal purchase, the Anti-Slavery
Circular, the Prince's Indian tour, and the augmentation of the Royal Title.   A valuable memorandum[1] by
Northcote on the Eastern Question shows the views
expressed in Parliament by the leaders of Opposition.

Parliament approved our course, Lord Granville and Lord
Hartington seeming a little jealous of our following the lead
of Austria, and putting in a word on behalf of the ' independence of the Ottoman Empire,' Gladstone, on the other
hand, cordially approving our acting with the other Powers,
and expressing his hope that we were going seriously to press
for Turkish reforms.   I remember Disraeli's wondering what
he meant by his rather curious speech, which at the moment
seemed somewhat uncalled for; but it is worth looking back
to as containing the germ of much that he has said since.

The acceptance by the Powers of the Andrassy note
gave diplomacy a respite.   The Porte, as usual, was
profuse in promises; time must be given to see the outcome.   In the interval of waiting, Bismarck, conscious
of the entry of a disregarded Power into the diplomatic
arena, made overtures to England for common action.
After the threat to France in the preceding spring his
proposals were naturally regarded with caution.

Lord Derby to Queen Victoria.

Feb. 10.—Lord Derby, with his humble duty, submits to
your Majesty that he has received your Majesty's letter

[1] Several extracts from this memorandum, written after the close of the
1874-1880 Government, were printed in Chapter 14 of Andrew Lang's
Life of Sir Stafford Northcote, published in 1890.   The 2nd Lord Iddesleigh
kindly sanctioned the use of further passages, which it would have been
indiscreet to make public a generation ago.

on the subject of the wish expressed by Prince Bismarck for free and unreserved interchange of ideas on Eastern affairs.

Lord Derby respectfully ventures to agree in the view taken by your Majesty of this offer: that it is one to be accepted, as the assistance of Prince Bismarck in carrying into effect English views on Eastern subjects might under certain circumstances be of incalculable value.

Lord Derby accordingly proposes to meet Prince Bismarck's overtures in the same spirit of cordial friendship between the two Governments in which they seem to be made. He must, however, bear in mind that more may be intended by this communication than meets the eye. He cannot possess implicit confidence in Prince Bismarck's desire of peace, remembering the events of last spring. And he would like to see more clearly than he does what assistance England is expected to give in return for that which is offered.

These necessary reservations need not, however, interfere with the reception of Prince Bismarck's proposal. If sincere, it cannot be too cordially met: if designs are kept in the background which may not be compatible with English interests, they will be most easily discovered by an apparent absence of all suspicion.

To Lord Derby.

2, WHITEHALL GARDENS, S.W., *Feb.* 15, '76.—I will not return the drt. despatch to Mr. V. Lister, but to yourself.

After reading it several times, I have not altered a word of yr. composition, for I find it is something that is wanting, not what is present, that jars a little on me. It ends with a matter of detail instead of closing with the chief theme, so that the effect is rather chilling.

You have to deal with a man who is dangerous, but who is sincere; and who will act straightforwardly with an English Minister whose sense of honor he appreciates; a man, too, very sensitive and impulsive.

The step he is now taking is one wh., I believe, he has long and often meditated, but he was piqued by our doctrinaire non-intervention, and all that.

I send a sketch of a concluding paragraph wh. you can adopt or alter, as you like.

[Sketch of concluding Parag.]

In conveying to you these remarks, I would, however, observe, that, tho' the fall of Count Andrassy and some other contingencies wh. I need not now dwell on, might be events, the tendency of which would certainly not be favorable to

the maintenance of peace, still, if a concerted action on public
affairs between Germany and England be established, as
intimated by Prince Bismarck, and wh. wd. meet the views
of H.M. Government and, as I believe, would be responded
to by the feelings and convictions of both countries, the
chances of so great a calamity as a general, or even considerable, war would, in my opinion, be infinitely reduced.

From Lord Derby.

Private.   F. O.   F[eb.] 15, '76.—I like your paragraph very
well, but with your consent would prefer to make it, or
the substance of it, into a separate draft.   The draft sent
to you was never intended as an answer to Bismarck's overtures, which I reserved until I could get from Russell an
answer to questions put to him in a private letter, these
questions being what you and I agreed upon.

The draft I sent you is a mere record of a conversation
which took place, and which I thought it as well to set down.
If you will let that go as it stands, I will supplement it in
the way you suggest.

Even when drafted according to Disraeli's suggestions,
Derby's reply to Bismarck's overtures did not prove
to be sufficiently encouraging to detach the German
Chancellor from his co-operation with Gortchakoff and
Andrassy; and the Imperial Powers continued on their
own way without taking any special account of this
country.   The Andrassy note produced as little effect
as the consular intervention of the autumn.   The revolt
continued to spread; Serbia and Montenegro prepared to
support their Slav brethren; and the situation was made
more acute by the murder, early in May, of the French
and German consuls at Salonika by Mohammedan rioters.
These events moved Bismarck, Gortchakoff, and Andrassy
to meet again, and draw up, mainly under Russian
inspiration, fresh proposals at Berlin; while France and
Germany sent ships of war to Salonika in order to exact
punishment, and to secure their interests in the future.

To Lord Derby.

Confidential.   HUGHENDEN MANOR, *April* 19, 1876.—. . . I
say nothing about Turkish affairs.   You are a younger man

than yr. friend and correspondent, and will have eno' to do for the rest of yr. life in these matters.

April 20.—. . . Altho' I am not very surprised at the position of Turkish affairs, I confess there is something cynical about Gortchakoff's treatment, wh. I think is not exactly respectful to us, after his representations. But with no Russian Ambassador here, and a mere Polonius at St. Petersburg, it is difficult to ascertain with precision the situation.

The illimitable trust wh. all the Great Powers have in Andrassy, while, apparently, they do everything to counteract his efforts, would be amusing were it not so dangerous. . . .

May 8.—. . . It appears to me, that we are hardly taking as much advantage as we might of Bismarck's original overture to us. Odo writes, as if it were something that had happened in a dream.

We ought to have revived the feeling previous to the arrival of Gortchakoff and the Austrian, so that Bismarck shd. take no step with[ou]t apprising and consulting us.

If the projected understanding between Germany and us is only a mirage, the sooner we ascertain that the better.

Confidential. W[HITEHALL] G[ARDENS], *May 15.*—I must, I am sorry to say, again complain of the want of order and discipline in your office.

The Queen sent to me twice on Saturday to enquire, whether there was news from Berlin, and wrote to me on her point of departure, requesting that I wd. forward the expected information immediately.

I did not go to the German Embassy on Saturday, but I have since heard, that the communication made to the excluded Ambassadors was generally known there.

Nothing had reached me, and on Sunday morning, when the messenger went to Windsor, I had to inform the Queen that Her Majy's Govt. knew nothing.

At one o'ck. I received Odo Russell's tel., wh. left Berlin at 5 o'ck. on Saturday, and wh. ought to have been here before you left town!

I sent instantly to the 'Resident Clerk' for an explanation, and with an enquiry (to have in writing) at what hour the Berlin tel. reached him. The 'Resident Clerk' was not in residence!

I believe yr. office is very badly managed—the clerks attend there later, than any other public office, witht. the excuse of being worked at night as they were by Palmn.[1]

---

[1] There seems to be no doubt that the Foreign Office was at this period understaffed, so that at times of crisis the Permanent Under-Secretary of State and the clerks in the political departments were overworked. The staff was, accordingly, shortly afterwards enlarged.

It is only a default at a most critical moment like the present, that the negligence becomes insufferable—and so one complains. I say nothing here of the contents of the tel., respecting wh. we can confer when you like.

The Queen complains that she never receives tels. direct; only in a bag when they are stale.

The Berlin memorandum, which reached Disraeli in the manner described in the last letter, contained proposals considerably in advance of the Andrassy note. An armistice of two months was to be insisted on, during which terms should be discussed between the Porte and the insurgents on the following basis: materials to be furnished by the Porte for the reconstruction of houses and churches destroyed; relief to be distributed in consultation with a mixed Commission representing both Christians and Mussulmans; Turkish troops to be concentrated, to avoid collisions; Christians as well as Mussulmans to retain arms; the consuls or delegates of the Powers to preside over the application of reforms. The importance of the memorandum, however, lay, not so much in these detailed suggestions, as in its conclusion that, if the armistice expired without the objects of the Powers being obtained, it would be necessary to reinforce diplomatic action by ' efficacious ' measures. To Disraeli the detailed proposals appeared to be impracticable or injudicious, and the final threat, in which he recognised the hand of Russia, incompatible with the British policy of maintaining the integrity and independence of Turkey. He resented, moreover, on his country's behalf, the peremptory demand for immediate adhesion to proposals from the framing of which Great Britain had been excluded. He drafted a note embodying his views, and read it to the Cabinet on Tuesday, May 16. His manner, Northcote says, was of ' unusual solemnity,' and he spoke of the question as by far the most important that had come before the Cabinet since its formation. This was the note:

Most Confidential. 10, DOWNING ST., *May* 16, 1876.— Mr. Disraeli fears, that we are being drawn, step by step, into participating in a scheme, which must end very soon in the disintegration of Turkey.

Though we may not be able to resist the decision of the three Military Empires, he does not think that we ought to sanction, or approve, their proposals.

It is almost a mockery for them to talk of a desire, that the Powers should ' act in concert ' and then exclude France, Italy, and England from their deliberations, and ask us by telegraph to say yes or no to propositions, which we have never heard discussed.

Moreover it is asking us to sanction them in putting a knife to the throat of Turkey, whether we like it or not.

Although the three Northern Powers have acted in a somewhat similar way twice during the last eight months, we had upon those two occasions no great difficulty in joining them, as we were asked to do so by the Porte.

Can we expect Turkey to make us the same request now ? Mr. Disraeli thinks not, and that it would be impolitic for us to agree if she did, and for these five principal reasons:

(1) He believes it is impossible for the Sultan to reconstruct the houses and churches of the insurgents, or to find food for the refugees.

(2) The distribution of relief by means of such a Commission as that proposed, would be a huge system of indiscriminate almsgiving, totally beyond the power of the Porte to effect, and utterly demoralising to any country.

(3) The concentration of troops in certain places would be delivering up the whole country to anarchy, particularly when the insurgents are to retain their arms.

(4) The ' consular supervision ' would reduce the authority of the Sultan to a nullity; and, without a force to support it, supervision would be impossible.

(5) The hope of restoring tranquillity by these means being, in Mr. Disraeli's opinion, groundless, we should then be asked to ' join in taking more efficacious measures in the interests of peace,' which, it is supposed, means taking more efficacious measures to break up the Empire.

In Mr. Disraeli's opinion it would be far better for Turkey to give up Bosnia and Herzegovina altogether, as Austria gave up Italy, than to acquiesce in the new proposals, and it would also be better for us that she should do so, than adopt the alternative now offered.

He would say, if Turkey agrees, we are ready to recommend an armistice and a European Conference based upon the territorial *status quo*.

One word as to the first part of the project which was not

even alluded to in the telegram from Berlin. He thinks that we ought to take care that neither we, nor any other Power, send ships of war to Constantinople on the pretence of protecting the Christians.

But above all it is taking a leap in the dark to act in this matter before we know what Turkey herself thinks of the new programme, and it would seem that we may fairly tell the three Northern Powers that a general concert cannot be attained by the course they are adopting.

The Cabinet came to a unanimous decision not to adhere to the Berlin proposals; and telegrams to this effect were immediately despatched to the Ambassadors abroad. In one respect the policy recommended by Disraeli to his colleagues was almost immediately modified. Lest the fanaticism, which had broken out at Salonika, should spread to Constantinople, the British fleet was ordered on May 24, not indeed to Constantinople, but to Besika Bay, just outside the Dardanelles, as a measure of precaution. The orders were given on representations received from the diplomatic body at Constantinople, and other nations took similar action.

Gladstone and others have maintained that the refusal to adopt the Berlin memorandum was the initial mistake of the Government; that it broke up the Concert of Europe, and encouraged the Porte to rely on the support of Great Britain against pressure from the Powers on behalf of the oppressed Christian nationalities. If so, hardly anyone in England except Gladstone himself objected to it at the time. The action of the Government was accepted as a prudent and dignified course by the country and by the leaders of Opposition. Hartington, as already noted, said on June 9, ' I do not believe there exists in the country any distrust of the proceedings of Her Majesty's Government.' And Granville not only expressed, on June 26, provisional approval of the non-adherence to the Berlin memorandum, but also, after two months' reflection, said on July 31, the day on which Gladstone attacked Ministers in the House of Commons on this very point: ' I agree that it would not have been wise to accede to that document. . . . As a whole it was not acceptable.' The only question that was raised here at the time—and it was raised both in Cabinet and in Parliament—was whether it would not have been advisable for England to put forward an alternative, or at least to have advocated the calling of a Conference or Congress. The idea of a Conference was constantly before Disraeli's mind, to be convened at the proper moment. When it was suggested before the end of May by the Queen, who was at first uneasy about the rejection of the memorandum, he replied that the idea was excellent but premature. 'There has been a full meal, and a little digestion is required.' As to alternative proposals generally, there was force in his argument in Parliament on July 31, that there would have been little chance of their acceptance by three Great Powers who had just given all their intelligence and influence to the production of their own scheme for settlement

Their self-love, their just pride, their somewhat mortified feeling at the course which we had taken, all would have impelled them to reject our proposition. And my own opinion is that it is not a wise thing for a country, and a country like England, to make proposals which it has not the means of carrying into effect, and to sketch a policy, which is never difficult to do, but which a country like this ought certainly not to entertain unless it entertained it in a serious, practical, and determined manner.

But, if no serious objection was raised at home to Disraeli's policy, undoubtedly England's refusal to endorse the Berlin memorandum surprised and disturbed the European chanceries, accustomed as they had become to take their cue from Bismarck. France and Italy, who had themselves hastened to accept, forwarded remonstrances. Lord Odo Russell telegraphed from Berlin that the refusal would have 'serious consequences,' and followed up his telegram by letters to the same effect. Disraeli was not impressed. 'Whatever is done now,' he wrote to Derby on May 18, ' the consequences will probably be serious.' And on May 29, 'I do not like Lord Odo's letter, or anything, so far as I can gather, he has done. He was not originally justified in offering his personal opinion, that our Government would accept the Russian note—an unheard-of step ! . . . He does not seem even now to comprehend the situation. I have myself no doubt that, if we are stiff, we shall gain all our points, because no one is really adverse to them, except Russia.'

The immediate course of events seemed to justify Disraeli's confidence. The Sultan Abdul Aziz, whose half-insane extravagance had been largely responsible for Turkey's internal and external difficulties, was deposed on May 29 by a palace revolution in favour of his nephew Murad; a deposition followed by the expected, if not arranged, suicide. As the *coup d'état* had been, in great part, the work of Midhat Pasha, who had a programme of constitutional reform and of friendly co-operation with foreign Powers, and especially with England, and as the new Sultan made similar professions, there was little difficulty in persuading the three Empires to withdraw the memorandum. Disraeli was accordingly able to announce in the House of Commons on June 9, ' There is a complete understanding between us and the Great Powers that there should be no undue pressure put upon the new Sovereign of Turkey; that he and his counsellors should have time to mature their measures.' All the Powers, he added, were agreed in affording the new Sultan immediate recognition. In fact, England's isolation was over; her policy had prevailed. ' Derby gets much credit, but he has needed pressure,' wrote Hardy in his diary for June 9. ' Disraeli has really been the mainspring.'

Disraeli's letters, just before and after the *coup d'état* at Constantinople, show the anxieties which weighed upon him, owing to the disorders in Turkey, Russia's suspicious policy, and the presence in Turkish waters of British and foreign ships of war. He never forgot how a policy of drift landed us in the Crimean War, and determined that we should preserve a clear and straight course now. 'Whatever happens,' he wrote to Lady Chesterfield on May 29, ' we shall certainly not drift into war, but go to war, if we do, because we intend it, and have a purpose which we mean to accomplish. I hope, however, Russia, at the bottom of the whole affair, will be sensible, and then we shall have peace.'

To Lord Derby.

2, WHITEHALL GARDENS, S.W., *May* 25, '76.—As the Ambassador[1] and Admiral[2] have come together naturally, without any intimation from us, I think we had better wait and learn the results of this spontaneous conference before we trouble them any further.

I am well satisfied with what we have done since Monday— and so far as I can judge, or learn, public opinion ratifies our course.

10, D. S., *May* 28.—. . . We must remember what is taking place in the Turkish waters is unprecedented. All the navies of Europe assembled: two of Powers never before known, and England with a novel force which she has never tried in battle; while at Constantinople itself there is in numbers a formidable fleet, but without ammunition and without crews.

These Turkish waters have been the frequent scene of *coups de main*. Even in our own time, among others, we have the abduction of the fleet by Egypt, Unkiar Skelessi, and Sinope.

The Turkish fleet is at present, in everybody's mind, a prize the possession of which may influence the fate of nations. The imminent danger—*i.e.*, a few weeks ago—was in my opinion from the side of the Bosphorus. Had Ignatieff succeeded in inducing the frightened Sultan to admit a Russian garrison and place his fleet under the guardianship of Russia, the difficulties would have been great. It is to be hoped that the personal influence of our Ambassador acting on changed circumstances may prevent any repetition of such efforts, if, as is believed, they were ever made.

The danger from the Dardanelles is of another kind. The Treaty of 1841 must not be violated. That should be a cardinal principle with us. But, if violated, there is but little compensation to be found in the consciousness that we have made a protest.

---

[1] Sir Henry Elliot.　　　[2] Sir James Drummond.

What if secret instructions were given to the Admiral that if any of the naval forces assembled propose to violate the Treaty of 1841 he should warn them that it must be on their responsibility and that he is instructed to maintain that Treaty by force ?

Before we decide on anything, it might be as well to hear the result of the interview between the Ambassador and the Admiral. After all, at a conjuncture like the present almost everything depends on the Ambassador. He must not depend too much on his instructions; he must rely on good information, on his own quickness of perception, resolution, and fertility of resource.

May 31.—Elliot tells us nothing as to who brought all this[1] about. It is always one man who does these things. It ought to have been Elliot himself, but that I fear is not the case.

What will happen ? Until we know we can hardly, I fear, shape our course. If the Turks were to establish ' a Constitution,' they would go up in the market of Europe, which is always liberal, and perhaps get a new loan.

But pray think of our last conversation as to possible Congress. I feel convinced it is the only practical solution in the long run. Conference or Congress on the basis of *status quo ;* admitting creation of new vassal States, but *sine qua non*, no increase of the territory of any existing vassal State. If Bismarck agrees to this, the affair is finished and for a generation.

I am very anxious about Besika Bay and its contents.

Instructions as I intimated mean, you say, ' war.'

That depends entirely on the men instructed. With a competent Ambassador and Admiral it should mean *peace* not *war*.

The Ambassador and Admiral under existing circumstances must be in confidential communication with the other envoys and commanders, and it is their principal duty to make these colleagues aware of contingencies.

Instructions may lead to war, but non-instructions may bring about catastrophes. Witness Navarino ! The circumstances were very similar, and the British Admiral was left entirely without instructions.

To Lady Bradford.

HUGHENDEN MANOR, *June* 6, 1876.—. . . I can say nothing about affairs, wh. no one can penetrate at this moment. I will only say that I see not the slightest cause of regret for

[1] The *coup d'état* at Constantinople.

the course I have taken. It requires calmness, wh. no one
I have to deal with possesses in an eminent degree, except
Derby, who takes things coolly enough: but I am not so
sure of his firmness as of his salutary apathy. However, I
think we shall do, and that Prince Gortchakoff has found
out by this time that he is not always to have his own
way. . . .

June 7.—. . . We have not had much leisure here, for
tels. from all quarters of the globe are showered on us, but
one can bear it when things go well. I like the look of things,
and shd. not be surprised if I accomplished exactly, and
entirely, all I intended. That ought to satisfy a man.

But the stakes are high. Generally speaking, there is no
gambling like politics; but when you have to deal only with
Emperors and High Chancellors, and Empires are on the
main, the excitement, I suppose, a little increases. . . .

Breathe nothing to any human being of my general feeling
as to affairs, except of course to B[radford], who is, always,
I know, discreet. . . .

To Lord John Manners.

HUGHENDEN MANOR, June 7, '76.—. . . It is a source of
great satisfaction to me, that you are with the Queen at this
trying moment. It is of the last importance, that H.M.
should have with her a trusty counsellor and a man of the
world, and one who possesses my entire confidence.

I see nothing to regret in the course we have followed;
indeed much the reverse.

The refusal to sanction the Berlin note: the sending the
Queen's fleet to the Turkish waters: the friendly warning to
the Governments of the assembled navies to remember and
respect treaties: all this forms a policy of determination, and
yet is consistent with a sincere love of peace, which, I believe,
it will secure.

I look upon the tripartite confederacy to be at an end.
It was an unnatural alliance, and never would have occurred
had England maintained, of late years, her just position in
public affairs.

I think not only peace will be maintained, but that Her
Majesty will be restored to her due and natural influence in
the government of the world. . . .

In spite of Odo Russell's forebodings, the independent
line taken by the British Government only strengthened
Bismarck's respect for Disraeli and his Cabinet.

To Lady Bradford.

HOUSE OF COMMONS, *June* 13, 1876.—. . . The great man at Berlin has completely realised my expectations. He is in the highest spirits and good humor. He delights in the whole affair, and particularly praised ' Disraeli's speeches' to Odo Russell, ' and his sending the fleet to the Dardanelles !' and then he fell into a fit of laughing at Gortchakoff—but I think I must tell you to burn this letter : at any rate, I will stop my pen.

Schou. was with Lord Derby yesterday, as I had arranged— and they had a very interesting conversation. I think things look as well as possible; but we must be prepared yet for stranger vicissitudes and trials of our mettle. So much the better ! These are politics worth managing. . . .

To Anne Lady Chesterfield.

2, WHITEHALL GARDENS, *June* 18.—It is not very easy, dear darling, to write letters when one's mind is entirely absorbed, and with an awful weight of responsibility on one's shoulders : so that Lord Derby said to me yesterday, that he cd. scarcely attend to general business, and really thought at all times of only one subject. You say ' everybody is at my feet.' Yes ! it may be so—but the thing is to keep them there. Gortchakoff won't give up his game easily. I see before me a period of great danger, agitation, and difficulty. I am pretty well, and if I cd. save myself from those terrible late nights in the H. of Commons shd. be able, perhaps, to guide the ship a little longer. . . .

Representations were constantly reaching the Queen during the last week of May and the early weeks of June from the Emperor William, the Crown Princess, and the Crown Prince, to the effect that Berlin had no special interest in the Eastern Question, and only co-operated with St. Petersburg and Vienna in virtue of an agreement between the three Empires in 1872, under which all important political questions were to be discussed, as far as possible, *à trois ;* that Germany under Bismarck was anxious for co-operation with England; that, if England would give the lead, Germany would follow. Disraeli, at the Queen's request, sent her this letter, describing British policy, to be forwarded to the Crown Prince :

To Queen Victoria.

June 18, 1876.—Mr. Disraeli . . . has read with deep interest the letter of the Crown Prince. Mr. Disraeli will say at once, simply and clearly, that your Majesty's Ministers are ready and willing to act with Prince Bismarck. They have endeavoured to convey that wish and resolution on their part frequently, and as they thought unmistakably, to His Highness. It is not to encourage controversy, when he wishes to lay the foundation of permanent and powerful co-operation, that Mr. Disraeli ventures to observe that, if Prince Bismarck is so anxious for these ends, it is to be regretted that he should have joined in the Berlin note without even stipulating that England should have a voice in the matter.

However, this is not a reproach: only a remark. Ready to act with Prince Bismarck, Mr. Disraeli would observe that, at this particular moment, your Majesty's Ministers have nothing to propose in the way of pacificatory measures. All have agreed that the new Sultan must have time to negotiate with the insurgents, and, if he fail, and they persist in continuing the struggle with the avowed object of achieving their independence, Mr. Disraeli does not see what kind of mediation is possible. We can in that case only see that there is fair play. . . .

Derby, a couple of days later, explained in more detail the policy which he and Disraeli were pursuing. The language in which he described the extreme difficulties of England's diplomatic situation recalls the terms of Disraeli's letter to Lady Bradford of September 6 in the previous autumn.[1]

Lord Derby to General Ponsonby.

F. O., *June* 20, 1876.—I quite agree—if I may venture to say so—in the view which Her Majesty takes of the existing state of things. We shall have to be on our guard against appearing as the supporters of Turks against Christians in the East. This is the danger, and neither Mr. Disraeli nor I are blind to it. All we have done, and all we ought to do, is to see fair play. We are very far from being out of the difficulty: indeed if the report be true that the Prince of Servia has asked for the Governorship of Bosnia, the real troubles are just about to begin. The demand is so absurd that it can be put forward only as an excuse for a quarrel;

[1] See above, p. 885.

and I doubt whether even Russian influence could prevent war, if it were made and refused.

I agree that we ought to have no antagonism with Russia. I do not believe the Czar or his responsible advisers desire to break up the Turkish Empire at present.

But the conduct of their agents in all places is absolutely at variance with the language held at Petersburg: showing either great duplicity or great administrative weakness. I believe in the existence of both, but more especially of the latter. I am as anxious as anyone to keep well with the Russians, but there is no acting with people when you cannot feel sure that they are telling truth.

In one word; I assent to everything contained in your letter, and am, and have been, endeavouring to follow the line which it indicates.

But the difficulties are many: not the least being the impossibility of relying on any one outside England.

Andrassy does not know his own mind for a week together. Bismarck wants us just now, but he is not exactly the person whom one can implicitly confide in: what I think of the Russian policy has been said above: France will do whatever Russia wishes. It is scarcely possible for us to be too cautious.

The steadiness and independence of British policy under Disraeli and Derby, the general support it received at home, and the tendency of Bismarck to rally to it, were not without their effect on Russia, and she showed herself disposed to moderate, or at least minimise, her own designs and those of her Balkan *protégés*.

To Lord Derby.

Confidential. 2, WHITEHALL GARDENS, *June* 24, '76.—I met Schou. last night at dinner, and he got me in a corner before he went to Beust's Ball.

He was full of matter: clear, for him calm, and not at all claret-y. This is the upshot, wh. I thought you ought to know.

The affairs must be settled: there must be a thoro' good understanding between Eng. and Russia. The despatch was one of *confiance* and *bon vouloir*. This he repeated often: at last, he asked me whether I did not think it so ? Obliged to speak, I said I cd. not doubt it, but he must admit, that with all its *confiance*, etc., it suggested, or proposed, a great deal.

'Really,' he replied, ' not more than, we believe, you wish

and is for your interest. But, if you disapprove, propose yourselves and we will follow you.'

Now this is the important part.

'England is under a false impression about autonomy: we do not propose, or wish, a military or political autonomy; only an administrative one. The Sultan may have his troops, his fortresses, his political officers, provided the people may manage their own affairs.

'As for Montenegro, it has got about that Russia is intriguing for a port under the pretence of increasing the territory of Montenegro. No such thing: we renounce the idea, Montenegro need have no port, only a little garden to grow cabbages and potatoes. We do not care for Servia as we do for Montenegro, but what Servia wants is not much: and I believe the Sultan has more than once been on the point of granting what they wish.' . . .

To Queen Victoria.

H. OF C., *June 29, '76.*—Mr. Disraeli . . . has the honor to acknowledge the receipt, forwarded by General Ponsonby, of the copy of a letter from H.R.H. the Princess Louis of Hesse, dated the 27th of June, on which Mr. Disraeli ventures to make one or two observations.

With respect to the remark that His Imperial Majesty and Prince Gortchakoff appear surprised that England, always so philanthropic, has no sympathy to assist the oppressed Christians, Mr. Disraeli would observe that the probable cause of the comparative coolness of the English people, and certainly of your Majesty's Government, in this respect, arises from the fact that they are in possession of incontestable evidence that the so-called insurgents are not natives of any Turkish province but are simply an invasion of revolutionary bands, whose strength lay in the support afforded to them by Servia and Montenegro, acting on the instigation of foreign agents and foreign committees. All this is evident from the report of your Majesty's Consuls, who are, Mr. Disraeli believes, without exception, men whose general sympathies are in favor of the Christian population. With regard to the alleged 'extremely anti-Russian feelings' of Sir H. Elliot, your Majesty's Ambassador at Constantinople appears to Mr. Disraeli to be a man of great calmness of judgment and feeling, and free from prejudice. Indeed for some time, Mr. Disraeli rather apprehended that Sir Henry was too much under the influence of the Russian Ambassador, with whom, Mr. Disraeli has heard, he was intimate and maintained confidential relations. . . . Mr. Disraeli trusts

that the despatch of Lord Derby, in reply to that of Count
Schouvaloff, which Mr. Disraeli is at this moment revising,
will remove any misconception from the minds of the Emperor
and his distinguished Minister; that they will feel that their
views are fully appreciated by your Majesty's Government,
and that your Majesty's Ministers are prepared to co-operate
with them, in every legitimate effort, not only to secure the
peace of Europe, but to improve the condition of the Christian
subjects of the Porte.

If the Russian Government was ready to co-operate
loyally with the other Powers, there was hope that the
war which Serbia and Montenegro were threatening
would be prevented. Even if it broke out, as Northcote
wrote in his memorandum, ' it was pretty sure to end
in [Servia's] defeat if she were not secretly supported
by a stronger Power. The great object was, therefore,
to bring the influence of the Powers to bear on Servia to
induce her to keep the peace.' Disraeli was ready to
use strong measures with this object.

To Lord Derby.

Confidential.   2, WHITEHALL GARDENS, S.W., *June* 28, '76.
—If war takes place between Turkey and Servia, and the
Porte is victorious, and seeks the legitimate consequences of
victory, as, for example, the restoration of Belgrade, it
shd. at once be distinctly signified to Russia, that if Russia
interfere under these circumstances, the position of affairs
will be considered by England as most grave.

Servia will not move, unless she is confident that Russia
will step in, in case of Servia being worsted, and so save her
from the consequences of her headstrong audacity.

At present, it's heads I win, tails you lose.

If this declaration, on our part, is simultaneously accompanied by a determined effort to detach Montenegro from
Servia, war will not take place—but this decided course
ought to be taken to-day. Even hours are precious.

The efforts of the Powers were unsuccessful. Serbia
declared war on Turkey on June 30; Montenegro followed
on July 1. But, though there was anxiety both in the
Ministry and in the country, the general lines of British
policy commanded confidence abroad and at home. A
deputation headed by Bright waited on Derby at the

Foreign Office on July 14, and assured him that there was no disposition to suspect or blame the Government. All that was wanted was strict neutrality, except so far as it might be possible to interpose friendly offices to bring the fighting to an end—a policy entirely in harmony with Derby's own feeling. The Government would see fair play, he said. ' We undertook, undoubtedly,' he added, ' twenty years ago, to guarantee the Sick Man against murder, but we never undertook to guarantee him against suicide or sudden death.' Disraeli's letters show his confidence, coupled with his disgust at what he conceived to be the unjustifiable action of Serbia.

To Anne Lady Chesterfield.

2, WHITEHALL GARDENS, *July* 9, 1876.—. . . I am sanguine enough to believe that, before the month terminates, the infamous invasion of the Servians will have been properly punished. All the Great Powers, Russia included, seem anxious to defer to England, and something like the old days of our authority appear to have returned.

To Lady Bradford.

2, WHITEHALL GARDENS, *July* 13.—. . . As the Emperors have now entirely adopted our policy of non-interference and neutrality, I am in great hope that the insurrection may be soon subdued, and some tolerable settlement brought about. . . .

To Queen Victoria.

2, WHITEHALL GARDENS, *July* 31.—. . . This is a terrible day of labor and some anxiety, as we have the Eastern debate to-night, and it is said that Mr. Gladstone is going to make one of his greatest efforts against your Majesty's Government, although his party have refused to support him in a vote of censure. . . .

To Lady Bradford.

2, WHITEHALL GARDENS, *Aug.* 1.—Last night went off very well. It was to have been an adjourned debate, and a great attack on Ministers, but Granville and Hartington were too sensible to indulge Gladstone's vagaries, and he so impetuous that he rose the first night, wh. gave me an opportunity to follow him; and the affair then collapsed, as I wd. not, nor could not, give them another day, as they declined

bringing forward a vote of censure. I did not speak at all
to my own satisfaction, wanting energy, and therefore fluency,
and clearness and consecutiveness of ideas, but it did well
enough, as I got out my principal thoughts, and the latter
part, not ill-reported, will be read by the country, I hope
profitably. . . .

Disraeli was justified in the satisfaction which he
expressed about this debate on July 31—the final debate
of the Session upon the general Eastern policy. ' I have
no desire,' said Hartington at its close, ' to place upon
record any condemnation of the conduct of the Government. I think that in the main the policy which they
have adopted is right, although I may have had objections
to the means they may have adopted to carry out that
policy.' Gladstone had been the only prominent speaker
who was definitely hostile; and he had combined a defence
of the Crimean War with a criticism of the rejection of the
Berlin memorandum, and a demand for ' prompt action '
which should at once preserve the territorial integrity
of Turkey and promote the free local government of the
subject races. The latter part of Disraeli's reply, on
which he relied for the enlightenment of the country,
was as follows :

I believe that the Governments of Russia and Austria have
from the first . . . sincerely and unreservedly endeavoured
to terminate these disturbances in Turkey. They felt that
it was their interest to do so, and they have been most anxious
to maintain the *status quo*. But, unfortunately, the world
consists not merely of Emperors and Governments, it consists also of secret societies and revolutionary committees;
and secret societies and revolutionary committees have been
unceasingly at work in these affairs, and they do bring about
in an Empire like Turkey most unexpected consequences,
which may have a most injurious effect on British
interests.

When we are told that we sent our fleet to the Dardanelles
in order to maintain the Turkish Empire, I deny it. . . .
The Turkish Government were never deceived on that point.
. . . They were told they must reform their course and
conduct; they must fulfil their engagements and obligations;
and that our arrival in their waters was to maintain the

interests of England and the British Empire, not to bolster up any Power that was falling into decrepitude from its own weakness.

The Turkish Government is engaged at this moment in a civil war . . .; but I cannot say that I have seen any cause at present why we should suddenly interfere. The right hon. gentleman used the expression 'prompt interference'; but at the same time he tells us he has nothing himself to propose. . . . In my opinion, it would be in the long run a very unsatisfactory interference if you did not know when you interfered what you intended, what you wished to accomplish. Her Majesty's Government have shown no disposition to avoid the liabilities which are attached to a great country like England, and which she must not shrink from. I am perfectly aware of our duties, not merely arising from treaties into which the country has entered, but the duties generally which we owe to civilisation; you cannot, however, settle these things by making speeches at public meetings. . . .

We have said from the first that we were in favour of non-interference; we have said from the first that we should observe a strict neutrality if that strict neutrality were observed by others. There has been a difference of opinion between us and the other Powers; there has been some controversy; in what has it all ended? It has all ended by the other Powers adopting our policy. . . . When I am told by the right hon. gentleman that we have lost our position in the European Concert, I am bound to say that is not the opinion of Her Majesty's Government. I believe the other Powers are most ready and prepared to act with us. . . .

The course which we have taken is the one which we believe we were called upon to pursue for the sake of our interests and for the sake of our Empire; it was the course which, in the second place, we were called upon to pursue because we believed it was most conducive to the maintenance of peace; and thirdly, also, the one which we believed would lead to the progressive improvement of the population of the Turkish Empire. If there is to be nothing but confusion, if we are to have nothing but struggles and war, if secret societies and revolutionary committees are to ride rampant over those fair provinces, I shall cordially deplore such a result as much as gentlemen who attack me very often for my want of sympathy with the sufferers by imaginary atrocities. . . .

When the occasion arrives we shall be ready to take our responsible part in what I hope may be the pacification of these countries, their advancement in civilisation, and their general improvement.

The hostile amendment was withdrawn without be'ng exposed to the risks of a division; Parliament accepted, without serious question, the general Eastern policy of the Government. Salisbury was justified in writing to Disraeli on July 27: 'It is quite evident, from the quiescence of Parliament and the country on the subject, that very general confidence is felt in the present conduct of our foreign policy; and in the shaping of that policy, the largest share is generally, and justly, attributed to you.' [1]

[1] See p. 834.

CHAPTER II.

THE BULGARIAN ATROCITIES.

1876.

The general Eastern policy of the Government was accepted; but before the debate of July 31 a side-issue had arisen, which was for some months largely to obscure the main question, and to deflect the opinions and action of men and parties, and even of nations. The unrest in European Turkey had spread before the close of April to Bulgaria, where an insurrection broke out which began with a massacre of the local Turkish officials, and which, as it was the outcome of a wide-spread conspiracy, fomented from beyond the frontier, might well have proved formidable. It was in the mountainous district round Philippopolis, in the country afterwards known as Eastern Rumelia, that this uprising occurred; not, as before, in the remote north-western corner of the Turkish Empire in Europe, but in a central province on the highway to the West. The Porte, with Bosnia and Herzegovina in revolt, and Serbia and Montenegro threatening war, determined to protect its armies from a flank attack by the ruthless suppression of the Bulgarian insurgents. Not only was a consider-able force of regular Turkish troops employed, but, before their arrival, irregulars, Bashi-bazouks and Cir-cassians, who were already settled in the country, were armed and let loose upon a mostly unarmed peasantry, committing on them terrible atrocities. The massacres and outrages which had marked the insurrection were avenged a hundredfold. Thousands perished and many villages were ravaged and destroyed. Peculiarly heinous atrocities were perpetrated at the hill town of Batak; every house in it was burnt, and five thousand people were slaughtered, neither age nor sex being spared.

These events took place in the first three weeks of May; but only very inadequate reports reached Ministers or the British public. There was no British consul at Philippopolis, the centre of disturbance; the worst horrors were perpetrated in secluded townships in the Balkan and Rhodope mountains; and such information as filtered through to Constantinople and London came either by way of Adrianople, over a hundred miles off, or from Rustchuk on the Danube, in the extreme north of the country. To what extent Sir Henry Elliot, the British Ambassador in Constantinople, was ill served, and to what extent he was deficient in energy and initiative, may be open questions; but he certainly failed to bring home to Downing Street at the time the terrible nature of the Turkish atrocities. The first detailed account appeared in the *Daily News* of June 23, a month or more after the perpetration of the crimes. It was a most lurid story, decorated with extravagant particulars which it was difficult for the judicious to believe, and which turned out eventually to be serious exaggerations.

Disraeli, with his wide knowledge of men and things, was well aware how stories of this sort tended to exaggeration; and he had shown at the time of the Indian Mutiny how sceptical in this respect was his habit of mind. That ferocity had been manifested both in the rising and in the suppression was certain from the whole history of warfare in the Balkan highlands. But he might reasonably suppose that, had the horrors perpetrated been out of the common even for that wild country, he would have received from Constantinople more detailed reports. The *Daily News*, founded in the forties, and at first edited by Charles Dickens, had won for itself by the seventies an honourable reputation; but Disraeli was not so much alive to this as to the fact that it was the leading Liberal organ, which had throughout been particularly hostile to himself and devoted to Gladstone. 'They appear,' he wrote of the horrors to Lady Bradford on July 13, 'in that journal alone, which is the real Opposition journal, and, I believe, are, to a great extent, inventions. But their object is to create a cry against the Government.' When he was questioned in the House of Commons on June 26, he said that undoubtedly there had been great ferocity shown on both sides, but that the information which the Government had received did not justify the statements made in the *Daily News*. That journal, however, continued to publish horrifying details, which were confirmed in a measure by *The Times* and from other quarters. When questioned again on July 10, Disraeli maintained substantially the same position.

With respect to the reports of the terrible atrocities to which the right hon. gentleman has referred, I would still express a hope that, when we become better informed—I would express this hope for the sake of human nature itself—when we are thoroughly informed of what has occurred, it will be found that the statements are scarcely warranted. . . . Sir Henry Elliot is not a man to be insensible to such terrible proceedings. On the contrary, he is a stern assertor of humanity, and I know no man who would more firmly and energetically interfere if he were aware of events such as those to which the right hon. gentleman has referred. . . . That there have been proceedings of an atrocious character in Bulgaria I never for a moment doubted. Wars of insurrection are always atrocious. These are wars not carried on by regular troops—in this case not even by irregular troops—but by a sort of *posse comitatus* of an armed population. We know in our own experience that one of our Colonies, an ancient colony of England—Jamaica—was the scene of transactions and of a panic which always accompanies insurrection, which no one can look back upon without horror. I cannot doubt that atrocities have been committed in Bulgaria; but that girls were sold into slavery, or that more than 10,000 persons have been imprisoned, I doubt. In fact, I doubt whether there is prison accommodation for so many, or that torture has been practised on a great scale among an Oriental people who seldom, I believe, resort to torture, but generally terminate their connection with culprits in a more expeditious manner.

At these last words there was a laugh in the House, always expectant of some humorous sally in the Prime Minister's utterances. A most unscrupulous use was made of this incident by the baser and more uncritical among his opponents. Over and over again in the next few months it was asserted that Disraeli, one of the most humane and tender-hearted of men, was so cynical as to make a public jest of unspeakable horrors inflicted by the Turks upon their Christian victims. All he meant to say, though he unfortunately employed sonorous Disraelian language, was that he could not believe the detailed accounts of the *Daily News*. Northcote has told us that he was sitting next his chief at the time he spoke, ' and heard him say to himself rather angrily, " What is there to laugh at ?" ' [1]

Disraeli, in this matter of the Bulgarian atrocities, had reason to complain, not merely of indifferent information supplied from Constantinople, but also of a carelessness in the Foreign Office, which did not see that he was provided with such information as it had.

To Lord Derby.

Confidential.   2, WHITEHALL GARDENS, *July* 14, '76.—I must again complain of the management of your office, and request your personal attention to it.

It is impossible to represent F. O. in the House of Commons, in these critical times, with[ou]t sufficient information. What I receive is neither ample, nor accurate.

---

[1] The following is an example of the latitude which clerical agitators permitted themselves to use in this controversy. The High Church Bishop of Bombay, Dr. Mylne, preaching in his Cathedral on Sept. 24, 1876, said: ' A pitiful sneer about exaggeration, a wretched jest about the murderous proclivities of those whom to our shame we call allies, is the response of the Premier of England to the wail of Christian Turkey. There was an England once, my friends, that would have brooked no cynical buffoonery in the man who directed her policy, when the question was the burning of homesteads and the ravishing of women.' Called to account by Corry, the Bishop replied on Dec. 3: ' The grounds on which I then felt warranted in making these charges . . . do not appear to me after an interval of two months to have been such that I can plead them in justification of my words. . . . I have no course open to me but to ask Lord Beaconsfield to accept such amends as can be made by my expression of regret. I should use the word " apology " instead of " expression of regret " had my original words been uttered in any other place than the pulpit.'

After I had made the declarations, wh. I did on yr. authority, respecting the Bulgarian ' atrocities,' I find a despatch from our Consul at Rustchuk, received, if I remember right, on the 28th June, and which reached me a fortnight afterwards, wh., if it do not confirm them as facts, refers to them as rumors, wh. are probable, and refers to them in some detail.

Last night Mr. Baxter gave notice of a question to be put on Monday to me—whether the Bulgarian outrages, referred to in the *Daily News*, were not regularly communicated, at the time, by our Consul at Adrianople, and whe[the]r our Ambassador at Const. had not consequently remonstrated with the Turkish Govt.

This was pretty well giving me the lie in the Ho. of Commons, and under ordinary circumstances, I shd. have at once risen, and not waited for Monday for the reply. But I have no confidence what[eve]r in yr. office, and I was obliged to submit in silence to the indignity, and, for ought I know, Monday may increase the pain of my position.

When Consul Reade's report reached Disraeli, he did not think it afforded sufficient ground for crediting the extravagant details of the newspaper correspondents:

A Consul hears, and no doubt truly, that there has been some extremely wild work on the part of some of the Bashi-bazouks, and he engages someone to go to a coffee-house frequented by these ruffians, where he listens to the reports of the wild work that has been going on. One present says, ' 5,000 or 6,000 must have perished innocently,' when another answers, ' If you had said 25,000 or 26,000 you would have been more correct,' as if exulting in the carnage. Now we know very well how difficult it is even in civilised nations with a well-organised police to obtain accurate information on such points, and how frequently we hear of 100,000 men being assembled on a public occasion when subsequent enquiry showed that the number was not more than 10,000. I was not justified for a moment to adopt that coffee-house babble brought by an anonymous Bulgarian to a Consul as at all furnishing a basis of belief that the accounts subsequently received had any justification.[1]

Disraeli was right; it *was* ' coffee-house babble '; and while it furn shed ground for investigation, it afforded no proof of the detailed charges. Indeed, the suggested

[1] House of Commons, July 31.

numbers of 25,000 to 26,000 were more than double those
which investigation ultimately showed to have perished.
But it was an indiscreet phrase, and was used by his
political opponents to deepen the impression created by
the previous incident.

Though Disraeli was sceptical, he was anxious to
discover the truth; Elliot's activities were repeatedly
st mulated from home; and a special envoy, Walter
Baring, was sent to investigate the facts. Public feeling,
however, shocked by the steadily recurrent, unrepudiated
tales of atrocity, began to take fire; and there was a
debate in the House of Commons which damaged the
Government. Even the phlegmatic Hartington said at
its close that, unless some complete defence of these
horrors could be put forward, the Porte would lose all
trace of the sympathy of England, and that it was the
duty of the Government to make the Turks understand
this.

To Lord Derby.

Confidential. H. of C., *Aug.* 7, '76.—We have had a very
damaging debate on Bulgarian atrocities, and it is lucky for
us, in this respect, that the session is dying.

Had it not been for an adroit and ingenious speech by
Bourke, who much distinguished himself, the consequences
might have been rather serious.

But two grave results are now evident:

1st. That Elliot has shown a lamentable want of energy
and deficiency of information throughout; and

2nd. That our own F. O. is liable to the same imputations.
The F. O. misled me in the first replies wh. I gave on their
voucher, and had I seen that despatch of Consul Reade,
which never reached me, I wd. never have made those answers,
and, what is more, shd. have pressed it on you to follow up
Reade's revelations.

I write this now, because Hartington wants more papers,
and wants them before Prorogation, that he may have more
damaging debates.

It is a very awkward business, and, I fear, a great exposure
of our diplomatic system abroad and at home.

Finally, on August 11, just before the close of the
Session, there was for the first time a real attack on the

Government, led by Evelyn Ashley, Shaftesbury's son,
and supported, from the front bench, by Forster in a
moderate and weighty speech, and by Harcourt in a
reckless and slashing one. Gladstone made no sign.
Harcourt ' hoped to God they had at last done with the
Turk.' European opinion, he affirmed, would support
any Power that ' would emancipate Europe from the
curse which afflicted her, and redeem Christendom from
the shame by which she had been too long dishonoured.'
By this time Baring's preliminary report had been received, fixing the number of Bulgarian victims at 12,000;
and Disraeli was able, with considerable reason, to maintain that his scepticism had been justified. The slaughter
of 12,000 individuals was certainly, he said, ' a horrible
event which no one can think of without emotion.' But
was it sufficient reason to make the British Empire, as
Harcourt demanded, denounce its treaties and change
its traditional policy ?

We are always treated as if we had some peculiar alliance
with the Turkish Government, as if we were their peculiar
friends, and even as if we were expected to uphold them in
any enormity they might commit. I want to know what
evidence there is of that, what interest we have in such a
thing. We are, it is true, the allies of the Sultan of Turkey;
so is Russia, so is Austria, so is France, and so are others.
We are also their partners in a tripartite treaty, in which
we, not only generally, but singly, guarantee with France
and Austria the territorial integrity of Turkey. These are
our engagements, and they are the engagements that we
endeavour to fulfil. And if these engagements, renovated
and repeated only four years ago by the wisdom of Europe,
are to be treated by the honourable and learned gentleman
as idle wind and chaff, and if we are to be told that our
political duty is by force to expel the Turks to the other
side of the Bosphorus, then politics cease to be an art, statesmanship becomes a mere mockery, and instead of being a
House of Commons faithful to its traditions, and which is
always influenced, I have ever thought, by sound principles
of policy, whoever may be its leaders, we had better at once
resolve ourselves into one of those revolutionary clubs which
settle all political and social questions with the same ease as
the honourable and learned member.

In the peroration of this, his last speech in the House of Commons, Disraeli sounded once again the imperial note.

What may be the fate of the eastern part of Europe it would be arrogant for me to speculate upon, and if I had any thoughts on the subject I trust I should not be so imprudent or so indiscreet as to take this opportunity to express them. But I am sure that as long as England is ruled by English parties who understand the principles on which our Empire is founded, and who are resolved to maintain that Empire, our influence in that part of the world can never be looked upon with indifference. If it should happen that the Government which controls the greater portion of those fair lands is found to be incompetent for its purpose, neither England nor any of the Great Powers will shrink from fulfilling the high political and moral duty which will then devolve upon them.

But, Sir, we must not jump at conclusions so quickly as is now the fashion. There is nothing to justify us in talking in such a vein of Turkey as has been, and is being at this moment, entertained. The present is a state of affairs which requires the most vigilant examination and the most careful management. But those who suppose that England ever would uphold, or at this moment particularly is upholding, Turkey from blind superstition, and from a want of sympathy with the highest aspirations of humanity, are deceived. What our duty is at this critical moment is to maintain the Empire of England. Nor will we agree to any step, though it may obtain for a moment comparative quiet and a false prosperity, that hazards the existence of that Empire.

In this speech, as in all his other statements in the House on the question, Disraeli chivalrously defended Elliot from the attacks very generally made on his negligence and inefficiency. But he was only too well aware of how seriously the Government at home had been damaged by the conduct of their representative at Constantinople.

To Lord Derby.

Confidential. 10, DOWNING STREET, *Aug.* 15, '76.—I am off, but I send a line, which I would rather have said than written. I had the pleasure, however, of seeing our dearest friend yesterday afternoon, and tried to say it to her.

We are on the eve, probably, of difficult negotiations, which require men who combine both tact and energy. The two principal places in these coming transactions will be Constantinople and Vienna—and in both posts we are singularly weak.

Elliot has many excellent qualities, both moral and intellectual, but he has no energy. This is probably the consequence of his wretched health; but, what[eve]r the cause, the result is the same. His conduct has seriously compromised, and damaged, the Government, and the more that is done now by him to redeem the situation, the more evident he makes it, that all this shd. have been done months ago.

Exertions, wh. are made in August, to counteract the mistakes of May, can achieve no reputation; as a public servant, the nation has utterly condemned him.

His hopeless health might, however, be a plea for a course on our part, wh., otherwise, might be painful. He might yet remain at his post, and assist an Extraordinary Envoy adapted to the present position of affairs. I think, myself, that Layard is the man for such a mission.

As for Buchanan, that is a hopeless case. He has been a public servant for ½ a century, and I knew him almost at the commencement of that time—at Constan[tinopl]e in 1830; I, therefore, can testify, that it is not age, which has enfeebled his intelligence or dimmed his powers. He was, and ever has been, a hopeless mediocrity.

Andrassy wants a guide—a man of quick perceptions and iron will—about him. I think Vienna more important than Constantinople. You ought to have no false delicacy in the business. Buchanan should be confidentially communicated with, and told that he should resign. . . .

Adieu ! cher camarade ! I wish you success and fame—and believe you will obtain both; but, in great affairs, to succeed you must not spare the feelings of mediocrities.

After his farewell to the Commons the new peer went for a short visit to the Queen at Osborne, and then spent a 'happy week' with the Bradfords at Castle Bromwich. 'The weather,' he wrote to Corry, 'was worthy of the "Castle of Indolence"; we sate under bowery trees surrounded by cooing doves, and, as mankind is mimetic, we cooed ourselves. At six o'clock, we went for some amusing drive, and Miladi generally drove me alone. I visited Drayton—a very fine place, full of art and all on a great scale.'   His host and hostess, when he left, took him to the station at Birmingham, where he had ' what is called " an ovation " . . . I was cheered through the streets, and at the station the demonstration was " intense." '   To Lady Bradford he wrote from Hughenden that evening, August 22: ' They were very tumultuous at Brummagem after we separated; perhaps you heard them.   And there was a party collected at every station till we got to Banbury with vociferous ejaculations and congratulations to " the noble Hurl of Beaconsfield." '   Two days later he added, ' I continue to receive innumerable letters of congratulation, occasionally mixed with 1 or 2 of menace.'

It is strange that Beaconsfield had not a larger proportion of menacing letters.   For that enthusiasm of the English people, which he had often signalised and admired, was keenly stirred in reprobation of the Bulgarian atrocities; and throughout the early autumn months a furious agitation raged, following the lines of Harcourt's call to a crusade.   It was assumed, in spite of obvious evidence of exaggeration, that the worst stories of horrors were true; and it was demanded that the Government guilty of permitting, if not decreeing, such atrocities should be forced to evacuate, certainly the provinces in which they had occurred, if not European territory altogether.   Public meetings were held all over the country, of wh'ch the keynote was that grave wrong had been done, and that the wrongdoers must be punished and the wrong righted, regardless of British interests or even of British treaty obligations.   It was further claimed that the issue of true rel'gion was at stake, that the followers of Christ must be rescued from the domination of the followers of Mahomet; and accordingly Nonconformist ministers on the one hand, and on the other H'gh Church clergy, suspicious of Beaconsfield ever since the Public Worship Regulation Act, took a prominent part in agitation.   In the background, despite the fact that Granville and Hartington were known to view the movement coldly, and that Gladstone had as yet made no sign, the strings were pulled by Liberal and Radical wirepullers, and there was an increasing tendency to throw the blame, for the horrors which were so hotly denounced, on the British as much as on the Turkish Government. The refusal to accept the Berlin memorandum and the despatch of the fleet to Besika Bay were shamelessly perverted into direct encouragements to the Porte to oppress and massacre its Christian subjects.

Beaconsfield, carrying on the business of government from his quiet Buckinghamshire home, was fertile in ideas for turning to account an agitation which he deprecated.

To Sir Stafford Northcote.

HUGHENDEN MANOR, *Sept.* 2, 1876.—We must be careful about ' demonstrations.' Nothing of that kind will do, which is not very effective. Unless it hits the nail on the head, it will be looked on as weak and hysterical. Elliot's stupidity has nearly brought us to a great peril. If he had acted with promptitude, or even kept himself, and us, informed, these ' atrocities' might have been checked. As it is, he has brought us into the position, most unjustly, of being thought to connive at them.

But when we have committed a mistake, or find ourselves in difficulties, the best thing is to turn them into ' commodities,' as Falstaff says, or something like it.[1] The ' atrocities ' will permit us to dictate to the Porte. That was the meaning of the telegram respecting which you wrote to me. It is to be hoped, that the leading part, which England may take, in obtaining an armistice, and afterwards in the preliminaries, will make the excited ' Public ' forget, or condone, the Elliotiana.

I hope this may be effected long before your meeting.

To Lord Salisbury.

HUGHENDEN MANOR, *Sept.* 3.—. . . I am here, tied to my post. Indeed I ought to be at Whitehall, but that really, in August and Septr., would be too dreary. Even Derby gets back every night to his ' placens uxor.' But still even here, with endless telegrams and ceaseless messengers, I find myself, every now and then, behindhand.

---

[1] ' A good wit will make use of anything; I will turn diseases to commodity.' 2 *King Henry IV.*, Act I., Sc. 2.

Affairs are most critical. Had it not been for those un-happy 'atrocities,' we should have settled a peace very honorable to England, and satisfactory to Europe.

Now, we are obliged to work from a new point of departure, and dictate to Turkey, who has forfeited all sympathy. . . . Derby is behaving with energy, and I hope will be up to the mark—it will not be from want of bottle-holding. It is the most difficult business I have ever had to touch.

To Lord Derby.

Confidential. HUGHENDEN, *Sept.* 4.—I have been thinking much about the present state of affairs and our new point of departure—wise and inevitable, and wise because inevitable. But it is difficult to conceal from ourselves that it is a course which will probably bring about a result very different from that originally contemplated.

I cannot help doubting whether any arrangement, though I have confidence in your skill and your fortune, a quality as important as skill, is now practicable. I fear affairs will linger on till the spring, when Russia and Austria will march their armies into the Balkans, either simultaneously and with a certain understanding, or one following the other's example from jealousy and fear.

As Count Andrassy observed to Sir Andrew Buchanan, 'there is no alternative between the notes of this year and the "solution" of the Eastern Question.'

I think the probability is that it will be 'the solution of the Eastern Question,' and, if so, it is wise that we should take the lead in it. Our chance of success will be greater because from us it will be unexpected.

If old Brunnow were here, the work, so far as Russia is concerned, might be shorter than with others. Perhaps Schouvaloff may be equally handy, but certainly Palmerston with Brunnow managed in 1840 the solution of the Eastern Question in the other direction most admirably.

Whatever the jealousies of Austria and Russia, they would prefer a division of the Balkan spoil under the friendly offices of England to war between themselves certainly, and perhaps with others. Constantinople with an adequate district should be neutralised and made a free port, in the custody and under the guardianship of England, as the Ionian Isles were.

I fancy there would be no difficulty in the enlargement of Greece. Nature indicates, and policy would not oppose it.

And now about Germany? When I am told its Prime Minister is in solitude and cannot be disturbed, and that the

Queen's Ambassador is here because it is of no use being at
his post, I listen to eccentricities, which must not be permitted to regulate events affecting the destiny of generations
and Empires. If Prince Bismarck won't see the Queen's
Ambassador, he must see you, but I cannot doubt for a
moment, if he hears from you that there is real business
afloat, he will be seen as much as we desire.

But what does he want? Does he want 'compensation'?
Is it to be in Austrian or even Russian Germany? Or would
he feel, without now demanding it, that such compensation
would naturally accrue to Germany in the course of events
from the Slavist development of Austria and perhaps Russia?

Or would he desire, as a remote and maritime Power, to
place himself on the level of England, and share with us the
guardianship of the Hellespont and the Symplegades, like
the *garnison confédératif* of Mainz and other places after the
peace of 1815?

I write this on the assumption that the present attempt
at peace will fail. God grant it may not! But, if it do, I
humbly think we cannot act too powerfully and too promptly.

Decision and energy will render the work practicable;
hesitation and timidity will involve us in infinite difficulty
and peril, in the whirlpool of which we should disappear.

Sept. 6.—. . . I sent you Northcote's letter, because he
has an ingenious mind, with popular sympathies, but timid,
unwisely timid—which timidity always is, tho' caution has
many charms.

What I wish to impress upon you, at this moment, as
regards home, is not to act, as if you were under the control
of popular opinion. If so, you may do what they like, but
they won't respect you for doing it.

After all, all this tumult is on a false assumption, that we
have been, or are, upholding Turkey. All the Turks may be
in the Propontis, so far as I am concerned, and the first thing,
after we had declined the Berlin mem., that you did, was
to tell Musurus so.

If the thing goes well and we get what we want, all this
row will subside, and be forgotten before our first Cab. Council,
and we shall get the credit of the arrangement; but if an
arrangement takes place, and it is supposed that we have
acted under the pressure of this Hudibrastic crew of High
Ritualists, Dissenting ministers, and 'the great Liberal
party,' we shall be contemptible.

Now—what is going on? You talk of 'if we get the
armistice.' Well, you cd. hardly expect that the Turks
wd. assent to such a naked proposition, tho' it was a very
wise thing for you to make it. But if you had a man at

Constantinople, by this time he wd. have fashioned 3 or 4 prelims. of peace, got them sanctioned by the Powers, and the Porte wd. have accepted the armistice. They wd. of course be vague—but definite eno'.

1. *Status quo*, etc.

2. Govt. of the Provinces (Bulgaria included ?) to be settled hereafter.

3. Indemnity from Servia, to be settled hereafter.

I fear there must be a Congress, tho' I hate it, and I am quite confident we cd. have managed without it, had it not been for this Bulgarian bogey. . . .

At this juncture, the atrocity agitation being in full swing, but comparatively ineffective because leaderless, Disraeli's great rival returned in good earnest ' from Elba ' to put himself at its head. Gladstone had taken no part in the Parliamentary debates on the subject, and had only made a cursory allusion to it when attacking in the House the general Eastern policy of the Govern-ment. But now, finding, to use his own words, ' that the question was alive,' he realised that his opportunity had come, and he took it without hesitation or scruple

To Lady Bradford.

HUGHENDEN MANOR, *Sept.* 5.—. . . Ld. Russell, having his brother-in-law Ambassador at Constantinople, halts and hesitates in his dotage. All his latter years he has been swearing by Ld. Derby and Elliot: and now he is going to call Parlt. together in Novr. to denounce them both. Glad-stone, ' who had retired from public life,' can't resist the first opportunity, and is going to declaim at Blackheath, having preliminarily given the cue to public opinion in a pamphlet. I wonder what Hartington thinks of all this activity. He is quietly killing grouse at Bolton Abbey, and, this very morning, sent me four brace—good fellow![1] The state of affairs is not one very favorable to the nervous system; but mine is not yet shaken.

---

[1] Writing on Sept. 6 to Hartington to thank him for the grouse, Beacons-field said: ' It is very kind of you to remember me, one likes to be remem-bered. I am sorry I shall not meet you so often in future, but we may meet perhaps more frequently in those secret societies where we sometimes encounter each other, when we ought to be, as Madame de Staël said, "conspiring on the public place." ' See Holland's *Devonshire*, Vol. I., p. 174.

Lord Mor'ey, in his great *Life of Gladstone,* treats his hero's retirement after the reverse of 1874 as not merely whole-hearted and sincere in its conception, in the resolve to find fitter occupation than politics for the interval between the age of sixty-five and the grave this may be conceded; but also as, for two years and a half, practically effective in execution. He mentions, indeed, in an inadequate and perfunctory manner that at the close of the session of 1874 Gladstone engaged—unwillingly, it is strangely suggested—in ecclesiastical debates over the Public Worship Regulation Bill, the Scotch Patronage Bill, and the Endowed Schools Bill. But, with that exception, the whole of his Parliamentary activity of nearly three sessions, till the summer of 1876, is dismissed in four words as ' occasional visits to Westminster,' the inference being that the occasions were of such slight importance as not to be worth chronicling. Immersed in pamphleteering controversies about Ritualism and Vaticanism, in theological and classical studies, in the simple delights of the Hawarden park and library, it was, we are given to understand, only with the utmost reluctance, and on the imperative call of duty and of humanity, that the statesman, who had put Parliament behind his back, came forth to lead an impassioned crusade against the Government and particularly against the Prime Minister.

The facts do not bear this picture out. It was thus, perhaps, that they presented themselves to Gladstone himself; W. E. Forster once said of him in the House of Commons, ' He can persuade most people of most things, and, above all, he can persuade himself of almost anything.' But those who have read the frequent references to Gladstone's Parliamentary appearances in Chapters 9, 10, and 12 of V., will be disposed to think that all from which he retired, after the first few months, was the daily drudgery of leadership. Not merely when he was lured by the ecclesiastical bait, but whenever any question of moment was raised, whenever,

especially, there was an opportunity for a vehement
party attack upon the Government, he appeared on the
Opposition front bench, and almost always, when he
appeared, he spoke. Listen to the friendly testimony
of Sir Henry Lucy's diary in the middle of the session
of 1875 and early in that of 1876.

May 7, 1875.—Gladstone's retirement from the leadership
of the Liberal party is much such another withdrawal from
the conduct of affairs as the captain of a ship effects when
he turns in for the night. The first mate is left in charge of
the ship, but on the slightest emergency the captain is to be
called.

Feb. 14, 1876.—For a man who, as he wrote to ' My dear
Granville ' more than a year ago, ' at the age of sixty-five
and after forty-two years of a laborious public life,' thought
himself ' entitled to retire,' Gladstone is uncommonly regular
in his attendance at the House, and is singularly ready to
fling himself into debate.

It might have been expected that, on these reappear-
ances, the retired veteran of more than forty years'
service would have played the part of a Nestor; would
have moderated by his mature experience the rash
counsels and reckless daring of younger men. On the
contrary, on all the most conspicuous occasions, he
returned, not to moderate but to aggravate, not to still
the spirit of faction but to evoke it; to spur the constituted leaders of the Liberal party into attacks on the
Government which they deprecated, or, failing success
in this, to launch out himself into vehement denunciation
—' like the Dragon of Wantley breathing fire and fury,'
as Disraeli wrote in one of his letters. Take, for example,
in 1874, Gladstone's attack on the Scotch Patronage
Bill, and his threat of resulting disestablishment if a
measure was passed which his Presbyterian friend Argyll
warmly commended; in 1875, his violent assault on
Northcote's Sinking Fund proposals—a scheme entirely
in harmony with his own financial doctrine; and more
particularly, in the early months of 1876, his association
with Lowe in denouncing the Suez Canal Purchase, and

the leading part he took in forcing the Opposition, against Hartington's better judgment, into a prolonged and factious fight over the Imperial Titles Bill. These spasmodic and unbalanced irruptions into politics are, with the trifling exception noted above, not merely slurred over, but absolutely ignored, in Lord Morley's *Life;* yet they surely must profoundly affect the final opinion to be passed on the singleness of heart and soundness of judgment with which Gladstone plunged into his furious ' Atrocity' crusade.

The available evidence certainly suggests that by 1876 Gladstone, like Cowper's retired statesman, had grown weary of his self-imposed exile, was feeling ' a secret thirst for his renounced employs,' and was, it may be only half consciously, on the lookout for a fitting occasion on which to burst from his retreat in order to save ' a sinking State.'[1] His Parliamentary activities in that spring were noticeably greater than in the previous two years; they consisted of strenuous attacks on Government about matters of foreign and imperial politics, in regard to which a patriotic Opposition is loth to take the offensive. This restlessness was as observable at Hawarden as at Westminster. Early in the year Sir Louis Mallet told Lord George Hamilton: ' A great friend of mine and a first-rate judge of men and affairs has just come back from Hawarden. He says Gladstone is in a most restless frame of mind—so much so, that if he gets his opportunity he will become the great demagogue of the century.'[2]

And there was little doubt as to the quarry whom the old hunter, once more sniffing the scent, was preparing to stalk. His mind was full of his successful rival, and of deep suspicions of that rival's character and policy. He wrote at this time to Hartington: ' Dizzy has never wanted courage, but his daring is elastic, and capable of any amount of extension with the servility

---

[1] See Cowper's *Retirement,* lines 473-480.
[2] Lord G. Hamilton's *Parliamentary Reminiscences,* p. 131. "Absolutely contrary to the fact," declares Lord Gladstone in *After Thirty Years,* p. 75.

of the times. He has fallen upon a period singularly
favourable to its exercise.'[1] That ' malignity '[2] wh.ch
Disraeli noted in Gladstone's attitude towards himself
during a quarter of a century, and which is suffered occasionally to peep out in Lord Morley's *Life*, was now to
be given a free course. Lady Beaconsfield, with her pacificatory and mollifying influence on the relations between
the two men, was gone. Gladstone, in his private letters
during this period, indulged in the wildest and most
absurd charges against the rival who was, in his opinion,
pursuing ' the most selfish and least worthy ' policy he
had ever known. ' What [Dizzy] hates,' he wrote to the
Duke of Argyll, ' is Christian liberty and reconstruction.
He supports old Turkey, thinking that if vital improvements be averted, it must break down; and his fleet is
at Besika Bay, I feel pretty sure, to be ready to lay hold
of Egypt as his share.' It is difficult to discuss with
patience such extraordinary nonsense. Besika Bay, a convenient anchorage enough for a fleet destined to protect
Christians in Constantinople against Mohammedan fanati-
c.sm, or to save Constantinople from Russian attack,
would of course be ridiculously out of the way for operations against Egypt, if any were contemplated. But, as
a matter of fact, Beaconsfield, far from contemplating
separate action in Egypt, was during this autumn promoting, by a benevolent attitude towards the Goschen-
Joubert mission, that joint French and English action in
Egyptian affairs, which was the consistent policy of his
Government, and which was only departed from—under
pressure of events, no doubt—by the Gladstone Ministry
which succeeded him. Again, Gladstone told the Duke
of Argyll, ' I have a strong suspicion that Dizzy's crypto-
Judaism has had to do with his policy. The Jews of the
East *bitterly* hate the Christians; who have not always
used them well.' There is no trace of Beaconsfield's
specially Judaic feeling in his Eastern policy. The race

[1] Holland's *Devonshire*, Vol. 1., p. 167.
[2] See p. 701.

which that feeling would have led him to support would have been, as was shown in *Tancred*, the Arab, and not the Turk. What Beaconsfield was endeavouring to carry through, amid enormous difficulties, was the traditional policy of England, to which she was bound by treaty, of supporting the independence and integrity of the Turkish Empire.

In fact, Gladstone's attitude towards Beaconsfield, during the last three years and a half of the Beaconsfield Government, amounted very nearly to a personal vendetta. He avowed that his energies were entirely applied to counterworking the Prime Minister. So notorious was his feeling among his intimates that Lord Acton, by the indirect method of a letter to Mrs. Drew, Gladstone's daughter, vehemently remonstrated with him, at the time of Beaconsfield's death, for proposing a public monument to a man of whose policy and character he thought so ill. Gladstone, it was confidently asserted by Acton, considered Beaconsfield's 'doctrines false, but the man more false than his doctrine'; believed 'that he demoralised public opinion, bargained with diseased appetites, stimulated passions, prejudices, and selfish desires, that they might maintain his influence'; and deemed him, in short, 'the worst and most immoral Minister since Castlereagh.'[1] To the four elements, which Lord Morley enumerates, 'in the mighty storm that now [August, 1876] agitated Mr. Gladstone's breast' —the rejection of the Berlin memorandum, the Bulgarian atrocities, the responsibilities incurred by the Crimean War, and sympathy with the Eastern Church[2]—there must be added two more: impatience of longer retirement from the forefront of politics, and a burning determination to pull down a too successful rival.

Gladstone's pamphlet on *The Bulgarian Horrors*, which appeared on September 6, was couched in superlatives. He would not wait for Baring's detailed report which

---

[1] *Letters of Lord Acton to Mary Drew*, p. 78. The words in inverted commas in this sentence are of course Acton's, though he imputes the sentiments to Gladstone.

[2] *Gladstone*, Bk. VII., ch. 4.

appeared a fortnight later; but based his invective on the most horrifying stories of the unverified newspaper reports. He denounced the Turkish race as 'the one great anti-human specimen of humanity'; he wrote of 'fell satanic orgies'; he averred that the crimes which had been committed would move the indignation of European gaol-birds and South Sea cannibals. These were wild and whirling words, indeed; the present generation, who have supped full of greater horrors, can realise better than his contemporaries how false was the perspective. He abused the Government for what he assumed to be their sole policy, the *status quo.* He invited his countrymen to insist on a change which, in concurrence with other States, should bring about 'the extinction of the Turkish executive power in Bulgaria. Let the Turks now carry away their abuses in the only possible manner—namely, by carrying off themselves. Their Zaptiehs and their Mudirs, their Bimbashis and their Yuzbashis, their Kaimakams and their Pashas, one and all, bag and baggage, shall, I hope, clear out from the province they have desolated and profaned.'

Let us see how this outburst was regarded by Beaconsfield.

To Lord Derby.

HUGHENDEN MANOR, *Sept.* 8, '76.—. . . Gladstone has had the impudence to send me his pamphlet, tho' he accuses me of several crimes. The document is passionate and not strong; vindictive and ill-written[1]—that of course. Indeed, in that respect, of all the Bulgarian horrors, perhaps the greatest.

Dss. of Manchester said to me, just before we broke up, 'That gentleman is only waiting to come to the fore with all his hypocritical retirement.' She hates him, for good reason. She showed her discrimination; however, I think he will have to go back, if we are firm and prudent, and Hartington may remain at Doncaster.

---

[1] On second thoughts Beaconsfield modified this opinion. Writing next day to Lady Bradford he describes the pamphlet as 'quite as unprincipled as usual, tho' on the surface apparently not so ill-written as is his custom. The reason why, because it is evidently dictated; so it is not so involved and obscure, but more wordy and more careless and imprudent.'

To Lady Bradford.

HUGHENDEN MANOR [? *Sept.* 8].—. . . A friend of mine
writes he went the other night to Haymarket Theatre. There
were three empty stalls before him. The play *Heir-at-Law*,
and the actor, to see a Mr. Clarke. Probably you know all
about him. Into one of the stalls came Ld. Granville; then
in a little time, Gladstone; then, at last, Harty-Tarty !
Gladstone laughed very much at the performance; H.-T.
never even smiled. 3 conspirators. . . .

10, DOWNING ST., *Sept.* 9.—I write you a line from
D. S., where I unexpectedly find myself. . . . I have had
a satisfactory morning with the great Secy.,[1] and as we are
agreed I think we shall conquer. Tho' when all the world
is mad, and there are only two keepers, the latter shd. be in
danger. . . .

The Fairy is very nervous about the Bucks election, wh.
won't come off for a fortnight. All that I can tell her is
that every gentleman, and every leading farmer, is on Fremantle's Committee, and only two landlords of any mark,
Ld. Chesham and Sir H. Verney, support Rupert [Carrington].
I hope the general insanity may have subsided in a fortnight;
if not, I really can't answer what may be the result of popular
passion and the ballot. . . .

To Sir Stafford Northcote.

HUGHENDEN MANOR, *Sept.* 11, 1876.—I am sorry to hear
you have to attend a public meeting.

The first and cardinal point, at the present moment, is,
that no member of the Government should countenance the
idea that we are hysterically ' modifying ' our policy, in
consequence of the excited state of the public mind. If such
an idea gets about, we shall become contemptible.

Derby, whom I saw on Saturday, is deeply impressed with
this principle, and it will entirely guide him in his reply to
a deputation, which he receives this morning.

When I was in town on Saturday, Baring's Report had
not yet arrived !

None of these brawlers propose anything practical or
precise. Even Gladstone has greatly exposed himself. He
writes a pamphlet, in which, for ethnological reasons, he
counsels the expulsion of the Turkish race from Europe, and
England rapturously assembled at Greenwich to hear the
statesmanlike development of this wise proposition. But,

[1] Derby.

the day before, having become alive to his folly, he writes a letter to *The Times*, saying he did not mean the expulsion of the Turkish nation—only of the Turkish Ministers. That he meant the expulsion of some Ministers, I have little doubt, only I think they were not Turks.

I am told his speech was a blank disappointment to the infuriate and merciless humanitarians, who looked upon it as a sort of revival of the Andrassy note.

Generally speaking, when the country goes mad, which it does every now and then—*e.g.*, Cardinal Wiseman and Queen Caroline—I think it best, that one should wait till everything has been said and frequently in one direction, and then the country, tired of hearing the same thing over and over again, begins to reflect, and opinion changes as quickly as it was formed. Fortunately for England, it is only the beginning of Septr.; so there is time.

Our case is a complete case, if people would only listen to argument, but I doubt whether they will—except perhaps from a Cabinet Minister.

Our policy, supported by the country, was non-interference. We objected to the Berlin note because it insured interference. All the Powers then adopted our view, which showed it was the sensible one.

We sent our fleet to B[esika] B[ay] to defend H.M. subjects and their property, and to prevent Xtian massacres, and to guard over British interests; and the consequence has been that there has been tranquillity instead of anxiety, and that too in the midst of revolutions, and our Ambassador has received the thanks of all the Xtian communities for our having saved them. Nothing can describe the alarm of the Xtian population of Constantinople, and its contiguous territories, at the rumor of our fleet being withdrawn.

But then, the ' moral and material aid given to the Turks,' by the refusal of the Berl. note, and the sending of the fleet, has so emboldened the Porte, that these ' atrocities ' have taken place !

The ' atrocities ' occurred before either of these great events.

Don't mix yourself up with punishing Agas and compensation. What ought to be done, will be done.

Derby, who was in hearty agreement with his chief, showed, as Beaconsfield wrote again and again, unusual rigour and decision, both in speech and in diplomacy, this autumn. He told the deputation of working-men who waited on him on September 11 at the Foreign

Office that, to judge by the abuse showered on the
Government, it would appear ' that there are a great
many people in England who fancy that Lord Beaconsfield is the Sultan and that I am the Grand Vizier.'
Whereas, in fact, ' with regard to acts connected with
the internal administration of Turkey, we have exactly
the same rights that are possessed by every other Great
Power, neither more nor less; and I do not learn that
in France, or Austria, or Italy, or Germany people are
crying out as they do here, and denouncing their Government as being in complicity with those answerable for
these atrocities.' There were two questions, he pointed
out, essentially distinct. One was the territorial integrity
of the Ottoman Empire, and the other the relationship
between the Turkish Government and the subject races.
The territorial integrity meant, at bottom, the possession
of Constantinople. ' No Great Power would be willing
to see it in the hands of any other Great Power. No
small Power could hold it at all. And as for joint occupation, and other ingenious schemes of that kind, they
are, at best, dangerous and doubtful expedients. . . .
Any attempt at partition would, in all probability, be
the signal for a European war.' So the territorial *status
quo*, which had been the policy of Gladstone's Government
as well as of Beaconsfield's, and was guaranteed by treaty,
should be preserved. But the relations between the
Turkish Government and the subject races had often
been modified and might be modified again. The
Beaconsfield Government had no objection in principle
to any further extension of constitutional changes which
the guaranteeing Powers might think necessary. They
were doing all they could, in conjunction with these
Powers, to bring about first an armistice and then peace.
The Bulgarians had a right to expect reparation, exem-
plary punishment of the offenders, and security against
the recurrence of outrage. If humanity was a virtue,
so was justice—justice to Turks and Mohammedans, as
well as to Bulgarians and Christians. Other Powers were

not looking at the question solely from the humanitarian
point of view, however that standpoint might predominate in England

This presentment of the case showed admirable common
sense; and there were members of the Opposition who
recognised the fact, as appeared from a conversation
which took place between Goschen and the Queen.

From Queen Victoria.

BALMORAL, *Sept.* 13, '76.—. . . Lord Derby seems to have
spoken remarkably well, and no doubt his speeches will do
good, but whether they will stop the agitation she does not
feel sure.   Mr. Goschen, who is staying at Braemar, and who
dined here yesterday, spoke with great good sense and
moderation, greatly deprecating the wild, senseless agitation
of the country, and the dangerous and absurd extent to
which the philanthropy is carried. . . . He said that he
thought it most unnecessary and ill-judged that 'we should
perform the part of sister of charity to the rest of Europe,'
which is an excellent mode of putting it.   The Queen told
him that, without wishing to injure a person, it was Sir
H. Elliot who had been the cause of this trouble and
that he had never ascertained the truth till long after he
should have known it.   He regretted this, as if Parliament
had been sitting it would have been easy to put a stop to
these misrepresentations.   He said he felt how very difficult
the task of the Government was, but he hoped that events
might remove this.   But how are we ever to reconcile the
obstinacy of the Turks and Servians ? . . .

The Queen, who had been horrified at the Bulgarian
reports, more than once pressed upon Beaconsfield the
advisability of speaking out more strongly in denunciation
of the crimes and their perpetrators.   Some of his colleagues also urged that the public would not be satisfied
without some such utterance.   But Beaconsfield would
not be persuaded.   He had shown, he thought, his
horror at atrocities sufficiently in Parliament; he would
forfeit his self-respect if, in deference to outside clamour,
he said more now.   He had to attend an agricultural
dinner at Aylesbury on September 20, the eve of the
poll for the vacancy in the representation of Bucks

created by his acceptance of a peerage. He had just
had rather a sharp attack of gout, and wrote on the
previous day to Lady Bradford: 'I got downstairs
to-day, free from all pain, but a little weak, as one must
always become from an imprisonment of four or five
days or more. I shall go to the dinner to-morrow, and
make a remark or two, if I have a good opportunity.'
In the speech which he delivered there was nothing of
the sentimental kind at all, but strong condemnation
of the unpatriotic character of the agitation. The
Foreign Secretary was in the midst, he said, of most
difficult negotiations, with the object of securing British
interests of the highest importance and also the peace
of Europe.

Under ordinary circumstances a British Minister so placed,
whatever might be his difficulties, would have the consolation
of knowing that he was backed by the country. It would be
affectation for me to pretend that this is the position of Her
Majesty's Government at this moment. . . . Unhappily a
great portion of the people of this country, prompted by
feelings which have drawn their attention to extraneous
matters, have arrived at a conclusion which, in the opinion
of Her Majesty's Government, if carried into effect, would
alike be injurious to the permanent and important interests
of England, and fatal to any chance of preserving the peace
of Europe.

Beaconsfield expressed his admiration for the enthusiasm and the noble sympathy shown by the English
people; but he feared that ' designing politicians might
take advantage of such sublime sentiments, and apply
them for the furtherance of their sinister ends.' He
continued:

I do not think that there is any language which can denounce
too strongly conduct of this description. He who at such a
moment would avail himself of such a commanding sentiment
in order to obtain his own individual ends, suggesting a
course which he must know to be injurious to the interests of
the country, and not favourable to the welfare of mankind,
is a man whose conduct no language can too strongly condemn. He outrages the principle of patriotism, which is the

soul of free communities.   He does more—he influences in
the most injurious manner the common welfare of humanity.
Such conduct, if pursued by any man at this moment, ought
to be indignantly reprobated by the people of England, for
in the general havoc and ruin which it may bring about it
may, I think, be fairly described as worse than any of those
Bulgarian atrocities which now occupy attention.

This attack on Gladstone's agitation as worse than the
Bulgarian atrocities infuriated his partisans and has
been condemned by more dispassionate critics.   But a
policy which gratuitously provoked the ' havoc and ruin '
of a general European war might surely be not unfairly
spoken of in these terms; and such a war, in Beaconsfield's opinion, was inevitable if Gladstone's policy was
carried through.   Gladstone, he wrote to Lady Bradford
a few days later, would ' avenge Bulgarian atrocities by
the butchery of the world.'   The speech proceeded :

The country in some of its exhibitions has completely out-
Heroded the most extravagant conceptions.   They tell us
that nothing will satisfy them but the expulsion of the Turks
from Europe, and the institution of Slavonic governments—
whether imperial, royal, or republican, I am at a loss to know.
Now Her Majesty's Government, and as I believe the Government of every country, are perfectly aware that, if such plans
are attempted to be carried into effect, we shall be landed in
a European war of no slight duration. . . .   Let us remember
that the sending a million Moors and Jews out of Spain a
good many years ago so convulsed that nation that it has
never recovered itself, and Europe suffers even at this moment
from that act.   I am quite convinced that Mr. Gladstone on
reflection never intended anything of the kind.   If he had
gone to the House of Commons and had proposed to the
House of Commons and the Speaker to attend Greenwich
Fair, and go to the top of Greenwich Hill and all roll down to
the bottom, I declare he could not have proposed anything
more absurdly incongruous.

In Beaconsfield's private letters the condemnation of
Gladstone's conduct was still more severe.   That he
should emerge from retirement to lead this demagogic
crusade against the foreign policy of the country—a policy
in essentials identical with that which, when in office, he

had pursued himself—appeared to Beaconsfield, and also
to the Queen, to be outrageous. In the letters to Lady
Bradford Gladstone is frequently called 'Tartuffe'; 'the
willing victim of every delusion that may bring him
power.' To Derby Beaconsfield wrote in October:
'Posterity will do justice to that unprincipled maniac
Gladstone—extraordinary mixture of envy, vindictiveness, hypocrisy, and superstition; and with one commanding characteristic—whether Prime Minister, or
Leader of Opposition, whether preaching, praying,
speechifying, or scribbling—never a gentleman!'

The Queen congratulated Beaconsfield on his 'masterly
speech'; and he himself was satisfied with the effect
produced.

To Lady Bradford.

HUGHENDEN MANOR [*Sept.* 21, 1876].— . . . Physically, I
got over yesterday fairly well: at least I am not worse to-day.
It was rather a remarkable meeting: 500 persons—but all
the notables of the county of both sides. That made it
peculiar. And it was very difficult to make a speech, political
but not party.

All I can say is, if I cd. judge from the enthusiasm, and
take it as a fair index of county sentiment, we ought to be
pretty sure of the struggle that is going on at this very hour.
. . . Charley C[arrington] looked very white all the time
I was speaking—just an hour. He felt, as it were, caught
in a trap.

At any rate the speech was successful in keeping the
Bucks seat for the Government. A member of the Carrington family endeavoured to win it for the Liberals; and
Beaconsfield had written to Derby two or three days before:
'I believe they are all waiting for the Bucks election—to
decide the fate of the Government and the policy of England. Gladstone has been down to Wycombe Abbey, and
Granville took £200 to £1[00] from Ld. Alington that we
shd. be beaten. Charley Carrington asked Granville
to let him have half the bet, and said, "What I want is
to get it in thousands!" They are cocksure. I retain
my opinion that Mr. Fremantle will be returned by a

good majority.' Fremantle's majority was under 200;
but it was sufficient; and, in spite of the impetus given
to agitation by Gladstone's emergence, the tide began
to turn in favour of the Government. 'Let nothing
shake you,' wrote Beaconsfield just before the poll to
Derby. 'The more I think and see, the more sure is
my conviction that this outcry is all froth, except where
it is faction.'

To Lord Derby.

HUGHENDEN MANOR, *Sept.* 23, '76.—. . . If it will give
you the slightest satisfaction, that I shd. come up to town
and 'assist' you in receiving the Russians,[1] I shd. be more
than ready.

Only understand: I say this out of true *camaraderie,* and
that you shd. not feel isolated, or deserted by your colleagues,
at this trying moment.

I have no wish to take any lead, and I wd. leave everything to your consummate tact with complete confidence.
Therefore, say just what you feel.

You can't be too firm. What the public meetings want
is nonsense, not politics: something quite shadowy, speculative, and not practical. They must recur to common sense
and the possible.

The result of an attempt to put their plans into operation
wd. be war by England alone against Turkey, and then the
Porte allying herself with Russia for protection.

There is nothing bet[wee]n our plan and partition.

To Lady Bradford.

HUGHENDEN MANOR, *Sept.* 27.—. . . I think things look
pretty well, but there will be many ups and downs before
all is finished. This is a critical day. I think I told you
why I did not go up to town to-day to receive the City Address.
It wd. have made them of too much importance, but I have
settled with D[erby] what to say, and, I doubt not, he will
say it well. He has such a repugnance to enthusiasm, and his
clear, callous, common sense is so shocked by the freaks of
the foolish, and so contemptuous of the machinations of the
factious, that he quite enjoys discharging a volume of cold
water on their unprotected persons.

The Times, as you must have observed yesterday, is ratting

---

[1] Beaconsfield is referring to a City deputation in favour of Gladstone's
policy.

fast, like a thaw after a very great frost. As for myself, I delight in the whole *débâcle*, having never bated an inch, and being quite as ' cynical' and ' heartless,' and everything else, as I was at the beginning. As for Gladstone—as your sister always properly styles him, ' that rascal Gladstone '—he is nowhere. The ' favorite' has broken down. . . .

I forgot to tell you all this time, while I am receiving indignant resolutions about Bulg. atrocities, I am equally receiving emblazoned, and some very pretty, addresses of congratulation on what is called my ' elevation.' This morning came one from Chester (I wish I cd. send it to you), a beautiful work of art, in many colors, and resplendent with much gold. The initial letter is a very pretty Cupid, worthy of Albano, lifting up, with pride and delight, an earl's coronet ! It is almost the only signal of my new order I possess. I was much amused with yr. acct. of the Wharncliffe achievements in this respect. I literally have done nothing in that way, and my plate and my linen are still plebeian. Had not a fairy dropped a paper-cutter from Mt. Olympus into my library, I shd. not know really how to sign my name I shd. still consider myself ' Christofero Sly.' . . .

Derby told the City deputation that, as soon as Baring's detailed report had been received and considered, the Government had sent a strong despatch to Elliot, directing him to obtain an audience of the Sultan, to lay all the proved facts before him, to denounce the chief authors of the atrocities by name and demand their punishment, and to represent the urgent necessity of immediate relief for the innocent sufferers. But he strongly deprecated a crusade to turn the Turk out of Europe, a crusade in which England would probably receive no support, and which would be resisted in arms by at least one Great Power, Austria He pointed out that there was no homogeneity of religion or race in the Balkan peninsula, and he therefore rejected the idea of creating a fresh group of tributary States; but he was anxious to extend local government in that region. He added, ' I do not at all wish to disguise the fact that what has happened in Bulgaria has to a certain extent changed the position, not only of our own Government, but of every European Government.'

Beaconsfield had, similarly, himself written to Derby
of ' the new departure ' of the Government; but he was
always anxious to emphasise that it did not constitute
a new 'policy.' The method might be different; the
policy, that of maintaining the integrity and independence of Turkey, remained. In this sense he wrote to
Salisbury, in answer to a letter in which the Indian
Secretary showed himself particularly sensible of the
necessity of change.

From Lord Salisbury.

Private. [DIEPPE], *Sept.* 23, '76.—The *Pall Mall* of
yesterday says that a Cabinet was summoned for to-day.
As I have received no summons, I presume your secretary
thought I was out of reach. This is not so. Whenever you
give 24 hours' notice to the India Office I can be present,
and can come over at any time if wanted. . . .

The Bucks election shows that the agitation has not been
without effect on our party. It is clear enough that the
traditional Palmerstonian policy is at an end. We have not
the power, even if we have the wish, to give back any of the
revolted districts to the *discretionary* government of the
Porte. The proposal in Derby's letter of the 21st, to send a
Commissioner to Bulgaria known to be friendly to the Christians, is very good for the emergency: but as a permanent
arrangement more will be required.

I should like to submit for your consideration whether the
opportunity should not be taken to exact some security for
the good government of the Christians generally throughout
the Turkish Empire. The Govt. of 1856 was satisfied with
promises: but they were promises extending to all the Christian subjects. We must have something more than promises:
but it will not do for us to cover a less extensive area of
relief than was covered by the Hatts referred to in the Treaty
of 1856. Would some such arrangement as this be possible ?
Let there be an Officer of State established at Constantinople
who shall be in fact, if not in name, Protector of Christians.
He should be nominated in concert with the Powers: and for
a term of years. He should always have access to the Sultan:
and it should be his duty to call the attention of the Turkish
Government to any breach of the decrees which have been
issued in protection of the Christians. He should not be
removable except with the consent of the Powers; and he
should be freely in communication with the Ambassadors.

It should further be his duty to submit to the Turkish Government a list of persons fit to hold office as Governors of Bosnia,
Herzegovina, and Bulgaria; and the Porte should be bound
to choose the Governors from that list. These Governors
should not be removable except with the Protector's assent;
and should hold office for a term of years. Subsidiary arrangements for councils might be necessary: but they would be of
less importance. The problem is solved, if you can get good
Governors for these oppressed provinces—men who will be
just to the Christians, but not disloyal to the Porte—and
who cannot be driven or dismissed by the corrupt intrigues
of the seraglio.

I was very glad to read the cordial language you used
towards Russia in your Aylesbury speech. Our best chance
of coming to a peaceful issue of these perplexities is—in my
belief—to come to an early understanding with Russia. Our
danger is that we should make that result impossible by
hanging on to the coat tails of Austria. Austria has good
reasons for resisting the faintest approach to self-government
in the revolted provinces. Her existence would be menaced
if she were hedged on the south by a line of Russian satellites.
But her existence is no longer of the importance to us that
it was in former times. Her vocation in Europe is gone.
She was a counterpoise to France and a barrier against
Russia; but France is gone, and the development of Russia
is chiefly in regions where Austria could not, and if she could
would not, help to check it. We have no reason, therefore,
for sharing Austria's tremors: and if we can get terms from
Russia that suit us, it would be most unwise to reject them
because they are not to the taste of Austria.

I venture to press this point, because I see that Austria
is urging a return to a state of things in which the lives and
property of the Christian populations of the three provinces
will be dependent on the promises of the Porte: and that in
this policy she will be backed by the advice of Buchanan
and Elliot. I feel convinced that such an arrangement,
though conformable to the pure Palmerston tradition, is not
suitable for the exigency; and that it would not be supported
in Parliament.

To Lord Salisbury.

HUGHENDEN MANOR, *Sept.* 26, 1876.—. . . The 'Cabinet'
was a hoax, or rather, perhaps, *un paragraphe hasardé*.

Notwithstanding the hullabaloo in which we still live,
there really has been no question to submit to the Cabinet,
and to have called them together unnecessarily, would have
much injured us on the Continent, and even at home would

only have given the impression that we were frightened and perplexed.

Derby has really only been working on the lines agreed on when we separated: the only difference is that, whether it were that he was piqued by being described as a Minister who never did anything, or whether he saw that golden opportunity, that, every now and then, occurs in public life, he has suddenly taken the conduct of affairs out of the hands of the other Powers, who, from various reasons, were indisposed to move, and has shown an energy and a resource and a firmness of purpose, wh. cannot be too highly praised, and for wh., much as I appreciated his many great qualities, I did not entirely give him credit.

But all that he has done as yet, or rather which he is still trying to do, is to carry thro' a successful mediation, and to obtain an armistice, and, in the shape of a protocol, to establish a basis of peace.

When he has done this, he will call us together, and then we will consider the means by which the preliminaries can be carried into effect. We are not, however, yet out of the wood. All depends upon Russia, and Russia cannot be trusted. It won't do, however, to tell her so, and I am working in the vein wh. you approve.

I think your idea well worthy of the deepest consideration as to some great officer at the metropolis to look after the interests of the rayahs.

Our great object, wh. Derby and myself have had during what Ld. Overstone calls 'a frantic ebullition of public excitement,' has never been to admit that we have changed our policy, and that we have adopted the views of the Opposition. This greatly irritates them, and *The Times* writes articles to prove that Lord Derby has changed his policy without knowing it. The force of impudence can't go much further.

If we had indulged in Bulgarian philippics, etc., etc., we might, to a certain degree, have checked the 'frantic ebullition,' but we should have become contemptible, and have soon fallen. You will see soon a great reaction. The conduct of the foreign Powers will alone occasion it, for they are all opposed to violent change. All the moneyed and commercial classes in all countries are against war: notably in London, where nobody will subscribe to the City Bulgarian Fund.

The new Sultan, I hear, really promises. He has got the Commons' blue book translated for him—and Forster's speech on 'atrocities.' He has only one wife: a *modiste* of Pera; a Belgian; he was in the habit of frequenting her shop, buying gloves, etc., and much admired her. One day he

said, ' Do you think you would marry me ?' and she replied
' Pourquoi non ?' And it was done. It is she who has set
him against seraglio life and all that: in short a Roxalana.
Will he be a Solyman the Great ?

A reign of three months had been sufficient to show
that Sultan Murad was incompetent, if not insane; and
on the last day of August a second palace revolution at
Constantinople had deposed him in favour of his brother,
the notorious Abdul Hamid. The hopefulness with which
Beaconsfield regarded Abdul Hamid's elevation appears
to us now to be extraordinarily shortsighted. But, after
all, the whole European world, and in particular the
Liberal party in England, committed a similar mistake
when they welcomed the rise of the Young Turks to
power in 1908; and Abdul Hamid not only made the
usual fair professions, but was obviously a man of capacity
and vigour.

Diplomacy, during August and September, waited on the
issue of the fighting in the Balkans. Montenegro, as ever,
maintained its cause bravely against the Turks. But,
unless Serbia could make good, little Montenegro's effort
would be of small avail. And the military adventure
of Serbia, though it achieved some success at first, broke
down in a few weeks before the superior power of the
enemy. Accordingly she was ready in August for the
armistice which England managed to secure for her in
September. But the Porte, successful in the field, was not
willing to grant easy terms to its foes, or more than a
short suspension of hostilities. Derby proposed as a
basis for discussion the kind of terms he had outlined to
the City deputation, the *status quo* in Serbia and Montenegro, and local self-government for Bosnia and Bulgaria.
Russia proceeded to show her hand by suggesting a
military occupation of Bulgaria by Russia, and of Bosnia
by Austria, together with a demonstration by the united
fleets in the Bosphorus. As if in concert with this large
demand, the Serbians renewed hostilities, and the situation became perceptibly more serious. There can be

little doubt that both Russia and Serbia were misled by
the clamour of the atrocity agitation in England, and
expected a support here for extreme measures which was
not forthcoming. As Beaconsfield said at Guildhall on
Lord Mayor's Day :

> An indignant burst of feeling in this country, excited by
> horrible events, created such a sensation and excitement that
> the people of Servia, and the friends of the people of Servia,
> really believed that the people of England had suddenly
> determined to give up the traditionary policy of the country
> which the eminent statesmen of Europe only five years ago
> —including the members of the late Government—thought
> so highly of; and Servia was induced to retract what she had
> expressed, and once more to engage in a sanguinary struggle
> which every friend of humanity must lament.

To Lord Derby.

Confidential. HUGHENDEN MANOR, *Sept.* 29.—The Queen
sent cyphered tel. yesterday, reverting to an idea, wh. she
started some time ago, but wh. I did not encourage, of sending
special envoy from herself, with a letter to E[mperor] of
R[ussia]. . . .

She now recurs to it: my answer cyphered was brief. . . .
I impressed upon Her Majesty, that the person to consult
was yourself; because a diplomatic visit, however secret and
private, or even a letter from her, might conflict with yr.
plans and movements, who have all the threads in your
hands.   This reasoning was not cyphered.

I distinctly said to her, that if the E. of R. would be as
peremptory with Servia, as he proposes to be with the Porte,
all would be well.

I think you, and you alone, can decide upon the point.
What[eve]r your decision, I shall, of course, support it, and
you may assume, therefore, in yr. reply, that anything like
a special Mission is not expedient.   Whether it wd. do good,
that she shd. write a letter to the Emperor, as she wrote to
the Emperor of the French before the Italian war, is another
thing.   It wd. please her, and might do no harm : but what-
[eve]r you think, I think.

I had written you a long letter yesterday congratulating
you on yr. speech—wh. was perfect; and wh. induced *The
Times* to throw over both Lowe and Gladstone specifically,
showing, after all, we were exactly right.

But the Serv. tel. upset me. I don't see my way. If

Austria step in to put an end to the conspiracy, the same reason that prevents Russia interfering herself, will force her to oppose Austria. There is war and a long one. France wants yet three years, and she will be delighted that those three years shd. be spent in the exhaustion of other Powers, and then she will come in fresh with ½ million of men.

I don't think we ought to join in the war, but I think, with an understanding with the Porte, we shd. occupy Const[antinop]le as ' a material guarantee.'

Everybody will be wanting something: even Italy. It is now or never with Bismarck, if he really wants peace.

Lord Derby to Queen Victoria.

FOREIGN OFFICE, *Sept.* 29, '76.—Lord Derby, with his humble duty, submits to your Majesty that the rupture by Servia of the suspension of hostilities agreed upon has introduced a new element of difficulty into the negotiations.

If the telegram in *The Times* is true, a general engagement is taking place on this day.

The Russian Ambassador speaks in strong terms of the want of good faith and respect to the Powers shown by Servia in this matter. He declares his belief that Prince Milan has been helpless in regard to it, General Tchernayeff being practically independent, and the Army so largely officered by Russians. Lord Derby owns he finds it hard to believe that the Russian volunteers, who have of late poured in at the rate, in one case, of 300 in a day, come without the tacit or implied consent of the Emperor. It is necessary at present to act as if we trusted Russia, for the present state of popular feeling makes all action in an anti-Russian sense practically impossible: but everything points to the probability that the Russian Government, while ostensibly promoting peace, are by indirect means making it impossible. Such is evidently the view entertained in Austria, and, Lord Derby thinks, to some extent in Germany also. But while Lord Derby states this as a matter of fact, and expresses his opinion, he must own that he has nothing to suggest Appeals to the Emperor would produce assurances of goodwill and peaceable intentions; which are seldom wanting: but the agents of General Kaufmann are at work in Cabul, and probably there is no place where Russian influence can be used to weaken that of other Powers where similar means are not being employed.

Lord Derby had written so far when your Majesty's telegram of to-day reached him. He had telegraphed to Lord Beaconsfield on the subject of it, on receiving the telegram of yesterday, and awaits Lord Beaconsfield's answer:

but he is bound to say that he has not much faith in the result of personal appeals. It is simply inconceivable that the Emperor of Russia—though he may choose to shut his eyes to details—can be ignorant of all that is doing in his name.

Lord Derby may add that he believes the officers who join Tchernayeff have received informal, but sufficient, promises that the commissions which they are obliged to resign on taking foreign service will be given back to them on their return. This cannot be done without the Emperor's knowledge.

To Lord Derby.

Private. HUGHENDEN MANOR, *Sept.* 30, 1876.—I will come up to you, when it is ripe. I only asked you here, as I thought it might be a beneficial change for yourself. .

I know you are bored going to any place, wh. is natural, but I was quite alone, or shd. not have asked you.

The Russians have behaved very badly. In future, they must have not only Ambassadors for their Emperors, but for their adventurous Generals, who have secret orders—but it is never any use to complain. We must see whether we may not be able to make a move, wh. may checkmate Gortchakoff.

I assume that, somehow or other, European Turkey will be invaded—but they must make a proposal first, and the Cabinet must decide upon it. That's quite clear.

I wrote in the sense you mention to the Queen this afternoon: I inferred you wished me. But a line from you would be acceptable; you are in great favor, which pleases, and amuses, me.

Keep up yr. spirits. You have shown some of the highest qualities of public life, and I believe the great mass of the nation believe in you.

We may yet confound their politics.

From Lord Derby.

Private. KESTON, *Oct.* 1, '76.—A thousand thanks for your cordial note. One really wants encouragement just now. I sometimes feel like the juryman who complained of having been sitting along with eleven of the most obstinate men he ever met. But we are fairly well supported in the press, which I suspect is a better test than provincial meetings, *Pall Mall, Telegraph, Post,* and *Standard*—for; *Times* uncertain and trimming; only *D. News* and *Echo* against us.

Foreigners don't know what to make of the movement; and I am not surprised. . . .

To Sir Stafford Northcote.

HUGHENDEN MANOR, *Sept.* 30.—. . . Derby has shown, throughout this business of the negotiations, the utmost energy and resource. A clear head, the clearest, and a sound judgment I always gave him credit for; but I feel I never did him sufficient justice—much and long as I have appreciated him—for his vigor, his action, and his fertility. I fear all thrown away. His hands have been fatally weakened by the lowest arts of faction abusing the noble enthusiasm of a great portion of the people. But we must be patient. The solution of this vast question will be long, the English people will come to their senses, and we may yet retrieve and regain our position.

You have made some capital speeches, and so far as the agitation is concerned, it has well introduced you to the country in your new position.[1] . . .

[1] Of Leader of the House of Commons.

CHAPTER III.

The Constantinople Conference.

1876-1877.

As summer passed into autumn, Beaconsfield's and Derby's diplomacy became more and more concentrated on a policy of armistice first, and conference afterwards. It was of the highest importance to put an end to hostilities between Turkey and Serbia, with so much combustible material about. On the one hand was Russia, proposing, not to say threatening, armed occupation of Turkey; and, on the other, the Porte, determined to exploit the favourable position of its victorious armies to the utmost. The Cabinet met at the beginning of October, and decided, while rejecting the Russian proposal, to put strong pressure upon the Porte to grant at once that substantial armistice which Serbia and her friends had demanded. An armistice once granted, it was proposed that arrangements should be made for the meeting of a European Conference.

To Lady Bradford.

Hughenden Manor, *Monday morning* [*Oct.* 2, 1876].— . . . I have summoned the Cabinet for Wednesday; I go up to town to-morrow. Whitehall Gardens are in the hands of workmen, painters especially, wh. wd. kill me; so I have ordered a camp-bed in D. S., and, like a true leader, shall sleep on the field of battle.

It is likely the Turkish reply will arrive before, or about, Wednesday, and the Cabinet therefore will be at hand: but it is necessary that it shd. meet irrespective of that contingency. The position of affairs never was more critical or more difficult. I don't believe the Russians have any money to make war, but they cannot resist what, according to their own language, 'they never had before; England on their side.'

Is it ?   As Hamlet saith, 'that is the question.'   All I know
is that England won't subscribe.   The City meeting, wh.
was to produce instantaneously £50,000, after weeks of tout-
ing does not count much more than £5—and that produced
by the knaves, or fools, who got up the gathering: even . . .
Lady Strangford shrieks at the ineffective answer to her
appeal, . . . while Monty's righteous uncle, . . . Lord
Shaftesbury, who began the nonsense, announces that after
two or 3 months of agitation his fund only amounts to
£147 6 0, and that there is no hope of more. . . .

10, DOWNING STREET, *Oct.* 5.—. . . Nothing can be more
critical or more interesting than the position.   Gortchakoff,
misled by Gladstone and Co., has made a false move, and his
proposal for Russia to occupy Bulgaria, the very heart and
most precious portion of European Turkey, with Constantinople almost in sight of the contemplated frontier, has roused
and alarmed John Bull.   Your friend, *The Times*, ratted this
morning.   It was like the verdict after the long trial of the
Claimant.[1]

England looks upon the proposed occupation by Russia as
a real Bulgarian atrocity.   When he sounded Austria on the
point, Austria enquired, What will England say ?   G[or-
tchakoff] answered instantly, ' England will certainly agree.'
Instead of that, I sent Schouvaloff off with a flea in his ear;
told him it was a double violation of treaties, etc., etc., and
that Russia must take the consequences, wh. wd. be most
grave.   Austria gave another kick, and the thing has collapsed.   But what will happen next I can't tell you.   Constantinople is in such a state of excitement that I fear the
people won't obey the Sultan, who seems, as I anticipated,
a real man. . . .

HUGHENDEN MANOR, *Oct.* 7.—. . . I came down yesterday,
and Derby went to Keston, a cottage he has, ten miles or
less from town: we can be there in a moment. . . .

Oct. 10.—. . . I can't give you good news.   I think, in the
most favorable view, it's a toss up.   If Turkey accepts our
proposal, Russia wd. be at least for the time checkmated.
But if Turkey refuse, I think Russia will declare war.   I think
Gortchakoff wants war.

The only good thing is the improved feeling in England;
but, I fear, it's too late.

I read an amusing private letter from Const. this morning.
Hartington, it seems, highly disapproves of Gladstone's
pamphlets and Lowe's speeches.   He, and the Duke of
Manchester, were on the following day to have their audience

---

[1] The Tichborne Claimant.

of the Sultan, and the Dss. was to see all the palaces. The day before there had been a grand dinner at Safvet Pasha, the Secy. of State for For. Affairs, and who speaks English. The Duchess dined there, tho' there was no other lady. The letter-writer, who was one of the guests, says that did not seem at all to embarrass her Grace; ' she lit her segar from that of Midhat Pasha, and showed the utmost *aplomb*.' To the life ! . . .

Confidential. Oct. 12.—. . . I could not write yesterday. I was so anxious and so uncertain. It was a neck-and-neck race.

We had taken a decided step—many thought a rash one. Elliot was to tell the Porte that the recommendation of the armistice by England was England's last step; that, if refused, she shd. attempt no longer to arrest the destruction of the Turkish Empire, but leave her to her fate; and that our Ambassador wd. leave Constantinople.

There were great, and just, objections to this course, because, when an Ambassador retires, he cannot reappear. All personal influence is lost, and in 1829, the last time when the Embassies left Constantinople, war between Russia and Turkey instantly ensued.

And yet affairs had come to such a pass, thro' the conduct of Gladstone and Co., that it was necessary to try this last card—and it succeeded ! But I did not know, till late last night, that Servia had accepted. I think now all is safe for some time.

The Porte has been crafty, I shd. rather say very wise and clever, in enlarging the proposal, and making the arm[isticet for 5 or 6 months. This will give us breathing time. I don'] think any Power will dare to disturb the European peace while an arm. exists. By that time, too, the people of England will have quite recovered their senses, and I hope Gladstone will be shut up. I feel much relieved, and tho' there are plenty of difficulties before me, the great oppression of the last six or seven weeks is removed. . . .

Beaconsfield's satisfaction and relief were altogether premature. Serbia, and Serbia's great friend, Russia, refused to accept a half-year's armistice, on the plausible ground that the Principality could not keep its army on a war footing for such a length of time without putting too severe a strain on its resources.

Looking round during this autumn for a stable basis for British policy amid all the shifting sands of diplomacy,

Beaconsfield came to the conclusion that a clear understanding with Bismarck, and a treaty with Germany, on the basis of the *status quo*, was the best available means of calming the disquiet of Europe, and preventing constant alarms and probable wars. He wrote in this sense to the Queen, to Derby, and to Salisbury; and their reception of his idea was generally sympathetic.

To Lord Derby.

Confidential.   HUGHENDEN MANOR, *Oct.* 17.—Nothing can be more unsatisfactory, than the whole state of Europe—and Asia too—in a great degree.

Russia is full of mischief, and yet ' willing to wound and yet afraid to strike.' That's her finance: still, she will go trying it on, trusting to no physical opposition, till she, as before, commits herself.

Can't we take advantage of the delay, and make some arrangement, wh. will put an end to these *misères*, and set the world to rights ?

What if we could negotiate a treaty with Germany to maintain the present *status quo* generally ? Not an alliance offensive and defensive, as Brunnow offered to yr. father in 1852—and wh. was wisely and promptly declined; but a treaty for the maintenance of the *status quo*.   This wd. make us easy about Constantinople, and relieve Bismarck of his real bugbear, the eventual alliance of England and France, and the loss of his two captured provinces. We don't wish France to be weaker than she is; but when she was stronger, she gave us plenty of trouble.

The objection, or rather difficulty, in bringing this about, wd. be, perhaps, the old German Emperor, who, I heartily wish, were in the same cave as Friedrich Barbarossa; but tho' he might shrink from a war with his nephew, or anything obviously hostile, with time, and management, and firmness, Bis. cd. succeed, I think, in the *status quo* treaty

The difficulty is to get hold of Bis. I counted on Odo Russell, but he might as well be at Bagdad. And Münster is not a genial nature to work on.   He is suspicious and stupid.

Still, I think, the thing ought to be done, and it wd. settle everything for our lives, and immortalise yourself.

Here we have the germ of the policy which was brought into actual working by Beaconsfield at the Congress of

Berlin, and which was pursued by him, and by Salisbury after him, until at the close of the nineteenth century the ambitious aims of the German Empire made further co-operation on the same footing impossible. There was never, of course, any alliance, and it is strange that Beaconsfield should have contemplated a formal treaty— a step which would have involved a permanent estrangement from France, whom he always preferred, and had long cherished, as an ally. But there was a steady reliance by the British Foreign Office on the Central Powers; a working arrangement which, so long as Russia was aggressive and France restless, and so long as Germany was content with industrial and commercial development, preserved peace in Europe, at least among the greater States.

But Bismarck, though he never forgave Gortchakoff for interfering to save France in the spring of 1875, was not yet disposed to weaken the bonds which united Germany to Russia. Moreover, it was by no means clear to foreign observers whether Beaconsfield could maintain his ground against Gladstone's agitation. Accordingly, in answer to Derby's appeal to him to use the influence of Germany ' in order to procure the acceptance of some compromise,' Bismarck replied that, though an armistice of six months seemed acceptable to the German Government, he could not put pressure on any other Power to secure its sanction.

To Queen Victoria.

(*Telegraphed in Cypher.*)   10, DOWNING ST., *Oct.* 19, '76.— The Cabinet decided, that they would take no further steps in negotiations for armistice, tho,' if Turkey assented to a proposal to shorten it, they would make no opposition. They decided, that Lord Derby should draw up a despatch reciting that Servia had appealed to us to mediate, that we undertook the office and succeeded, that then Servia rejected the armistice which we had solicited for her; that we should protest against the military emigration of Russia into Servia, and end by warning Russia that a violation of the Treaty of Paris by the occupation of Bulgaria would lead to serious consequences.

To Lady Bradford.

10, DOWNING ST., *Oct.* 20, 1876.—. . . We had a Cabinet yesterday, wh. then dispersed, from wh. the world infers we are unanimous, and that there is no split. . . .

In a talk with a political and personal friend Beaconsfield expounded his view of the present situation and his hopes for the future.

Memorandum by Lord Barrington.

Oct. 23, 1876.—I had an interview with Lord Beaconsfield this evening at 5.30. He entered rather fully into the details of the present crisis in the East. Alluding to his speech at Aylesbury, he utterly repudiated having ever said that the ' Government was opposed to the feelings of a majority in the country.' The report of that speech in *The Times* of Sept. 21, ought to be enough to show the utter fallacy of such a statement. Yet this has constantly, and persistently, been asserted by Messrs. Gladstone and Lowe, and this assertion has done immense harm in retarding negotiations with Foreign Powers on this question. Lord Beaconsfield's statement that the Government had not the ' unanimous ' support of the country, but that a large party in the country was using the ' atrocity cry ' for party purposes (or words to that effect), was quite true.

The present state of affairs in the East is that England advised ' an armistice of *not less* than a month or six weeks.' The Turks replied that six weeks was too short, and proposed ' five or six months.' This the Russians refused to accept, and reverted to what they termed the English proposal of ' six weeks.' But England had put no extending limit, and had guarded herself by ' not less.' Consequently England accepted the Turkish proposal. Russia never imagined that Turkey would accept any armistice, and therefore finds herself in a difficulty. The Turks have now, in all probability at the instance of our Ambassador, Sir H. Elliot, averred themselves willing to accept the English proposal, with the understanding that the six weeks' armistice may be prolonged if necessary.

Lord Beaconsfield has great hopes of being able to settle this great question, but of course guarded himself against any opinion as to Peace or War. Supposing the Russians to enter Bulgaria, said I. That, he answered, would be an entirely new phase of the question. He is evidently quite determined that the Russians shall not directly, or indirectly, become possessed of Constantinople.

Many in England say, Why not ? England might take Egypt, and so secure our highway to India.

But the answer is obvious, said Lord B. If the Russians had Constantinople, they could at any time march their Army through Syria to the mouth of the Nile, and then what would be the use of our holding Egypt ? Not even the command of the sea could help us under such circumstances. People who talk in this manner must be utterly ignorant of geography. Our strength is on the sea. Constantinople is the key of India, and not Egypt and the Suez Canal.

The mendacity of the Russians is the same as ever. They say, ' We do not wish to hold Constantinople.' Perhaps not, but for all that their game is to have someone there who is more or less dependent on them. . . .

The grand political duel between Lord Beaconsfield and Prince Gortchakoff has now lasted some months, and, up to the present time, the latter has got the worst of it. That England should be victorious in diplomacy (and war if necessary, as a matter of course), is Lord B.'s grand object, and will be a splendid consummation to his wonderful career. He appears to me to have no doubt that, whatever present appearances may be, Germany will eventually go against Russia. . . .

The six months' armistice which Turkey proposed having been rejected, the Turkish armies continued their advance and, in spite of all the efforts of the Russian General and the Russian Volunteers who organised the resistance to them under the banner of Serbia, won success after success until Belgrade itself was in danger. Beaconsfield flattered himself that these Turkish victories, coupled with the firm attitude of the British Cabinet, had produced a moderating effect on the counsels of the Russian Government, as Gortchakoff began to express interest in the Conference which Derby had suggested, and Ignatieff at Constantinople seemed to be ready for a reasonable compromise about the length of armistice Appearances were deceptive. The Turkish successes convinced the Emperor Alexander that, if Serbia was to be saved, he must interpose at once, and on the last day of the month his Ambassador presented an ultimatum at Constantinople, demanding, under the threat of a total severance of diplomatic relations, the acceptance by Turkey, within forty-eight hours, of the armistice limited to a month or six weeks. Under the menace of force Turkey agreed.

To Lady Bradford.

10, DOWNING STREET, *Oct.* 28, 1876.—There is a streak of light on the horizon. Whether it be the victory of the Turks, or whether it be that the Russians commence to comprehend that England will stand no nonsense, but a great change occurred last night—and for the better. . . .

Oct. 30.—We are not out of the wood, but we sometimes think we see light in the distance—I hope not a mirage. I have had now nearly a quarter of a year of it, and feel a good deal older. Certainly, it has not been a dull life, but a very hard one. . . .

Schou. called on me with a message of horror and indignation from the Emperor of R. about the *Golos.* I said I was under the impression that the press was not free in Russia. He assured me that he had been libelled himself in the *Golos,* and accused of having sold himself to Germany. I remarked that the press was free in England, but that if such an article had appeared in a respectable paper agst. Prince Gortff., I wd. undertake to say I wd. have made the editor apologise.[1]

Nov. 1.—Yesterday (Tuesday) I received two tels. when I woke: they had arrived in the night. One was from our Ambassador at Livadia saying that P. Gortchakoff considered the armistice now settled, and making suggestions about ulterior points—and much more important ones: the basis of the Conference. The other telegram was from our Ambassador at Constantinople, dated Monday night $\frac{1}{2}$ past 10 o'ck. (Therapia), saying that the armistice was settled—very satisfactorily and honorably to the Turks, that Ignatieff had

---

[1] The *Golos* had had the effrontery to accuse Beaconsfield of having, in conjunction with the firm of Erlanger, amassed a colossal fortune by speculating on the various phases of the Eastern Question! Whereas, as Rose, who had been familiar with Beaconsfield's pecuniary dealings for thirty years, wrote indignantly to Corry on Oct. 25, 'if ever a man lived who was pure as snow in money matters, and more scrupulous than any living man in everything that concerned his pecuniary interests, it is Lord B[eaconsfiel]d: as history will prove.' In spite of Schouvaloff's assurances, the *Golos* felt it so necessary to damage the reputation of the most determined opponent of Russia's Turkish policy, that it reiterated its scandalous charges. 'The fact,' wrote Corry to Schouvaloff. 'that this repetition is made after the gracious message wh. on behalf of the Emperor of Russia you last week conveyed to Lord Beaconsfield much aggravates the calumny.'

been conciliatory throughout, and that he was to execute it formally in the morning, having an appointment with the G. Vizier to that effect.

So I thought my cares were over, and I remembered what your friend Delane said to me on Sunday, ' that the Minister who opened Parliamt. with an announcement of peace in the Queen's Speech, wd. be in a prouder position than any Minister since Mr. Pitt.'

A little after noon came the awful news that Genl. Ignatieff had received orders from Livadia to deliver the offensive and hostile ultimatum you are now well acquainted with !

This was the consequence of the Turkish victories, and the humiliation the Emperor felt at the probability of the Turks reaching Belgrade. The pretext that the Turks carried on hostilities during negotiations for armistice is quite hollow. The Russo-Servian army has never ceased attacking and harassing the Turks during the whole time. Besides, negotiations for armistice never suspend hostilities as a matter of public law.

What will happen now ? I think it looks as black as possible. The whole affair has been a conspiracy of Russia from the beginning, and she has failed in everything—even in active warfare the Porte has defeated her. I don't think she can stand it, and she will rush to further reverses.

Yesterday I dined at S[tafford] House—with the little Duchess, and the ' bride and bridegroom ' [1] and Ronald; and then they took me to the play, a new comedy that is making some noise, *Peril*—an adaptation from the French *Nos Intimes*—not over-moral, but fairly transmogrified from the original, and cleverly acted in the chief part—a woman[2] whom, I doubt not, you, an *habituée* of the drama, know very well, but quite new to me. Now she is married, but she was a sister of Robertson, the playwright. She had evidently studied in the French school. The whole was good, and the theatre was ventilated; so I did not feel exhausted, and was rather amused, and shd. rather have enjoyed myself, had not the bad news thrown its dark shadow over one's haunted consciousness. . . .

Nov. 2.—As I have often told you ' there is no gambling like politics '—and here we are with the armistice signed ! . . . I can't write any details: until this moment, I have not had a moment of pause—4 and 20 hours indeed of awful crisis.

' How can we ever trust the Russians ?' was the Queen's comment to Beaconsfield on what she termed

---

[1] Mr. (afterwards Viscount) and Lady Florence Chaplin.
[2] Mrs. Kendal.

the Emperor's ' rash and intemperate act.'   The Emperor
must have felt the need of reassuring English opinion,
for on November 2 he pledged his word at Livadia to
the British Ambassador that he had not the smallest
wish or intention to acquire Constantinople, and that
any occupation of Bulgaria to which necessity might
drive him would be only provisional.   Derby telegraphed
the satisfaction of the Cabinet at these assurances, but
Beaconsfield was more impressed by the obvious preparations which Russia was making for independent
military action, and by Gortchakoff's hectoring tone
about the proposals for autonomy to be submitted to the
Porte.   For, now that the armistice was signed, Beaconsfield and Derby proposed to issue invitations to the Conference which they had for some time contemplated—
a step which was taken by a Cabinet Council on
November 4.   For the chief representative of Great
Britain at the Conference the Prime Minister selected the
ablest of his younger colleagues, overcoming his reluctance by friendly pressure.   Among the Beaconsfield
papers there is preserved an undated sheet of Downing
Street writing-paper, with the words, in Beaconsfield's
handwriting: ' Conf[identia]l.   I want you to go.   That
is my idea.   A great enterprise, and wd. not take much
time.   B.,' followed by Salisbury's response, ' Of course
I will do what the Cabinet wishes, but it is essential that
your policy should be settled first.'   These notes were
almost certainly interchanged at this meeting of the
Cabinet.

To Lord Derby.

Confidential.   10, DOWNING ST., WHITEHALL, *Nov.* 3, '76.—
I shall call to-day latish, on the chance of seeing you, as I
think we ought to confer together before the Cabinet.

In the meanwhile, reflection has only confirmed me in my
conviction, that it wd. be most unwise for us to be hurried
into any proceedings; that we shd. principally be represented
by someone of great authority, not mixed up with the previous
transactions; and that we shd. come to an agreement, before
the meeting of the Congress, as to the basis of our negotiations.

I foresee endless chicanery on the part of Russia, who is. at present, somewhat baffled and mortified.

I think a *sine qua non* on our part shd. be, that no interference shd. be sanctioned with the military arrangements of the Porte in Bulgaria, or indeed Bosnia, etc.

Turkey cd. maintain 200,000 men between the Danube and Constantinople, and with this force, and the command of the sea, she is, so far as Russia is concerned, invincible. This is consistent with her maintaining 100,000 men on her Asiatic frontier.

. And now, again, I must impress upon you the importance, if we wish to secure a long peace, of coming to some understanding with some European Power.

The difficulties of negotiating any satisfactory understanding with Germany may be great, but Odo Russell ought to be instructed to lose no opportunity of conferring with Bismarck in this sense. By the bye, I do not at all believe Ignatieff's 'confidential' communication to Elliot about the German Chanr.

But without the trouble, and the risk, of any new treaties, we have a course open to us, wh. I think it imprudent, and scarcely justifiable on our part, to neglect. It is not only our right, but, in my opinion, our duty, to enquire of France and Austria, what, in the event of the failure of the Congress, are their views and feelings with reference to their engagements under the Tripartite Treaty ?

This will give Austria, if she wishes it, an occasion to unburthen or unbutton herself—and may lead to important consequences. I do not understand from you, and I do not hear from any other quarter, that you have ever made to her, howr. guarded, any overture for joint action. I believe it has been expected. If made, it shd. be expressed thro' Buchanan, not Beust, but it wd. be more conveniently managed with reference to keeping existing engagements: the Tripartite.

It is probable that France, at this moment, wd. avoid action, but that reserve on her part will not subsist as long as she thinks, if troublous times arrive. And she wd. be gratified by the enquiry and the appeal, and if it did nothing else, with regard to both France and Austria, I think it wd. have an advantageous effect on both of them in influencing their conduct in the Conference.

I have no hesitation myself in saying, that it wd. be most desirable to arrive at a clear agreement with Austria for joint action, and that, if the Conference fail, and Russia is arrogant and menacing, it shd. at once be intimated to Russia that the integrity of the Turkish dominions shd. not be violated.

Nov. 4.—I do not think that Gortchakoff's insolent announcement to Loftus, that, if the Russian propositions respecting autonomy are not agreed to, Ignatieff is to withdraw, ought to pass unnoticed.

This was not said after dinner, like the Emperor's sentimental ebullition—but it was said in the morning, and was an announcement to us.

It shd. be noticed we gain nothing with Russia by conciliation or concession.

If Gortchakoff's position is a genuine one, then there is no use in conferring. At any rate, he shd. privately inform us what are his views.

Loftus, tho' a mere Livadian parasite, and afraid even of G.'s shadow, will, I suppose, still obey absolute orders, and I think you ought to send him a rattler.

Your complaints of Andrassy are echoed back from Vienna as against us. There, it is the fashion to say that England will do nothing and join them in no action.

Nothing can secure the success of the Conference but firmness on our side, and we cannot be firm, unless we are prepared for the future.

Our policy hitherto has secured the first object proposed by us: viz., the maintenance of the integrity of the Ott. Empire. The refusal of the Berlin note, and the fleet, have hitherto accomplished that. There has been no ' occupation.' For the second object proposed, the amelioration of the condition of the rayahs, we ought to arrive, among ourselves, at some clear conception of your definition of autonomy with[ou]t loss of time.

A catalogue of the proposals in the Andrassy note, in language as little technical as possible, shd., if possible, be before the Cabinet this morning.

To Lady Bradford.

10, Downing St., *Nov.* 4.—Cabinet just over; very tired, and a little harassed—but I won't let the post go without a line.

We have agreed to invite the Powers to a Conference; the place, Constantinople; and each Power to be represented by two Plenipotentiaries. I assume the Ambassador at Constantinople, and six greater men, what you call *swells.* Who is to go for England ? I have a good mind to go myself.

How will it all end ? So many plots and counterplots and such Machiavellian brains to deal with ! . . .

Nov. 8.—The appointment of Ld. Salisbury as Ambassador Extra[ordinar]y to the Conference seems to give great satisfaction. I do not despair, if the Conference take place, that we may succeed in our main purposes, but what I dread is that Russia will secretly encourage and invite the Porte to refuse the Conference, and then privately arrange with her. I have detected some traits of this intrigue and Ignatieff is equal to anything.

By proposing a Conference on a broader basis—*i.e.*, two Ambassadors or Plenipotentiaries from each State—a certain delay has been obtained, and a proportionately greater importance has been given to the Conference—wh. may balk him. But if his original proposition of an immediate council of the Ambassadors at Constantinople and none else had been agreed to, I think he wd. have succeeded. He may yet.

Ld. Mayor's Day.—. . . Yes, it is the fatal day, that always makes me ill—when I have to make a speech wh. is ever strictly scanned and wh., on this occasion, will be criticised by all Europe: sent on the wings of the lightning to the old coxcomb at Livadia (wh. he has left by-the-bye) and the fox at Varzin.

It is about as nervous an affair as can fall to the lot of man—particularly when it is to be accomplished in a heated hall, full of gas and aldermen and trumpeters, after sitting for hours talking slipslop to a defunct Lady Mayoress, and with every circumstance that can exhaust and discomfort man. I think I will never do it again, and should not be able to do it now, were it not for the hope of seeing you to-morrow.

To Queen Victoria.

10, DOWNING STREET, WHITEHALL, *Nov.* 9, 1876.—. . . To-day is 'Lord Mayor's Day,' always the most distressful day in the year to Lord Beaconsfield, but, this year, his sense of discomfort and nervousness are aggravated. He must speak on the great question, and every word he utters will be criticised throughout Europe. However, it is something, that he can mention even a prospect of peace. He feels, at this moment, as if he should hardly get through the day, and the only thing which sustains him is the desire not to disgrace your Majesty's service and confidence. . . .

It is noteworthy that Beaconsfield should have written to the Queen of the speech which he was about to deliver at Guildhall as one suggesting a prospect of peace. Such, fairly construed, it seems in historical retrospect to have been, but his domestic critics at the time insisted that its tone was one of warlike defiance. Undoubtedly it contained a grave warning, which can hardly be thought unjustified in view of the policy of combined intrigue and menace which Russia had pursued during the year. But he was careful to speak of her with due respect, and to attribute to her a cordiality and a readiness to accept reasonable proposals of which she had in fact shown little sign. He described the great objects which the Government had set before themselves to be, first, to maintain the general peace of Europe by the due observance of the Treaties of 1856 and 1871, which laid down as the best security for peace the preservation of the independence and territorial integrity of the Turkish Empire, and, secondly, to secure such an amelioration of the condition of the subjects of Turkish provinces as, by increasing their prosperity, would promote that independence and integrity. He expressed his satisfaction at the armistice; ' an armistice is certainly not peace any more than courtship is wedlock; but in general it is the auspicious harbinger of a happy future.' As to the ' ultimatum' by which it was obtained, ' that is an ugly word when we are endeavouring to bring about a pacific settlement.' But in this case the ultimatum was something like ' bringing an action for debt when the whole sum claimed had previously been paid into court.'

Beaconsfield dwelt with satisfaction on the Conference and on its acceptance by all the Powers, and paid a generous compliment to Salisbury, who, he said, possessed the complete confidence of his colleagues.

They have confidence in his abilities, in his grasp of the subject, and in the tact and firmness of his character; and I have no doubt that he will use and exercise all his abilities to bring about that permanent peace in Europe which all statesmen agree can best be secured by adhering to the treaties which exist, knowing well—and none knows better than my noble friend—that the independence and territorial integrity of Turkey are not to be secured by mere pen-and-ink work. Unless the great body of the people find that they are under a Government which studies their welfare and is proud of their prosperity, even the independence and integrity of a country must themselves vanish.

Then followed the passage which excited so much attention and provoked so much criticism.

I am hopeful, in the present temper of Europe, we shall be able to accomplish the objects we have in view without those terrible appeals to war, of which, I think, we have heard too frequently and too much. . . . There is no country so interested in the maintenance of peace as England. Peace is especially an English policy. She is not an aggressive Power, for there is nothing which she desires. She covets no cities and no provinces. What she wishes is to maintain and to enjoy the unexampled empire which she has built up, and which it is her pride to remember exists as much upon sympathy as upon force. But although the policy of England is peace, there is no country so well prepared for war as our own. If she enters into conflict in a righteous cause—and I will not believe that England will go to war except for a righteous cause—if the contest is one which concerns her liberty, her independence, or her empire, her resources, I feel, are inexhaustible. She is not a country that, when she enters into a campaign, has to ask herself whether she can support a second or a third campaign. She enters into a campaign which she will not terminate till right is done.

It was not Beaconsfield, but Russia, who had made the ' appeals to war ' of which he spoke. And his reply only restated, in grave and forcible fashion, the permanent conditions which those who challenge this country must face. He had recounted them in almost identical language in 1862, when he was in opposition. He had then said that ' England is the only country which, when it enters into a quarrel which it believes to be just, never ceases its efforts until it has accomplished its aim '; that ' it was not a question of one, two, or three campaigns, but that, as we have proved in old days, our determination, supported by our resources, would allow us to prepare for an indefinite struggle when we had an adequate and worthy object in view.' [1] The words remain as true now as when they were spoken in 1862 and in 1876; and most Englishmen to-day will heartily endorse them. Whether the occasion in 1876 was a fitting one on which to repeat

[1] See pp. 44, 45.

them as Prime Minister at Guildhall is, of course, an arguable question. But Russia's menacing attitude undoubtedly suggested that she had either forgotten England's historic power and persistence, or believed that the ancient spirit was dead. The very next day the Emperor Alexander, in an address to the nobles and communal council of Moscow, caused a sensation in Europe by saying that, if the Conference failed to bring peace, and if he could not obtain the guarantees which he desired from the Porte, he was firmly resolved to take independent action and that he was convinced that Russia would respond to his summons. The leaders of the atrocity agitation saw in this threat the natural, and indeed legitimate, retort to what they considered to be Beaconsfield's wanton provocation. In actual fact, the Emperor, when he spoke, had no cognisance of Beaconsfield's words, and was only saying openly what Gortchakoff, his Chancellor, had already intimated to the British Ambassador; and the Russian Government proceeded to mobilise a considerable force and to issue a new loan for 100,000,000 roubles. 'What an infamous *lie* that was,' wrote the Queen to Beaconsfield on November 21, ' to say the Emperor Alexander's speech at Moscow was in consequence of Lord Beaconsfield's excellent one at the Mansion House [? Guildhall].'

While those responsible for the atrocity agitation were indignant with Beaconsfield for his Guildhall speech, they cordially approved the appointment of Salisbury as British representative at the Constantinople Conference. They remembered the deep-seated distrust of Disraeli which Salisbury had long cherished; they knew that he was a High Churchman, a friend of those High Churchmen, such as Liddon, who took a leading part in the agitation; they noticed that Carnarvon, who had formerly acted with Salisbury in breaking from Disraeli, made no secret of his general sympathy with the agitators; and they hoped, if not for an open breach between Beaconsfield and his Indian Secretary, at least for action by Salisbury at Constantinople in fundamental agreement with Gladstone and his policy. Undoubtedly Salisbury was keenly alive to the duty of securing tolerable government for Christians in Turkey—that was a main reason for his appointment; but some selections from Ministerial correspondence will show how far his course in the Ministry was from justifying the exaggerated expectations of Gladstone's partisans.

To Lord Salisbury.

HUGHENDEN MANOR, *Oct.* 17, 1876.—. . . As you are a particular friend of Carnarvon's, I will make a confidential observation. He is distinguished by his hospitality, but is not always, perhaps, so discreet in its exercise, as might be desired.

Poor dear Lady Chesterfield, when she was much under his roof, was very annoyed at constantly dining with the editor of the *Spectator*, who, she said, wrote weekly libels on her dearest friend (myself); but I, being used to that sort of treatment, mitigated her feelings, and, I believe, prevented any serious *esclandre.* But now, no less a personage than the stoic Derby is annoyed, and more than annoyed, by the same cause.

It seems that Liddon made a ' most acrimonious ' attack on Derby, and he is now a cherished guest at Highclere ! I believe it was in a sermon, and I was, of course, included in it, but, tho' I see most things, it escaped me, and I should not have noticed it, had I encountered it, except perhaps a little rap some day. . . .

From Lord Salisbury.

Confidential. HATFIELD HOUSE, *Oct.* 18, '76.—. . . I agree with you that it is unfortunate that Carnarvon should have asked Liddon at this particular time, when everyone is on the watch for the slightest indication of division of opinion in the Cabinet—as it may be misconstrued. But the friendship is a very old one: and Liddon usually goes to Highclere just before the Oxford term. I don't suppose the construction which might be put on it ever occurred to Carnarvon's mind. . . .

To Lord Derby.

Confidl. 10, DOWNING ST., WHITEHALL, *Nov.* 1, '76.— I return you Carnarvon's letter, and your reply, wh. is *admirable.* You pierced the Jesuits. What with Manning and

Lyddon (*sic*),[1] and the Archbishop of Belgrade, our colleague is getting a little insufferable.

It is a gang of Jesuits that he lives amongst, in many guises, from priests to journalists.

The only authentic *mot* of Gladstone, that I have ascertained, was that he said the other day, that he was confident that Carnarvon, Salisbury, Hardy, and Northcote wd. never support our policy. I believe no one is the least hesitating except Carnarvon, and ultimately he is ruled by Salisbury. . . .

Nov. 19.—I hear from Salisbury, that there is great discontent and disturbance at the 'Instructions'[2] having been sent down for the Queen's signature when Ld. Carnarvon, Ld. Chancellor, and others did not consider, that they had passed the Cabinet. What is to be done? They understood they were to be again considered on Thursday.

I have sent Mr. Corry to Ld. Chanr. to explain, that I doubted not you were under the impression that the general Instructions were approved, and that the supplementary ones were those to be considered on Thursday. But it is difficult to argue with men under the influence of strong religious feeling, and it wd. appear that the heresy of Photius, commonly called the Greek Church, and Moody and Sankey, have coalesced against us. . . .

From Lord Derby.

Private. FAIRHILL, TONBRIDGE, *Nov.* 19, '76.—There can be no mistake as to what passed in Cabinet yesterday. It was clearly understood that the instructions were approved, the cause of nearly all the difficulty having been removed by the insertion of the words suggested by Cairns, which only excluded from discussion *in the Conference* the question of military occupation, leaving it an open question whether such occupation might not be agreed upon by the Powers in certain possible contingencies. This was to be made clear by a supplementary instruction which was to be considered at the Cabinet of Thursday. I heard all that passed, and naturally attended more closely than anyone, the business concerning my department. It had never occurred to me, till I received your letter, that any of our colleagues could be under a different impression. . . .

I was prepared for Carnarvon taking the line he has taken, but regret the Chancellor having followed his lead. The question at issue is really serious: and I do not see how we can give way upon it. . . .

[1] Beaconsfield, never very accurate in his spelling of proper names, seems to have written indifferently 'Liddon' or 'Lyddon.'

[2] For the Constantinople Conference.

To Lord Derby.

Confidential. **2,** WHITEHALL GARDENS, *Nov.* 20.—You wisely got away, in legitimate dudgeon, to a distant fortress; but I was obliged to meet the storm, and therefore sent for the Ld. Chancellor, and, after some time, concluded a satisfactory interview.

He had no previous concert, or conversation, with that little Carnarvon, and when I explained to him the mysteries of the heresy of Photius, and that he had, I was sure unintentionally, lent himself to a sacerdotal intrigue, he turned quite pale.

I told him, that if the sentiment of religious enthusiasm, or the principle of ecclesiastical supremacy, were brought into play, the satisfactory settlement of a purely political question, wh. referred to the distribution of power, was impossible.

Then I sent for the little Carnarvon, who was out of town, and so I telegraphed for him, and he will probably attend me to-morrow, accompanied by Liddon.

Confidential. HUGHENDEN MANOR, *Dec.* 9.—You must keep the Ld. Chanr. quiet—at least for the nonce. His scheme of occupation is that of a pettifogger—joint stock and limited liability.

It is best not to harass Salisbury with instructions. He has enough. Affairs will develop themselves, and he seems not unequal to the situation. If the ' Eastern Xtians ' will be tolerably tranquil—sensible on such matters they never can be—I by no means despair of ultimate success.

I shall be in town on Monday at 3 o'ck., being tempted to prolong my stay here by these golden morns of expiring autumn.

Since he had returned from Castle Bromwich in August, Beaconsfield had pursued his anxious labours at Hughenden and in London, without interruption or change. But he spent a week-end at Sandringham immediately after the Guildhall banquet, and then went for a day or two to Ingestre, where Lady Bradford was a guest. Early in December, also, he got away from London for the inside of a week to Crichel, where the Granvilles were included in a large party to meet him.

To Lady Bradford.

2, WHITEHALL GARDENS, *Nov.* 20.—. . . Salisbury went off this morning, about eleven. Monty accompanied him to the station. He had several secretaries and, I think un-happily, several members of his family; Lady Salisbury, and his eldest son, and his daughter! I fear these latter will not be as serviceable as his secretaries. The French papers say the Conference is delayed because M. de Salisbury is accompanied by Mme. de Salisbury, and seven children! It was not quite so bad as that, but bad eno'.

Pss. Mary wrote to me and begged me to call on her, wh. I did yesterday. . . . Pss. Mary was amusing; she had been living in a Russian circle and retailed all their gossip, wh. showed they were counting on many things wh. will not happen. . . .

10, DOWNING ST., *Nov.* 29.—. . . I am very busy trying to make a Bishop of Truro. Nothing gives me more trouble than the Episcopacy. There are so many parties, so many 'schools of thought' in the Church.

Cornwall is full of Dissenters, like a rabbit warren. And any high jinks there wd. never do. And yet the dissenting pastors, particularly the Wesleyans, the most numerous, are no longer popular with their flocks. So there is an oppor-tunity for an adequate man. . . .

'I think I have got a good man' for the Bishopric of Truro, wrote Disraeli to Lady Chesterfield on Decem-ber 3. He was quite right. Benson's gifts both of organising capacity and of spiritual leadership proved so fruitful in his newly created diocese that when, six years later, the metropolitan see of Canterbury fell vacant, he was promoted to it on the recommendation of Disraeli's rival and successor, Gladstone. Hardy had strongly urged Benson's appointment to Truro: 'You have made a bishop,' wrote Disraeli to him on the day on which the offer was sent.

To Anne Lady Chesterfield.

CRICHEL, WIMBORNE, *Dec.* 8.—. . . The party here is very large, and ought to be very brilliant, if persons were as agreeable as their rank and fashion, their dresses and their looks. But then they are not. The fine ladies here are all below par, and as S. was not here the first two days, I had every opportunity of tasting them. The vintage was very insipid; and had it not been for your ever agreeable friend Lady A.,[1] I shd. have been much bored. Things are better now, as I get a walk with S., and a rubber in the evening with herself and Lady A., and Lord Granville. . . .

To Lady Bradford.

10, DOWNING ST., *Dec.* 8,[2] 1876.—Great despatches arrived last night from Constantinople, and the Cabinet has been sitting on them this long morning. I think there is a chance of my getting down to you on Saturday.

I sate next to Prince Hal[3] at dinner yesterday—at Ferdinand de R[othschild]'s. . . .

After dinner there was whist, and Rosebery came up to me, and talked very well—just come from America—his 3rd visit, and full as an egg of fun and quaint observation.

The dinner was really exquisite and served with incomparable taste. I was so much amused with the menu, that I stole it for the first time in my life; but I stole it for you.

The preliminary Conferences are closed, and I hope we have given the formal Conference, wh. commences on Thursday, eno' work to give us a tolerably tranquil Xmas week.

2, WHITEHALL GARDENS, *Dec.* 13.—All the world is talking now of a private meeting yesterday at Stafford House, the Duke[4] in the chair, to commence a subscription for the Turkish soldiers, who are fighting for their country, and bravely—without pay, or food, or clothes. . . . The Lord Blantyre gave 1,000 guineas. There shd. be a report of all this.

Beaconsfield was properly anxious, throughout this critical autumn and winter, not to let diplomacy outrun military preparation. On September 30 he wrote to Hardy, the War Secretary, in view of what appeared then to be the probability of an immediate invasion of Turkey by Russia, and perhaps by Austria also, to make enquiries as to the practicability of sending a British

[1] Maria Marchioness of Ailesbury.

[2] There must be some mistake about the date, as Beaconsfield was at Crichel on Dec. 8.

[3] In Beaconsfield's private letters of this period, the Prince of Wales, afterwards King Edward VII., is often called 'Prince Hal,' in obvious reference to Prince Henry in Shakespeare's *Henry IV.*—a Prince who eventually became, as Beaconsfield believed that Prince Albert Edward would become, an excellent and popular king.

[4] Of Sutherland.

force, with the Porte's consent, to hold and defend Constantinople. Hardy at once set to work with his professional advisers; but Beaconsfield found it difficult to induce Derby to contemplate the possibility of military action.

To Lord Derby.

Confidential.   10, DOWNING STREET, WHITEHALL, *Oct.* 21.— It appeared to me yesterday, from yr. remarks in Cabinet, that you hardly cared to consider the military elements of the question that absorbs our thought.

We don't live in the times of Marshal Diebitsch,[1] when his troops were exhausted, half famished, and diseased, by the time they had reached only the frontier. We live in the times of Odessa and Rumanian railways.

General Fadéef has laid a plan before the Russian Government, ' in order to settle the fate of European Turkey in spite of the maritime Powers.'

It is at the War Office, in their confidential archives, with a study by experts, assisted by all the secret intelligence from Wellesley as to position of troops, wh. appears always to have been accurate.

From this, and other documents, all of wh. shd. be known to you, I conclude the invasion of Turkey, and conquest of Constantinople, may be rapid.

If so, our determination as to our ultimate course cannot be too soon decided on. Constantinople occupied by the Russians, while the British fleet was in Besika Bay, would be the most humiliating event, that has occurred to England, since the surrenders of Whitelocke and Burgoyne and Cornwallis, but infinitely in its consequences more important and disastrous.

Oct. 22.—I am anxious about the state of affairs.

There seems to me no doubt that, after the passage of the Pruth, Russia may reach Constantinople in sixty days—at the most 64.

The Danube, from some of the strong places being now in Rumania and other causes, is no longer a barrier, and the crossing of the Balkans may be calculated almost to a nicety.

Any possibility of defence under these circumstances depends upon Turkey possessing the command of the sea, as in that case the Russians would be deprived of their heavy artillery, their siege trains, which cannot pass the Balkans; but if a Russian squadron reaches the Black Sea and captures Varna her siege trains would then be at her disposal.

[1] Who gained his fame in the Russo-Turkish War of 1828-9.

Any movement on our part, whether we fortify the Peninsula by Lake Durkos or the Chersonese, would be sixteen days too late if delayed till the Russians cross the Balkans.

But what alarms me is that Turkey, feeling she is utterly deserted, may make some mad compact with Russia, opening the Straits, and giving her complete control over the Asiatic shore.

As for compensation to England by having Egypt and Crete, this is moonshine. If Constantinople is Russian, they would only be an expensive encumbrance.

I have asked Hardy to come up to-morrow, that we may have the military details clear, and then after a consultation of all three together, I think we ought to have a Cabinet. . . .

Hardy's diary gives the result of his long talk with Beaconsfield on October 23. ' We discussed eventualities and came to some conclusions; to send officers to survey the ground behind Constantinople, and to look forward to guarding it in case of need.' Beaconsfield also concerted naval preparations with Ward Hunt, the First Lord of the Admiralty, but found Derby resolutely opposed to giving hypothetical instructions to the Fleet to pass the Dardanelles in the event of Russian aggression on the Straits.

Lord Derby to G. Ward Hunt.

Private. FOREIGN OFFICE, *Oct.* 24, '76.—The step of ordering a British fleet to pass the Dardanelles (the consent of the Porte not having been asked) is not one to be taken offhand, nor without the fullest consideration. I cannot sanction the order which has been suggested to you as matters now stand. If a Russian vessel went through—which I do not consider as probable—there would be plenty of time to send the order by telegraph. But I repeat that I do not expect the contingency to occur, since the passage would be resisted, and, as we know, the Russians have no fleet to match that of Turkey.

The open preparations for war made by Russia in November caused Beaconsfield to press forward our own military plans for the preservation of Constantinople and the two Straits from sudden seizure, the one great military object which he always kept before his eyes. The Beaconsfield papers contain an interesting manuscript, partly in his own handwriting, and partly in Corry's, headed ' November, 1876. Notes for Cabinet—Russo-Turkish Question.' It is not clear for which of the November Cabinets this was prepared, perhaps for one of which Richmond wrote to Cairns on November 19: ' A most interesting Cabinet. I do not think I ever saw the For[eign] Sec. so " stiff." . . . I suspect it will be necessary to keep him up to the mark. I was surprised to find the P[rime] M[inister] so much with him.'

If order given for mobilising Eng. army it may be practically ready for embarkation in 21 days and at Const. in 42.

If given at passage of the Pruth, Eng. army will be in position 22 days before arrival of Russian.

If given at passage of Danube *one* day before.

If at passage of Balkans 16 days too late.

Can the period for mobilising be diminished ? Yes—by taking certain steps.

By moving war material to the points where the troops will assemble prior to embarkation and gradually moving the troops to those places—but a strong hand required for this.

Malta may be strengthened with Artillery and Engineers and the armament for the lines shipped ready to be pushed on.

The neck of land at Boulair is $4\frac{1}{2}$ miles across. Works to render the Chersonese practically impregnable would be accomplished in 14 days by 6,000 men. These men need not be English. A force of 20,000 men would be required to hold the works Without the works a fleet, however powerful, could not arrest, scarcely delay, the march of an army along the Chersonese by Boulair. This might be said even were the country level. There are in fact hills wh. would practically shelter an army from attack from the sea.

Bosphorus—the distance between Lake Durkos, Byyk, Tcheckmeje is 11 miles. Works to render this line practically impregnable could be accomplished in 21 days by 6,000 men. These men need not be English. A force of 40,000 men would be required to hold the works.

It is obvious that, to attain her object, England would have to seize both the Bosphorus and the Dardanelles, and to hold the land approaches to each.

To accomplish both operations would not demand, necessarily, so large a force as the numbers combined (20,000 +40,000)—which have been stated as required respectively for either operation by itself; and this, because a flank of each of the suggested positions would rest on the shore of the Sea of Marmora, each from the other only about *100* miles. It may be said that England could at once despatch an Army sufficient to occupy and hold both positions.

Given the means of transport, and given that there shall be no hastily conceived reforms, nor disturbance of the mobilisation scheme, England can place on board ship, in 21 days, a force of *46,000,* and *practically* ready for the field, of which, about *34,000* men would be men now serving in the Army, about *5,000* men of the Army reserve, and the rest men of the Militia reserve.

About this time Beaconsfield obtained the consent of his colleagues to a policy of detaining for the time in this country as a precaution eight guns, of hitherto unprecedented size and power, which were being built by a famous firm in England to the order of a foreign Government. He further elucidated his views in a conversation with Hardy at the end of the month. On the assumption of the failure of the Conference and a Russian occupation of Bulgaria, he suggested, as recorded by Hardy in a memorandum at the time, the following policy:

He would, on the application of the Porte, send up the fleet, but would not assent to send it at the instance of the Powers or Russia, as some quarrel would be got up, and it used to destroy the Turkish fleet and play into Russian hands. Then he would occupy the lines behind Constantinople and at Gallipoli, but whether at the crossing of the Pruth or later—he inclines to the former. He says that, although partition has not been intended, it will come, and in that case offers will be made to us. Constantinople not likely to be offered, nor would it be desirable to accept. He would like to buy a port in the Black Sea from the Porte, as Batoum, . . . or Sinope. . . . He said Egypt would be offered as before, but he did not see what we should gain. . . . What he wants is a Malta or Gibraltar, which would prevent the Black Sea being a constant threat to our maritime power in the Mediterranean. He is clearly full of anxiety for the future.[1] . . .

Beaconsfield developed his ideas still further in a couple of letters to Salisbury, who very wisely took Paris,

[1] Gathorne Hardy, Vol. I., p. 377.

Berlin, Vienna, and Rome on his way to Constantinople, and held long conversations in each capital with Sovereigns and statesmen.

To Lord Salisbury.

10, DOWNING ST., *Nov.* 29, 1876.—. . . The visits to the Continental Courts have not been fruitless: it was a serviceable reconnaissance, and when you have seen men, you can judge better of their conduct. So far as the Conference is concerned, the result seems to be this: it will consist of a meeting between you and Ignatieff. It is possible that meeting may have results. It is possible that Russia may wish to avoid, honorably, a struggle, wh. the state of her finances, the unpreparedness of her armies, and her want of naval power, may make her desirous to postpone.

It was always one of her principles never to engage the Porte except she had a command of the sea. Now, that condition is just reversed. Nevertheless, 1st, the bankruptcy of the Porte; 2ndly, the assumed alienation of England from the Turks, partly produced by the Bulgarian outrages, and partly by the non-payment of Turkish dividends, have prevailed on her, apparently, to take a step at wh. she first hesitated.

Any peace, the conditions of wh. do not involve foreign occupation, would be a triumph for England.

It is wise, however, to assume, that there will be an invasion of Turkey by Russia. I do not think that would necessitate any declaration of war against Russia on our part. Protesting against the passage of the Pruth, as a violation of the revised Treaty of Paris (1871), I think the Porte should then be advised to solicit the presence of our fleet at the capital and, of course, if expedient, in the Black Sea. At the same time, at the expense of the English Government, the works on the Peninsula of Constantinople should be completed.

If the Danube, as I will apprehend, is passed without effective opposition, the Russians leaving a sufficient force behind them to mask the fortresses (this, however, would require 100,000 men), the next step of England would depend on their progress in Bulgaria, and in the prospects of resistance on the Balkans.

Upon such circumstances should depend whether, and when, we may decide to send a *corps d'armée* to the Peninsula of Constantinople. We could send our troops there in three weeks, and all will have been prepared for their reception.

Generally speaking, the situation is very similar to the state, wh. preceded the partition of Poland; Austria protesting against a deed, and really disapproving of it, which she afterwards joined with others to consummate. It is highly probable that Austria will assemble a powerful force in Transylvania, and I believe that, in so doing, her object is to coerce Russia, but it will end by Russia having her own way, and Austria seeking consolation not only in the possession of Bosnia, wh. she will have previously occupied, but in Herzegovina, and, not unlikely, Servia.

It is a most critical moment in European politics. If Russia is not checked, the Holy Alliance will be revived in aggravated form and force. Germany will have Holland; and France, Belgium, and England will be in a position I trust I shall never live to witness.

If we act in the manner I have generally indicated we shall, probably, in the conclusion, obtain some commanding stronghold in Turkey from wh. we need never recede. It will be for the interest of the Porte itself that we should; and if they would sell to us, for instance, Varna, the supremacy of Russia might for ever be arrested.

I am surprised that Bismarck should go on harping about Egypt. Its occupation by us would embitter France, and I don't see it would at all benefit us, if Russia possessed Constantinople. I would sooner we had Asia Minor than Egypt.

In regard to home politics as influenced by the foreign situation, there are two points worth noticing.

1st. An organised attempt to revive agitation under the title of a Conference in London on Turkish affairs, wh. is to sit while the real Conference is holding its session. Several leading members of the Liberal party have declined to be members of this intolerable assembly, but Lord Shaftesbury, who believes he is preparing a great career for Evelyn Ashley, is of course a leading member, and the Gladstone influence has prevailed on the Duke of Westminster to be President. The Queen told me, that G. could command the Duke of Westminster and the Duke and Dss. of Argyll.

The second point is our Parliamentary position, wh. is very favourable. It is not merely that our own men are unanimously staunch, but the whole of the Irish party has been instructed to support the Government, and there is a decided anti-Russian section in the English Liberals. It is said not less than sixty. . . .

Dec. 1.—I wrote to you yesterday by F. O. messenger. You will receive this by a private hand, almost as soon. It refers to the most serious matter: the question of occupation, on wh. some information has reached me, wh. throws a new and strange light on that crux.

If the question of occupation be immediately introduced into the Conference, the position, that you might well take, would be this: England will not say, that she is unequivocally opposed to the occupation of Turkey for a temporary purpose, but she cannot agree to such a step except at the instance, and with the full consent, of the Porte—as in the Syrian case, now so quoted.

This attitude would prevent Conference breaking up, and would allow the critical examination of the measures of Reform independently of the question of Guarantee.

When ultimately submitted to the Porte, this position might be assumed by the Sultan: the Porte will consent to the occupation provided it is not effected by conterminous Powers, which will lead to war; and she may suggest, that England should occupy. Having taken this position, she must be inexorable.

I am prepared to propose such a measure to the Cabinet, and cannot doubt, especially with your aid and approval, that they would adopt it, and that it would be cheerfully accepted by Parliament, and be popular outside: as alike preventing war, effecting our object, and maintaining the authority of this country.

We have a force of 40,000 men ready, and I cannot doubt that, if 6,000 French were sufficient for Syria, 40,000 English would be ample for European Turkey: say 10[000], or 15,000 for Bosnia, etc., and 25[000] or 30,000 for Bulg[ari]a. Besides, we should have the aid, if necessary, of the Turkish regular army, which would be under our supreme command.

Of course, it must be the last card to be played, and it must be so done, that we must seem almost unwillingly to consent.

Turkey would consent when she found, as the negotiations proceed, that occupation was inevitable, and, that too, by Russia.

Russia would faintly oppose, perhaps at once agree, assuming that England has neither the ability, nor the inclination, for such a step.

I think it would suit Austria, who shrinks from the expense of occupying Bosnia, and only would do it out of jealousy of Russia.

If this view of affairs be correct, it seemed to me, that no delay should occur in your having it in your mind, as it would be a polestar to guide you, and a great end always to be working up to. So I have sent you this by a private and trusty hand. And have not, and shall not, breathe a word

tontents to a single human being. Let it come to us,
a approve it, in due course as your proposal, which I
immediately support in the Cabinet.

A joint occupation with Russia I look upon as highly
objectionable, and I don't believe the Porte would take that.
They would prefer fighting.

I need not repeat, what I have said more than once in
Cabinet, that the Russian scheme of occupation; Bulgaria
to Russia, Bosnia to Austria, and our fleet to Constantinople,
would be most perilous, if not fatal. It would insure another
Navarino, and probably was so intended. We must never
attempt to occupy Constantinople, but at the instance of the
Porte. . . .

To Montagu Corry.

2, WHITEHALL GARDENS, *Dec.* 13, 1876.—. . . The ' Intelligence Dept.' must change its name. It is the department
of Ignorance. Instead of 40,000 men for the entrenched
camp to defend Constantinople, they now require 65,000,
and that does not include 10,000 more for Gallipoli.

It is the same with guns and everything. 50 per cent.
more men and guns of a heavier calibre—a railway for stores,
and telegraph lines from Malta to Crete, etc.: in short, a
very big business, in which the present state of affairs hardly
justifies us in embarking.

The Conference is in full swing. You could hardly get out
of the park gates at Crichel, when telegrams came pouring
in: two huge ones when we were at tea, in Gussie's[1] little
room, which made Granville's mouth water. Since I arrived,
they have rained—3 yesterday from Salisbury. . . .

The London Conference to which Beaconsfield referred
in his letter to Salisbury was the answer of the pro-
Russian or anti-Turkish agitators to the Guildhall speech.
It was held in St. James's Hall on December 8, under
the presidency of the Duke of Westminster in the afternoon, and of Lord Shaftesbury in the evening, and was
attended by Gladstone himself and some prominent
Radical politicians, as well as by many men of distinction
in different walks of life. While some speakers used
moderate language and only deprecated any policy
wh ch might commit the country to fighting on behalf
of Turkey, the keynote of the Conference was struck

[1] Lady Alington.

at the outset by a demand from the Duke in the chair that the fleets and armies of England should be sent to Constantinople to coerce the Turk. Liddon, the great preacher, expressed a fervent hope for armed intervention in Turkey on behalf of the subject races, preferably by an English army of 50,000, 80,000, or 100,000 men; and Freeman, the historian, exclaimed, ' Perish the interests of England, perish our dominion in India, sooner than we should strike one blow or speak one word on behalf of the wrong against the right.' The extravagance of these sentiments and proposals, which received no countenance from the Liberal leaders, Granville and Hartington, or from their immediate followers, assisted that revulsion of public feeling in favour of the Government which had been visible for some weeks. Scotland and the north of England were still under the spell of Gladstone's agitation, but London and the south largely shared the indignation with which the Queen regarded the proceedings at St. James's Hall.

To Lady Bradford.

2, WHITEHALL GARDENS, *Dec.* 16, 1876, 6 *o'ck.*—I have just returned from Windsor, wh. has taken up the whole day. I found the Faery most indignant about the St. James's Hall ' Conference.' . . . She thinks the Attorney-General ought to be set at these men; it can't be constitutional. . . . I said a good word for Granville and Harty-Tarty—to whom, I was sure, she might look, if necessary, with confidence. She is sure the country is right, and that when Parliament meets, we shall be triumphant. ' It has gone on for 6 months—this noise; and suppose a mistake had been made, what then ? But I will never admit that any mistake has been made from first to last.' Bravo! . . .

The hopes of the country, and of Europe, were fixed on the Constantinople Conference, which was formally to open just before Christmas. Salisbury, who, while on his way, had explored the ground so far as the other Powers were concerned, had long and amicable conversations, when he reached Constantinople, with the

..ntative of Russia, Ignatieff. The general out-
.ome appeared to be that, while Russia maintained her
view that military occupation was the only really effective
guarantee, the Powers as a whole endorsed Salisbury's
programme, which deprecated military occupation and
the creation of tributary States, favoured the *status quo*
in Serbia and Montenegro, and proposed a large measure
of administrative autonomy for Bosnia and Bulgaria,
together with guarantees for the due carrying out of the
reforms by the Porte. But it was already apparent to
the far-sighted that the principal obstacle to the success
of the Conference would be the obstinacy of Turkey. In
that case what would the Government do?

To Lady Bradford.

10, Downing St., *Dec.* 20, 7 *o'ck.*—I have just returned from
Windsor, and after a long conference with Ld. Derby, and
an order for a Cabinet next Friday, I steal a moment for you.

Salisbury has succeeded in all the great points of his mission
as regards Russia. There is to be no Russian occupation of
Bulgaria; Bulgaria is to be divided into two provinces,[1] wh.
will, or rather would, strengthen the Porte; the Circassians
are not to be banished; the population generally are not to
be disarmed, wh. wd. create a civil war—and other things;
but we understand, and believe, that the Porte will accept
nothing and wishes to fight.

There was a change of Government yesterday at Constantinople, but I doubt whether that will help us. . . .

To Lord Derby.

2, Whitehall Gardens, *Dec.* 21, '76.—Remember you
kindly offered to dine with me to-morrow. I think we had
better be alone: it is years since we have had such a *tête-à-tête*
— and there is plenty to talk about.

But there is one thing we ought to talk about before our
meeting and before the Cabinet.

We—that is you and I—ought to have clear and distinct
views about our course as to the suspension of diplomatic
intercourse with the Porte under certain circumstances. I
shd. like to talk this over with you to-day. I am engaged

---

[1] An anticipation of the arrangement secured by the Congress of Berlin.

the earlier part of this morn.—but at yr. service anywhere after 3 o'ck.

Schou. said to me last night, that Russia did not care a pin for Bulgaria, or Bosnia, or any other land—what it really wanted was 'the Straits'—the only thing they wanted. I said, I knew that.

Friday, [*Dec.* 22].—. . . The tel. of this morning from S[alisbury] shows, that it will be wise to come to a very clear decision to-day.

We shd. resolve, that H.M. Gt. can participate in no coercive measures agst. the Porte, nor sanction them.

That if the proposals of the Conference are declined, Ld. Saly. is to leave Const., Sir Henry Elliot to avail himself of his leave of absence, but that diplomatic relations not to be suspended.

The Beaconsfield papers contain notes for this Cabinet of Friday, December 22, written partly in his own hand, partly in Corry's, as follows:

Policy to be recommended in event of Turkey proving obstinate at Conference.

Principle—not to coerce the Porte or to sanction coercion by others, but to use every means of friendly influence and persuasion.

Russian system—always to induce England to join in coercion of the Porte.

Mr. Canning's experience and its consequences.

Different effect on England from that on other Powers of suspension of diplomatic relations with the Porte.

The Cabinet decided in the sense desired by Beaconsfield, but the moral persuasion which was all that their regard for the integrity and independence of Turkey permitted them to employ did not prove sufficient. Midhat Pasha, the Turkish statesman principally associated with the demand for a Constitution, was appointed Grand Vizier immediately before the Conference met; and on the very day of its assemblage, a Constitution was solemnly promulgated by the Sultan containing on paper all the rights and liberties that reasonable men could desire. It was a clear intimation that the Porte intended to maintain that the Conference and its proposed reforms were superfluous, as the Sultan had already granted by the Constitution all that was necessary. In vain did the representatives of the Powers whittle down their demands, which had at first been somewhat stringent and involved the creation of either a Belgian or an international *gendarmerie* to superintend the execution of the reforms. Even the minimum finally presented for acceptance in the middle of January was definitely rejected on the 18th of the month by a Grand Advisory Council which the Sultan had summoned for its consideration.

We get from Beaconsfield's letters an insight into his feelings and policy during this disapppointing time. The Queen's request and the urgency of public business kept him in London for Christmas, which he had hoped to spend as Lady Bradford's guest at Weston, but he went to Windsor on New Year's Day to celebrate the occasion of Her Majesty's proclamation as Empress in India,[1] and immediately afterwards contrived to run down to Weston for the inside of a week.

To Lady Bradford.

10, DOWNING ST., *Dec.* 22.—I sent you a horrid tel. this morning, and am too much upset to write anything now that cd. amuse or interest you. Last night the Queen wrote to me that she thought it an act of great imprudence that myself and Ld. Derby shd. be absent from London at such a critical time, and that she must express her anxious and extreme desire that we should not depart.

Ld. D. never intended to leave town: his wife has gone to Knowsley to do what is necessary at this season of the year.

I can't doubt the Queen was right: indeed my conscience had pricked me more than once, and probably I shd. not have stayed with you over Xmas Day. Still I had counted on this visit—more than I care to express. It wd. have been the only happy week during this laborious and anxious year—except dear C[astle] Bromwich.

It was, of course, impossible not to remain; and we have had a Cabinet to-day, and probably things will turn up every hour. Affairs are most critical. . . .

2, WHITEHALL GARDENS, *Xmas Day.*—. . . We had some other offerings yesterday. . . . In the evening came a

[1] See pp. 825-827.

Xmas card from the Faery, and signed V.R. & I. (*Regina et Imperatrix*), the first time I have received that signature. And an enormous packet. Unfolded, it took the shape of a large folio volume—*Faust*, illustrated with a weird and romantic pencil, by a German artist. . . . The binding of this volume exceeds in work and splendor all the treasures wh. Dr. Schliemann has disinterred at Mycenæ. . . .

This is Xmas Day and I dine quite alone. . . .

I can give you no absolute information as to affairs; 99 out of a 100 will tell you that war is certain between R[ussia] and T[urkey]. But when everybody wishes for peace, and, most of all, Russia, I can't help hoping that some golden bridge may be constructed, even if it be gilded, to extricate R. from its false position. To-day, when we were to have heard so much, nothing has yet arrived, which makes me wildly think that, at the last, something has been devised. . . .

To Lord Derby.

Confidl. 2, WHITEHALL GARDENS, *Dec.* 28.—Sal.'s tel. received last night, and wh. I have just read shows, I fear, that he is much duped by Ig.

Remember, for example, his information that war wd. take place on Russian Xmas Day, and that the Proclamation was signed, and, I think, he had even seen it.

Now we are equally confidentially informed, that the Russians don't wish war till April. This he is permitted to know after he has unnecessarily bullied the Turks.

Really this thing ought to be put an end to. Lyons cd. have done it. Odo Russell ought to do it at Berlin. . . .

It is a case for *mezzo termine*. The Russians shrink from war: the Porte cannot accept the preposterous proposals. Could not Pomposo[1] with Gort[chakoff] communicate a mitigated scheme? wh. might be proposed by Austria, or even ourselves, after previous arrangements with Porte?

Confdl. *Dec.* 30.—I am greatly distressed by Sal.'s tel. of this morning It is clear, that Elliot had never communicated to him Elliot's interview with Midhat, or Sal. wd. never have made the observation, that he did not believe the Turkish Plenipos. had ever read the papers.

Sal. seems most prejudiced, and not to be aware, that his principal object, in being sent to Const., is to keep the Russians out of Turkey, not to create an ideal existence for Turkish Xtians.

He is more Russian than Ignatieff: *plus Arabe que l'Arabie!*

---

[1] Lord Augustus Loftus.

While Russia, I believe, is meditating and preparing compromise, and the Porte not disinclined to that, Sal. sees only obduracy and war.

Is he informed of the reports of Loftus, of Lyons, of all, even the Russian courtier Odo, showing the necessity and wish for peace ?

We ought to be asked whe[the]r he was aware of the Midhat interview ? You *must* take him in hand, confidentially and cordially.

To Anne Lady Chesterfield.

10, DOWNING STREET, 7 o'ck. [? Jan. 2, 1877].—I have just come back from Windsor. The Queen is imprisoned— like the Pope: all the country about is under water, and she cannot go to Osborne because there is scarlet fever, or measles, or some other ill that flesh is heir to, in her curtilage. . . .

Ld. Salisbury has succeeded in everything as regards the Russians, and much distinguished himself; but now it is said, and feared, and believed, that the Turks will fight. I wish they were all—Russians and Turks—at the bottom of the Black Sea.

2, WHITEHALL GARDENS, *Jan. 7, 1877.*—I arrived here yesterday afternoon. . . . You left us [at Weston] on Wednesday morning, and from that moment the pressure began: two messengers every day. However, I was resolved to remain, tho' Royalty herself was ' quite surprised ' that I had left town ! I knew the cut of the Conference better than Her Majesty, and that affairs are never precipitated at Stamboul, tho' Emperors may threaten, and Plenipotentiaries be positive. They are to meet again to-morrow, when everything is to be ' settled,' one way or the other; nevertheless, I shall not be astonished that the Conference will again adjourn. The fact is, Russia would give a good deal to get out of the scrape into wh. her blustering has entrapped her; and the Porte knows this, and seems resolved to make the Emperor and his princely Minister eat the leek: very difficult to digest, if not impossible. So you may be prepared for anything, except the humiliation of the Turks.

To Lady Bradford.

10, DOWNING STREET, *Jan. 8, 1877.*—. . . I think, myself, the Conference is on its last legs.[1] Salisbury succeeded in moderating the Russians, and I have done my best to moderate the Turks; but we have found out that Bismarck is resolved

[1] Hardy wrote in his diary under the same date that the Conference was rendered futile by ' Russian falsehood, Turkish evasion, German treachery.'

that Russia shall go to war, or that Gortchakoff, whom he hates and a little despises, and yet [is] very jealous of, shall endure ineffable mortifications by retreating, without the honors of war, after all his blustering.

2, WHITEHALL GARDENS, *Jan.* 10.—. . . I took a little walk this morning, but it was an easterly wind. I met Malmesbury, walking very well, and looking very well, tho' he says he has the Roman fever wh. has knocked him up again. . . . M. was skilfully rouged. People say, that resource is effeminate. M. is manly enough, and the two most manly persons I ever knew, Palmerston and Lyndhurst, both rouged. So one must not trust too much to general observations.

Jan. 20, 1877.—. . . I am a prisoner.[1] . . . It is harassing —much more than any Eastern Question, wh. by no means appals me, I assure you. We shall have a time no doubt of some trouble and suspense, and much that will require both pluck and prudence. . . . I think it probable that the Russians will keep their army on the Turkish frontier for some time, to veil their discomfiture and really ignominious position; and then, after a while, the Emperor of Germany, or some such being, will address a Xtian appeal to the Tsar, who will be becomingly magnanimous, and sacrifice everything to the peace of the world. I only hope the Turks won't get too bumptious, and do something silly. . . .

To Lord Derby.

2, WHITEHALL G'DNS, *Jan.* 15, '77.—It is most unfortunate that you are away.

Last night there came to me a tel. from Salisbury of the most pressing nature. He says ' all Ambass. have agreed to announce, that, if our reduced terms are not accepted on Thursday, we shall declare the Conference broken up, and leave Const. But Sir H. E. refuses to promise to leave at the same time we do.

' This will make our success much more unlikely. It will be treated as justifying the rumors that he represents a different pol. from the Conf. and that Brit. Govt. will not support me.'

' Earnestly urges ' that Elliot should be instructed to leave at the same time. ' No time to be lost,' etc., etc., etc. ' Perhaps the best form will be a joint instruction to me and E. to leave at the same time, directly after Conf. broken up.'

This is a grave and doubtful matter and requires our counsel. . . .

[1] With an attack of gouty bronchitis.

The last sitting of the Conference was on January 20. Elliot was recalled on leave, and Salisbury came quietly home. Disraeli held that Salisbury had perhaps been unduly influenced by Ignatieff; but he did not underestimate either the considerable success which Salisbury had achieved in keeping the European Concert in harmony during a trying period, or the remarkable impression which his massive personality, hitherto unknown to the Continent, had produced. He was very anxious that his colleague should not take too much to heart the failure of the Conference to persuade the Porte to be reasonable.

To Lord Salisbury.

2, WHITEHALL GARDENS, *Feb.* 6, 1877.—. . . I hope you will not permit the immediate result of the Conference unduly to depress you.

Trust me, before very long, you will bless the day, wh. permitted you to obtain such a mastery of men and things, and especially as connected with the East, as this momentous enterprise has afforded to you. I feel, stronger than ever, that all that is occurring portends—and that not remotely— partition. Then, you will feel the inestimable advantage of yr. recent labors, and, then, all will appreciate your invaluable services.

CHAPTER IV.

War and Cabinet Dissension.

1877.

The outcome of the Constantinople Conference was to leave Russia and Turkey face to face, with no apparent prospect of immediate support, from any other Power, for the extreme position which each occupied. Turkey, while vaunting her new Constitution and professing her readiness to reform her administration, had definitely refused the minimum of autonomy for her Christian provinces which united Europe had pressed upon her. Russia had insisted that nothing but military occupation of Turkey by a European Power, or Powers, would be efficacious for Christian protection. But Europe as a whole, under England's leadership, had refused to associate itself with this policy of force. Would Russia, now that Turkey had chosen to isolate herself, await the issue of Turkish professions, or proceed to enforce her will in arms, as Alexander had threatened in November ?

Beaconsfield thought, as did apparently the Turks, that Russia would hesitate and draw back. He did not know that Alexander had taken precautions in advance to secure the benevolent neutrality of the Power best situated geographically for intervention in a Russo-Turkish War. On July 8 of the previous year, at Reichstadt in Bohemia, the Emperors and Foreign Ministers of Austria and Russia had come to a private understanding; and on January 15 of 1877, while the Conference was still in being at Constantinople, a definite treaty was signed at Vienna between the two Powers, delimiting their spheres of interest in the Balkans, and specifying the terms on which Austria would consent to remain neutral if Russia invaded Turkey. The treaty was concealed from Europe as the understanding had been concealed, and even now its actual provisions are in dispute. But there is no doubt that it was based on that policy of partition which Beaconsfield anticipated, and that Austria claimed, and was conceded, the right, in certain eventualities, to occupy Bosnia and Herzegovina. By this treaty Russia had secured herself against a flank attack, and it is difficult to regard her various diplomatic manœuvres between January, when the treaty was signed, and April, when she declared war, as anything but playing for position and for time, until the snows should melt in the Balkans and the season for campaigning should open.

Her principal political opponent in Europe, the British Prime Minister, was once more attacked this January by gout.

To Lady Bradford.

2, WHITEHALL GARDENS, *Jan.* 30.—. . . I hope I have turned the corner, but have had a severe attack. . . . I forgot to tell you that your friend the P. of Wales came and sate with me a good hour last Sunday, hearing I was in quarantine. He did not want anything: only chitter-chatter: so you see I am almost as much in favor, as your agreeable *bête noire*, Granville. . . .

Beaconsfield was naturally anxious to present his case to Parliament in the most convincing manner, and was dissatisfied with his Foreign Secretary's draft of the paragraphs of the Queen's Speech dealing with the Eastern Question. He himself drafted an alternative, which he asked Derby to treat as ' brute matter.'

To Lord Derby.

2, WHITEHALL G'DNS, *Jan.* 29.—My paragraphs were only drawn to show you what was passing in my mind; raw material for you to work upon. The time is, however, now so pressing, that, chastened by your criticism, I will insert them in the drt. speech, and then all may have a shot at them.

I think we cannot deny that our policy preceding the Conference, and our efforts in it, were to maintain the integ. and indep. of the Ott. Emp. The declaration refers only to the past, and it appears to me, I confess, of vital importance, for reasons which it would weary you to listen to in writing.

Great fallacies exist on this famous phrase of integ. and indep.

When we speak of maintaining the integ. of a Kingdom, we mean the integrity as then existing. England, and Austria, and France, will assert their integrity, and expect it to be acknowledged, tho' they have all of them lost more provinces than Turkey.

Then again as to independence, we mean by maintaining the independence of a State that we acknowledge and contemplate the continuity of its sovereign power, even while we may be suggesting limitations of that power for a temporary purpose.

Prussia was subject at the beginning of this century to far more humiliating conditions, than those proposed for Turkey: its fortresses were occupied, and its power of enlistment limited—to as low an amount as 40,000 men—and so on.

These are rough mems. I would send them to nobody but yourself: but they are, I hope, suggestive.

The special Envoy's[1] letter alarms me. I am a little less alarmed, that he twice applied, 1st, for increased assistance to Colonel Home in his fortifications of Constantinople, and 2nd, for his survey of the Turkish ports—Batoum, Rhodes, Cyprus.

The Cabinet accepted Beaconsfield's draft, after some inaccuracies had been corrected by Derby. To Salisbury, who did not return from Constantinople in time to take part in the discussion, he wrote, 'I am, and I alone, responsible for the notice of Eastern affairs. . . . The remarks pledge us to nothing, for we are now indeed as free as air; but they state the past—*i.e.*, since the prorogation—in a manner which, I trust, will show the country that our course, instead of being vacillating and capricious, has been clear and consistent.' The Speech explained how the Government had anxiously

[1] Salisbury.

waited for an opportunity to interpose their good offices in the war between Turkey and Serbia; how, in the course of the negotiations, they had laid down, and obtained the acceptance of the Powers for, the bases upon which not only might peace be brought about, 'but the permanent pacification of the disturbed provinces, including Bulgaria, might be effected'; how they had denounced to the Porte 'the excesses ascertained to have been committed in Bulgaria'; how an armistice had been arranged, and a Conference assembled 'for the consideration of extended terms in accordance with the original bases.' The Speech proceeded:

In taking these steps, my object has throughout been to maintain the peace of Europe, and to bring about the better government of the disturbed provinces, without infringing upon the independence and integrity of the Ottoman Empire.

The proposals recommended by myself and my allies have not, I regret to say, been accepted by the Porte; but the result of the Conference has been to show the existence of a general agreement among the European Powers, which cannot fail to have a material effect upon the condition and government of Turkey.

In the meantime, the armistice between Turkey and the Principalities has been prolonged, and is still unexpired, and may, I trust, yet lead to the conclusion of an honourable peace.

The debates on the Address in both Houses mainly turned on an attempt by the Opposition to convict the Government of a change of front on the Eastern Question. There, as we have seen, Granville and Hartington had a case, not so far as the end was concerned, but as to the means employed to reach it. As to the immediate policy there was little or no condemnation, but, rather, tacit acquiescence. But, in the Lords, the Duke of Argyll, one of the few Opposition leaders in full sympathy with Gladstone's crusade, denounced Ministers with rhetoric and passion. 'I say distinctly,' he burst out, 'in this high place, on this housetop of Europe, that every insurrection under [the Turkish] Government is a legitimate insurrection. Human beings under that Government owe it no allegiance.' Much as Derby might despise sentimentality in politics, the Duke predicted that sentimentality would be too strong for him, for sentiment, on which all moral feeling was founded, ruled the world. The Government, he averred, had been the drag upon Europe. This outburst elicited a brief reply from Beaconsfield, who had only taken his seat in the House that day, and who had meant to leave the defence of the Government in Derby's hands. In a few words he pointed out that the position of the Christian subjects of Turkey was not the only question to be considered, and that, even if it were, the attempted coercion of the Porte would probably only worsen it. The Eastern Question involved some of the elements of the distribution of world power; it involved the existence of empires. He pleaded for calm, sagacious, and statesmanlike consideration of a question affecting the great interests of England.

In spite of the general belief of the public that the Government were steering a safe middle course between extreme policies which would drag England in to fight against her will for either Turkey or Russia, the Duke of Argyll raised another debate ten days later.[1] He was concerned at the prospect of the Turkish question being left entirely to Russia, owing to British weakness and vacillation. The one obstacle, in his view, to firm and effective action by the European Concert had been the resolve of the Government not to sanction the coercion of Turkey. Would not Ministers persevere in the policy which Salisbury advocated at Constantinople ? Would not Beaconsfield connect the history of his Government with some determined measure in favour of the Christians in Turkey, which should guarantee them alike from Turkish barbarism and from Russian autocracy ?

The debate gave Derby the opportunity of maintaining the peaceful tendency of Ministerial policy, and

[1] Feb. 20.

Salisbury of justifying his proceedings at the Conference, and especially his refusal to be a party to the coercion of Turkey. It was also productive of a speech by Kimberley in the old Whig spirit, proclaiming his continued adherence to that Palmerstonian Eastern policy against which Gladstone's assaults were directed. That was a policy, Beaconsfield maintained in his speech at the close of the debate, not merely Palmerstonian or even English, but traditional and European. These were the Prime Minister's words:

> Let us for a moment take a broad view of what has been the situation and the conduct of the Government. We have been called upon, somewhat unexpectedly, to deal with the largest and the most difficult problem of modern politics. We have been called upon, as many eminent statesmen have been called upon before, to consider this—whether the Ottoman Empire could maintain itself; or whether, after long and sanguinary wars, its vast possessions might be doomed to partition, which probably might affect, without any exaggeration, the fate of Empires. My lords, the policy of Europe on this question has been distinct, and is almost traditional. I say absolutely the policy of Europe, and not merely the policy of England, as it is sometimes described, has been this—that by the maintenance of the territorial integrity and independence of the Ottoman Empire great calamities may be averted from Europe, wars may be prevented, and wars of no ordinary duration, and such a disturbance of the distribution of power as might operate most disadvantageously to the general welfare. The phrase, ' the territorial integrity and independence of the Ottoman Empire,' has been frequently referred to to-night, and in language of derision. . . . But your lordships will remember it embodies a principle which has always been accepted by statesmen; and the proof of it is seen in this very Conference. . . . The basis on which my noble friend (Lord Derby) achieved the great feat, which has been admired by the noble duke and his friends, of bringing all the Powers to consent to this Conference, was their recognition of the territorial integrity and independence of the Ottoman Empire.

Beaconsfield then explained the meaning of this historic phrase on the lines of his letter to Derby of January 29, elaborating the argument with numerous

illustrations.   He pointed out that the traditional policy
had been reaffirmed at the Congress of London in 1871,
only six years before, when Gladstone, being then in
power, saw no reason for a fresh departure.

After reciting and vindicating the various measures
taken by the Government in the autumn, Beaconsfield
in a weighty passage called attention to the dangers to
the traditional policy involved in Russia's plan for the
benefit of the Balkan Christians.

Now there were two great policies before us with regard
to the Christian subjects of the Porte.   There was the Russian
plan, and it was one deserving of all respect.   It was a plan
for establishing a chain of autonomous States, tributary to
the Porte, but in every other sense independent.   No one
can deny that was a large scheme worthy of statesmen and
worthy of the deepest consideration.   But the result of the
deepest consideration which Her Majesty's Government could
give to it was that they were forced entirely to disapprove of
that scheme.   The scheme of a chain of autonomous States
in the Balkan country, and indeed in the whole of the country
that during the last half-century has been known as European
Turkey, is a state of affairs that has existed before.   The
Turks did not slip down from Asia and conquer Constantinople, as is sometimes mentioned in speeches at national
conferences.   It was very gradually that they entered and
established themselves in Europe.   As a rising military
Power they obtained territories near the Black Sea, and ultimately entered into Thracia, and there they remained for
some time in company with all these independent and autonomous States.   There was, of course, an Emperor at Constantinople; there was a King of Bulgaria; there was a King
of Servia; there was a hospodar of Wallachia; there was a
duke of Athens, and there was a prince of Corinth.   And
what happened ?   The new military Power that had entered
Europe gradually absorbed and conquered all these independent States; and having conquered these independent and
autonomous States, these kingdoms and duchies, the Empire
of Constantinople being now limited to its matchless city,
and to what in modern diplomatic language is called 'a
cabbage garden,' was invested and fell.   And it did occur
to us that, if there were a chain of autonomous States, and
the possessors of Constantinople were again limited to 'a
cabbage garden,' probably the same result might occur. . . .
Against this plan of the Russian Court we proposed what was

II.   32*

called administrative autonomy, and we defined that administrative autonomy to be institutions that would secure to the Christian subjects of the Porte some control over their local affairs, and some security against the excesses of arbitrary power.

If the Conference, which, it had been hoped, would secure for the Christians this desirable autonomy, had failed, it was, Beaconsfield declared, from no fault of Salisbury, with whose proceedings at Constantinople he identified himself. Salisbury had succeeded in obtaining the withdrawal of the extreme Russian proposals for an armed occupation of Bulgaria. His only error was that ' he gave too much credit to the Turks for common sense, and he could not believe that, when he made so admirable an arrangement in their favour, they would have lost so happy an opportunity.' Beaconsfield ended on the note which he had been attacked for sounding at Guildhall:

It has been said that the people of this country are deeply interested in the humanitarian and philanthropic considerations involved in [the Eastern Question]. All must appreciate such feelings. But I am mistaken if there be not a yet deeper sentiment on the part of the people of this country, one with which I cannot doubt your lordships will ever sympathise, and that is—the determination to maintain the Empire of England.

For the policy of this speech Beaconsfield had a strong supporter in the Queen, as extracts from her letters to him just before and just after it will show.

From Queen Victoria.

OSBORNE, *Feb.* 14, '77.—The Queen has seen Sir H. Elliot and must say she thinks what he says is very sensible. He is perfectly astounded at Mr. Gladstone, his wildness, folly, and fury! What the Queen is most anxious for, for the interests of this country, is that in any debate which may take place in Parliament it should be clearly stated that we will not be a party to coerce Turkey, and that Russia must not (and we cannot allow her to) go to Constantinople. It is necessary that this should be demonstrated in Parliament, for else Russia may be found advancing and we shall be unable to stop her. No one can fathom Russian duplicity and skill in deception. . . .

Feb. 22.—The Queen congratulates Lord Beaconsfield (as much as she does herself) on the very successful debate in the House of Lords on Tuesday and on his admirable speech. She thinks Lord Beaconsfield will be gratified to hear that the Duke of Richmond wrote *purposely* to the Queen to tell her how admirably Lord Beaconsfield ' had acquitted himself, feeling that he may not himself have done justice to his efforts.' Considering the Duke's former position, the Queen thinks it very handsome and loyal of him.

The Opposition's conduct has done them no good, but it was necessary there should be these debates.

She thinks Bismarck is making much mischief. We may be driven to draw closer to France.

This was the only speech which Beaconsfield made during the session on the Eastern Question. Though, as his correspondence proves, his attention was directed during the whole period almost exclusively to foreign affairs, he left to the Foreign Secretary the parliamentary exposition, in the House of Lords, of the policy of the Government. For an effacement which naturally provoked public comment there were many reasons. It had been his practice, from his first days of leadership in office in 1852, to leave departmental matters to be dealt with in Parliament by the departmental chiefs; he admired Derby's capacity and authority in addressing the House of Lords; and, at any rate in the earlier months of the session, he was not dissatisfied with the attitude which his Foreign Minister took up. Then, in spite of the agitation in the country, there was in the Lords comparatively little question of Government policy, and therefore not much reason for Government defence. In the Commons, where vehement attacks were made by Gladstone and the Radicals, Beaconsfield could not be present to answer, and adequate defence, supported on occasion by large majorities, was offered by Northcote, Hardy, and Cross. Besides, after war had begun between Russia and Turkey, there was general approval of the policy of neutrality adopted by the Government; and

Beaconsfield, in view of the divergent tendencies of his colleagues, strongly deprecated discussion as to eventual action in certain contingencies.

But the weightiest and most compelling reason of all for silence and inaction in the Lords was the reason which had already driven him from the Commons— ill-health. Constant attacks of gout, bronchitis, and asthma throughout the year, till he obtained some relief from Dr. Kidd, whom he consulted for the first time in November, made it necessary for him to husband his little strength for the direction of policy in Cabinet. Even the speech just quoted was delivered during illness, and resulted in an aggravated return of his complaint.

To Lady Bradford.

(*In pencil.*) 2, WHITEHALL GARDENS, *Monday* [? *Feb*. 26, 1877].—Your letter is most welcome to me, and I send you the first line I have written, for my correspondence with the Great Lady, tho' frequent, is telegraphic.

I have had a fair night, and the first one with[ou]t pain.

The attack has been very severe, and unexpected, as I have been guarding against its contemplated occurrence for the last six weeks. It has always been menacing: in fact I spoke in the gout on D. of Arg.'s motion, and that settled it.

I hope I have nothing now to fight against but weakness, for I can scarcely walk across the room; but I have the rallying power—or had, I shd. rather say.

What ought to rally me now is the prospect of having defeated Gort[cha]k[off] and baffled Bismarck, and secured European peace, and, greater than defeating G. and B.— keeping the Cab. together ! . . .

To Queen Victoria.

2, WHITEHALL GARDENS, *Feb*. 27, 1877.—Lord Beaconsfield . . . thanks your Majesty for your Majesty's gracious letter.

He should be quite unhappy, if he had not the honor and gratification of waiting on your Majesty, when your Majesty is in London. He thinks if he did not see your Majesty, he should never get quite well.

There is much to confer about, and, perhaps, by that time,

some important issues will have been decided, and decided to your Majesty's pleasure.

The Parliamentary collapse of the 'Eastern Question' agitation is almost unprecedented: so rapid and so complete.

Lord Beaconsfield wishes to consult your Majesty also about Church affairs. The hostility of the Ritualists to your Majesty's Government, but especially to himself, is rancorous. They never will pardon the 'Public Worship Act.' Lord Beaconsfield thinks it one of the most memorable Acts of your Majesty's reign, and it shows how great is the power of the Sovereign in this country, if firm and faithfully served: for the Act would never have passed, nay, would never have been introduced, had it not been for your Majesty.

The 'Titles' Act the same. Both Bills, certainly the first, were passed without the support of the Cabinet. And yet both are great Acts, and most efficacious. . . .

Turkey and Russia both occupied the winter months in proceedings which were meant to impress the world with their good faith and moderation, but which failed in each case to produce the desired result. The Sultan affected to put the new Constitution into operation, and in opening the Ottoman Parliament in great state in March declared that his disagreement with the Powers and their wishes was rather one of method than of substance. But he had previously dismissed and degraded Midhat Pasha, the author of that Constitution, and had appointed a reactionary as Grand Vizier in his place. The Tsar, on his side, professing a desire still to work in accord with the rest of Europe, inquired through Gortchakoff what were the intentions of the Powers in view of the Porte's refusal to meet their wishes—a refusal which touched 'the dignity and peace of Europe.' He desired to have this information, he significantly added, 'before deciding on the course which he may think it right to follow.' One anxiety was removed from Europe by the signing of a definite peace between Turkey and Serbia.

Beaconsfield was anxious to gain time, and so to prevent the outbreak of hostilities, and his suggestions to Derby were inspired by that idea.

To Lord Derby.

10, DOWNING ST., *Feb.* 9, '77.—You must pardon the roughness of this communication, but I am in the gout, which is fatal to finished composition, and penmanship.

The position of affairs is most critical, and requires decision.

I believe that, at no moment, was Russia more anxious for peace, than the present. She is perfectly conscious of the intrigues of Bismarck to involve her in a struggle, which, whatever the ultimate result, must be materially disastrous to her; but she must have a golden bridge. The Moscow speech, and the host on the Pruth, render this necessary.

If war begins, I think it will end in partition. I cannot learn that Turkey has any adequate resources: no money; not many men. In that case we must have a decided course, and seize, at the fitting time, what is necessary for the security of our Empire. No one will resist us, either at the time, or afterwards.

But can war be avoided ? Only by a reply to Gortchakoff's note, or a negotiation with Russia through the Ambassador here, which will construct the golden bridge.

The last *coup d'état* at Constantinople may assist us.

If the Porte concedes the three following points, what we desire might be obtained.

Midhat could not, or would not; the Sultan can and may.

1. That the Vali should be appointed for a fixed term, removable only on recommendation of some Turkish authority independent of the Minister of the day: say, a vote of their Senate.

2. That the Provincial Assembly should have the control over the raising and spending of some considerable portion of the direct taxes. Query, tithes ?

3. That there should be a police and a Militia containing Xtians in proportion to the population.

I think if the Porte would concede these, they might have a fixed term to carry them into full effect: say, eighteen months.

He who gains time, gains everything. By that period, France will be armed.

I think something like this would be accepted at St. Petersburg.

I don't fancy the country will stand *laisser faire*, but they will back us, I believe, in whatever we do, provided we are doing.

2, WHITEHALL G'DNS, [*March* 2, '77].—You must pardon an unhappy correspondent, who, in addition to other sufferings, has gout in his eye !

If the genl. draft, in its present form, is to prevail, there can be no doubt that your drt. conclusion is infinitely the preferable one.

But I frankly tell you, I don't like the general draft. I say nothing about its style—what I call ' the carrying out ' style—which is too common in F. O., and which has this merit, that it contrasts with the terse and lucid corrections of the chief, which always makes me wish that, on eminent occasions like the present, he should trust to no pen but his own.

It is the general conception of the reply to which I object.

There runs throughout all Gort.'s circular an assumption which ought to be corrected—an assumption as to the *raison d'être* of the Conference.

The Powers were mediators: they were invited by the Porte to mediate: by no one was the position of the Powers, as mediators, and the character and object in which, and for which, they made these proposals to Turkey, more clearly defined than by the Plenipos. of Russia at the Conference.

As we were all mediators only, the refusal of the Porte to adopt our recommendations was no offence to the dignity of Europe.

Time would not allow me to attempt a sketch, even were I physically capable, but I throw out these rough lines.

If the draft is to remain, see that the word reform, etc., do not occur too often, and too slangishly.

The Tsar was not content with merely issuing Gortchakoff's circular, but reinforced it by a special mission to the various Courts of Europe.   The chosen envoy was Ignatieff, long Russian Ambassador at Constantinople, whose Pan-Slavonic intrigues had contributed so materially to produce the Eastern crisis, and whom, accordingly, Beaconsfield was by no means disposed to welcome when in the course of his tour he reached England in March. Salisbury, however, who had established friendly relations with Ignatieff at the Conference, invited him, to Beaconsfield's dismay, to be his guest at Hatfield, and Beaconsfield subsequently thought it proper himself to give a banquet in honour of the special envoy and his wife.

To Lady Bradford.

2, WHITEHALL GARDENS, *March* 16.—. . . The Ignatieff arrival is a thunderbolt; nothing cd. be more inopportune, and

nothing more awkward than his going to Hatfield. I am
asked to meet him there Saty. and Sunday, and was very
glad I cd. conscientiously refuse both days, being engaged to
Ld. D. to-morrow, and to the Peels on Sunday.

Absolute dismay at headquarters about the visit: telegrams
and letters about it every hour. It seems that Ld. Salisbury
wrote to him a week ago, suggesting that ' when all this
turmoil was over ' he shd. pay Ld. S. a visit at Hatd. . .

March 19.—. . . I have been out of sorts, as you know,
for these three months. I attended the Cabinet on Saturday
morning pretty well, but in the afternoon felt very ill with
feverish catarrh.   cd. hardly get thro' the dinner, of wh.
I did not partake, and stole away as soon as I possibly
could. Yesterday I was very ill; but last night I had a fair
rest, and got rid of my fever, tho' I feel dreadfully weak. I
cd. not put off my guests, and think I shall get thro' it pretty
well. But I shall not go to the H. of Lords to-day, tho' I
have some business there. . . .

March 22.—. . . hardly thought the day wd. ever end,
or that myself shd. last as long. The dinner was successful,
tho' I cd. not partake of it, or contribute to its grace and
gaiety. Prince Hal,[1] who had invited himself, and for the
sake of the Ignatieffs, took out Madame, as arranged by
himself. His [other] neighbour [was] Lady Londonderry. . . .
Dss. Louise[2] sate on my right; we had a longer table than
usual, and I sate in the middle. . . . Monty sate on the
other side of Madame [Ignatieff] . . . and got on very well
with the greatlady, who is pretty and, they say, very agreeable,
except when he recommended to her some Apollinaris water.
Not the custom of the Russian ladies. When they offered
her wine, ' Sherry or Manzanilla ? etc., etc.,' she always
answered, ' Any one,' but never refused 'any one.' But is
very calm and collected, and must have had therefore an
early training at it. . . . The fine ladies, who had heard
that Mme. Ig. was even finer than themselves, and gave herself airs, determined not to yield without a struggle. Ly.
Londy. staggered under the jewels of the 3 united families
of Stewart and Vane and Londonderry, and on her right arm,
set in diamonds, the portrait of the Empress of Russia—an
imperial present to the great Marchioness. Mme. Ig. had
many diamonds, and a fine costume, but paled before this.
As for Louise, she set everything on fire, even the neighbouring
Thames; her face still flushed with the Lincoln race-course,
her form in a spick-and-span new dress, scarcely finished, and
her hair *à la* Marie Antoinette, studded with diamonds, wh.

[1] See above, p. 970.   [2] Of Manchester.

by the bye were stuck in every part of her costume. 'Lady Bradford ought to be here,' she said. 'Why is not Lady Bd. here?' And echo answered, Why? . . .

I continued very ill yesterday and had a bad night; but they thought it better not to send for Gull to-day. . . .

March 24.—. . . Two hours after noon, I shall be at Hughenden. They say I must go out of town, even if it be only for 8 and 40 hours. . . .

Yesterday was the most important meeting of the Cabinet which has yet been holden, and I trust we shall never hear any more Bathism,[1] Lyddonism (*sic*), really Gladstonism, within those walls. . . .

HUGHENDEN MANOR, *March* 27, 1877.—. . . I made my voyage to Windsor yesterday in a brougham with closed windows, and so returned. Nor was I kept loitering in the corridor, wh. is a most windy place, but found rooms for me ready with good fires: so I think I have escaped all perils. . .

My audience was most agreeable, and the longest I ever had. It exceeded the hour, and was never dull, or flagged for a moment. She wanted very much to know all about the Ignatieff dinner party. . . .

She talked to me a great deal about Hughenden; she has quite made up her mind to pay me a visit. 'But it must be in the summer; now you are in H. of L. you will always be free.' . . . I think you will have to come down to receive her. At any rate she will see your portrait in the library. . . .

April 5.—. . . [The equinox] has a debilitating effect on many persons; on myself especially; I am not the same person I was 8 and 40 hours ago; my appetite waning, and weak and chilly. I thought we had escaped these, I concluded necessary, but disagreeable gales. Every year, the same illusion, or rather every half-year, for, vernal or autumnal, they equally upset me. . . .

April 9.—. . . The change of air has entirely relieved me of my cough, wh. had harassed me, more or less, for 3 months, but my eyes trouble me much, and I think my retirement from society a necessity. Whe[the]r I can go on steering the ship, I hardly know, but I may be turned out of office, wh. will solve that diff[icult]y. . . .

Ignatieff's mission had some effect on those members of the Cabinet who were especially interested in the cause of the Eastern Christians, as appears from a royal letter to the Prime Minister.

[1] Lord Bath, a leading Tory, sympathised with the 'Atrocity' agitation.

From Queen Victoria.

WINDSOR CASTLE, *March* 21, '77.—The Queen . . . trusts
the Cabinet will be very firm, and Lord Derby seemed so
yesterday. She is prepared to speak or write to good but
nervous and somewhat weak and sentimental Lord Carnarvon,
if necessary, as well as to Lord Salisbury. This mawkish
sentimentality for people who hardly deserve the name of
real Christians, as if they were more God's creatures and our
fellow-creatures than every other nation abroad, and forgetting the great interests of this great country—is really
incomprehensible.

Only say if the Queen can do anything. . . .

The Russian proposal which so moved the Queen
appears to have been that Turkey should be invited to
disarm while Russia retained her troops mobilised on
the frontier. Beaconsfield's tact and good management
of his colleagues prevented any weakening on this point;
and on March 31 the Powers made yet one more effort
to get the Eastern Question in train for settlement
without war. On that day, at the instance of Russia,
a protocol was signed in London by Derby, as Foreign
Secretary, and by the representatives on the spot of all
the Treaty Powers. They took cognisance with satisfaction of the peace concluded by Turkey with Serbia
and of the arrangement in process of completion with
Montenegro, and invited the Porte to proceed at once
to reduce its army to a peace footing, and to put in hand
without delay the reforms promised for the Christian
populations. If the Porte accepted and showed signs
of acting on this advice, and would send an envoy to
St. Petersburg to treat of disarmament, the Tsar, his
Ambassador was authorised to declare, would also consent to disarm. The Powers proposed to watch carefully
through their ambassadors and local agents the manner in
which the Porte's promises were carried out. If their hopes
were disappointed, they announced that such ' a state
of affairs would be incompatible with their interests and
those of Europe in general '; and in that case they reserved
to themselves ' to consider in common as to the means

which they may deem best fitted to secure the well-
being of the Christian populations and the interests of
the general peace.' Derby added to the protocol on
behalf of the British Government an emphatic declaration that, as they had only signed it in the interests of
European peace, it should be regarded as null and void
if reciprocal disarmament and peace were not attained.

'So the protocol is signed, and everybody writes to
me about our triumph and the humiliation of Russia!
I can't yet quite make head or tail of it.' This was
Beaconsfield's own comment, next day, in a letter to
Salisbury. To Lady Bradford he wrote, ' I think affairs
look well, and should be more certain, did they not seem
incredible.' It hardly appears as if he expected much
result from the protocol. If so, he was not disappointed.
Turkey, though warned by Derby of the unwisdom of
refusing this friendly overture, energetically protested
against the tutelage and supervision which it would
impose upon her, and appealed to the provisions of the
Treaty of Paris guaranteeing her integrity and independence. Russia—in spite of her responsibility for a
protocol which was in no sense an ultimatum to the
Porte, but contemplated that it should have time to
carry out reforms, and in case of failure that there should
be a further consultation of the European Areopagus—
continued and perfected her preparations for war; and
on April 21 the Tsar announced that his patience was
exhausted, and ordered his armies to cross the frontier.
The season for campaigning had come.

Derby had regarded war as ' inevitable' ever since
the Porte had rejected the protocol, but neither he nor
the Government regarded it as therefore justifiable. To
the Pan-Slavonic party in Russia, and to their counter-
parts in England, the supporters of Gladstone's agitation,
Russia's invasion of Turkey appeared to be a righteous
and unselfish crusade, in which the more extreme fanatics
in this country only regretted that England had not
taken a share. But disapproval and anxiety were

necessarily the sentiments of those statesmen who, like Beaconsfield, bore in mind the persistent and unscrupulous advance of Russia both in Europe and in Asia over a long period of years, who realised the importance to British and imperial interests of Constantinople and the Straits, of Egypt and the Suez Canal, and who held that the stability and orderly progress of Europe depended on the observance of treaties which Russia's isolated action disregarded. The Queen was passionately of this opinion. Before the Tsar had completely exposed his hand she wrote, on April 17, to Beaconsfield: ' The Queen feels more and more anxious lest we should be found powerless and receive a slap in the face from these false Russians, and wishes the Cabinet to consider seriously what measures we should take to show that we are not going to follow Mr. Gladstone's view of giving up all to the beneficent and tender mercies of Russia.' Her Majesty composed a letter to be read to the Cabinet, and in a private note accompanying it told Beaconsfield that ' she has made it firm, general, and conciliatory, but to him she will say (and he may make use of it) that, if England is to kiss Russia's feet, she will not be a party to the humiliation of England and would lay down her crown. She did say as much to Lord Carnarvon the other day.' Here is the letter, which was read to the Cabinet on Saturday, April 21, and which, Beaconsfield told the Queen, ' produced a marked effect ':

From Queen Victoria.

OSBORNE, *April* 19, '77.—The present moment is one of great gravity, and requires to be met with calmness, firmness, and complete unanimity. Any difference of opinion if known would be most serious and would encourage the Opposition in their harassing, tho' hitherto fruitless, attacks on the Government.

It is natural that everyone should have their own opinion, especially on religion; but, when the policy of Great Britain comes into consideration and her greatest if not vital interests (viz., our Indian Empire) are involved, *all* private feelings should be overruled, and the one desire should be to agree on the policy most likely to conduce to the welfare of the country. While it is obviously necessary to be extremely cautious and prudent, this must not be carried too far, so as not to have the appearance of feebleness and vacillation.

The Queen appeals to the feelings of patriotism which she knows animate her Government, and is certain that every member of it will feel the absolute necessity of showing a bold and united front to the enemy in the country as well as outside it.

No time should be lost or wasted in deliberating on the best steps to be taken in this momentous crisis.

It is not the question of upholding Turkey; it is the question of Russian or British supremacy in the world !

When the war broke out, Her Majesty's indignation was great, and she had no doubt as to the kind of policy which Beaconsfield and his Cabinet ought to adopt.

From Queen Victoria.

WINDSOR CASTLE, *April* 25, '77.—The news from Mr. Layard is very important. We must not submit tamely to Russia's advance and to the dangers in Egypt. Whatever we intend to do ought to be clearly explained to the other Powers. The Russian circular is not exact even as to facts. The recollection of the facts connected with the Crimean War and what led to it are fresh in the Queen's memory, and the contrast to the present moment with the feeling of indignation which filled everyone then is very painful to the Queen. She wishes no general war—God knows ! for no one abhors it more than she does: but then there ought to be an under- standing that we cannot allow the Russians to occupy Con- stantinople, and that we must see that this is promised or the consequences may be serious. To let it be thought that we shall never fight and that England will submit to Egypt being under Russia would be to abdicate the position of Great Britain as one of the Great Powers—to which she never will submit, and another must wear the crown if this is intended.

The Queen may very well have been echoing in her letter the sentiments which she had frequently heard from Beaconsfield. He was at any rate clear what the course of the British Government ought to be. It should express its disapproval of the Russian action, as inconsistent both with the Treaty of Paris and with the London protocol. It could not intervene, as in the Crimean War, on Turkey's behalf, owing to her misconduct and the consequent alienation from her of popular sympathy in Britain. It should therefore adopt a position of neutrality in the war, but of watchful and conditional neutrality, and should at the outset obtain a pledge from Russia to respect British interests in Turkey, such as Constantinople, Egypt, and the Suez Canal. At the same time it should make preparations to enforce its claims, in case victory should tempt Russia to evade her promises. Moreover. it should look out for, and seize, any favourable opportunity for mediation, so that the war might be brought to an end before the Russian armies approached any of the vital points. It was in this sense that he counselled the Cabinet on May 1. Corry has left a note of this meeting: ' Lord B. suddenly taken ill, while Cabinet sitting: had to go to bed. I wrote to inform H.M. of his inability to attend H.M. at 6, and was summoned to report what had occurred in Cabinet. The occasion was the *first real* unfolding, by Lord B., of his policy in the East.' Corry reported to his sick chief the result of his audience.

From Montagu Corry.

BUCKINGHAM PALACE, *May* 1, '77. 7.10.—I have been more than twenty minutes with the Queen, who was more gracious and condescendingly charming than words can express.

My tidings, I need hardly say, gave her great satisfaction, and she bids me tell you so.

I am to send her to-morrow morning a *résumé* of what I told her, and, if you are not materially better, I am to come in your place to report the result of to-morrow's Cabinet.

She spoke freely of Gladstone, the Duchess of Edinburgh, and so on, as if I had been her favourite Prime Minister !

She sends you her anxious hopes that you will have a good night, and injunctions to have the Cabinet at your house, if you are not better to-morrow.

To Queen Victoria.

2, WHITEHALL GARDENS, *May* 5, 1877.—Lord Beaconsfield
with his humble duty to your Majesty:

The Cabinet settled to-day the despatch to Russia, warning
that Power of the circumstances which would render it
impossible for your Majesty's Government to continue a
policy of abstention and neutrality. Lord Beaconsfield hopes,
and thinks, your Majesty will not be displeased with it. It
seems to him to be spirited, and though courteous, and even
conciliatory, most decided and unmistakable. . . .

Thus, though the Cabinet by no means considered
themselves bound to the forceful action which Beaconsfield in certain circumstances contemplated, they were
ready to take the first step. In a despatch which Beaconsfield afterwards described as ' the charter of our policy,'
' the diapason of our diplomacy,' Derby definitely warned
the Russian Government off the Suez Canal, the Persian
Gulf, and the Bosphorus as points where British interests
arose; and Gortchakoff, in reply, as definitely promised
to respect these points. It was not, however, enough to
have a policy; it was necessary to have a man of ability,
character, and resolution to carry it out at the danger
spot, Constantinople. Beaconsfield insisted that Elliot
could not go back. ' What we want,' he wrote on
April 10 to Lady Bradford, ' is a man of the necessary
experience and commanding mind, at this moment, at
Constantinople—and one not too scrupulous. But such
men are rare everywhere.' Beaconsfield's choice fell on
Layard, whose strength of character he had experienced
over the Spanish Question, and who, as an old Foreign
Under-Secretary in Palmerston's Government, had every
sympathy with the Palmerstonian and traditional method
of treating the Eastern Question. The Queen, who was
far too great to bear a grudge, was much pleased, she
told Beaconsfield, with Layard's ' tone ' in conversation.
' He is very strong upon the vital interests of this country,
which Mr. Gladstone and some of his followers have
entirely forgotten.'

The Opposition had utilised the pause after the signing of the protocol and before the outbreak of war to raise debates in both Houses, but without much profit to themselves or damage to the Government.

To Lady Bradford.

10, DOWNING STREET, *April* 14, 1877.—My third *séance* to Von Angeli [1] this morning. It is said to be a great success. And then a Cabinet, wh. is just over. And in a few minutes, the head of the engineer officers, whom I sent to Constantinople nearly a year ago, will be with me, with maps, and plans, and estimates, and all sorts of things, wh. perhaps will never be wanted; for it is very clear that Russia does not like the war at all wh. she has brought about by her own intrigues and miscalculated swagger.

Last night the great Whig reconnaissance ended very disastrously for its concocters. The House of Commons was crammed full; Harty-Tarty did very well, but Hardy blew the whole thing out of the water, like a torpedo ! Harcourt who had got up the whole scheme, rose to answer him, with an immense speech and endless papers; but was so mortified by everybody rushing to dinner, except the habitual bores, who never dine—at least at late hours—that he broke down, quite demoralised; and the debate never rallied, except when Roebuck fired a well-aimed and destructive shot. We are to have the same farce in the House of Lords on Monday, if Granville still has stomach for it.

Von Angeli's studio is the Queen's private dining-room. and it is furnished, and entirely fitted up, with the Pagoda furniture of the Brighton Pavilion. The fantastic scene, the artist himself, very good-looking, picturesque, and a genius, the P. Minister seated in a crimson chair on a stage, and the Private Secretary reading the despatches, with his boxes, would make a good *genre* picture !

April 17.—. . . The great debate in the Lords collapsed. Granville made a speech, wh. entered on no great questions

---

[1] The Queen had asked her favourite Minister to have his portrait painted for her by her favourite artist. She wrote from Osborne, March 29: 'The Queen has now a favour to ask of Lord Beaconsfield. It is that he should be painted for her, for Windsor, by the great artist Angeli, who painted herself, who is coming to England immediately. It would only be the head, and as he is wonderfully quick he would require but very few sittings. Lord Beaconsfield's career is one of the most remarkable in the annals of the Empire, and none of her Ministers have ever shown her more consideration and kindness than he has.' A replica of the picture, which is not a pleasing likeness, was given by the Queen to Beaconsfield, and is still at Hughenden.

of policy, but was a tissue of verbal criticism and petty points. Derby, who, to my pleased surprise, is a first-rate debater in the Ho. of Lords, wh. he never was in the Ho. of Commons, answered him on every point, so completely that it was impossible to sustain the debate, wh. after some ordinary remarks of Ld. Lansdowne, and some nonsense from the maniac, Dudley, like the Rhine never reached the sea, but vanished in mud.

So I went home to a dinnerless hearth, and feasted on sandwiches wh. were to have been my banquet in the H. of C. [? H. of L.].

To Anne Lady Chesterfield.

2, WHITEHALL GARDENS, *April* 29, 1877.—. . . Gladstone and the real leaders of the Whigs seem at length to have separated, and he is going to take his own line, and move a vote of censure on the Government, wh. they will not support. I am not afraid of his motions, and believe he loses, every day, weight with the country, but the mischief he has done is incalculable.

The attacks on the Government in the Commons culminated, after the war had begun, in a series of resolutions, submitted by Gladstone, which amounted in effect to a policy of joining Russia in her crusade. This programme could not well be supported by the Opposition leaders, who were on the whole satisfied with the Ministerial policy of watchful neutrality; but a compromise was patched up between them and their former chief, under which, while they merely asked the House to disengage British interests from the maintenance of the Ottoman Empire, Gladstone was free to advocate, in eloquent language, the coercion of the Porte, in alliance with Russia, for the liberation of the subject Christian races in Turkey. But, after Cross, in a convincing speech, had pointed out that no British Government could be indifferent to a threat to the Suez Canal, to Egypt, to the Dardanelles, or to Constantinople, the House, by the large majority of 131, declined, at this critical moment, to entertain any resolution which might embarrass Ministers in the maintenance of peace and the protection of British interests.

By this vote, which was taken on May 14, the Parliamentary situation was regularised, and there was little further trouble for Ministers from outside attack for the remainder of the session. But the stress of war aggravated the tendencies to internal disagreement which had already appeared in the Cabinet during the Bulgarian agitation and the Constantinople Conference. The complicity of Turkish civil and military authorities, if not of the Porte itself, in the Bulgarian atrocities, its neglect to punish the culprits, and its stubborn refusal to accept the reforms demanded by the united representatives of the Powers, had produced in the Cabinet, as in the country, a strong indisposition again to be allied in arms with so barbarous and purblind a State. Quite half of the Cabinet were more or less affected by this feeling, and particularly Carnarvon, Salisbury, Northcote, and Derby. The whole Cabinet, indeed, were convinced, with their chief, that there was a point at which Russia must be checked, beyond which she must not be permitted to advance. But not only were there differences as to where this point ought exactly to be fixed; there was also a reluctance, amounting in individual cases to a refusal, to recognise that, in the possible, if not probable, contingency of victorious Russia's defiant persistence, this accepted policy involved war, or at least an unmistakable threat of war—and war, as in the Crimean days, by Turkey's side. They would not realise that it was necessary, not merely to proclaim a policy, but to convince Russia, by deeds as well as words, that the British Ministry were in earnest in their resolve to carry it out, even, in the last resort, by taking up arms on Turkey's behalf.

This prospect was clearly envisaged by Beaconsfield, and he devoted his energies throughout the year, with masterly skill and patience, to bringing his colleagues to recognise facts as he recognised them, and to make, however tardily, the necessary preparations. Constantly hampered as he was by their hesitations, and racked,

moreover, by incessant gout, he never allowed himself
to be permanently discouraged. He was warmly supported and heartened by the Queen, whose indignation
at Russia's conduct was indeed of so burning a character
as to be even embarrassing to a Minister who was bound
to take care not to venture beyond the point where he
could definitely count on public support.

Northcote gives us in his memorandum a vivid picture
of Ministerial divergences.

It cannot be denied that there were real, though suppressed,
differences of opinion and feeling among the members of the
Cabinet with regard to our Eastern policy. We never came
to an actual division, and we may be held to have agreed to
each step as it came; but the ultimate views of some of us
differed from those of others, and we more than once, after
adopting a particular measure one day, found ourselves on
the next adopting another wholly inconsistent with the
intentions, at all events, of the day before. The Prime Minister
was most anxious to keep us all together. Lord Derby was
chiefly bent on keeping us out of war, but was ready to go
almost any length which his colleagues desired in writing
despatches, apparently not perceiving that the strength of
his language would be held to involve, under possible and
probable circumstances, the necessity for corresponding
action. In the earlier days of our difficulties the peace party
in the Cabinet may be said to have consisted, under Lord
Derby, of Cairns, Cross, the Duke of Richmond, Salisbury,
Carnarvon, and myself. As time wore on, Cairns, Cross,
and Richmond seemed somewhat to modify their views. I
was much in communication with Salisbury and Carnarvon,
and I was also in communication with Derby, between whom
and the other two there was some coldness. Carnarvon was
strongly impressed with the belief that the Prime Minister
was desirous of war. Derby, judging more correctly, said
to me: 'I don't think he desires war; he desires to place
England in a "commanding position."' The Prime Minister
himself said to me more than once that his great fear was
that Derby's policy would lead us to war; and, looking back,
I am more and more convinced that there was much ground
for the apprehension.

It was in this spring that Beaconsfield began to be
seriously uneasy as to the adequacy of Derby for the
Foreign Secretaryship at a time of national stress. In

the previous autumn he had admired the strong stand which his colleague had taken against the enthusiasts who were eager to drive England into the forcible coercion of Turkey. Now, when it was necessary to put a limit on the advance of Russia, he saw the same temperament, which produced the autumn attitude he admired, responsible for a policy which, save for excellent despatches, was purely passive. A belated attempt was indeed made to secure the real co-operation of Austria; but, as she was already secretly bound to Russia, nothing for the moment came of it.

To Lord Derby.

HUGHENDEN, *May* 22, '77.—I think affairs look very bad for us, and that some other body will yet fall before the Ottoman Empire tumbles. The tactics of the Opposition are clear: they were laid down by Harcourt in the debate. He distinctly laid the ground for an appeal to the people against the Ministry, whose want of foresight and courage will have compelled us to acquiesce either in a ruinous war, or a humiliating peace. Having successfully acted on a nervous and divided Cabinet, and prevented anything being done, they will now turn round and say, ' This is the way you protect British interests!' They will probably turn us out in this Parliament, or they will force us to a dissolution under the influence of a disastrous defeat abroad.

When do you expect the answer from Austria? I never thought anything would come of it, but there is a strong party in the Cabinet which does, and would agree to nothing till it was tried. I think you ought to press, and press hard, for a reply. Every moment is now golden. Austria never acts, only writes despatches, as the Duke said of Metternich in very similar circumstances to the present.

Even Loftus sees thro' Gortk. and Schou. I am sorry you gave such free warren to the latter, but, as you mentioned, we are not bound by those words. . . .

A Government can only die once: it is better to die with glory, than vanish in an ignominious end. The country would still rally round British interests: in three months' time, Brit. interests will be in the mud.

I have written this with difficulty, for my hand has relapsed.

From Lord Derby.

KNOWSLEY, PRESCOT, *May* 24, '77.—I am very sorry for your renewed attack of the enemy—knowing from home recollections what an infliction it is—and not less so that you take a desponding view of the situation. You have been so often right when others were wrong that I hardly like to express dissent: but I am quite sure that in the middle class at least the feeling is so strong against war that you would lose more support by asking money for an expedition than you could gain by the seizure of an important military position. . . .

To Lord Derby.

HUGHENDEN, *May* 25, '77.—The same messenger, who brings me your letter, brings me a box from the Lord Chancellor. It is a very distressing one, as he does not see affairs in the light you do, and foreseeing great disgrace to us as a Government, attacks from the Opposition and repudiation by our own friends, he shrinks from encountering a position of ignominy tho' he detests ' the appearance of a selfish disloyalty to the colleagues of my whole public life.'

The situation he thinks deeply critical. ' We have defined Brit. interests, and said we would protect them, and we are not taking any real step for their protection. It is quite apparent, that Russia is trying to bridge over the few weeks, which will make her safe against any action of ours. She will then be potentially master of Constantinople and will arrange the passage of the Straits, as she and Germany please, and will snap her fingers at us. Then the Opposition will turn upon us, and our own friends will join them.'

I must say that all this expresses very much my own views, and indeed I often ask myself, if you had resolved to do nothing, why not have accepted Bismarck's offer ?

Nothing can justify isolation on the part of England but a determination to act.

The Lord Chancellor wants the Cabinet to be called together and to review the situation again, preliminarily to a final decision. I suppose it will break up.

Altho' I expect nothing from Austria, I feel we must wait for the reply, provided it is not postponed, and some of our colls. are even abroad. I don't think we could meet before a week.

I hope you will be able to make this out, but I am very suffering, feet and hands.

From Lord Derby.

FOREIGN OFFICE, [? *May* 26, 1877].—I will do as you like, but I do not see what there is to discuss in the present state of affairs. And I doubt as to the wisdom of ' talking over ' things when no action is possible. Men only work each other up into a state of agitation, and are then ready to rush into anything rash to relieve it.

Why does not Cairns tell us the points which he wants considered ?

Beaconsfield's personal views as to the precautions which the British Government ought to take are clearly set out in a ' secret ' letter which he wrote at this period to the new Ambassador at Constantinople. The vigorous action which he suggested was as unwelcome to the Sultan as to the majority of the British Cabinet. Gladstone's agitation, Derby's despatches, the Constantinople Conference, and the London protocol, had made the Sultan nearly as suspicious of England as of Russia, and it was some months before Layard could make the Porte understand that Beaconsfield sincerely desired to preserve Turkey's integrity and independence.

To Austen Henry Layard.

Secret. 2, WHITEHALL GARDENS, *June* 6, '77.—I find, at the last moment and on a busy day, I have the opportunity of communicating with you by a trusty hand. Understand, this is not an official communication, but one strictly personal, and of the utmost confidence.

The campaign has hitherto realised my anticipations: disastrous in Asia; on the Danube, doubtful, but big with menacing consequences.

Are there no means, notwithstanding the paralysing neutrality in vogue, which might tend, if effected, to maintain generally the *status quo*, and, at the same time, place England in a commanding position when the conditions of peace are discussed ?

Is it impossible for the Porte to invite the presence of our fleet at Constantinople, and for us to accede to the invitation, still asserting our neutrality, on the ground, that we are taking a material guarantee for the observance of existing treaties ?

A maritime movement of that kind could not be hazarded without securing our communications; otherwise, the Russians might be at the Dardanelles before they occupy Constantinople, and our fleet might be caught in a trap. The material guarantee, therefore, should also consist of a military occupation of the Peninsula of Gallipoli by England   Twenty thousand men would secure this. We should engage to evacuate this position on the termination of the war.

If such a proposal came from the Porte, I would recommend its adoption by the Cabinet, but the proposal must come from Constantinople.

I wish you would consider these matters, and communicate with me in entire confidence. Time is of inestimable value, as I should think the preparation and despatch of the military portion of the expedition might require ten weeks. It could hardly be delayed later than the passage of the Danube by the Russians, and it would be most appropriate, if that event were the occasion of the appeal to us of the Porte.

I cannot refrain from mentioning my sense of the skill and energy with which your Excellency is conducting the Queen's business at your Court.

The hesitations of the Cabinet caused the greatest distress to the Queen.

From Queen Victoria.

Confidential. BALMORAL, *June* 7, '77.—Since writing to Lord Beaconsfield last night the Queen has had a great deal of very interesting and important conversation with Lord Odo Russell, who she is very sorry to hear has not seen Lord Beaconsfield—and Lord Derby only for a very short time—who said to him he supposed *he had 'nothing'* to *say* to *him ! ! !* Before saying anything else, the Queen must tell Lord Beaconsfield in strict confidence that Lord Odo was (as Sir S. Northcote likewise was) struck with the extreme imperturbability of Lord Derby, who actually said—it was enough to say we would not allow certain things and he hoped we should not have to do more! The Queen owns that she is greatly alarmed, and all Lord Odo tells her of the extreme readiness of the Russians and of the dangers of letting them go on makes her tremble lest we should *un beau matin* find them on their way to Constantinople. Lord Odo says that our position abroad and the respect in which everything coming from us is held never was greater, and that they only wait for us to move! He says that he is certain that Russia won't on any account quarrel with us, and that if we speak out very firmly they will stop.

There is, he says, an intimate understanding of some kind or other between the three Powers, which Lord Derby won't believe, as he sometimes is very slow at that, and this it is which makes the Queen suspect Austria. While she has carefully abstained from saying anything about our Austrian communications to Lord Odo, she feels sure that Bismarck will hear of it, and that it would be unwise not to try to carry him with us. Pray see Lord Odo and hear all he has to say, which is so clear and well defined. Only let us be firm and hold strong language to Russia and the rest of Europe will follow! Lord Derby must be *made* to move. The Queen feels terribly anxious about this.

Pray be firm in the House of Commons. . . .

Lord Odo quite bears out the Queen's very strong conviction, as well as that of our other Ambassadors, that the language of Mr. Gladstone and others in the autumn and even early part of the session has done the greatest possible mischief, and that Russia has been encouraged to go ahead and go to war thereby. The Queen has taken the opportunity of stating this in strong terms to the Duke of Argyll in replying to a letter of congratulation on her birthday, and of adding at the same time that it is not yet too late ' to act a patriotic part and to desist.'

The Queen thinks the Prince of Wales should know what we hear of the plans and proceedings of Russia and of the extreme danger of being deceived by them. . . .

Pray for God's sake *lose no time* and be *prepared* to act, tho' we may never have to do so. But to threaten, and intend to do nothing, will never do.

Make any use of this letter, only take care not to let Lord Derby see what the Queen says of him. Sir S. Northcote might see it. Should the Queen write to Lord Derby? Pray cypher or telegraph on receiving this and see Lord Odo when he returns to London.

June 9.—The Queen writes a few lines to say she wrote fully and strongly to Lord Derby and told him to show the letter to Lord Beaconsfield. . . .

The Queen is feeling terribly anxious lest delay should cause us to be too late and lose our prestige for ever! It worries her night and day.

To Lord Salisbury.

2, Whitehall Gardens, *June* 14, 1877.—Derby saw Beust yesterday; the conference was long, and, so far as I can understand, D. faithfully made the proposition, as to active alliance, wh. the Cabinet sanctioned. D. pressed for a reply without delay, and said it was, if possible, most desirable it should be laid before Cab. on Saturday next. I think it best, therefore, to have no Cab. till that time, and I will fix it at 3 o'c., so that we may have the morning for the chance of the arrival of the Austrian answer.

Beust promised to telegraph instantly.

It is but ingenuous to tell you, that the Queen is ' greatly distressed ' about ' the very wavering language of Ld. Salisbury, wh. will encourage Russia and the Russian party.' This, with a reply from Ld. Derby, which ' fills her with despair,' ' greatly moves ' her. ' Another Sovn. must be got to carry out Ld. Derby's policy.'

Sa isbury was no dupe of Russia, but his personal experience, at the Constantinople Conference, of the utter impracticability of the Turkish Government, made him strongly desirous of finding some accommodation with the northern Power which would prevent the hateful possibility of having to fight on Turkey's side. Accordingly, though no one was more impressed than the Indian Secretary by the real menace which Russia's Asiatic advance constituted to the Indian Empire, he, somewhat unwisely, endeavoured during this session to calm public alarm by inviting critics to use large maps, which would magnify, instead of minimising, the distance between Russianised Turkestan and the north-west frontier of India. Beaconsfield was, it appears, unduly apprehensive of Salisbury's anti-Turkish tendency, and he made the first of a series of impassioned appeals to Derby, his colleague from early years, to support him in a policy of active preparation for eventualities. The Queen, never an admirer of Derby's methods, was already looking for a change at the Fore gn Office, but Beaconsfield, though sympathising with Her Majesty's feelings, determined to carry Derby with him to the utmost possible distance. Chancellor Cairns told the Queen early in July that Derby ' would go any length, short of declaring war.'

To Lord Derby.

Confidential.　2, WHITEHALL G'DNS, *June* 17, '77.—I hope you will support me at this juncture. It is necessary, that I should take this issue to decide the existence of the present Cabinet. It is quite evident to me, that Lord Salisbury wishes the Russians to enter, and indefinitely occupy, Constantinople, acting, as he has done throughout, under the influence and counsel of Lyddon.

II.　　　　　　　　　　　　　　　　　　　　　33

It is the Conference over again, in which, unquestionably, he much compromised us, tho' both you, and myself, then, treated him with generous magnanimity, which however was thrown away on his sacerdotal convictions.

The Ministry will not be weakened by his secession, and, I think, I can supply his place, and, if necessary, that of others, in a manner, which would commend itself to the country at this exigency.

But your course, on this occasion, is not that of an ordinary colleague. My heart is as much concerned in it as my intelligence, and I wish not to conceal, how grievous would be to me the blow, that severed our long connection and faithful friendship.

My colleagues are bound to no particular course by the vote [1] I am suggesting. I should be sorry to take any future step, which, after mature reflection, did not meet with your particular sanction, and their general approval. All I want now is, to reassure the country, that is alarmed and perplexed; to show, that we are in a state not of puzzled inertness, but of preparedness for action; so to assist negotiations, which will be constantly cropping up, and place ourselves in a position, if there be eventually a crash, to assume a tone, which will be respected.

I write with great difficulty, but am Yours ever, D.

From Lord Derby.

Private. FOREIGN OFFICE, *June* 17, '77.—I will write, or (better) speak to you to-morrow on the whole question. Enough for the present to say that, as far as you and I are concerned, I do not think we shall have any difficulty in agreeing, at least in the present stage of the affair. It seems to me that the vital question is not yet raised; and I hardly anticipate a disruption until it is raised. No doubt, Salisbury's language was ominous, but he did not absolutely declare himself against preparation.

I need not add that a political separation between us two would be as painful to me as it could possibly be to you.

To Queen Victoria.

2, WHITEHALL GARDENS, *June* 23, '77.—Lord Beaconsfield with his humble duty to your Majesty.

The Cabinet was quite satisfactory. It resolved to take a firm tone on Monday, and, to prevent mistakes, we agreed upon, and recorded in writing, the answer to be given to the

---

[1] A vote of credit.

'interpellation' of Mr. Gladstone, or his followers.   The assembling of the Cabinet immediately on Lord Beaconsfield's return from the royal audience, was food for the quidnuncs, and Lord Beaconsfield is told, that the Ball at the Palace was rife with rumors.   Lord Beaconsfield was not present, being obliged to avoid, as much as possible, late hours and hot rooms.   He saw Lord Derby and made the remarks to him which your Majesty wished. . . .   He defended and not unsuccessfully his language to the Austrian Ambassador, as he said the great object of Austria was to see England accomplish what was necessary—unaided: and that, if Austria suspected that England would not act alone, there might be an increased inducement to join us.

Poor Mr. Hunt goes to Homburg to-night.   His case seems very bad.   Lord Beaconsfield gave him a kind message from your Majesty, which seemed to light up his eyes for a moment.   He has behaved bravely and truly in the great business, and redeemed some peccadilloes which, besides, it is not likely he will ever have the opportunity to repeat.[1]

From Queen Victoria.

WINDSOR CASTLE, *June 25, '77.*—The Queen thanks Lord Beaconsfield for his letter of yesterday and for the copy of the terms in which the answer is to be given to-day.   They are excellent.

The reports in Mr. Layard's last letter of the 13th inst., which the Queen saw yesterday, are very alarming !   Surely Lord Derby cannot be indifferent to the dangers expressed therein ?   Warning after warning arrives and he seems to take it all without saying a word ! !   Such a Foreign Minister the Queen really never remembers !

The news to-day continues very unpleasant and makes the Queen very anxious.   The feeling against Russia is getting stronger and stronger !   Only *do* not delay. . . .

The Queen has been thinking very much of what Lord Beaconsfield told her, and she thinks that in fact public affairs would be benefited if Lord Lyons replaced Lord Derby, as the former has such knowledge of foreign countries.   Lord Clarendon had the same, and Lord Granville also to a great extent: so had Lord Malmesbury.   But unfortunately Lord Derby has *not*.   If he and Lord Salisbury want to resign, however, the Queen thinks they should be told that she could not accept their resignations now, but that they should be relieved later.   Could not that be done ? . . .

[1] Ward Hunt died on July 29, 1877; and W. H. Smith was appointed First Lord of the Admiralty in his place.

To Queen Victoria.

Confidential. 2, WHITEHALL G'DNS, *June* 26, '77.—. . . It would not be possible to retain the services of Lords Salisbury and Derby in the manner your Majesty suggests. But they would not think of resigning at present. They are prepared to support the vote of credit, tho' they may shrink from applying the proceeds of that vote to the purposes which your Majesty and Lord Beaconsfield approve. But some time must necessarily elapse before that issue is to be decided. At present, it is quite evident from the Austrian note, that Vienna sees no objection to the Gallipoli expedition, and if Germany can arrive at an understanding with us on the same head, Lord Beaconsfield believes that the existing Cabinet will sanction the expedition; and that will put all right very soon. It would bring peace. Lord Beaconsfield has had a satisfactory interview with Lord Odo this morning. . . .

To Lord Derby your Majesty would do well to repeat your Majesty's earnest desire and purpose, that the Russians should not be permitted to ' occupy ' Constantinople, or to enter it. Your Majesty need not, at this moment, enter into details. Lord Beaconsfield is giving ceaseless attention to affairs, and will come down, one morning, and ask for an audience, when matters become ripe.

From Queen Victoria.

Confidential. WINDSOR CASTLE, *June* 27, '77.—The Queen must write to Lord Beaconsfield again and with the greatest earnestness on the very critical state of affairs. From so many does she hear of the great anxiety evinced that the Government should take a firm, bold line. This delay—this uncertainty, by which, abroad, we are losing our prestige and our position, while Russia is advancing and will be before Constantinople in no time! Then the Government will be fearfully blamed and the Queen so humiliated that she thinks she would abdicate at once. Be bold ! Why not call your followers together, of the House of Commons as well as of the House of Lords; tell them that the interests of Great Britain are at stake; that it is not for the Christians (and they are quite as cruel as the Turks) but for conquest that this cruel, wicked war is waged, that Russia is as barbarous and tyrannical as the Turks ! Tell them this, and that they should rally round their Sovereign and country—and you will have a large and powerful majority. And only say Russia *shall not* go farther and she will stop But if this be not done and done quickly it will soon be too late; and we shall then have to do much more than we shall have to do now.

The Queen was so alarmed and horrified at Lord Derby's language last night, and at poor Lady Derby's distress at his not doing what he ought, that she could hardly rest. The Prince of Wales was frantic about it, Prince Leopold equally so, and everyone puts the blame on the 3 Lords—Derby, Salisbury, and Carnarvon. The Opposition will be the first to turn round on you, if you don't at last act, and delay of weeks or days only may be—mark the Queen's words—fatal !

Pray act quickly ! The Austrian note is fair enough, but also weak and procrastinating.

Could Lord Beaconsfield not summon Lord Lyons over to say what the feeling in France is, and then confidentially ascertain whether he could not, in case Lord Derby resigns (and really his views and language make him a danger to the country)—you could reckon sure on him as a successor [*sic*] ! Lord Derby praises him and Mr. Layard to the skies—but goes on as if they wrote nothing ! The Queen's anxiety from her knowledge of the past and of foreign Governments is unbounded.

To Queen Victoria.

Confidential and secret. 2, WHITEHALL G'DNS, *June* 28, '77. —Lord Beaconsfield . . . has had the honor of receiving your Majesty's letter of yesterday. Sympathising entirely with all your Majesty's feelings in the present critical state of affairs, it is his duty to lay before your Majesty two important facts: 1. It is impossible to obtain a vote of money and men, until the War Estimates are passed, that is to say, so long as we may remain in a state of neutrality. 2. If we had men and money, we could not despatch them to any part of the Turkish Empire without the permission of the Porte, and the Porte will not grant that permission, unless we occupy the Dardanelles, or otherwise, as their avowed allies. All these difficulties would be removed, if we declared war against Russia: but there are not three men in the Cabinet, who are prepared to advise that step.

Lord Beaconsfield has placed the Army Estimates again first on the paper to-morrow, and if we succeed in passing them, he will make proposals to the Cabinet on Saturday.

In the meantime, he is working privately at Constantinople and with Count Bismarck, with the view of inducing the Porte to request the occupation of the Dardanelles by England as a material guarantee, and of prevailing on Count Bismarck, in some way, to co-operate with that step.

The progress of the war strengthened Beaconsfield against his dissentient colleagues. Though the Russians made no great headway in their attack on Armenia, their invasion of the Balkans proceeded without pause. The Danube was crossed before the end of June; on July 7 Tirnova, the chief city of the northern Bulgarian province, was captured; and in the middle of the month the Russian General Gurko seized two passes in the Balkans, and his light troops began to raid the Thracian valley of the Maritza, the Bulgarians in his train exacting a bloody vengeance from their Turkish persecutors. An advance to Constantinople became at once an immediate possibility of the war; and the Cabinet, fortified by representations to the same effect by Austria, took steps to make Russia aware of the seriousness with which they would regard any occupation of the imperial city. As Layard had advised prompt application to the Sultan for permission to the British to occupy the Gallipoli peninsula in arms, the decision of the Cabinet fell short of what the Prime Minister desired, and very far short indeed of what the Queen regarded as the imperative necessities of the situation. Her Majesty's feverish anxiety added much to her Prime Minister's labours. 'The Faery writes every day, and telegraphs every hour; this is almost literally the case,' he told Lady Bradford in June.

To Queen Victoria.

2, Whitehall G'dns, *July* 12, '77.—Lord Beaconsfield with his humble duty to your Majesty. The important Cabinet is over, and the Lord Chancellor will have the honor of communicating in detail its general conclusions, and submit them to your Majesty's pleasure. Subject to that, we have decided to address a note, of a very formal and authoritative character, to Russia in the vein sketched in a previous letter of Lord Beaconsfield to your Majesty. Anxious, sincerely anxious, to meet the Russian views in other matters, the occupation of Constantinople, or attempt to occupy it, will be looked upon as an incident, which frees us from all previous engagements, and must lead to serious consequences.

The phrase *casus belli* is not used, but reserved for a subsequent occasion, if necessary.   The Secretary of State for War, and the (*pro tem.*) First Lord of the Admiralty, are to examine Admiral Commerell and others on the approaches of Constantinople, and the Cabinet will, at its next meeting, decide the question whether the appearance of your Majesty's fleet at Constantinople will be sufficient to effect our object. . . .

July 16.—Lord Beaconsfield . . . deeply regrets the distress which your Majesty experiences, and so naturally experiences, in the present critical state of affairs: but he trusts, on reflection, that distress may be softened, if not altogether removed; and he believes that the vessel of the State, tho' no doubt there will be perils and vicissitudes, may be steered into a haven, safe and satisfactory.

And, in the first place, with regard to the Russian outrages and ' atrocities.'   He has not neglected the subject, especially since your Majesty has so repeatedly, and so forcibly, called his attention to it.   He is, at present, in communication with a member of Parliament, who has a position, and speaks well, to bring the subject before the House of Commons by enquiries, and, subsequently, by a motion on going into Committee of Supply, and he, some days ago, took active measures, that the transactions in question should be placed before the public eye and feeling by the Press.   With regard to diplomatic interposition by your Majesty's Government, there is an important difference between the instances of ' Turkish atrocities ' and the Russian outrages.   The Turkish atrocities were investigated by a judicial tribunal, by which many of the chief delinquents were found guilty—yet no punishments were inflicted.   There was a clear miscarriage of justice, and a firm ground on which your Majesty could rest your indignant remonstrance.   That is not yet the case in the Russian instance, and if we make a protest founded on hearsay and anonymous communications, we should only leave ourselves open to the cynical criticism, and the impertinent incredulity, of Prince Gortchakoff.

And now with respect to the still more important question of the occupation of Constantinople.   Lord Beaconsfield experiences great difficulty in appearing to comment on your Majesty's remarks on this matter, because he entirely agrees with your Majesty in your Majesty's views and sentiments upon it, and should, long ago, have asked permission to retire from the difficult and not very agreeable office of attempting to guide a discordant and unwilling Cabinet on the most important conjuncture in the politics of this half-century, had he not been restrained by the conviction, that it was his duty to stand by your Majesty as long as there was a chance of your Majesty's policy being accomplished. And he was quite prepared, on Saturday late, to have advised your Majesty to accept the resignations of Lord Salisbury and Lord Derby, had they alone been the obstacles: but when he found the Lord Chancellor, hitherto his right arm in affairs, followed by the Duke of Richmond, and every other member of the Cabinet except Lord John Manners and Sir Michael Beach, shrink from the last resort, he felt it best (waiting to the very end before he spoke) to bring about the arrangement ultimately agreed to—which was still a step in advance, and which may lead to all that is required. The Cabinet agreed to make something like an ultimatum notice to Russia; Lord Derby went so far as to say, that, whatever others might feel, he had no objection to be the ally of Turkey, provided that alliance was for English interests: and even Lord Salisbury declared, that he had no objection to the English fleet going to Constantinople, if such a move would prevent the Russian invasion. To-morrow, the Cabinet meets early, and it will have to consider the report of the naval authorities as to the efficiency of the fleet to prevent occupation. Lord Beaconsfield believes that, alone, the fleet would not be sufficient. On all these matters, Lord Beaconsfield proposes to confer with your Majesty after the Cabinet—to-morrow at Windsor, at 3 o'clock, unless commanded otherwise.

There is one point which Lord Beaconsfield would humbly place before your Majesty. Lord Beaconsfield ventures to remark, that he has never at any time, represented to your Majesty, that, if the present state of neutrality were maintained, your Majesty could prevent the Russians from occupying Constantinople. That would require war with Russia, a force of 60 to 80,000 men at Constantinople, and the British fleet. What he always recommended was, that the Dardanelles should be occupied, while still professing neutrality, and held as a material guarantee for the obligations and respect of treaties. This would not have prevented the occupation of Constantinople were the Russians strong enough to effect it, but it would have given us a commanding position at the time of negotiations for peace, which would have ensured the restoration of Constantinople by the Russians and maintained untouched England's present position in the Mediterranean.

From Queen Victoria.

WINDSOR CASTLE, *July* 16, '77.—The Queen has only time to thank Lord Beaconsfield for his kind long letter, and she must say—and she does not care if he repeats it—that she is shocked and bitterly disappointed at the conduct of the

Chancellor, the Duke of Richmond, and others! We ought to have acted when Lord Beaconsfield originally proposed it, long ago, and those who opposed it will bitterly rue it some day. However, that is now no longer the question, but, What can be done, as a material guarantee and as an assertion of our position, if Russia goes on as she does? The crossing of the Balkans makes a great difference, and nothing should prevent our sending the fleet to Constantinople, and being prepared for action, for we shall have to act. These are very important points. Lord Derby, to whom the Queen has also telegraphed about the cruelties answers that he will, at once, speak to Count Schouvaloff. For the protection of the Christians at Constantinople the fleet would seem necessary. . . .

OSBORNE, *July* 20.—To-day's telegram from Mr. Layard is very alarming. What the Queen fears is an outburst of (just) indignation at Constantinople, in which all Christians will suffer and our last hold on our poor Allies whom we (to the Queen's feeling) so cruelly abandon to a shameful and detestable enemy and invader! She is distressed too not to see anything acted upon which Lord Beaconsfield tells her is to be done. He told her on Tuesday that in 3 days 5,000 men could be sent to increase the garrisons, and that every effort should be made to be prepared, even for Gallipoli if the Russians did not make a dash at Constantinople. But she hears of no troops moving or going, and becomes more and more alarmed. The Queen always feels hopeful and encouraged when she has seen Lord Beaconsfield, but somehow or other, whether intentionally or thro' want of energy on the part of those under him or at the offices, nothing material is done!! It alarms her seriously.

For fear of any mistake she wishes to recapitulate what he said in answer to her serious question, 'What are we to do, and how are we to assert our position if the Russians succeed in getting to Constantinople?' The Queen understood Lord Beaconsfield to answer: 'If I am your Majesty's Minister I am prepared to say to Russia that if the Russians do not quit Constantinople at a given day, which I would name, I will declare war.' And Lord Beaconsfield added that Lord Salisbury on his (Ld. B.'s) putting the same question had himself said, 'Declare war.' Is this correct? The Queen hopes that there will be an opportunity for Lord Beaconsfield soon to state strongly in Parliament that the Government will never stand anything which would injure the interests and lower the honour and dignity of this country.

How can Lord Granville hold such equivocal language? He who was cheated about Khiva, how can he speak as he

II.   33*

does ? And the language — the insulting language — used by the Russians against us ! It makes the Queen's blood boil ! What has become of the feeling of many in this country ?

The Queen rejoices to hear how completely the unjust attack on Lord Beaconsfield about Mr. Pigott's[1] appointment has been refuted. But she is sorry for the annoyance it must have caused him. . . .

The Queen most earnestly urges on Lord Beaconsfield to hold very strong language to the Cabinet to-morrow and to insist on the speedy despatch of the troops to increase the garrisons, as speedily as possible.

Beaconsfield took care that the serious representation to Russia should be seen to be no mere empty threat; and he succeeded in carrying his Cabinet with him in further measures of precaution.

To Queen Victoria.

(*Telegram in cypher.*) *July* 21, 1877, 2.30 *p.m.*—The Cabinet has agreed unanimously, if Russia occupies Constantinople, and does not arrange for her immediate retirement from it, to advise your Majesty to declare war against that Power. Orders have been given to strengthen the Mediterranean garrisons.

2, WHITEHALL G'DNS, *July* 22, '77.—Lord Beaconsfield . . . deeply regrets that your Majesty should suppose for a moment, that he makes any representations to your Majesty which he does not sincerely intend to effect: even with the short-sighted view of sparing your Majesty anxiety, [that] would be, in his mind, dishonorable conduct, and almost amount to treason. He errs, perhaps, in being too communicative to your Majesty, in often imparting to your Majesty plans which are in embryo, and which, even if apparently matured, occasionally encounter unforeseen difficulties: but it relieves his mind, and often assists his judgment, to converse, and confer, with your Majesty without the slightest reserve, and this necessarily leads to your Majesty sometimes assuming that steps will be taken, which are necessarily delayed, and sometimes even relinquished.

The opposition to the increase of the Mediterranean garrisons, and the procrastination, have entirely arisen from the

---

[1] See below, pp. 1035-1040.

military authorities, that is to say, the ' Confidential Committee ' of General Officers, who would be as powerful as the Council of Ten, and outvote always the Doges. It is they who have opposed every military move, that has been suggested from the beginning—Mediterranean garrisons, expeditions to Gallipoli, and so on. What they want, and what they have ever tried to bring about, is a great military expedition, like the Crimean; but such a step would be utterly inconsistent with the policy of neutrality adopted by the Cabinet, and cannot be countenanced unless there is an avowed and public change of that policy.

Yesterday, the Cabinet in a decided manner declared, that they would receive no further protests from the ' Confidential Committee,' and ordered steps to be taken immediately for strengthening the Malta garrison by 3,000 men, and will follow this up, according to circumstances. So great is the influence of the ' Confidential Committee,' that the Secretary of War, who had been in favor of the measure, advised the Cabinet not to adopt it, and ultimately agreed only with a protest.

Yesterday, also, in the most formal, and even solemn, manner, the question was placed before the Cabinet, What they were prepared to do, if Russia occupied Constantinople ? They unanimously agreed, no one stronger and more decided than Lord Salisbury, that the Cabinet should advise your Majesty to declare war against Russia.

It is Lord Beaconsfield's present opinion, that in such a case Russia must be attacked from Asia, that troops should be sent to the Persian Gulf, and that the Empress of India should order her armies to clear Central Asia of the Muscovites, and drive them into the Caspian. We have a good instrument for this purpose in Lord Lytton, and indeed he was placed there with that view.

Lord Salisbury will attend your Majesty on Wednesday, and Lord Beaconsfield purposes soon, perhaps on the Saturday following, to have the honor, and great delight, of seeing your Majesty. He continues pretty well, but has been, and still is, a little harassed by this impertinent nonsense about Mr. Pigott.[1] These affairs take up precious time, and, if the time is not given, the most unfounded calumnies get afloat.

Strangely enough, at this point Beaconsfield was faced with the threat of secession, not by his anti-Turkish colleagues, but by the most stalwart representative in the Cabinet of the Palmerstonian pro-Turkish tradition.

[1] See below, pp. 1035-1040.

To Lord John Manners.

2, WHITEHALL G'DNS, *July* 24, '77.—Your letter is a great blow to me, and most unexpected. I really don't exactly understand what decision of the Cabinet you refer to.

I must beg you, at all events, to keep your resignation secret, until I can communicate it to the Queen personally, as a written announcement would lead to much excitement. Her Majesty, of all my colleagues, most depended on your supporting me, and now, when, for the first time, her Cabinet has unanimously and heartily agreed to declare war against Russia, if she evinces the slightest intention to fortify, or remain in, Constantinople (if she ever get there), the Queen will be greatly distressed and surprised at your determination.

I most earnestly request, therefore, that all may be suspended until I see Her Majesty, which I will try to effect on Saturday next.

What Manners objected to was the apparent abandonment to Russia of Batoum, the great seaport on the south-east coast of the Black Sea. But of course the Cabinet were concentrating on the vital point of Constantinople and the Straits, leaving minor matters for subsequent consideration, according to the progress of the war; and Beaconsfield was able to persuade his old comrade-in-arms to withdraw his resignation. No sooner was this difficulty settled than Beaconsfield had to act once more as lightning-conductor between the Queen and Derby, with whose conduct of foreign affairs Her Majesty became daily more utterly dissatisfied. With Salisbury, on the other hand, who was invited at this period to Osborne, the Queen was much better pleased. She wrote to Beaconsfield on July 25 of the Indian Secretary's ' sound views.' ' He is deeply impressed with the extreme importance of our being completely prepared for eventualities which may shortly arise.'

From Queen Victoria.

OSBORNE, *July* 26, '77.—The Queen saw with pleasure last night the emphatic denial of Lord Derby and Count Beust to the extraordinary and very alarming assertion made to the latter and reported—of our not objecting to the temporary occupation by the Russians of Constantinople. But she is bound to say in confidence to Lord Beaconsfield that the language of Lord Derby to Count Beust as described in the draft of July 21 to Sir A. Buchanan is of a very doubtful nature on the subject; and when the Queen read it just after seeing the alarming telegram she felt very painfully impressed with the conviction (which Lord Salisbury she found shared) that Lord D. did not truly and properly carry out the decisions of the Cabinet, and still more did not conduct foreign affairs as they ought—for the Cabinet must do that. The time is come when our policy must be clear and decided. Always—as Sir S. Northcote and Lord Derby do —explaining away every act which is intended to show Russia and Europe that we are not passive spectators of the former's shameful aggressive conduct—is disastrous, and injures the Government in the eyes of the country and makes us contemptible in the eyes of Europe. . . .

To Queen Victoria.

(*Telegram.*) WHITEHALL G'DNS, *July 26, '77.*—There was a Cabinet this morning to consider the question. We have decided on two resolutions, and the Chancellor of the Exchequer has sent them to Lord Hartington, who wishes to act in concert with your Majesty's Government.

From Queen Victoria.

(*Telegram in cypher.*) OSBORNE, *July 28, '77.*—Greatly alarmed at Mr. Layard's appeal, which can no longer be disregarded if British interests are not to suffer most seriously. A decided answer must be given, Gallipoli must be occupied. You will be fearfully blamed if you let Constantinople be taken, and without declaring to Russia what the consequences will be. If there is a horrible massacre of the Christians we shall be held responsible for it. You should bring this at once before the Cabinet.

The Queen sent an identical message to Derby, and received a reply whose studied calm only added fuel to her indignation

Lord Derby to Queen Victoria.

FOREIGN OFFICE, *July 28, '77.*—Lord Derby, with his humble duty, submits that he has been honored by your Majesty's telegram received to-day. The subject of it has been discussed in Cabinet, but the telegram did not arrive

till after the Cabinet was over. Lord Beaconsfield will have
given your Majesty the fullest details as to what has passed.
Lord Derby cyphered that it would be too late to occupy
Gallipoli, even if that step were desirable. Lord Derby is
quite aware that there will be an outcry, indeed there is one
already—from the party which does not conceal its wish for
war with Russia. But he believes that party to be small
in numbers, though loud and active. He is quite satisfied
that the great bulk of the nation desires nothing so much, in
connection with this question, as the maintenance of peace.
If they have not spoken out, it is, in his belief, because the
declarations of the Ministry have satisfied them that there
is no danger of its being disturbed.

Beaconsfield was at Osborne for a week-end visit when
Derby's letter to the Queen arrived. Her Majesty
immediately submitted it to him.

To Queen Victoria.

OSBORNE, *July* 29, '77.—Lord Beaconsfield with his humble
duty to your Majesty. This is a mere *boutade* of [Lord
Derby's] bad temper at being obliged by the Cabinet to
send the telegram to Mr. Layard.[1] It is quite intolerable, and
is as much addressed to your Majesty's humble Minister as
to your Majesty. Your Majesty will not deign to notice it,
Lord Beaconsfield feels quite sure. Lord Beaconsfield hopes,
that the great objects of your Majesty's imperial policy may
be secured without going to war: but if war is necessary he
will not shrink from advising your Majesty to declare it, and,
in that case, he very much doubts whether Lord Derby,
with all his savage and sullen expressions, will resign.

But the Queen's indignation was too great to suffer
her to adopt her Minister's advice and take no notice;
and ultimately he consented to draft a reply for her
which she described as ' admirable,' and which she forwarded without alteration.

Queen Victoria to Lord Derby.

OSBORNE, *July* 29, 1877.—The Queen regrets to hear from
Lord Derby, that it is now too late to undertake the Gallipoli
expedition. It is much to be deplored, that it was not under-

---

[1] See below, pp. 1032, 1033.

taken at the time when it was proposed by the Prime Minister, and entirely approved and supported by the Queen. There seems a general concurrence in all parties, now, in its favour, and it is not improbable that it would have prevented this horrible war. The Queen does not know from what sources Lord Derby gathers his opinion, that the British people are in favour of Russian supremacy. She is convinced of the contrary, and believes there will soon be no controversy on the subject.

CHAPTER V.

Conditional Neutrality.

1877.

The tension of Queen and Ministers was appreciably relieved at the close of July by the serious and unexpected check which the Russians suffered before Plevna—a great centre of roads on the right flank of their advance. It soon became evident that there was no longer any immediate prospect of a Russian occupation of Constantinople — the danger which had dominated the counsels of Ministers for many months. Beaconsfield was able to give some attention to the troubles of his former theatre of fame, the House of Commons, where Parnell and his small following had taken advantage of the great leader's withdrawal to organise a most formidable course of systematic obstruction.

To Queen Victoria.

2, WHITEHALL GARDENS, *Aug.* 1, 1877.—. . . With reference to an observation in your Majesty's cyphered telegram of this morn., Lord Beaconsfield would ask leave to remark, that the telegram in question was sent to Mr. Layard, not to the Sultan; and that, in due time, it will have to be printed and presented to the House of Commons, and that great care must be taken, lest we be accused of changing our policy without due public notice. The state of neutrality, which has been adopted, renders the conduct of affairs extremely delicate, and difficult. Lord Beaconsfield, however, has much confidence in the secret telegram, which he forwarded to Mr. Layard from Osborne last Sunday.[1]

If the battle, described in the second edition of the *Telegraph*

---

[1] This telegram from Beaconsfield to Layard ran as follows: ' Osborne, July 29. *Personal and most confidential.* The telegram sent you yesterday from the Cabinet opens a prospect of recurring to the wise and ancient policy of England. The British Fleet in the Turkish waters with the

of this day, has really taken place, and with the results described, the position of the Russian armies, both north and south
of the Balkans, will be perilous—24,000 Russians *hors de combat* !
So far as the opinion of the Porte is concerned, a telegram
from Mr. Layard would seem to confirm this ' wondrous
tale.'   There is a Cabinet to-morrow at two o'ck., after which
Lord Beaconsfield will communicate to your Majesty. . . .

Almost as great an affair as the battle in Bulgaria is the
signal triumph of Constitutional principles and Parliamentary
practice in the House of Commons this day.   A session of
26 unbroken hours !   There is nothing like it on record.   It
was the triumph of British pluck and British gentlemen, and
will have a great effect on the conduct of public affairs.

Lord Beaconsfield made a visit to the House of Commons
this morning.   It was the first time he had been able to visit
it since he left it, after having sate in it for nearly forty years,
and having been its leader—one side or the other—for nearly
a quarter of a century.   The House gave him a cheer when
he appeared in the gallery, and the cheer commenced on the
Liberal benches, which first observed him

This is one of the comparatively rare references in the
Beaconsfield correspondence of this period to domestic
politics.   From the summer of 1876 to that of 1878 the
Eastern Question was, for him, the Aaron's rod which
swallowed all minor, and particularly all domestic,
interests—sometimes with unfortunate results.   One of
the sanitary measures of this Government of Social
Reform was a much-needed Bill, introduced in the Lords
in 1877, for consolidating the Burials Acts and providing
additional cemeteries.   Here, it seemed to the Queen and
to Archbishop Tait, was an opportunity for a settlement
of the vexed question of Dissenters' burials, and Beaconsfield was not indisposed to move in that direction.

To Queen Victoria.

2, WHITEHALL GARDENS, *Feb.* 20, 1877.—Lord Beaconsfield with his humble duty to your Majesty.

---

consent of the Sultan may be the first step in the virtual preservation of
his Empire.   I much depend upon your energy and skill, in both of which
I have the utmost confidence.'   But the Sultan was still suspicious of
British intentions, and, as the threat to Constantinople was no longer
immediate, it was not until the following February that the Fleet entered
the Sea of Marmora.

The Burials Bill, to be introduced into the House of Lords, is only a Consolidation Bill, simplifying in one Bill the various Acts on the subject of Burials.

There has been an attempt to introduce a few original clauses, which it was thought might facilitate the resistance to Mr. Morgan's 'Burials Bill' in the House of Commons. They will not satisfy the Dissenters, but may perhaps aid a little our Borough Members, as giving an excuse for opposing him.

But the clauses are not yet drawn, and hang fire, so it is impossible to send them to your Majesty.

The clergy are quite inexorable on the subject: 'all schools of Church thought.'

In the meantime, the Sacerdotalists are moving every influence, divine or much the reverse, against your Majesty's Ministers. . . .

But the resistance of the clergy to change was strongly reflected in the attitude of churchmen in the Cabinet. Accordingly, the additional clauses went no further than to permit silent burials of Dissenters in consecrated ground; and even this concession was withdrawn by the Government after the second reading had been secured. The Archbishop was indignant, and many lay churchmen in the House of Lords shared his feelings. Lord Harrowby, whose son, Lord Sandon, was himself a Minister, gave notice of an amendment in Committee permitting, not merely silent burials, but Nonconformist services by the open grave. Beaconsfield realised that the time had come to evacuate a position which could not be much longer held. On Saturday, May 12, the Archbishop called on him, and records in his diary that the Prime Minister was 'quite in accord with me, and as acute as possible respecting the best way of proceeding. "The question ought to be settled." Agreed to bring it before the Cabinet.' But on the follow ng Monday Beaconsfield had to confess to the Archbishop that ' he could not manage the Cabinet, but he hoped I would persevere in the course I had sketched out.' Harrowby moved his amendment on the Thursday, and with the Archbishop's help reduced the Government, despite their assiduous whipping, to a tie. ' It was somewhat absurd,' writes the Archbishop, ' to be dividing the House against them, knowing that their chief was all the time on my side. . . . It was amusing to see him sitting quietly throughout the debate, without saying a word, and voting with his colleagues, while hoping they would be beaten.' On Report Harrowby absolutely carried his amendment by a majority of sixteen, and the Government abandoned the Bill.[1] Beaconsfield's acquiescence in this somewhat humiliating procedure was undoubtedly due to his determination not to lose from his Cabinet one of his most stalwart and capable supporters in Eastern questions. Other churchmen among his colleagues might be disposed to compromise on this church question; but Hardy, the representative of the Oxford clergy, made it clear that, if Harrowby's amendment were accepted by the Government, he would resign.[2] This was a loss which, in view of the dubious attitude, in regard to Russia and Turkey, of Derby, Salisbury, and Carnarvon, Beaconsfield was not prepared to face. He preferred to risk the inconveniences and dangers of postponing the settlement of the burials question. It is difficult to maintain that he was wrong.

There was, during this session of 1877, one striking episode, which, after apparently threatening a serious blow to Beaconsfield's reputation, proved in the end to be the means of confirming and consolidating it. A vacancy had arisen in the office of Comptroller, or permanent head, of the Stationery Office. It was a post which had been held by literary men of some distinction, such as McCulloch, the economist, and W. R. Greg, the essayist and reviewer; but a Select Committee of the House of Commons had condemned the waste and mismanagement of the department, and had recommended that its head should in future be a man ' practically as well acquainted with the trade as if he were a stationer.'

---

[1] See *Life of Archbishop Tait*, ch. 29.
[2] See Gathorne Hardy, Vol. II., p. 23.

Beaconsfield disregarded this recommendation and appointed Thomas Digby Pigott,[1] a clerk n the War Office of eighteen years' standing.   The transaction was brought before the House of Commons on July 16, and denounced by the Opposition free lances as a 'job.'   On what ground, they asked, was the report of the Committee ignored, and this important post of £1,500 a year conferred upon a man who was 'one of a hundred and one jun or c'erks in the War Office, being 69th on the list ?' Was it because Mr. Pigott's father had been vicar of Hughenden, and, with his family, had rendered valuable assistance to Disraeli in his electoral contests in Bucks ? Such was the insinuation; and it had a very plausible air.   The Prime Minister could no longer appear in that House to answer for himself; his colleagues, imperfectly informed, gave only the usual official reply that their chief had duly considered public interests in making the appo ntment.   This was not convincing to the House at large; Knightley, now almost the solitary unconverted member of the anti-Disraeli Tory clique,[2] aired his virtue by speaking and dividing against the Government; the Whips were caught napping; and what amounted to a personal vote of censure upon Beaconsfield was carried by four votes.   The press and public ratified the censure; *The Times* describing the appointment as 'too splendidly audacious.'

And yet the whole affair was, to use the title under which those of the Beaconsfield papers which concern it were docketed, a 'great mare's nest.'   Three days later (July 19) Beaconsfield rose in the House of Lords to defend his action.   The speech, besides being a complete vindication, was a masterpiece of stage effect.   'Never shall I forget,' writes Redesdale,[3] who was present, ' the air of dejection, the hang-dog look, with which he entered the House.   His head was bent, his ga t uncertain, and he sat down wearily ' on the front bench.   It was amid

---

[1] Afterwards Sir Digby Pigott.   [2] See pp. 543, 544.
[3] *Memories*, ch. 35.

chilling silence that he began to narrate the reasons
which had actuated him in the appointment. The recommendations of the Select Committee, he explained,
had been by no means disregarded by the Government.
Many had been adopted; but the suggestion that the
head of the stationery department should have technical
knowledge appeared to him, on consideration, to be
impracticable, as no one connected with great commercial
transactions would be tempted to accept a post, the
salary of which hardly exceeded that of the manager
of a first-class establishment. To carry out the recommendation, 'I should have had to appoint some person
who had retired from business, or some person from
whom business had retired.' What was wanted for the
discharge of the duties of Comptroller was not technical
knowledge, which could be supplied by subordinates in
the office, but administrative ability, official experience,
and capacity for labour, together with the educational,
moral, and social qualities necessary for presiding over
a great public department. Accordingly he had decided
to give the post to a young member of the Civil Service
as a reward for merit and industry. Mr. Pigott was no
'mere War Office clerk'; he had served as private secretary
to various Secretaries of State, and he had especially
distinguished himself as secretary to more than one Commission. He had now, owing to the vote of the Commons,
resigned; but to accept his resignation would be to leave
an able and deserving Civil Servant to absolute desti-
tution. Beaconsfield therefore hoped that the House of
Commons would yet reconsider the case in a milder and
juster spirit.

So far Beaconsfield had preserved the subdued and
deprecatory air with which he began his speech. But,
having justified the appointment on public grounds, he
now turned with brightening face and more confident
tones to the personal attack on himself. 'My lords,'
he continued, 'it has been said, in an assembly almost
as classical as that which I am addressing, that the

appointment was a job.' 'A job!' writes Sir Henry Lucy,[1] who watched the scene from the gallery; ' it was worth being crushed and crowded and hustled to hear Beaconsfield simply pronounce those two words. His indignant shoulders went upwards in dumb appeal to his sympathising ears. His still plump hands were held out, palm upwards, that noble lords might see how clean they were. His eyes were widened to their utmost capacity, in astonishment at the supposition that he might be thought capable of this thing charged against him, whilst his cheeks puffed out to emit, in an almost horrifying whisper, the fearsome words, " a job !" ' It had been said, Beaconsfield proceeded,

that the father of Mr. Pigott was the parson of my parish, that I had relations of long and intimate friendship with him, that he busied himself in county elections, and that in my earlier contests in the county with which I am connected I was indebted to his exertions. My Lords, this is really a romance. Thirty years ago there was a vicar of my parish of the name of Pigott, and he certainly was father to this gentleman. He did not owe his preferment to me, nor was he ever under any obligation to me. Shortly after I succeeded to the property Mr. Pigott gave up his living and retired to a distant county. I have never had any relations with him. With regard to our intimate friendship and his electioneering assistance, all I know of his interference in county elections is that before he departed from the county of Buckingham he registered his vote against me. And, my Lords, it is the truth—it may surprise you, but it is the truth —that I have no personal acquaintance with his son, Mr. Digby Pigott, who was appointed to this office the other day. I do not know him even by sight.

As Beaconsfield pronounced these last sentences he drew himself up to his full height, and his assured and triumphant tones ' galvanised ' the House of Lords ' into something like life.' The general cheers and laughter which greeted the conclusion of his speech showed that he had won his cause with his audience; and, adds Redesdale, ' the Lord Beaconsfield who walked out of

[1] *Diary of the Disraeli Parliament*, ch. 21.

the House that evening with a firm step was twenty years younger than the poor old man, broken down with care and the weight of years, who had shuffled into it so feebly an hour earlier.' Redesdale dwells on the histrionic success of the performance, but the attentive reader of this biography will realise that in these latter years, save when under the stimulus of direct political excitement, Beaconsfield was never far from the border of physical collapse. The public and the press, even the Liberal press, followed the Lords in accepting the defence as complete, and the next week the Commons rescinded their censure without a division, Hartington, the Opposition leader, and the irreconcilable Knightley joining in the generous apologies offered to the Prime Minister.

To Lady Bradford.

2, WHITEHALL GARDENS, *July* 20.—. . . There has been a meeting of the Speaker, the Cr. of the Exchequer, and Hartington, and they have come to an unanimous conclusion, that steps must be immediately taken to rescind the resolution of the Ho. of Commons. It takes a great deal to elate me, but I confess I am not insensible to such a triumph !

It may be added that the suggestion that Beaconsfield had any · special obligation to, or tenderness for, the Pigott family was absurd. The Rev. J. Pigott was only his vicar for three years, from 1848 to 1851, when he accepted a living in Norfolk; and in this short time the relations between squire and parson were not unfrequently strained. One instance has been mentioned in III., ch. 6, when the vicar took upon himself to reprove the squire for Sunday travelling; another concerned a question of right of way. The vicar appears to have been a Whig, and if he travelled from his Norfolk living to vote for Bucks in 1852 (which, in spite of Beaconsfield's confident assertion, seems uncertain) would naturally have supported the Whig candidate, Cavendish. Mr. Digby Pigott's principal work for the State had been as secretary to the important Commission on Army promotion, which had recently reported. For this he had been publicly thanked by Gathorne Hardy, the Secretary of State, and had been warmly recommended for promotion by the Chairman of the Commission, Disraeli's old colleague, Pakington, now Lord Hampton. Few statesmen were more vitally interested in securing a competent head for the Stationery Office than Beaconsfield, who had made frequent complaint of official pens, ink and paper; and it is satisfactory to know that his new Comptroller justified the confidence placed in him, and sensibly improved the methods of his office.

Beaconsfield's private correspondence shows that, though his sufferings during this spring and summer were great, he managed in the intervals of his attacks to make occasional appearances in society. He seems to have felt that, as his chest complaint rendered him, in his words to Lady Chesterfield, ' quite incapable of addressing a public assembly,' it was incumbent on him to make it clear to the world that an almost absolute silence in the House of Lords was compatible with a vitality which could dominate the Cabinet at a period of crisis.

To Anne Lady Chesterfield.

2, WHITEHALL GARDENS, *June* 22.—. . . My colossal American dinner—forty guests, all men, except the hostess and Mrs. Grant: the room full of flowers and strong perfumes, which, afterwards mixing with the fumes of tobacco, did not at all benefit my bronchial tubes, wh. are not in very good order.

I sate next to the General,[1] more honorable than pleasant. I felt so overcome that I escaped as soon as possible, and did not go to Grosvenor House, where I might have seen S., whom I never see. . . .

To Lady Bradford.

2, WHITEHALL GARDENS, *Sunday, July* 1, 1877.—. . . Gull is all froth and words: what you heard, he also said to me,

---

[1] Ex-President Grant was then on a visit to Europe. Beaconsfield, at Derby's suggestion, asked Grant to his official banquet on the Queen's birthday, but the visitor was engaged.

but yesterday he was evidently perplexed and disappointed, and came twice.

They are all alike. First of all, they throw it on the weather: then there must be change of scene: so Sir W. Jenner, after blundering and plundering in the usual way, sent me to Bournemouth, and Gull wants to send me to Ems. I shd. like to send both of them to Jericho. . . .

I shall be very disappointed if Monty sees your dear orange-tinted eyes and I am not to have that pleasure.

The only good thing in all these troubles is that I am to drink port wine. After 3 years of plebeian tipples, this amuses me. . . .

To Anne Lady Chesterfield.

2, WHITEHALL GARDENS, *July* 14, 1877.—. . . It is raining cats and dogs, wh. it fortunately did not do on Thursday, when there was a garden party at Marlboro' House. I was there for a moment, having been to a wedding, and then to a wedding festival—hard work; but it is, sometimes, necessary to show oneself, or else the *Daily News* says I am dead, or dying, wh. is the same. I am pretty well, but shd. be glad to hear that you were better.

Garden parties in London are wells; full of dank air. Sir W. Gull tells me that if the great garden parties in future are held at Buckingham and Marlboro' House instead of Chiswick and so on, his practice will be doubled.

Afterwards on Thursday, I dined with the Duke of ——. I like to go, as a rule, to a house for the first time. I rarely go a second. I shall not dine with the Duke of —— again. The Duchess, attractive at the first glance, is not so when you sit next to her; an ordinary mind and a squalling voice. The claret, wh. Sir Gull [*sic*] orders me to drink, was poison. When I dine out now, I am at the mercy of these criminal landlords. They shd. be punished like Signora Tofana and the Marchioness of Brinvilliers. An Englishman, incapable otherwise of a shabby action, will nevertheless order inferior claret at dinner, wh. is the only time at which a real gentleman drinks wine. At Lord Northbrook's last Tuesday, the table claret was of the highest class, but then he is a Baring, and the sons of princely merchants look upon bad wine as a damnable heresy. The P. and Pss. of Wales dined there, but did not arrive until ¼ past 9 ! ! ! Too soon for supper, too late for the sublimer meal. . . .

To Lady Bradford.

2, WHITEHALL GARDENS, *July* 26.—. . . 'Gussie' has asked me to dine there on Sunday—to meet you. It is exactly four years ago—the Sunday before Goodwood—that I met you dining at that very house. I shd. like much to have celebrated that anniversary, tho' anniversaries are not much to my taste. . . .

July 28.—Not a moment—and yet it is a farewell! How terrible it shd. be so perfunctory. I think of other ones—and sigh. . . .

Four years ago! It makes one very sad. I gave you feelings you could not return. It was not your fault: my fate and my misfortune.

I leave a dismayed Cabinet to encounter a stormy Court; but have faith in my star.

OSBORNE, *July* 29.—. . . Yesterday, almost the moment I arrived, I had to plant a tree—a pinsapo. P. Leopold had to attend at the ceremony. He is clever. . . . Monty takes to him very much. Monty had the honor of dining with the Queen—a strictly family circle. I sate next to Pss. Beatrice. They were all full of my visit to Zazel, whom the Pss. Beatrice had been promised she was to see. 'You also,' sd. the Queen, 'paid a visit to somebody else, the Gorilla.' 'Yes, Madam, there were three sights; Zazel, Pongo, and myself.' And then I told her how we moved about as if in a fair.

To Mrs. de Burgh.

2, WHITEHALL GARDENS, *Aug.* 16, '77.—I am grieved I did not see you before you left town—but I have been very ill, and continue very ill, and am really quite incapable of walking upstairs—gout and bronchitis have ended in asthma, the horrors of wh. I have never contemplated or conceived. I have seen more than one person die, but I don't think they suffered the oppression and despair, wh. I have sometimes to encounter—and, sometimes, I am obliged to sit up all night, and want of sleep at last breaks me down.

Nothing but the critical state of affairs has kept me at my post, but if I die at it, I cannot desert it now. I have managed to attend every Cabinet, but I can't walk at present from Whitehall to Downing St., but am obliged to brougham even that step, wh. I once could have repeated fifty times a day. . . .

Beaconsfield had very wisely deprecated and evaded discussions in Parliament about the possibilities of future policy in the Near East. But, before separating for the recess the Cabinet had a general talk about the situation —a talk which shows how Beaconsfield's policy was gaining ground with his colleagues.

To Queen Victoria.

2, WHITEHALL G'D'NS, *Aug.* 10, '77.—Lord Beaconsfield
with his humble duty to your Majesty. Assuming that
affairs will not now be concluded in one campaign, and that,
consequently, our policy has become more precise and decided,
and that we cannot consent even to an occupation of Constantinople, however definite and temporary the purpose,
he has prevented discussions in Parliament. Had they
taken place, and ambiguous and uncertain language been
used about ' the occupation,' it would have been supposed
that your Majesty's Government was vacillating and infirm:
had, on the contrary, our ultimate and real purpose been
expressed, the Porte would have felt that we were already
virtually her allies, and taking advantage of our having
committed ourselves, we should have been unable to make
those conditions, and use that influence, which it will be
necessary to exact and exercise, in order to obtain a satisfactory settlement.

The Cabinet to-day was solely busied with considering the
Speech from the Throne: but they agreed to have a meeting
before separation to decide upon what steps should be taken
in the event, which it is hoped is now not probable, of a
sudden recurrence to that dangerous position, which was
threatened a fortnight ago, and that Constantinople might
be endangered. It was also settled that, while Lord Derby
and Lord Beaconsfield should remain in town, or in its immediate vicinity, the rest of the Cabinet must be prepared
to reassemble frequently, and at a few hours' notice.

Note on the Cabinet of 15th August, '77.

OSBORNE.—After settling the answer to the Austrian note,
Mr. Secretary Cross said there was an important, and as he
thought, an urgent question for the decision of his colleagues.
The unexpected course of events had relieved us from an
embarrassing position with respect to the occupation of
Constantinople by the Russians; but a similar state of affairs,
as that from which we had been relieved, might recur, and
in the separation of the Cabinet. The question was, What was
the Cabinet prepared to do, in the event of the Russians
again threatening to occupy Constantinople ? Mr. Secretary
Hardy, after a general pause, said he assumed that the
Cabinet would act in the spirit they had previously decided
on; that they would send up their fleet to Constantinople,
and occupy all necessary positions. Lord Carnarvon asked,

With or without the consent of the Sultan ? General assent, with such consent. Whereupon Lord Carnarvon said 'that opened a large question—an alliance with Turkey, to which he could not agree.'

Prime Minister said, the first question was to decide, whether we should permit the occupation of Constantinople with impunity by the Russians. The means of prevention must be considered afterwards, and the consent of the Sultan was only one of these means. All agreed, with the exception of Lord Carnarvon, that, if the tide of affairs changed and that the occupation by the Russians of Constantinople this year appeared to be on the cards, the Cabinet should meet immediately, and take such steps as the exigency required, and of a similar character as previously contemplated. Lord Salisbury, however, did say, that he did not think the country was at present prepared to ally itself with Turkey. Prime Minister again observed, 'Sole question now to decide was, Would we interfere if Russians again menaced Constantinople ?' There was no dissent except from Lord Carnarvon.

After this, Prime Minister said, there was another, and not less important, question to decide; that was, assuming the Russians could not overcome Turkey in one campaign, would England permit a second ? This was a war of extermination.

Irrespective of English interests concerned, he doubted whether a system of strict neutrality should be maintained in a war avowedly, and practically, of extermination. He did not wish to bind the Cabinet by an immediate decision, but his own opinion was strong—that we, and Europe, ought not to tolerate another campaign. He wished the Cabinet now to discuss, and eventually to consider, our policy under these circumstances, and he should propose, that when it was apparent, and avowed, that the first campaign could not be decisive, the Cabinet should meet, and consider the course to be adopted to prevent a recurrence to arms in the spring.

There was much and general discussion on this matter, and a general, if not universal, opinion, that the British policy, under such circumstances, would be to prevent a second campaign.

Lord Derby said we should remember we had no allies.

Prime Minister observed, that in his opinion no other ally than Turkey was required; that, as for large armies, it was not for us to reconquer Bulgaria; that we were masters of the sea, and could send a British force to Batoum, march without difficulty through Armenia, and menace the Asiatic possessions of Russia.

These views were favorably received.

In August an opportunity offered for one of those private negotiations outside the usual Fore'gn Office channels on which Beaconsfield throughout his life was disposed to place a somewhat excessive reliance.   Colonel Frederick Arthur Wellesley, son of the first Earl Cowley, who was British military attaché in Russia, came to England from the Tsar's headquarters with personal assurances for the Queen and British Government from Alexander of the purity of his motives and the innocence of his intentions.   His sole object was the amelioration of the lot of the Christians in Turkey; he had no thought of annexation save perhaps in Bessarabia and possibly in Asia Minor; a temporary occupation of Bulgaria would be inevitable, but he would only occupy Constantinople if such a step was rendered necessary by the march of events; he would in no wise menace British interests, either there or in Egypt, the Suez Canal, or India.   Beaconsfield saw his chance of direct communication, and determined that Wellesley should carry back more than the official reply.   In that document, he told him, it would, of course, not be possible to make use of language which could in any way be interpreted as a threat; and consequently it would necessarily be of a somewhat formal character, couched of course in conciliatory terms.   He added, however, that Wellesley, having been made acquainted with the opinions both of the Queen and of the Prime Minister, would be in a position to explain to the Emperor the actual policy of Great Britain.   Both Queen and Minister sincerely desired the re-establishment of peace, and would welcome any arrangement that would conclude the war that year in a manner honourable and satisfactory to Russia   At the same time they feared that the neutrality of England could not be maintained, if the war were not soon terminated; but that, if there were a second campaign, England must necessarily take her place as a belligerent. ' This,' said Beaconsfield, ' is the policy of Great Britain; and as you have been told so both by the Queen and

by myself, you are at liberty to put the case clearly
to the Emperor in the manner you consider the most
advisable.' He charged Wellesley, further, to impress on
His Majesty's mind the perfect harmony of opinion
existing between Queen and Minister, and the strength
of the Beaconsfield Government.

On August 17 Wellesley supplied Corry with a memorandum explaining how he conceived his mission.

Memorandum by Col. the Hon. F. A. Wellesley.

The subject of the correspondence and conversations which
have passed between the Queen, Lord Beaconsfield, and Col.
Wellesley, to be considered secret and on no account to be
mentioned at the Foreign Office.

Col. Wellesley is the bearer of an answer from Her Majesty's
Government which he will communicate officially to the
Emperor. Although Col. Wellesley has no orders from Lord
Beaconsfield to make any further statement to His Majesty,
it is thought advisable in the interests of Russia as well as
of England, that the Emperor be informed with regard to
the future attitude of this country under certain contingencies.

His Lordship has therefore communicated to Col. Wellesley
his views and intentions, which coincide entirely with those
of the Queen, and which it is left to Col. Wellesley's discretion
to make known to the Emperor, should a favorable opportunity present itself.

The policy of the Government is as follows:

The Queen and H.M. Government have a sincere desire
to see the speedy re-establishment of peace on terms honorable
to Russia and would be glad to contribute to such a result;
should, however, the war be prolonged and a second campaign
undertaken, the neutrality of England could not be maintained
and she would take her part as a belligerent.

In bringing the above facts to the knowledge of the Emperor
it is most important that Col. Wellesley should disabuse His
Majesty's mind of certain misconceptions which could only
lead to a false appreciation of the actual state of affairs.

It has been stated that there are dissensions in the Cabinet
which would prevent active intervention on the part of
England. This is entirely false. The Cabinet is led by one
mind and has the entire support of the Sovereign.

There exists perfect harmony of opinion between the Queen
and Lord Beaconsfield respecting the foreign policy of the
country. The Government is as strong as ever, and possesses

the confidence of the people; which is proved by the present tranquil attitude of the public, who are convinced that the interests of England are safe in their hands.

It must not be thought that the policy of Lord Beaconsfield is one of hostility to Russia, and it might fairly be asked who has proved himself the greatest friend of Russia, Prince Bismarck or Lord Beaconsfield; the Chancellor who has done all in his power to urge Russia to undertake this disastrous war, or the Prime Minister who has endeavoured to save her from it ?

It is commonly supposed in Russia that the mind of the English public is poisoned against Russia by Lord Beaconsfield, and that His Lordship is responsible for the present relations which exist between the two countries. Col. Wellesley is in a position to deny these statements, and to show that on the contrary it is Lord Beaconsfield who has recently discouraged discussions in Parliament with a view to avoiding the possibility of leading Turkey to believe that sooner or later England may be on her side, a belief which would no doubt have been created had the Government been compelled to make a distinct statement with regard to their future policy.

A private letter from Lord Beaconsfield to the Queen, which Her Majesty showed Col. Wellesley, proved that Lord Beaconsfield has checked Parliamentary discussion as well as anti-Russian public meetings with the object of avoiding all encouragement to Turkey.

However much Lord Beaconsfield may desire peace he is equally determined to uphold the honor and defend the interests of England, and Russia should not indulge in any erroneous impressions as to the weakness or vacillation of the British Government, which, Colonel Wellesley knows, enjoys the support of the Sovereign and the confidence of the nation.

Col. Wellesley should not fail to point out to the Emperor that the influence of the English Government at Constantinople is not by any means such as His Majesty appears to think, and that as a matter of fact the influence which Mr. Layard can bring to bear on the Porte is far more personal than official.

Col. Wellesley has had the exceptional advantage of two interviews with the Queen as well as frequent conversations with the Prime Minister, which has enabled him to obtain the most correct information with regard to the policy of England; and he is authorised, if necessary, to make use of the name of the Queen and that of Lord Beaconsfield in making this confidential communication to the Emperor of Russia.

Wellesley carried out his mission with skill and tact. The Emperor, far from showing annoyance, expressed his thanks for the frankness with which he had been treated; and there can be little doubt that the vigour with which he prosecuted the war during the autumn and winter of 1877–8 was partly due to his knowledge that a second campa'gn would involve too much risk.

It was a questionable proceeding, no doubt, to send a message of this character to the Tsar behind the back of the Foreign Minister, and to intimate as the fixed resolution of the British Government a policy which had indeed the firm support of the Queen and the Prime Minister, but which had been only outlined to the Cabinet without being even definitely offered for their acceptance. The situation, however, was abnormal, and gave much excuse for abnormal treatment. There were British interests of great importance threatened by a victorious Russian advance and by the Pan-Slavonic feeling in Russia which victory would enhance; and Parliament and the country expected that those interests would be respected. But the only security we had was the assurance of a Government which had for years allowed the pressure of circumstances and of popular feeling to override and annul its assurances; and it was obvious to Beaconsfield that the binding value of this particular assurance would depend on our ability to convince the Russian Government that in the last resort England would fight. In the last resort he was resolved to fight; so was the Queen; and so, he believed, when the moment came, would the country be. But Derby's attitude and language, and the attitude and language of others of their colleagues, conveyed quite a different impression. The Queen wrote to Beaconsfield on August 1, urging strongly once more ' the importance of the Tsar knowing that we will not let him have Constantinople. Lord Derby,' Her Majesty continued, ' most likely says the reverse, right and left, and Russia goes on ! It maddens the Queen to feel that all our efforts are being destroyed by the Ministers who ought to carry them out. The Queen must say that she can't stand it!' Moreover, Gladstone's agitation was still powerful in the country, encouraging Russia to believe that in her invasion of Turkey she would always have the sympathy, and never the resistance, of the British people. Beaconsfield might know his own mind; he might feel sure that, when the time came, he could dominate, or dispense with, his colleagues, and rally the country round him; but how was he to bring this home to the Tsar and the Russian Government through the ordinary Foreign Office channels? And for obvious reasons he was anxious to secure Derby's services down to the latest possible moment.

Beaconsfield spent the last half of August and the whole of September at Hughenden. He told Lady Bradford that he could not pay any country-house visits. ' The truth is that this place is now the headquarters of the Government, and I can't be away for more than an hour or two even if I wished. It rains telegrams morn, noon, and night, and Balmoral is really ceaseless. If I were not here, I must be at Whitehall.' From his Bucks home he watched with satisfaction the growing reaction throughout the country against the pro-Russian agitation; a reaction stimulated alike by the unpatriotic excesses of the agitators, and by the vigorous resistance which Plevna under Osman Pasha continued month after month to offer to the Russian advance. He was anxious to make Derby realise the significance of this development.

To Lord Derby.

HUGHENDEN MANOR, *Sept.* 1, 1877.—I observe you have to go to some meeting in your county. I suppose it will be necessary to say something on public affairs, though silence is golden.

Let me impress upon you not to mistake the feeling of this country. It is for peace, but it is, every day, getting more Turkish.

It is for peace because it has confidence in our policy—*i.e.*, peace with British interests all safe.

But we know this is a mere delusion, and that, had it not been for our good luck, British interests would not have been safe, the Russians would virtually have been at Constantinople, and Her Majesty's Government nowhere.

Opinion is getting more pro-Turkish every day, because the country recognises that the Turks have the vigor and the resources and the national spirit which entitle them to rank and to remain among the sovereign Powers of the world, and that there is no clear evidence that a better Government than the Ottoman can be established in the regions in question.

There is also to be noted that there is a deep feeling of discontent growing up about Servia. Its interference in the war would be greatly resented here, and I doubt whether it will be considered that we have denounced such a step with sufficient strength and earnestness.

It is to Russia and to Austria that we ought to have addressed ourselves, and to have warned those Powers that if they wish to preserve the neutrality of England, they must be careful in this matter.

The feeling is, that our honor is concerned in the issue—and I cannot say I think the feeling unfounded.

Pardon these rough hints.

Sept. 13.—I have reopened your box, to say that I have received your letter and entirely approve of your projected appointments. It will be a great thing to have got rid of Harris and Buchanan. I wish we could get rid of the whole lot. They seem to me to be quite useless. It is difficult to control events, but none of them try to. I think Odo Russell the worst of all. He contents himself with reporting all Bismarck's cynical bravadoes, which he evidently listens to in an ecstasy of sycophantic wonder.

Why does not he try to influence Bismarck, as the Prince controls him ? Why does not he impress upon Bis., for instance, that if Germany and Austria police Poland, in order that Russia should add 50,000 men to her legions, England will look upon that as a gross breach of neutrality ?

Why does he not confidentially impress upon Bismarck, that Turkey has shown such vigor and resource, that she has established her place among the sovereign Powers of Europe, and that if they continue to play their dark game of partition they must come in collision with England, who will not permit the breaking up of the Ottoman Empire ?

As for the argument that Russian compensation is to be found in Armenia and so on, an English Army, 40,000 men, with the Black Sea and Batoum at our command, could march to Tiflis.

We want no allies.   We are not going to fight in Bulgaria.
The situation is much the same as when Wellington went to
the Peninsula, except that a Turk as a soldier is worth 20
Spaniards.   What allies had we then ?

The private correspondence of this month of September
is of much and varied interest.

To Lady Bradford.

HUGHENDEN MANOR, *Sept.* 6.—. . . I heard from Mr.
Layard to-day.   His date is Aug. 29, and much has happened,
and is perhaps happening, since then.   He seems to have
completely re-established our influence at Constantinople,
and to have entirely gained the Sultan's confidence, whom
he continually represents to me as one of the most amiable
men he ever knew; with nothing but good impulses.   One
result of the influence of Mr. Layard is that he has got rid
of all the Ministers who were jealous of foreigners and so
deprived the Sultan of the services of many distinguished
English officers, now all employed ; Baker Pasha among
others.

Do not mention this letter of Mr. Layard, as ours is a
' secret ' correspondence.

I am almost thinking of perpetrating a sort of atrocity
here, and massacring the peacocks.   They make a sorry
show at this time of the year, with[ou]t their purple trains; a
' ragged regiment ' on the terrace every morning, and all the
flower-beds full of their moulting plumage, rarely with an
Argus eye.

Perhaps you remember the church here.   I was obliged,
when I arrived, to have the pony chair to take me home—
so slight a steep.   Now, I can walk back.

Sept. 8.—. . . Windermere you had not seen of late, and
it is redolent of romance, and poetry in its brightest form:
romance of feeling I know from experience, for I recall my
hours there with a sweet delight.   But how you can every
year repeat the dull monotonies of Longshaw and the conventional ceremonies of Sandbeck, I confess, astounds me;
but I suppose miserable necessity binds you in its iron chain,
and what is inevitable becomes, in a certain degree, natural.
Yet life is very short, and to spend so much in the monotony
of organised platitude is severe. . . .

Sept. 24.—. . . Pray give Laddo[1] a kiss for me, and try to
see if he *really* remembers me.   I like always experiments

---

[1] Lady Bradford's grandson, now the Earl of Bradford.

on dawning intellect and memory. You must not give him the slightest clue, or any leading question. Talk about whips; ask, if he like them; whether he ever had any ? and so on. If he remembers me *really*, give him two kisses; and, if he forget me, give him one. . . .

Sept. 29.—The Hardy visit was satisfactory—very. The Cabinet is summoned for Friday next; and after that we shall know better where we all are: but I don't think the state of affairs is dark. The only drawback is my health. I really don't see how I can meet Parlt. unless some change takes place. It wd. be impossible for me to address a public assembly. There is no one to consult. Gull, in whom I have little confidence, is still far away, and Dr. Kidd, whom all my friends wish me to consult, and who, of course, like all untried men, is a magician, won't be in town till the middle of Octr., and is such a swell that, I believe, he only receives, and does not pay, visits—convenient for a Prime Minister !

I can't conceive at my time of life miracles can be performed: still one must cling to hope, or rather patience, wh., as Horace Walpole says, is a good substitute for hope—when you are 70.

I did very well when I came down here, drank port wine, seemed to get quite strong, and got free of all bronchial distress: but after 3 weeks they [*sic*] reappeared in the aggravated form of asthma, and this destroys my nights and makes me consequently shattered in the day.

I think of going to Brighton, but dread the hardships of hotel life, where they give you only one sitting-room, and all your papers are moved, even when you eat an egg, or a slice of dried toast. I must have a sitting-room for myself; and they tell me it is not to be got. We live, I know, in more barbarous ages than we imagine, but this seems impossible !

It is, at this moment, difficult, almost out of mortal power, to retire from public life: and so far as Cabinets, and correspondence, and all that, are concerned, one can yet manage, and it all falls, and rightly, on me; but when it comes to speaking in public, one must have the physical ability, wh. I entirely lack—and have no chance of remedy, except sea air, or change of scene, or other commonplaces, in wh. really I don't in the least believe. . . .

Oct. 3.—Here is Robinson Crusoe on his island—with[ou]t even a parrot, only a peacock. What can he tell you, what say ? Nothing, nothing; from Dan to Beersheba, all is barren. I really, literally, have not opened my mouth for two days, and shall not probably till Monty arrive at 6 o'ck. —if then he do arrive. . . .

What you say about Gladstone is most just. What rest-

lessness! What vanity! And what unhappiness must be
his! Easy to say he is mad. It looks like it. My theory
about him is unchanged: a ceaseless Tartuffe from the beginning. That sort of man does not get mad at 70.

His *vanitas vanitatum* is to be a literary character, like
Cardinal Richelieu, who was a great statesman, but never
content unless he was writing a tragedy, sure to be applauded
by his parasites. Now, there is not a form of literature wh.
this man is not attempting, except a work of fiction—the
test of all talents—for the greatest books are works of fiction,
and the worst; as for instance *Don Quixote*, *Gil Blas*, *Wilhelm
Meister*—and Mrs. [*sic*] Braddon, and the endless fry who
imitate even her.

Gladstone, like Richelieu, can't write. Nothing can be
more unmusical, more involved, or more uncouth than all his
scribblement; he has not produced a page wh. you can put
on yr. library shelves. . . .

Beaconsfield utilised the lull produced by the heroic
resistance of Plevna for a further endeavour to bring
his colleagues into line, and to keep them steadfast in
upholding the national cause. The Queen used all her
influence in the same direction.

From Queen Victoria.

BALMORAL, *Sept.* 26, 1877.—. . . The Queen will not fail
to speak fully and strongly to the Chancellor. She has done
so to Mr. Cross, who shares her views respecting a 2nd campaign and Constantinople. She is glad to hear that Lord
Beaconsfield is going to have Mr. Hardy at Hughenden, and
to prepare for eventualities. She trusts, however, that he
will also see Sir S. Northcote. He may be a little nervous
(he has had a terribly trying session) and disinclined for
action, but he is sure to see things in the right light, if Lord
Beaconsfield explains everything to him. She cannot overrate the importance of complete confidence between himself
and the Leader of the House of Commons. If Lord Beaconsfield does not tell him anything before he learns it in the
Cabinet, she fears he may feel hurt and discouraged, for he
it is, who must defend and explain the foreign policy in the
House of Commons. Lord Beaconsfield has so often asked
her to give her opinion, that she trusts he will excuse her
from mentioning what she thinks of such importance.

How well everything worked when Lord Beaconsfield acted
as Leader in the House of Commons, and enjoyed the com-

plete confidence of Lord Derby! It is so important that the Cabinet should present a united front, which she trusts and thinks it will (except in one or two instances), that the Queen has spoken out thus strongly and feels sure Lord Beaconsfield will appreciate it.

As the letters we have quoted show, Beaconsfield summoned Hardy, perhaps the one of his colleagues whose point of view most nearly coincided with his own, to a conference at Hughenden; and then, when agreement was obtained, he convened the Cabinet, writing a special appeal at least to Derby and to Salisbury. He urged the former, as Foreign Secretary, to take the lead in an active policy; but he urged in vain.

To Lord Derby.

HUGHENDEN MANOR, *Sept.* 28, '77.—I have summoned the Cabinet for next Friday.

I wish to place before it this proposal:

It being of the utmost importance that there should not be a second campaign, the only object of which would be the seizure of Constantinople, it is proposed that Her Majesty's Ambassador should sound the Porte as to the terms of peace it is prepared to offer.

If they include the settlement of Bulgaria on the basis of the Protocol of London, and the restoration to Russia of the portion of Bessarabia, forfeited by the Treaty of Paris, it would seem that the honor of Russia would be sufficiently vindicated.

It is assumed, that the Porte would agree to these, or any other reasonable terms, provided England, if empowered, as mediator, to make them to Russia, and they being rejected by that Power, would assure the Porte, that, under such circumstances, we should depart from our present position of neutrality, and inform Russia, that, if Constantinople be menaced, England would afford material assistance to Turkey to prevent its seizure.

This is a clear and precise policy; it gets us out of all the embarrassing distinctions between temporary and permanent occupation, which harassed, and nearly humiliated, us last session; and, if rejected by Russia, would put her more in the wrong in the eyes of Europe, while it would place H.M. Government in an honorable, an intelligible, and popular position.

What I should like most is, that the proposal should be made by yourself—the natural organ of the Government on these high matters; and it will be a source of the highest satisfaction to me, if, on reflection, you will comply with my wishes.

From Lord Derby.

KNOWSLEY, PRESCOT, *Sept.* 29, '77.—I am not sorry that you mean to call the Cabinet; both for the sake of the effect out of doors, and also because after two months, or nearly that time, it is well to compare notes.

There can be no harm in trying to find out what terms of peace the Turks would accept, when once the campaign of this year is over. I doubt whether they would give any opinion now, as they may still hope for successes that will alter their position.

I am not prepared to support the proposal which you suggest, still less to put it forward; but a preliminary discussion will be of use as showing how far, and on what points, there is likely to be agreement among us as to the course which we ought to take.

The Cabinet was held on October 5, and Beaconsfield found a general support for his views from Cairns, Hardy, Manners, Beach, and Richmond, and not so much opposition as he had feared from Derby and Salisbury.

To Queen Victoria.

(*Cypher Telegram.*) 10, DOWNING ST., *Oct.* 5, '77.—The Cabinet on the whole seemed indisposed to mix up the question of mediation with anything like a threat, but with the exception of Lord C. there seemed a general concurrence of opinion, that at the close of the campaign a formal, tho', if required, a secret engagement should be obtained from Russia, that she would not occupy that capital, while at the same time we should offer to Russia our offices to obtain favorable terms of peace from the other belligerent.

If she refused this engagement, then we must open Parliament with a vote of men and money. . . .

Secret. Oct. 6.—. . . Lord Beaconsfield is not, in any way, dissatisfied or disappointed by the Cabinet of yesterday. On the contrary, he looks forward with confidence to accomplishing, in due season, all your Majesty's wishes, which he himself entirely approves and sanctions, and so does the very large majority of the Cabinet. It was generally felt, and naturally, that it was impossible to take any active step in the prosecution of the proposal while the campaign was not concluded, as a simple military event might disturb all the calculations on either side.

Lord Beaconsfield was prepared for this objection, but was of opinion, that even a hypothetical discussion on the subject was preferable to prolonged silence and inertness. No inconsiderable effect was also produced by the intimation of Lord Derby, that he had had a confidential conversation with Count Schouvaloff at Knowsley, the upshot of which was, that His Excellency would not be surprised if, in the course of the winter, both belligerents might appeal to Great Britain. Lord Derby, who had been very cold, and evidently offended, in his previous correspondence with Lord Beaconsfield, spoke in the Cabinet with moderation, a due deference to the views of others, and in a view highly conciliatory.

Lord Salisbury was rather sharp, but made immense admissions towards the end of the discussion, of which the Lord Chancellor, who is a tower of strength to Lord Beaconsfield both for his intelligence and fidelity, made great use, and prepared the way for the decision of the next Cabinet on the subject.

Lord Carnarvon said little, but they were the words of a weak enthusiast dreaming over the celebration of High Mass in St. Sophia.

Lord Beaconsfield thanks very much your Majesty for your Majesty's kind enquiry as to himself. He cannot give a very brilliant bulletin of his condition, as he has had some relapse of late. It was unreasonable to expect that years of illness should be suddenly cured, but man is unreasonable, and, were he not, life would probably be intolerable. Lord Beaconsfield is going to Brighton to-day to escape the fall of the leaf in his own bowers. All he aspires to, is to secure sufficient health to be able to see your Majesty conclude your Majesty's present arduous labors and anxieties with honor and glory; and he shall then be quite content to say 'Nunc dimittis.' The crisis is one that requires unceasing thought and vigilance, and his attributes, in these respects, are not what they were, but so long as your Majesty has confidence in him, and assists him, as your Majesty has, throughout these great affairs, with your Majesty's counsel and active influence and support, the labor is most interesting, and even delightful. He heard from more than one of his colleagues, with much satisfaction, that your Majesty was looking so well, and full of spirit and energy. Your Majesty's demeanor has a beneficial effect on a timid or hesitating Minister, tho' that is not the character of any, who have had the honor of being your Majesty's guests.

Beaconsfield spent three weeks at Brighton—' a tree-less,' or ' a leafless Capua,' as he called it. He arrived on a Saturday, and on the front on the Sunday met an unexpected but not unwelcome acquaintance, the Russian Ambassador. He gave Lady Bradford a humorous account of the scene. ' Yesterday on the Prado, Schou. rushed up to me, full of overflowing affection, but doubt-ful how he wd. be received. Of course I returned all his effusion and took his arm (Monty having my other and Deym[1] hanging about Monty). The world seemed astonished by the spectacle and no doubt it has been telegraphed over Europe—and even Asia. Schou. wd. see me to my hotel door, and asked leave to call on me, etc., etc. Not the slightest allusion was made to public affairs.' But Schouvaloff came on the Tuesday for a political talk, and Beaconsfield gave the Queen a most interesting report of what was said. It will be seen that by this time the British Government had been informed that Austria had bound herself to Russia.

To Queen Victoria.

Secret. BRIGHTON, *Oct.* 10, '77.—. . . Count Schouvaloff called on me yesterday, at his desire, and ' to talk together like two private gentlemen, who are friends, and in the utmost confidence on public affairs,' which seemed to him ' dark.'

He called at one o'clock and stayed exactly one hour. With the exception, at the right moment, of a remark or two of mine respecting Sir Henry Havelock (having received your Majesty's cypher anent that morning) and once my strongly expressed opinion, that if there were a second campaign, it would be impossible for England to continue her state of neutrality, His Excellency occupied the whole time—about 55 minutes out of 60. He said, ' I have nothing to do; nothing can be done. Diplomacy has ceased. The position of Gortchakoff at Bucharest is humiliating. Nobody writes to him, nobody notices him. He says himself, " I am shelved." This combination of the three Imperial Courts was an invention of Prince Bismarck. You know what a state we find ourselves [in]; Austria is dying for peace, but Bismarck, who does nothing, and suffers nothing, is complete

---

[1] Austrian Ambassador.

master, Andrassy only his Viceroy ; and Russia and Austria
are moved about by him like pieces at chess.'

He insisted, notwithstanding the assurance given by Count
Andrassy to Lord Derby, thro' Buchanan and Beust, to the
contrary, that there was a secret convention between Russia
and Austria. He had seen it. He had been severely called
to account, on his last, fruitless visit to St. Petersburg, for
having ' let the cat out of the bag,' as it was agreed that it
should be kept a secret from Beust. Schouvaloff defended
himself on the ground that it was only by such a communication he could induce the English Government to act with
energy on Turkey. He thought there would not be, what
was called, a second campaign; that they would continue the
present one; that something might occur in the late autumn,
or the early winter, which might afford an opening. ' Much
depended on the Emperor, who takes sudden resolves.
Russian Government has credit always for deep designs:
which sometimes helps them; but in truth very often, perhaps
generally, it is a " Government of caprice," as all Governments must be which depend on the will of an individual
surrounded by 2 or 3 hangers-on.' The Emperor, startled
at the situation in which he finds himself, may take some
sudden resolve. When Lord Beaconsfield, *àpropos* to a
remark of the Count's, had very distinctly said, that our
neutrality must cease if the war continued, His Excellency
said, that he had in the most solemn and serious manner
already impressed that upon the Emperor; that the whole
tendency of affairs was to a war between Russia and England;
that Bismarck desired it—and for this among other reasons:
the whole commerce of Russia, which is a commerce mainly
of exports, in the event of the Baltic and the Black Seas
being blockaded, must be carried on by the German railways;
and the impulse to business of Germany would be great.
That impulse too was wanted. It would seem that Prince
Gortchakoff and Gen. Ignatieff are both in disgrace, tho'
Count S. was reserved on these points. It had been the
common saying of Ignatieff, when they were discussing the
war at Livadia, that ' Turkey has no soldiers.' The Emperor, therefore, is a little surprised at the military reception
that has greeted him in Bulgaria. These are some of the
principal, but only a portion, of the singular monologue of
yesterday, Ld. Beaconsfield believes sincere and straightforward: a deliverance of a pent-up diplomatic spirit amid the
sounds and shocks of that war, which has ' shelved ' him. . . .

Letters to Lady Bradford show the difficulties under
which Beaconsfield carried on his work at Br.ghton.

To Lady Bradford.

[BRIGHTON], *Oct.* 11.—. . . Monty leaves me to-day, and to my great annoyance. He certainly has been with me a couple of months, but I certainly shd. not have come here, had I not understood he was to remain with me. One requires someone in this bustling, idle, place, to guard one from ' third parties ' who are ever attacking and invading you in every form. But what am I to do ? He says he is ill: as Sir Charles Bagot wd. say—his old complaint. . . .

It comes at a moment of great public anxiety, for I have no substitute for him. The other two are faithful, and able, and gentlemen; but I can't live with them, as I do with Monty: so I am obliged to have one of them down, every other day, to clear the decks; and the telegraph and the messengers seem never to cease coming and going. . . .

B., *Oct.* 13.—. . . Whenever Monty leaves me, having convinced himself that nothing can happen for a while, the most pressing business always immediately prevails. It has happened remarkably so this time. Lord Tenterden comes down to me this afternoon, and dines and sleeps here. I have given him Monty's room, so he is my guest. Poor Algernon Turnor, who, unbidden, would come down out of pure devotion, and thinks it ' horrid ' that Monty has left me, is at the Bedford, and has to call in the morning for orders and all that. . . .

Beaconsfield interrupted his sojourn at Brighton to pay a visit, for the second time, to the great Whig magnate, the Duke of Bedford,[1] at Woburn Abbey. When announcing his intention to Lady Bradford, Beaconsfield had written: ' It is rather a bold step in the Duke of Bedford to have a Tory party at such a place; but I am to meet Derby there, and it looks like it. The world goes round.' But it was hardly a Tory party after all, as Derby was prevented from going by a bad cold, and, with the exception of Lady Derby, the remainder of the guests had a distinctly Whiggish flavour. Beaconsfield described the social aspect of the gathering in his letters to Lady Bradford, and its political value in a report to his Sovereign.

[1] The ninth Duke (Hastings), who at the time of the previous visit, though he already occupied Woburn, had not succeeded to the title. See p. 155.

To Lady Bradford.

WOBURN ABBEY, *Oct.* 17, 1877.—. . . Our party, Ld. Lyons, the Odos, Lady Derby, Dean of Westminster, Henry Cowper, Jowett, and the family, Tavistocks and all. One of the daughters I like, Lady Ela. She is very good-looking and intelligent. Lady Cowley also here.

Arrived before six o'ck. tea; glad to have it, as I was cold and voiceless. Duke, whom I always like, and who received me with cordial ceremony, soon suggested that I might like to go to my rooms, but I had not had my tea, and did not want to be dismissed for two hours. Still he hung about me, and, in due season, tho' once repulsed, and tho' nobody else was moving, he 'still harped upon my daughter,' and would insist upon showing me to my room. It seems the State suite was prepared for me, wh. is very gorgeous, and he wished, I suppose, personally to witness the effect produced upon his guest. I sleep in a golden bed, with a golden ceiling, and walls covered with masterpieces of modern art—Landseer, Linton, Newton and Leslie, and, in the right place, the picture of the trial of Ld. Russell by Hayter. Then I have a writing-room, not less magnificent, and that opens into a third long gallery room, 'where,' the Duke said, 'you are to receive yr. Ambassadors,' they being, I suppose, Odo and Lyons. . . .

BN., *Oct.* 21.—. . . The visit to Woburn was not so irksome as I feared. It was not too long—but I feel, every year more, that country-house visiting is very irksome: it is too conventional. In this case, however, there was business to be done. . . .

To Queen Victoria.

2, WHITEHALL G'D'NS, *Oct.* 18, '77.—Lord Beaconsfield . . . has just returned from Woburn, and writes this between the two railroads, on his way to Brighton. The defeat of the Turks seems complete, and is a disaster. Tho' a striking success, being in Asia, it is feared it will not be considered by the Emperor as sufficient for a basis of negotiation: while, at the same time, it may revive the contemplated claim for Batoum, which it was impossible for Russia to urge, or even mention, a week ago.

Lord Beaconsfield has had long conferences at Woburn with Lord Odo and Lord Lyons. They are both absolutely cowed by Prince Bismarck. Lord Lyons even fears the Prince coquetting with the Gambetta party, and promising Egypt to France, as a compensation for Alsace and Lorraine. If there were any fear of that, of which we should no doubt have advice in time, your Majesty must occupy Egypt. Prince Bismarck cannot be more formidable than the first

Napoleon. Then we were told we had no allies, which was quite true; nevertheless, we were victorious. Lord Lyons sighs over the absence of our prestige. The best way, if it is lost. Pressed very hard, Lord Odo admitted that Prince Bismarck would consent to peace, provided Russia had obtained some signal success. He did not wish her to be too much humiliated. According to him, nothing is decided either at St. Petersburg or Vienna, without consulting the Prince. He is an autocrat. But Lord Odo thinks, under no circumstances will he send German troops into Turkey, which the Emperor of Germany wishes; public opinion in Germany is strongly against that, and against increased military expenditure generally.

The Duke of Bedford has had great havoc in his elm avenues from the storm, but ' at any rate, my house is not burnt down,' he adds. Since the Inveraray calamity, he has had Shaw down, who told him that a single spark, and Woburn Abbey would burn like paper, not a scrap would remain. So they have an internal, and external, watchman at night. The Duke is a strange character. He enjoys his power and prosperity, and yet seems to hold a lower opinion of human nature than any man Lord Beaconsfield was ever acquainted with. He is a joyous cynic.

Box opened to say Lord Beaconsfield has seen Lord Derby, a cynic also, but not a joyous one. Lord Derby did not go to Woburn, as he had a cold so savage, that it incapacitates him for ' society.' He thinks the Asian victory, tho' probably very decided, will lead to no results, as it is too late in the year to campaign in Armenia. All depends now on Plevna, where the Russians are determined to make a great effort; if defeated, the Asian victory will be forgotten, or altogether be a barren triumph; if successful, the Russians will, he thinks, open negotiations, or cause them to be opened directly. Does not foresee any great difficulties about territory, and feels convinced that Constantinople is in no danger, but anticipates difficulties, and vast difficulties, as to the Government of Bulgaria. The Porte will not, and cannot be expected to, give up the military and civil supremacy of that province. He was mild, moderate, and conciliatory. What he will be in the November Cabinet, remains to be seen.

Your Majesty must pardon these rough lines. They are, as it were, from your Majesty's ' own correspondent,' and written, as it were, in the saddle.

The victory of the Russians in Armenia added to the depression felt by Beaconsfield in consequence of his total inability to rally in Brighton air. He ended his seaside sojourn in very low spirits.

To Lady Bradford.

B[RIGHTON], *Oct.* 23.—. . . I am very ill. . . . If I could only face the scene wh. would occur at headquarters if I resigned, I would do so at once; but I never cd. bear scenes, and have no pluck for the occasion.

Schou. called on me on Saty. afternoon (late) and stayed a long while. I knew he came to talk about the victory, and I was resolved not to help him, so he was obliged to break it at last.

He was 'candid,' as usual, but not 'gay': evidently depressed. He said it was a decided victory: the only real battle since the war (not true, for 2nd Plevna was a real battle and a great one), 'but it was not in the right place.' 'The Danube must decide the course of events, and he feared that his countrymen had already been repulsed again at Plevna.' This turned out to be true: but I think his depression was occasioned by something more serious than a military defeat. He knew then, what I only knew last night, that the collapse of the Russian army is complete. They acknowledge to have lost (dead) 50,000 in war; but they have 20,000 in nominal hospitals at Plevna, housed in worse than pigsties, and perhaps 30,000 on the Lom and Shipka: all these will die. The Imperial Guard, just arrived, in a horrid state. Half their horses are already dead. The only fodder prepared for them being compressed hay, wh. was damp, or in a state of effervescence, and the horses won't touch it. Literally half the horses that first arrived, dead! Our informant seems to think that, instead of a winter campaign in Bulgaria, we may perhaps look out for a 'retreat-from-Moscow catastrophe.' And all this is concealed from the Emperor and the Russian nation—the only two influences that could bring about peace. .

The people here are asking me to dinner, wh. is pestiferous. I send their invitations up to town, to be answered by Mr. Algernon Turnor. I hope this will sicken them. . . .

Oct. 25.—. . . I speak the truth to you on some matters, tho' I may not, on such, to others. When I say I am ill, I mean it. I leave this place, wh. I do on 29th, in no degree better, as regards the main and only suffering—asthma. I am now inhaling, night and day; a last desperate effort, and futile.

It is quite impossible I can go on, because the Constitution

of this country is a Parliamen[tar]y Govt.—'c'est un gouverne-
ment qui parle.' I can't lead a House of Pt., even H. of L.,
witht. a voice—witht. health. And Lord Mayor's Day, when
my words may govern the world, what am I to do? If it
were not for the Faery, I certainly wd. at once retire, but
I wait her return before it is broached.

On his way back to London he paid a two days' visit
to Lord Abergavenny at Eridge. There he met, and
did 'some good business' with, Cairns and Hardy. He
also tells Lady Bradford: 'I was shown the tree I planted
in '68, with an inscription: "Prime Minister, etc." Now
this morning I have planted another tree, which I shall
not see after another nine years.' He did not go to
Whitehall Gardens, but to the official residence in
Downing Street, 'to avoid,' he told Lady Bradford, 'my
terrible steep Whitehall stairs, which I cannot manage.'
For the remainder of his Premiership he lived, when in
London, at 10, Downing Street. He had the November
Cabinets before him, and the Lord Mayor's banquet.
'I have not accepted the Lord Mayor's dinner yet,' he
told Corry on October 28, 'for I shrink from an occasion
which will be like a roarer entering for the Derby. And
yet if I don't go, I shall feel dishonored.' Happily he
at last found a physician, Dr. Kidd, who seemed to
understand his case, who patched him up for the Guildhall banquet, and who afforded him some prospect of
more than temporary relief.

To Lady Bradford.

10, DOWNING STREET, Nov. 1.—. . . To-day I saw Dr.
Kidd, who cured the Ld. Chancellor. I like him much. He
examined me as if I were a recruit—but reports no organic
deficiency. My complaint is bronchial asthma, more distressing than bronchitis, but curable, wh. bronchitis is not,
and I am to be cured—and very soon![1]
This is a ray of hope, and I trust I may get to the Lord
Mayor's dinner, for if I do not Europe will be alarmed,

---

[1] Dr. Kidd also diagnosed Bright's disease, which gave him great trouble,
as Beaconsfield would take no exercise save a slow saunter. See article by
Dr. Kidd in *Nineteenth Century* for July, 1889, 'The last illness of Lord
Beaconsfield.'

England agitated, and the Tory party frightened. There is egotism for you ! . . .

Nov. 6.—Very hard work: Cabinet every day and another to-morrow; the Lord Mayor's fell banquet haunting me, if I be a moment idle—and an M.D. coming every day to try to get me up for Friday ! What a picture of horrors to write about, but I have nothing else to say, and you don't like silence. . . .

I fear the Turks are annihilated in Asia; that the Russians are already at Erzeroum and that Kars will fall. . . .

Plevna is our only chance. Osman Pasha is a real general— even the English officers say so; but no one really knows the elements of the position: whether he has troops enough, or rations enough, or whether the weather will smash the Russians, these are the points. . . .

Nov. 7.—. . . Affairs in France are grave. There will be no riot—but the Marshal[1] must resign; people laugh at him —and that is fatal at Paris. Playing at being a hero and not doing it, does not answer Nothing justified his conduct, but the predetermination of a *coup d'état*. . . .

Nov. 13.—. . . I had made up my mind never to breathe a word as to my progress, or the reverse, until I had given my new man a fair and real trial: but, as you press me, and I can refuse you nothing, I will tell you that I entertain the highest opinion of Dr. Kidd, and that all the medical men I have known, and I have seen some of the highest, seem much inferior to him, in quickness of observation, and perception, and in the reasonableness, and at the same time originality, of his measures. I am told his practice is immense, and especially in chest and bronchial complaints. The difficulty is in seeing him, as he does not like to leave his house. . . .

Beaconsfield said little of moment at Guildhall, but he made it clear that he was resolved that British interests should be respected, and that he sympathised with the plucky resistance which the Turks were making. He defined the policy of the Government as having been throughout one of conditional neutrality—neutrality, that is, so long as British interests were not assailed or menaced. 'Cosmopolitan critics, men who are the friends of every country save their own, have denounced this policy as a selfish policy. My Lord Mayor, it is as selfish as patriotism.' The war had shown, he maintained, that the Turkish Government was no fiction, nor were

[1] Macmahon, President of the French Republic.

the Turkish people effete; the independence of Turkey was no longer a subject of ridicule.   As to the prospects of peace, he recommended patience and hope.

Meanwhile his letters to the Queen show the progress he was making in bringing his   abinet to view the situation with his eyes.

To Queen Victoria.

10, DOWNING ST., *Nov.* 1, '77.—. . . The circumstances have become more complicated, and difficult, but, he thinks, he sees his way.   What the Cabinet will have to decide on their meeting is, whether they shall make an immediate— but secret—conciliatory communication to Russia, requiring a written undertaking from Russia that she will not, under any circumstances, even occupy Constantinople.   Lord Beaconsfield has had an interview with Lord Derby on this matter, and it was not discouraging.   Lord Beaconsfield is to see Lord Salisbury upon it to-morrow.   Lord Beaconsfield thinks he shall succeed in carrying this important point. He has impressed Lord Derby with the fact, that it is only carrying into effect the policy for which the country gives him credit.

What we should do in case of Russia's refusal is clear to Lord Beaconsfield, and he will take an early opportunity of laying it before your Majesty, but he does not think it wise that the primary step, which he wishes the Cabinet to adopt, should be involved with any consideration of merely hypothetical circumstances.   What he is now about to say has no reference to his policy; or to the measures, which, if necessary, he contemplates: but he would remark to your Majesty that, so far as a march on Constantinople is concerned, there is now no fear of a *coup de main*.   Constantinople itself is now strongly fortified; both Peninsulas, Gallipoli and Durkos, being in a state of defence which, with sufficient troops, would render them impregnable, and, with insufficient troops, would offer a long resistance.   Adrianople, too, which was an open town, is now as strong as Plevna. . . .

He hopes your Majesty will not misconceive this letter, or think for a moment that he is reserved in communicating with your Majesty; he wishes never to have a thought on affairs, which your Majesty should not share, but he has been suffering a great deal of late and is physically incapable, to-day, of putting his views before your Majesty. . . .

Secret.   Nov. 3.—Lord Beaconsfield with his humble duty to your Majesty.   Government in Cabinet are about to reassemble, in order to consider their general policy, and the measures to be submitted to Parliament.   Lord Beaconsfield thinks your Majesty should be made accurately acquainted with the views and feelings of the various members of the Cabinet, with respect to the Eastern Question, in which your Majesty, naturally, takes so deep an interest.

In a Cabinet of twelve members, there are seven parties, or policies, as to the course which should be pursued.

1st, the War Party pure and simple: which is of opinion that the time has arrived when material assistance should be afforded to the Porte.   This party is headed by Mr. Secretary Hardy, supported by Lord John Manners, Sir M. Beach, and, before his untimely end, by the late First Lord of the Admiralty [Ward Hunt].

2nd, the party which is prepared to go to war, if Russia will not engage not to occupy Constantinople.   The party consists of the Lord Chancellor, Mr. Secretary Cross, the present First Lord of the Admiralty [W. H. Smith], and the Duke of Richmond.

3rd, the party that is prepared to go to war, if, after the signature of peace, the Russians would not evacuate Constantinople.   This party consists of the Marquis of Salisbury.

4th, the party of ‘ peace at any price ’ represented by the Earl of Derby.

5th, the party, which disapproves of any policy avowedly resting on what are called ‘ British interests,’ which is considered ‘ a selfish policy ’ (almost as selfish as patriotism), and is in favor of an address to the four other neutral Powers, inviting them to join us ‘ in making some kind of appeal to the belligerents.’   These are the views, very briefly, of the Chancellor of Exchequer.   They are utterly futile, and assuming as they do that Prince Bismarck, who is master of the situation, would join with the other neutral Powers in such a step, they approach silliness.[1]

The 6th policy is represented by Lord Carnarvon, who did not conceal, at the last meeting of the Cabinet, his inclination, that Constantinople should be permanently acquired by Russia.   These are the views of Lyddon, Freeman, and other priests and professors, who are now stirring in favor of the ‘ freedom of the Dardanelles.’

The 7th policy is that of your Majesty, and which will be

[1] In talking to Northcote Beaconsfield gave a similar account of the parties in the Cabinet, save that, in compliment to his interlocutor, he associated him with himself as desiring to see something done.   But Northcote himself wrote about his views to Beaconsfield from Balmoral on Nov. 16: ‘ As you know, mine are not wholly in unison with those of anybody else in the Cabinet.’

introduced, and enforced to his utmost by the Prime Minister:
—viz., that, in the first place, the Cabinet shall decide upon
something, and if so, that the something shall consist of a
notification to Russia, that the present state of British
neutrality cannot be depended on for another campaign
unless your Majesty's Government receives a written engagement from Russia, that under no circumstances will she
occupy Constantinople or the Dardanelles. The engagement
on the part of Russia, of course, to be secret.

Lord Beaconsfield has been active since his arrival in town,
and seeing and conferring with some of his most important
colleagues, and he believes he shall carry his proposal, unanimously, with the exception of Lord Carnarvon, who will
probably resign. What course should be pursued if Russia
refuses, has been enquired by several, but, as the notification
would at once break up the Cabinet, Lord Beaconsfield has
declined to enter into the consideration of hypothetical
circumstances. When the reply of Russia is received, the
Cabinet will then have the opportunity of considering again
the situation. Lord Beaconsfield is far from believing that
Russia will decline our proposal, but, in that case, there is,
according to his view, only one step to take. For your
Majesty, in your Majesty's Speech from the Throne, to notice
in a becoming manner the situation, and a considerable
increase of the army to be immediately proposed. The Lord
Chancellor and Mr. Secretary Hardy both agreed in this, when
it was intimated to them at Eridge.

(*Cypher.*) FOREIGN OFFICE, *Nov.* 5, '77.—I proposed the
policy agreed upon, which Lord Carnarvon immediately
opposed, but as, to his evident surprise, it was supported
both by Lord Salisbury and then Lord Derby, he was
routed. . . .

Throughout the later autumn months the Russians
continued their successes in Asia, and it became more
and more evident each day that, if Plevna fell, Turkey
would lie at the mercy of her foe, and the road would be
open to those regions where British interests were centred.
The agitation of the Queen increased, and Beaconsfield
found it difficult to satisfy her; while, on the other hand,
Derby, now that the moment for action appeared to be
approaching, became more obstinately set than ever
on a purely passive policy. 'I gather from my lady
D[erby]' wrote Corry to his chief on October 31, 'that

our friend is as resolute as ever to keep his hands
in his pockets.' On a deputation which waited on him
at the Foreign Office on November 28 to advise ' a bold
course at a critical moment,' Derby poured a plentiful
douche of cold water, making light of possible danger to
British interests, and reminding his hearers that the
French Minister who in 1870 went to war with a light
heart ' did not come out of it with a light heart—neither
he, nor his master, nor his country.' It could no longer
be doubted that he and his chief were drifting apart.
Meanwhile Beaconsfield, while he anxiously watched
events, took advantage of the respite which Kidd procured
him from his malady to appear somewhat more frequently
in society.

To Lady Bradford.

10, DOWNING STREET, Nov. 19, 1877.—. . . The fall of
Kars is a great blow, the more so as I saw Musurus yesterday,
or rather received him, for he came with a telegram from the
Sultan to thank me for my Guildhall speech, and Musurus
told me to be quite easy about Asia, that they cd. not take
Erzeroum, and that Kars was provisioned for months !

Nov. 21.—. . . I was much amused at Gorhambury—a
very fine collection of portraits of the Baconian age. Except
my host, there was no one of my generation: more than that,
there was no one of Monty's, who still figures as a young
man. There were six heirs-apparent, whose collected ages
could hardly secure them, on an average, of having completed
their majority: Mountcharles, Wiltshire, Newark, Grimston,
Duncombe, and Scudamore-Stanhope. When they were presented to me, I had to tell them that I had sate in Parliament not only with their fathers, but the race before them.
They were all men (or boys), who may, and must, exercise
considerable influence in this country, and it was amusing to
watch them. They went out shooting, and shot each other,
and a beater or two—but it was kept a secret from the ladies.

I arrived at Pancras station this morning at ½ past ten,
and, my brougham waiting, got to the Oratory, late, but in
time.[1] There was as great a crowd from Hyde Park Corner to
Brompton as on Lord Mayor's Day. When I arrived, it was
supposed to be the bride, and the whole church, very long
and very full, rose, and were sadly disappointed when it was

---

[1] For the marriage of the 15th Duke of Norfolk to Lady Flora Hastings.

only I, in a fur coat and your rustic stick, wh. I had taken with me to Gorhamy. The ceremony was long, and all the severest Gregorian music. I confess I like a little more florid music, which Bute gave us.

I was one of the witnesses summoned to the vestry: and afterwards there was a breakfast at the bride's father's, and I had to propose her health. This latter business, as well as my speech, was not too long, as, tho' the repast was most elaborate, it was necessary for the bride and bridegroom to arrive at Arundel in full daylight, as there was an immense reception prepared there for them.

I got to business at ½ past two, saw Lord Derby with whom I had an appointment, and am now waiting to see Schou., who has an appointment also—tho' later. . . .

Dec. 6.—. . . The victory of Suleiman Pasha is a great affair, and if he can follow it up and take Tirnova, the experts think that Osman in Plevna is saved. But that seems too good to be true. . . .

Dec. 7—Just returned from [Windsor]. The audience lasted from 12.30 to luncheon time, when I joined that lively and interesting being the Duchess of —— and three younger female courtiers, who vied with her in loveliness, and fascinating manners. Nothing cd. be more formal than the hushed tones of their conversation, and it was impossible to assert one's share in it. I was fairly famished, and was ashamed of my silence. At last, I said I had a special train, and, if they liked, I wd. take them all up to town with me. They seemed shocked and terrified, and when, in reply to what wd. then happen, I promised to give them a dinner at a café, and take them all to the play, I thought the ceiling wd. have fallen down. The Duchess took it all quite *au sérieux.* . . .

To Queen Victoria.

10, DOWNING ST., *Nov.* 16, '77.—Lord Beaconsfield . . . is distressed by the telegram received from your Majesty yesterday, and by the letter of this morning. He entirely sympathises with all your Majesty feels, but he cannot but believe that, on continued reflection, your Majesty may be of opinion, that, however vexatious and disheartening the occurrence of certain possible contingencies in Bulgaria may be to your Majesty, neither the honor of your Majesty, nor of your Crown, Government, or people, could be involved in them.

Unquestionably the fall of Plevna, which has not yet fallen, would be a calamity to this country, but it would not be a disgrace. If the relations of Russia with England were the same as in the Crimean War, it would be our duty to exert our utmost to prevent the fall of Plevna, but they are not so, Then the passage of the Pruth was a *casus belli*, and we were justified in resisting the invasion of the Principalities and Bulgaria. Now, we have adopted and announced a different policy: one of neutrality, conditional on no British interest being menaced or attacked. We have defined those British interests. The occupation by Russia of Constantinople, or the Dardanelles, would assail one of those interests, and the honor of your Majesty's Crown, of your Government and your people would then be forfeited, if your Majesty, by all the means in your Majesty's power, did not endeavor to guard your Majesty's Empire from such a result.

Lord Beaconsfield has wished to place the position of affairs before your Majesty in as clear and terse a manner, as in his power, but he does not wish to conceal his great regret at even appearing to differ in opinion from your Majesty, not merely from his relations, as one of your Majesty's servants, but from his unfeigned confidence in your Majesty's judgment.

Lord John Manners to Queen Victoria.

Dec. 4, 1877.—Lord John Manners with his humble duty to your Majesty. At the Cabinet, after a short statement by the Prime Minister, Lord Derby explained why the preparation of the note to Russia, which had been determined upon by a previous Cabinet, had been postponed, and then read the draft as he had originally drawn it, consisting of two parts—the 1st, asking Russia in courteous terms for a definite answer to our conditions of neutrality as to Constantinople and the Dardanelles; the 2nd containing an assurance that if her reply on those two points was satisfactory we should take no steps to oppose her further advance in Europe, or Asia. Lord Derby went on to say that, while the second part was drawn according to his notes taken at the time, he understood that the recollection of some of his colleagues was of a different character. He ended by suggesting that the note, instead of the form of a question, should assume that of a warning to Russia that if her armies appeared to menace Constantinople or the Dardanelles, Great Britain would reserve her liberty of action; omitting the second part altogether.

Lord Cairns stated his recollection to be at variance with that of Lord Derby as to the 2nd part of the proposed note, and proceeded to suggest that a tentative effort at mediation should now be made on the basis of the Russian note of June 8th; and that the Porte should be informally sounded as to its disposition in that respect. Most of the Cabinet

Lord Derby at first dissenting, were of that opinion, and all agreed that a note of warning would be preferable to one of enquiry. Ultimately on Lord Beaconsfield's suggestion the two ideas were combined and Lord Derby was requested to draw up a note, for consideration at the next Cabinet, which should couple the warning to Russia with an intimation that your Majesty's Government would gladly tender its good offices for a pacification. . . .

To Lord Derby.

10, DOWNING ST., *Dec.* 5, '77.—I have to be at Windsor on Friday, at noon, and I don't anticipate a very agreeable audience.

I consented to change, yesterday, the form of the note to Russia, which the Cabinet had previously agreed to, in compliance with your wishes, which I always wish to meet if possible, but I prefer the original proposal.

I trust by Friday your colleagues may be in possession of the dr't note, so that they may well consider it, before Saturday morning.

Its tone cannot be too firm and clear. Whatever may be told to you, I believe that Russia, generally, is more ready for peace than her journals pretend, but the war party is encouraged by our presumed supineness.

I was sorry to hear you say yesterday, that you were not prepared to make the occupation of Constantinople, or rather the menaced occupation of that city, a *casus belli.* I hope I misunderstood you. I hold, myself, both this event, if impending, as well as the simultaneous opening of the Straits to Russia and their closing to other Powers, should decidedly be *casus belli* for this country, with or without allies. And with regard to this last consideration, we should remember that Turkey herself is now a powerful ally. In the Crimean War, she literally had no army. After a fierce campaign, she has still 400,000 men in the field, armed with admirable weapons; her arsenals are well supplied, and it is not impossible, by any means, that the loan, which she has opened at Bombay and Calcutta, may be subscribed to the amount of some millions.

CHAPTER VI.

DERBY'S FIRST RESIGNATION.

1877–1878.

Plevna fell on December 9. Beaconsfield recognised immediately that the moment had come for public action, which should show unmistakably to the world that England was in earnest in her resolve to protect her interests. He telegraphed to the Queen from Hughenden, on the 11th, that he had summoned a Cabinet for Friday the 14th, and that he would propose ' that Parliament should meet as soon as practicable, and that the Speech from the Throne should announce a large increase in your Majesty's armaments, and also the undertaking, on the part of your Majesty, at the invitation of the Sultan, to mediate between the belligerents.' The Queen, who had long pressed for definite action, warmly seconded her Minister; and on the eve of the meeting urged him once more to be firm, ' and not give way to anyone, even if Lord Derby should wish to resign.'

To mark the definiteness of his resolve and his intention to advance regardless of the possible defection of individual colleagues, Beaconsfield made no attempt, as on other occasions, to secure support for his proposals beforehand, nor did he solicit, as he had during the past months solicited, and solicited in vain, the Foreign Secretary to assume the responsibility of putting forward the policy as his own. The proposals were, indeed, not exactly a novelty to his colleagues, as he had often indicated measures of the kind as those which must be taken when the critical moment came. But, before he moved their adoption now in Cabinet, he had taken no one into his confidence save his Sovereign. To her he reported what passed,

To Queen Victoria.

MEMORANDUM OF THE MEETING OF THE CABINET HOLDEN ON DEC. 14, 1877.

HUGHENDEN, *Dec.* 14, '77.—Lord Beaconsfield, calling the attention of his colleagues to the critical state of affairs in the East, and to the absolute necessity of adopting means to secure the conditions on which the policy of neutrality, hitherto pursued, was founded, concluded by proposing that your Majesty should be advised to summon Parliament immediately; that a considerable increase of your Majesty's forces should be proposed; and that your Majesty should simultaneously commence negotiations, as mediator, between the belligerents. No previous intimation to any one had been given of these proposals, and when they had been made there was a dead silence, broken, at last, by Lord John Manners, who supported them with much energy and ability.

Then Lord Carnarvon, after many cavils, enquired for whom was England to hold Constantinople in the event of our succeeding in defeating the attempt of the Russians to occupy it?

The Lord Chancellor spoke at some length; said Lord Carnarvon had involved a simple question with fallacies. What we had to decide, was whether, now that the contemplated circumstances were at hand, we were prepared to support the policy which we had announced as the only course efficient to prevent these circumstances. In his opinion, the measures recommended by the Prime Minister were not only adequate, but the only ones left open to us.

Mr. Secretary Hardy spoke in the same vein, and entered into some military details.

The Marquis of Salisbury saw no abstract objection to the proposals of the Prime Minister, but, practically, they would lead to an alliance with Turkey, to which he could not assent. The Chancellor of the Exchequer asked Lord Salisbury what then was the alternative? Some course must now be taken. What other course was there? No one could ever answer this question. The C. of Ex'r said he was not only for a vote of men and money, but for a large vote, as the best means to secure peace.

Mr. Secretary Cross said one thing was quite clear, that it was necessary the Government should make up their minds about what they would do before they met Parliament. He thought they had decided to prevent the occupation of Constantinople by the Russians, but it would seem, from what had fallen from Lord Carnarvon, and, in some degree, from Lord Salisbury, that was not the case.

Sir Michael Beach spoke shortly, but very strongly, in the same vein. The Duke of Richmond had done so previously.

The First Lord of the Admiralty [W. H. Smith] was in favour of calling Parliament together, and of large increase of force, but wished the mediation to commence immediately, as, if the attempt failed, the position of the Government, in asking for increased supplies, would be stronger.

Then Lord Derby spoke at length. He had been taken by surprise, and had not had time to give due consideration to the proposals, but, as at present advised, he entirely disapproved of them. We had sent a note to Russia, and should await her answer. There was no *casus belli* in that note, and he wished distinctly to say, that he was not prepared to look upon the occupation of Constantinople by the Russians as a *casus belli*. Lord Derby spoke at some length, and with unusual fire. The general tenor of his observations was that any active interference in Eastern affairs by England was to be deprecated.

There was a good deal of sharp remark from several members of the Cabinet, as he spoke and after he had concluded.

The Prime Minister said, that he did not wish to hurry the Cabinet into a resolution, which was the most important they had yet been called upon to adopt, but affairs were pressing. He should like Parliament to be summoned as soon as practicable in the next month. With regard to the Russian Note, his present proposals were perfectly consistent with that and all our previous steps. He desired peace, anxiously, but he wished the country to be placed in a position, which would give her authority in arranging and settling the terms of that peace. The Cabinet adjourned till Monday, when every effort will be made to bring the question to a conclusion.

Before the Cabinet resumed the discussion on the following Monday, they and the country and the world had a proof of the exceptional confidence which the Queen reposed in her Prime Minister, of the exceptional friendship with which Her Majesty honoured him. The royal visit to Hughenden which had been first suggested in the spring was paid on Saturday, December 15; and was intended no doubt to emphasise the support which the Sovereign extended to the Eastern policy of the Minister.

In one respect the date chosen was unfortunate. It was the anniversary of Lady Beaconsfield's death.

From Queen Victoria.

WINDSOR CASTLE, *Dec.* 15.—The Queen is anxious to express her concern at having inadvertently fixed this day of such sad recollections to Lord Beaconsfield for her visit to Hughenden; and she wishes he should know that she only found out what she had done, when it was too late to alter it. But it has annoyed her very much.

'The contiguity of a largish town,' as Beaconsfield told Lady Bradford, converted the visit into 'a regular function.' The Queen, accompanied by Princess Beatrice, came by special train to High Wycombe, where she was met, not only by Beaconsfield and Corry, but by the Mayor, who presented an address; and it was through cheering crowds and beflagged streets that she drove to Hughenden. At the house all was simple. No one was present but the Queen, the Princess, and two or three members of Her Majesty's Household in attendance; Beaconsfield had only his secretary to assist him. The Queen stayed a couple of hours, and she and the Princess took lunch with their host, each planting before their departure a tree on the south lawn. Beaconsfield was the third Prime Minister, Melbourne and Peel being the previous two, to whom Her Majesty paid the special honour of accepting his hospitality during his term of office.

To Queen Victoria.

HUGHENDEN MANOR, *Dec.* 16, 1877.—Lord Beaconsfield . . . hopes he may be permitted to take this occasion of offering to your Majesty his grateful, and heartfelt, thanks for the honor, which your Majesty conferred on him, yesterday, by deigning to visit his home: where your Majesty left a dream of dignified condescension and ever-graceful charm.

To Lady Bradford.

10, DOWNING STREET, *Dec.* 17.—I am here with another Cabinet, and another to-morrow at twelve ! I can't conceal, and don't wish to conceal, from you, that affairs are most critical, and I have so much to do and think of, I really cannot write.

The visit of Saturday a great success: fine day, and with some gleams of sunshine. The Faery seemed to admire, and be interested in, everything, and has written to me a very pretty letter to that effect.

I have got to go to Windsor to-morrow ' to dine and sleep,' rather a tax in these busy times, and with my feeble health.

The Faery took away my statuette by Trentanova as a memorial of Hughenden. I had for the Princess the most beautiful *bonbonnière* you ever saw or fancied—just fresh from Paris. I cd. tell you many things to amuse you, but they must keep for more tranquil times.

Monday's Cabinet produced no agreement; and Beaconsfield, in pursuance of his fixed resolve to carry his policy through, announced that, in default of agreement, he should resign. This gave his colleagues pause, and they requested and obtained a day's reprieve.

To Queen Victoria.

10, DOWNING ST., *Dec.* 17, '77.—. . . A stormy meeting of two hours and $\frac{1}{2}$. Nothing settled, the Cabinet having adjourned till to-morrow at twelve o'clock, after Lord Beaconsfield had announced that he should place his resignation in your Majesty's hands. It was then requested that they should adjourn until to-morrow. He thinks the three peers will retire, tho' the Lord Chancellor has hopes of Lord Salisbury. The Lord Chancellor is engaged to go down to Hatfield to-night, and will, therefore, have an opportunity of conferring with Lord Salisbury alone.

The conspirators had got hold of the Chancellor of the Exchequer and Mr. Smith, in Lord Beaconsfield's absence, and had influenced them both, but Lord Beaconsfield feels little doubt, that he shall put all right in those quarters.

What broke up the Cabinet was not so much the 3 propositions of Lord Beaconsfield, viz., (1) To call Parliament together immediately, (2) To vote considerable increase of forces, and (3) To negotiate alone between the belligerents, but rather the startling truth, that became revealed in the discussion, that not one of the three peers ever really intended either to resist Russia, or to assist Turkey. . . .

The Queen, failing entirely to grasp her Minister's resolve, was startled at the suggestion that he might resign. She could understand the resignation of his three dissentient colleagues; but his own! 'Under any circumstances,' she wrote, ' the Queen would never accept Lord Beaconsfield's resignation which he says he said he would tender to her, but which she hopes is not in earnest. That the Queen will not accept.' Beaconsfield explained.

To Queen Victoria.

10, DOWNING ST., *Dec.* 17, '77.—. . . He is sorry to have caused your Majesty any unnecessary anxiety, when your Majesty has unhappily so much.

He thought he expressed an usual, and constitutional, practice when he found half his Cabinet at that moment arrayed against him, in saying that if not supported he should feel it his duty to resign to your Majesty the trust, which your Majesty had, so graciously, bestowed on him. But that would not prevent your Majesty, if your Majesty graciously thought fit to entrust to him the formation of a new ministry, and certainly, in that case, he would do his utmost to form one. . . .

Night brought reflection and appeasement. Derby showed next morning a great reluctance to push differences to extremes; Cairns returned from Hatfield with a favourable report of Salisbury's disposition. Indeed, from this moment Salisbury, who felt that a testing time was approaching for British statesmen, began to range himself more and more by Beaconsfield's side. The Minister could report after the Cabinet to his Sovereign that his policy had prevailed without provoking any resignation. The only change made was one of date. Beaconsfield had suggested January 7 for the meeting of Parliament; it was fixed for January 17.

From Lord Derby.

FOREIGN OFFICE, *Dec.* 17 [? 18].—I will call on you a little after eleven, and happy indeed I shall be if we can see our way out of this mess. We all want to keep together: and no one in the Cabinet will feel as I shall if circumstances separate me from my old friend and teacher in public life.

To Queen Victoria.

On the preceding day, the Cabinet was about to close by the virtual resignation of three ministers, and the announcement of the Prime Minister that he should lay before the Queen his inability to carry on Her Majesty's affairs with his present colleagues and to ask Her Majesty's commands in consequence, when the Lord Chancellor requested that the Cabinet should adjourn until the next day at noon.

Lord Beaconsfield conferred with the Lord Chancellor after the Cabinet.

On Tuesday morning Lord Derby called on the P. Minister at 11 o'clock, an hour before the Cabinet met, and, to the great surprise of Lord Beaconsfield, expressed his deep regret at the dissolution of your Majesty's Government, and asked, whether there was no *modus vivendi* possible. Lord Beaconsfield said no compromise was possible. Lord Derby then sketched his view how the *modus vivendi* might be secured.

That he would agree to earlier meeting of Parliament, say 24 January; and some increase of force; but, under no circumstances, any attempt at mediation, which must fail.

Lord Beaconsfield held out no hope of accepting this plan, but Lord Derby, with many expressions of regard, said he should offer it to the consideration of his colleagues before an absolute rupture was decided on.

In the meantime, the Lord Chancellor arrived from Hatfield, and reported Lord Salisbury as very amenable and said that he had drawn up three resolutions, which embodied Lord Beaconsfield's proposals, and that he had no doubt Lord Salisbury would accept them.

The Cabinet met: the Lord Chancellor brought forward his resolutions: Lord Derby introduced his *modus vivendi:* Lord Salisbury answered Lord Derby and said that, if anything was done, he preferred the proposals of the Prime Minister, as more effective.

There was a general assent to these views.

Lord Derby said he would not contend with the unanimous opinion of the Cabinet, when the contest was only a question of degree. Then Lord Carnarvon, who had hitherto been silent, screamed out that, altho' he accepted these resolutions, he begged it to be understood that their acceptance, on his part, involved no assent to any expedition to any part of the Turkish Empire or any alliance with the Porte.

The Prime Minister replied, that no such question was now before the Cabinet: what they wanted now was to secure sufficient forces for the Queen; what was to be done with those increased forces depended on the circumstances which we should have to meet; at present he held the Cabinet unanimous in adopting his measures and he should report the three resolutions accordingly to the Queen.

He omitted to mention, that the Lord Chancellor and Lord Salisbury were very strong on the expediency of accompanying announcement of the meeting of Parliament with a direct communication to Russia as to mediation between the belligerents. And the Lord Chancellor sketched the form of such a despatch. Lord Derby strongly opposed but ultimately accepted this.

10, Downing St. *Dec.* 19, '77.—. . . . The Cabinet to-day was subdued, and chiefly considered domestic affairs, but also considered the Russian despatch, of which he believes your Majesty will have a copy, for your Majesty's approbation, this evening.

All this is another proof of what may be done when the Sovereign and the Minister act together.

Witness the Public Worship Act. Witness your Majesty's Imperial Crown. . . .

To Lady Bradford.

Most Private. 10, Downing Street, *Dec.* 19.—The great struggle is over, and I have triumphed.

On Monday night there was virtually no Government, but on Tuesday the recusants fell upon their knees, and surrendered at discretion.

Parliament is to meet 17th next month. There is to be a large increase of force, and England is to mediate directly betn. the belligerents.

I was at Windsor yesterday, and sate at dinner next to the Faery, who is delighted with all that has happened.

I have been talking and writing now for several days without interruption; therefore you must excuse this brief and hurried line.

The following letters give us a picture of a statesman's Christmas, as it might have been, and as it was.

To Lady Newport.[1]

Hughenden Manor, *Dec.* 13, '77.—There is no one I should like so much to pass my Xmas with as you and yours—but alas ! that cannot be.

The state of affairs is so urgent and critical, that I doubt

[1] Now the Countess Dowager of Bradford.

very much, whether I shall be able to remain even here. Probably my sarcastically 'merrie' Xmas will be passed in London.

It is a great disappointment to me, for I should like very much to have seen B[1] and M,[2] who must by this time have forgotten me. Laddo[3] has an advantage over them in that respect, for we met recently at a country house. But I want to make the acquaintance of those he describes as his ' little sisters.' It is time.

To Lady Bradford.

10, DOWNING STREET, *Dec.* 23.—Here we are with all the business in the world to be transacted, and everybody away. Even Derby must go down to his home at 5.30. I believe Knowsley is held by the tenure of its lord eating roast turkey on Xmas Day on the spot. Fortunately Monty is here, whom I am obliged to send about to Ambassadors and make write to Ministers of State.

I was at Windsor yesterday, and the Faery will remain there for a week: at least, till Friday. I have got to go down there again, and, I fear, more than once. All is well as long as I can keep to my room, or a morning walk, but toilette, and evening mannerisms, destroy me.

The J[ohn] M[anner]s asked me to dine with them on Xmas Day. It is impossible; but having the largest pineapple sent to me yesterday, I forwarded it, with my refusal, to Janetta[4]—a golden apple of the Hesperides. I hope it will stop their mouths from abusing me for not going.

I suppose you know Bretby is in town, and I will call there this afternoon, tho' I am really quite incapable of conversation, and wish most ardently the world would leave me alone to my business wh. is hard eno'. I want nothing else except letters from you.

Xmas Day.—I wear my new muffetees to-day, wh. I believe is etiquette, tho' I discard, for a moment, another pair, which served me pleasantly, tho' they have not been with me very long. I change my colors according to the season, like a ritualist priest. . . .

The 3rd vol. of the Prince's *Life*[5] is one of the most interesting and one of the most important works that has appeared for a long time. Its predecessors did not, and could not, prepare us for anything so striking and so excellent. All the incidents and characters are great, and wonderfully appo-

---

[1] Now Lady Beatrice Pretyman.   [2] Now Duchess of Buccleuch.
[3] Now Earl of Bradford.
[4] Lady John Manners, afterwards Duchess of Rutland.
[5] Sir Theodore Martin's *Life of the Prince Consort.*

site to the present hour. I am delighted that you delight in it. . . . The main subject of course at this moment is invested with peculiar interest, but the book has charms irrespective of the main subject. . . .

To-morrow I go to Windsor, and remain till the next day, when I come up to a Cabinet. . . .

Dec. 28.—Yesterday was a hard day. Had to get up at 7 o'ck. at Windsor—dark and cold: was at D.S. by ten—many interviews, and then a long Cabinet, and then writing to the Faery—so it was quite impossible to write to some one else. . . .

As you want to know something about Peace and War, you will be glad to hear that the Sultan has solicited our kind offices for peace with Russia, and that H.M.'s Government have accepted the trust.

God knows what will happen, but it is a good answer to that vain maniac Shaftesbury, and your simple friend Westminster, who, at the instigation of Gladstone, are getting up an agitation against the Government because it is going to war.

If Russia refuses, it will put her still more in the wrong, and if the weather on the Danube be as damnable as it is at St. James's, perhaps Russia will be prudent and reasonable. . . .

In the circle (in the corridor) the three Princesses,[1] who were grouped together, sent for me, on the plea that I was standing in a draught, etc. They wanted a little amusement. When I came up to them I said, ' Three goddesses—to wh. am I to give the golden apple ?' . . .

Dec. 29.—. . . The announcement of the application of the Porte makes a great sensation.

The meeting of Parlt. was the 1st Act in the Drama. This is the second. What will be the 3rd ?

Beaconsfield saw with satisfaction, as December wore on, that Salisbury was beginning to realise that, in the Eastern Question, he had more in common with his chief than with Derby or with Carnarvon. One factor in bringing the two men together was the sympathetic indignation they felt over the leakage of Cabinet secrets which marked the year 1877. Cabinet decisions —or indecisions—were, it was discovered from Colonel Wellesley's reports and from other sources, immediately and regularly reported by Schouvaloff, the Russian Am-

---

[1] Princesses Helena, Louise, and Beatrice.

bassador, to his government. At the end of December
Beaconsfield sent Salisbury a letter from Wellesley
showing the mischief that was being done; and at the
same time distinguished him from amongst his colleagues
by taking him into his confidence over the secret message
to the Tsar.

To Lord Salisbury.

Very Private. [? *Dec.* 25, 1877.]—I enclose you a letter
which I have not shown to any of my colleagues and probably
never shall, but which requires and deserves your deep
attention.

When Col. W. last left England and had his final interview
with me, I advised him to impress upon the Emperor that
England was unwilling to depart from its neutrality, that it
wished to assist in bringing about a settlement honorable
and fairly advantageous to Russia, but that I could not conceal from myself that if the Emperor was obliged to enter
into a second campaign it would be difficult for England to
rest in her present inertness. The Emperor accepted this
statement with confidence, and in the conciliatory spirit in
which it was conceived: and he acted on it.

I have myself been convinced, both from thought and
information, that a firm front shown by England would
terminate the war without material injury to our interests.
I think I could persuade you of this, but I will not dwell
upon the matter here. What I wish to show you is that if
the present system of the Cabinet is persisted in, and every
resolution of every council is regularly reported by Count
S[chouvaloff], it seems inevitable that our very endeavors to
secure peace will land us in the reverse.

I have endeavoured to arrest this evil by some remarks
I made in Cabinet. . . . But more decisive means are
requisite.

We must put an end to all this gossip about war parties
and peace parties in the Cabinet, and we must come to
decisions which may be, and will be, betrayed, but which
may convince Russia that we are agreed and determined.
You and I must go together into the depth of the affair and
settle what we are prepared to do. I dare say we shall not
differ when we talk the matter over together as becomes
public men with so great a responsibility: but unless we
make an effort to clear ourselves from the Canidian spells
which are environing us, we shall make shipwreck of alike
our own reputations and the interests of our country.

Salisbury, in his reply, still manifested his great repugnance to any step which might involve us in war with Russia; and the reasons he gave were certainly such as to demand grave consideration.

From Lord Salisbury.

INDIA OFFICE, *Dec.* 26, '77.—I return the enclosed most interesting and disquieting letter, with many thanks.

I sympathise fully in the solicitude this information causes you. Throughout the last anxious year, the apparent ease with which a knowledge of our councils has leaked out has placed us at a constant disadvantage. I hardly see in what way you, or the Cabinet as a body, can do anything to check the evil. It is a question of honour for each member of the Cabinet individually; but the public mischief of any such breach of our implied engagement as that to which you refer is enormous.

I do not think Wellesley's advice ' to fight Russia now ' is sound. She is exhausted in the sense that she cannot go on fighting without great sacrifices. But she is not so exhausted as to be unable to make head against any great national danger—such as a war with England. Nor would the Turks be of any great value as allies. Enrolled as troops under our officers they would fight admirably: but such an arrangement on an extensive scale will never be permitted, so long as the Turkish Government retains a shadow of independence. Under their own officers, they would be of little use. I see therefore no reason for agreeing with Wellesley that this is a good moment for seeking to bring on the inevitable collision with Russia, if it be inevitable.

And there are particular circumstances in our own case that make it unsuitable. Owing to financial difficulties our Indian Army is in a less efficient state than will probably be the case some years hence: and the position of Cabul is a difficulty. Our English Army has not had time to accumulate reserves under Cardwell's system. Our manufacturing industries are depressed: and profoundly averse to war. And, owing to the peculiar condition of the Continent, Austria, our natural ally in such a question, has been seduced from us, at least for the moment.

The national feeling here, though strongly partial to the Turk, shrinks from war; and I think with a true instinct. Of course, it is possible that events may take such a turn as to force us into war ultimately: but it will be unpopular, and unprofitable. . . .

To Queen Victoria.

10, Downing St., *Jan.* 2, '78.— . . . Cabinet resolved to
reply to the Russian message. Substance of that reply;
that Turkey had never asked for an armistice; nevertheless,
if Russia deemed an armistice indispensable to the commencement of negotiations for peace, England would convey the
wish of Russia to Turkey: at the same time remarking, that
the armistice should be settled by the two Governments,
not by the commanders of forces in the field. Military men
decide on truces, not on armistices. The exchange of prisoners,
the surrender of a post, are fit subjects for truces, but when
we have to decide on the affairs of Empires—on a state of
conditions both in Europe and Asia, there were political
considerations involved which Cabinets could alone decide.

This must be answered and will keep the negotiations
going, and accustom Courts, and people in general, to the idea
of peace. After this, we discussed the amount of the vote,
and the manner it should be raised, and then Lord Salisbury
raised the question, What we should say we were going to do
with the money ? Hereupon a discussion took place, which
was highly satisfactory. Even Lord Carnarvon did not cavil.
And Lord Salisbury got into an argument as to the respective
advantages of occupying Gallipoli or Constantinople.

On the whole well pleased, but so tired, having been at
ceaseless work all day, that he must apologise for this un-
gainly and imperfect note. He is not without hope of making
some arrangement with the Irish Members. They are Anti-
Russian, and pleased with the release of some Fenian prisoners.
Will write more at another time—but a good chance.

The situation with which the Cabinet had to deal at
the end of 1877 and the beginning of 1878 was full of
difficulty. The Russians, having cleared out of their way
the obstacle of Plevna, had taken Sofia and were steadily
advancing on Constantinople; they claimed, as the
masters of victorious troops, the full right of action, and
showed no disposition to accept the offer of mediation,
made by the British Government. The Turks, on the
other hand, first applied to the Powers in general to
intervene on their behalf, and then, being met by an
ostentatious refusal on the part of Germany, appealed
especially to England. It was obviously an extremely
delicate situation and one in which Ministers, if they

committed themselves to any public utterance, ought
to measure their words. But one Cabinet Minister, whose
attitude on the Eastern Question had from the first
caused Beaconsfield grave uneasiness, had no doubts; and
on his way to the Cabinet of January 2, just described,
'without seeing a single colleague,' as his chief wrote to
Lady Chesterfield, made a speech which had a lamentable
effect. Replying to a deputation of South African
merchants, Carnarvon expressed his total dissent from
the idea that Russia's rejection of our peace overtures
conveyed 'any affront or insult' to England. He hoped
we should not 'lash ourselves up into a nervous apprehension for so-called British honour and British interests.'
Nobody, he added, in this country was 'insane enough
to desire a repetition' of the Crimean War.

Beaconsfield had long resented Carnarvon's dissentient
attitude in Cabinet, and he condemned the speech
very plainly next day, making no secret of his indifference
whether his colleague went or stayed.

To Queen Victoria.

10, DOWNING STREET, *Jan.* 3, '78.—. . . Lord Beaconsfield
felt it his duty to commence the proceedings of the Cabinet
to-day by calling its attention to the speech of Lord Carnarvon,
made yesterday to a deputation of the S. African merchants,
and which might have proceeded from Mr. Gladstone. Lord
Carnarvon attempted but feebly to justify every expression
he had used, and ended by saying that, after the grave censure
of the Prime Minister, he must consider, whether he could
continue his connection with the Administration.

There was a silence; then the Lord Chancellor, in a concilia
tory spirit, regretted the speech of Lord Carnarvon.

Lord Derby trusted he would not retire at this moment, as
a false interpretation would be placed on his conduct, and
that no one was justified in retiring in the midst of negotiations, except on a strong ground, and clear principle.

Lord Salisbury vindicated his friend on every head, especially
in thinking the Crimean War 'an insane policy.' He spoke
very warmly and incisively. Lord John Manners answered
him with great spirit, showing that this speech was a continuation of the same system, which had dictated the telegram of

Count Schouvaloff to the Emperor, mentioned by Wellesley, and that it was one entirely encouraging to Russia in all her designs. Mr. Secretary Hardy spoke shortly, but well. The Chancellor of the Exchequer more at length, and in a most satisfactory manner.

Lord Derby made another effort to obtain from Lord Carnarvon, that he would not persist in his withdrawal. This was not encouraged by the Prime Minister, and the matter dropped. The Cabinet then considered, and settled, the armistice reply to Prince Gortchakoff, which was telegraphed this afternoon, and then Lord Carnarvon had to rise and leave the Cabinet for Osborne. . . .

To Lady Bradford.

10, DOWNING STREET, *Jan.* 3, 1878.—Grateful to you for yr. letter wh. I did not deserve from my silence; but Cabinets every day, unceasing labor otherwise, and much anxiety really prevent one—I shd. say disqualify one—from doing anything so agreeable as to communicate with you.

Carnarvon, when I thought all was right, has made a terrible escapade, a speech worthy of Gladstone. . . .

He has gone to-day, after the Cabinet, to Osborne. I don't envy him his audience. It is some time since he has been at Court, the Queen being greatly offended with him, and I asked H.M., as a personal favor to myself, to invite him ! Alas ! he is in the hands of Lyddon and Froude ! and consults them on all occasions and on all matters. . . .

I have been obliged to speak my mind to him at last, and do not know whether I shall meet him again as a colleague, and do not much care. . . .

Jan. 6.—Nothing is yet settled : all confused and perplexing. But, as there is a Cabinet to-morrow, it is impossible that the decision shd. be delayed.

Tho' all his colleagues think his conduct indefensible, and calculated to produce the utmost evil, nearly all of them are on their knees to him not to resign. They fear further ruptures, and think, with cause, that only one interpretation can be placed on such an incident—that we are going at once to war with Russia ! At this moment, Parliament on the eve of meeting, there wd. be of course the most factious agitation in the country, and instead of being welcomed by the H. of C., carrying our measures, and securing peace, we shd. probably be defeated or weakly supported, and have to dissolve Parliament ! . . .

Jan. 7.—I have not a moment, but you will like to know, that all is well arranged. The Cabinet remains unbroken,

and can show a front at this critical time.   The mischief done
cannot be recalled, but a break-up on the eve of Parlt. wd.
have been perilous and perhaps fatal. . . .

The Queen expressed herself very strongly to Carnarvon,
both in speech and in writing; and Salisbury, whose
defence of his friend in Cabinet sprang from chivalry,
and not from approval, did his best to persuade him to
reasonableness.   'Except brave John Manners and
haughty Sir Michael,' wrote the Prime Minister to the
Queen, 'Lord Beaconsfield believes all his colleagues
are on their knees to Lord Carnarvon to stay.   The
Cabinet wants a little of your Majesty's fire.'   The
difficulty was accordingly patched up for the moment.

To Queen Victoria.

10, DOWNING ST., *Jan.* 7, '78.—. . . On the opening of the
Cabinet this morning, Lord Carnarvon made some graceful,
slightly conciliatory remarks on the scene which occurred at
the last meeting; and, then, he asked leave to read a paper
which he had drawn up, so that his views might not be misunderstood in the future.

When he had finished, Prime Minister said, that Lord Carnarvon had not withdrawn from his colleagues, for two reasons.
1st, That in the present critical state of affairs, his secession
might be injurious to the Queen's service: 2nd, that we appreciated a colleague, whose administration of his office had
added to the reputation of Her Majesty's Government: but
that Lord Beaconsfield could not now enter into any criticism
or controversy on the points contained in a carefully prepared
paper, but that, if Lord Carnarvon furnished him with a copy
he would, of course, consider it, and in a friendly spirit.

There the matter ended with a sympathetic murmur from
all, and with some incoherent but well-meant expressions from
Lord Derby.   Then the reply to Prince Gortchakoff was
settled, and sent to your Majesty for approval.

Then, after some feeble opposition from Lord Derby, the
Cabinet resolved on the amount of the vote of credit, viz.,
five millions.

Lord Beaconsfield very much thanks your Majesty for the
copies of the Carnarvon correspondence.   He thought your
Majesty's letter admirable, and he has no doubt it influenced
the person to whom it was addressed. . . .

This Carnarvon incident was only one of many difficulties in the Cabinet, which were not finally overcome
till the end of March. 'Cabinets every day, and unceasing anxiety and toil,' wrote Beaconsfield to Lady Bradford
on January 14; 'the confusion is so great that it seems
the end of the world' was his despairing wail three days
later; to Lady Chesterfield on January 22 he wrote,
'The Cabinet really sits *en permanence.*' In reading
Beaconsfield's letters to the Queen describing the deliberations over which he presided we should, however, make
some allowance for his artistic and impressionable temperament, prone to exaggerate both failures and successes.

To Queen Victoria.

10, DOWNING ST., *Jan.* 9, '78.—. . . The draft of your
Majesty's speech was submitted to the Cabinet this day,
having been in their hands for four and twenty hours previously.

Lord Derby attacked it in every way, in a very elaborate
address. He said it was a menace to Russia. Lord Salisbury
followed in the same vein. To the consternation, but concealed consternation, of the Prime Minister, the Lord Chancellor too much agreed with them. Mr. Secretary Cross gave
a faint note and dwelt on the depression of trade, and the
fearful decline in the revenue, which was continuous.

Mr. Secretary Hardy touched only on some technical military points, but gave no assistance on the great issues. The
Chancellor of the Exchequer was able and true.

Lord Derby then proposed that the draft should be withdrawn and another prepared.

Lord Carnarvon supported him. They receded from all
the engagements, which they had accepted three weeks or so
ago.

It was, then, necessary for the Prime Minister to make a
great effort, and to say, that, late as it was, he would not meet
Parliament unless they were prepared to fulfil their engagements. Why had they agreed to call Parliament together ?
Why was it meeting ?

A sharp half hour, but, ultimately, they adopted the speech,
exchanging words, but still adhering to the three great points :
1. Negotiations for peace, 2. Meeting of Parliament, 3. Increase
of Armaments.

Lord Beaconsfield will not be able to get a becoming copy
of the Speech for your Majesty's consideration and sanction.

by this post.   He will send it to-morrow with his original draft. He was nearly alone in the Cabinet, Lord John Manners and Chancellor of the Exchequer alone really supporting him. It is evident, that, besides the opposition we have always had to encounter from the Russian party in the Cabinet, Lord Beaconsfield's colleagues generally are much affected by the depressed state of trade and the great fall in the revenue last week, the commencement of a quarter in which it was hoped it would rally.   It only shows, we ought to have met Parliament on the 7th of this month, as Lord Beaconsfield originally proposed.   He doubts whether, if the resolutions he brought forward some few weeks ago were now recommended to his colleagues, they would adopt them.   They take a dark view of the condition and prospects of the country.   But they cannot now recede.

From Queen Victoria.

OSBORNE, *Jan.* 10, '78.—The Queen is really distressed at the low tone which this country is inclined to hold.   She thinks every opportunity ought to be taken and every effort made to show them that the Empire and even their low sordid love of gain will suffer permanently and most seriously if this goes on.   The country should be frightened as to the results. Could not Lord Beaconsfield get something to be written, tho' the *Daily Telegraph, Pall Mall* and *Post* are very strong in the right sense, to instruct the blinded country in this respect ?   She feels she cannot, as she before said, remain the Sovereign of a country that is letting itself down to kiss the feet of the great barbarians, the retarders of all liberty and civilisation that exists.   Her son feels more strongly than herself even.   She is utterly ashamed of the Cabinet, but delighted to see and hear Sir Stafford is so right and sound. . . . Be firm and you will rally your party round you.   The Queen means to speak very strongly to Count Beust.   It can do no harm; it may do good.   Oh, if the Queen were a man, she would like to go and give those Russians, whose word one cannot believe, such a beating !   We shall never be friends again till we have it out.   This the Queen feels sure of.

The Queen is so grieved at these constant annoyances to which Lord Beaconsfield is exposed and at the trouble which yesterday's Cabinet caused him, which he so well describes in the letter received to-day, for which she thanks him very much.   Lord Derby is the real misfortune; another Foreign Secretary, who felt as he ought, would support the Prime Minister, [and] would carry the others with him. . . .

II.   35*

'It is something to serve such a Sovereign!' wrote Beaconsfield on receipt of this 'spirited' letter. He, no less than the Queen, felt that, in view of the rapid advance of Russian troops in Thrace,[1] some definite step in the nature of armed precaution must be taken on the spot; and he summoned the Cabinet on January 12 to decide whether, considering Layard's despatches, the time had not come for England to occupy the Dardanelles. Her Majesty wrote a memorandum to impress on the Cabinet the importance of the occasion. The meeting was noteworthy, as Salisbury then, for the first time, took a lead among his colleagues in support of his chief's policy.

Memorandum by Queen Victoria.

OSBORNE, *Jan.* 11, '78.—The state of the Eastern Question has become most serious and events are following each other with such rapidity and developing such fearful proportions, that what was decided even two or three days ago seems no longer of much avail.

The news of the surrender of the Turkish Army at Shipka yesterday and of the intention not to defend Adrianople to-day show that Constantinople may be attacked very soon, and if there is a panic, *not* defended!!

We must therefore stand by what we have always declared, viz., that any advance on Constantinople would free us from our position of neutrality. Were these mere empty words? If so, England must abdicate her position and retire from having any longer any voice in the Councils of Europe and sink down to a third-rate power!

But the Queen feels sure that there is not one amongst her Ministers who, whatever their individual feelings for Turkey and against war may be, would wish us not to support the honour and dignity of Great Britain, and in that case she calls upon them to determine at once what means should instantly be taken to prevent Constantinople from being attacked, which we have repeatedly stated would be tantamount to a *casus belli.*

There is not a moment to be lost or the whole of our policy of centuries, of our honour as a great European Power, will have received an irreparable blow! The Queen has not a

---

[1] 'The Turks have lost another army—that of the Shipka Pass,' Beaconsfield told Lady Bradford on January 10; '40 battalions surrounded and surrendered! I think the curtain will now fall.'

doubt what the feeling of the nation would be, if the real danger is known and explained.

The Queen wishes Lord Beaconsfield to read this to the Cabinet to-morrow.

To Queen Victoria.

10, DOWNING ST., *Jan.* 12, '78.—. . . A Cabinet of three hours, most stormy.   The proposition was to send fleet to the Dardanelles and forces to Boulair, if Sultan permitted.   Lord Derby violently opposed the proposition.   Ultimately Lord Salisbury proposed that Mr. Layard should be instructed to ask permission of the Sultan for 'the fleet to anchor in the Straits,' the language used by Mr. Layard; and that in reply to P. Gortchakoff's unanswered note on the subject of 'British Interests' and their more complete definition, the Prince should be requested to give an assurance to the English Government, that the Russians would not occupy Gallipoli.

After long reflection, and extreme stubbornness, Lord Derby rose from his seat, and said 'that he could not sanction any projects of the kind, and that he must retire from the ministry.' Lord Salisbury said then, that, if Lord Derby retired, he must retire too, as he felt the differences of opinion in the Cabinet were insurmountable; that the P. Minister, by his powers of conciliation, had kept them together for four years, but he felt it was hopeless; that he had only suggested the compromise to keep them, if possible, together at this moment, as he felt it would be disastrous to the Queen's service to break up now.

The Lord Chancellor asked Lord Derby what he proposed as an alternative answer to Mr. Layard, but as usual Lord Derby had nothing to propose.   He opposes everything, proposes nothing.   The P. Minister said that Lord Derby and those who agreed with him, ought to have retired three weeks ago, and not consented to the summoning of Parliament. By their remaining, but retiring now, they had deceived the Queen.

Lord Beaconsfield ought to have told your Majesty that the proceedings commenced by his reading your Majesty's letter.   The whole of the Cabinet, with the exception of Lord Carnarvon, much supported the P. Minister.

Lord Derby at length accepted the proposal of Lord Salisbury, but Lord Carnarvon had the impertinence of violently protesting against it, even after that.

As the telegrams in discussion were most urgent, Lord Beaconsfield sanctioned their being sent from the Council-chamber, on the ground, that he was sufficiently acquainted, from hourly correspondence, with your Majesty's pleasure and opinions on the subject, to venture on that step. If he erred, he trusts humbly your Majesty will pardon him.

Layard's despatches were not the only appeals which reached England from Constantinople. On January 10 the Sultan telegraphed personally to the Queen, begging Her Majesty for her mediation with a view to arranging an armistice and the discussion of the preliminaries of peace. The Queen, accordingly, with the unanimous approval of the Cabinet—'almost the only occasion,' wrote Beaconsfield, ' on which they have been unanimous ' —telegraphed to the Tsar on January 14, communicating the fact of the Sultan's appeal, and expressing the hope that Alexander, as one sincerely desirous of peace, would accelerate the negotiations. The Tsar must have resented this direct approach, as he replied next day with a message which the Queen and Beaconsfield not unnaturally found ' unsatisfactory,' ' rude,' and ' vulgar '; but which the Minister thought indicated that Russia was finding unexpected obstacles in her path.

The Emperor Alexander to Queen Victoria.

Your Majesty does me justice in saying that I desire peace, but I wish it to be serious and lasting. The Commanders-in-Chief of my armies in Europe and Asia know the conditions on which a suspension of hostilities can be granted.

The Emperor's reply was not calculated to reassure the Cabinet as to the intentions of the Russian ruler and his victorious Generals. Beaconsfield accordingly pressed forward in the Cabinet of Tuesday, January 15, the scheme of sending the fleet to the Dardanelles, though by the Cabinet of the following day, mainly in consequence of the Sultan's objections, the order was held in abeyance. Carnarvon tendered to Beaconsfield a provisional resignation, to take effect directly the order was sent; and Derby also, who at this critical time was laid up with illness, and unable to attend Cabinets, wrote from his sickbed, strongly protesting against the policy. ' More I think of

the Dardanelles business, less I like it,' he wrote on
January 15; and again next day, 'I cannot put too
strongly the objections which I feel to the sending up of
the fleet.' He forwarded a minute which was read at
the Cabinet on January 16, and in which he summed up
his objections in the sentence, ' I object to the proposed
step as contrary to Treaty, as increasing the risk of collision with Russia, as tending to irritate rather than to
conciliate, and as being, so far as I can judge, useless,
if not dangerous, in a military point of view.'

Hardy's diary gives us succinct accounts of the varying
decisions of these two Cabinets, and of the motives which
inspired them. ' Jan. 15.—We agreed to communications to Austria to draw closer to her, to Loftus to urge
an answer about Gallipoli, to Austria as to association
with us in entering the Dardanelles. Salisbury, worn out
by Russian duplicity, was more eager than anyone for
the last action.' ' Jan. 16.—Beust's communications as
to Austria, the Grand Vizier's to the fleet, backed by
Layard—Russia's more than half promise not to go to
Gallipoli—changed all our purposes of yesterday. Austria
is shaky, but we must go with her as she urges.'

Beaconsfield was very impatient with Carnarvon and
his provisional resignation.

From Lord Carnarvon.

16, Bruton St., Jan. 18, '78.—On Monday last, the 14th
inst., I wrote to you requesting you to be good enough to submit my resignation to the Queen, as soon as the order for
moving the fleet to the Dardanelles should be given. I afterwards received a message from you through Mr. M. Corry to
the effect that subsequent telegrams had induced you to
change your mind; and on attending the Cabinet on Tuesday,
the following day—as I did to prevent any rumours which
might be injurious to the Government arising—I understood
that they, as well as you, saw reason to abandon the course
which had been agreed upon.

I am very glad that so sound a decision has been come to—
whatever the reasons on which it may have been founded—
but looking to the fact that my resignation, though provisional,
is in your hands, and to the serious nature of such a fact,

I think it is my duty to state, in a manner which cannot be mistaken, what I conceive to be my present position.

When at the last Cabinet held I stated the course which I had taken in placing my provisional resignation in your hands, no opinion was expressed or comment made by you, or as far as I remember by any other member of the Cabinet; and therefore it is the more necessary that there should be no room for misapprehension as to my past or present action.

I have no desire to separate myself from colleagues with whom I have acted on terms of great personal regard and goodwill: I am sensible of the public inconvenience which would arise from discord or open difference of opinion at this moment; and I am ready now, as I hope I have been on former occasions, to modify or concede my views on points of detail, in order to secure a general harmony of action among the members of the Government.

But I have been led to consider carefully the events of the last few weeks and the divergences of opinion which have unfortunately developed themselves amongst us; and I cannot conceal from myself that those differences have been very considerable on a question, where it is of the utmost importance to the country that the Government should be one and undivided.

Taking therefore all this into account I avail myself of this opportunity to place clearly on paper the opinion—even though you and my colleagues are already familiar with it— that I am not prepared in present circumstances, or in circumstances similar to them, to agree to any armed intervention or any course of a similar nature. I see no reason as yet why the question at issue should pass out of the realm of diplomacy. Further, the vote of credit or the increase in Army and Navy estimates (whichever it may be) is a measure which I consider useful as a means of strengthening our diplomacy at this juncture; but I do not contemplate the application of any aid granted by Parliament to the purposes of a foreign expedition, unless circumstances should change in a manner and to a degree wholly beyond my present anticipations. The anxiety which I own to have felt on this subject has been greatly relieved by the explicit language of the Chancellor of the Exchequer, in which he explained that the Government would not, until it was clear that the Russian conditions are unsatisfactory, make any proposals for the increase of armaments.

Relying therefore upon this as a trustworthy exposition of the views of the Government I feel that I may for the present content myself with the statement, which I have endeavoured to express as clearly as possible in reference to my own position.

1878]   MEETING OF PARLIAMENT   1095

But it remains for you to consider whether this view, which is satisfactory to me, and on which my continuance in office depends, is also satisfactory to you and my colleagues. I shall be glad to hear from you at your convenience.

To Lord Carnarvon.

10, DOWNING STREET, *Jan.* 18, '78.—I cd. not answer your letter this morning, as my carriage was at the door, and I was obliged to keep an engagement.

You are in error in supposing that you wrote to me on Monday last, the 14th. It was on Tuesday, the 15th, that you wrote to me a letter wh. I received on Wednes[day], the 16th, just before the early meeting of the Cabinet.

As yr. letter was founded on assumed circ[umstanc]es wh. did not exist, or wh. had been removed, I thought it was only a friendly act—and it was in a spirit of thoro' comradeship I did it—to send to you a gent[leman] who possessed my entire confidence, and who was an intimate acquaintance of your own, to apprise you of this, and to beg you to consider the letter *non avenue,* and therefore not to mention the subject to our colleagues, already sufficiently harassed with such matters.

You took another course, wh. I regret, if only for the cause of its occasioning you to write so many letters and I to answer them.

There is no adequate cause for yr. tendering the resignation of yr. office at this moment, and I shd. be quite unable to inform the Queen what was the reason of yr. retirement. These are not times when statesmen shd. be too susceptible. We have enough to encounter without wasting our energies in contests among ourselves.

I shall not therefore submit yr. resignation to H.M. Such a step wd. deprive me of a colleague I value, and at any rate it shd. be reserved for a period when there is a very important difference of opinion between us, wh. at present does not seem to be the case.

While Cabinet councils were thus distracted, Ministers were forced to make declarations in the open by the meeting of Parliament on Thursday, January 17. The Queen's Speech, on the draft of which the Cabinet had found so much difficulty in agreeing, narrated the progress of Russia's victorious arms in Europe and Asia, the appeal of the Porte to England, and the fact that, through British

mediation, Russia and Turkey were in communication as
to peace.   Then followed the critical paragraph.

Hitherto, so far as the war has proceeded, neither of the
belligerents has infringed the conditions on which my neutrality is founded, and I willingly believe that both parties
are desirous to respect them, so far as it may be in their power.
So long as these conditions are not infringed, my attitude
will continue the same.   But I cannot conceal from myself
that, should hostilities be unfortunately prolonged, some
unexpected occurrence may render it incumbent on me to
adopt measures of precaution.   Such measures could not be
taken without adequate preparation, and I trust to the libera-
lity of my Parliament to supply the means which may be
required for that purpose.

This warning was enforced by Beaconsfield in his
peroration when he spoke in the debate on the Address.
'If we are called upon to vindicate our rights and to
defend the interests of our country; if our present hopes
and purposes of peace are baffled; if there be circumstances which demand that we should appeal to Parliament again and again for means to vindicate the honour
of the realm, and to preserve and maintain the interests
of the empire, I am sure that Her Majesty's Government
will never hesitate to take that course.'   But, in general,
the Duke of Connaught's report of the speech to the
Queen was well founded: 'When he sat down everybody
was as wise as they were before and the Opposition were
terribly nettled.'   His main theme was to show how
absurd was the lament of the Opposition about England's
isolation and want of influence.   Why, he pointed out, the
only Power which had done anything was England.   It
was she who defeated the Berlin memorandum, who called
the Constantinople Conference into existence, who obtained an armistice for Serbia, and who had interfered
to bring about the present negotiation between Russia
and Turkey.   A peppery attack which Argyll made upon
Beaconsfield gave Salisbury an opportunity, in Derby's
absence from illness, to defend the policy of his chief.
He challenged Parliament either to give its implicit

confidence to the Government, and so enable it to act with force in these great issues, or to replace it.

To Queen Victoria.

10, DOWNING STREET, *Jan.* 18, '78.—. . . It seems universally admitted, that last night in Parliament redounded much to the credit of your Majesty's Government.   The debate in the Lords was well sustained, and its not least remarkable feature was the vigorous, loyal and uncompromising support given to the Prime Minister by Lord Salisbury.

The observations of the Chancellor of the Exchequer, to which your Majesty refers, have attracted remark, but the general interpretation of them by the House of Commons and the country, is, that they were a challenge to Russia, that if the terms of peace were not such as England had a right to expect, we should be prepared to go to war with that Power, and this is the interpretation that Sir Stafford accepts !

The communications with Austria are constant, and promising, and Lord Tenterden informs Lord Beaconsfield that M. de Harcourt [1] intimated to-day, that France was disposed to move and apprise Russia, that the Danube and the Straits were European questions.

Lord Beaconsfield hopes that your Majesty may not suffer from all this anxiety, and absolute and extreme labor, which your Majesty undergoes.   He wishes, often, he was at your Majesty's side to soothe and to aid and to be your Majesty's Secretary as well as your Minister.   That cannot be, but let him hope that his distant devotion is not without solace, and, even tho' removed and apart, his humble energies may, in some degree, aid.

In the midst of this agitated time the Queen was anxious to follow up the mark of confidence in Beaconsfield which she had given in her December visit to Hughenden by a further striking act of favour.   'Let Lord Derby and Lord Carnarvon go, and be very firm,' she wrote on January 20, from Osborne.   'A divided Cabinet is of no use.   The Queen would wish to confer the vacant Garter on Lord Beaconsfield as a mark of her confidence and support.   She and the country at large have the greatest confidence in him.'   But Beaconsfield felt at once that this was a very unsuitable moment for him to accept

---

[1] French Ambassador.

honours and decorations. Besides, as he told Lady
Bradford, he had Melbourne's reason for declining, that
he did not want to bribe himself. Her Majesty thought
her Minister's letter declining the honour ' a beautiful
one—she almost expected it; but hopes to bestow it on
some future occasion.'

To Queen Victoria.

10, DOWNING ST., *Jan.* 21, '78.—He is deeply touched,
almost overcome, by the gracious expression of your Majesty's
wish to confer on him the high dignity of the Garter, and
especially as a mark of your Majesty's confidence and support.

But with the profoundest deference he would venture to
observe that this great distinction would only add to the
jealousy and envy of which he is already the object and that
it might be better to reserve it for some one on whom your
Majesty could less depend than on himself, and whose support
might add strength to your Majesty's Government.

There is no honor and no reward that with him can ever
equal the possession of your Majesty's kind thoughts. All
his own thoughts and feelings and duties and affections are
now concentrated in your Majesty, and he desires nothing
more for his remaining years than to serve your Majesty or,
if that service ceases, to live still on its memory as a period
of his existence most interesting and fascinating.

The Queen's gracious offer reached Beaconsfield on
the morning of a day—Monday, January 21—when he
had determined to put his authority to the test, and
obtain his colleagues' assent to a definitely forward
policy. For the first time during these troubles, there
was a prospect for England of a serious ally in resisting
Russian advance. Neither in the Reichstadt understanding of 1876, nor in the Vienna Treaty of 1877, had
Austria carried her policy of hypothetical partition so
far as to admit of Russian occupation of Constantinople
and the Straits. She, like England, was at last gravely
alarmed that this danger was imminent, and she seemed
to be ready to join England in preventing it. Russia
still concealed her terms while daily advancing her
military position. Beaconsfield accordingly felt that the

moment had come to burst the shackles that had bound
his Cabinet, and in three sittings on Monday, Tuesday,
and Wednesday, the 21st, 22nd, and 23rd, he pressed for
and obtained a decision.

To Queen Victoria.

10, DOWNING ST., *Jan.* 21, '78.—Lord Beaconsfield . . . proposed to-day to the Cabinet that we should offer to Austria
a defensive alliance with this country; if necessary, a pecuniary aid, provided she would mobilise a sufficient force upon
her frontier, and join us in an identic note to Russia. Our
fleet, of course, to go up to Constantinople.

The discussion was fiery. Ten members of the Cabinet
warmly adopted the proposals, Lord Derby fiercely opposing
them, and Lord Carnarvon feebly.

No one supported them with more energy than Lord Salisbury, whose conduct throughout was admirable.

Ultimately, Lord Derby agreed to the identic note, and a
draft of it was drawn up and telegraphed to Vienna, and the
Cabinet is to meet and decide to-morrow on the main question, at 2 o'clock, when we expect an answer from Sir [*sic*]
Buchanan. Lord Beaconsfield will see Count Beust this evening,
and has great hopes, that he shall be able to settle everything.

He shall not hesitate to undertake to His Excellency, that
your Majesty's Government will adopt these measures, and if
Lord Derby cannot approve them, he must at once resign.

The Austrian reply, which was of an indecisive character,
came in time for the Council of Wednesday the 23rd;
and Beaconsfield, recognising that important results
must follow from the meeting, obtained that morning
by telegram in advance the Queen's authority to accept
resignations in order 'to prevent second thoughts.'
Before six he reported to Her Majesty that the fleet
had been ordered to proceed immediately to Constantinople; that the Chancellor of the Exchequer would give
notice in the House of Commons of a Vote of Credit; and
that the Cabinet was resolute, except Derby and Carnarvon, whose resignations he expected at once. His
expectations were fulfilled in both cases. Derby's letter
was manly and touching.

From Lord Derby.

FOREIGN OFFICE, *Jan.* 23, 1878.

MY DEAR DISRAELI,—After our repeated discussions in Cabinet on the question of sending up the fleet to Constantinople, and the decision which was come to this afternoon, you will feel as I do that only one result is possible so far as I am concerned.

The question on which we were unable to agree is obviously one of grave importance; it is certain to be eagerly and frequently discussed both in and out of Parliament; the Foreign Secretary more than any other Minister would in the ordinary course of things be charged with the duty of defending the decision taken; and as I cannot think it, or say that I think it, a safe or wise one, it is clear that no alternative is left me except to ask you to allow me to retire from the post I hold.

I deeply and sincerely regret that we should differ on any point of policy; but two considerations reconcile me in some measure to a step which is quite as painful to me personally as it can be to you. You will get on better with a thoroughly harmonious Cabinet; and you are so strong in the Lords that the loss of two colleagues will not practically affect you there. I may add that the incessant anxiety of the last two years has made me often doubt of late—all questions of political difference set aside—whether I should long be capable of even moderately efficient service in an office which at times like these admits of no rest from responsibility and labour.

It is needless to say that whatever I can do, out of office, to support your Government will be done by me, both as an obligation of public duty and from feelings of private friendship which no lapse of time or change of circumstances will alter. Believe me always most sincerely yrs., DERBY.

Beaconsfield immediately obtained the Queen's permission to offer the succession to the Foreign Office to Salisbury, whose thoroughgoing adhesion to his chief's policy had been a marked feature of recent Cabinets; and Hicks Beach, who had been a stalwart throughout, became Colonial Secretary. The orders were sent to the fleet to enter the Dardanelles, and Layard was instructed to inform the Sultan, and secure that the forts did not fire on the ships. Northcote duly notified the House of Commons of a Vote of Credit to be moved on the following Monday. Beaconsfield felt he could now go full steam ahead; and his Royal Mistress was immensely satisfied and relieved.

Robert Third Marquis of Salisbury
from the portrait at Hughenden

To Queen Victoria.

10, DOWNING ST., *Jan.* 24.—Lord Beaconsfield . . . encloses letters received this morning from Lord Carnarvon and Lord Derby. It is the policy of Lord Salisbury that they oppose. Until Lord Salisbury was permanently detached from these noble Lords, it was impossible to bring the Cabinet to any firm or general decision. Directly Lord Salisbury declared, which he did in a most uncompromising view, against Russian aggression, the Cabinet divided ten to twelve in favor of a decided policy. Lord Salisbury is most firmly anti-Russian. His experience in the India Office has taught him this. His diplomatic promenade last year in Europe has given him personal acquaintance with all its leading statesmen. He is a man of commanding ability and station and Lord Beaconsfield thoroughly believes that your Majesty will find in him a most efficient, devoted and agreeable Minister. He therefore earnestly prays your Majesty to appoint him Secretary of State. It will show that your Majesty's Government is determined.

Lord Beaconsfield is touched by Lord Derby's letter. It closes a public connection of a quarter of a century, softened too by much private intimacy. Lord Salisbury also is detached from his intimate friend.

These are trials of public life, but everything must yield to duty, especially at an imperial crisis like the present.

He begs your Majesty to have the kindness to telegraph permission to the two retiring Ministers to make their parliamentary statements to-morrow.

He thanks your Majesty for your Majesty's gracious messages and enquiries. He is glad to say he is fairly well, but the tension of the present moment is extreme, and the thought and labor are unceasing. He would willingly write more, but he must now hurry down to the House of Lords, and has been the whole morning in conference and consultation.

From Queen Victoria.

OSBORNE, *Jan.* 24, '78.—The Queen must write a few lines to Lord Beaconsfield, to express her immense satisfaction and relief at the intelligence conveyed in his two cyphers. To the last, she feared Lord Derby would stay and she really believes that next to the agitation and behaviour of the Opposition, he has been the chief obstacle to all action and moreover has tried Lord Beaconsfield dreadfully, and often paralysed the whole Government, in the most lamentable way. His inaction and delay on every occasion and total want of energy and purpose, have been such that, irrespective of this question, he had become totally unfit to be Foreign Secretary.

What has led to this, at the last, after the scenes which Lord Beaconsfield described ? The announcement in the House of Commons is also most important.

In short the Queen cannot sufficiently thank her wise and kind Prime Minister, for the firmness and energy displayed, which will yet carry us on to where we should be.

Under these circumstances, Lord Salisbury is no doubt an excellent appointment and his great ability and readiness as a speaker will make him invaluable as Foreign Secretary. She wonders whom he will submit as Secretary for the Colonies.

The Queen trusts Lord Beaconsfield will not be the worse for all this excitement and anxiety. . . .

These resignations and Lord Salisbury's appointment with other strong measures will have an immense effect in Russia.

The satisfaction and relief of Queen and Minister were premature. Carnarvon's resignation was indeed final; but, after a few days' uncertainty and confusion, Derby, at Beaconsfield's request and with Her Majesty's reluctant acquiescence, resumed the seals of the Foreign Office, which he held for a couple of months longer. It is a curious story. On Thursday, January 24, the day after the decisive Cabinet, when the orders to the fleet had only just been despatched, there came a telegram from Layard announcing that the terms or bases of peace had been agreed to, and that the last of them was that the question of the Straits should be settled between ' the Congress and the Emperor of Russia.' Northcote has given us, in his memorandum, a vivacious account of the way in which this news affected Ministers.

This fell amongst us like a bombshell. Our justification for sending up the fleet was that we feared that a private arrangement would be made about the Straits between the Turks and Russians, to the exclusion and the detriment of other Powers; and here were the Russian terms of peace, by which this question was to be reserved to be settled by a Congress ! What could we say to justify ourselves ? And how much would not the difficulty of the situation be increased by the emphatic dissent and resignation of Lord Derby ? After a little hasty consultation with those of our colleagues who were in the House of Commons, I went up to Downing

Street, taking Smith[1] with me. We found Lord Beaconsfield
in bed, but quite able to talk the matter over with us. The
result was that we agreed to stop Admiral Hornby before he
entered the Dardanelles, where he had been led to expect that
he might find orders. Smith despatched an Admiralty telegram at once. It was not in time to stop the fleet, but it
brought it back again to the entrance of the Straits. Looking
back, I think this was the greatest mistake we made in the
whole business; but at the moment we were all agreed on it.
The next day came a correction of the telegram; it was not
between the Emperor and the Congress that the question of
the Straits was to be settled, but between the Emperor and the
Sultan ! How we gnashed our teeth !

The original impression of the moderation of Russia's
terms, which Ministers derived from the mistake in
Layard's telegram, was confirmed on the Friday morning
by a minimising statement of them which Schouvaloff—
'no doubt,' wrote Beaconsfield, 'in consequence of the
Parliamentary movements of yesterday '—handed to
Derby. They were considered by the 'Council of Ten,'
as Beaconsfield called the Cabinet minus Derby and
Carnarvon, and were thought more studious of British
than of Austrian interests; but Ministers naturally determined to proceed with the Vote of Credit as a measure of
precaution. Then came Layard's correcting telegram,
which caused the Queen to telegraph at once to her Prime
Minister, ' Do not you agree with me in thinking it highly
desirable that the fleet should still be sent to Constantinople, else we are sure to be duped, which would be fatal ?'

But it would hardly have been dignified to send the fleet
a third order within twenty-four hours, countermanding
the second order and restoring the first. Moreover, the
firm attitude of the Ministry in announcing an immediate
Vote of Credit had already abated Russian pretensions,
and made her produce her terms of peace. The movement of the fleet might perhaps wait for the developments of the next few days; especially as the mere rumour,
as yet unconfirmed, of Derby's resignation had produced
serious domestic difficulties for the Government which

---

[1] First Lord of the Admiralty.

1104   DERBY'S FIRST RESIGNATION   [6, vi

it is strange that Beaconsfield and his colleagues had not foreseen and allowed for. Not only was the head of the house of Stanley a name to conjure with in his native Lancashire, a county which had made a marvellous rally to Conservatism in recent years. But also, throughout the middle classes and in the eyes of the plain man, Derby stood for prudence and commonsense in politics;[1] and the Whips represented to Beaconsfield and Northcote that his defection would shake the confidence of the country and of the party in the soundness of Ministerial policy, and would certainly diminish, and might even imperil, the Government majority on the coming Vote of Credit. Almost the whole of the Ministry, with Northcote and Cairns at their head, pressed these views upon Beaconsfield, who had no choice but to yield to them. It was pointed out that the recall of the order to the fleet gave an obvious opening for accommodation. Carnarvon had resigned because he opposed both the movement of the fleet and the immediate Vote of Credit. Derby had based his resignation on the movement of the fleet alone; and he had left himself a loophole that very Friday afternoon, by abstaining at Beaconsfield's request from any announcement, when Carnarvon gave the House of Lords the detailed story of his own disagreements with his colleagues in the past three weeks. Beaconsfield, when questioned by Granville on the current rumours of Derby's action, could only say that he 'always thought it a high, valuable and ancient privilege of anyone retiring from a Government that he should announce the fact to Parliament himself in the first instance.'

Convinced though he was that Derby's return was in the circumstances desirable, Beaconsfield did not feel that, after the increasing friction of the last eight or nine months, he could make a personal appeal to his old friend. Northcote has told us that a curious reserve had

[1] 'His name affects the country, which does not know his indecision and timidity,' wrote Hardy in his diary on January 28.

lately sprung up between the two men, once so intimate;
' they became shy of speaking directly to each other, and
I was frequently employed as a medium of communication between them.'   It was so now.   ' The chief told
me,' writes Northcote, ' that he could say nothing to
[Derby], but that if I could persuade him to stay he would
be very glad.   He did not think I should succeed. . . .   I
spent the whole of Saturday in negotiation, and have kept
the letters which passed between us, besides writing
which I had one or two long conversations, and on Sunday
morning I was able to report my success.'   It was a difficult job that Northcote undertook; for Salisbury, to the
satisfaction of his colleagues, was prepared to take over
the Secretaryship of State, and yet Derby would accept
no other post.   Only a sense of public duty could have
induced Derby to return; though he spoke of his action
next week in the House of Lords as the most natural
thing in the world; he had resigned because the Cabinet
had taken a decision with which he could not agree, but,
the cause of the difference having disappeared, he had no
hesitation in withdrawing his resignation.

There was one high authority in the State to whom
Derby's return would be very unwelcome.   For many
months the Queen had insisted, with no little reason, in
her communications with Beaconsfield, that the one
indispensable preliminary to a courageous and steadfast
foreign policy was the substitution of another Secretary
of State for Derby, whose person and policy had been
antipathetic to her from early days.   Beaconsfield had
to use all his diplomacy to overcome Her Majesty's
reluctance; his most effectual argument being that Derby's
position, after his return without Carnarvon, would be
one of vastly less influence and importance.

To Queen Victoria.

10, DOWNING ST., *Jan.* 26, '78.

MADAM, AND MOST BELOVED SOVEREIGN,—I fear your
Majesty will never pardon me for writing to your Majesty this

letter, but my duty to your Majesty impels me, and I entreat
your Majesty to deign to extend to me your Majesty's
commanding judgment and infinite indulgence.

It is represented to me, by all the great authorities on these
matters, that the retirement of Lord Derby is producing
disastrous results on the Conservative party, both in Parliament and out of doors. A general disintegration is taking
place.   The vote of Monday next, which would have originally
been carried by a large majority, and on which I depended
as exercising a great influence on Austria and Russia, is, with
this disruption of the Cabinet, not only endangered, but even
problematical.

All the Lancashire members, and others who represent
the chief seats of manufactures and commerce, cannot any
longer be relied on, and our friends in Lancashire, who were
organising public meetings on a large scale to support your
Majesty's Government, and answer the mechanical agitation
of the last month, have telegraphed that, in consequence of
the assumed resignation of Lord Derby, they must relinquish
the attempt.

Almost every member of the Cabinet has pressed strongly
on me to advise your Majesty to retain him, especially the
Lord Chancellor, who has conferred with my leading colleagues
privately. The policy of your Majesty's Government cannot
be changed one whit; and neither Lord Derby, nor anyone else,
can join your Majesty's Government, who is not immediately
prepared to support the vote of six millions, which will be
proposed on Monday.

The Lord Chancellor and others seem to think that Lord
Derby regrets his withdrawal, to which he was induced by the
personal representations of Lord Carnarvon, himself suffering
under depressing illness. Lord Beaconsfield has had no communication with him, and his resignation in the House of Lords
last night was not announced, because, it is believed, he did
not wish to connect that act with the resignation of Lord
Carnarvon.

The Lord Chancellor is of opinion that in this state of affairs,
and indeed in future, the conduct of Lord Derby may be
powerfully controlled by the Cabinet. They will dictate the
instructions to your Majesty's Ministers at the Conference,
and there too your Majesty would be careful to be represented
by those your Majesty can entirely trust.

The Lord Chancellor, also, pointed out that Lord Derby
would now be alone in the Cabinet, for Lord Salisbury is now
entirely in everything with the Prime Minister, and of Lord
Carnarvon we have for ever got rid.

I place, with much agitation and disquietude, these statements before your Majesty for your Majesty's gracious consideration. We are dealing with great and pressing affairs, and the attitude of Austria is critical. If your Majesty deigns to empower me to communicate with Lord Derby, I will obey your Majesty's commands.

I have not over-stated, or colored, anything.

I am greatly distressed in mind, but I am ever your Majesty's devoted BEACONSFIELD.

P.S.—I ought to mention to your Majesty, that if, as some good judges suppose, war, and a dissolution of Parliament, are inevitable, it would be important to retain Lord Derby until the dissolution is over, and then, if necessary, he could retire with impunity.

From Queen Victoria.

OSBORNE, *Jan.* 27, '78.

MY DEAR LORD BEACONSFIELD,—I answer you as you kindly addressed me and as I hope you will do, whenever it is easier, which it undoubtedly is. I will not pretend to conceal from you that I was a good deal startled and annoyed at the contents of your letter. But I have no other object but that of maintaining the dignity and interests of this country, and therefore I am ready to withdraw my acceptance of Lord Derby's resignation, if, in doing so, you are certain of carrying the vote, which is all-important, and if you continue in a firm and decided line. The changes (of course in many cases unavoidable) of purpose, and the necessary silence on the communications with other Powers give an appearance of vacillation and mystery to our conduct which weakens our position in Parliament, and it would be of immense advantage if we could announce to Parliament that we are acting with Austria. The telegrams from Sir A. Buchanan, reporting what the Emperor of Austria said as well as what Count Andrassy said, seem to me so very distinct as to their strong objection to the terms of the Peace (which are outrageous), that she [? I] should think there ought to be no difficulty for the two Governments to act together.

The telegram just received saying that the Porte dare not divulge the bases of Peace, as Russia threatens her, is really an insult to all the Powers who signed the Treaty of Paris and took part in the Conference at Constantinople. Surely something will be done on our part as soon as possible to effect this object ?

To return to Lord Derby: if he would take another office, like Privy Seal—as he says himself he feels unequal to the labour of his present office and his great dilatoriness was one of the most alarming features in his very peculiar character all throughout these two very trying years—it would be far the best. But I offer no objection to any arrangement you think best for the welfare of the country and to strengthen and support the Government. The great dislike to go to war arises no doubt from the ignorance of people, who do not see that, if Russia has all her own way, we shall suffer also in a commercial point of view, and shall still less avoid it in future. A dissolution would be much to be deprecated as it would cause such excitement and agitation and things would be said which would show a division of feeling in the nation of which Russia would take great advantage.

I am so truly grieved at all your trouble and anxiety and at Mr. Corry's illness which at this moment is most unfortunate.

What I want especially to lay stress on, is the necessity of not losing time, and thereby not letting any opportunity slip which might prevent matters getting still worse. So many telegrams seem to require answering. You must I am sure feel that, if you had been listened to 6 months ago, this present complication might have been avoided.

The countermanding of the fleet at the very entrance of the Dardanelles is most unfortunate I think. . . .

Hoping to hear soon, believe me, with the sincerest regard, Yours aff'ly, V. R. & I.

The reconciliation was effected by Sunday morning, and a strenuous and agitated week was followed by that unusual portent, a Sunday Cabinet. To Salisbury, on whose judgment in foreign affairs, rather than on Derby's, Beaconsfield had now begun to rely, and whose helpfulness and disregard of self-interest during the crisis had been conspicuous, his chief sent a letter of warm acknowledgment.

To Lord Salisbury.

10, Downing St., *Jan.* 27, 1878.—I inferred from your significant remark, at yesterday's Cabinet, respecting Derby, that you desired his return.

I have succeeded in accomplishing that, tho' a Pyrrhic victory: at least I feel I have not sufficient energy remaining to go through another such trial.

The Cabinet is called to-day at 5 o'c. It is necessary for Northcote's sake, but I thought it desirable, as the most effective mode, to-morrow, of answering the rumors afloat respecting D.

I must express my sense of the cordial co-operation and

confidence I have received from you throughout this affair.
It is a good omen for the Sovereign and the country; and I
can assure you, and I ought to assure you, that your behavior
at headquarters is entirely understood and completely appreciated.

The continuation of the correspondence with the Queen
describes the Council of that Sunday, January 27. It will
be seen that Derby marked, by his attitude in Cabinet,
the distrustful and unconciliatory spirit in which he
resumed office. He had made it clear in his final letter
to Northcote, that, as he wrote in his diary, 'I remain
rather in the hope of preventing mischief as long as
I can, than from sympathising with the views of my
colleagues.'

To Queen Victoria.

10, DOWNING ST., *Jan.* 27, '78.—. . . The Cabinet, which
had principally to consider the statement of the Chancellor
of the Exchequer to be made to-morrow, met late, and sate
long, and therefore Lord Beaconsfield cannot write at the
length he could wish. He received your Majesty's gracious
telegram, and, cannot, on this occasion, attempt to express
his deep sense of all your Majesty's goodness in the almost
overpoweringly difficult position in which he finds himself.
Lord Derby was offered Indian Sec'y, Colonies, Privy Seal,
or Lord Presidency, but no arrangement could be made.
He held that his honor required the Foreign Office or nothing,
which of course he said he preferred. His attending the
Cabinet, which will appear to-morrow, will equally astonish,
and disappoint, the Opposition, who looked upon the days
of the present Administration as numbered. That may not
be the case, but its days will be days of terrible toil and danger,
and it will have to encounter great crises in affairs.

Lord Beaconsfield saw the Austrian Ambassador to-day.
They are terribly alarmed, and believe they have been entirely
deceived by Russia.

In this projected Austrian alliance, Lord Beaconsfield was
much helped by Mr. Corry, whose services he has now lost.
It is a great blow. Mr. Corry has broken down from over-
work and over-anxiety. His nervous system has given way.
His loss to Lord Beaconsfield cannot be estimated. He has
fine talents, a sweet temper, wonderful energy, and a noble
disposition. Besides, he understood, and appreciated, your
Majesty's character, which was a bond of sympathy between

them, and a source of constant consolation. Mr. Corry will have to travel abroad.

Lord Derby did not resume his usual seat in the Cabinet, which was next to Lord Beaconsfield, but sate far apart in the vacant seat of Lord Carnarvon. This was very marked. He is evidently in a dark temper, but all must be borne at this moment. When we have carried the six million vote, we shall be freer and more powerful. . . .

Jan. 28.—. . . Ld. Beaconsfield thanks your Majesty for your Majesty's gracious letter received last evening.

He will not attempt to express his sense of your Majesty's kindness and of the graceful terms in which that kindness is conveyed.

During a somewhat romantic and imaginative life, nothing has ever occurred to him so interesting as this confidential correspondence with one so exalted and so inspiring.

To Lady Bradford Beaconsfield observed a becoming reticence about Derby, but he made no secret of his feelings about Carnarvon.

To Lady Bradford.

10, Downing Street, *Jan.* 27.—. . . Yesterday I cd. not even send the 'two lines.' And now, in less than an hour, there is to be a Cabinet, a Sunday Cabinet! and, after that, much to do.

Lord Derby remains with us, as his presence at the C. to-day will prove. Ld. Carnarvon's was a very ungentlemanlike speech, with details which ought never to have been mentioned; the Faery much disgusted at what she considers an abuse of her permission to refer to Cabinet affairs necessary to elucidate his conduct. They only elucidated his peevish and conceited temper. Besides it was vain and egotistical, and, worse than all, prosy. He must be immensely astonished to find himself detached from Salisbury, and that Derby has left him in the lurch!

Jan. 28.—. . . I am private secretary for poor dear Monty, who is not equal to writing a letter, and goes to-morrow to South of France. What a calamity! And at such a moment!

I am now going to H. of L. I don't know what will happen. They will hardly leave Derby alone. Nothing would have been known of his temporary aberration had not . . . Carnarvon revealed it. . . .

Feb. 1.—. . . I am glad you had time to read G.'s speech. What an exposure! The mask has fallen, and instead of a pious Xtian, we find a vindictive fiend, who confesses he has, for a year and a half, been dodging and manœuvring against an individual—because he was a successful rival! . . .

The reference is to a speech that Gladstone made at Oxford on January 30, in which he said that his purpose had been, ' to the best of my power, for the last eighteen months, day and night, week by week, month by month, to counterwork as well as I could what I believe to be the purpose of Lord Beaconsfield.'

CHAPTER VII.

FINAL PARTING WITH DERBY.

1878.

The more the Russian terms were examined, the less possible it seemed to accept them as a satisfactory basis of peace. They included the creation of a big Bulgaria ' within the limits of the Bulgarian nationality '—a most indefinite phrase—and practically independent of the Porte; the complete independence of Rumania, Serbia, and Montenegro; the autonomy of Bosnia and Herzegovina; an indemnity for Russia of unspecified amount, in a form, pecuniary, territorial, or other, to be hereafter determined; and an understanding to safeguard the interest of Russia in the Straits. Though the Opposition professed to regard these provisions as not incompatible with British interests, and therefore opposed Northcote's motion for a Vote of Credit of £6,000,000 to increase the national armaments, public opinion, especially in London and the South of England, rallied to the support of the Government. It was felt that, in face of terms so elastic, and with the Russian forces steadily advancing on Constantinople, it was imperative to make Russian generals and statesmen realise that England was in earnest in her resolve to defend her interests. It was believed by the plain man, as well as by the Prime Minister, that, if a determined front was shown, Russia would yield to our just demands. The music-hall refrain of the moment, which enriched political vocabulary with the term ' Jingo,'—

> We don't want to fight, but, by Jingo, if we do,
> We've got the ships, we've got the men, we've got
>   the money too,—

however vulgar in expression, gave vent to a real political truth; namely, that England, devoted to peace as she was, meant to make her decisions respected, and possessed the necessary material force for doing so. This was the spirit in which Beaconsfield had acted throughout. Even the cautious and pacific Derby was not unaffected by the popular current. He admitted in the House of Lords that it was very conceivable that circumstances might arise in which the sending up of the fleet to Constantinople would be entirely justified, and would not in any manner endanger the public peace. When the question was raised again in Cabinet on February 2, and the suggestion was made that the Italian and British fleets might combine for such a movement, in case the Russians directly threatened Constantinople, Derby, Beaconsfield told the Queen, ' did not seem adverse to this plan, and appears less scrupulous now that the country begins to speak out. He had evidently persuaded himself that the country was adverse to any interference.'

That Beaconsfield was the mainspring of Government action, that, though another held the seals of the Foreign Office, he was really his own Secretary of State, was generally understood by the country; and the Opposition accordingly directed their onslaughts in the debate against the person of the Minister, drawing a clear distinction between him and his colleagues. The Queen was ' indignant and shocked ' at these ' disgraceful attacks '; and Beaconsfield, in response to Her Majesty's sympathy, wrote that such efforts at dividing a Prime Minister from his colleagues were in old days ' not only deemed unfair and unjust and unconstitutional, but ungentlemanlike.' But they could not daunt him; indeed, they only hardened his resolution and increased his power.

After the debate had begun an armistice was at last (on February 1) signed between Russia and Turkey; but Beaconsfield, with good reason, suspected, as he told the Queen, ' that the whole affair of the armistice is a comedy, and that Russia will advance.' Russia did advance; and on Thursday, February 7, the last day but one of the debate, her armies were, or were reported to be, in such close and threatening proximity to Constantinople that there was something like a panic on the London Stock Exchange; that the approaches to Westminster were thronged with excited and patriotic crowds cheering Beaconsfield; and that the opposition to the Vote of Credit suddenly collapsed. Beaconsfield described the events of the day to his great friend.

To Lady Bradford.

10, DOWNING STREET, *Feb.* 7.—This has been a terrible day of excitement. Last night there came news from Constantinople that all the wires were cut by the Russians, so that our intelligence had to reach us *via* Bombay, that the Russians were on the very point of reaching both Const. and Gallipoli, and that they occupied the principal position in the defensive works of Const., so that the city was at their mercy.

Cabinet at 11 o'ck., rather hard work for those of my colleagues who had been to Münster's ball (to the Austrian Prince) and from wh. I prudently refrained.[1]

The funds fell nearly 2 per ct., and all the Russian stocks, that had been rising, tumbled down—but there seems to be a chance of the situation being exaggerated, and Schou. called Ld. Derby out of the H. of Lords to give him a tel. just received from Gort., declaring the rumors were false. I am not so sure of that, but we are in the thick of great events, and something will happen every day.

The crowd was so great, from this street to H. of Lords, to escort me, that it was very difficult to reach my point of destination, tho' piloted betn. the forms of the daring Abergavenny and the beauteous Abercorn. You wd. have been amused.

---

[1] Dr. Kidd's treatment enabled Beaconsfield to take some share in the entertainments organised in connection with the visit of the Austrian Crown Prince Rudolph to England. But, while he attended several dinners, he shunned evening receptions and balls. Here are extracts from his letters of this month to Lady Bradford: '*Feb.* 10.—I dined yesterday with Lady C., rather an agreeable party, and I dine to-day with P. Hal to meet the Austrian heir. I could not go to Ct. Beust's reception, and really, tho' Saturday, ball last night, for the same reason I did not go to Münster's, and wh. I gave him, *i.e.*, I die about eleven o'ck. every evening, and am always buried before midnight.' '*Feb.* 13.—. . . I dined at Clarence House on Sunday, and was amused. . . . I dine (D.V.) at the Duke of Cam.'s and also D. of W[ellington]'s, which is a charming future. . . .'

The Queen's indignation at what she considered Russia's 'monstrous treachery' was extreme; and so was her anxiety that her Ministry should act at once. She wrote Beaconsfield no fewer than three hortatory letters on that one day.

From Queen Victoria.

OSBORNE, *Feb.* 7, '78.—The Queen writes her third letter, but the state is so serious and so critical that she must exhaust every argument to put him in possession of her views—her very strong and decided views. The proceedings in the House of Commons are very satisfactory and the Government must be firm and decided, or the honour as well as the interests of this country and the Throne will be sacrificed, and we shall never be safe from Russia's false, hypocritical intrigues and proceedings. Whether they have got to Constantinople (for in spite of Gortchakoff's answer and denial, the Queen is sure they are there or are nearly so, for Reuter states it, who generally knows, as well as Mr. Layard) on an agreement with Turkey or in spite of the Porte, it is equally a case of breach of faith, and we have told them again and again so.

As early as July 22, '77, Lord Beaconsfield writes:

' Yesterday also in the most formal and even solemn manner the question was brought before the Cabinet what they were prepared to do if Russia occupied Constantinople. They unanimously agreed, and no one stronger and more decided than Lord Salisbury, that the Cabinet should advise your Majesty to declare war against Russia.'[1]

Then in the annexed extract from an account by the Chancellor of the Cabinet held at the beginning of October, the language was equally decided; and on November 16, Lord Beaconsfield writes:

' We have defined those British interests. The occupation of Constantinople or the Dardanelles by Russia would assail one of those interests, and the honor of your Majesty's Crown and of your Government and of your people would then be forfeited if your Majesty by all the means in your Majesty's power did not endeavor to guard your Majesty's Empire from such a result.'[2]

These are only a few extracts out of many letters, and the Queen considers that she has a right to expect that these oft-repeated assurances are carried out. She cannot speak strongly enough, for Great Britain's safety and honour are at stake; and she cannot for a moment doubt [? think] that Lord Beaconsfield, or any of her present Ministers, would sacrifice them.

[1] See above, p. 1027.   [2] See above, p. 1070.

She cannot rest by day or night till she hears that strong measures are taken to carry out these principles. She hopes Italy will be pressed to join. Oh! if her faithful ally and friend King Victor Emmanuel were still alive, she would at once write to him and her appeal would not have been in vain!

How strange that the poor old Pope should also have gone to his rest now, only four weeks after his opponent.[1]

Beaconsfield required no spur; but Her Majesty's exhortations no doubt helped him with his Cabinet, who next day, without any dissent, adopted once more, and finally, the measure which, little more than a fortnight before, had produced two resignations. Even so, the Queen was hardly appeased; and Beaconsfield found it necessary to proffer a formal defence of the course which the Government had pursued.

To Queen Victoria.

10, DOWNING ST., *Feb.* 9, '78.—Lord Beaconsfield with his humble duty to your Majesty. Just returned from the House of Lords and scarcely time to enter into length upon the incidents of an important day.

He conveyed to the Cabinet the contents of your Majesty's last letter, and read in detail the extracts from his own correspondence and the statement drawn up by the Lord Chancellor at Balmoral; and then he called upon the Cabinet to fulfil their engagement to their Sovereign.

The fact of the armistice being now in our possession, and, that apparently, by its provisions, the Russians could not actually enter Constantinople, obliged him to modify his proposal, but after a long and animated discussion, the Cabinet resolved to send a division of the fleet up to the Turkish capital, and invite all the neutral Powers to join with them in a similar act.

Lord Beaconsfield is told the announcement was received with much cheering in the House of Commons, where the division of last night[2] shows the tone and temper prevalent.

The country is greatly stirring at last; if we only had a *corps d'armée* at Gallipoli, the Crowns of Great Britain and India would be not unworthy of the imperial brow which they adorn.

---

[1] King Victor Emmanuel died on Jan. 9, and Pope Pius IX. on Feb. 7, of this year, 1878.

[2] The Vote of Credit was carried by 328 to 134 votes.

From Queen Victoria.

OSBORNE, *Feb.* 9, '78.—The Queen thanks Lord Beacons-field for his two letters and cypher.   She feels deeply, keenly, the way in which—thanks to the . . . conduct of Lord Derby and Lord Carnarvon, acting as it did upon their colleagues— he has been unable to fulfil his engagement to her !

She feels deeply humiliated and must say that she thinks we deserve great censure for the way in which we have aban-doned our standpoint; her own first impulse would be to throw every thing up, and to lay down the thorny crown, which she feels little satisfaction in retaining if the position of this country is to remain as it is now.   But she thinks in the Conference we may reassert our position, and with Austria (who does not behave well, for she held a fortnight or 3 weeks ago far stronger language than ourselves) and Italy, and any others who will join us, we may come to an agreement, in which to insist on our and European interests being maintained, and to fight for them alone, if we are not supported. . . .

She sends copies of two letters from Lord Derby, who now writes continually, and she will be obliged to answer the second and rather strongly.   The country should know who has dragged them down.

The Queen sends some camellias grown in the open air and primroses for Lord Beaconsfield. . . .

To Queen Victoria.

10, DOWNING ST., *Feb.* 10, '78.—Lord Beaconsfield is deeply distressed, indeed feels real unhappiness, at the letter receivep from your Majesty last night.   But tho' he entirely sympa-thises with your Majesty, and would willingly take any step, or endure any sacrifice, for your Majesty's service and relief, for your Majesty's interests and personal feelings are dearer to him than life, he still ventures to hope, that, on further reflection, it may be felt, that neither the situation of affairs, nor the conduct of your Majesty's Government, need be viewed in so dark a light.

It is not . . . Lord Derby, or even Lord Carnarvon, that has mainly brought about the present, no doubt lamentable, state of affairs: it is the necessary consequence of a policy of neutrality.   Vain now to argue whether that was, or was not, a right policy.   Enough to say, that an alliance with Turkey was, at the time that policy was adopted, impossible.

In the second place the effects of neutrality have been aggravated by the total and rapid collapse of the Turkish Armies.   With regard to the Conference, Lord Beaconsfield does not feel sure it will ever take place, and if it do, he doubts whether it will secure peace, but it will give an opportunity for the development of the views of the various Powers, which may lead to practical consequences.

The use of the six million vote is this: it will put your Majesty's forces, now on a peace establishment, on a war footing, so that they will be ready for action when the time arrives, *i.e.*, on the break-up of the Conference, or some analogous event. The present state of affairs is not a conclusion, or a catastrophe. It is not the beginning of the end; it is the end of the beginning.

He had a long conversation yesterday with Col. Wellesley, on the subject of war with Russia without allies. Col. Wellesley does not fear it. The Baltic and the Black Sea both blockaded, Russia would never know where the military attack would take place, whether in Central Asia, or the Euxine, or any other part, and she would have to keep her armies in exhausting restlessness.

If your Majesty's Government have from wilfulness, or even from weakness, deceived your Majesty, or not fulfilled their engagements to their Sovereign, they should experience the consequences of such misconduct, and the constitutional, and becoming, manner of their punishment is obvious. They cannot with their present Parliamentary majority in both Houses, and the existing difficulties, as men of honor, resign, but your Majesty has the clear, constitutional right to dismiss them.

Nor is there any doubt, notwithstanding the apparent dislocation of party in the present Opposition, that your Majesty would be able to find adequate advisers. Lord Beaconsfield indeed impressed this view on the Cabinet yesterday, and pointed out to them, that such a step on the part of your Majesty would not only be a strictly constitutional course, but the obvious solution of many difficulties.

At the same time, Lord Beaconsfield must observe, with the utmost and profound deference, that he is not conscious of having failed in any engagement to your Majesty. It was never in the power of a neutral State to prevent the entry of the Russians into Constantinople. All that a neutral Power could do was [*sic*] that such a step should terminate its neutrality, and it would then feel at liberty to take such measures, as it might deem expedient to counteract the Russian course.

That was the engagement of Lord Beaconsfield, and he is prepared to fulfil it.

Lord Beaconsfield is deeply touched by your Majesty's **gracious kindness** in deigning to send him some flowers from

your Majesty's island home. Truly he can say they are
' more precious than rubies'; coming, as they do, and at such
a moment, from a Sovereign whom he adores. . . .

From Queen Victoria.

OSBORNE, *Feb.* 10, '78.—The Queen thanks Lord Beaconsfield for his very kind and interesting letter.

He must not for a moment think she would wish to change
her Government.

Her only comfort is that Lord Beaconsfield and his Government are so secure and that the country is so thoroughly
roused and supports them.

The Queen has perfect confidence in him and great confidence in all his colleagues *but one*, and it was only to urge
him on to support him in a bold, firm, decided course that she
wrote as she did. . . .

The Queen thinks a policy of neutrality is fatal. It has not
kept the Russians in check, and yet we have offended and
thwarted them, while we have estranged the Turks with whom
we could have done anything, and have lost all power over
them. . . .

The Cabinet, having taken the plunge and ordered the
fleet into the Sea of Marmora, showed a disposition to
support all the forward movements which Beaconsfield
suggested. Derby assumed in Ministerial councils an
air of detachment rather than of opposition; and apparently made no serious objection to the consequential
measures proposed, though he intimated his personal
dissent from some of them. Ever since the crisis at the
end of January, Beaconsfield had been in regular private
consultation about foreign affairs with Salisbury and
Cairns, rather than, as in old days, with Derby; and
the Prime Minister himself openly conducted the Eastern
policy of the country in Cabinet, leaving to the Foreign
Secretary the part, for which he was pre-eminently fitted,
of critic-in-chief, sometimes captious, but often helpful.
Derby, in fact, during this last couple of months of
office, was reduced in regard to the Eastern Question,
apparently without protest if not with his own consent,
almost to the position of an under-secretary, serving
the Prime Minister and the Cabinet, seeing Ambassadors

and writing despatches on their behalf, but without independence or initiative of his own. His discharge of even these subordinate functions was by no means always to the satisfaction of his chief.

To Queen Victoria.

10, DOWNING ST., *Feb.* 16, '78.—Lord Beaconsfield . . . grieves he has not been able, the last two days, to keep your Majesty informed of affairs as much as he could wish, but he has been physically incapable of doing what, in general, is not only a duty, but a delight.

Cabinets every day, and sometimes—indeed generally— of unusual length, the necessity of private conference with his colleagues, to keep affairs in proper train, and the general conduct of business, have so absorbed and exhausted him, that towards the hour of post he has not had clearness of mind, and vigor of pen, adequate to convey his thoughts and facts to the most loved and illustrious being, who deigns to consider them.

In addition to this, he has been obliged to conduct the secret and unofficial negotiations with Austria, which he hopes he has now brought to a conclusion, and that she will put into the field immediately at least 300,000 men, and join Great Britain in an identic note to Russia, which will announce, that we cannot consent to go into conference unless Russia retires from Constantinople, or places Gallipoli, and the fortresses of the Straits, in the custody of Great Britain, or of garrisons of the neutral Powers.

Mr. Corry greatly helped him in the conduct of this important affair, but alas! there is no Mr. Corry now, and, sometimes, Lord Beaconsfield feels that he can scarcely stem the torrent. It truly makes him miserable, that your Majesty should ever feel yourself neglected, and yet he is conscious all day, that, notwithstanding his heart and brain are at your Majesty's service, your Majesty must be sensible of some difference in the frequency and fulness of his communications. He humbly hopes your Majesty will be indulgent to him in this respect. He feels there is no devotion that your Majesty does not deserve, and he only wishes he had youth and energy to be the fitting champion of such an inspiring Mistress as your Majesty.

To-day, the Cabinet discussed the Sultan's offer, contained in Mr. Layard's tel. despatch, and empowered your Majesty's Ambassador to purchase, if possible, the chief ships of the Turkish fleet, promising their best offices to prevent the

Russians entering Constantinople, and offering hospitality if necessary, in your Majesty's fleet, to the Sultan.

Then they resumed the consideration of the means for securing the Dardanelles.

And then they considered the Austrian alliance, the negotiations for which had been hitherto conducted, unofficially, by the Prime Minister, and sent instructions to Sir Henry Elliot, which Lord Beaconsfield hopes may bring them to a formal conclusion. After that they examined Sir Lintorn Simmons on military questions, chiefly with reference to the Straits.

Lord Derby offers little resistance to all these plans and proposals; indeed only that occasional criticism, which is not only justifiable, but salutary. Whether this disposition will continue, Lord Beaconsfield knows not, but there is no chance he thinks now, of any relaxation in the determination of the Cabinet. They meet every day, and every day seem more resolute.

To Lord Derby.[1]

10, DOWNING ST., *Feb.* 28, '78.—I must point out to you how insufficient, in my opinion, is the manner in which F.O. has expressed the resolutions of the Cabinet about the preliminaries of peace.

The enclosed tel. means, that H.M. Government wish to know, as soon as possible, the terms of the peace made between Russia and Turkey,

No one ever doubted, that we should hear this quite as soon as we could wish.

What the Cabinet wanted to know was, What are the terms, which Russia proposes to Turkey, and as to which Turkey hesitates to accept? It is very likely, that Russia will refuse to tell us, and will not allow Turkey to tell. But we can, then, say, we have asked, and have been refused.

I don't think we are justified, in the present crisis, to be sending to Russia civil messages. 'We shall be obliged to you, as soon as you have made your terms with Turkey, to let us know what they are.'

I am very anxious about this matter, as the Cabinet counts, when it meets again, on a reply from Russia, on which they would be prepared to shape their course.

Depend upon it, the uneasiness and dissatisfaction of the country on this head are great, and Parliamentary action, from our own side, will be the disastrous consequence.

---

[1] This letter to Derby was based on a private remonstrance which Beaconsfield had received from Cairns.

[ENCLOSURE.]

Ld. Derby to A. H. Layard.

Telegram. F.O., *Feb.* 27, '78. 6 p.m.—I have to-day
stated to the Russian Ambassador that, in the opinion of
Her Majesty's Government, it is essential that they should be
informed, with as little delay as possible, of the terms of
peace now being negotiated. Your Excellency should address
the same request to the Porte.

From many quarters there came warnings that, in
spite of all assurances, it was the Russian intention to
occupy Constantinople, at least to the extent of marching
their troops through the town in order to embark them
for home from the port. The Crown Princess of Prussia
told her mother Queen Victoria on February 8 that the
Emperor William I. had always understood that to be
one of the terms of the armistice; and a telegram arrived
from St. Petersburg on February 11 that Loftus learnt
from a secret authentic source that orders had been
sent to the Russian commander-in-chief to occupy Constantinople with the consent of the Sultan. Beaconsfield
was not dismayed, and entreated the Queen 'not to
indulge in unnecessary anxiety.' 'The difficulties and
dangers, no doubt, are numerous and considerable,' he
told Her Majesty on February 13, ' but Lord Beaconsfield has no fear of ultimately overcoming them, now that
he has the support alike of his Sovereign, the Parliament,
and the nation. England alone can do it, but he feels
we have powerful allies.' There was reason to believe
that Bismarck was secretly encouraging Austria to join
England in resisting Russia.

Beaconsfield's confidence was not misplaced. The
fleet came unharmed through the Dardanelles, though
the Sultan, with the invader at his gates, refused to grant
the firman for the passage; and Russia, now that the
British ships lay ready for action in the Sea of Marmora,
shrank from taking any extreme step which might provoke
war with a further foe. She neither entered Constantinople nor attacked the lines of Boulair and the penin-

sula of Gallipoli. We on our side made no attempt
to land. Meanwhile Beaconsfield hurried forward the
arrangements for a military expedition from England,
should such be required; and Woolwich and Chatham
hummed with warlike preparation. He approved the
choice of Napier of Magdala to command, with Wolseley
as chief of the staff, telegraphing for the former to Gibraltar and insisting that a preliminary consultation should
at once be held with the latter. 'There is no time to be
lost,' he wrote to Hardy on February 17; ' much depends
upon the power to act, when we do act, with promptness.'

The military preparations which the Cabinet undertook
impressed forcibly upon Ministers the desirability of
having some place of arms in the Levant, either port
or island, where British troops might assemble in force,
and British ships might anchor and coal in safety. Malta
was too far off Constantinople and Egypt, and was too
small in area. 'Over and over again,' Northcote tells
us, ' did we curse Gladstone for having given up Corfu,
which would have been invaluable to us.' Beaconsfield
had foreseen this necessity for many months and had
realised how the acquisition of such a place of arms might
indirectly give Turkey the financial help which she sorely
needed, but which her own maladministration and
bankruptcy had made it impossible to afford by way
of loan. He had sketched out his idea in a letter to
the Ambassador at Constantinople.

To Austen Henry Layard.

Most Secret. 10, DOWNING STREET, *Nov.* 22, '77.—Musurus
has more than once, of late, anxiously enquired, whether
there was any chance of financial assistance from England.
I have not given him encouragement; but have told him,
that the suspension of payments, on the part of his Government, has deprived a person in my position of the plausible
proposition of a Turkish loan with the guarantee of Great
Britain for the interest. Any proposal of that kind, now
offered to Parliament, would be looked upon as a vote of a
gross sum to Turkey, and nothing more; and it would scarcely
be listened to.

It has occurred to me, that some substantial assistance might be afforded to the Porte, if we could contrive to purchase some territorial station conducive to British interests. Anything in the Mediterranean might excite general jealousy, unless it figured as a coaling station, and that would not involve a sufficiently large sum. A port in the Black Sea once occurred to me, but difficulties might arise from the Straits treaty, etc.

At present, I apprehend Turkey might invite us to navigate the Euxine, but she might refuse. If the freedom of the Straits to all nations were ever conceded, our possession of Batoum, for example, might be alike advantageous to her and ourselves.

Again, a commanding position in the Persian Gulf might be a great object to us, if Armenia is lost to the Porte.

I wish you would consider this matter, and advise me thereon.

If a sum could be secured to the Porte, which would render it possible to enter into a second campaign, the result, as to after negotiations, might be great. If we could combine with it the presence of the English fleet in the Bosphorus, and a British army corps at Gallipoli and Durkos, and all this without a declaration of war against Russia, I think the Ottoman Empire, though it may have lost a province or two, which every Power has in its turn, might yet survive, and, tho' not a first-rate Power, an independent and vigorous one. . . .

I ought to tell you . . . that six months ago, the present Grand Vizier was in communication with an Englishman at Constantinople, one Bright, since dead, with the view of raising a large sum from England by the sale of Turkish possessions; all this on a large scale—the *suzeraineté* of Egypt for example, or Crete, etc., etc. This Bright was in communication with Colonel Gordon, a subordinate of the War Office, who sent his letters to the Government, but no step was taken.

The idea was first broached in Cabinet, Beaconsfield told the Queen, on February 27; and it was soon associated with a superficially attractive scheme, which, however, was never realised, of a Mediterranean league. From the first Derby protested against the acquisition of a fresh place of arms; and Beaconsfield recognised that, when that step was definitely accepted and acted on, Derby's final resignation was inevitable. In spite of the Foreign Secretary's protests, however, the policy was, it will be seen, provisionally and hypothetically adopted on March 8, by formal Cabinet resolution. As the resolution was only provisional and hypothetical, and a definite proposal to occupy Mytilene was at the same time abandoned, there was no occasion then for resignation, unless Derby were to follow Carnarvon's unfortunate precedent of provisional and hypothetical resignation.

Sir Stafford Northcote to Queen Victoria.

WINDSOR CASTLE, *Mar.* 2, '78.—Sir Stafford Northcote presents his humble duty to the Queen, and has the honour, in obedience to your Majesty's commands, to report what passed at the Cabinet to-day.

Lord Beaconsfield began by observing that whatever might be the truth as to particular demands, the general character of the Russian conditions of peace was sufficiently known to enable us to form a judgment.

There were three points on which we ought to feel anxious:

1st. The military position of the country, as affecting its communications with the East.

2nd. The financial situation.

3rd. The question of our trade with the Black Sea and Asia.

As regarded the first point, the Lord Chancellor expressed a wish that something in the nature of a Mediterranean league could be formed, embracing Greece, Italy, probably Austria, and France. The object should be to secure the trade and communications of Europe with the East from the overshadowing interference of Russia. The Powers might agree on the points to be secured. . . .

The points suggested for possible occupation in the event of any action being necessary were Mytilene, St. Jean d'Acre, and a post on the Persian Gulf. This would give a strong chain of communication with India.

Lord Derby entered a sort of protest against the principle of an occupation.

A committee was appointed to consult the military and naval authorities as to the best course of action.

To Queen Victoria.

Most Secret. 10, DOWNING ST., *Mar.* 2.—. . . A most interesting Cabinet. Lord Beaconsfield brought his plans forward again, which were supported by everyone except Lord Derby.

Lord Beaconsfield feels convinced, that Lord Derby will retire, perhaps not immediately, but in a week's time or so.

The Cabinet has sent for Lord Lyons, that they may consult as to temper of French Government about Egypt, etc., etc.

' The plot thickens.' . . .

Mar. 6.—. . . Lord Beaconsfield is much pleased with the First Lord of the Admiralty [W. H. Smith], who is both calm and energetic. With respect to affairs in general, Lord Beaconsfield wishes to remove a misapprehension from your Majesty's mind, that the presence of Lord Derby in the Cabinet, at this moment, is the cause of delay and weakness in your Majesty's councils. That is not the case. It is highly probable, that Lord Derby, when Lord Beaconsfield proposes his measures for the adoption of the Cabinet, will retire, but, at present, these measures are not sufficiently matured to be introduced to the consideration of the Cabinet, tho' unceasing attention is given to their preparation by Lord Beaconsfield himself. But it is not sufficient to be bold, one must also be prudent; and the number of points to consider is considerable. . . .

Lord Beaconsfield hopes to bring about a league of the Mediterranean Powers to secure the independence of that Sea. But this is a secret of secrets, and its success greatly depends on inviolable confidence. It must be managed, a great deal, by private communications with colleagues, and not be brought, at least at present, before the entire Cabinet. . . .

He entreats your Majesty not to be unnecessarily anxious and not to write too much at night. If your Majesty is ill, he is sure he will himself break down. All, really, depends upon your Majesty.

Mar. 8.—Lord Beaconsfield . . . is now going to the Cabinet. The question of occupying a station on the Asiatic coast is necessarily mixed up with consideration of the request of the Sultan to withdraw our fleet from Marmora, in case the Russians will withdraw from Constantinople. It is a difficult business, but Lord Beaconsfield thinks he sees his way. But there is another matter still more pressing, for Parliament is going to ask questions about it—the Congress, its locality, its object, etc., etc. Lord Beaconsfield thinks, with regard to the latter point, that there are two conditions on which we should insist.

1. That every clause in the Treaty of Peace between Russia and Turkey should be submitted to the Congress.

2. That no territorial change of any kind shall be sanctioned which is not also submitted to Congress.

He is obliged to write all this hurriedly, but he wishes your Majesty, if possible, to know everything that is going on, even if your Majesty is told it so roughly.

The violets and primroses came to him when he was in a

somewhat exhausted and desponding mood, and he felt their magic influence.

(*Later.*) . . . A very long but most interesting Cabinet. . . . In the first place, most gratifying and most important intelligence from the Admiral. He finds his position in the Sea of Marmora much more satisfactory than he contemplated. He has reconnoitered well the Bosphorus, and is quite prepared to force it when necessary, and to enter the Black Sea. He is not panic-struck by torpedoes at all. He seems to have no doubt of ample supplies, and of fuel.

He says, if the Russians occupy Boulair and the lines, he can manage it: a little damage perhaps, but nothing serious. He has, Lord Beaconsfield thinks, six iron-clads (perhaps five) and five other craft. He could cut off the Russians from all their supplies *via* Black Sea. Experience has so changed his views, that he does not wish to leave his station.

This alters everything: we are in a commanding position.

As there was some difficulty started about a rock in the channel to the harbour of Mytilene, which we intended to occupy, we have appointed a Committee of three of the Cabinet to report on the matter, and on any other preferable position, if there be one. The altered state of affairs in Sea of Marmora gives us time for this.

But in order to pledge the Cabinet to a positive policy, and to have no further debate on the point, the Cabinet came to a formal resolution drawn up by the Lord Chancellor, which Lord Beaconsfield encloses.

Lord Derby would not concur. Whether he immediately resigns or not, Lord Beaconsfield cannot say, but the Cabinet has taken the management of the F.O. into its own hands.

To-morrow, early, they will consider our relations with Greece, and an invitation to Italy to join in a Mediterranean League. The resignation of Crispi, a creature of Bismarck, will help us. The Cabinet will launch the League with Italy and Greece alone, if the other Mediterranean Powers decline. We count as such France and Austria. If the League is floated, they will soon join.

Lord Beaconsfield fears, that having agreed to Vienna (a capital) for the Congress, we cannot well decline Berlin, but we shall be stiff to make stipulations. Austria is on her knees to us to go to Berlin, and vows she will be faithful. ' Methinks the lady doth protest too much.'

He ought to say much more, but he cannot. He hopes your Majesty remembers your gracious promise not to write at night, at least not so much. He lives only for Her, and works only for Her, and without Her, all is lost. . . .

[*Drawn up by the Lord Chancellor.*] ' The Cabinet agree

that in the event of the Treaty of Peace between Russia and Turkey, after its revision by the Conference, or in default of any Conference taking place, compromising the maritime interests of Great Britain in the Mediterranean, a new naval station in the east of the Mediterranean must be obtained, and if necessary by force.'

HOUSE OF LORDS (*still later*).—. . . With respect to Berlin, every other Government, except your Majesty's, has accepted that city as the scene of the Congress, and if your Majesty declines to be represented there, the Congress will probably be held without the presence of your Majesty's representatives, which would not be desirable.

Austria is on her knees to us to agree to Berlin, giving the most solemn assurance that she has no secret treaty or understanding with Russia; that Germany will support her, and that, with the aid of Great Britain, Russia may be seriously checked.

Lord Beaconsfield is of opinion, that, throughout the transactions of the last two years, much too much consideration has been given to the disposition of other Powers. England is quite strong enough, when the nation is united as it is now, to vindicate and assert her own rights and interests. There have been terrible opportunities lost, and terrible acts of weakness committed, by us during these two years, but the nation was perplexed, bewildered, and half-hearted. The nation is so no longer. She is fresh, united, and full of resources, and a state of affairs must be substituted for that which has been destroyed and displaced. We must think less of Bismarcks and Andrassys and Gortchakoffs, and more of our own energies and resources. We must rebuild, and on stronger foundations than before, for doubtless they were nearly worn out. Your Majesty will soon have a navy superior to all the navies united of the world, and, in a short time, an army most efficient, not contemptible in number, and with a body of officers superior to that of any existing force.

Your Majesty must pardon this scrawl. He writes with great difficulty where he is now sitting, with no light but gas, and metal pens, which he abhors. He entreats your Majesty to take a more cheering view of affairs. He has no fear, if he be spared, of conducting them to a satisfactory, and even triumphant, end.

In the diplomatic controversy with Russia, Beaconsfield's main contention, in which he was supported by Derby no less than by the rest of his colleagues, was that Russia must submit her terms of peace with Turkey to

the judgment of Europe.   The affairs of the Near East
had been regulated by Europe in the Treaties of 1856
and 1871; and no modification of those treaties, the
British Government maintained, could be regarded as
valid except with the assent of the Powers who had been
parties to them.   This demand was put forward by
Derby early in January, as soon as it was understood
that Russia and Turkey were in negotiation; and was
repeated categorically to the Russian Government on
several subsequent occasions.   Russia's response was
evasive; but she acknowledged at the close of January
in general terms that questions bearing on European
interests should be concerted with European Powers; and
accordingly agreed to the assembling of a European conference at Vienna, as proposed by Austria on February 3.
The Austrian proposal was heartily welcomed by Beaconsfield and his Cabinet; and they showed themselves
equally complaisant, when it was suggested that the
Conference should be magnified into a Congress, and
should sit at Berlin and not at Vienna.   But they insisted
on the categorical acceptance of their demand as the
condition of British participation.   As Derby put it in
the middle of March, ' Her Majesty's Government desire
to state that they must distinctly understand, before
they enter into Congress, that every article in the treaty
between Russia and Turkey shall be placed before the
Congress, not necessarily for acceptance, but in order that
it may be considered what articles require acceptance
or concurrence by the several Powers and what
do not.'

   This condition was all the more necessary, as Russia, in
spite of her acceptance of the Conference proposal, had
compelled Turkey, by threats of occupying Constantinople,
to sign on March 3 at San Stefano a definitive treaty,
much more stringent in its provisions than the preliminary
terms had led Europe to expect.   Beaconsfield thus
described, on April 8 in the House of Lords, the effect of
the treaty on Turkey-in-Europe.

The Treaty of San Stefano completely abrogates what is known as Turkey-in-Europe; it abolishes the dominion of the Ottoman Empire in Europe; it creates a large State which, under the name of Bulgaria, is inhabited by many races not Bulgarians.   This Bulgaria goes to the shores of the Black Sea and seizes the ports of that sea; it extends to the coast of the Ægean and appropriates the ports of that coast.   The treaty provides for the government of this new Bulgaria, under a prince who is to be selected by Russia; its administration is to be organised and supervised by a commissary of Russia; and this new State is to be garrisoned, I say for an indefinite period, but at all events for two years certain, by Russia.

Besides the creation of a huge Bulgaria, the treaty provided for the complete independence of Rumania, Serbia, and Montenegro, with a slight extension of territory for the two latter, and for Rumania the acquisition of the Dobrudscha, but in exchange for the forced retrocession to Russia of Rumanian Bessarabia which had been assigned to Rumania by the Treaty of Paris; the autonomy of Bosnia and Herzegovina; and the application of an organic law, to be settled by arrangement between Russia and Turkey, to the districts of Thessaly and Epirus.   In Asia Turkey was to cede to Russia, in lieu of an enormous indemnity, all the eastern portion of Armenia, including Batoum, Kars, Ardahan, and Bayazid; and in addition to pay an indemnity of 45 millions sterling.   The question of the Straits was left untouched save by guaranteeing the right of passage of merchant ships at all times; but Beaconsfield argued in the Lords that by the treaty ' the Sultan of Turkey is reduced to a state of absolute subjugation to Russia, and, either as to the opening of the navigation of the Black Sea or as to all those rights and privileges with which the Sultan was invested as an independent Sovereign, he would be no longer in the position in which he was placed by the European treaties. We therefore protest against an arrangement which practically would place at the command of Russia, and Russia alone, that unrivalled situation and the resources which the European Powers placed under the government of the Porte.'

The Treaty of San Stefano was negotiated in the strictest secrecy, the Turks being bound by threats to silence; and, though its provisions soon began to leak out, it was not delivered to the British Government till March 23, three weeks after signature. Meanwhile, Russia continued to evade acceptance of the British condition for the Congress, Gortchakoff maintaining that it was sufficient that the treaty should be communicated to the Powers before the meeting, and that each Power should have in the Congress itself ' the full liberty of appreciation and of action.' ' Delphi itself could hardly be more perplexing and august,' said Beaconsfield. Whatever the phrase about liberty of appreciation and action meant, it was clearly not categorical acceptance; and that the Russian attitude was much nearer to categorical refusal was shown by the arrogance of the final reply which reached the Cabinet on March 27. The Russian Government, it ran, ' leaves to the other Powers the liberty of raising such questions at the Congress as they might think fit to discuss, and reserves to itself the liberty of accepting or not accepting the discussion of these questions.'

While waiting for Russia's decision, the Cabinet continued to elaborate the measures of precaution which Beaconsfield had laid before them. His report to the Queen of the meeting of March 16 says: ' They discussed *corps d'armée*, new Gibraltars, and expeditions from India, in great fulness. Lord Derby said nothing.' It will be seen that the idea of a Mediterranean league, which was not received with much favour abroad, had been dropped; and that we have here the first intimation of the project of bringing Indian troops to European waters—a project entirely in harmony with Beaconsfield's policy of magnifying the place of India in the British Empire. At last, on March 24, Beaconsfield obtained confidential information of Russia's definite refusal, and he at once prepared

for action. His will was indomitable, but, as his letters
to Lady Bradford show, he had little health or strength
during the critical days.

To Queen Victoria.

Most Secret. 10, DOWNING ST., *Mar.* 24, '78.—. . . The
Russian answer has arrived, but will not be delivered, or
made known, to anyone, until to-morrow; if then. It rejects
our conditions, and will not submit the treaty to the consideration of Congress.

There will be no Congress, as all agree there can be no
Congress without England—Russia says this. Russia will,
in all probability, immediately commence a direct negotiation
with your Majesty's Government.

After all their taunts about isolation, and about being ' left
out in the cold,' this is interesting ! No Congress and direct
negotiations with England.

This information comes to Lord Beaconsfield under such a
seal of confidence that Lord Beaconsfield cannot tell it even
to his colleagues, but his conscience and his heart alike assure
him, that he can have no secrets from his beloved Sovereign.

To Lady Bradford.

10, DOWNING STREET, *Mar.* 22, 1878.—You were prophetic
last night, for I have a regular influenza cold—constant
coughing and streaming eyes.

I have just had my audience, tho' I was scolded for coming
out in such a plight—but my Royal Mistress was not much
better than her Minister. The Kingdom was never governed
with such an amount of catarrh and sneezing.

I'm too ill and achy to be out later; I have written to D.
of Richmond that I can't be in my place. . . .

Mar. 24.—I am still a prisoner, but must, if possible, appear
in the H. of L. to-morrow—and I think I shall. . . .

The Russian ultimatum, for so we must call it, has not
yet arrived, altho' promised on Saturday. It will come this
evening, probably, or to-morrow morn. I think they will
not accept our terms, or rather conditions, and we shall not
yield an inch. People are very alarmed and think war instan-
taneous. I do not, and am not at all alarmed. I hold it is
much more likely that as Russia finds England firm, and
preparing for conflict, she will end by offering separate negotiations with us. . . .

Mar. 25.—Nothing to tell you. Then why do you write ?
Difficult to answer.

I am somewhat better, but ought not to go out. Then why do you ? Because, plea indisposition, I did not reply to some notice of Granville's on Friday, and have heard since of nothing but my illness. So, at great inconvenience and some risk, I go down to H. of Lords, because I wd. not ask G. again to postpone his motion.

Tels. come every quarter of an hour from a certain place, to know how I am—full of sympathy when sent, and full of anger when not answered. . . .

No news from Russia, tho' I have reason to believe Schou. has the answer, and has had for days.

Mar. 26.—I can only send a little, and a hurried, line.

Nothing can be more critical than the situation, and you must prepare, I think, for great events.

I could not get down to the Windsor Council to-day, as I had promised—but it was impossible. I am suffering very much from my influenza, which my visit to the Ho. of Lords did not improve yesterday—and yet I must repeat it to-day. . . .

Mar. 27.—. . . It is impossible that affairs could be more critical than they are. . . .

Except two days, when I went in a close carriage to H. of L., I have not been out since last Thursday, and this alone makes one nervous.

The spirit in which Beaconsfield approached the fateful Cabinet meeting on March 27, which brought about Derby's resignation, was shown by a letter which he sent on that morning to Hardy. ' Rest assured,' he wrote, ' the critical time has arrived when we must declare the emergency. We are drifting into war. If we are bold and determined we shall secure peace, and dictate its conditions to Europe. . . . On you I very mainly count. We have to maintain the Empire, and secure peace; I think we can do both.'[1] Beaconsfield had probably discussed his plans in detail with Hardy. He had certainly, according to his habit since Derby's first resignation, discussed them with Cairns and Salisbury; and also with Northcote, as Northcote himself tells us. Here are Beaconsfield's reports to the Queen of what he proposed on this occasion and what was decided.

[1] Gathorne Hardy, vol. ii., p. 36.

To Queen Victoria.

10, Downing St., *Mar.* 26, '78.—. . . The Russian answer, tho' it arrived here on Saturday, has not yet been delivered to your Majesty's Government.

Yesterday afternoon, Count Schouvaloff called on Lord Derby, and began feeling his way, to give the answer *viva voce*, but Lord Derby said that, as the English conditions were in writing, the reply must be in the same form. Whereupon Count Schouvaloff seemed to be shut up, and murmured that he would send the reply in writing, but it has not come yet.

Lord Beaconsfield has summoned the Cabinet for to-morrow at noon.

The Russian reply has been seen by some members of the Opposition. It is a categorical refusal.

Therefore, to-morrow, Lord Beaconsfield will propose to the Cabinet the measures which he has long matured, and which he trusts will be equal to the occasion. He will recommend immediately calling out the Reserves, which will place immediately at our command two *corps d'armée*, and at the same time will direct the Indian Government to send out a considerable force, thro' the Suez Canal, and occupy two important posts in the Levant, which will command the Persian Gulf and all the country round Bagdad, and entirely neutralise the Russian conquests and influence in Armenia. . . .

Mar. 27. Lord Beaconsfield . . . has carried all his measures this morning unanimously, with the exception of Lord Derby, who will, no doubt, resign.

When he asks your Majesty's gracious permission to make a statement, etc., your Majesty must be very cautious and reserved in granting the permission, for, otherwise, the statement may tell things to the world, which it is absolutely necessary, for success, should be kept secret: as, for example, the Indian expedition.

It will be necessary that the Mutiny Bill should be passed, before a message is sent down to Parliament and a proclamation issued.

The Cabinet meets again to-morrow at noon to frame the materials for a circular to the different Courts of Europe on the present situation.

It will be our case in the face of Europe and our own country. He [Beaconsfield] has had a good night and feels at this moment much relieved by what has just occurred. . . .

Later.—. . . Lord Derby has tendered his resignation, and wishes to make his announcement to-morrow.

It should be kept quite secret at this moment, as they have

a reception at the F.O. to-night, and their position, were the resignation known, would be painfully ludicrous. Lord B. conceals it therefore even from his colleagues. Lord Beaconsfield requests from your Majesty authority to receive the resignation and also to arrange with Lord Derby as to his statement. He seems perfectly loyal, and desirous of saying nothing disagreeable to his colleagues, or injurious to the public service. . . .

The only military plans of Lord Napier are in the hands of H.R.H. the F.-M. Commanding in Chief. They seemed to Lord Beaconsfield meagre.

From Queen Victoria.

WINDSOR CASTLE, *Mar.* 27, '78.—. . . The Queen must own, that she feels Lord Derby's resignation an unmixed blessing. . . . His name had suffered and was doing great harm to us abroad: and the very fact of his becoming a mere cypher and putting his name to things he disapproved, was very anomalous and damaging. . . . The Queen, therefore, without a moment's hesitation, sanctions Lord Beaconsfield's acceptance of his resignation, but will keep it secret till to-morrow. Pray tell him from the Queen that she relies on his loyalty to his colleagues, as well as to his Sovereign, and feels sure he will join in no factious opposition. But he must be very cautious in what he says, for fear of letting out important measures, which we must keep secret.

Now who is to succeed him ? Lord Salisbury or Lord Lyons ? . . .

It will be noticed that Beaconsfield does not specify the two important posts in the Levant which were to be occupied by the proposed Indian expedition, nor indeed does he definitely say that the names were given to the Cabinet. But there can be no reasonable doubt that the names were given, and that the posts were Cyprus and Alexandretta (Scanderoon), as mentioned by Derby in confidence, immediately on coming out of Cabinet, to his private secretary, now Lord Sanderson. Besides Beaconsfield's letters to the Queen, there are, as Hardy's diary is apparently silent,[1] no other contemporary records extant, so far as is known, of the proceedings of this decisive Council, except two papers in Derby's hand-

---

[1] Gathorne Hardy, vol. ii., p. 56.

writing: one the note which, in accordance with his usual practice,[1] Derby jotted down in Cabinet, and which he sealed up separately; the other a shorter statement which he entered in his private diary, either that evening or the next morning. In view of the discrepant accounts which were afterwards given from memory by Cabinet Ministers, the late Lord Sanderson felt justified in authorising, with the concurrence of the present Lord Derby, the publication of these confidential documents. The following is the note in Cabinet :

D[ERBY] reads answer of Schouvaloff. It is a refusal.

LORD B. wishes a circular to be addressed to all the Powers, stating our views.

This is talked over and not dissented from in principle.

D. proposes to lay papers at once and explain in Parliament. This is agreed to.

LORD B. We must now decide our policy. Our objects have been the maintenance of the Empire, and the maintenance of peace. Peace is not to be secured by 'drifting.' All our attempts to be moderate and neutral, and avoid collision with Russia, have lessened our influence, and caused it to be thought that we had no power. Our position is impaired since Parliament met. Austria is more deeply concerned than we are. Austria and Russia are now in a position of great mutual difficulty. Russia has really desired a congress. She has strained her resources, her armies are suffering from disease, etc. Thinks a bold policy will secure peace: one of conciliation will end in war. An emergency has arisen: the balance of power in the Mediterranean is in danger; every State must now look to its own interests. The time is now come when we should issue a proclamation declaring emergency, and be ready to put a force in the field. An expedition from India should occupy Cyprus and Scanderoon. We shall thus neutralise the effect of the Armenian conquest. Influence of England in the Persian Gulf will be maintained. These points are the key of Asia. Proposes to communicate

---

[1] Writing to Beaconsfield on July 14, 1877, Derby says: 'The notes which I generally take at Cabinets . . . have been kept merely for purposes of convenient reference; those of old dates have been from time to time destroyed, and all will be. I have always understood it to be an unwritten rule of administrative practice, that no permanent record should remain of what passes in Cabinet. But to temporary memoranda kept, while they exist, for personal use, I know of no objection.'

with the Porte, to guarantee the revenues now received, so
that they shall not lose. This does not involve alliance with
the Porte. Nor is it inconsistent with anything we have done.
Thinks it important that these two steps shall be taken.
Wishes to call the resources of India into play, and show that
from England also we can send forth our hosts. Time has
come, the emergency has arisen.

CAIRNS. Great and grave emergency has arisen. We have
been neutral, but we always said we meant to have something
to say to the peace. Russia now tells us we shall not. Thinks
the time is come to make our resources available. We want a
counterpoise to what is doing in Armenia. Position in India
will be shaken if we do nothing.

SALISBURY was always against interference in the war
and therefore feels especially responsible. Policy of neutrality
was dangerous, though right. Russia refuses to allow our
voice to be heard. We must put ourselves in a position to
assert our views by force if necessary. It is necessary therefore
to declare an emergency at once. If this opportunity is lost,
it will not recur. As to Scanderoon, it commands the route
both to Suez Canal and to the Persian Gulf. We must be
ready to defend both these routes. It also gives as little
offence to France as any occupation can. It also maintains
our influence over the Asiatic populations. Their feeling
towards us will be changed, if there is not a visible exertion
of our power. They will look to Russia. Doubts as to first
obtaining the consent of Turkey. Wishes not to do anything
hostile to Turkey, but it is hardly fair to ask her. Would
do it first. The question of Cyprus is less urgent than that
of Scanderoon. Would act at once as to that.

HARDY. We have now no choice except to maintain our
own interests. Comments on the Russian answer. The whole
Treaty concerns us. Time has come as to declaring an emergency. As to Scanderoon leaves that to be judged by military
men.

J. MANNERS agrees in general policy. Would send Mussulman regiments if possible.

NORTHCOTE. Is it necessary to go to Parliament ? (Answer—
yes, for a vote.) Asks as to course of proceeding.

RICHMOND entirely agrees that time is come to take some
action.

(Some general talk.) Necessity of secrecy as to the expedition insisted upon by Lord B. and agreed to. (Some talk.)

D. declares dissent on grounds of general policy—come to
point where two roads part.

SALISBURY does not see that compromise is possible.

RICHMOND. We can't go drifting on.

CAIRNS. We are driven out of Congress.

NORTHUMBERLAND can see no step except this to take Security of the road to India is all-important.

CROSS. Question is which course is most likely to lead to peace.

LORD B. Austria will bring about a settlement of the Bulgarian situation. It is the Armenian danger which is to be guarded against.

(Some more talk, but not to any purpose.)

The following is Derby's entry in his diary:

Wednesday, Mar. 27.—Cabinet at 12, sat only till 1; but the business done was important both nationally and to me in particular. Lord B. addressed us in a set speech, to the effect that we must now decide our policy; that our objects have been the maintenance of the Empire, and of peace, but peace is not to be secured by 'drifting'; that our attempts to be moderate and neutral have only lessened our influence, and caused our power not to be believed in. He dwelt on the weakness of Russia, with finances ruined, and armies suffering from disease. An emergency had arisen; every State must now look to its own resources; the balance of power in the Mediterranean was destroyed. He proposed to issue a proclamation declaring emergency, to put a force in the field, and simultaneously to send an expedition from India to occupy Cyprus and Scanderoon. Thus the effect of the Armenian conquests would be neutralised, the influence of England in the Persian Gulf would be maintained, and we should hold posts which are the key of Asia.

Cairns and Salisbury both supported the Premier, showing clearly by their language that they were aware of the plan now proposed and had discussed it with him in detail; others supported more vaguely. I declared my dissent in a brief speech, referring to what I had said before, and agreeing with an expression that fell from Salisbury that we must now decide, and that no compromise was possible. We had come, I said, to the point where the roads diverged, and must choose one or the other. I intimated that I could not agree, and it was understood that my resignation was to follow.

These accounts add much interesting and valuable detail to the outline given by Beaconsfield to the Queen; but the reports of the two statesmen are in complete accord, both as to the proposals made, and as to the approval with which they were regarded by the whole Cabinet except Derby. As to the exact nature of that approval there is one further scrap of contemporary evidence. Salisbury asked Northcote in Cabinet in writing whether it was agreed that the cost of bringing the Indian troops should be defrayed by the British Exchequer; and he preserved the note which Northcote wrote on the same sheet and passed across to him in reply. It ran thus: ' The agreement absolutely involves a decision in favour of sending such an expedition. I am not opposed to it in principle, but I think we ought to have more than 10 minutes to decide on it. If it is decided to send the expedition, I agree to place the cost on imperial revenues.' [1] It would appear from this interchange of opinion that Salisbury regarded the decision to send the Indian expedition as more definitely taken than Northcote did, but that even Northcote was prepared to accept it in principle. There was, at any rate, no outward dissent, save Derby's, from Beaconsfield's policy; and both the protagonists, Beaconsfield and Derby, came away from the Cabinet with the same impression. Derby told Lord Sanderson, that proposals had been discussed and approved by his colleagues, he alone dissenting, for proclaiming an emergency and calling out the Reserve, and for a secret expedition of troops from India to occupy Cyprus and Scanderoon, and that, in consequence, he intended to resign. Beaconsfield, on his part, as we have seen, told the Queen that all his measures were carried unanimously, save for Derby's dissent; and he specifically mentioned, in the following sentence, the Indian expedition as one of those measures. Indeed, it is clear, both from Beaconsfield's letters and from Derby's note and diary, that the Prime Minister presented his policy as one whole; and orders for the preparation of the Indian force, and for the survey of the necessary landing-places, were immediately despatched.

That Derby would resign when definite steps were

[1] A copy of this note was forwarded by Northcote to Derby in a letter dated July 22, 1878. In writing his subsequent memorandum, Northcote quoted the note inaccurately from memory.

taken towards acquiring a place of arms in the Levant
had long been foreseen by his chief and his colleagues;
and he said that day in Cabinet that they had come to
a parting of the ways. But he did not actually give in
his resignation there and then; and both he and Beaconsfield were glad to make use of Northcote as a means of
communication, to avoid alike the awkwardness of writing,
and any direct personal clash between old friends. Northcote found Derby, after the Cabinet ' most friendly, and
I thought really relieved by getting rid of the " tin kettle,"
as he called the Foreign Office. He would not, however,
write to the chief, but asked me to do so in his name.'
Hence there is no letter in existence from Derby, detailing,
as at the end of January, the cause of his resignation.
When he made his explanation next day in the House of
Lords, he was naturally unable to reveal Cabinet secrets;
though he had received, in accordance with Beaconsfield's second thoughts, Her Majesty's permission to
make ' such statement as you, in your discretion, in which
the Queen has entire confidence, may think fit.' He
merely stated that the Cabinet had decided on certain
measures of a grave and important character in which
he had been unable to concur—measures not inevitably
tending to bring about war, but not, in his opinion, prudent in the interests of European peace, or necessary for
the safety of the country, or warranted by the state of
affairs abroad. Any further explanation, should it become necessary, he reserved for a later date. His references to his colleagues, and especially to his chief, were
friendly. Every personal motive and every private
feeling urged him, he said, to remain with them. ' No
man would willingly break, even for a time, political and
personal ties of long standing; and in the public life
of the present day there are few political and personal
ties closer or of older date than those which unite me
with my noble friend.'

Beaconsfield fully reciprocated the ' personal respect
and regard ' in which Derby averred that he held him.

His emotion as he rose to follow his resigning colleague in debate was very visible.   He said:

> The Queen has lost to-day the services of one of the ablest of her counsellors.   Those only who have served with my noble friend can sufficiently appreciate his capacity for affairs, the penetrating power of his intelligence, and the judicial impartiality of his general conduct.   My lords, I have served with my noble friend in public life for more than a quarter of a century, and during that long period the cares of public life have been mitigated by the consolation of private friendship. A quarter of a century is a long period in the history of any man, and I can truly say that, so far as the relations between myself and my noble friend are concerned, those years have passed without a cloud. . . .   These wrenches of feeling are among the most terrible trials of public life. . . .   I have felt of late that the political ties between myself and my noble friend must soon terminate; but I believed they would terminate in a very different and a more natural manner—that I should disappear from the scene and that he would remain, in the maturity of manhood, with his great talents and experience, to take that leading part in public affairs for which he is so well qualified.

These public courtesies were repeated in private.   The Queen wrote Derby a gracious letter of thanks for his services, adding: ' The Queen is also certain that she can entirely rely on his loyalty to herself and his former colleagues, especially the Prime Minister; and she is sure that he will never join in any factious opposition to the Government of which he has been so long so distinguished a member.'   Derby responded in the same spirit.   ' He has left office with no personal feeling, except one of goodwill towards his former colleagues, especially to his very old friend Lord Beaconsfield, from whom it is a real pain to be separated.'   He added that he had no desire to oppose, and would leave the disagreeable task of criticism, as far as possible, to others.

Beaconsfield showed his abiding goodwill by the offer of the Garter—an unprecedented act of generosity by a Prime Minister to a colleague who had left him in a crisis; and Derby, though he could hardly accept, was obviously touched by so much magnanimity.

To Lord Derby.

10, DOWNING ST., *Mar.* 31, '78.—I hope you will allow me
to offer you the vacant Garter. I always intended it for you,
but there were difficulties in my way. I hope you will now
accept it, in memory of our long friendship; if of nothing else.

I suppose you and Miladi are in the country. I have not
had a sniff of provincial air for five months.

From Lord Derby.

Private. FOREIGN OFFICE, M[ar]. 31, '78.—I am touched
and gratified by your offer; by the time and manner of it
far more than by the thing itself. Give me till to-morrow to
consider as to acceptance. In any event, my sense of your
kindness will not be less.

Private. April 1.—On thinking fully over the matter, I
have decided against accepting the Garter which you so
kindly offer me. You will I am sure understand that my
refusal is not dictated by any reluctance to accept an honour
at your hands, or by any diminution of our old friendship.
I shall not forget the offer, nor the time and circumstances
of its being made.

There was one more friendly letter, before the intimate
correspondence of five and twenty years came to an
abrupt close.

From Lord Derby.

23, ST. JAMES'S SQUARE, *April* 3.—When Schouvaloff called
to take leave of me, on Monday, he expressed a wish that I
should communicate with you on the subject of a report which
he said had reached your ears, and which he supposed that
you believed to be true.

It was to the effect that he had been in the habit of talking
over official matters with members of the Opposition, especially with V[ernon] Harcourt.

He denies having ever held any private conversations with
them, or having talked about pending negotiations with anyone except members of the Government.

I told him he had better address his denial direct to you,
but he preferred doing it through me, and I could not civilly
refuse.

No answer is necessary.

In the course of his speech Beaconsfield, while com-
mending the 'prudence and perfect taste' which had

prevented Derby from referring in detail to the reasons
of his resignation, announced, in order to avoid ' unnecessary mystery,' that the Government, in view of the
failure to reach agreement about the Congress, and of
the disturbance of the balance of power in the Mediterranean, had decided to call out the Reserve. This was
the only part of the Beaconsfield policy, as expounded
in the Cabinet of March 27, which it was possible for
the Prime Minister to reveal; as the Indian expedition
and the acquisition of posts in the Levant, though approved in principle, depended on time and circumstances
for execution, and secrecy till the moment of execution
was essential for their success. It was also inevitable
that he should make the announcement in such a way
as to leave the impression that this was the whole pre-
cautionary policy so far accepted, in order that the secret
might be preserved, and that public opinion at home
and abroad might not be set agog as to further measures
hinted at but not revealed.

The world naturally concluded, and was presumably
meant to conclude, that the calling out of the Reserve
was the sole cause of Derby's resignation; and, as that
measure of precaution was generally welcomed not only
by his own party, but by moderate men in opposition,
the seceding Minister met with little or no sympathy
or support outside the ranks of the pro-Russian agitators.
Conscious that it was the resolve to acquire ' new Gibraltars ' in the Levant rather than the summoning of the
Reserve to the colours that had decided his action, he
was galled by what appeared to him the injustice of the
public condemnation, and by what he considered the
unfairness of his treatment by his colleagues. He may
also have been irritated by the Prime Minister's very
natural method of supplying his place in Cabinet. In
the shuffle of offices succeeding the resignation, Beaconsfield took the opportunity to secure, so far as might
be, in spite of Derby's defection, the continued confidence
of Lancashire and the adhesion of the house of Stanley

by promoting Frederick Stanley, Derby's brother and heir-presumptive, to Cabinet rank as Secretary of State for War. In these circumstances Derby allowed himself, for once, to be governed by his feelings rather than by his cool judgment; and in the Lords debate of April 8 on the calling out of the Reserve he offered a further explanation which, however intelligible and in a sense excusable, violated his obligation not to reveal Cabinet secrets and the duty incumbent on a patriotic ex-Foreign Secretary not to embarrass the country's policy at a crisis. Beaconsfield thus described to the Queen Derby's intervention.

To Queen Victoria.

10, DOWNING STREET, *April* 9, '78.—. . . Lord Derby made a disagreeable and unauthorised speech, for he divulged the proceedings of the Cabinet of which he had been a member, with an absence of discretion and reserve, very unusual under such circumstances, and which will produce a painful effect on public opinion. He will perhaps justify himself by arguing that Lord Beaconsfield made an unnecessary reference to his conduct.

Lord Beaconsfield, who was somewhat wearied, may have erred in this respect, but quite unintentionally, and Lord Derby, if this be his excuse, misunderstood the allusion of Lord Beaconsfield. . . .

Certainly Beaconsfield's reference to Derby in his speech on this occasion was not only unnecessary but also unfortunate. He said that he could not conceive that any responsible person could for a moment pretend that, when all were armed, England alone should be disarmed. He proceeded: ' I am sure my noble friend, whose loss I so much deplore, would never uphold that doctrine, or he would not have added the sanction of his authority to the meeting of Parliament and the appeal we made to Parliament immediately for funds adequate to the occasion of peril, which we believed to exist. No, I do not think such things of him '; and he suggested that only a lunatic could take up such a position. As Derby had strongly objected originally to the earlier summoning of Parliament and the Vote of Credit, and had only consented in order to prevent the break-up of the Government, the reference was hardly fair. Derby therefore had some provocation; but it was rather petty not to accept in silence responsibility for the Cabinet actions in which he had finally concurred instead of making public the fact of his original objection; and it was hardly patriotic to inform the world, for the purpose of self-justification, that there were other secret decisions of the Cabinet which he deemed of a still more serious and unjustifiable character than the calling out of the Reserve. It is not surprising that Salisbury should have denounced with some warmth such disloyalty to country and to colleagues. These were Derby's actual words about his resignation:

I have been referred to by my noble friend at the head of the Government, and by newspaper writers and others, as having resigned office in consequence of the calling out of the Reserves. Now I feel bound to tell your Lordships that, whatever I may have thought of that step, it was not the sole, nor indeed the principal, reason for the differences that unfortunately arose between my colleagues and myself. What the other reasons are I cannot divulge until the propositions of the Government, from which I dissented, are made known.

Events, as we shall see, modified Beaconsfield's policy, and the programme of March 27 was never carried out in its fulness. The Indian expedition came to Malta, but proceeded no farther. Alexandretta was not occupied, and Cyprus was acquired, not by force, but by lease from the Porte. But, in spite of these modifications, when European peace had been signed at Berlin nearly four months later, in July, Derby considered himself justified, without obtaining any further permission either from the Queen or from his late chief, in revealing what that programme was from which he dissented. It had become, he thought, ' historical fact,' and he availed himself of ' that discretion which is allowed to an outgoing Minister to state what has really happened.' This was his statement.

When I quitted the Cabinet in the last days of March, it was on account of the decision then taken—namely, that it

was necessary to secure a naval station in the eastern part
of the Mediterranean, and that for that purpose it was necessary to seize and occupy the island of Cyprus, together with
a point on the Syrian coast.   This was to have been done by
a secret naval expedition sent out from India, with or without
the consent of the Sultan; although undoubtedly a part of the
arrangement was that full compensation should be made to
the Sultan for any loss of revenue which he might sustain. . . .
My lords, I endeavoured to induce the Cabinet to reconsider
this determination, and from whatever cause the change took
place I am heartily glad that that unfortunate resolution was
modified.

Derby's old colleagues naturally resented these unli-
censed ' revelations from the dark interior of the Cabinet,'
to use Salisbury's expression in reply. A settlement
had only just, and with difficulty, been effected between
Russia and Turkey; and it was distinctly embarrassing
to the policy of Great Britain to have a disclosure made
of projected measures of precaution, which, however
reasonable and right at a moment of acute tension, could
hardly be agreeable to either of the recent belligerents,
and which, as circumstances had prevented them from
being executed, ought to have been kept secret until the
lapse of years had rendered their divulgation harmless.
Moreover, the Cyprus convention was as yet unratified
by the Sultan, who was making difficulties and reservations; a fact which was not indeed known to Derby, but
which, from his official experience of Turkish procrastination, he might perhaps have anticipated. But Salisbury
allowed justifiable resentment to carry him to unjustifiable lengths. He compared Derby's progressive revelations to the successive fragments of disclosure made by
the notorious Titus Oates in regard to the Popish plot;
which was tantamount to charging Derby with a particularly mean form of mendacity. He proceeded to a categorical denial of what Derby had said. ' The statement
which my noble friend has made to the effect that a resolution had been come to in the Cabinet to take the island
of Cyprus and a position on the coast of Syria by a secret
expedition, with or without the consent of the Sultan,

and that that was the ground upon which he left the Cabinet, is a statement which, so far as my memory goes, is not true.' Cries of ' Order ' caused him to declare that he did not necessarily impugn Derby's veracity, and to substitute the words ' not correct ' for ' not true.' He added that, in his denial of Derby's statement, he was supported by the Prime Minister, the Lord Chancellor, the Secretaries of State for India and the Home Department, the President of the Council, the Chancellor of the Exchequer, and the First Lord of the Admiralty.

No doubt, the international situation made it desirable that Derby's account should be discredited. But the connected history which has been given here from original documents forces us to the conclusion that what Derby said was substantially correct, and that the denial can only be justified on narrow and technical grounds. In support of this denial there have been published not only an extract from Northcote's memorandum, drawn up after the close of the Ministry, but also a short note by Cross, evidently written in later life, and an extract from Hardy's diary of July 19, 1878.[1] None of these is contemporary with the Cabinet meeting, even Hardy's testimony being nearly four months after date; and they do not agree among themselves. Take the question of Cyprus. Hardy and Cross are quite certain that Cyprus was not mentioned on March 27; but, while Hardy admits that there was a discussion about Alexandretta, Cross declares that, as the Cabinet were at that time contending for the integrity of Turkey, they could never have contemplated the dismemberment of that empire—which would, of course, have been equally begun by the seizure of Alexandretta as by that of Cyprus.[2] Northcote,

---

[1] These documents are all set out at length in Gathorne Hardy, vol. ii., pp. 73-77.

[2] The value of Cross's note is discounted also by a suggestion made in it, for reconciling the conflicting statements of his colleagues, that ' Lord Beaconsfield may have whispered to Lord Derby, who always sat at his left hand: " What do you say as to Cyprus ?" ' Now we know both from Beaconsfield's letter to the Queen (see above, p. 1110) and from Hardy's diary (Gathorne Hardy, vol. ii., p. 50) that, when Derby returned to the Cabinet after his first resignation, he did not resume his old seat by his chief's side.

however, states definitely and categorically that 'the Prime Minister . . . proposed to us the despatch of a force from India, which should occupy Alexandretta and Cyprus, and should so sever the Euphrates route and cut off the Russians from an advance on Egypt.' With this explicit corroboration of Derby's note and diary and of Beaconsfield's letters to the Queen, the question of Cyprus seems to be concluded.

The only point really open to controversy on the facts is the exact nature of the reception given by the Cabinet to Beaconsfield's proposals, other than that for the calling out of the Reserve. Hardy's recollection some months after—he tells us he has no 'record'—is that there was a discussion, and inquiries were to be made, but no action was settled. Northcote, writing more than two years afterwards, says that the matter was far too serious to be hastily decided on, though most of the Cabinet appeared to be pleased with it; and that it was accordingly laid aside. He adds that Derby, being in a state of much excitement, did not distinguish between the 'conversation' about the Indian troops and the 'decision' about the Reserve. But this minimising description is not entirely borne out by his contemporary note, already quoted, written to Salisbury during the Cabinet. Acceptance of the expeditionary policy 'in principle' is there implied; an acceptance which was reiterated by him in a letter to Derby after the July debate. 'I remember,' he wrote on July 20, 'that in the conversation I had with you immediately after the Cabinet, you asked me when the expedition would start, and that I replied, "I don't know that it will ever start at all—I for one agreed to it in principle when (or if) a conjuncture arises to make it necessary; but I don't think such a conjuncture has arisen yet, and perhaps it never will."' It is important to observe that none of the accounts suggests that there was any audible dissent, save Derby's, from Beaconsfield's proposals; and, that being so, it is difficult to maintain that there was no approval in principle.

On the whole, there is nothing in these recollections
of colleagues which seriously affects the impression
derived from Beaconsfield's contemporary letters and
Derby's contemporary note and diary. Memory was
obviously not quite trustworthy when dealing with plans
which were never completely carried out, but which met
with general assent in Cabinet and for which preliminary
preparations were at once put in hand. Derby, however,
went perhaps somewhat beyond the actual stage arrived
at, when he used in his speech the words ' decision,'
' determination,' and especially ' resolution '; and thereby
gave an opportunity for a technically accurate denial.
Readers will doubtless have noted that this is only the
last and most serious of several misunderstandings in these
years as to the exact results of Cabinet Councils;[1] misunderstandings which were almost inevitable so long as
the venerable but unbusinesslike tradition was observed
which forbade the preservation of minutes of the proceedings. Many will draw the conclusion that one at
least of Mr. Lloyd George's constitutional reforms was
long overdue—that which has established a definite
record of what is done in Cabinet Councils, with a permanent secretary to keep that record.

Not only Derby's old colleagues, but the Queen strongly
resented his July speech. When Her Majesty read it
in the newspapers, she telegraphed from Windsor at once
in cypher to Beaconsfield, ' Don't you think I should write
a few strong lines to Lord Derby telling him that it was
contrary to all precedent and all constitutional usage
to divulge what passed in the Cabinet to which he belonged
only three months ago ? Ministers always ask permission
to make explanations, and it will be a very dangerous
precedent for the future if this is to pass unobserved.'
Beaconsfield expressed his entire approval. In reply
to the Queen's remonstrances, Derby pleaded Her
Majesty's original permission of three months before,
which he did not think could be held to be extinguished

---

[1] See above, pp. 967, 1070.

because it could not be acted upon at once. The Queen replied, through her secretary on July 26, that she expected that, whenever a Privy Councillor made any statement in Parliament respecting proceedings in Her Majesty's Councils, the Queen's permission to do so should be first solicited and the object of the statement made clear; and that the permission thus given should only serve for the particular instance and not be considered an open licence.

Derby, though he loyally bowed to Her Majesty's decision and never reopened the question in public, nevertheless thought that the royal intervention was not spontaneous, but was undertaken at Beaconsfield's suggestion. Here, as we have seen, he did his old friend a wrong. Her Majesty's telegram shows that she acted on her own initiative, although with Beaconsfield's approval; and the principles she laid down appear to be unimpeachable. Indeed, with the exception of giving authority for the Cabinet denial, Beaconsfield carefully avoided putting himself in any sort of personal opposition to one with whom he had been so intimate. It was Salisbury in each debate who gave the stinging reply, who launched the wounding taunt. Beaconsfield, who felt deeply the severance of the old ties, never alluded in public during this period to his former pupil and friend save in terms of respect. It was indeed a very real political loss to him to part with a colleague whose plain common sense was a wholesome corrective to his chief's daring imagination. But in the circumstances of the moment it was an inevitable loss; and indeed the Queen was right that it would have been better for the policy of the country had the resignation been offered and accepted earlier. So long as Derby remained at the Foreign Office, it was impossible for Russia to believe that the British Government would be ready to run the risk of war in order to enforce their will. It is perhaps somewhat strange that Derby should have been so anxious to bring to light what was the exact stroke of policy which caused his resignation, seeing that he had steadily resisted every decisive measure which Beaconsfield had proposed, outside the ordinary diplomatic course, since the outbreak of the Russo-Turkish War, only yielding occasionally at the last moment in order to avoid a break-up of the Cabinet. It was absolutely necessary to convince Russia that Great Britain and its Prime Minister were in earnest and meant what they said. The mere fact that Derby could no longer remain in the Ministry was almost as eloquent and convincing a proof of national determination as the votes for money and men, the movements of fleets and troops, and the large majorities by which these measures of precaution were sustained in Parliament. Within a very few weeks of his departure, Russia, as Beaconsfield anticipated, abandoned her unyielding attitude, and opened direct negotiations with the Power whom she had failed to bluff.

Derby's definitive resignation made way for the appointment of a successor who was to hold the seals of the Foreign Office for thirteen years in all, and to be the dominating influence in British foreign policy for the whole of the final period of the nineteenth century. The transfer of Salisbury from the India Office was followed by a number of further changes, among them Hardy's removal to the Lords as Viscount Cranbrook; and the Cabinet, which had persisted unaltered until Disraeli's acceptance of a peerage in the summer of 1876, had undergone by April, 1878, a considerable renewal and transformation. From that date till the close of the Ministry it was constituted thus:

First Lord of the Treasury	..	EARL OF BEACONSFIELD.
Lord Chancellor ..	.. ..	EARL CAIRNS.[1]
Lord President ..	.. ..	DUKE OF RICHMOND AND GORDON.[2]
Lord Privy Seal ..	.. ..	DUKE OF NORTHUMBERLAND.

[1] Cairns was not created an Earl until September 27, 1878.
[2] Richmond received the additional Dukedom of Gordon on January 13, 1876.

Home Secretary ..	.. ..	RICHARD A. CROSS.
Foreign Secretary	.. ..	MARQUIS OF SALISBURY.
Colonial Secretary	.. ..	SIR MICHAEL HICKS BEACH.
War Secretary ..	.. ..	COL. HON. F. A. STANLEY.
Indian Secretary	.. ..	VISCOUNT CRANBROOK.
Chancellor of the Exchequer	..	SIR STAFFORD NORTHCOTE.
First Lord of the Admiralty	..	W. H. SMITH.
President of the Board of Trade		VISCOUNT SANDON.
Postmaster-General	.. ..	LORD JOHN MANNERS.

It was still a strong Cabinet; for, though it had lost
Derby, it had gained Beach and Smith, both destined in
due course to lead the House of Commons. Smith had
served under Disraeli's immediate observation as Secretary to the Treasury; and the chief, Lord George Hamilton
tells us, had been especially struck by his rare business
aptitude and sense of justice. 'Whenever there was any
departmental or other difficulty of a business character
which required unravelling, [Disraeli] simply said or
wrote, " Refer it to Mr. Smith for his decision "; and his
decision was always accepted without demur.'[1] Sandon's
promotion was due to his successful conduct of the Ministerial Education Bill of 1876; and a suitable office was
found for him by giving Adderley the peerage of which
there was talk in the discussions about the Board of Trade
in 1875.[2] Of Northumberland's appointment as Lord Privy
Seal, Hardy wrote in his diary, ' a strange choice surely.'
Though he had sat for many years as Lord Lovaine in the
House of Commons, and had held subordinate office in
the Derby-Disraeli Ministry of 1858–9, the Duke was not
a leading politician. It was, no doubt, as the head of the
Percies that Beaconsfield took him into his Cabinet.
He had lost the head of the house of Stanley and of the
younger branch of the Herberts; he himself and Cairns
and Cranbrook were new men; it was not, to his mind,
fitting that a Tory Cabinet should lack on its front bench
in the Lords a due representation of the old families;
so, to redress the balance, he added Northumberland
to Salisbury and Richmond.

[1] Lord G. Hamilton's *Reminiscences*, p. 77.　　　[2] See p. 735.

In the opportunities given to young men by these changes and promotions Beaconsfield took, as ever, an especial interest.

To Queen Victoria.

10, Downing St., *April* 24, '78.—. . . The Und.-Secretary for India is Hon. Edward Stanhope, recently Secretary to the Board of Trade. He is a young man of great abilities, and a capital speaker. He entered public life early as one of your Majesty's Inspectors of Factories. He has great knowledge, much official experience, and is altogether very bright. He is succeeded as Secretary to the Board of Trade by Mr. John Talbot, also an excellent speaker, and highly cultivated. Sir Matthew White Ridley becomes Under-Secretary of State for the Home Department.

These are young men who, with George Hamilton,[1] will mount, and be faithful and most efficient servants to your Majesty in due course. . . .

---

[1] Who succeeded Sandon as Vice-President of the Committee of Council on Education.

CHAPTER VIII.

AGREEMENTS WITH RUSSIA AND TURKEY.

1878.

Lord Salisbury signalised his entry into the Foreign Office by the drafting and publication of a masterly despatch, which explained, and justified, to the whole world the diplomatic position of the British Government. The demand that Russia should submit the Treaty of San Stefano to the judgment of Europe was one that Derby had made as absolutely as Salisbury now made it. But it was Salisbury who drove home the reasonableness of the contention in paragraphs of luminous directness; and the active measures which the Cabinet had already taken gave a special weight to his words. Beaconsfield claimed, no doubt with truth, a share in the credit for the circular.

To Queen Victoria.

10, DOWNING STREET, *April* 2.—. . . Lord Salisbury and Lord Beaconsfield are responsible for the circular, but it was submitted to the Cabinet, and critically examined by them.

Lord Beaconsfield thinks it does Lord Salisbury great credit, and that it will produce a considerable and beneficial effect. It is an attempt also to take the composition of important despatches out of the manufactory of the Hammonds and the Tenterdens, who have written everything, in their F.O. jargon, during the last ten years. Mr. Canning wrote his own despatches on great occasions, and also Lord Palmerston. . . .

April 3.—. . . Lord Beaconsfield assures your Majesty that he is prudent in his social movements. He never goes out in the evening, and only to such dinners where it is necessary for him to appear. There is a certain tact in the management of even great affairs which only can be acquired by feeling the pulse of society. Mr. Corry, who went everywhere, used to perform this office for him, but now he is alone !

Lord Salisbury comes to him at eleven o'clock to consult over affairs before the Cabinet; and this is to be a regular rule without exception.

The circular has done wonders. . . .

To Lady Bradford.

10, DOWNING STREET, *April* 4, 1878.—. . . I think the circular has put the country on its legs again. I wonder what Harty-T. thinks of it.

The French dinner,[1] on Tuesday, was a menagerie, from Royalty down to a Miss Henniker! In the interval, some second-rate fashionables. I sate next to Pss. Mary. . . .

The dinner yesterday at P[ercy] Wyndham's was of an æsthetical character; Pss. Louise, De Vescis (of course), etc., etc., and Browning, a noisy, conceited poet; all the talk about pictures and art, and Raffaelle, and what Sterne calls ' the Correggiosity of Correggio.'

I dine at the Lornes' to-day in case I return in time, wh. is doubtful. . . .

Beaconsfield was justified in his satisfaction with the impression produced by the circular. Both Houses of Parliament proceeded to endorse the calling out of the Reserve, the Lords without a division, the Commons by the huge majority of 310 to 64.

To Queen Victoria.

10, DOWNING ST., *April* 9, '78.—. . . He moved the address in answer to your Majesty's message yesterday in the Lords, and endeavoured to place clearly before the country what was the engagement Russia had entered into with the Powers, and which was the foundation, not to say cause, of their neutrality in the late war.

Lord Granville, not disputing the general accuracy of the statement, could only have recourse to critical observations of a desultory kind. . . .[2]

The debate, tho' there was no amendment, was continued till 1 o'clock a.m., and, on the whole, well sustained. Lord Salisbury spoke with vigor. Lord Beaconsfield had the privilege of a reply, on which he had counted, when he framed his original speech, but when the hour had arrived, the house, which, when he opened the discussion, was crowded in every nook and corner, with overflowing galleries and benches

---

[1] Apparently a dinner at the French Embassy.

[2] Here follows the passage about Derby's speech quoted on p. 1144.

entirely filled, had dwindled into two or three peers, and all
the Opposition chiefs had vanished. So it was inopportune
and useless. There will be other occasions. . . .

Beaconsfield's speech need not detain us. His docu-
mented review of Anglo-Russian diplomatic correspondence about the submission of Russo-Turkish agreements
for European sanction, and his destructive criticism of
the Treaty of San Stefano, have already been drawn upon
in Chapter 7.[1] His peroration dwelt on the peculiar
character of that Empire which British statesmen have
in charge.

No Cæsar or Charlemagne ever presided over a dominion
so peculiar. Its flag floats on many waters; it has provinces
in every zone; they are inhabited by persons of different
races, different religions, different laws, manners, and customs.
Some of these are bound to us by the ties of liberty, fully
conscious that without their connection with the metropolis
they have no security for public freedom and self-government;
others are bound to us by flesh and blood and by material
as well as moral considerations. There are millions who are
bound to us by our military sway, and they bow to that sway
because they know that they are indebted to it for order and
justice. All these communities agree in recognising the
commanding spirit of these islands that has formed and
fashioned in such a manner so great a portion of the globe.
My lords, that Empire is no mean heritage; but it is not an
heritage that can only be enjoyed; it must be maintained.
And it can only be maintained by the same qualities that
created it—by courage, by discipline, by patience, by determination, and by a reverence for public law and respect for
national rights. My lords, in the East of Europe at this
moment some securities of that Empire are imperilled. I
never can believe that at such a moment it is the Peers of
England who will be wanting to uphold the cause of their
country.

The circular was well received abroad no less than at
home. In particular, it made an effective appeal to the
whole of the peoples interested in South-eastern Europe,
except the Russians and their *protégés* the Bulgarians.
The Treaty of San Stefano, overriding as it did the claims
of every Balkan race save the Bulgarians, whom it aggran-

---

[1] See pp. 1129-1131.

dised beyond measure, provoked strong local protests.
Not merely the Turks, but the Greeks, the Serbians,
and the Rumanians saw in it the deathblow of their
hopes. Serbia and Rumania had both fought against
Turkey, and Greece had only been restrained from prosecuting the invasion of Thessaly by the protests and
promises of the Powers. And yet Russia imposed a
solution which, on the one hand, placed large communities
of Serbians and Greeks under the sway of Bulgaria, whose
liberation had been effected not by her own efforts, but
by Russian armies; and which, on the other hand, forced
Rumania to restore to Russian rule the Rumanian population of Bessarabia that had been redeemed in 1856.
Moreover, Austria and Hungary were aroused at last;
and their forces were mobilised in the Carpathians in
order to keep Russian pretensions within bounds. Bismarck, who in February had ostentatiously disclaimed
any German interest in the Balkans, but had expressed
his readiness to welcome a European Congress to Berlin
and to play himself the part of an ' honest broker,' began
to show increased friendliness to this country; and there
was a growing tendency in French opinion to decline
to support Russia in extreme courses.

In this favourable atmosphere Beaconsfield pressed
forward the arrangements for that Indian expedition to
the Mediterranean, which should impress the imagination
of Europe in general, and Russia in particular, both with
the extensive military resources and with the firm resolution of Great Britain; and which should be ready, if
need be, to seize Cyprus and Alexandretta in accordance
with the policy approved in principle on March 27.

To Queen Victoria.

10, Downing St., *April* 12, '78.—. . . The Cabinet considered this morning the subject of the introduction of your
Majesty's Indian Army into the Mediterranean and made
many arrangements. Lord Beaconsfield believes this to be
a matter of supreme importance. After all the sneers of our
not having any great military force, the imagination of the

Continent will be much affected by the first appearance of
what they will believe to be an inexhaustible supply of men.

Lord Derby's speech has benefited your Majesty's Government abroad. It marks still more decidedly the difference
between the late and the present politics of your Majesty's
advisers. All that Lord Beaconsfield devised, and contemplated, will now be carried into effect, and England already
occupies again a leading and soon a commanding position.

Lord Salisbury, in every respect, is qualified for the Garter,
but it would be rather premature to confer it on him at this
moment. Lord Beaconsfield wishes it to be the recognition
of his merits in the now impending negotiations; and when
they are concluded, whether by peace or war, Lord Beaconsfield will advise your Majesty to confer on him this paramount
distinction. . . .

The new Foreign Secretary found, it will be seen,
immediate favour with his royal mistress; and Beaconsfield was untiring in his efforts to promote and maintain
cordial relations between the Palace and the Foreign
Office.

From Queen Victoria.

OSBORNE, *April* 14, '78.—The Queen is much interested by
the account of the Cabinet. Most truly is Great Britain in
her right position again, thanks to Lord Beaconsfield and to
the departure, not an instant too soon, of Lord Derby.

Lord Salisbury keeps her continually informed of what
is going on, which is an immense relief. Now that terrible
strain of constant watching is over, which affected the Queen
and she has no doubt Lord Beaconsfield also—from the
extraordinary habit of delay and neglect which existed when
Lord Derby was at the Foreign Office. . .

To Queen Victoria.

10, DOWNING STREET, *April* 15, '78.—Lord Beaconsfield
. . . is gratified that Lord Salisbury is keeping your Majesty
quite *au fait* to all that is going on. He impressed upon
Lord Salisbury that, in conducting your Majesty's affairs,
he was to look upon your Majesty as an exalted friend, whose
support and sympathy would lighten his labors, and whose
judgment would not infrequently assist them. He is a man
of feeling and some imagination, and can therefore appreciate
your Majesty, which the cold-blooded or the dull cannot. . . .

The announcement that 7,000 native Indian troops were under immediate orders for Malta was made a few days before Easter, and the troops themselves arrived before the end of May. It was a final and decisive stroke. There could no longer be any doubt of the determination of the Beaconsfield Government; and Parliament, in spite of some passionate protests, steadily supported them. The policy indeed was not seriously challenged. For, though there were debates in both Houses, they turned mainly upon legal questions—the exact scope of Ministers' powers, without special sanction of Parliament, under the Mutiny Act; the exact meaning of the clause in the India Act which forbade, save on sudden or urgent necessity, the application of Indian revenues, without the previous sanction of Parliament, to military movements beyond Indian frontiers. Even out of the legal debates the life was largely taken by the consent of the Treasury to place the cost of transport on the British Exchequer. In the Commons the Government were sustained on the legal and constitutional questions by a majority of 121. In the Lords, Granville would not risk the disclosure of the barrenness of the land by taking a division, thus exposing himself to Beaconsfield's taunt: ' You will never be in a majority if your nerves are so very delicate. You must assert your opinions without fear and with perseverance; and if they are just and true and right, you will ultimately be supported by the country.' Of Parliamentary courage of this kind, Beaconsfield was himself a shining example.

To support his Parliamentary case, Beaconsfield quoted numerous precedents. He was able to show that troops had been despatched from India in the past to the Cape, the Straits Settlements, Hongkong, and Abyssinia. But these, of course, were small matters; and none of them involved service in Europe. In essentials Beaconsfield's action constituted a new policy, as wholesome as it was dramatic; though a policy springing naturally from the Queen's assumption, under his advice, of the title of

Empress of India. He thereby established the principle, welcome to India and in the long run to Great Britain, that it is the right and duty of India to support, if necessary, by military force, even in Europe, an imperial policy undertaken for India's benefit. This great principle of imperial solidarity for defence has since Beaconsfield's day, and largely owing to the precedent which he set, taken such firm hold of the British mind, that even the Liberal Government in power at the outbreak of the Great War did not hesitate at once to bring over a powerful Indian army to fight for the imperial cause on the battlefields of France. Of the quibbles with which Liberal speeches abounded in 1878 nothing was heard in 1914. Public approval was enthusiastic and unanimous.

It was never necessary in 1878 to take the Indian troops at Malta into action in Europe or Asia Minor. Russia was at last convinced, and began to consider how far she could meet, instead of defying, the British Government. The Salisbury Circular, while unmistakable in its assertion of the right of the Powers to be consulted and in its refusal to accept the Treaty of San Stefano, had frankly admitted that, after the events of the past couple of years, large changes would be requisite in the treaties by which South-eastern Europe had hitherto been ruled. In response to this admission, Gortchakoff, while combating in detail Salisbury's arguments, invited the British Government to state not merely what it did not wish, but what it did wish. Schouvaloff, the Ambassador, immediately began to prosecute inquiries in this sense at the Foreign Office. The first negotiations, entered into on Bismarck's suggestion,[1] concerned the removal of the threat to Constantinople caused by the presence of Russian armies

---

[1] Northcote, in his memorandum, writes that Bismarck, after long being inscrutable, 'at length conveyed to us pretty clearly that he would support a Congress if he could be assured beforehand that it would not end in a failure; and for this purpose he was anxious that Russia and England should have some kind of understanding as to the points which each would regard as so essential that, sooner than yield on them, they would break up the Congress at the risk of bringing about war.'

in its close neighbourhood. How matters developed and how British policy took a concrete shape appears from Beaconsfield's letters.

To Queen Victoria.

10, Downing St., [*April* 19,] '78. *Good Friday.*—. . . First he must thank your Majesty for the gracious kindness, which sent to him, shut up in a city, the only consolation under such circumstances, beautiful flowers, and of all flowers, the one that retains its beauty longest, sweet primrose, the ambassador of spring.[1]

He is much touched by your Majesty deigning to remember him in a manner full of nature and grace.

His *villegiatura* has not yet commenced, and he fears never will. First of all, he is quite alone, Sir W. Gull having again banished Mr. Corry, tho' not from England, but from London and business. Secondly, affairs are so critical at this moment, that it is impossible to be absent. Lord Salisbury is at Hatfield, but he comes up every day; and indeed we are in the very pith of the most important work.

Lord Beaconsfield has the greatest hopes that, in the course of 8 and 40 hours, we shall have arranged, that the Russians shall evacuate Turkey as far as Adrianople on condition that your Majesty's fleet will return to Besika Bay. Constantinople and Gallipoli will then be in the entire and complete possession of the Sultan.

But this proposition, made by P. Bismarck, would never have been made, unless the Emperor of Russia was determined on peace, for he can make no other concession so great and complete. The next fortnight will be one of intense interest.

Northumberland [2] is not lost, but it should have been won.

Lord Beaconsfield hopes that your Majesty is well; that your Majesty is enjoying the burst of spring, and that Spithead is looking like the Mediterranean, rolling blue at your Majesty's feet.

April 21.—. . . Yesterday was an active and critical day. If we can trust Bismarck, affairs might be concluded in a manner very honorable to England, but Lord Beaconsfield has not a very strong conviction on this head; and altho' the new attitude of this country has evidently greatly affected Bismarck, and made him feel that England must have a voice in the final settlement, Lord Beaconsfield does not feel sure

[1] The Queen had written from Osborne that she sent 'some primroses picked by the Princesses and the ladies yesterday here.'

[2] A by-election which resulted in a tie. On a scrutiny the Conservative was declared elected.

that the Prince can withstand the temptation of embroiling
and exhausting both Great Britain and Russia. Otherwise,
if the fleets and armies of the two nations are withdrawn from
Turkey, the future arrangements scarcely seem so difficult.

If the territory south of the Balkans be restored to the
Porte, Turkey may be as strong to guard the Straits, as
Denmark is in a similar position.

With regard to Armenia, it would be well to propose that,
if Batoum is a free port, we will not question the possession
of Kars, etc., but if Batoum is to be Russian, we must occupy
some island or station on the coast of Asia Minor, which will
neutralise the presence of Russia in Armenia.

Lord Beaconsfield goes to Hatfield to-morrow afternoon.
He could not succeed in his Wimbledon plan. . . .

These two letters were written on Good Friday and
Easter Day. The crisis had come at the holiday season,
just when Beaconsfield, after a long period of strain,
was fondly hoping (he told Lady Bradford) to get a house
out of town for a month ' somewhere near—Richmond,
Roehampton, Wimbledon, that sort of thing; a pretty
villa with some flowers and conifers '; ' so that I may at
least sleep in the country air, which, they say, fairies
favor.' With Corry still away, however, he could not
face the household cares involved, and had to content
himself with a short visit to Hatfield beginning on Easter
Monday. It was his first real acquaintance with the
Cecil family, and he enjoyed the society of his new friends.

To Lady Bradford.

10, DOWNING STREET, *Easter Sunday,* [*April* 21,] 1878.—. . .
I tried to go and hear Mr. Fleming at St. Michael's to-day,
Lady Macclesfield having given me her pew; but, tho' in good
time, I cd. not enter the sacred precinct. I tried three doors,
but found a mob, as, in old days, when the drama flourished,
was found at the pit door. The church wd. not be taken—
a regular Plevna; and [I] was obliged ignominiously to retreat,
Fleming having of course prepared a rich discourse for my
edification. . . .

I go to Hatfield to-morrow afternoon, but shall come up
every day.

HATFIELD HOUSE, *April* 23.—I must write you a line, tho'
I am almost incapable of doing so. I feel stunned and
stupefied by, I suppose, the country air, and the unnatural

quiet around me. I am quite unhinged; the machinery has stopped . . . I have a complete day in the country, but I doubt whether I shall repeat it. The reaction is too painful. . . .

10, DOWNING STREET, *April* 24.—. . . I came up this morning, and am returning in an hour's time to Hatfield, where will be Münster. . . .

Nobody at Hatfield: literally the family, wh. however is large, singular, and amusing. The two girls, whom I never spoke to before, are very intelligent and agreeable; they are women, and yet not devoid of the grace of childhood, tho' highly cultivated. . . .

The weather was detestable at Hatfield, and I have had quite eno' of country air: a north-east blast, with a sprinkling of hail.

To Queen Victoria.

10, DOWNING ST., *May* 5, '78.—. . . If Cyprus be conceded to your Majesty by the Porte, and England, at the same time, enters into a defensive alliance with Turkey, guaranteeing Asiatic Turkey from Russian invasion, the power of England in the Mediterranean will be absolutely increased in that region, and your Majesty's Indian Empire immensely strengthened.

Cyprus is the key of Western Asia.

Such an arrangement would also greatly strengthen Turkey in Europe, and altogether she would be a stronger barrier against Russia than she was before the war.

If this policy be carried into effect, and it must be carried, your Majesty need fear no coalition of Emperors. It will weld together your Majesty's Indian Empire and Great Britain. As Lord Beaconsfield is soon to have the honor of an audience of your Majesty, he will reserve this great subject until that time.

Francis Knollys [1] to Montagu Corry.

HOTEL BRISTOL, PARIS, *May* 7, '78.—The Prince of Wales desires me to ask you to let Lord Beaconsfield know that, since H.R.H. wrote to him, he has met Gambetta. He was at M. Waddington's evening party last night, and was presented to the Prince by Lord Lyons. They had a long conversation together, in the course of which Gambetta expressed his hearty approval of every step taken by Lord Beaconsfield in connection with the Eastern Question, and his strong dislike to

---

[1] Afterwards Viscount Knollys.

the doctrine that nations having large armies at their command might upset all treaties in defiance of protests from those concerned and contrary to public law. . . .

It was not difficult for Schouvaloff to discover from Salisbury in general terms what the British Government did wish. There was, of course, no pretension that Turkey should emerge from an unsuccessful war, largely attributable to her own obstinacy, without serious loss and serious territorial curtailment; that victorious Russia should be asked to forgo all the fruits of her lavish expenditure of blood and treasure. But from Salisbury's despatch and from Beaconsfield's speech in the Lords it was obvious that their aim was to preserve for Turkey a compact and considerable territory, with a defensible frontier, both in Europe and in Asia; to prevent Russia from securing such a territorial rearrangement as would place Turkey permanently at her mercy, and as, in particular, would give her control of Constantinople, the Straits, the Black Sea, and the route through Mesopotamia to the Persian Gulf. In other words, Russia must abandon the plan of a big Bulgaria, a Russianised province extending from the Black Sea to the Ægean and almost to the very gates of Constantinople, embracing many Greek and Serbian localities and communities, and cutting the territorial connection between the Porte and its Greek, Albanian, and Slavonic provinces; and either Batoum and the Armenian conquests of Russia in Asia must be relinquished, or the effect of their loss must be neutralised in some other fashion.

Fully apprised of the points to which Beaconsfield's Government attached vital importance, and also of the unshakable firmness of its resolution, Schouvaloff started in the second week of May for St. Petersburg in order to obtain the consent of his imperial master and of Gortchakoff to an arrangement on the British terms. Beaconsfield told him in his last conversation before parting ' that it was only fair to state distinctly that we could not, in the slightest degree, cease from our plans of preparation; and that they must go on, even if there were a Congress.'[1]   He knew that

> The same arts that did gain
> A power, must it maintain.

It was this readiness of Great Britain for war that had brought Russia to reason.   Writing to the Queen half a year later, on November 29, in regard to the change in Russian policy, Beaconsfield claimed that ' it was the confidential announcement to the Sultan, Andrassy, and Rumanian Government, that, even if we were alone, we were ready on the 3rd May to effect the withdrawal of the Russians from E. Rumelia by force, that produced this great change.   The Sultan, sworn to secrecy, of course told his Greek physician; Andrassy, equally bound, of course, as we intended, revealed it to Bismarck; and Rumania, of course, to Russia.'   Helped, no doubt, by Beaconsfield's frank warning,   Schouvaloff's mission was on the whole successful.   The Emperor and his Chancellor consented in the main to such a curtailment of the big Bulgaria as Beaconsfield demanded; but about Batoum and Kars they were stiff, and Beaconsfield had to have recourse to other means to secure his purpose.

To Queen Victoria.

10, DOWNING ST., *May 23*, '78.—. . . No change whatever has occurred about the Cyprus scheme: but nothing could be done actively, till we saw our way, somewhat, as to Bulgaria and the European question.

Count Schouvaloff has returned. Lord Beaconsfield has not yet seen him, but Lord Salisbury's account is highly satisfactory, as regards European Turkey.

The Cabinet is to be summoned for noon to-morrow, when Lord Salisbury will make his statement, and if the Cabinet agrees, of which Lord Beaconsfield cannot doubt, a telegram (already prepared, for it is of great length) will be sent to Mr. Layard, who has been, all along, confidentially prepared for the proposal to the Porte.

No delay can be permitted in the negotiations with the Porte.   We shall offer a guarantee, a British guarantee, of all

[1] Letter from Beaconsfield to the Queen, May 7.

the Asiatic provinces to Turkey, and [we shall offer] Rumelia in Europe, tho' this, or any portion of Turkey-in-Europe, is not to be guaranteed. The result, if all be carried, as planned, into effect, will be that Turkey will still be an independent Power, with large possessions and resources. She will be as independent, and more powerful, than the Scandinavian kingdoms, and now, under the protection of England, will be the most effective, and indeed only possible barrier against an aggressive Russia.

If all is agreed to by the Cabinet, there must be an exchange of notes between Great Britain and Russia as to the terms agreed on, and a treaty or convention between Great Britain and Turkey.

With these documents we should be prepared to go into Congress, which will not be of long duration, and probably may meet in the middle of June.

May 26.—. . . He was disappointed in writing to your Majesty yesterday, not only from the bustle of the day, but because he did not feel able to place before your Majesty the state of affairs in as clear and precise a manner as was necessary.

On Thursday last Count Schouvaloff had his interview with Lord Salisbury, having arrived, himself, from St. Petersburg, the previous afternoon.

The Ambassador communicated to his Court the result of this interview in a telegram of 8 pages, and received an answer accepting all the modifications of the Treaty of S. Stefano, except one proposed by England, referring to the military occupation of Rumelia by Turkey.

All this was made known to the Cabinet on Friday, who are anxious not to press the point which was not conceded, as they are of opinion that the country would not approve of their refusing to go into Congress on a subject not of the first importance, especially when so much had been conceded.

Lord Beaconsfield not sanctioning these views, the matter is at present suspended after further discussion in the Cabinet of yesterday.

Count Schouvaloff had his interview with the Prime Minister yesterday at five o'clock.

The result of none of these negotiations will be made known at present, nor until they are formally sanctioned by the Congress. What will be made known to the country, if we come to a general agreement on all the main points, is that England has agreed to enter into the Congress to consider the Treaty of S. Stefano in all its bearings.

We have gone perfectly straight with Austria, and have agreed to support her in all her declared points of policy, except in insisting, that the Montenegrins shall not have the port of Antivari.

We do not think that this country could make of such a question a *casus belli*.

None of these negotiations have yet touched the Asiatic portion of the question. Nothing has, as yet, been said about Batoum and Kars, and we do not wish to enter into that till we have our answer from Constantinople about Cyprus. It may arrive to-day.

What does your Majesty think of making Mr. Roebuck a Privy Councillor ? Lord Beaconsfield believes he is a true patriot, and, tho' now very advanced in age and infirmity, such a distinction from his Sovereign would approve and adorn an honorable life. Perhaps, if your Majesty does approve of this suggestion, your Majesty would be so gracious as to telegraph to Lord Beaconsfield accordingly.[1]

The Congress is now looming in the immediate distance. P. Bismarck wishes it to be a Congress without *ad referendum*, or, he says, nothing will be really done. Such a Congress must be attended by Ministers of State, who can act on their own responsibility.

Lord Salisbury urges Lord Beaconsfield himself to go, as he is the only person who can declare with authority the policy of England : what she requires and what she will grant. He is pleased to say the Continental statesmen are afraid of Lord Beaconsfield.

This is a grave issue. . . .

Beaconsfield found, as he hoped, that the Sultan was ready to allow Great Britain to occupy Cyprus in return for a guarantee of his Asiatic dominions; and, as he expected, that the Tsar was extremely indisposed to relinquish Kars and Batoum. The way was therefore clear for the agreements with Russia and Turkey which his letters to the Queen had outlined. The memorandum embodying the agreement with Russia was signed by Salisbury and Schouvaloff in London on May 30; and the Cyprus Convention with the Porte was signed by Layard and Safvet at Constantinople on June 4.

Under the memorandum Russia made a fairly complete surrender of that ' Big Bulgaria ' which was the outstand-

---

[1] The Queen expressed approval, and Roebuck was consequently sworn of Privy Council.

ing feature of the Treaty of San Stefano. She consented
to the exclusion of Bulgaria from the Ægean coast; to the
rectification of its proposed western frontiers upon the
basis of nationalities, so as to exclude non-Bulgarian
populations; and to its division into two provinces,
separated by the Balkan range, of which only the province north of the Balkans should have political autonomy
under the government of a Prince, while that south of
the Balkans should receive a large measure of administrative self-government, with a Christian governor.
Thus the Balkan range, and not the southern frontier of
a big Bulgaria, would become the frontier of the effective
Turkish empire; though the provisions as to Turkish
military action in the southern province, to which
Beaconsfield naturally attached great importance, were
left in rather a vague condition. The Turkish army was
to retreat from that province, but Turkish troops were
to be allowed to re-enter to resist insurrection or invasion.
Moreover, ' England reserves to herself to insist at the
Congress on the right of the Sultan to be able to canton
troops on the frontiers of Southern Bulgaria '—a proposition as to which Russia also reserved complete liberty
for herself in the Congress discussion. The British
Government further demanded that the superior officers
of the militia in the province should be named by the
Porte, with Europe's consent. Owing to the ' warm
interest ' which England felt in the cause of the Greeks,
it was arranged that the Treaty of San Stefano should be
modified so as to give the other Powers, and notably
England, as well as Russia, a consulting voice in the
future organisation of Thessaly and Epirus and the other
Christian provinces under the Turkish dominion. The
retrocession of Rumanian Bessarabia to Russia was
accepted ' with profound regret '; but, as the other signatories of the Treaty of Paris were not prepared to fight
to preserve the boundaries therein assigned to Rumania,
England could not incur alone the responsibility of opposing the change.

Thus, with the exception of Bessarabia, England secured under the memorandum nearly all the changes her Government desired in that part of the Treaty of San Stefano which affected Europe. In regard to Asia it was otherwise. Bayazid the Tsar consented to return, and he gave an assurance that there should be no further extension of the Russian frontier in Asiatic Turkey; but in regard to Kars and Batoum he continued adamant. In the text of the memorandum the Beaconsfield Government did not disguise what appeared to them to be the gravity of the decision, and at the same time gave an intimation of their own resolve to secure British interests in these regions in another fashion. These were the words used:

In consenting not to contest the desire of the Emperor of Russia to occupy the port of Batoum and to guard his conquests in Armenia, the Government of Her Majesty do not hide from themselves that grave dangers—menacing the tranquillity of the populations of Turkey-in-Asia—may result in the future by this extension of the Russian frontier. But Her Majesty's Government are of opinion that the duty of protecting the Ottoman Empire from this danger, which henceforth will rest largely (*d'une mesure spéciale*) upon England, can be effected without exposing Europe to the calamities of a fresh war.

It is clear from this passage, as well as from his letters to the Queen, that Beaconsfield would not have sanctioned the signature of the memorandum, had he not seen his way to safeguard by other means the Asiatic dominions of the Porte. He was greatly disturbed by the power which her Armenian conquests had given Russia, not only of dominating the Black Sea, but also of attacking at will, overland, either Palestine and Egypt on the one hand, or the Baghdad route to the Persian Gulf on the other. A successful advance in either direction would be a menace to India, whose security was the principal aim of his Eastern policy. In this region, too, England must act alone. 'We had felt from the beginning of the war,' writes Northcote, ' that, while several nations were quite as much interested as ourselves in the results of a possible overthrow of Turkey-in-Europe, or even more so, and while we might therefore reckon on their co-operation in that part of the Empire, none of them were likely to care much what happened to Turkey-in-Asia, which to us was even more important than the other.   We were convinced that Russia would try to console herself for any diplomatic defeat she might sustain in Europe, by making good terms for herself in Asia.' Russia had already shown this tendency in the negotiations which resulted in the memorandum.   It was impossible, after the experience of the brittle nature of Russian pledges about Turkestan, to place much reliance on the Tsar's engagement not to extend the Russian frontier farther in Asia Minor.   Hence the necessity of a convention with Turkey.

The convention was very short, containing only one operative clause.   It provided that, if Russia retained Batoum, Ardahan, Kars, or any of them, the British Government would defend by force of arms the Sultan's Asiatic dominions, as demarcated by the Congress, against any fresh Russian attack.   In order to be in a position to execute this engagement the English were to be allowed to occupy and administer the island of Cyprus, paying annually to the Sultan (under an annex to the Convention) the excess of income over expenditure in the island— the sum being calculated on the basis of the previous five years.   Further the Sultan promised to England ' to introduce necessary reforms, to be agreed upon later between the two Powers, into the Government and for the protection of the Christian and other subjects in these [the Asiatic] territories.'

Thus was the policy of the Cabinet of March 27 in effect carried out, only with such modifications as the regained goodwill of Turkey would fortunately permit. The ' new Gibraltar ' was secured by arrangement with the Sultan.   The idea of Melos or Mytilene had long been abandoned. and Cyprus had been definitely selected

as, in Northcote's words, ' a place of arms in the Levant,
where our ships could lie in bad weather, and troops
and stores could be held ready for action.' Situated
as it is in the far north-east corner of the eastern Mediterranean, between Syria and Asia Minor, no position in
that sea could be more handy for checking Russian
advances on Egypt or the Persian gulf. With Cyprus
occupied by consent and a defensive alliance contracted
with the Porte, it was obviously unnecessary to occupy
Alexandretta, the natural landing-place of troops collected
in the island for the protection of Turkey-in-Asia. The
choice of Cyprus was probably Beaconsfield's own.
Nearly thirty years before, he had represented one of
the Jerusalem gossips in *Tancred* as saying, ' The English
want Cyprus, and they will take it as compensation ';
but it is quite certain that, until he arranged for its
acquisition, very few people in England indeed had ever
cherished the slightest wish for it. To an imaginative
mind, like his, which had long brooded over the problem
of the Levant, the possibilities of this romantic island
were familiar. He had spent a day there in 1831; but
then he professed, in whimsical fashion, to find a ' land
famous in all ages ' more delightful as the residence of
Fortunatus, in the fairy tale of *The Wishing Cap*, ' than
as the rosy realm of Venus or the romantic kingdom
of the Crusaders.'[1] Phœnicians and Ptolemies, Greeks
and Romans, Templars and Lusignans, Venetians and
Turks were among the motley throng who at one time or
another had there borne sway. It must have given
Beaconsfield's historical sense a real satisfaction to provide in the nineteenth century for the establishment of
British administration in a land which had been won
in arms in the twelfth century by Richard Cœur de Lion.

The responsibility incurred by England in giving a
guarantee, against Russian attack, of the curtailed Turkish
dominion in Asia, was no doubt serious. But it added
very little to the responsibility which the Beaconsfield

[1] See Vol. I., p. 175.

Government, confident of the support of public opinion, had already accepted; namely that of preventing in arms a southern advance of Russia from Armenia down the Tigris or along the Syrian coast. The two responsibilities dovetailed into each other; the same force, applied in the same direction, would go far to accomplish both aims. Moreover, Turkish dominion rested on a much firmer foundation in Asia than in Europe. In European Turkey a minority of Mohammedans kept in subjection a majority of Christian Serbs, Bulgars, and Greeks. But Asiatic Turkey was, broadly speaking, a Mohammedan country; Christian Greeks, Armenians, and others, though constituting a local majority in some districts, were on the whole largely outnumbered by the Mohammedan population. Beaconsfield never forgot that England, in India and elsewhere, was a great Mohammedan Power; and it seemed to him reasonable and natural that such a Power should be ready, where India's security was at stake, to guarantee the Mohammedan core of an empire whose ruler was the Caliph.

Not that, in signing the convention, Beaconsfield and his Cabinet showed any neglect of Christian interests in Asiatic Turkey. It was, no doubt, a comparatively small, though not unimportant, matter that the occupation of Cyprus ensured the fair treatment of the Cypriot Greeks, the large majority of the inhabitants of the island. But the convention further gave England special rights and responsibilities in regard to the whole Christian and subject population of the Asiatic territories of the Porte; and Beaconsfield and his colleagues took measures to secure that the Sultan's promises of better government and due protection should really be carried out. To this end they appointed as British military Consul-General for Anatolia Sir Charles Wilson, an engineer officer whose labours in surveying and exploring Palestine and the Sinaitic peninsula had given him a wide knowledge of Near Eastern conditions and a sympathy with the subject peoples of Asiatic Turkey. Fixing his headquarters at Sivas, he divided Anatolia into four consulates, with a military vice-consul in each. For these posts young officers of promise were selected, one of them being Lieutenant H. H. Kitchener, afterwards the famous Field-Marshal. With assistants of this calibre, and full of energy himself, Wilson in less than a couple of years effected considerable improvements in local government, securing the dismissal of some of the worst Turkish officials, and making Greeks and Armenians realise that they had powerful protectors against oppression. These results could not, of course, have been obtained without the goodwill of the Porte, which was actively displayed so long as Beaconsfield was in power and so long as Layard represented Great Britain at Constantinople. But when Gladstone ousted Beaconsfield in 1880, and Goschen was sent to Constantinople to threaten and coerce rather than to offer friendly advice, the efforts of the consuls in Anatolia were largely nullified; and at length in 1882, on the pretext of the outbreak of war against Arabi, these officers were all transferred from Asia Minor to Egypt. British influence, which had been making rapid headway, disappeared from Anatolia, to be replaced almost immediately by German penetration. There was no longer any disinterested protection on the spot for oppressed Christians; and in course of time Bulgarian atrocities were reproduced on an enormously magnified scale in Armenia. Some share in the responsibility for these horrors must rest with the statesman who clamoured when in opposition for a foreign policy based on humanity, but who yet, when in power, while retaining the material gage, Cyprus, which was acquired for England by what he denounced as an ' insane covenant,' destroyed the machinery set up under that covenant for securing better government for Asiatic Christians.

Both the memorandum and the convention were preliminaries to the Congress, and were to be kept secret at least till they had served their purpose in Congress. When they became known, strong objection was taken both to the policy of making preliminary agreements, and to the secrecy in which they were shrouded. But, as Bismarck saw no less than Beaconsfield, it would be absurd for Powers who were in serious diplomatic conflict, threatening war, to enter into Congress without having examined the ground beforehand, and ascertained whether there was a chance of mutual understanding. A rupture in open Congress would much more certainly lead to war than a mere diplomatic difference uncomplicated by the immense publicity and the personal vanities and jealousies inseparable from a Congress. If preliminary agreements are admitted to be reasonable and in some cases inevitable, temporary secrecy follows almost as a matter of course. It has been suggested that Russia would not have signed the memorandum had she known of the convention, nor Turkey the convention had she known of the memorandum. But if both agreements were in themselves reasonable, the objection has little force in it; moreover, the suggestion is probably quite unfounded. Russia, indeed, had received in the very language of the memorandum a hint of England's resolve to take special charge of Asiatic Turkey; and there was nothing in the convention which abated a jot of Russia's material gains under the Treaty of San Stefano, as modified by the memorandum. As for Turkey, though the memorandum did not regain for her all for which she may have hoped, she owed the reconstitution of her power in Europe to British exertions; and in that reconstitution and in the guarantee of her Asiatic dominions she obtained an amply adequate return for the surrender of Cyprus—a surrender, moreover, which was entirely in the interest of her own defence.

The secrecy which Beaconsfield rightly thought important was broken, and broken in the most mischievous manner; because one instrument became known to the public without the other, and thus the world obtained a very one-sided impression of British policy, which could only be fairly appreciated on a comparison of both documents. Through carelessness at the Foreign Office, which put a secret paper in the power of a temporary copying clerk, the *Globe* was enabled to publish the Anglo-Russian Memorandum, just as the Congress was beginning its labours. Naturally a considerable sensation was caused by the discovery that England and Russia had come to a private agreement covering most of the points of controversy; and, in the absence of all knowledge of the Cyprus Convention, there was strong comment on the apparent surrender of British interests in Asiatic Turkey. The Government vented its vexation in some-what random denials, and in the abortive prosecution of the clerk, Marvin, at Bow Street. This step was taken, Northcote assures us, on Salisbury's direct order from Berlin. Beaconsfield, who suspected that Cross, the Home Secretary, was responsible, rated the colleagues whom he had left at home for the fatuity of their pro-ceedings.

To Sir Stafford Northcote.

BERLIN, *July* 2, '78.—. . . What in the name of Heaven, or rather Hell, and all the infernal regions of all religions, could have induced you all to arrest, and prosecute, that poor wretch Marvin? This is the dirtiest linen that was ever washed in public by any family on record. You will not, probably, be able to punish him, and, if you do, he will have general sympathy—this sad wretch entrusted with secrets of State with a salary of 8d. an hour! Before this we were supposed to be the not contemptible victims of an imperial misfortune; now we are ridiculous. I never was so astonished in my life, as when P. Gortchakoff gave me his telegram from London with the police examination. . . .

Throughout these spring weeks of anxious negotiation and preparation, Beaconsfield kept up his appearances in society, not without some detriment to his precarious health.

To Lady Bradford.

10, DOWNING STREET, *April* 29.—. . . I am glad you approve of the Bishop.[1] It seems a success with all 'schools of Church thought,' *alias* Church nonsense.

---

[1] The appointment of Maclagan, afterwards Archbishop of York, to the bishopric of Lichfield.

May 4.—A long Cabinet, only just over, much to do in a short space, and then that terrible Academy dinner, wh. some day will be my death. Oh ! how many social taxes there are worse than the income tax !

May 9.—. . . I think Gladstone's speech exceeds any of his previous performances. What do you say ?

May 10.—. . . I dined yesterday at Gloster Ho.: a little round table—only Pss. Mary, and some generals, . . . but it was pretty agreeable.

To Anne Lady Chesterfield.

10, DOWNING STREET, *May* 13.—I have hardly time to write. I saw S. yesterday, who looked better. They wanted me to dine there, but I was engaged, to De la Warrs, same time. I am grateful to anyone, who asks me to an agreeable dinner on Sunday. It is a terrible day in this lone, rambling house: no secretaries to enliven the scene, scarcely a servant visible, for it's their holiday. . . .

May 15.—Forgot to tell you I went to St. Anne's, Soho, on Sunday last with Ld. Barrington. Service a little too long, but, on the whole, good. Out of the great choir of more than fifty persons, the chief performances were by a little boy, who reminded me of S.'s piping bullfinch.

Notwithstanding the ceaseless inspections of the Guai under my windows, and the magnificence of their bands, wh. are superior even to the cathedral service of the Soho Church, peace is said to be in the ascendant. England, however, goes on with its warlike preparations all the same. . . .

I dine to-day with the Clevelands, and meet the Duke of Cambridge, my warlike colleague. . . .

To Lady Bradford.

10, DOWNING STREET, *May* 16.—. . . I was obliged to leave my dinner yesterday at the Clevelands at ten o'ck., being wretchedly ill: but a vapour bath last night, and my doctor this morning, have patched me up. . . .

With the memorandum signed, the meeting of the Congress was assured. Russia had ascertained and, in the main, accepted the modifications on which England insisted in what is called in the memorandum the *Preliminary* Treaty of San Stefano; and England in return, fortified by the Cyprus Convention, had promised not to dispute the remaining terms of that treaty, if after due discussion Russia persisted in maintaining them.

Being thus in a position to know with tolerable certainty what she must surrender and what she might hope to keep, Russia found herself able to comply with what had been England's unvarying demand, that the whole of the peace terms should be submitted to the judgment of the Congress, so that the ultimate treaty should be a genuine European pact.

The Congress would therefore meet, armed, at Bismarck's suggestion, with full powers to act without reference home. Whom should England send to this great assize at Berlin ? There could be but one answer. Salisbury was unquestionably right in urging that Beaconsfield should himself act as her chief representative. Who but he could cope, face to face, with statesmen of the European reputation of Gortchakoff, Andrassy, and, above all, Bismarck ? He was clearly not very difficult to persuade. So entirely did the idea of representing his country in an important international assembly fall within the scope of his political ambition, that he had even at one moment contemplated going to the Constantinople Conference. There he would have been out of place; but all considerations pointed to his attendance at Berlin, save those of age and health. The Queen, in her affectionate concern for her faithful servant, was disposed to think these drawbacks prohibitive, unless the venue of the Congress were transferred to some city much nearer England than Berlin. The Prince of Wales took an active share in promoting Beaconsfield's appointment.

The Prince of Wales to Queen Victoria.

MARLBOROUGH HOUSE, *May* 28, '78.—I had occasion to see Mr. M. Corry to-day on several matters, and in course of conversation we discussed the chances of a Congress becoming daily more likely and as to who was going to represent England. I said, of course Lord Beaconsfield was the only man who could go, as however clever Lord Salisbury undoubtedly was, still after his fiasco at Constantinople he really would not do. Then Lord Lyons is not a Cabinet Minister and if he went it would be almost an affront to Lord Odo Russell, and then he would have to refer everything home. I understand that P. Bismarck particularly begs that there should be no *ad referendum*.

Under these circumstances, it strikes me more forcibly than ever that the Prime Minister is not only the right man to represent us at a Congress but the only man who can go, as he would show Russia and the other Powers that we were really in earnest. . . .

It struck me that if you wrote a mem. which was to be laid before the Cabinet, in which you expressed your positive desire that Lord B. should go, the matter would then be settled. . . .

Queen Victoria to the Prince of Wales.

BALMORAL, *May* 30, '78.—. . . . The subject of Lord Beaconsfield attending the Conference has been before me, and if it were to be at Brussels, The Hague, or Paris . . . I should (and I have done so) urge it, but you know that Lord Beaconsfield is 72 and $\frac{1}{2}$,[1] is far from strong, and that he is the firm and wise head and hand, that rules the Government, and who is my great support and comfort, for you cannot think how kind he is to me, how attached ! His health and life are of immense value to me and the country, and should on no account be risked. Berlin is decidedly too far and this is what I have said. I wrote to him on the subject two days ago, and have not had an answer yet. . . .

To Queen Victoria.

10, DOWNING ST., *May* 31, '78.—Lord Beaconsfield . . . could not ' answer about attending the Conference,' for nothing had been sufficiently settled to place before your Majesty until to-day.

There is no possibility of changing the venue of the Congress. As the Prime Ministers of the other Powers will represent their respective States, we must not employ, for that purpose, mere professionals. Men like Bismarck treat them with little consideration, as they fancy, or choose to fancy, that they know nothing of the real feelings of the country that sends them.

What we propose for your Majesty's consideration is, that your Majesty should be represented at the Congress by your Majesty's chief Minister and also by your Majesty's Secretary of State. Lord Beaconsfield will travel to Berlin by himself and with his personal suite, and he will take four days for this operation, so that he will arrive quite fresh. Then, he will

---

[1] He was really 73$\frac{1}{2}$.

have interviews with all the chief statesmen, so that there will be no mistake as to the designs, and the determination, of this country. Lord Beaconsfield proposes to attend the first meetings of the Congress, and exhibit his full powers, and then return to England, leaving Lord Salisbury to complete all the details of which he is consummate master.

Lord Salisbury highly and entirely approves of this arrangement, which will prevent all mischievous and malignant rumors of two parties in the Cabinet, and will, as he is pleased to say, give great weight and authority by the presence of Lord Beaconsfield to the proposals and policy of your Majesty's Government.

From Queen Victoria.

BALMORAL, *May* 31.—. . . The Queen again cyphered about Lord Beaconsfield's going to the Congress if it takes place. There is no doubt that no one could carry out our views, proposals, etc., except him, for no one has such weight and such power of conciliating men and no one such firmness or has a stronger sense of the honour and interests of his Sovereign and country. If only the place of meeting could be brought nearer!

On June 1 the Cabinet definitely decided to enter the Congress, and appointed Beaconsfield and Salisbury as British Plenipotentiaries, with whom was associated Odo Russell, the Ambassador in Berlin. Beaconsfield's final arrangements for his journey, his provision for carrying on the Government at home in his absence, and the spirit and hopes with which he entered the Congress, sufficiently appear from his letters to the Queen before his departure.

To Queen Victoria.

10, DOWNING ST., *June* 3, '78.—Lord Beaconsfield . . . has just received your Majesty's telegram of this morning. Lord Salisbury has, he believes, communicated to your Majesty, why we did not insist on the removal of the Russian army before the Conference took place.

We never made a *sine qua non* of this condition, because it also involved the withdrawal of the British fleet. But we insisted strongly on the point, because the policy was proposed by P. Bismarck, and we thought he might have been offended by its withdrawal.

Lord Beaconsfield believes that some communication has taken place with the German Chancellor, and that the withdrawal of the Russian army will be the first question which Congress will have to discuss.

Lord Beaconsfield contemplates departing on Saturday and arriving in four days at Berlin. Lord Salisbury will quit London on Tuesday night and travel all through.

Lord Beaconsfield will travel with Mr. Corry, a fair linguist in more than one tongue, and his personal attendants. There will also be immediately attached to him his second private secretary, Mr. Algernon Turnor, to attend to home business, as it arrives and accrues, and Mr. Austin Lee (of the Foreign Office), who is an accomplished linguist and experienced in affairs. They will follow Lord Beaconsfield, and the mass of the Embassy will arrive with Lord Salisbury.

Three years ago or so Lord and Lady Salisbury prepared a fête of great splendor at Hatfield in honour of their guests, the Crown Prince and Princess of Germany. Four thunderstorms destroyed everything except Hatfield House itself.

The Crown Princess, remembering that day of magnificent disaster, expressed on this occasion her wish to pass two days at Hatfield in comparative quiet.

Nothing could be more complete than the reception, on which the sun never ceased to smile, but the Fates had decided against a tranquil visit, and the party was broken up in alarmed disorder.[1]

June 7.—. . . Your Majesty must pardon a somewhat rambling despatch, but really until your Majesty appointed him your Majesty's Plenipotentiary, he had no idea how many things there were to do, and how many persons to see, and all in so short a time !

The treaty with Turkey is so drawn, that it will fall to the ground in the case of Russia not taking Batoum and surrendering Kars : and this will be clearly placed and strongly urged when the occasion offers. If Russia chooses to retain her prey, Lord Beaconsfield has no fear but that our country will approve of, and sanction, the Cyprus policy.

He has arranged, subject to your Majesty's sanction, that the Chancellor of the Exchequer should be the Minister in general communication with your Majesty. It adds, in his case, to great labors and responsibilities, but he is the Minister who, from the variety of his knowledge of what is going on, will be most qualified to inform and assist your Majesty. . . .

Lord Beaconsfield was tempted to take the gorgeous fish with him to Berlin and feed the Congress, which it could well

[1] By the news of the attempt of Nobiling on the German Emperor's life.

do, but, on soberer reflection, he has been persuaded to dine on a small portion of it this evening, and his housekeeper, who is a countrywoman of Mr. Brown, is to kipper (he thinks that is the word) the great mass, so he will breakfast on it when he returns, and so he will be under a double obligation to its skilful captor, and owe two meals to your Majesty's faithful attendant.

There was a Cabinet to-day settling and completing the instructions of the Plenipotentiaries. It was a satisfactory Cabinet. They are to meet twice a week as usual, and as often besides as they like, so that the country may not consider them as ' cyphers.'

He will observe all your Majesty's commands about writing and telegraphing.[1] He is not too sanguine as to the result, but shall do his utmost to achieve success. In all his troubles and perplexities, he will think of his Sovereign Lady, and that thought will sustain and inspire him.

June 8.—. . . Your Majesty's box this instant arrived as he was about to write a few last lines to Balmoral.

The Socialist movement[2] requires the utmost vigilance and preparation. The moment we have concluded our treaty, we must give up our whole mind to it.

Lord John Manners, the most faithful of colleagues, and one of the best of men, errs in one respect. He views the pending negotiations as if they referred to a Treaty of Peace between Great Britain and Russia. That would be comparatively very easy work: but, in truth, we are only critics of a treaty between two other Powers and their belligerents, and we must take care not to be in the position of maintaining our own opinions by withdrawing from the negotiations. The other Powers might persist in their labors, and arrive at a settlement without us.

He will not now dwell upon these great affairs, as in three hours he departs, and is distracted by many claims and calls. These are literally his last lines, addressed to one whose imperial courage has sustained him in immense difficulties, whose kindness has softened labor, and who possesses the utmost devotion of his brain and heart.

---

[1] The Queen had asked for frequent telegrams and letters, both about Beaconsfield's health and about the progress of the Congress. If he could not write or telegraph himself, Her Majesty hoped Corry or Salisbury would do so.

[2] The Queen had written anxiously about the developments of the Socialist movement in Germany.

CHAPTER IX.

The Congress of Berlin.

1878.

The Congress of Berlin, with its resulting treaty, is a landmark in the diplomatic history of the nineteenth century; but of the real value and importance of its work there have been very varying appreciations. One thing, however, is certain. It marked the zenith of Beaconsfield's career. It revealed him finally to the world as a great international figure; a statesman capable of reducing for the moment the redoubtable Bismarck himself to a secondary place in a European assembly held in Bismarck's own capital. Here were gathered, to name only the principal actors—for Russia, Gortchakoff, the wily Chancellor, suffering now from the infirmities of age, and jealous of his brilliant second, Schouvaloff; for Austria-Hungary, Andrassy, the Magyar statesman, who restored, temporarily at least, the tarnished prestige of the Hapsburg Empire, accompanied by Karolyi, afterwards popular in London as Austrian Ambassador; for France, the Anglo-Frenchman Waddington, a product of English education and French commerce, a blend of archæologist and statesman; for Italy, Corti; for Turkey, Carathéodory; for Great Britain, along with Beaconsfield, Salisbury,[1] destined to loom large in the world's eyes as the century waned, and Odo Russell, the experienced diplomatist; while Bismarck, the President of the Congress, was supported by the distinguished names of Hohenlohe and Bülow, one a future Chancellor of the

[1] With Salisbury as private secretary was Mr. Arthur Balfour, so that both Beaconsfield's successors as Conservative Prime Ministers were present with him at Berlin.

German Empire, the other the father of a future Chancellor[1] and himself Minister of State. Among all these renowned and forceful personalities, one figure stood out pre-eminent. He arrested attention immediately by a strange and picturesque distinction of personal appearance; he enforced respect and achieved a diplomatic success by the manifestation of a clear purpose, a dexterous intellect, and an inflexible will. The Empress Augusta wrote to Queen Victoria before the end of June that she could clearly see that Beaconsfield formed the real centre of the Congress and represented the greatest authority there. The general voice of the Plenipotentiaries would readily have echoed, before they had sat many days, the historic words in which Bismarck expressed his own estimate: ' Der alte Jude, das ist der Mann' (' the old Jew, that is the man ').

The personal impression which Beaconsfield made on his fellow-Plenipotentiaries was heightened by the practice, which he followed throughout, of addressing the Congress, not in the usual language of diplomacy, French, but in his native English. This was not his original intention, and Odo Russell was fond of relating how the change was brought about. The story has been often printed, and has been told in recent years, with some variations of detail, in Redesdale's *Memories*, ch. 35, and in G. W. E. Russell's *Portraits of the Seventies*. Corry and the other secretaries were horrified lest, by speaking, as he proposed, in French, their chief should become the laughing-stock of Europe. They knew that, in spite of a few winters spent in Paris in middle life, his French was so completely of the Stratford-atte-Bowe type that he pronounced the French word for ' grocer ' as if it rhymed with ' overseer.' They dared not remonstrate with him themselves, but applied to the Ambassador, who was accustomed to deal with delicate situations, for his help. It was the evening before the Congress met, and Odo Russell caught the great man as he was retiring to bed

---

[1] Who was present at the Congress in a subordinate capacity.

A dreadful rumour, he said, had reached him, that Beaconsfield would address the Congress next day in French.
That would be, said Lord Odo, a very great disappointment to the Plenipotentiaries. ' They know that they
have here in you the greatest living master of English
oratory, and are looking forward to your speech in
English as the intellectual treat of their lives.' Beaconsfield gravely promised to give the matter due consideration; and the result of a night's reflection was that he used
English in Congress next morning and always afterwards.
Lord Odo, Redesdale tells us, was wont to declare that
he never knew whether Beaconsfield took the hint or
accepted the compliment.

The British Prime Minister came to Berlin with the
prestige of the statesman who had determined the basis
on which alone the Congress could assemble. All the
terms of the Treaty of San Stefano must be submitted
to the judgment of Europe—such had been throughout
the claim which his Cabinet had put forward. He
had made it clear that, rather than accept Russia's
Eastern settlement, England was, in the last resort, prepared to fight. Accordingly other Governments had
followed England's lead, and Russia had capitulated.
' England,' Disraeli's sometime Radical foe, Roebuck,
said, ' now holds as proud a position as she ever held;
and that is due to the sagacity, and power, and conduct
of the despised person once called Benjamin Disraeli,
but now Lord Beaconsfield.' ' You would hardly believe,'
wrote Sir Henry Elliot to Beaconsfield from Vienna on
June 11, ' the change in the position of England in Continental estimation that has been operated within the
last two months; but it would be gratifying to those who
have brought it about if they could see it as much
as we do, who live abroad.' Bismarck's opening words
in Congress, as President, registered Beaconsfield's
success. The object, he said, for which the Congress
was assembled, was to submit the work of San Stefano
to the free discussion of the Governments which signed

the treaties of 1856 and 1871. 'La Russie est sur la sellette,' is the caustic expression in which M. Hanotaux [1] sums up the situation.

Moreover, Beaconsfield and Salisbury came prepared in a sense in which no other attendants at the Congress were prepared. They had concluded an agreement on essentials with their principal opponent, Russia; they had supplemented this agreement by a convention with Turkey, Russia's defeated foe; they had achieved an understanding with Austria, whose geographical position and prudent reserve must give her an enormous influence in Balkan arrangements; and they were on excellent terms with France and Italy. The policy of Germany was a mystery. Whom would she favour, Russia or England ? She would be very loth to irritate her great Eastern neighbour, with whom her relations were those of ostentatious intimacy; at the same time it was essential to keep Austria, now recovering from her humiliation in 1866, in line with the German movement. It was not without significance that, in consequence of the recent serious attack on his life, the Emperor William was incapacitated during the sittings of the Congress for the performance of his State duties; and that the royal and imperial welcome and hospitalities to the Plenipotentiaries had to be undertaken on his behalf by the Crown Prince as regent. By position and temperament the Emperor William was disposed to attach peculiar importance to the preservation of close relations with his brother autocrat at St. Petersburg. The Crown Prince, himself of mildly liberal tendencies, and the devoted husband of an accomplished English princess, naturally inclined rather to a system of co-operation with England. In these circumstances both Bismarck and Beaconsfield felt the advisability, if not of a preliminary understanding, at least of a preliminary conversation in which soundings could be taken. It was not delayed

---

[1] See two articles on the Berlin Congress by M. Hanotaux in *Revue des Deux Mondes*, September 15 and October 1, 1909.

Beaconsfield journeyed to Berlin in the leisurely manner which he had indicated to the Queen, spending four days on the way. He left London on Saturday, June 8, with Montagu Corry and his own personal attendants, and (he told Lady Chesterfield) 'with couriers *en avant*, who will arrange about hotels and beds and other botherations.' He crossed the Channel that afternoon, the passage being ' as still as the Dead Sea itself,' and slept at Calais. Next day, Sunday, he travelled no farther than Brussels where, as he wrote to Queen Victoria, ' the King and Queen of the Belgians entertained him right royally. Lord B. sate between them at their banquet, and was struck and gratified by the considerable culture, and the quiet good taste, of the Queen.' Monday night was spent at Cologne, and, as the result of this unhurried progression, he reached Berlin at 8 o'clock on Tuesday evening (June 11) ' as fresh as if he was taking his seat in the House of Lords.' He took up his quarters, not at the British Embassy, but at an hotel, the Kaiserhof.

It was fortunate that he was fresh, as Bismarck at once proposed a personal meeting. Beaconsfield, realising the full importance of seeing the Chancellor before the other Plenipotentaries, due on the morrow, arrived, went to his house the same evening after dinner.

To Queen Victoria.

BERLIN, *June 12*, 1878.—. . . [Lord Beaconsfield] arrived here last night about 8 o'clock and while dining received a visit from the chief secretary of Prince Bismarck inviting an immediate visit. Accordingly, at a quarter to ten o'clock Lord Beaconsfield waited on the Chancellor. They had not met for sixteen years; but that space of time did not seem adequate to produce the startling change which Lord B. observed in the Chancellor's appearance. A tall, pallid man, with a wasplike waist, was now represented by an extremely stout person with a ruddy countenance, on which he is now growing a silvery beard. In his manner there was no change, except perhaps he was not quite so energetic, but frank and unaffected as before. He was serious throughout an interview which lasted one hour and a quarter, and apparently sincere. He talked a great deal, but well and calmly: no attempt at those grotesque expressions for which he is, or has been, celebrated.

The interview was not unsatisfactory, and Lord B. arrived at the conclusion that the Prince was anxious for a peaceful settlement. He suggested to Lord B. that, as, probably, President of the Congress, he should, in his initial speech on Thursday, group the questions according to their importance, and that he should like to begin with Bulgaria, as perhaps the most weighty, 'Tho' we need not avoid a single article of the Treaty of San Stefano, if we took them in their regular order, many days, and the freshness of the Congress, would be expended on such insignificant topics as the port of Antivari, "a cavern in a rock," and the borders of Montenegro and Servia, and places of which no one ever heard before this war. All these concern Austria and he wished to serve Austria, but Austria is not going to war with Russia. Let us therefore deal with the great things that concern England, for England is quite ready to go to war with Russia.' . . .

The order of business which Bismarck proposed was in itself reasonable; and it was thoroughly congenial to Beaconsfield, who regarded the undoing of that provision of the Treaty of San Stefano which constituted the new Bulgaria as the most urgent and indispensable duty of the Congress. Before, however, coming to grips with this vital question on the following Monday at the second session, there was much inevitable formality, including the formal opening of the Congress on Thursday the 13th, and many receptions, including a week-end visit to the Crown Prince and Princess at Potsdam. Beaconsfield was indefatigable, throughout these early days, in making himself acquainted with the personalities of the statesmen with whom he had to deal, in gauging their purposes and their power to enforce them. We possess happily very full evidence of the impression which the Congress and its characters, its negotiations and its festivities, produced on his mind. Besides writing numerous letters to the Queen, describing his actions and experiences, he also kept a diary for Her Majesty, which he forwarded to her in instalments, and for which he apologised as 'rough notes,' 'rough journal for One Person only.' He reported, moreover, at intervals to Northcote, as acting head of the home Government; and, of course, the Berlin visit did not interrupt the correspondence with Lady Bradford and Lady Chesterfield, though his letters to these ladies often merely reproduced the phraseology of those to the Queen. From the diary and the letters to the Queen it has been possible, by a little dovetailing and rearrangement, to compile a fairly continuous narrative in his own words, the extracts from the letters being indicated by the letter *L* and those from the diary by the letter *D*; supplementing this narrative occasionally by his letters to his other correspondents. Here is the story of the opening days.

To Queen Victoria.

L. BERLIN, *June* 12.—The Congress will certainly meet to-morrow, but the non-arrival of the Turkish envoys, who have been shipwrecked in the Black Sea, may retard decisions, as there would be scandal in coming to any absolute conclusions in their absence.

Lord B. had an audience of State from the Crown Prince this morning[1] at ½ past three o'clock. The Prince received himself and Lord Salisbury at that hour; the other Ambassadors at four.

Count Andrassy, Prince Hohenlohe, and ultimately Schouvaloff, thinking that Lord B. was not going to the Palace until four o'clock, all called as he was on the point of girding on his sword, and would come up tho' it was only 'serrer la main.' Count Andrassy is a picturesque-looking person, but apparently wanting calm. He expressed his determination to stand by England, and said, had we known each other sooner, affairs would have been more satisfactory. He is to call on Lord B. to-morrow morning, so as to have a full conversation before the Congress.

Lord B. and Lord S. were received by the Prince at ½ past three, and were ushered at once into the closet by the Master of the Ceremonies, without the form of presentation.

The others were received at four o'clock, and were all formally presented. The English Ambassadors were half an hour with the Crown Prince in easy and agreeable conversation. It was like a continuance of the Hatfield visit. The manner

---

[1] Used for 'afternoon,' as in 'morning call,' '*matinée*.'

of the Crown Prince singularly natural and cordial. His remarks full of sense, and not devoid of humor.

The Crown Prince and Princess have showered kindnesses on Ld. B. during his visit to Berlin, and what makes them more delightful is, that he feels they must be, in no slight degree, owing to the inspiration of one to whom he owes everything. He found a most fanciful basket of flowers on his arrival, so vast that it nearly covered the table, and crowned with a bed of delicious strawberries environed with orange flowers and roses.

After his 'gala' audience he paid a visit to the Crown Princess; a very agreeable one. He was pleased by her second son, a young sailor about to sail for Japan; a spirited youth with a frank, merry countenance.[1]

In the evening he dined at the British Embassy, one of the finest mansions in Berlin: a quiet party.

He hopes his most beloved Sovereign is well and happy. Distant from your Majesty in a foreign land, and with so awful a responsibility, he feels more keenly than ever, how entirely his happiness depends on his doing his duty to your Majesty, and on your Majesty's kind appreciation of his efforts.

He heard by tel. from the D. of Cambridge this morning of the death of the King of Hanover at Paris. It was not known here until he mentioned it at Court to the Crown Prince.

June 13.—Count Andrassy called on him by appointment this morning at eleven o'clock, and remained upwards of an hour. He covered the floor with maps, and his chief object seemed to be to persuade Lord B. that the line of the Balkans, which he had signed a memorandum to support, was inferior to another one which he was anxious should be substituted for it. Lord B. thought that, the question being once settled, it had better not be disturbed. In truth, common persons understand what the line of the Balkans means, but the complications of Count Andrassy, all arising out of little interests and obscure influences of his own, would only convey an impression, that we were surrendering something intelligible and substantial.

At two o'clock the Congress met in the Radzivill Palace— a noble hall just restored and becoming all the golden coats and glittering stars that filled it.[2] Ld. B. believes that every day is not to be so ceremonious and costumish. P. Bismarck, a giant, 6 feet 2 at least, and proportionately huge, was chosen President. In the course of the morn. P. Gortchakoff,

---

[1] Prince Henry of Prussia.

[2] The hall is, I think, too large for business,' wrote Beaconsfield to Lady Bradford. 'At least no one's voice, except my own, was, I understand, heard.'

a shrivelled old man, was leaning on the arm of his gigantic rival, and, P. Bismarck being seized with a sudden fit of rheumatism, both fell to the ground.   Unhappily, P. Bismarck's dog, seeing his master apparently struggling with an opponent, sprang to the rescue.   It is said that P. Gortchakoff was not maimed or bitten thro' the energetic efforts of his companion.

The business of the Congress was chiefly formal, except that Lord B. brought forward the question of the retirement of the Russian troops from Constantinople, which, after some discussion, was adjourned till Monday, when the Congress meets again.   The P[leni] P[otentiaries] are arranged at the table according to the letters of the alphabet—Austria first, and so on.   Lord B. sate between the 3rd Austrian P.P. and Lord Salisbury.

At seven o'clock was a gala banquet at the old Palace: a scene of extraordinary splendor.   It is a real Palace, but, strange to say, all the magnificent rooms and galleries of reception are where, in the days of Queen Anne, poor poets used to reside: the garrets.   It must have been much more than 100 steps before Lord B. reached the gorgeous scene, and he thinks he should have sunk under it, had not, fortunately, the Master of the Ceremonies been shorter-breathed even than himself, so there were many halts of the caravan.

It was, on the whole, the most splendid scene that Lord B. ever witnessed.   The banquet was in the White Hall.   The costumes were singularly various and splendid.   Lord B. sate between Count Andrassy and the Russian Ambassador (Count Schou.) and Andrassy was next to Bismarck.   All were opposite the Royal Family.   The Crown Princess encouraged him by many kind glances, and the C. Prince and Princess drank to the health of the Queen of England, which Lord B. acknowledged with some agitation.   It was the health of one of whom he was almost always thinking.   After the banquet, the guests assembled in the gallery.   He made the acquaintance of the Gd. Duke and Duchess of Baden, the father, and the grandfather of our future Princess,[1] and many other notables.   In appearance, the grandfather is a remarkable man: he said he was nearly eighty, but he looked scarcely its moiety.   Lord B. mistook His Royal Highness for the father of the bride, who soon appeared as 'The Red Prince.'

The Duke of Connaught, in consequence of the death,[2] did not dine at the White Hall and, therefore, his *fiancée* declined, tho' her sister, and P. Henry of the Netherlands, were present.

[1] The late Duchess of Connaught, daughter of Prince Frederick Charles of Prussia, ' the Red Prince.'
[2] Of the King of Hanover.

But after dinner, the Duke of Connaught invited Lord B. to visit him at the Palace of the Crown Prince, and there introduced him to his bride. Lord B. told her Royal Highness that your Majesty was a little jealous of my seeing her first, which amused them. The Crown Princess was present, and we passed half an hour in merry talk.

June 14.—This morning he had a long interview by request with Count Schouvaloff, who, it appears, was rather frightened by the tone, or reported tone, of Lord B. The point was respecting the political and military control by the Sultan over the southern province of Bulgaria. The Russians propose that the Sultan should not be permitted to employ his own army in the government of this part of his dominions. This is outrageous, and to give the Sultan the line of the Balkans for his frontier, and not permit him to fortify and defend them, is monstrous and a gross insult to England. Lord B. spoke thunder about it. It will be given up by St. Petersburg.

Afterwards, an interesting visit to the Empress. She was very kind, remembered Lord B. at Windsor, and her last words to him at the Duke of Cambridge, etc., etc.

D. NEUES PALAIS, POTSDAM, *June* 16.—Arrived here yesterday afternoon. A most kind reception, and every comfort. Charming suite of rooms, in one of which Crown Prince born, and fire in every chamber. So much care about my not taking cold, that I sometimes fancy, on this and other occasions, that a benignant, tho' distant, influence deigns to guard over me.

Palace, described by Lord Malmesbury in his journals as the most hideous of existing structures, pleased me: probably the last erection of the Rococo: reminded me a little of the Palace at Wurzburg. Lord Salisbury was my companion, and we dined alone with the Crown Princess and Her Imp. Highness's immediate attendants. Conversation animated— as Dr. Johnson would say, ' good talk.'

Before I went down to Potsdam, I had, by his invitation, an interview with Prince Bismarck, which lasted upwards of an hour. What his object was, or is, I have not yet discovered. There was no business done: it was a monologue; a rambling, amusing, egotistical autobiography. As His Highness had requested the interview, I would not open on any point. Lord Salisbury, equally invited, had an audience almost immediately after me, and of the same surprising character. Lord Odo had warned me, that the interview would probably be to ascertain how squeezable I was with respect to Russia— my interview with Count Schouvaloff having alarmed that personage. But not a word of business from Prince Bismarck, either to Lord Salisbury or myself. Perhaps when he made the appointments he had counted on having certain proposals from Russia, which, however, were not ready.

Before interview with Ct. [*sic*] Bismarck, had a long one with Carathéodory, the 1st Turkish Plenipotentiary, a perfect Greek of the Fanar: good-looking, full of finesse, and yet calm and plausible: a man of decided ability.

This morning at eleven we took a delightful drive with the Crown Princess and saw the famous orangery and Sans Souci with all its fountains playing. Sans Souci was one of the places I always wished to see, and never expected. It was deeply interesting, and the library of the great man [1] highly characteristic. I was prudent, and declined the afternoon drive to Babelsberg, and instead am writing this and many other things.

There is to be a grand banquet here this evening to the English Mission and the Royal Family. The Crown Prince, who came down from Berlin, paid me a visit in my rooms, which has just finished, and we all return by a special train, and the Congress meets to-morrow at two o'clock.

BERLIN, *June* 17.—The banquet yesterday was bright and agreeable in a splendid Rococo hall, which would have driven old Lord Malmesbury, with his frigid Ionic taste, quite crazy. I sate next to the *fiancée* of our English Prince, and having made only a superficial observation before, with my poor near-sight, determined to profit by the opportunity, as if I were 'our own correspondent.' She is delicate and has an extremely interesting appearance and quite pretty. She has a beautiful complexion, a fine brow, lovely eyes, a short upper lip, and singularly beautiful hands. Confirmed in my first impression, that she was not, as reputed, shy but extremely modest; but calm and quite self-possessed. She conversed freely and most naturally. All her remarks were sensible; her inquiries, as to her new home, pertinent and in good taste. I should say of a sympathising, affectionate nature, and winning from her innocence and gentleness of manner. I think she will be a source of happiness to my beloved Sovereign, and adorn and animate the Royal circle.

On Monday, June 17, the real business of the Congress began, with the question of the constitution of the new Bulgaria; and, before the week was over, Beaconsfield, after a short but severe struggle, had imposed his will, and secured the solution he demanded. The Schouvaloff memorandum was by this time public property, but

[1] Frederick the Great.

Beaconsfield did not allow himself to be disturbed by this vexatious revelation. 'The publication,' he wrote to Northcote, ' was, and is, a mortifying incident, but it can only injure us with our own friends at home, and it is to be hoped that what we are doing here will, when fairly known, remove all this annoyance. The publication was calculated to injure us with Austria and Turkey, but we had made our book with Austria, and Turkey is in our pocket. People here never mention Batoum or questions of that calibre. There is only one thought— Bulgaria. The sixth article of the Treaty of S. Stefano is the real point for which the Congress is assembled. . . Upon its treatment depends whether there shall be a Turkey-in-Europe or not.' Under the memorandum it will be remembered that, while Russia consented to the division of Bulgaria into two provinces, of which only the northern should have political autonomy but the southern should remain as a portion of Turkey with a large measure of self-government, she did not accept, but remitted to the Congress, the British contention that the Sultan should have full military rights in this southern province, and especially the right to canton troops on its frontiers. Beaconsfield had hesitated about going into Congress at all with this important point unconceded; he was determined now to obtain it, and had already spoken 'thunder' about it to Schouvaloff. His claim was that the province south of the Balkans should be under the political and military control of the Sultan, and that it should be known by the name of Eastern Rumelia. Let us see how he described this eventful week to the Queen.

To Queen Victoria.

D. *June* 17.—Second meeting of Congress. Boundaries of Bulgaria treated by P. Bismarck as the most important question before Congress, and the most difficult.

The 6th article of the Treaty of San Stefano being read, the English P.P. proposed two resolutions.

1. That the chain of the Balkans should be the new frontier of Turkey.

2. That in the country south of the Balkans, the Sultan should exercise a real political and military power.

The Russian P.P. disputed both these propositions: recommended a division of Bulgaria by a longitudinal line, and that the Turkish troops should not be permitted to enter the province, which the Russian P.P. styled 'South Bulgaria.'

After discussion, P. Bismarck adjourned the question till Wednesday, remarking that, in the interval, the Powers most interested should confer together. This is the system on which His Highness manages the Conference, and it is a practical one. All questions are publicly introduced, and then privately settled.

In the afternoon at 6 o'clock great dinner at P. Bismarck's. All these banquets are very well done. There must have been sixty guests. The Princess was present. She is not fair to see, tho' her domestic influence is said to be irresistible. I sate on the right of P. Bismarck and, never caring much to eat in public, I could listen to his Rabelaisian monologues: endless revelations of things he ought not to mention. He impressed on me never to trust Princes or courtiers; that his illness was not, as people supposed, brought on by the French War, but by the horrible conduct of his Sovereign, etc., etc. In the archives of his family remain the documents, the royal letters, which accuse him after all his services of being a traitor. He went on in such a vein that I was at last obliged to tell him that, instead of encountering 'duplicity,' which he said was universal among Sovereigns, I served one who was the soul of candor and justice, and whom all her Ministers loved.

The contrast between his voice, which is sweet and gentle, with his ogre-like form, striking. He is apparently well read, familiar with modern literature. His characters of personages extremely piquant. Recklessly frank. He is bound hand and foot to Austria [? Russia], whether he thinks them right or wrong: but always adds 'I offered myself to England, and Lord Derby would not notice my application for 6 weeks and then rejected it.'

Afterwards a reception at Lady Odo's.

June 18, *Waterloo Day.*—At twelve o'clock to-day, Count Schouvaloff and Baron d'Oubril for Russia, Count Andrassy and Baron de Haymerle for Austria, Lord B. and Lord Salisbury for England, met on the two English resolutions.

I introduced the matter fully, and in the same decided tone in which I had previously in a long interview addressed Count Schouvaloff. He, with little hesitation, tho' with regret announced that he accepted the line of the Balkans, but the second resolution was so serious, that he could not act on his powers, but must refer to the Emperor. Throughout the discussion Austria entirely supported England; it lasted four hours, wh. were nearly the severest four hours I can well recall.

Much mortification among Russians at our understanding with Austria. I declared the English proposals as to what is called 'Delimitation of Bulgaria' an ultimatum. Consternation in the Russian camp.

At half-past five I called on Prince Gortchakoff at his desire, and had a most important conversation with him.

June 19.—An anxious day. The Congress met, but did nothing, as Count Schouvaloff had received no instructions.

Banquet at the Italian Ambassador, Count de Launay. I sate next to Count Corti. Knowing my man: that he was a favourite of Bismarck, who talked freely to him, and that, as the Ambassador of an almost neutral State, he had the ear of everyone, I told him, in confidence and as an old friend, that I took the gloomiest view of affairs, and that, if Russia would not accept our proposals, I had resolved to break up the Congress.

June 20.—On this day, by appointment, Great Britain, Austria and Russia met again at our Ambassador's, when Count Schouvaloff stated that they had been unable by telegraphic communication to arrive at any results, and that the Russian P.Ps. had despatched a Colonel to St. Petersburg, and that his return might possibly occur on Friday evening.

L. Russia has asked for 4 and 20 hours for the Emperor's answer, as they have not sufficient powers in regard to this important point and have been obliged to send an envoy to St. Petersburg. I have no fear about the result, as I have intimated in the proper quarter, that I shall break up the Congress if England's views are not adopted. When this change in the Treaty of San Stefano occurs Russia will be again entirely excluded from the Mediterranean, the object of the last, and all their wars. Much attention is now paying to Greece.

The Congress continues to make progress, and P. Bismarck wants much to take the waters of Kissingen, and sometimes dreams of finishing in a few days: but Greece, the Straits, Batoum, and some others, are massy matters.

P. Bismarck's plan is, when we have settled all the great questions, to execute a treaty to that effect, and to leave to a local commission consisting of the resident Ambassadors, and some experts, the research and settlement of what he calls the little questions, involving no great political interest or divergence of general opinion. When these are satisfactorily arranged, they will probably be annexed to the Treaty of *Haute Politique* which the P.Ps. will have previously executed.

The great heat has been favorable to Lord Beaconsfield's menace of gout. It has disappeared—and he is very fairly well.

D. Friday, June 21.—I was engaged to-day to dine at a grand party at the English Embassy: but, about 5 o'clock, Prince Bismarck called on me and asked how we were getting on, and expressed his anxiety and threw out some plans for a compromise, such as limiting the troops of the Sultan, etc., etc.

I told him that in London we had compromised this question, and in deference to the feelings of the Emperor of Russia, and it was impossible to recede. ' Am I to understand it is an ultimatum ?' ' You are.' ' I am obliged to go to the Crown Prince now. We should talk over this matter. Where do you dine to-day ?' ' At the English Embassy.' ' I wish you could dine with me. I am alone at 6 o'clock.'

I accepted his invitation, sent my apology to Lady Odo, dined with Bismarck, the Princess, his daughter, his married niece, and two sons. He was very agreeable indeed at dinner, made no allusion to politics, and, tho' he ate and drank a great deal, talked more.

After dinner, we retired to another room, where he smoked and I followed his example. I believe I gave the last blow to my shattered constitution, but I felt it absolutely necessary. I had an hour and ½ of the most interesting conversation, entirely political; he was convinced that the ultimatum was not a sham, and, before I went to bed, I had the satisfaction of knowing that St. Petersburg had surrendered.

Accordingly next morning, Saturday, June 22, at half-past ten, Beaconsfield was able to telegraph to the Queen and to the Chancellor of the Exchequer: ' Russia surrenders, and accepts the English scheme for the European frontier of the Empire, and its military and political rule by the Sultan. B[ismarc]k says, "There is again a Turkey-in-Europe." ' ' It is all due to your energy and firmness,' was the Queen's reply.

The Queen was right; the result *was* due to Beaconsfield's energy and firmness. ' I have to hold terribly firm language,' he told Northcote. ' I have had a hard time of it, as I am brought forward as the man of war on all occasions, and have to speak like Mars.' But he regarded his success as ' breaking the back ' of the business of the Congress. It meant the exclusion of Russia from the Mediterranean, ' to settle herself upon whose shores was the real object of the late war. P. Gortchakoff says, " We have sacrificed 100,000 picked soldiers, and 100 millions of money for an illusion." ' Bismarck said to Beaconsfield, ' You have made a present to the Sultan of the richest province in the world; 4,000 square miles of the richest soil.' ' We have gained a great victory here,' Beaconsfield told Lady Chesterfield on June 28, ' the extent of which is hardly yet understood in England.' Some, however, in England understood it. ' Joe Cowen,' wrote Barrington to Beaconsfield from the House of Commons on June 24, ' said to me just now in the lobby, " Well, when he comes back the nation ought to give him another Blenheim " ! So you will see at all events that some Radicals appreciate your capacity as a statesman.'

Beaconsfield did not rely solely on the firmness of his language; on his mere declaration that he would break up the Congress rather than give way. He took the practical step of ordering a special train to be in readiness to carry the British mission back to Calais. Corry received the instructions while his chief leant, after his wont, on his arm during a morning walk *unter den Linden* on Friday the 21st, the day on the evening of which the delay granted to Russia for her answer expired; and Bismarck's hurried and unexpected call at the Kaiserhof in the afternoon was due to his knowledge of the order. Bismarck was determined to bring the Congress to a successful conclusion, and to avoid a war which could not fail to embarrass Germany. He must find out in person whether the ultimatum was final, and he persuaded Beaconsfield to throw over his engagements and dine with him quietly, in order that he might thoroughly explore his mind and intentions. Bismarck was that evening convinced himself, and he made it his business to carry conviction to the Russian Plenipotentiaries; and the victory was won.

Corry was wont, in later life, to recount the proceedings of this fateful Friday with picturesque detail; but perhaps, for the purposes of history, it is better to rely on a contemporary letter which he wrote to a friend.

Montagu Corry to Lady Ilchester.[1]

KAISERHOF, BERLIN, *July* 2.—. . . When Lord B. told Russia that, unless Turkey had the Balkan line with all rights of defending it accorded to her, and unless this new Bulgaria shd. be so reduced that its most southern part shd. be many and many a mile from the coveted Mediterranean, we shd. leave Berlin, or in other words go home to prepare for war with Russia, men were aghast. Bismarck was as alarmed as annoyed, Russia frantic, France and Italy astonished, Andrassy delighted but incredulous ! The acute crisis lasted from Lord B.'s distinct avowal of his intention at one of the private *séances* of the chief Plenipotentiaries on Tuesday the 18th till 5 p.m. on the 21st. At one moment all looked as if Russia could not give in, and I had made arrangements for a special train for England at a few hours' notice, when *the* incident of the Congress occurred, which I make no secret of though it is not known.

At 3.45 [2] on the 21st Bis. called, and I showed him, dressed in general's uniform, into my chief's room—he (Bis.) charging me to know when it was 3.55, as he had an appointment at 4 ! And so this meeting between the two great men lasted about 7 minutes. But the business did not take long. ' Is this really the ultimatum of England,' said P. Bis. ' Yes, my Prince, it is,' replied Lord B. Just one hour after that, we learnt that the Tsar agreed to the entire English scheme. . . .

The week's struggle, ending in an excited meeting of Congress on the Saturday to register Beaconsfield's victory, brought on an attack of gout, and so prevented him from spending a second week-end at Potsdam.

To Queen Victoria.

L. *June* 23.—I hear nothing about the Emperor which does not reach the ears of your Majesty in the bulletins. I have tried to obtain fuller information, but have not felt justified in saying anything to your Majesty which might have distressed and perplexed your Majesty. I have heard contrary

[1] Now the Dowager Lady Ilchester.
[2] It will be noticed that Corry gives the hour of Bismarck's famous call as 3.45, whereas Beaconsfield told the Queen that it was about 5 o'clock.

accounts to those of the bulletins, but inquiry has made me, I am glad to say, doubtful of their accuracy.

I should say Mr. Waddington looks like an *épicier*, and I think his looks do not bely his mind and general intelligence.[1]

With regard to myself, I am a little suffering from gout: it came on the night before last. I could have cured it, but there was an important and rather excited Congress yesterday, and I had to speak, and that always develops the complaint, so I remain a prisoner, which prevents my passing the day at Potsdam. It is a great loss, but the gentle Princess, who reigns in that fairy-land of Rococo, has forgiven me for my absence, and has graciously sent me fruit and flowers to tell me so.

I have just observed, that in the hurry of writing, in order to gain the messenger, I have violated all etiquette, and addressed my beloved Sovereign in the first person. My first impression was to destroy the letter, and write again by to-morrow's messenger. But a day lost is dreadful, and on the whole, I think it best to throw myself on your Majesty's ever prompt indulgence, and venture to describe myself with all duty and affection, your Majesty's devoted BEACONSFIELD.

June 24.—The Conference sate three hours to-day. Satisfactory progress. The Russian proposals as to occupation rejected, and greatly reduced.

D. In the evening Lady Odo's reception; very full and a splendid house. She is quite out and out the leader of fashion in Berlin—plays her part admirably. It is absolutely necessary to go to these receptions, but the late hours try me. I begin to die at ten o'clock and should like to be buried before midnight. But, in a Congress, absence from any influential assembly of human beings is a mistake. So much more than the world imagines is done by personal influence.

The Countess Karolyi receives on Wednesdays. She is very pretty and pleasing and I believe irreproachable for all the duties of life. Remarkably unaffected. I sate next to her at dinner, and as she had the menu in her hand, in order to say something, I asked her whether she was studying her campaign. She said quite innocently, ' Oh no—I never refuse a dish.'

I watched her and it was literally true. I watched her with amazement, that so delicate and pretty a mouth could perform such awful feats.

June 25 and 26.—Meetings of Congress both days, and pro-

---

[1] The Queen had asked for Beaconsfield's opinion of Waddington. To Baron Lionel de Rothschild Beaconsfield wrote a more favourable description —' an *épicier*, but a good man—not what the French call *méchant*. He thinks he talks English, but it is American.'

gress well kept up. P. Gortchakoff, who is reported in the newspapers as having retired from the Congress, is seldom absent, and never ceases talking. P. Bismarck says ' Gortchakoff thinks he was made for a great parliamentary debater. It is our misfortune.' Prince Gortchakoff observed to me, on the contrary, that P. Bismarck was a very bad President, as he had no experience of Congresses, and conducts business ' as if he were in a Parliament.' P. Gortchakoff has only been two days absent: one at an early sitting, really from gout: the other, after the Balkan victory, when he did not show from chagrin.

Beaconsfield found time, now that the back of the business was broken, to send Lady Bradford a descriptive account of his experiences.

To Lady Bradford.

BERLIN, *June* 26.—. . . This is a wondrous scene; life in its highest form; and the interest wh. *la haute Assemblée* (our technical title) excites seems to increase every day.

Mine passes in attendance on the Congress; not very severe —from two till five: and in interviews with the great guns, which is far more important. Prince Gortchakoff reappeared to-day, the first time since my great victory. He is the most courteous gentleman, quite caressing, and it is quite painful to me to occasion him so much annoyance :[1] particularly as he tells me he only came to the Congress to make my acquaintance, Frances Anne of Londonderry having always mentioned me in her letters, said she thought I shd. be Minister, and, if so, hoped we shd. be friends. And, now, we meet under such terrible and trying circumstances.

Ct. Andrassy is a very picturesque gentleman. I have gained him quite, and he supports me in everything. In fact the northern Alliance is broken up.

Schou. fights a difficult and losing battle with marvellous talent and temper. He is a first-rate parliamentary debater, never takes a note, and yet in his reply never misses a point.

Bismarck soars above all: he is six foot four I shd. think, proportionately stout; with a sweet and gentle voice, and with a peculiarly refined enunciation, wh. singularly and strangely contrasts with the awful things he says: appalling from their

[1] ' He entreated me,' wrote Beaconsfield of Gortchakoff to Baron Lionel de Rothschild, ' not to change the name of South Bulgaria into Eastern Rumelia, which he said would be the greatest humiliation to Russia which could be devised. It is quite distressing to refuse anything to this dear old fox, who seems melting with the milk of human kindness.'

frankness and their audacity. He is a complete despot here, and from the highest to the lowest of the Prussians, and all the permanent foreign diplomacy, tremble at his frown and court most sedulously his smile. He loads me with kindnesses, and, tho' often preoccupied, with an immediate dissolution of Parliament on his hands, an internecine war with the Socialists, 100's of whom he puts daily into prison in defiance of all law, he yesterday exacted from me a promise that, before I depart, I will once more dine with him quite alone. His palace has large and beautiful gardens. He has never been out since I came here, except the memorable day when he called on me to ascertain whe[the]r my policy was an ultimatum. I convinced him it was, and the Russians surrendered a few hours afterwards.

The weather here is a midsummer night's dream. Banquets and receptions every day and eve—but they don't clash with each other, as the hours are earlier, and the dinners, tho' sumptuous, are not long. People go to the theatre in the interval, or drive in the Thiergarten, wh. is a vast and most beautiful park, half forest; 1500 acres in size, wh. is exactly double of Hyde Park and Kensington Gardens together. . . .

The arrangements for the new Bulgaria and for Eastern Rumelia having been made, Beaconsfield, in his reports to the Queen, treated the discussions and conclusions of the next ten days somewhat summarily, dwelling more on the social than on the political side of his doings.

To Queen Victoria.

D. June 30.—No Congress on Thursday, as Russia requested a *relâche* in order to prepare for the difficult questions which have engaged us on Friday and yesterday. The boundaries of Servia, Montenegro, and the exchange with Rumania, not yet settled.

I went to the French reception last night (Saturday). It was male only; but I had never been, and, as I am to dine there to-day, it was necessary. I did a good deal of business, and find Count Andrassy a manageable man.

On Thursday, I called on Madame de Schleinitz, who appears to be one of the greatest ladies here. She is not very young, but still pretty, and as eloquent as Madame de Staël, tho' not at all priggish or ' superior.' She is highly cultivated and most animated, agreeable and amusing. In her chief tastes and thoughts, she told me, without reserve, that she was an enthusiastic Wagnerite, and a Pessimist !

L. July 1.—Congress sat 3 hours to-day. Rumanian deputies

were heard. Russia made them an offer which it is supposed they will accept. The boundaries of Montenegro were then settled, chiefly according to the wishes of Austria. The Danube and indemnity will be taken to-morrow, Greece on Wednesday, and it is contemplated that Batoum will be taken on Thursday; which engrosses Lord B.'s mind.

D. The Turkish Plenipos. gave their banquet this day at the Turkish Embassy. There was a disposition—too frequent on other occasions and in other things—to treat the Turkish invitation somewhat contemptuously, and to expect a not very satisfactory reception. It was just the reverse. It was impossible for anything to be better served than the dinner; there were a number of attendants in superb dresses, and one or two national dishes, especially a huge *pilaff*, created much interest. The French Ambassador, Mr. Waddington, expressed his wish to be helped twice to this dish, and mentioned incidentally that he had travelled for three years both in Asiatic and European Turkey.

Tuesday, July 2, was the Austrian banquet. Ladies were invited. I sate between the Countess Karolyi and the Princess Radzivill, both very pretty and very agreeable women. It was a most graceful dinner. We dined in the conservatory, surrounded by exotic trees and the murmur of fountains, and looking into a beautiful garden. There was a reception in the evening—very successful.

July 3.—The great banker of Berlin is Mr. Bleichröder. He was originally Rothschild's agent, but the Prussian Wars offered him so great opportunities, that he now almost seems to rival his former master. He has built himself a real palace, and his magnificent banqueting hall permitted him to invite the whole of the Plenipotentiaries and the Secretaries of Embassy and the chief Ministers of the Empire. All these last were present, except P. Bismarck, who never appears, except occasionally at a Royal table. Mr. Bleichröder, however, is P. Bismarck's intimate, attends him every morning, and according to his own account, is the only individual who dares to speak the truth to His Highness. The banqueting hall, very vast and very lofty, and indeed the whole of the mansion, is built of every species of rare marble, and, where it is not marble, it is gold. There was a gallery for the musicians, who played Wagner, and Wagner only, which I was very glad of, as I have rarely had an opportunity of hearing that master. After dinner we were promenaded thro' the splendid saloons and picture galleries, and a ballroom fit for a fairy tale, and sitting alone on a sofa was a very mean-looking little woman, covered with pearls and diamonds, who was Madame Bleichröder and whom he had married very early in lif, when he was penniless. She was unlike her husband, and by no means equal to her wondrous fortune.

July 4.—I dined with the Minister of State, Bülow; a small party, about sixteen. An accomplished and apparently most amiable family. Bülow himself attractive from his experience, highly courteous tho' natural manners; his wife, lively and well informed, and two or three sons at table, who I really think were the best-looking, the best-dressed, and the best-mannered young gentlemen I ever met. They were all in the army, but she has 7 sons, equally engaging it is said.

What amuses me rather at Berlin, is that almost everybody, certainly all the ladies, are reading my novels, from the Empress downwards. The ladies are generally reading *Henrietta Temple*, which being a 'love story' and written forty years ago, is hardly becoming an Envoy Extraordinary. The Bülow family generally are very deep in my works, but P. Bismarck seemed very familiar with them.[1]

July 5.—I dined with [Bismarck] alone, *i.e.*, with his family, who disappear after the repast, and then we talked and smoked. If you do not smoke under such circumstances, you look like a spy, taking down his conversation in your mind. Smoking in common puts him at his ease.

He asked me to-day whether racing was still much encouraged in England. I replied never more so; that when I was young, tho' there were numerous race meetings, they were at intervals and sometimes long intervals—Epsom, Ascot, Doncaster, Goodwood—and Newmarket frequently; but now there were races throughout the year—it might be said, every day of the year—and all much attended.

'Then,' cried the Prince eagerly, 'there never will be Socialism in England. You are a happy country. You are safe, as long as the people are devoted to racing. Here a gentleman cannot ride down the street without twenty persons saying to themselves, or each other, "Why has that fellow a horse, and I have not one?" In England the more horses a nobleman has, the more popular he is. So long as the English are devoted to racing, Socialism has no chance with you.' This will give you a slight idea of the style of his conversation.

---

[1] One Wednesday night during the Congress Odo Russell sent Beaconsfield the following note: 'At the Austrian Embassy this evening I was told by the Ministers of Public Instruction, of the Interior, and of the Police, that your presence here has produced boundless excitement in the "reading world." The circulating libraries, unable to meet the demands of the public, have bought up all the Tauchnitz editions of your works, both here and at Leipzig, while the booksellers have been obliged to telegraph to England for more copies of all your novels. The newspapers who publish *feuilletons* are all advertising translations for the coming quarter of your earlier books, etc., etc., etc.'

His views on all subjects are original, but there is no strain, no effort at paradox. He talks as Montaigne writes. When he heard about Cyprus,[1] he said: ' You have done a wise thing. This is progress. It will be popular; a nation likes progress.' His idea of progress was evidently seizing something. He said he looked upon our relinquishment of the Ionian Isles as the first sign of our decadence. Cyprus put us all right again.

L. The Rumanians have made a very good bargain for themselves, which was at the bottom of all their importunity. It is also an arrangement favorable to Turkey and Great Britain, for it gives them a seacoast[2] which would have been Bulgarian (Russian) but which now belongs to an Anti-Slav race.

Lord Beaconsfield can say nothing yet positive about Batoum, tho' its fate will probably be decided to-morrow. He thinks it, however, not impossible, that he shall succeed in getting it made a free port. This would do very well, if this be effected to-morrow. No time will then be lost in announcing the treaty with Turkey, and the occupation by your Majesty's forces of Cyprus.

This is going by an unexpected morning messenger, which is the reason that these lines are brief and hurried. He thinks there is a chance of his getting back before the 17th. If only a day, he will hasten instantly to Windsor: but he must bring the treaty, signed and sealed, with him, and that may take time.

It is evident, not only from this narrative, but from Beaconsfield's whole attitude in the negotiations both before and during the Congress, that he concentrated his personal attention on what he considered the two vital issues: first and foremost, that of Bulgaria, and, secondarily, that of Batoum and Armenia; and that he treated all the other points as of minor importance. It is also clear that, while he kept the general direction in his own hands, he left the spadework of the Congress, even in regard to the major issues, almost entirely to Salisbury, whose ' consummate mastery ' of detail he greatly admired, and whose assistance at Berlin he always treated as invaluable. The British Plenipotentiaries had no

---

[1] Beaconsfield obviously told Bismarck confidentially about the Cyprus Convention a few days in advance of its publication to the world.
[2] The Dobrudscha.

serious difficulty in carrying through their arrangement with Austria, by which that Power was to occupy and administer Bosnia and Herzegovina in the interests of the peace of Europe—a change which could not fail to improve the condition of their inhabitants. The understanding of Reichstadt and the Treaty of Vienna made Russia's consent to this occupation inevitable, though it was obviously reluctant. The only protest came from the Ottoman delegates; but it was clear that, after the range of the Balkans had been accepted as the northern limit of Turkey in the eastern half of the peninsula, the Sultan could not hope, in the remoter western half, to exercise any effective authority north of the Balkan parallel of latitude. To persist, as Carathéodory and his colleagues did, in passionate remonstrance, was only, as Beaconsfield and Salisbury told them, to call attention to the lack of wisdom and of regard for its true interests which marked the policy of the Turkish Government.

The smaller Powers interested in the Balkans were not members of the Congress, but representatives of their interests were permitted to plead their cause. The three States which had fought in Russia's interest—Rumania, Serbia, and Montenegro—had been scurvily treated in the Treaty of San Stefano; and though their position was improved by the Treaty of Berlin, owing largely to the efforts of the British Plenipotentiaries, the clauses which affected them were such as to inspire a doubt of both the power and the fair dealing of their great Slav champion. Russia insisted on the retrocession of Bessarabia from Rumania; Beaconsfield pleaded eloquently against this unnatural dismemberment, but he had recognised in the memorandum that England could not insist on the point as vital. He was instrumental, however, in securing compensation for Rumania, and additional territory for Serbia, at the expense of the bloated Bulgaria which Russia had endeavoured to create; and for Montenegro, Antivari. Beaconsfield was not altogether sorry that what he had always regarded as the ill-advised warlike adventures of these States should fail to realise the hopes in which they were undertaken. This appears in a letter which he wrote to the Queen for transmission to the Princess of Wales, to justify his treatment of the one small Balkan State which, on the urgent recommendation of the Powers, had desisted from its threatened invasion of Turkey.

To Queen Victoria.

OSBORNE, *July* 20, 1878.—Lord Beaconsfield is distressed to hear that Her Royal Highness the Princess of Wales should be under the impression, that Her Royal Highness, or her brother His Majesty the King of Greece, were injuriously misled by your Majesty's Government in the advice, which, when solicited, they offered to Her Royal Highness and her brother during the late war between Russia and Turkey.

That advice was not to interfere in the contest; and for these reasons.

The war would terminate either by the partition of the Ottoman Empire in Europe or by a peace in which the Powers would feel it necessary to re-establish the general authority of the Sultan.

In the first instance, which Lord Beaconsfield did himself not anticipate, the claims of Greece for a share of the partitioned Empire could not be resisted: indeed they would be probably anticipated by the arrangements of the Great Powers, as no satisfactory settlement could be made without their recognition and concession. No expenditure of blood and treasure would in all probability have strengthened the position of Greece under these circumstances.

In the event of the re-establishment of the authority of the Sultan, it was Lord Beaconsfield's opinion that the compensation allotted to the rebellious tributary States for their alliance with Russia would be as meagre as practicable; and the subsequent discontent of Rumania, Servia and Montenegro proves this. As the assistance of Greece was not as necessary to Russia as that of the tributary States, it is probable that she would have shared [? fared] even worse, nor is it likely that she would have obtained more than what the Congress has recommended that the Sultan should grant to her, and which was drawn up and recommended to the Porte by your Majesty's Government before it was adopted by the Congress.

This was the general view on which the advice of Lord Beaconsfield was founded, and the soundness of which he has had no subsequent reason to doubt; but in the instance

of Greece, there were other cogent reasons in favour of a
policy of reserve.

The rebellious tributary States could only be assailed by
Turkey on land, where they had many advantages; but Greece
possessed a considerable and wealthy seaboard, and Turkey
[had] at all times during the war a powerful and irresistible
maritime force. It is true that it is probable that your
Majesty's Government would not have permitted the bombardment of Athens, but they could not interfere to prevent the
belligerent rights of the Porte without stipulating at the same
time for the retirement of Greece from a contest which she
would in all probability have found equally unequal and
destructive.

The Greeks, whose cause was championed by Waddington, based their pretensions on the theory that
the business which the Powers had taken in hand at
Berlin was to partition the Turkish Empire among the
subject nationalities. What was being decided in regard
to Bulgaria, Bosnia, and Armenia, gave some colour to
their theory; and, if a general liquidation of a bankrupt
estate were in progress, their claims were undoubted
and considerable. But it is certain that no such view of
the duties of the Congress was entertained by the Powers
as a whole; and Beaconsfield, in particular, regarded its
especial work to be that of consolidating and restoring
the authority and stability of Turkey, after such outlying
portions of her territory had been lopped off as Russia's
victories made no longer defensible. While, therefore,
expressing warmly the traditional friendship between
Great Britain and Greece, he declined to go farther than
to recommend to the Porte a moderate rectification,
in favour of Greece, of the Turco-Greek frontier in Thessaly
and Epirus. He urged upon Turks and Greeks the
advisability of a good understanding between them, in
view of Pan-Slavonic ambitions.

These questions of the smaller Balkan States disposed
of, the Congress came, in its later sittings, to the critical
questions of Batoum and the Russo-Turkish frontier
in Asia. Beaconsfield had been anxious throughout
to reduce, as far as possible, Russian control over the

Black Sea; and he was no doubt influenced, to some extent, by the outcry of his friends in England at the failure of the Government to secure Batoum and Kars for Turkey under the Anglo-Russian Memorandum. The terms of that document with reference to Asiatic Turkey were that the Tsar 'consented to restore' to Turkey the valley of Alashkerd and the town of Bayazid, 'that valley being the great transit route to Persia'; while the British Government consented 'not to contest the desire of the Emperor of Russia to occupy the port of Batoum and to guard his conquests in Armenia.' Not only were these terms of an elastic nature as to the actual lines of demarcation to be drawn between Russia and Turkey; but the ' occupation' of Batoum was obviously a vague expression, by no means necessarily implying complete incorporation in the Russian dominions or complete subordination to Russian sovereignty. Beaconsfield therefore set himself to win Russia's consent to a considerable limitation of the occupation of the port; and, further, to such a frontier line as should give Asiatic Turkey a reasonable chance of defence against future attack. In both his aims he had an appreciable success, in spite of the fact that, during his final negotiations with Gortchakoff, his health broke down, and Kidd had to be hurriedly summoned to his patient from London. In consequence Beaconsfield's diary for the Queen was wound up in a few sentences. 'On Saturday [July 6],' he told her Majesty, 'I gave my dinner to the British Embassy, ordinary and extraordinary. I gave the hotel-keeper *carte blanche*, and he deserved it. It was well done, but I felt very ill, and the effort to welcome my guests brought affairs rather to a crisis. I called on P. Gortchakoff next morning on the Batoum affair, which I was fast bringing to a satisfactory settlement, and when I returned home I had a shivering fit.' He was asked to Potsdam again on this Sunday, and again had to decline the Crown Princess's invitation and to keep his room. But his indomitable resolution rose superior

to illness. He called once more on Gortchakoff on the
Monday, and attended Congress both that day and on
Tuesday, when the questions of Batoum and of the
Asiatic frontier of Turkey were finally settled. Only
when he had obtained the Tsar's promise that Batoum
should be a free and merely commercial port, and when
he had secured an unexpectedly favourable boundary
line for Turkey, did he succumb and retire to bed.

A temporary misunderstanding in the negotiations
between Beaconsfield and Gortchakoff about the boundary
line was responsible for something of a scene at one of the
last sittings of Congress. Schouvaloff was fond of telling
the story, and it is quoted by M. Hanotaux in his articles.
The President, threatening to leave for Kissingen if the
whole business was not wound up in twenty-four hours,
placed the two old statesmen side by side to explain
the agreement at which they had arrived. Each solemnly
produced a map with a line traced upon it, which he
alleged to be the line to which the other had agreed.
But the lines were different ! Whereupon Gortchakoff,
Schouvaloff said, turned to him in agitation and cried,
' Il y a eu trahison ; ils ont eu la carte de notre état-major '
—a secret map on which was drawn the line that marked
the extreme limit of Russian concession. Schouvaloff
used to intimate that what had really happened was that
Gortchakoff, through age and incompetence, had made
a muddle, and had himself handed to Beaconsfield during
their conversations the confidential map. Corry, on the
other hand, was in the habit of declaring that the tricky
Russian Chancellor endeavoured to get the better of the
British Prime Minister by sending him, after the boundary
had been fixed between them, a second map with a less
favourable line. As both statesmen were old, and both
ill, at the time of the interviews, it is perhaps most
charitable to assume a *bona fide* misunderstanding.
According to Schouvaloff, the discussion in Congress
became so warm between Beaconsfield and Gortchakoff
that Bismarck suggested the matter should be left for

final settlement to Salisbury and Schouvaloff, assisted
by Hohenlohe. There seems to be no doubt that, if
Beaconsfield did not get all he hoped for, he got decidedly
more than Schouvaloff was originally disposed to concede.

To Queen Victoria.

(*Telegram*) BERLIN, *July* 6, 6.35.—Russia, at the personal
instance of the Emperor, to show his anxiety to meet the wishes
of England, offers to make Batoum a free port. England has
reserved its opinion, otherwise the Congress might have
virtually closed to-day.

(*Telegram*) *July* 9, 1.30 *p.m.*—The affair of Batoum is just
arranged between myself and Prince Gortchakoff, which he
particularly desired me to tell to your Majesty. Russia
restores to Turkey the districts in question, which contain
one hundred and fifty thousand Mussulman population.
Russia retains the port, which is to be free and exclusively
commercial.

Montagu Corry to Queen Victoria.

BERLIN, *July* 9, '78.—Mr. Montagu Corry with his humble
duty to your Majesty. Lord Beaconsfield has, since the
change, last week, to almost wintry weather, been complaining
of a return of the throat affection, which has so often troubled
him, and of feeling unwell generally. On no occasion, however,
has he had to remain away from Congress, or to avoid a single
necessary act of business. But yesterday at the close of the
longest sitting of Congress which has yet taken place—lasting
four hours—Mr. Corry found Lord Beaconsfield to be so
suffering and prostrate that he despatched a telegram to
Dr. Kidd, asking him to come to Berlin at once.

Mr. Corry has to-day received a message that Dr. Kidd is
on his way and will reach Berlin to-morrow. To-day Lord
Beaconsfield is undoubtedly better, in every respect, and has
closed his day's work, which has included a sitting of the
Congress, without a return of the severe difficulty of breathing
which overpowered him yesterday. Your Majesty shall have
by telegram, after Dr. Kidd's arrival, a report of Lord Beaconsfield's condition.

July 11 (*Thursday*).—. . . Mr. Corry is happy to say that
Dr. Kidd finds no evil existing which may not be removed
entirely before the journey home. He will remain and accompany Lord Beaconsfield. . . .

Friday, July 12.—. . . This morning the gout is more
developed, and Dr. Kidd wishes Lord Beaconsfield to remain,
for the day, in a recumbent position, and to be as quiet as

possible, so that Lord Beaconsfield once again has to forgo the honour of writing to your Majesty with his own hand. At the same time Dr. Kidd finds very considerable improvement in all the symptoms, especially in the chest affection, and entertains no doubt whatever that Lord Beaconsfield will be well able to leave on Sunday morning and confidently hopes that he will reach London—on Tuesday—in better condition than for some months past.

Lord Beaconsfield desires Mr. Corry to let your Majesty know that Prince Bismarck called upon him at about 10 o'clock last evening and remained with him an hour talking over Hanoverian affairs. Lord Beaconsfield believes that the Prince is personally anxious for a settlement—but he detailed reasons which showed that, in His Highness's opinion, a *mezzo termine* was impossible. Prince Bismarck said Lord Beaconsfield might maintain a confidential correspondence with him on the subject whenever he liked.

Beaconsfield's efforts to secure more favourable terms for the Hanoverian Royal Family, in whom Queen Victoria, as their near relative, was much interested, were constantly met by Bismarck with the reply that restitution depended on absolute abdication—a condition with which the new King would not comply. Two letters that passed between the Chancellor and the Prime Minister in the following year, in pursuance of the arrangement for confidential correspondence, may be given here.

From Prince Bismarck.

BERLIN, *April* 16, 1879.

MY DEAR LORD,—I received your letter of the 6th inst., and feel very grateful to you for having diverted the subject to which it refers from the intended channel to that of a confidential correspondence between us.

Considering the painful position of Her Majesty Queen Mary and her daughters I think it proper that an adequate provision should be found for them, though I have distinctly to deny any kind of obligation on the part of the Prussian Government. The will of His late Majesty King George, of which you have been kind enough to send me an extract, rests on an erroneous supposition; from the memoir I beg to enclose you will see that there is under our administration no fund to pay the legacies. Nor is the settlement made in November, 1842, in favour of Queen Mary and her future progeny binding [on] the Prussian Government.

But, as the private property of the late King, existing in England and elsewhere, has gone to His Royal Highness the Duke of Cumberland exclusively, I am prepared to propose to the Prussian Ministers, and, after having obtained their consent, to His Majesty, that sums amounting approximately to those of the above-mentioned settlement should be paid to Queen Mary and her daughters during their respective lifetime. If in consequence of the attitude assumed by His Royal Highness the Duke of Cumberland in issuing his manifesto of June last the sequestrated property should return to the Prussian exchequer, I am, further, disposed, in a sense of equity, to exert myself for the purpose of securing the continuance of the said annuities and not allowing the three Royal ladies to become victims of an act they were unable to prevent.

While you kindly remember my house, I think with sympathy of the policy you are pursuing towards those unruly wasps that annoy the British lion in some of his dominions. My wife and my daughter, thanking you for your kind words, tell me to say that they will, like myself, be very happy to meet your lordship once more round a mahogany of moderate size. Believe me, my dear Lord, in true attachment, your faithful servant, v. BISMARCK.

To Prince Bismarck.

10, DOWNING STREET, *July* 13, 1879.

MY DEAR PRINCE,—I should have thanked you for your letter of true friendship long before this, but I postponed doing so while the affairs of the unhappy family seemed unsettled, as the members of it in this country were a little more restless than those on the Continent. I assume now, however, that everything is concluded: at any rate, my interference is formally terminated.

I will, therefore, only thank you for the cordiality with which you responded to my appeal, and I was gratified to feel, that I had not counted on your friendship in vain.

You seem to have got over your principal difficulties with your accustomed energy and resource; I have, also, little to complain of. The Afghan campaign realised all that I had contemplated, and I expect good and conclusive news from Africa, very shortly.

Your honor, and mine own, were concerned in carrying out the Treaty of Berlin, for it is not for a man like you to preside over a Congress, and see its provisions evaded. I wish we were smoking a pipe together, and could talk over the Greek affairs. The Janina question is not one of Turkish *amour propre*, at which we should all laugh. It involves

an Albanian war, which would probably be long and devastating, and precipitate results which it is the interest of Germany
and England to postpone.

The conduct of the Greek Govt., assuming certain conclusions in the Treaty of Berlin, which can't be found there, and,
simultaneously, declaring that they will not negotiate except
upon this imaginary basis, really arrests diplomacy.

A larger share of Thessaly to Greece would be a prudent and
satisfactory settlement. Think of this, my dear Prince !

I can't make out about our good friend Schouvaloff, who
is most popular with all of us. Will he return here ? I hope
so, for the sake of his society, tho', for public reasons, many
would be glad to see him in the first place.

Remember me, I pray, to the dear kind Princess, and to
your charming daughter, who, I hope and feel sure, is as happy
as she deserves.

I hope also that you yourself are well. The successful
should really enjoy good health, for chagrin is the origin of
most disorders. Though I fear there is little chance of our
meeting again, we must cherish good relations. That is not
difficult for me, since I remember our intimacy always with
pleasure, and entertain for you a sincere affection.—BEACONS-
FIELD.

Beaconsfield's diary and letters have shown how marked
was the attention Bismarck paid him; how he constantly
treated him as the pivot on whom the Congress turned.
There can be no doubt of the strong impression that the
Prime Minister made on the Chancellor. Besides the
well-known sentence about the ' old Jew,' there is a conversation reported by Poschinger in which Bismarck
described Beaconsfield as ' a capable statesman, far
above Gortchakoff and many others.' He recognised
in him not merely a finesse which he could well appreciate,
but also a directness, when business was in question,
which matched his own. ' It was easy to transact business
with him; in a quarter of an hour you knew exactly how
you stood with him; the limits to which he was prepared
to go were clearly defined, and a rapid summary soon
precised matters.'[1] To the Crown Princess Bismarck
said that Beaconsfield fulfilled all his ideas of a great

---

[1] Poschinger's *Conversations with Prince Bismarck.*

statesman, besides being personally agreeable and charming. Those who penetrated to Bismarck's private cabinet in Berlin, in the times immediately following the Congress, found that Beaconsfield's was one of three portraits there displayed; 'my Sovereign, my wife, and my friend,' the Chancellor explained. 'How I should have liked to have seen you and him [Bismarck] together !' wrote the Prince of Wales to Beaconsfield.

Beaconsfield, for his part, found that his experience in the Congress and his frequent talks with its President confirmed him in the view which the course of events, in spite of his original reluctance, had forced upon him—that a good understanding with Bismarck and Germany was for the time the best foundation of British foreign policy. But he was well aware of the dangers of Bismarck's statecraft, which carried out in action the old maxim, 'Divide et impera.' He knew that throughout the European negotiations of the last two years, the German Chancellor had played off England against Russia, and Russia against England, though he finally came out on England's side. Accordingly Beaconsfield declined entirely to entertain the insidious suggestion that England should take Egypt—a suggestion made with the view of permanently dividing England and France. He had been compelled to abandon for the present the idea of an Anglo-French alliance; but he was determined not to wound French feelings by aggressive action in regions where French interest was strong. On the suggestion that France should have free scope in Tunis he seems to have hesitated. He was shrewd enough to realise that the main object was to alienate Italy from France. But he was ready to gratify the French desire for expansion, and he agreed with Bismarck that it would be well if it should be gratified outside Europe. Accordingly Salisbury intimated to Waddington that no objection to a forward policy in Tunis would come from England.

Beaconsfield concentrated the attention of the Plenipotentiaries on himself at the close, as he had at the beginning, of the Congress. As soon as the question of Batoum was settled the Cyprus Convention was given to the world; and was recognised everywhere as a daring stroke with the obvious mark of Disraelian inspiration. Though there was some grumbling in France and a little in Italy, the general feeling in Europe was one of admiration of an instrument so well calculated to restore British prestige in the East. 'The traditions of England are not quite lost,' wrote the *Journal des Débats;* 'they still survive in the hearts of a woman and of an aged statesman.' Nowhere was there more applause and appreciation than among the diplomatists assembled at Berlin. If there was any annoyance felt in Russia, there was no suspension or even weakening of the good relations in Congress between Beaconsfield and Gortchakoff, Salisbury and Schouvaloff. At home the terms of the Convention reassured those of Beaconsfield's friends who had been dismayed at the concessions made to Russia in the memorandum; and, though many Liberals protested against the acquisition of fresh territory and fresh responsibilities, they recognised that public opinion was here decidedly against them. Barrington wrote on July 11, ' Charles Villiers tells me his friends have been raving a good deal to him about the awful crime you have committed, that it is unconstitutional, etc., etc.; but that his reply was that, although it might all be true, he thought his friends had better not drive the Government to a dissolution, as the Liberals would fare but badly in the country !'

With the blushing honours of the Cyprus Convention thick upon him, Beaconsfield rose from his sick-bed to sign the treaty which he had taken so considerable a part in arranging, and was even able to write to his Sovereign with his own hand an account of the historic day.

To Queen Victoria.

BERLIN, *July* 13, '78.—Lord Beaconsfield with his humble duty to your Majesty. Treaty signed to-day at four o'clock, at the Radzivill Palace. It was a full-dress meeting. Lord Beaconsfield was present, his first appearance for some days. All the Secretaries of Legation were permitted to witness the act.

He leaves Berlin to-morrow morning at 9 o'clock, and intends to sleep at Cologne, and at Calais next night, and hopes to reach London on Tuesday. Wednesday will be a day of rest, and it is his present purpose to address the House of Lords on Thursday. Papers will be presented, and the Opposition will of course ask for some time—ten days or so —to digest them. During this interval Lord Beaconsfield will ask permission to wait upon your Majesty at Osborne.

After the treaty was signed, Lord Beaconsfield had an audience of the Empress, an interesting one—not a mere formal one—and after that he paid a farewell visit to the Crown Princess, whose kindness to him while at Berlin has been extreme. All this has exhausted the little strength he has, and therefore he has asked permission not to attend the great banquet to-night in the White Hall. He regrets it, as it will be an historic occasion: but he consoles himself by the recollection, that he has assisted in bringing about a settlement which will probably secure the peace of Europe for a long time, and will certainly not disgrace your Majesty's throne.

How shall he thank sufficiently your Majesty for your Majesty's gracious letter of this morning and its enclosures, and many other passages of condescending sympathy and kindness! He cannot very well guide his pen, but yet will try to say how deeply and finely he feels the privilege of being the trusted servant of a Sovereign whom he adores!

King Leopold to Queen Victoria.

(*Translation*) *July* 14, '78.—. . . Allow me to offer you my most sincere and my warmest congratulations on the occasion of the great triumph of English policy.

The line of the Balkans assured to Turkey, the treaty guaranteeing her Asiatic possessions, and the occupation of the Island of Cyprus, are great events, which have made a great impression on the world and greatly rejoiced the friends of England. Bright pages have been added to the history of a splendid reign. Honour to Lord Beaconsfield, honour to you, dear Cousin, who have sustained and encouraged him and have given him the necessary support to render immense services to your Empire. . . .

The Crown Princess to Queen Victoria.

NEUES PALAIS, POTSDAM, *July* 16, '78.—I am all impatience to hear from you after the event of the Turko-English Convention and the occupation of Cyprus. I think it such a great event, and, as I already wrote, one which must give such pleasure to all friends of England! Lord Beaconsfield has indeed won laurels, made himself a name, and before all restored to his country the prestige of honour and dignity it had lost on the Continent, thanks to Lord Derby and Mr. Gladstone; and you must feel intense gratification after all the anxiety and worry you went through!

I was very sorry to take leave of Lord Beaconsfield, who certainly has a great charm when one sees more of him, and of Lord Salisbury, who is such a truly amiable man! The others, alas, I saw little or nothing of!

Schouvaloff is much pleased at the result of the Congress. Prince Gortchakoff went away deeply disappointed and dejected. . . .

King Leopold wished to do Beaconsfield honour on his return to England, as on his outward journey; but the gout-ridden statesman had to husband his resources to meet the calls that must be made upon them at home. He had not strength even to pay his devoirs to his own Sovereign before making his public explanation in the House of Lords. He arrived in England with the treaty on Tuesday, July 16, and was welcomed with enthusiasm both in Dover and in London. The reception was popular rather than official.[1] Though the Lord Mayor and Sheriffs were present at Charing Cross, together with such few of Beaconsfield's colleagues as could be spared from their Parliamentary duties, the most notable persons to meet him were two eminent philanthropists, Lady Burdett-Coutts, an old friend, and Sir Moses Montefiore, the most respected member in England of that great race from which Beaconsfield sprang. When he reached his official residence he reported to the Queen that there had been a marvellous exhibition of public feeling from Charing Cross to Downing Street, and that the street was filled with a dense crowd, singing loyal songs. There was one marked feature in his home-coming. Whereas he had travelled out by himself, he

[1] So far as there was any organisation Lord Henry Lennox was responsible for it. He thus resumed his attitude of devotion to his old chief. See pp. 631 and 823.

returned with Salisbury by his side, and they drove together amid the cheering throng from the station; Beaconsfield insisting that his colleague—to whom, he said in one of his speeches, 'fell the labouring oar '—should be associated with himself in all public tributes of regard, and earnestly requesting the Queen to bestow like honours on them both. Both statesmen appeared at windows in Downing Street, when Beaconsfield proudly claimed that they had brought back from Berlin 'Peace with Honour.'

The Queen's welcome to her favourite Minister on his triumphant return was almost of a rapturous character. She gave him—and Salisbury on his recommendation—the Garter which he had refused in January; and would gladly have raised him to a marquisate or dukedom, and settled a peerage on his brother or nephew, could she have prevailed on him to consent. Beaconsfield did not forget his other colleague at Berlin, but recommended Odo Russell for a peerage; which he at first accepted, with his brother the Duke of Bedford's consent, but afterwards refused, because the Duke, on reconsideration, doubted the propriety of a Whig Ambassador, and a Russell, accepting honours from a Tory Prime Minister.

From Queen Victoria.

WINDSOR, *July* 16, '78.—The Queen thanks Lord Beaconsfield very much for his very kind letter of the 13th, and sends these lines with some Windsor flowers to welcome him back in triumph ! He has gained a wreath of laurels which she would willingly herself offer him, but hopes that the Blue Ribbon she may greet him with [*sic*] at Osborne. He must take 2 days there and of course bring Mr. Corry. The Queen is so grieved at his provoking indisposition. . . .

She will write again to-night.

What distinction should be given Lord Salisbury ?

(*Later*) The Queen is much grieved to hear from Lord Beaconsfield that he has been so suffering from his old enemy, but she trusts that by this time he is already much better. The exertions he has made have been so great that the Queen has always been living in fear of some such attack. But he has achieved so much that that will help to make him well.

He *must now* accept the Garter.   She must insist on it.

It will be a disappointment not to see Lord Beaconsfield so soon, but he must be very careful and husband his strength for Parliament.   The Convention and possession of Cyprus has given immense satisfaction to the country.   High and low are delighted, excepting Mr. Gladstone, who is frantic. . . .

To Queen Victoria.

10, Downing Street., *July* 16, '78.

Madam, and most beloved Sovereign,—I am scarcely capable of addressing your Majesty, and could indeed address no one else, but I could not let so gracious a letter remain for an hour unnoticed.

I envy Lord Salisbury seeing your Majesty first, yet, in spite of that, I will even on my knees entreat your Majesty to deign to bestow on him, also, the great distinction which your Majesty has proposed to confer on me.   He has been a faithful and a most able colleague, and his great talents, his historic name, and this signal public service indicate a worthy recipient of your Majesty's favor.

I hope to speak in the House of Lords on Thursday, and in that case, I should propose on Saturday, if this be not too early, which perhaps it may be, to wait on your Majesty, to tell your Majesty many things, but certainly to assure your Majesty, that of all your Majesty's faithful subjects, there is none that can exceed in duty and affection, Your devoted Beaconsfield.

From Queen Victoria.

Frogmore, *July* 17, '78.—The Queen was much touched by Lord Beaconsfield's very kind letter.   Would he not accept a Marquisate or Dukedom *in addition* to the Blue Ribbon ? And will he not allow the Queen to settle a Barony or Viscounty on his Brother and Nephew ?   Such a name should be perpetuated !

The Queen would be delighted to see Lord Beaconsfield on Saturday but really thinks he ought to delay it until Tuesday or Wednesday next week, and she hopes to see him again before leaving for Scotland, which she does not think of doing before the 23rd of August. . . .

The Queen will have much pleasure in giving the Blue Ribbon to Lord Salisbury.

To Queen Victoria.

10, Downing St., *July* 18, '78.—Lord Beaconsfield with his humble duty to your Majesty.   He was too unwell to be able to acknowledge your Majesty's most gracious letter yesterday, but he is glad to say he is quite himself again, and shall be able to make his statement in the House of Lords this afternoon at five o'clock. He could not endure postponing his visit to your Majesty any later than Saturday. It is so very long since he has had the happiness of seeing your Majesty, and so much has happened in the interval.

He will not trust himself now in endeavoring to express what he feels to your Majesty's kindness. He thinks he is ennobled thro' your Majesty's goodness quite enough, tho' with infinite deference to your Majesty's gracious pleasure, he would presume to receive the Garter; but, as he always feels, your Majesty's kind thoughts are dearer to him than any personal distinction, however rich and rare. The belief that your Majesty trusts, and approves of, him is 'more precious than rubies.'

From Queen Victoria.

WINDSOR, *July* 18, '78.—The Queen thanks Lord Beaconsfield for his most kind letter. She asks and counts on his making no exertion when at Osborne, and doing what is good for him and what he likes.

She hopes he will certainly stay 2 and she hopes 3 days at Osborne.[1] This heat tries the Queen. . . .

The Queen and Beatrice wish we could hear you speak to-night.

There was joy and relief in the country that European peace had been secured, to all appearance, for many years; and there was general satisfaction both with the terms of the Treaty and with the distinguished part that British representatives had played in Berlin. But two extreme parties, at opposite poles, were critical. The special friends of Turkey, who were, in the main, high Tories, complained that, instead of preserving Turkey's independence and integrity, Beaconsfield and Salisbury had ruthlessly partitioned her territory amongst her foes and her false friends. A Macaronic poem of the day sadly asked:

---

[1] Beaconsfield wrote to Lady Bradford from Osborne on Monday, July 22: 'At three o'clock I am to be inve ted with the Garter: a sort of ceremony I fear.'

> Ubi sunt provinciæ
> Quas est laus pacâsse ?
> Totæ, totæ, sunt partitæ;
> Has tulerunt Muscovitæ,
> Illas Count Andrassy.

On the other hand, the friends of Russia and advocates of the claims of oppressed nationalities, who were mostly Radicals or high Anglicans, complained that the partition of Turkey had not been more thorough; and were indignant at the comparatively moderate satisfaction which Bulgaria, Rumania, Serbia, Bosnia, Montenegro, and, above all, Greece received under the provisions of the Treaty. Headed by Gladstone, they deplored that British Plenipotentiaries should have spoken and acted at Berlin rather like Metternich than like Canning— both of them, by the way, statesmen whom Beaconsfield's catholic taste enabled him to admire.

Both sets of critics were met and dealt with by Beaconsfield in his speech in the House of Lords on laying the protocols of the Treaty on the table. His main contention was, he said, that by the Congress of Berlin and the Cyprus Convention the menace to European independence contained in the Treaty of San Stefano had been removed, and the threatened injury to the British Empire averted. That preliminary Treaty had reduced the Sultan to a state of subjection to Russia. Now the Congress had restored to him two-thirds of the territory that was to have formed the great Bulgarian State, and had given him in the Balkans a defensible frontier, which he had power to guard with all his available force. Beaconsfield explained that he had effected a change in the name of the new province south of the Balkans, from South Bulgaria to Eastern Rumelia, so as to prevent constant intriguing to bring about a union of the two provinces; and he went into some detail in regard to the improvements proposed in Turkish administration there.

He justified the policy of entrusting Austria with the administration of Bosnia by pointing out that this distant province was in a state of chronic anarchy; that Turkey could only restore order by an army of 50,000 men; that it was probable that such an effort would absolutely ruin the Porte, at a time when the statesmen of Europe were attempting to concentrate and condense Turkish resources with a view to strengthening them. Austria was the neighbour clearly fitted by position to undertake the duty of restoring order and tranquillity. Thereupon the cry of ' partition of Turkey ' had been raised. On the contrary the object of the Government was restoration, not partition. There was a school of statesmen who advocated partition, but the Government had resisted them because, ' exclusive of high moral considerations, they believed an attempt, on a great scale, to accomplish the partition of Turkey would inevitably lead to a long, sanguinary, and often-recurring struggle, and that Europe and Asia would both be involved in a series of troubles and sources of disaster and danger of which no adequate idea could be formed.' It was remarkable that the whole Powers of Europe, including Russia, had come to the unanimous conclusion that the best chance for the tranquillity and order of the world was ' to retain the Sultan as part of the acknowledged political system of Europe.' Once more Beaconsfield explained in detail how the mere loss of provinces did not imply partition.

After a great war like this, it is utterly impossible that you can have a settlement of any permanent character without a redistribution of territory and considerable changes. But that is not partition. My lords, a country may have lost provinces, but that is not partition. We know that not very long ago a great country—one of the foremost countries in the world—lost provinces; yet is not France one of the great Powers of the world, and with a future—a commanding future ? Austria herself has lost provinces—more provinces even than Turkey, perhaps; even England has lost provinces—the most precious possessions—the loss of which every Englishman must deplore to this moment.[1] We lost them from bad government. Had the principles which now obtain between the metropolis

---

[1] Quoting this passage, M. Hanotaux interposes a query; ' S'agit-il de Calais ?' But of course Beaconsfield was referring to the American Colonies.

and her dependencies prevailed then, we should not perhaps have lost those provinces, and the power of this Empire would have been proportionally increased. It is perfectly true that the Sultan of Turkey has lost provinces; it is true that his armies have been defeated; it is true that his enemy is even now at his gates; but all that has happened to other Powers. But a Sovereign who has not yet forfeited his capital, whose capital has not yet been occupied by his enemy and that capital one of the strongest in the world—who has armies and fleets at his disposal, and who still rules over 20,000,000 of inhabitants, cannot be described as a Power whose dominions have been partitioned.

Connected with this question of partition was that of the claims of Greece. It was on the desire of the British Government that Greek representatives were heard at the Congress; but their demands were extravagant, not stopping short of Constantinople, though, indeed, ' they were willing to accept as an instalment the two large provinces of Epirus and Thessaly, and the island of Crete. It was quite evident at the Congress that the representatives of Greece entirely misunderstood the objects of our labours; that we were not there to partition Turkey and give them their share of Turkey, but for a very contrary purpose; as far as we could, to re-establish the dominion of the Sultan on a rational basis, to condense and concentrate his authority, and to take the opportunity—of which we have largely availed ourselves—of improving the condition of his subjects.' In spite of this misunderstanding the Government had done what they could for Greece. They had urged Turkey and Greece to come together to defend their common interests against the overpowering Slav current in the Balkans; and they had recommended Turkey to grant a rectification of frontier, which would add considerably to Greek strength and resources. ' Greece is a country so interesting,' added Beaconsfield, ' that it enlists the sympathies of all educated men. Greece has a future; and I would say, if I might be permitted, to Greece, what I would say to an individual who has a future, "Learn to be patient." ' It was good, but unpalatable, advice.

Summing up the first portion of his speech, Beaconsfield pointed with some pride to the fact that—omitting, of course, Serbia and Rumania, now independent; omitting Bulgaria, still a tributary principality; and Bosnia, in Austrian occupation—European Turkey still retained a dominion of 60,000 square miles, with a population of 6,000,000, ' and that population in a very great degree concentrated and condensed in the provinces contiguous to the capital.' Moreover, Great Britain had secured this satisfactory result without war, and without more than comparatively trifling expenditure.

You cannot look at the map of [European] Turkey as it had been left by the Treaty of San Stefano, and as it has been rearranged by the Treaty of Berlin, without seeing that great results have accrued. If these results had been the consequences of a long war, if they had been the results of a struggle like that we underwent in the Crimea, I do not think they would have been even then unsubstantial or unsatisfactory. My lords, I hope that you and the country will not forget that these results have been obtained without shedding the blood of a single Englishman; and if there has been some expenditure, it has been an expenditure which, at least, has shown the resources and determination of this country. Had you entered into that war, for which you were prepared, and well prepared, probably in a month you would have exceeded the whole expenditure you have now incurred.

Turning to Asia, Beaconsfield recognised that one of his most difficult tasks would be to justify the assignment to Russia of Kars and Batoum. His defence was, if not absolutely convincing, at least difficult to answer. Russia had fairly won this territory in war, by no means for the first time, and the Turks had accepted her title in the Treaty of San Stefano. Kars had been conquered by Russia three times, and three times she had been forced to relinquish it, mainly owing to English efforts. Were we to make it a *casus belli* ? And Batoum ? Was it a Portsmouth, or was it not rather a Cowes ? (This suggestion, considering the importance which Beaconsfield had always attached to Batoum, did not lack boldness.) It could only be made a first-class port by great and

expensive engineering works. Should we be justified in
going to war with Russia for Batoum ? Especially as we
had secured for Turkey the caravan route to Persia
through Bayazid and the Alashkerd Valley, and so,
though Beaconsfield tactfully omitted to say this, cut off
Russia from pushing her advantage to the south. It
seemed to the Government that the time had come for
an arrangement which should put an end to these perpetually recurring wars between Russia and the Porte;
and which should secure tranquillity and order in Asiatic
Turkey, and so terminate British anxieties about India.
This was the object of the Cyprus Convention. Beaconsfield explained how careful they had been to show consideration for France—' a nation to whom we are bound
by almost every tie that can unite a people, and with
whom our intimacy is daily increasing.'

We avoided Egypt, knowing how susceptible France is with
regard to Egypt; we avoided Syria, knowing how susceptible
France is on the subject of Syria; and we avoided availing
ourselves of any part of the *terra firma*, because we would not
hurt the feelings or excite the suspicions of France. France
knows that for the last two or three years we have listened
to no appeal which involved anything like an acquisition of
territory, because the territory which might have come to us
would have been territory which France would see in our
hand with suspicion and dislike.

But I must make this observation to your lordships. We
have a substantial interest in the East; it is a commanding
interest, and its behest must be obeyed. But the interest of
France in Egypt, and her interest in Syria, are, as she acknowledges, sentimental and traditionary interests; and, although
I respect them, and although I wish to see in the Lebanon and
Egypt the influence of France fairly and justly maintained,
and although her officers and ours in that part of the world—
and especially in Egypt—are acting together with confidence
and trust, we must remember that our connection with the
East is not merely an affair of sentiment and tradition, but
that we have urgent and substantial and enormous interests
which we must guard and keep. Therefore, when we find
that the progress of Russia is a progress which, whatever may
be the intentions of Russia, necessarily in that part of the
world produces such a state of disorganisation and want of

confidence in the Porte, it comes to this—that, if we do not interfere in vindication of our own interests, that part of Asia must become the victim of anarchy, and ultimately become part of the possessions of Russia.

Russia, Beaconsfield admitted, could not be blamed for availing herself of the anarchy in Asiatic Turkey. ' But, yielding to Russia what she has obtained, we say to her, " Thus far, and no farther." Asia is large enough for both of us. There is no reason for these constant wars, or fears of wars, between Russia and England.' He had said before, and repeated now, that there was room enough in Asia for both Russia and England. But the room that we required we must secure. ' In taking Cyprus the movement is not Mediterranean, it is Indian.' It was for the preservation of the Empire in peace, and secondarily for the development of civilisation in Asia, that the Cyprus Convention was signed. It was on this note that he ended.

We have no reason to fear war. Her Majesty has fleets and armies which are second to none. England must have seen with pride the Mediterranean covered with her ships; she must have seen with pride the discipline and devotion which have been shown to her and her Government by all her troops, drawn from every part of her Empire. I leave it to the illustrious duke [Cambridge], in whose presence I speak, to bear witness to the spirit of imperial patriotism which has been exhibited by the troops from India, which he recently reviewed at Malta. But it is not on our fleets and armies, however necessary they may be for the maintenance of our material strength, that I alone or mainly depend in that enterprise on which this country is about to enter. It is on what I most highly value—the consciousness that in the Eastern nations there is confidence in this country, and that, while they know we can enforce our policy, at the same time they know that our Empire is an Empire of liberty, of truth, and of justice.

In this speech Beaconsfield touched but lightly upon the increase of British responsibilities incurred under the Cyprus Convention; but his few words were pointed. ' A prudent Minister certainly would not recklessly

enter into any responsibility; but a Minister who is afraid
to enter into any responsibility is, to my mind, not a
prudent Minister. We do not wish to enter into any
unnecessary responsibility, but there is a responsibility
from which we certainly shrink; we shrink from the
responsibility of handing to our successors a weakened or
a diminished Empire.' A much fuller defence on this
point was extracted from Beaconsfield by on attack which
Gladstone made upon him in a public speech at Southwark.
Gladstone complained that British engagements had
been enormously extended, and British taxation vastly
increased, without British assent, even without British
knowledge. No despotic power would have dared to do
what Beaconsfield had done. No statesman he had
known would have put his name to such an arrangement
as the Convention. It was an 'insane covenant,' and its
secret negotiation an 'act of duplicity.' Beaconsfield
took advantage of a banquet given him at Knightsbridge
on July 27 to reply to this vehement onslaught.

It is said that we have increased, and dangerously increased,
our responsibilities as a nation by that convention. In the first
place, I deny that we have increased our responsibilities by
that convention. I maintain that by that convention we
have lessened our responsibilities. Suppose now, for example,
the settlement of Europe had not included the convention
of Constantinople and the occupation of the isle of Cyprus;
suppose it had been limited to the mere Treaty of Berlin, what
under all probable circumstances might then have occurred ?
In ten, fifteen, it might be in twenty years, the power and
resources of Russia having revived, some quarrel would again
have occurred, Bulgarian or otherwise, and in all probability
the armies of Russia would have been assailing the Ottoman
dominions both in Europe and Asia, and enveloping and
enclosing the city of Constantinople and its all-powerful
position.

Well, what would be the probable conduct, under these
circumstances, of the Government of this country, whoever
the Ministers might be, whatever party might be in power ?
I fear there might be hesitation for a time, a want of decision,
a want of firmness; but no one doubts that ultimately England
would have said, 'This will never do; we must prevent the
conquest of Asia Minor; we must interfere in this matter and

arrest the course of Russia.' . . . Well, that being the case, I say it is extremely important that this country should take a step beforehand which should indicate what the policy of England would be; that you should not have your Ministers meeting in a council chamber, hesitating and doubting, and considering contingencies, and then acting at last, but acting perhaps too late. I say, therefore, that the responsibilities of this country have not been increased; the responsibilities already existed. Though I, for one, would never shrink from increasing the responsibilities of this country if they are responsibilities which ought to be undertaken, the responsibilities of this country are practically diminished by the course we have taken.

My lords and gentlemen, one of the results of my attending the Congress of Berlin has been to prove, what I always suspected to be an absolute fact, that neither the Crimean War, nor this horrible devastating war which has just terminated, would have taken place if England had spoken with the necessary firmness. Russia has complaints to make against this country that neither in the case of the Crimean War nor on this occasion—and I don't shrink from my share of the responsibility in this matter—was the voice of England so clear and decided as to exercise a due share in the guidance of European opinion. Well, gentlemen, suppose my noble friend and myself had come back with the Treaty of Berlin, and had not taken the step which is to be questioned within the next eight and forty hours, could we with any self-respect have met our countrymen when they asked, What securities have you made for the peace of Europe ? How far have you diminished the chance of perpetually recurring war on this question of the East by the Treaty of Berlin ? Why, they could say, all we have gained by the Treaty of Berlin is probably the peace of a few years, and at the end of that time the same phenomenon will arise, and the Ministers of England must patch up the affair as well as they can.

Beaconsfield then fastened on Gladstone's phrase ' an insane covenant.' He would not pretend to be as competent a judge of insanity as his opponent.

But I would put this issue to an English jury. Which do you believe most likely to enter an insane convention, a body of English gentlemen honoured by the favour of their Sovereign and the confidence of their fellow-subjects, managing your affairs for five years, I hope with prudence, and not altogether without success, or a sophistical rhetorician, inebriated with the exuberance of his own verbosity, and gifted with an egotistical imagination that can at all times command an interminable and inconsistent series of arguments to malign an opponent and to glorify himself ?

Gladstone's unmeasured language, the climax of a violent campaign carried on for two years against the foreign policy of his country, justified a crushing rejoinder; but there was not much evidence of happy inspiration or of statesmanlike dignity in the phrases which Beaconsfield actually used. Gladstone, however, was perhaps not well advised when he wrote to ask Beaconsfield for particulars of any personal attacks made in the course of a campaign which derived much of its piquancy from the personal *animus* which was clearly interwoven with its political idealism. Beaconsfield's reply pointed this out.

To W. E. Gladstone.

10, DOWNING STREET, *July* 30, 1878.—Lord Beaconsfield presents his compliments to Mr. Gladstone, and has the honor to acknowledge the receipt of his letter of this day's date, referring to some remarks made by Lord Beaconsfield last night in the House of Lords, and requesting to be supplied with a list of epithets applied, not merely to Lord Beaconsfield's measures, but to his person and character, and with a note of the times and places at which they were used.

As this would involve a research over a period of two years and a half, during which Mr. Gladstone, to use his own expressions at Oxford, has been counterworking ' by day and by night, week by week, and month by month,' the purpose of Lord Beaconsfield, Lord Beaconsfield, who is at this moment much pressed with affairs, is obliged to request those gentlemen, who are kind enough to assist him in the conduct of public business, to undertake the necessary researches, which probably may require some little time; but that Lord Beaconsfield, by such delay in replying to Mr. Gladstone, may not appear wanting in becoming courtesy, he must observe with reference to the Oxford speech referred to in the House of Lords, and which was one long invective against the Government, that Mr. Gladstone then remarked that, when he spoke of the Government, he meant Lord Beaconsfield, who was alone responsible, and by whom ' the great name of England had been degraded and debased.'

In the same spirit a few days back at Southwark, Lord

Beaconsfield was charged with 'an act of duplicity of which
every Englishman should be ashamed, an act of duplicity
which has not been surpassed, and,' Mr. Gladstone believed,
'has been rarely equalled in the history of nations.' Such an
act, however, might be expected from a Minister who, according to Mr. Gladstone, had 'sold the Greeks.'

With regard to the epithet 'devilish' which Lord Beaconsfield used in the House of Lords, he is informed that it
was not Mr. Gladstone at Hawarden who compared Lord
Beaconsfield to Mephistopheles, but only one of Mr. Gladstone's friends, kindly enquiring of Mr. Gladstone how they
were 'to get rid of this Mephistopheles': but as Mr. Gladstone
proceeded to explain the mode, probably the Birmingham
caucus, Lord Beaconsfield may perhaps be excused for
assuming that Mr. Gladstone sanctioned the propriety of the
scarcely complimentary appellation.

Whatever Gladstone may have said or thought of
Beaconsfield during these tumultuous years, he had the
greatness and the impartiality—when his object was
accomplished, the 1874-80 Government destroyed, himself
seated in his rival's place, and that rival dead—to select
this moment of the return from Berlin as the culminating
point of Beaconsfield's renown. A friend, he said, might
in July, 1878, have fairly applied to him the stately lines
of Virgil—

> Aspice ut insignis spoliis Marcellus opimis
> Ingreditur, victorque viros supereminet omnes.

The enthusiasm of the crowds which welcomed
Beaconsfield at Dover and Charing Cross was succeeded
by other tributes of popular appreciation and admiration.
Parliament endorsed the Treaty, the Lords without a
division, the Commons by the great majority of 143, in
spite of all Gladstone's efforts and eloquence. Indeed,
Hartington did not venture to submit a purely hostile
resolution; only what Beaconsfield happily described as
'a string of congratulatory regrets.' Congratulations
poured in from legislative bodies and great public meetings
in all parts of the British Empire; particularly in Australasia, which realised the importance of Beaconsfield's
success in providing for the security of the imperial high-

way through the Levant.　The Prime Minister's colleagues
welcomed him with open arms, the Duke of Richmond
sending him a Garter badge [1] as a token of his esteem and
regard; and if there was a certain disposition in the literary
world, always critical of the pyrotechnics of their literary
statesman, to stand aloof, Beaconsfield was gratified by
the receipt of some Latin verses on the return from Berlin,
written by the scholarly Bishop Charles Wordsworth,
and translated into English verse by Dean Stanley; and
admiration was wrung from one of the finest spirits of
the age, John Henry Newman.

To the Bishop of St. Andrews.

HUGHENDEN MANOR, *Aug.* 26, 1878.—It is the happiest
union since Beaumont and Fletcher.　I am deeply gratified
by such an expression of sympathy from men so distinguished
by their learning and piety.

Cardinal Newman to Lord Blachford.

THE ORATORY, *July* 22, 1878.—. . . As to Disraeli's
firework, I confess I am much dazzled with it, and wish it
well.　It is a grand idea, that of hugging from love the Turk
to death, instead of the Russian bear, which, as a poem or
romance, finds a weak part in my imagination.　And then it
opens such a view of England, great in the deeds of their
forefathers, shewing that they are not degenerate sons, but
rising with the occasion in fulfilment of the ' Tu ne cede malis,
sed contra audentior ito.'　And then it is so laughably clever
a move, in a grave diplomatic congress—and then it opens
such wonderful views of the future—that I am overcome by it.
Nor do I see the hypocrisy you speak of.[2]

To the Duke of Richmond.

10, DOWNING STREET, *July* 23, 1878.—I am deeply touched
by your letter, and by the interesting and graceful offering,
which accompanied it.

We have known each other, now, for more than thirty years,
and, often, in trying times; and under any circumstances, it
would be agreeable to remember, that there has never been
a cloud between us.

---

[1] Sir Richard Wallace also presented to Beaconsfield the Garter insignia
worn by the 3rd Marquis of Hertford (' Lord Monmouth ').
[2] Quoted in the *Life of Dean Church*, p. 269.

But it is ony of recent years, that I have had an opportunity of becoming duly acquainted with your great and good
qualities; your aptitude for public affairs, your quick intelligence, and that delightful absence of selfishness in your character, which distinguishes your relations with your colleagues.

As for myself, I am proud of your friendship, and can truly
subscribe myself, with great affection,—Yours, BEACONSFIELD.

The Conservative party entertained Beaconsfield and
Salisbury to dinner in the Riding School at Knightsbridge
on July 27; on August 3, the Corporation of the City of
London conferred its freedom on them, and held a banquet
in their honour. On each occasion Beaconsfield's reception was of the most enthusiastic character, suggesting
that he possessed the confidence not only of his own
party, but of the people at large. Of his speech at the
Riding School we have already quoted the principal
passages; in the City he claimed that the outcome of the
Berlin Congress had been a general, and, he believed, an
enduring, peace in Europe, and he spoke with justifiable
hopefulness of the prospects of good government in Asia
Minor under the Cyprus Convention.

Montagu Corry to Queen Victoria.

10, DOWNING STREET, *July* 29.—Mr. Montagu Corry presents his humble duty to your Majesty. . . . The Banquet
in the Duke of Wellington's Riding House was one of the best
arranged, though, at the same time, one of the most genuine
exhibitions of public feeling ever seen. It was a glorious sight
to see five hundred of the proudest peers and sturdiest squires
of England accord their fervent welcome to the man who had
maintained their country's honour ! *He* spoke with extraordinary force and power, and well earned the ringing cheers
which again and again—for minutes—burst forth after he
had sat down.

Lord Salisbury made an admirable speech, and carried to
every heart the conviction, most welcome and important, that
your Majesty's two Ministers were entirely of one mind as to
the present and future. His reception showed how well he is
gaining the confidence of the party ! . . .

Mr. Corry feels sure, from what he learns, that this remarkable meeting, and the speeches made there, will have a powerful
influence upon the debate and the division in the House of

Commons this week. He has sometimes of late, heard Conservative Members complain, that they ' never saw their Chief now-a-days.' They have now seen and heard him, and it is already obvious that, with even increased confidence and determination, they will uphold the policy of your Majesty's Government.

To Lady Bradford.

HOUSE OF LORDS, *Aug.* 1.—. . . I can't give a good bulletin of myself, as I suffer from Bradford's enemy, asthma, the present of the east wind. I meant to have kept at home to-day, but . . . Carnarvon posted up from the country to vindicate his highly susceptible character from an imaginary attack wh. he fancies I made on him the other night. He has just got my answer, and I hope he likes it.

I dined yesterday at the Salisburys', and miladi had a reception in the evening, notwithstanding Goodwood. There were a good many people and the dinner was more amusing than might have been supposed. I sate betn. Mme. Harcourt and Lady Maud. . . .

Lord Salisbury had his blue ribbon and regulation star on, but his solicitor has written to him to say that in some box at the banker's there is a diamond star of the Garter which belonged to his father or some ancestor. I told him he must have it ready by Saturday. . . .

To Queen Victoria.

Aug. 6.—Saturday was a day of triumph. Lord Beaconsfield managed to get thro' it tho' greatly suffering. He is much influenced by the electric fluid, and three days of thunderstorms quite prostrated him. He could have wished, that your Majesty even could have witnessed the scene at Guildhall. It was very picturesque, and admirably arranged. From Charing Cross to the Guildhall, there was a continuous and enthusiastic crowd, and quite spontaneous; no organisation, no committee work.

To day thero has been a most extraordinary scene at the Foreign Office : 700 deputies from nearly 1,000 Conservative Associations, and they passed Lord Salisbury and myself, and they [Lord Salisbury and Lord Beaconsfield] had to shake hands with every member from every part of England, and then to address them, exhausted as Lord Beaconsfield was by standing more than an hour.

To Lady Bradford.

10, DOWNING STREET, *Aug.* 6, '78.—. . . Monty and I are going to the play to-night to see some nonsense, wh. everybody

is going to see—*Parasol* or *Pinafore*—a burlesque, a sort of
thing I hate, but I got into the scrape on Saturday at H[olland]
House, with Pss. Mary. She is patroness and we go in her box.

Yesterday's dinner was amusing, as Louise[1] looked her best
and talked her best. I sate on her right hand, and D. of Cam.
on her left, and Harty-Tarty not too near with Lady Westmor-
land, the only other lady there. Louise talked a good deal
about you, and pretends to love you very much, and I hope
she is sincere. She does not think you look so well as she
cd. wish, and wishes you wd. take more care of yourself, and
lead a quiet life. But who can lead a quiet life with two
daughters to attend to ! . . .

Aug. 8.—. . . I am quite exhausted. . . . I want to go
to bed for a week, or lie on the summer grass, if it wd. not
rain.

Except at Wycombe fair, in my youth, I have never seen
anything so bad as *Pinafore*. It was not even a burlesque,
a sort of provincial *Black-eyed Susan*. Princess Mary's face
spoke volumes of disgust and disappointment, but who cd.
have told her to go there ?

The Treaty of Berlin is Beaconsfield's main international work; by it his reputation as a European statesman must stand or fall. At one time it was the fashion
to conclude that, because his vaunted division of Bulgaria
into two provinces, of which only one was given political
autonomy, lasted no longer than seven years, and was
then terminated with England's cheerful acquiescence,
therefore the Treaty was a failure, and Beaconsfield's
diplomacy was proved to be a futile sham. This judgment has long been abandoned as superficial; it may
seem strange that it was ever widely accepted, seeing that
the British statesman, who acquiesced in the union of the
two provinces in 1885, was Salisbury, Beaconsfield's
colleague at Berlin in 1878. The separation of Eastern
Rumelia from Bulgaria was in Beaconsfield's mind a
means, and not an end. The danger to be guarded
against was the complete Russian dominance of the
Balkan Peninsula by means of a huge Russianised Bulgaria, which should frustrate the aspirations of all the
other Balkan peoples, and should reduce Turkey-in-Europe

---

[1] Duchess of Manchester, afterwards Duchess of Devonshire.

to a state of vassalage to Russia. That danger was removed by the provisions of the Treaty. The seven years' delay, which Beaconsfield's insistence on division interposed, gave time for the growth of a national spirit which by 1885 had transformed the Bulgarians from clients and tools of Russia into a people with a strong sense of individuality and independence. This development was hastened by Russia's foolish and shortsighted conduct towards Bulgaria. Having already lost to a large extent the sympathy of Greeks, Serbs, and Rumanians by her neglect of their interests at San Stefano and Berlin, she now contrived, by high-handed and incessant interference in all the affairs of her *protégés*, to alienate even the Bulgarians; and it was to be expected that united Bulgaria—united by her own motion, and in Russia's despite—would in consequence prove rather a bulwark of Turkey against Russia than an outwork of Russia against Turkey. It should also be noted that the united Bulgaria of 1885 was much smaller in extent than the 'big Bulgaria' of the Treaty of San Stefano; that it nowhere reached the Ægean coast, nor did it include Macedonia; and so neither prejudiced Greek and Serbian claims in those regions, nor broke the continuity of Turkish dominion in Europe. The aims of Beaconsfield's policy were therefore secured by the rearrangement of 1885, though the means differed.

The Treaty unquestionably had many imperfections, and not a few of its clauses were never seriously put in force. Still, if we look broadly at its aims and its results, it is impossible not to recognise that what Beaconsfield determined to secure—the safety of the British Empire from the threatening advance of Russia, and the continuance of European peace—he did secure. So far as peace is concerned, whereas, in the months preceding the Treaty, on the top of a desolating struggle between Russia and Turkey, war between Great Britain and Russia appeared to be imminent and war between Austria and Russia probable, none of the six great European Powers—

Austria, France, Germany, Great Britain, Italy,[1] Russia— was at war in Europe during the thirty-six years which intervened between the Treaty and the outbreak of Armageddon in 1914. Russia certainly fought Japan in the Far East, Great Britain engaged in wars in India, Egypt, the Sudan, and South Africa, and France, Germany, and Italy all conducted military operations in connection with their African colonies; but European peace among the Great Powers, though sometimes imperilled, was never broken. A steady continuance of peace in the Balkans was, however, not secured. No arrangement that was possible in the conditions of 1878 could have effected that; it remains indeed to be proved whether the settlement made in the immeasurably better conditions of 1919 and 1920 will be permanently satisfactory.[2] But, at any rate, Balkan conflicts were confined for nearly forty years to the Balkan States themselves; and the dispute of Austria with Serbia in 1914 was rather the pretext than the cause of the Great War.

As regards the threat to the British Empire and its communications by the advance of Russia through European Turkey towards the Mediterranean, and through Asia Minor towards Syria and Egypt on the one hand and Mesopotamia and the Persian Gulf on the other, Beaconsfield's success was complete. These movements were definitely stopped, and have never been renewed in arms. That the corresponding Russian advance from Turkestan towards India was stimulated for a while by the check in Europe and Asia Minor is hardly a reflection on the Treaty or on Beaconsfield's work at Berlin, as he was fully alive to the danger and had directed his policy since he came into office towards the attainment of a more 'scientific' north-west frontier for India, the foundations of which he laid before his retirement.

If Cyprus has not been utilised as Beaconsfield intended

[1] Italy's war with Turkey over Tripoli was rather an African than a European struggle.

[2] Written in 1920. An entire rearrangement of Turco-Greek frontiers has taken place since then.

and expected, it has been partly because there has been
no renewal of Russian activity in Asia Minor, and partly
because Egypt, which, from regard for French interests,
he deliberately put out of his consideration at Berlin,
was subsequently thrown upon our hands owing to French
renunciation. That he fully realised British interests
in Egypt his actions, speeches, and letters prove; that he
anticipated and welcomed a great extension of British
influence there in the future may fairly be deduced from
his purchase of the Suez Canal shares; but he could not in
1878 have acquired exclusive control of Egypt as a place
of arms in the Eastern Mediterranean without a direct
breach with our joint controller, France, which would
have gravely affected our international position. None
who remember the excessive irritation which prevailed
in France for twenty years on account of a British occupation of Egypt, in which she had been pressed originally
to take a share, will join in the reproaches sometimes
thrown on Beaconsfield's memory, even in Liberal
quarters, for not having occupied Egypt in 1878, in
France's despite, instead of Cyprus.

The principal obstacle which Beaconsfield interposed
by the Treaty in the way of Russian ambitions was, of
course, a concentrated and strengthened Turkey. For
few would now endorse the criticism much heard at the
time that Beaconsfield, who claimed to be a friend, had
dealt Turkey more mortal blows than her professed
enemies. It is now generally recognised that her
effective power was increased by the lopping off of outlying provinces which she could neither govern nor
defend, and which constituted an unceasing drain upon
her resources; which provinces, moreover, might well
be turned eventually into buffer States to protect her
frontier. But was not this strengthening of Turkey,
however excusable from the standpoint of British imperial defence, treason to the general interest of Europe
and to the cause of humanity? Did not these demand
the withdrawal, to the utmost possible extent, of Christian
nationalities from Turkish rule, and the strictest European

supervision of those whose actual enfranchisement could not for the moment be enforced ?

The answer is that the Treaty, though not satisfactory to extremists on either side, did find a means of largely reconciling apparent incompatibles. Far from neglecting the emancipation of Christian nationalities, the Treaty and the Cyprus Convention withdrew from effective Turkish government both the Bulgarias, in different degrees, the whole of Bosnia and Herzegovina, parts of Thessaly and Epirus, a large portion of Armenia, and the island of Cyprus. The transfer of Eastern Armenia to Russia, and the administration of Bosnia and Herzegovina by Austria, were calculated in both cases materially to improve the condition of the inhabitants. And, when the Treaty is condemned for prejudicing the establishment of a great South Slavic kingdom by putting the Slavs of Bosnia and Herzegovina under Austria, it has to be remembered that this reinforcement of the already numerous Slavs of Austria-Hungary might well have led to the merger of a Dual in a Triple Empire, in which Slavs should have an equal place and equal rights with Magyars and Austrian Germans.

The Christian nationalities still left under Turkish rule had much to hope from the restored influence of Great Britain in the counsels of the Porte. Those in Asia were benefited directly by the establishment of military consuls under Sir Charles Wilson's leadership; those in Europe would profit indirectly by the ascendency of the British Ambassador at Constantinople, where Layard bade fair to occupy the place once filled by Stratford de Redcliffe. These prospects were ruined by the abrupt change in British policy when Gladstone returned to power in 1880. British threats did indeed wring from a reluctant Turkey overdue concessions to Greece and Montenegro. But that was a small gain to set against the permanent alienation of the Porte, the disappearance of British influence at Constantinople, and the cessation of British power to protect persecuted Christians, either in Asia

Minor or in European Turkey. In this respect Beaconsfield's policy is open to the serious reproach that it
assumed the continuance of his party in office for, at least,
another Parliament, so that a reversal would become
difficult, if not impossible. And yet no one should have
known better than he the mutability of the British
electorate.

The place of authority at Constantinople and in Asia
Minor vacated by Great Britain was gradually occupied,
not by Russia, but by Germany; and the renewed strength
which Beaconsfield had given to Turkey came eventually
to be used under German direction to hamper and not
to promote British interests. But he can hardly be
blamed for this. Statesmen must deal with the evils
before them. In the middle of the nineteenth century
the danger to the free development of, at any rate, the
Eastern World was Russia. She was, of course, nothing
like so formidable nor so destructive of human liberties
as Napoleon at the beginning of that century or Germany
at the beginning of the next; but she kept Europe generally
in constant uneasiness, while to the British Empire she
was a serious menace. She was foiled principally by
two British statesmen, Palmerston and Beaconsfield;
and by Beaconsfield she was foiled without resort to arms.
It has been the duty of later statesmen to provide against
the German threat, and they must bear the responsibility.

Looking back at the work of the British Plenipotentiaries at the Berlin Congress after two and a half years'
experience, Beaconsfield wrote to Drummond Wolff on
November 4, 1880: 'Next to making a tolerable settlement for the Porte, our great object was to break up,
and permanently prevent, the alliance of the three
Empires, and I maintain there never was a general diplomatic result more completely effected. Of course, it
does not appear on the protocols; it was realised by personal influence alone, both with Andrassy and Bismarck.'
These are pregnant sentences, which may well be pondered
by those who accuse Disraeli of having destroyed the

concert of Europe by refusing the adherence of Great
Britain to the Berlin Memorandum in May, 1876. There
was, in fact, at that time no concert of Europe in any real
sense. There was a concert of three autocrats—the
Emperors of Russia, Austria, and Germany, inspired by
Bismarck—which was gradually assuming the direction
of free Europe, in the belief that Italy was absorbed
in internal development, France crushed and helpless,
and England wedded to a policy of non-interference on the
Continent. In regard neither to the Andrassy note, nor to
the Berlin Memorandum, did the three Empires seek the
assistance of the rest of Europe in concerting their policy.
They framed their policy by themselves first, and demanded the assent of the popularly governed States
afterwards. Such a method of conducting European
affairs, if tolerated, would have led to the subordination
of the progressive to the non-progressive elements in
Europe, of the free to the subservient nations. France
and Italy seemed for the moment to be willing to accept
this dictation; England, under Disraeli, was not. There
could be no real concert of Europe unless the Western
Powers took a large share in directing it. That seems a
truism to-day; but it was Beaconsfield's policy and personal influence at Berlin which claimed and secured for his
country as large a share in directing European affairs as
that of any of the three autocrats, and which drove a
wedge between the three Empires, making it impossible
for them in future, in spite of all Bismarck's dexterous
diplomacy, to hold together with sufficient coherence to
dictate to Europe. In fact Beaconsfield at Berlin—with
no aid from triumphant arms, such as sustained Castlereagh at Vienna and Mr. Lloyd George in Paris—retrieved
for Great Britain the right to a potent voice in the settlement of Europe. It was a victory for free institutions
in a continent which had been drifting for some years
towards autocracy. It was also a vindication of that
sane imperialism which he had been returned to power
in 1874 to promote.

CHAPTER X.

THE AFGHAN WAR.

1878.

At the close of the first session of 1878 Beaconsfield was at the height of his renown and popularity. It was the common opinion that a dissolution at that time would have confirmed the Tory Government in power by a substantial majority for another period of five or six years. The adventure must have had its attractions, as time was needed to ensure the permanence of Beaconsfield's Eastern policy just embodied in treaty form. But he and his Cabinet decided, on August 10, not to endeavour to snatch a party victory out of a success in foreign policy. There was no constitutional excuse for dissolving a Parliament which steadily supported Ministers by large majorities, and which had still two years and a half to run. 'It would be like throwing up a rubber at whist,' wrote Sir William Hart Dyke, the Whip, 'whilst holding nothing but good cards.' But virtue was indeed in this case its own, and only, reward. Partly through their own fault, but mainly through disasters abroad and distress at home, for both of which their responsibility was slight, Ministers perceptibly declined in public favour during the remainder of their term of office.

The abounding trade of the early seventies had, in the normal cycle, been succeeded, soon after the change of Government, by a period of depression, which the wars and rumours of wars of the last year or two had no doubt helped to deepen. Wages had to be reduced in one industry after another, with the natural result of serious conflicts between capital and labour, prolonged and

repeated strikes being sometimes accompanied by out-
breaks of lawless violence. Much of the savings of the
country was lost by speculative investment in unsound
foreign loans; and in the October of this year the failure
of the City of Glasgow Bank brought widespread disaster
to Scotland and the North of England. Our imperial
and foreign trade suffered heavily owing to famines in
India and China; and there was now felt fully the back-
wash caused by the destruction of capital and temporary
inflation of trade due to the wars of the sixties and early
seventies—the Civil War in America, the Austro-Prussian
War of 1866, and the Franco-German War of 1870-71.
More serious still in some ways, the ruin which Disraeli
and his friends foresaw for the agricultural interest as
the result of Peel's corn law legislation, but which had
been hitherto postponed by various accidental causes,
came at last with full force, grievously aggravated by a
succession of bad harvests. Owing to the unlimited entry
of cheap food from abroad—which, of course, on the other
hand, enabled the artisan better to support his own
industrial troubles—agricultural prices tumbled headlong
down, neither rents nor wages could be paid, and farms
were being thrown up all over the country.

Then, though European peace was secured, the ordinary
man was disturbed to find that within a few months
Great Britain had two wars on her hands, one in India,
and one in South Africa; and he was still more disturbed
when disaster befell our troops in Zululand and our
Mission at Cabul. The great imperial questions, out of
which these two wars sprang, were what mainly occupied
Beaconsfield's attention during the last year and a half
of his Ministry. But his relation to them was not nearly
so close, his direction of them not nearly so complete,
as had been the case with the Eastern question. He
undoubtedly charged the Viceroy, whom he selected for
India, to secure the north-west frontier by a more forward
policy than had been recently pursued, and he adopted
a policy of confederation for South Africa and authorised

the annexation of the Transvaal. But the methods of procedure, the times and places for decisive strokes, were in both cases usually chosen by the servants of the Government on the spot, Lytton or Shepstone or Bartle Frere, and chosen in some instances either without communication with the Home Government, or in actual disobedience to its wishes, if not its orders, and without any particular regard for its difficulties in other parts of the world. Beaconsfield and his Cabinet found themselves more than once in the awkward position of having either to accept and support policies which they disapproved and men who had disobeyed or disregarded them, or else to visit great servants of the Crown, strenuous defenders of imperial interests, with reproof or recall. It cannot be maintained that Beaconsfield always emerged from dilemmas of this kind with dignity or success. He had but a short space for rest before he was confronted with the first of these difficulties.

Owing to the labours of Berlin and the excitements of the welcome home, he was, early in August, more than usually eager to get away to the repose and quiet of Hughenden. ' Dr. Kidd sent me out of town to-day,' he wrote to Lady Bradford on Saturday, August 10, ' but that was impossible. I do go, however, on Monday. All I want, I fancy, is quiet and fresh air. We had a Cabinet to-day, wh. lasted more than three hours—the longest I ever knew. But it was our last.' From Hughenden in the following week he told the Queen that he felt the advantage of the comparative calm; ' but, unfortunately, very little upsets [Lord Beaconsfield], and tho' his energy is generally equal to the occasion, there is no longer that continuous flow of power, which becomes the servant of an Empress and a Queen.'

To Anne Lady Chesterfield.

HUGHENDEN MANOR, *Aug.* 25.—. . . I am extremely un-well, having the bronchitis worse than ever. It exhausts and disgusts me with life. Going to Osborne did me harm, as I knew it would. The slightest social excitement injures me, but the visit was inevitable, and the Queen is greatly disappointed that I did not go for a fortnight to Balmoral! It was impossible. My only hope is in a very quiet life, solitude, regular hours, and no talking. I am now quite alone and therefore ought to ensure the latter condition. Monty went from Osborne to Scotland, and I don't expect to see him again for months. I have given orders that none of my other secretaries, and no messenger, except on urgent and critical business, shall come near me. . . .

To Lady Bradford.

HUGHENDEN MANOR, *Aug.* 29, '78.—. . . You ask me where I generally lived. In my workshop[1] in the morning, and always in the library in the evening. Books are companions, even if you don't open them. They are at least proof that there are, or were, human beings in the world besides yourself; tho' I cannot say I fear solitude or find it irksome. It is the next best thing to being with those you like very much. . . .

Beaconsfield's anxieties this autumn were largely concerned with the proper execution of the Treaty of Berlin. Neither Russia nor Turkey showed any undue haste in carrying out provisions to which they had originally objected but ultimately agreed. But Beaconsfield was clear that both must be assumed to be acting *bona fide* until the contrary was proved, and that consequently full time must be allowed to both before the Powers resorted to diplomatic or other pressure. He successfully resisted a proposal which, apparently at Austria's instance, Bismarck made for an identic note to the Porte.

From Lord Salisbury.

Private. CHÂLET CECIL, PRÈS DIEPPE, *Sept.* 2, '78.—I enclose a note I received from Waddington two days ago. The marked passage seems to show that the Egyptian business has not excited him. . . . His power of doing harm does not extend far.

At the opposite pole of the horizon the weather looks uglier. Either Kissingen baths have disagreed seriously with Bismarck or the Russians are up to some mischief. I do not profess to guess what; for I can't see what advantage they will get. Anyhow, Bismarck's note, when it comes, must be looked at with suspicion; and my present impression is that we ought

---

[1] The small study on the first floor. See Vol. I., III., ch. 6.

not to accede. To begin bullying the Porte is hardly reasonable when the ratifications have hardly been exchanged a month. Probably I shall run over if the note really makes its appearance.

To Lord Salisbury.

HUGHENDEN MANOR, *Sept.* 3, 1878.—It gave me great satisfaction to hear from you this morning.

I think Waddington, tho' he may not always intend it, a somewhat dangerous animal to deal with. Harcourt[1] has taken Harleyford, Sir Wm. Clayton's seat near Marlow, for the season, and, some little time ago, came here in great excitement, with a letter from W., directing him to see you, or me instantly, about the contemplated marriage of P. Napoleon and the P'ss Thyra, wh. he looked upon as a probable revolution in France. If necessary, Harcourt was to read to me their confidential despatches on this subject. I thought I would let him do so, and more frivolous gossip I have seldom perused. When it was over, I told him, which, by an accident, it was in my power to do, that there was not the slightest foundation for his narrative, wh. W. evidently entirely credited.

A week ago, Harcourt drove here with Mme. H., on the pretence of seeing the place, etc., 'not a word of politics to be spoken': but he got me at last in a corner', and was evidently frightened out of his, or Waddington's, wits, about Rivers W[ilson] being Finance Minister in Egypt. I told him, that I had no official information that the post was yet offered to R. W. or, if offered, whether he could, or would accept it, but I hoped, equally for the sake of France and England, that it would be offered and accepted, for it seemed to be the best, if not the only, chance of the two nations getting back any of their money.

I have not the slightest confidence in Waddington; he is feeble and sly, wh. feeble men often are. . The only point on wh. I don't agree with you is as to his inability of doing harm. He can do harm enough, and has done a great deal already about Greece. I should not be at all surprised, that he has been stimulating Bismarck. Waddington wants to convey to the world, that France is yet a great Power, tho' it can't, or won't, do great things. All this at the expense of the Porte, alias at our own expense.

I am clear myself, that if we do not take up a very firm and decided line about the Porte, we shall have serious difficulties arise. I think, we must, on no account, join in any note, such as I hear referred to in the journals.

---

[1] The French Ambassador.

I think we ought to do more: deprecate altogether its transmission, and say that, while we shall use our utmost efforts to induce the Porte to fulfil the spirit of her engagements, and at this moment, believe she will act accordingly, we feel that her engagements are so large, so, at the same time, extensive and difficult, that the utmost forbearance and indulgence must be extended to her during her operations.

I don't think our fleet should leave the Turkish waters at present, and if it does, I don't think our naval force in the Mediterranean should be reduced. Waddington is quite capable, in that case, of sending a French fleet to Greece, or 'demonstrating' in some manner or other. At present, he will do anything but fight, but his tactics are dangerous, and should be discouraged; if necessary, by a little confidential frankness. We intend to see the Treaty of Berlin fulfilled, but, so long as the Porte is acting *bona fide*, we cannot sanction any recourse to compulsion. . . .

Aug. [*Sept.*] 8.—I have received yr. box, and read its contents with entire satisfaction. It is always a real pleasure to me to find ourselves in accord, wh. will help us in the difficulties, which, I doubt not, we shall have to encounter.

I feel your time at this moment is more valuable than mine, and I certainly should have offered to come up to town, but I have no home there. Downing St. is in the hands of the painters; the first time, probably, since Sir Robert Walpole; and therefore, my visit would be a hurried one, between two trains. I like to consult, and, if possible, sleep over our thoughts, before we come to a decision in the morning. I should, therefore, be delighted to see you here, for the statistics of travel are convenient for such a purpose. . . .

To Lady Bradford.

HUGHENDEN MANOR, *Sept.* 7, '78.—. . . I really have nothing to tell you. Solitude mitigates my sufferings, and I have nearly got rid of my bronchitis, but any social excitement, anything wh. breaks the mechanical regularity of my habits, upsets me in a moment. Yesterday I was obliged to have Mr. Turnor down to transact business till four o'ck., when I bid him adieu, with a blessing and a hope I shd. never see him, or any other secretary, again—when I again heard the sound of chariot wheels, and there was the 1st Lord of the Admiralty who had driven over 18 miles, and was obliged to see me. I th[ough]t I shd. have sunk under it, and it led to great labors, all of wh. I had to accomplish myself.

I fear, also, that I shall be otherwise troubled, as Salisbury has come over ! This bodes business ! . . .

Sept. 10.—. . . The Faery complains that I have not

written a letter to her for a fortnight, and have communicated only by telegrams. . . .

Sept. 12.—. . . Ld. S[alisbury] came down here on Tuesday, and left the following morn—affairs being most pressing; but as for myself, I have not had a moment since even for meals or sleep—so much to do and so much coming. It is worse than the Congress. . . .

Salisbury came to an agreement at Hughenden with Beaconsfield that they would have nothing to do with the proposed identic note; but subsequently Austria's eagerness in pressing England to join caused the Foreign Secretary for a moment to waver. The Prime Minister, however, stood firm. As he told the Queen, he had ' had anxious moments about the identic note. Fortunately, he knows more now of the character of Continental statesmen, and of some of his own colleagues, than he did before the Berlin Congress. There had been an attempt to override his decision, but he was inexorable; and the result is that Prince Bismarck has absolutely adopted our view, and says we are right.' The following was Beaconsfield's reply to a letter in which Salisbury expressed his uneasiness and hesitation.

To Lord Salisbury.

HUGHENDEN MANOR, *Sept.* 20, 1878.—. . . Our joining in the identic note, after having declined to do so, and declined for good reasons, would have the worst effect, and convey an impression of vacillation and perplexity on our part; two qualities which we should always avoid.

Success would hardly justify such a step. But would it succeed ? Is it in the power, even if it be in the will, of Turkey, to control events in Bosnia ? An identic note, and no results, would be humiliating.

But let us assume that it is in the power of Turkey to manage Bosnia; then England ought to be able to induce her to take the necessary steps without joining in identic notes. You may bully with impunity the Turks in private, provided you uphold them publicly; but strong remonstrances accompanied by identic notes, and such machinery, always fail with them. If the Turks can control the Bosnian insurrection, let our Ambassador point out to them all the evils of their neglecting to do so, and the eventual necessity of England acting with their foes.

I am ready and willing to give any proof of the sympathy of England which you can recommend—I should not shrink myself from a tripartite treaty such as you intimate. It would not displease Germany; it would please France; and Russia could do nothing.

The situation at present allows, and demands, bold action. Every Power is too embarrassed to act except England. It is a moment when what is called prudence is not wise. We must control, and we must create, events.

As for the rumours about Todleben and his mate, and the Rumanian plébiscite, I should utterly disregard such bugbears. A plébiscite in E. Rumelia, occupied by a Russian army, would only excite indignation.

As for Afghanistan, Russia, in my opinion, will get out of the business as soon, and as well, as she can. There will be no continuity of military operations, and the Russian Mission, instead of being permanent, will ultimately take the form of an Embassy extraordinary and temporary. But we must act with firmness there, as everywhere.

I am rather disgusted about the Egyptian delay. The affair is in the hands of Lingen ! who has drawn up, I understand, a great piece, ' grandis et verbosa,' wh. is to be sent to me.

However, the main object will be obtained, and all we can hope is, that Cr. of Exr. Wilson may not find an Egyptian Lingen.

The same policy of patience and hope which Beaconsfield was resolved to pursue as regards Turkish action in Europe, he also desired to extend to Russian action in Central Asia. It was natural, he felt, that when we brought Indian troops to the Mediterranean as a reminder to Russia of our power and determination, Russia should retaliate, as she did, by sending a formal mission to Cabul, and by preparing columns of troops in Turkestan to threaten India. He believed that, now that peace was signed, Russia would recall the mission and the troops; and he was confirmed in this view by Gortchakoff's somewhat general assurances.

From Prince Gortchakoff.

Confidential. BADEN, *Sept.* 16, 1878.—This morning I received your confidential letter of the 11th September. I fully persevere in the conviction that every step which tends to terminate unwise jealousies between two great States consolidates the peace which is in both our wishes. No continuity of military demonstrations in the direction of Afghanistan is contemplated on our part. We don't research any particular influence, but merely good relations which should in no way inspire any apprehension to England.

I confirm the wishes we exchanged at Berlin, and persevere in the hope that they will come to a practical conclusion by the assistance of an elevated mind.

Accordingly, Beaconsfield was anxious that the Indian Government should take no precipitate action. Lytton, the Viceroy, on the other hand, with perhaps a truer appreciation of the Afghan problem, was convinced that the time had come for a forward movement in fulfilment of the charge entrusted to him when Disraeli selected and sent him out to India in 1876. That charge, as we have seen,[1] was to provide for the permanent security of the north-western frontier, which was endangered by the steady advance of Russia in Turkestan, and by the growing intimacy of the relations between General Kaufmann, the Russian Governor of Turkestan, and the Ameer of Afghanistan, Sher Ali. The map might suggest that the barren and rugged mountains on this frontier were a sufficient protection. But history taught us that invader after invader had penetrated their barrier and overrun the Indian plains; and, indeed, that it was only the British conqueror who had reached India by any other approach than that across or beside Afghanistan. Accordingly ' the Prime Minister,' writes Lytton's daughter, ' strongly impressed upon the new Viceroy his opinion that the policy of Russia gave cause for extreme anxiety and watchfulness, and that it was essential, even at the risk of failure, the possibility of which could not be denied, that an attempt should be made to induce the Ameer of Cabul to enter into more satisfactory relations with our Government; or, if such a result proved impracticable, that he should at least be compelled to show clearly the attitude which he intended to hold towards Russia and towards ourselves. Anything, Mr. Disraeli thought,

[1] See V., ch. 11.

was better than the state of absolute uncertainty and suspicion in which our relations with Afghanistan were involved.'[1]

The instructions which Lytton, on taking up his post, received from Salisbury, the Secretary of State, were to endeavour to obtain the assent of the Ameer to the reception of a friendly mission; and, in case of success, he was authorised to give him assurances as to subsidies, recognition of the *de facto* succession of his favourite son, and material assistance in the event of a clear case of unprovoked aggression. But, in order that such assistance might be effectual, the Ameer must admit British agents to frontier positions. Should the Ameer refuse to receive the mission, his estrangement would be beyond a doubt, and the Government of India might have to reconsider their whole policy towards Afghanistan.

The first year of Lytton's Viceroyalty was largely occupied with repeated but unavailing efforts to come to an understanding with the Ameer on these lines. Lytton was given a wide discretion; and he tried every means to get into friendly relation, culminating in a conference held at Peshawur in the early months of 1877 between Sir Lewis Pelly and two of the Ameer's principal Ministers. This conference, however, finally broke down on the absolute refusal of the Ameer, who claimed British material support, to give British officers access to his frontier posts. The reception of a permanent British agent in Cabul was never even asked of him, so careful was Lytton of Afghan susceptibilities. But Sher Ali was by this time deeply committed to Russia, and he even endeavoured, with little result, to stir up a holy war against British India among the wild tribes bordering on the Punjab. In spite of this failure to bring the Ameer to reason, Lytton's policy in these early days added enormously to the strength of the north-west frontier of India by the Treaty of Jacobabad, concluded with the Khan of Khelat in December, 1876; by which the great

[1] *Lord Lytton's Indian Administration*, pp. 28, 29.

province of Baluchistan, lying between Afghanistan and the Indian Ocean, was brought within the orbit of Great Britain, and the right was obtained to station British troops at Quetta, a mountain bastion on the southern flank of Afghanistan, over against Candahar. Moreover, the defiance thrown out by the Ameer in calling the frontier tribes to a holy war was met by arrangements for strengthening British influence among them, especially at Chitral and Gilgit in the north. These arrangements involved both risks of serious complications, and also military operations against the Jowakis; but Beaconsfield was decided in his support of the Viceroy.

To Lord Salisbury.

HUGHENDEN MANOR, *April* 1, 1877.—. . . I have no doubt whatever, as to our course; we must, completely and unflinchingly, support Lytton. We chose him for this very kind of business. Had it been a routine age, we might have made, what might be called, a more prudent selection, but we foresaw what would occur, and indeed saw what was occurring; and we wanted a man of ambition, imagination, some vanity, and much will—and we have got him. He reminds me of Ld. Wellesley, physically and morally, and may have as eminent a career. Wellesley wrote Latin verses instead of English ones; that was the fashion of the day. . . .

After the failure of the Peshawur Conference all communications with the Ameer ceased, and Lytton began to contemplate the breaking up, rather than the consolidation and support, of the Afghan power as the proper aim of British policy. In this extreme development of the 'forward' theory, however, he met with decided discouragement from home; and, in the absence of further provocation from Cabul, he bided his time. He warmly seconded, if he did not suggest, the despatch of troops from India to the Mediterranean in order to remind Russia, at the critical moment in the spring of 1878, of the solidarity and material strength of the Empire, and he busied himself with preparations against a possible Russian attack; but he took no action on the frontier, till the Russian Mission under General Stoletoff appeared at

Cabul in July. To Lytton this was a decisive event. He could not regard it merely as the natural Russian reply to British preparations, but rather as an open breach by the Ameer of his obligations to British India. It is true that the Ameer protested against the coming of the Mission, but he took no military action to prevent its advance, he received Stoletoff at Cabul with honour, and there is no doubt that he signed some sort of treaty or convention with him. Conduct of this kind could not be tolerated in a ruler who looked to Britain for the protection of his independence and who yet had for years evaded or declined the reception of any Mission from the Viceroy of India. Lytton decided at once that the only suitable course for the Indian Government was to despatch a Mission of its own to Cabul, and, this time, to insist on its reception with becoming honours. He obtained the sanction of the India Office, selected a competent and experienced officer, Sir Neville Chamberlain, and sent the Mission forward, taking care that the public in India and outside should realise the serious importance of this new departure in policy. Beaconsfield, and still more Salisbury, deprecated this haste, in view of Russia's disposition to retreat. Cranbrook, the Indian Secretary, supported the Viceroy; and Beaconsfield, though annoyed by Lytton's tendency to force the hand of the Home Government, admitted the strength of his case and admired the ability with which he defended his action.

To Lord Cranbrook.

Confidential. HUGHENDEN MANOR, *Sept.* 12, '78.—I have read with some alarm the V-Roy's telegram. It appears, that Lord Lytton cd. not have been kept *au fait* to the communications, that have taken place, and are taking place, betn. H.M.'s Government and that of Russia, on the subject of Afghanistan. If this be the case, I think it is deeply to be deplored.

As far as they have proceeded, and as far as I can now judge, the explanations of the Russian Govt. are satisfactory, and the whole matter would have quietly disappeared, the Russian projects having been intended for a contemplated war with this country, wh., I trust, is now out of the question.

What injurious effect Lytton's policy, ostentatiously, indiscreetly, but, evidently, officially announced, in the Calcutta correspondence of *The Times* of yesterday, may produce, I cannot presume to say. But I am alarmed, and affairs require, in my opinion, your gravest attention.

If Ld. Lytton has ventured on these steps with full acquaintance with our relations with Russia on the subject of Afghan[ista]n, he has committed a grave error; if he have been left in ignorance of them, our responsibility is extreme.

I won't go into any details as to his views, assuming, for argument's sake, that some course was necessary; but I must remark, that the unconditional guarantee of the Afghan territories ought to be well considered before sanctioned. . . .

Private. Sept. 13.—Our despatches crossed. I should not have written mine, had I previously received yrs.

I have read all yr. documents, printed and MS. Lytton grapples with his subject, and grasps it like a man. I always thought very highly of his abilities, but this specimen of them elevates my estimate. With his general policy I agree, in great measure—but the all-important question, wh. disturbs me, immediately arises—is he acquainted with the negotiations now going on with Russia ?

And if he be not, will the announcement of his views and projects in *The Times* injuriously affect our position with that Power ?

Confidential. Sept. 17.—I have yours of the 13th, and, by this post, return all the Lytton papers, which I have read with the utmost attention.

I have not yet seen the answer from Livadia, but from the tel. of its contents, forwarded by Mr. Plunket, it is unsatisfactory. You have no doubt also received this tel.

I am convinced the country requires that we shall act with decision and firmness on this Afghan question. So far as I can judge, the feeling is strong, and rising, in the country. So long as they thought there was ' Peace with Honor ' the conduct of the Government was popular, but if they find there is no peace, they will soon be apt to conclude there is also no honor.

With Lytton's general policy I entirely agree. I have always been opposed to, and deplored, ' masterly inactivity.'

As to his instructions to our Envoy, I shd. leave them to your sound criticism, and good sense, and experience in public affairs, but I think there is no doubt that there shd. be no delay in the Mission. . . .

Confidential. Sept. 22.—There can be no Cabinets now,

and matters must be settled by myself, and the Secretaries of State for For. Affr. and India.

Under these circumstances, when you and the V-Roy agree, I shall, as a general rule, always wish to support you.

No doubt Salisbury's views, under ordinary circumstances, would be prudent; but there are occasions when prudence is not wisdom. And this is one. There are times for action. We must control, and even create events.

No doubt our Envoy will make the best terms he can. He will, of course, not show all his cards at once, but I am clearly of opinion that what we want, at this present moment, is to prove our ascendency in Afghanistan, and, to accomplish that, we must not stick at trifles. . . .

Confidential. Sept. 26.—Yours of the 24th reached me this morning. I am not satisfied with the position, as nothing could justify Lytton's course except he was prepared to act, and was in a situation wh. justified the responsibility of disobeying the orders of H.M. Government.

He was told to wait until we had received the answer from Russia to our remonstrance. I was very strong on this, having good reasons for my opinion. He disobeyed us. I was assured by Lord Salisbury that, under no circumstances, was the Khyber Pass to be attempted. Nothing would have induced me to consent to such a step. He was told to send the Mission by Candahar. He has sent it by the Khyber, and received a snub, wh. it may cost us much to wipe away.

When V-Roys and Comms.-in-chief disobey orders, they ought to be sure of success in their mutiny. Lytton, by disobeying orders, has only secured insult and failure.

What course we ought, now, to take is a grave affair.

To force the Khyber, and take Cabul, is a perilous business. Candahar we might, probably, occupy with ease, and retain.

These are only jottings. I have the utmost confidence in yr. judgment and firmness, but I shall never feel certain, now, whether your instructions are fulfilled.

To the Duke of Richmond.

HUGHENDEN MANOR, *Sept.* 24.—You are very kind to me; you make much of me; you feed me with delicate cates; and I am very ungrateful for not sooner acknowledging all your gifts; but you must pardon a hermit, who lives in entire solitude, and gets every day more incapable of the private duties of life.

To call the Cabinet together would agitate all Europe, and I should think the V-Roy was quite prepared for the probable incident that has occurred. I telegraphed yesterday to Hardy, but I have not yet his answer. It is unfortunate, at such a moment, that the Sec. of S. for For. affairs should be at Dieppe and Sec. for India at Balmoral. We are terribly scattered; naturally in Sept., but events happen every day. They have no recess and no holidays. I think with firmness we shall settle all the other things and this too.

To Lord Salisbury.

HUGHENDEN MANOR, *Oct.* 3, 1878.—I have been obliged to summon the Cabinet. I found they were talking all sorts of nonsense over the country; especially some in whose prudence I still had some lingering trust; and there were already 'two parties in the Cabinet,' and 'all that.'

I have given the deepest attention and study to the situation and read with becoming consideration all Lytton's wonderful MS. pamphlets; wh. are admirable both in their grasp and their detail; and this is my opinion. His policy is perfectly fitted to a state of affairs in which Russia was our assailant; but Russia is not our assailant. She has sneaked out of her hostile position, with sincerity in my mind, but scarcely with dignity, and if Lytton had only been quiet and obeyed my orders, I have no doubt that, under the advice of Russia, Shere Ali would have been equally prudent.

However, it is not so, and we have received a *coup*, which was needlessly encouraged. We can't let the matter remain as it is, but our retort, tho' dignified and authoritative, ought to be moderate. It is not a *casus belli*, after the withdrawal of Russia, and if we had been quiet, we need have done nothing. I fear you will smile at my specific for the occasion, and that it will remind you of my ancient proposals about Gallipoli, but I think it is a case for 'material guarantee.' That will gain time, and that is, in my opinion, all that is required.

But can we take a material guarantee without calling Parliament together ? That would be terrible The Act is now under the consideration of the Ld. Chancellor, and he will enlighten us. . . .

Beaconsfield's last three letters were written after receipt of the news of the forcible stoppage of Chamberlain's Mission by order of the Ameer at Ali Musjid, the fort at the entrance of the Khyber Pass. It was a deliberate affront, and the Viceroy desired to meet it with a declaration of war. But neither Beaconsfield nor the majority of his colleagues were prepared for so drastic a course. A meeting of the Cabinet on October 4 was indecisive, and Beaconsfield invited Cranbrook to Hughenden to discuss the problem. The guest wrote in his diary that his host was 'disturbed about India because Russia is taking advantage of our embarrassment in India, and, as Corry says, it is a " black moment." '

To Lady Bradford.

HUGHENDEN MANOR, *Oct.* [? 9 or 10].—. . . The news this morning is so black that I do not at present well see how a November meeting [of Parliament] can be avoided. Monty has gone up to town to-day and will see Ld. Cranbrook, who is also there to-day, and I hope will succeed in sending him down here. It is terrible for all of us to be so scattered. This critical state of affairs need not have happened, and cd. not have, if my orders had not been disobeyed. This makes it more grievous. I wrote to you, a month ago I shd. think, that I hoped I had settled the Afghan business, but alas ! I did not reckon on distant and headstrong counsels. . . .

To Queen Victoria.

HUGHENDEN, *Oct.* 11, '78.—. . . Mr Corry went up to town yesterday to make a reconnaissance about Mr. Leighton[1] and his prospects, and Lord Beaconsfield will inform your Majesty of the result as soon as he receives it. He is desirous himself, for the honor of English Art, that Mr. Leighton should succeed to an office for which his personal accomplishments highly qualify him. . . .

Oct. 15.—. . . The state of affairs as regards Russia is more harassing than perilous. If strong protests are made and continued against the conduct of the Russian Government, and the affairs of Afghanistan terminate to the satisfaction of your Majesty, Russia will recede from this new position.[2] If, on the other hand, the Afghanistan settlement be not as speedy and decisive as is hoped and expected, it will still be expedient to continue negotiations with Russia, while, at the same time, we shall be maturing some great stroke, which will effectually vindicate the provisions of the Treaty of Berlin.

The situation is similar to that of the occupation of Syria and Asia Minor by the Egyptians, backed by France, and in the teeth of the remonstrances of Y.M. Government. Lord Palmerston continued his negotiations with M. Thiers, thro'

[1] The reference is to Leighton's candidature for the Presidency of the Royal Academy, which was successful.
[2] Russia was showing a disposition to delay the evacuation of the Turkish territories she occupied in Europe.

M. Guizot, until he had concluded alliances which allowed him to drop the diplomatic mask, and to sweep the Egyptians, in the teeth of France, from the countries which they persisted in occupying. The state of Europe is such that Lord Beaconsfield believes that combinations may, in due time, be realised, which will bring about an analogous result.

Lord and Lady Odo Russell have been here on a visit of explanation, and to receive condolences on their cruel disappointment in their not being able to receive the honors which your Majesty was graciously pleased to express your Majesty's readiness to confer on them. It seems that the Duke of Bedford has revoked the promised endowment of the peerage, as he is advised that it is improper for a member of the House of Russell to accept a distinction on the advice of a Tory Minister. There is no doubt, as Lord Beaconsfield assured the Ambassador, that the acceptance of a peerage for distinguished public service, such as the winning of a battle, or the signature of a treaty, involved no political relations with the Minister of the time. According to the reverse doctrine, had the Whig party been in office, Sir Arthur Wellesley would have continued only a Knight of the Bath during the whole of the Peninsular Campaign. The Duke of Bedford is the wealthiest of your Majesty's subjects, his income absolutely exceeding £300,000 *per annum;* but, as he observed to a friend of Ld. Beaconsfield, very recently, that His Grace considered accumulation was the only pleasure of life and that he never retired to rest satisfied, unless he could trace that he had saved, that day, at least a five pound note, Lord Beaconsfield fears it may not be easy to remove the Duke's constitutional objections. However, Lord Beaconsfield advised Lord Odo not to deem the affair concluded, and said that he should not formally advise your Majesty at once of what had taken place, in the hope that the difficulty, so unjustly raised, might be removed.[1]

Lord Beaconsfield had long and exhaustive conversations with Lord Cranbrook, and hopes that he left Hughenden in a profitable state of mind.

Since Lord Beaconsfield wrote thus far, the first Lord of the Admiralty has driven over to this place. It is evident that he is very anxious about Cyprus, and altho' he had relinquished all intention of going there, and has sent his Admirals to examine Malta, which was necessary, the question of some member of the Ministry visiting Cyprus may arise. He will consult the Secretaries of State for F.O. and India on Thursday morning next, and if they are of opinion that he should go,

---

[1] The difficulty was not removed; but, when Gladstone returned to power, the peerage (Ampthill) was again offered and accepted.

he will submit the case to your Majesty for your Majesty's consideration. His absence would hardly exceed three weeks, as he can reach Cyprus in five days.[1] Lord Beaconsfield reminded him that he was on the Balmoral roster. . . .

WESTON,[2] SHIFNAL, *Oct.* 18, '78.—. . . It is wise that the fountain of honor should flow freely in the Colonies. . . .

Lord Beaconsfield is deeply interested your Majesty is reading *Coningsby.* It would be presumption in him to hope that your Majesty would ever deign to make any critical remarks to him on its pages, but perhaps, some day, when he may have the honor and happiness of being in your Majesty's presence, your Majesty may allude to the subject. . . .

A Cabinet was held on October 25, to come to a final decision about Lytton's Afghan policy; and Beaconsfield gave the Queen a lively account of what he characterised as ' one of the most remarkable meetings ' that he remembered.

To Queen Victoria.

HUGHENDEN, *Oct.* 26, '78.—Meeting of the Cabinet yesterday on the affairs of Afghanistan. Lord Beaconsfield, after a few preliminary observations, the object of which was to prevent recurrence in the discussion to what was passed and inevitable, called upon Secretary Lord Cranbrook to lay before the Cabinet the present position of affairs, which he did, and concluded by recommending the Cabinet to adopt the proposals of Lord Lytton. He was followed by the Lord Chancellor, who said that the projected proclamation, proposed by Lord Lytton, was a declaration of war; that Parliament must be called together, and the first question that would be asked would be, What was the *casus belli ?* Lord Cairns saw none. The Lord Chancellor then analysed the papers before the Cabinet, and showed that the Ameer had acted towards the Russians with the same reluctance to receive them as he had exhibited to the envoy of the Viceroy; that it was a fair inference from the papers that the Ameer, when he had got rid of the Russians, would have received the English; that inference would certainly be drawn by Parliament. He spoke with great power, earnestness, and acuteness, and was evidently highly displeased with the conduct of the Viceroy.

[1] Smith and Stanley, the ministers for the Navy and the Army, paid a short visit to Cyprus this autumn.

[2] Beaconsfield paid short visits in the middle of this month to the Bradfords at Weston, and to Lady Chesterfield at Bretby, and Lady Bradford came to Hughenden for a day or two at the end of the month.

The Leader of the House of Commons followed the Lord Chancellor, and said he was about to ask the same question—What was the *casus belli ?* As at present advised, he could find none, and was sure our party would not support us in the Commons. He spoke at length and very earnestly.

Mr. Secretary Cross entirely agreed with the Leader of the House of Commons. He saw no case.

The Marquis of Salisbury said that the Viceroy was 'forcing the hand of the Government,' and had been doing so from the very first; he thought only of India, and was dictating, by its means, the foreign policy of the Government in Europe and Turkey. He had twice disobeyed orders: first in acting on the Khyber Pass; 2nd, in sending the Mission contrary to the most express and repeated orders that he was not to do so, till we had received an expected despatch from Russia, and never without the precise instructions of the Ministry in England; that, even now, he was not prepared to act even if we permitted him to do so. He spoke with great bitterness of the conduct of the Viceroy, and said that, unless curbed, he would bring about some terrible disaster.

Lord Cranbrook spoke in answer to the preceding speakers, taking the strong Indian view of affairs, and said the *casus belli* was formed by an aggregate of hostile incidents on the part of the Ameer.

In this critical state of affairs, there being now silence, Lord Beaconsfield gave his opinion. He said it would doubtless be dangerous to summon Parliament to sanction a war, if our *casus belli* was not unimpeachable; but he was of opinion that a demonstration of the power and determination of England was at this moment necessary; that instead of the proposed manifesto of the Viceroy, which the Lord Chancellor informed them was a declaration of war, he would propose that a strong column should pass the frontiers and occupy the Kurram Valley, all our preparations in other quarters simultaneously proceeding, and that the Viceroy should issue a note, declaring that this invasion was not intended as an hostile act, but as the taking of a ' material guarantee ' that justice should be obtained for the English demand. The occupation of the Principalities by Russia before the Crimean War was quoted as a precedent. It was shown such a step was in the nature of ' reprisals ' and which were sanctioned by public law, and not considered as active hostilities.

The Duke of Richmond strongly approved of these remarks. Lord Salisbury said such a course would content him—in demonstrating power, and not necessarily leading to any disaster. The Lord Chancellor and the House of Commons members, following him, murmured approbation, when suddenly Lord Cranbrook startled us all by saying, that he would not undertake the responsibility of such a course; that his own opinion was for war, immediate and complete; that he believed it inevitable sooner or later, and very soon; that the 'material guarantee' project was a half measure, and would be looked upon as an act of timidity; and secondly, that he would prefer continuing our preparations, postponing the inevitable campaign, to any middle course, and the more so because he would frankly confess that he was not altogether satisfied with the military preparations of the Viceroy; that Lord Lytton was acting in opposition to the military members of his Council—first in not employing as they thought sufficient English troops, and secondly in refusing to retain the reliefs, which Lord Cranbrook on his own responsibility, and in opposition to the opinion of Lord Lytton, had ordered to remain.

After this extraordinary statement on the part of the Secretary of India, in addition to the fact that none of the forces had as yet arrived at their stations, and that all was matter of calculation and estimate, there seemed only one course to take. The military preparations were ordered to be continued and completed, and even on a greater scale, while, in order to strengthen our case for Parliament, it was agreed that another message to the Ameer, to be submitted, before transmission, to the Cabinet, should be prepared and sent.

This is not a complete, and perhaps a feeble, but a faithful, sketch of one of the most remarkable meetings of a Cabinet that Lord Beaconsfield well remembers. It is certainly unfortunate that the Afghan business should have been precipitated, which was quite unnecessary, for we have much on our hands at this moment, and the utmost energy and resources of the country may have to be appealed to by your Majesty's Government; but Lord Beaconsfield himself, tho' anxious, looks forward to the future without dismay, and Lord Salisbury is prepared to support Lord Beaconsfield in some steps, which, if necessary, will be of a very decided character.

This letter shows the great reluctance with which the Cabinet, and even its chief, entered upon the Afghan War. They felt that they had been unduly hustled by Lytton, though they were eventually convinced that his policy must be supported—and supported, as the Queen urged and Beaconsfield agreed, with as much cordiality as if there had been no initial difference of opinion. The ultimatum to the Ameer, which the Cabinet authorised, demanded an apology in writing for the affront at Ali Musjid, and the reception of a permanent British Mission in Afghanistan; and it gave him till November 20 to reply. In the interval came Lord Mayor's Day, and Beaconsfield went to stay at Hatfield at the beginning of the month to consult with Salisbury on the line to be taken in the Guildhall speech.

To Queen Victoria.

HUGHENDEN, *Oct.* 31, '78.—Lord Beaconsfield . . . goes to Hatfield to-morrow, and will remain there, more or less, until Lord Mayor's day is past. It is necessary that some unmistakable expression of the policy of your Majesty's Government should be made on that day, and Lord Beaconsfield must be in daily communication with Lord Salisbury on its nature. . .

Lord Beaconsfield hopes your Majesty will graciously confer the honor of Knighthood on the Lord Mayor. There is some murmuring in the city as to the scanty honors which have been granted to the municipality, but, in truth, when Lord Mayors began to believe that they had a vested interest in the honorable and territorial title of Baronet, it became necessary to check their unreasonable ambition. But Knightbood in the City Lord Beaconsfield thinks should be rather encouraged. . . .

To Lady Bradford.

[HATFIELD], *Nov.* 4.—I came down here on Friday and have done much business. They wish me to remain permanently during the month of Cabinets, but tho' they are most kind, and there is some convenience in daily intercourse with the Secretary of State, I sigh for 'my crust of bread and liberty,' and return to town to-morrow, Monty's house being my home. . . .

There is no party here at present, but somebody comes every day and stays for 8 and 40 hours. Monty is of course here, and is, I perceive, a great favorite with all the members of the family. . . . The daughters of the house keep everybody alive; always on horseback, and in scrapes, or playing lawn tennis even in twilight. The evening passes in chorus singing —all the airs of *Pinafore*. It's a distraction both for Salisbury and myself from many cares.

Your letter pleased me very much, and I was glad the H[ughende]n visit was not a failure. I wish you to like my home, to use a mild word.

10, DOWNING STREET, *Oct.* [*Nov.*] 8.—. . . I dined on Wednesday at Lady Marian's, a farewell dinner to the beauti-

ful Louise and Lorne.[1] Marian just arrived to a long un-
inhabited house, all her heating apparatus out of gear and
wouldn't work—never knew a house so cold, and feeble wood
fires. The company never got over it. . . . I got home and
drenched myself with hot cognac and water, and was not so
much injured on the morrow as I expected.

'Yesterday a Cabinet and afterwards a real farewell dinner
at the Lornes'; house very warm (to make up for the former
day), exquisite dinner, tho' I cd. not partake of it, and there
were too many luxuries; a very small party, but rather
amusing. Prince Leopold was there, in his blue ribbon, and full
of talk. I sate betn. our hostess and him. The Coutts Lind-
says, Abergavenny (your Hughenden friend), the Bertie
Mitfords. . . . Lorne the most genial of hosts, and directed
his conversation much to yr. humble servant, who cd. not
keep up the ball, for I never for a moment understood what
he was talking about. . . .

It was clearly impossible to say much at Guildhall
about the Afghan dispute, as we were awaiting a reply
to the ultimatum. But most Prime Ministers in Beaconsfield's place would probably have justified Ministerial
action by a short statement of the wrongs which we had
suffered at the Ameer's hands, culminating in the repulse
of a British Mission by force after the reception of a
Russian Mission with honour. Commonplace of this
sort, however, was uncongenial to Beaconsfield. His
attention was fixed, as he assumed that of the nation to
be, on safeguarding the north-west frontier. The danger
of invasion of India from Asia Minor and from the valley
of the Euphrates had been averted, he maintained, by
the Cyprus Convention, which gave us 'a strong place
of arms,' and secured the Sultan in the possession of
his Asiatic dominions, providing for their regeneration
under our influence. On the 'matter of immediate
interest' what he said was this:

Our north-western frontier is a haphazard and not a
scientific frontier. It is in the power of any foe so to embarrass
and disturb our dominion that we should be obliged to maintain
the presence of a great military force in that quarter, entailing
on the country a proportionate expenditure. These are

[1] Lord Lorne had been appointed, on Beaconsfield's recommendation,
Governor-General of Canada.

unquestionably great evils, and former Viceroys have had their attention called with anxiety to the state of our frontier. Recently, however, some peculiar circumstances have occurred in that part of the world, which have convinced Her Majesty's Government that the time has arrived when we must terminate all this inconvenience and prevent all this possible injury. With this view we have made arrangements by which, when completed, in all probability at no distant day, all anxiety respecting the north-western frontier of India will be removed. We shall live, I hope, on good terms with our immediate neighbours, and not on bad terms, perhaps, with some neighbours that are more remote.

Several of Beaconsfield's colleagues, and particularly Cranbrook, the Indian Secretary, realised the imprudence of this passage while their chief uttered it. Northcote wrote to Lady Northcote next day: ' The chief spoke very well, and was very well received. We were, however, rather dismayed by what he said as to Indian frontier policy; and Cranbrook, Salisbury, and Cross pulled very long faces over the "rectification" passage.' It would be only too easy to represent it—and the Liberal party and press hastened to do so—as an admission that we were wantonly making war in order to establish a scientific frontier. Undoubtedly it was the policy both of Beaconsfield and of Lytton to secure, after the defeat of Sher Ali, a line of frontier more defensible than the existing one. But it was no quest of a scientific frontier, but the intolerable conduct of Sher Ali towards the British Government, culminating in the insolent stoppage of Chamberlain's Mission, which had produced the ultimatum, and which, if the Ameer refused to comply with the ultimatum, would bring about war.

This passage, however, was merely an episode in a speech which dealt mainly with the European situation and the execution of the Treaty of Berlin. Difficulties in Bosnia, Albania, Eastern Rumelia, and Rumania, and the refusal hitherto of Turkey to revise her frontier with Greece, had given opportunity for criticism to suggest that the Treaty on which the British Government had prided itself was so much waste paper. In reply to this shallow carping, Beaconsfield pointed out that time was always allowed for the fulfilment of a treaty's terms, and that in the present case not half, not much more than a third, of the period prescribed had elapsed. Nevertheless, already, under the provisions of the Treaty, Russia had retired from Constantinople and from the Straits of Gallipoli, and had restored Erzeroum to the Porte, while the Sultan had surrendered the fortresses on the Danube and Batoum had been given up without the shedding of a drop of blood; moreover, international commissions were actively at work arranging the new lines of demarcation created at Berlin. These were the most considerable points of the Treaty; and all this had been done in three months. No intimation had been received from any of the signatories that it was their desire or intention to evade the complete fulfilment of its conditions. It was the policy and determination of Her Majesty's Government that the Treaty should be carried out in spirit and to the letter; and they would, if necessary, appeal to the people of this country to support them in that policy with all their energy and all their resources. But he did not believe that could be necessary. He disregarded current gossip to a contrary effect. 'The government of the world is carried on by Sovereigns and statesmen, and not by anonymous paragraphers, or by the hare-brained chatter of irresponsible frivolity.' On Lord Mayor's Day there was a 'chance of hearing the voice of sense and truth.'

On September 15 Beaconsfield had written to the Queen, in reference to 'Lord Palmerston's "dangerous man,"' Gladstone: 'The article in the N[orth] American Review, disparaging his own country, the country of which he was chief Minister, and acknowledging its decline and fall, fills Lord Beaconsfield with amazement.' It was clearly this article that Beaconsfield had in his mind in composing the fine peroration of his Guildhall speech; and subsequent history has vindicated his confidence in the imperial capacity of his countrymen.

I know there are some who think that the power of England is on the wane. We have been informed lately that ours will be the lot of Genoa and Venice and Holland. But, my Lord Mayor, there is a great difference between the condition of England and those picturesque and interesting communities. We have, during ages of prosperity, created a nation of 34,000,000; a nation who are enjoying, and have long enjoyed, the two greatest blessings of civil life—justice and liberty. A nation of that character is more calculated to create empires than to give them up; and I feel confident, if England is true to herself, if the English people prove themselves worthy of their ancestors, if they possess still the courage and determination of their forefathers, their honour will never be tarnished and their power will never diminish. The fate of England is in the hands of England; and you must place no credit on those rumours which would induce you to believe that you have neither the power nor the principle to assert that policy which you believe is a policy of justice and truth.

To Lady Bradford.

S. Audley St.,[1] *Nov.* 11, '78.—. . . Saturday was a great, I believe I might say a complete, success. The party is what is called on its legs again, and jingoism triumphant ! In a very mixed assembly, as Guildhall ever is, there was enthusiasm as far as concerned me, not merely cheering, but rising in their places of a 1,000 guests, and waving of kerchiefs and all that, napkins included.

My voice was queer in the morning, but remedies got it all right, and the Ld. Chan[cello]r says it was never more powerful or clear. All our people, all people, and the foreign Ambassadors esp[eciall]y, in high spirits. Quite ashamed to write this egotistical trash, wh. is only for your dear eyes.

Nov. 13.—. . . Our accounts from the Continent to-day are all favorable, and the Guildhall speech seems to have done what I intended. . . .

Nov. 16.—Going to Sandringham. . . . The Faery has just telegraphed that she highly disapproves of my going: 'most imprudent, running great risk, cold stormy weather. . . .' Go to S. I must. I can't tell the Faery the exact reason, but you will remember last year and what occurred.[2] . . .

Nov. 19.—There was rather an agreeable party at S[andringham]. The Manchesters, Salisburys, D. of Sutherland, Beust, Mrs. Standish, ourselves, Leighton, Oliphant. . . .

---

[1] Corry's house.
[2] Beaconsfield excused himself in 1877 from going to Sandringham, and then went to Weston.

Prince Hal was very gracious, agreeable, and in high feather; and very proud of having four Knights of the Garter at dinner. . . .

The Cabinet meets to-morrow, and will have to decide whether Parliament is to be summoned. It is vexatious, for the reason is only technical, for tho' the language of the Act of Parliament is ambiguous, I can't help feeling myself that an interpretation favorable to not meeting might be fairly given to it. There are some, however, who fancy that the cry of the Opposition of our governing without Parliament may take the fears and fancy of John Bull, who is sometimes apt to be hastily headstrong.

Sir Stafford Northcote to Lady Northcote.

11, DOWNING STREET, *Nov.* 19.—. . . The Chief has written a saucy letter, declining to receive the deputation of thoughtful Liberals, and remarking that he has already had ample opportunities of making himself acquainted with Lord Lawrence's views. . . .

Lord Odo Russell to Montagu Corry.

Private. BRITISH EMBASSY, BERLIN, *Nov.* 23, '78.—. . . I am rejoiced to say that Ld. Beaconsfield's great speech at the Mansion House [? Guildhall] has produced a most excellent impression in Berlin and indeed throughout Germany. It is most remarkable and refreshing to see how the Oriental policy of H.M.G., in, and since, the Congress, has elevated England in the eyes of the Continent.

What a marvellous and delightful change for the better, since the day when I first had the satisfaction of an exchange of ideas on this subject with you after the Londonderry dinner at Holdernesse House on the 19th of June, 1877! . . .

To Lady Bradford.

SOUTH AUDLEY ST., *Nov.* 21.—Hardly a moment to write. These are agitated and agitating times. Nothing was decided yesterday as to meeting of Parliament, but the Cab. meets to-morrow at noon, and will settle it—one way or the other. I think the meeting will take place, as the House of Comm. Ministers are in favor of it, and they bear the strain, and their opinion therefore carries double weight. The army has entered Afghn. at three points this morning. . . .

Nov. 26.—. . . Schou[valoff] has just been here, and had his interview—a long one, and to me satisfactory. I think we shall triumph in all quarters, and not only get our Berlin

Treaty successfully carried into effect, but that the Ameer is what the Yankees call ' a dead crow '! . . .

Nov. 28.—. . . I cd. not go to the Faery yesterday—to Council—my old enemy being on me. . . . I was obliged to go to the Cab. to-day, but have just returned, quite unable to call in Hill St., or do anything but write to you.

The consequence is that I shall have to go down to Windsor, if possible, again by a spec[ial] train; and on Wednesday I must go to the Council besides, if possible—and Thursday, Parliament ! . . . Things look well, but I am not.

Dec. 2.—. . . I fear I never told you, and I only tell it quite in secret, that the Faery wanted Monty to succeed Biddulph, £2,000 *pr. ann.*, and the head place of the Household ! What a strange thing had it happened ! . . .

To Queen Victoria.

10, DOWNING ST., *Nov.* 27, '78.—. . . *Secret.* To-morrow he understands your Majesty will give audience to Lord Salisbury on the occasion of Count Beust's farewell.

Lord Beaconsfield is entirely satisfied with the conduct of Lord Salisbury; his personal loyalty to himself, his remarkable capacity of labor, and his fertile resource; but Lord Beaconsfield a little fears the cajoling influence of Count Schouvaloff over him. He would, therefore, humbly entreat your Majesty to impress upon the Secretary of State, while appreciating his labors and ability, the absolute necessity and wisdom of the utmost firmness in our relations with Russia. We may be, and ought to be, quite conciliatory in tone, but we must concede nothing. If we are firm and decided, Russia will surrender every point in dispute, present or future dispute. All is going right. Cyprus will be a marvellous success, and Hamley says that Famagusta will turn out a harbor, which will conveniently receive all your Majesty's ironsides. The Sultan is certainly with us, since our announcement of our determination as to Bulgaria and E. Rumelia; and Austria, influenced much by the same cause, every day more inclined to act with us. All that is required is—that England should be conscious of her own strength. . . .

Beaconsfield's language at Guildhall confirmed the Liberal party in its resistance to his Afghan policy. The Ameer left the ultimatum unanswered, and on November 21 the British forces advanced through the passes. The Opposition, once more under the *de facto* leadership of Gladstone, immediately proclaimed that we

had entered on an ' unjust ' war. They adopted eagerly
the doctrines of the old Anglo-Indian school, whose spokesman was Lord Lawrence, and who deprecated any intermeddling whatever with the affairs of Afghanistan. They
failed to see that the Russian conquest of Turkestan,
and the imminent inclusion of Afghanistan within the
Russian sphere of influence, had entirely altered the
problem; which, ever since Gladstone's refusal of Sher
Ali's request for definite support and protection in 1873,
had been urgently demanding a fresh solution. This
was fully recognised by many of the ablest Anglo-Indians,
of whom Sir Bartle Frere and Sir James Fitzjames Stephen
were the most powerful voices. But the Liberals shut their
eyes to the facts, insisted on regarding the Ameer, who
was deep in Russian intrigue, as a would-be friend whom
Lytton had treated ill, and vehemently protested that the
forcible stoppage of a British Mission after the honorific
reception of a Russian Mission was no sufficient ground
for a punitive expedition.

Once more, as at the time of the Bulgarian atrocities,
it was claimed that a great moral issue was involved;
and so much were men's minds inflamed that the chronicler of the *Annual Register* for 1878, whose duty it was
to register facts and not to pass judgments, was moved
solemnly to record the grave opinion that this was ' a very
wanton and a very wicked war,' undertaken in pursuance
of a ' deliberately aggressive ' policy, and deserving
therefore of ' most emphatic condemnation.' These
expressions read very foolishly now side by side with the
judgment of a man who was as alive as Gladstone to
moral issues but who knew the facts. Lord Roberts,
after gathering first-hand information on the spot, wrote
at Cabul on November 22, 1879: ' Our recent rupture
with Shere Ali has, in fact, been the means of unmasking
and checking a very serious conspiracy against the peace
and security of our Indian Empire.' A modern historian
of good judgment, Dr. Holland Rose,[1] who recognises

---

[1] *The Development of the European Nations*, 5th ed., p. 393.

that the action of the British Government in the situation
existing in 1878 was justifiable, is yet inclined to maintain
that that situation would never have existed but for the
rejection of the Berlin Memorandum and for Beaconsfield's anti-Russian policy.   He writes that ' as far as can
be judged from the evidence hitherto published (if we
except some wild talk on the part of Muscovite Chauvinists),
Russia would not have interfered in Afghanistan except
in order to paralyse England's action in Turkish affairs.'
Surely he forgets that it was in 1870, six years before
the rejection of the Berlin Memorandum, that Russia's
intervention in Afghanistan began; when General Kaufmann, the Governor of Turkestan, opened communications
with the Ameer, which steadily increased from year to
year in frequency and intimacy.   The danger existed,
and was ever growing, many years before the Eastern
Question was reopened in Europe.

In spite of the Liberal outcry, the Afghan policy was
successful both in the field and in Parliament.   One
British division took Ali Musjid and occupied the Khyber
Pass as far as Jellalabad; another, under General Roberts,
operating by the Kurram Pass, routed the Afghans in a
brilliant action at Peiwar Kotal; a third, starting from
Quetta, occupied Pishin, and early in January reached
Candahar.   Parliament met on December 5, while the
news of these successes were coming in, and Northcote
wrote next day to his wife: ' Roberts's great victory has
taken the wind not only out of the sails, but out of the
bodies of our opponents. . . . Poor Hartington is in
lamentable case, and is reduced to asking my advice
as to the best mode of attacking us, without hurting us.'
In both Houses Ministers, in spite of some initial anxiety,
had large majorities.   The Lords supported their action
by 201 to 65; the Commons by 328 to 227.   The following
were Beaconsfield's reports to the Queen:

To Queen Victoria.

10, DOWNING ST., *Dec.* 6, '78.—Lord Beaconsfield with his
humble duty to your Majesty, must offer his congratulations

to his beloved Sovereign, on the signal triumph of your Majesty's arms. The letter of the Ameer, which Lord Beaconsfield underlined some days ago, in a telegram which he forwarded to your Majesty, has just been received by the Secretary of State, and it is clear we may demand any terms we like. Of course, he offers to receive your Majesty's Envoy at Cabul.

The check to Russia, to use a very mild expression, is complete. Lord Beaconsfield has no doubt, that expectations were held out by Russia of military aid to the Ameer.

Lord Beaconsfield has summoned the Cabinet to meet at three o'clock to-day, to consider the Ameer's letter, and the situation generally. The debates proved last night that the Opposition is broken into pieces on the great question of the war. They dare not face it, but take refuge in mere squabbling about sentences in despatches. Lord Beaconsfield closed the debate in the House of Lords to his satisfaction, and is not worse for what was a considerable, tho' not very prolonged, physical exertion. He hopes your Majesty is well on this bright morning, which is as bright as your Majesty's imperial fortunes. . . .

Dec. 7.—. . . The Cabinet decided that Major Cavagnari or some one of his standing should reply to the Ameer, that the terms of the ultimatum must be accepted, but that your Majesty's Government were ready to conclude peace on just conditions. The military operations, in the meanwhile, not to be suspended. He would, and meant to, have written this at length to your Majesty, but was summoned to the House of Lords from the Cabinet, and on arriving at the Houses of Parliament, found everything in agitation and confusion. The legitimate leaders of the Opposition, influenced, at the last moment, by the violent section of their supporters, had suddenly changed their front and had given notice of Votes of Censure on your Majesty's Government, for Monday, in both Houses. The Opposition are sanguine of success in the House of Lords, the members of which are not prepared to give up their shooting parties, and other pursuits popular at this season. The Peers are independent, and cannot be acted upon like the members of the House of Commons thro' their constituencies. Lord Beaconsfield was detained until a late hour in the Lord Chancellor's room, considering the situation, and writing incentive letters to apathetic Peers.

The House of Lords will divide—perhaps even some days before the House of Commons, and the effect, it is feared, of an adverse, or feeble, vote in the Upper Chamber, on the decision of the Lower, may be very injurious. All influences and efforts are necessary. . . .

Dec. 9.—Lord Beaconsfield . . . will not trouble your Majesty at this moment with business, for he knows your Majesty's heart is disturbed.[1] There is no agitation like that of the affections, and he can truly say, that the thought of your Majesty's suffering haunts him amid all his affairs. He thought on the whole, however, that it might perhaps be a little relief to your Majesty to know that the prospects of your Majesty's Government in the impending struggle seem not unfavorable. He has very good accounts from the House of Commons, and his personal appeals to the House of Lords have brought some unexpectedly favorable results. With all duty and affection.

Dec. 11.—. . . Your Majesty is, of course, aware of the division last night in House of Lords: the greatest majority on record. Dukes of Sutherland and Somerset and Lord Fitzwilliam, and several other Whigs, voted with your Majesty's Government, and others stayed away. Lord Beaconsfield could not write to your Majesty before, as he did not retire last night, or rather this morning, until past four o'clock, having sate in the House of Lords for nearly twelve hours continuously. He is rather shattered, but managed to speak at $\frac{1}{2}$ past 2 o'clock this morning, an exhausted orator, he fears, to a jaded House. However, the deed is done, and the House of Lords has adjourned for a week, until next Tuesday. This division must have a considerable effect on that of the Commons. If good news could come from Darmstadt, he should feel content, but those thoughts prevent his writing more, and perhaps he ought to ask your Majesty's gracious pardon for saying so much. . . .

The speech delivered in these unpromising circumstances was a successful effort which extorted admiration even from hostile critics. Beaconsfield occupied the earlier part of it with an ingenious defence of his Guildhall indiscretion. He repudiated the idea that rectification of frontier necessarily implied annexation or spoliation. It might be managed by an exchange of equivalents. Treaties for rectification of frontiers had been quite common in the recent history of European diplomacy. In any case he never said that the substitution of a scientific for a haphazard frontier was the object, but only a possible consequence, of the war. When he spoke he had in mind the wild ideas then prevalent, that we were about

[1] Owing to Princess Alice's illness.

to conquer Afghanistan and annex it to our Empire; whereas a scientific rectification would give us all the results we required, and enable us to garrison the frontier with a comparatively small number of men. He quoted Lord Napier of Magdala as a high military authority who confirmed his view.

The sudden appearance of Russia in the immediate vicinity of Afghanistan, said Beaconsfield, had necessarily changed our policy. He held that Russia's military and political preparations in Central Asia against India, at a time when war between Britain and Russia seemed to be impending, were perfectly justifiable. But, now that the crisis was past, the Tsar was prepared to meet our wishes. He had given orders to his troops to retire; and his Ambassador would be merely considered as on a mission of courtesy, and would soon return. Russia's conduct was satisfactory; but after Russian armies had been almost in sight of Afghanistan and a Russian embassy had been within the walls of Cabul, our relations with the Ameer could not remain as they were, and we could not fancy our frontier to be secure. It was said that we ought to have appealed to the Ameer and treated him with courtesy and kindness. That was what we had done. ' Really the Ameer of Afghanistan has been treated like a spoiled child. He has had messages sent to him, he has had messengers offered to him. He has sent messengers to us who have been courteously received. We have written him letters, some of which he has not answered, and others he has answered with unkindness. What more could we do ?' Yet the Government were reproached for not fighting Russia rather than the Ameer. ' Remember,' said Beaconsfield, ' Russia has taken every step in this business so as to make honourable amends to England, and her conduct presents the most striking contrast to that furnished by the Ameer.'

Beaconsfield impressed on the House the magnitude and gravity of the issue it had to decide. ' It is not a question of the Khyber Pass merely, and of some small cantonments at Dakka or Jellalabad. It is a question which concerns the character and the influence of England in Europe.' He developed this train of thought in his peroration.

What I see in the amendment is not an assertion of great principles, which no man honours more than myself. What is at the bottom of it is rather that principle of peace at any price which a certain party in this country upholds. It is that dangerous dogma which I believe animates the ranks before me at this moment, although many of them may be unconscious of it. That deleterious doctrine haunts the people of this country in every form. Sometimes it is a committee; sometimes it is a letter; sometimes it is an amendment to the Address; sometimes it is a proposition to stop the supplies. That doctrine has done more mischief than any I can well recall that have been afloat in this century. It has occasioned more wars than the most ruthless conquerors. It has disturbed and nearly destroyed that political equilibrium so necessary to the liberties of nations and the welfare of the world. It has dimmed occasionally for a moment even the majesty of England. And, my lords, to-night you have an opportunity, which I trust you will not lose, of branding these opinions, these deleterious dogmas, with the reprobation of the Peers of England.

To Lady Bradford.

[SOUTH AUDLEY STREET], *Dec.* 15.—This terrible death[1] has thrown us into endless distress and confusion. . .

The Parliamentary campaign may be said to have ended. It lasted six weeks, and I made three speeches. The first, at Guildhall, put an end to the silly stories about the failure of the Berlin Treaty. The others were the pitched battles in the Lords. I can truly say of all three, *Veni, vidi, vici.*

Beaconsfield's satisfaction with the course of events in Asia seemed, during the early months of 1879, to be justified. No further military operations against the Afghans were found to be necessary. Sher Ali fled to Russian Turkestan; his appeals for help to those with whom he had intrigued, though they met with sympathy from some local representatives of Russia, were disregarded by the Tsar; and he died in exile before the close of February, 1879. Yakub Khan, his son, who had been

[1] Princess Alice.

long kept in prison by his father, at once made overtures
to the Indian Government. Both Lytton and the Cabinet
at home thought that they had found in Yakub a man
who would have the power to rule the Afghans, and the
will to rule in friendship with British India. By a treaty
concluded at Gandamak near Jellalabad on May 26 the
Ameer accepted British control of his foreign policy and
consented to receive a British Resident at Cabul, obtaining
in return a promise of support against foreign aggression.
He recovered Candahar and Jellalabad; but he ceded the
frontier districts of Kurram, Pishin, and Sibi, the British
Government also retaining control over the Khyber and
Michnee Passes, which had never acknowledged Afghan
rule. Thus apparently all that Beaconsfield and Lytton
desired was cheaply secured; a scientific frontier giving
command of the passes, and the guidance of Afghan
policy though a resident agent. *Dis aliter visum.*

To return to December, 1878.—Again public affairs
kept Beaconsfield hard at work during the holiday
season; and again he ate a solitary Christmas dinner at
Hughenden.

To Lady Bradford.

S[OUTH] A[UDLEY] ST., *Dec.* 20, '78.—Yesterday was a day
of terrible pressure. A sudden Cabinet at ½ pt. 11—a Golden
Casket Deputation at one, and then, after seeing many colleagues, an early audience at Windsor—*i.e.*, six o'ck. So I
could not write to you, wh. annoyed me.

And all this with a most oppressive attack of my great
enemy, wh. quite disqualified me for a royal audience, during
wh., strictly, I believe you may not even blow your nose!
Nothing cd. be worse than going to Windsor, but it was inevitable and put off till the last moment.

We arrived in London this morning in a black fog, and I
found alarming letters on my table, preparing me for the
failure of banks, ' another black Friday,' and begging me to
telegraph to the Cr. of Exchequer, who, I believe, left London
last night, that it may be necessary to suspend the Bank
Charter! A pleasant Xmas! and my birthday to-morrow!
And to-morrow Monty goes to Melbury! . . .

I had a long audience—more than an hour. . . .

I have kept this open, and wd. have wished to write more,

but am busied, harassed, and ill.   London is as black as night.
I am ordered out of town to-morrow, and shd. have gone some
days ago, but this Windsor visit hung over me. . . .

HUGHENDEN MANOR, *Dec.* 22.—I got down here yesterday
—a white world. . . .

I forgot to tell you I met Manning, after ten years' and more
non-acquaintance.   He called on me the day before yesterday,
and sate with me a long time.   He is a fervent supporter ! ! !

Xmas Day.—. . . It is not my throat that ails, it is my
breast; and one always feels, with complaints of this kind,
that we are in dangerous vicinage of the lungs.   Hitherto I
have escaped in that department, but my present attack is
a severe one, and out of door life is almost impossible. . . .

The snow is falling fast and thick on a crust of ½ a doz.
inches.   There only want snowballs to recall one's youth.

I have two secretaries in London.   Mr. Turnor, my hunting
secretary, is frostbound.   He has seven hunters !   Private
secretaries are different from what they were in my days,
when I was Lord Lyndhurst's, and hunted in Vale of Aylesbury
on one horse ! at the hazard of my life !   I cd. afford no more.
Exactly thirty years afterwards, when Lord Lonsdale was
leaving the field, but did not like breaking up his stable at
Tring, he offered me the complete control and enjoyment of his
stud there—as long as I liked.   But it was too late.   Everything, they say, comes too late.   It is something if it comes.
However, I can't complain of life.   I have had a good innings,
and cannot at all agree with the great King that all is vanity.

Dec. 27.—. . . I have now been here a week to-morrow, and
have not spoken to anyone.   I woke this morning to a green
world, and went out on the terrace: this is my third time.   I
think the change of weather must bring me relief, but it has
not come yet.   I found the peacocks all mounted on the marble
vases (with their tails reaching to the earth), wh. vases are
now, of course, emptied of flowers.   There were not vases
enough for them, so the rest had flown up to the pergola, and
one or two were looking into the windows of yr. rooms, and
seemed much disappointed at not finding you.   I was not so
disappointed, but, I am sure, more sorry. . . .

You are right in supposing that the business, wh. now takes
up so much of my time, is the general distress; but it is one
most difficult to deal with.   There are so many plans, so many
schemes, and so many reasons why there shd. be neither plans
nor schemes.

What I fear is that the Opposition, who will stick at nothing,
may take up the theme for party purposes.   If we then don't
support them, we shall be stigmatised as unpatriotic: if we
do, they will carry all the glory.

And yet—what is the cause of the distress ? And, if permanent, is there to be a permanent Committee of Relief ? And the property of the nation to support the numbers of unemployed labor ? Worse than socialism.

To hoist the flag of distress, when there has been no visible calamity to account for it, like a cotton famine, no bread and meat famine, no convulsion of nature, is difficult and may not be wise.

There are 1,000 other things to be said (on both sides)—but after all starvation has no answer. You will see, however, how difficult is my present position with constant correspond-ence (and no Secs.) of equal and contradictory character—impossibility of calling a Cabinet, for that, at Xmas, wd. frighten the world—and everybody agreeing with nobody, but throwing the respon[sibilit]y on my shoulders. . . .

To Anne Lady Chesterfield.

HUGHENDEN MANOR, *Dec.* 26, '78.—I must thank you for my Xmas dinner, tho' I have only a moment. . . .

The Parliamentary campaign was brilliant and triumphant. Why the Opposition insisted upon one, I can only account for by the want of judgment which distinguishes human nature: still, in my own case, it will not do to make speeches on bronchitis.

Dec. 30.—. . . [Lord Grey de Wilton] is insipid. Somebody offered him £50 for the original of the Bath letter,[1] wh. I wrote to him from Weston. He stared, but said he had not kept it. He was worthy of the most famous state-paper of modern times, and wh. destroyed a Ministry. . . .

[1] See p. 602.

CHAPTER XI.

The Zulu War.

1879.

The year 1879 was marked by British disasters in two continents, which contributed materially to the downfall of Beaconsfield's Government. But it opened well. On New Year's Day Sher Ali was in precipitate flight, and the British armies were completely successful in their advance on Afghanistan. It was known that trouble was brewing in South Africa, but few believed it to be serious; and the one dark patch, in the picture that Beaconsfield painted for the Queen, was the domestic distress, which his optimism regarded as transient.

To Queen Victoria.

HUGHENDEN MANOR, *New Year's Day*, 1879.—Lord Beaconsfield with his humble duty to yr. Majesty. He had not heart enough to congratulate yr. Majesty at Xmas, and why does he do it now? when only a few days have elapsed since that season left us in sorrow. Because, tho' it seems somewhat irrational that an artificial arrangement of time should affect our feelings, yet it is so. A new year is a new departure in life; and Hope, rather than Care, is its harbinger.

Indeed, if yr. Majesty would, or could, for a moment throw a veil over the anguish of private sorrow, there is much in yr. Majesty's state that may be looked upon with more than content. The authority of yr. Majesty's throne stands high again in Europe. Yr. Majesty's counsellors have taken a leading, and successful, part in the most important diplomatic meeting since the Congress of Vienna, and yr. Majesty's arms have achieved, in Asia, a brilliant and enduring success.

One public care remains, no doubt, in the great industrial distress, which, in common with all countries, has fallen on yr. Majesty's kingdom, but it is not in the nature of things that it should long endure, tho' its progress requires the utmost vigilance and judgment.

Lord Beaconsfield, with all his good wishes for yr. Majesty's happiness, both public and private, cannot refrain, on such an occasion, from expressing his own gratitude to yr. Majesty for the condescending and unshaken kindness, which yr. Majesty has ever extended to him; lightening, as it does, every care, and lending a charm to labor.

From Queen Victoria.

OSBORNE, *Jan.* 1, 1879.—Tho' the Queen has telegraphed her New Year's wishes to Lord Beaconsfield she desires to repeat them, earnestly hoping that he may see many more, and also to thank him for his *very* kind letter. The Queen wishes to thank Lord Beaconsfield for all his kindness to her, and for the great services he has rendered to the country. May he long continue to guide its destinies! The prospects—as regards foreign affairs, our position in the world, our successes in India and our general policy at home—are very cheering. The distress is, of course, a cause of great concern and of a certain amount of anxiety—but she trusts that that will soon improve. . . .

Beaconsfield's own health was far from satisfactory, and his New Year letter to Lady Bradford was couched in a more despondent tone than that to the Queen.

To Lady Bradford.

HUGHENDEN MANOR, *Jan.* 1, 1879.—. . . You talk, in yr. last, of a 'tendency to bronchitis'! Alas! it is not a tendency; it is bronchitis absolute, and in its most aggravated form. Nothing else wd. have prevented my going to Weston. It began in town: more or less, I had it all the last month. I see people die of it every day. I don't see why I don't. Nobody can do me any good. I have tried 'all schools of thought,' as they say. . . .

My present physicians are Dr. Solitude, Dr. Silence, Dr. Warmth, and two general practitioners, Regular Hours, and Regular Meals. I mention this, that you shd. not think I was neglected. I don't want any companion, unless it were you.

The Prime Minister was well enough to preside over the usual Cabinets held to prepare the programme of the session. His interest, however, this month was largely

taken up by two appointments: that of the Whig Lord
Dufferin as Ambassador to St. Petersburg, where the
presence of a first-rate man was essential, and that of
Lightfoot to the bishopric of Durham. The Queen,
though she herself suggested Lightfoot as a suitable
addition to the episcopate, would have preferred to
fill the See of Durham by the translation of Magee.

To Queen Victoria.

HUGHENDEN MANOR, *Jan.* 17, 1879.—No one can deny,
and Lord Beaconsfield does not wish to deny, the abilities of
the Bishop of Peterboro,' but no party has any confidence in
him; his judgment cannot be relied on, he is vehement in
opposite directions; and above all, he is wanting in dignity
of manner and mind. Lord Beaconsfield is quite satisfied
about Dr. Lightfoot, but he doubts, whether he has the personal
gifts, particularly as to preaching and public speaking, which
are necessary for Durham. . . .

10, DOWNING STREET, *Jan.* 27, 1879.—. . . Yr. Majesty's
appointment of Canon Lightfoot to the see of Durham will
add lustre to yr. Majesty's reign. The University of Durham,
under his guidance, will exercise great influence on the ecclesiastical future, and on the formation of the religious mind
of the rising generation. It is of great importance, to yr.
Majesty's Government, that some mark of respect and recognition should now be shown to that powerful party of the Anglican
Church, which Lord Beaconsfield would describe as the 'right
centre': those, who, tho' High Churchmen, firmly resist, or
hitherto have resisted, the deleterious designs of Canon
Lyddon, and the Dean of St. Paul's,[1] who wish to terminate
the connection between the Crown and the Church, and ultimately, unite with the Greek Church. The Church Union is
entirely under their control, and now, at every election, that
Union systematically votes against yr. Majesty's Government,
on the main ground, among others, that Lord Beaconsfield
virtually carried the Public Worship Act. No effort should be
spared in preventing the orthodox and loyal High Church
party being absorbed by these dangerous malcontents, who
would support any candidate, even Bradlaugh, against yr.
Majesty's Government. For this reason Lord Beaconsfield
much wishes, that yr. Majesty should confer the vacant
Canonry of St. Paul's on Professor Stubbs,[2] Regius Professor
of Modern History at Oxford, a man of European reputation.

---

[1] Church. [2] Afterwards Bishop of Oxford.

From Prince Gortchakoff.

Confidential. St. Petersburg, *Jan.* 30 (*Feb.* 11), 1879.—
I have received your lordship's letter of February 6.
Your friend, Lord Dufferin, will be welcome. I shall be the
more happy to see him as he is entrusted by your lordship
to communicate me all your efforts for the maintenance of
peace and the foundations of a sincerely good understanding
between our two Empires. The achievement would be worthy
of your superior intelligence.

For my part, I entertain entire confidence in the words we
exchanged at Berlin. But I must candidly avow that the
conduct of the majority of your agents abroad does not confirm our mutual hopes.

I am sure you will not grudge me for this frankness—frankness is the highest proof of esteem—and that you allow me this
appeal to your personal power and loyalty.

To Lady Bradford.

10, Downing Street, *J*[*an*]. 24, '79.—It is difficult to write:
even the Faery is forgotten. But Cabinets—and languor, every
day, and interviews—unceasing—afterwards, exhaust and at
last almost confuse me. I came up with great care; in an
express train, and in a small saloon carriage, which had been
warming for me at Wycombe for a week, and I have never left
this house for a minute, and yet the enemy has caught me.
Dr. Kidd comes to me to-morrow morning, and I hope we may
arrest it, but I have no great hopes till this savage weather
changes.

All the world, I hear, is skating. I do not hear of any
human being of the civilised order being in town. . . .

Jan. 27.—. . . I am suffering, and a prisoner now of ten
days, but still I have held five Cabinets in a week, wh. no
P. Minister ever did before.

Jan. 29.—. . . I have just had a visit from the new Bishop.
I was prepared for a very ill-looking man; I was told by the
Faery, the most ill-looking man she knew. He is ugly, but
his ugliness is not hideous; a good expression in short, wh.
is enough in a man. . . .

Feb. 6.—. . . This change to Favonian breezes is a great
relief and delight. I have been here three weeks next Saturday, and only went out for the first time this early morn—and
not alone. I am very tired, but still it is a first step out of
quarantine, and later in the day I go to Hatfield for a change
of air and scene, and shall remain there till Parliament. . . .

I hope Dufferin's appointment to St. Petersburg will produce results. I wanted a first-rate man there. I conclude the Whigs will be sulky about it; that can't be helped. . . .

HATFIELD HOUSE, *Feb. some day or other* [? *Feb.* 8].—I offered myself here when the wind changed, but [they] did not tell me their house was full. I met, among others, Lady Cornelia Guest, whose letter, written in the heat of the British election, I had never answered! and Janetta.[1] . . . The crowd is very miscellaneous—Lady Marian and the Harcourts, and Schou., and the Cranbrooks . . . and *Pinafore* Smith[2] and his wife and daughter . . . and Count Piper, and Ct. Montebello, and a good many others. Our hostess is admirable from her unflagging energy and resource, and the daughters of the house are always delightful, from their extreme intelligence and natural manners; but it requires all their gifts to carry the thing through, but they succeed.

To-day, they had the meet here, and, with a Favonian breeze and frequent gleams of sunshine, the scene was bright with scarlet coats and the promise of ½ a doz. foxes in the Park—but alas! not one was found there; but the *chasseurs* have not returned, and, it is to be hoped, have been more fortunate in more distant regions.

I shd. have remained here till Tuesday, but have a Cabinet on Monday, and, of course, will not return. After two months of imprisonment, the bland atmosphere must be beneficial.

Monty is here, and seems in high force—with endless tennis, in courts, or lawns, and in the evening singing, dancing—a new Swedish dance quite excellent wh. you shd. see and learn, and introduced by Count Piper, who is the Swedish Minister. At ½ pt. 11—with great difficulty, much preparation, and seizing the select opportunity—I manage to escape, but no one else does, and I am told, before they disperse, the small hours sound; in short, quite orgies!

Parliament was to meet on Thursday the 13th, and Beaconsfield came to town on the Monday to make final preparations for what appeared likely to be a quiet session. Next day all his hopes were shattered by the news of the disaster at Isandhlwana to part of the British force invading Zululand under Lord Chelmsford's command. Eight hundred white soldiers and nearly five hundred natives had been surprised by the enemy, and cut off to a man. The tidings fell like a thunderbolt on the unprepared

---

[1] Lady John Manners.
[2] W. H. Smith, First Lord of the Admiralty.

British public, and produced a shock and disturbance unmatched since the Indian Mutiny.

Hitherto no large amount of public attention had been attracted to the Colonial policy of the Government. Disraeli had originally selected as Secretary of State for the Colonies the one man among the Conservative leaders who had made a continuous study of Colonial problems; whose views, moreover, corresponded with that consolidating and unifying policy which he himself had propounded at the Crystal Palace in 1872. Carnarvon had signalised his first tenure of the seals of the Colonial Office in 1866–67 by carrying through the great Act for the confederation of Canada. On returning to Downing Street, he embraced with eagerness the view of his Liberal predecessor in the office, Kimberley, that South Africa, owing to the native peril, was ripe for a similar measure; and he was encouraged to proceed by his chief as well as by a large body of opinion, both Dutch and English, on the spot. Subsequent history has shown that the policy was in itself a right one for a large country with a comparatively small and scattered white population, divided into several colonies, states, and territories, and surrounded and interpenetrated by a vast mass of natives, many of them imbued with the fighting spirit. But reconsideration of the conditions of 1874 certainly suggests that the policy was then premature, if only because two of the principal states, the Transvaal and the Orange Free State, were at that date recognised by the British Government as independent. It would be only with the utmost reluctance, and owing to the pressure of hard necessity, that the Boers who had gone out of the British Empire to found these states would come again within it. But if they remained independent, South African federation, being confined to British territories, would be a very imperfect instrument of government; unless, indeed, it was contemplated to make a new departure and embrace in the Confederation, not only countries which acknowledged allegiance to the British Crown, but also countries which repudiated such allegiance. Such a hybrid experiment, it may be confidently asserted, could not have been permanently workable.

Whatever Carnarvon's expectations may have been, the first measures which he took to promote his policy were hardly judicious. It was only a few years since the Cape Colony had been granted responsible government, and it was naturally tenacious of its privileges. But Carnarvon, in a despatch to Sir Henry Barkly, the Governor, not merely deprived it of the initiative by himself suggesting a conference on the spot to discuss federation, but actually named the persons in his opinion best fitted to represent the constituent States. The Colony took umbrage, which the Governor felt to be justified; and a resolution was carried in the Assembly that any movement in the direction of federation should originate in South Africa and not in England. Besides offending a considerable section of South African feeling by this despatch, Carnarvon also made unhappy use of a diplomatic weapon of which his chief was too fond, the semi-official mission of a personal friend. In this case the friend was J. A. Froude, the historian, who was a master of English prose, but who was singularly lacking in practical political insight. He made two tours in South Africa, in successive years (1874 and 1875), as in some sort Carnarvon's personal representative. He returned from the first tour with much more sympathy for the Dutch than for the British point of view in South Africa. Nevertheless Carnarvon sent him back as one of his nominated members of the proposed federation conference. Though the resolution of the Cape Assembly had killed the conference before he arrived for the second time, Froude was ill-advised enough to carry on a campaign in the Cape Colony and the Orange Free State on behalf of his friend's policy; and Carnarvon failed to realise the impropriety of this defiance of the responsible authorities at Capetown.

The Froude mission produced a very different impression upon Disraeli. His frequent recurrence to the blunder in his private letters shows that it seriously shook his confidence in Carnarvon's judgment. Carnarvon himself discovered before long that Froude's picture of an enthusiastic and unanimous South Africa backing the Minister in Downing Street against the responsible Government in Capetown was a work of imagination. He dropped his original proposal, substituting for it an invitation to a conference in London; which, however, attracted only a limited attendance and did not materially advance federation.

In other respects Carnarvon's administration in these early years reflected credit on the Minister and the Government, and frequently elicited the commendation of his chief. He carried through the annexation of the Fiji Islands, the sovereignty over which had been offered to Great Britain over and over again by native kings and white settlers during more than twenty years. He was responsible also for an extension of our dominion in the Malay Peninsula, whereby Perak was pacified and the foundation laid for our protectorate of the neighbouring Malay States; though the principal credit here is due to the Governor of the Straits Settlements, Sir William Jervois, whose vigorous campaign in Perak was looked upon coldly both by Carnarvon and by Disraeli until it was successful. On the West Coast of Africa, Carnarvon began his administration happily by the stamping out of the slave trade and the emancipation of the slaves in British Colonies. On the other hand, he failed in an attempt to make an exchange of territory in that region with France, involving the cession of our isolated Colony of Gambia. The project was finally upset by the protests of the Gambia traders; and Disraeli did not consider that the negotiation, which was protracted over many months, was well managed.

But South Africa was Carnarvon's chief preoccupation throughout his ministry, and he was able to contribute in many ways to the improvement of a tangled situation. For Natal the native question was always acute, and, after Langalibalele's rebellion in 1874, Carnarvon sent out Wolseley as Special Commissioner, who was able to establish a better and more humane policy. Then the discovery of diamonds north of the Orange River, in Griqualand West, in land claimed both by Cape Colony and by the Orange Free State, produced a serious dispute with one of the independent Dutch States, which was happily settled by Carnarvon in July, 1876, by the payment to the Free State of £90,000 in consideration of the abandonment of their claim. But it was the condition of the other Dutch State, the Transvaal Republic, and its relation with its native neighbours, which presented the most difficult problem for Carnarvon's solution. The Transvaal, of course, was at that time, some years before the discovery of the Rand goldfield, an almost purely pastoral State, with a scattered population of *voor-trekkers*, who had left British territory and gone north into the wilderness, in order to escape the restraints of British rule and to preserve their absolute independence. That independence had been definitely recognised by the Sand River Convention of. 1852; but the Dutch farmers, sprinkled at wide intervals over the high veld, had failed to establish an organised or cohesive or self-supporting State. The internal anarchy of the Republic was a scandal throughout South Africa; and externally it was constantly threatening, and generally fighting, some one or other of its coloured neighbours, who detested the Boers for their uniformly harsh treatment of natives. Khama and Lobengula in the north implored the protection of the Queen against Boer aggression; Cetywayo, the king of the great fighting tribe of Zulus, was only restrained from attacking his hereditary enemies by the British authorities in Natal; while in the summer of 1876 war broke out between the Transvaal and a native chief called Sikukuni, whose location was near Lydenburg. The Boers suffered defeats, but the fighting dragged on and was exasperated through the employment by the Republic of bands of filibustering scoundrels.

The whole native population of South Africa became dangerously excited, and there was in the minds of those who knew the situation best, such as Barkly, the Governor of the Cape, and Shepstone, Secretary for Native Affairs in Natal, a serious fear of a general Kaffir war. Carnarvon shared this fear, and at the same time saw, as he thought, a real opportunity of pushing forward, in spite of recent rebuffs, his great panacea of federation. 'My hope,' he wrote to Beaconsfield on September 15, 'is that by acting at once, we may prevent war and acquire at a stroke the whole of the Transvaal Republic, after which the Orange Free State will follow, and the whole policy in South Africa, for which we have been labouring, [will be] fully and completely justified.' He developed his policy in a couple of letters during the next few weeks.

From Lord Carnarvon.

Private and very Confidl. COL. OFFICE, *Sept.* 20, '76.— Matters at the Cape are extremely critical, but they are up to my last advices going as I desire. But they need very prompt handling, and the loss of a mail now may be irretrievable.

The Dutch army is apparently *in extremis*, and I have received information that a meeting has already been called by a certain part of the people to ask for our intervention and to take over the Govt. of the country. Some even of the Dutch authorities appear to be consenting parties.

It is on every ground of the highest importance not to lose this opportunity, and I propose to send out by the mail of Friday Sir Theoph. Shepstone—the man who has the most intimate knowledge of S. African affairs and the greatest influence alike over natives and Dutch—with a secret despatch empowering him to take over the Transvaal Govt. and country, and to become the first English Governor—if circumstances on his arrival render this in any way possible. Should any now unforeseen change have occurred—as unfortunately is possible, though I hope not likely—he will hold his hand, and I shall try to give him instructions suitable to the case. But I have every confidence in his judgment and capacity and courage; and, knowing my mind, he will under almost any circumstances I believe act rightly.

Will you send me back by the messenger a few lines to convey your concurrence in what may seem a sudden, but is not a hasty or ill-considered measure? There is every reason for it both on the ground of policy and in order to prevent a great S. African war which—if there is any want of decision at home or on the spot—will be the consequence. . . .

Private. HIGHCLERE CASTLE, NEWBURY, *Oct.* 15, '76.— The progress of events in S. Africa seems to bring a possible annexation of the Transvaal Republic and the consequent confederation of the various colonies and states within sight. Much, however, will depend upon every preparation being now made to enable us to take advantage of the feeling of the time.

Under these circumstances I am preparing a *permissive* Bill to allow these colonies and states to confederate. My next step must be, without loss of time, to bring S. African opinion to bear upon it in such a way as to secure some criticism and expression of feeling on it. If this is, as I hope, favourable, there will be no difficulty in passing the measure through Parliament,[1] but, owing to the length of time required for communicating with the Cape and to the critical state of affairs there, I do not like to delay my movements for the meeting and discussion of the matter in Cabinet. Though the Bill will not be immediately ready it seems to me desirable to give an intimation of my intentions at once: and every day is of value.

If, therefore, you concur in this general line, which I believe is safe and expedient, I will act as I have described.

It is clear from these letters that Carnarvon's policy was the annexation of the Transvaal, that he expected and hoped that Shepstone would find no other course possible; not, as has been sometimes represented, that he hoped to avoid it and gave Shepstone authority to annex only in the last resort. He had realised by this time that the existence in South Africa of two states not owing fealty to the British Crown was an almost insuperable obstacle to federation. He saw his way to bringing one of them immediately within the Empire, and believed that the other would necessarily follow. Beaconsfield, though a strong believer in federation for South Africa, appears to have had his doubts of this very forward policy; but his mind in this autumn of 1876 was occupied with the Eastern Question, and he deferred,

---

[1] The Bill was passed in the session of 1877, after being seriously obstructed in the House of Commons by the Parnellites.

as he seems to have done throughout Carnarvon's
tenure of the Colonial Office, to his colleague's expert
knowledge, and accepted, with whatever hesitation,
his proposals. On April 6, 1877, he wrote to him: 'I
approve of the Permissive Bill; indeed, I don't see we
have any other course to take. . . . Paul Kruger is an
ugly customer.' Subsequently in the House of Lords
Beaconsfield defended the annexation as 'a geographical
necessity.'

Shepstone spent eleven weeks in Pretoria in investigation of the problem on the spot before he acted. He
found the Republic bankrupt, trade at a standstill,
the white men split into factions, Sikukuni threatening
one frontier and the Zulus massed, ready to attack, on
another. The President and the Volksraad had no
suggestion to make other than vague schemes of Constitutional reform. Annexation seemed to him to be the only
adequate cure for the evils of the State; and it was accordingly publicly proclaimed on April 12, 1877. There was
no suggestion of force; Shepstone, whose coming to the
Transvaal had been welcomed by the residents, had with
him only a staff of seven or eight officers, and an escort
of 25 Natal Mounted Police; to all appearance public
opinion acquiesced, if it did not rejoice, in the change.
But the assent of the Volksraad was not sought; the
President made a formal protest, retiring to the Cape
on a pension; and the Executive Council sent Vice-
President Kruger and another ex-official to England to
plead, on behalf of the recalcitrant back-veld Boers, for a
reversal of Shepstone's act. Carnarvon, while of course
maintaining the annexation, promised that the wishes
and interests of the Dutch population should be fully
consulted; which was a repetition and endorsement of
pledges given by Shepstone himself. In spite of these
promises, however, no Constitution was granted for two
years and a half; and then the Boers, whose discontent
had been steadily increasing, and who naturally desired
responsible government through their Volksraad, were

put off with Crown Colony administration. Shepstone clearly had not the same insight into the Dutch mind and character as he had into the native. It is impossible not to blame both the Government at home[1] and their agents on the spot for this unnecessary delay and this insensibility to the needs of the situation. Had a free Constitution as well as material advantage immediately followed annexation, the Boers might perhaps have settled down quietly under British rule, and some of the darkest pages in recent South African history might never have been written.

Carnarvon accompanied the despatch of the Shepstone mission by another decisive move in the direction of South African federation and of a forward policy to secure it. He prevailed on Sir Bartle Frere, one of the foremost Anglo-Indian administrators of the day, a man of the highest character and ability, to accept the Governorship of Cape Colony and the High Commissionership for South Africa. He selected him as 'the statesman who seems to me most capable of carrying my scheme of confederation into effect'; and, assuming that the work of union would not take more than two years, he expressed the hope that Frere would stay on for a year or two after union 'to bring the new machine into working order, as the first Governor-General of the South African Dominion.' It was a task thoroughly calculated to appeal to the patriotic ambitions of a great Proconsul, one of the leading apologists of a forward policy on the north-west frontier of India, a man exceptionally self-reliant, accustomed by his official experience to take serious decisions without direction from Downing Street. No better choice could have been made if Ministers at home had determined on a forward policy in South Africa, and were prepared for the risks involved. But there can be little doubt that the main desire of the Cabinet, and especially of the Prime Minister, was, in view of the reopening of the Eastern

[1] It should, of course, be remembered that Carnarvon only remained in the Government for nine months after the annexation.

Question in Europe and Asia, to keep things as quiet as possible in South Africa. They accepted the policy of confederation as being, what it ultimately was, a policy of peace; they shut their eyes to the probability that, in existing conditions, the desired end could hardly be attained without war.

Frere reached the Cape almost simultaneously with Shepstone's hoisting of the British flag at Pretoria; and he was confronted immediately by a South Africa whose conditions were materially affected by that historic act. In particular, the general Kaffir war, to avert which was one of Carnarvon's reasons for annexation, appeared to be more imminent than ever. There was no longer a balance of power in which the English held the scales between the Dutch and the natives. Where there had been two white Governments, there was now but one; as the Free State might be expected to follow the Transvaal, and in any case it constituted an enclave which hardly affected general policy. Roughly speaking, the English power confronted the native face to face throughout the land. The warlike Zulus, in particular, who had a blood-feud, handed down from father to son, with the Boers, but who were friendly with the English, found there was now no opening for that ' washing of their spears ' for which they lusted. Cetywayo, their king, ' could no longer go to war in any direction without coming into collision with the English or those whom the English protected. In his mind there grew up the idea that he was being surrounded like a wild beast in its lair, and like a wild beast he prepared for his last fight.'[1] Frere was prevented from dealing with the Zulu danger for several months owing to Kaffir wars with Gaikas and Galekas in the Transkei on the eastern frontier of Cape Colony. When he had brought these to a satisfactory conclusion and was able to turn his attention to Cetywayo, Carnarvon had resigned and there was seated at the Colo-

---

[1] Sir Charles Lucas's *Historical Geography of the British Colonies, South and East Africa*, Part I., ch. 8.

nial Office Hicks Beach, who had no special knowledge of South Africa or enthusiasm for his predecessor's ideals, but who was impressed by the importance of the Eastern crisis, and was especially anxious to avoid military complications in other quarters of the world.

Frere, on the other hand, brought away from his experience of the Gaika and Galeka wars the conviction that there was spreading throughout South African Kaffirdom a spirit of general revolt against white civilisation; and that the natives everywhere were looking to the Zulus, as the strongest race, to try conclusions with the white men.   When he came to study the Zulu question on the spot in September, 1878, he formed the conclusion that Natal had been living on a volcano for years, and he was profoundly astonished at the insensibility of the colonists to their peril.   It seemed to him that there could be no peace and safety in South Africa, and especially in Natal, until Cetywayo's power was broken.   It was likely that the Zulus, who had already violated the frontier and committed isolated acts of defiance and outrage, would themselves open war upon the white men.   But, if they refrained, Frere resolved to force the issue, terminate a paralysing condition of suspense and dread, and bring on at once a struggle which he was convinced could not be postponed for long.   ' It is generally bad diplomacy,' writes a still greater Empire-builder, Cromer, ' to force on a conflict even when it seems inevitable.' [1]

Beaconsfield began to get uneasy about the state of affairs in South Africa just at the time when the Eastern Question was in a crucial stage.   The Kaffir wars of 1877 and 1878 were not at all the result he expected from Carnarvon's policy of confederation.

Montagu Corry to Sir Henry Ponsonby.

Confidential.   10, DOWNING ST., *May* 13, '78.—. . . Ld. B. is extremely dissatisfied with all that has taken, or is taking, place at the Cape.   The troubles commenced by Lord Carnarvon, who, he says, lived mainly in a coterie of editors of

[1] *Abbas II.*, p. 17.

Liberal papers who praised him and drank his claret, sending
Mr. Froude—a desultory and theoretical *littérateur* who wrote
more rot on the reign of Elizabeth than Gibbon required for
all the *Decline and Fall*—to reform the Cape, which ended
naturally in a Kaffir War. . . .

Then Shepstone's failure to appease the Transvaal
further alarmed Beaconsfield in the autumn. Lanyon
was sent from Griqualand West to take Shepstone's
place. It was no more convenient to have complications
in South Africa while trouble was brewing in India than
when the Eastern Question was acute.

To Lady Bradford.

HUGHENDEN MANOR, *Sept.* 27, 1878.—. . . I am not in a
state of consternation about Afgh[anista]n, and if anything
annoys me more than another, it is our Cape affairs, where
every day brings forward a new blunder of Twitters.[1]

The man he swore by was Sir T. Shepstone, whom he looked
upon as heaven-born for the object in view. We sent him out
entirely for Twitters' sake, and he has managed to quarrel with
Eng., Dutch, and Zulus; and now he is obliged to be recalled,
but not before he has brought on, I fear, a new war. Froude was
bad enough, and has cost us a million; this will be worse. . . .

Soon there came strong appeals from Chelmsford, the
General in command in Natal, backed by Frere, for reinforcements. Beach was reluctantly disposed to agree;
but Beaconsfield, in view of our other commitments,
demurred to any action which might encourage war in
South Africa; and the Cabinet decided to send out the
' special service ' officers asked for, but no more troops
for the present. Beach, in writing to Frere, expressed ' a
confident hope that by the exercise of prudence, and
by meeting the Zulus in a spirit of forbearance and reasonable compromise, it will be possible to avert the very
serious evil of a war with Cetywayo.' This was in the
middle of October, but at the beginning of November
further urgent demands for troops made reconsideration
inevitable. Beach, and the Cabinet with him, were by

[1] Lord Carnarvon.

no means satisfied that a Zulu war was necessary; or
that, if one should break out, a sufficient force, out of
the 6,000 troops in South Africa, could not be concentrated in Natal to bring it to a successful termination.
'I have impressed this view,' wrote Beach to Beaconsfield on November 3, 'upon Sir B. Frere, both officially
and privately, to the best of my power. But I cannot
really control him without a telegraph.[1] (I don't know that
I could, with one.) I feel it is as likely as not that he is
at war with the Zulus at the present moment; and if his
forces should prove inadequate, or the Transvaal Boers
should take the opportunity to rise, he will be in a great
difficulty, and we shall be blamed for not suppporting
him.' These last considerations prevailed over the
Cabinet's reluctance to encourage their agent's forward
policy, and the reinforcements were sent before the end
of November, with the instruction, however, that they
were only to be used for defensive purposes.

Frere seems to have been taken aback by the hesitation
of the Cabinet to send reinforcements and by their evident
anxiety to avoid war. He had frequently, in his letters
to the Imperial Government, expressed in general terms his
view that Great Britain should be the sole sovereign, on
both South African coasts, up to the Portuguese frontiers,
and that she should not evade the clear responsibilities of
sovereignty, but make the native tribes realise that she
was master. As this view had not been controverted from
home, he appears to have conceived that he had a right to
claim Cabinet support for the detailed measures, including
a declaration of war, which were necessary, in his judgment, for carrying it out. The present exhortations of the
Cabinet to moderation came, he considered, too late; he
had, in reliance on their acceptance of his policy, committed
himself too far, and the peril to white men in South Africa
was too imminent, for any hesitation now. And yet there

---

[1] At that time there was no cable to South Africa, and telegrams were
brought to Capetown by steamer from the Cape Verde Islands. Accordingly
telegrams then took between two and three weeks, letters between three
and four weeks, in transmission.

seem to have been some of the elements of a possible
compromise. Cetywayo had consented to accept arbitration on the vexed question of the boundary between
Zululand and the Transvaal, and a Commission appointed
by the Lieutenant-Governor of Natal had reported that
most of the disputed territory belonged rightfully to the
Zulus. Frere, as High Commissioner, had to make the
award. He thought that the report was too partial to
the Zulus, but that nevertheless, in spite of the disgust
which its acceptance would cause the Boers, it must in
the main be accepted.

With a communication of this agreeable kind to make,
it ought, one would think, to have been possible for Frere
to come to an arrangement with the Zulus which would
comply with his instructions from home and, while securing the Colony from immediate danger, postpone, in
deference to imperial difficulties in other continents,
a South African war. He saw his duty differently, and
he may have been right. He disregarded the instructions
which had been in his hands for some weeks, and, without
reference to the Home Government, delivered on December 11, along with the award, an ultimatum which he felt
sure Cetywayo would not accept and which would therefore involve immediate hostilities. He required the
king, as was obviously proper, to make good, by fine or
surrender, the outrages which his people had committed;
but he went farther and demanded that he should abolish
the military system of a celibate soldiery which made
the Zulus a terror to their neighbours, that he should
receive back and protect the missionaries whom he had
expelled, and that he should agree to the appointment of
a permanent British Resident in his country. No answer
was returned within the stipulated time, and early in
January, 1879, the war began.[1] Frere was apparently
satisfied that Chelmsford had sufficient force, and that
success would be speedy and complete. Beach also was
sanguine.

[1] For Frere's own view, see Martineau's *Life of Sir Bartle Frere*, Vol. II.

From Sir Michael Hicks Beach.

WILLIAMSTRIP PARK, FAIRFORD, *Jan.* 13, '79.—. . . There is, I hope, a good prospect . . . of the war being short and successful, like the Afghan campaign. The reinforcements would arrive just about in time to take part in it; Frere and Thesiger[1] seemed, from the last letters I have received, very confident, though these letters were written at a time when they thought no reinforcements were coming; the Zulus are reported to be much divided in opinion, likely to be rendered more so by some of the demands which Frere has made, so that Cetywayo's position may be very similar to that of Shere Ali; and the Boers, who might place us in a very difficult situation by rising in the Transvaal while we are engaged with the Zulus, are said to be perfectly passive, according to their nature, waiting to see what will turn up. When the Zulus have submitted or are beaten, the Boers will be afraid to move—and Carnarvon's acquisition should then settle down under our rule in a way which has not, as yet, seemed probable since we took it.

So that, on the whole, though Frere's policy—especially in the matter of cost—is extremely inconvenient to us at the present moment, I am sanguine as to its success, and think we shall be able, without much difficulty, to defend its main principles here. I think it most fortunate that we sent out the reinforcements when we did. Frere had made up his mind not to be stopped by the want of them; but if the weakness of his forces had led to any failure at first, a most serious war might have resulted, and we should have had to bear all the blame. Now he has got all the force he asked for, in time to finish off the affair easily and quickly, if his calculations as to what he is undertaking are at all accurate.

Frere's calculations had not taken sufficiently into account those characteristics of British Generals, when fighting in South Africa, which have so often resulted in the opening of our campaigns there with a serious check if not with disaster: namely, over-confidence, disregard of local advice, and under-estimate of the enemy. All these contributed their share to the fatal day of Isandhlwana, January 22, 1879. The Cabinet were, therefore, as unprepared as the public for the news; and to Beaconsfield himself it was a crushing blow, as he saw at once how injuriously it must affect England's position abroad, and his Cabinet's position at home.

[1] Lord Chelmsford.

To Queen Victoria.

10, DOWNING STREET, *Feb.* 11, 1879.—Lord Beaconsfield
with his humble duty to yr. Majesty. It has been a very
agitating day with this terrible news from S. Africa, which to
Lord Beaconsfield is very unintelligible. The Cabinet met,
and have sent five regiments of Infantry instead of three asked
for by Lord Chelmsford, and all the Cavalry, and Artillery,
and stores which he requested. It is to be hoped, that he may
be equal to the occasion, but it is impossible not to feel, that
this disaster has occurred to the Headquarters column, which
he was himself commanding. This sad news has come when,
by indefatigable efforts, everything was beginning to look
bright. It will change everything, reduce our Continental
influence, and embarrass our finances.

From Queen Victoria.

OSBORNE, *Feb.* 12, 1879.—. . . [Lord Beaconsfield] must not
be downhearted for a moment, but show a bold front to the
world. This ought, however, to be a lesson *never* to reduce
our forces, which was just going to be done; for, with our
enormous Empire, we must always be prepared for such contingencies. . . .

To Lady Bradford.

10, DOWNING STREET, *Feb.* 12, '79.—I could not write
to you yesterday, and am equally incapable to-day. I am
greatly stricken; and have to support others, which increases
the burthen; almost intolerable. I know not which I dread
most, the banquet to-day, or the Senate to-morrow. The
Prince of Wales comes to me in half an hour. He is from
Osborne; yesterday the D. of Cambridge was with me.
Everybody was congratulating me on being the most
fortunate of Ministers, when there comes this horrible disaster !

It is not surprising that this blow should have prostrated Beaconsfield physically; and it is clear that he had
a serious relapse during the remainder of this month,
when the energies of the Government were mainly directed
to retrieving, as quickly as possible, the position in South
Africa.

To Queen Victoria.

10, DOWNING ST., *Feb.* 18, 1879.—Lord Beaconsfield . . . is
greatly distressed at not having the honor and the happiness
of an audience of yr. Majesty to-day, but he is really quite

prostrate, tho' Dr. Kidd assures him his malaise will pass away, and even speedily. Still he cannot shut his eyes to the fact, that he has rarely left his roof for the last three months, and he feels that so great a Sovereign as yr. Majesty should not have a sick Minister. This is the anniversary of the fifth year of the existing Administration. He hopes he has not altogether failed in devotion to yr. Majesty, and in some accomplishment of Yr. Majesty's policy, but he feels deeply how much in any efforts he owes to yr. Majesty's support and expression of confidence. . . .

From Queen Victoria.

WINDSOR CASTLE, *Feb*. 18, 1879.—The Queen has just received Lord Beaconsfield's kind letter. She is so grieved to hear that he is not well, but hopes it will soon pass off, and that he will for long yet continue to direct the councils of his Sovereign, which he has done so ably and firmly, and to whom he has shown such great personal devotion and kindness. . . .

The public outcry against both Frere and Chelmsford was very loud and very widespread. The general view was that the one, by ignoring his instructions from home, had needlessly precipitated the war which had begun so disastrously; that the other had shown carelessness and incompetence in the field. That they should both be recalled was the popular demand. The Cabinet were naturally more incensed against Frere, who had disregarded their wishes, than against Chelmsford, of whose professional adequacy they could not well judge. Beaconsfield, though resenting Frere's disobedience, had the highest opinion of his abilities and character, which he believed to be a tower of strength in South Africa. With regard to Chelmsford he felt himself to be in a delicate situation. He had left Chelmsford, the father, out of his Cabinet in 1868 because he thought him an incompetent Lord Chancellor; it would be distressing to him to have to supersede Chelmsford, the son, as a not sufficiently competent General. It would be fair, at any rate, to allow him a certain time in which to retrieve what had been lost. Beaconsfield did not easily carry the

Cabinet along with him. He told the Queen that the feeling against both men was very strong, and required ' considerable private handling.' It was decided to take no step against Chelmsford for the present, but to rebuke Frere for his disobedience while at the same time continuing him in a post for which he was pre-eminently qualified.

The despatch of March 19, from Beach to Frere, containing the considered judgment of the Cabinet, stated that ' they have been unable to find in the documents you have placed before them that evidence of urgent necessity for immediate action which alone could justify you in taking, without their full knowledge and sanction, a course almost certain to result in war, which, as I had previously impressed upon you, every effort should have been used to avoid.' But they gladly recorded ' their high appreciation of the great experience, ability, and energy which you have brought to bear on the important and difficult task you have undertaken'; and they concluded by stating that ' they have no desire to withdraw, in the present crisis of affairs, the confidence hitherto reposed in you, the continuance of which is now more than ever needed to conduct our difficulties in South Africa to a successful termination.' The decision represented the exact feelings of the Prime Minister towards Frere; but it was a very illogical one, as the Opposition, who, by resolution in both Houses, demanded Frere's recall, pointed out. How could a man who is publicly censured continue to command the confidence essential to the efficient performance of Frere's high duties ? To that question the Prime Minister's speech in debate afforded no answer. He said:

What we had to determine is this: Was it wise that such an act on the part of Sir Bartle Frere as, in fact, commencing war without consulting the Government at home, and without their sanction, should be passed unnoticed ? Ought it not to be noticed in a manner which should convey to that eminent person a clear conviction of the feelings of Her Majesty's

Government; and at the same time was it not their duty to consider, were he superseded, whether they could place in his position an individual equally qualified to fulfil the great duties and responsibility resting on him ? That is what we had to consider. We considered it entirely with reference to the public interest, and the public interest alone, and we arrived at a conviction that on the whole the retention of Sir Bartle Frere in that position was our duty, notwithstanding the inconvenient observations and criticisms to which we were, of course, conscious it might subject us; and, that being our conviction, we have acted upon it.

It is a very easy thing for a Government to make a scape-goat. . . . If Sir Bartle Frere had been recalled in deference to the panic, the thoughtless panic, of the hour, . . . no doubt a certain degree of odium might have been averted from the heads of Her Majesty's Ministers, and the world would have been delighted, as it always is, to find a victim. This was not the course which we pursued, and it is one which I trust no British Government ever will pursue. We had but one object in view, and that was to take care that at this most critical period the affairs of Her Majesty in South Africa should be directed by one not only qualified to direct them, but who was superior to any other individual whom we could have selected for that purpose. The sole question that we really have to decide to-night is: Was it the duty of Her Majesty's Government to recall Sir Bartle Frere in consequence of his having declared war without our consent ?

Beaconsfield proceeded to declare that the policy of the Government in South Africa was still what it had always been, and what Carnarvon selected Frere to carry out—a policy of confederation, and emphatically not one of annexation. ' I myself regard a policy of annexation with great distrust.' If they had annexed the Transvaal, it was because the circumstances were peculiar; that was ' a territory which was no longer defended by its occupiers.' But, while he trusted we should shortly defeat the Zulus in a significant manner, he altogether disclaimed any intention either of exterminating them or of annexing their country. Though Ministers had a majority of 95 in the Lords, they were only supported in the Commons by a majority of 60.

To Lady Bradford.

HOUSE OF LORDS, *April* 4.—I hope you like our popular Budget ! ! !　Gladstone, Childers, and Goschen are furious and frantic.　Rylands goes about roaring 'There never was such a sell.'[1] . . .

10, DOWNING STREET, *April* 14, '79.—. . . Two baskets of primroses, made up into little bouquets, have just arrived from Osborne.　The head g[ardene]r there has orders, he says, to send them every week.

Prince Hal is sanguine—nay, sure—that Bartle F. and Chelmsford will come out triumphant.　I wish I shared his convictions. . . .

April 21.—I found the post wd. not allow my writing to you from Hatfield, or rather the Sabbath-stricken trains, which are as immovable as in Scotland.

I went down there[2] with the hope that I might combine business and frequent tels. with the burst of spring; but that has been a failure.　The sun appeared on Saturday, but with a cutting easterly wind, in wh. I am sorry to hear that you sat out.　And on Sunday it poured, and now I am in London again, black and terribly cold.

There was literally nobody at Hatfield save the family—but that is a numerous and amusing one.　Five boys, the youngest quite an urchin, hardly breeched but giving his opinion on public affairs like his brothers.　The *Standard* is his favourite paper, but he did not approve of its leading article on Russia of that day, 'the tone too sarcastic' ! ! !

The course of events in South Africa and the despatches and letters received from Frere and Chelmsford tended to strengthen the current setting against both of them in the Cabinet.　'Sir Bartle Frere,' wrote Beaconsfield to the Queen on April 8, 'persists in vindicating his conduct to the alarm of the Cabinet, the majority of whom is decidedly in favour of his recall; but Lord Beaconsfield feels that such a step, after the recent discussions in Parliament, would be as damaging to yr. Majesty's Government as to Sir Bartle.'　But a month later he felt that matters could not be left to drift on without a change.　'The news from the Cape very unsatisfactory,' he wrote to Lady Chesterfield on May 8.　'Chelmsford

---

[1] Because there were no new taxes.　　[2] For the Easter holiday.

wanting more force, tho' he does nothing with the 15,000 men he has. He seems cowed and confused.' The long delay on the spot in taking steps to retrieve the disasters of the beginning of the year exasperated the public at home as well as the Prime Minister; and the Cabinet came to the conclusion that it was necessary to have a new man as their representative in the theatre of South African war. They had three sittings in rapid succession, and Beaconsfield thus reported their decision to Her Majesty.

To Queen Victoria.

10, DOWNING STREET, *May* 19, 1879.—. . . The Cabinet sat for more than two hours on the affairs of South Africa, which they found most unsatisfactory; no despatches by this packet, either from the Lord High Commissioner, or the Commander-in-Chief, tho' an abundance of private information, which would show that the expenditure for transport was enormous, and aggravated by the misunderstanding which appears to subsist between the Commander-in-Chief, and Sir Henry Bulwer, the Governor of Natal. Lord John Manners, Dukes of Richmond and Northumberland, Mr. Secretary Stanley, and Sir H. Beach, supported Lord Chelmsford, but all acknowledged that yr. Majesty's Government were left in a state of great darkness, and that no one seemed clearly to understand what we were aiming at, and what terms would satisfactorily conclude the war. The Cabinet adjourned their decision, but the prevalent, not to say unanimous, opinion seemed to be, that without superseding either Sir Bartle or Lord Chelmsford, a 'dictator' should be sent out, intimately acquainted with the views and policy of yr. Majesty's Government, who should be able to conclude peace, when the fitting opportunity occurred, and effect a general settlement. . . .

What may be called the preliminaries of peace have been signed by the Ameer of Afghanistan. This will be announced to both Houses to-night, a great event. . . .

May 23.—The third consecutive Cabinet has just closed on the affairs of South Africa. . . . The Cabinet is of opinion that the civil and military commands in S. Africa should be rearranged. The authority of Sir B. Frere to extend over the Cape Colony and the territories adjacent (Sir B. F. will be 1,000 miles from the seat of war). Sir Garnet Wolseley to be yr. Majesty's High Commissioner, and Commander-in-Chief for Natal, Transvaal, and territories adjacent, including Zululand, and to have within that area supreme civil and mili-

tary authority under yr. Majesty. Sir Garnet having superior
rank, the present Commander-in-Chief will become second
in command. If yr. Majesty approves these arrangements,
perhaps, as time is precious, yr. Majesty may telegraph yr
Majesty's answer, or do so indeed if yr. Majesty wishes further
information immediately.

The Queen telegraphed at once strongly deprecating the
arrangement. Perhaps it was in view of the storm of
royal opposition which he was evidently about to encounter
that Beaconsfield couched his congratulations on Her
Majesty's birthday next day in his highest vein of extravagance.

To Queen Victoria.

10, DOWNING STREET, *May* 24, 1879.—To-day Lord Beaconsfield ought fitly, perhaps, to congratulate a powerful Sovereign
on her imperial sway, the vastness of her Empire, and the
success and strength of her fleets and armies. But he
cannot, his mind is in another mood. He can only think of
the strangeness of his destiny, that it has come to pass, that
he should be the servant of one so great, and whose infinite
kindness, the brightness of whose intelligence and the firmness
of whose will, have enabled him to undertake labors, to which
he otherwise would be quite unequal, and supported him in all
things by a condescending sympathy, which in the hour of
difficulty alike charms and inspires.

Upon the Sovereign of many lands and many hearts, may
an omnipotent Providence shed every blessing that the wise
can desire, and the virtuous deserve ! If this year has been
a year of gloom, may the bright shadow of the coming hours
illumine her with their happiness, sustain her in her state,
and touch with an enchanting ray the hallowed influences of
her hearth !

The Queen was not placated by these compliments,
but sent a reasoned remonstrance well worthy of
consideration.

From Queen Victoria.

BALMORAL, *May* 26, 1879.—The Queen telegraphed in
cypher twice to Lord Beaconsfield in answer to his cypher and
letter. She can only repeat in the very strongest terms her
opinion on this all-important subject of S. Africa. Whatever
fault may have been committed in declaring, (perhaps) too
hastily, war, Sir B. Frere seems to have succeeded, by his per-

sonal influence, in conciliating those important portions of the Colonies, who were considered to be disaffected.[1] To reward his efforts therefore by sending out an officer with the powers proposed, instead of encouraging him, will be a public mark of want of confidence—at a moment of great difficulty—which will have a most disastrous effect both at home and abroad; and will make it almost impossible for any public man to serve his country if on the 1st misfortune occurring he is to be thrown over ! The case of Lord Chelmsford may, perhaps, be less certain, but he also seems to have been successful of late.

And the Queen most strongly protests against the use of private information, than which nothing more injurious to discipline and good government can exist. This was one of the causes of our suffering in the Crimea and led to every sort of evil. No Commander or Governor can stand against or submit to that; and the Queen can only attribute this to the inexperience of public life in some of his colleagues.

If it is absolutely necessary to prevent any peace being concluded which the Govt. would disapprove, send someone out with messages to Sir B. Frere and Lord Chelmsford to explain exactly what the Govt. wish and what they object to. But do not upset everything—which will be the case if an officer, whoever he may be, is sent out with the powers proposed.

The Queen would sanction the proposal submitted if her warnings are disregarded, but she would *not approve* it. This is confidential, but Lord Beaconsfield can read any portion of it, he thinks proper, to the Cabinet.

The Cabinet persisted, in spite of royal disapproval.

To Queen Victoria.

10, Downing Street, *May* 27, 1879.—. . . Yr. Majesty's cyphered telegram, dated 23rd inst., was received on the birthday. It gave yr. Majesty's sanction to the proposed arrangements in S. Africa if the Cabinet was really of opinion, that they were absolutely necessary, tho', then, yr. Majesty could not approve them. Lord Beaconsfield passed Sunday, there being no Cabinet on the birthday, in attempting to consult with his colleagues in detail, and in seeing H.R.H. the Duke of Cambridge, with whom he had already conferred on the main business some time ago, and who only differed from yr. Majesty's Govt. on the personal point, wishing Lord Napier of M[agdala] to be selected instead of Sir G. Wolseley.

[1] Frere had held conversations with the Transvaal Boers, which for the moment somewhat lessened their discontent.

It was only yesterday that the Cabinet could be again called together. Lord Beaconsfield read to his colleagues, the two cyphered telegrams of yr. Majesty, and they received a long and deep consideration, but the deliberation ended by the Cabinet unanimously adhering to their previous decision and also urging the appointment of Sir G. Wolseley instead of Lord Napier; among other grounds, on his local experience of the scene of war. More than one member of the Cabinet declared that they could not undertake the responsibility of affairs, if some great and similar change were not agreed to.

It was with much difficulty that Lord Beaconsfield secured the arrangement, that Sir Bartle Frere should remain as High Commissioner of the Cape Colony and its dependencies. These are more than 1,000 miles from the seat of war.

No one upheld Lord Chelmsford. Even the Secretary of War gave him up, and spoke as if the military authorities had done the same. His quarrel and controversial correspondence with Sir H. Bulwer seemed the last drop. Perhaps also the dissensions in his own staff. The Cabinet throughout has not been influenced by private information, a private letter has been rarely introduced, and only in the case of its being written by persons in high acknowledged public place and responsibility.

The Cabinet scarcely closed its labors yesterday, until the Houses of Parliament assembled; and it was absolutely necessary that the public announcement of their labors should be made, as the House of Commons adjourns to-day for the holidays, and had they been allowed to disperse without being apprised of the intentions of yr. Majesty's Ministers, there would have been the usual outcry of *coup d'état*, and customary complaint that important measures are always taken when Parliament is not sitting.

Lord Beaconsfield is pained that yr. Majesty disapproves of the policy of yr. Majesty's servants, but he is himself deeply convinced that the measures in question were necessary for the honor and welfare of yr. Majesty's subjects, and the highest interests of their Sovereign.

The Queen was not convinced. She thought Wolseley unconciliatory, ambitious, and too junior in military standing for the commission; and she recorded her conviction that ' yielding to a cry, and superseding (for it is that, though under a disguised form) so distinguished and able as well as excellent a man as Sir B. Frere is deeply to be regretted; for it will discourage all public servants in distant parts, and forms a bad precedent.' The decision once taken, however, the Queen, in accordance with her regular constitutional practice, did everything to smooth the way for the new policy, and to avert the bad consequences which she anticipated. Frere, much to her satisfaction, did not resign.

From Queen Victoria.

BALMORAL, *June* 3, 1879.—The Queen . . . sees and admits the force of the arguments, especially as regards Lord Chelmsford, but regrets anything that might discourage poor Sir Bartle Frere, who seems to have been so very successful with the Boers. However, the instructions seem very properly worded and not in a spirit to hurt Sir Bartle's feelings, she hopes. She has received an interesting letter from him which she encloses and would ask Lord Beaconsfield to send to Sir M. H. Beach, and to ask him to return it to her. She thought of replying to him merely thanking him, expressing her feeling for the great anxiety he must have gone through as well as her satisfaction at the news respecting the Boers; and she thought of adding that she trusted that the arrangements just concluded, and which were necessitated by the great distances and the importance of having a general officer to act both in the military and civil capacity, would prove an assistance and relieve him from much anxiety as well as from bodily fatigue. If Lord Beaconsfield approves would he telegraph? She will also mention this to Sir M. H. Beach. The Queen will then send Sir B. Frere the 4th Volume:[1] and thank him for his congratulations, and she hopes in this way that he may remain, tho' she is fearful that the attacks in the press and in Parliament may make it more difficult. . . .

Beaconsfield had to face opposition from the military authorities as well as from the Queen, as appears from his private letters.

To Anne Lady Chesterfield.

10, DOWNING ST., *May* 28, '79.—We have had a terrible time of it: six Cabinets in eight days. I believe it never happened before. However, Sir Garnet Wolseley goes to S. Africa, and goes to-morrow night, tho', between ourselves, the Horse Guards are furious, the Princes all raging, and every mediocrity

[1] Of the *Life of the Prince Consort.*

as jealous as if we had prevented him from conquering the world.

As for domestic affairs, the Empress[1] has departed, having presented me with her framed portrait. I met her at dinner last Wedy. at the Salisburys', and on the next day at Marlboro' House. And then she went. There are a good many royalties still lingering about, looking as if they wanted a dinner.

On the birthday, S. and Ida and the little ones came here to see the trooping of the colors, a pretty sight, with a fine day, wh. we fortunately had. S. looks better. They go to Weston on Friday. I am very tired and hope on Saturday to reach Hughenden. . . .

May 31.—. . . The Horse Guards rage furiously, but Sir Garnet has departed. They all complain of the hurried manner in wh. the affair was managed. I dare say. If there had not been a little hurry, he never wd. have gone. They wd. have got up some conspiracy wh. wd. have arrested everything.

All the world now is thinking and talking of a new French actress, Sarah Bernhardt; places, boxes, and stalls taken for more than two months. Lord Dudley gives a great banquet in the midst of Whitsun week, and she is to play in the evening. He invited me, and I declined, as I cd. not forgo country air. I met him at dinner at the Cadogans' on Thursday, and he was stiff and said, ' Not yet departed, I see.' I replied, ' No, I go for my holidays, and they have not yet commenced.' 'Holidays are a convenient word.' Huffish. . . .

It was a small circle, but a perfect repast. Our host (Cadogan) a very rising man. With Edward Stanhope, and George Hamilton, he will make some day a future Minister.

HUGHENDEN MANOR, *June* 3.—. . . We came down here (Monty and myself) on Saturday,[2] but it has scarcely ever ceased raining.

I cannot write any more. I have just received a tel. announcing the death of Baron Rothschild, one of my greatest friends, and one of the ablest men I ever knew. I am greatly shocked. Very sudden and ' short the illness.' I presume a fit.

To Lady Bradford.

HUGHENDEN MANOR, *June* 5, '79.—. . . The country is lovely, now that great gilder and varnisher, the sun, has touched up the picture; bloom and blossom still behindhand, but this delay compensated for by the extraordinary luxuriance of the foliage. I never knew my beeches so heavy with leaf. . . .

---

[1] Of Germany.　　　[2] June 1 was Whitsunday.

10, DOWNING STREET, *June 6.*—. . . To-morrow there is a Cabinet at eleven, and a meeting of the party immediately afterwards. Affairs have got into such a mess in the House of Commons that I am obliged to call the party together.[1] It is the first time since I left the House of Commons, and only the second time since the existence of the present Ministry, wh. shows how loyal and true the party has run. . . .

June 13.—. . . Cardinal Manning paid me a long visit yesterday, followed by M. Lesseps, who wants to cut thro' the Isthmus of Panama; it can be done in eight years, and wd. cost only forty millions (sterling). . . .

Wolseley's appointment gave general satisfaction to opinion at home; but, before he could take over the command of the forces in the field, Chelmsford had once more made a general advance into Zululand and had gained on July 4, six days after his successor's arrival in Natal, a complete victory at Ulundi, which practically brought the war to an end. Wolseley's main work was consequently of a civil character. He made a temporary settlement of Zululand by dividing it up among a series of petty chieftains; and he gave a Crown Colony constitution to the Transvaal, solemnly assuring the disaffected Boers that the annexation would never be revoked. But he reckoned without Gladstone; and he could not foresee Majuba Hill.

Wolseley was a favourite with Beaconsfield, though the statesman was not blind to the soldier's foibles, as a letter to the Queen in this autumn shows.

To Queen Victoria.

HUGHENDEN MANOR, *Aug. 24, 1879.*—. . . With regard to Sir G. Wolseley, Lord Beaconsfield will write to yr. Majesty with that complete and unlimited confidence which, he trusts, has always distinguished the remarks he has had the honor of submitting to his Sovereign.

It is quite true that Wolseley is an egotist, and a braggart. So was Nelson. Mr. Pitt always treated him to the last as a charlatan, and doled out the honors of the Crown, when rewarding him for his magnificent exploits, with a parsimony

---

[1] The meeting was successful in rallying the party to the support of the Army Discipline Bill.

which posterity has unanimously condemned. He advised the Crown, for example, to make Jervis Earl for the battle of St. Vincent, which was mainly won by Nelson, then second in command, while an Earl's coronet was only bestowed on the corpse of Nelson, and this after Aboukir and Copenhagen and Trafalgar.

Men of action, when eminently successful in early life, are generally boastful and full of themselves. It is not limited to military and naval heroes, and if Lord Beaconsfield, with many other imperfections, has escaped these two imputations, it is, probably, only due to the immense advantage, which he has enjoyed, of having been vilified and decried for upwards of forty years, and which has taught him self-control, patience, and some circumspection. . . .

One distressing incident of the Zulu War caused Beaconsfield much worry and anxiety. The ex-Prince Imperial of France, who since the fall of the Second Empire had lived with his mother, the Empress Eugénie, in exile in England, and who had undergone a thorough military training at the Royal Military Academy, Woolwich, pressed, as any spirited soldier of twenty-three in his position would have pressed, to be allowed to join the British Army in South Africa. The Queen, at the Empress's request, was disposed to consent. Ministers objected. ' I did all I could to stop his going,' Beaconsfield told Redesdale afterwards. ' But what can you do when you have to deal with two obstinate women ?'

To Lord Salisbury.

10, DOWNING ST., *Feb.* 28, 1879.—I am quite mystified about . . . the Prince Imperial. I thought we had agreed not to sanction his adventure ? Instead of that, he has Royal audiences previous to departure, is reported to be a future staff officer, and is attended to the station by Whiskerandos himself, the very General who was to conquer Constantinople.

I have to go to Windsor to-morrow after the Cabinet, and, as I have not seen our Royal Mistress for three months, shall have to touch on every point. What am I to say on this ? H.M. knows my little sympathy with the Buonapartes.

Though the Prince went out, not as an officer in the British army, but in some undefined capacity, he was attached to the staff in the theatre of war, and at the beginning of June was killed by the Zulus in a small outpost affray.   Beaconsfield, on receipt of the news, wrote to the Queen, who was bitterly grieved: ' The death of Prince Louis with its consequences is a tragedy, equalled only by the death of the Emperor Maximilian of Mexico and the consequences of that heartrending event.   In a certain sense the two catastrophes are connected, and would form materials for a series of Greek tragedies.' To Lady Chesterfield he expressed his anxiety lest this unfortunate affair, and the inordinate sympathy felt and expressed by the Queen, might lead to a misunderstanding between England and France, now on friendly terms.   Happily the correctness of the Ministerial attitude prevented trouble.

To Anne Lady Chesterfield.

10, DOWNING STREET, *June* 22, '79.—This affair of Prince Louis Napoleon occasions great perplexities.   Her Majesty's Government disapproved of his going to Africa, and when he persisted in his purpose, would not permit him to be enrolled in Her Majesty's forces.   He went, therefore, as a mere traveller, but I fear, tho' I do not, as yet, absolutely know it, that some indiscreet friends, in very high places, gave him privately letters to Ld. Chelmsford, begging that General to place the Prince on his staff.

The Queen, who returned to Windsor only yesterday, is much affected by this sad event; but if we do not take care, in endeavoring to pay respect to his memory and express sympathy with his unhappy mother, we may irritate and offend the French people and Government.   After all, he was nothing more nor less than a pretender to the throne of France, supported by a well-organised and very active clique, but representing numerically only a small minority of the people.   The Queen, who is much agitated about the affair, wh. she learnt as she was leaving Balmoral, telegraphed to me frequently during her route, and I am now going down to Windsor to see Her Majesty, and expect a distressing scene, for I cannot sanction, or recommend, much that Her Majesty, in the fulness of her heart and grief, would suggest to express her sympathy and that of her people at this moment.

The Wiltons gave one of the most successful and prettiest entertainments I easily remember on Thursday last: a dinner to the Prince of Wales, which I attended: and afterwards, the principal saloon, turned into a charming theatre, received the world to witness the heroine of the hour, Sarah Bernhardt. Nothing was ever better done, not marred even by the mournful but exciting news of the death of Prince Louis, which arrived in a telegram to H.R. Highness.

On Friday Prince Leopold dined with me at his own suggestion. . . . S. dined with me and some other pretty or agreeable, and pretty and agreeable ladies: Lady Lonsdale, who is now looked upon as our chief beauty, and Lady Clarendon, much admired, and Lady Archie Campbell, who is a spiritualist and looks one, and some others. The dinner was remarkable for one thing—the return to society, after six years of ill-health and solitude, of the Duchess of Abercorn.

I ought to have told you that the Duchess Louise[1] was on my right hand, the soul of everything, tho' she had a patch on her eye ! . . .

June 28.—. . . The gout attacked me on Wednesday very sharp but not unkindly, and I have been a close prisoner to my bed, or sofa, since; but the remedies, tho' safe and simple, have been effective, and I quite expect to be out, and in my place in the House of Lords, on Monday.

S., who is going to-day to the Rosslyns in Essex, has just paid me a visit, and she paid me also a visit the day before yesterday with Ida.

Public affairs look well. The Egyptian business[2] has been admirably managed. And the very day that Harty-Tarty was about to commence a campaign against us on the subject, the news arrived that we had completely gained our purpose. A telegram has just arrived dated Capetown, the 10th June, from Sir B. F. saying that the Prince Imperial's body was expected there on the 15th per *Boadicea*. 'No forward move in Zululand, but suggestions for peace conference continue. The sincerity of the Zulu King doubtful.' Sir B. F., who ought to be impeached, writes always as if he were quite unconscious of having done anything wrong !

I was with the Queen on Monday last: a very long audience, nearly an hour and a half; and H.M. talked only on one subject, which seems greatly to have affected her. The body is to be received by the Duke of Cambridge, who will place, on behalf of the Queen, the Grand X of the Bath on the coffin.

I was to have gone to Windsor again on Thursday as the Queen 'had so much to say to me, and had said nothing.' I could not, of course, go, or even move. I am very free from pain to-day, but wonderfully weak, and can scarcely write these feeble lines.

---

[1] Of Manchester.   [2] See below, p. 1313.

July 12.—I have just got a tel. from the Queen, who had returned to Windsor and who seems highly pleased at all that occurred at Chislehurst[1] this morning. I hope the French Government will be as joyful. In my mind, nothing cd. be more injudicious than the whole affair. . . .

Besides the Zulu and Afghan wars there were other serious external questions pressing during this session upon Beaconsfield. The disinclination of Russia to evacuate Turkey-in-Europe caused him many anxious moments; but the mission of the conciliatory Dufferin to St. Petersburg synchronised happily with a more reasonable spirit in Russian counsels. The Cabinet at home met the Tsar's advances by ordering the British Fleet to leave Constantinople.

To Queen Victoria.

10, DOWNING STREET, *March* 11, 1879.—Lord Beaconsfield . . . is distressed at having to trespass on yr. Majesty at a moment, when yr. Majesty has so many claims on yr. Majesty's thoughts and feelings, but the matter on which he addresses yr. Majesty is as urgent as it is critical. In the last ten weeks, he might say three months, the Court of St. Petersburg has been working sincerely with yr. Majesty's Government, in their efforts to accomplish the Treaty of Berlin, and to secure peace; of this Lord Beaconsfield himself has reason to have no doubt. Unhappily the previous period was differently employed by the Russian Government, and the mischief, then prepared, it is most difficult now to counteract. But it can, and must be counteracted.

The Emperor is a great influence in bringing about this result, and it assists him, in struggling with the Pan-Slav party, to soften, as far as possible, his evacuation of the conquered provinces. He wishes it to be done in a manner which will prove that England has no suspicions of his loyalty.

The enclosed telegram from Mr. Malet will show the opinion of the Porte as to the sincerity of Russia; and we know, from private sources of authenticity, that the Turks have already occupied Adrianople in force. It is quite believed that the complete evacuation will be accomplished in ten days more. If we meet the feeling of the Emperor on this head, Lord Beaconsfield believes that we may count on his cordial co-operation with respect to the paramount difficulty of Eastern

---

[1] Where the funeral of the Prince was held.

Rumelia, the successful management of which involves probably the peace of Europe; certainly the existence of the present English Ministry.

What is desirable is that Lord Dufferin, in his audience to-day, may lay the foundation of a satisfactory settlement of every ' burning' question between the two Governments of yr. Majesty and the Emperor. It is most important, that this settlement should not be delayed—if possible not even a day—for the condition of the Turkish Empire is such, that we must contemplate the possibility of a catastrophe in that quarter. Lord Beaconsfield therefore earnestly entreats yr. Majesty to support him at this moment with yr. Majesty's sanction as to the course which he is taking. . . . Lord Beaconsfield observes, in reading over these pages, that he has omitted to assure yr. Majesty, that there will be no difficulty whatever in yr. Majesty's fleet returning, if necessary, to the Turkish waters, and in that event taking up its position at Bourgas, if possible a still more commanding one, than it previously occupied.

After many vicissitudes the situation was sufficiently relieved by May to render comparatively harmless a vehement assault by the Duke of Argyll in the House of Lords on the Government's whole Eastern policy. Beaconsfield's defence was weighty, but it followed the lines of his speeches on returning from Berlin. His rebuke to Gladstone and Argyll was well merited when he expressed his regret that after united Europe had executed ' so solemn an act as the Treaty of Berlin ' for the maintenance of peace, ' certain members of the Opposition should, not once, twice, nor thrice, but month after month habitually declare to the world that the Treaty was utterly impracticable, and have used such external influence as they might possess to throw every obstacle and impediment in the way of carrying that Treaty into practical effect.'

To Lady Bradford.

10, DOWNING STREET, *May* 17.—. . . Yesterday we had a warmish debate in H. of Lords, but I don't think the enemy gained much. It impresses on the public that the Russians are actually evacuating Bulgaria and Rumelia, wh. John Bull never believed they wd., but wh. I always declared wd. be the case. . . .

This year British diplomacy under Beaconsfield took a distinct step forward in Egypt; and the dual control of France and England, which had been in force in a tentative form since 1876, was definitely established and recognised. Both nations had interests of many kinds in Egypt: traditional, sentimental, and material. To France Egypt was the theatre of Napoleon's most romantic expedition, and the land which a great Frenchman had dowered with one of the most magnificent engineering works in the world, the Suez Canal. To England she recalled Nelson's victory of the Nile, and she had of late years become the halfway house to the British Empire in the East; situate on the banks of the great imperial highway, nearly a moiety of the shares in which were now British.   Moreover, it was mainly in France and England that Ismail had contracted those loans, the interest on which he found it increasingly difficult to provide.   It was vital to the British Empire not to permit exclusive control of Egypt by France; it would be a grievous blow to French pride to accept exclusive control of Egypt by Great Britain.   But some sort of interference and support from the outside was inevitable for a country which, according to Stephen Cave's report in March, 1876, was grossly misgoverned and was plunging headlong into bankruptcy. Beaconsfield acted on the common-sense view that, in whatever was done for Egypt, France and England must for the time being go hand in hand.

On April 8, 1876, the Khedive suspended payment of his Treasury bills. The bondholders in both countries, and indeed in Europe generally, took action at once for the protection of their interests; and the Khedive showed himself ready and willing to accept European officials, mainly French and English, to set his house in order. Thus we had the Goschen-Joubert Mission, the appointment of two Controllers-General, Mr. Romaine and Baron de Malaret, and of four Commissioners of the Public Debt, of whom the English Commissioner was the future Lord Cromer and the French M. de Blignières.   A

Commission of Enquiry followed, in which de Blignières and Cromer and another Englishman, Sir Rivers Wilson, took a prominent part. This Commission recommended the establishment of responsible Government and the limitation of the Khedive to a definite Civil List. Ismail professed acquiescence, and appointed in the autumn of 1878 a responsible Ministry, with Nubar Pasha at its head and with Rivers Wilson and de Blignières as Ministers. These changes began to work a serious improvement both in the Egyptian finances and in the condition of the downtrodden fellah. But before long the Khedive chafed under the restrictions placed on his power; he overthrew Nubar in February, 1879, by the aid of a mutiny of Egyptian officers, which he had tolerated if not fomented; and then, a few weeks later, finally upset the European Ministers by means of a carefully stage-managed ' national ' protest against foreign interference.

What was the Beaconsfield Government to do ? Technically the Khedive's action was not such a slap in the face to England as to France. The French officials in Egypt had, generally speaking, been nominated by their Government; the English officials by the bondholders, or by Goschen, or by the Khedive, the British Foreign Office ostentatiously disclaiming responsibility, though the Prime Minister kept a watchful eye on the selections made. Directly he heard of the *coup d'état* Beaconsfield told the Queen that ' we must act with France,' though ' it does not seem, however provoking may be the result, that the Khedive has as yet done anything illegal, or in violation of any agreement with yr. Majesty's Government.' ' We have not only never acknowledged Wilson,' he wrote in his next letter ' as an agent of yr. Majesty's Government, but have always studiously and repeatedly disclaimed his being so.' The first proposals of Waddington, the French Minister, did not commend themselves to Beaconsfield.

To Lord Salisbury.

10, DOWNING STREET, *April* 13, 1879.—I can't help thinking
that Waddington's scheme is both weak and wild.

It will never do, however indirectly, to threaten the Khedive,
unless we are sure of our position with the Sultan.   What if
he be already squared ?

If, therefore, you act on Waddington's suggestion, we ought
to make all things safe first at Stamboul.

Then, again, I doubt the wisdom of insisting on the restoration of Wilson and Blignières.

We might fairly insist upon two European Ministers with
equal powers and similar duties as the late ones.   But, I
think, the sooner Wilson disappears from the scene the better.

April 16.—I entirely agree with every word in your mem.
received last night.   After reading all the papers and correspondence, I had arrived at exactly the same result as yourself.
Waddington would have been a blind guide, and notwithstanding all his timidity, would have landed us in an untenable
position.

The Khedive has treated two great Powers with discourtesy,
and he must be made to feel that they are sensible of it.

What would be desirable, I venture to think, is that he should
notify to us, that he wishes to appoint again two European
Ministers with the same privileges and powers as the late ones.

But how is this to be brought about ?   No doubt our
diplomatic agent on the spot, if equal to the occasion, by
watching and managing, might accomplish this. . . .

An intimation from the Sultan to the Khedive would,
probably, on such a point, be decisive—and, tho' the Khedive
may have squared Stamboul, the belief of the Sultan, that, until
our financial relations with Egypt be accommodated, no hope
exists of a Turkish loan, might settle the business. . . .

The two Cabinets determined, after consultation, to
try the effect of a grave remonstrance before resorting
to extreme measures.   Salisbury's despatch expressed
a hope that the Khedive's attitude towards European
Ministers was not final.   If, however, he persisted in
renouncing the friendship of France and England, the
two Cabinets would 'reserve to themselves an entire
liberty of appreciation and action.'   It must have
amused Salisbury, and Beaconsfield too, to employ
towards the Khedive the phrase which the British Government had resented, and which Beaconsfield had covered

with sarcasm, when it was used by Gortchakoff in an
attempt to evade the submission of the Treaty of San
Stefano to the judgment of Europe.[1]

The Khedive was obdurate, and his fate was finally
sealed by a brutally frank declaration by Germany that
she regarded his recent decree, resuming full control of
the Debt, as an open and direct violation of his international engagements. Europe was clearly ready to co-
operate with France and England in strong measures.
Ismail must go.

To Lord Salisbury.

HUGHENDEN MANOR, *June* 6, 1879.—. . . Egypt must be
grappled with. No wonder you can't go to Dieppe. It is a
most dreadful nut to crack.

None of the propositions satisfy me: the Sultan's the best;
but I suppose, a romance, an affair of the 1000 and 1 nights.
Secrecy and promptitude could alone secure its success, and
I daresay everything would be known at Cairo, as soon and as
long, as the Spanish Armada was with us. All the other
schemes are bricks without straw, a process not unknown to
the Egyptians.

June [? 8].—The Cabinet is summoned for Wednesday at
noon. I should like to have had some, not hurried, talk with
you before we met our colleagues respecting Egyptian affairs,
the consideration of which, I apprehend, cannot be delayed.
They have occupied my thought much during this wet Whitsun,
and I have a strong conviction we must grapple with them.

The situation appears to me to be not very unlike that which
long perplexed Palmerston with reference to the same country,
and which he ultimately, and successfully, encountered by the
Convention of 1840.

His difficulty was to induce the European Powers to join him
in interference. That difficulty you, apparently, will not
experience, for the European Powers seem quite desirous of
contributing to the settlement.

Then, again, tho' France may have preferred that the intervention should be confined to herself and us, the financial
interests she has at stake are so great, and so urgent, that,
with any fair prospect of these being settled, she would probably not hesitate in joining any combination which might
have that result.

In France, finance, and even private finance, is politics.

It is true, that Mehemet Ali set the Convention, at first, at

[1] See above, p. 1131.

defiance, but that was because he counted on France being his active ally. He has no chance, now, of France or any other Power, assisting him, and I, therefore, believe he would yield to the summons of the great Powers, if made in a formal and determined manner.[1]

What he should be summoned to do, is another question, but we need not discuss that now.

I commend these remarks to your good judgment, in which I have much confidence, and to your energy, which is unrivalled.

This, or any other, plan ought not to be placed before the Cabinet until it is matured, so that we should not lose time in desultory criticism. . . .

June 24.—. . . I should be glad to see you about Egypt to-day, but am always loth to trespass on your time, which is most precious. The Government should put its foot down on Thursday and, while expressing its general policy, should firmly decline entering into details of negotiation.

My own feeling is that, if we speak out, and declare that our policy involves not merely the abdication of the Khedive, but the liquidation of Egypt, the House and the country will support us. It must not be, and it is not, a mere bondholders' policy.

On June 19 England and France invited the Khedive to abdicate in favour of his son Tewfik; and Ismail's natural hesitations were terminated a week later, on June 26, by a telegram from Constantinople in which the Sultan, who had been subject himself to the diplomatic pressure of united Europe, announced that he had nominated Tewfik as Khedive in his father's place. The two Powers, having thus changed the ruler, proceeded further to appoint two Controllers, Cromer and de Blignières, under the condition that the new Khedive should have no power to dismiss them without the consent of their respective Governments. It was a definite subjection of Egypt to the joint supervision of France and England. The Dual Control worked well at the beginning because both Controllers were men of high character and capacity, and had already proved by experiment that they could act in harmony. We may perhaps doubt whether, in the

[1] Beaconsfield wrote to the same effect to the Queen, adding: 'Lord Beaconsfield mentions these views to yr. Majesty in secrecy, for they are only known to Lord Salisbury, whose opinion upon them has not yet been given; but in life one must have for one's secret thoughts a sacred depository. and Lord Beaconsfield ever presumes to seek that in his Sovereign Mistress.'

long run, the system would not have been wrecked by the jealousies and suspicions of individuals and Governments. It was probably well for Egypt that, after two or three difficult years, the renunciation of one Controlling Power left her to the exclusive care of the other. The Dual Control was an expedient rather than a policy; but it was at the time a necessary expedient, in Beaconsfield's mind, in order to preserve a good understanding between England and France.[1]

To Lady Bradford.

HATFIELD, *July* 20.—. . . The weather here has destroyed everything. One cannot but feel for our hosts, remembering the fête, five years ago, of the four thunderbolts. . . .

The banquet yesterday was effective, but I pitied those who had to leave a late dinner for a special train at eleven o'ck. There was a long table in the hall, and two small round tables, wh. were called the Prince's and the Princess's table. I dined at the last, taking out Lady Castlereagh, and there were Salisbury himself, Princess of Wales and Princess Mary, Sweden and Norway, Duchess of Marlboro' and Karolyi. At the Prince's, Harty-Tarty, Dss. of Manchester, Css. Karolyi, Hereditary Baden, Lady Salisbury . . . Lady Spencer. . . Dinner good.

The illustrious guests did not arrive until six o'ck. The day guests at 2.40. . . .

The weather was bad yesterday, but not so bad as to prevent a good deal of damp lawn tennis. Monty, however, prudently played in the tennis court. But to-day is hopeless; a real wet Sunday, and the projected amusement of a fête in the Vineyard utterly vain.

The day I came down, Friday, there was nobody here. It was beautiful: sun and blue sky. I went to the Vineyard, and we had a row on the river, with banks of ancient yews down to the water. They were full of hope for fine weather. . . .

10, DOWNING STREET, *July* 30.—. . . We have still blazing weather, and people begin to talk of better harvests than they imagined. No dinner parties for me. . . . The effort is too great, and I have been obliged to accept the Lord Mayor for 6th—a horror, but it is demanded by party interests, wh. no one can resist. . . .

---

[1] See Cromer's *Modern Egypt*, Vol. I., Part I., for a detailed account of these transactions.

Aug. 4.—. . . The storm was terrible here and in the valley of the Thames generally. It has destroyed a great deal—and to-day looks as black as usual. . . .

At the close of the session there was rather a warm discussion in Cabinet on the method of meeting the bill for the Zulu War. Beaconsfield was determined not to increase taxation at a time of distress and bad trade, in order to pay for a war that was forced on against his wishes by his agent. Northcote, however, who was somewhat of a financial purist, proposed to increase the duty on tea, regardless of the unpopularity that such a measure must bring upon a Government shortly about to face a general election. But Beaconsfield carried his Cabinet with him; and Northcote had recourse to Exchequer Bonds. Beaconsfield considered that it was sufficient that half the additional military expenditure of these troubled years should have been provided out of taxation.

To Queen Victoria.

10, DOWNING STREET, *July* 24, 1879.—. . . The Cabinet this morning discussed the question of the Irish University, which will be introduced to-night, or rather its second reading, by Mr. Secretary Lowther. Lord Beaconsfield is not without hope, that this measure may be carried. The news from Zululand, with the long-awaited sunshine, fill everyone with sanguine hopes. . . . It has fallen to Lord Beaconsfield's lot thrice to advise yr. Majesty on the question of peace or war, and thrice it has been decided for the latter; but neither Abyssinia, nor Afghanistan, nor Zululand, has deteriorated [*sic*] from yr. Majesty's arms. These wars have been brief, and complete and successful. Yr. Majesty threw down your glaive [? glove] in the Levant, but it was not taken up. . . .

July 27. —. . . He assumes that Lord Cranbrook has given to yr. Majesty a sketch of the proceedings in the Cabinet yesterday. . . .

The disturbance in our councils was occasioned by the unexpected exposition of the expenditure of the Zulu War, and of the ways and means proposed to provide for it by the Chancellor of the Exchequer. It seems that the immediate expenditure has not been less than five millions, and further demands are anticipated; of this little sum more than a million and a half have been provided by the House of Commons, and this was borrowed. The Chancellor of the Exchequer said, that he could not propose to borrow any more, and that the balance must be supplied by taxation; and as an increased income tax had supplied our previous military expenditure, he proposed now to have recourse to a considerable increase of the duties on tea.

It is impossible to name a tax more unpopular. Tea is an article which, above all others, has entered into the life of the people. They have introduced it into their principal meal—their dinner. Its consumption is the basis of the great Temperance movement. The Cabinet was alarmed and its principal members were the strongest in their comments.

We are placed in this painful position by a war, which, if not in time unnecessary, was unwisely precipitated, weakening us thereby in our settlement of the Levant, and which, but for singular energy, would have embarrassed us in the arrangement of our Indian frontier—a war, which, had we had the prudence to prepare the indispensable transport before we declared it, might have been concluded in a month, nor required more than two or three thousand men.

Seeing that the Cabinet could come to no conclusion, and symptoms of acerbity were developing, Lord Beaconsfield adjourned the subject till Tuesday morning, and must do what he can, in the interval, to bring things to bear.

We may be said to have carried on four wars, for our movements in the Levant entailed a war expenditure, and we have done it all at a cost of 11 or 12 millions. A moiety of this has been supplied by taxation, and it would seem to me, that that other moiety might be left to posterity. Mr. Pitt would not have hesitated to bequeath the whole of it in that direction. But alas! there are no longer Mr. Pitts, but a leader of the House of Commons, who, tho' one of the most amiable and gifted of men, thinks more of an austere smile from Mr. Gladstone, or a word of approval from Mr. Childers than the applause and confidence of a great historic party, and a Prime Minister, who, it seems to me, can do nothing in his troubles, but fly to a too gracious Sovereign, and whimper over his own incompetence.

(*Telegram.*) *July* 29.—Prime Minister recommended as alternative to the new taxation proposed by the Chancellor of the Exchequer that the Sinking Fund should be suspended for a short and specified time. The whole of the Cabinet approved this plan except Chancellor of the Exchequer, who has not yet adopted it. Cabinet must meet again to-morrow unless Chancellor of the Exchequer expresses his adhesion in the interval.

(*Telegram.*) *July* 30.—. . . Chancellor of Exchequer without accepting the alternative suggested by the Prime Minister consents to borrow the necessary sum by Exchequer Bonds. The sum required is only one million two hundred thousand pounds. To have increased the tea duties 50 per cent. for such an amount would have been insane pedantry. Chancellor of the Exchequer is much disturbed, but the Prime Minister has endeavoured to convey to him how greatly he is esteemed and regarded by his colleagues.

Aug. 1.—. . . The Cabinet yesterday was brief, and was only called to give the Chancellor of the Exchequer an opportunity of imparting his new measures to his colleagues with becoming dignity. Lord Beaconsfield trusts that his (Chancellor of Exchequer) self-respect is restored, especially by the reception of his announcement in the House of Commons, where it seemed generally to be held to be a prudent and inevitable course. The scheme of adding 50 per cent. to the tea duties, for the sake of supplying a deficiency of little more than a million, could only be accounted for by what Lord Beaconsfield fears is the sad truth, that Sir Stafford's nervous system has been greatly strained and exhausted by his almost unparalleled labors during this session. Take him for all in all, Lord Beaconsfield doubts whether any other person could have gone thro' so much and so well. If he wants a little backbone, as some say, the sweetness of his temper gains him friends, even among his opponents, and when there was a rumor that he had met with a severe accident, even Jacobins and Home-Rulers seemed depressed and sad. He has only a fortnight more, and he says he thinks he can last a fortnight without breaking down. . . .

With the general results of the session Beaconsfield was satisfied.

To Lady Bradford.

10, DOWNING STREET, *Aug.* 6.—Horrid weather and dispiriting for a City feast, where I eat nothing, and where, after three or four hours of gas, inane conversation, and every other species of exhaustion, I have to get up, with a confused brain and exhausted body, to make a speech, every word of which will be criticised for a month.

As to S. Africa, I shall be disappointed if the next news does not tell us the war is virtually finished. I have confidence in Wolseley, but I believe Chelmsford committed at the last as many mistakes as are consistent with what is called success.

. . Some Canadian Prime Ministers, etc., have arrived in town, and ought to be fêted. I really can do no more, but have been obliged to agree to meet them at dinner at Sir Beach's on 9th.

Aug. 12.—Visit to Osborne rather lighter than usual. H.M. most gracious and agreeable, and made up for the stupidity and mysterious whispering of the courtiers. . . . By rising at ½ past 6, I got to London yesterday in good business time, having much to do. . . .

Aug. 14.—The Ld. Chanr. and D. of Richmond, and others, have gone down to Osborne to-day with the Queen's Speech, and to-morrow Parlt. will be prorogued. An arduous, but on the whole glorious, session, for, besides our external triumphs, the world will be surprised at the weighty domestic measures wh. we have carried; notably the Army Discipline Act wh., for length and difficulty, was equal to three great measures, and the Irish University Act, solving a difficulty wh. had upset two previous Ministries.

I never had a harder task than to write the Queen's Speech, for the domestic measures were not passed when I attempted to record their being carried—and it was a hard task to carry them. It required a physical effort of no mean character, and if on Monday the House had not sate firmly till 7.10 into Tuesday morn, the faction wd. have beaten us. But that night of terrible determination and endurance cowed them. Mine was not a very gracious effort, when I did not, and could not, share them; but it was not a moment for false delicacy, and I was as ruthless as Ld. Strathnairn in India.

We have a Cabinet to-morrow at 11 o'ck.; prorogation at two; and then I go down to Hughenden; Monty with me till Monday, and then he goes to Scotland. . . .

CHAPTER XII.

BEACONSFIELD AND THE QUEEN.

1874–1880.

A Prime Minister under a Constitutional Monarchy such as prevails in this country owes to a certain extent a divided allegiance. He is at once a servant of the Crown and a servant of the people. He has a duty to the permanent Head of the British Empire, who appoints him, and appoints him sometimes with a real liberty of selection, and who has the power in the last resort to dismiss him, subject to ratification of his act by the people through Parliament. He has a duty to the people through Parliament, where he cannot maintain his position unless he can command the support, or at least the toleration, of a majority of the House of Commons. As this country becomes increasingly democratised, and as general elections assume more and more the shape of a direct choice of the Prime Minister by the people, there is a tendency to dwell almost exclusively upon the last-mentioned duty, and to ignore, or at least to minimise, the first. Happily, in spite of some glaring instances to the contrary, there has been since the accession of the House of Hanover, and more particularly since the accession of Queen Victoria, such a general harmony between the Crown and the people that the two duties seldom clash. Happily, also, when there is a divergence, the Crown has definitely recognised the obligation to defer in all matters of moment to the will of the people constitutionally expressed; and in consequence to accept, now and again, with a good grace unwelcome advice or an unwelcome Minister.

Disraeli, when in office, never forgot for a moment that, if he was a servant of the people, he was also the Minister of his Sovereign. ' So long as by the favour of the Queen I stand here ' was a notable phrase used by him in the House of Commons as Prime Minister during the constitutional crisis of May, 1868. Though it drew down upon his head storms of indignant protests from shocked Liberals, it was a true and constitutional, if incomplete, representation of the facts. When Derby resigned two or three months previously, the Queen, who might have called upon Stanley, the Foreign Secretary, or the Duke of Richmond, an important Minister in the Lords, to take his place, chose instead to entrust the charge to Disraeli, the Leader in the Commons. Though it was the natural, it was not the inevitable, choice; he was, not only in the technical sense, but actually Minister by the Queen's favour; and Parliament showed no disposition to withdraw its confidence in him under penalty of dissolution.

The Whigs, as a close family corporation whose business, so to speak, it was during many decades to administer our public affairs, and the Radicals, nourished on philosophic theories of popular government, both tended to conceive of the Sovereign as a mere puppet whose strings were pulled at will by the Minister; and they were both impatient of being reminded of his undoubted prerogatives. Disraeli saw in the Sovereign not merely the Chief Magistrate of a selfgoverning nation—a magistrate sprung from a German stock which it had suited the Whigs to put upon the throne of England; but the heir to the historic monarchy of Alfred, of William the Conqueror, of the great Henries and Edwards, of Elizabeth, of the Stuarts, and of the wrong-headed, but sturdy and national, George III. He realised that it was the Sovereign who, owing to historical and personal causes, was the chief unifying influence, not merely in the nation at home, but, even more, in an empire of extraordinary diversity and extent. He recognised, moreover, in the actual Sovereign whom it was his privilege to serve, one who had by the

Queen Victoria
from the portrait at Hughenden by Von Angeli
Presented by Her Majesty to the Earl of Beaconsfield

seventies a larger mastery of State affairs, domestic and foreign, than any conceivable Minister; one, therefore, of whose judgment and experience the fullest possible use should be made in the government of the country.[1] He was confirmed in this view by noting, in the successive volumes of the *Life of the Prince Consort* then in course of publication, the influence for good on British politics which in the earlier part of the reign the Prince had exercised behind the scenes. The Prince was, of course, seriously handicapped by his highly anomalous position. The Queen, as the actual head of the State, had unquestionable and extensive rights and prerogatives; and Disraeli held that her influence should be felt throughout the administration. There ought, in his own words, to be ' a real Throne.'

It might, indeed, almost be said that Disraeli treated the government of the country as a kind of partnership between the Sovereign and the Minister: a partnership in which each should bring to bear on their common business his accumulated store of knowledge and experience, and in which not merely conclusions should be communicated, but there should be a free interchange of mind and mind before conclusions were reached. The Constitution requires that important decisions of the Minister and Cabinet must be submitted to the Sovereign for his sanction; but there has been a great elasticity in practice as to the extent to which the Sovereign is kept in touch with the trend of the Minister's mind, and with the progress of important transactions while they are still unconcluded. The traditional attitude of the Minister towards the Sovereign, due largely to George III.'s extraordinary treatment of Ministers whom he disliked, has been rather one of reserve, or economy of information. No one can have read the correspondence between Disraeli and the Queen without seeing that his method was very different. He kept his royal mistress constantly informed of the direction his own thoughts were taking in regard

[1] See pp. 483, 484.

to current politics, and sought her opinion before
decisions were come to in Cabinet. He kept her also
informed of the disposition and tendencies of the Cabinet
as a whole, and even of individual members of it in par
ticular, while great affairs were in process of discussion.
Here Gladstone, who was eminently of the traditional
school in constitutional matters, was aghast at his rival's
practice. He told Sir Robert Phillimore emphatically
that if Beaconsfield mentioned to the Queen any of his
colleagues who had opposed him in the Cabinet, ' he was
guilty of great baseness and perfidy '; and that he himself
had never once, in writing to the Queen, referred to the
opinion of his colleagues expressed in Cabinet.[1]

Obviously, in Gladstone's view, the report of Cabinet
meetings made by the Minister to the Sovereign should be
limited to the decisions arrived at, and the reasons on
which they were based. But why should the Sovereign
be deprived of the knowledge that Ministers A and B
opposed on such and such grounds the general view of
their colleagues ? He knows the Ministers individually,
and talks to them of their work, and can form a shrewd
judgment of the value of their opinion in Cabinet. That
opinion must necessarily weigh with him in making up
his own mind whether to encourage his Prime Minister
in the policy proposed, or to warn and caution him and
endeavour to get the policy modified; the right not
merely to encourage, but to warn and remonstrate, being
undoubtedly his by the Constitution. Where do the
'baseness and perfidy' come in ? Gladstone talked as
if, by mentioning dissentients to the Queen, Beaconsfield
ipso facto designated them for execution on Tower Hill.
Far from undermining his colleagues in the Queen's
favour, we have seen Beaconsfield, again and again,
shielding individuals, like Derby and Salisbury, from what
appeared to him to be unfair depreciation on Her
Majesty's part, and doing everything in his power to bring
her to recognise and value their strong qualities.

[1] Morley's *Gladstone*, Book XII., ch. 5.

This intimate association of the Queen, which Beaconsfield encouraged, with the development of opinion in the
Cabinet, did not imply that he worried her with the
tedious detail of controversial business.   He would have
been quite incapable of pressing upon her attention, as
Gladstone did, the minute provisions of a lengthy Bill,
accompanied by an elaborate explanation extending over
a dozen quarto pages of close writing.   Beaconsfield,
while keeping her in touch with the principles on which
Government were acting in various departments, spared
her the drudgery of detail as far as possible.   There is so
much formal business of ceremony and signature which
must occupy the time of the Sovereign that he felt it to
be cruelty to add to it unnecessarily.

The close relations between the Sovereign and her
Minister did not, of course, escape public attention; and
Beaconsfield was in consequence accused by his critics
of abuse of the Constitution in a twofold fashion.   On
the one hand, he was charged with unduly magnifying
the prerogative—the sphere, that is, in which a Minister
could act with the sanction of the Sovereign but without
the direct authority of Parliament.   On the other, he
was reproached with encouraging the Queen to exercise
a personal authority in government which was admired
in the Tudors, resented in the Stuarts, and no longer
permitted to the Sovereign by the modern development
of the Constitution.

The principal instances in which Beaconsfield was said
to have strained the prerogative were the summons of
Indian troops to the Mediterranean and the Cyprus
Convention; in both of which affairs Parliament was
presented with an accomplished fact, and given no
opportunity of previous discussion.   The first case, as
we have seen, was treated in Parliament as if it was
governed by the proper legal construction of the Mutiny
Act and the India Act.   If Government under these Acts
had the power by law, as Ministers contended and Parliament accepted, then the question of prerogative did not

arise; but in general it may be said that the movement
of troops at a critical moment in foreign affairs must
obviously lie within the discretion of Ministers with the
Sovereign's sanction. In the case of the Cyprus Convention the ordinary constitutional course was followed.
The treaty-making power of the Crown is unquestionable;
and in matters of high policy the negotiations have
generally been secret. The two vital instruments, which
governed our foreign policy in the ten years before the
Great War, the treaty with Japan and the entente with
France, were negotiated in the same secret fashion as the
Cyprus Convention; and no serious politicians have ever
suggested that thereby Mr. Balfour and Lord Lansdowne
made an undue use of the prerogative. In all these
cases Parliament might have expelled the treaty-makers
from office and repudiated the treaties; but there, constitutionally, its power ended. The strange thing is that
Gladstone, who was largely responsible for these accusa-
tions, had himself made a very questionable use of the
prerogative in 1871, when he invoked its aid to carry
through that abolition of purchase in the Army which he
had endeavoured, but failed, to effect by Bill.

There seems to be no substance in the charge of
straining the prerogative; but there was some excuse,
no doubt, for the charge of enlarging the Sovereign's
personal power. It was Disraeli's aim to associate the
Sovereign with the work of government to an ampler
extent than had recently been customary. He did not,
indeed, desire to push to their logical conclusion the
theories of a monarchical counter-revolution with which
he had dallied in his 'Young England' days. But he
did most decidedly intend to raise the prestige of monarchy
in the public mind; to keep well before the public eye and
well within the public recollection the person of the
Sovereign and the important work done by the Chief
Magistrate of the nation. In pursuance of this aim he
induced Her Majesty to emerge more frequently from her
retreat to perform her public ceremonial duties; and he

rather stimulated than repressed the natural longing of a Sovereign, and a woman, to leave the impress of her personality on the current of events.   Derby, the incarnation of common sense, wedded, like Gladstone, to the traditional attitude of reserve towards the Crown, perceived early in the Ministry the drift of Disraeli's mind, and warned him against an excessive complaisance to the Queen's personal wishes.   'Is there not,' he wrote to Disraeli in May, 1874, 'just a risk of encouraging her in too large ideas of her personal power, and too great indifference to what the public expects ?   I only ask; it is for you to judge.'[1]   It may be that Disraeli, before he had conquered an unassailable position in his Sovereign's regard, made no objection, at any rate in matters of small account, to a possibly undue exercise of personal volition. It is certain that, whenever, as happened more often than not, he and the Queen were in cordial agreement over a public question, it was his instinct as a courtier addressing his Sovereign, and as a man addressing a woman, to attribute to her an undue share in the authorship of the policy, and to write about it to her as 'your Majesty's policy.'   But the whole record of the unique relation in which he stood to the Queen shows that, in affairs of moment, he never forgot that constitutionally the responsibility was his, and that, unless his royal mistress could convince him and the Cabinet of their error, the policy to be pursued must be his and theirs, not hers.

The one case in which he may be fairly said to have yielded, in a question of importance, his judgment, supported by that of his colleagues, to hers was the introduction of the Royal Titles Bill.   But, even there, the concession was only on the matter of time.   He was as convinced as she was that there should be an assumption by the British Crown of the imperial title in India, and that the act would confirm the stability and permanence of the British Raj.   But it was inconvenient for him, from a Parliamentary point of view, to have the

[1] See p. 754.

question forced on in the session of 1876. Doubtless, however, he reflected that, if there was one matter in which a Constitutional Monarch had every right to have her personal wishes respected, it was that of her title; and, in any case, he had the reward that the troubles and abuse which he underwent in the process of steering through the two Houses of Parliament the Bill on which Her Majesty had set her heart, finally secured for him her unlimited confidence and a place in her favour that no subsequent disagreements could affect.

For there were many disagreements on details of policy, though there was harmony in the broad outlook. On the Eastern Question the documents we have quoted have abundantly shown the difficulty which Beaconsfield experienced in keeping Her Majesty to that middle course which alone had a chance of support in public opinion. In 1879, over the Zulu War, the disagreement was very serious. Her Majesty, in her laudable desire to support those of her servants who were engaged in difficult civil and military duties on the outposts of empire, resisted, as we have seen, in a determined manner any suggestion to supersede Frere and Chelmsford. It was only with the utmost reluctance that she accepted the proposal to send Wolseley out, although his commission was drawn up in such a fashion as to spare, as far as might be, the susceptibilities of both High Commissioner and General. The climax of disagreement was, however, reached in the autumn, when the fighting leaders returned home from Zululand.

Chelmsford's final victory at Ulundi obliterated in the mind of the generous British public all his earlier mistakes, and he and other South African captains were welcomed in England enthusiastically, and presented with swords of honour suitable to a great war and an untarnished record. The Queen shared the enthusiasm, but Beaconsfield thought it very ill-judged. Her Majesty pressed him to receive Chelmsford at Hughenden, in order to hear his account of his proceedings in South

Africa. But the Minister would not consent to accord the returning General anything more than an official interview in Downing Street. He gave the Queen his reasons.

To Queen Victoria.

HUGHENDEN MANOR, *Aug.* 30, 1879.—. . . . With regard to Lord Chelmsford, Lord Beaconsfield feels that it would be hardly becoming, in their relative positions, for Lord Beaconsfield to receive him, except in an official interview. Lord Beaconsfield, by the advice he had the honor to offer yr. Majesty, has virtually recalled Lord Chelmsford from his command, and for reasons which appeared, and still appear, to Lord Beaconsfield to be peremptory.

He mixes up Lord Chelmsford, in no degree, with the policy of the unhappily precipitated Zulu War, the evil consequences of which to this country have been incalculable. Had it not taken place, your Majesty would be Dictatress of Europe; the Sultan would be in military possession of the line of the Balkans; the Egyptian trouble would never have occurred; and the Grecian question would have been settled in unison with our views.

Lord Beaconsfield charges Lord Chelmsford with having invaded Zululand 'avec un cœur léger,' with no adequate knowledge of the country he was attacking, and no precaution or preparation. A dreadful disaster occurred in consequence, and then Lord Chelmsford became panic-struck; appealed to yr. Majesty's Govt. frantically for reinforcements, and found himself at the head of 20,000 of yr. Majesty's troops, in order to reduce a country not larger than Yorkshire.

Having this unwieldy force, he was naturally unable to handle it. The release of Colonel Pearson was not accomplished until further delay would have become an infamy; and, had he not been furtively apprised by telegraph that he was about to be superseded, Lord Chelmsford would probably never have advanced to Ulundi. His retreat from that post was his last and crowning mistake, and the allegation, that he was instructed to do so by Sir G. Wolseley, has been investigated by Lord Beaconsfield, and found to be without foundation.

It is most painful for Lord Beaconsfield to differ from yr. Majesty in any view of public affairs, not merely because he is bound to yr. Majesty by every tie of duty and respectful affection, but because he has a distinct and real confidence in yr. Majesty's judgment, matured, as it is, by an unrivalled political experience, and an extensive knowledge of mankind.

In Sir Evelyn Wood and Colonel Buller, Lord Beaconsfield believes yr. Majesty has officers worthy of your colors, and who will hereafter worthily maintain the interests of yr. Majesty's Empire, and the honor of yr. Majesty's Crown.

This was, as Ponsonby told Her Majesty, 'a tremendous indictment'; but it did not alter the Queen's opinion in the least.

From Queen Victoria.

BALMORAL CASTLE, *Sept.* 1, 1879.—The Queen has to-day received Lord Beaconsfield's letter, which she must say has grieved and astonished her. Her wish that he should see Lord Chelmsford, as also Lord William Beresford, was that he should hear everything from them who know all and who have gone through endless difficulties, and not to decide on condemning people in most difficult and trying positions *from* the Cabinet, pressed by an unscrupulous Opposition (at least a portion of it) and still more unscrupulous press— without allowing them to state their own case and defend themselves ! How *can* civilians decide in a Cabinet on the causes for movements and the reasons for defeat ? Lord Beaconsfield himself so strongly condemned the Aulic Council that she *is* surprised at his severity, unmerited to a great extent, against Lord Chelmsford. *He* has obtained the decisive victory at Ulundi, which has paralysed Cetywayo. . . .

To recall a General whenever he is not successful is to act as the French used to do formerly. The Queen maintains that the war was imminent and that the Colonies might have been attacked, people murdered, and horrors committed, which would have ended in a very different way, to what it will do, it is to be hoped, now; but [for] which we shall have to thank those who were engaged in it. There was just as great an envy against Lord Lytton at the time of the Afghan War, and if he had met with reverses probably the same course might have been suggested. The Queen does not pretend to say that Lord Chelmsford has not made mistakes, but she cannot bear injustice, a want of generosity towards those who have had unbounded difficulties to contend with, and who ought to be supported from home and not condemned unheard.

Beaconsfield, distressed as he was at this acute difference with his Sovereign, nevertheless maintained his position, though he sent simultaneously with his reply a letter to Lady Ely, meant no doubt for Her Majesty's eye, in which he protested the depth of his distress, because he 'loved' the Queen.

To Queen Victoria.

HUGHENDEN MANOR, *Sept.* 4, 1879.—Lord Beaconsfield with his humble duty to yr. Majesty. He is grieved that some remarks he recently felt it his duty to make have incurred the displeasure of yr. Majesty, and in that respect, whether his remarks were just or erroneous, he should be equally grieved. Lord Beaconsfield will not presume to enter into a controversy with his Sovereign, but he will ask yr. Majesty's gracious permission to make one or two observations, which may remove misapprehension.

Lord Beaconsfield entirely agrees with yr. Majesty about the pernicious interference of Aulic Councils in warfare, and he never would permit any criticism in the Cabinet either of Sir B. Frere, or Ld. Chelmsford, when the war had commenced There was an occasion when Lord Beaconsfield, on this head, was absolutely alone among his colleagues, and they had to withdraw their otherwise unanimous views, to prevent the disruption of the Cabinet.

Throughout these anxious times, Lord Beaconsfield endeavoured to form his opinion solely from the letters, public and private, of Lord Chelmsford, and it was only when those letters became confused, he might say incoherent, vacillating and apparently without resource, that he felt it his duty to offer that advice to yr. Majesty, which ultimately led to Lord Chelmsford's return to England. Lord Beaconsfield feels it his duty to say that, before he took that step, he communicated confidentially with the military authorities, and they were unquestionably of opinion, then, that a new commander should be appointed.

Lord Napier was the General whom they wished to select. It was a selection agreeable to Lord Beaconsfield, and he made the proposition accordingly in the Cabinet. It would be wearisome now to trouble yr. Majesty with the circumstances why this appointment did not ultimately take place, and why Lord Napier's name was not submitted to yr. Majesty. Lord Beaconsfield feels conscious, that neither the unprincipled opposition in the House of Commons, which, he hopes, he never shrinks from encountering, nor the equally unprincipled and ignorant press which he has always despised, influenced him in the advice, which he had the honor to offer to yr. Majesty, and he was only moved to it by a pure sense of duty to his Sovereign.

The course of events, however, has released Lord Chelmsford from a painful position, and Lord Beaconsfield sanctioned without hesitation the great distinction[1] yr. Majesty is about

[1] G.C.B.

to confer on that officer. It had been, perhaps, better, therefore, that Lord Beaconsfield should not have expressed opinions, which have disquieted in any degree yr. Majesty, but the system which he has hitherto pursued, of communicating everything to yr. Majesty without reserve, may be pleaded, he hopes, as some extenuation of his indiscretion.

To the Dowager Lady Ely.[1]

HUGHENDEN MANOR, *Sept.* 4, '79.—. . . I am grieved, and greatly, that anything I should say, or do, should be displeasing to Her Majesty. I love the Queen—perhaps the only person in this world left to me that I do love; and therefore you can understand how much it worries and disquiets me, when there is a cloud between us. . . .

The Queen received Chelmsford herself at Balmoral, and was favourably impressed by his explanations; and once more urged Beaconsfield to be 'generous' and receive him at Hughenden as well as Wood and Buller. But Beaconsfield was obdurate and only extended his invitation to the two subordinate officers; and no insistence by the Queen could prevail on him to do more than go up to town to give Chelmsford an official audience in Downing Street. He fully realised how seriously he had hurt Her Majesty's feelings by refusing her entreaty. He wrote humorously to Salisbury on September 20: 'My greatest [trouble] is from my having refused to receive Lord Chelmsford at Hughenden. I am quite in disgrace, and may probably have to follow Andrassy's example.[2] If so, you will know the truth, and that the cause is not the Afghan War, but only Mrs. Masham's petticoat.'

It has been worth while to give this Chelmsford episode at considerable length to dispel the absurd idea that the Queen's attachment to her favourite Minister, instead of being based on the solid ground of confidence begot by experience, was mainly due to the flattering language in which he addressed her, and to the unworthy compliance which he showed with her every wish. This

---

[1] Letter quoted in Meynell's *Disraeli*, p. 539.   [2] *I.e.*, resign.

myth has sprung largely from Beaconsfield's ingrained habit of attributing to himself, in his hatred of cant, lower motives than those from which he really acted. Two delightful sayings of his are quoted. He told Lord Esher that, in talking with the Queen, he observed a simple rule: 'I never deny; I never contradict; I sometimes forget.' And to Matthew Arnold, in a conversation shortly before his death, he said: 'You have heard me called a flatterer, and it is true. Everyone likes flattery; and, when you come to royalty, you should lay it on with a trowel.' But the Queen was too much inured to flattery to care for it. Indeed those whom she suspected of concealing their true sentiments to adopt hers speedily lost her good opinion. She was downright and honest herself; and respected downrightness and honesty in others. But she was a woman as well as a Queen; and Disraeli was her only Minister since Melbourne who always bore the fact in mind. To women, as we have seen, his attitude throughout life was one of chivalrous devotion. 'What wonder,' as Lord Esher has well written, 'that his chivalrous regard for the sex should have taken a deeper complexion when the personage was not merely a woman, but a Queen?'

To Disraeli his whole life was a romance: and nothing in it seemed to him more romantic than his relation to Queen Victoria. Take his letters to Her Majesty in 1875 after receiving gifts from her of spring flowers. The flattery is, indeed, laid on 'with a trowel'; but what is most noticeable is the spirit of high romance in which they are written.

To Queen Victoria.

2, WHITEHALL GARDENS, *Feb.* 25, 1875.—Mr. Disraeli with his humble duty to your Majesty:

Yesterday eve, there appeared, in Whitehall Gardens, a delicate-looking case, with a royal superscription, which, when he opened, he thought, at first, that your Majesty had graciously bestowed upon him the stars of your Majesty's principal orders. And, indeed, he was so impressed with this graceful illusion, that, having a banquet, where there were

many stars and ribbons, he could not resist the temptation,
by placing some snowdrops on his heart, of showing that he,
too, was decorated by a gracious Sovereign.

Then, in the middle of the night, it occurred to him, that
it might all be an enchantment, and that, perhaps, it was a
Faery gift and came from another monarch: Queen Titania,
gathering flowers, with her Court, in a soft and sea-girt isle,
and sending magic blossoms, which, they say, turn the heads
of those who receive them.

They certainly would turn Mr. Disraeli's, if his sense of duty
to your Majesty did not exceed, he sincerely believes, his
conceit.

HOUSE OF COMMONS, *Friday, midnight* [*April* 16, 1875].—
Mr. Disraeli . . . returned home late last night, somewhat
anxious and wearied, when he found his room blazing, and
perfumed, with the gems and jewels of Nature; and presenting
in its appearance, and its associations, the most striking
contrast to the scene he had just quitted.

He could not refrain from blessing the gracious tenderness
that had deigned to fill his lonely home with fragrance and
beauty !

Such incidents outweigh all earthly honors: they sustain
energy, sweeten toil, and soften many sorrows.

The letter of February 25 is particularly interesting
and enlightening. If he could tell the Queen herself that
her flowers seemed like ' Faery ' gifts from Queen Titania,
it is not strange that in writing and talking to his intimates he should use the word ' Faery,' a term of romance
if ever there was one, as a synonym for Her Majesty.
But it was not only Queen Titania and her court that
Disraeli had in mind when he envisaged his Royal Mistress
as ' the Faery.' Still more was he thinking of the great
Queen who presided over the heroic and romantic age of
English adventure and literature, and of the famous
poem, one of his own favourites, dedicated to her—the
Faery Queen. It was after the romantic fashion of
Raleigh's service to Queen Elizabeth that Disraeli
conceived of his own service to Queen Victoria.

Queen Victoria, without having any of Queen Elizabeth's
inordinate relish for courtly and fantastic adoration,
would have been more or less than a woman if she had
been insensible to Disraeli's attitude; especially after

she had proved his wisdom and tested his patriotism
in public affairs.   The outcome was an unprecedented
intimacy and mutual confidence between Sovereign and
Minister.   Disraeli exhausted his resources of humour
and wit, his stores of epigram and anecdote, for Her
Majesty's amusement.   The article in the *Quarterly
Review* for April, 1901, already quoted, gives a pleasant
picture of their social relations.

He was never in the least shy; he did not trouble to insinuate;
he said what he meant in terms the most surprising, the most
unconventional; and the Queen thought that she had never
in her life seen so amusing a person.   He gratified her by his
bold assumptions of her knowledge, she excused his florid
adulation on the ground that it was 'Oriental,' and she was
pleased with the audacious way in which he broke through
the ice that surrounded her.   He would ask, across the
dinner-table, 'Madam, did Lord Melbourne ever tell your
Majesty that you were not to do this or that?' and the Queen
would take it as the best of jokes. . . .   She loved the East,
with all its pageantry and all its trappings, and she accepted
Disraeli as a picturesque image of it.   It is still remembered
how much more she used to smile in conversation with him
than she did with any other of her Ministers.

Of the letters which he used to write her, blending
business with sympathy, and affairs with romance, these
volumes are full.   Here is an attractive specimen, giving
an account of Beaconsfield's conversation with the
young Prince Alexander of Bulgaria, in whom and
whose fortunes Her Majesty was peculiarly interested.

To Queen Victoria.

10, DOWNING STREET, *June* 13, 1879.—. . .   Lord Beaconsfield saw a good deal of the Prince of Bulgaria, considering
the brevity of his visit.   Lord Beaconsfield was pleased and
satisfied with him.   Lord Beaconsfield met the Prince in
society, and had a very long and interesting private interview
with him.   He solicited Lord Beaconsfield's advice as to his
general conduct, and it was conceded to him sincerely and
simply.

Lord Beaconsfield reminded him that he had youth on his
side, which he should never forget.   He was called upon to
exercise dominion in a part of the world, where probably, at

least, sooner or later, there would be considerable changes; that this almost inevitable lot of the Levant would give rise, as it has given rise, to endless intrigues, combinations, offers of alliance, even conspiracies; that what is contemplated rarely occurs, and never exactly as was anticipated, it is the unexpected that always occurs; that he should confine his efforts to making himself esteemed, and beloved by his subjects, and tho' civil to all his neighbours, he should keep himself aloof from their machinations which probably would be disastrous; that being only twenty-two, he could afford to wait the natural development of affairs, which would do for him much more than forced alliances. To be young is a great thing, to be young and wise is irresistible. Finally Lord Beaconsfield recommended him to take the late King of the Belgians for his model, and study his career from the time that Prince was offered the throne of Greece to his illustrious end. In this interview the Prince of Bulgaria showed intelligence and sympathy, and seemed natural and sincere.

Lord Salisbury, who had to give him a banquet at 4 and 20 hours' notice, managed well. As it was Ascot week, independent of other difficulties, it was impossible to invoke the presence of ladies, so he invited the diplomatic corps and yr. Majesty's Ministers. Lord Salisbury was afraid it would be very dull, and male dinners necessarily must be—but it was not dull to the Prince of Bulgaria. He met exactly the persons he wanted to see. He mentioned to Lord Beaconsfield what an immense advantage it was to him, that he should thus have become personally acquainted with so many distinguished public men, who, otherwise, would only be to him words in newspapers.

Lord Beaconsfield also had the honor to meet the Prince at the Golden Wedding Banquet given at Prussia House. This really, if the locale had been equal to the occasion, would have been a striking affair. Forty guests in gorgeous uniforms, glittering with decorations, with many Princes, and all celebrated, were materials for a great effect, if there had only been room. It was like looking too close at a picture.

The weather here is tantalising, and tho' there is yet time to rally, the prospects can scarcely be called favorable. Lord Beaconsfield found his own county, tho' backward, yet flourishing, but he has had bad accounts from the great Midland counties. He himself, if he may venture to mention such a subject, is fairly well; and, having in his London garden fine trees of pink may, all in full bloom, he is not disposed to quarrel with his lot, or to believe that spots on the sun have obliterated from the earth all the promise of spring and all the splendor of summer. He remembers, when he first

served yr. Majesty nearly thirty years ago, having mentioned
his passion for pink may, there came the next morning from
Windsor a whole thorn tree in rosy bloom. It was a gift
worthy of Queen Elizabeth, and of an age when great
affairs and romance were not incompatible. All things
change, they say, even pink may, but what he thinks will
never change—at least to yr. Majesty—is your devoted
BEACONSFIELD.

The special favours which the Queen bestowed on the
Minister of her preference were many and great. Besides
the earldom and the Garter, she pressed, but pressed in
vain, higher honours in the peerage on him, and would
willingly have let him have any honour or decoration in
her power. In addition to countless gifts of flowers, she
constantly, on birthdays and other anniversaries, gave
him presents, and received presents from him. Him
alone of her Prime Ministers from the thirties to the
eighties did she invite to sit down when he had an
audience. She excused him, while he was still in the
Commons, from sending her the nightly letter in which
the Leader had been wont to give the Sovereign an
account of the proceedings, and permitted him to
devolve the duty on Lord Barrington, who occupied a
post in the Household. She excused him also, during nearly
the whole of his Ministry, from attendance at Balmoral.
She paid him the notable compliment of visiting and
lunching with him at his country home at a time when he
was a special target of Opposition abuse. For him, more
often than for any other Minister since the Prince Consort's
death, did she undertake the heavy duty of opening
Parliament in person. To him she gave, in December,
1879, the Windsor uniform, a special dress worn by the
Royal Family and the members of the Household in
personal attendance. She gave it, she wrote, as 'a mark
of personal regard and friendship. Lord Melbourne had
it, the Duke of Wellington, and Lord Aberdeen. The
Queen is not quite sure about Sir R. Peel.[1] But no other
Premier had it.' After Beaconsfield's day Lord Salisbury

---

[1] Sir R. Peel had the Windsor uniform.

received it from Queen Victoria; Mr. Balfour from King Edward; and Lord Rosebery from King George. Beaconsfield, in acknowledgment, wrote of the dress as connecting him, 'in a certain sense, permanently with your Majesty's service. It will always be a link.'

Here is the manner in which he thanked the Queen, on Christmas Day, 1879, for the latest of a long series of beautiful books.

To Queen Victoria.

HUGHENDEN MANOR, *Xmas Day,* 1879.—. . . Your Majesty has again added to the chamber where [Lord Beaconsfield] will probably pass the greater part of the future days, that may yet await him, a beautiful volume, fair alike in form and subject, and one of those books, which one may recur to, again and again.

Lord Beaconsfield is infinitely touched by this act. It is not merely that the sight of many beautiful volumes in his library will remind him, that he has had the honor of being the confidant and counsellor of a great Sovereign, and that too at a critical period of her Empire; but that the gracious Mistress, to whom he was thus bound by the highest sense of duty, was a being, who deigned to acknowledge, between herself and her servant, other sources of sympathy than the cares of Empire, and found them in that mutual love of the fine arts, of which yr. Majesty is instinctively appreciative, and in which yr. Majesty's tastes were trained and developed by one, who in that, and almost in every department requiring intelligence and sensibility, was himself consummate.

Lord Beaconsfield ventures to send, from this home which yr. Majesty has honored, his earnest wishes for yr. Majesty's private happiness, and for the fame and glory of your reign.

From Queen Victoria.

OSBORNE, *Dec.* 26, 1879.—The Queen thanks Lord Beaconsfield so very much for his very kind letter and good wishes. Most truly does she pray that he may be long spared in health and strength as her valued and trusted Minister! She is glad the book pleases him. . . .

And here is his tactful pleading with the Queen, which persuaded her to open the last session of the Beaconsfield Parliament in person.

To Queen Victoria.

HUGHENDEN MANOR, *Jan.* 10, 1880.— . . . He has much considered the question of yr. Majesty opening Parliament in person. Remembering that the military operations, in Asia and Africa, have both been brought to a satisfactory conclusion, with great credit to your Majesty's arms, and much individual distinction in your Majesty's troops; that the present Parliament has shown on every occasion patriotism and loyalty, always supporting your Majesty's Government in their external policy, by majorities largely consisting of the Liberal party; recollecting also that this loyalty was singularly exemplified, when your Majesty assumed the Imperial Crown of India: Lord Beaconsfield cannot resist the conviction, that on an occasion, which, probably, may be the last when yr. Majesty could personally address your Majesty's Parliament, it would be a gracious welcome, and popular act, for your Majesty to ascend yr. Majesty's throne on the 5th of next month.

From Queen Victoria.

OSBORNE, *Jan.* 12, 1880.—The Queen, having received Lord Beaconsfield's telegram, will no longer delay answering him about the Opening of Parliament. She will make the sacrifice (for there is nothing she dreads and dislikes more) ever ready to do what she can to support the present Govt.— and to gratify her people. . . .

Beaconsfield, for his part, took the warmest interest in the private concerns and in the family joys and sorrows of the Queen. The principal sorrow during his Ministry was the death, in December, 1878, of the Princess Alice, 'the first break,' as Her Majesty wrote to him, 'in my circle of children.' His speech on the Vote of Condolence, in which G. W. E. Russell, an acute but sometimes superfine critic, detected 'inconceivable bathos,' was thought by the Queen to be 'beautiful.' The Princess died of diphtheria, from which all her family were suffering, through kissing her sick boy, after she had been warned by the physicians of the danger of such an embrace. Beaconsfield held the circumstances to be, as they indeed were, 'wonderfully piteous,' and his language, though florid, would appeal to the heart of many besides the Queen.

It became [Princess Alice's] lot to break to her son, quite a youth, the death of his youngest sister, to whom he was devotedly attached. The boy was so overcome with misery that the agitated mother, to console him, clasped him in her arms—and thus received the kiss of death. My lords, I hardly know an incident more pathetic. It is one by which poets might be inspired, and in which the artist in every class, whether in picture, in statue, or in gem, might find a fitting subject for commemoration.

In spite of her sorrow, the Queen sent Beaconsfield her wonted Christmas letter.

To Queen Victoria.

HUGHENDEN, *Dec.* 26, 1878.—Lord Beaconsfield . . . has received this morning your Majesty's gracious letter. He cannot have a happy Xmas when your Majesty is in grief. . . .

He is always afraid of obtruding himself in such matters. In truth it is shyness, not inadvertence, that makes him often appear negligent.

Ever since he has been intimately connected with your Majesty, your Majesty has been to him a guardian Angel, and much that he has done that is right, or said that was appropriate, is due to you, Madam. He often thinks how he can repay your Majesty, but he has nothing more to give, having given to your Majesty his duty and his heart.

Beaconsfield was profoundly and rightly convinced of the importance of the Queen's life to the Empire, and was rendered anxious by a desperate attempt made on the Tsar's life in 1879. Her Minister, he wrote to Her Majesty, was 'a bubble who will be succeeded by other bubbles, but on your Majesty's life depends perhaps the fate of an Empire—in times of great trial.' He therefore implored her, popular and beloved as she was, not to disdain taking all reasonable precautions, whether walking or driving, 'for human nature is mimetic, and the crazy are often tempted to commit crimes not so much from innate wickedness as from a diseased self-consciousness, which upsets their reasoning powers.' And he impressed on Sir Henry Ponsonby, her secretary, the necessity of having 'adequate experts hovering over the towers and terraces of Windsor.'

In spite of the fact that the Queen looked with a somewhat jealous eye upon any incursions of the Heir-Apparent into the field of politics, Disraeli's relations with the Prince and Princess of Wales were friendly and cordial; the gracious lady who became Queen Alexandra especially distinguishing him on more than one occasion with her kindly regard.   He told Lady Bradford a pretty story of a dinner at the Hertfords' on May 22, 1875.   He there sat next to the Princess of Wales, whose quickness in conversation and ready sense of humour he greatly admired.

I said something about her 'orders,' all of which she wore. She said it was a shame I had no decoration, and she gave me her 'menu,' which was a pretty one, to wear instead.   I said, 'Your Royal Highness will not be able to select your dinner.'   She replied, 'We will exchange menus, and I will wear yours as an additional order.'

In the last days of December, 1879, the Prince of Wales, who had often been Beaconsfield's host at Sandringham, intimated his desire to be the Prime Minister's guest at Hughenden, and to meet there, as Beaconsfield whimsically put it in writing to Lady Bradford, 'some grave, but agreeable, signiors.'   Hughenden was a small house in which to entertain royalty, and, besides Corry, Beaconsfield could only accommodate four other guests.   The Prince selected Lord Salisbury and Sir William Hart Dyke, the Whip, from the world of politics; and Lord Rosslyn and Lord Orford, two of Beaconsfield's particular friends, from the world of society.   Orford could not come, being ill at Bath; and the Prince suggested Bernal Osborne, another of his host's old friends, as a substitute. The party lasted from the afternoon of Monday, January 12, 1880, to late on the following afternoon, and was most successful.   Beaconsfield gave accounts of the visit both to the Queen and to Lady Bradford.

To Queen Victoria.

10, DOWNING ST., *Jan.* 14, 1880.—. . .   The royal visit to Hughenden, he hopes he may say, was not altogether unsuccessful. A Prince, who really has seen everything, and knows everybody, is a guest one might despair of interesting and amusing even for a passing hour, but His Royal Highness was so gracious, and so agreeable, that one hoped he was not wearied.

The conversation was grave as well as gay; and His Royal Highness, Lord Beaconsfield can say with the utmost truth, maintained his part with felicity and even distinction.

His Royal Highness had the opportunity of speaking alone with Lord Salisbury, and also with Lord Beaconsfield, and at more social moments Lord Rosslyn and Mr. Osborne expressed and elicited many a flashing phrase.

To Lady Bradford.

HUGHENDEN MANOR, *Jan.* 13.—The visit has been, all say, a great success, but H.R.H. does not depart until late this afternoon, and I can only get hold of ten minutes to write to you by messenger, who must depart immediately. He praised the house, praised his dinner, praised the pictures, praised everything: was himself most agreeable in conversation, said some good things, and told more.

When I found out that both Rosslyn and B[ernal] O[sborne] had been his companions at Cumberland Lodge, I was afraid they must have exhausted all their resources; but I was wrong. Success inspired them, and the dinner was like a pantomime, where there are two clowns, and both capital ones. . . .

We played at whist in the evening—his own choice. I had hoped to have induced them to play nap, which wd. have left me alone, for I don't understand that mystery. But he wd. not have it, and insisted on playing with B. O. against Salisbury and myself at whist. He beat us, which does not displease him.

To-day he rambled about the grounds, and then took a drive in a snowstorm and in an open carriage to Wycombe and about. . . .

10, DOWNING ST., *Jan.* 15.—. . . They returned from their barouche drive in a snow storm in high spirits; his companions, Monty, and the two clowns; B. O. affecting seriousness and sense of hardship, his Grace the Lord Commissioner, on the other hand, rollicking.

H.R.H. disappeared then for an hour, and told me he had been writing an account of Hughenden to the Princess. Then there was a very successful, but very long, luncheon, and then, after a little wandering about the house, he departed, having, he said, ' greatly enjoyed himself.'

Salisbury behaved very well, and helped me much. . . .

Beaconsfield showed a shrewd appreciation both of the social gifts and of the political promise of the future King Edward, in writing of him to his intimates as ' Prince Hal,' after the merry Prince who developed, upon the throne, into the heroic victor of Agincourt.

It was natural that a Minister for whom the Sovereign entertained an exceptional regard should receive many marks of attention from the Royal Family. A special compliment was paid him, early in his last Ministry, by the Duke and Duchess of Edinburgh, who asked him to their house-warming dinner-party at Clarence House; a party at which there were none but royalties present, except Disraeli and Dr. Quin, the homœopathic physician and wit—even equerries and ladies-in-waiting being excluded. The attentions, indeed, which he received from Princes and Princesses were so numerous as to be sometimes embarrassing, and were not always considerate. He declined altogether to oblige a Princess who, at a time of political crisis, asked the Prime Minister to call on her at a quarter to ten in the morning. ' Had I been as idle as a ploughboy sitting on a gate,' he told a friend, ' I would not have gone. A liberty to ask me to derange my day for such frivolity !' Outside the Queen, and the Prince and Princess of Wales, the member of the Royal Family whom he most highly appreciated, and whom he was most pleased to meet in society, was undoubtedly the vivacious Princess Mary of Cambridge, Duchess of Teck. With her brother, the Duke of Cambridge, he was on friendly terms, but he came, by the end of his period of office, to distrust the influence of the Horse Guards under the Duke's control.

To Lady Bradford.

HUGHENDEN MANOR, *Dec.* 26, 1879.—. . . Sir Garnet Wolseley has not disappointed me. He is one of those men who not only succeed, but succeed quickly. Nothing can give you an idea of the jealousy, hatred, and all uncharitableness of the Horse Gds. against our only soldier. The Horse Guards will ruin this country, unless there is a Prime Minister who will have his way, and that cannot be counted on. Fortunately he has the power, if he have only the determination. You cannot get a Secy. of War to resist the cousin of the Sovereign, with whom he is placed in daily and hourly communication. I tremble when I think what may be the fate of this country if, as is not unlikely, a great struggle occur, with the Duke of Cambridge's generals. . . !

Though Beaconsfield sometimes wrote to his friends impatiently of courtiers, he always showed the greatest courtesy and consideration to those about the person of the Sovereign; and was consequently more popular at Court than statesmen are wont to be. With Lady Ely, General Grey, and Sir Henry Ponsonby he maintained very friendly and confidential relations. Here is the tribute paid to him on his retirement by the Queen's shrewd and faithful secretary, who was, be it observed, a Whig.

From Sir Henry Ponsonby.

WINDSOR CASTLE, *April* 19, 1880.—. . . I have to thank you sincerely for recommending my name to the Queen for the honour of being appointed a Privy Councillor. . . . I should be most ungrateful if I did not thank you most heartily for the very kind manner you have always treated me, and for permitting me to have free and unrestricted intercourse with you, which has made my duty an easy and agreeable one under your Administration. But however grateful I am for your kindness to me, may I be allowed to add my deep sense of the service of friendship you have rendered to the Queen personally, which has undoubtedly softened her difficulties and alleviated her troubles? Your retirement from office therefore is not only the resignation of a Minister but the loss to the Queen of a true and faithful friend, and my position here allows me, I hope, to share the Queen's real regret at such a separation.

CHAPTER XIII.

LAST MONTHS OF THE GOVERNMENT.

1879–1880.

When Beaconsfield went down to Hughenden in August, 1879, for rest and refreshment after the session, he was able to regard public affairs with satisfaction save for the continuance of bad trade and bad harvests.

To Lord Lytton.

Confidential. 10, DOWNING STREET, *Aug.* 14, '79.—. . . I write to you now at the end of a long and laborious campaign, which has terminated triumphantly for H.M.'s Government. It is not merely that our external affairs figure well in the Queen's Speech; that not a single Russian soldier remains in the Sultan's dominions; that, greatly owing to your energy and foresight, we have secured a scientific and adequate frontier for our Indian Empire; and that our S. African anxieties are virtually closed; but we have succeeded in 'passing' some domestic measures, in spite of factious obstruction, of first-class interest and importance—notably our Army Discipline Act, a measure of magnitude and gravity, equal in range and difficulty to three great measures, and our Irish University Act, a question which had upset two Administrations.

Although we have entered ' the sixth year of our reign,' our parliamentary majority, instead of diminishing, has increased, and notwithstanding the rumors that may reach you, I see no reason, scarcely a right, to dissolve Parliament—though this, of course, must depend on circumstances. . . .

The only danger and difficulty which the present Ministry has to encounter are natural. 'The stars in their courses have fought against' me. After four bad harvests in this country, we are apparently about to meet a fifth dearth, and one not confined to this country. There can be no substantial revival of trade unless the earth gives us an abundant increase. We have had to struggle against four bad harvests and four wars, and it is difficult to carry through a commanding policy with a failing Exchequer. The spirit of England is yet so high, that, I believe, it would endure any amount of taxation if its imperial position were at stake; but taxes, without that sentiment of glory and patriotism, will pull down any Ministry. However, in this respect, things may yet mend, and, whatever happens, it will always be to me a source of real satisfaction that I had the opportunity of placing you on the throne of the Gt. Mogul.[1]

In three weeks' time, before Lytton had even received his chief's optimistic letter, the second disaster of this fatal year had befallen, and had wrecked the Afghan settlement on which the Government prided themselves. Not a suspicion, however, of coming trouble from Afghanistan is to be discerned in Beaconsfield's private letters in the interval.

To Lady Bradford.

HUGHENDEN MANOR, *Aug.* 19.—. . . We came here on Friday (Sal[isbur]y going same day to Dieppe), rode over the new estate on Saturday, a finish day, with the agent, and the chief tenant, who complained of nothing and asked for nothing, and is a furrier at Wycombe and is worth £30,000, so I suppose he means to pay under all circumstances. The old tenants think me quite mad in buying land in this county, and evidently intend to decamp: but they have got to Xmas now ! . . .

Aug. 20.—. . . This place is desolate, and except on Saturday, wh. I have described to you, I have never been able to get out. It has rained night and day The peacocks have no tails and are yet still moulting. They persist in showing themselves, like Falstaff's ragged regiment. They have eaten all the flowers, and have no beauty to substitute for that which they have destroyed. Nothing can now save the harvest. . . .

Aug. 22.—. . . Dufferin writes that he attended the grand review by special invitation, and that in the course of the morning [the Emperor] held the most friendly and amiable conversation with him. The Emperor wonderfully pleased by what I said of him at the Mansion House, and all the generals did nothing but praise Ld. Beaconsfield and England ! Quite a new thing ! from wh'ch I infer that their expedition to Merv has failed, and that the heat, and the want of water,

---

[1] This letter is quoted, in part, in *Lord Lytton's Indian Administration.*

and the desert, have floored them.   Duff[erin] was particularly
to impress upon Ld. Beaconsfield that the Emperor had no
intention, and never had one, of going to Merv.   Probably
not, now.

I have not read a word that Gladstone has written, or
spoken, for nearly a year; but I like your criticism, and hope
your judgment is correct, tho' I think the agricultural bankruptcy must finish us.

Aug. 25.—. . . The peacocks look better; crouching in
the sun which lights up their purple necks, while the loss of
the rest of their splendor is not so obvious.   One of the
ladies presented me on Saturday with a family of four: an
almost unprecedented event, as they seldom exceed 1 or 2,
and these are hatched always in wild places and mysterious
woods.

Aug. 30.—. . . Wolseley writes in good spirits, and
evidently thinks that he shall make a good and quick job of
it. . . .

Sept. 2.—The P[rime] M[inister] of the Dominion of Canada[1]
arrived yesterday and departed by early train this morning,
having given me a bad night and leaving me very exhausted.
He is gentlemanlike, agreeable, and very intelligent: a considerable man, with no Yankeeisms except a little sing-song
occasionally at the end of a sentence.   It is a pity these
people always come when everybody is scattered.   It wd. not
have been half as exhausting to have given him a London
dinner, or more.   But it was necessary, for many grave
reasons, that he should not depart and feel on his return,
like the Dss. of Marlboro', ' that she had had no attention paid
to her.'   Considering that the Princess Louise is V[ice] Queen
of Canada, it is to be regretted that Lorne's Prime Minister,
the head too of the English and Conservative party, shd. not
have been invited to dine with our Sovereign the day he was
sworn in of the Privy Council at Osborne. . . .

By the bye, the Canadian chief is said to be very like your
humble servant, tho' a much younger man.   I think there is
a resemblance.   He says the Princess is a great success in
Canada, which was a toss up: but she is extremely gracious,
speaks to everybody and is interested in everything, and
skates divinely ! . . . I fear that Lorne, tho' he tries hard,
has not made them forget Dufferin.

Haymerle, it is settled, is to succeed Andrassy, tho' it will
not be announced at present.   This is an anti-Russian appointment, and will suit England well.   He is not a great noble:
I believe a plebeian, and looks one; nor will he set the Danube

---

[1] Sir John A. Macdonald.

on fire; but he has great experience in affairs, thoro'ly knows his business, and is honorable.

Upon these quiet autumn days at Hughenden there burst, on September 6, the terrible news that the British Envoy, Mission, and escort at Cabul had been treacherously attacked by Afghan soldiers, and had all perished. The presence of a British Envoy in Cabul had long been held by Beaconsfield, Salisbury, and Lytton to be most desirable; but, in view of Sher Ali's notorious objection, no proposal of the kind had been made in any of the numerous negotiations with him since Lytton's arrival in India. When, however, Sher Ali had fled and died in exile, and Afghanistan, owing to the victorious advance of our three columns, lay open, from north to south, to British troops, it was natural to include the reception of a British Envoy among the conditions presented at Gandamak to Yakub Khan, the new Ameer, for his acceptance. It was Yakub who suggested Cabul as the place of the Envoy's residence, as it was only there, he said, that he himself could protect him Sir Louis Cavagnari, a brilliant and experienced frontier officer, who had negotiated the Treaty of Gandamak, was appointed Resident; and by his own wish his staff and escort were reduced to the smallest possible dimensions. They were received with due respect and honour on their entry into Cabul on July 24; and, during the six weeks that their mission lasted, Cavagnari, though he noted several unsatisfactory features in the Afghan situation, never showed any apprehension of danger, and on the last day of his life, September 2, telegraphed to the Viceroy 'All well.' Nevertheless next day mutinous Afghan troops stormed the Residency and massacred all its defenders, while the Ameer, if he did not connive at the treachery, at any rate took no steps to safeguard those who were peculiarly under his care.

It was a crushing blow to Beaconsfield. 'I am quite overcome,' he telegraphed at once to the Queen, 'and was trying to write to my Sovereign, but I am unequal to it.'

The Queen urged immediate action, which the Minister was not slow to carry out. 'We must act with great energy,' Her Majesty telegraphed from Balmoral on September 6, 'and no hanging back, or fear to be found fault with, must deter us from strong and prompt measures. . . . Pray urge this on the Viceroy, and assure him of support and confidence.'

To Queen Victoria.

HUGHENDEN MANOR, *Sept*. 7, 1879.—Lord Beaconsfield . . . had the honor to receive this afternoon yr. Majesty's gracious telegram. . . . He will, yr. Majesty may be sure, act on its spirit. The whole Afghan question is now *tabula rasa* and, if necessary, we may march to Herat. It is fortunate that Parliament is not sitting: there is nothing to paralyse us.

He has confidence in Lytton. It is a situation which befits his courage, resource, and imagination.

Alas! for the brilliant Cavagnari! and his friends and companions, whose names Lord Beaconsfield does not yet know, and dares not to think of. And yet such is the high spirit of the service, that Lord Beaconsfield doubts not that there are men ready to take the same post. They serve under an Empress who may well inspire them. . . .

Cranbrook, the Secretary for India, hurriedly summoned back from a Scottish holiday but just begun, came to Hughenden at once; and the Viceroy was assured of the complete support of the home authorities for vigorous measures.

To Lord Salisbury.

HUGHENDEN MANOR, *Sept*. 9, 1879.—This is a shaker, and it is difficult, at the first breath, to recognise all the consequences of such a disaster. I fear they will be extensive and manifold. We are all scattered, of course. The unhappy Cranbrook left town on Friday night, to find, on his arrival at Murthly, in the land of Athole, that he would have to return immediately. He will be in town this morning: I hope—and trust—he will be with me by the 5 o'c. train. . . .

I have telegraphed to Cranbrook in favor of the most decided and instant action. Is that in our power ? We may be only five days' march from Cabul, but that would be as bad as the great desert, if we have no transport and inadequate commissariat. As for transport, I remember, with alarm, that

50 or 60 thousand camels have already been wasted. However, these are points on wh. Cranbrook, I trust, will throw much light. . . .

(*Later.*) Our friend arrived here this afternoon. He brought no fresh news from the Ind. Office, nor had he been able to see any member of his Council. The result of our deliberations was a telegram to the Viceroy, assuring him of the support of H.M. Government in a prompt and vigorous advance on Cabul, assuming that his communications were all secured; requesting immediate information as to the amount of troops available for such a movement, as the forces, I fear, are much scattered in cantonments; what was his amount of transport for the operation, wh. he could immediately command; whether his commissariat was adequate ?

As to future movements, and general policy, after the occupation of Cabul—that we would not, at present, touch upon.

Of course, that must be decided by the Cabinet, but, in the meantime, I will to you roughly touch upon the course I think we ought to pursue.

No annexation, generally speaking: military occupation for a time absolutely necessary .

I look upon our engagements under the Treaty as null and void, as the Ameer has been unable to protect our Envoy, whose presence at Cabul he himself suggested, as it was the only place where the Ameer could answer for his safety.

If the Ameer himself is still in existence, if we are satisfied of his fidelity, and if the principal Sirdars rally round him, and this turn out to be a merely military revolt, a mutiny of the Herat troops, then, I think, it will be impossible for us to throw over Yakub; but if he is dead or disappears, I don't think we ought to set up another Prince, that, then, we should content ourselves by consolidating our military frontier (retaining Candahar, wh. we must now, probably, under any circumstances) and let the rest of the country quarrel among themselves, and after a certain course of violence, plunder, treachery and massacre, become apportioned among various chiefs. This was Lytton's original plan, but the Cabinet did not then relish it.

What alarms me is the state of the Indian Army, as revealed in a letter from Lytton written to Cran. before the catastrophe. Except Roberts, who he believes is highly gifted, and who certainly is a strategist, there seems no one much to rely on: Stewart respectable; Massey promising; but all the persons, with slight exceptions, to whom we have voted Parliamentary thanks, and on whom the Crown has conferred honors, utterly worthless.

As for General Sam Browne, according to Lytton, he ought

to have been tried by a court martial, and he goes thro' them all with analogous remarks.

And these are the men whom, only a few months, or weeks, ago, he recommended for all these distinctions !

I begin to think he ought to be tried by a court martial himself; but I have confidence, still, in his energy and resource.

Poor Cranbrook, dead beat with his travel and this great chagrin, has gone to bed, tho' it has not struck ten, so I write this, which he will take by the earliest train to-morrow. 'Tis rough stuff, but I hope may convey a fair view of the situation to you.

Any hurried or immediate meeting of the Cabinet seems unnecessary, and Cranbrook to-day will see Maine[1] about the Parliamentary point of law. He seems to have confidence in Maine about such matters.

Beaconsfield did not permit these external anxieties to interfere with a party at Hughenden of his intimate friends, which was arranged for the end of the month, and which included Lady Chesterfield as well as the Bradfords.

To Lady Bradford.

HUGHENDEN MANOR, *Sept.* 10, '79.—It has been quite out of my power to write to you, my attention being entirely absorbed by the awful catastrophe of Cabul, and the necessary measures to take in consequence. . . .

I have heard from Bradford (on the 9th), and have written to him by this post. I do not see why friends shd. not meet, because there has been a national disaster, and therefore I have fixed the 23rd inst. for yr. arrival here, and I hope you will stay at least till the end of that week. I hope the young ladies will accompany you. I have no party of any kind, and fear they will not be amused; no dancing, no charades, no lawn tennis ! A dreary prospect ! . . .

Sept. 11.—. . . I have had a sharp 8 and 40 hours or so, but am perfectly calm. It is a horrible business, because the Queen has lost some admirable servants, but for no other reason. It will not, in the slightest degree, change, or affect, the policy of H.M.'s Government, but, on the contrary, confirm and consolidate it.

I have good accounts this morning of the state of our troops and of their preparedness. I was a little nervous about transport, but am not now. . . .

Sept. 19.—. . . You will meet Sir Evelyn Wood on Tuesday, who, the Queen tells me, is extremely agreeable.

---

[1] Sir Henry Maine, the jurist, who was then on the India Council.

The British power was promptly re-established in Afghanistan by the energy of Roberts, who pressed on rapidly by the Kurram to Cabul, winning a complete victory over the rebels at Charasiab on the way, while in the south Stewart re-occupied Candahar.   Yakub, who had early fled to Roberts's camp, abdicated when the General entered Cabul.   By the middle of October, we had the *tabula rasa*, of which Beaconsfield wrote, for our Afghan policy.   He was wisely in no hurry to take final decisions, though the Viceroy desired to proceed at once with his scheme of disintegration, involving the permanent annexation of Candahar and the neighbourhood.

The Opposition, with Harcourt as their fugleman, claimed that the Cabul disaster showed the justice of their contentions.   Nothing was to be expected but disaster if you forsook in any particular the strict Lawrence doctrine of non-interference in Afghanistan. Lytton's mad policy, the Liberals averred, had only produced its natural fruits.   In view of the approval of the Mission by the best frontier authorities, such as Cavagnari himself, this criticism did not sound very impressive.   A truer criticism, perhaps, would be that Lytton's error lay in misjudging his Ameer.   Yakub was both weak and treacherous; and the policy of the Mission postulated, for its success, a strong and reasonably straightforward ruler.

To Queen Victoria.

HUGHENDEN MANOR, *Oct*. 23, 1879.—Lord Beaconsfield . . . was content with the tone of his colleagues generally, and believes that the unanimous decision of the Cabinet was a wise one.   It may be, that the proposals of Lord Lytton may eventually have to be adopted, and even more than his Excellency suggests; but looking, not merely in an Indian aspect, at the situation, they were premature.   What we have first to effect, is to establish our military authority throughout Afghanistan, by the occupation of its strongholds.   Doing this, and when we have done this, no one will suspect us of 'hesitation and feebleness.'   We shall then be in a position to dictate according to circumstances.   We have had too many fits and starts in our history, as far as Afghanistan and Central Asia are concerned. We must accustom the world a little to the permanence and stability of our authority there. In the military occupation of the country, we can march to Herat if the Russians advance to Merv, we can deal with Persia without being embarrassed by the claims or pretences of any Afghan Sovereign; we can, in short, if we are not in a hurry, consolidate yr. Majesty's Empire, and inflict such a check on any rival Power, which will influence the conduct of all Eastern States. No longer bound by the Treaty negotiated by the gifted Cavagnari, we may make arrangements with Persia, for example, which may tend to the restoration of her influence in Asia, and save her from the ravenous maw of Russia.

Lord Beaconsfield conferred with Lord Salisbury much on this matter yesterday, which had often occupied their thoughts. The Cavagnari Treaty was an obstacle to all this, which, if successfully carried into effect, may greatly affect the position of Russia in Turkey.

The speech of Lord Salisbury at Manchester was of the highest class of eloquence. It has much influenced public opinion, and is a striking contrast to the brilliant flippancy of Sir W. Harcourt, and its utter refutation. . . .

Beaconsfield did not give any hint, in his speech at Guildhall on Lord Mayor's Day, of the nature of the future settlement of Afghanistan. But he seized the opportunity to rebuke the hostile and depreciatory criticism to which Lytton had been subjected by the Opposition orators and press, and to pronounce an emphatic eulogy of his conduct. 'For my own part, I have rarely met a man in whom genius and sagacity were more happily allied than in Lord Lytton, a man of greater resource, or one possessing in such degree that highest quality of public life—courage in adversity, and firmness and constancy in difficulty and danger.' It was to Lytton's policy of disintegration that, in the apparent absence of any chief strong enough to hold Afghanistan together, the Cabinet came gradually round. But Beaconsfield and Salisbury desired, in addition, to negotiate an agreement with Persia, under which, in accordance with that policy, Herat should be held by the Shah as the feudatory of the British Crown. This scheme, to which the Queen objected,

with some reason, as unduly increasing British responsibilities, was never carried through.

To Queen Victoria.

HUGHENDEN, *Dec.* 5, 1879.—Lord Beaconsfield with his
humble duty to yr. Majesty. With the utmost deference, he
begs to assure yr. Majesty, that yr. Majesty's Ministers in any
line, which they may advise yr. Majesty to take, about the
Russian Letters,[1] will not in their opinion show weakness, but
strength; strength in their cause, and confidence in the commanding position, which in this affair they occupy. Lord
Beaconsfield does not contemplate eventual 'silence or
concealment' in this matter. But the occasion, and the
manner, require much consideration. Lord Cranbrook, on
Wednesday, talked of further letters, in private to Lord
Beaconsfield; but no information of that kind has reached him,
and he has written in consequence to Lord Cranbrook on the
subject.

And now with regard to the 'other, larger and more difficult
subject.' Here are the views of Lord Beaconsfield personally
and which he ventures to hope, that yr. Majesty, after consideration, may be pleased not to disapprove.

It is clear, that Lord Lytton would like to fall back on the
Treaty of Gandamak, but feels that it is impossible; he therefore contemplates a group of quasi-independent chieftains
under the influence of the imperial Crown of India, but
combining this, for some time, with adequate military occupation of the country by yr. Majesty's forces. If this were
effected, and Candahar, for example, in possession of yr.
Majesty's army, and in two years' time connected by a railway
with Herat, Lord Lytton would not be unwilling to see the
Shah of Persia Lord of Herat, on the same terms as the chiefs
of Candahar, Cabul, Ghuznee, etc. Such arrangements cannot
be made off-hand.

Lord Salisbury, on the other hand, tho' not disapproving
of this general policy, wishes to close with Persia at once, for
the fear that Russia will forestall us. Lord Cranbrook,
who from his office, as well as his character, naturally exercises
much influence on this question, looks upon the disintegration
of Afghanistan as inevitable, and is in favor, generally, of the
Viceroy's views; but more strongly in favor of the Persian
Convention than Lord Lytton, and wishes to hasten the
general settlement of Afghanistan, so that we may meet
Parliament with a distinct policy.

[1] Correspondence between Sher Ali and Russian agents, found at Cabul.

After the Cabinet unanimously agreeing that the Treaty of Gandamak should be looked upon as abrogated, and that disintegration must be accepted as a fact by yr. Majesty's Government, Lord Beaconsfield guided the Cabinet to a decision on Wednesday which substantially adopted the views of Lord Cranbrook, but authorised Lord Salisbury to continue negotiating with Persia. It is the opinion of Lord Beaconsfield that Persia will wait; and so, that we may be able to effect a safer and more satisfactory arrangement, than the Shah now would propose or accept.

Russia can offer nothing at present to Persia. She can only menace, and she menaces while she herself is under great difficulties. We are now more at hand, as regards Persia, than Russia is. Russia could not move against Persia under two years, and then, with a railway from Candahar to Herat, your Majesty could immediately display a military power against which Russia could not contend. Lord Salisbury proposes, in his contemplated convention, many engagements on the part of Persia, which would practically make the Shah yr. Majesty's feudatory; not as Shah of Persia, but as Lord of Herat, as in the case of the K. of the Netherlands, who is a feudatory, it is believed, of the German Empire, as Grand Duke of Luxembourg.

Yr. Majesty justly enquires, What guarantees have we that the Shah will observe these conditions ? The same guarantees that made him observe the Treaty of Paris for 30 years, and, in addition, the increased guarantee arising from his increased proximity to yr. Majesty's Empire, and its military resources, while the Persian Gulf is at all times open to your Majesty's Fleet.

Only one important step was actually taken in the process of disintegration. A chieftain, independent of Cabul, but under the protection of England, was set up in Candahar. Before any definite decision had been reached in the north, there appeared out of Turkestan a claimant to the Afghan throne, Abdul Rahman, nephew of Sher Ali. There was reason to think that he might prove the strong ruler who was desired; and negotiations had been begun with him when the Beaconsfield Government left office. Ministers had acquired for India an enormously strengthened frontier, and had beaten down, for the time, opposition in Afghanistan; the final settlement had to be left for their successors.

The temporary disasters in South Africa and Afghanistan, however they might disaffect voters at home to Beaconsfield's Government, did not lead competent foreign observers to doubt England's power or the value of her goodwill. For in September of this year the friendly relations which had existed since the Treaty of Berlin between Great Britain and Germany culminated in what appeared to be a serious overture from Bismarck. He sent Münster, the German Ambassador in London, direct to Beaconsfield at Hughenden, to propose, confidentially and for the moment unofficially, a defensive alliance between Germany, Austria, and England. Beaconsfield, who insisted that the confidence should be extended to his Sovereign and his colleague, the Foreign Secretary, submitted to the Queen the following account of this important conversation; forwarding at the same time an almost verbally identical report to Salisbury.

Memorandum for Queen Victoria.

Secret. HUGHENDEN MANOR, *Sept.* 27, 1879.—Count Münster arrived here yesterday at half-past six o'clock, and departed early this morning. . . . Absolutely before he sat down, he said, ' I disturb you in your retirement with reluctance, but I obey the order of Prince Bismarck, and I come to make you a proposal of the gravest character. It must be made, however, in complete confidence; not looked upon, at this stage, as an official communication, but one of private friendship of Prince Bismarck, with the hope that it may lead to official communication.' Then I said: ' I must stop you at once to say that, while I engage that the confidence shall be respected, it is impossible for me to listen to anything on public affairs, which I am not free to communicate to my Sovereign and the Secretary of State.'

Count Münster: ' Prince Bismarck feels that and knows that it is not possible, nor desirable, for you to converse with me except on those conditions; but why he insists, for the moment, that his confidence should be limited to yourself, is that he has not yet communicated his purpose to the Emperor, and if the Emperor hears of it from another quarter—we will say from royal correspondence or otherwise—before Prince Bismarck has told him—the result might be highly disadvantageous.'

I, however, persisted in my view, saying that Lord Salisbury and myself were the same, and that, from long experience, I could answer with my head for the discretion of my Sovereign. After some demurring, Count Münster made his statement. It was long, but interesting. The principal points are thus condensed.

The relations of Russia and Germany are in their nature essentially unsatisfactory, and since the union of Germany have become more so. The Russians hate the Germans, and have succeeded, during late years, in removing almost every eminent German from their public service, altho' German statesmen really made this Empire. The Pan-Slavic sentiment now entirely absorbs them, and the reason why Schouvaloff is shelved is that, altho' a Russian, he is enlightened, and would follow the policy of the great Russo-German statesmen who preceded him.

This chronic state of affairs induced Prince Bismarck to make an effort to rid Germany of the Russian thraldom under which Germany has so long groaned, and to follow up the comparative emancipation which had been effected by the union of Germany. In this spirit, he made, at an early period of Lord Beaconsfield's administration, a proposal to Lord Odo Russell proposing an alliance with Gt. Britain. That proposal was not only rejected by the English Secretary of State, but was only notified by him to his colleagues accompanied by his opinion, that it could not for a moment be entertained. Had that proposal been accepted, there would have been no Turkish war, and none of the complications that now embarrass us. Thrown back on himself, Prince Bismarck was forced to rely on Russia, and by the invention of the alliance of the three Emperors, which was never realised, and by the reciprocal regard of the two Emperors of Germany and Russia, the Prince managed for a time to keep affairs tolerably straight.[1]

Now, all the old and organic rancor has reappeared. All the complaints of Germany having thrown over Russia, are false and mere pretexts. So also the pretended personal difference of Gortchakoff and Bismarck, and the articles in the Russian newspapers. What is true, is, that Pan-Slavism is entirely paramount in Russia, and that the Emperor of Russia has at last given in entirely to it. The meeting of the two Emperors, the other day, was an entire failure. The Emperor of Germany said and did many things on that occasion which his friends regretted, but the Emperor himself is now convinced, that these sacrifices were in vain, and that his influence with his nephew has vanished.

---

[1] This, of course, was an audacious inversion of the order of events. The understanding between the three Emperors began in 1872; Bismarck's overtures to Odo Russell and Derby were made in 1876.

Russia is preparing to attack Austria; the peace of the world will be disturbed; it is in the nature of things that it will not be a localised war; it will be a great and general war. Peace is necessary to Germany; no country desires or requires peace more. To secure it, she proposes an alliance between Germany, Austria and Great Britain. But before he mentions this to the Emperor, Prince Bismarck wishes to know from Lord Beaconsfield, whether he may consider England as favorable to such a scheme, as he does not wish to embark on fruitless negotiations, and, if Lord Beaconsfield does not favor the idea, he will proceed no further.

Lord Beaconsfield said he regretted the original proposition of P. Bismarck some years ago had been so abruptly dismissed. Had it been made the subject of negotiation, between the two Courts, it might have assumed a practical shape. He agreed with Prince Bismarck, that it probably would have prevented the war, but in considering the new proposal, tho' himself favorable, and always favorable, to an understanding with Germany, he could not conceal from himself, that any step on the part of Gt. Britain, that would seem hostile to France, might now be viewed with suspicion and dislike by the people of England, the commercial and social, and, in some degree, the political relations of the two countries being so intimate.

Count Münster said that Prince Bismarck had foreseen this; that the alliance he contemplated would not be incompatible with cordial relations with France; that their relations with France were of that description; and that the Prince had reason to believe, that neither the present French Ministry, nor Gambetta and his friends, would commence a war of aggression against Germany; that any danger of that kind could only come from the old clerical and monarchical parties, and that France under any circumstances would never stir if Gt. Britain and Germany were united.

The two leading features of such co-operation would naturally be, to guard Germany from such aggression, and to support in the Levant, and the East generally, the policy and interests of England.

The conversation had gone on now for an hour, when the gong conveniently sounded for dinner.

After that the conversation was resumed. Lord Beaconsfield said, that he had always been, and still was, favorable in public affairs to the principle of an alliance or good understanding with Germany, but much depended on the application of that principle, and it could not be satisfactorily carried into effect except with the Secretary of State. He should advise Count Münster to convey this his opinion to

P. Bismarck, and ask his Highness's permission to place himself in personal communication with Lord Salisbury.

Ultimately Count Münster said he should write to Prince Bismarck to that effect; that it was too great and grave a business to be hurried; but that, probably, about the time Lord Salisbury had returned to England, Count Münster would have received a reply from the Chancellor.[1]

The Queen in her reply took strongly the point which Beaconsfield had at once raised with Münster. Bismarck should certainly, Her Majesty thought, not be entirely discouraged, 'but we must not alienate France. . . . If we ally ourselves with Germany and Austria, France might join with Russia and Italy, which would be very serious.' Salisbury was disposed to think that, in then existing circumstances, we should have to aid Austria if she were attacked by Russia, whether we were allied, or not, to the Central Powers.

To Lord Salisbury.

HUGHENDEN, *Oct.* 1, 1879.—. . . What B.'s game may exactly be, I venture not to say, but, no doubt, he is a man who, if he have cards in his hand, will play them. The question is, whether, at this moment, his game is not ours ?

There is a preponderant impression here, that the general policy of our Government may be good, but that we have been unskilful or unfortunate in managing its details, so that we have not adequately achieved our purpose.

That purpose, in the mind of the country, is the maintenance of our Empire, and hostility to Russia. Notwithstanding the general depression, a fear of Russia, as the Power that will ultimately strike at the root of our Empire, is singularly prevalent, and is felt even by those, who do not publicly, or loudly, express it. I believe that an alliance between the three Powers in question, at this moment, might probably be hailed with something like enthusiasm by the country. It would explain many passages, that are now ambiguous or unsatisfactory. They would, then, be treated as parts of one coherent whole. I will not use the poet's more ambitious epithet: I will leave that to the country.

The great difficulty, if we adopt this policy, is how to make

[1] Count Münster's version of this conversation, which differs markedly from Beaconsfield's, especially in attributing to the latter the first mention of an 'alliance,' is published in *German Diplomatic Documents*, Vol. I., ch. 10.

it known.   I carefully avoided using the word ' treaty ' in my
conversation with M[ünster].   Yet it might be worth considering, whether some treaty between the three Allies, not formally
and avowedly for the great object, but with reference to some
practical point connected with it, might not be expedient;
but these matters are too vast and intricate to write about,
and we shall soon meet. . . .

I would just observe, however, that supposing I am wrong
in my assumption as to the effect of this alliance on the
immediate opinion of England, and we retire from office, we
shall retire as the representatives of a strong and intelligent
policy, and the advantage of this will be felt by the Tory
party hereafter

I think you would gain nothing by pumping Waddington.
We know what is in that well.   Were it, otherwise, worth
while to do so, you would gain nothing.   France could not,
in reason, object to our assisting Austria, if attacked by
Russia; particularly if she remember the Tripartite
Treaty. . . .

Presumably Bismarck was not satisfied with Beaconsfield's friendly but indecisive attitude.   At any rate,
Münster about a fortnight later had a general talk with
Salisbury in the Foreign Office without making any
reference to the proposal submitted at Hughenden.
Beaconsfield was determined, very rightly, to explore
the situation, and urged Salisbury himself to open the
matter with Münster.

To Lord Salisbury.

HUGHENDEN MANOR, *Oct.* 14, 1879.—. . . What I would
suggest for your consideration is, that you should see M. before
his departure, and frankly open on the whole matter.

Make any use of my name you like, and throw any blame
upon me, wh. may be expedient, as to my clumsiness in the
negotiation.

We gain nothing by reserve, as it seems to me.   If Bismarck
sees, which it is desirable that he should see, that it is our
determination, in the event of European complications, not
to be neutral and non-interfering, but to act, and to act with
allies, he will fear, what he does at present, probably, a little
fear, that we should ally ourselves with France, and, it might
be, Russia too.   After he has once broken his mind to us
and so confidentially as he has done, it is our interest, I think,
to fathom the affair.

From Lord Salisbury.

Confidential.   HATFIELD, *Wednesday, Oct.* 15, '79.—Münster is here now, and I have had a long talk with him about our matter. . . .

I stated to him our view—that Austria's position in Europe was a matter in which we took deep interest, and considered essential: that, if Russia attacked Germany and Austria, Germany might rely on our being on her side. I said, ' I suppose the service you would want of us would be to influence France and Italy to observe neutrality.' He replied that was their object : that Metz and Strasburg made them tolerably safe from all attack on the south part of the frontier; but that they were open through Belgium, and they wished to feel confident that we should not tolerate an attack through Belgium. Of that, I said, he might feel confident; and I was pretty sure that we could prevent any French Government from joining Russia against him; but that he might rely on our goodwill and assistance in the contingency of an attack on Austria and Germany.

It was all very much in the sense and tone of his conversation with you: but it left the impression on my mind that since he had spoken to you there had been a slight change of mind: and that B. is not so keen now as then. . . .

Nothing further came from Berlin about the proposed triple alliance between Germany, Austria, and England. But on October 27 Karolyi, the Austrian Ambassador, announced to Salisbury the conclusion of the famous Austro-German Alliance, without any allusion to the possibility of including England as a third party. The memorandum which Salisbury drew up for the Queen shows the manner in which this covenant was originally represented by its framers.

Lord Salisbury to Queen Victoria :

Memorandum of interview on October 27, 1879, *between Lord Salisbury and Count Karolyi.*

Most Secret.   The Austrian Ambassador formally announced to-day (though under pledge of the strictest secrecy) a defensive alliance between Germany and Austria. He said that its object was purely the maintenance of the general peace and of the state of things established by the Berlin Treaty. It had been proposed by Prince Bismarck to Count Andrassy: the

Prince having become 'frightened' by the attitude of the Russian Government. The two Empires had agreed that for the little matters which still remained to be executed by the Berlin Treaty (chiefly questions of delimitation) they would observe a most conciliatory attitude, so long as Russia did the same: but if on them, or for any other causes, Russia were to attack either Empire, they had agreed to treat it as an attack on both of them. He insisted that it was an alliance having for its object the maintenance of peace and the *status quo*: that Austria having obtained Bosnia was satisfied and entertained no projects of *convoitise*: that if Turkey were to fall, an event which he did not affect to regard as very distant, Austria would neither desire to take her place, nor would suffer Russia to do so; but would do her best to strengthen the 'little States,' and the actual inhabitants, whoever they were, in their resistance to invasion. He concluded by saying that this communication had been made to England only; and that the two Empires earnestly hoped that it would be a gratifying one to your Majesty's Government.

Lord Salisbury replied that the intelligence would be received by your Majesty and the Cabinet with great gratification as they would see in it a pledge for European peace. He expressed a confidence that, if in the lapse of years the Turkish Empire should fall, the difficult questions arising out of that result would be settled only after an intimate consultation between the three Powers, and he asked whether the agreement was a written one. To this question Count Karolyi would give no direct answer: but only said that it was a 'serious engagement,' and if the events it provided against took place, it would be followed by acts.

He said that the German Emperor had been brought to approve of it with great difficulty and only after great pressure from Prince Bismarck. He concluded by repeating his exhortations to secrecy.

Probably the 'great gratification' which Salisbury expressed to Karolyi at the receipt of the news, and his public description of the mere rumour of it as 'glad tidings of great joy,' gave Bismarck all he wished. 'The German Empire in alliance with Austria,' Bismarck wrote to the King of Bavaria, 'would not lack the support of England.'[1] He had found it difficult enough to obtain the consent of his pro-Russian master, the German

[1] See Grant Robertson's *Bismarck*, p. 346.

Emperor, to the Austrian treaty; he would have encountered still more opposition from him to the inclusion of
England in it. Moreover, so long as England, at that
time Russia's principal antagonist on the stage of the
world, was omitted from the treaty, there was room for
that 'reinsurance' with Russia which he always kept
before his mind as desirable.

Bismarck's omission to prosecute his overture relieved
the Cabinet from a difficulty. Both the Queen and
Northcote, who was at this period Minister in attendance
at Balmoral, felt very strongly the danger of alienating
France. Her Majesty feared, she wrote, that Bismarck's
proposal was meant ' to paralyse France as much as against
Russia; and that we may be drawn into a trap.' Even
Beaconsfield, though he considered that danger to be
over-estimated, held that it was not unfortunate that the
affair should have ended without forfeiting the sympathy
either of the Central Powers or of France.

To Queen Victoria.

10, DOWNING STREET, *Nov.* 5, 1879.—Lord Beaconsfield . . .
duly received the letter of the Chancellor of the Exchequer expressing yr. Majesty's views on the subject of the alliance
with Austria and Germany. . . .

When Count Münster left Hughenden, it was with the intention of communicating to Prince Bismarck the result of his
conference with Lord Beaconsfield, and to ask the Prince's
authority to speak on the subject to Lord Salisbury. Count
Münster then calculated that he should receive an answer
from Prince Bismarck in about a week or ten days. Whether
the Prince was disappointed by the reserve shown on the
general subject by Lord Beaconsfield, or was offended by
Lord Beaconsfield insisting on immediate communication of
the proposal to yr. Majesty and the Secretary of State, or
whether some sudden change had taken place in the circumstances at Berlin, or whether Count Münster blundered from
the first, or whatever the cause, the fact remains, that P.
Bismarck never wrote to Count Münster and has never
subsequently written to him, nor has the Prince seen Count
Münster during his last visit to Germany; in fact, the Prince
declined to see him. The secret note from Count Andrassy
was a communication from Austria, not from Germany, and,

though Count Münster, on Monday last, read a similar note to Lord Salisbury, the two identical notes only announced a defensive alliance between Austria and Germany, in no sense inviting, or soliciting, the adhesion of England.

This is all very strange, but, in Lord Beaconsfield's opinion, by no means unfortunate. It would have been a difficult, and even dangerous, affair to have altogether rejected the contemplated alliance; and, although from the interviews of M. Waddington and Lord Salisbury at Dieppe, an estrangement from France would not have, necessarily, occurred, still it would have been an event, which might have chilled the reciprocal feelings of yr. Majesty's Government and that of Paris. At present yr. Majesty is as free as air, and that, too, without showing any want of sympathy with the Austro-German views.[1] . . .

An hour was occupied [at the Cabinet yesterday] in discussing the question of dissolution. With one exception, every Minister was in favour of postponing the dissolution, provided no new tax were proposed. The Chancellor of the Exchequer observed silence, which Lord Beaconsfield will not describe as ominous. All, however, depends on his decision. If he will only do what Mr. Pitt did—what a humbler man, Lord Beaconsfield, did in 1858—and not attempt an artificial sinking fund in the teeth of new taxes, all would be right. The best way, however, with Sir Stafford is not to press him prematurely. He will have good advice from many quarters, and Lord Beaconsfield thinks will feel the impropriety of levying fresh taxation, when the industry of the country is only just recovering from almost unprecedented depression.

The Cabinet meets again to-day, the subject, Ireland. . . .

It was, no doubt, with recollections of this overture from Bismarck in his mind, that Beaconsfield vindicated, in the most striking passage of his Guildhall speech, England's place and high responsibility in the councils of Europe.

In assuming that peace will be maintained, I assume also that no Great Power would shrink from its responsibilities. If there be a country, for example, one of the most extensive and wealthiest of empires in the world—if that country, from a perverse interpretation of its insular geographical position, turns an indifferent ear to the feelings and the fortunes of Continental Europe, such a course would, I believe,

---

[1] ' We are well out of it ' wrote the Queen in reply.

only end in its becoming an object of general plunder. So long as the power and advice of England are felt in the councils of Europe, peace, I believe, will be maintained, and maintained for a long period. Without their presence, war, as has happened before, and too frequently of late, seems to me to be inevitable. I speak on this subject with confidence to the citizens of London, because I know that they are men who are not ashamed of the Empire which their ancestors created; because I know that they are not ashamed of the noblest of human sentiments, now decried by philosophers—the sentiment of patriotism; because I know they will not be beguiled into believing that in maintaining their Empire they may forfeit their liberties. One of the greatest of Romans, when asked what were his politics, replied, *Imperium et Libertas*. That would not make a bad programme for a British Ministry. It is one from which Her Majesty's advisers do not shrink.

In this speech Beaconsfield had the satisfaction of being able to congratulate the City on the signs of a revival in trade, after a depression which had lasted nearly as long as his Government. With his customary shrewdness he singled out for notice, ' as significant of the general prosperity of commerce,' the manufacture of chemicals, an industry which, he said, was then so active that it was difficult to execute the orders which were pouring in. The laughter and scorn, with which contemporary critics greeted this selection of an apparently obscure trade as typical, appear very foolish now, when chemists and chemistry are universally recognised as dominating manufacture.

But, though Beaconsfield could point to a revival of commerce, he said nothing, as there was no cheering news to give, about agriculture, an industry which touched him more nearly. T. E. Kebbel has truly said that the landed interest of England was, to the day of Beaconsfield's death, ' the object of his devotion; and on it he constantly maintained that the greatness of England had been reared.' What was its condition now ? ' No one,' he had said in Parliament in the spring of this year,[1] ' can deny that the depression of the agricultural interest

---

[1] March 28.

is excessive. Though I can recall several periods of suffering, none of them have ever equalled the present in its intenseness. . . . The remarkable feature of the present agricultural depression is this—that the agricultural interest is suffering from a succession of bad harvests, and that these bad harvests are accompanied for the first time by extremely low prices. . . . In old days, when we had a bad harvest, we had also the somewhat dismal compensation of higher prices. That is not the condition of the present; on the contrary the harvests are bad, and the prices are lower. ' This was because of the foreign competition which was the inevitable result of Peel's action in 1846. ' The immense importations of foreign agricultural produce have been vastly in excess of what the increased demands of our population actually require. And that is why such low prices are maintained.'

There had consequently arisen from the agricultural interest loud demands for the removal of the burdens on real property, for reciprocity, and finally for full-blown Protection; and landlords and farmers naturally quoted in favour of these policies what Beaconsfield called in the House of Lords 'speeches which I myself made, in another place, and in another generation,' ' musty phrases of mine forty years ago.' In two speeches in Parliament, on March 28 and April 29, Beaconsfield explained why none of the suggested remedies could now be adopted. The first policy, the relief of the burdens on real property, had largely been carried out under his own Government: the rates had been relieved of pauper lunatics, registration, police, and prisons. No serious relief for land could be obtained from further readjustment. As for reciprocity, when he himself advocated it, there were elements on which treaties of reciprocity could be negotiated. Now there were none.

At that time, although the great changes of Sir Robert Peel had taken place, there were 168 articles in the tariff which were materials by which you could have negotiated, if that was a wise and desirable policy, commercial treaties of

reciprocity.   What is the number you now have in the tariff ?
Twenty-two.   Those who talk of negotiating treaties of
reciprocity—have they the materials for negotiating treaties
of reciprocity ?   You have lost the opportunity.   I do not
want to enter into the argument, at the present moment,
whether this was wise or not; but the policy which was long
ago abandoned you cannot resume.

Reciprocity, whatever its merits, was dead.   England
had lost the power of building up a reciprocal system of
commercial treaties.

Still less could general Protection be resumed.   A whole
session had been devoted to the discussion before the
Corn Laws were repealed.   The distress which followed
repeal kept the controversy alive for several years, but
all efforts to obtain from the constituencies a verdict in
favour of the reversal of the policy of 1846 failed.   ' Under
these circumstances it was impossible for public men,
whatever might have been their opinions upon these great
commercial questions when these important changes were
first introduced, to have had an open controversy for a
quarter of a century.   The Government of the country
could not have been carried on.   It was necessary to bow
to the decision of Parliament and the country, expressed
by its representatives in both Houses, and ultimately
by an appeal to the whole nation itself.'   In other words,
Protection, like reciprocity, was, for the Victorian epoch,
dead; and practical statesmen would not waste time in
discussing its virtues.   But it must be supposed that
Beaconsfield was still of opinion that Protection, if
practicable, would have been the only policy to restore
the landed interest, as he appeared to be bankrupt of
other ideas on the question.   He certainly propounded
no remedy of his own for the woeful state of agriculture,
except a vague reliance upon ' the energy of this country.'
He was not disposed in April even to grant a Royal
Commission, but subsequent debates in the House of
Commons caused him to change his mind, and such a
Commission was appointed at the end of the session under
the chairmanship of the Duke of Richmond.

II.

44

As the Tory leader had no specific, the Radicals were the more emboldened to press for revision of the land laws in the direction of eliminating landowners and setting up peasant proprietors in their place. And even the Whig Hartington said that, if Mr. Chaplin and his friends had made out their case, the land system of England had broken down—that unique system under which 'the cultivation of the soil is carried on by a class of men who are not the owners of the soil, and who are not the actual cultivators of the soil.' Beaconsfield at once rallied to the defence of that ordered scheme of country life, landlord, farmer, and labourer, which he admired: and evolved a noteworthy theory about the three profits necessarily derived from the land. This he propounded to the world in his speech at the Mansion House at the close of the session. Here is the crucial passage.

Look at the peasant proprietor. The peasant buys a farm, ten, fifteen, or twenty acres, and pays for it out of his earnings previously invested in the public funds of his country, or, as is often the case, with money borrowed from a banker in his neighbourhood. The interest paid to the banker, or that which represents what the peasant derived from his previous investment, is the first income of the soil, and may be said to represent rent. Then the peasant proprietor has to stock his farm and to supply the machinery which is to cultivate the soil. He has to buy, if not a plough, many spades, barrows, and other instruments; he has to build a cart, purchase a horse, whose manure is necessary for the due cultivation of the soil; he has to raise some building, however modest; a barn, at least a shed. All this floating capital and its wear and tear demand and receive the second income from the soil, and represent the farmer's return. Having purchased his farm and then stocked it, the peasant proprietor, and probably his sons, proceed to cultivate the soil, and during their labours they must be fed and clothed, and nurtured and lodged, and that is an income which in this country we should call wages. But it is the third income which the land is obliged to produce under the tenure of peasant proprietorship. I wish it then to be impressed on the sense of this nation that the three incomes which land must, under any circumstances, produce are in England distributed among three classes, and on the land where peasant proprietorship prevails they are

devoted only to one class. The number and variety of classes
in England dependent on land are sources of our strength.
They have given us the proprietors of the soil, the constructors
of our liberty in a great degree, and the best security for local
government; they have given us the farmers, who cultivate
and improve their estates, and lastly the agricultural peasant,
whose lot is deplored by those not acquainted with it, but who
has during the last forty years made more continuous progress
than any other class in Her Majesty's dominions.

Beaconsfield developed this ingenious, if somewhat
fanciful, theme in a long speech which he made on September 18, after his frequent autumnal custom, to his
county Agricultural Association at Aylesbury. The
occasion weighed heavily on him in prospect, as he told
Lady Bradford on September 2: 'I have another
affair hanging over me, which horribly distresses and
depresses me; to be President, in about a fortnight, of
the Royal Bucks Agricultural Association; at all times
a painful effort, but at this moment, so critical in the
agricultural world, entailing on me more thought and
labor than if I had to bring forward a great measure in
Parliament.' He would not admit, he said, that the
agricultural system of England had broken down. There
was distress, but not decadence. He maintained that
the distribution of the three profits from the land gave us
three valuable classes on the land instead of one; and
quoted statistics to show that production per acre in
England under the triple system was double that of France
under the system of peasant proprietors. He discussed
the uncertain conditions of transatlantic competition
with a view of discouraging precipitate action; at home,
moreover, bad harvests would before long be replaced by
good ones. But there was ample reason for rent reduction
by landlords, who he was sure would be ready to stand by
their farmers. Then full use should be made of his own
Agricultural Holdings Act, which secured compensation
to the farmer for unexhausted improvements. Finally
he bade his country hearers beware of Cockney agitators
sent out by the party which always viewed the agricul-

tural interest with hostility. ' But a year ago, they were setting the agricultural labourers against the farmers; now they are attempting to set the farmers against the landlords.' These men were opposed to our 'free and aristocratic government. You may get rid of that government, gentlemen; but if you do you will have either a despotism that ends in democracy, or a democracy that ends in despotism.'

Patience, liberal reductions of rent, compensation for tenants' unexhausted improvements—these constituted Beaconsfield's prescription for the immediate trouble. He had manifested his own belief in the future of agricultural property by adding at this season to his Hughenden estate; but his letters show the straits to which his friends among the big landlords were driven.

To Lady Bradford.

10, DOWNING STREET, *Oct.* 7.—I hope you have won the race,[1] wh. is possible, as they say ' everybody has his turn,' tho' I have heard the apophthegm in coarser tongue.

They say now, however, as the consequence of the landed break-up, that there are to be no more turf, and no more London seasons. All our friends have shut up their houses, or are to do so. It will be an excuse for some, who ought to have done so under any circumstances.

There is no doubt of one; Burghley ! But this, I think, must be her ladyship's temper as much as his l[ordshi]p's ruin. A good many more were mentioned at the Council yesterday, but I have forgotten them, so I hope they may not be true.

To my surprise, how[eve]r, your friend Duke of R[ichmond] and G[ordon], who throughout has been quite sceptical of smash, announced that his news, from Sussex, was the very worst, and that his men, with leases, were throwing up ! I am sorry for the country, still more for him, whom I like. . . For myself, I could live in a garret provided it was well white-washed, and very clean.

I came up yesterday early to see S[alisbury], a very long con-ference, and then Cab., still longer—and now I am returning, in 10 mins., to H[ughenden] with[ou]t any news from Cabul. It looks as if there had been, or rather was, a battle, for they may be still fighting. So much the better. . . .

[1] The Cesarewitch, which was won by Lord Bradford's horse, Chippendale.

HUGHENDEN MANOR, *Oct.* 9.—I smelt gunpowder in my last letter, and it has come.[1] I wish Roberts had more force. It is clear that, from the first, we have suffered from want of transport, and, tho' there are troops eno', they are still at too great a distance.

However, I will only think of yr. own victory, which is very triumphant. I wrote a line of congratulation to Bradford yesterday, who, being Master of the Horse, deserves to win. My household is much excited by the event. I suspect B.'s valet must have 'put them on.' I fear they are all on the turf—even Mr. Baum.

The peacocks are beginning to get proud again, their tails developing as the leaves fall. . . .

The Aylesbury and Guildhall speeches were Beaconsfield's only contributions to the oratory of the autumn. But in view of the fact that the Parliament had completed six out of a possible seven sessions and that therefore dissolution could not be far distant, the outpouring this year was immense on both sides. All other efforts, however, paled beside Gladstone's Midlothian 'pilgrimage of passion,' with its herculean programme, its undiscriminating denunciation of the Beaconsfield Government and all their works, its arrogant claim to be fighting the battle of 'justice, humanity, freedom, law'[2] against the powers of darkness. This outburst, which occupied the last week of November and the first week of December, did not disturb Beaconsfield's autumn routine of incessant work at Hughenden and in London, varied by an occasional visit for a day or two to friends. At the close of Gladstone's campaign he wrote to Cranbrook: 'It certainly is a relief that this drenching rhetoric has at length ceased; but I have never read a word of it. *Satis eloquentiæ, sapientiæ parum.*'

To Lady Bradford.

HATFIELD HOUSE, *Nov.* 1.—. . . I believe the only foundation for the sudden surmise of a dissolution was Willie Dyke paying his annual visit to Hughenden, and Charley Carington,

---

[1] The Battle of Charasiab.
[2] Quoted from Gladstone's Diary for December 28, 1879. Morley's *Gladstone*, Book XII., ch. 6.

that genius, immediately telegraphing to Sir Wm. Harcourt that all was arranged, and dissolution instant. I have heard no single valid reason why a loyal Parliament shd. be submitted to such an injury and insult as a reward for their faithful services and support. . . .

10, DOWNING STREET, *Nov.* 5.—As you say, a heavy, a very heavy week. I'd be very glad were it as short as that. Cabs. every day. I have just come up from the Cabt. and was told that poor Schou[valoff], who called on me yesterday to say farewell, was waiting for me in the reception room. He is recalled, and alas ! not to be Minister or anything : his successor Prince Lobanoff. . . .

This is incoherent; as Schou. said, ' You are breathless and exhausted with your Cabinet; so I will be short.'

Nov. 9.—. . . The City dinner to-morrow is always an exhausting affair, and I am sorry to say I am not free from my old foe. It always attacks me about this time, and after two months of health, I began to think I was immortal. I feel very much the reverse at this moment. . . .

To Anne Lady Chesterfield.

10, DOWNING STREET, *Nov.* 13, '79.—I am very sorry about your dog. I have a collie of Monty's standing on his hind legs, and begging to be noticed, by me at this very moment. His shaggy coat is beautiful in texture and color, and his eyes like precious stones, yet full of intelligence and humanity : a most sensible and agreeable companion. But then they die too soon, and, in their youth, are apt to meet mischances like yours. Distemper is a terrible mystery. I had a collie once, who suffered terribly, but I saved his life by frequent, but very slight, doses of port wine, recommended by a vet. at Beaconsfield.

The dinner at the Guildhall was very successful. It was the most crowded banquet that Gog and Magog ever looked down upon. . . .

To Lady Bradford.

10, DOWNING STREET, *Nov.* 16, '79.—. . . We seem to be in for a premature hard black frost, and I cannot venture out, but I am pretty well. . . .

Of course, you know they expelled Labouchere from the B[eef]steak Club. I doubt the justice of the Committee and their friends in this particular instance, but they did rightly in seizing an occasion to show the disgust of society at the originator of what are called ' society ' papers. There is no excuse for Labouchere. Born with, or to, every advantage, good abilities, large fortune, first-rate education, a member of an illustrious profession, and, while quite young, member for the metrop. county, he sacrifices England for Bohemia, and lives with bravoes and ruffians, whose natural business it is to poison society. . . .

Nov. 24.—I am writing to you by candlelight, and so it has been for these days past; with no change, except to-day, they say, there is a dreary thaw, and that the hard black frost has gone, or is going. . . .

Schou. luncheoned here, I think on Friday. . . . I have succeeded in getting him his farewell audience for Thursday next, for wh. he seems greatly obliged to me. I hope the Queen may invite him to dine. After all, he is the only Russian who at least pretends to be our friend, and his disgrace at his own Court is attributable to his supposed friendliness to this country. Really it means his friendship to peace and common sense, neither of wh. are popular at St. Petersburg.

I offered Henry Lennox the Deputy Governorship of the New Forest, wh. half the world is candidate for. All my colleagues, to whom I broke my intention, protested against my madness in so doing. Will you believe it, that Henry declined the post, and also, if it became vacant, a Commissionership of Customs, wh. he understood I was reserving for him. He will not leave the House of Commons, or take anything but a high post: he absolutely intimated the Cabinet ! ! Don't say anything about this. . . .

Nov. 26.—I am now going to have my audience at Windsor —at $\frac{1}{2}$ past two, tho' our Sovereign does not arrive until betn. 9 and 10 this morning ! What nerve ! what muscle ! what energy ! Her Minister is very deficient in all three. The fogs and frosts of this harsh November have terribly knocked me down. . . .

HUGHENDEN MANOR, *Nov.* 28.—. . . You are quite right. I have not read a single line of all this row,[1] but Monty has told me something, and has promised me to make notes, in case it fall to my lot to notice his wearisome rhetoric. What a waste of powder and shot ! Because all this was planned on the wild assumption, that Parlt. was going to be dissolved, whereas, as Sir George Bowyer, apparently from authority, has just informed the world, Parlt. will probably not be dissolved till the year after next. . . . Monty is of great use to me, and therefore goes off to-morrow ! Such is life. . . .

Nov. 29.—. . . I have had not a moment to look at the papers to-day, save glancing at *The Times:* most amused at their quoting my description of the oratory of the Impetuous Hypocrite, wh., when it was first uttered, they disapproved !

---

[1] Gladstone's Midlothian campaign.

Dec. 1.—. . . There is a Cabinet on Wednesday. . . . Awful to go up, and return, in this dreadful weather; the snow now falling fast, and the frost continuing. . . .

Poor Roebuck gone! His Privy Councillorship made his last hours tranquil, if not content. Never was such an unsuccessful career except poor Joseph Hume's, who, tho' he was perpetually making, or saving, Ministries, was not even made a P. Councillor. I was more generous.

Dec. 8.—Your letters are most agreeable to me, and tho' they are not a compensation for yr. society at Crichel, wh. I shall probably never see again, they are a solace.

My visits there, and at most places, are rather artificial. I always feel there is nothing in common between me and the other guests, and tho' in theory we are living, when you are a guest, under the same roof, in practice our companionship is very slight. A forced walk in the morning at a disagreeable hour, always necessarily short, and then come carriages, in wh. I never enter, and wh. you always do—and must always do—and I am alone, while you are luncheoning with sporting heroes. I think, therefore, I shall never leave my own roof again: no one can be offended, for, unless there is a change, wh. it is difficult to foresee, I have told the Faery the same thing, and will not go now even to Windsor, tho' I believe from the top of my highest hill the Castle is in sight.

I read a despatch yesterday from Odo Russ[ell], very curious: not a private letter to Ld. S[alisbury], but a regular despatch, ' very confidential.' It gives an account of a very confidential conversation with Cte. St. Vallier, the French Ambassador at Berlin, as to his recent visit to Bismarck at Varzin.

He found the great man in much better health than the newspapers report, ' reading over again all Lord Beaconsfield's novels.' He told St. Vallier that a first-rate work of fiction was the only thing that gave him distraction; that riding, shooting, farming, planting, and hunting, even wolves and wild boars, he still was thinking of politics; but with a fine novel, he was quite lost.

He said he had never written works of fiction, because he cd. not do two things at the same time; that all the *creative* power that he had, he gave to politics, otherwise he shd. probably write novels; and he said a good deal more. He was very frank and satisfactory, according to St. Vallier, as to general politics.

What Bismarck says as to writing fiction is perfectly true. I have told you the same thing. I never cd. do two things at the same time; at least 2 wh. required the creative power.

When I was made Leader of the Opposition, I was obliged

to leave off writing; from *Tancred*, my last then, to *Lothair* 23 years, and from *Loth.* nine years, being a Minister.

Dec. 17.—. . . Visit to the Faery very agreeable. It was a perpetual audience, and, at last, daughters tapped at the door at ¼ to 9 before dinner to break up the charming flow. . . .

Once more Beaconsfield spent a solitary Christmas at Hughenden, waiting for news of Roberts, whom a sudden rising of the tribes had beleaguered at Sherpur, near Cabul. He was not well. 'The fact is,' he told Lady Bradford, 'I have scarcely been out of the house for six weeks, in order to save my chest, and have knocked up one's nervous system a little in consequence.' Happily his anxiety was relieved by Indian telegrams on December 28. 'I believe,' he told his friend, 'the smash of the enemy is complete, nor do I think they will again rally. I expect to meet Parliament, both as regards Asia and Africa, with a clean bill of health.' Accordingly he began the new year in fair spirits and, he told the Queen, in better health owing to the quiet life which he had led.

To Lady Bradford.

HUGHENDEN MANOR, *Jan.* 1, '80.—I hate anniversaries as much as you do: but you wd. be amused with the various 'kind wishes' I have received this morning. I won't dwell on Sandringham, or Bruxelles, tho' one was a Princess, and the other a Queen, but I think you would be diverted by one from the Prince of Bagdad, my 'devoted, tho' distant, admirer.' I remember him in this country, when he made one of those civilising visits the Orientals are fond of.

Osborne has sent me, as an *étrenne,* a most beautiful book, so rich in illustrations of the Teutonic, Italian, and English schools of art that, I am sure, it will occupy and delight you on your next visit here.

Our news is very good this morning from the seat of war. Baker has returned from a successful expedition, and the ascertained loss of the enemy on the 23-4 was 3,000: ours not half 300. There has been nothing like it in point of numbers since Agincourt.

After the visit of the Prince of Wales to Hughenden, Beaconsfield went up to town to prepare for the opening of Parliament, and, in spite of his indifferent health, resumed his practice of dining out. Perhaps as the result, he was once more confined to his room by illness —a misfortune which he shared with Salisbury and other important colleagues.

To Lady Bradford.

10, DOWNING ST., *Jan.* 19.—As you have seen, business is very pressing: Cabinets every day since I came up, and we only do not meet in the morning, because the expected Indian mail has not yet arrived. . . . I dined on Saturday at Gloucester House—a royal party, but very agreeable, and a first-rate dinner, wh. even Prince Hal, very curious in such matters, noticed with much praise. The Tecks were there: Princess Louise to whom the dinner was given. . . .

Yesterday I dined at Stafford House: a dinner also given to Pss. L[ouise]—a farewell one, as she departs[1] on Wedy. . . . P. Hal was there, but no other royalties, but a miscellaneous and an æsthetical crew, to interest and amuse the Queen of Canada. . . .

Jan. 23.—. . . I have not been out since Monday, and been obliged to ask Dr. Kidd to call on me, which is a bore. The worst is that Salisbury has knocked up; and in the very heat and crisis of affairs, with daily Cabinets, Queen's Speeches and new Russian Ambassadors, is ordered not to attend to business; a feverish attack, which always frightens one. . . . Don't say anything to the world about Salisbury, as the enemy will triumph. . . .

Jan. 25.—. . . Lady Salisbury writes a better acc[oun]t of her husband. The fever much diminished, and nearly gone, but very weak. We have a Cab. to-morrow, the second he cannot attend, at a time, too, when I most want him.

(*In pencil*). *Thursday* [*Jan.* 29].—I am unable to move; Salisbury is confined to his room at Hatfield, and must do no work; the Ld. Chancellor, attacked by asthma for the first time, was so frightened that he rushed to Bournemouth, where he found the fog blacker than here; the Chr. of the Exchequer is in bed with influenza; Sandon is at Liverpool;[2] where John Manners' broken bones are I hardly know. But if there had been a Cabinet to-day, *six* wd. have been absent. . . .

Feb. 5.—. . . I was obliged to give up any share in the ceremony,[3] wh. with the dinner of yesterday and the debate of this evening was beyond my physical powers. So the

---

[1] For Canada.
[2] Where there was a by-election in progress.
[3] Of the opening of Parliament by the Queen.

sword of state was carried by yr. friend the Duke of R. and G., and the D. of Northumberland was consoled by [? for] his never having anything to do, by bearing the Crown—rather a weighty and difficult office. . . .

I hope to be in my place in H. of L. in two hours' time, but I have not yet put on a boot, and am as shaky as a man can be, who has been shut up for two weeks.

Feb. 6.—. . . I had great difficulty in speaking last night, and what I did say I said very badly. . . .

Altogether an ill-omened beginning for the final session of the 1874 Parliament.

CHAPTER XIV.

DISSOLUTION AND DEFEAT.

1880.

When Ministers met Parliament, they had come to no conclusion as to the date of dissolution. The choice lay between the spring and the autumn; and their disposition, in which their chief concurred, was on the whole to allow the Parliament to run its course, and hold the elections in the autumn. A dissolution in the spring was hardly even possible until certain measures had been passed to relieve distress in Ireland. Once more the affairs of that unhappy country, which had dominated the General Election of 1868 and the Parliament then elected, but which had occupied a more moderate share of Ministerial and Parliamentary attention since 1874, forced themselves insistently upon the Cabinet, though they had by no means as yet similarly affected the public mind.

Froude has blamed Disraeli for not seizing in 1874 'the opportunity to reorganise the internal government of Ireland.' He suggests that the land question might have been adjusted on equitable lines, the authority of the law restored, nationalist visions extinguished, and a permanent settlement arrived at, but he gives us no clue to the scheme by which these desirable results might have been achieved. Froude's is a perverse judgment, which takes no account of the conditions in which Disraeli was called to power. One of the causes which produced the Conservative majority was resentment at the disproportionate preoccupation of Government and Parliament with Ireland. The desire and intention of the electorate were to give heroic legislation a pause, and to proceed with social reform.　Gladstone had passed two great and revolutionary Irish measures, the Church Act and the Land Act, which, with a University Bill still to be passed, were to bring appeasement to a distracted country. Disraeli had not agreed with the policy of these measures; but they were now in force, and it was the obvious duty of his Government to give them time to work and to produce all the healing effects of which they were capable, while maintaining the authority of the law and assisting social improvement.　Such was the policy of Abercorn and Hicks Beach, Disraeli's first Lord-Lieutenant and Chief Secretary—a policy continued by their successors, Marlborough and James Lowther.　They even succeeded in completing Gladstone's original scheme by passing in 1879, in addition to other educational measures, a University Act, which went a considerable way to meet the demands of Irish Roman Catholics for University privileges; and they administered the law with courage, and on the whole with success.　Though these proceedings hardly fulfilled Disraeli's expressed hope of governing Ireland ' according to the policy of Charles I. and not of Oliver Cromwell,' their aim was distinctly ameliorative; and perhaps the amelioration might have been quickened, had he been able to carry out the intention of visiting Ireland in person, which he had so much at heart in the first recess after his return to office in 1874.

Gladstone's legislation failed to effect its object, as Disraeli had said from the first that it was bound to fail. Instead of appeasing Irish discontent, it revived the old Repeal movement in a new guise.　Beginning as a constitutional agitation in which all might well join, the movement gradually took on a revolutionary form, as its guidance fell more and more under the direction of Parnell, acting on parallel lines with Davitt, a Fenian convict on ticket of leave.　The failure of the harvests in Ireland, as in England, gave the agitators a dangerous leverage on which to act.　Obstruction in the House of Commons, and in Ireland the withholding of rent—the

only interest in the land left by the Act of 1870 to the
Irish landlord—were creating in the autumn of 1879 a
dangerous situation, which was temporarily relieved by
a few judicious arrests. Beaconsfield, there is reason to
believe, was prepared to consider some sort of Federal
Constitution for Ireland—'your damnable, delightful
country,' as he called it in talking with David Plunket.
But, along with all British statesmen of his day, including
even the Gladstone of that epoch, he was profoundly
convinced that the United Kingdom, as the heart of the
Empire, must be preserved intact, and therefore strongly
resisted an agitation which in his opinion must, if successful, result in separation

To cope, however, with the real distress produced by a
succession of bad harvests, he and the Irish Government
promoted immediate relief legislation, which should
meet the many cases of undeserved misfortune not provided for by a great voluntary fund organised in Ireland
under the direction of the Duchess of Marlborough, the
Lord-Lieutenant's wife. He was resolved to prevent
the possibility of the recurrence of such a calamity as
befell Ireland in 1848. Other Irish measures which were
under discussion in the Cabinet during the winter, but on
which no final decision had been taken, were the placing
of the surplus from the Disestablished Church Fund in
the hands of Commissioners as a Reproductive Loan Fund,
and the expansion of the Purchase Clauses of the Land
Act. The relief Bills, in spite of the benefits conferred
by them on suffering Irish agriculturists, were at once and
persistently obstructed by Parnellite members; and this
factious spirit threatened to make the continuance of the
Parliament impossible. But Ministers were at first still
loth to precipitate dissolution. Beaconsfield's correspondence with the Queen shows what considerations were
uppermost in his and their minds. The Queen feared,
she wrote, that the Irish Home Rule members would
make it impossible to go on with the Session. But would
they be better in another Parliament ?

From Queen Victoria.

OSBORNE, *Feb.* 12, 1880.—. . . Ought you not to come to some agreement with some of the sensible, and reasonable and not violent men on the other side, to put a stop to what clearly is a determination to force the disruption of the British Empire ? It is a serious Constitutional question. Can the Queen personally do anything to facilitate matters ?

To Queen Victoria.

10, DOWNING STREET, *Feb.* 13, 1880.—. . . Even if it were advisable to dissolve Parliament, that is not so easy a process as seems upon the surface.

Yr. Majesty's Govt. might fairly hold, that the conduct of the Opposition exempts yr. Majesty's Ministers from the pledges, which they have given, to pass several measures of urgency—such as the 'Corrupt Practices Bill,' the 'Vacant Seats in the H. of Commons Bill'—before they advise yr. Majesty to empower them to go to the country. But even with this justifiable disregard of their engagements Parliament could not be dissolved without arranging the finances of the country, and passing the Mutiny Act, and this would place it in the power of the Opposition, greatly to delay the dissolution. . . .

Lord Beaconsfield believes that the time may come, when the interposition and personal influence of yr. Majesty may most beneficially be exercised in bringing about a more satisfactory state of the H. of Commons than now prevails. But Lord Beaconsfield fears, that nothing can be effected in this vein, until there is a new Parliament. There are no 'sensible and reasonable, and really not violent men' in the ranks of the Opposition on whom your Majesty might now act. The nominal leaders have no authority; and the mass, chiefly under the guidance and authority, or rather inspiration, of Mr. Gladstone, who avoids the responsibility of his position, are animated by an avidity for office such as Lord Beaconsfield, after more than forty years' experience, cannot recall.

Whether yr. Majesty's present Ministers have a majority at the impending election, or whether they have to cross the House, yr. Majesty's interposition might be equally efficacious, and the leading men of both parties would, then, be more free to carry your Majesty's patriotic intentions into effect.

Feb. 14.—. . . The Cabinet to-day considered the question of dissolution in all its forms and contingencies. They unanimously agreed, that nothing but a very critical state of affairs, such as menaced during the first week of the session, could authorise such a step, as it would justly be reproached to them, that, if dissolution were desired, it should have occurred in the late autumn.   If however the factious spirit were continued, or revived, then they would recommend yr. Majesty to appeal to your people at all risks.

The Chancellor of the Exchequer was in good heart, and said, tho' his plan was not yet strictly matured, it was his intention to make a financial proposition which would involve no additional taxation.   This declaration on his part will be worth more than, even, the elections at Liverpool and the Borough. . . .

Feb. 21.—. . . The debate in the House of Lords last night, it is to be hoped, will finish discussions on Afghanistan, until new events and circumstances happen and occur.   The Duke of Argyll made a most able review of matters on which the House of Lords had long ago decided.   Lord Beaconsfield endeavored to put an intelligible issue to the country.   The intrigues of Russia determined yr. Majesty's Govt. to secure the gates of India.   They have accomplished their purpose. Their policy has never changed, and the unsatisfactory accidents that have occurred have nothing to do with that policy, but are those casualties, which are inseparable from human affairs.

The state of business last night in the House of Commons augurs important events.   The Chancellor of the Exchequer gave notice of the intention of yr. Majesty's Govt. to grapple with the Obstructionists. . . .

Thus, in spite of Ministers' hesitation, the prevalence of faction in Parliament, which had obliged them at once to strengthen the Speaker's hands to deal with it, was bringing their minds round to contemplate the advisability of an immediate dissolution.   Other considerations pointed in the same direction.   Urgent legislative necessities were met by the passage of the Irish relief Bills into law early in March.   But, in the face of faction, it would be difficult to secure the renewal of the Peace Preservation Act, just about to expire.   And yet that, without such a renewal, Ireland, in the throes of an anti-rent agitation, would be ungovernable, Beaconsfield and the Irish Government were well assured, and the measure was drafted.   An immediate dissolution would provide a new Parliament, fresh from contact with the people's will, in sufficient time to deal with this imperative matter. In another respect dissolution would relieve the situation in the House of Commons, as a Home Office scheme for the purchase of the London Water Companies had met there with severe criticism on account of its apparently excessive generosity to existing shareholders. After Roberts's victories in Afghanistan, there was no serious difficulty in imperial or foreign affairs to stand in the way; and the recent revival of trade had put the business community in a better position to sustain the necessary disturbance of a General Election.

The electoral omens, moreover, seemed to be good. During the years of crisis in foreign affairs the Government had lost on balance some seats in the by-elections; but the House of Commons had supported them unswervingly, both moderate Liberals and Irish Home Rulers being often found in the Ministerial lobby; and three recent elections had suggested that the period of danger had passed. At Sheffield in December the Liberals had only retained by a small majority the seat to which Roebuck, who supported Ministers in foreign affairs, had been originally elected as a Radical. At Liverpool in February a Conservative held the seat by a majority of 2,000 in spite of a large Irish vote which was captured by the popular Liberal candidate on a Home Rule platform. And at Southwark in the same month a barrister, then unknown to political life, but whose eloquence and character must have won him many friends and votes— now Sir Edward Clarke, K.C.—captured for the Conservatives, contrary to all expectation, a seat with a long Liberal history.

If Government stood well with typical urban constituencies in Yorkshire, Lancashire, and London, there seemed no reason to hesitate; and accordingly at a Cabinet on March 6, held in Arlington Street on account of Lord Salisbury's illness, the fateful decision was taken to dissolve as soon as current business could be wound up.

To Queen Victoria.

10, Downing Street, *March* 6, 1880 —Lord Beaconsfield with his humble duty to your Majesty:

The Cabinet, just concluded, sate two hours and a half, and every member of it was requested to give his opinion: the members of the House of Commons having the priority.

There were various views, and some differences of opinion, but the ultimate result was unanimity.

The question, after exhausting arguments, really resolved itself to this: whether your Majesty should be advised to dissolve Parliament now, or in the late autumn.

The latter alternative was thought to involve too many risks; and perhaps was altogether impracticable, for the excitement of the existing House of Commons could hardly be restrained till that later period.

There is some difficulty about the day of dissolution, in consequence of the embarrassments of Easter,[1] and the hallowed claims of Passion Week. Your Majesty's visit to Baden may without difficulty be protracted, but your Majesty might perhaps graciously deign to consider the day of your Majesty's departure.

Lord Cranbrook, who will have the privilege of attending your Majesty this evening, will explain these matters, which now might weary your Majesty.

The Cabinet was held at Lord Salisbury's house, who looked better.

The announcement was made in both Houses on Monday, March 8, and next morning there appeared a manifesto from the Prime Minister, in the shape of a letter to the Lord-Lieutenant, in which he endeavoured to focus the attention of the electorate on the question of Ireland, and the dangers involved in the furious agitation there in progress. It will be remembered that at that period it was still held to be unconstitutional for peers to take any part in elections; and therefore it was only in some such indirect fashion as Beaconsfield adopted that the Prime Minister, if a peer, could appeal to the constituencies to support his Government.

To the Duke of Marlborough.

10, Downing Street, *March* 8, 1880.—The measures respecting the state of Ireland, which Her Majesty's Govern-

[1] March 28.

ment so anxiously considered with your Excellency, and in which they were much aided by your advice and authority, are now about to be submitted for the Royal Assent, and it is at length in the power of the Ministers to advise the Queen to recur to the sense of her people. The arts of agitators, which represented that England, instead of being the generous and sympathising friend, was indifferent to the dangers and the sufferings of Ireland, have been defeated by the measures, at once liberal and prudent, which Parliament has almost unanimously sanctioned.

During the six years of the present Administration the improvement of Ireland and the content of our fellow-countrymen in that island have much occupied the care of the Ministry, and they may remember with satisfaction that, in this period, they have solved one of the most difficult problems connected with its government and people, by establishing a system of public education open to all classes and all creeds.

Nevertheless a danger, in its ultimate results scarcely less disastrous than pestilence and famine, and which now engages your Excellency's anxious attention, distracts that country. A portion of its population is attempting to sever the Constitutional tie which unites it to Great Britain in that bond which has favoured the power and prosperity of both.

It is to be hoped that all men of light and leading will resist this destructive doctrine. The strength of this nation depends on the unity of feeling which should pervade the United Kingdom and its widespread dependencies. The first duty of an English Minister should be to consolidate that co-operation which renders irresistible a community educated, as our own, in an equal love of liberty and law.

And yet there are some who challenge the expediency of the imperial character of this realm. Having attempted, and failed, to enfeeble our colonies by their policy of decomposition, they may perhaps now recognise in the disintegration of the United Kingdom a mode which will not only accomplish but precipitate their purpose.

The immediate dissolution of Parliament will afford an opportunity to the nation to decide upon a course which will materially influence its future fortunes and shape its destiny.

Rarely in this century has there been an occasion more critical. The power of England and the peace of Europe will largely depend on the verdict of the country. Her Majesty's present Ministers have hitherto been enabled to secure that peace, so necessary to the welfare of all civilised countries, and so peculiarly the interest of our own. But this ineffable blessing cannot be obtained by the passive principle of non-interference. Peace rests on the presence, not to say the

ascendancy, of England in the councils of Europe. Even
at this moment, the doubt, supposed to be inseparable from
popular election, if it does not diminish, certainly arrests
her influence, and is a main reason for not delaying an appeal
to the national voice. Whatever may be its consequences
to Her Majesty's present advisers, may it return to West-
minister a Parliament not unworthy of the power of England,
and resolved to maintain it !

With the exception of the characteristically Disraelian
phrase,[1] 'men of light and leading,' this was not a very
happily worded document. Besides noticing a misused
' and which' in the third paragraph—a constantly
recurring inelegance of the writer's style—criticism justly
pounced on the clumsiness of a ' tie which unites ' nations
in a 'bond,' of ' to consolidate co-operation,' of ' challenge
the expediency of the imperial character of this realm.'
A more serious matter was the maladroit claim for England
of ' ascendancy ' in the councils of Europe. Challenged
in the House of Lords, Beaconsfield explained that he
meant, not supremacy, but only moral ascendancy. Most
serious of all was the definite assertion in the letter that
Ireland occupied once more, and must inevitably occupy,
the forefront of politics. The ordinary English and
Scottish elector was certain to resent the suggestion that
the attention of Parliament should be largely monopolised,
as it was ten years before, with Irish affairs. On the
whole, it is not surprising that the manifesto proved in the
electoral fight to be rather a welcome target for Beaconsfield's foes than an inspiriting banner for his friends.
It lost him the Irish vote at the English elections. ' Vote
against Benjamin Disraeli,' rang the Home Rule clarion,
' as you would vote against the mortal enemy of your
country and your race.' It did not rally to the Government the Anti-Home Rule Liberals; they trusted, and
with some reason, in Hartington's pledges. And yet in
substance, in his two main points, Beaconsfield was right
and his warnings were soon justified. Ireland was at that
moment the danger-point, as he, with official knowledge
of its state to guide him, told his countrymen. And the

---

[1] Borrowed, however, from Burke's *Revolution in France.*

experience of the last six years, especially of the Russo-Turkish War and the Berlin Congress, only confirmed the lesson taught by the Crimean War of 1854, and the Danish War of 1864, that, in order to preserve European peace, England must take a leading part in European councils, and speak in them with a firm and unambiguous voice. In the late autumn Beaconsfield had the melancholy satisfaction of saying, ' I told you so.'

To Lord Beauchamp.

HUGHENDEN, *Nov.* 21, '80.—. . . You are kind in recalling my letter to the Duke of Marlborough. Our enemies said, at the time, that I had fixed on the only two subjects on which they could have no difficulty: that Mr. Gladstone would settle Turkey by an European concert, and that Ireland only required a truly Liberal Government. The European concert is a ' fiasco,' and nearly landed us in war, which I intimated ! and Ireland is—anarchy !

I must say I thought my friends, at the time I wrote the letter, seemed very much to agree with the then Opposition, and evidently thought I had blundered. I don't count you among them: you are always faithful, and have a good political nose ! . . .

At the moment the Opposition treated the Irish portion of the manifesto as a barefaced attempt to divert the attention of the electorate from the blunders and wrong-doing of the Government, Gladstone in particular describing Beaconsfield's warnings as ' baseless ' and ' terrifying insinuations.' Four years later, on September 1, 1884, Gladstone made a curious apology. ' I frankly admit,' he said, ' I had had much upon my hands connected with the doings of the Beaconsfield Government in almost every quarter of the world, and I did not know, no one knew, the severity of the crisis that was already swelling upon the horizon, and that shortly after rushed upon us like a flood.' Beaconsfield knew, and had warned the country in impressive tones, but Gladstone was too headstrong to listen. Here are the counts on which Gladstone asked the constituencies to condemn the Beaconsfield Government.

At home the Ministers have neglected legislation; aggravated the public distress by continual shocks to confidence, which is the life of enterprise; augmented the public expenditure and taxation for purposes not merely unnecessary but mischievous; and plunged the finances, which were handed over to them in a state of singular prosperity, into a series of deficits unexampled in modern times. . . . Abroad they have strained, if they have not endangered, the prerogative by gross misuse; have weakened the empire by needless wars, unprofitable extensions, and unwise engagements; and have dishonoured it in the eyes of Europe by filching the island of Cyprus from the Porte, under a treaty clandestinely concluded in violation of the Treaty of Paris. . . . They have aggrandised Russia; lured Turkey on to her dismemberment, if not her ruin; replaced the Christian population of Macedonia under a degrading yoke, and loaded India with the costs and dangers of an unjustifiable war. . . . From day to day, under a Ministry called, as if in mockery, Conservative, the nation is perplexed with fear of change.

This was the theme which Gladstone elaborated in another whirlwind campaign in Midlothian. Readers of this biography, who have followed Beaconsfield's policy from the inside, may rub their eyes and marvel how even self-righteousness and jealousy could so pervert the doings and aims of Ministers. Far from neglecting legislation, Ministers had placed on the Statute-Book a whole series of valuable measures of social reform. They had carried the country safely through a threatening crisis in foreign affairs, without European war, and, in spite of bad trade and bad harvests, with only a slight increase of expenditure and taxation. In many ways, but especially by the purchase of the Suez Canal shares, by the substitution of the Treaty of Berlin for the Treaty of San Stefano, and by the rectification of the north-west frontier of India, they had materially strengthened the defensive position of the Empire. Finally they had greatly raised the reputation of their country in the eyes of Europe and of the world.

Extravagant, however, as Gladstone's denunciation was, it could hardly fail of effect in the absence of any adequate reply. Not only Beaconsfield himself, but the two hardest hitters among his colleagues, Salisbury and Cranbrook, were debarred by being peers from taking part in the fray. And Northcote, Cross, and Beach were outmatched in platform oratory by Hartington, Bright, and Harcourt. The moderation, too, as well as weight with which Hartington stated his case kept the moderate Liberals, in spite of their disgust at Midlothian methods, true to their party. While outrageous abuse of Beaconsfield formed the staple of Liberal orations throughout the country, Hartington prefaced his condemnation of the policy of the Minister by the following chivalrous tribute to the man.

It may be said that Lord Beaconsfield is ambitious. I should like to know what man who has attained to the position to which he has attained in the political life of his country is not actuated by motives of ambition. No one can, certainly, attribute any mean or unworthy motive to Lord Beaconsfield. We may disagree with his politics, but we must admire the genius which the man has shown under the disadvantages that he has laboured under. I firmly believe that Lord Beaconsfield has had in view what he believes to be the greatness of his country and the power of the Sovereign whom he serves.

Not only were Ministers outmatched on the platform, but they had lost their previous advantage in organisation. While the Liberals had been stimulated by defeat to perfect the Birmingham caucus, the Tories had parted with their manager, Gorst, whose organising capacity had paved the way to victory in 1874. A correspondence between him and Beaconsfield in 1877 shows how party interests had been neglected and mismanaged in three years. He told Beaconsfield that in order to renovate organisation ' you must put a stop to that which has been the chief cause of all the mischief that has occurred— the system . . . of managing elections at the Treasury.' He pointed out that ' the established principle of non-interference with the local leaders has in many instances been neglected; and those leaders have been constantly offended and alienated both in the distribution of patronage and in other matters.' He was certain that ' unless some energetic measures are speedily adopted, our organisation, whenever the election does take place, will be as inferior to that of our opponents as it was superior in 1874.' The measures taken in 1877 were not sufficiently energetic, probably because Beaconsfield, with the burden of government on his weakening shoulders, was unable to give personal superintendence to the work; partly, perhaps, because he was less in touch with popular and party feeling than when he led the House of Commons. At any rate the event proved, when the General Election of 1880 came, that the Conservative Central Office was quite ignorant of the mind of the electorate. Its representative advised the dissolution in March, and calculated that the party would lose 6 or 7 seats in Scotland, 5 or 6 in Ireland, and 5 on balance in England, but would return with a working majority for the Government.

It is, however, only fair to the Conservative managers to say that the bulk of the Liberal managers did not look forward to any very dissimilar result. Brand, the Speaker, who had been a Liberal Whip himself, came to an understanding with Beaconsfield as to the Speakership in the next Parliament, on the assumption that the General Election would not produce a change of Government. The interchange of ideas was creditable both to Prime Minister and to Speaker.

Memorandum by Mr. Speaker Brand.

March 9, '80.—Saw Ld. B. accordingly, and informed him that I waited on him because in a few days the Speaker's chair would be vacant. I said that I was very sensible of the difficulties which every Prime Minister must have in the conduct of affairs, and that it had occurred to me that he might desire on public grounds to make a new appointment. If so, I said, I should have no ground of complaint, on the contrary, I would willingly facilitate such an arrangement by withdrawing from Parl't; adding, that having worked hard for many years, and feeling the effects of work more as I grew older, I should be thankful for rest.

Ld. B. said that I had been nominated by one party, and

adopted by another, and that I could not be regarded as a partisan Speaker, being approved by both sides.

He was frank and cordial as to the estimation in which I was held; and added that the question of retirement should be left entirely to my own convenience.

I replied, that in that case I should consider it my duty to go forward in the service of the House, and that I was led to that conclusion mainly by the consideration of the new powers and responsibilities lately cast upon the Speaker by the House.—H. B.

It was with some such expectations as those of the Speaker and of the Tory Central Office that Beaconsfield awaited the elections, though he was haunted by the fear of a defection of county voters owing to the prolonged agricultural distress. He was also depressed by the open opposition of his old colleague Derby, who announced his adhesion to the Liberal cause shortly before the formal dissolution of Parliament. Beaconsfield spent Easter and the electoral period, of which Easter was the centre, at Hatfield, which had been placed at his disposal by his colleague the Foreign Secretary, who had gone to the South of France to recover from his illness, along with Lady Salisbury and other members of the family. 'At this awful pause my mind is a blank,' he told Lady Bradford; but one letter to her gives a picture of his surroundings and his anxieties.

To Lady Bradford.

HATFIELD HOUSE, *March* 29.[1]—. . . I have not written before, for I have not a word to say. As for news about the elections, that no longer exists. All you hear now is mere speculation and gossip. The seed is sown, and we must wait for the harvest: I hope our electoral one will be better than our agricultural. We are in the hands of the ballot.

The petty boroughs of the West seem our weakest point in England. Alington ought to have kept Dorchester right, and Lady W[estminster] Shaftesbury. Poole, Xchurch, were always weak horses; but I fain hope we have a chance in both.

I hope the Yorkshire mess may yet be cooked to our satisfaction. Wharncliffe is very wroth anent, but rather sanguine about Sheffield.

[1] Easter Monday.

I am here quite alone, except Monty, who occasionally goes up to town to dine with Princes and Princesses. The eldest son of the house, an agreeable youth, is assisting his brother-in-law[1] in canvassing Hertford, where they are unexpectedly pushed. He sometimes gets home for dinner. Then another son comes for a day with his tutor, and one evening two ladies arrived (an aunt and cousin) and so on. Everybody seems to do what they like—an extraordinarily freeand easy house.

I drink Grand Château Margaux of 1870—exquisite—by special orders; but, as it is not given to anyone else, I feel awkward, but forget my embarrassment in the exquisite flavor. All this because I mentioned once my detestation of hosts who give you an inferior claret at dinner, when alone sensible men drink wine; and reserve their superior *crus* for after the repast.

To-day a brilliant sun, wh. we have had every day, and a blue sky; but what we have not had every day, instead of a blasting east, a delicious soft, wind. This will do me good.

With the exception of Gladstone and some enthusiastic Radicals, nobody expected a sweeping victory for either side; and the general opinion, especially in London and the South of England, was that Ministers would be able to maintain their position. Accordingly, the result of the first day's polling, on Wednesday, March 31, was a dramatic surprise: the Conservatives lost, on balance, no fewer than 15 seats in 69 constituencies. By Saturday 50 seats had been lost; and all hope of a Ministerial majority had been abandoned. Such was the result of the urban polling. Next week, the farmers in the counties, as Beaconsfield had feared they might, added to the Ministerial discomfiture. In the final result it was reckoned that, whereas the old Parliament contained 351 Conservatives, 250 Liberals, and 51 Home Rulers, the new Parliament would number 349 Liberals, 243 Conservatives, and 60 Home Rulers. Prolonged depression in trade, a series of bad harvests, warlike adventures in Asia and Africa which, though in the main victorious, had been marked by unexpected and apparently avoidable disasters, and, of course, the swing of the pendulum—all had their share

---

[1] It was his first cousin, Mr. Arthur Balfour

in bringing about the catastrophe.   But undoubtedly the chief factor was Gladstone's success in instilling into the minds of many of the most serious, and more of the most ignorant, of the electorate, the conviction that Beaconsfield's policy, even granting that it might have safeguarded British interests, was nevertheless morally wrong.

Under this crushing and unexpected disaster Beaconsfield bore himself with unruffled dignity and composure; but he did not conceal from his intimates that he felt its bitterness.

To Lady Bradford.

HATFIELD, *April* 1.—Alas! Alas! I cannot write a letter, and almost thought of sending you a blank sheet, which, at least, wd. have shown my sympathy.   In the general discomfiture, the success of Francis[1] wd. have been to you a consolation.

I can [no] more at present.   With great affection, Yrs., B.

April 2.—I return to town to-morrow and remain there while the dreadful ceremonies are performed.   I suppose it may take six weeks—6 weeks as disagreeable as can be easily conceived.

Never was so great a discomfiture with a cause so inadequate.   I think, as far as I can collect, ' hard times ' was the cry against us.   The suffering want a change—no matter what, they are sick of waiting. . . .

We have an account by Barrington of a talk with his chief, showing the equable temper in which the beaten Minister met his fate.

Memorandum by Lord Barrington.

CARLTON CLUB, *April* 4, 1880.—With Lord B[eaconsfield] at luncheon and afterwards till 3.30.   He is not cast down by adversity and never has been, but looks forward to the next month rather with annoyance, because of holding responsibility without power, and being pestered by all who want honours showered on them by wholesale, which is of course impossible. He was never very sanguine, but rather expected a small majority either way which would have led to a weak Government, which would have gone out ingloriously in a short time hence.   He will not hear of anyone being blamed for ignorantly advising him to dissolve.   All trouble to ascertain

---

[1] Hon. F. Bridgeman was defeated at Bolton.

what would happen had been taken, tho' perhaps some of the
sub-agents in the country held out unjustifiable hopes.   In
Cabinets the Peers thought it was not for them to judge the
proper time for dissolving, and no one was more enthusiastic
in favour of its taking place immediately than cautious
Northcote, also Cross.   Beach and J. Manners were not of
their opinion, but only Beach spoke out as far as he remembered.   The chief proof that the principal wire-pullers of
the party were not to blame, lay in the ignorance of the other
side, for no one anticipated this wonderful Radical *pronun-
ciamiento.*

For his own part he was not sorry to have some rest, and
pass the spring and summer in the woods of Hughenden,
which he had never been able to do, and longed for.   At the
same time he would gladly have gone on managing England,
especially with reference to foreign affairs, which, although
partially settled, still wore a grave aspect.   He chiefly
deplored his fall from power, on account of M. Corry, who
in his opinion was fitted to fill any *Cabinet* office.   This was
said with genuine warmth.

What would follow ?   The Queen would certainly send for
Granville, and he and Hartington would certainly form a
Government whether Gladstone liked it or not.   After a year
or so, G[ladstone] might upset Granville, and then the moderate Liberals might have to come to us for support, and we
should give it.   But at all events Granville would have the
opportunity this time of being Prime Minister.   He did not
think Gladstone would serve under him.   Perhaps Derby
would, but the Foreign Office would never be conducted by
anyone like Salisbury, who acted for himself, and did not
leave it all to the permanent officials, which had been, and
would again be the case now.   The Queen is in despair, but
that she will get over. . . .

Lord B. spoke very strongly against Gladstone, and said
his conduct in ' chucking up the sponge ' as Leader, and
spouting all over the country, like an irresponsible demagogue,
was wholly inexcusable in a man who was a statesman. . . .

It is pleasing to see how well D[israeli] is, and with what
charming temper he takes this evil stroke of fortune in the
sunset of his great career.   So many of his friends, especially
ladies, send to enquire how he is.   'As well as can be expected,'
says he, as if he had been confined !

No one took Beaconsfield's defeat in the Election more
to heart than his Sovereign.   Her Majesty had been
sanguine, more sanguine than her Minister, that he

would secure a majority. She had accepted the Southwark victory as a sign. 'It shows,' she had written to
him, 'what the feeling of the country is.' She had been
confident that the factiousness of the Opposition in the
Commons, and the crude appeal of Gladstone to humani-
tarianism and ignorance in regard to delicate questions
of foreign affairs, must disgust her people as they had
disgusted herself. And now she saw before her the prospect of an immediate wrench, more painful than any
since the fall of Melbourne, her early friend and political
mentor. Moreover, when Melbourne resigned, she was
only twenty-two and had the speedy rallying power of
youth; and she was a happily married wife, with a husband
to turn to for support. Now she was over sixty, and a
widow; and the complete confidence and warm affection
which her mature judgment had bestowed on Beaconsfield
could not be uprooted and transferred. As early as
April 2 he telegraphed to her at Baden that the results
so far announced left no doubt of the defeat of the
Ministry. She could hardly believe the news; but telegraphed back her great distress. 'Nothing more than
trouble and trial await me. I consider it a great public
misfortune.' And again the next day she expressed her
'intense astonishment, distress, and annoyance.' The
correspondence which followed clearly showed both his
view of the catastrophe which had overwhelmed him and
the depth of her feelings at the approaching parting. His
own sorrow at the severance of the intimate personal
relation has a very genuine ring.

To Queen Victoria.

HATFIELD, *April* 2, 1880.—Lord Beaconsfield with his
humble duty to your Majesty. He has already, by a cyphered
telegram this morning, had the honor to apprise your Majesty
of his general view of the result of the election. He believes
that the counties, by their decision, will ensure to your
Majesty, in the Govt. of your Majesty's Dominions, the advantage of a powerful Opposition. It is true the farmers are
suffering and are discontented, but they always have difficulty
in moving and combining. On the present occasion events

have been too quick for them, and, with returning prosperity, they will, in a season or two, revert to their ancient loyalty and love of order. Lord Beaconsfield attributes the cause of the present disaster to that sympathy for change which is inherent in man. Small communities are capricious, and are not affected by strong national feeling to the degree which influences cities where there is a vast population. The immense majority in the City of London in favor of your Majesty's Govt., the considerable numbers in Westminster, and in Greenwich (the only poll of a Metropolitan district, which, as yet, has reached Lord Beaconsfield), the return of Mr. Wortley for Sheffield, and the nearness of the numbers in a vast amount of polls, indicate the existence of a substantial and powerful party in the towns. Surely the enlightened opinion of the country is in favor of the policy which has been pursued. The suffrage of the City of London is a proof of that, as well as the circumstance that every powerful newspaper, save those known to be under the influence of Russia, has upheld your Majesty's Govt. Lord Beaconsfield leaves Hatfield for Downing St. to-morrow morning.

From Queen Victoria.

VILLA HOHENLOHE, BADEN-BADEN, *April* 4, 1880.—The Queen has received Lord Beaconsfield's letter with the deepest interest. There is not a doubt that $\frac{1}{2}$ of these ' Liberals' cannot be considered an acting majority, and the majorities in so many cases are so very small, whereas those in London, at Sheffield, and others in favour of the Govt. are so overwhelming. The newspapers, except the really violent ones, are all so strong in support of Ld. Beaconsfield that the Queen feels sure that there will be the very greatest difficulty in forming a Govt. The grief to her of having to part with the kindest and most devoted as well as one of the wisest Ministers the Queen has ever had, is not to be told, tho' she feels sure it will be but for a very short time. She won't, however, contemplate this at present. . . .

To Queen Victoria.

DOWNING STREET, *April* 8, 1880.—Lord Beaconsfield . . . had the honor to receive yesterday your Majesty's most gracious letter, the receipt of which he acknowledged. He cannot conceal, nor wishes he to conceal, that the present state of affairs costs him a pang; not for the country, for, having done his duty to it with ceaseless effort and entire fidelity, he leaves its fortunes to Providence.

But his separation from your Majesty is almost over-whelming. His relations with your Majesty were his chief, he might almost say his only, happiness and interest in this world. They came to him when he was alone, and they have inspired and sustained him in his isolation. Your Majesty's judgment and rich experience often guided him, and in the most trying moments he felt he served a Sovereign who was constant and consistent, and who never quailed.

Then, again, the brightness of those conversations, in which your Majesty occasionally deigned to blend domestic with imperial confidence, had a charm to him quite inexpressible, and their recollection will be to him a source of frequent consolation.

Thanking your Majesty for all your goodness to him, he remains with all duty and affection, Your Majesty's grateful and devoted BEACONSFIELD.

(*Same date*).—. . . Lord Beaconsfield in *six* years, has advised your Majesty to create fifteen peers.

His predecessor in *five* years, advised your Majesty to create thirty-seven peers.

Lord Beaconsfield has no wish to place himself in compe-tition with his predecessor in this respect. He has always studiously refrained from pressing your Majesty on the sub-ject of honors, the distinction of which he wished to prevent being depreciated by their becoming too general. . . .

He hopes your Majesty may be pleased to confer some distinguished mark of your Majesty's favor on the Viceroy of your Majesty's Indian Empire. Never was a Viceroy so ill-treated by an Opposition. Lord Lytton is a first-rate man, and, being a real orator, his presence in the House of Lords will be invaluable. He has telegraphed to Lord Beaconsfield to place his resignation in your Majesty's hands when Lord Beaconsfield tenders his own. . . .

From Queen Victoria.

VILLA HOHENLOHE, BADEN-BADEN, *April* 9, 1880.

DEAR LORD BEACONSFIELD,

I cannot thank you for your most kind letter, which affected me much, in the 3rd person—it is too formal; and when we correspond—which I hope we shall on many a *private* subject and without anyone being astonished or offended, and even more without anyone knowing about it—I hope it will be in this more easy form. You can be of such use to me about my family and other things and about great public questions. My great hope and belief is, that this shame-fully heterogeneous union—out of mere folly—will separate

into many parts very soon, and that the Conservatives will
come in stronger than ever in a short time. Possibly a
coalition first. But you must promise me for the country's,
as well as for my sake, to be very watchful and very severe,
and to allow no lowering of Gt. Britain's proud position!
It must not be lowered. The Army and Navy *not* diminished,
and I look to you for that. Give me that firm promise. I
do not care for the trouble of changes of Govt. if it is to have
a secure and safe one, which the new one cannot be. I am
shocked and ashamed at what has happened. It is really
disgraceful. . . .

The sort of mad and unreasoning *flow* of Liberal success is
so unnatural that I feel certain it can't last. It is not like
as if the Govt. had had a succession of defeats; the Opposition
never the least expected it. Of course I shall not take any
notice of . . . Mr. Gladstone, who has done so much mischief.
It is most essential that *that* should be known and that is
why I cyphered to you. . . . You must not think it is a
real parting. I shall always let you hear how I am and what
I am doing, and you must promise to let me hear from and
about you. I have many about me who will write to you and
I hope you will to them—so that we are not cut off. That
would be too painful. The Liberal Opposition has been
very factious; Sir M. H. Beach is inclined to be too generous.
Do not be indulgent but make them feel what they have
brought on themselves. Indulgence and forbearance after
such disgraceful and unpatriotic attacks would not be right.
It is not like an ordinary change of Govt.—if so it must be!
It was the bad beginning which led to the whole mischief.
If the Elections had been favourable that day, *all* the rest
would have followed as a matter of course.

Hoping that you are well,

Ever yours affly. and gratefully,

V.R.I.

The Queen was very anxious to testify in some public
manner her high appreciation of her favourite Minister.
'The Queen wishes it were in her power,' she wrote on
April 9, 'to confer any other mark of her gratitude and
admiration on Lord Beaconsfield. Will he not allow her
now—to let a barony be settled on his nephew in remembrance of the great services of Lord Beaconsfield?'
While refusing for his nephew on the same grounds as he
had given in 1876, Beaconsfield recommended his private
secretary, who was also his intimate friend, for the honour

—a unique distinction, which no private secretary had received before, and which few indeed had been in a position to support. The Queen's only hesitation about granting the request was that she feared that it might not be 'advantageous' for Beaconsfield and Corry; but on being reassured she gladly consented.

To Queen Victoria.

DOWNING STREET, *April* 11.—Lord Beaconsfield . . . is most touched by your Majesty's gracious proposal respecting his heir. In asking leave still to decline this gracious offer, he would express his most grateful sense of its repetition.

He doubts not that, in due time, his countrymen will give an opening in public life to his nephew. If he be equal to the occasion, he may yet serve your Majesty, for your Majesty, thank God, is really yet young.

Personally, all that Lord Beaconsfield can desire for himself is, that your Majesty may deign sometimes to remember him.

There is one point on which he would ask permission yet to trouble your Majesty. It refers to the position of Mr. Corry. Mr. Corry has served Lord Beaconsfield for fourteen years with great advantage to Lord Beaconsfield, and with absolute devotion. He has refused every preferment[1] that Lord Beaconsfield has offered to him, and Lord Beaconsfield has offered to him the highest in his power. He has refused the uncontested representation of his own county of Shropshire, as his duties as an M.P. were not consistent with those to your Majesty's Prime Minister.

A great change in the social position of Mr. Corry has taken place since your Majesty left England. He has come into possession of Rowton Castle, and a domain of seven thousand acres in Shropshire. His income will exceed ten thousand per annum.

---

[1] The principal offer that Disraeli had made to Corry was that of Clerk of the Parliaments, on March 9, 1875. 'I think it is the best post in my gift,' wrote Disraeli, 'both in matter of dignity, agreeable duties, and income. Although you have hitherto refused everything I have offered you, I make one more effort to accomplish some material evidence of my personal regard for you, my appreciation of your abilities, and my gratitude for your faithful services. The office is one for which, both from your legal training, and now considerable experience of public life, you are eminently qualified. You need not hurry your decision. Think well over it. I shall ever lament, I feel sure, my loss, but shall find some consolation in the thought that I have advanced the fortunes of a dear and devoted friend.' It was at this time that Disraeli secured for his brother Ralph the post of Clerk-Assistant in the House of Lords.

Mr. Corry is of noble birth on either side: his parents were both the children of Earls. His maternal grandmother was a daughter of the then Duke of Marlborough.

He is now forty years of age, with a great fund of political knowledge and experience in addition to talents of a high class. He possesses the confidence of leading men to an extraordinary degree.

It is impossible that such a man will be content to fall back into the crowd of dismissed private secretaries. He will probably become absorbed in that fashionable world where he is a favorite.

Is it possible that your Majesty might make him Baron Rowton of Rowton Castle in the county of Shropshire ?

He knows nothing of this request, being away from me on private affairs, of which your Majesty has been apprised.

It would be for him a link to public life, and he would be of great use to Lord Beaconsfield in keeping him *au fait* to all going on in the House of Lords in Lord Beaconsfield's occasional absence, for nature tells Lord Beaconsfield he must sometimes rest.

Not only Mr. Corry knows nothing of this suggestion, but Lord Beaconsfield does not wish to press it on your Majesty in any sense. He would not wish it to occur, unless your Majesty thought it a wise and becoming arrangement.

April 17.—Lord Beaconsfield . . . has had the honor to receive your Majesty's most gracious letter from Flushing, but in vain does he endeavor to express his sense of the favor which your Majesty has conferred on him.

He does not anticipate much hostile criticism on the elevation of Mr. Corry, as Lord Beaconsfield proposes that it shall not be mixed up with the other honors, nor known until Lord Beaconsfield's resignation is announced. When his opponents have got rid of him, Lord Beaconsfield's offences will be forgotten, and perhaps take the most charitable shape of a sincere, though mistaken, duty to his Sovereign and his country.

Lord Beaconsfield looks forward with the greatest interest to his audience of your Majesty. There is much, comparatively formal, business to transact, when the greater theme, and all its probable and possible consequences, have been considered, or decided on. . . .

While waiting for his Sovereign to return, Beaconsfield occupied himself with winding up the affairs of his Government, especially with dealing with those whom he called on a docket ' pesterers of the 11th hour '—the applicants for honours, rewards, and appointments. The following letter shows how he dealt with one such ' pesterer.'

To —— ——.

April 16, 1880.—I doubt not you would make an excellent peer, and, had my Ministry continued, I should in due time in all probability have had the pleasure of submitting your name to Her Majesty; but I am obliged to consider the claims of those who, while they have made great sacrifices, both of time and treasure, for the Government, have received hitherto neither office nor honors.

You have received the first and obtained reputation by the discharge of its duties; and tho' the post you fill is not a high one, you must remember that you continued there at your own desire, and that I was always ready to promote you.

How is the Opposition to be carried on if all those, who have had the advantage of official experience, desire to leave the House of Commons ?

I have been obliged this morning to ask this question of one of your colleagues, as good a man of business as yourself with an estate not less important.

To Lady Bradford.

DOWNING STREET, *April* 8.—I have nothing to say: a most dreary life and labor mine ! Winding up a Government as hard work as forming one, without any of its excitement. My room is filled with beggars, mournful or indignant, and my desk covered with letters like a snowstorm.

It is the last, and least glorious exercise of power, and will be followed, wh. is the only compensation, by utter neglect and isolation.

April 10.—I only write to you because I think you would prefer having a blank sheet to nothing. This is a blank sheet.

My life continues the same. Discomfited, defeated, and, if not disgraced, prostrate, by a singular anomaly and irony of fate I pass my life now in exercising supreme power—making peers, creating baronets, and showering places and pensions on a rapacious crew.

The Faery arrives on the 17th, and I am to be with her on the morning of 18th, and stay a day or so. . . .

April 13.—. . . John Manners has done well and pulled his man thro' too—on wh. I did not count. John is to have the red ribbon.[1] He is the only one of the present Cabinet

---

[1] Northcote and Cross also were given the G.C.B., and Cranbrook the G.C.S.I.

who was in the original Derby Cabinet of '52 and has been in every one since of wh. I have been a member. . . .

DOWNING STREET, *April* 18.—I do not know when I wrote to you: I cannot count days in the dreary excitement in which I live. That, however, must soon cease, at least I hope so, tho' until I see my Sovereign I can say nothing absolutely positive. . . .

I have given Henry Lennox a place of £1,500 *per ann.:* but I fear the first achievement of the H. of Commons will be to take it from him. However, I have given him a chance. . . .

This offer to Henry Lennox is an example of the excessive lengths to which Beaconsfield's devotion to old friends sometimes led him. The post was that of Chief Civil Service Commissioner, and the Cabinet, with Northcote at their head, had great difficulty in persuading their chief that such an appointment could not possibly be justified in Parliament and must be abandoned.

As soon as the trend of the elections was beyond a doubt Beaconsfield despatched one of the junior members of the Cabinet, Hicks Beach, to Baden in order to reconcile the Queen, so far as might be, to the inevitable change. Beach reported on April 6: 'I endeavoured to put before H.M. the view of the present position of affairs, and of the prospect before us, which you had impressed upon me; and I hope with some success, as I hear, from those who have seen H.M. since, that she is less disturbed and more hopeful as to the future.' She almost immediately raised the question of Beaconsfield's successor.

From Sir Michael Hicks Beach.

HOTEL DE L'EUROPE, BADEN-BADEN, *April* 9.—. . . I may mention that H.M. spoke to me to-day upon the choice of the person who should be entrusted with the formation of a Government: and expressed a decided preference for Lord Hartington over Lord Granville. I remarked that the latter was the older, and more experienced: but H.M. said she . . . thought he would be too pliable to Radical influence: saying that he had been very bitter lately. I remarked that Mr. Gladstone's position would then be, as it seemed to me, a very dangerous one: as supposing Lord H. to be Prime Minister, and Mr. G. outside the

Govt., the latter would control public affairs without responsibility. H.M. said that she could not believe that Mr.
Gladstone would take any, but the principal post, in a Government: and that she interpreted his recent speeches as intimating that he would not accept even that. I said that I thought
they might have a very opposite interpretation. But I
am pretty certain that the Queen will not send for Mr. Gladstone in the first instance: and will only be induced, if she is
induced at all, to do so in the end by the greatest possible
pressure. H.M. spoke very strongly on this point. . . .

The Queen had apparently a wider liberty of choice
on the present occasion than at any crisis during her
reign, except perhaps in 1859 and subsequently in 1894.
Gladstone had definitely resigned the Liberal leadership
five years before, and Hartington had been elected by
the party in the House of Commons as their leader,
Granville remaining leader in the House of Lords. There
was no single leader of the whole party, though Gladstone,
in his memoranda on this crisis, appeared to maintain the
very undemocratic doctrine that, as he had 'resigned
his trust' to Granville in 1875, he had thereby constituted
him his successor.[1] The natural course for the Queen
to take was to send for either Granville or Hartington.
Granville had the advantage of length of service, Hartington that of leadership in the Chamber which made and
unmade Ministries. But the situation was complicated
by Gladstone's vehement reappearance, a few years after
his retirement, in the forefront of politics, and by his
Midlothian speeches, which were the main feature of the
election. But for his fiery zeal, there could hardly have
been the political upheaval disclosed by the polls. He
had, in fact, taken the lead; but he had himself protested,
when entering on the campaign, that it was his hope that
'the verdict of the country will give to Lord Granville
and Lord Hartington the responsible charge of affairs.'
The selection of a statesman to be entrusted with the
formation of a Government is one of the very few public
acts which the Sovereign can constitutionally perform

---

[1] See Lord Morley's *Gladstone*, Bk. VII., ch. 9.

without his responsibility being covered by Ministerial advice. It lies entirely within his discretion whether he shall or shall not consult the outgoing Minister. Queen Victoria clung to her prerogative in the matter, and usually acted on her own judgment, only consulting the outgoing Minister when, as happened with Melbourne and Aberdeen, she had special confidence in him. In the present case the Queen was parting with a Minister in whom her confidence was absolute, and she acted under his advice throughout what proved to be a difficult and delicate negotiation. Her own decided inclination was to send in the first place for Hartington; and her Minister advised her that this was, constitutionally speaking, the right course. He had apparently changed his mind as to the relative claims of Granville and Hartington since his talk with Barrington. Her Majesty returned to England on Saturday the 17th and commanded her Minister's presence the next morning. She made a memorandum of what passed at the audience.

Memorandum by Queen Victoria.

WINDSOR CASTLE, *April* 18, 1880.—I saw Lord Beaconsfield this morning at ½ pt. 12. After remarks on the sad and startling result of the elections which no one was in the least prepared for, I asked him what he advised me to do for the real good of the country, which we both agreed was inseparable from my own; and he replied that, irrespective of any personal feeling which I might have respecting Mr. Gladstone, the right and constitutional course for me to take was to send for Lord Hartington. He was in his heart a conservative, a gentleman, and very straightforward in his conduct. Lord Granville was less disinterested and looked more for his own objects. That Mr. Gladstone had formally given up the leadership, and was only clung to by the Radicals. That he (Lord Beaconsfield) could tell me something which he thought more hopeful for the future, viz., that, tho' some dreadful people like Bradlaugh had been elected, a great many of the respectable and moderate old Whigs had also been. There were 200 of them, he thought, and 240 of the Conservatives— a very compact and united body—returned, while the Home Rulers and extreme Radicals only amounted to 190. By calling upon a Whig to form a Government, these moderate

Liberals would rally round and support him, and the Radicals would be harmless.

He did not wish to meet Parliament, but to resign before, as in 1868 and as Mr. Gladstone did in 1874; that it was a mockery to have to prepare a Queen's Speech; that an amendment would be proposed of want of confidence in the House of Commons, in which all the Moderates and Radicals would have to join, which was to be deprecated; while in the House of Lords any amendment would be defeated, Lord Beaconsfield having a very large majority there; and this would bring the two Houses into collision, and the Lords would be humiliated by having to yield to the House of Commons. . . .

I said that it would be impossible for me to send for Mr. Gladstone, as . . . I considered him to be the cause of all the mischief that brought on the Russian war, and that he had done everything he could to vilify and weaken the Government in times of the greatest difficulty . . . and could he be my Minister under such circumstances ? I myself felt sure he would not expect or wish it. India would be a great difficulty. Foreign affairs equally so. What could Lord Hartington be ? First Lord of the Treasury ? . . .

I repeated what I had written, viz., that this was no ordinary change of Government, but had been brought about by the most unjust and shameful persecution of Mr. Gladstone, that therefore I hoped that he (Lord Beaconsfield) would be very watchful and very severe upon them, and prevent any mischief, which he could and said he would do. But he has great confidence in Lord Hartington. . . .

I have omitted mentioning that Lord Beaconsfield said that certainly the Conservatives had been too confident, and that they had not had that same organisation or worked as hard as the Liberals had. That the Liberals had worked on that American system called caucus, originated by the great Radical, Mr. Chamberlain.

Beaconsfield seems seriously to have thought that the Whigs and moderate Liberals had been returned to the House of Commons in sufficient strength to make a Hartington Administration feasible. He may very well have had some communication to that effect from his friend Harcourt, who was at this time pressing Hartington to go forward and form a Government if the Queen should ask him to undertake the task.[1] At any rate he repeated his advice to the Queen, three days later, enforcing it

[1] See Holland's *Life of the Duke of Devonshire*, Vol. I., ch. 12.

by forwarding, no doubt in good faith, a report about
the intentions of the Liberal leaders which was only
true of Granville and Hartington, and quite unfounded
in regard to Gladstone.

To Queen Victoria.

DOWNING STREET, *April* 21, 1880.—Lord Beaconsfield . . .
was assured last night by a person of authority, that the
Triumvirate had met, and agreed that they would serve under
the individual of the three, whom your Majesty should
graciously appoint.

Nothing has occurred to change the opinion which Lord
Beaconsfield had the honor to express to your Majesty.

Even if your Majesty wished Mr. Gladstone to be chief,
the Constitutional course would still be to send for an acknowledged leader of opposition.

Lord Beaconsfield is informed, that the Whigs in the new
Parliament amount to 237.   Lord Hartington must be aware
of this.

Lord Beaconsfield earnestly advises your Majesty to make
no conditions when the person sent for arrives: merely
enquire whether he is prepared to form an Administration.
Conditions may develop afterwards.

He has not five minutes to write this, and he is anxious it
should reach your Majesty without delay.

This letter was sent to the Queen on the last morning
of the existence of the Beaconsfield Administration.   The
programme of the day, as the retiring Minister told Lady
Bradford, was: ' This morning a Cabinet, and then to
Windsor for final operation.   H.M. insists upon softening
the catastrophe by my dining and sleeping at her Castle.'
The Cabinet had resolved, at its meeting in the previous
week, to resign at once, without waiting for the opening of
Parliament; and this meeting, having only to ratify that
decision, was rather, as Hardy tells us, ' conversational.'

[Beaconsfield] thanked us all for the cordiality and harmony
with which we had worked with him. The Chancellor
expressed briefly what we all felt, and Northcote, Cross, and
Salisbury added a few words; the last saying that there had
never been a cloud between him and the Prime Minister,
through all their arduous work. All assented heartily to the
expressions of good feeling, and I can record without hesitation

my belief that a more united Cabinet than the one that has now been dissolved has never sat.

Beaconsfield went from the Cabinet to the Queen at Windsor and tendered his resignation, which was accepted. Her Majesty at once sought his advice on the nature of the statement she should make to Hartington, whom she summoned for the following afternoon.

From Queen Victoria.

WINDSOR CASTLE, *April 21, 1880.*—Will this do ?

Pray make any suggestion or alteration as this is only a draft.

Would it be well perhaps to say after ' Leader of the Opposition ' ' who have been the cause of the defeat of her Govt.' or not ?

There are times when people should have no hearts or feelings; for *what* can be more cruel than for a female Sovereign no longer young, severely tried—without a husband or any *one* person on whose help (when her valued Minister leaves her) she can securely rest—to have to take those people who have done all they could to vilify and weaken her Govt. ? *Can* she have confidence in them ?

To Queen Victoria—Memorandum.

WINDSOR CASTLE, *April* [21], 1880.—It would seem expedient to address the individual called upon to form a new Ministry in this manner:

' The Opposition having successfully appealed to the country to turn out my Ministry, I now wish to know, whether you, the Leader of the Opposition, will undertake the administration of my affairs; and, in that case, how you propose to form your Cabinet ?'

This preamble will oblige the individual summoned to enter into details, both as to policy and persons, and then will be the time and the occasion for your Majesty to make remarks on individuals, and, without a too absolute or peremptory tone, which might be made by the person summoned an excuse to resign the task, for your Majesty to intimate any conditions which your Majesty may deem expedient.

The Queen conducted her conversation with Hartington in accordance with her outgoing Minister's counsel; but Hartington grievously disappointed both of them by telling Her Majesty that no Liberal Government could

II.   45*

stand unless Gladstone was a member, and that he did
not believe that Gladstone would accept any position
but the first. Accordingly, in spite of her pressure and
her insistence upon the want of confidence she felt in the
Midlothian campaigner, he advised her to send for
Gladstone. He consented, however, at Her Majesty's
request, to put the question directly to Gladstone whether
he would serve under either Granville or himself, and
received the reply he expected. With Granville he
returned to Windsor on the following day; and the two
Whig leaders convinced the Queen that there was no
other course but to apply to Gladstone, for whose personal
devotion to Her Majesty they vouched. The Queen
sent Beaconsfield a full memorandum of what passed at
each of these two audiences; and when she was driven,
in spite of her extreme reluctance, to accept Gladstone in
the end as Prime Minister, sought and obtained her old
friend's advice as to how she should treat him.

To Queen Victoria.

DOWNING STREET, *April* 23, 1880.—Lord Beaconsfield,
with his humble duty, returns to your Majesty one of the
most interesting State papers that he has ever perused.[1]

He has entire confidence, at this moment of terrible trial,
in your Majesty's courage and wisdom.

(*Same date*).—. . . If the leaders of the Opposition shrink
from the responsibility of their position, and confess their
inability to form a Ministry, your Majesty should fix them
with the responsibility of advising your Majesty to send for
Mr. Gladstone.

If he have an audience, your Majesty should say:

' The Opposition having succeeded in defeating my Government, I have, in the spirit of the Constitution, sent for their
leaders, who have confessed their inability to form a Ministry,
and have advised me to send for you. I wish therefore to
know, whether you are prepared to form an Administration ?'

Lord Beaconsfield would advise your Majesty, in the first
instance, to confine yourself to this question. Mr. Gladstone
will, probably, be diffuse in his reply, which will give your
Majesty advantage in ascertaining his real intentions.

---

[1] The account of Hartington's audience on April 22.

If he be not diffuse, then your Majesty, if he replies in the affirmative, may proceed to enquire as to the policy he recommends, and the persons he will propose to carry it into effect.

April 24.—Lord Beaconsfield has read with the deepest interest the picturesque and living description of an interview, which will always form an important chapter in your Majesty's memorable reign and life.[1]

May Omnipotent Providence guide, guard, and sustain, your Majesty, at this trying moment !

Lord Beaconsfield, with his humble duty, received the cyphered telegram last evening, and the box afterwards—at night.

This is his last day in Downing Street. He goes to Hatfield to-morrow, until Tuesday, and then to Lord Beauchamp's if necessary still to remain in town.

After his final audience, he will endeavour to find repose in the woods of Hughenden; consolation he will find, always, in the recollection of your Majesty, and all your goodness to him.

While the Queen had thought it right to keep her outgoing Minister completely *au courant* of all the negotiations down to the acceptance of office by Gladstone, she appears to have been too constitutional to do more than send the bare results of her new Minister's audience, now that he had kissed hands. Here is the text of the telegram to which Beaconsfield's letter refers and of a short supplementary note which followed it.

From Queen Victoria.

(*Telegram*). WINDSOR, *April 23.*—I have seen Mr. Gladstone, who has accepted and kissed hands. He says he accepts all facts; and that bitterness of feeling is past.

(*Letter, same date*).—The Queen is touched by Lord Beaconsfield's kind words. Her trial is great. She forgot to say 2 things, 1st, that Mr. Gladstone looks very ill, very old and haggard and his voice feeble. 2ndly, That he said twice he looked to his not being long in office as it was too much for him, and being Leader and Chancellor of the Exchequer as well as Prime Minister is utterly too much for a man of 70 !

On Sunday, April 25, Beaconsfield finally quitted Downing Street. He went that afternoon to Hatfield for a couple of days, and then, as he no longer had a house

[1] The account of the audience of Hartington and Granville on April 23.

in town, stayed till the following Saturday as his friend Beauchamp's guest in Belgrave Square before retreating to Hughenden. From Hatfield he was summoned to Windsor for his farewell audience, ' to kiss hands on abdication,' as he wrote to Lady Chesterfield.

Memorandum by Queen Victoria.

WINDSOR CASTLE, *April* 27, 1880.—Saw Lord Beaconsfield at 3 and gave him a parting gift, my statuette in bronze, and the plaster casts of the group of Brown, the pony, and ' Sharp,' and the statuettes of Sharp and William Brown, all of which he had never seen and with which he expressed himself much delighted. We then talked of the new Government, which he thought very moderate, but which I told him I heard the Radicals were very indignant at! His intention, he said, was to impress upon his party, of whom he should have a large meeting before the opening of Parliament, not to attack the Government excepting when extreme measures were proposed, or any change in foreign policy. Otherwise they should let them alone. . . .

He would not come to town or to the drawing-room, and wished to ' keep out of sight,' only coming up when it was necessary for him to be in the House of Lords.

I then took leave of him, shaking hands, when he kissed mine. I would not consider this as a leave-taking, as I said I was sure to see him again before we left for Scotland, and that I begged he would always let me know his whereabouts so that I could always give him news of myself.

To Lady Bradford.

13, BELGRAVE SQUARE, *April* 28.—. . . Yesterday morning I was summoned to Windsor from Hatfield; a long, cold drive, but I picked up Lord Rowton *en route*.

My audience was very long, and everything was said that cd. be said; but what was news yesterday is scarcely so to-day, and I arrived back too late for post.

I cd. perceive there was something concealed from somebody, and hinted that; but the delusion existed that all was safe, and that no danger was to be apprehended of the presence of Lowe or Dilke. Instead of them, with[ou]t the slightest preparation for the catastrophe, she will be told that she must take this morning an avowed republican[1] for a Cabinet Minister, quite inexperienced in official life, and little known

[1] Chamberlain.

in Parliament. It wd. have been better to have permitted
Dilke to be one of her counsellors.

I shall leave town on Saturday, but latish, so that if you
have a festival I will attend it, tho' I shd. have preferred
saying Adieu alone.

To Anne Lady Chesterfield.

13, BELGRAVE SQUARE, *April 29.*—. . . I had not seen
the article you sent me. I avoid newspapers which it was
once my business to scan. I see only *The Times*—just to
keep me *au fait* to what is going on. . . .

I am naturally a terribly bad letter-writer, and only the
breath of official life kept me at all in epistolary cue. I am
no longer *responsible* in any sense.

The audience on April 27 was only a farewell audience
in name, as the Queen had her fallen Minister as her
guest at Windsor three times in the remaining eight
months of the year; during five of which months the
Court was absent at Balmoral or Osborne. The first
visit was on May 17-18, when the Queen, to whom he
sat next at dinner, said, ' I feel so happy that I think
what has happened is only a horrid dream.' The next
was on July 15-16, when the Queen had returned from her
spring visit to Balmoral, but had not yet started for
Osborne. The visit, he told Lady Bradford, ' was most
interesting and agreeable. I went there early and saw
a great deal of my late, and gracious mistress. She
looked ten years younger, and, as you say, quite pretty.
She confessed she was perfectly well.' The third occasion
was in December, after the Court had come south from its
autumn sojourn in the Highlands. He was at Windsor
from Wednesday to Friday, December 8 to 10, and he
made the acquaintance there of a distinguished man
whose exploits he had long admired.

To Lady Bradford.

WINDSOR CASTLE, *Dec.* 10.—The Lyttons here, who are
always agreeable, because they are intelligent; and the great
hero, Sir Fred. Roberts, a little wiry man, not unlike poor
Sir John Pakington at a distance, but a more determined

countenance when you approach him.　Yesterday he departed, and there came Genl. Ross, the second in command during the great march—a smaller man even than Sir Fredk., wiry little men who can mount and dismount with rapid ease. Somebody told me, however, that Roberts was so exhausted and unwell that he was obliged to be carried in a litter into Candahar, and having to fight a battle almost directly, he was on horseback during the fray, and cd. only sustain himself in his saddle by the beneficial aid of champagne. . . .

The Queen looks well, and is well, notwithstanding the danger of her realm. . . .

It was not only by frequent invitations to Windsor that the Queen showed her warm affection for Beaconsfield.　She constantly kept up with him, as with no other ex-Minister since Melbourne, a confidential correspondence from which politics were by no means excluded; and she sought her trusted friend's counsel and consolation in the difficulties into which she was plunged by her new advisers. Her Majesty's letters were no longer in the formal third person traditionally employed between Sovereign and Minister, but were written as from friend to friend; beginning 'Dear Lord Beaconsfield,' and ending 'Ever your affectionate and grateful friend,' or 'Ever yours affectionately, V.R.I.'　Constitutionally, it was a perilous experiment, as the Sovereign should accept advice on public affairs only from the Minister in office.　But he must be a hardened Constitutionalist indeed who would refuse his sympathy to a widowed Queen, forced by what she held to be a sorely misguided public opinion to accept a Minister in whom she had little confidence; and Ministerial resentment and public scandal were prevented by Beaconsfield's prudence and discretion, and, it may be, by his death a year after his fall from office.　A small selection from Her Majesty's letters will show their nature.

From Queen Victoria.

WINDSOR CASTLE, *May* 4, 1880.—I . . . cannot refrain from saying a few words on what is passing.　The Council was extraordinary yesterday. . . . The other Ministers seem very anxious to be agreeable and not to reverse things. Mr. Childers has given the Duke of Cambridge satisfaction—

as well as the other appointments to that office. Lord
Northbrook—most amiable and desirous to meet my wishes.
Lord Granville very desirous of acting in the present line.
Sir H. Layard will probably have leave of absence and then
not return; but Lord Salisbury himself advised *this*. There
is great difficulty to find a successor. No one should be
removed. Mr. Gladstone . . . is very desirous of being
respectful and obliging. He looks very ill—walks with and
leans on a stick. He laments his Cabinet is not as small as
yours, which he considered most wise.

I enjoined the all-importance of secrecy in the Cabinet
and instanced the mischief which had been done *formerly*
by the reverse.

I often think of you—indeed constantly—and rejoice to see
you looking down from the *wall* after dinner.

May 9 —. . . I think you may be easy about Foreign
Affairs. Lord Granville manages them entirely and the P.M.
never even names them to me, and I watch very carefully;
he consults me very much. . . .

BALMORAL CASTLE, *Sept.* 1.—Your last kind letter interested
me very much and I thank you warmly for it. You have the
position fortunately still very much in your hands, and
you *can* exercise, as you have done, a most beneficial influence
over everyone.

Lord Granville also told me of the little dinner,[1] and how
well you looked and seemed ! This is a great pleasure for
me to hear. . . .

Oct. 7.—Since I received your kind and interesting
letters I have seen Lord Rowton, twice if not 3 times. . . .
The complications in the East are most distressing. Turkey
is very obstinate and dilatory, as we all know, but formerly
she believed us to be her friend; now she thinks the very
reverse, and much more so than really is the case. But
Mr. Gladstone's language is the cause of all the evil. He is
now seriously alarmed about Ireland and determined to proceed against the Land League if it is found possible. Lord
Hartington is particularly strong about it. I am glad to say
a great change is perceptible in their views about Afghanistan.
There will be no rash or hasty action and the advice of really
competent people will be heard, and I believe followed. . . .

Oct. 31.—It was a great pleasure to receive 2 kind letters,
which are a proof that this dreadful gout has done your health
no harm. May you continue as well through the winter, of
which we had a most extraordinary unnatural foretaste !
Such a long touch of it is quite unprecedented in Oct. here.

I am very much interested to hear of your new book[2] !

[1] See below, p. 1462.   [2] *Endymion.*

With so active a mind as yours and having for 6 years been so continually employed and overwhelmed with work, comparative idleness must have been very trying. I shall look anxiously forward to the promised copy which you so kindly say you will send to me.

As regards affairs they are sad indeed, and I hardly trust myself to speak of them—they are so confused and so dreadful ! Oh ! if only I had you, my kind friend and wise councillor and strong arm to help and lean on ! I have *no one*. Lord Dufferin said to me, ' I feel so much for you, you never were so alone.' And it is so ! . . .

OSBORNE, *Dec*. 20.—I trust I may be one of the first to wish you joy and many happy returns of your birthday—on which day I trust the sun will shine, which it did beautifully yesterday. To-day we have had, as well as last night, a fearful amount of very heavy rain, and I just hear of a heavy fall of snow at Windsor !

The state of Ireland continues to get worse and worse. But I may tell you that the Govt. are quite determined to bring in a Coercion Bill the very first thing and to push it through before anything else is proposed. Mr. Forster would have wished for measures far earlier and is terribly anxious. He made, as we had well known, terrible mistakes last session, but he is fully alive to the great dangers and difficulties of the case and wishes for powers to put it down. He is an honest man. . . .

He is not a man of the world—and his present office quite overwhelms him. The P. Minister was also far more impressed with the dangers of the position than I have yet seen him. But it ought never to have come to this pass. . . .

These letters are a forcible reminder that the change of government brought in its train few or none of those blessings which Gladstone had led the electors to expect. There was no cessation of foreign and imperial adventure; there was a marked increase in disastrous incidents. Domestic legislation had to be thrust aside to make way for the tragic necessities of Ireland; and the principal achievement in this sphere was the extension of household suffrage to the counties—an extension the principle of which Beaconsfield had accepted. An increase by the Beaconsfield Ministry of national expenditure from some seventy to some eighty millions a year had been denounced as profligate finance; it was a strange irony that

there was a Budget of a hundred millions before the
second Gladstone Ministry fell. Gladstone was even
ready, over a frontier post in Afghanistan, to incur that
risk of war with Russia which he had made it matter of
grave reproach against Beaconsfield to have incurred
over the fate of Constantinople and the Straits. And,
throughout the five years that the new Ministry lasted,
the foreign reputation of the country, which Beaconsfield had raised so high, was gradually frittered away—
only to be restored, towards the close of the century, by
the sagacious counsels of Beaconsfield's lieutenant and
successor, Salisbury.

In short, subsequent history has gone far to justify
the view which the Queen and most contemporary
foreign statesmen took of the election of 1880; that it
was a blunder of the democracy, misled by the almost
apostolic fervour with which Gladstone arraigned Beaconsfield's Eastern and Indian policy as not merely ill-judged
but absolutely wicked. This was perhaps the most conspicuous instance of Gladstone's tendency, in the latter
half of his life, to believe and to preach that all the most
important political questions involve moral issues. It
was from this angle that he had treated the franchise and
the Irish Church, and it was from this angle that he was,
after Beaconsfield's death, to treat Home Rule. As a
matter of fact, and as Disraeli saw, political questions
seldom present clear-cut moral issues, so that you can
definitely say that one course is morally right, the other
morally wrong. But the politician who, like Gladstone
and, in some measure, Bright, can persuade a serious and
religious people like the English, and still more the
Scotch, that such an issue is involved, has a tremendous
electoral and Parliamentary advantage. This method
of conducting political controversy was repugnant to
Disraeli, who despised it as savouring of cant; hence, no
doubt, came much of the suspicion and misconstruction
which he was never able altogether to dispel. He took
the common-sense view that in politics it is generally a

question merely of the more expedient course; and that the prime duty of a British statesman is to regard British honour and promote British welfare.

Beaconsfield's achievements during his great Ministry in the furtherance of social reform and of imperial consolidation have been sufficiently expounded in the course of our narrative. But something may be added as to his methods as Prime Minister, though these stand out clearly enough from his correspondence with his Sovereign and with his principal colleagues. There was an extreme, an Eastern, ceremoniousness, as of one who respected alike his office and his audience; a ceremoniousness which was so marked in his latter days as to lead Lord Rosebery to describe those days as majestic. He never forgot the dignity of the office he held, or underestimated the importance of the decisions at which his Cabinet might arrive. In his demeanour, as in his attire, he played the part to the full. While he spared no pains to meet the difficulties and satisfy the scruples of individual colleagues, yet more and more, as the years went on and as he realised that it was on him rather than on them that the country placed its reliance, it became his practice in Cabinet to lay down a policy which he asked his colleagues to support, and from which in essentials he would not budge, rather than —as some Prime Ministers have done—to throw the burden upon them, and count heads to ascertain their disposition. He combined immense consideration with unshakable firmness.

But the firm grip which he kept on the aims of policy was compatible with an unfailing readiness to adopt new means. A man of infinite imagination, he abounded in fresh ideas and novel, if sometimes fantastic, expedients. As a rule he did not broach these crudely in Cabinet, but tested them in the first place in intimate converse with his most trusted lieutenants—Cairns, Derby, Salisbury, Hardy, or Northcote; and he showed no hesitation in yielding if convinced of their impracticability. But so penetrating was his insight, so keen his intuition, that, over and over again, he would light at once on the solution which had evaded the patient labour and logical faculty of a competent colleague. Contemptuous as he was of detail, and constitutionally unskilled in its manipulation, he could immerse himself in it, if necessary, with ardour and success, as he proved in his conduct of the Reform Bill of 1867 through the House of Commons. He had, indeed, a hawk's eye for what was really important, and shrank from no exertion or discomfort when he deemed it necessary to be prompt and vigorous. The reader cannot fail to have been struck with the keenness and thoroughness as well as the courage and resolution with which he faced each critical situation during his great Ministry.

In his individual dealings with his colleagues he was particularly happy. There is no surer test of a chief than his attitude towards a colleague who, acting in good faith, has made a blunder. Whether it was in Parliament or in administration, his instinct was always to support his lieutenant, however mistaken his view, and however awkward the Parliamentary difficulties in which the defaulter might have involved him and his Government. In spite of that defaulter's readiness to be thrown over, Beaconsfield would again and again take the blame on himself, chivalrously ignoring the temptation to sacrifice a scapegoat; and often, by his brilliant sally, would extricate the Government with credit from an apparently hopeless muddle. ' A chief like that commands loyalty,' was the tribute of colleague after colleague. Not only would he take on his own broad shoulders the blame for the mistakes of under-secretaries; but he would not allow promising youngsters in his team to be overridden, when they had a good case, by the Cabinet or the Treasury. Lord George Hamilton, in his *Parliamentary Reminiscences*, tells a delightful story of how, on his representation as Vice-President of the Committee of Council on Education, Beaconsfield prevented the Cabinet and the Treasury from hampering the education of the country in a frantic desire to produce a popular Budget on the eve of a General Election. Lord George's estimates had been seriously mutilated early in 1880 behind his back by the Chancellor of the Exchequer with the connivance of the Lord President. The young Vice-President, failing redress from his immediate chief, carried his grievance direct to the Court of Appeal—that is, the Prime Minister.

I went to [Lord Beaconsfield] and described exactly what had occurred. He listened intently, and after a minute's reflection said: ' Is there not a thing that you call the Committee of Council upon Education ?' ' Yes,' I said, ' there is.' ' Am I on it ?' ' Yes.' ' Very well, then, tell the Lord President I wish it to be summoned at once.' It was summoned, and, I should think, for the first and last time in [its] existence, all the official members of this heterogeneous body met. We sat in a semicircle, Lord Beaconsfield in the centre, and I at the extreme outside. ' I understand,' said Lord Beaconsfield, ' that the Vice-President has a statement to make to us.' I then proceeded to state my case as best I could, letting down the Lord President and the Chancellor of the Exchequer as much as possible. When I had finished, there was a dead silence, whereupon Lord Beaconsfield remarked: ' I move that the Committee of Council on Education do agree with the Vice-President.' There was not a word of opposition to this motion, both the Chancellor of the Exchequer and the Lord President looking rather foolish.[1]

Beaconsfield was a careful dispenser of Crown patronage and honours; and he prided himself upon avoiding what he considered to be Gladstone's lavishness in their distribution. There was often, as might have been expected, an imaginative touch about his selections, as in the offer of the G.C.B. to Carlyle, and in the appointment of the poet and diplomatist, Lytton, to the Viceroyalty of India, and of the Sovereign's son-in-law, Lorne, to the Governor-Generalship of Canada. In his ecclesiastical patronage during his second Ministry he observed the rule of fair division and comprehensiveness which he had laid down in 1868, but without that eye to immediate electoral advantage which was noticeable when the fate

[1] Lord G. Hamilton's *Parliamentary Reminiscences*, pp. 152-154.

of the Irish Church was at stake.[1] He had been responsible for the promotion of Tait, Magee, Mansel, Merivale,
and Christopher Wordsworth in 1868; between 1874 and
1880 the same tradition was preserved by the advancement of Benson, Maclagan, Lightfoot, Stubbs, Farrar, and
Ryle.   In regard to patronage Fraser makes a most surprising charge against his hero.   He writes: ' No rewards
awaited those who had sacrificed everything in their support of him ; no thought was given to them ; they had
served their purpose; and, except personal courtesy, they
received no recompense of any sort or kind.'[2]   Fraser
must have been thinking of himself, but he was a gossip
and a bore, not at all a suitable candidate for office.   If
Disraeli is open to any reproach, it is, as we should have
expected in so stanch a friend, that he was perhaps too
indiscriminate in rewarding those who had served him.
Fraser can only think of the offer of a lordship-in-waiting
to Lord Exmouth.   He forgets that Disraeli secured
appointments in the public service for both his brothers
Ralph and James; that he obtained a baronetcy for Rose;
that the Lyttons, father and son, were promoted to high
office in the State; that he took John Manners, his
' Young England ' comrade, into all his Cabinets, and
gave him a red ribbon at the close, while gratifying another ' Young England ' associate, Baillie Cochrane, with
a peerage; that a peerage and a baronetcy were the
rewards of Yarde Buller and Miles, two of his stoutest supporters for the Conservative leadership; that he promoted
Lord Abergavenny from an earldom to a marquisate;
that he braved public opinion by appointing his society
friend, Lord Rosslyn, High Commissioner for the Church
of Scotland; that he offered a peerage to Andrew Montagu;
that he gave Earle office, and Corry a peerage; and that
he astonished his colleagues in the Cabinet by the high
positions in the public service for which he thought Henry
Lennox was suitable.   The list might be largely extended.
    One creditable mark of Beaconsfield's great Ministry

[1] See pp. 397-413.   [2] Fraser, p. 34.

should not pass unrecorded. It was the first Cabinet to concern itself seriously with imperial defence, which had been neglected ever since the withdrawal of imperial forces from the Colonies. Here the Prime Minister was in complete harmony with Carnarvon, who had made a special study of the subject.

To Lord Carnarvon.

CRICHEL, *Dec.* 8, '75.—. . . I look upon the restoration of our military relations with our Colonies as a question of high policy, which ought never to be absent from our thoughts. The question involves social, and political, as well as military, considerations; and you may rely on my earnest support of any steps, on your part, to accomplish this great end.

The near approach of war in 1878 forced the question to the front; and Beaconsfield appointed in the next year a strong Royal Commission, with Carnarvon, no longer a member of the Government, at its head, to consider the protection of British possessions and commerce abroad. The Commission, in the expert opinion of Lord Sydenham, the first Secretary of the Committee of Imperial Defence, ' marked a new departure in the national history.' Its three exhaustive Reports constituted the foundation whereon was gradually built that system of imperial defence which was ultimately tested in the Great War, and not found wanting.

CHAPTER XV.

ENDYMION.

1880.

At the time of his final farewell to power Beaconsfield was in his seventy-sixth year, and for long had maintained a desperate fight with the gout, asthma, and bronchitis which ever threatened to lay him low. But his spirit was still undefeated. Not content with the continuing labours of political leadership, he set to work at once to finish the novel which he had planned and begun as a consequence of the success of *Lothair*, but which he had abandoned for many years owing to engrossing political avocations. There was little for a Leader of Opposition in the House of Lords to do for some months; and Beaconsfield applied himself to composition with such steadiness that the manuscript was practically complete early in August. The negotiations with Longmans for its publication were placed entirely in Rowton's hands; and so successfully did he conduct them that the firm, whose original offer was £7,500, finally agreed, before even seeing the manuscript, to give for all rights in *Endymion* what they believed to be the largest sum ever till then paid for a work of fiction—£10,000: £2,500 on the delivery of the manuscript, and £7,500 on April 1, 1881—less than three weeks, as it happened, before Beaconsfield's death. The manuscript was delivered in September, 1880, and *Endymion* appeared on November 26. Rowton told Beaconsfield of the success of the negotiation when they were both attending a debate in the House of Lords.

From Lord Rowton.

HOUSE OF LORDS, *Aug.* 4, '80.—There are things too big to impart in whispers! so I leave your side, just to write these words.

Longman has to-day offered *Ten Thousand Pounds* for *Endymion*.

I have accepted it! I cannot tell you what a pleasure it is to me to see my ardent ambition for you gratified!

And you have an added honor which may for ever remain without precedent.

To Lord Rowton.

HUGHENDEN, *Sept.* 14, 1880.—L[ongman] arrived here yesterday by 5 o'clock train, and proposed that 'our little business' should be transacted before dinner. I was ready: the MS. had been carefully revised, and the printer much assisted, so I hope I shall not have to trouble him much for revises. . . . The receipt was ready and the cheque drawn, or else I should have thought it this morning all a dream. I know no magic of the Middle Ages equal to it! And you are the Magician, best and dearest of friends! . . .

The first proof will arrive this day—no—yesterday week, and it will all be consummated, I understand, by the first week of October. . . .

Since I wrote this, L[ongman] has departed (10 o'clock train) with our young friend. Three businesslike packages, all in his portmanteaus . .

Mr. Norton Longman kindly allows me to quote, in a slightly shortened form, from a memorandum which he drew up at the time, his humorous description of the fashion in which the momentous transaction was carried through. It was his second visit to Hughenden, as he had stayed there, after the conclusion of the agreement, for a week-end in August, and had then, under Rowton's guidance, inspected the manuscript. This time he found Beaconsfield quite alone, without either secretary or visitor, and in capital spirits.

Knowing I had to leave rather early the next morning, I ventured to suggest that it might be convenient for us to do our little business before dinner. The business *I* alluded to was connected with our bankers, but it is certain Ld. B.'s idea of the business was the formal delivery of the MS. to

me. 'Oh yes, certainly,' was the reply to my suggestion
'Of course, much better to get our business done, the sooner
the better. Ah, let me see, how shall we manage?' I confess
I did not quite understand his lordship's meaning, because
everything seemed to me to be simple enough, so I said
nothing, and waited for another cue, as it was clear to me Ld.
B. was a little fidgety and rather excited. The formal
delivery of his precious child appeared to be too much for
him. 'Well, Mr. Longman,' continued the author in a
somewhat low tone of voice, 'shall I ring for Mr. Baum, and
have my study lighted?' Of course, I agreed and said,
'Yes, certainly,' but to my surprise his lordship turned to
me and said, 'No, no, Mr. Longman, stop a minute. Mr. Baum
knows nothing of this, and we must not excite his suspicion.[1]
We must light the candles ourselves.' Feeling quite equal
to this responsibility I simply said, 'Oh yes,' in rather a cheery
voice, endeavouring to remove the idea, which appeared to
be so prominent in his mind, that we were about to rob a
church or do some such dreadful deed.

I followed him upstairs to his own apartment. He is very
shortsighted, and I had to render him a great deal of assistance
in finding and lighting the candles. 'We must light ALL the
candles, Mr. Longman; I can't get on without plenty of light!'
said Lord B., and continued; 'but we must have your room
lighted also. But Mr. Baum can do that.' So Mr. B. was
summoned and instructed to light my room. No sooner had
Mr. Baum left us and the door been closed with special care
than the distinguished author proceeded to lay open three
red despatch boxes. Each volume was carefully tied up in
red tape, and each in its own box. These well-known recep-
tacles of secret information being emptied of their valuable
contents, I felt a little anxious to know what was to come
next. After a moment's pause he turned to me and said,
'Are you ready?' 'Oh yes,' I replied, 'I am quite ready, are
you?' What was going to happen? Were we really going
to rob a church? The air was full of mystery. 'Can you
carry two?' he continued. 'Yes,' I replied, not saying one
word more than was absolutely necessary. The door being
opened—slowly, solemnly, carefully, mysteriously I followed
the ex-Premier as he trod lightly along the passage, to my
apartment! Having arrived safely, and closing the door
with extra precaution, he remarked, 'I am most anxious

---

[1] Beaconsfield once described to Rose his experience of an old retainer—
almost certainly Baum—thus: 'For the first five years he was with me I
found him a most excellent servant; for the next five years he was a faithful
and interesting friend; and for the last five years he has been a most indulgent
master.'

none of my servants should know anything of this; that is why I am so careful.'

'Well,' thought I to myself, 'so far, so good, but what is to come next ?' This was the evening before dinner, and I did not of course leave the house until the next morning. The valuable burden having been deposited on the table, Ld. B. with a sigh of relief remarked, 'There; but what are you going to do with it ?' This was a regular poser, as I had not the slightest idea what to do with so precious an article for some fifteen hours or so. A happy thought flashed across my mind. 'My Glad——' I luckily stopped in time— 'bag !' But this notion only created fresh complications. My bag was nowhere to be found. It had simply vanished. Awful idea ! Had Mr. Baum done this on purpose ? Of course we could not ring to ask Mr. Baum what had become of it, as no doubt he would guess something was going on. We looked under the bed, in the wardrobes, in every corner; but no, nothing could be found until a brilliant idea came to the mind of the great statesman. 'Perhaps it is in the dressing-room, just outside here,' he said; and much to our relief it was. I immediately carried it off to my room, and there under the very eye of the author deposited the three volumes in my little portmanteau. After placing the 3rd volume in its temporary resting-place Lord B. turned to me and said, 'But, Mr. Longman, how about your wardrobe ?' 'Oh, there will be plenty of room for that,' I replied. But this did not satisfy my host at all, and he pressed me to allow him to be of service. 'Mr. Baum can supply you with any variety of portmanteau, if you only ask him,' continued Lord B., but I assured his lordship it was quite unnecessary for me to trespass on his hospitality.

Having thus accomplished the solemn and complicated task of the formal delivery of the MS., but not without some difficulty, we returned to his lordship's room, and in a very few minutes I finished my part of the affair by paying him a cheque and taking his receipt.

The dominant idea in *Endymion* is the enormous, indeed decisive, importance of women in directing and moulding the life of man, and, particularly, political man. Looking back over his own career Beaconsfield realised all that he owed to his sister's discerning sympathy, to Mrs. Austen's encouragement and criticism, to his wife's devotion—and income, to Lady Blessington's and Lady Londonderry's friendship, to Mrs. Brydges Willyams's benevolence, and to the atmosphere of sympathy and appreciation which had been provided for his declining years through his intimacy with Lady Bradford and Lady Chesterfield and through the gracious indulgence of his Queen. His debt to women was no doubt great; but his inherent genius, his patient labour, and his indomitable will were, after all, the main factors in his astonishing success. It pleased him, in certain moods, to say, as he did once in a letter to Lady Bradford, ' I owe everything to woman'; but, of him, it was not true. Of Endymion, the hero of his last novel, however, it is true. Had it not been for Myra, his virile sister; for Lady Montfort, the leader of society who marries him; and, in a lesser degree, for Adriana Neuchatel, the banker's daughter, and for Lady Beaumaris, transformed by a fortunate marriage from a lodging-house keeper's daughter into a Tory *grande dame*, Endymion would have spent his days in a second-rate Government office, rising gradually by a good address and a punctual discharge of duty to an assistant-secretaryship and a pension. Thanks to the influence of these women, he becomes, at about the age of forty, Prime Minister of Great Britain.

His story may be told in few words. Born in 1819, the grandson of a successful Civil Servant, and the son of a politician at one time of much promise—who, having lived far beyond his means and having made the mistake of attaching himself to Wellington rather than to Canning or to Grey, was hopelessly ruined and driven ultimately to suicide by the Reform Act of 1832—Endymion Ferrars could get no better start in life than a clerkship in Somerset House at the age of sixteen. But he has a twin sister, Myra, who is depicted as the embodiment of irresistible will, and who determines from her girlhood to devote her life to promoting her brother's career. ' I shall be in the world,' she says when rejecting as a girl of seventeen her first suitor, ' whatever be my lot, high or low— the active, stirring world—working for him, thinking only of him. Yes: moulding events and circumstances

in his favour.' Though left, like her brother, penniless
at their parents' death, she, by a turn of fortune's wheel,
meets, and wins the affections of, an elderly statesman of
great distinction, then Foreign Secretary, and at the age of
nineteen marries him, largely with the object of advancing
her brother's interests. 'Our degradation is over,' she
tells Endymion. 'I see a career, ay, and a great one;
and what is far more important, I see a career for you. . . .
We have now got a lever to move the world.' Her new
status, as Lady Roehampton, gives her brother at once
the entry into society, and her influence procures him,
first, the private secretaryship to one of her husband's
colleagues, together with a transfer to a Government
office of a higher class, and afterwards, at the age of twenty-
six, the under-secretaryship for foreign affairs under her
husband. The opening having been provided by his
sister, the rest of Endymion's rise to greatness is mainly
due to Lady Montfort, 'the famous Berengaria, Queen of
Society, and the genius of Whiggism.' This powerful
personage takes him up from his first appearance in
society, pushes him both socially and politically, finds
him a seat in Parliament, and finally, when her immensely
rich husband has conveniently died and left her everything
except the settled estates, bestows herself and all her
possessions on her *protégé*, thus giving him an unassailable
position, 'a root in the country.' Meanwhile his sister,
early left a widow, has become by her second marriage
the Queen Consort of a friendly Sovereign. No wonder
that before long Endymion is appointed Foreign Secretary
and that when the curtain is rung down he has just
kissed hands at Windsor as Prime Minister. Towards
the seat in Parliament, it should be added, Endymion
received substantial assistance from the two other ladies.
Lady Beaumaris, from the Tory camp, staved off an
opposition that might have proved fatal; and the wealthy
Adriana Neuchatel, by a timely but anonymous investment of £20,000 on his behalf in Consols, put him in a
pecuniary position to avail himself of the opportunity.

A hero of this kind could hardly fail to be colourless and insipid.   We are told that, besides being good-looking and pleasant-mannered, he was 'intelligent and well informed, without any alarming originality or too positive convictions'; that he was 'prudent and plastic'; that he 'always did and said the right thing.'   He is, indeed, the industrious apprentice *in excelsis;* but he has no resolution, no *élan,* no sparkle, no genius, and is as different as well can be from the brilliant and adventurous heroes of Disraeli's earlier novels, such as Vivian Grey, Contarini Fleming, and Coningsby.   It is rather surprising that Dilke should have been gratified by the belief that Endymion's political career had been largely modelled on his own; a belief which Beaconsfield himself encouraged in conversation.   For the story of Endymion's progress to the helm of State is a fairy tale which cannot be accepted as possible or credible; it can make no converts to the theory of the omnipotence of female influence in the world.

Myra, Endymion's resolute sister, is also a failure; but Lady Montfort, his other principal patroness, is alive and charming.   Some of her characteristics may have been derived from recollections of Mrs. Norton, Lord Melbourne's friend; in a few particulars Beaconsfield seems to be drawing on his experiences with Lady Bradford. Lord Montfort, her husband, is also a well-conceived and well-presented character.

Lord Montfort was the only living Englishman who gave one an idea of the nobleman of the eighteenth century.   He was totally devoid of the sense of responsibility, and he looked what he resembled. . . .
No one could say Lord Montfort was a bad-hearted man, for he had no heart.   He was good-natured, provided it brought him no inconvenience; and as for temper, his was never disturbed, but this not from sweetness of disposition, rather from a contemptuous fine taste, which assured him that a gentleman should never be deprived of tranquillity in a world where nothing was of the slightest consequence.

In spite, indeed, of the unconvincing presentation of the main argument, *Endymion* is full of interest.   It contains much brilliant writing and characterisation; and it throws many informing sidelights on its author's point of view and on society and politics in the second quarter of the nineteenth century. For the book is a curious blend of history and fiction. In his old age, Beaconsfield looks back with fondness to the period of his vigorous manhood, and places the creations of his fancy in the world which was familiar to him when he was in the twenties, thirties, and forties. Starting from Canning's death in 1827, the story wends its way with a background of the authentic domestic politics of the time down to the defeat of the Coalition in 1855. From that point—which is not, however, reached till the last dozen pages—the whole becomes romance, and neither Sidney Wilton's premiership, nor Endymion's succession to him, has any counterpart in the history of the late fifties. To the historical portions of the book it is unnecessary to refer at length, as they have been abundantly quoted in the first three volumes of this biography. It may, however, perhaps be said that the opening chapters, dealing with the effects of Canning's death and with the troubled politics of the next five years, are particularly striking and vigorous, having been written presumably before the pressure of public work compelled the author, in 1872 or 1873, to lay the manuscript aside. There are, moreover, some admirable sketches of social movements, the recollection of which had almost faded away even in 1880: the agitation in 1850-51 over the Papal aggression; that high fantastical show, the Eglinton Tournament (called here the Montfort Tournament) of 1839, about which Disraeli obtained information in 1872 from Jane Duchess of Somerset, who had, as Lady Seymour, presided over the tournament; and the railway mania of the forties, when 'a new channel' was found for capital and labour, and gigantic fortunes were made—and lost.

Though Endymion is not in the least like his creator in character or career, he is given in the latter chapters, somewhat incongruously, qualities, feelings, and habits which Beaconsfield had observed in himself. 'The power and melody of his voice'; his readiness without excessive fluency in debate; his power of keen sarcasm, 'that dangerous, though most effective, weapon,' held in severe check; his complete control of his temper—for these Disraelian qualities the earlier history of Endymion had little prepared the reader. And Beaconsfield was surely thinking of himself rather than of Endymion when he wrote: 'there was nothing for him to do but to plunge into business: and affairs of State are a cure for many cares and sorrows. What are our petty annoyances and griefs when we have to guard the fortunes and the honour of a nation?' Intimate and family dinners during the session with the Bradfords and with Lady Chesterfield must have been in his mind when he wrote of Endymion's difficulties in getting away from the House when in office: 'No little runnings up to Montfort House or Hill Street just to tell them the authentic news, or snatch a hasty repast with furtive delight, with persons still more delightful.'

The experience of the statesman who has taken his full share in the direction of great affairs pervades the book. The importance, for the art of government, of personal knowledge of foreign statesmen comes with effect from one who played a leading part at the Congress of Berlin. There, as his Lord Roehampton at Vienna, 'he learned to gauge the men who govern the world.' 'Conducting affairs without this knowledge is, in effect, an affair of stationery; it is pens and paper who are in communication, not human beings.' To the retrospective statesman, 'the finest elements in the management of men and affairs' seem to be 'observation and perception of character.' He blames Peel for not trusting youth: 'it is a confidence which should be exercised, particularly in the conduct of a popular assembly.' He himself had shown it in many cases, notably those of Lord George Hamilton and Edward Stanhope. He looks, almost with complacency, on the confusion of his private affairs which

had pursued him throughout life. 'That seems almost
the inevitable result of being absorbed in the great business of governing mankind.' He does not neglect in his
reflections, as he did not in his life, the question of dress.
Mr. Vigo tells Endymion, 'You must dress according to
your age, your pursuits, your object in life. . . . In youth,
a little fancy is rather expected, but, if political life be
your object, it should be avoided, at least after one and
twenty.' Disraeli himself had postponed the change till
he was forty. Other personal touches may be noted.
He ascribes to his heroine Myra that 'passion for light,'
even when alone, which he felt himself; the belief that
brilliant illumination had a beneficial moral effect on the
temperament. He had his own talk in mind when he
defined the art of conversation thus: 'to be prompt
without being stubborn, to refute without argument, and
to clothe grave matters in a motley garb.' His own
ambition, his belief in the power of will, and in the
utilisation of opportunity, find extreme and uncompromising utterance in Myra's words: 'A human being with
a settled purpose must accomplish it.' 'Nothing can
resist a will that will stake even existence for its fulfilment.' 'Power, and power alone, should be your absorbing object, and all the accidents and incidents of life should
only be considered with reference to that main result.'
'Great men should think of Opportunity, and not of
Time. Time is the excuse of feeble and tired spirits.
They make time the sleeping partner of their lives to
accomplish what ought to be achieved by their own will.'
There is also, no doubt, something of Beaconsfield's own
sentiment about religion in the views which he borrows
from the wits of the past and puts into the mouth of
Waldershare: 'Sensible men are all of the same religion.'
'And pray, what is that?' 'Sensible men never tell.'[1]
An absolute reticence as to his personal religion was one

---

[1] Lord Fitzmaurice, in his *Life of Lord Granville*, points out that this
passage is a reproduction of Speaker Onslow's footnote to Burnet's character
of Shaftesbury in his *History of His Own Time*, Vol. I., p. 164.

of Beaconsfield's marked characteristics, though he has told us much of his ideals in this sphere in *Tancred* and *Lord George Bentinck.*

Though not so full of 'quotations' as *Lothair, Endymion* yet contains many sententious phrases of the right Disraelian mintage. In the political sphere we hear of 'the commonplaces of middle-class ambition, which are humorously called democratic opinions'; in the social sphere, of 'a Knight of the Garter or a member of White's —the only two things an Englishman cannot command.' And here are two admirable aphorisms: 'Inquirers who are always inquiring never learn anything'; 'A dinner of wits is proverbially a palace of silence.'

The Queen was puzzled to find the hero of the Tory leader's last novel a Whig. And, indeed, it is a mark of the detachment with which the book is written, that the history of from 1827 to 1855 is treated from the Whig standpoint, and, so to speak, from within the Whig camp; and that in Waldershare the opinions of the 'Young England' party, with which Disraeli himself sympathised, are put forward in a bizarre and extravagant manner, calculated rather to provoke laughter than to win acceptance. Take Waldershare's dogma about foreign policy: 'All diplomacy since the Treaty of Utrecht seems to me to be fiddle faddle.' Or his lament over the disappearance of 'pottles' of strawberries: 'I believe they went out, like all good things, with the Stuarts.' Or his paradoxes about the navy—

I must say it was a grand idea of our kings making themselves Sovereigns of the sea. The greater portion of this planet is water; so we at once became a first-rate power. We owe our navy entirely to the Stuarts. King James the Second was the true founder and hero of the British navy. He was the worthy son of his admirable father, that blessed Martyr, the restorer at least, if not the inventor, of ship money; the most patriotic and popular tax that ever was devised by man. The Nonconformists thought themselves so wise in resisting it, and they have got the naval estimates instead !

II.   46

Not indeed that the Whig conventions are too seriously
respected.. 'The cause for which Hampden died on the
field, and Sidney on the scaffold' is identified, not with
the liberties of the subject, but with 'the Whig Government of England'; and the typical magnate of this great
historical connection would be, we are given to understand,
'a haughty Whig peer, proud of his order, prouder of
his party . . . freezing with arrogant reserve and condescending politeness.' Of Melbourne's dissolution in
1841 Beaconsfield writes: 'It was unusual, almost unconstitutional, thus to terminate the body they had
created. Nevertheless, the Whigs, never too delicate in
such matters, thought they had a chance, and determined
not to lose it.'

More perhaps than in any other of his novels did
Beaconsfield in *Endymion* draw his characters from the
life.[1] That Waldershare was a full-length portrait of
George Smythe has been already pointed out.[2] Smythe's
very words in a speech at Canterbury in 1847, reprinted
in 1875 in the memoir of him prefixed to his novel *Angela
Pisani*, about the Tory party being a succession of heroic
spirits, are put into Waldershare's mouth in *Endymion*,
so that no concealment whatever was affected. Then
Lord Roehampton, so far as his public action as Foreign
Minister is concerned, was, as we have seen, a flattering
portrait of Palmerston. Zenobia, 'the queen of London,
of fashion, and of the Tory party,' was drawn from Lady
Jersey. Sidney Wilton, Endymion's Ministerial chief.
'a man of noble disposition, fine manners, considerable
culture '—' a great gentleman '—inevitably recalled, by
name and character, Sidney Herbert, the Peelite statesman.
The great financial family, the Neuchatels, represent the
Rothschilds under a thin disguise, though the Jewish
element is dropped, and the founder described as a Swiss

---

[1] It is impossible to take very seriously Disraeli's frequent protests against
the identification of his characters with living individuals. 'When I write,'
he once told Lady Chesterfield, 'I never introduce photographs of any
living character, tho' it is impossible, when dealing with human nature, not
to appropriate some human traits.' See Vol. I., pp. 95-97.
[2] See Vol. I., p. 560.

Hainault House, with its magnificent stables, park, gardens, and conservatories, and a *chef* who was the 'greatest celebrity of Europe'—all within an hour's drive of the City—is a glorified reflection of Gunnersbury. There Beaconsfield had often enjoyed such week-end parties and dinners as are depicted in *Endymion*. Adrian Neuchatel himself, who combined the financial genius of the family with culture and political ambition, is painted pretty directly from the author's friend, Baron Lionel. In Nigel Penruddock, the Anglican clergyman who, despairing of the 'chance of becoming a Laud,' submits to Rome and becomes a Cardinal, Disraeli repaired any injustice he may be thought to have done Manning in his picture of Cardinal Grandison in *Lothair*. 'A smiling ascetic,' he 'was seen everywhere, even at fashionable assemblies'; but the conversion of England was 'his constant purpose and his daily and nightly prayer.' In Job Thornberry there are touches both of Cobden and of Bright; and fleeting memories of the brothers Bulwer in that amusing pair, Mr. Bertie Tremaine and Mr. Tremaine Bertie. Mr. Vigo is an incongruous blend of Poole, the tailor, and Hudson, the 'railway king.'

Thackeray fares as badly at Beaconsfield's hands in *Endymion* as Croker had fared in old days in *Coningsby*. Thackeray had burlesqued Disraeli's style in *Novels by Eminent Hands*, 'Codlingsby by D. Shrewsberry Esq.'— a skit which was originally published in *Punch*. It was not a very happy or satisfying performance, although thoroughly in harmony with *Punch's* whole attitude to Disraeli in his earlier days. But Thackeray had subsequently, in two speeches at the Royal Literary Fund dinner in 1851 and 1852, shown appreciation of the credit which Disraeli's career reflected on the whole profession of novel-writing. What he said in 1852 has been already quoted.[1] In 1851 he said:

If you will but look at the novelists of the present day, I think you will see it is altogether out of the question to pity

[1] Vol. I., p. 1163.

them. We will take in the first instance, if you please, a great novelist who is the great head of a great party in a great assembly in the country. When this celebrated man went into his county and proposed to represent it, and was asked on what interest he stood, he nobly said he stood on his head. And I want to know who can deny the gallantry and brilliancy of that eminent crest of his, and question the merit of Mr. Disraeli.

Thackeray himself sent a copy of the speech to Mrs. Disraeli as a proof ' that some authors can praise other authors behind their backs.' After these handsome compliments, it was perhaps rather ill-natured of Beaconsfield, in his turn, to burlesque Thackeray as St. Barbe, ' the vainest, most envious, most amusing of men.' That there was something of the snob in the immortal author of the *Book of Snobs* himself may be admitted. But the exaggeration of this quality in St. Barbe makes the caricature almost unrecognisable. On the other hand, few characters in the book are in themselves more vivid and diverting.

Two characters represent, with more or less fidelity, the two most eminent foreign statesmen with whom Disraeli had to deal, Napoleon III. and Bismarck. The plots and vicissitudes which diversified Louis Napoleon's exile are reproduced in the career of the pretender, Prince Florestan, who first appears in London society as Count Albert, a mysterious, silent, and solitary figure. An inveterate and shifty conspirator from his boyhood, he excuses the breach of his solemn parole by the plea that he is ' the child of destiny,' that his action was ' the natural development of the irresistible principle of historical necessity '; but he is a romantic personality who interests women, being gifted with tender and gentle manners, and ready with unobtrusive sympathy, save when lost in profound abstraction. When he set up house in London in his own name, ' it was the fashion among the *crème de la crème* to keep aloof from him. The Tories did not love revolutionary dynasties, and the Whigs being in office could not sanction a pretender, and one who, they significantly intimated with a charitable shrug of the shoulders

was not a very scrupulous one.' He promoted his cause
by political dinners, at which he 'encouraged conversation,
though himself inclined to taciturnity. When he did
speak, his terse remarks and condensed views were
striking, and were remembered.' The year of revolution,
1848, gave him back his father's throne; and, like Louis
Napoleon, he established a Government 'liberal but
discreet, and, though conciliatory, firm'; declared for an
English alliance; and tried, but failed, to marry into a
Continental reigning house.

Both Florestan and Count Ferroll, who stands for
Bismarck, were at the Montfort Tournament, as Louis
Napoleon certainly attended the Eglinton Tournament;
and they were the most successful knights in the jousting.
The Prince recognised that Ferroll and he would have
to contend for many things more precious than golden
helms before they died. Ferroll, said the Prince, 'is a
man neither to love nor to detest. He has himself an
intelligence superior to all passion, I might say all feeling;
and if, in dealing with such a being, we ourselves have
either, we give him an advantage.'

Florestan's attitude of detached admiration is the
attitude which Beaconsfield preserves himself towards
his Bismarck-Ferroll—'a man of an original not to say
eccentric turn of mind,' 'a man who seldom makes a
mistake.' There is a vivid presentment of the great man's
appearance in early middle age. 'Though not to be
described as a handsome man, his countenance was
striking; a brow of much intellectual development, and a
massive jaw. He was tall, broad-shouldered, with a
slender waist.' At that time he was 'brooding over the
position of what he could scarcely call his country, but
rather an aggregation of lands baptised by protocols, and
christened and consolidated by treaties which he looked
upon as eminently untrustworthy.' Ferroll reveals in a
conversation with Lady Montfort the Bismarckian
methods by which this unsatisfactory state of things
was to be remedied.

'My worthy master wants me to return home and be Minister; I am to fashion for him a new constitution. I will never have anything to do with new constitutions; their inventors are always the first victims. Instead of making a constitution, he should make a country, and convert his heterogeneous domains into a patriotic dominion.'

'But how is that to be done ?'

'There is only one way; by blood and iron.'

'My dear Count, you shock me.'

'I shall have to shock you a great deal more, before the inevitable is brought about.'

Europe, Ferroll told Endymion on another occasion, 'is a geographical expression. There is no State in Europe; I exclude your own country, which belongs to every division of the globe, and is fast becoming more commercial than political, and I exclude Russia, for she is essentially Oriental, and her future will be entirely in the East.' As for Germany, he could not find it on the maps. It was practically as weak as Italy. 'We have some kingdoms who are allowed to play at being first-rate powers; but it is only play.' 'Then is France periodically to overrun Europe?' asks Endymion. 'So long as it continues to be merely Europe,' is the answer.

Rowton tells us that *Endymion* is named after Endymion Porter—the royalist friend of Davenant, Dekker, and Herrick—whom Lady Beaconsfield claimed as an ancestor. It is possible that the original suggestion arose in this way. But it may be pointed out that the choice of *Endymion* for the title of a book written to glorify female influence over male careers, and for the name of its hero, was a kind of cryptic dedication of the volumes to 'Selina Bradford'; as, of course, in Greek mythology, Endymion was the human lover of Selene, the Moon Goddess. The selection must have appealed to Beaconsfield's ironical humour; as one of the few imperfections he found in Lady Bradford was an inability to appreciate his novels, and she would almost certainly fail to understand the compliment unless he pointed it out to her.

To Lady de Rothschild.[1]

HUGHENDEN MANOR, *Nov.* 21, '80.—I always think there is something very egotistical in a writer presenting his work to another person. It is an offering that should be reserved for our dearest friends, for they will not misinterpret the motive, or attribute to arrogance what springs from affection.

Do me, therefore, the honor of receiving *Endymion*, when he calls to-day, or to-morrow; and if I might venture to do so, I would ask the favor, at your convenience, of conveying to me some of your impressions in reading it. I particularly ask this, not only because I have confidence in your intelligence and always welcome criticism, but because this is the first work wh. I ever published without the preliminary advantage of a female counsellor, an advantage which, I know from experience, is inestimable.

I fear the young gentleman will not reach you till Tuesday

From the Princess of Wales.

SANDRINGHAM, NORFOLK, *Nov.* 29*th*, 1880.

DEAR LORD BEACONSFIELD,

It is not from want of appreciation of your most interesting and valuable present, that I have delayed some days thanking you for it—but I was absent from home when your book arrived and only found it here on my return Saturday afternoon.

I cannot, I am afraid, flatter myself at having had any share in the book beyond having suggested years ago 'the title,' 'Sympathy,' which I see, however, you have *not* adopted, so, alas! I have no claims whatever to go down to posterity as joint author of *Endymion*.

But, joking apart, I am looking forward to spending many most agreeable hours with one of the best authors of the century. May I only ask you still further to enhance the value of the book by writing your name in it when we next meet?—Believe me, dear Lord Beaconsfield, Yrs. sincerely,—ALEXANDRA.

High appreciation of *Endymion* was expressed by both the distinguished men who had served under Beaconsfield as Foreign Secretary. Derby told Northcote at Grillion's that 'there were three remarkable things about it. (1) He knew no other novel in English written by a man of 75,

[1] Now Lady Rothschild, widow of Nathaniel, 1st Lord Rothschild, Disraeli's friend and executor.

or (2) published 50 years after a former novel by the same author, or (3) written by a man after he had been Prime Minister (except, of course, *Lothair*).' And Salisbury wrote gracefully to Beaconsfield on December 1: 'You must let me congratulate you on the universal popularity of *Endymion*. Many people think it the best you have written—a judgment in which I should agree, if I ventured upon an opinion in matters critical.' But the book, like others of Disraeli's writings, displeased many a serious reader. Archbishop Tait confided to his diary, 'I have finished *Endymion* with a painful feeling that the writer considers all political life as mere play and gambling.' And a valued correspondent of W. H. Smith wrote: 'The reader cannot refrain from the disagreeable conclusion that the writer holds the world as a mere plaything, for his special amusement and contempt by turns.' There was, of course, much of this sardonic humour in Disraeli, and free vent is given to it in *Endymion*. The hero, in particular, seems to have no political views save those which are pumped into him by others. But that Disraeli had high ideals, and the will to make them prevail, was shown by many previous books, especially the trilogy of *Coningsby*, *Sybil*, and *Tancred*, and by the administration and legislation for which he was responsible. It is not unnatural that, in the evening of life, he should have written in a lighter, even in a trifling, vein.

In accepting Messrs. Longmans' 'truly liberal offer' of £10,000 for *Endymion*, Beaconsfield wrote, on August 7, that he was convinced that the firm would have no cause to regret the enterprise. The interest which the book excited appeared to justify this hope. Mudie put his name down for 3,000 copies, which Mr. Longman believed to be unprecedented; and the number of copies printed for the first edition was 10,500, which the publisher thought 'simply gigantic.' But on the day of publication, November 26, Beaconsfield was less sanguine. He wrote to Lady Bradford: 'I confess I accepted [the £10,000]

with a scruple, such a sum never having before
been given for a work of fiction, or indeed any other
work. I fear it will prove rather the skill of Monty's
diplomacy than Mr. Longman's business acumen. If so,
my conscience will force me to disgorge.' The premature publication of a review, in the *Standard,* greatly
annoyed both author and publisher, and may have
interfered with the sales. But the reviews were generally
favourable. Beaconsfield reported progress to Rowton
in Algiers.

To Lord Rowton.

HUGHENDEN, *Dec.* 6, '80.—. . . As for private affairs, I
can't give you the definite information I could wish. His
[Longman's] original plan of the campaign turned out to be
a right one. The response was enormous, but something
happened about the *Standard,* which, according to his view,
has played the devil. I can't attempt to go into the story.

As for literary verdict, very generally in favor.

But as for society, I can say nothing. I am a hermit and
see nobody. Those, the very few, to whom it was given,
send, of course, mechanical applause. All the gossips, who
would have told us the talk of the town . . . are silent,
because they are sulky at not having received it. . . .

By March, 1881, Beaconsfield had definite reason to
fear that the novel had not been a commercial success;
and he therefore generously volunteered, through Rowton,
to cancel the agreement, and fall back on the arrangement
made in the case of *Lothair,* a royalty of 10s. in the £ on all
copies sold. This proposal amounted, in the publisher's
opinion, to making the firm a present of £3,000. Mr.
Longman at once replied that it was true that the three-
volume edition of *Endymion* had not been the commercial
success that the three-volume edition of *Lothair* was;
but that the firm had made their offer with their eyes
open and the result had quite answered their expectations;
and that they could not think of availing themselves of
Beaconsfield's liberal and considerate suggestion. The
story, creditable in a high degree to both author and
publisher, had an appropriate and felicitous sequel.

The popular 6s. edition of *Endymion*, which was on sale
during the early months of the year, was more successful
even than the popular edition of *Lothair* had been.   On
March 24 Mr. Longman was able to report to Beaconsfield that over 8,000 copies had been disposed of; and early
in April the debt on the book had been completely worked
off.   Beaconsfield had by this time been overtaken by his
fatal illness; but Mr. Longman sent the facts to Rowton,
who was able to brighten one of his dying friend's last
days with the good news.   'This was the last business
transaction I ever had with my dear chief,' was Rowton's
endorsement on Mr. Longman's letter.

Beaconsfield did not lay down his pen when he had
finished *Endymion*.   He promptly started a new novel,
of which he had completed nine short chapters before
his death.   This unfinished work is printed as an
Appendix.   It promised to be a story rather in the
manner of *Lothair* than in that of *Endymion*.   There was
no return to the memories of the author's youth and
middle age; but the action was represented as taking
place in the present or the immediate past, Lothair himself
being mentioned, and his friends Lady Clanmorne and
Hugo Bohun being introduced.   Detailed critical comment
on a work in which Beaconsfield had only posed the
characters, and had hardly yet begun to set them in
motion, would be absurd.   But it may confidently be
said that this fragment bears no sign of failing power;
the peculiar qualities which give their savour to the
Disraeli novel are all present.   Attention may be
specially directed to two points.   The central figure was
unmistakably drawn from the rival who had just pulled
Beaconsfield down, and seated himself in triumph in his
place.   Joseph Toplady Falconet, sprung from a well-to-
do commercial family; a young man with a remarkable
power of acquisition, a vigorous and retentive memory,
a disputatious and arrogant temper, an immense flow of
language, and no sense of humour whatever; who carried
all before him at public school and University, and then

was immediately brought by the noble patron of a small
borough into Parliament; who, ' firm in his faith in an age
of dissolving creeds, wished to believe that he was the
man ordained '—but only as a lay champion—' to vindicate the sublime cause of religious truth ' :—can there be a
doubt that we have here a picture of the youthful Gladstone, only with his birth post-dated by nearly half-a-
century ? It is indeed a loss that we can never know
how Falconet's character was intended to be developed,
and what adventures were to be his in love, politics, and
religion.

The other point that cannot fail to attract the reader's
notice is the prominence given to a sort of philosophy of
despair, destruction, and anarchism. No fewer than four
of the characters profess it in some form or another; a
Great Unknown, a personage near akin to the unique
Sidonia; a German millionaire of philosophic tendencies;
a charming, but hopelessly impracticable, heir to a
peerage; and a Buddhist missionary from Ceylon. These
all accept, in differing degrees, the doctrine that the
future must be secured by destroying the present, that
the human race is exhausted, that destruction in every
form must be welcomed. We may perhaps trace here the
profound impression made on Beaconsfield by the Nihilist
conspiracy in Russia, which succeeded in murdering
Alexander while this unfinished novel was in the making.
It was a movement that carried to a further pitch that
political and religious Revolution in Europe, of which we
know from *Lothair* that he was a keen observer. One
sentence, which falls from the lips of the Buddhist
Kusinara, represents a sentiment that may well have been
in the writer's mind in his last days : ' Death is only
happiness, if understood.'

With the close of the first paragraph of chapter 10 the
pen dropped from Beaconsfield's hand. It was fifty-six
years since his first publication, a pamphlet on American
mining companies, and fifty-five years since the appearance
of *Vivian Grey*, which brought him public notoriety. The

story goes that someone asked Disraeli in later life what
had become of Vivian Grey, and received the delightful
reply: 'There was no inquest; it is believed that he
survives.' In a sense most of his heroes survived in him
—Vivian Grey, Contarini Fleming, Coningsby, Tancred,
and the rest. It is this aspect of his novels that has made
it necessary to analyse them at greater length than is
usual in biographies. Without a study of his books, it
is impossible to understand his life. They all abound
in illustrations of distinctive qualities of his mind and
character; they all, with hardly an exception, are closely
interwoven with the experiences of his personal or his
political career. 'My books,' he once wrote to Lady
Bradford, ' are the history of my life. I don't mean a
vulgar photograph of incidents, but the psychological
development of my character. Self-inspiration may be
egotistical, but it is generally true.' Remarkable as
Disraeli's books are as literary creations, they are
indispensable to the biographer as emanations from the
creative artist behind them.

Perhaps this quality of these unique works has been
responsible for their under-valuation as literature. Few
critics have been able to regard them with a single eye
for their literary merits. Sir Leslie Stephen writes
enthusiastically of some of their features, especially of
the irony which pervades them. 'This ambiguous
hovering between two meanings,' he says, ' this oscillation
between the ironical and the serious, is always amusing,
and sometimes delightful. . . . The texture of Mr.
Disraeli's writings is so ingeniously shot with irony and
serious sentiment that each tint may predominate by
turns. Mr. Disraeli is not exactly a humourist, but
something for which the rough nomenclature of critics
has not yet provided a distinctive name.' Yet even
Stephen, with all his appreciation, suggests that the
novels represent promise, rather than performance; and
are only an earnest of what might have been creative
work of permanent value, had not their writer unfor-

tunately subordinated his literary to his political career.
This judgment seems to be demonstrably mistaken. The
novels of Disraeli's first period, while he was largely
supporting himself by his pen, and hesitating as to his
ultimate career, would hardly, interesting as they are,
secure for him of themselves a permanent place in literary
history. That place is his as the creator, and to some
minds the sole really successful practitioner, of a new
genre, the Political Novel. It was only in his second
period, after he had become an active politician, that he
could have produced *Coningsby, Sybil,* and *Tancred;* only
in his third period, when he had garnered the experience
of a statesman, that he could have written *Lothair* and
Endymion. On the basis of this performance we can
definitely claim for him, apart altogether from his
political eminence, a durable place as—in Sir Edmund
Gosse's phrase—a minor classic of English Literature.
A graceful tribute, associating Disraeli's work with that
of one of the brightest luminaries of letters, was once
paid him by a doughty antagonist in the Lords, himself
with some claim to the title of a literary statesman.
The Duke of Argyll wrote to Beaconsfield on January 1,
1878: ' You have written enough, I hope, to last me for all
the assaults of that foe [the gout]; I used to keep Scott's
novels as my *vis medicatrix,* and now I keep yours.'

What Disraeli himself particularly appreciated in
literature was style—a quality which distinguished some
portions of his own work, but of which unfortunately his
command was limited and uncertain. He elaborated his
views at some length in a letter written while he was
reading J. A. Symonds's *Renaissance in Italy.*

To Lady Bradford.

BRETBY, *Sept.* 4, 1875.—. . . I have now read ⅔rds of the
Renaissance volume with unflagging interest. I do not know
that it tells me anything wh. I did not absolutely know before;
but then, early in life, I was rather deep in Italian Literature,
and the Hughenden Library is rich in Renaissance. But the
writer is a complete Italian scholar, and has a grasp of his

subject, wh., from the rich variety of its elements, can never be one of simplicity, and yet wh., from his complete hold, he keeps perspicuous.

As he warms with his theme, he even evinces some spark of that divine gift of imagination, in wh. he appeared to me at first deficient. . . .

What he fails in is style; not that he lacks vigor but taste. He writes like a newspaper man, 'our own correspondent,' but wants the stillness and refinement and delicacy and music, wh. do not fall to the lot of the active journalist.

He talks, for example, of two great statesmen 'playing a game of diplomatic *Écart*!' Independent of the familiarity and triteness of such an image, there is something offensive in a grave historian illustrating his narrative by referring to a transient game. He might as well have illustrated his battles by croquet, or that lawn-tennis in wh. you excel. He is perpetually speaking of certain opinions and feelings as being very *bourgeois*—and so on.

In letters, the first, and greatest, condition of success is—style. It is that by wh. the great authors live. It is a charm for all generations, and keeps works alive, wh. would be superseded from the superior information obtained since they were first composed, by the magic of the language in wh. the original statements and conclusions are conveyed.

Works of imagination, whether in prose or verse, have this advantage over other literary compositions—they cannot become obsolete from their matter being superseded; but then they cannot live unless they fulfil the great condition of style in the highest degree. This makes Shakespeare and Goethe and Byron and Dante immortal—and not less so, the authors of *Don Quixote* and *Gil Blas*. We have no English novel like them, for style is not the forte of Walter Scott.

It is style wh. is the secret and spell of the classic authors. Both Greek and Roman had a power of expression, wh. was then their characteristic. . . .

CHAPTER XVI.

THE LAST YEAR.

1880–1881.

Beaconsfield survived his downfall exactly one year; and during all the time, in spite of age and illness, he refused either to seek the ease of retirement, or to give himself wholly to those literary pursuits which he loved and with which he filled his leisure hours. He was moved by a sense of chivalry and duty to the country, to the Queen, and to his party. He would do his utmost to ward off from the country those evils which he feared the new régime would bring upon her; to help and comfort the Queen, compelled to accept a Minister of whose conduct she disapproved and whose policy she distrusted; and to reinvigorate and reorganise his own creation, the modern Tory party. His conception of his duty to the party which he had led first to victory and then to defeat was quite different from his rival's; and his cheerful shouldering, at the age of seventy-five, of the thankless political burden laid upon him in 1880 contrasts very favourably with Gladstone's evasion, at the age of sixty-four, of similar difficulties in 1874. It was at a party meeting of Tory Lords and Commons in Bridgwater House on May 19 that Beaconsfield formally intimated that his services were still at the disposal of his political friends; and Rowton gave the Queen an account of a function from which the Press had been excluded.

Lord Rowton to Queen Victoria.

71, SOUTH AUDLEY STREET, *Wed., May* 19, 1880.—Lord Rowton, with his humble duty to your Majesty.

The meeting at Bridgwater House this afternoon was a conspicuous success, in numbers full beyond expectation, in spirit excellent, while Lord Beaconsfield's observations met with deep attention and constant applause, which leave no doubt as to the unanimous feeling of the Conservative party.

Lord Beaconsfield, on entering the Picture Gallery, in which there were some 500 Peers and Members of Parliament, past and present, was received with enthusiastic cheering, and at once began to speak from a dais in the centre of the Gallery.

Enjoining strict confidence as to all that might be said there, he compared the position of the party with the far worse one which it occupied after the Election of 1832, pointing the moral to be drawn from Lord Grey's early fall, and citing other precedents and reasons for not taking an exaggerated view of the present defeat.

He ascribed it to two principal causes. First the state of general social distress, commercial and agricultural, which really arose from natural causes, and not, as was alleged by 'travelling agitators,' from neglect of beneficial legislation by your Majesty's late Government. This he proved very successfully by dwelling on their many good social measures in redress of real grievances.

The second cause he described as the 'new foreign political organisation' of the Liberal party—a system demanding most minute criticism and consideration, which duty had been undertaken by a small Committee of his late colleagues, with the Rt. Hon. W. H. Smith as Chairman.

As to the future his advice, mainly addressed to the House of Commons, was to watch especially the party of revolution, perhaps 100 in number; and to support the Government with all their force, when resisting, as they must at first, any violent proposals. Such a course would infallibly win for the party the respect and confidence of the country.

'The policy of the Conservative party is to maintain the *Empire* and preserve the *Constitution*.'

The Empire was especially in risk of being threatened in the regions of the Mediterranean, where it was of supreme importance that England should have such a stronghold as Cyprus could easily be made to afford—a remark which was received with strong assent. The Empire moreover depended much on the maintenance of the tie with the Colonies—a tie which he believed to be at this moment a growing one, in proof of which he cited amid great applause the offer of Canada, when war seemed probable lately, to furnish your Majesty with a contingent of 10,000 troops.

As to the Constitution, he would not criticise the probable domestic action of the party in power as to particular measures.

But there could be no doubt that the first step towards any organic change must be a revolution in the tenure of land—in other words the pulling down of the aristocracy, which was the first object of the revolutionary party. All their propounded schemes should be examined with reference to that key-note.

Lord Beaconsfield ended by saying that, had the result of the elections been different, he might have felt himself justified, in view of many years' service, in seeking repose and asking them to follow the leaders of great ability who were to be found among his colleagues; but in the hour of failure he would not withdraw, but would still place at their service whatever advice his experience might enable him to afford.

This announcement was cheered again and again; and he sat down after speaking an hour and forty minutes.

Lord Carnarvon then rose and expressed his wish to act with the Conservative party in its moment of trouble, whatever may have been the course which, two years since, he felt himself reluctantly obliged to adopt, and gave his general warm approval to what Lord Beaconsfield had said.

The Duke of Buccleuch spoke in strong support of Lord Beaconsfield, and his advice to-day given.

Sir Robert Peel in a characteristic vigorous speech declared his complete adhesion to the Conservative party and Lord Beaconsfield: and the Duke of Richmond and Sir Stafford Northcote expressed the complete confidence of your Majesty's late Ministers in Lord Beaconsfield, and their gratification that he still proposed to lead the Conservative party.

This meeting was on the day before the opening of the new Parliament for business. Beaconsfield had retired to Hughenden on Saturday, May 1—in a state of coma, he told Lady Bradford; and there, in the country home of which he was so fond, he lived quietly for the remainder of the year, only coming up to London for a few nights when the stress of politics demanded his presence in the House of Lords, and paying occasional visits to his Sovereign. With the loss of Downing Street, he was entirely without a London house, as he had given up Whitehall Gardens when he moved into the official residence. In this difficulty, Alfred de Rothschild, Baron Lionel's second son, came tactfully to his rescue; and placed at his disposal 'a suite of independent rooms' in his beautiful house in Seamore Place, and, Beaconsfield told Lady Bradford, 'everything else that I want, and, as far as he is concerned, leaves me quite alone.' There could have been no greater kindness, and the old statesman was delighted with his quarters. ' I think it is the most charming house in London,' he told Lady Chesterfield; 'the magnificence of its decorations and furniture, equalled by their good taste.'

To Lady Bradford.

HUGHENDEN MANOR, *May* 9.—Your letter was most agreeable—your letters always are. You said you had a great deal more to tell me. Pray tell it, and don't wait for responses from the eremite, who hears nothing, and is absorbed in his own thoughts.

Except the first two days when I lived in the air, the N.E. wind, which then arrived, as Gladstone did, after me, has brought back my asthma and kept me much a prisoner. . . .

May 14.—. . . It is hot here, but a fatal blast all the same, and I suffer much from my enemy. I have a terrible week before me. On Monday we[1] go to Windsor ' dine and sleep,' and on the following day I have a sort of council in Seamore Place. Then, on Wednesday, Bridgwater House: a fine occasion for an asthmatic Demosthenes.

The only consolation I have is to remember that William 3rd was a victim like myself; but then he had only to counsel and fight, and not to talk. And I have heard my father say that his friend the great Kemble (John) used to enchant the world with his Coriolanus, and when he came behind the scenes, fell into the arms of men who carried him to a sofa, where he panted like a hippopotamus for an hour.

I tried to write yesterday, but cd. not spell, and feel now half idiotic.

[SEAMORE PLACE], *May* 19.—A fine meeting in a palace worthy of one. I was in hopes to have called on you afterwards, but the affair was late and longer than I had expected, and I was exhausted, tho' I hope I did not show it.

Now I am going to the dinner, with the Speech,[2] just received from the A.V.;[3] 'tis dull and mischievous, but won't set the Thames on fire. . . .

---

[1] Rowton went with Beaconsfield.

[2] *I.e.*, the Queen's Speech.

[3] ' A. V.,' short for ' Arch Villain,' is often used at this period in Beaconsfield's familiar letters to denote Gladstone.

I believe they will not be content with[ou]t my head, as Strafford said.

To Anne Lady Chesterfield.

[SEAMORE PLACE], *May* 24.—. . . On Friday I shd. have returned to Hughenden, but H.R.H. Prince Hal kept me in town for a Sunday luncheon. This has inconvenienced me, as I want to get back to my woods, and watch the burst of spring.

The Ministry seems in all sorts of difficulties, but I don't think scrapes signify to a Government in their first year.

Lord Hartington dined here last night, and was friendly and agreeable, with[ou]t any affectation. He told me he thought the Govt. wd. be beaten about Bradlaugh.

To Lady Bradford.

HUGHENDEN MANOR, *May* 27.—. . . My week, beginning with Windsor and ending with Seamore Place, was too much for me, and I have been very unwell ever since. In spite of westerly winds, my asthma has returned.

I am here quite alone,wh. for an invalid is the best medicine.

While enjoying the summer at Hughenden, and working daily at his desk to finish *Endymion*, Beaconsfield kept a keen watch on the developments of Ministerial policy. Gladstone was checked at the outset by a miserable squabble about the propriety of allowing Bradlaugh, the militant atheist, to take the oath or affirm his allegiance in the House of Commons; and before long he found himself involved in those serious difficulties in Ireland, the imminence of which, in spite of Beaconsfield's warnings, he had obstinately refused to contemplate. He allowed the Peace Preservation Act to lapse which the Beaconsfield Government would have renewed; and, in the face of a growing anti-rent agitation, proposed to secure social order by suspending for eighteen months the right of eviction for non-payment of rent. This was the one right of the landlord left untouched by the Irish Land Act of 1870; and Disraeli had then predicted that, as a result of the Act, Irish agitators would fix upon the payment of rent as a new grievance, to be abated by the old methods of lawless violence. But he had never contemplated that a British Government would admit the agitator's claim; and he took a substantial part in advising the Lords to throw out a Bill, for which a majority was obtained in the Commons only by the Parnellite and Home Rule vote.

To Anne Lady Chesterfield.

HUGHENDEN MANOR, *June* 2.—. . . . Last Thursday Newport and his brother Francis came down here for a day's fishing in my water, and did well. Newport bagged nine trout, and one twopounder. I sent him up to town with all of them, and they were to be divided bet[wee]n S. and Ida.

These two ladies came down and lunched here yesterday; but the day was not one of brilliant sunshine as awaited Newport, for the rain came at last. Hitherto, it has rained in every parish except this.

I go up to town to-morrow for the 2nd reading of the Burials Bill in the Lords. I think it an odious Bill, and cannot see, on the grounds the concession is to be made, why the Dissenters shd. not have their share of the churches as well as their yards. I shall oppose it, but with little hope, since I understand the two Archbishops, and half the bench, vote for it ! This feebleness and false conciliation gain neither regard nor respect. . . .

To Lady Bradford.

HUGHENDEN MANOR, *June* 8.—. . . . When I am in solitude, and mine is complete, for I have not interchanged a word with a human being since we parted, I get absorbed in studies and pursuits, wh. render letter-writing almost impossible to me—quite impossible except to you. . . .

My Lady of the Isle presented me yesterday with four fine cygnets.

There are $\frac{1}{2}$ a doz. peacocks now basking at full length on the lawn, motionless. I prefer them in these attitudes to their nourishing unfurled their fanlike tails. They are silent as well as motionless, and that's something. In the morning, they strut about, and scream, and make love or war.

All my hopes are on Chippendale.[1]

June 11.—Your letter was delightful—what they call graphic. I am glad I have been to Ascot, and have royally lunched, and lounged on lawn; as I see it all in your bright page to the very life.

---

[1] Lord Bradford's racehorse. See above, p. 1372.

All my household were on Bradford's stable, and I believe well backed their opinion. The coachman on these matters is the great authority, greater even than Baum. He has backed the stable systematically for some time. At first, to use his lingo, because he thought it ' respectable to Ld. B.,' as a friend of his Lord's; but for the last year from a conviction that Ld. B.'s stable had at length got right. I fear, however, he has been hit on the Cup. We cd. have beaten anything but Isonomy. . . .

June 14.—. . . I shall be in the Ho. of Lords to-morrow evening D.V., but shall depart by an early train the next day. I cannot resist the fascination of the sultry note of the cuckoo, the cooing of the woodpigeons, and the blaze of the rosy may. . . .

About the Budget, I don't think it a Conservative budg. It is another attempt to divert and separate the farmers from the gentlemen, and will be successful. I think the Game Bill, with this view, much the most devilish of the A. V.'s schemes. In time the farmers will find out that Rep[eal] of M[alt] T[ax] will do them no good, but they will stick to the hares and rabbits, and there will be a chronic cause of warfare.

To Anne Lady Chesterfield.

HUGHENDEN MANOR, *June* 27.—. . . If the Eviction Act passes, there will not be many more seasons. It is a revolutionary age, and the chances are that even you and I may live to see the final extinction of the great London season, wh. was the wonder and admiration of our youth. . . .

July 7.—. . . I have had the honor of receiving this importunate guest[1] in most of my limbs. It began with my right hand, and there it lingers; all rest well. My only compensation, and it is a great one, is that it appears to have driven away my asthma, of which I have long been the victim this year. . . .

To Lady Bradford.

HUGHENDEN MANOR, *July* 4.—. . . I have no faith whatever in the Whig defection on the Land Bill—the most dangerous thing that has happened in my time—now a long experience. The Fenian members will, by their numbers, compensate the A. V. for the Whig defection. The Whigs may be indignant, but they are pusillanimous. There is no one in the Cabinet equal to the emergency, or qualified for it. Spencer is weaker than water; Granville has not an acre; Kimberley not much; Argyll will only kick for Scotland;

[1] The gout.

Westm[inste]r a creature of the A. V., and, I fear, we know the length of Hart[ingto]n's foot. Alas! Alas!

July 7.—. . . I really think the country is going to the devil, but I have resolved to oppose the Land Bill, in the House of Lords, on its principle, and we must be fools and cowards if we do not win. So Bradford, and no one, must go away. I am trying not to make it a mere party move, but an effort to keep property still sacred. The D. of Somerset will oppose the Bill, and, if he wd. move its rejection, I think we should be safe. . . .

I shall appeal personally to every peer who owes his creation to the late Ministry.

Northcote came down to consult his chief about the obnoxious Bill; and his diary gives a pleasing picture of the old statesman's life in the country.

From Sir Stafford Northcote's Diary.[1]

July 11, 1880.—I went down to Hughenden in the afternoon. Lord Beaconsfield sent his carriage to meet me at Maidenhead, and I had a most charming drive of 12 miles. . . . Found the chief very well and delighted to see me. He has been quite alone with his peacocks, and revelling in the country, which he says he has never seen in May or June before. I gave him an account of the Parliamentary situation. His general view was, that we ought, above all, to avoid putting our Whig friends into any difficulty by making them appear to be playing a Tory game. We must keep as clear as possible of any Home Rule alliance and we had better not move amendments on the [Compensation for Disturbance] Bill. . . . We ought to make a strong effort to defeat the Bill on the Third Reading. The Lords, he said, were determined to throw it out, whatever might be its shape when it came up to them, and he hoped they would do so by a very large majority, a hundred or so. This would show that they saw it in its true light, as not merely an Irish measure but as the opening of a great attack on the land, and that they were determined to stand upon their defence. The effects of the proceedings upon next year would be salutary.

He spoke strongly of Gladstone's vindictiveness, an element never to be left out of sight in calculating the course of events. It was a great fault in the Leader of a party, who ought to be above personal feelings. He said the Queen had told him, even before the Bradlaugh affair and these further troubles, that Gladstone found the House unmanageable. We talked

---

[1] Part of this extract was printed in Lang's *Northcote*, ch. 16.

over the party arrangements and could arrive at no better conclusion than I had already reached. . . .

After dinner, we chiefly talked books; the Chief is always at his best in his library, and seemed thoroughly to enjoy a good ramble over literature. He was contemptuous over Browning (of whom, however, he had read very little) and the other poetasters of the day, none of whom he thought would live except Tennyson, who he said was a poet though not of a high order. He was much interested in my story of Sir Robert Peel's consulting Monckton Milnes on the relative merits of Tennyson and Sheridan Knowles when he had a pension to dispose of. He talked of Lord Derby's translation of Homer and said he had given his opinion against rendering him in blank verse. It was Ballad poetry. Pope's style was better suited to it, but was not the right thing. Walter Scott would have done it better than anyone. I told him of Tennyson's telling me that Burns originally wrote ' Ye banks and braes ' with two syllables less in the 2nd and 4th lines and that he had spoilt it to fit a particular tune. This was like, or rather the reverse of, Scott's treatment of the heroic couplet. The chief was warm against the Homeric unity, and considered that everything Gladstone had written on Homer was wrong. He agreed with my theory that no poet could be well translated except by a superior (or at least an equal) poet. I said Coleridge's *Wallenstein* was the most satisfactory translation I knew, but then Coleridge was quite equal to Schiller. ' Yes,' he said, ' and better.' He instanced Moore's *Anacreon* as a success, and considered the translation there quite equal to his original. He was very laudatory of Theocritus, and quoted his line on Galatea coquetting for the kiss[1] as the most musical he knew in any language. He used to be fond of Sophocles, and to carry him about, but did not much care for Æschylus. Euripides had a good deal of fun in him. Lucian was a great favorite, and he gave me the *True History* to read in bed. He was very fond of Quinctilian, and said it was strange that in the decadence of Roman Literature, as it was called, we had three such authors as Tacitus, Juvenal, and Quinctilian. Horace, of course, he delighted in, and Virgil grew on one; he was a great admirer of Scaliger and of Bentley; Porson he did not think much of. He agreed with me in being unable to see the point of ' Now Hermann's a German.' He mentioned Bentley's correction of ' rectis oculus ' as a good piece of criticism. Ben Jonson he did not care for. I did battle for him, and he promised to read him again. He gave me a good deal of information about editions,

---

[1] καὶ φεύγει φιλέοντα καὶ οὐ φιλέοντα διώκει.

and as to which were rising in price. Giffard's *Ben Jonson* was one which was going up wonderfully. We lamented the disuse of classical quotations in the House of Commons. He said he had at one time tried to revert to them but the Speaker (Denison) had asked him not. 'Why? Do you think they don't like it?' 'Oh no! the House rather likes it; but you are making John Russell restless, and I am afraid of his taking to it too. He gave us six or seven lines of Virgil the other night, which had not the smallest connection with his speech or with the subject.'

July 12.—Stayed at Hughenden till 12, and had a pleasant walk in the garden with the chief. He said reflection only made him feel more sure that we ought to handle the Whigs carefully, making them seem to take the initiative, and supporting them; rather than taking it ourselves, and putting them in the distasteful position of having to desert their own party and join the Tories. The Whigs ought to come out and assert their *raison d'être* as upholders of the landed interest. The history of 1834 was repeating itself, and we ought to avoid the mess made of the 'Derby Dilly' secession, when Stanley and Graham joined the Conservatives too late. He said of the present crisis: 'A Government with a large majority may do almost anything with impunity in its first session. The errors of the present Government may be condoned and forgotten, but Lansdowne's resignation remains. That is the great fact we have to look to, and it will produce a great and lasting effect. People generally don't know that he is a young man. Many will think it is his grandfather. Anyhow, it is a great name, and as a fact, he is a devilish clever fellow who ought to be in the Cabinet.' He reverted again to Gladstone's vindictiveness and said Cardinal Manning had once told him that he knew Gladstone well, and that he thought him the most revengeful man he ever knew.

· He talked over the state of the House and asked me many questions, as to the progress of Harcourt, Chamberlain, Dilke, James, Herschell, etc., and also as to our own bench He lamented the uncertainty of Sandon's remaining in our House, and Smith's inferiority in speaking, which was much to be lamented as he was so valuable in many respects. . . .

To Lady Bradford.

HUGHENDEN MANOR, *July* 18.—. . . Here we are absolutely ruined. The series of never-ending storms has destroyed all our hopes. A plentiful hay harvest drowned, and the finest crops we have had for ten years laid. It is a scene of ravage; of havoc like a conquered country. No amount of caloric, of which there seems little prospect, could now rally things. It is quite heartrending, and, coming from church to-day, my best tenants told me that they could struggle against it no longer. Wheat in Wycombe market on Friday, from New Zealand, and very fine, sold at 42s. pr. quarter—sold by samples, and guaranteed to be delivered in August.

This will be 'nuts' to Gladstone, who will never rest till he has destroyed the landed interest. If he were younger, the Crown would be in peril.

1, SEAMORE PLACE, *July* 30.—The terrible news from Afghanistan,[1] the defeat of Chippendale, and some other matters so knocked me up yesterday that I felt physically incapacitated to write. . . . I believe myself that this military disaster wd. never have occurred, had it not been for the rash announcement of Ripon, that England was only too anxious to quit Af[ghanista]n. Immediately every chief tried to make his fortune so that he might be the future Sovereign. . . .

Ld. Cairns arrived on Wedy., and called on me at once. He looks well and full of fight. Saly. also much improved. . . .

I am suffering from 'mine old familiar foe'—asthma; not very agreeable with a great debate before me.

Aug. 4.—A hurried line before I leave for Hughenden . . .

Last night, after a great debate of two days, an overwhelming majority showed that there was yet something to rally round in this country, tho' we have trying times before us.

The speech of Ld. Cairns was overwhelming, and one of the most extraordinary performances of sustained power in rhetoric that I ever listened to. Tho' nearly 3 hours, it was not too long, as it was our complete case for the country—not a point omitted.

The gem of the debate was Ld. Lansdowne's speech the first night, wh. only proved how very deficient Gladstone is in his perception of character and knowledge of human nature—in not placing Lans[down]e in the Cab. and offering him a subordinate office wh. he nearly declined. However, he has now taken his position as the ablest man of the Whig party—the most important, I shd. perhaps say, because, besides ability, one must look to his other great qualities, his rank, above all his name, and even superior to that—his youth.

I did not speak at all to my own satisfaction, wh. I rarely do; but, considering I had a bad asthma and it was two o'ck in the morn, I must be content. . . .

[1] The defeat of General Burrows at Maiwand.

Beaconsfield was successful in his political strategy; the Whigs took the lead in resisting the Bill in the Lords. Lord Lansdowne left the Government rather than support it; the rejection was moved by Lord Grey, the son of the Whig Premier of 1832; and in the majority of 282 who condemned the Bill there were more professing Liberals than the 51 who were all that could be collected to vote in its favour. Beaconsfield's speech was considered rather tame; but, apart from the asthma, he chivalrously abandoned a direct attack on Gladstone, because the Prime Minister was then lying seriously ill in Downing Street. The objections which Beaconsfield formulated to the Bill were three: that it imposed the burden of what was a national misfortune upon a specific class, that it introduced insecurity into all kinds of transactions, and that it delegated to a public officer the extraordinary power of fixing the rents of the country. He could not understand, he said, that the best way of relieving the agricultural distress in Ireland was by plundering the landlords. He regarded the Bill as 'a reconnaissance in force' to test the feeling of Parliament and the people on the constitutional position of the landed interest; and he concluded with a passage, which legislators in a democratic country might well bear constantly in mind, about the difference between public opinion to which the Legislature should defer, and public sentiment or passion, which it was often desirable they should resist.

Beaconsfield held that the Compensation for Disturbance Bill was a matter of principle on which the Lords should take a firm stand. But he was anxious that they should avoid collisions with the Commons on minor matters, and in particular that they should not reject a Bill which the Government had introduced to allow tenants to protect their crops from injury by killing hares and rabbits. Here the interests of landlords and farmers were opposed, and Beaconsfield insisted that the House of landlords should show due consideration to the farmers. His efforts had to be the more energetic, as many Tory leaders in both

Houses treated the prolongation of the session through August as an excuse for deserting Parliament. By example, as well as by precept, their chief, in his seventy-sixth year, did his best to rally them to the call of duty.

To the Duke of Richmond and Gordon.

Private. HUGHENDEN MANOR, *Aug.* 18, 1880.—I am in frequent communication with our friends in the Ho. of Lords, and shall be in my place to oppose the Hares and Rabbits Bill.

I think it would be unwise to oppose the 2nd reading in our House, for, I believe, we should not succeed in our attempt. But it does not do to announce that we are going to assent to the second reading, and that prevents my sending out at present, a whip for attendance on the Committee on the Bill. . . .

Private and Confidential. 1 *o'c.*, *Aug.* 20.—. . . There is a general *émeute* against the absolute desertion of the Front bench, when the Government is pushing most important Bills. When men like the Duke of Buccleuch seriously remonstrate with me about the absence of myself and colleagues—'Nobody to guide us, nobody to confer with. As for myself (Duke of B.) I at least, shall remain here to the last' etc., etc.—it is time to look to our p's and q's, if the party is really to be kept together.

The complaints of the absence of Lord Cairns are very marked. They say he has had long holidays, and much leisure this year, and while many of the peers are great employers of labor, in mines especially, they have not their Lord Chancellor to advise them—not a lawyer on our side. I go up on Monday and shall stay till the end. . . .

When I wrote to you last, I was not aware of the situation being so critical as regards the party, but that night Sir Stafford Northcote came down to me in a state of great perplexity and peril—and earnest remonstrances about the desertion of the Lords in a most difficult and critical session.

He is obliged to call the party together, to-day I believe, and looks forward to very troublous scenes. . . .

To Lady Bradford.

HUGHENDEN MANOR, *Aug.* 20.—I go up to London on Monday to take the command of the troops. It was necessary, as the greatest dissatisfaction was expressed, by our friends in both Houses, at our front bench, in the House of Lords.

being deserted, and that in the Ho. of C. feebly attended. Stanley and John Manners seemed to have run away. Discontent very general. . . .

There is some reason in my being absent, for I have no roof of my own in town, but that is not the case of Cairns, D. of R. and G., and Ld. Cranbrook, who sneaked off with[ou]t saying a word. I have summoned them back, and they swear, at least the first two, most horribly, but they must eat the leek. Cranbrook behaves better, and will be up on Monday. I have ordered a stout whip to be sent everywhere.

I don't see why you think it will not last. So long as Hartington remains, and he gets deeper in with them every day, the Whigs will never move with effect; in fact, they can't; they are not strong enough.

CARLTON CLUB, *Aug.* 25, 6 *o'ck.*—I did not come up till Tuesday, the H. of L. having unexpectedly adjourned till that day. Yesterday, and to-day, pressing business. I had a meeting yesterday, and afterwards H. of L., and to-day another meeting of bewildered peers. It will be difficult to steer thro' all their difficulties.

To-day I had my late colls., Duke of Buccleuch, Bradford, Aveland, Carnarvon! The latter will surprise you. It was at his own request. I have the meetings in the golden rooms,[1] wh. are now in my sole possession.

I went this morning to the H. of Comm. and saw Mr. Chamberlain, who looked, and spoke, like a cheesemonger, and the other new lights: Mundella, who looked like an old goat on Mount Hæmus, and other dreadful beings. . . .

I am very tired, having walked too much, and too far, with Arthur Balfour for my equerry, who piloted me to the H. of C. . . .

This was Beaconsfield's much-talked-of visit to the House of Commons 'to see the Fourth Party.' That band of Tory free lances, consisting of Randolph Churchill, Drummond Wolff, and Gorst, with Mr. Arthur Balfour as a semi-attached member, had made their mark from the very first days of the Parliament by their untiring and effective militancy, regardless of the convenience alike of Ministers and of their own leader. They were all well known to Beaconsfield, and Churchill, their moving spirit, was a son of two old friends, and had attracted his

---

[1] At Seamore Place.

favourable notice by his maiden speech. The puckish audacity and defiant independence of the party reminded him of his own youthful career; and he encouraged them to persevere, provided they did not carry their natural restiveness under the quiet methods of Northcote's leading into sheer rebellion. 'I fully appreciate your feelings and those of your friends,' he told Drummond Wolff; 'but you must stick to Northcote. He represents the respectability of the party. I wholly sympathise with you all, because I was never respectable myself. . . . Don't on any account break with Northcote, but defer to him as often as you can.' Gorst represents Beaconsfield as palliating disobedience, provided it came short of rupture. 'We should always courteously inform Northcote, through the Whip, of any step we are about to take in the House of Commons, and listen with respect and attention to anything he may say about it; his remarks, even when we disagree with him, will be well worth attention. But just at present we need not be too scrupulous about obeying our leader. An open rupture between us would, however, be most disastrous.'[1] It is possible that Gorst exaggerated the encouragement which he received. Beaconsfield wrote to Northcote from Hughenden on December 1 after this talk: 'I have had Gorst down here, and have confidence in his future conduct. I will assist you, as much as I possibly can, in looking after the Fourth Party.'

To Lady Bradford.

1. SEAMORE PLACE, *Aug.* 28.—. . . We are here in the thick of the Parly. campaign, and no one knows what may be its course or consequences. On Monday we have the 2nd reading of the Game Bill, and I have no idea of what the Lords will do; they seem very much inclined to cut their own throats. Unfortunately, many find a respectable leader in Lord Redesdale,[2] who has many excellent qualities and talents, but who is narrow-minded, prejudiced, and utterly unconscious of what is going on in the country, its wishes, opinions, or feelings.

[1] Winston Churchill's *Lord Randolph Churchill*, Vol. I., pp. 184-187.
[2] Chairman of Committees in the House of Lords, 1851-1886.

I dined last night with Granville *en petitissième comité*. Hartington was there, and Spencer, and D. of Richmond, Hardwicke, and Bradford. Miladi made the 8th at a table wh. wd. rather have suited the Graces than the Muses. There ought to have been good conversation with such guests: but it was not so. Their talk was all shop, and I was greatly bored.

HUGHENDEN MANOR, *Sept.* 3.—I came down here on Wedy. afternoon and am prostrate with asthma—the consequence of a week of spouting. Not that the public jabber was so much the cause, for that, tho' frequent, was brief, but the constant and lengthened homilies of private discussion did the mischief, and strained my feeble instrument beyond its power. . .

Beaconsfield might have exhausted himself by his exertions and brought on asthma; but he had succeeded in preventing the peers from perpetrating the folly of throwing out the Game Bill, and thus losing, as he told Lady Chesterfield, 'the only classes on wh. we once thought we cd. rely—the landed interest in all its divisions.' The argument which he found effectual in the House was that it would be a mistake for the Lords to take up a feeble position on the eve of a great constitutional struggle.

Beaconsfield's correspondence gives us a clue to his thoughts and feelings during the autumn; an autumn in which he had a peculiarly acute and prolonged attack of asthma and gout.

To Lady Bradford.

HUGHENDEN MANOR, *Sept.* 6.—. . . Here I am in perfect solitude: I hate driving, and I can't walk, until I get rid of my asthmatic demon.

Roberts is a first-rate man, as I always believed. I understand it was quite on the cards that he was not dismissed by the new Administration. They instantly put Stewart over him, and contemplated, I am told, his supersession in due course. . . .

The march[1] was the march of Xenophon, and the victory that of Alexander.

Sept. 10.—. . . I don't give my mind to politics, but it

---

[1] From Cabul to Candahar.

seems to me that the A. V. has carried everything before him, and has completely detached from us our old allies, the farmers. The clergy he had corrupted before.

We have been so unlucky that I think we ought to take the hint that Providence has given us. A ruler of England, who has to encounter six bad harvests, ought to retire from public life; if only on the plea of being *infelix*—the worst of epithets.

Sept. 17.—. . . You ask me about reading and new books, and reproach me rather for not recommending some. I never read, and scarcely see, a new book. All these new crotchetty reviews I am obliged to see—to catch not the Cynthia, but the nonsense of the minute, of which the Leader of a party must be master; and when they are exhausted, I take refuge in my classics, and try to restore the tone of the mind.

To Anne Lady Chesterfield.

HUGHENDEN MANOR, *Sept.* 17.—. . . My farmers have in-gathered an exuberant harvest, for wh. they say they cannot get a paying price. The rain suits them, as they abound in turnips and other roots.

Sept. 26.—. . . I have not been generally a pessimist, but am by nature somewhat too sanguine. I confess, however, that I feel evil times are falling on this land. I heard, yesterday, from a high quarter, that to-morrow the Great Powers, with the exception of France who withdraws from the Concert, will bombard Dulcigno ! A sheer act of madness, and more calculated eventually to bring about a general war, than any piece of mischief that could be devised.

Oct. 10.—I am hardly capable of writing a line, for, last Monday, having the day before been quite well, I was fiercely and suddenly attacked by my old enemy, the asthma, and am really prostrate with, yesterday, incipient gout, which, tho' it adds to my sufferings, may eventually prove my friend.

It is very unfortunate that this shd. happen on the only time this year I have asked a few friends to Hughenden. . . .

I have seen, therefore, little of Selina during this visit,[1] tho' I hope she has been amused, as there were several agreeable men, Lytton, Sandon, and others, and yesterday arrived the great Monty, the favorite of Courts and Queens, and whom Her Majesty invited to dinner the same day as she did Hartington !

---

[1] Lord and Lady Bradford came to Hughenden on Friday, Oct. 8.

To Lady Bradford.

HUGHENDEN MANOR, *Oct.* 22.—A few feeble words—my first—to tell you I have left my room this morning, and am shaven and shorn, and dressed and sofaed and in my writing-room after a terrible ten days or more. My right leg is yet bound up, and I dare not have recourse to any tonics while the enemy still lingers, or it would probably flare up again like the asthmatic powders, when all seems extinguished.

Oct. 26.—. . . I think I never knew the country in a worse state. There is only one thing worse, and that is the Tory party.

Oct. 29 —. . . I can't walk—even on the terrace, and it is too cold to sit out. But I am quite relieved from that awful asthma. . . .

Monty was to have gone this afternoon to Claremont and from thence to Sandringham for a week, and so on; but I hear his sister is ill, and he will have to take her probably to Biarritz at once. He is a devoted brother, and I believe he wd. even sacrifice Prince Hal for her, but sisters shd. marry and not require such sacrifices.

Lord Mayor's Day, '80.—. . . This is now the 5th week of my imprisonment, for tho' I am carried downstairs to sit in the sun, that is all I can manage, for I cannot use my legs. But the freedom from asthma is so vast a relief that I scarcely grudge the sort of coma into which my life has fallen. I have never had a fit of gout like it. It has attacked me with renovating ferocity. It reminds me of poor Ld. Derby. My hands are now pretty free, but the gout is in my face, etc. . . .

This voyage, and I fear prolonged visit, of Monty to Biarritz is most unfortunate, otherwise he wd. now have been here. . . .

1, SEAMORE PLACE, *Nov.* 15.—I am here rather unexpectedly, but many things combined to call me, among them to see my M.D. If he continued his visits to H[ughende]n, I shd. have to execute a mortgage on my estate, if indeed land be any longer a security. . . .

HUGHENDEN MANOR, *Nov.* 21.—. . . Yesterday I learnt that Tankerville had accepted my offer;[1] so I am settled, in that respect, for the rest of my life: it being a nine years' lease. I don't think I cd. have done better, particularly as Monty, who undertook to do all this, was away. . . .

Nov. 26.—. . . I liked the *Cors[ican] Brothers*[2] as a melo drama, and never saw anything put cleverer on the stage. Irving, whom I saw for the first time, is third-rate, and never

---

[1] For his house in Curzon Street.

[2] Which he saw when last in London.

will improve, but good eno' for the part he played, tho' he continually reminded me of Lord Dudley. . . .

Endymion is only published to-day. . . .

Nov. 28.—. . . Why you call this 'a tottering Govt.' I am entirely at a loss to comprehend. It appears to me one of the strongest Ministries we have had, and unhappily, and I speak, I am sure, with[ou]t prejudice, its strength will be, and must be, exercised against all those institutions, laws, manners, customs, wh. we have hitherto revered and tried to cherish.

The Queen has been horribly deceived; she was told, as I believe, that the present arrangement was the only one that wd. preserve her from the Radicals, guarded, as she wd. be, by a firm Whig element in the Cabinet. The Whig element dare not say Bo to a goose—much less to Gladstone, who certainly [is] not a goose. He is now really the head of the Radicals, and sets the Whigs at defiance, who will swallow anything, if only to conceal their insignificance, which resignation would demonstrate.

As for the Crown, it is not much better off than the Whigs. . .

To Anne Lady Chesterfield.

HUGHENDEN MANOR, *Dec.* 2.—. . . This Epiphany session very inconvenient, and, I think, a little blasphemous. I can't get into my house by the 6th Jany., and shall have to lie in the streets. . . .

Dec. 7.—I am going to Windsor to-morrow, and shall return here on Friday afternoon. . . .

The weather here is delicious. As yet, December has beaten even our soft and sunny November. What fools they are to go to Cannes, and Nice, and Algiers! when they might stay at home with every comfort, and with as bland an atmosphere ! . . .

Private. Dec. 22.—I am not a pessimist: rather the reverse: but, I confess, the present state of affairs makes me tremble. Old England seems to be tumbling to pieces. I believe that, if Constantinople were occupied by a foreign Power to-morrow, we shd. not stir a foot. Could we ? With Ireland in revolution, S. Africa in rebellion, and the Radicals and Jacobins in England so intent on the destruction of the landed interest, wh. is the backbone of the State, that no one will spare any energies to external dangers and vigilance. I never thought that, in my time, it wd. come to this.

I receive letters every day, asking me to write a manifesto, and make a speech; that I am the only man who cd. do so with effect; and all that.

II.   47

Why shd. I ? I warned the country about Ireland before the General Election, and told them to be vigilant, or there wd. something happen there 'worse even than famine or pestilence.' It has happened. And there have been elections since the Irish Revolution in England, Wales, and Scotland, and they have supported the policy of imbecility and treason that has brought about all this disaster.

Beaconsfield's last Christmas was once more spent in solitude at Hughenden. His anxieties, public and private, were serious. His prophecies of the troubles which a change of Government would entail had proved to be only too true. Ireland was in revolution, the Transvaal in revolt, while England had lost the Continental sympathies and respect that he had secured for her. Parliament was to meet early in the New Year in order to cope with Irish disorder; but Rowton, instead of returning to watch over his chief, had been compelled to take his sick sister to winter in Algiers. 'Your absence is a calamity,' Beaconsfield wrote to him. Looking round for help he had recourse to another friend of some standing to take his secretary's place.

To Lady Bradford.

HUGHENDEN MANOR, *Dec.* 17.—. . . Affairs are most critical, and my labors intolerable—the mere letter-writing etc. too much even for youth. I have written to George Barrington to take Monty's place. He is not a Monty, but he has good talents, great experience of the pol. world, having been priv. secy. to Ld. Derby, and one too on whose honor and devotion I can rely.

The problem of providing for a successor in the leadership of the Lords, if not of the party, had occupied much of Beaconsfield's thoughts in the autumn. He had experienced considerable trouble in the management of the Lords over the Hares and Rabbits Bill, and his acute attack of the gout in the autumn and the steady deterioration of his health during the winter, warned him that his time might not be long. 'I hope my successor will soon appear,' he had written to Sandon on October 1. And in December, when writing to the Duke of Buccleuch, who, having been Peel's colleague in the forties, was the veteran of the Tory party, he said: 'I had hopes that our friends in the House of Lords would by this time have found a leader more competent in many respects than your correspondent. But I have been foiled in effecting this.' His choice was, of course, Salisbury, to whom, by letter to his retreat on the Riviera, he confided his sentiments on this and other political matters on the eve of the session.

To Lord Salisbury.

HUGHENDEN MANOR, *Dec.* 27, 1880.—Your letter reached me on Saturday. On the 20th of this month I heard[1] that the Ministry is agreed, 'quite determined,' to bring in a Coercion Bill the first thing, and to proceed with it *de die in diem* until passed. So much for intelligence. Now for other matters.

One of my dreams was, that, in Feby., I should be sitting behind you in the Ho. of Lords, and that you would be leading H.M.'s Opposition. I thought the publication of *Endymion* would have much facilitated this. But this Epiphany session, and your letter of to-day, add to my embarrassments.

I have communicated my general wish, among other matters, to the Duke of Buccleuch, but I have not got his answer, which is long due. We are so driven for time, that, I suppose, I must appear in my place.

Now as to immediate business: Lytton will not lose a day in bringing forward the Afghan policy. Your presence in such a debate would be desirable, but is not absolutely necessary. I should think that Cranbrook and myself could sufficiently sustain the debate.

But what about Turkish questions? There is to be a blue book, and notwithstanding the absorbing interest of Ireland, the world will expect to be illumined on the Eastern situation, and will naturally look to the Ho. of Lords for it. What do you propose in this matter? You might study the papers at Nice, and come over specially for the debate? If there be one.

I pause, in the midst of this troublesome letter, to touch on the nemesis, that made Derby subscribe to Boycott,[2] and

---

[1] From the Queen. See above, p. 1416.

[2] Captain Boycott was, in Ireland this winter, the most conspicuous victim of the system which in consequence was named 'boycotting.'

Carnarvon denounce Bright, on the same day, or almost. And for this, they left their real friends !

I shall be in town permanently on 31st Decr. I wish to see many people, and to use myself to the human face divine. It is no easy thing to step out of the profound solitude in which I live—often not speaking to a human being the whole day—and walk into the House of Lords and make a speech on a falling Empire. I have telegraphed to Gibson, and Cairns, to see me as soon as possible—I have had correspondence with Donoughmore, whose sensible letter only explains that wh. it does not alter. It seems that this Orange movement is a continuation of some nonsense of that whipper-snapper——, wh. he promulgated to save his seat, and wh. seat he lost—as most of the others, who made the same disgraceful sacrifice of common sense and honesty.

Now I must tell you that nothing will induce me to support the 3 F's[1]—three fiddlesticks. During a long parliamentary life, and long before I was in Parliament, I have been profoundly convinced, that the greatness and character of this country depended on our landed tenure. All the rest, I look upon, and have ever looked upon, as ' leather and prunella.' I fear the pass is sold, but I shall make every effort to rally the troops and restore discipline. And then, if I fail, I must be content with the position of Cassandra, and prophesy what no one will credit.

I have formally, and even solemnly, warned the house in wh. I now sit, that the landed system of this country would be attacked and invaded by the revolutionary party, and if, after that, they relinquish their outposts without a struggle, I think it would be as impertinent in me as useless, to attempt to guide their decisions.

I have tried to convey to you the state of affairs—I can give you no counsel as to your movements. I think your absence deplorable, but your presence, at the sacrifice of your health, would be calamitous. You have got good councillors. I wish I had such. I hope they are well, and send to them 1,000 kind thoughts.

With the money which he received for *Endymion* Beaconsfield had taken a house in Curzon Street; but it was not ready for his occupation when the ' Epiphany ' session of Parliament brought him to town. Once more, therefore, he availed himself of Alfred de Rothschild's hospitality, and went up to Seamore Place on the last

[1] Fixity of tenure, fair rents, and free sale—the principles which were embodied in the Irish Land Act of 1881.

day of the year. For the few days that elapsed before
Parliament met he was so indisposed that he scarcely
left his room. But he was able to be in his place for the
debate on the Address on January 7, and to denounce
the Government on the general lines of his political
letters of December. He pointed out that the old
tradition, which introduced a certain magnanimity into
public life, was that, when a change of Administration
took place, there should be no more alteration in the
general conduct of affairs than was absolutely necessary.
But, when Gladstone's Ministry was formed, 'in every
manner and on every occasion it was announced that a
change of Government meant a change in every part
and portion of the Government; that everything which
had been concluded was to be repudiated; that everything
consummated was to be reversed. . . . Perpetual and
complete reversal of all that had occurred was the order
that was given.' So a Conference had been convoked at
Berlin to modify and supersede the decisions of the
Congress of Berlin. The Congress had brought European
peace; but the result of this new Conference was that the
war in the East was on the point of being revived, ' and
England was near being a belligerent, and a belligerent,
too, against our old ally.' So in Afghanistan, which would
form a subject of special debate later. In Ireland, too,
Beaconsfield's solemn warning had been slighted, it was
asserted that the country was crimeless and satisfied, and
the Peace Preservation Act which the late Government
was about to renew was dropped. Now Ministers had to
change their course on a great scale, because nothing less
would suffice. ' Your lordships know the condition of
Ireland at the present time. Europe knows it, Asia
knows it. It is no longer, unhappily, a merely " English
question." The honour, perhaps the existence, of England
depends upon our rallying our forces, not only with
regard to Ireland, but with regard to other scenes of
disquietude and danger which have been created by what
has occurred in Ireland.' Nothing would be more

justifiable than an amendment censuring the Government
for not taking measures in time to meet the Irish crisis.
But the occasion was too serious for party considerations,
and therefore he would not move; but would support
the measures to be proposed to restore, in Ireland,
peace and order, and to re-establish there the Queen's
sovereignty.

'I had much to say,' he told Lady Bradford next day,
'which I was physically unable to express—and I left
the House. I had been suffering from my great enemy
for a week, and, tho' relieved from it, the remedies had
terribly weakened me.' But, in spite of this constant
ill-health, and of the most severe winter for many years,
Beaconsfield was indefatigable, whenever he could muster
sufficient strength, in dining out; and in his letters, and
in the diaries and letters of others, we have frequent
mention of dinner-parties which he attended in the ten
weeks before his fatal illness began. On many of these
occasions he seems to have been in large measure his
old self, and to have delighted those who met him by the
sententious piquancy of his talk. But at other times he
sat silent and deathlike, a mummy at the feast; and his
fellow-guests carried away an impression of deafness and
decrepitude. One thing was evident. Wherever he
appeared, he was the centre of interest. He might have
lost his political supremacy: he remained the most
commanding figure in London society. After the first
fortnight of January he got into his new house in Curzon
Street, in a district which he loved as being above the
fogs of Westminster and in close neighbourhood to
the 'sylvan joyance' of that Arcadia, Hyde Park. Of
the street itself he had written affectionately in *Tancred*[1]
as having a semi-rural character; starting almost out
of 'what is still really a lane,' Park Lane, skirting the
gardens of Chesterfield House where the rooks could be
heard cawing in the trees, and, 'after a long, straggling,
sawney course, ceasing to be a thoroughfare, and losing

[1] Ch. 1.

itself in the gardens' of Lansdowne House and Devonshire House.

To Lady Bradford.

1, SEAMORE PLACE, *Jan.* 10.—. . . My hostess [Lady Lonsdale] told me she had invited you. It was very well done; the house beautiful, full of everything fair and precious, but owing its mansion character entirely to the staircase, wh. I devised. Before that, it was two houses, and a failure. Louise dined there and Harty-T., and the Lathoms, Cadogan, Dorchesters, Claud Hamiltons, Monty, B. O. . . .

The preceding day my host had a little dinner, wh. was amusing, the Lyttons, Randolph Churchills, Harry Bourkes, Louise, and some men, B. O., Dupplin and Co.

I am very nervous to-day about Lytton's *début* in the Lords, on Candahar, etc. . . .

Jan. 12.—Lytton made a great success on Monday, and at once mounted into the first class of present Parliamentary speakers. He had been so traduced, and so depreciated by the Government and Co.; they had circulated so many ill-natured stories about his preparations and certain and ludicrous failure; that his triumph was proportionately increased. Now he is master, and can give on any occasion even his bitter opponent the D. of Argyll much more than he receives.

It is a white world here, and deep. I dine at Louise's to-day; also Monty, but feel very sleepy. Harty-Tarty, they say, made a very effective speech last night. Hitherto we have done well in the debate, but chiefly owing to two Irishmen, Gibson and Plunket; the former, they say, quite excellent. But I wish Northcote wd. bring forward a little more his young English members—Stanhope and G. Hamilton for example. . . .

19, CURZON STREET, *Jan.* 17.—I was very sorry that I could not write to you on Saturday, and announce my having again a London home, but the weather had so completely paralysed me that I cd. do absolutely nothing. . . .

Louise's was amusing. I asked Hartington 'how the miscreants were,' wh. seemed not to displease him. But it is really too cold for society. I had fires for nearly a month in every room in my house every day, and I have hot air besides. I was glad to get away from Alfred's. He is the best and kindest host in the world, but all the marriage festivities[1] are now taking place, and one must have been in the way. I

---

[1] Leopold de Rothschild's marriage on Jan. 19, 1881. When congratulating him on his engagement, Beaconsfield wrote: 'I have always been of opinion that there cannot be too many Rothschilds.'

dined there on Saturday at a great banquet, and sate by Lady Dudley, whom I always like; she is very intelligent. The garden was illumined by electric light: magical. They danced aft[erwar]ds, but I escaped at 11 o'ck.: Monty tells me the affair was late. On Wedy. there will be a real ball, wh. I shall not attend, as I shall be in my first sleep before the first guest arrives. Then, some other day, there is to be a great Sassoon ball. P. of W[ales] goes to Alfred's ball on Wednesday.

Politics are more confused than ever: no one sees light.

To Anne Lady Chesterfield.

19, Curzon Street, *Jan.* 20.—I did not get out on Tuesday, being in a state of stupor, and only capable of lying on a sofa by the fire. I cannot write in these moods. I suppose there never was a severer day in this great city. I was not much better yesterday, and could not possibly go to the wedding, but I did manage to appear at the later ceremonial, tho' quite unfit for it. To-day my room is full of sunbeams, but I am told they do not portend a thaw. . . .

Jan. 26.—The weather has completely upset me, and I really cannot fight against it any more. As they say, it would kill a horse.

I was in hopes to have called on you to-day, but the moment I breathe the air, even in furs and a close carriage, the asthmatic seizure comes on. I was obliged to return, and shall, if possible, not go out again till the wind changes. . . .

During this month there was in progress, in the House of Commons, a vehement struggle by Parnell and his followers against the measures introduced by the Government—a Protection of Person and Property Bill and an Arms Bill—to restore order in Ireland. These Irish irreconcilables held up all the proceedings of the House by the most flagrant obstruction, culminating in a sitting of over forty-one hours, from the afternoon of Monday, January 31, to nine o'clock on the morning of Wednesday, February 2, when it was only terminated by resolute and unprecedented action on the part of the Speaker. Some form of closure of debate was felt to be inevitable; but the Conservatives, under Beaconsfield's guidance, insisted on confining its operation within narrow limits. To Rowton, who had returned for a few weeks from Algiers and was on a visit to Sandringham, Beaconsfield wrote about the difficulty of coming to any arrangement in these matters with Gladstone.

To Lord Rowton.

19, CURZON STREET, *Jan.* 29, '81.—I got your letter with pleasure, and merely send this line, that you may have the satisfaction of knowing, that my going down to the *Clôture* Meeting did much good, and saved the ship from the breakers.

Gladstone is trying it on, with every art of Jesuitry, on his former pupil, but all is so tied up—'strictly tied up' as B. Hope would say—that N[orthcote] can do nothing without consulting me. To-day, Ponsonby called from our ever gracious Mistress, with a view of ascertaining whether H.M. could 'do anything'; mediate between the parties, etc. The Cabinet is now sitting on the matter.

It was easy to settle affairs with Palmerston because he was a man of the world, and was, therefore, governed by the principle of honor: but when you have to deal with an earnest man, severely religious, and enthusiastic, every attempted arrangement ends in unintelligible correspondence and violated confidence.

To Lady Bradford.

19, CURZON STREET, *Feb.* 1.—The H. of C. is still sitting, having had a whole night of it, and, as yet, half of this day. I don't see the end of it. We are the laughing-stock of Europe.

I dined on Saturday at Granville's; a pleasant party. I sate next to Pss. Louise who never looked prettier; and on Sunday I dined with Lady Lonsdale, my lord away—very amusing. Louise and Harty-Tarty were there—the Cadogans, H. Chaplins, Sir Charles Dilke; all very good company and talked well: Harty-T. particularly, who is a clever fellow, and with some humor.

I am suffering, however, very much from asthma, wh. is detestable.

Monty has come back from Sandringham. . . .

[*Feb.*]—. . . We have had a feverish week here, and wonderful events in the House of Commons, recalling the days of Charles the 1st and the Commonwealth, the 5 members and Pride's Purge. Nobody, as yet, has got any credit except the Tory party, wh. carried with triumph yesterday its amendments to the Government scheme, amendments which were approved at my house, at a large meeting, called at a moment's notice, and attended by all the crotcheteers of the H. of C.

My house received them with ease, and cd. at any time

accommodate 200. It is agreeable and convenient in every respect.

Feb. 9.—There is to be a great battle in the Lords on Candahar on the 24th inst.,[1] and I have some hope that the Government may be forced to 'repudiate' their rash and malicious decision on this subject.

I saw your sister to-day, driving in the Park, so she is better, but still suffering. The westerly wind and the sunbeams allowed me also to move and breathe, but my sufferings have been also great during the last month, tho' I have not wearied you about them. . . .

Feb. 12.—. . . Alas! Alas! Monty leaves me again, and for quite an indefinite time. Indeed I think the prospect is that he will remain at Algiers, or some similar place, for the whole of the spring and summer. His sister cannot get rid of her fever, and her physician writes that he had better join her as soon as possible.

In the midst of preparation for a great debate, having to see crowds of people, and to hold meetings, I lose the chief of my staff; my correspondence alone will overwhelm me. It is impossible to teach a new secretary his work. . .

Rowton's return to Algiers meant that Beaconsfield, from now onwards till the closing stage of his illness, had to depend entirely upon Barrington, who was comparatively new to his chief's methods of work, but of whose devotion the association of December and January had made him well assured. While preparing for the Afghan debate, Beaconsfield continued to find relaxation in dining out. We have accounts of three dinners at the end of the third week in February, at Lady Airlie's on Friday the 18th, at Lady Stanhope's on the Saturday, and at Alfred de Rothschild's on the Sunday. After dinner at Lady Airlie's he had a talk with Matthew Arnold, by whose skill in coining unforgettable phrases he had long been attracted; and whom he complimented now as the only living Englishman who had become a classic in his lifetime.

The dinner at Alfred de Rothschild's was to meet the Prince of Wales. Among others present was Sir Charles Dilke, who thus met, for the second time within a month,[2]

---

[1] The debate was postponed till March 3 and 4. [2] See preceding page.

the statesman whom he considered ' the most romantic
character of our time.' On the first occasion Beaconsfield
admitted that he had borrowed from Dilke's career traits
for *Endymion*, and Dilke recorded that he ' thought him
very polite and pretty in all his ways and in all he said.'
On the second occasion he mentions that when Beaconsfield was offered a cigar he said: ' You English once had
a great man who discovered tobacco, on which you
English now live; and potatoes on which your Irish live;
and you cut off his head !'—a very foreign and comical
way of regarding Raleigh.[1]

On the last day of February Beaconsfield dined with
the Queen, and, in what was to be his last talk with her
Majesty, received her thanks for the help his party had
given in supporting her Government against obstruction.
With the beginning of March, his activities in the House
of Lords were resumed. On Tuesday, the 1st, he made a
speech in support of the second reading of the Government Bill for the Protection of Person and Property in
Ireland—a speech that was notable for the attention it
called to the ' organised conspiracy of foreigners, living in
a foreign country,' America, which sent emissaries to
preach in Ireland ' the doctrine of assassination, of confiscation, and of the explosive patriotism of dynamite.'
On the following Thursday and Friday, there came the
Candahar debate, in which he made the last serious
deliverance of his life on policy. Ministers had decided to
give up Candahar, as had been Beaconsfield's own intention at the time of the Treaty of Gandamak. But he
thought now that the situation had altered, and he
strongly supported Lytton's motion that Candahar should
be retained. The speech was made late on the second
night of debate, in circumstances afterwards explained by
Granville when, two months later, he was pronouncing a
Parliamentary eulogium on his dead opponent.

I think it was at about twelve o'clock that Lord Beaconsfield sent me a message that he purposed speaking directly.

---

[1] *Life of Dilke*, Vol. I., pp. 410, 411.

I sent him a strong remonstrance, saying that two peers who had been in office, and a third peer, one of the most remarkable speakers in the House, desired to take part in the debate. But Lord Beaconsfield persisted, and I thought I was justified in making a rather strong complaint of his having done so. I have since learned with regret that Lord Beaconsfield, just before he received the message, had swallowed one drug and had inhaled another drug, in quantities so nicely adapted as to enable him to speak free from the depression of his complaint, during the time that that speech required for delivery.

Though not up to the level of the best Disraeli orations, the speech had passages which deserve recall. The negotiations which the Government, who had previously been stiff, entered into with the Boers as soon as British troops had been beaten in the field prompted the gibe at Northbrook that ' one would suppose that the noble earl was not only a pupil in the peace-at-any-price school, but that he was also graduating for higher honours in the more refined school which would wage war and at the same time negotiate, more especially if our arms had been defeated.' And for once he turned sharply on his old friend, the deserter Derby, who had made a ' very animated ' speech: 'I do not know that there is anything that would excite enthusiasm in him except when he contemplates the surrender of some national possession.' But the most memorable passage in his speech dealt with the 'keys of India.'

There are several places which are called the keys of India. There is Merv. . . . Then there is a place whose name I forget [presumably Herat]; there is Ghuznee, then there is Balkh; then Candahar. My opinion is that, although such places may not be essential to us, yet I should regret to see any great military Power in possession of them. I should look upon such an event with regret, and perhaps with some degree of apprehension; but if the great military power were there, I trust we might still be able to maintain our Empire. But, my lords, the key of India is not Herat or Candahar. The key of India is London. The majesty and sovereignty, the spirit and vigour of your Parliament, the inexhaustible resources, the ingenuity and determination of your people— these are the keys of India. But, my lords, a wise statesman

would be chary in drawing upon what I may call the arterial
sources of his power. He would use selection, and would
seek to sustain his empire by recourse to local resources only,
which would meet his purpose. You have always observed
that system in this country for the last hundred years. You
have skilfully appropriated many strong places in the world.
You have erected a range of fortifications; you have overcome
countries by the valour of your soldiers and the efforts of
your engineers. Well, my lords, I hope that we shall pursue
the same policy. If we pursue the same policy, Candahar
is eminently one of those places which would contribute
to the maintenance of that empire.

Redesdale in his *Memoirs*[1] relates a curious story about
this classical phrase, 'The key of India is London.'
Prince Lobanoff, Russian Ambassador in London in 1881,
told Redesdale, three years later, at Contrexéville, that
the day before the delivery of the speech he called in
Curzon Street and had a long talk with Beaconsfield over
the whole question; and that he himself had countered
Beaconsfield's argument, that British troops could not
evacuate Candahar as it was the key of India, by the
reply : ' No, London is the key of India.' ' Le lendemain,'
Lobanoff continued, ' il a reproduit mon mot dans son
fameux discours.'   Lobanoff's claim may, of course, have
no better origin than in the besetting weakness of retailers
of conversations to ascribe to themselves, regardless of
accuracy, the best phrases struck out by the meeting of
wits. But probably we have here a superlative instance
of Beaconsfield's extraordinary power of appropriating
phrases of others which had hitherto made no mark, and
using them in so apt a fashion and on so wide a theatre
that they can never in future be dissociated from his fame.

Beaconsfield had received since his resignation much
hospitality from others;[2] he determined, now that he had
a London house, to entertain once more in his turn,
little fitted though he was in health for such an exertion.
His principal guests were to be the Granvilles, a becoming

[1] Ch. 35.
[2] One of his last dinner-parties was at Harcourt's house in Grafton
Street on Sunday, March 6.

courtesy to the Leader in the Lords and his wife. In order that they might not feel ' isolated ' in a Tory house, he asked their colleagues, the Spencers, to meet them. Lady Bradford was not in town; but he had Bradford and Lady Chesterfield; the Duke[1] and Duchess of Sutherland, Lady Dudley,[2] Lady Lonsdale,[3] the Cadogans, the Barringtons; Leighton, the President of the Royal Academy; Alfred de Rothschild, recently his generous host, and Henry Manners, his old friend Lord John's eldest son, afterwards eighth Duke of Rutland. Thus the party— Beaconsfield's first and last in his new house—contained several of the most distinguished and agreeable men and of the most beautiful and accomplished women in the London society of the day. The guests were asked for Thursday, March 10. On the Tuesday and Wednesday Beaconsfield was in bed with the gout—' very weak and shattered,' he told Rose. He had to put off ' Apelles,' as he playfully called Millais, to whom he was sitting for a portrait destined never to be finished;[4] and he feared he might have to put off the party also. But rest and care enabled him to play respectably his part as host.

To Lady Bradford.

19, CURZON STREET, *March* 11.—. . . The dinner yesterday went off, I believe, very well, but I was obliged to receive my guests with a stick, and while they enquired after my gout, required their sympathies for greater sufferings of which they knew nothing. As the gentlemen smoked after dinner, tho' not long, that gave me an opportunity of inhaling some of my poison in the form of a cigarette, and nobody found it out.

My gout is not worse, and I must hope the sun and the western breeze may mitigate my greater evil; but they have not yet.

Your arm will be agreeable to me in our morning walks, wh. I hope are at hand.

The day after the dinner-party he had to deal with a minor political crisis. He woke to find a letter from

---

[1] The 3rd Duke.
[3] Afterwards Marchioness of Ripon.
[2] Wife of the 1st Earl.
[4] See Frontispiece.

Northcote, telling him that Gladstone wanted to apply to the ordinary business of Supply the new rule of Urgency, which had been framed to overcome the Parnellite obstruction to Peace Preservation Bills. The Tory leaders met at once in Curzon Street, and were inspired by Beaconsfield to resist this excessive demand. Here are his comments to the Queen.

To Queen Victoria.

19, CURZON STREET, *March* 12, 1881.

MADAM AND MOST BELOVED SOVEREIGN,—No Sovereign could decorate a subject with a new order, which could have conferred greater pleasure, than the box, which contained yesterday the harbingers of spring, and which now adorn my writing table. . . .

Here matters are most serious. Last night the Minister astounded the world with an announcement which, if carried into effect, would occasion the greatest revolution in the country since 1688.

He must have counted on the fears of the Tory party, and felt convinced that he could frighten them into submission. He has reckoned without his host. There is no one so indignant and determined as Sir Stafford Northcote, and, at a meeting this morning, all his followers pledged themselves to support him.

No one can foresee what your Majesty may be advised to do in 8 and 40 hours !

March 14.—. . . Your Majesty has doubtless seen the manifesto of Sir Stafford Northcote, addressed to the Electors of Devon, and in all the journals of this morning. I think it a masterpiece; his conduct, indeed, throughout this session, has shown equal skill and courage, and I have never found him falter in any advice which I have given him.

If the Minister persist in what has been styled an attempt at a revolution greater than anything since 1688, he will certainly be defeated. At the Cosmopolitan Club, last night, which both parties frequent, and where there is a philosophic latitude and license of political speculation, some of the Minister's intimates announced, that, if he were thwarted in this enterprise, he would take a ' decided step '; probably advise your Majesty to appeal to the country. This I doubt: but I should not be surprised, if your Majesty were favored with a mock resignation, as in 1873.

I foresee that the whole feeling of the country will be

against him in this matter.—Ever, Madam, With all duty and affection, Your Majesty's devoted BEACONSFIELD.

'The House wouldn't stand it,' wrote Beaconsfield, narrating the upshot of the crisis to Rowton. 'Northcote greatly distinguished himself, and in spite of the tears of Walpole and the stern remonstrances of Sir John Mowbray, who is now treated by the Whigs as if he were a Bart. of James I., absolutely marshalled his forces, and inflicted an ignominious discomfiture on the great enemy.' To Northcote himself he said, in the last letter which he was to write to him, 'I most heartily congratulate you on your triumph. The Capitol never was ascended with more deserved glory!'

The sands of Beaconsfield's life were now running low, and he felt his powers of resistance to be failing him. On Tuesday, March 15, he made his last appearance in the House of Lords; and there supported, in moving terms, a Vote of Condolence to the Queen on the recent murder of the Tsar. He had long and often contended against Alexander, but he could now generously call him 'the most beneficent prince that ever filled the throne of Russia.' He described Europe as united in alarm and indignation at the crime; but said that no country was more horrified and sympathetic than Great Britain. The words, in their simplicity and sincerity, were worthy to be the farewell of a statesman to the Parliament which he had adorned.

His last letter to Lady Bradford was written on the following day.

To Lady Bradford.

Wednesday, [*March* 16].—A hurried line, for I hardly think this will reach you before your departure, just to say that I trust I shall see you to-morrow, if I call, as I hope, about six o'ck.

The P. of W. . . . has seen a great deal in his fortnight's absence: all the great men and, I suppose, some of the famous women—Bismarck, who in two hours did not give him the oppor[tunit]y of 'getting in a word,' and Gambetta, with whom he breakfasted, 'quite private,' alone, and who seems to have been as loquacious as his German rival. . . .

I am very unwell, and go about as little as I can, but, after an engagement of five weeks, have a great diplomatic banquet to-day, wh. will finish me. I thought when I was obliged to accept it the five weeks never wd. elapse.

Mrs. Goschen met him at the party mentioned in this last paragraph, and thought that, though brighter after dinner than before, and as courteous as ever to women, he had lost his old spirit and seemed very aged. 'I am blind and deaf,' he told her. 'I only live for climate and I never get it.'[1] In his failing health he felt Rowton's absence acutely. He wrote to him, on this same March 16: 'Barrington is very kind and sedulous, but I want you. My health has been very bad, and I have really been fit for nothing, but perhaps the spring, which commences in a week, may help me.'

The spring, to whose coming he looked for relief, delayed much longer than a week, and he never got the climate for which he sighed. On the heels of a winter of unusual severity there followed a March and an April of bitter and incessant east winds. We have a record of one more dinner-party with the Prince of Wales at Marlborough House, on Saturday, March 19, and then on the following Wednesday Beaconsfield succumbed and went to bed with a chill, and a further attack of the asthmatic symptoms which had troubled him so long. Dr Kidd was in attendance, as in recent years; the patient was nursed by his valet Baum and Baum's wife under Barrington's supervision, and for some days there seemed to be nothing to distinguish this attack from others which the usual remedies had after a while subdued. On the Saturday he had a talk with Salisbury, Cranbrook and Cairns about Majuba and the Transvaal, and on the Sunday (March 27) Barrington took Dilke, whom he had met in Curzon Street, in to see him. Dilke found him lying on a couch, breathing with difficulty, but ' still the old Disraeli,' and ' his pleasant spitefulness about " Mr.

---

[1] Elliot's *Life of Lord Goschen*, Vol. I., pp. 247, 248.

G." was not abated.'[1]   Lady Bradford, writing to Rowton on April 11, claimed to have been the recipient of Beaconsfield's last visit, and to have been the last person, outside of Rowton, Barrington, and Rose, to have seen him in his own house.   Beaconsfield continued his confidential correspondence with his Sovereign from his sickroom, and his last letter to Her Majesty was scrawled five days after the beginning of the illness.

To Queen Victoria.

19, CURZON STREET, W., *March* 28, 1881.—With duty. It would be better for your Majesty to communicate directly, as there seems little prospect of my being visible before Easter. I am ashamed to address your Majesty not only from my room, but even my bed.

About the title and the time, your Majesty is the best judge of such matters, but I should be able, I hope, to write to your Majesty on any point that may arise, in a day or two.

At present I am prostrate, though devoted.—B.

That evening the Queen became anxious, and expressed to Barrington, who was dining at Buckingham Palace, her strong desire that further medical advice should be obtained; following up her conversation with a letter in which she told him that it was his duty to require Dr. Kidd to call in someone else, and that he was incurring a grave responsibility in not doing so. The same judgment was formed independently on the next morning by Beaconsfield's old friend, and confidential adviser, Rose; who was shocked at the patient's appearance and his difficulty in breathing, and obtained his consent, subject to Barrington's approval, to call in the best chest doctor available, such as Dr., afterwards Sir Richard, Quain. Kidd readily agreed, but there was a serious professional difficulty in the way. Kidd was a homœopathist; and the regular practitioners were bound by their trade union rules not to meet homœopathists in consultation. Barrington and Rose only obtained Quain's consent by representing that it would be disloyalty to the Queen to refuse, and by procuring from Kidd a written promise to

[1] *Life of Dilke*, Vol. I., p. 411.

act strictly under Quain's advice and an assurance that
he had not been treating Beaconsfield homœopathically
but allopathically. In these circumstances Quain was
advised by the leader of his profession whose advice he
sought that he ought to take the case; the first consultation was held on that afternoon, and a trained nurse
procured. A few days later another physician—Dr.
Mitchell Bruce, of the Brompton Hospital—was called
in to relieve Kidd of the night work, and a second nurse
was provided, so that the skilled attendance might never
be interrupted.

Quain and Kidd, in the early stages, were both hopeful;
but Beaconsfield seems never to have varied in his belief
that this was the end. On Rose's first visit he said,
'Dear friend, I shall never survive this attack. I feel
it is quite impossible. . . . I feel this is the last of it.'
And two days later, when Rose saw him next, and
received his final instructions as to the future, he said in
the most clear and distinct tones, 'I feel I am dying.
Whatever the doctors may tell you, I do not believe I
shall get well.' When he read one day the bulletin, 'Lord
Beaconsfield's strength is maintained,' he remarked, 'I
presume the physicians are conscious of that. It is more
than I am;' and he demurred to the word 'well,' in a
statement that he had 'taken nourishment well.' The
disease took the form of violent spasms at intervals; and
the doctors insisted on the extreme importance of keeping
their patient quite quiet and free from visitors. This
system, on the whole, chimed in with his own inclination,
for he even looked forward to the prospect of Rowton's
return with dread. But occasionally in the early part
of the illness, on his good days, he resented the cordon
drawn round his room, and would not be denied a little
conversation with his intimate friends, such as Rose and
Barrington. 'It does me good,' he said once to Rose,
'and distracts me and helps me to get through the day.'
His kindness and consideration to doctors, nurses,
and servants never failed; and there was, now and again,

a recrudescence of the old ironic wit. When they sought
to ease his recumbent attitude by a circular air-cushion,
from which any casual puncture would drain the life,
he waved it off, saying, ' Take away that emblem of
mortality.'

His mind does not seem to have dwelt at all continuously
on public affairs, but it amused him on March 31 to correct
the proof of his last speech in Parliament for Hansard.
'I will not go down to posterity,' he explained, ' talking
bad grammar.' Again, when Rose saw him on April 1
he showed much interest in hearing about the debate in
the House of Lords on the negotiations with the Boers
after Majuba, and especially about Cairns's great speech
which finished with the quotation:

> In all the ills we ever bore,
> We grieved, we sighed, we wept; we never blushed before.

' Capital,' he said. ' But this is all my arrangement.
I settled it all. I felt that the eyes of the country ought
to be opened, and that there was no one who could do it
like Cairns.'

Rose told him, on this occasion, of the general sympathy;
of a postcard that had come from a working man—'Don't
give up, old man, we can't spare you.' Indeed, ever
since the summons to Quain and the issue of regular
bulletins had made people aware that Beaconsfield's
illness was serious, there had been an extraordinary
manifestation of public feeling in his favour. During
the three weeks of his ceaseless fight with death the whole
country seemed to be waiting anxiously for the latest
news from his sick-bed; and the occasional intimations of
progress made, showing that his physicians had not yet
lost hope, were everywhere hailed with unfeigned relief.
In London, where he was perhaps best known and best
liked, sympathy was peculiarly acute; the inquiries in
Curzon Street were ceaseless. Nor was it only in this
country that the daily bulletins were eagerly scanned.
Throughout the British Empire and in foreign countries

men followed with painful interest the details of the illness
of the great imperial and international statesman.

No one was more sympathetically anxious than the
Queen. Her telegrams and letters to Barrington came
day after day. She kept the sick-room supplied with
spring flowers from Windsor and Osborne, and wrote
occasionally direct to the patient himself. On March 31
she sent a 'little note' and primroses, and 'perhaps
Lord Barrington will let her know if he [Beaconsfield] is
pleased with them.'

From Queen Victoria.

WINDSOR CASTLE, *March* 30, 1881.

DEAR LORD BEACONSFIELD,—I am so thankful to hear you
are better and more comfortable, and send these few lines to
say how grateful I am for your little note of Monday.

I send some Osborne primroses and I meant to pay you a
little visit this week but I thought it better you should be
quite quiet and not speak. And I beg you will be very good
and obey the doctors and commit no imprudence. . . .

Hoping to hear a good report of you to-night and that
Lord Rowton will be back very soon, Ever yours very
affly., V.R.I.

Everyone is so distressed at your not being well. Beatrice
wishes I should say everything kind to you.

Her Majesty longed to pay her friend a personal visit,
but responded loyally to the desire of the doctors to keep
their patient quiet. She wrote to Barrington from
Windsor on April 3: 'If he continues to improve, she will
not propose to visit him, as it is clear that quiet had done
good and it would, she fears, agitate him. Unless, therefore, dear Lord B. expressed a wish to see the Queen
(when of course she would be delighted to go up and see
him), or should he get much worse (which, please God,
is not now very likely), when she would wish to see him
for a moment, she will not propose to go up before going
to Osborne.' Before she left for the Isle of Wight on
April 5 she prevailed on her own physician Jenner to
ignore the professional difficulty, and to go and see
Beaconsfield if Quain called him in, which Quain did on

three occasions. She also sent a special messenger with
flowers and a letter which was to be read to the patient,
if he could not read it himself; ' there is nothing,' she
assured Barrington, ' agitating in it.' On receiving the
letter the old statesman poised it in his hand and, after
consideration, said, ' This letter ought to be read to me by
Lord Barrington, a Privy Councillor,' and Barrington
was duly summoned for the task. At the close Beaconsfield desired the letter should be locked up in the table
by his side where he kept his most private papers.

From Queen Victoria.

WINDSOR CASTLE, *April 5,* 1881.

DEAREST LORD BEACONSFIELD,—I send you a few of your
favourite spring flowers—this time from the slopes here. I
will send more from Osborne.

I wd. have proposed to come to see you, but I think it is
far better you shd. be quite quiet, and that I may then have
the great pleasure of coming to see you when we come back
from Osborne, wh. won't be long. You are very constantly
in my thoughts, and I wish I could do anything to cheer you
and be of the slightest use or comfort.

With earnest wishes for your uninterrupted progress in
recovery, Ever yours affectionately, V.R.I.

You shall hear of our safe arrival at Osborne as usual.

It was the final letter of a most voluminous correspondence. Before the Queen returned from Osborne, he was
dead.

There were the usual fluctuations in the course of the
disease. But the physical strength of the patient
gradually diminished, and there was a progressive failure
of the nerve power, on which, rather than on physical
strength, he was long supported. Rowton, when he
heard the bad news, came hurrying back from Algiers.
But Beaconsfield showed himself, both to Rose and Barrington, very apprehensive of the meeting. 'I cannot see
him,' he kept saying. 'Surely Monty, who is so fond of
you—you would like to see him when he arrives,' Barrington pleaded. 'You and Rose must arrange it gradually;
it would be too great a shock,' he replied. It was on
Thursday, April 7, that Rowton joined Rose and Barring-

ton in Curzon Street. But, three days later, his meeting with his chief had not yet taken place, and he sent a despairing report to the woman who was the dying man's most cherished friend.

Lord Rowton to Lady Bradford.[1]

19, CURZON STREET, *Sunday* 10*th* [*April* 1881].—I have indeed, not had the heart to write !

I know how you are feeling for the poor sufferer here, and with us ! The doctors have just pronounced almost their one favorable word since I came on Thursday mg., and say 'there is a slight improvement of strength' this afternoon.

But when one sees how weak he is, and how little real nourishment he is taking, the words scarcely raise in one a hope.

God grant I am wrong ! It *may* well be ! for the doctors are by no means hopeless. But somehow I feel as if I knew better than they ! A new mechanical bed has relieved him much, and his suffering is chiefly when difficulty in expectoration comes.

He still shrinks from seeing me ! He knows I am always here, day and night, and I have begged him to give no thought to me till we can meet without effort to him. The doctors wish him to be as quiet as possible, and, I think, even were you here, would combat your seeing him ! He does not try to read letters.

I have seen *him* often, and do not see any bad change in his face. But the weakness ! and how can we overcome it ? He is being wonderfully nursed, and, they say, is so gentle and clear and kind. All about him are charmed.

He begs to be told the worst—if it is to be: and I have told the doctors they must do so, should it become evident. He talks of death without a shade of fear. . . .

The reunion of the two men came naturally in a day or two, when Rowton quietly entered Beaconsfield's room and read him a Parliamentary debate for which he had asked; and for the last week Rowton took his natural place as the principal watcher, with Rose and Barrington, by the bed of the dying statesman. Even during these last days there were gleams of hope. On April 15, four days before the end, we find the Queen telegraphing to Barrington: 'Thank God for this good

---

[1] During the latter portion of Beaconsfield's illness, Lady Bradford was at Weston, nursing her husband through a bad attack of asthma.

news, which overjoys us; but the care must in no way be
relaxed.'   The coming Sunday, April 17, was Easter Day,
and Rose, an earnest Churchman, remembering that it
was Beaconsfield's regular custom to receive the Sacrament
on that day in his parish church at Hughenden, wished
that he should be reminded and given the opportunity
of communicating once more.   Rowton and Barrington
agreed, but Quain peremptorily forbade the suggestion
being made, on the ground that the patient would realise
at once that his case was hopeless and would turn his face
to the wall and die.   ' To myself sitting by his bed at
night,' writes Kidd, ' he spoke twice on spiritual subjects,
in a manner indicating his appreciation of the work of
Christ and of the Redemption.'   Two of his last recorded
utterances, eloquent, the one of his sufferings, the other
of his fearlessness in presence of the Hereafter, were:
' I have suffered much.   Had I been a Nihilist, I should
have confessed all,' and ' I had rather live, but I am not
afraid to die.'

   At Eastertide his drowsiness gained on him and passed
into stupor; and in the early morning of Easter Tuesday,
April 19, it was clear to his friends and physicians gathered
round his bed, that he was sinking.   Rowton and Barrington clasped his right hand; his left was laid in Kidd's.
' A quarter of an hour before his heart ceased to beat, a
strangely affecting movement of the dying man was
observed by [his] two devoted political friends . .
The Minister, his ministering over, half raised himself
from his recumbent posture, and stretched himself out,
as his wont was when rising to reply in debate.   Then his
lips moved; but no words came to the acutely listening
ears about him.   Only Death heard.'[1]   Here are the
simple terms in which Rose described the end to his
son, the second Sir Philip Rose: ' He passed away without

---

[1] Meynell's *Benjamin Disraeli*, p. 199.   I am indebted to this ' unconventional biography' for several details, derived apparently from Barrington, of Beaconsfield's last illness.   Dr. Kidd's article in the *Nineteenth
Century* for July, 1889, has supplied others.   But my account is mainly
based on a memorandum, unfortunately incomplete, drawn up by Rose.

suffering, calmly as if in sleep, at 4.30 in the presence of Lord Rowton, Lord Barrington, myself, and the physicians. We kissed his fine noble forehead. . . . I never saw anything more fine and impressive than his peaceful and tranquil expression, and his appearance is one of the greatest dignity and repose.' A Power had passed from the earth.

Rowton sent a detailed account of the last days to Lady Bradford.

Lord Rowton to Lady Bradford.

19, CURZON STREET, *Friday night, April 22,* '81.—Since that dreadful morning I may say I have been unable to write. To-day I have been better: but I had not a moment. When I was at Osborne, when I had hoped for time to send you a few lines, I found my every moment taken up by the Queen, with whom I passed hours telling her all she wished to know of her loved friend. And she did love him.

The last day and hours were distressing from his laboured breathing, but the last minutes and moments were very quiet and evidently quite painless. The very end was strikingly dignified and fine, and as I looked on his dear face, just at the moment when his spirit left him, I thought that I had never seen him look so triumphant and full of victory.

In all those last days he was so brave and gentle, so wonderfully considerate and good to all, that I felt I should have loved him more than ever, had he lived.

He often said he knew he had no chance, and seemed to wish almost that the doctors would tell him so. But they did not know—or would not tell him, and so he glided on till the ship of his life got among the clouds and the breakers, and he began to sink without knowing where he was. And so it came that he had not the opportunity of sending a word to some, to whom, as I thought I could see, he would have sent a loving message had he known what was so near. I never doubted what the end must be. I knew too well, how little of reserve force for long past was left in him.

I am very unhappy! but I won't dwell on that. My life is dreadfully changed. But I have often thought of you and Lady Chesterfield, and known how your dear kind hearts were aching. Will you give her my love and ask her to forgive my not writing to her?

Indeed, till to-day I have scarcely been physically able to do so. Day and night was I with him trying to help him over all his pains and troubles, as each arose, or to dispel some of the confusions which came over his poor tired brain. It was weary work that sitting, with my hand in his, in the night watches, trying to guide that mighty mind, as a child's has to be led—that trying to be cheerful, when I could scarcely help weeping! And I was thankful, more than I could ever have deemed possible, when the great peace came over him.

Will you let me know when you come to London? It will be a real comfort to see you; there is none greater than to give and receive sympathy.

How Lady Chesterfield will miss him! I feel for *her* so deeply.

Lady Chesterfield, now quite an old woman, survived Beaconsfield only four years. Lady Bradford lived till 1894, cherishing always as one of her greatest treasures a framed miniature portrait of Beaconsfield, specially designed for, and presented to, her by the Queen, after his death, in memory of their common friend.

Deep and sincere and almost universal was the national mourning for the national loss. It was felt, even by those who had lightly rejected him the year before, that the country was infinitely the poorer for his death; that a true lover and faithful servant of England was gone. Great as he had been in his day of power, he had seemed even greater in the manly fashion in which he had accepted the decision of the polls, neither whining nor sulking, but still, in spite of age and illness, labouring for his country's good. Abroad it was everywhere recognised that indeed a prince and great man had fallen in Israel.

The Queen's grief was profound; in some of her letters she said she was 'heart-broken.' She summoned Rowton to Osborne to tell her everything and answer all her questions; but she did not wait for his arrival before giving expression to her deep feeling. She wrote with her own hand the notice in the Court Circular: ' The Queen received this morning, with feelings of the deepest sorrow, the sad intelligence of the death of the Earl of Beaconsfield, in which Her Majesty lost a most devoted friend and counsellor, and the nation one of its most distinguished

statesmen.' And this was her first outpouring of sorrow
to Barrington:

Queen Victoria to Lord Barrington.

OSBORNE, *April* 19, 1881.—The Queen meant to write to
Lord Barrington before she received his sad and touching
letter giving the details—so painfully interesting—of the last
hours and moments of the life of her beloved and valued
friend and counsellor. She feels very keenly not having
seen him, or even looked at him once more, but then she
feared the great agitation for him, and it might have been
painful to all. And she grieves now to think she cannot see
him even in his last sleep—as she has so many valued friends.
But it is too far off and the weather too uncertain.

Words are too weak to say what the Queen feels; how
overwhelmed she is with this terrible, irreparable loss—which
is a national one—and indeed a great one to the world at
large! His kindness and devotion to the Queen on all and
every occasion—his anxiety to lighten her cares and difficulties she never, never can forget, and will miss cruelly.
Queen feels deeply for all dear Lord Beaconsfield's friends,
and for his many followers who have lost so admirable and
wise a Leader. The Queen would wish to thank Lord Barrington for his constant attention in telegraphing to her. All
is silent now, and still; and the terrible void makes the heart
sick. What three weeks of anxious watching—of hopes and
fears—these have been; just three weeks yesterday since Lord
Barrington dined with the Queen and first expressed anxiety!

No one felt the blow more keenly than those who,
now that Beaconsfield was gone, were left to be the
standard-bearers of the Conservative cause. Northcote
wrote to Rowton on hearing the news:

I can't write about the dear Chief. The last twenty years
come back upon me too strongly just now to let me realise
the end of a long and close friendship. The sun has been
taken out of our political system; but that is not all our
loss. There was such a wonderful power of sympathy in
him that one felt sure of his understanding all sorts of feelings
and giving comfort and counsel in all sorts of difficulties.

And Salisbury, in a letter to H. C. Raikes on April 26,
said, 'I have just returned from the old chief's funeral.
It was a very striking sight, and to me inexpressibly sad.

It seems like the passing away of an epoch.   What is it
that lies before us ?'

On the day of Beaconsfield's death Gladstone, as Prime
Minister, offered, by telegram and letter, the honour of a
public funeral,[1] feeling assured that, in so doing, he was
' acting in conformity with the general expectation and
desire.'   Such a national tribute had been amply earned;
but the old statesman had left with Rowton and Rose, and
inserted in his will, definite instructions that he was to
be buried at Hughenden with his wife and that his funeral
was to be conducted with the same simplicity as hers was.
Any hesitation that his secretary and executors may
have felt was finally set at rest by finding in their chief's
private despatch box Lady Beaconsfield's touching letter[2]
of farewell to her husband, desiring that he and she, who
were so united in life, should lie in the same grave after
death.   It might seem more fitting that one who delighted
in gorgeous ceremonial, and who always carried himself
with picturesque distinction through the pageant of life,
should be borne with stately ritual through mourning
crowds to a resting-place among his peers in the historic
Abbey.   But there was another side to his character, which
suited well with his own quiet country churchyard.   Artificial as he was in many ways, few men have more relished
the simpler sources of happiness : wife and home, reading
and writing, trees, flowers, and birds, old friends and
small kindnesses.

So it was the man, rather than the statesman and
author, who was uppermost in the thoughts of the
illustrious assemblage which gathered on April 26 at
Hughenden.   There the Prince of Wales and the Duke
of Connaught were in attendance; and Prince Leopold,
representing the Queen whom Beaconsfield had so
devotedly served.   Thither came the Ambassadors of
Germany, Austria, and Turkey, and Russell Lowell,

[1] Beaconsfield had, as Prime Minister, made a similar offer to Lady
Russell on her husband's death; but it was Russell's desire, as it was
Beaconsfield's, to rest in Bucks—among his ancestors at Chenies.
[2] Quoted on p. 572.

at once the Minister of the mighty Anglo-Saxon State
across the ocean and a literary man of high distinction.
There, with the exception of Cranbrook, who was in
Italy, were almost all Beaconsfield's old colleagues—
conspicuous among them Salisbury, of late his right-
hand man and destined successor; Northcote, stanchest of
lieutenants and friends; John Manners, lifelong comrade
in political action; Cairns, the weightiest in counsel
of all; and Derby, present to bury in the grave the
discords of the last three years and to revive the memories
of a political discipleship of a quarter of a century.   Nor
were there wanting worthy representatives of his political
opponents.   If Gladstone was kept away by business and
Granville by illness, Hartington, between whom and
Beaconsfield there had been much mutual liking and
respect, attended, along with other leaders of the future,
such as Harcourt and Lord Rosebery, who both had
recollections of visits to Hughenden in happier days
and of pleasant saunter and converse with its master.
Personal as well as political friendship of long standing
brought Abergavenny and Henry Lennox.   Art was represented by Leighton and Millais.   Lytton followed to the
grave the chief who had raised and upheld him; and it was
fitting that the Duke of Portland,[1] head of the Bentincks,
should come to show respect for the coadjutor and
biographer of his cousin Lord George.   Bradford's
presence recalled the tenderer intimacies of recent years.
Prominent among the mourners were the faithful three
who had kept vigil in Curzon Street, Rowton, Barrington.
and Rose; and associated with Rose was the other
executor, Sir Nathaniel de Rothschild, afterwards Lord
Rothschild, Baron Lionel's eldest son.   The family
mourners were only two, Ralph Disraeli, Clerk Assistant
in the House of Lords, the sole surviving brother, and his
son, Coningsby, his uncle's heir, as yet but a boy.   Among
the wreaths which covered the coffin and the bier were
two from the Queen, one being entirely of fresh primroses,

[1] Beaconsfield had accepted an invitation to Welbeck for this very Easter.

with the legend, 'His favourite flowers, from Osborne, a tribute of affection from Queen Victoria.' After a simple service conducted by the vicar in the village church, the remains of Benjamin Disraeli, Earl of Beaconsfield, borne by the tenants of the estate, were laid to rest by the side of his wife in the vault which he had had constructed just outside the eastern wall; and with him in the coffin, next his heart, was buried the farewell letter which that wife had written him five and twenty years before. In the same vault had long reposed in death Mrs. Brydges Willyams, his friend and benefactress;[1] and his last brother, Ralph, filled, some years later, a neighbouring grave.

Four days after the funeral, on April 30, Beaconsfield's royal mistress came to Hughenden to bid a personal farewell to her favourite Minister in his tomb. His last stay of some days as her guest at Windsor had been in the previous December. At the close of that visit he had driven home by Rose's house of Rayners at Penn, and had lunched there, entering Rayners park by Loudwater gate and leaving by Criers-hill. The Queen determined to follow the same route in her pilgrimage to Hughenden churchyard; and accordingly the royal carriages were conducted by Rose's servant through the park from lodge to lodge by the exact way that Beaconsfield had taken. Similarly at Hughenden, Her Majesty trod in the path by which his body had been borne to the grave; and the vault was reopened that she might lay on his coffin yet another wreath. Nor could the Queen's loyalty to him who had been so loyal to her be satisfied till, from her privy purse, she had erected in Hughenden Church, over the seat in the chancel which he had been wont to occupy, a personal monument in marble to his memory. It is in three compartments, with his arms on top, his portrait in profile in the centre, and below the following inscription: 'To the dear and honored

[1] See Vol. I., III., ch. 13.

memory of Benjamin, Earl of Beaconsfield, this memorial is placed by his grateful Sovereign and Friend, Victoria R.I. "Kings love him that speaketh right," Proverbs, xvi. 13. February 27, 1882.'

The death came in the Easter recess. When Parliawent reassembled, both Houses voted, in accordance with precedent, the erection, at the public expense, of a statue of the great Minister and consummate Parliamentarian in Westminster Abbey, the Lords with unanimity, the Commons with a dissenting minority less in proportion than that which, at Fox's instance, had disputed a similar public honour to Pitt. Gladstone, the Leader of a House of Commons elected to overthrow Beaconsfield's Government and reverse his policy, was in a delicate position, as the proposer of such a resolution; but he acquitted himself with taste and dignity. He impressed upon the House that not only had Beaconsfield sustained a great historical part but that his actions had received at the time the full constitutional authority of Parliament. Besides the happy quotation, already mentioned,[1] about the return from Berlin, he dwelt on his unique career, on his loyalty to his race, on his pure domestic life, and on the absence of personal animosity in his dealings with political opponents. The following passage was felt to be alike absolutely true and absolutely sincere:

There were certain great qualities of the deceased statesman that I think it right to dwell upon . . .—qualities immediately connected with conduct—with regard to which I would say, were I a younger man, that I should like to stamp the recollection of them on myself for my own future guidance, and with regard to which I would confidently say to others who are younger than myself that I strongly recommend them for notice and imitation. They were qualities not only written in a marked manner on his career, but possessed by him in a degree undoubtedly extraordinary. I speak, for example, of such as these—his strength of will; his long-sighted persistency of purpose, reaching from his first entrance upon the avenue of life to its very close; his remarkable

1 See above, p. 1230.

power of self-government; and last, but not least, of all, his great parliamentary courage—a quality in which I, who have been associated in the course of my life with some scores of Ministers, have, I think, never known but two whom I could pronounce his equal.

But it was in the House of Lords that the most delicate appreciation was shown, that the aptest and truest eulogies were delivered. Granville, socially a friend though politically a foe,[1] touched with deft grace on many salient points of the dead leader's character and career. He spoke of his rare and splendid gifts, of his force of character, of his long and continuous service. He reminded the peers that Beaconsfield's great personal success had been achieved by his own strong individuality, without any adventitious circumstances. He dwelt on his mastery, in writing and speaking and conversation, of censure and of eulogy; on his 'singular power of coining and applying phrases which caught the popular mind and which attached praise or blame to the actions of the great parties in the State.' He singled out for notice the tolerance and fairness and forbearance which he had shown to his political opponents and especially to himself in that House, notwithstanding the remarkable power of destructiveness which he possessed and sometimes exercised. He added a tribute to his good nature and kindheartedness in private life, and in particular to his sensitiveness to kindnesses shown him by others. One sentence deserves to be especially remembered: 'The noble earl undoubtedly possessed a power of appealing to the imagination, not only of his countrymen, but of foreigners, and that power is not destroyed by death.' In his peroration Granville dwelt on the cordial reception which Beaconsfield had met with in that House, representative though it was of a proud,

---

[1] 'Happy Sydney! to be your neighbour!' was Beaconsfield's graceful reply to Granville's announcement that he, as Lord Warden, living at Walmer Castle, had appointed Lord Sydney Captain of Deal Castle—Walmer and Deal forming one continuous town. Even politically Disraeli had, early in 1868, made tentative overtures through Dr. Quin for a working understanding with Granville. See Fitzmaurice's *Granville*, Vol. I., pp. 519, 520; Vol. II., p. 130.

powerful, and wealthy aristocracy. 'I can conceive
no brighter and no more brilliant example of the way in
which the portals of this assembly smoothly roll back
to admit eminent and distinguished men and welcome
them to the very first ranks in the assembly that they
so entered, than the example of the late Lord Beaconsfield.'

Salisbury's tribute was at once more weighty and
more moving. His close political connection with
Beaconsfield was, he reminded the House, comparatively
recent. 'But it lasted through anxious and difficult
times, when the character of men is plainly seen by
those who work with them; and on me, as I believe on
all others who have worked with him, his patience, his
gentleness, his unswerving and unselfish loyalty to his
colleagues and fellow-labourers have made an impression
which will never leave me so long as life lasts.' The
impression, he said, which Beaconsfield made on the mass
of his countrymen was, of course, due to other causes;
partly to the peculiar character of his genius, the wonderful combination of qualities rarely found together;
partly to the splendid perseverance by which he overcame all obstacles and proved that there was for every
Englishman, however humble, an open career leading to
the highest positions under the Crown. There was yet
another cause.

Lord Beaconsfield's feelings and principles with respect
to the greatness of his country, more and more as life went
on, made an impression on his countrymen. Zeal for the
greatness of England was the passion of his life. Opinions
might differ, and did differ deeply, as to the measures and
the steps by which expression was given to that dominant
feeling; but, more and more as his life went on and drew
near its close, as the heat and turmoil of controversy were
left behind, as the gratification of every possible ambition
negatived the suggestion of any inferior motive and brought
out into greater prominence the purity and the strength of
this one intense feeling, the people of this country recognised
the force with which this desire dominated his actions, and
they repaid it by an affection and reverence which did not

depend on, and had no concern with, opinions as to the
particular policy pursued. This was his great title to their
attachment, that above all things he wished to see England
united, and powerful, and great.

Even so, we may well believe, would the dead man have
desired to be praised.

It is a satisfaction to reflect that Beaconsfield's later
years were free from those pecuniary troubles which
had grievously afflicted his youth and middle age. It is
true that he never paid off in his lifetime the mortgage
which Andrew Montagu held on Hughenden for £57,000—
the enormous sum which represented Disraeli's accumulated indebtedness. But since 1873, owing to
Montagu's generosity, he had been paying interest at
only 2 per cent. on this mortgage; and during the last
twenty years of his life he had received some £35,000
under the wills of Mrs. Brydges Willyams and his brother
James, and had made nearly £20,000 by *Lothair* and
Endymion and the popular reprint of his novels. Most
of this money he had prudently invested in Consols,
where there were £40,000 standing in his name at his
death. Moreover, he had almost doubled the acreage,
and in consequence considerably increased the rental
value, of the Hughenden estate. Then, although he had
lost by his wife's death £5,000 a year and a house in
London, he had enjoyed from 1874 to 1880 an official
income of the same amount[1] and an official residence
which he occupied for about a couple of years; and,
when he was out of office, he had received since 1859 a
pension of £2,000 a year. Accordingly at his death his
financial position was found to be satisfactory. His
will was proved originally at £63,000, subsequently
increased to £84,000; and the executors were easily able
to pay off the mortgage on Hughenden. Owing to the
considerable sum realised by the sale of Beaconsfield's

[1] For a year and a half—from August, 1876, to February, 1878—
Beaconsfield held the office of Privy Seal (£2,000 a year) in addition to that
of First Lord of the Treasury (£5,000 a year), but he only drew his salary
as Privy Seal for about half that period.

personal effects, and to the accumulations of a long
minority, continued under the provisions of the will until
his nephew attained the age of twenty-five, the estate
passed to his heir not merely unembarrassed by mortgage,
but also in excellent condition. With pardonable pride in
the association of the name and the place, Beaconsfield
directed that any future tenant in possession of Hughenden under the entail, who should happen to be otherwise
named when he succeeded, should take at once the
name of Disraeli. Even in these revolutionary days,
there will be a widespread hope that it may be long
before the lord of the manor of Hughenden is of any
other blood or bears any other name.

CHAPTER XVII.

The Man and His Fame.

A politician who looms very large to his own con-temporaries is frequently forgotten almost before the grass has grown on his grave. Even a veritable statesman sometimes undergoes temporary oblivion in the years immediately following his death, and is only resuscitated and placed in his proper niche in history by a subsequent generation. Disraeli's fame was never forgotten nor obscured. It was kept alive from year to year through a popular observance and through the development of a popular political organisation.

The legend, ' his favourite flowers,' attached by the Queen to the wreath of primroses which she sent to be laid on his coffin, surprised and puzzled the world. Surely, people said, there must be some mistake. A man whose pet bird was a peacock must have had a corre-spondingly flamboyant taste in flowers. To so bizarre and sophisticated a statesman, a primrose, even if the gift of a Queen, could but have been a yellow primrose, and nothing more. Had he sung the praises of primroses in his novels ? They were only mentioned, it appeared, in *Coningsby* as a suitable natural object to which to compare a dish of hissing bacon and eggs, and in *Lothair* as making a capital salad ! So unaccountable did the Queen's statement seem that the far-fetched suggestion was hazarded, that by ' his ' Her Majesty meant the Prince Consort's—a suggestion which was even accepted in quarters which should have known Disraeli better. Those intimates who noticed how he relished simple country pleasures—though he preferred trees to any flowers—were not surprised, nor will the readers of this biography have been. It may be impossible to prove that he honoured the primrose above all other flowers; but it is certain that he gave Queen Victoria, and several of his friends, excellent reasons for believing so. Year by year, in March and April, the Queen, as we have seen, sent her Minister spring flowers, mainly primroses and violets, from Windsor and Osborne; and his acknowledgments generally singled out the primroses —ambassadors, as he called them, of spring—for especial admiration. Some of his phrases have been quoted already. Here are more extracts from his letters. On April 21, 1876: 'He likes the primroses so much better for their being wild; they seem an offering from the Fauns and Dryads of the woods of Osborne.' On March 28, 1878: 'Some bright bands of primroses have visited him to-day, which he thinks shows that your Majesty's sceptre has touched the Enchanted Isle.' Guests who dined with him just after one of these consignments had arrived remembered how he would say with pride when they admired the heaped-up bowls of primroses that formed the table decoration: 'They were all sent to me this morning by the Queen from Osborne, as she knows it is my favourite flower.' And he told some of those who condoled with him on his loss of power in April, 1880, that he was looking forward now to enjoying his favourite primroses at Hughenden. For at Hughenden he cultivated them freely in the German Forest and the Park, and gave the woodmen strict orders to protect the wild plants. More than most men did the ageing Beaconsfield welcome each year the approach of spring, as, owing to recurrent asthma and bronchitis, it was only in 'Favonian' airs that he could freely breathe; and his affections were naturally attracted to the typical spring flower.

The controversy had definitely connected Beaconsfield with the primrose in the public mind, and, as the first anniversary of his death drew near, without any notably successful exploits having been performed by his rival and successor to dim the lustre of the departed leader, both the man and the flower were much in people's thoughts. A letter in *The Times* of April 14 crystallised the vague sentiment of the public and led directly to the observance of April 19 as Primrose Day.

To the Editor of 'The Times.'

It is an interesting fact worth noting that during the last day or two a demand has arisen at florists' in London, at least in every part of the West End, for what are called 'Beaconsfield buttonholes'—that is, small bunches of primroses, for wearing on the anniversary of Lord Beaconsfield's death on the 19th inst. It will be remembered that the primrose was his favourite flower. This spontaneous expression of popular sentiment is, so far as it has come under my own observation, altogether apart from party feeling, any exhibition of which, on such an occasion, would, indeed, be a desecration of Lord Beaconsfield's memory. It has always been a popular practice, as classical mythology, Church history, and heraldry prove, to associate great names with particular flowers; and it is still in full force. . . .

The purpose of my letter . . . is . . . to place on open record the small beginnings of what may gradually grow into a settled popular custom, more honouring in its simple, unbought loyalty to Lord Beaconsfield's memory, and more truly English, than the proudest monument of bronze or marble that could be raised to his name.

The letter was signed 'Out of the Hurly-Burly'; but the writer was the eminent Anglo-Indian, the late Sir George Birdwood, who, in his enthusiasm for his brilliant idea, had himself been largely responsible for those preparations for an outbreak of primroses on April 19 which he recounted so objectively. In spite, or perhaps partly because, of the tactless sneers of the Liberal press, the idea appealed at once to the popular imagination. Buttonholes of primroses were very noticeable in London on the day in 1882; and next year, stimulated by a further letter in *The Times* from Birdwood, under the signature this time of 'Hortus Siccus,' and by the ceremony of the unveiling on April 19 of the

Beaconsfield statue in Parliament Square, there was a general floral observance of Primrose Day, which thenceforward was definitely established as a popular institution. This wearing of the primrose suggested in that year of 1883 to the ingenious mind of Drummond Wolff the further idea of a great organisation to popularise the Tory principles of which Beaconsfield was the exponent; and the scheme was enthusiastically worked out by the Fourth Party and by Borthwick of the *Morning Post*. Thus out of Primrose Day grew the Primrose League, with its glittering array of knights, dames, and associates, and its profitable adaptation of social influences to political ends—a League which has long taken rank as one of the most numerous and most efficient political organisations in existence. Never had a dead statesman so marked a tribute paid to the persistence of his fame. Even the Great War has not brought the observance of Primrose Day to an end. The statue in Parliament Square is still decorated on that day with ' his favourite flower ' in honour of a statesman who has been dead nearly fifty years; still a considerable proportion of the population, male and female, appear in the streets on April 19 wearing bunches or buttonholes of primroses.

What qualities in Disraeli, what political achievement of his, gained him this unique position in the affection and recollection of his countrymen ? Why has honour been paid to him which was never offered to Chatham or Pitt, to Peel, Palmerston, or Gladstone ? Something, no doubt, is to be attributed to the flower, so pretty, so popular, so abundant throughout the English countryside; and to the happy coincidence of the date of the anniversary with the season at which the primrose is in fullest bloom. Some influence, too, in the building up of a Disraeli tradition may be ascribed to the cruel disillusion of the performances of the second Gladstone Government; to the associations called up by the names of Bradlaugh, Majuba, Boycott, Kilmainham, Phœnix Park, Penjdeh, and Gordon. But the main grounds for

the enduring reputation to which the general observance
of Primrose Day bears witness are, of course, to be found
in the man himself and in his career.   Not, indeed, that
the public mind has fastened on any of his particular
strokes of policy—Reform Bill, Suez Canal purchase,
augmentation of Royal title—great and fertile as many of
them are proved to have been.   Not mainly by these has
his permanent fame been secured; but by his marvellous
rise from the midst of a then despised race to the summit
of power, by his mysterious and romantic personality,
by the high and imperial patriotism of his ideas, and by
that imaginative quality in him which fired the imagination of others.   Though these features of his life and
character are writ large over this and the preceding
volumes, something more may perhaps be said here in
conclusion about each of them.

The progress from a middle-class Jewish literary home
to Downing Street and the Congress Hall of Berlin could
not be better portrayed than in some striking lines from
Tennyson's *In Memoriam;* lines which, nevertheless,
were in no sense suggested by Disraeli's career, and were,
indeed, composed at a time when his public course was
not half run.   The extraordinary manner in which they
fit that career was first pointed out by Sir John Skelton,
one of Disraeli's most judiciously appreciative admirers
Tennyson writes of ' a divinely gifted man,'

> Who breaks his birth's invidious bar,
>   And grasps the skirts of happy chance,
>   And breasts the blows of circumstance,
> And grapples with his evil star;
>
> Who makes by force his merit known,
>   And lives to clutch the golden keys,
>   To mould a mighty state's decrees,
> And shape the whisper of the throne;
>
> And, moving up from high to higher,
>   Becomes on Fortune's crowning slope
>   The pillar of a people's hope,
> The centre of a world's desire.[1]

[1] Tennyson's *In Memoriam*, canto 64.

The first two stanzas would not need the alteration of a syllable to meet the case, so absolutely do they mirror the facts of Disraeli's ascent; and even the swelling words of the last stanza would be felt not greatly to exaggerate his achievements ' on Fortune's crowning slope.' In 1874 he might well seem to be ' the pillar of a people's hope'; and to describe the leading figure of a great European Peace Congress as ' the centre of a world's desire' would be a poetical licence of no excessive kind.

Here in Disraeli's career there was the realisation in fact of the vision which has floated before the eyes of many an ambitious youth; a clear proof that there is no eminence to which genius, aided by courage, resolution, patience, industry, and ' happy chance,' may not attain in this free country of ours. And though it was attained in this case, as in most others, ' by force,' it was in fair and open Parliamentary fight; and, as regards the main struggle, in what looked at first like a hopeless defiance hurled by a pigmy at a giant. It is nonsense to talk as if Disraeli betrayed Peel; if there was any betrayal, it was by Peel of his party. Peel may have been right in his change of front, and the Victorian age thought he was; but Disraeli, who championed the principles on which he and the rest of Peel's followers had been elected, no more betrayed Peel than Hartington betrayed Gladstone, when Gladstone suddenly adopted Home Rule, and Hartington, with a remnant of Liberals who were true to their pledges, withstood and routed him. Not only was Disraeli's political advancement won in fair fight. It was also uncontaminated by any suspicion that he was in politics for pecuniary gain. Had that been in any degree his object, he must be reckoned most unsuccessful, as he enjoyed office for only one quarter of the forty years and more during which he sat in Parliament Moreover, none of his success was due to demagogy; he made no ' pilgrimages of passion' among the electorate;[1] nor did he ever appeal for support to private cupidity, but only to public and patriotic principle.

In one respect Disraeli's success was more striking and complete than that suggested in Tennyson's lines. He not only scaled the political ladder to the topmost rung, and 'shaped the whisper of the throne'; he also conquered Society. He dominated the dinner-tables and what he would call the saloons of Mayfair, whenever he cared or could find time to attend them, as well as Downing Street and the Houses of Parliament; and his social triumph, whatever may be thought by philosophers of its intrinsic value, was certainly not less difficult of achievement for a despised outsider than his political, and was perhaps the sweeter to his palate. It is clear from his papers and letters that he was accepted in the last half-dozen years of his life as a competent arbiter in delicate questions arising in what delights to consider itself the Great World.

To the attraction of the dazzling brilliance of Disraeli's rise there was added the further attraction of his mysterious character and strange appearance. Mentally and physically he was quite unlike the traditional type of the British statesman. Hence the unvarying interest and zest with which his sentiments and his action were awaited at any time of crisis. Others might follow a humdrum rule of thumb; whatever Disraeli did, it would not be that. 'What will Dizzy say?' 'What will Dizzy do?' men asked. 'How like Dizzy!' would be the cry, when the witty aphorism had been launched, the unconventional and unexpected step taken. Indeed, the universal use of the pet name 'Dizzy,' recalling the familiar 'Pam' of another popular statesman, was a testimony to the way in which his personality had been taken to the people's heart. At first employed in a spirit

---

[1] The story goes that when, on some occasion after Berlin, he was wildly cheered by a tumultuous crowd as he drove to Downing Street in an open carriage, he sat quite unmoved and took no notice; alighted and walked up to the door in apparent unconsciousness; and, just as it opened to admit him, turned half round and touched his hat with his hand before disappearing.

of not always tolerant contempt, it became long
before his death a mark of kindly and humorous attachment.

The fundamental fact about Disraeli was that he was
a Jew. He accepted Christianity, but he accepted it as
the highest development of Judaism. He had inherited
from his father a profound interest in English history,
literature, society, and tradition, which his own reading
and experience had deepened. But he seemed throughout his life never to be quite of the nation which he loved,
served, and governed; always to be a little detached when
in the act of leading; always to be the spectator, almost
the critic, as well as the principal performer. 'No
Englishman,' writes Greenwood, ' could approach Disraeli
without some immediate consciousness that he was in the
presence of a foreigner.'

It was, indeed, a strange and impressive figure that you
might meet, any day, in the late seventies during the
session, sauntering slowly on Corry's arm down Whitehall. A frame, once large and powerful, now shrunken
and obviously in physical decay, but preserving a conscious dignity, and, whenever aware of observation,
regaining with effort an erect attitude; a countenance of
extreme pallor set rigidly like a mask ; a high, broad
forehead, and straight, well-formed nose; eyes deeply
sunken and usually lustreless, but capable of sudden
brightening in moments of excitement; a wide, flexible
mouth, and firm chin; the whole face in a setting of still
abundant hair, kept perennially as black as coal, and
arranged with a remnant of curliness over the ears, with
one conspicuous curl in the centre of the forehead, and
with a small tuft under the chin. A letter of Northcote's
to his wife at the opening of Parliament in 1862 dates the
origin of the chin-tuft: ' Dizzy,' he writes, ' has set up a
small peaked beard.' The curl on the forehead, which
came naturally in youth, was a work of careful art in age.
' It was kept in its place,' writes one who, when young,
was admitted to the great man's intimacy, ' by being
damped and then a yellow bandanna tied tightly round

it in front, with the ends down his back, till it was dry. I have thus seen him in his bedroom, attired in addition in a dressing-gown of many colours and a silk cord round his waist.'

His mental processes were as unusual as his physical appearance was peculiar. He did not form his opinions by amassing facts, but by some intuitive process of imagination. And so dramatic was the quality of his mind that he seems never to have been conscious of an opinion or conviction without being simultaneously conscious of the effect which its expression would produce. Hence the epigrammatic character of his talk and writing; to which a cynical flavour was added owing to the mask which he seldom put off in public. *Lothair* and *Endymion* recapture and repeat his table-talk, which was uttered with deliberate and impressive sententiousness. The stories told of it were endless. People heard of the royal lady who, indignant at the hesitation shown by Ministers on the Eastern Question, asked him at dinner what he was waiting for, and was told, 'For peas and potatoes, ma'am;' of the charming neighbour whose insidious attempts to wheedle political secrets out of him were met by a pressure of the hand and a whispered 'You darling;' of the public dinner at which the food was poor and cold, and at which Disraeli, when he tried the champagne, remarked with fervour, 'Thank God, I have at last got something warm;' of his grandiloquent excuse for inability to recommend a novel to a neighbour, 'When I want to read a novel, I write one;' of his judgment on a leading politician, nearly as well known in Mayfair as in Parliament, 'He has a fine presence, ancient descent, a ready wit, and no principles; he must succeed.' But silence and self-absorption grew upon Beaconsfield in society along with age and disease; so that Fraser could jestingly maintain that he was, in reality, a corpse which only at intervals came to life.

Beaconsfield could, on occasion, make capital out of his physical infirmities. A bishop of his acquaintance, of an unusually touchy disposition, thought that the Prime Minister had intentionally cut him on two public occasions in one day, and wrote a would-be dignified letter to say that, although quite unaware of having given offence, he would accept the intimation that the acquaintance must cease. Beaconsfield's reply was delightful.

10, DOWNING STREET, *May* 5, 1879.—I sincerely regret that I had not the gratification of recognising you at the Levée or the Academy, since it reminds me of the most unfortunate incident in my life—viz., that I am, perhaps, the most short-sighted of H.M.'s subjects.

My friends who are aware of my infirmity treat me with tenderness, and always address me first. Even our most gracious Prince, the Heir Apparent, with whom I have the honor of being in frequent communication, habitually deigns to pardon me for my default. Let me hope that a Christian Bishop will not be less charitable !

The bishop extricated himself with some dexterity from an awkward situation by explaining that he had not been in the habit of associating the idea of infirmity of any kind with the name of Lord Beaconsfield.

When Beaconsfield went down to Hughenden in these later years, the statesman and social oracle became the literary recluse of country tastes. Though often alone there for long periods and, after his release from office, without any pressure of public work to keep him busy, he declared that he never felt dull. He told Barrington that he 'peopled the air with imaginary personages'—person-ages, no doubt, whose acquaintance, in many cases, we too have made in *Endymion*. Over his solitary and simple dinner he would read one of his favourite authors, mostly classics of either Latin, Italian Renaissance, or English eighteenth-century literature, pausing for ten minutes between each course. He found constant interest in attending to the proper upkeep of his house and park, and to the seemly condition of his estate. We see him, in his letters to his agent, Mr. Arthur Vernon, provident and anxious about the due warming of his library so as to preserve the books, and about the necessity of postponing painting so that there might be no smell during the Queen's visit. In one letter he calls attention to the fences of a farm. 'I never in my life saw hedges in a more disgraceful state; absolute gaps, and some filled up by a strong hurdle: the whole presenting a picture which might have been expected in Ireland, but not in the county of Buckingham, and least of all on the Hughenden estate.' Ill-treatment of his beloved trees moves him to quick wrath. He writes to Mr. Vernon in 1879: 'I perceive to my amazement that Mr. ——— has horses in the park, contrary to his written engagement to your father, after the great injury that was occasioned to the trees, some years ago, by these animals. There are many trees which were taken out of their cradles last autumn, which are now not secure. I must call your immediate attention to this gross infraction of his agreement by Mr. ———, by which I feel as much aggrieved as injured.' His anxiety, both to secure the comfort of his people and to preserve and improve the amenities of the property, comes out in yet another letter.

To Arthur Vernon.

Private. HUGHENDEN MANOR, *April* 3, 1877.—Going to Q. Sess. yesterday, I left Hughenden by the Aylesbury lodge. I was pained, and distressed, at the scene of desolation I witnessed on the Park Road, near the Church. There was some excuse, in old days, for permitting a stack near that building, for it was beggarly and hideous; but now the nuisance seems to have been removed, in consequence of the restoration of the structure, is advanced to the roadside, and is guarded by rough pales.

After the great trouble I have taken to civilise this approach, I really cannot endure the present aggravated state of affairs.

I require that there shall be no more stacks permitted in that part of the park; that the place shall be entirely cleared, and sown with the best grass seed; so that we may have in time a good sward.

I visited the cottages, but was amazed to find that the dwellers therein were plagued with smoky chimneys. This pest destroys all the comfort and beauty of home. Is it impossible to build a cottage without smoky chimneys?

Hughenden Manor
from a photograph

I remember our great annoyance and trouble at the principal lodge, but, there, the discomfort was ultimately overcome.

I am anxious to know that the new cottagers are comfortable, and I wish their abodes to be more than comfortable: their gardens should be assisted with flowers, and there shd. be some trees planted in them. Gibbons must have some in the nursery, conifers and plants and trees of that kind.

Lytton wrote to Rowton after Beaconsfield's death: 'What stranger or what unborn biographer will have any means of knowing, in their right proportion to his whole character, all the lovable sides of it—the warmth of his heart, his domestic tenderness, his filial piety, his loyalty to friends, his complete freedom from malice and vindictiveness?' A constant, if imperfect, attempt has been made throughout this biography to bring out these lovable qualities, and to show the depth of feeling concealed beneath the cynical mask. Some lighter touches may be added.

Disraeli, who never had the happiness of a family of his own, always enjoyed himself in the company of children and young people, and made himself much liked in the families of his friends. 'The young ones think Dizzy the most charming playfellow they ever met,' wrote his host to him at the close of a country-house visit in 1855. His letters to Lady Bradford and Lady Newport show how devoted he was to Lady Bradford's grandchildren. And, during the last three years of his life, he was a very welcome guest in the family party at Hatfield. He took a constant interest in the development of his nephew Coningsby. 'I am glad you can give me so good an account of yourself,' he wrote to the boy in 1876, 'and that you have gained prizes both in Latin and in French. Next to your own, these are the two languages which will be most useful to you.'

At a dinner at Lord Wilton's house on June 19, 1879,[1] Beaconsfield had the misfortune, when cutting bread, to cut a finger of his left hand rather badly. The Princess of Wales bandaged it for the moment with her handker-

[1] See above, p. 1309.

chief. 'I asked for bread and they gave me a stone,' Beaconsfield murmured, 'but I had a princess to bind up my wounds.' After dinner a very junior local practitioner was, in the absence of his chief, called in to strap the finger up in proper fashion. He was treated with Beaconsfield's invariable courtesy, playfully called his 'guardian angel,' told to come round and complete his treatment next morning in Downing Street, and there shaken hands with and cordially thanked.

G. W. E. Russell tells the following story:

A well-known and delightful lady tried to make him read *The New Republic*, and write a favourable word about it for the author's encouragement. He replied: 'I am not as strong as I was, and I cannot undertake to read your young friend's romances; but give me a sheet of paper.' So then and there he sate down and wrote: 'Dear Mrs. S——, I am sorry that I cannot dine with you next week, but I shall be at Hughenden. Would that my solitude could be peopled with the bright creations of Mr. Mallock's fancy!' I have always thought that 'bright creations,' as an epitome of a book which one had not read, was a stroke of genius.[1]

A final instance must be given of Beaconsfield's capacity for playful unbending among his intimates. In his last years he united his especial women friends into a fantastic fellowship or order; and he gave each member as a badge a small brooch of insect shape. At first, in presenting the brooch, he wrote of it as a 'fly'; but after a while, apparently with a punning reference to the initial of his title, as a 'bee'; and the order was termed the Order of the Bee (B). Princess Beatrice, with the Queen's approval, accepted one of these brooches on her twenty-first birthday. The other members of the order appear to have been Lady Bradford, Lady Chesterfield, Lady Newport, Lady Beauchamp, and the Ladies Maud and Gwendolen Cecil, with perhaps one or two more 'I am much flattered,' wrote a neophyte, on receipt of the badge, 'at being enrolled among the distinguished ladies

[1] G. W. E. Russell's *Portraits of the Seventies*.

whom you delight to honour.' Montagu Corry was dubbed C.B., Chancellor of the Order of the Bee. To institute a female fellowship of this kind was a congenial relaxation to a statesman who could write to Lady Bradford: ' I hate clubs, not being fond of male society.'

Among the papers left by Mr. Monypenny there were found several stray paragraphs in his handwriting, apparently composed after he had worked through his material, and obviously meant for incorporation in some form in his final estimate of Disraeli's character and career. It is of course impossible to say whether he might not have modified his judgments on further consideration; but it has been a real satisfaction to his successor to collect and edit the most noteworthy and most finished of these fragments, and to include them in the last chapter of a work which will always bear his name on the title-page. Here is what Mr. Monypenny has written:

I have sometimes been asked if my book would at last dispel the mystery that surrounds Disraeli; and my answer has invariably been that, unless the mystery remained when I had finished my labours, I should have failed in my task of portraiture; for mystery was of the essence of the man. Yet to those who want, not portraiture but explanation, not synthesis but analysis, there is really no mystery at all except in the sense in which every personality is mysterious. Given his complex character and genius, and his peculiar origin and environment, everything naturally follows, correspondence, works, and career.

In the first period of his life we see the real Disraeli before he was trammelled by party connection; in the last, again, after he had mastered party. In the middle period—and it is the reason of its comparative lack of interest—he had to pay his tribute to convention; and we only get occasional if startling glimpses of the real Disraeli behind the mask which he had adopted. It is in this period that the legend of the mystery-man grew up.

A recent work insists that will is the distinctive characteristic of the Jewish race, and rightly points out that highly developed will-power tends to dwarf imagination. The will that swoops on its object and makes for success usually goes with a choice of material objects and success of the worldly kind. On the other hand, the brooding temperament that is essential to high imagination makes for ineffectiveness and dispersion of will-power. Where the two are combined we get a man of genius. Disraeli had the will of his race in its highest expression; but he had also in a high degree the quality which Houston Chamberlain denies them, imagination.

We read in *Coningsby* : ' What wonderful things are events; the least are of greater importance than the most sublime and comprehensive speculation !' Disraeli had that strong grip and profound appreciation of fact and reality, and that imaginative insight into their significance, to which only the man of ideas and imagination can ever attain. Those who are immersed in facts and cannot look on them from the outside fall short in these mental qualities; and still more, of course, the second order of idealists—those who cannot see the superiority of fact to their own subjective fancies.

How far was he in earnest, how far was he true in his motives, disinterested in his aims, of moral rectitude of character ? That in Disraeli there was from the beginning a certain worship of self, not so much in a small or merely selfish sense, but with something that was sincere and almost artistic in the motive, must be obvious to all who have read these pages from the beginning; and this self-worship was often, no doubt, in conflict with that surrender to a great purpose which we associate with the highest greatness. Yet it is easy to exaggerate the importance of this element of self. There is always something impersonal in genius. In his case, no more than in that of a far greater egoist, Napoleon, will self explain everything. There was profound insight in Napoleon's saying, ' I am not a person but a thing ;' and in Disraeli's case also the political genius of the man often drove him on regardless of self, and equally regardless, no doubt, of the consciously moral motives of lesser men, and gave to his character an elevation and a self-abandonment almost in his own despite.

Was he sincere ? The question seems at once to lead us back into the atmosphere in which Disraeli lived his life, to set up a standard which is inapplicable in his case, to refer the artist to the judgment of the conventicle. There is no absolute sincerity, for no man can be faithful to the truth in all its aspects, and a man may be sincere as an artist, and in a lofty sense, without being conspicuous for the virtue of truthfulness in its elementary form, and without possessing beliefs or convictions in the practical affairs of life, religion, ethics, or politics. Disraeli, however, though an artist, descended into the practical sphere, and must come to judgment at the bar of the practical spirit. We can then see that, though not more untruthful than the mass of mankind, and not wanting in high convictions to which he resolutely held, he too often dealt with the lesser convictions in the artist's light-hearted spirit, and so created distrust and marred his own influence. Intellectual sincerity he possessed in a high degree, but he allowed his mind to play too freely and sincerely over everything that came before it to possess moral earnestness in the conventional sense.

Apart from any laxity of principle or anything in his political conduct that might account for his reputation, Disraeli seems to have been one of those men who have the unfortunate knack of inspiring even more distrust than they deserve. From individuals with whom he was brought into intimate relations, whatever the dislike or suspicion with which they began, he would nearly always succeed in winning confidence and esteem; but in that gift, which defies analysis, of inspiring confidence in bodies of men he was curiously deficient—deficient even as compared with men essentially less earnest and less honest.

Disraeli was habitually inaccurate in trifles. His memory was not of the kind that makes faithfulness in such matters easy, nor his conscience of the quality that impels a man to spend effort in attaining it.

In the human tragi-comedy there are few things more diverting, when it is not also provoking, than, in exploring the morals of the past, to find the man of genius, about whom alone we now care, excluded from the coteries of the unmemorable great, or patronised by the petty social potentates of the hour; frowned on by the crowd of merely respectable people whose respectability has not availed to save them from oblivion, or condemned by the multitude of small righteous men, whose righteousness, though it was too much present to their own thoughts, the world has long ago forgotten. Through every phase of Disraeli's career we are confronted every day with these little affectations—these little envies, malices, judgments, rectitudes, and reprobations, which have fallen with those who harboured them; while he, with all his faults, stands there for ever serene and erect, an ironic smile playing about his lips the only reminder of the spleen from which he suffered.

Disraeli was in English politics the embodiment of the counter-revolution, the political creed which does not shrink from democracy nor even from the revolution on its salutary constructive side, but which opposes to the destructive tendencies of both a fuller and wider reconstruction. His Act of 1867 helped to restore to the English Constitution that balance which has almost invariably marked it and which had been disturbed since 1832 by the undue predominance of

the *bourgeoisie*. With the emergence of the people, the monarchy also re-emerged.

Disraeli's conception of Toryism anticipates the ideal to
which we shall attain when the destructive work of Liberalism
is fully accomplished, and we have reached that age of stability or reconstruction which calls for a really national party.

Oddly enough, Disraeli, with all his wide interest in, and
curiosity about, history, seems never to have cared about the
Middle Ages, that great and fascinating period in which the
foundations were laid of Western civilisation in its distinctive
form and, above all, of Western Christianity. But, perhaps,
when we consider his race, the attitude of the Middle Ages
towards the Jews, and the extent to which they deprived
Christianity of the special colour derived from its Jewish
origin, there is nothing odd about it at all.

Both Disraeli and Salisbury had sharp tongues which
raised up enemies for them; but both had extraordinary
kindness of heart. The Beaconsfield papers abound with evidence of gratitude, alike from intimate friends and from slight
acquaintances, for Disraeli's tactful sympathy, thoughtful
kindness, willingness to take pains to oblige, and remembrance
of his friends and their families when in misfortune, and long
after they had lost the power in any way to return his favours.
'Knowing how chivalrously true you always are to your
friends,' is the opening of one letter, in 1868. In another,
of 1875, we read, 'If anything could have enhanced in my
eyes what you have done for me, it is the way in which you
have done it, and the note by which you inform me of your
decision.'

In the case of Gladstone,[1] and in his case alone, the invincible detachment and tolerant insight, with which Disraeli
was wont to estimate the characters of friends and enemies
alike, were sometimes conspicuously wanting. In his later
years especially, he sometimes failed to understand the
motives or to show a just appreciation of the really great
qualities of his rival. And yet, even if the following judgment
is unkind, what could be more truly the last word as an
estimate of Gladstone's literary achievements ? 'Mr. Gladstone is an excellent writer, but nothing that he writes is
literature.'

---

[1] Disraeli was, however, always elaborately civil to the Gladstone
family. Talking to one of the daughters at some reception, where one of
the principal guests was a foreign diplomatist of very varied political
career, 'That,' he said in response to her inquiry, 'is the most dangerous
statesman in Europe—except, as your father would say, myself, or, as I
should prefer to put it, your father.'

Disraeli's place is not among the greatest of all, the supreme statesmen who lay the foundations of many generations, the supreme poets or men of letters whose works are perennial fountains of wisdom and beauty, the supreme teachers who awaken the conscience and elevate the mind and are an inspiration to mankind in every age. But he remains a unique and fascinating figure with a grandeur of his own which, if strictly neither the grandeur of memorable action on the one hand nor of moral force or intellectual insight on the other, is yet subtly blended of all, has its roots deep down in character, is armed with wide and penetrating vision, and finds expression in spacious and picturesque achievement.

Mr. Monypenny's paragraphs have carried us on from Disraeli's career and personality to his ideas and his imagination,[1] the other potent qualities that have assured his fame. We rather pride ourselves as a nation on our inaccessibility to ideas and take no shame for deficiency in imagination. We are guided, we say, by common sense and not by theories. The Whigs, who governed the country so long, and on the whole so successfully, were eminently distrustful of ideas outside the traditional Whig shibboleth, and were always disposed to compromise and a middle course. The other historical connection, the Tory party, had forgotten, till Disraeli reminded it in forcible fashion, that it had its origin in high and national ideas, and did not represent mere stagnation. But, for all our proclaimed devotion to common sense, there is a deep vein of romance and idealism in the English people, which Disraeli perceived and which he was wont to call enthusiasm. Its workings in politics have been often erratic, and sometimes almost ruinous. But it recognised, more perhaps after death than during life, the kindred nature of Disraeli's spirit, saw that there was a divine spark in him which was commonly wanting in British political leaders, and rescued him from the oblivion which has overtaken most of these in the popular mind.

[1] 'My book opened with personality, ideas, and imagination. With imagination, ideas, and personality it shall close' (Walter Sichel's *Disraeli*, p. 326).

It is needless, and it would be tedious, to recapitulate here, in the last pages of our detailed story, the multitude of fertile ideas on life in general, and in particular on the political and social past and future of Great Britain and the Empire, which Disraeli's active imagination poured forth throughout his long life in novel and treatise, in letter and speech.   Frequently paradoxical, sometimes apparently inconsistent, but always expressed with memorable incisiveness, they penetrated again and again to the heart of a misunderstood situation. Received often at the time of their utterance with scoffing and contempt, they appear in retrospect to have shown, in several instances, an astonishing amount of prophetic insight. Many of them are alive and move the minds of men to-day. And where, even now, we may find it difficult to believe that he was in earnest in the theories he propounded, some of us cannot resist the conviction that a subsequent generation may well accept what we still reject.

The ideas on politics by which he lives group themselves round two broad lines of thought, dealing on the one hand with the consolidation of our far-flung Empire and the assertion of its due influence on the world at large, and on the other with the consolidation of the commonwealth at home by promoting the moral and physical improvement of the people and by welding all classes into an harmonious whole. He sought union, not disintegration, of empire; class co-operation, not class competition and strife, at home; the reconstruction and development, not the destruction, of ancient institutions; abroad, neither selfish isolation nor indiscriminate meddling, but the assumption of a worthy place in the international Areopagus. His famous catchwords, such as ' Imperium et Libertas,' ' Sanitas Sanitatum,' ' a real Throne,' ' the key of India is London,' may appear on a superficial glance to be either paradoxes or truisms; but they embody a wealth of sound political doctrine which repays thorough exploration, and they have profoundly influenced, and continue profoundly to influence, political development. Moreover, we must never forget that, though he abhorred cant and was wont in consequence to affect a cynicism in speech which belied his real aims, nevertheless the whole of his teaching was directed against a material view of life either for the individual or for the State.

Although it is through his ideas and his imagination that Disraeli will live, he showed on more than one occasion that, when he set his mind to the task, he could rival the practical statesman in legislative achievement. Among the more fruitful Acts of Parliament of the Victorian era a high place is taken by the India Act, the Canada Act, the Reform Act of 1867, the Artisans' Dwellings Act, and the Masters and Workmen Act; all of them passed when Disraeli was either the first or the second person in the Government, and some of them mainly carried through his personal exertions. All of them, too, had the note of construction—the building up of empire or of society; in this resembling other less conspicuous but salutary legislation in which he had a share—such as the London Main Drainage Act, and the Consolidating Acts for Public Health and for Factories.

But there is no need to labour further what is written broadly over the record which has been here presented, largely in his own words, drawn from sources new and old. The evidence is before the reader; it is for him to judge whether the claim for Disraeli of exceptional greatness, only just short of supreme mastery, has been made out. To the present writer, as to his predecessor, looking back over the Victorian age from the disinterested standpoint of to-day, Disraeli appears a grand and magnificent figure, standing solitary, towering above his contemporaries; the man of fervid imagination and vision wide and deep, amid a nation of narrow practical minds, philistine, Puritan-ridden; his life at once a romance and a tragedy, but a splendid tragedy; himself the greatest of our statesmen since the days of Chatham and of Pitt.

APPENDIX.

AN UNFINISHED NOVEL,

BY THE EARL OF BEACONSFIELD, K.G.

Published, in Three Instalments, in "The Times" of January 20, 21, and 23, 1905.

Chapter I.

Of all the pretty suburbs that still adorn our metropolis, there are few that exceed in charm Clapham Common. An unenclosed park of 200 acres, well turfed and timbered, and, though free to all and without a paling, so well managed that a domain in a distant county could scarcely be more orderly and refined.

Those who live about this agreeable spot have shown, by the solid convenience and rich comfort of their dwellings, that they appreciate the pleasant place where their lot has been cast, and do not contemplate that they or their posterity should quit or desert it. Many of the red-brick structures have the true character of the manor-house, and are varied now and then by buildings of a more ornate and villa style, but still firm and compact, in the manner which the brothers Adam introduced at the beginning of this century. All of them are surrounded by ample and old-fashioned gardens; of late, however, much modernized, and so losing something of their picturesque stateliness, though they now abound with houses of glass of every form and for every purpose.

The dwellers in these homes have, generally speaking, a peculiar character. They have an idiosyncrasy. They are chiefly rich merchants, directors of the Bank of England, men whose fathers were directors of the East India Company, or chairmen of the great docks that were built in the Port of London during the great war. The new class of railway magnates are rarely found here. Their fortunes have been made in modern times, and by means which allow them to live much further from the City and yet find themselves as early every morning at their boards and counting-houses as the old families at Clapham, who, after all, are only four miles from Cornhill. But the very fact that, comparatively speaking, they are old families, and that there is no inglorious tradition among them of philanthropy and piety, of good and great works, and of some names that are even illustrious, binds them to the sacred soil by that local spell which is one of the most powerful influences over mankind.

Mr. Falconet was the head of one of the most considerable of these families. His father, an East Indian director, had been an intimate friend and companion of Mr. Wilberforce, who lived in his immediate neighbourhood and who was the godfather of his son. He had supported Mr. Wilberforce in all his great enterprises with his purse as well as his personal energy. His son, Mr. Wilberforce Falconet, had married, according to the Clapham custom, at an early age, a young lady who lived at Lavender Hill, and whose father was another friend of Mr. Wilberforce. Even in the enthusiastic world in which she was born, the bride was remarkable for the exaltation of her ideas. She was the founder of many institutions and the soul of all. Schools and hymns and Bible classes and tract distributions and industrial homes engrossed her life. But she was pretty, and Wilberforce Falconet lost his heart to her. He himself quite sympathized with all her pursuits and purposes, and had, indeed, been born and bred in a similar religious and moral atmosphere to her own. This, however, did not prevent him from having the reputation of being a first-rate man of business. Indeed, he was sometimes thought to be a little too sharp in his transactions, in which a fuller and larger degree of Christian forbearance, some intimated, might be desirable. As it was, at the head of one of the most considerable East India houses, he succeeded, on the death of his father, to a large realized fortune and was so wealthy that he need not have been appalled by the large family of both sexes which the pretty and enthusiastic partner of his life had presented to him.

It was not the thirty thousand pounds with which he endowed each of his daughters when they married that was the sole or even principal cause of their soon quitting the paternal roof. It was really the custom of the county; and as they were all pretty, like their mother, and full of enthusiasm, they quickly captivated young gentlemen of the neighbourhood, who were generally about the same age and yielded to the blended spell of religious devotion, female charms, and the most comfortable and piously luxurious domestic establishment in the whole neighbourhood.

The sons, though stalwart youths, had not inherited the fair mien of their mother. They resembled, and strongly, their other parent, who, it was the custom to aver, was descended from a Huguenot family. In truth, his father was the son of a Genevese watchmaker, and he had himself been a clerk to an eminent English firm, where his talents and knowledge of foreign tongues were appreciated. The revocation of the Edict of Nantes with the rich middle-class of this country occupies the same position as the conquest of England by the Normans does with our patricians. It throws a halo of imagination over many a humble or obscure origin.

The countenance of Mr. Wilberforce Falconet was austere, and its expression would have been saturnine had it not been in a state of constant mitigation from his thrilling sense of domestic happiness, worldly prosperity, and religious satisfaction. In the management of his family, Mr. Wilberforce Falconet was a despot, but he was an affectionate one. He often required sacrifices, but he occasionally made them, and, in either case, he was satisfied he was acting in a manner becoming the patriarchs.

His two elder sons were in his counting-house, and were soon to be his partners, when they both were engaged to marry young ladies who were the bosom friends of their sisters and were members of the same committees and distributors of the same tracts. Another son was a sailor. Permission to enter the naval profession had been long contested, but with the prospect that his services would be confined to the South African squadron had at length been obtained. Another son, who seemed inclined to be a soldier, was turned by the panic-stricken family into a clergyman without delay, and there only remained the youngest son for whom a career was to be provided.

Joseph Toplady Falconet had been a child of singular precocity. His power of acquisition was remarkable, and, as he advanced in youth, his talents were evidently not merely those which ripen before their time. He was a grave boy, and scarcely ever known to smile; and this not so much from a want of sympathy for those among whom he was born and bred, for he seemed far from being incapable of domestic affection, but rather from a complete deficiency in the sense of humour, of which he seemed quite debarred. His memory was vigorous, ready, and retentive; but his chief peculiarity was his disputatious temper, and the flow of language which, even as a child, was ever at command to express his arguments. In person, with a commanding brow, his countenance was an exaggeration of that of his father; austere even to harshness, and grave even to melancholy.

A learned man, who had guided his early studies, struck by his acuteness and his powers of rapid attainment, had, after much difficulty, persuaded his father to send him to a public school. This decision cost Mrs. Falconet great sorrow, who believed a public school was a place of much wickedness and cruelty. Her fears and anxiety were, however, unnecessary, for her son was at once placed in a position in the school which exempted him from the servitude which she dreaded, while a very short time elapsed before, even with so many competitors, his singular powers began to be remarked and admired.

His success at school secured for him the University. He was always the favourite son of his father, though that feeling on the part of the parent was never acknowledged or evinced. Secretly, however, the elder Falconet began to muse over the future of this gifted child, and indulge in dreams, which he never communicated to his wife. It was agreed, in due course, that Joseph should study for the Bar, having left the University in a blaze of glory as Senior Wrangler, and recognized as the unrivalled orator of its mimic Parliament.

And what were the dreams of the youth himself ? Had he any ? Though of an eager and earnest temperament, his imagination was limited, and quite conscious of his powers, being, indeed, somewhat arrogant and peremptory, aspired only to devote them to accomplishing those objects which, from his cradle, he had been taught were the greatest, and the only ones, which could or should occupy the energies of man.

Firm in his faith in an age of dissolving creeds, he wished

to believe that he was the man ordained to vindicate the sublime cause of religious truth. With these ardent hopes, he had renounced the suggestion which he had once favoured of taking Orders. It was as the lay champion of the Church that he desired to act, and believed that in such a position his influence would be infinitely greater than in that of a clergyman whatever his repute. The career of Mr. Wilberforce, ever before the eyes of the domestic circle in which he moved, doubtless much influenced him. It certainly did his father, for the secret scheme of the elder Falconet over which he mused alone was to obtain a seat in Parliament for his son.

No easy matter in these days, when men think themselves fortunate to reach the House of Commons with a grey or a bald head. And yet men of influence by pondering over an affair generally strike fire at last. If they be not men of influence the luminous particle generally will not appear and they are called visionaries, crotchety, or adventurers.

CHAPTER II.

The house of Falconet held a mortgage on the West Indian property of a noble lord, who was also a Minister of State. It was not in itself a good security, but the noble lord possessed ample property of a more substantial character, and so the firm was safe. The firm had taken a leading part in that abolition of West Indian slavery which had seriously reduced the value of the property in question. Whether the memory of this fact entailed some remorse, or whether they were influenced by the recollection of happier times, when, for a long series of years, they had been the agents of the noble lord, and had received in consequence a considerable income in the shape of commissions and interest on advances, there is no doubt that the existing relations between the peer and his former factors were always friendly, and, on the part of the commercial firm, frequently obliging.

Now this noble lord was so fortunate as to have an interest in a borough which his opponents always denounced as a nomination borough, though in truth he had no property whatever in it and could not command a single vote. But he and his wife, being wise and good people, were very civil and courteous to the inhabitants of this borough, which reached almost to their park gates; gave them every year a ball or two, went to theirs, asked them to shooting-parties, subscribed to their charities, presided over their meetings, religious and horticultural, supplied all the wants of the great house from the borough instead of from co-operative stores—and so the lord and lady were what is called "adored," and the borough always asked leave to return their sons or nephews to Parliament.

It seems that the son and heir-apparent of the noble lord, who was at present member for this grateful community, had thought fit to change his politics—what are called the family politics—a great sin, and being a gentleman of honour and spirit, nothing would content him but making this known in an address unnecessarily offensive, and then resigning his seat. Mr. Falconet, through the solicitor of the noble lord, had been aware of all this some time before it was publicly known, and had let the noble patron of the borough become aware that if it could be arranged that his son Joseph could succeed to the representation he should not only be singularly grateful, but should be very happy to prove that his gratitude was not shadowy, but of a substantial character, and so it came about that Mr. Falconet and his son were invited to spend the Whitsun week at the great house, and a public meeting in the borough, on the revival of the slave trade in the Red Sea, having been arranged, Mr. Joseph Toplady Falconet had the opportunity of making a speech, which literally electrified the audience. The speech, indeed, became not only famous in the place where it was delivered, it was reported in the London papers, and leading articles were written, attesting its commanding eloquence, and announcing the advent of a new and powerful candidate for the honours of public life. True it was that it subsequently appeared that there had been no revival of the slave trade in the Red Sea, but that the misapprehension had occurred from a mistake in the telegraph, manipulated by a functionary suffering from a *coup de soleil* or *delirium tremens*. But this did not signify and made no difference whatever in the eloquence of Mr. Joseph Toplady Falconet, or the result which that eloquence was to accomplish.

There was a dinner to be given at "the Common" to

celebrate the return of Joseph. There was a good deal of mystery about this coming event; some little hesitation for some time, and then immense preparations. The truth is Mr. Falconet had conceived the idea of asking the noble lord to be his guest on the occasion, and it was a long time before he could induce Mrs. Falconet even to comprehend his purpose, much less to sanction or encourage it. The Falconet gave many dinner-parties, but their guests were always their own family or intimate connexions, or persons who entirely sympathised with their chief thoughts and pursuits. In short, their banquets generally led to some religious ceremony, and were always accompanied by psalmody. Though he regretted the necessity, Mr. Falconet felt that it was possible his noble guest was scarcely accustomed to such pious practices, and as the noble lord would be the only one present who was unused to them, he could not but feel that a due consideration of all the circumstances might justify him in this instance of finding refuge in a compromise by a grace, both before and after the meal, of unusual length.

At length all was settled, the invitation was accepted and the day was fixed. It was a fine summer afternoon, and the noble guest asked permission to arrive an hour before dinner so that he might " enjoy the country a little and see their place." All were a little uneasy, and some were quite frightened, but Mr. Falconet himself felt he must make an effort and his demeanour was outwardly calm. But there was not the slightest necessity for this embarrassment. The noble lord was the personification of tact and polished sympathy. His eyes smiled with gentle kindness when he was presented to Mrs. Falconet, and his general bow was so skilful that everyone appropriated it to him or herself. He was almost enthusiastic about the Common, which, it seems, he had seen for the first time, and said it was worthy of *As You Like It*. He much praised the conifers in the private grounds, and intimated he had never seen any so fine; though the truth was he was himself unfortunately lord of the most rare and extensive arboretum in England. He visited several of the glasshouses and hinted that there could be few in England equal to them, though he had at home acres of these structures which he had unhappily inherited, and which it cost him annually thousands to maintain.

The dinner was quite a family party. Three married daughters and their husbands were present; the two sons in the business and the young ladies to whom they were engaged; two unmarried daughters; the clergyman brother, who had travelled all night to be there, and was to return at dawn so that he might assist at a Bible class, from which he never had been absent. Of course, the new M.P. was there, and the only child away was the sailor, but then, as a compensation, Mrs. Falconet had just received from him a letter on very thin paper and crossed, and which gave a most animated account of the capture by his vessel of one of the most terrific slavers in the Bight of Benin. She wished their noble guest to read this epistle, which he took with much courtesy, and then glancing at its calligraphy with a somewhat humorous expression put the letter in his pocket, saying he should like to show it to the Secretary of State.

The dinner was, of course, too elaborate, and much too long. The dessert itself lasted as long as a dinner ordinarily ought to do, but nothing would satisfy Mr. Falconet, on these occasions, but a procession of all his wondrous fruits—golden pines of vast shape, green melons like gigantic emeralds, rare figs of all sizes and colours, and bananas which in form and flavour beat Egypt. Indeed he had on this occasion some from that sultry land handed round, in order to prove the pre-eminence of Clapham Common.

The evening was short and went off pretty well. The young ladies had sweet voices and were skilful musicans. They did sing some psalms, but his lordship did not find it out. He sat on a sofa in the evening between Mr. and Mrs. Falconet, Joseph Toplady on a chair opposite to them, looking earnest and rather grim. They discussed his new life in the House of Commons, and Joseph took the opportunity of remarking that he had received some new information respecting the s ave trade in the Red Sea and thought of bringing the matter forward. "I think I would leave the Red Sea alone," said the Earl. "It was a miracle that saved us from being drowned in it before."

Mrs. Falconet looked grave, and her husband quickly turned the conversation by remarking that there was great difficulty in settling the habitation of Joseph now that he had become a Parliament man. He wished to live at home, but that seemed incompatible in the long run with the late hours of the House of Commons.

"When I was a young man," said the Earl, "I had to rough it, for I started as a cadet with no great allowance and with little prospect of my inheritance. I found the Albany a very suitable place for a young man, convenient and inexpensive. Why not try the Albany?"

"We had hoped," said Mrs. Falconet, "that Joseph might have found an abode with some serious family."

"Ah!" said the Earl, "I fear that serious families are rarer than they were in Westminster, and he must not be too far from the House. And now I will say Good-night. I have enjoyed myself greatly, and I only wish I had asked permission to bring Lady Bertram with me."

CHAPTER III.

There are few things more striking than arriving in the Port of London on a Sunday and then proceeding to some distant hotel. An enormous and illimitable city stretches out before you, apparently without an inhabitant. The windows are closed, the shops shuttered up, and in mighty thoroughfares, groaning on week-days with the weight of wains and carts and carriages, and streaming with population, perhaps the hansom cab that you have been fortunate enough to secure when you disembarked is the only vehicle visible—and no voice is heard except perhaps your own giving unintelligible directions to some obstinate or silently supercilious driver.

In the present case, however, the individual who had secured the cab had a companion, for when they had landed he had courteously offered a seat in his vehicle to one whose acquaintance he had only made during a short voyage, but whose conversation and manner had interested him.

"There is nothing to me so striking and so unexpected as this appearance of London," said his guest. "I came here with the persuasion that the English were rapidly renouncing, not only their own religion, but the religious principle altogether, and I find a scene which, for the cessation of labour, could only have been equalled in old Jerusalem."

"Manners and customs outlive superstitions," said his

companion, a man who, if he had lost his youth, was in the prime of middle age—of middle stature, still slender, with an inscrutable countenance, for the colour of his eyes seemed to change while he spoke. On the whole, it might be described as a compact face, the features regular but inclined to delicacy; the brow square and the mouth resolute. In these days costume is little guide to a man's station, except to the very practised, and after a voyage the most fashionable and fastidious are somewhat soiled and shattered. Nevertheless, it would be at once felt that the manner of this person was high-bred; natural, easy, and yet dignified.

" I do not disapprove of the Sabbatarian institution," said his companion; " on the contrary, I approve of it. It was a step in the right direction. It secured repose for one day in the week. True religion would secure repose for every day."

" That would be the Kingdom of Heaven," said his companion, " with which you were just saying these English people were not so content as in old days."

" When we were talking together on deck," replied the other, " I told you that I was a missionary, and I saw that you despised me, though you were too polite to express such a sentiment. I am a missionary, and of a faith held by many millions. It will some day, and perhaps sooner than is generally credited, be professed by all, and then there will be an end of all our troubles. I am a subject of Her Majesty and an inhabitant of Ceylon. I have heard much of late of the decay of faith in England, and the evil consequences which may ensue from this. Being independent, and long educated in these high matters, I resolved to visit Europe, and especially England, and see whether steps might not advantageously be taken to advance the great remedy which can alone cure the evils of the human race."

" And establish the Nirvana ?" said his companion with a scrutinising glance.

" I see you are not altogether unacquainted with the truth."

" I am myself in favour of a Sabbath of seven days," said his companion, " of a real Nirvana, but my perpetual Sabbath can only be celebrated in a city of the dead."

" Death is only happiness, if understood," said the Buddhist

" We are at your hotel. This is Blackfriars. Can I be of service to you ? Have you friends ?"

" I have a private letter to my banker, besides my letter of credit, and I am assured he will take care of me. Falconet and Co.—they are eminent, I understand. Do you know them ?"

" No," replied the other carelessly, " but bankers, if you have a good letter of credit, are generally obliging. What is your name ?"

" My name is Kusinara—and yours ?"

" I have no name," said the unknown.

CHAPTER IV.

The receptions of Lady Bertram were distinguished; almost amounted to being celebrated. An illustrious foreigner, for example, after the Thames Tunnel and the Crystal Palace, noted among his agenda, during his London visit, the opportunity, if possible, of making his bow to that great lady. Invitations were not a matter of course even to her own political friends, and murmurs were not infrequently heard by expecting, but omitted, guests that their room seemed to be occupied by " the other side." No individuals, however, foreign or domestic, experienced any difficulty in entering her saloons, provided they were famous or even eminent, and provided they properly appreciated the transcendent qualities of their hostess.

Claribel, Countess Bertram, was a very young widow when she consented to become the second wife of her present husband. Herself a member of one of our most ancient and noblest families, beautiful, highly jointured, and with an only child who was a great heiress, if the world did not exactly express their wonder at her union with Lord Bertram, they still, with frequent kindness, would observe that he was the most fortunate of men. But Lord Bertram was one of those who understand women, and he was a favourite with them.

Tall, pale, and somewhat fragile, but of a distinguished mien, her large dark eyes full of inscrutable meaning, while a profusion of rich brown hair, all her own, veiled in a straight line her well-moulded brow, and shaded with rich masses her oval cheeks, Claribel received her guests; her voice low, but musical, and quite distinct, though she scarcely condescended to raise it beyond a whisper. She listened, rather than conversed, but could seem deeply, or what is styled intensely, interested with her companion, and generally herself summed up with an epigram, or what sounded as such. Then the favoured guest might retire, and record the words of wit and wisdom in his journal, if he kept one.

It was amusing, unobserved, to watch the various modes with which she welcomed her guests. Generally speaking, the mass, of either sex, passed by her absolutely in fear and trembling. The beautiful head, grave almost to sadness, with a slight touch of celestial pride in the recognition, just divinely inclined itself; but occasionally her countenance became animated, a phosphoric flame shot forth from those eyes of Olympian repose, and she held forth the most beautiful hand in the world for them to touch, and even to press. These favourites were almost always men: statesmen of both sides, who habitually consulted her, neological professors from foreign Universities, or wild Radical poets, who found occasion, notwithstanding their screaming odes to coming men and coming times, privately to indite impassioned sonnets to the queen of beauty, of fashion, and of genius.

With her own sex she was courteous, but rarely cordial, except with some young ladies who were her worshippers and certainly except with her own family, whom she habitually welcomed with a courtly embrace. It was a divine condescension, and meant to intimate, what she was in the habit of asserting, that there was no family in the peerage which, for blood and historical achievement, could for a moment be classed with her own.

The daughter of Lady Bertram, the Lady Ermyntrude, had just been presented, though young even for such an initiation. Her future was a subject of frequent discussion in what is called "society." Whom she would marry, and when she would marry? Large questions—and then there were some who fancied she would never marry, and why? Because she was eccentric. Eccentric in what? Well, they say, she has ideas of her own. That is certainly serious. To-night, it might have been expected, that she would have been by the side of her mother, as Lady Bertram received her guests; but Lady Ermyntrude had an instinctive feeling that Lady Bertram was not particularly anxious for her contiguous presence, and she found it more amusing to move in her own orbit—but not unattended. There was a German lady, Fräulein von Weimar, who was her official and inseparable companion, and generally one of her guardians; a Bishop of captivating gifts, sufficiently serious yet of a lusory mind, a prelate who ever remembered how much the Church owed to holy women, contrived to hover round her, and was usually welcomed and encouraged by her smile.

It must not be supposed, however, that Lady Bertram was not a devoted mother. She was a perfect parent—in theory. She wished her daughter to have every advantage and enjoy every delight that was alike proper and practicable, only she was too much interested about herself to be able to spare any time to carry her theories into practice. Fortunately she had become acquainted with Fräulein von Weimar, who had gained her confidence and her heart by her appreciation of Lady Bertram's genius and her wondering recognition of Lady Bertram's resistless influence over men. This last ascendant power, however, was of so fascinating a character and it absorbed the life of Claribel to such a degree that, in due course, she found it was impossible to spare any longer any portion of her existence even to the sweet tongue and subtle mind of Fräulein von Weimar. So, after some scenes and much unnecessary diplomacy on both sides, this lady became the guide, the preceptress, and inseparable companion of the Lady Ermyntrude.

Her pupil had not the lustrous beauty of her mother, and yet her appearance was hardly less striking. She had a beautiful figure: rare to see anyone more shapely, and she moved as if she were conscious of her symmetry. Her countenance was delicate, aquiline, with grey eyes, but there was a want of mobility about her features, and it seemed doubtful whether their habitual expression were a simper or a sneer. Fräulein, although very few years older than Lady Ermyntrude, had the mien and carriage of a matured woman. She was rather under the middle size, and her stature was scarcely redeemed by grace, but she had a bright complexion, beautiful teeth, a commanding brow, and a large blue eye of searching power.

It was rather late in the evening; Lord Bertram, who, at its commencement, as was his custom, had assisted his wife in the reception of her guests, and then wandered about the crowded saloons talking with those he wished or cared to meet, had quietly stolen away to his red boxes. The rooms were still full, though thinner. Mr. Chatterley was standing by the side of Lady Bertram. He was one of the favoured, though never welcomed with enthusiasm, and sometimes scarcely treated with consideration. He was Lady Bertram's man of letters and, as he flattered himself, the only one of his class really in society. His chief business was to carry to her gossip, and to take care that she was properly worshipped in the lettered world. Servile to her and adulatory, he vindicated his independence by his arrogance in the inferior circles which he sometimes deigned to re-enter, and where his quotation of great personages made his conversation somewhat resemble the columns of the *Court Circular*.

"Lady Ermyntrude is looking charming to-night," observed Mr. Chatterley.

"Dearest Ermyntrude !" exclaimed her mama.

"She has just had a joust with the Bishop," said Mr. Chatterley, "and I do not think had the worst of it."

"Indeed," murmured Lady Bertram, with a vacant look "Have you no news to give me to-night ?" She could not for a moment suppose that Mr. Chatterley had ventured to stop by her side merely to praise her daughter.

"All the world is talking of young Mr. Falconet's speech," said Mr. Chatterley.

"Yes; he seems a considerable person. He dined here to-day."

"I am told he is a great admirer of Lady Bertram," said Mr. Chatterley.

"He knows very little of me," said the lady, trying to veil her curiosity.

"He knows what all know, and feels what all feel, who have the honour and delight of Lady Bertram's acquaintance; only what we feel or know goes for nothing; we alas ! who are not orators, or poets and statesmen."

"What did he say ?" said Lady Bertram in a hushed voice.

But before he could answer, he was obliged to retire, for a young man quickly and unceremoniously approached and addressed Lady Bertram.

He was handsome; the highest order of English beauty;

the Norman tempered by the Saxon; his complexion bright, his dark blue eye delicately arched, regular features, the upper lip short, and with hyacinthine locks of auburn hair.

"I thought I was not to see you to-night, Gaston," said the lady of the house.

"Well, I do not know whether I ought to be here. I have not been exactly cut by some of your friends, but they were rather queer. I suppose being in my father's house they could scarcely refrain from noticing me."

"I have made the acquaintance of your successor," murmured Lady Bertram. "He dined here. I have had much conversation with him."

"Ah!" said Lord Gaston. "Then I suppose you are in an orthodox mood."

"The English are essentially a religious people," said Lady Bertram.

"You did not think so the last time we talked about these matters."

"I think I might now sit down," said Lady Bertram, as if his words had not reached her; and she took his arm before even it could be offered, and they were soon seated on a sofa.

"This Mr. Falconet is an extraordinary man," said Lady Bertram. "I never knew anyone so eloquent. He talks, of course, too much, but that will wear off. I am sorry now that you left Parliament."

"I am not. Parliaments are worn out."

"But you say that of everything," said Lady Bertram.

"And it is true of everything; but of the whole affair nothing is so exhausted as the human race itself."

"But what, then, is to happen?" inquired Lady Bertram.

"Many things may happen. I do not suppose that because man is worn out even this little planet which we call ours has not yet some future. The mistake which our self-conceit has always made has been to suppose that this planet was made for man. There never was any foundation for such a belief, and now we know it is mere folly. The fact is that man has really never very much taken to this globe. And no wonder. It clearly was never intended for him. It consists of more water than land, and of that land a great portion is uninhabitable desert. Look at the miserable amount of population that, after millions of years, he has just contrived to procreate ! Scarcely equal to the spawn of a shoal of her-rings."

"Then you think the world was made for herrings?" sweetly whispered Lady Bertram. .

"I cannot tell what it was made for, but I think I can tell what it was not made for."

"Then you can have no interest in life ?"

"Yes; I have in you."

"If you begin talking nonsense I will go and fetch my lord."

"I suppose it is only Mr. Falconet who may talk nonsense."

"Mr. Falconet has none but the most exalted ideas. His life is devoted to the vindication and the triumph of religious truth."

"I am also capable of devotion," said Lord Gaston, "and that is to the happiness of my species. For that reason I wish it to become extinct."

Two young ladies with very long trains bowed to Lady Bertram from a distance and kissed their hands. "I must say a word to them," she said, as she returned their salute. "You do not mind ?"

"No, I like them both. They have more sense than half the girls I know."

The ladies approached. "I was so sorry, Lady Bertram," said one of them, "not to meet Professor O'Galaxy here to-night. We were at his lecture to-day at the Royal, and I wanted so much to ask him a question. I see my way so far as Protoplasm clearly; but there I stop. I think we ought to be satisfied; but Blanche De Grey says, No; that will not satisfy her; she must go further."

"If Lady Blanche goes further she will not get rid of her difficulties," said Lord Gaston.

CHAPTER V.

Though in the formation of our character the influence of individuals cannot be doubted or denied, nevertheless there are some persons born with a predisposition so strong that it is difficult to believe that, under any circumstances, that native vein would not have asserted itself. Lord Gaston was of this kind and class. Even as a child he was inquisitive, sceptical, and eccentric; doing things which were forbidden. or, if too original to have been contemplated, anticipated by the censure of others, when done, disapproved. He had the awkward habit of asking questions which could not be easily answered, and expressing opinions which perplexed and sometimes shocked. Nevertheless he was a favourite, and at first universally so; and this was owing to two causes—his good looks and his good temper. Nothing could disturb the last, and his first glance fascinated. Still it was a lamentable fact that, in the long run, he could not, as the phrase goes, "get on" with anybody. At a great public school he was soon idolised, but it ended by the authorities privately communicating with his father that they thought, on the whole, it would be advantageous that his son should be withdrawn from their control. Not that he ever did anything disgraceful, mean, or ignominious, or even committed violent or rebellious acts, but he was in the habit of circulating opinions which injuriously affected the discipline of the school; was in the habit of reading and advising others to read books which, while affecting to be philosophical, could not for a moment be tolerated, as tending, in the opinion of the masters, to the destruction of morals and religion. What, however, brought affairs to a crisis was a motion which he made in the boy's debating society condemning the system of public education. Had he not been the son of a great noble, who himself in his day had been one of the bright ornaments of their institution, he would probably have been expelled, but, as it was, he surrendered and marched out with all the honours of war.

Lord Bertram was such a complete man of the world that he resolved never to quarrel with his son, and he endeavoured by indirect means to guide him in the right path and counteract these evil tendencies. He thought Oxford would remove them, and he sent him there at an unusually early age. But the Oxford of Gaston was no longer the Oxford of his father, and Lord Bertram, who had many things to think about, was not sufficiently aware of this. A spirit almost as inquisitive as that which influenced his son had begun to pervade the great University, and it unfortunately happened that the head of the house of which Gaston had become a member was one of those distinguished divines who do not believe in divinity. Of this Socrates he soon became the favourite pupil, and, considering his rank, his fine looks, his fine temper, and the reputation for talents which was soon circulated about and easily and eagerly accepted, Oxford came to believe that it cherished in its bosom one who in due season would become its most brilliant ornament and its shining light.

Nevertheless, when he had exhausted all the nebulous interpretations of his master, which would prove that things, though entirely profane, were yet essentially sacred, Gaston engaged in a controversy on the origin of evil which terminated by his somewhat abruptly quitting his Alma Mater and informing his father that he should not return to Oxford, which he looked upon as a nest of sacerdotal hypocrisy.

This was a great disappointment to Lord Bertram, who, however, was a man never without resource, and Lord Gaston was soon gazetted as an attaché to one of our most important Embassies. This seemed a successful arrangement. Nobody could be more popular than Lord Gaston in his new world. All the great ladies were enchanted with him and invited him to their tea-parties. He was called the handsome Englishman, and then he was so kind and obliging, too. He was as good-natured as he was beautiful. Apparently he was well pleased with his new life. Two years passed away and he never asked for leave of absence, though he wrote charming letters to his father, who read extracts from them sometimes to his colleagues, and sent the most exquisite presents to Claribel, whom he called Mama. Unhappily, one morning he appeared without notice at Bertram House, and ordered breakfast as calmly as if he never had left his home. He had travelled night and day, for he had been ordered by the Government of the country to leave it at an hour's notice, some correspondence having been discovered between the noble British attaché and a revolutionary leader. A secret communication was made to Lord Bertram, but it was the interest of all parties that the affair should be hushed up.

"There is nothing to be done for him now but to push him into Parliament," said his father. "If anything can get the nonsense out of a man, it is the House of Commons."

The reader will have seen that this last expedient had not been quite successful. Lord Bertram forgot his annoyance in the pressure of public business, and Lady Bertram found a substitute for the sceptical confidences and revolutionary principles of her stepson, with which she was beginning to sympathise, in the unflinching orthodoxy and ultra-Conservatism of his Parliamentary successor, urged as they were by him with irresistible dialectics and a torrent of words which no improvisatore could excel, and to which Lady Bertram in veiled ecstasy listened as she would to a cataract in the Alps.

On a certain day in every week it came to be understood that Mr. Joseph Toplady Falconet would probably be drinking a cup of tea at Bertram House and expounding his schemes of regeneration for a society which he was resolved to save, though he admitted its condition was somewhat desperate. He had already achieved success in the House of Commons, where rapid success is difficult. Very shortly after his entrance into that still fastidious and somewhat incredulous assembly he took up the Sabbatarian question, and the notice of his motion was received with contemptuous respect. But the feeling was far otherwise when they had listened to him. The old hands at once recognised that this was a man who would mount and looked forward with interest to the occasions when he might deliver himself on some practical subject and not on such moonshine as that with which he had favoured them. But here the old hands, as they often do, made a mistake. There was a great, though latent, fund of Religionism in the House; much of it sincere, a large portion, no doubt, inspired by the constituencies; but the members who acknowledged these sentiments, were, generally speaking, not of a class calculated to enthral listening Senates. They were respectable men, usually opulent, and their opinions on matters of trade and taxation always commanded deference, but they were quite incapable of grappling with the great questions that touch the convictions and consciences of nations, and they hailed with satisfaction a commanding expounder of opinions which in their hands they felt would have assumed a character of feebleness which they were persuaded was undeserved. These men, sitting on both sides of the House, rallied round Falconet. He gathered other allies. With all his abilities and acquirements, Joseph Toplady Falconet was essentially a prig, and among prigs there is a freemasonry which never fails. All the prigs spoke of him as of the coming man.

Lady Bertram always returned from her daily drive at five o'clock, and she was always at home. There never had been formal invitations, but the initiated came—a small, refined circle. There were always a few ladies of great fashion, sometimes a Royal Duchess, an Ambassador, a dandy or two— for Lady Bertram could even command dandies—and half a dozen other men, native or foreign, but of European celebrity. When it was in his power Falconet was there, but that was uncertain, for the House of Commons is a jealous mistress and will not grant success without due attention. The greatest compliment you can pay to a woman is to give to her your time, and it is the same with our Senate. A man who is always in his place becomes a sort of favourite. But there were other means of communication between Claribel and her new prophet; books were mutually lent to each other, and every day there were letters exchanged: on her part, little emblazoned notes; on his, treatises, pamphlets, where everything was divided under heads and every question exhausted and settled.

CHAPTER VI.

The clubs, which, in their fanciful invention, are only inferior to the Arabian Nights' Entertainments, speculated much on the future of the Lady Ermyntrude. Some thought her so matured in her mind and manner that she would marry immediately; others, on the contrary, held that she would hesitate for a long time before she decided; a third party ventured on an opinion that she would probably never marry at all.

The names of some persons, however, were already intimated as the possible, or even probable, partners of her life and fortune. Gaston, from his connexion with the lady, was always the first mentioned, and yet his name was almost invariably dismissed as that of a man who had no thought of marriage. Then there was Lord Fitz-Alb. He was supposed to have a very good chance, being the great favourite of the Bishop, and quite fit, though youthful, to be a prelate himself. The Bishop was one of Lady Ermyntrude's guardians, who, it was understood, consulted him on all occasions. Some thought that Hugo Bohun would be the lucky man. Heiresses, somehow or other, always seemed to like him, though somehow or other eventually they had hitherto never united their fate with his. Hugo Bohun was an ostentatious pauper, and had a theory that rich women like to marry paupers, particularly if they were personages so *comme il faut* as himself. The knowing ones on the whole backed Lord Warrener against the field. It was circulated that Lady Ermyntrude in one of her morning rides had more than once inquired whether Lord Warrener was in the Park, and seemed disappointed he was not at her side.

Lord Warrener was a good-looking, accomplished cosmopolitan. He ostentatiously announced, though of ample estate, that he cared for nothing but money, but it was generally held that he would prefer obtaining it by a race or a rubber rather than by the aid of an heiress, however wealthy or distinguished.

There was a ball, and the Lady Ermyntrude had danced twice with Hugo Bohun; he had even attended her to the tea-room.

"This is one of the happiest nights of my life," he said to her. "Do you know, I think it wonderfully kind of you to dance with such a miserable wretch as I am."

"One meets with so many happy people," said the Lady Ermyntrude, "I rather like sometimes to meet a miserable wretch."

"What other miserable wretch do you know except myself?" asked Hugo.

"I know several wretches," replied the lady, "but I am not at all sure they are miserable wretches."

"Well, what is your idea of a wretch?"

"I think a man who is discontented with his lot in life is a wretch."

"Everybody is discontented with their lot in life."

"I thought just now you said you were most happy."

"So I am when I am with you."

"Then, after all, you are not a real wretch," said the lady.

"Do you think Gaston is?" inquired Hugo.

"His wretchedness is on so great a scale that it amounts to the sublime."

"I should think you were contented with your lot in life," said Hugo.

"I have not yet considered that question so deeply as it deserves," said Lady Ermyntrude. "At present my thoughts are limited to these walls and to the cotillon which I am now going to dance."

"Alas! not with me?"

"No," said Lady Ermyntrude, withdrawing her arm, and taking that of Lord Warrener, who at that moment joined her, and bowed.

"Now I feel this is the most miserable night of my life," murmured Hugo.

The lady, departing, looked over her shoulder and smiled.

Chapter VII.

One of the most important neighbours of Mr. Falconet died about this time. He was a German gentleman, and lived at Lavender Hill in a mansion situated in unusually ample grounds for a villa residence, and approached through lodges and by roads ingeniously winding. Mr. Hartmann was a bachelor; the firm a distinguished one—Hartmann Brothers. They were bankers to more than one European potentate, and whenever any member of the Royal or Imperial families paid a visit to England they spared one day to be entertained at Lavender Hill with much magnificence; banquets and balls in colossal tents, and all the bowers and groves of Lavender resonant with musicians and illumined with many lamps of many colours.

It was understood that Mr. Hartmann had died very wealthy, and that the bulk of his large fortune had been bequeathed to his brother, who resided in a foreign capital. It was still more interesting news when it began to be rather authoritatively rumoured that in future England was to be the residence of the heir, and not only England but Lavender Hill.

In due time, architects and builders and workmen arrived at the spot, and it was said that great alterations were making there, with that disregard for expense which became the proprietor of means so ample. Among other changes, it was said that a library had arrived from Germany, rich and rare, and which was to be housed in a new chamber becoming such treasures.

Mr. Falconet had great respect for the house of Hartmann Brothers, and took the earliest opportunity of personally paying his respects to the newcomer. His arrival among them was rendered not less interesting by the circumstance of his not being a bachelor. He was a widower, but with an only child, a daughter still in her teens, yet already, it was understood, recognized as the head of his establishment. The arrival of the Hartmanns, therefore, created no little excitement in the Falconet family, both among the sons and the daughters. Especially was there no lack of speculation as to the character and appearance of Miss Hartmann.

The first visit was made and returned, and the first impression of their new neighbours on the Falconet family highly favourable. Mr. Hartmann was a man singularly calm, with an intellectual countenance; reserved, a little shy, perhaps, but not dull. As for his daughter Angela, all the young ladies fell immediately in love with her, and, after having walked twice round their own grounds with her, were quite prepared to vow eternal friendship. Their brothers were less vehement, restrained, perhaps, by their engagements to their sisters' coadjutors in the Bible class, but their glance betrayed their appreciation of the charms and manner of their new acquaintance.

Not that Angela Hartmann was an ideal beauty—a Phryne to be painted by Apelles or modelled by Praxiteles, or a Titian's Flora, or even a Madonna of Raffaelle; but there were a sweetness in her voice and a softness in her demeanour which at once attracted, while, though the habitual expression of her mild cheek and pencilled brow was grave, it was, at the same time, not rigorous but sympathetic. Nevertheless, as time flowed on, the enthusiasm of the Falconet family in her behalf, and especially of its female portion, abated. They embraced her when they met, but they did not meet very often; they still much talked of her when she was not present, but amid varying comments and criticism there seemed a general agreement that they could not quite make her out. She had sweetly declined to assist them in their Bible classes; and had softly refused to teach at their Sunday schools. She was not uninterested in hymnology, but her songs of adoration were different from those in their orthodox collection. Miss Hartmann regularly attended Divine service at their parish church, but unfortunately she was never accompanied by her father. This greatly disquieted Mrs. Falconet, who at first wished Mr. Falconet to speak to him, and eventually did send him a sheaf of tracts. Mr. Falconet, however, though as devout as his better half, was still, to a certain degree, a man of the world, which truly every merchant must be, and he intimated to his wife that Mr. Hartmann was probably a German philosopher; a difficult kind of animal in these matters to deal with. "He was showing to me his library the other day," said Mr. Falconet, "and there were two portraits in it, very fine pictures; one was of Spinoza, the other of Kant.'

"Good gracious!" exclaimed Mrs. Falconet.

"You need not be too much alarmed, my dear, for I said to him—I thought it just as well to say to him—'You have two advanced thinkers there, Mr. Hartmann.'"

"Yes," he replied, "I owe them much; they did their work in their time, and I am grateful to them, but I have long ceased to share their opinions."

"I feel greatly relieved," said Mrs. Falconet.

Chapter VIII.

It was a Bank holiday, and Mr. Hartmann was absorbed in a new work of a friend of Schopenhauer which had just arrived, when a visitor was announced. He looked at the card which his servant brought in to him, and the spleen which, for a moment, was excited at being disturbed vanished instantly as he glanced at the superscription. So the servant was ordered to usher in the guest, and there entered the room the same gentleman who had behaved kindly at the beginning of this history to the Indian who landed on a Sunday at the Port of London.

"My first visit to your new home," said the guest, "a pleasant quarter."

"I might have chosen a more picturesque spot, and one equally convenient," said Mr. Hartmann, "but I passed my childhood here and had a weakness here to close my life."

"The local influences are the strongest," said his companion. "It is almost vain to struggle against them, though they are exceedingly mischievous. I see you have a new book. He has also sent me a copy."

"I do not know that there is anything new in it," replied

Mr. Hartmann, " but what is old to us is new to the world. He is one of the few men who can write on an abstruse subject with clearness."

" They never really answer him," said the visitor.

" So they call him a visionary," said Mr. Hartmann.

" A visionary !" exclaimed his friend. " So are you a visionary; so am I; so was Mahomet; so was Columbus. If anything is to be really done in this world, it must be done by visionaries; men who see the future, and make the future because they see it. What I really feared about him was that he had the weakness of believing in politics, of supposing that the pessimism of the universe could be changed or even modified by human arrangements."

" I heard he was a Communist."

" He might as well be a Liberal or a Conservative—mere jargon; different names for the same thing. You and I know that in attempting to terminate the misery of man, there is only one principle to recognize, and that is the destruction of the species. You and I hold the same tenets, and we desire the same end. We differ only in our estimate as to the time required; but that is of no import. You think that centuries must elapse before the consummation. I would fain believe our release and redemption were nearer; but you are a sedentary man, a man of books. Action and some instinct have taught me what you have derived from pondering on your own observations and the thoughts of others. All that is happening in the world appears to me to indicate a speedier catastrophe. These immense armies, these new-fangled armaments—what do they mean ? In the Thirty Years' War they would have depopulated Europe. What commissariat can support these hosts ? I trust more to the disease and famine of campaigns than to the slaughter of battles."

" Remember what Condé said when he lost his best troops," remarked Mr. Hartmann. " One night at Paris will supply their place."

" Ah ! but a night at Paris is different now from what it was in the days of the Condés. The French are the most civilized nation and the most sterile. But, reverting to what I was saying, there are indications of habitual dearth in this globe which are encouraging."

"Surely these are comparatively slight means to achieve such a result as the total destruction of the human species."

"Not so slight as you may imagine. Besides, we must accept all means. Destruction in every form must be welcomed. If it be only the destruction of a class it is a step in the right direction. Society is formed of classes, and it may be necessary to destroy it in detail."

"What I fear will be the great obstacle to accomplishing our end," said Hartmann, "to which, as you really know, I am not less devoted than yourself, is the religion of Europe, and which has unhappily been colonially introduced into America."

"It has many assailants," said his companion.

"And in its time it has defeated many assailants," replied Hartmann. "I doubt whether my neological countrymen will be more fortunate and effective than the French encyclopædists."

"Ah, but you do not sufficiently allow for the influence of science at the present day."

"Query, whether science was less influential at the end of the eighteenth century than at the present moment. D'Alembert, and Diderot, and Holbach (? Lamarque) were no mean authorities, and as for mathematics, the French were always supreme. No, the more I ponder over this religious question, the more I am convinced that we shall never succeed in our mighty aim unless we contrive to enlist some religious faith in our resources. If it be true that the confidence of Europe and her colonies in their creeds is falling away, cannot our principle of extermination be clothed in a celestial form?"

"Secure the future by destroying the present," said his companion musingly.

"You know I have always had some views of this character," said Mr. Hartmann, "but they are fresh in my mind at this moment from some conversations I have recently had with an Indian gentleman, who has been visiting in this neighbourhood, and whom I met at a house certainly not renowned for its philosophy. This Indian gentleman, a man of great culture, is from Ceylon. He is a Buddhist and a self-appointed missionary of that faith, which, if imbibed in its pure and original spirit, would consummate our purpose."

"I fancy I know your friend, and have regretted that the

pressure of affairs has prevented me from cultivating his acquaintance. You are speaking, I am sure, of Kusinara. I came over from Rotterdam with him some little time ago; a remarkable man."

" 'Tis the same person," said Mr. Hartmann.

" He might give lectures. Lectures are grains of mustard seed. Or, what would be better, we might give him a chapel, and let him celebrate, at the same time that he expounded his doctrine, the services of his sect. There must be among the Chinese about the Port of London and other places the elements of a congregation. The English like a congregation. The moment there is a congregation, they think the affair practical."

" There is no doubt," said his friend, " that if we could enlist the religious principle on our side, it might produce great effects. There is nothing to be compared to it in power except the influence of women—and they generally go together. I once thought I had gained one of the greatest ladies in Europe to our creed; I gave, I might say, years to the effort and travelled thousands of miles. I should think nothing of going to the Brazils to-morrow were there a chance of enlisting the sympathies in our cause of any woman of influence. In these matters, they are stronger than armies."

" Here comes my daughter," said Mr. Hartmann. " She wants to give you some luncheon. She is not one of those women who are stronger than armies, but she is a dear girl."

CHAPTER IX.

There was an assembly at Lady Clanmorne's, a popular person, a friend of Lothair. Lady Bertram was present, and moved about with the consciousness of her irresistible fascination. She had received the homage of all the illustrious who were present with a mystical glance from her soft rich eyes, and occasionally had deigned to breathe forth a sentence worthy of a Sibyl. Then, as was rather her wont, she retired from the principal saloons, and seated herself alone on a sofa in a chamber less frequented, meditating on the variety of her charms and her magical influence over mankind. Self-introspection was ever the delightful and inexhaustible pursuit of Claribel, and she never closed these bewitching reveries without increased admiration of her own idiosyncrasy.

A gentleman approached her of distinguished mien. He was young, but of matured youth; his fine countenance serene, but commanding. His costume, though simple, was effective, and, though he wore no ribbon, he was decorated by a star in brilliants.

"Lady Bertram," he said, "I am commanded by Lady Clanmorne to attend you to the tea-room, where you will find Lady Clanmorne, who particularly wishes to see you."

Claribel a little lost her presence of mind. She did not know the envoy of her friend, and yet she ought to know everybody who was anybody. And this, too, a stranger so distinguished! He seemed made to appreciate her. She was already contemplating her irresistible influence over him, though certainly before she commenced her mystic charms she would have liked to have known exactly who he was. But aspiring to control, she felt herself controlled. She rose and with a slight bow took his offered arm.

He gave her some tea, observing Lady Clanmorne had not arrived, and then, without any formal suggestion on his part, she found herself seated, and the stranger by her side.

"I owe Lady Clanmorne much," he said, "but am most grateful to her for giving me this opportunity of speaking to Lady Bertram."

"And why should you be grateful for that?" murmured Claribel, with a glance of voluptuous penetration.

"Because it has been the object of my life that I might have the opportunity of conversing with one of the most gifted of women."

"The most gifted woman, I fear, can do little."

"She can do everything."

"There is much to be done," replied Claribel mysteriously, but as she really had nothing to suggest she only looked like a high priestess bound to betray no secrets of the initiated.

"Certainly there is much to be done," said the stranger. "Society is resolving itself into its original elements. Its superficial order is the result of habit, not of conviction. Everything is changing, and changing rapidly. Creeds disappear in a night. As for political institutions, they are all challenged, and statesmen, conscious of what is at hand, are changing nations into armies."

"What you say is true," said Lady Bertram moodily; and then she added with a subtle, knowing look, and in a cadenced whisper, "but is it the whole truth?"

"Those who know the whole truth are the lords of the world," said the stranger; "and it is because I feel that I am perhaps speaking to one of such Sovereigns that I hail this night, which has given me the advantage of listening to her counsels."

"We must think," said Lady Bertram.

"Pardon me, Madam, but I am mistaken, if you have not exhausted thought. There are thinkers, I know many, not unequal to the times in which we move, but they are all of opinion that what we require now is not so much further thought as a transcendent type of that thought alike to guide and inspire us."

Claribel unfurled her fan and gracefully waved it. There was a gentle tumult in her frame which indicated an increased action of the heart, her cheek slightly glowed. It was delicious to hear, and, as she could not refrain from believing, from high authority, that her mission was to guide and inspire. She had been trying to do this all her life, but, not knowing the way, she had found it difficult to direct what path to follow, and instead of inspiring others she generally imbibed the last ideas which were infused into her. Now it was absolutely necessary to say something, and so she said in a tone of mystical decision, "It is impossible to resist one's destiny."

"Impossible—and yours is a commanding one."

"You were speaking of your friends and some peculiar views of theirs?" remarked Lady Bertram, vanity and curiosity combining in an effort to discover who were these unknown admirers of her consummate self.

"Their views are peculiar only because they are conscious, and have long been conscious, that the pretended principles upon which society is formed have ceased to exist, and that they are merely conventional phrases which, for the moment, are convenient to employ."

"We must resist conventionalism," observed Lady Bertram with much authority.

"These are good tidings from such lips," said the stranger

" It will give courage to those who would extricate us from the blunders of ages."

At this moment, smiling, yet with an air of curiosity blended with her smiles, Lady Clanmorne entered the tea-room and approached Claribel. Her attendant, murmuring that he had now fulfilled his mission, rose, and, bowing to both ladies, left the room.

" I am most anxious to know who is your friend. I saw you from a distance on his arm," said Lady Clanmorne. " I thought he must have come with one of the Princes and yet I should have remembered him had he been presented to me."

" He brought to me a message from you," said Lady Bertram, amazed, " and a rendezvous in the tea-room."

" From me ! Let us follow him !"

The two great ladies returned to the ball-room, but the stranger was not there. They walked through the other saloons. He was not visible. Lady Clanmorne, describing her unknown guest, made inquiries about him of the attendants. They agreed that he had just quitted the house. He was for a moment in the cloak-room, but there he had only figured as a number. There was a scribe in the hall making a catalogue of the guests. It seemed that the stranger had avoided giving his name, and, as he was decorated with a diamond star, the scribe thought all must be right.

Chapter X.

In the meantime, Kusinara, the gentleman from Ceylon, became very intimate with the Falconet family. He had been invited at once to Clapham, for his letter of credit also announced that he was a man of considerable station and distinction. Mrs. Falconet soon discovered that he was also half a Christian, and resolved, that he should become a whole one. The expected neophyte was extremely docile, was interested in all he heard, and if not at once a convert, was always a candid, and often an admiring, listener. . . .

INDEX

PRINTED IN GREAT BRITAIN BY
BILLING AND SONS LTD., GUILDFORD AND ESHER